CASES AND MATERIALS ON COMBATING RACISM IN CRIMINAL PROCEDURE

Cases and Materials on Combating Racism in Criminal Procedure

LeRoy Pernell and Omar Saleem

Published by:

 Vandeplas Publishing, LLC – March 2021

801 International Parkway, 5th Floor
Lake Mary, FL. 32746
USA

www.vandeplaspublishing.com

ISBN 978-1-60042-525-7

CASES AND MATERIALS ON COMBATING RACISM IN CRIMINAL PROCEDURE

LEROY PERNELL

Professor of Law
Florida Agricultural and Mechanical University
College of Law
Professor Emeritus, Northern Illinois University
College of Law

OMAR SALEEM

Professor of Law
Florida Agricultural and Mechanical University
College of Law

TABLE OF CONTENTS

INTRODUCTION

Most text implicitly foster a disconnect between the history of the significance of race in American society and the implementation and the development of modern, constitution-based criminal procedure

While brilliant work has been done on the impact of race on specific stages of the criminal process, such as jury selection and racial profiling, this work looks at the causal and pervasive impact of what W.E. B. Dubois termed as (the "color line") the most significant problem of the twentieth century.

Racism and criminal procedure did not develop along two separate paths that occasionally crossed each other, but instead grew intertwined as a cause and effect that is only now seeing the full light of day.

As an organizational framework for this book it will first look at the functioning of the criminal justice system as part of American Slavery and race-based suppression. From there we will look at how race during reconstruction, the criminal justice implementation of Black Code "Jim Crow" laws, lynching, race-based terrorism, prior and during the civil rights movement, and finally, as context and prelude to an examination of due process implications of specific stages of criminal process and the current challenges of mass incarceration.

Along the way and as appropriate discussion of issues of race and criminal procedure will expand beyond the pervasive issue of racial treatment of African Americans to include the significance of race in the criminal process treatment of other non-whites including Latinos/ Hispanics, Asians and particularly more recently Arab/Muslim American citizens.

One final word on the goal of this text. It is our hope that these cases and materials will not only serve as a way of understanding the intersections of race but will offer ideas for practical application in order to combat and minimize the impact of race in our criminal justice system.

CHAPTER ONE: RACE AND CRIME IN AMERICA

The Presence of Race in the Criminal Justice System Before and after the Civil War

No case decided by the United States Supreme Court involving race and racial justice, has been treated with such odium as the 1857 decision of *Dred Scott v. Sanford*. While historians still debate whether this was the final match which lit the Civil War, there is little debate that its most infamous statement is the conclusion "they had no rights which the white man was bound to respect.."

Many saw this as a rejection of the orientation of the Supreme Court reflected in its 1841 decision in *The United States v. The Libellants and Claimants of the Schooner Amistad*, 40 U.S. 518 (1841). In *Armistad* the question was whether an African, kidnapped and made a slave, could be a person, for purposes associated with criminal prosecution. Fifty-three Africans were purchased, illegally, in Cuba as slaves. They were to be transported from Cuba aboard the Spanish-built schooner Amistad. The Africans successfully overcame their captures and took command of the ship, killing the captain and a cook. Certain crew were spared with the understanding that they would steer the ship to Africa. By changing the ship's course at night, the crew members instead sailed the Amistad to a position of the coast of Long Island where an American ship intercepted the vessel. The two remaining Spaniard crew members were freed, and the Africans taken into custody. Public outcry from abolitionist and other prevailed against extradition of the Africans to Spain and instead a trial before an American court was held. After a finding by a federal district court that the Africans were not liable because they had been illegally enslaved, the case proceeded ultimately to the United States Supreme Court. The Court, with only one dissent, found that the Africans were free citizens of another country and their return to Africa was ordered immediately.

The *Dred Scott* decision produced nine separate opinions, however, it is the opinion of Justice Taney, speaking for the Court that is most remembered.

Dred Scott sued for his freedom from slavery. He maintained that in 1834 he was transported as a slave first to Illinois, a free state, and then to Wisconsin a territory which pursuant to the Missouri Compromise, prohibited slavery. Although Dred Scott was subsequently transported back to Missouri, a slave state, he maintained that he had been freed pursuant to his extended time in Illinois and Wisconsin, and by virtue of that freedom he was a free citizen of both Illinois and Wisconsin and as a consequence a citizen of the United States.

DRED SCOTT V. SANFORD
60 U.S. (19 How.) 393 (1857)

Mr. Chief Justice TANEY delivered the opinion of the court.

This case has been twice argued. After the argument at the last term, differences of opinion were found to exist among the members of the court; and as the questions in controversy are of the highest importance, and the court was at that time much pressed by the ordinary business of the term, it was deemed advisable to continue the case, and direct a re-argument on some of the points, in order that we might have an opportunity of giving to the whole subject a more deliberate consideration. It has accordingly been again argued by counsel, and considered by the court; and I now proceed to deliver its opinion.

....

The question is simply this: Can a negro, whose ancestors were imported into this country, and sold as slaves, become a member of the political community formed and brought into existence by the Constitution of the United States, and as such become entitled to all the rights, and privileges, and immunities, guaranteed by that instrument to the citizen? One of which rights is the privilege of suing in a court of the United States in the cases specified in the Constitution.

It will be observed, that the plea applies to that class of persons only whose ancestors were negroes of the African race, and imported into this country, and sold and held as slaves. The only matter in issue before the court, therefore, is, whether the descendants of such slaves, when they shall be emancipated, or who are born of parents who had become free before their birth, are citizens of a State, in the sense in which the word citizen is used in the Constitution of the United States. And this being the only matter in dispute on the pleadings, the court must be understood as speaking in this opinion of that class only, that is, of those persons who are the descendants of Africans who were imported into this country, and sold as slaves.

....

We proceed to examine the case as presented by the pleadings.

The words 'people of the United States' and 'citizens' are synonymous terms, and mean the same thing. They both describe the political body who, according to our republican institutions, form the sovereignty, and who hold the power and conduct the Government through their representatives. They are what we familiarly call the 'sovereign people,' and every citizen is one of this people, and a constituent member of this sovereignty. The question before us is, whether the class of persons described in the plea in abatement compose a portion of this people, and are constituent members of this sovereignty? We think they are not, and that they are not included, and were not intended to be included, under the word 'citizens' in the Constitution, and can therefore claim none of the rights and privileges which that instrument provides for and secures to citizens of the United States. On the contrary, they were at that time considered as a subordinate and inferior class of beings, who had been subjugated by the dominant race, and, whether emancipated or not, yet remained subject to their authority, and had no rights or privileges but such as those who held the power and the Government might choose to grant them.

It is not the province of the court to decide upon the justice or injustice, the policy or impolicy, of these laws. The decision of that question belonged to the political or law-making power; to those who formed the sovereignty and framed the Constitution. The duty of the court is, to interpret the instrument they have framed, with the best lights we can obtain on the subject, and to administer it as we find it, according to its true intent and meaning when it was adopted.

In discussing this question, we must not confound the rights of citizenship which a State may confer within its own limits, and the rights of citizenship as a member of the Union. It does not by any means follow, because he has all the rights and privileges of a citizen of a State, that he must be a citizen of the United States. He may have all of the rights and privileges of the citizen of a State, and yet not be entitled to the rights and privileges of a citizen in any other State. For, previous to the adoption of the Constitution of the United States, every State had the undoubted right to confer on whomsoever it pleased the character of citizen, and to endow him with all its rights. But this character of course was confined to the boundaries of the State, and gave him no rights or privileges in other States beyond those secured to him by the laws of nations and the comity of States. Nor have the several States surrendered the power of conferring these rights and privileges by adopting the Constitution of the United States. Each State may still confer them upon an alien, or any one it thinks proper, or upon any class or description of persons; yet he would not be a citizen in the sense in which that word is used in the Constitution of the United States, nor entitled to sue as such in one of its courts, nor to the privileges and immunities of a citizen in the other States. The rights which he would acquire would be restricted to the State which gave them. The Constitution has conferred on Congress the right to establish an uniform rule of naturalization, and this right is evidently exclusive, and has always been held by this court to be so. Consequently, no State, since the adoption of the Constitution, can by naturalizing an alien invest him with the rights and privileges secured to a citizen of a State under the Federal Government, although, so far as the State alone was concerned, he would undoubtedly be entitled to the rights of a citizen, and clothed with all the rights and immunities which the Constitution and laws of the State attached to that character.

It is very clear, therefore, that no State can, by any act or law of its own, passed since the adoption of the Constitution, introduce a new member into the political community created by the Constitution of the United States. It cannot make him a member of this community by making him a member of its own. And for the same reason it cannot introduce any person, or description of persons, who were not intended to be embraced in this new political family, which the Constitution brought into existence, but were intended to be excluded from it.

The question then arises, whether the provisions of the Constitution, in relation to the personal rights and privileges to which the citizen of a State should be entitled, embraced the negro African race, at that time in this country, or who might afterwards be imported, who had then or should afterwards be made free in any State; and to put it in the power of a single State to make him a citizen of the United States, and endue him with the full rights of citizenship in every other State without their consent? Does the Constitution of the United States act upon him whenever he shall be made free under the laws of a State, and raised there to the rank of a citizen, and immediately clothe him with all the privileges of a citizen in every other State, and in its own courts?

The court think the affirmative of these propositions cannot be maintained. And if it cannot, the plaintiff in error could not be a citizen of the State of Missouri, within the meaning of the Constitution of the United States, and, consequently, was not entitled to sue in its courts.

It is true, every person, and every class and description of persons, who were at the time of the adoption of the Constitution recognized as citizens in the several States, became also citizens of this new political body; but none other; it was formed by them, and for them and their posterity, but for no one else. And the personal rights and privileges guaranteed to citizens of this new sovereignty were intended to embrace those only who were then members of the several State communities, or who should afterwards by birthright or otherwise become members, according to the provisions of the Constitution and the principles on which it was founded. It was the union of those who were at that time members of distinct and separate political communities into one political family, whose power, for certain specified purposes, was to extend over the whole territory of the United States. And it gave to each citizen rights and privileges outside of his State *407 which he did not before possess, and placed him in every other State upon a perfect equality with its own citizens as to rights of person and rights of property; it made him a citizen of the United States.

It becomes necessary, therefore, to determine who were citizens of the several States when the Constitution was adopted. And in order to do this, we must recur to the Governments and institutions of the thirteen colonies, when they separated from Great Britain and formed new sovereignties, and took their places in the family of independent nations. We must inquire who, at that time, were recognized as the people or citizens of a State, whose rights and liberties had been outraged by the English Government; and who declared their independence, and assumed the powers of Government to defend their rights by force of arms.

In the opinion of the court, the legislation and histories of the times, and the language used in the Declaration of Independence, show, that neither the class of persons who had been imported as slaves, nor their descendants, whether they had become free or not, were then acknowledged as a part of the people, nor intended to be included in the general words used in that memorable instrument.

It is difficult at this day to realize the state of public opinion in relation to that unfortunate race, which prevailed in the civilized and enlightened portions of the world at the time of the

Declaration of Independence, and when the Constitution of the United States was framed and adopted. But the public history of every European nation displays it in a manner too plain to be mistaken.

They had for more than a century before been regarded as beings of an inferior order, and altogether unfit to associate with the white race, either in social or political relations; and so far inferior, that they had no rights which the white man was bound to respect; and that the negro might justly and lawfully be reduced to slavery for his benefit. He was bought and sold, and treated as an ordinary article of merchandise and traffic, whenever a profit could be made by it. This opinion was at that time fixed and universal in the civilized portion of the white race. It was regarded as an axiom in morals as well as in politics, which no one thought of disputing, or supposed to be open to dispute; and men in every grade and position in society daily and habitually acted upon it in their private pursuits, as well as in matters of public concern, without doubting for a moment the correctness of this opinion.

And in no nation was this opinion more firmly fixed or more *408 uniformly acted upon than by the English Government and English people. They not only seized them on the coast of Africa, and sold them or held them in slavery for their own use; but they took them as ordinary articles of merchandise to every country where they could make a profit on them, and were far more extensively engaged in this commerce than any other nation in the world.

The opinion thus entertained and acted upon in England was naturally impressed upon the colonies they founded on this side of the Atlantic. And, accordingly, a negro of the African race was regarded by them as an article of property, and held, and bought and sold as such, in every one of the thirteen colonies which united in the Declaration of Independence, and afterwards formed the Constitution of the United States. The slaves were more or less numerous in the different colonies, as slave labor was found more or less profitable. But no one seems to have doubted the correctness of the prevailing opinion of the time.

The legislation of the different colonies furnishes positive and indisputable proof of this fact.

It would be tedious, in this opinion, to enumerate the various laws they passed upon this subject. It will be sufficient, as a sample of the legislation which then generally prevailed throughout the British colonies, to give the laws of two of them; one being still a large slaveholding State, and the other the first State in which slavery ceased to exist.

The province of Maryland, in 1717, (ch. 13, s. 5,) passed a law declaring 'that if any free negro or mulatto intermarry with any white woman, or if any white man shall intermarry with any negro or mulatto woman, such negro or mulatto shall become a slave during life, excepting mulattoes born of white women, who, for such intermarriage, shall only become servants for seven years, to be disposed of as the justices of the county court, where such marriage so happens, shall think fit; to be applied by them towards the support of a public school within the said county. And any white man or white woman who shall intermarry as aforesaid, with any negro or mulatto, such white man or white woman shall become servants during the term of seven years, and shall be disposed of by the justices as aforesaid, and be applied to the uses aforesaid. '

The other colonial law to which we refer was passed by Massachusetts in 1705, (chap. 6.) It is entitled 'An act for the better preventing of a spurious and mixed issue,' &c.; and it provides, that 'if any negro or mulatto shall presume to smite or strike any person of the English or other Christian nation, such negro or mulatto shall be severely whipped, at the discretion of the justices before whom the offender shall be convicted.'

And 'that none of her Majesty's English or Scottish subjects, nor of any other Christian nation, within this province, shall contract matrimony with any negro or mulatto; nor shall any person, duly authorized to solemnize marriage, presume to join any such in marriage, on pain of forfeiting the sum of fifty pounds; one moiety thereof to her Majesty, for and towards the support of the Government within this province, and the other moiety to him or them that shall inform and sue for the same, in any of her Majesty's courts of record within the province, by bill, plaint, or information.'

We give both of these laws in the words used by the respective legislative bodies, because the language in which they are framed, as well as the provisions contained in them, show, too plainly to be misunderstood, the degraded condition of this unhappy race. They were still in force when the Revolution began, and are a faithful index to the state of feeling towards the class of persons of whom they speak, and of the position they occupied throughout the thirteen colonies, in the eyes and thoughts of the men who framed the Declaration of Independence and established the State Constitutions and Governments. They show that a perpetual and impassable barrier was intended to be erected between the white race and the one which they had reduced to slavery, and governed as subjects with absolute and despotic power, and which they then looked upon as so far below them in the scale of created beings, that intermarriages between white persons and negroes or mulattoes were regarded as unnatural and immoral, and punished as crimes, not only in the parties, but in the person who joined them in marriage. And no distinction in this respect was made between the free negro or mulatto and the slave, but this stigma, of the deepest degradation, was fixed upon the whole race.

We refer to these historical facts for the purpose of showing the fixed opinions concerning that race, upon which the statesmen of that day spoke and acted. It is necessary to do this, in order to determine whether the general terms used in the Constitution of the United States, as to the rights of man and the rights of the people, was intended to include them, or to give to them or their posterity the benefit of any of its provisions.

The language of the Declaration of Independence is equally conclusive:

It begins by declaring that, 'when in the course of human events it becomes necessary for one people to dissolve the political bands which have connected them with another, and to assume among the powers of the earth the separate and equal station to which the laws of nature and nature's God entitle them, a decent respect for the opinions of mankind requires that they should declare the causes which impel them to the separation.'

It then proceeds to say: 'We hold these truths to be self-evident: that all men are created equal; that they are endowed by their Creator with certain unalienable rights; that among them is life, liberty, and the pursuit of happiness; that to secure these rights, Governments are instituted, deriving their just powers from the consent of the governed.'

The general words above quoted would seem to embrace the whole human family, and if they were used in a similar instrument at this day would be so understood. But it is too clear for dispute, that the enslaved African race were not intended to be included, and formed no part of the people who framed and adopted this declaration; for if the language, as understood in that day, would embrace them, the conduct of the distinguished men who framed the Declaration of Independence would have been utterly and flagrantly inconsistent with the principles they asserted; and instead of the sympathy of mankind, to which they so confidently appealed, they would have deserved and received universal rebuke and reprobation.

....

Upon the whole, therefore, it is the judgment of this court, that it appears by the record before us that the plaintiff in error is not a citizen of Missouri, in the sense in which that word is used in the Constitution; and that the Circuit Court of the United States, for that reason, had no jurisdiction in the case, and could give no judgment in it. Its judgment for the defendant must, consequently, be reversed, and a mandate issued, directing the suit to be dismissed for want of jurisdiction.

Note

One way of viewing the role of race as seen through the eyes of courts such as Dred Scott is to consider the perspective addressed by Professor Charles W. Mills. Professor Mills has suggested that the racial balance in America can be seen in the context of a "Racial Contract" wherein there exists a "racial juridical system" with a clear division based on race dictated by both law and custom. The purpose of such a "contract" is to reproduce a racial order that secures privileges for white citizens by subordination of non-whites. This contractual concept requires that in order to maintain and secure these privileges White citizens must fulfill their roles as dominators. As such, support of racism becomes a civic duty and those white citizens who fail to fulfill their duties in this regard are to be considered derelict and by extension risk no longer being entitled to the rights and privileges of being "white". For a fuller discussion see, Charles W. Mills, THE RACIAL CONTRACT, P. 13-14, (Cornell University Press 1999)

The view, adopted by the Supreme Court in *Dred Scott*, that a slave was not a person but property became somewhat twisted in regard to criminal prosecution where the slave was a person for purposes of inflicting punishment under the criminal law but not a person for purpose of rights and privileges within the criminal justice system, as reflected in the below subsequent opinion of Judge Taney.

.....

UNITED STATES V. AMY
24 F. Cas. 792 (1859)

Opinion
TANEY, Circuit Justice.

The prisoner (Amy) in this case was indicted for stealing a letter from the post-office, containing articles of value, particularly described in the indictment. It appeared in evidence on the trial that she was at the time the offence was committed, and at the time of trial, a slave, and her counsel therefore prayed the direction of the court to the jury that the prisoner was not embraced in the description of persons to which the law in question applied, and upon whom it intends to inflict punishment. The motion was overruled by the court, and the prisoner, under its direction, was found guilty by the jury, as charged in the indictment; and a motion is now made to set aside the verdict, and grant a new trial, upon the ground that the instruction asked for ought to have been given, and that the court erred in refusing it. The act of March 3, 1825 (section 22), under which the prisoner is indicted, provides that, if any person shall steal or take a letter from the mail, or any post-office, the offender shall, upon conviction thereof, be imprisoned not less than two, nor more than ten, years.

It has been argued in support of the motion that a slave, in the eye of the law, is regarded as property; and, as the act of congress speaks only of persons, without any reference to the property of the master, and makes no provision to compensate him for its loss, it was not intended, and does not operate, upon slaves.

It is true that a slave is the property of the master, and his right of property is recognized and secured by the constitution and laws of the United States; and it is equally true that he is not a citizen, and would not be embraced in a law operating only upon that class of persons. Yet, he is a person, and is always spoken of and described as such in the state papers and public acts of the United States. Thus, the two clauses in the constitution which point particularly to property in slaves, and sanction its acquisition and provide for its protection, both speak of them as persons, without any other or further word of description. The clause which authorized their importation declared 'that the migration or importation of such persons as any of the states now existing shall think proper to admit shall not be prohibited by congress prior to the year one thousand eight hundred and eight.' And the clause intended to protect the right of property in the master provides 'that no person held to service or labor in one state, under the laws thereof, escaping into another, shall, in consequence of any law or regulation therein, be discharged from such service or labor; but shall be delivered upon claim of the party to whom such labor or service may be due.' And the third clause of the second section of the first article, which apportions the representation in congress among the several states, describes them by the same word, and provides 'that representation and direct taxes shall be apportioned among the several states which may be included within this Union, according to their respective numbers, which shall be determined by adding to the whole number of free persons, including those bound to service for a term of years, and excluding Indians not taxed, three-fifths of all other persons'; and under this description slaves have always been enumerated in the census, and the slave-holding states represented in congress according to their numbers, in the proportion specified, and no one has ever questioned the right of the slave-holding states to this representation, or doubted the meaning of the words 'all other persons.' It is evident, therefore, that the word 'person' is used in the constitution to describe slaves, as well as freemen, and a court of justice would not be justified in refusing to give the same word the same construction when it is used in an act of congress, unless there was something in the object and policy of the law, or in the provisions with which the word was associated, which manifestly indicated that it was used in a different and narrower sense, and intended to be confined to persons who are free.

There is certainly nothing in the object and policy of the law in question from which it can be inferred that slaves were not intended to be punished for the offences therein enumerated. The offences were as likely to be committed by slaves as by freemen, and the mischief is equally great whether committed by the one or the other; and, if a slave is not within the law, it would be in the power of the evil disposed to train and tutor him for these depredations on the mails and post-offices, and, as the slave could not be a witness, the culprit, who was the real instigator of the crime, would not be brought to punishment. And if the slave himself is not within the law, the crime might be committed daily, and with perfect impunity, and all of the safeguards which congress intended to provide for the protection of its mails and post-offices would be of no value. Such a construction would defeat the whole evident object and policy of the law, and would rather tempt to the commission of these offences by the certainty of impunity, than to prevent them by the fear of punishment.

In expounding this law, we must not lose sight of the twofold character which belongs to the slave. He is a person, and also property. As property, the rights of the owner are entitled to the protection of the law. As a person, he is bound to obey the law, and may, like any other person, be punished if he offends against it; and he may be embraced in the provisions of the law, either by the description of property or as a person, according to the subject-matter upon which congress or a state is legislating.

It is true, that some of the offences created by this act of congress subject the party to both fine and imprisonment, and it is evident that the incapacity and disabilities of a slave were not in the mind and contemplation of congress when it inflicted a pecuniary punishment; for he can have no property, and is also incapable of making a contract, and consequently could not borrow the amount of the fine; and a small fine, which would be but a slight punishment to another, would, in effect, in his case, be imprisonment for life, if the court adopted the usual course of committing the party until the fine was paid. And we think it must be admitted that, in imposing these pecuniary penalties, congress could not have intended to embrace persons who were slaves, and we greatly doubt whether a court of justice could lawfully imprison a party for not doing an act, which, by the law of his condition, it was impossible for him to perform; and to imprison him, to compel the master to pay the fine, would be equally objectionable, as that would be punishing an innocent man for the crime of another.

The case before us, however, does not involve this question, and we must not be understood as expressing a decided opinion upon it. The offence of which the prisoner has been found guilty is punished by the law by imprisonment only, and that punishment is, without doubt, looked to with as much apprehension and fear, and felt as severely, by the slave as it is by the freeman. But, although the difficulty above mentioned will arise in passing the sentence of the law where both fine and imprisonment are imposed, yet that circumstance will not justify the court in departing from the sense and meaning in which the word 'person' is used in the constitution; especially when it is obvious that the whole object and purpose of this act of congress would be defeated if the word 'person,' as used in it, was held not to embrace a person who was a slave. Nor do we doubt the authority of congress to pass this law. It is true that no compensation is provided for the master for the loss of service during the period of imprisonment. But the clause in the 5th amendment of the constitution which declares that private property shall not be taken for public use without just compensation cannot, upon any fair interpretation, apply to the case of a slave who is punished in his own person for an offense committed by him, although the punishment may incidentally affect the property of another to whom he belongs. The clause obviously applies to cases where private property is taken to be used as property for the benefit of the government, and not to cases where crimes are punished by law. And if, in one of those contingencies which sometimes arise in time of war, a slave is pressed by the proper authority into the public service, in order to be employed as a laborer or teamster, or in any other manner, this clause of the constitution undoubtedly makes it the duty of congress to compensate the master for the loss he sustains. In such cases, and in all other cases where the slave is taken and used as property for the benefit of the government, the government acts directly and exclusively upon the master's right of property, without any reference to the personal rights or personal duties of the slave towards the government. It deals with him as property only, and not as a person, and, as it takes property to be used for the public emolument, it must pay for it.

But punishment for crime stands upon very different principles. A person, whether free or slave, is not taken for public use when he is punished for an offence against the law. The public, in such cases, acts in self-defence, to preserve its own existence, and protect its members in their rights of person and rights of property; and the loss which the master sustains in his property is incidental, and necessarily arises from its twofold character, since the slave, as a person, may commit offences which society has a right to punish for its own safety, although the punishment may render the property of the master of little or no value. But this hazard is unavoidably and inseparably associated with this description of property, and it can furnish no reason why a slave, like any other person, should not be punished by the United States for offences against its laws, passed within the scope of its delegated authority.

It is not for the court to say whether the government is or is not bound, injustice, to compensate the master for the loss of service during the time the slave shall be imprisoned. The question does not depend upon any provision in the constitution, nor has it been provided for by any act of congress; and, as the matter now stands, it is a question for the decision of the political department of the government, and not for the judicial; and, consequently, is one upon which this court forbears to express an opinion. It would seem, from the statements in the argument at the bar, that in different slaveholding states different opinions upon the subject have been adopted and acted on by the constituted authorities.

In maintaining the power of the United States to pass this law, it is, however, proper to say that, as these letters, with the money in them, were stolen in Virginia, the party might undoubtedly have been punished in the state tribunals, according to the laws of the state, without any reference to the post-office or the act of congress; because, from the nature of our government, the same act may be an offence against the laws of the United States and also of a state, and be punishable in both. This was considered and decided in the supreme court of the United States in the case of Fox v. Ohio, and the punishment in one sovereignty is no bar to his punishment in the other. Yet in all civilized countries it is recognized as a fundamental principle of justice that a man ought not to be punished twice for the same offence; and, if this party had been punished for the larceny in the state tribunal, the court would have felt it to be its duty to suspend sentence, and to represent the facts to the president, to give him an opportunity of ordering a nolle prosequi, or granting a pardon. But there does not appear to have been any proceeding in the state tribunals, or under the state laws, to punish the offence, and, as the prisoner has been proceeded against according to the laws of the United States, and found guilty by a jury selected and impaneled according to the act of congress, we see no ground for setting aside the verdict or suspending the sentence, and the motion is therefore overruled.

Daniel John Flanigan, THE CRIMINAL LAW OF SLAVERY AND FREEDOM, 1800-1868, a Thesis Submitted in Partial fulfillment of the Requirements for the Degree of Doctor of Philosophy, Rice University, 1973, Chapter II *From Master to Magistrate* [excerpt reprinted by permission of Dr. Daniel John Flanigan, phD]

....

Southern states adopted various methods of trial for slaves accused of minor crimes, but the central figure in all of these proceedings was the justice of the peace, the jack-of-all-trades of county government. Though these officials were never lauded for their legal acumen, it required small legal talent to try slaves. The statutes, where they bothered to elaborate at all, usually prescribed a brief and summary process for disposition of such cases. The justice might proceed to trial on a written complaint or statement of the offense, and then continue unhampered by strict rules of evidence, juries, or in most cases, defense counsel. As Jeffrey R. Brackett has described the process in Maryland, the justice "might be called away from business or pleasure, when drunk or sober, to give sentence within a few hours perhaps of the commission of the offense, while the injured neighbors were still angry." Moreover, there was usually no appeal from the decision of justice of the peace. In many states a single justice tried and punished slaves and also free blacks for all manner of noncapital offenses from insulting whites to grand larceny. But whites did not always entrust their own fates to the mercy of the magistrates. While a Georgia justice of the peace handled the pre-trial proceedings, even in misdemeanor cases he did not preside at the trial, which proceeded before a higher court and a jury. Still, whites in the antebellum period did not and do not even now altogether escape the summary justice of magistrates. Efficiency militated against jury trials in minor cases. In Virginia, for example, four of the justices who composed the county or corporation court could try misdemeanor cases involving whites, but blacks still suffered discrimination since only one justice handled their cases. if a slave was accused of a noncapital offense of a higher grade than petit larceny, he was tried before a court of two justices of the peace, the judge of the probate court, and a jury. Texas provided fuller guarantees than any other slave state for blacks accused of non-capital offenses. There all blacks received a jury trial and slaves were provided with court-appointed counsel.

Since justice of the peace courts were seldom courts of record, it is difficult to determine the quantity and quality of justice they dispensed. That several states required the concurrence of other whites before a magistrate passed sentence evidenced an element of mistrust on the part of the slaveholders. On the other hand, justices of the peace may have been susceptible to the restraining influence of the master, but the written record provides little basis for more than speculation on this point. Though the role of the rural justice of the peace in disciplining blacks may never be fully understood because of lack of evidence, the urban versions of the justices' courts, the mayors' and recorders' or police courts, often left sufficient records of their proceedings or attracted enough newspaper reportage to provide insight into their role in the criminal justice system. Though the workings of the municipal courts might reflect in some degree the activities of rural justices, there were large differences between them. While urban life required a diminution of often corrupt, legal system served as much to open opportunities as to restrict them." Conflicts of jurisdiction between state and city courts, crowded dockets, and incompetence appears to have actually aided slaves. Ironically statutes and ordinances, by making slaves liable to punishment for such a large number of crimes, ensured that the courts would not be able to cope with the offenders.

Though justices of the peace in rural areas and mayoral and recorders' courts in the cities handled the bulk of criminal cases involving slaves, and though they constituted slaves' primary contact with the institutions of public justice, their importance should not be exaggerated. Whipping was a severe punishment, but the magistrates were seldom allowed to decide issues of life and death. Such crucial determinations usually were the province of higher courts, operating under much more elaborate and strict procedural rules. As slaves were accused of more serious crimes, they were more likely to escape the personal justice that the master, the private citizen, the patrol, and the magistrate in varying degrees represented. As with most other aspects of the law of slavery, however, Southern states adopted a variety of methods for trying slaves accused of capital crimes. At one extreme were Virginia and South Carolina, which placed a high premium on efficiency and speedy justice. At the other extreme were states like Alabama, Mississippi and North Carolina, which guaranteed substantial equality with whites.

In South Carolina two justices and three to five freeholders sat in judgment on all blacks accused of capital offenses. Guilty verdicts did not have to be unanimous. Until 1833 the only appeal allowed condemned blacks was in the nature of a writ of prohibition, which could not be addressed to errors committed during the course of the trial but only to the legality of the court's assumption of jurisdiction. The few cases that arose illustrated the importance of even this severely limited right of appeal. In 1820 a slaveowner sought to overturn a guilty verdict against his slave for an attempted poisoning. Not only did the court fail to notify the master that his slave was going to be tried, but the two "justices" and one of the "freeholders" were not legally qualified to preside at slave trials. Though a state law directed that slaves be tried within six days of the commission of the offense, the court had tried him after the allotted period. In addition, that eminent tribunal had allowed the alleged victim and even one of the presiding "justices" to testify against the slave without oath and in the absence of the accused. The South Carolina Court of Appeals overruled the decision because the inferior court was not legally constituted. "It is a case sui generis," the court said, "where a tribunal is created by act of assembly, to try cases of life and death,' and contrary to the rules of the common law. Every feeling of humanity and justice revolts at the idea, that any other mode of trial less formal and substantial than what the act has prescribed, should be sanctioned." But if the members of the inferior court would have possessed the requisite qualifications, notified the owner, and tried the case within the prescribed period, they could have flouted common law rules of evidence. In an 1824 case before the Court of Appeals the record revealed that the lower court had instructed defense counsel -that his efforts would avail nothing, as on the former trial of the prisoner for the same offense, they had heard the said counsel, and he had not made an alteration of the opinion they had formed.-The conviction was not overturned on this point but because proper warrants had not been issued the freeholders, and one of their Dumber did not reside in the county where the offense occurred.

Despite these cases the South Carolina Court of Appeals did not vigorously intrude upon the prerogatives of lower tribunals. In fact the high court was far more interested in convictions of guilty slaves than in the means by which trial courts obtained such convictions. In 1830, when a master objected that the magistrates had tried his slave more than six days after the offense, allegedly insurrection, and that other slaves were allowed to testify against him. without oath, the Court of Appeals was not disturbed. Judge Bay remarked that "when the dreadful ... consequences of the insurrection of slaves in South Carolina. are taken into consideration, it appears to me, that the judges of the superior courts ought to be extremely cautious in interfering with the magistrates and freeholders ... and that they ought not to be eagle eyed in ~viewing their proceedings, and in finding out and supporting every formal error or neglect, where the real merits have been duly and fairly attended to, and determined according to justice."

In the late 1820's and throughout the 1830's the method of trying blacks for capital crimes underwent considerable change. A special court was created for Charleston by a series of acts passed between 1827 and 1833. In 1831 the master received the right to challenge prospective freeholders for cause. In 1832 the legislature required unanimity for the conviction of Charleston free Negroes. For slaves only the consent of the freeholders and one of the magistrates was necessary. At the end of the decade the mode of trial for all blacks outside of Charleston was changed. After 1839 five freeholders and one magistrate presided at slave trials. The most important modification of previous law, however, was the grant of an expanded right of appeal in 1833. Advocating further protection of slaves accused of crime, Governor Robert Y. Hayne told the legislature:

> It is true that the moral sense of the community afford them, in general, protection from injustice, yet it is sufficient for us to know that the justices and freeholders are not unfrequently selected by the prosecutor, to perceive at once the liability of such a system to gross abuse. Capital offences committed by slaves, involving the nicest questions of the law, are often tried by courts composed of persons ignorant of the law and left without the aid of counsel.

The legislature heeded Hayne's message and allowed convicted slaves an appeal to a circuit judge or one of the judges of the Court of Appeals. Though there were various later attempts to seek appellate review from the Court of Appeals sitting en banc, such appeals were allowed only when the judge who heard the original appeal requested the high court to decide the case. Predictably, few judges doubted their own wisdom enough to seek the advice of their fellow jurists.

......

Though no other slaveholding states adopted procedural systems. that consistently weighed so heavily on accused slaves as those of Virginia and South Carolina, several opted for similar arrangements. Georgia did not extend equality to slaves until 1850. A tribunal of one magistrate and ten slaveowners, nine of whom constituted quorum, tried Louisiana slaves. A unanimous verdict was required for conviction or acquittal, but if the court could not reach unanimity, it could decree corporal punishment as a compromise. In 1849 this system was challenged as a denial of slaves' constitutional right to a jury trial, but the Louisiana Supreme Court predictably denied that slaves possessed any such constitutional right. In 1853 the high court declared that the law did "not demand on the trial of slaves..., an observance of the technical rules which regulate criminal proceedings in the higher courts." Still, the Supreme Court had ruled earlier that slaves had the important right of appeal, which helped to check the worst abuses. While Delaware and Maryland granted slaves a large measure of equality in criminal cases, no slaves' cases were appealed to those states' highest courts in the antebellum period, and though Kentucky slaves had the right to a jury trial, the Kentucky Court of Appeals did not rule on a slave's appeal until 1859'. As the experience of other appellate courts demonstrated. the right of appeal was crucial. Even where blacks enjoyed a substantial measure of equality, lower courts frequently committed serious errors. A Tennessee Supreme Court decision of 1826 revealed the importance that contemporary jurists placed on the right of appeal and demonstrated how a sympathetic appellate court could expand the rights of slaves.

Until 1835 Tennessee relegated accused slaves to special tribunals composed of three justices and twelve slaveholders. The legislature had not expressly provided for appeals from these courts. In 1826 a sympathetic master attempted to rescue his slave from the noose by appealing the slave's murder conviction to a circuit court, which refused to grant a writ of certiorari. On appeal the Supreme Court agreed with the master that the verdict was contrary to the evidence. The real question. however. was whether a remedy existed for the trial court's error, invoking the maxim "that there is no wrong without a remedy," Judge John Haywood overruled the circuit court. Though a writ of error would not lie in such a case, he argued, the writ of certiorari was peculiarly suited to review the proceedings of courts, such as the Tennessee tribunal for slave trials, which proceeded by rules other than those of the common law. "And in all conscience and justice," he asked. "is not this in itself right and proper? Shall it be said that a human being shall be condemned to death by a wrongful sentence, and that there is no power residing in the law to rescue him from it? Does the law delight in cruelty? Will it inflict punishment where it is not deserved? Will it have no power to avoid le unjust sentence? Then where is the justice of the law, and where is its boasted humanity?" In a concurring opinion Judge James Peck claimed that a different decision would furnish "a barbarous example of the execution of a human being, mocked on his trial by perhaps the introduction of illegal evidence, his triers, at intervals, mixing with the crowd, or, perhaps, some of the thousand accidental errors that are daily committed by higher courts, .. .

....

The equalitarian commitment in states where slavery was strongest suggests also that procedural fairness was compatible with slavery in its most rigid form. Southerners recognized that they were protecting property rights as well as human life. Arguing for more humane treatment of criminally accused slaves, the Charleston Mercury remarked, "Our policy as a slaveholding state requires that this species of property should be protected by a better system." Southern jurists also were able to use procedural fairness to fuel the pro-slavery fire. "[I]t is the crowning glory of our 'peculiar institutions,'" wrote Florida's Chief Judge, "that whenever life is involved, the slave stands upon as safe ground as the master." After the Georgia legislature finally extended equality to slaves in 1850, in the first Supreme Court case construing the act Judge Nisbet, dazzled by the generosity of his fellow citizens, exulted that "by this Act, as well as by numerous other provisions of the law, whilst they are in law and in fact, property, they are recognized as human creatures. For the justice and mercy of the slaveholding state of Georgia, an appeal well lies from the slanderous imputations of the ignorant, the fanatical, or the willfully base, ..." But Joseph Lumpkin, Chief Judge of the Georgia Supreme Court and the most polemical of Southern judges, best stated the equality-within-slavery paradox. Confronted with a slave's appeal from a rape conviction, Lumpkin wrote:

> I shall endeavor, as briefly and dispassionately as I can, to investigate the numerous points made
> by the record. The crime, from the very nature of it, is calculated to excite indignation in every
> heart; and when perpetrated by a slave on a free white female of immature mind and body,
> that indignation becomes greater, and is more difficult to repress. The very helplessness of the
> accused, however, like infancy and womanhood, appeals to our sympathy. And a controversy
> between the State of Georgia and a slave is so unequal, as of itself to divest the mind of all
> warmth and prejudice, and enable it to exercise its judgment in the most temperate manner.

While Lumpkin elevated the slave, he also drove him relentlessly down.

Of course, not all Southern courts shared the attitudes of the Georgia Supreme Court, which was so dominated by Lumpkin and his Gothic temperament. AS A. E. Keir Nash has forcefully argued, certain Southern judges not only solidified but extended statutory guarantees of procedural rights; however to designate the Georgia Supreme Court a "pro-slavery" court as opposed to other "libertarian" courts, as Nash has done, is misleading. Almost all Southern judges worked within the confines of the pro-slavery mentality, but some, given a legislative mandate of equality to build upon, realized that full recognition of the slave's. humanity in a criminal trial did not endanger his status as the master's property. In this respect Lumpkin's attitudes were widely shared by legislators as well as judge. Guarantees of procedural fairness did not represent "libertarian-assaults on the slave system but rather revealed the most generous dimension of the slaveholding mind as it expressed itself in law. By avoiding the tempting expedients of efficiency and speedy justice Southerners affirmed the noblest aspects of their common law heritage.

Just as the motives behind the equalitarian thrusts of the nineteenth century were highly complex, so were the effects of such actions. Though Southern states might guarantee slaves certain procedural rights, not all of these procedures worked toward the benefit of the slaves. The most striking example was the grand jury. For example, after examination of the activities of North Carolina grand juries, Richard D. Younger concluded that they were often exceedingly vigilant on matters of slave crime and harsh in their treatment of slaves. But whites as well as blacks were dubious about the protective functions of grand juries. Grand juries always played a dual role, prosecutorial as well as protective. Often the grand jury served merely as an arm of the prosecutor, or grand jurors used their considerable powers to harass citizens and indulge in personal vendettas against their enemies. In the latter part of the nineteenth century the grand jury as an institution came under serious attack, and many states abolished it altogether. If grand juries were frequently oppressive even to whites and if Younger's conclusions about North Carolina describe grand jurors' attitudes throughout the South, slaves gained little from this aspect of their equality.

Though it had its darker side, one aspect of the grand jury requirement worked in slaves' favor. In an age when grand juries and prosecutors were less sophisticated and deprived of the priceless form books that aid modern prosecutors, and where courts were still often wary of even the slightest flaws in indictments, the states paid the price in numerous new trials because of convictions based on faulty indictments. Not all Southern courts were disposed to view indictments with sharp eyes. When a slave objected to an indictment that did not charge him with rape upon a free white female and thus did not charge him with a crime he could have committed, Georgia Chief Justice Lumpkin lamented: "Will the age of technicalities never pass away? Shall the law, affecting the dearest interests of men. their property, life and character, 'coming home to their businesses and bosoms,' never become a popular science?" Still, the Georgia court generally followed tradition and granted new trials because of improper indictments. Usually the legislature had to require the court. to desist from invoking mere technicalities, though courts often responded favorably to legislative curtailment of their ability to overturn convictions on the basis of minor errors in form. When the Tennessee legislature acted to reduce the number of convictions set aside because of technicalities in the indictment, the Supreme Court gladly welcomed "the great reform". But few legislatures had taken steps to aid the courts in this matter before the Civil War, and courts were seldom inclined to innovation, especially where the rights of the accused were involved.

The rationale behind the insistence on carefully drawn indictments was that the accused had the right to know precisely the nature of the crime he had allegedly committed. This quite sensible requirement, however, when too rigidly applied, resulted in numerous reversals and new trials because of miniscule drafting errors. The North Carolina Supreme Court reached the most absurd results in its scrutiny of faulty indictments. In one case the court overturned a slave's conviction because the indictment did not conclude "*contra formam statui.*" Another slave received a new trial because the indictment concluded -against the form of the statutes" when the state was seeking conviction under one statute only.

......

Like the grand jury, the petit jury had a special significance for blacks. As abolitionists enjoyed pointing out, if a slave was truly equal, he must have a jury of his peers, in other words a jury of his fellow bondsmen. The great protection of trial by jury, so dear to the common law, gave less security to slaves than to whites. In his study of Virginia slavery J. C. Ballagh argued that trial by magistrates was actually a boon to the slave since the justices were far more select than a jury and one dissenting vote would result in an acquittal. Ballagh's contention has some merit. In the tight local communities of the antebellum South there were abundant possibilities for prejudice, especially in juries that included nonslave¬owners. A few states were sensitive to this problem. Louisiana required that those who assisted the magistrate in slave trials be slaveholders. Alabama and North Carolina, though they made slaves equal to whites in other respects, kept their requirements that the jury be composed of those who owned slave property. In an 1826 case before the North Carolina Supreme Court the state argued that if the slave was equal to whites in other areas, he must also be tried by the same juries, but the court preferred to continue the older policy. Judge John Taylor recognized that the slave, though legally a person in a criminal trial, remained a chattel. The requirement of the slaveowner jury

> was intended to surround the life of the slave with additional safeguards, and more effectually
> to protect the property of the owner, ... That the master could have assurance of an equitable
> trial by persons who had property constantly exposed to similar accusations, and who would
> not wantonly sacrifice the life of a slave, but yield it only to a sense of justice, daily experience is
> sufficient to convince us. The property of a man is more secure when he cannot be deprived of it
> except by a jury, part of whom, at least, have the like kind of property to 1ose.

Behind this reasoning were deep fears of the nonslaveholding class who might harbor a dangerous hatred of the masters' human property. Though Tennessee later abandoned its requirement of a slaveholder jury, an 1825 law governing slave trials frankly recognized these fears.

The statute allowed nonslaveholders as jurors if a sufficient number of slaveholders could not be obtained. But if the owner could show that the slaveless jurors had divided the jury, he had grounds for an appeal. This was actually a form of disfranchisment directed against nonslaveowners, but despite frank recognitions of class antagonism in some jurisdictions, most states were democratic enough to allow nonslaveowner juries. Still, the North Carolina Supreme Court's reasoning was quite sound, and if slaves were aware of such issues, they may well have regretted such democracy.

Whatever the composition of juries, they could not always be trusted to serve justice. The hysterical atmosphere that pervaded local communities in the wake of a particularly serious crime could make it almost impossible for a slave to secure an unbiased jury. The slave had limited weapons to combat jury prejudice in the form of peremptory challenges, challenges for cause, continuance, and change of venue. Peremptory challenges might be quickly exhausted, and then the slave had to depend on the skill of his counsel and the wisdom of the trial judge to protect him from biased jurors. Though appellate court. decided a few -cases on the qualifications of jurors, the small number of such cases indicated the difficulty of proving bias. Moreover, in the many sparsely settled counties it was difficult to find jurors who had not formed an opinion as to the guilt or innocence of the accused.

For example, Louisiana slaves were denied the right of peremptory challenge and could not apply for a change of venue. Thus challenge for cause was an especially important right. In an 1844 case before the Supreme Court the trial judge had overruled defense counsel's objection to a juror who had definitely made up his mind as to the prisoner's guilt. The court pointed to the immense difficulties of jury selection in certain communities:

> However desirable it may be to procure jurors whose minds are prepared to receive their impressions alone from the testimony submitted to them, yet the experience of almost every term of a district court held in the country parishes, teaches, that this is often impracticable. The ends of justice require, that such offenders should be brought to punishment, and they will not be permitted to shield themselves from the consequences of their crimes by perpetrating acts of such heinousness as to excite universal inquiry, which inquiry leads to the formation of an opinion.

Though the juror should have been rejected because he had formed a definite opinion, if his opinion would have been indefinite or formed with vague rumor, he could have been sworn. The high courts of Tennessee and Mississippi encountered similar problems.

Change of venue and continuance were also limited remedies. Since change of venue was a discretionary matter with the trial judge, it was difficult to prove that he had exceeded his discretion in refusing to grant the application." During one Tennessee trial 212 men were summoned in an effort to secure an impartial jury for a slave accused of killing his master. Though the eligible population of the county must have been nearly exhausted in the process, the trial judge denied the slave's application for change of venue. When the slave appealed his conviction on that ground, the Supreme Court had to admit that venue was so firmly in the discretion of the trial judge that "it is difficult to perceive how a case could exist, where this court could say the circuit judge erred in not changing the venue under this statute." A successful motion for continuance could at least prevent the trial from taking place in the midst of hysteria, but the slave would eventually be tried in the same county, and opinions once formed were hard to alter.

Once the jury was impaneled and avoided gross misconduct during the progress of the trial, it was difficult for appellate courts to overturn the verdict even if it was contrary to the evidence. A three-year battle in the 1850's that pitted Major, a Tennessee slave, and the state Supreme Court against several juries revealed the often illusory protection provided by white juries. Major was accused of attempting to rape a young white girl. Though Major had known the girl most of her life and had even slept in the same room with the girl and her mother, she accused him of assaulting her. First convicted in 1854, Major appealed, and the Supreme Court ordered a new trial because the record had omitted material portions of the evidence, and the girl had not satisfactorily identified Major as her assailant. When the case finally returned to the high court in 1857, there had been several changes of venue and three different convictions, two of which had been set aside, one because of jury misconduct.

When the Supreme Court reviewed the evidence, it discovered a maze of conflicting testimony. Almost all of the witnesses had contradicted themselves and each other. Several children who were supposedly present at the scene were not interrogated at all, and it appeared that the prosecutor had not even attempted to introduce them as witnesses. The girl's testimony was hopelessly inaccurate. At one point in the trial she was "asked if she did not have great feeling against the prisoner. She said she had; that she wanted him and his counsel, and all that would take his part and defend him, hung; that she could take him out and hang him herself, and saw his head off with an old saw, and would do so if they would let her, and also the counsel that defended him." Despite the chaos of the prosecution's evidence, the jury found Major guilty. The Supreme Court took the unusual step of directly aborting the jury's verdict and acquitting Major. By interfering with the verdict in that particular case, the court attempted to reaffirm the larger meaning of trial by jury. It wrote:

> This case strongly admonishes us of the necessity of a watchful vigilance and an unyielding firmness on the part of judicial officers to see that the invaluable right of fair trial by an impartial jury' should not be disregarded. ....This provision, securing to the accused the right of trial by an 'impartial jury' is not unmeaning—was not placed in our Bill of Rights without motive, and cannot be disregarded by the courts.

But the Tennessee decision was the exception rather than the rule.

In most states appellate courts were forbidden to review the facts, and jury verdicts were seldom questioned. Generally, if the courts were disturbed by a jury verdict, they could not directly attack it but were forced to use the more covert and devious method of criticizing the trial judge's charge to the jury rather than the verdict itself. Despite the limitations of the jury as a protective device for the accused slave, however, trial by jury was probably fairer than trial by magistrates. Justices of the peace depended on community support not only for reelection but also for the effective enforcement of their decrees. They could be as susceptible as private citizens to bias. A Virginia lawyer, protesting the murder conviction of a slave by a magistrates' court, told the Governor that "But for the excitement which prevailed, I could not have conceived such a sentence possible, by reflecting court." Moreover, in states where jury' trials were required slaves were more likely to benefit from the entire procedural system that protected whites, including the crucial right of appeal, while the magistrates were frequently courts of first and last resort.

. . . .

Of more importance to slaves than the master's testimony were the rules governing the admissibility of their confessions. In many instances whites employed coercion to extract admissions of guilt from slaves. Probably the most spectacular example occurred during the insurrection scare that swept through Kentucky and Tennessee in 1856. At the Cumberland Iron Works in Tennessee sixty-five slaves were tortured (one was killed in the process) until they admitted their complicity in the alleged insurrection scheme. In hundreds of other cases individual slaves endured similar treatment. The New Orleans police admitted publicly that they used strongarm methods to extract slaves' confessions. Confrontation with coerced confession cases required appellate courts to understand and take into account the slave's vulnerable position in Southern society as well as the dynamics of the master-slave relationship in applying the general law of confessions to slaves. Again courts were faced with the paradoxical condition of the slave—for him to be truly equal in law he required special treatment. In a brilliant argument before the Mississippi Court of Appeals a slave's lawyer stated this paradox.

> The man who is born a slave, raised a slave, and knows, and feels his destiny and lot is to die a slave; always under a superior, controlling his actions and his will, cannot be supposed to act or speak voluntarily and of his free will, while surrounded by fifteen or twenty of those to whom he knows he is subservient, and by the law bound to obey. Such a being, in his physical, moral, and intellectual faculties, is, and must ever be, more or less subservient to the will and wishes of the freeman...

. . . .

Slaves' appeals offered the courts ample opportunities for application of the subjective approach to unique fact situations because of the anomalous status of slaves both in law and in daily life, but the most basic question that courts had to answer was whether the rules concerning coerced confessions came into play when private citizens rather than public officials interrogated slaves. In the antebellum South, where the predominant mode of life was rural and where public institutions and officials were few, the maintenance of law and order depended upon the active participation of the citizenry. Posses were only the most obvious examples, but at least members of a posse were usually deputized. Frequently law enforcement was even more informal. Citizens sometimes acted in a wholly private capacity as detectives, and once a suspect fell under suspicion, as interrogators. Too little is known about the role of private citizens in apprehending and questioning white suspect, but when slaves committed serious crimes, private individuals usually played a more important role than public officials. Not only did the law encourage individuals to apprehend and sometimes administer punishment to slaves guilty of minor offenses such as illegal travel, but the absence of peace officers meant that the only effective law enforcement might necessarily be entirely private in nature. Thus, it was extremely important that the slave be protected against the impositions of overzealous citizen interrogators.

Three appellate courts confronted this issue directly. In North Carolina a slave accused of murdering his master was told by an angry white that he would be killed if he did not confess. The white also struck him in the face. Later another interrogator told him he would be hanged if he did not tell the truth. The slave persisted in his denials until a large angry crowd gathered when he admitted his guilt. The confession was admitted at trial, but the Supreme Court reversed. "It was the duty of every good citizen" said the court, "to do his utmost in order to find the perpetrators of the crime, but care should have been taken not to exceed the limits allowed by the rules of law." In a similar case the Louisiana Supreme Court designated the arresting whites "as public officers for the time being; ..." The most remarkable decision of this kind, however, issued from the Mississippi Court of Appeals. Two whites had bullied a slave into confessing by beating him with a stick and threatening to shoot him. The court ruled that the law applied equally to private individuals as to the state and went even further. The slave not only had the right "to preserve his entire silence in regard to the killing, but to resist force by force, ...".

While private individuals played a large role in the criminal law of slavery, the master was the most important authority figure for the slave and thus a confession to the master presented a special problem. A Virginia case involving a free black raised issues that also surfaced in slaves' cases. The defendant, suspected of rape, was apprenticed to a master who was also a justice of the peace. The master exhorted his apprentice to confess, telling him. 'I will save your neck if I can." This was clearly a promise of favor, but the court admitted the confession. Since the master was not taking part in the actual arrest or examination of the prisoner, the court did not consider him to be a person who had authority over his apprentice! Though claiming that it was not -insensible to the force of the argument ..., founded upon the status of the prisoner, (and] the extreme ignorance and dependence of that class upon those by whom they are held in service," the court felt that the jury could weigh such matters in assessing the worth of the confession. In other words the admissibility of such confessions was not a matter of law for the court to rule upon, but the jury could hear any such confession and supposedly disregard it completely if the jurors considered it coerced or untrustworthy. In addition the Virginia judiciary would not formulate special rules in accordance with blacks' inferior position in society. The case of an apprenticed free black man was an unusual one, but when other courts examined the conditions surrounding slaves' confessions to their masters, they arrived at a different estimate of the dependability of such admissions.

The first court to rule on the question apparently took the most advanced position. In an 1830 case two of the three judges of the North Carolina Supreme Court stated that a slave's confession to the master should never be admitted because of the essentially coercive nature of the master-slave relationship. But since there were alternate grounds for reversal, and each judge filed a separate concurring opinion, none of which was designated as the majority opinion, it was difficult to separate decisional law from dictum. Unfortunately, since the precise issue did not again come before the court (which may have indicated that trial courts in fact refused to admit such confessions), it is difficult to ascertain whether the lower tribunals adhered to the opinion of the two judges. Though other courts did not go so far, several did agree that confessions to the master should be carefully scrutinized. As the Florida Supreme Court observed, the "absolute control" that the master exercised over the slave "should induce the courts at all times to receive their confessions with the utmost caution and distrust." The particular case eminently justified this approach since the slave's confession was later revealed to be untrue. Still, courts. refused to reject all confessions made to the master. The paramount reason for admission of such confessions according to the Mississippi Court of Appeals was that slaves would otherwise often "go unpunished in the courts of justice. And the consequence of this would be, that a disposition would be created to punish slaves, otherwise than according to the rules and restraints of law, ...".

These decisions indicated that most courts would carefully examine the facts surrounding each case to detect a coercive atmosphere, no matter who was questioning the slave. However there were exceptions. The Georgia Supreme Court allowed a confession to go to the jury though the sheriff who questioned the slave thought it inadmissible.

In 1851 the Louisiana Supreme Court cynically adopted a different standard for judging slaves' confessions. The court insisted that the truth of the statement was the essential issue. "*In favorem vitae*," it said, -too much strictness has been observed on this subject as to free persons... We are not prepared to say the same strictness should be observed, so as to exclude the confessions of slaves as evidence; ...". In contrast to the Georgia and Louisiana Supreme Courts the high courts of Alabama and Mississippi insisted on more rigid standards for slaves' confessions precisely because they were a degraded class.

From the late' 1840' s to the end of the Civil War the Alabama Supreme Court struggled with a particularly thorny issue—if a confession was first obtained through fear or promise of favor, were subsequent confessions tainted by the first? In 1841 the court raised the issue, suggesting the possibility that once a confession was given under coercive conditions, "it would seem that no subsequent confession of the same facts, ought in the case of slaves, under any circumstances to be admitted, ...". In 1854 the court applied a Miranda-like standard to slave confessions. The judges rejected a confession made to the master and then to a magistrate because both had failed to advise the prisoner of the probable consequences of his admissions. "Ordinarily," said the court, "we would not exclude confessions which are clearly shown to be voluntarily made before a magistrate for the sole reason that the justice failed to caution the prisoner," but once the confession was obtained improperly by the master, the magistrate should have assured the slave that he would not be punished if he recanted. The Mississippi Court of Appeals had come to a similar conclusion a decade earlier. In an 1844 case several whites had captured a slave accused of murder and threatened to hang him if he did not admit his guilt. The slave wisely confessed and subsequently was carried before a magistrate when he confessed again. Judge Thatcher reminded the prosecution of the presumption that once a confession was obtained through promise or threat, a subsequent confession was equally objectionable. The justice should have warned the slave that he had nothing to fear if he denied his earlier statement: "Being a slave, he must be presumed to have been ignorant of the protection from sudden violence, which the presence of the justice of the peace afforded him, ...". In subsequent years the Mississippi court several times affirmed the principle it laid down in 1844.

Though the Alabama Supreme Court did not rule on the necessity of warnings after 1854, in 1858 it demonstrated that it would apply with unusual rigor the presumption that once a confession was coerced, the same conditions under which the first confession was obtained would negate later confessions of ~he same facts. In Bob v. State the slave had made a confession eight months after. he first confessed in reaction to a promise of favor. Though a white's confession would have been admissible under such circumstances, the situation of the slave called for a different outcome. The slave knew nothing. about judicial proceedings. He might fear punishment if he changed his story. And "When the slave had been assured by the jailor, who was his custodian, that it would be better for him to confess, ... who can say that an ignorant negro did not continue to indulge that expectation even to the gallows, unless he was informed that he had been deceived? "Though the members of the court may have been unduly contemptuous of the slave's intellect, their contempt greatly benefited the defendant. Though the court retreated slightly from this position in 1860 and 1861, in two wartime decisions the court indicated that it had not abandoned its extremely cautious approach to slaves'confessions.

It was fitting that during the final year of the Civil War, when slavery was on the verge of violent death, the Alabama Supreme Court continued to insist on strict procedural fairness in slave trials. Despite the deep commitment of its members to the perpetuation of slavery, at its best the court had helped to bring the slave within the law. The coerced confession cases were, perhaps, the most important that the court decided, for they involved the most troubling aspects of the slave's fragile position in Southern society. At the mercy of local passions. in danger of being dragged to the scaffold or worse without even the semblance of a fair trial, slaves badly needed the kind of even-handed justice that appellate courts in such states as Alabama, North Carolina, Tennessee. Texas, and Mississippi consistently dispensed. Unfortunately, these jurists apparently did not represent a very large segment of Southern opinion, and especially during the 1850's their influence was at an extremely low ebb.

An incident in Virginia in 1850 best illustrated the impotence of the judiciary in the face of opposition from the populace. A free black was found guilty and sentenced to death for the brutal murder of a white. Even though his hands were squeezed in a vise, he had refused to confess to the crime. The Virginia Court of Appeals ordered a new trial because the evidence was insufficient for a conviction. At the second trial the accused was again sentenced to death. On appeal the high court reversed again because the evidence "is hardly sufficient to raise a suspicion against him." Immediately below the written opinion of the court the reporter noted, "After the decision of the Court ..., an armed mob in the day time, took him from the jail and hung him: And thus to punish a man whom they suspected of murder, they committed murder.

Most striking is the wide extent of collusive practices and shared values that have united vigilantes and legal authorities. There are many instances of sheriffs and officials who have collaborated with vigilantes and lynch mobs. Distinguished lawyers and judges and notable Americans and the public have seen vigilantism as performing a necessary role in the over-all fabric of American justice. In the antebellum South the connections between law and lynch law were even more apparent.

Olmstead's comment is especially pertinent in this context. Effective law enforcement hinged "upon the constant, habitual and instinctive surveillance and authority of all the white people over the blacks. The law not only allowed the master wide authority over his bondsmen but permitted all whites to arrest and even punish slaves. Patrol laws further encouraged the citizenry to take an active part in disciplining slaves. Slaves became painfully aware of the effects of these measures during insurrection scares. During and after the tense election campaigns of 1856 and 1860 many slaves paid with their lives for the anxieties of the superior race. Often the prelude to these executions was a proceeding that ranked somewhere between pure mob violence and orderly procedures of law enforcement. For example, in Gallatin, Tennessee during the 1856 insurrection scare four blacks were arrested on a charge of conspiracy. At a town meeting, presided over by respectable citizens, a vote was taken. This rather large jury voted to convict, and the slaves were hanged. In his description of lynch law in The American

Commonwealth James Bryce emphasized how organized it often was. The "vigilance committee" was an example. During an insurrection scare in 1835 a Livingston, Mississippi vigilance committee sent five whites and more than a dozen blacks to the gallows. William Sharkey, later Chief Justice of the state supreme court and provisional governor in 1865, saved his cousin (a local justice of the peace) from a death sentence through a skillful argument to the committee in which he did not question its authority and conceded the inadequacy of the courts in such a "crisis." The members of the committee later attempted to justify their actions by claiming that the jail was not large enough to hold the offenders. Sensitive to the dynamics of insurrection scares, the Alabama legislature passed a remarkable statute in which it tried to strike a middle ground between due process of law and vigilante justice. In cases of actual or threatened rebellion two justices of the peace and a probate judge must try slaves within fifteen days of the commission of the offense. Two-thirds of the jury were to be slaveholders if possible, but if the number of veniremen summoned were exhausted by challenges, bystanders would be chosen. The prosecutor simply had to write out a brief statement of the offense and sign it. If the slave was found guilty, the authorities were to execute him immediately. Of course this allowed for no appeal.

Though the Alabama legislature restricted the rights of slaves in insurrection cases, the statute may well have been intended to ensure that the slave would receive at least some benefit from the law if he happened to be innocent. Unfortunately for many influential citizens, rather than seeking to temper the passions of the mob, actively participated in mob violence. Far more highly placed Southerners spoke out against lynch law in the antebellum period than they did after Appomattox, "but in a time of crisis or great public danger," wrote Clement Eaton, "a decided majority seemed to have approved of its use." When the pressures became even more intense after emancipation, that majority grew much larger. Though the appellate courts might insist that the rights of accused slaves be respected, other aspects of the legal system diminished the significance of their decisions.

An 1888 case in Tennessee provided a distressing example. A master had sued a group of whites who had lynched his slave. Since the slave was accused of rape and murder, the jury refused to award the master any damages. On appeal Judge Caruthers seized the occasion to deliver a scathing denunciation of mob violence.

> The case was one of extraordinary aggravation, in which all law was set at defiance, public justice insulted, and the life of a human being, already in manacles lawlessly destroyed... without a hearing—a fair and impartial trial. There is neither valor nor patriotism in deeds like these. ... No matter how great the malefactor may be,-whose life is thus taken without law, a feeling of alarm and insecurity pervades the whole community when one of these shocking deeds of violence is perpetrated. No man can tell what unfortunate concurrence of circumstances may raise the storm of popular fury against him, though he may be innocent, ... All good citizens, everyone

who values his own safety, or has any regard for law and order, should unite in rebuking, in all proper modes, these outrages upon the lives of men and obstructions of the course of law and justice. The courts and juries, public officers and citizens, should set their faces like flint against popular outbreaks and mobs, in all their forms.

The irony of this admirable statement of the rights of the slave and the shrewd assessment of the dangers that mob violence posed for the entire community was the setting in which it was uttered. The law had failed to hold the mob accountable for the murder of a human being; rather it was a civil suit to recover the value of a chattel.

Note

The association of freed African American slaves with criminality was continued and enhanced in the post-reconstruction period. The roots of much of what we now see as disproportionate mass incarceration may in large part be found in the adoption throughout the south of Black Codes (Jim Crow Laws). These "codes" took advantage of the poverty and disenfranchisement of many, if not most, freed slaves, by enforcement of criminal provisions designed either specifically against poor African Americans or disproportionately enforced. Such provisions and enforcement grew from a need to offset the economic loss of former slaveholders by first convicting African Americans of relatively minor offenses, sentencing those convicted to pay fines and costs that were beyond the means of freed Blacks and then sentencing those who could not pay to "work-off" their fines and costs as underpaid plantation workers. This form of slavery was believed to not be in violation of the Thirteenth Amendment because of language within the amendment that allowed slavery and servitude "as a punishment for crime".

The types of "crimes" permitting this type of involuntary servitude for impoverished African Americans included, in all southern states the arresting of Blacks without jobs as "vagrants", and in some states, such as Mississippi "handling money carelessly" and otherwise being idle. For a more detailed discussion of the relationship between Black Codes and race in criminal prosecutions, see Nadra Kareem Nittle, *The Black Codes and Why They Matter Today,* https://www.thoughtco.com/the-black-codes-41257447 (2018).

For an expansive treatment see Douglas A. Blackmon, SLAVERY BY ANOTHER NAME: THE RE-ENSLAVEMENT OF BLACK AMERICANS FROM THE CIVIL WAR TO WORLD WAR II (Anchors Book 2008)

BROWN V. MISSISSIPPI
297 U.S. 278 (1936)

Mr. Chief Justice HUGHES delivered the opinion of the Court.

The question in this case is whether convictions, which rest solely upon confessions shown to have been extorted by officers of the state by brutality and violence, are consistent with the due process of law required by the Fourteenth Amendment of the Constitution of the United States.

Petitioners were indicted for the murder of one Raymond Stewart, whose death occurred on March 30, 1934. They were indicted on April 4, 1934, and were then arraigned and pleaded not guilty. Counsel were appointed by the court to defend them. Trial was begun the next morning and was concluded on the following day, when they were found guilty and sentenced to death.

Aside from the confessions, there was no evidence sufficient to warrant the submission of the case to the jury. After a preliminary inquiry, testimony as to the confessions was received over the objection of defendants' counsel. Defendants then testified that the confessions were false and had been procured by physical torture. The case went to the jury with instructions, upon the request of defendants' counsel, that if the jury had reasonable doubt as to the confessions having resulted from coercion, and that they were not they were not to be considered as evidence. On their to the Supreme Court of the State, defendants assigned as error the inadmissibility of the confessions. The judgment was affirmed. 158 So. 339.

Defendants then moved in the Supreme Court of the State to arrest the judgment and for a new trial on the ground that all the evidence against them was obtained by coercion and brutality known to the court and to the district attorney, and that defendants had been denied the benefit of counsel or opportunity to confer with counsel in a reasonable manner. The motion was supported by affidavits. At about the same time, defendants filed in the Supreme Court a 'suggestion of error' explicitly challenging the proceedings of the trial, in the use of the confessions and with respect to the alleged denial of representation by counsel, as violating the due process clause of the Fourteenth Amendment of the Constitution of the United States. The state court entertained the suggestion of error, considered the federal question, and decided it against defendants' contentions. 161 So. 465. Two judges dissented. 161 So. 470. We granted a writ of certiorari. 296 U.S. 559, 56 S.Ct. 128, 80 L.Ed. 394.

The grounds of the decision were (1) that immunity from self-incrimination is not essential to due process of law; and (2) that the failure of the trial court to exclude the confessions after the introduction of evidence showing their incompetency, in the absence of a request for such exclusion, did not deprive the defendants of life or liberty without due process of law; and that even if the trial court had erroneously overruled a motion to exclude the confessions, the ruling would have been mere error reversible on appeal, but not a violation of constitution right. 161 So. 465, at page 468.

The opinion of the state court did not set forth the evidence as to the circumstances in which the confessions were procured. That the evidence established that they were procured by coercion was not questioned. The state court said: 'After the state closed its case on the merits, the appellants, for the first time, introduced evidence from which it appears that the confessions were not made voluntarily but were coerced.' 161 So. 465, at page 466. There is no dispute as to the facts upon this point, and as they are clearly and adequately stated in the dissenting opinion of Judge Griffith (with whom Judge Anderson concurred), showing both the extreme brutality of the measures to extort the confessions and the participation of the state authorities, we quote this part of his opinion in full, as follows (161 So. 465, at pages 470, 471):

'The crime with which these defendants, all ignorant negroes, are charged, was discovered about 1 o'clock p.m. on Friday, March 30, 1934. On that night one Dial, a deputy sheriff, accompanied by others, came to the home of Ellington, one of the defendants, and requested him to accompany them to the house of the deceased, and there a number of white men were gathered, who began to accuse the defendant of the crime. Upon his denial they seized him, and with the participation of the deputy they hanged him by a rope to the limb of a tree, and, having let him down, they hung him again, and when he was let down the second time, and he still protested his innocence, he was tied to a tree and whipped, and, still declining to accede to the demands that he confess, he was finally released, and he returned with some difficulty to his home, suffering intense pain and agony. The record of the testimony shows that the signs of the rope on his neck were plainly visible during the so-called trial. A day or two thereafter the said deputy, accompanied by another, returned to the home of the said defendant and arrested him, and departed with the prisoner towards the jail in an adjoining county, but went by a route which led into the state of Alabama; and while on the way, in that state, the deputy stopped and again severely whipped the defendant, declaring that he would continue the whipping until he confessed, and the defendant then agreed to confess to such a statement as the deputy would dictate, and he did so, after which he was delivered to jail.

'The other two defendants, Ed Brown and Henry Shields, were also arrested and taken to the same jail. On Sunday night, April 1, 1934, the same deputy, accompanied by a number of white men, one of whom was also an officer, and by the jailer, came to the jail, and the two last named defendants were made to strip and they were laid over chairs and their backs were cut to pieces with a leather strap with buckles on it, and they were likewise made by the said deputy definitely to understand that the whipping would be continued unless and until they confessed, and not only confessed, but confessed in every matter of detail as demanded by those present; and in this manner the defendants confessed the crime, and, as the whippings progressed and were repeated, they changed or adjusted their confession in all particulars of detail so as to conform to the demands of their torturers. When the confessions had been obtained in the exact form and contents as desired by the mob, they left with the parting admonition and warning that, if the defendants changed their story at any time in any respect from that last stated, the perpetrators of the outrage would administer the same or equally effective treatment.

'Further details of the brutal treatment to which these helpless prisoners were subjected need not be pursued. It is sufficient to say that in pertinent respects the transcript reads more like pages torn from some medieval account than a record made within the confines of a modern civilization which aspires to an enlightened constitutional government.

'All this having been accomplished, on the next day, that is, on Monday, April 2, when the defendants had been given time to recuperate somewhat from the tortures to which they had been subjected, the two sheriffs, one of the county where the crime was committed, and the other of the county of the jail in which the prisoners were confined, came to the jail, accompanied by eight other persons, some of them deputies, there to hear the free and voluntary confession of these miserable and abject defendants. The sheriff of the county of the crime admitted that he had heard of the whipping, but averred that he had no personal knowledge of it. He admitted that one of the defendants, when brought before him to confess, was limping and did not sit down, and that this particular defendant then and there stated that he had been strapped so severely that he could not sit down, and, as already stated, the signs of the rope on the neck of another of the defendants were plainly visible to all. Nevertheless the solemn farce of hearing the free and voluntary confessions was gone through with, and these two sheriffs and one other person then present were the three witnesses used in court to establish the so-called confessions, which were received by the court and admitted in evidence over the objections of the defendants duly entered of record as each of the said three witnesses delivered their alleged testimony. There was thus enough before the court when these confessions were first offered to make known to the court that they were not, beyond all reasonable doubt, free and voluntary; and the failure of the court then to exclude the confessions is sufficient to reverse the judgment, under every rule of procedure that has heretofore been prescribed, and hence it was not necessary subsequently to renew the objections by motion or otherwise.

'The spurious confessions having been obtained—and the farce last mentioned having been gone through with on Monday, April 2d—the court, then in session, on the following day, Tuesday, April 3, 1934, ordered the grand jury to reassemble on the succeeding day, April 4, 1934, at 9 o'clock, and on the morning of the day last mentioned the grand jury returned an indictment against the defendants for murder. Late that afternoon the defendants were brought from the jail in the adjoining county and arraigned, when one or more of them offered to plead guilty, which the court declined to accept, and, upon inquiry whether they had or desired counsel, they stated that they had none, and did not suppose that counsel could be of any assistance to them. The court thereupon appointed counsel, and set the case for trial for the following morning at 9 o'clock, and the defendants were returned to the jail in the adjoining county about thirty miles away.

'The defendants were brought to the courthouse of the county on the following morning, April 5th, and the so-called trial was opened, and was concluded on the next day, April 6, 1934, and resulted in a pretended conviction with death sentences. The evidence upon which the conviction was obtained was the so-called confessions. Without this evidence, a peremptory instruction to find for the defendants would have been inescapable. The defendants were put on the stand, and by their testimony the facts and the details thereof as to the manner by which the confessions were extorted from them were fully developed, and it is further disclosed by the record that the same deputy, Dial, under whose guiding hand and active participation the tortures to coerce the confessions were administered, was actively in the performance of the supposed duties of a court deputy in the courthouse and in the presence of the prisoners during what is denominated, in complimentary terms, the trial of these defendants. This deputy was put on the stand by the state in rebuttal, and admitted the whippings. It is interesting to note that in his testimony with reference to the whipping of the defendant Ellington, and in response to the inquiry as to how severely he was whipped, the deputy stated, 'Not too much for a negro; not as much as I would have done if it were left to me.' Two others who had participated in these whippings were introduced and admitted it—not a single witness was introduced who denied it. The facts are not only undisputed, they are admitted, and admitted to have been done by officers of the state, in conjunction with other participants, and all this was definitely well known to everybody connected with the trial, and during the trial, including the state's prosecuting attorney and the trial judge presiding.'

The state stresses the statement in *Twining v. New Jersey*, 211 U.S. 78, 114, 29 S.Ct. 14, 26, 53 L.Ed. 97, that 'exemption from compulsory self-incrimination in the courts of the states is not secured by any part of the Federal Constitution,' and the statement in *Snyder v. Massachusetts*, 291 U.S. 97, 105, 54 S.Ct. 330, 332, 78 L.Ed. 674, 90 A.L.R. 575, that 'the privilege against self-incrimination may be withdrawn and the accused put upon the stand as a witness for the state.' But the question of the right of the state to withdraw the privilege against self-incrimination is not here involved. The compulsion to which the quoted statements refer is that of the processes of justice by which the accused may be called as a witness and required to testify. Compulsion by torture to extort a confession is a different matter.

The state is free to regulate the procedure of its courts in accordance with its own conceptions of policy, unless in so doing it 'offends some principle of justice so rooted in the traditions and conscience of our people as to be ranked as fundamental.' The state may abolish trial by jury.

It may dispense with indictment by a grand jury and substitute complaint or information. But the freedom of the state in establishing its policy is the freedom of constitutional government and is limited by the requirement of due process of law. Because a state may dispense with a jury trial, it does not follow that it may substitute trial by ordeal. The rack and torture chamber may not be substituted for the witness stand. The state may not permit an accused to be hurried to conviction under mob domination—where the whole proceeding is but a mask—without supplying corrective process. Nor may a state, through the action of its officers, contrive a conviction through the pretense of a trial which in truth is 'but used as a means of depriving a defendant of liberty through a deliberate deception of court and jury by the presentation of testimony known to be perjured.' *Mooney v. Holohan.* And the trial equally is a mere pretense where the state authorities have contrived a conviction resting solely upon confessions obtained by violence. The due process clause requires 'that state action, whether through one agency or another, shall be consistent with the fundamental principles of liberty and justice which lie at the base of all our civil and political institutions.' Hebert v. Louisiana. It would be difficult to conceive of methods more revolting to the sense of justice than those taken to procure the confessions of these petitioners, and the use of the confessions thus obtained as the basis for conviction and sentence was a clear denial of due process.

It is in this view that the further contention of the State must be considered. That contention rests upon the failure of counsel for the accused, who had objected to the admissibility of the confessions, to move for their exclusion after they had been introduced and the fact of coercion had been proved. It is a contention which proceeds upon a misconception of the nature of petitioners' complaint. That complaint is not of the commission of mere error, but of a wrong so fundamental that it made the whole proceeding a mere pretense of a trial and rendered the conviction and sentence wholly void. *Moore v. Dempsey, supra.* We are not concerned with a mere question of state practice, or whether counsel assigned to petitioners were competent or mistakenly assumed that their first objections were sufficient. In an earlier case the Supreme Court of the State had recognized the duty of the court to supply corrective process where due process of law had been denied. In *Fisher v. State*, 145 Miss. 116, 134, 110 So. 361, 365, the court said: 'Coercing the supposed state's criminals into confessions and using such confessions so coerced from them against them in trials has been the curse of all countries. It was the chief iniquity, the crowning infamy of the Star Chamber, and the Inquisition, and other similar institutions. The Constitution recognized the evils that lay behind these practices and prohibited them in this country. * * * The duty of maintaining constitutional rights of a person on trial for his life rises above mere rules of procedure, and wherever the court is clearly satisfied that such violations exist, it will refuse to sanction such violations and will apply the corrective.'

In the instant case, the trial court was fully advised by the undisputed evidence of the way in which the confessions had been procured. The trial court knew that there was no other evidence upon which conviction and sentence could be based. Yet it proceeded to permit conviction and to pronounce sentence. The conviction and sentence were void for want of the essential elements of due process, and the proceeding thus vitiated could be challenged in any appropriate manner. *Mooney v. Holohan, supra.* It was challenged before the Supreme Court of the State by the express invocation of the Fourteenth Amendment. That court entertained the challenge, considered the federal question thus presented, but declined to enforce petitioners' constitutional right. The court thus denied a federal right fully established and specially set up and claimed, and the judgment must be reversed.

It is so ordered.

POWELL V. ALABAMA
287 U.S. 45 (1932)

Mr. Justice SUTHERLAND delivered the opinion of the Court.

These cases were argued together and submitted for decision as one case.

The petitioners, hereinafter referred to as defendants, are negroes charged with the crime of rape, committed upon the persons of two white girls. The crime is said to have been committed on March 25, 1931. The indictment was returned in a state court of first instance on March 31, and the record recites that on the same day the defendants were arraigned and entered pleas of not guilty. There is a further recital to the effect that upon the arraignment they were represented by counsel. But no counsel had been employed, and aside from a statement made by the trial judge several days later during a colloquy immediately preceding the trial, the record does not disclose when, or under what circumstances, an appointment of counsel was made, or who was appointed. During the colloquy referred to, the trial judge, in response to a question, said that he had appointed all the members of the bar for the purpose of arraigning the defendants and then of course anticipated that the members of the bar would continue to help the defendants if no counsel appeared. Upon the argument here both sides accepted that as a correct statement of the facts concerning the matter.

There was a severance upon the request of the state, and the defendants were tried in three several groups, as indicated above. As each of the three cases was called for trial, each defendant was arraigned, and, having the indictment read to him, entered a plea of not guilty. Whether the original arraignment and pleas were regarded as ineffective is not shown. Each of the three trials was completed within a single day. Under the Alabama statute the punishment for rape is to be fixed by the jury, and in its discretion may be from ten years imprisonment to death. The juries found defendants guilty and imposed the death penalty upon all. The trial court overruled motions for new trials and sentenced the defendants in accordance with the verdicts. The judgments were affirmed by the state supreme court. Chief Justice Anderson thought the defendants had not been accorded a fair trial and strongly dissented.

In this court the judgments are assailed upon the grounds that the defendants, and each of them, were denied due process of law and the equal protection of the laws, in contravention of the Fourteenth Amendment, specifically as follows: (1) They were not given a fair, impartial, and deliberate trial; (2) they were denied the right of counsel, with the accustomed incidents of consultation and opportunity of preparation for trial; and (3) they were tried before juries from which qualified members of their own race were systematically excluded. These questions were properly raised and saved in the courts below.

The only one of the assignments which we shall consider is the second, in respect of the denial of counsel; and it becomes unnecessary to discuss the facts of the case or the circumstances surrounding the prosecution except in so far as they reflect light upon that question.

The record shows that on the day when the offense is said to have been committed, these defendants, together with a number of other negroes, were upon a freight train on its way through Alabama. On the same train were seven white boys and the two white girls. A fight took place between the negroes and the white boys, in the course of which the white boys, with the exception of one named Gilley, were thrown off the train. A message was sent ahead, reporting the fight and asking that every negro be gotten off the train. The participants in the fight, and the two girls, were in an open gondola car. The two girls testified that each of them was assaulted by six different negroes in turn, and they identified the seven defendants as having been among the number. None of the white boys was called to testify, with the exception of Gilley, who was called in rebuttal.

Before the train reached Scottsboro, Ala., a sheriff's posse seized the defendants and two other negroes. Both girls and the negroes then were taken to Scottsboro, the county seat. Word of their coming and of the alleged assault had preceded them, and they were met at Scottsboro by a large crowd. It does not sufficiently appear that the defendants were seriously threatened with, or that they were actually in danger of, mob violence; but it does appear that the attitude of the community was one of great hostility. The sheriff thought it necessary to call for the militia to assist in safeguarding the prisoners. Chief Justice Anderson pointed out in his opinion that every step taken from the arrest and arraignment to the sentence was accompanied by the military. Soldiers took the defendants to Gadsden for safe-keeping, brought them back to Scottsboro for arraignment, returned them to Gadsden for safe-keeping while awaiting trial, escorted them to Scottsboro for trial a few days later, and guarded the courthouse and grounds at every stage of the proceedings. It is perfectly apparent that the proceedings, from beginning to end, took place in an atmosphere of tense, hostile, and excited public sentiment. During the entire time, the defendants were closely confined or were under military guard. The record does not disclose their ages, except that one of them was nineteen; but the record clearly indicates that most, if not all, of them were youthful, and they are constantly referred to as 'the boys.' They were ignorant and illiterate. All of them were residents of other states, where alone members of their families or friends resided.

However guilty defendants, upon due inquiry, might prove to have been, they were, until convicted, presumed to be innocent. It was the duty of the court having their cases in charge to see that they were denied no necessary incident of a fair trial. With any error of the state court involving alleged contravention of the state statutes or Constitution we, of course, have nothing to do. The sole inquiry which we are permitted to make is whether the federal Constitution was contravened; and as to that, we confine ourselves, as already suggested, to the inquiry whether the defendants were in substance denied the right of counsel, and if so, whether such denial infringes the due process clause of the Fourteenth Amendment.

First. The record shows that immediately upon the return of the indictment defendants were arraigned and pleaded not guilty. Apparently, they were not asked whether they had, or were able to employ, counsel, or wished to have counsel appointed; or whether they had friends or relatives who might assist in that regard if communicated with. That it would not have been an idle ceremony to have given the defendants reasonable opportunity to communicate with their families and endeavor to obtain counsel is demonstrated by the fact that very soon after conviction, able counsel appeared in their behalf. This was pointed out by Chief Justice Anderson in the course of his dissenting opinion. 'They were nonresidents,' he said, 'and had little time or opportunity to get in touch with their families and friends who were scattered throughout two other states, and time has demonstrated that they could or would have been represented by able counsel had a better opportunity been given by a reasonable delay in the trial of the cases judging from the number and activity of counsel that appeared immediately or shortly after their conviction.'

It is hardly necessary to say that the right to counsel being conceded, a defendant should be afforded a fair opportunity to secure counsel of his own choice. Not only was that not done here, but such designation of counsel as was attempted was either so indefinite or so close upon the trial as to amount to a denial of effective and substantial aid in that regard. This will be amply demonstrated by a brief review of the record.

April 6, six days after indictment, the trials began. When the first case was called, the court inquired whether the parties were ready for trial. The state's attorney replied that he was ready to proceed. No one answered for the defendants or appeared to represent or defend them. Mr. Roddy, a Tennessee lawyer not a member of the local bar, addressed the court, saying that he had not been employed, but that people who were interested had spoken to him about the case. He was asked by the court whether he intended to appear for the defendants, and answered that he would like to appear along with counsel that the court might appoint. The record then proceeds:

'The Court: If you appear for these defendants, then I will not appoint counsel; if local counsel are willing to appear and assist you under the circumstances all right, but I will not appoint them.

'Mr. Roddy: Your Honor has appointed counsel, is that correct?

'The Court: I appointed all the members of the bar for the purpose of arraigning the defendants and then of course I anticipated them to continue to help them if no counsel appears.

*54 'Mr. Roddy: Then I don't appear then as counsel but I do want to stay in and not be ruled out in this case.

'The Court: Of course I would not do that—

'Mr. Roddy: I just appear here through the courtesy of Your Honor.

'The Court: Of course I give you that right * * *.'

And then, apparently addressing all the lawyers present, the court inquired:
'* * * Well are you all willing to assist?

'Mr. Moody: Your Honor appointed us all and we have been proceeding along every line we know about it under Your Honor's appointment.

'The Court: The only thing I am trying to do is, if counsel appears for these defendants I don't want to impose on you all, but if you feel like counsel from Chattanooga—

'Mr. Moody: I see his situation of course and I have not run out of anything yet. Of course, if Your Honor purposes to appoint us, Mr. Parks, I am willing to go on with it. Most of the bar have been down and conferred with these defendants in this case; they did not know what else to do.

'The Court: The thing, I did not want to impose on the members of the bar if counsel unqualifiedly appears; if you all feel like Mr. Roddy is only interested in a limited way to assist, then I don't care to appoint—

'Mr. Parks: Your Honor, I don't feel like you ought to impose on any member of the local bar if the defendants are represented by counsel.

'The Court: That is what I was trying to ascertain, Mr. Parks.

'Mr. Parks: Of course if they have counsel, I don't see the necessity of the Court appointing anybody; if they haven't counsel, of course I think it is up to the Court to appoint counsel to represent them.

*55 'The Court: I think you are right about it Mr. Parks and that is the reason I was trying to get an expression from Mr. Roddy.

'Mr. Roddy: I think Mr. Parks is entirely right about it, if I was paid down here and employed, it would be a different thing, but I have not prepared this case for trial and have only been called into it by people who are interested in these boys from Chattanooga. Now, they have not given me an opportunity to prepare the case and I am not familiar with the procedure in Alabama, but I merely came down here as a friend of the people who are interested and not as paid counsel, and certainly I haven't any money to pay them and nobody I am interested in had me to come down here has put up any fund of money to come down here and pay counsel. If they should do it I would be glad to turn it over—a counsel but I am merely here at the solicitation of people who have become interested in this case without any payment of fee and without any preparation for trial and I think the boys would be better off if I step entirely out of the case according to my way of looking at it and according to my lack of preparation for it and not being familiar with the procedure in Alabama * * *.'

Mr. Roddy later observed:

'If there is anything I can do to be of help to them, I will be glad to do it; I am interested to that extent.

'The Court: Well gentlemen, if Mr. Roddy only appears as assistant that way, I think it is proper that I appoint members of this bar to represent them, I expect that is right. If Mr. Roddy will appear, I wouldn't of course, I would not appoint anybody. I don't see, Mr. Roddy, how I can make a qualified appointment or a limited appointment. Of course, I don't mean to cut off your assistance in any way—Well gentlemen, I think you understand it.

'Mr. Moody: I am willing to go ahead and help Mr. Roddy in anything I can do about it, under the circumstances.

'The Court: All right, all the lawyers that will; of course I would not require a lawyer to appear if—

'Mr. Moody: I am willing to go ahead and help Mr. Roddy in anything I can do about it, under the circumstances.

'The Court: All right, all the lawyers that will, of course, I would not require a lawyer to appear if—

'Mr. Moody: I am willing to do that for him as a member of the bar; I will go ahead and help do anything I can do.

'The Court: All right.'

And in this casual fashion the matter of counsel in a capital case was disposed of.

It thus will be seen that until the very morning of the trial no lawyer had been named or definitely designated to represent the defendants. Prior to that time, the trial judge had 'appointed all the members of the bar' for the limited 'purpose of arraigning the defendants.' Whether they would represent the defendants thereafter, if no counsel appeared in their behalf, was a matter of speculation only, or, as the judge indicated, of mere anticipation on the part of the court. Such a designation, even if made for all purposes, would, in our opinion, have fallen far short of meeting, in any proper sense, a requirement for the appointment of counsel. How many lawyers were members of the bar does not appear; but, in the very nature of things, whether many or few, they would not, thus collectively named, have been given that clear appreciation of responsibility or impressed with that individual sense of duty which should and naturally would accompany the appointment of a selected member of the bar, specifically named and assigned.

That this action of the trial judge in respect of appointment of counsel was little more than an expansive gesture, imposing no substantial or definite obligation upon any one, is borne out by the fact that prior to the calling of the case for trial on April 6, a leading member of the local bar accepted employment on the side of the prosecution and actively participated in the trial. It is true that he said that before doing so he had understood Mr. Roddy would be employed as counsel for the defendants. This the lawyer is question, of his own accord, frankly stated to the court; and no doubt he acted with the utmost good faith. Probably other members of the bar had a like understanding. In any event, the circumstance lends emphasis to the conclusion that during perhaps the most critical period of the proceedings against these defendants, that is to say, from the time of their arraignment until the beginning of their trial, when consultation, thorough-going investigation and preparation were vitally important, the defendants did not have the aid of counsel in any real sense, although they were as much entitled to such aid during that period as at the trial itself. *People ex rel. Burgess v. Riseley*, 66 How.Pr.(N.Y.) 67; *Batchelor v. State*, 189 Ind. 69, 76, 125 N.E. 773.

Nor do we think the situation was helped by what occurred on the morning of the trial. At that time, as appears from the colloquy printed above, Mr. Roddy stated to the court that he did not appear as counsel, but that he would like to appear along with counsel that the court might appoint; that he had not been given an opportunity to prepare the case; that he was not familiar with the procedure in Alabama, but merely came down as a friend of the people who were interested; that he thought the boys would be better off if he should step entirely out of the case. Mr. Moody, a member of the local bar, expressed a willingness to help Mr. Roddy in anything he could do under the circumstances. To this the court responded: 'All right, all the lawyers that will; of course I would not require a lawyer to appear if—.' And Mr. Moody continued: 'I am willing to do that for him as a member of the bar; I will go ahead and help do anything I can do.' With this dubious understanding, the trials immediately proceeded. The defendants, young, ignorant, illiterate, surrounded by hostile sentiment, haled back and forth under guard of soldiers, charged with an atrocious crime regarded with especial horror in the community where they were to be tried, were thus put in peril of their lives within a few moments after counsel for the first time charged with any degree of responsibility began to represent them.

It is not enough to assume that counsel thus precipitated into the case thought there was no defense, and exercised their best judgment in proceeding to trial without preparation. Neither they nor the court could say what a prompt and thorough-going investigation might disclose as to the facts. No attempt was made to investigate. No opportunity to do so was given. Defendants were immediately hurried to trial. Chief Justice Anderson, after disclaiming any intention to criticize harshly counsel who attempted to represent defendants at the trials, said: '* * * The record indicates that the appearance was rather pro forma than zealous and active * * *.' Under the circumstances disclosed, we hold that defendants were not accorded the right of counsel in any substantial sense. To decide otherwise, would simply be to ignore actualities. This conclusion finds ample support in the reasoning of an overwhelming array of state decisions...

It is true that great and inexcusable delay in the enforcement of our criminal law is one of the grave evils of our time. Continuances are frequently granted for unnecessarily long periods of time, and delays incident to the disposition of motions for new trial and hearings upon appeal have come in many cases to be a distinct reproach to the administration of justice. The prompt disposition of criminal cases is to be commended and encouraged. But in reaching that result a defendant, charged with a serious crime, must not be stripped of his right to have sufficient time to advise with counsel and prepare his defense. To do that is not to proceed promptly in the calm spirit of regulated justice but to go forward with the haste of the mob.

As the court said in *Commonwealth v. O'Keefe*, 298 Pa. 169, 173, 148 A. 73, 74:

'It is vain to give the accused a day in court, with no opportunity to prepare for it, or to guarantee him counsel without giving the latter any opportunity to acquaint himself with the facts or law of the case. * * *

'A prompt and vigorous administration of the criminal law is commendable and we have no desire to clog the wheels of justice. What we here decide is that to force a defendant, charged with a serious misdemeanor, to trial within five hours of his arrest, is not due process of law, regardless of the merits of the case.'

Compare *Reliford v. State*, 140 Ga. 777, 778, 79 S.E. 1128.

Second. The Constitution of Alabama (Const. 1901, s 6) provides that in all criminal prosecutions the accused shall enjoy the right to have the assistance of counsel; and a state statute (Code 1923, s 5567) requires the court in a capital case, where the defendant is unable to employ counsel, to appoint counsel for him. The state Supreme Court held that these provisions had not been infringed, and with that holding we are powerless to interfere. The question, however, which it is our duty, and within our power, to decide, is whether the denial of the assistance of counsel contravenes the due process clause of the Fourteenth Amendment to the Federal Constitution.

If recognition of the right of a defendant charged with a felony to have the aid of counsel depended upon the existence of a similar right at common law as it existed in England when our Constitution was adopted, there would be great difficulty in maintaining it as necessary to due process. Originally, in England, a person charged with treason or felony was denied the aid of counsel, except in respect of legal questions which the accused himself might suggest. At the same time parties in civil cases and persons accused of misdemeanors were entitled to the full assistance of counsel. After the revolution of 1688, the rule was abolished as to treason, but was otherwise steadily adhered to until 1836, when by act of Parliament the full right was granted in respect of felonies generally. 1 Cooley's Constitutional Limitations (8th Ed.) 698 et seq., and notes.

An affirmation of the right to the aid of counsel in petty offenses, and its denial in the case of crimes of the gravest character, where such aid is most needed, is so outrageous and so obviously a perversion of all sense of proportion that the rule was constantly, vigorously and sometimes passionately assailed by English statesmen and lawyers. As early as 1758, Blackstone, although recognizing that the rule was settled at common law, denounced it as not in keeping with the rest of the humane treatment of prisoners by the English law. 'For upon what face of reason,' he says 'can that assistance be denied to save the life of a man, which yet is allowed him in prosecutions for every petty trespass?' 4 Blackstone, 355. One of the grounds upon which Lord Coke defended the rule was that in felonies the court itself was counsel for the prisoner. 1 Cooley's Constitutional Limitations, supra. But how can a judge, whose functions are purely judicial, effectively discharge the obligations of counsel for the accused? He can and should see to it that in the proceedings before the court the accused shall be dealt with justly and fairly. He cannot investigate the facts, advise and direct the defense, or participate in those necessary conferences between counsel and accused which sometimes partake of the inviolable character of the confessional.

The rule was rejected by the colonies. Before the adoption of the Federal Constitution, the Constitution of Maryland had declared 'That, in all criminal prosecutions, every man hath a right * * * to be allowed counsel. * * *' Article 19, Constitution of 1776. The Constitution of Massachusetts, adopted in 1780 (part the first, art. 12), the Constitution of New Hampshire, adopted in 1784 (part 1, art. 15), the Constitution of New York of 1777 (article 34), and the Constitution of Pennsylvania of 1776 (Declaration of Rights, art. 9), had also declared to the same effect. And in the case of Pennsylvania, as early as 1701, the Penn Charter (article 5) declared that 'all Criminals shall have the same Privileges of Witnesses and Council as their Prosecutors'; and there was also a provision in the Pennsylvania statute of May 31, 1718 (Dallas, Laws of Pennsylvania, 1700—1781, vol. 1, p. 134), that in capital cases learned counsel should be assigned to the prisoners.

In Delaware, the Constitution of 1776 (article 25) adopted the common law of England, but expressly excepted such parts as were repugnant to the rights and privileges contained in the Declaration of Rights; and the Declaration of Rights, which was adopted on September 11, 1776, provided (article 14) 'That in all Prosecutions for criminal Offences, every Man hath a Right * * * to be allowed Counsel * * *.' In addition, Penn's Charter, already referred to, was applicable in Delaware. The original Constitution of New Jersey of 1776 (article 16) contained a provision like that of the Penn Charter, to the effect that all criminals should be admitted to the same privileges of counsel as their prosecutors. The original Constitution of North Carolina (1776) did not contain the guaranty, but chapter 115, s 85, Sess. Laws, N. Car., 1777 (N. Car. Rev. Laws, 1715—1796, vol. 1, 316) provided: '* * * That every person accused of any crime or misdemeanor whatsoever, shall be entitled to council in all matters which may be necessary for his defence, as well to facts as to law * * *.' Similarly, in South Carolina the original Constitution of 1776 did not contain the provision as to counsel, but it was provided as early as 1731 (Act of August 20, 1731, s XLIII, Grimke, S. Car. Pub. Laws, 1682—1790, p. 130) that every person charged with treason, murder, felony, or other capital offense, should be admitted to make full defense by counsel learned in the law. In Virginia there was no constitutional provision on the subject, but as early as August, 1734 (chapter 7, s 3, Laws of Va., 8th Geo. II, Hening's Stat. at Large, vol. 4, p. 404), there was an act declaring that in all trials for capital offenses the prisoner, upon his petition to the court, should be allowed counsel.

The original Constitution of Connecticut (article 1, s 9) contained a provision that 'in all criminal prosecutions, the accused shall have a right to be heard by himself and by counsel'; but this Constitution was not adopted until 1818. However, it appears that the English common-law rule had been rejected in practice long prior to 1796. See Zephaniah Swift's 'A System of the Laws of the State of Connecticut,' printed at Windham by John Byrne, 1795—1796, vol. II, Bk. 5, 'Of Crimes and Punishments,' c. XXIV, 'Of Trials,' pp. 398—399.1

The original Constitution of Georgia (1777) did not contain a guarantee in respect of counsel, but the Constitution of 1798 (article 3, s 8) provided that '* * * no person shall be debarred from advocating or defending his cause before any court or tribunal, either by himself or counsel, or both.' What the practice was prior to 1798 we are unable to discover. The first Constitution adopted by Rhode Island was in 1842, and this Constitution contained the usual guaranty in respect of the assistance of counsel in criminal prosecutions. As early as 1798 it was provided by statute, in the very language of the Sixth Amendment to the federal Constitution, that 'in all criminal prosecutions, the accused shall enjoy the right * * * to have the assistance of counsel for his defence * * *.' An Act Declaratory of certain Rights of the People of this State, section 6, Rev. Pub. Laws, Rhode Island and Providence Plantations, 1798. Furthermore, while the statute itself is not available, it is recorded as a matter of history that in 1668 or 1669 the colonial assembly enacted that any person who was indicted might employ an attorney to plead in his behalf. 1 Arnold, History of Rhode Island, 336.

It thus appears that in at least twelve of the thirteen colonies the rule of the English common law, in the respect now under consideration, had been definitely rejected and the right to counsel fully recognized in all criminal prosecutions, save that in one or two instances the right was limited to capital offenses or to the more serious crimes; and this court seems to have been of the opinion that this was true in all the colonies. In *Holden v. Hardy*, 169 U.S. 366, 386, Mr. Justice Brown, writing for the court, said:

> 'The earlier practice of the common law, which denied the benefit of witnesses to a person accused of felony, had been abolished by statute, though, so far as it deprived him of the assistance of counsel and compulsory process for the attendance of his witnesses, it had not been changed in England. But to the credit of her American colonies, let it be said that so oppressive a doctrine had never obtained a foothold there.'

One test which has been applied to determine whether due process of law has been accorded in given instances is to ascertain what were the settled usages and modes of proceeding under the common and statute law of England before the Declaration of Independence, subject, however, to the qualification that they be shown not to have been unsuited to the civil and political conditions of our ancestors by having been followed in this country after it became a nation. *Lowe v. Kansas*, 163 U.S. 81, 85. Plainly, as appears from the foregoing, this test, as thus qualified, has not been met in the present case.

We do not overlook the case of *Hurtado v. California*, 110 U.S. 516, where this court determined that due process of law does not require an indictment by a grand jury as a prerequisite to prosecution by a state for murder. In support of that conclusion the court (pages 534, 535 of 110 U.S.,) referred to the fact that the Fifth Amendment, in addition to containing the due process of law clause, provides in explicit terms that 'no person shall be held to answer for a capital, or otherwise infamous crime, unless on a presentment or indictment of a Grand Jury, * * *' and said that since no part of this important amendment could be regarded as superfluous, the obvious inference is that in the sense of the Constitution due process of law was not intended to include, ex vi termini, the institution and procedure of a grand jury in any case; and that the same phrase, employed in the Fourteenth Amendment to restrain the action of the states, was to be interpreted as having been used in the same sense and with no greater extent; and that if it had been the purpose of that Amendment to perpetuate the institution of the grand jury in the states, it would have embodied, as did the Fifth Amendment, an express declaration to that effect.

The Sixth Amendment, in terms, provides that in all criminal prosecutions the accused shall enjoy the right 'to have the Assistance of Counsel for his defence.' In the face of the reasoning of the *Hurtado* Case, if it stood alone, it would be difficult to justify the conclusion that the right to counsel, being thus specifically granted by the Sixth Amendment, was also within the intendement of the due process of law clause. But the *Hurtado* Case does not stand alone. In the later case of *Chicago, Burlington & Q.R. Co. v. Chicago*, 166 U.S. 226, 241, this court held that a judgment of a state court, even though authorized by statute, by which private property was taken for public use without just compensation, was in violation of the due process of law required by the Fourteenth Amendment, notwithstanding that the Fifth Amendment explicitly declares that private property shall not be taken for public use without just compensation. This holding was followed in *Norwood v. Baker*, 172 U.S. 269, 277.

Likewise, this court has considered that freedom of speech and of the press are rights protected by the due process clause of the Fourteenth Amendment, although in the First Amendment, Congress is prohibited in specific terms from abridging the right. *Gitlow v. People of State of New York*, 268 U.S. 652, 666,; *Stromberg v. California*, 283 U.S. 359, 368,; *Near v. Minnesota*, 283 U.S. 697, 707,.

These later cases establish that notwithstanding the sweeping character of the language in the Hurtado Case, the rule laid down is not without exceptions. The rule is an aid to construction, and in some instances may be conclusive; but it must yield to more compelling considerations whenever such considerations exist. The fact that the right involved is of such a character that it cannot be denied without violating those 'fundamental principles of liberty and justice which lie at the base of all our civil and political institutions' (*Hebert v. State of Louisiana*, 272 U.S. 312, is obviously one of those compelling considerations which must prevail in determining whether it is embraced within the due process clause of the Fourteenth Amendment, although it be specifically dealt with in another part of the Federal Constitution. Evidently this court, in the later cases enumerated, regarded the rights there under consideration as of this fundamental character. That some such distinction must be observed is foreshadowed in *Twining v. New Jersey*, 211 U.S. 78, 99, where Mr. Justice Moody, speaking for the court, said that: '* * * It is possible that some of the personal rights safeguarded by the first eight Amendments against national action may also be safeguarded against state action, because a denial of them would be a denial of due process of law. *Chicago, Burlington & Quincy Railroad v. Chicago*, 166 U.S. 226,. If this is so, it is not because those rights are enumerated in the first eight Amendments, but because they are of such a nature that they are included in the conception of due process of law.' While the question has never been categorically determined by this court, a consideration of the nature of the right and a review of the expressions of this and other courts makes it clear that the right to the aid of counsel is of this fundamental character.

It never has been doubted by this court, or any other so far as we know, that notice and hearing are preliminary steps essential to the passing of an enforceable judgment, and that they, together with a legally competent tribunal having jurisdiction of the case, constitute basic elements of the constitutional requirement of due process of law. The words of Webster, so often quoted, that by 'the law of the land' is intended 'a law which hears before it condemns,' have been repeated in varying forms of expression in a multitude of decisions. In *Holden v. Hardy*, 169 U.S. 366, 389, the necessity of due notice and an opportunity of being heard is described as among the 'immutable principles of justice which inhere in the very idea of free government which no member of the Union may disregard.' And Mr. Justice Field, in an earlier case, *Galpin v. Page*, 18 Wall. 350, 368, 369, said that the rule that no one shall be personally bound until he has had his day in court was as old as the law, and it meant that he must be cited to appear and afforded an opportunity to be heard. 'Judgment without such citation and opportunity wants all the attributes of a judicial determination; it is judicial usurpation and oppression, and never can be upheld where justice is justly administered.' Citations to the same effect might be indefinitely multiplied, but there is no occasion for doing so.

What, then, does a hearing include? Historically and in practice, in our own country at least, it has always included the right to the aid of counsel when desired and provided by the party asserting the right. The right to be heard would be, in many cases, of little avail if it did not comprehend the right to be heard by counsel. Even the intelligent and educated layman has small and sometimes no skill in the science of law. If charged with crime, he is incapable, generally, of determining for himself whether the indictment is good or bad. He is unfamiliar with the rules of evidence. Left without the aid of counsel he may be put on trial without a proper charge, and convicted upon incompetent evidence, or evidence irrelevant to the issue or otherwise inadmissible. He lacks both the skill and knowledge adequately to prepare his defense, even though he have a perfect one. He requires the guiding hand of counsel at every step in the proceedings against him. Without it, though he be not guilty, he faces the danger of conviction because he does not know how to establish his innocence. If that be true of men of intelligence, how much more true is it of the ignorant and illiterate, or those of feeble intellect. If in any case, civil or criminal, a state or federal court were arbitrarily to refuse to hear a party by counsel, employed by and appearing for him, it reasonably may not be doubted that such a refusal would be a denial of a hearing, and, therefore, of due process in the constitutional sense.

The decisions all point to that conclusion. In *Cooke v. United States*, 267 U.S. 517, 537, it was held that where a contempt was not in open court, due process of law required charges and a reasonable opportunity to defend or explain. The court added, 'We think this includes the assistance of counsel, if requested. * * *' In numerous other cases the court, in determining that due process was accorded, has frequently stressed the fact that the defendant had the aid of counsel. See, for example, Felts v. Murphy, 201 U.S. 123, 129,.; *Frank v. Mangum*, 237 U.S. 309, 344; *Kelley v. State of Oregon*, 273 U.S. 589, 591,. In *Ex parte Hidekuni Iwata* (D.C.) 219 F. 610, 611, the federal district judge enumerated among the elements necessary to due process of law in a deportation case the opportunity at some stage of the hearing to secure and have the advice and assistance of counsel. In *Ex parte Chin Loy You* (D.C.) 223 F. 833, 838, also a deportation case, the district judge held that under the particular circumstances of the case the prisoner, having seasonably made demand, was entitled to confer with and have the aid of counsel. Pointing to the fact that the right to counsel as secured by the Sixth Amendment relates only to criminal prosecutions, judge said, '* * * but it is equally true that that provision was inserted in the Constitution because the assistance of counsel was recognized as essential to any fair trial of a case against a prisoner.' In *Ex parte Riggins* (C.C.A.) 134 F. 404, 418, a case involving the due process clause of the Fourteenth Amendment, the court said, by way of illustration, that if the state should deprive a person of the benefit of counsel, it would not be due process of law. Judge Cooley refers to the right of a person accused of crime to have counsel as perhaps his most important privilege, and after discussing the development of the English law upon that subject, says: 'With us it is a universal principle of constitutional law, that the prisoner shall be allowed a defense by counsel.' 1 Cooley's Constitutional Limitations (8th Ed.) 700. The same author, as appears from a chapter which he added to his edition of Story on the Constitution, regarded the right of the accused to the presence, advice and assistance of counsel as necessarily included in due process of law. 2 Story on the Constitution (4th Ed.) s 1949, p. 668. The state decisions which refer to the matter, invariably recognize the right to the aid of counsel as fundamental in character. E.g., *People v. Napthaly*, 105 Cal. 641, 644,

In the light of the facts outlined in the forepart of this opinion—the ignorance and illiteracy of the defendants, their youth, the circumstances of public hostility, the imprisonment and the close surveillance of the defendants by the military forces, the fact that their friends and families were all in other states and communication with them necessarily difficult, and above all that they stood in deadly peril of their lives—we think the failure of the trial court to give them reasonable time and opportunity to secure counsel was a clear denial of due process.

But passing that, and assuming their inability, even if opportunity had been given, to employ counsel, as the trial court evidently did assume, we are of opinion that, under the circumstances just stated, the necessity of counsel was so vital and imperative that the failure of the trial court to make an effective appointment of counsel was likewise a denial of due process within the meaning of the Fourteenth Amendment. Whether this would be so in other criminal prosecutions, or under other circumstances, we need not determine. All that it is necessary now to decide, as we do decide, is that in a capital case, where the defendant is unable to employ counsel, and is incapable adequately of making his own defense because of ignorance, feeble-mindedness, illiteracy, or the like, it is the duty of the court, whether requested or not, to assign counsel for him as a necessary requisite of due process of law; and that duty is not discharged by an assignment at such a time or under such circumstances as to preclude the giving of effective aid in the preparation and trial of the case. To hold otherwise would be to ignore the fundamental postulate, already adverted to, 'that there are certain immutable principles of justice which inhere in the very idea of free government which no member of the Union may disregard.' *Holden v. Hardy*, supra. In a case such as this, whatever may be the rule in other cases, the right to have counsel appointed, when necessary, is a logical corollary from the constitutional right to be heard by counsel. Compare *Carpenter & Sprague v. Dane County*, 9 Wis. 274; *Dane County v. Smith*, 13 Wis. 585, 586, 80 Am.Dec. 754; *Hendryx v. State*, 130 Ind. 265, 268, 269, 29 N.E. 1131; *Cutts v. State*, 54 Fla. 21, 23, 45 So. 491; *People v. Goldenson*, 76 Cal. 328, 344, 19 P. 161; *Delk v. State*, 99 Ga. 667, 669, 670, 26 S.E. 752.

In Hendryx v. State, supra, there was no statute authorizing the assignment of an attorney to defend an indigent person accused of crime, but the court held that such an assignment was necessary to accomplish the ends of public justice, and that the court possessed the inherent power to make it. 'Where a prisoner,' the court said (page 269 of 130 Ind., 29 N.E. 1131, 1132), 'without legal knowledge is confined in jail, absent from his friends, without the aid of legal advice or the means of investigating the charge against him, it is impossible to conceive of a fair trial where he is compelled to conduct his cause in court, without the aid of counsel. * * * Such a trial is not far removed from an exparte proceeding.'

Let us suppose the extreme case of a prisoner charged with a capital offense, who is deaf and dumb, illiterate, and feeble-minded, unable to employ counsel, with the whole power of the state arrayed against him, prosecuted by counsel for the state without assignment of counsel for his defense, tried, convicted, and sentenced to death. Such a result, which, if carried into execution, would be little short of judicial murder, it cannot be doubted would be a gross violation of the guarantee of due process of law; and we venture to think that no appellate court, state or federal, would hesitate so to decide. See *Stephenson v. State*, 4 Ohio App. 128; *Williams v. State*, 163 Ark. 623, 628, 260 S.W. 721; *Grogan v. Commonwealth*, 222 Ky. 484, 485, 1 S.W.(2d) 779; *Mullen v. State*, 28 Okl.Cr. 218, 230, 230 P. 285; *Williams v. Commonwealth* (Ky.) 110 S.W. 339, 340. The duty of the trial court to appoint counsel under such circumstances is clear, as it is clear under circumstances such as are disclosed by the record here; and its power to do so, even in the absence of a statute, can not be questioned. Attorneys are officers of the court, and are bound to render service when required by such an appointment. See Cooley, Constitutional Limitations, supra, 700 and note.

The United States by statute and every state in the Union by express provision of law, or by the determination of its courts, make it the duty of the trial judge, where the accused is unable to employ counsel, to appoint counsel for him. In most states the rule applies broadly to all criminal prosecutions, in others it is limited to the more serious crimes, and in a very limited number, to capital cases. A rule adopted with such unanimous accord reflects, if it does not establish the inherent right to have counsel appointed at least in cases like the present, and lends convincing support to the conclusion we have reached as to the fundamental nature of that right.

The judgments must be reversed and the causes remanded for further proceedings not inconsistent with this opinion.

Judgments reversed.

Note

The case of the Scottsboro defendants, particularly as reflected in *Powell v. Alabama*, was not only a major turning point for criminal procedure as we know it today, but also represents the ongoing issues of race and the criminal justice system intersections. As we consider the significant concerns currently highlighted by scholars such Michelle Alexander in THE NEW JIM CROW: MASS INCARCERATION IN THE AGE OF COLORBLINDNESS (The New Press; 10th Anniversary ed. edition , January 7, 2020), consider also the national and even international attention that is now focus on American justice. In 1986 the United Nations established a Sentencing Project to examine whether the United States provides a fair and effective system of criminal justice in addressing racial disparity. Noting that in the United States African Americans are 5.9 times more likely to be incarcerated than whites and that Hispanics are 3.1 times more likely to incarcerated than whites, such racial disparity is in direct violation of Article 2 and Article 26 of the International Covenant on Civil and Political Rights. *Regarding Racial Disparities in the United States Criminal Justice System; Report of The Sentencing Project to the United Nations Special Rapporteur on Contemporary Forms of Racism, Racial Discrimination, Xenophobia, and Related Intolerance, March 2018.*

The report of the Sentencing Project makes seven broad-based recommendations for addressing racial disparity and its resultant mass incarceration:

• End the War on Drugs (by reduction of the volume of low-level drug offense prosecution and increased use of alternative to incarceration programs)
• Eliminate mandatory minimum sentences (thus restoring the discretion of trial judges to consider individual case characteristics)
• Reduce the use of cash bail (by implementing transparent risk-assessment instruments to determine flight risk)

- Fully fund indigent defense agencies (federal, state and local resources should both support training and technical assistance for indigent defense and monitor jurisdictions for compliance with legal profession standards).
- Adoption of requirements for the use of racial impact statements (by requiring that legislatures assess the disparate racial consequences of criminal justice legislation).
- Develop and implement training to reduee racial bias (training to mitigate the influence of racism at all levels of the criminal justice system; including police, public defenders, prosecutors, judges, jurors, and parole boards).
- Address collateral consequences (Restoration of voting rights for convicted felons who have served their sentence, while preserving public safety, removal or curtailing of conviction restrictions in employment opportunities, education, housing and social service safety net).

The full report of the Sentencing Project may be found at;
www.sentencingproject.org/publications/un-report-on-racial-disparities .

In 1999 the Union for Reform Judaism reached this similar conclusion:

> There is an increasing perception that we have two criminal justice systems, separate and unequal: one for affluent Whites and one for racial minorities and the poor. Foremost among the complaints are disparate application of the death penalty, police brutality, racial profiling, sentencing disparity, and disparate treatment of minorities by the juvenile justice system. https://urj.org/what-we-believe/resolutions/race-and-us-criminal-justice-system

CHAPTER TWO: RACE AND CONFESSIONS

Race, Interrogation, and the Use of Physical Torture and Coercion

LeRoy Pernell, *Racial Justice And Federal Habeas Corpus As Postconviction Relief From State Convictions,* 69 MERCER LAW REVIEW 453, 475-477 (2018) (footnotes omitted) (excerpt)(reprint by permission of Mercer Law Review)
....

Dating back at least to the late nineteenth century, police tactics in interrogating suspects have a long history of reliance on coercion and out-right torture. The infamous "third degree," associated with the infliction of physical and psychological pain to obtain confessions, became part of American culture and its perception of law enforcement. Media coverage in the closing decades of the 1800s, through at least the 1930s, recognized that police regularly engaged in tactics such as the sweat box, hanging suspects by the neck, and use of incommunicado detention.

Less prominent in the public acknowledgement of police torture was the connection between the use of torture and race. Police abuse of African-Americans was particularly prominent in southern, former slave states. The first example of such to reach the Court was *Brown*. Yet *Brown* was hardly alone in the Court's reporting or consideration of torture tactics used against African-American suspects. As noted by Professor Maclin, "In the eight years following *Brown*, the Court heard six more confession cases coming from southern state courts where [African-American] defendants alleged their confessions had been coerced."

This trail of cases involving confessions resulting from brutality ultimately led to official disavowal of the third degree as a sanctioned method of interrogation. The "Wickersham Report," commissioned by President Herbert Hoover, condemned the use of physical coercion and called for the adoption of alternative methods of interrogation.

Judicial response, keying in on the lack of reliability of confessions obtained from brutality, developed an "involuntary" or "coerced confessions" rule. Building on its handling of *Brown*, the Court, through a series of cases, crafted an approach to confessions derived from torture, depending less on disapproval of race-inspired violence and more on the probative value of statements gained through such mechanisms. Building on the common-law proscription against coerced confessions as unreliable, the Court developed a complex due process-based matrix to determine the constitutional permissibility of admission of statements derived from coercion on a case-by-case basis. Based on the totality of the circumstances, the Court weighed the probative value of such statements, along with whether the confession was the product of free will.

Concern regarding the effectiveness of torture-like tactics in producing usable confessions, growing judicial concern over reliability and voluntariness, and growing public distaste over reported brutal acts caused reform of the training and approach of police officers. Recognizing the recommendation for change in the Wickersham Report, police developed new techniques, using behavioral science and psychology, as an alternative to physical violence. Psychological manipulation became a cornerstone of modern interrogation. The police training manual became central to developing psychological manipulation skills.

In 1962, Professor Fred Inbau of Northwestern University, along with John E. Reid, published the first edition of what would become the standard text for police training. Professor Inbau, who was once the director of the Scientific Crime Detection Laboratory in Chicago, developed and taught interrogation techniques relying on deceit, deception, and tricks to produce incriminating statements. His method also relied on presenting the suspect with large amounts of damaging facts in order to persuade confession. The use of these psychological techniques was touted as a reform and replacement for the third degree. It was the coercive nature of these techniques in incommunicado interrogation settings that formed a large part of the concern expressed by the Warren Court in Miranda.

....

Note

As indicated above, the *Brown* case helped draw attention to the use of physical torture in the interrogation of African Americans. At the time of *Brown* national attention to such brutality had already been drawn by press reports and the Wickersham Commission report, as noted by the following:

> "After reviewing the evidence obtainable the authors of the report reach the conclusion that the third degree-that is, the use of physical brutality, or other forms of cruelty, to obtain involuntary confessions or admissions-is widespread. Protracted questioning of prisoners is commonly employed. Threats and methods of intimidation, adjusted to the age or mentality of the victim, are frequently used, either by themselves or in combination with some of the other practices mentioned. Physical brutality, illegal detention, and refusal to allow access of counsel to the prisoner is common. Even where the law requires prompt production of a prisoner before a magistrate, the police not infrequently delay doing so and employ the time in efforts to compel confession."

See, Edwin R. Keedy, The Third Degree and Legal Interrogation of Suspects, 85 UNIV. OF PENN. L. REV. 761-764 (1937)

Race and the Emergence of Psychological Coercion

CHAMBERS V. FLORIDA
309 U.S. 227 (1940)

Mr. Justice BLACK delivered the opinion of the Court.

The grave question presented by the petition for certiorari, granted in forma pauperis, is whether proceedings in which confessions were utilized, and which culminated in sentences of death upon four young negro men in the State of Florida, failed to afford the safeguard of that due process of law guaranteed by the Fourteenth Amendment U.S.C.A.Const.

First. The State of Florida challenges our jurisdiction to look behind the judgments below claiming that the issues of fact upon which petitioners base their claim that due process was denied them have been finally determined because passed upon by a jury. However, use by a State of an improperly obtained confession may constitute a denial of due process of law as guaranteed in the Fourteenth Amendment. Since petitioners have seasonably asserted the right under the Federal Constitution to have their guilt or innocence of a capital crime determined without reliance upon confessions obtained by means proscribed by the due process clause of the Fourteenth Amendment, we must determine independently whether petitioners' confessions were so obtained, by review of the facts upon which that issue necessarily turns.

Second. The record shows—
About nine o'clock on the night of Saturday, May 13, 1933, Robert Darcy, an elderly white man, was robbed and murdered in Pompano, Florida, a small town in Broward County about twelve miles from Fort Lauderdale, the County seat. The opinion of the Supreme Court of Florida affirming petitioners' conviction for this crime stated that 'It was one of those crimes that induced an enraged community And, as the dissenting judge pointed out, 'The murder and robbery of the elderly Mr. Darcy was a most dastardly and atrocious crime. It naturally aroused great and well justified public indignation.

Between 9:30 and 10 o'clock after the murder, petitioner Charlie Davis was arrested, and within the next twenty-four hours from twenty-five to forty negroes living in the community, including petitioners Williamson, Chambers and Woodward, were arrested without warrants and confined in the Broward County jail, at Fort Lauderdale. On the night of the crime, attempts to trail the murderers by bloodhounds brought J. T. Williams, a convict guard, into the proceedings. From then until confessions were obtained and petitioners were sentenced, he took a prominent part. About 11 P.M. on the following Monday, May 15, the sheriff and Williams took several of the imprisoned negroes, including Williamson and Chambers, to the Dade County jail at Miami. The sheriff testified that they were taken there because he felt a possibility of mob violence and 'wanted to give protection to every prisoner in jail.' Evidence of petitioners was that on the way to Miami a motorcycle patrolman drew up to the car in which the men were riding and the sheriff 'told the cop that he had some negroes that he taking down to Miami to escape a mob.' This statement was not denied by the sheriff in his testimony and Williams did not testify at all; Williams apparently has now disappeared. Upon order of Williams, petitioner Williamson was kept in the death cell of the Dade County jail. The prisoners thus spirited to Miami were returned to the Fort Lauderdale jail the next day, Tuesday.

It is clear from the evidence of both the State and petitioners that from Sunday, May 14, to Saturday, May 20, the thirty to forty negro suspects were subjected to questioning and cross questioning (with the exception that several of the suspects were in Dade County jail over one night). From the afternoon of Saturday, May 20, until sunrise of the 21st, petitioners and possibly one or two others underwent persistent and repeated questioning. The Supreme Court of Florida said the questioning 'was in progress several days and all night before the confessions were secured' and referred to the last night as an 'all night vigil.' The sheriff who supervised the procedure of continued interrogation testified that he questioned the prisoners 'in the day time all the week,' but did not question them during any night before the all night vigil of Saturday, May 20, because after having 'questioned them all day (he) was tired.' Other evidence of the State was 'that the officers of Broward County were in that jail almost continually during the whole week questioning these boys, and other boys, in connection with this' case.

The process of repeated questioning took place in the jailer's quarters on the fourth floor of the jail. During the week following their arrests and until their confessions were finally acceptable to the State's attorney in the early dawn of Sunday, May 21st, petitioners and their fellow prisoners were led one at a time from their cells to the questioning room, quizzed, and returned to their cells to await another turn. So far as appears, the prisoners at no time during the week were permitted to see or confer with counsel or a single friend or relative. When carried singly from his cell and subjected to questioning, each found himself, a single prisoner, surrounded in a fourth floor jail room by four to ten men, the county sheriff, his deputies, a convict guard, and other white officers and citizens of the community.

The testimony is in conflict as to whether all four petitioners were continually threatened and physically mistreated until they finally, in hopeless desperation and fear of their lives, agreed to confess on Sunday morning just after daylight. Be that as it may, it is certain that by Saturday, May 20th, five days of continued questioning had elicited no confession. Admittedly, a concentration of effort—directed against a small number of prisoners including petitioners—on the part of the questioners, principally the sheriff and Williams, the convict guard, began about 3:30 that Saturday afternoon. From that hour on, with only short intervals for food and rest for the questioners—'They all stayed up all night.' 'They bring one of them at a time backwards and forwards * * * until they confessed.' And Williams was present and participating that night, during the whole of which the jail cook served coffee and sandwiches to the men who 'grilled' the prisoners.

Sometime in the early hours of Sunday, the 21st, probably about 2:30 A.M., Woodward apparently 'broke'— as one of the State's witnesses put it—after a fifteen or twenty minute period of questioning by Williams, the sheriff and the constable 'one right after the other.' The State's attorney was awakened at his home, and called to the jail. He came, but was dissatisfied with the confession of Woodward which he took down in writing at that time, and said something like 'tear this paper up, that isn't what I want, when you get something worth while call me.'7 This same State's attorney conducted the State's case in the circuit court below and also made himself a witness, but did not testify as to why Woodward's first alleged confession was unsatisfactory to him. The sheriff did, however:

'A. No, it wasn't false, part of it was true and part of it wasn't; Mr. Maire (the State's attorney) said there wasn't enough. It wasn't clear enough.

'Q. * * * Was that voluntarily made at that time? A. Yes, sir.

'Q. It was voluntarily made that time. A. Yes, sir.

'Q. You didn't consider it sufficient? A. Mr. Maire.

'Q. Mr. Maire told you that it wasn't sufficient, so you kept on questioning him until the time you got him to make a free and voluntary confession of other matters that he hadn't included in the first? A. No, sir, we questioned him there and we caught him in lies.

'Q. Caught all of them telling lies? A. Caught every one of them lying to us that night, yes, sir.

'Q. Did you tell them they were lying? A. Yes, sir.

'Q. Just how would you tell them that? A. Just like I am talking to you.

'Q. You said 'Jack, you told me a lie'? A. Yes, sir.'

After one week's constant denial of all guilt, petitioners 'broke.'

Just before sunrise, the State officials got something 'worthwhile' from petitioners which the State's attorney would 'want'; again he was called; he came; in the presence of those who had carried on and witnessed the all night questioning, he caused his questions and petitioners' answers to be stenographically reported. These are the confessions utilized by the State to obtain the judgments upon which petitioners were sentenced to death. No formal charges had been brought before the confessions. Two days thereafter, petitioners were indicted, were arraigned and Williamson and Woodward pleaded guilty; Chambers and Davis pleaded not guilty. Later the sheriff, accompanied by Williams, informed an attorney who presumably had been appointed to defend Davis that Davis wanted his plea of not guilty withdrawn. This was done, and Davis then pleaded guilty. When Chambers was tried, his conviction rested upon his confession and testimony of the other three confessors. The convict guard and the sheriff 'were in the Court room sitting down in a seat.' And from arrest until sentenced to death, petitioners were never—either in jail or in court—wholly removed from the constant observation, influence, custody and control of those whose persistent pressure brought about the sunrise confessions.

Third. The scope and operation of the Fourteenth Amendment have been fruitful sources of controversy in our constitutional history. However, in view of its historical setting and the wrongs which called it into being, the due process provision of the Fourteenth Amendment—just as that in the Fifth—has led few to doubt that it was intended to guarantee procedural standards adequate and appropriate, then and thereafter,9 to protect, at all times, people charged with or suspected of crime by those holding positions of power and authority. Tyrannical governments had immemorially utilized dictatorial criminal procedure and punishment to make scape goats of the weak, or of helpless political, religious, or racial minorities and those who differed, who would not conform and who resisted tyranny. The instruments of such governments were in the main, two. Conduct, innocent when engaged in, was subsequently made by fiat criminally punishable without legislation. And a liberty loving people won the principle that criminal punishments could not be inflicted save for that which proper legislative action had already by 'the law of the land' forbidden when done. But even more was needed. From the popular hatred and abhorrence of illegal confinement, torture and extortion of confessions of violations of the 'law of the land' evolved the fundamental idea that no man's life, liberty or property be forfeited as criminal punishment for violation of that law until there had been a charge fairly made and fairly tried in a public tribunal free of prejudice, passion, excitement and tyrannical power. Thus, as assurance against ancient evils, our country, in order to preserve 'the blessings of liberty', wrote into its basic law the requirement, among others, that the forfeiture of the lives, liberties or property of people accused of crime can only follow if procedural safeguards of due process have been obeyed.

The determination to preserve an accused's right to procedural due process sprang in large part from knowledge of the historical truth that the rights and liberties of people accused of crime could not be safely entrusted to secret inquisitorial processes. The testimony of centuries, in governments of varying kinds over populations of different races and beliefs, stood as proof that physical and mental torture and coercion had brought about the tragically unjust sacrifices of some who were the noblest and most useful of their generations. The rack, the thumbscrew, the wheel, solitary confinement, protracted questioning and cross questioning, and other ingenious forms of entrapment of the helpless or unpopular had left their wake of mutilated bodies and shattered minds along the way to the cross, the guillotine, the stake and the hangman's noose. And they who have suffered most from secret and dictatorial proceedings have almost always been the poor, the ignorant, the numerically weak, the friendless, and the powerless.

This requirement—of conforming to fundamental standards of procedure in criminal trials— was made operative against the States by the Fourteenth Amendment. Where one of several accused had limped into the trial court as a result of admitted physical mistreatment inflicted to obtain confessions upon which a jury had returned a verdict of guilty of murder, this Court recently declared, Brown v. State of Mississippi, that 'It would be difficult to conceive of methods more revolting to the sense of justice than those taken to procure the confessions of these petitioners, and the use of the confessions thus obtained as the basis for conviction and sentence was a clear denial of due process.

Here, the record develops a sharp conflict upon the issue of physical violence and mistreatment, but shows, without conflict, the drag net methods of arrest on suspicion without warrant, and the protracted questioning and cross questioning of these ignorant young colored tenant farmers by State officers and other white citizens, in a fourth floor jail room, where as prisoners they were without friends, advisers or counselors, and under circumstances calculated to break the strongest nerves and the stoutest resistance. Just as our decision in Brown v. State of Mississippi was based upon the fact that the confessions were the result of compulsion, so in the present case, the admitted practices were such as to justify the statement that 'The undisputed facts showed that compulsion was applied.'

For five days petitioners were subjected to interrogations culminating in Saturday's (May 20th) all night examination. Over a period of five days they steadily refused to confess and disclaimed any guilt. The very circumstances surrounding their confinement and their questioning without any formal charges having been brought, were such as to fill petitioners with terror and frightful misgivings. Some were practical strangers in the community; three were arrested in a one-room farm tenant house which was their home; the haunting fear of mob violence was around them in an atmosphere charged with excitement and public indignation. From virtually the moment of their arrest until their eventual confessions, they never knew just when any one would be called back to the fourth floor room, and there, surrounded by his accusers and others, interrogated by men who held their very lives—so far as these ignorant petitioners could know—in the balance. The rejection of petitioner Woodward's first 'confession', given in the early hours of Sunday morning, because it was found wanting, demonstrates the relentless tenacity which 'broke' petitioners' will and rendered them helpless to resist their accusers further. To permit human lives to be forfeited upon confessions thus obtained would make of the constitutional requirement of due process of law a meaningless symbol.

We are not impressed by the argument that law enforcement methods such as those under review are necessary to uphold our laws . The Constitution proscribes such lawless means irrespective of the end. And this argument flouts the basic principle that all people must stand on an equality before the bar of justice in every American court. Today, as in ages past, we are not without tragic proof that the exalted power of some governments to punish manufactured crime dictatorially is the handmaid of tyranny. Under our constitutional system, courts stand against any winds that blow as havens of refuge for those who might otherwise suffer because they are helpless, weak, outnumbered, or because they are non-conforming victims of prejudice and public excitement. Due process of law, preserved for all by our Constitution, commands that no such practice as that disclosed by this record shall send any accused to his death. No higher duty, no more solemn responsibility, rests upon this Court, than that of translating into living law and maintaining this constitutional shield deliberately planned and inscribed for the benefit of every human being subject to our Constitution—of whatever race, creed or persuasion.

The Supreme Court of Florida was in error and its judgment is

Reversed.

Note

Following *Chambers* the Court considered whether to extend its disapproval of non-physical coercion – induced confessions to second statements derived after the coerced one but possibly the result of the broken will of the suspect. This concept of extension of what the Court viewed as "voluntariness" questions to statements that are subsequently obtained absent direct "coercion", will later manifest itself in a doctrine sometimes referred to as "the Cat Out of the Bag" See, United States v. Bayer, 331 U.S. 532,(1947), Oregon v. Elstad, 470 U.S. 298 (1985). And will largely be determined by an assessment of how independent of the first coerced statement is the subsequent statement. While the later cases focused more on this issue in the face of *Miranda* violations occurring in regards to the initial interrogation, it is not long after *Chambers* that the Court is asked to take up this question in regards to African Americans subjected to intense physical and non-physical coercion in the initial interrogation but who subsequently give a second incriminating statements. Such was the case in *Lyons v. Oklahoma*, 322 U.S. 596 (1944), which like *Chambers* was also argued to the Court by a young Thurgood Marshall.

LYONS V. OKLAHOMA.
322 U.S. 596 (1944)

Mr. Justice REED delivered the opinion of the Court.

This writ brings to this Court for review a conviction obtained with the aid of a confession which furnished, if voluntary, material evidence to support the conviction. As the questioned confession followed a previous confession which was given on the same day and which was admittedly involuntary, the issue is the voluntary character of the second confession under the circumstances which existed at the time and place of its signature and, particularly, because of the alleged continued influence of the unlawful inducements which vitiated the prior confession.

The petitioner was convicted in the state district court of Choctaw County, Oklahoma, on an information charging him and another with the crime of murder. The jury fixed his punishment at life imprisonment. The conviction was affirmed by the Criminal Court of Appeals, and this Court granted certiorari, , upon the petitioner's representation that there had been admitted against him an involuntary confession procured under circumstances which made its use in evidence a violation of his rights under the due process clause of the Fourteenth Amendment.

Prior to Sunday, December 31, 1939, Elmer Rogers lived with his wife and three small sons in a tenant house situated a short distance northwest of Fort Towson, Choctaw County, Oklahoma. Late in the evening of that day Mr. and Mrs. Rogers and a four year old son Elvie were murdered at their home and the house was burned to conceal the crime.

Suspicion was directed toward the petitioner Lyons and a confederate, Van Bizzell. On January 11, 1940. Lyons was arrested by a special policeman and another officer whose exact official status is not disclosed by the record. The first formal charge that appears is at Lyons' hearing before a magistrate on January 27, 1940. Immediately after his arrest there was an interrogation of about two hours at the jail. After he had been in jail eleven days he was again questioned, this time in the county prosecutor's office. This interrogation began about six-thirty in the evening, and on the following morning between two and four produced a confession. This questioning is the basis of the objection to the introduction as evidence of a second confession which was obtained later in the day at the state penitentiary at McAlester by Warden Jess Dunn and introduced in evidence at the trial. There was also a third confession, oral, which was admitted on the trial without objection by petitioner. This was given to a guard at the penitentiary two days after the second. Only the petitioner, police, prosecuting and penitentiary officials were present at any of these interrogations, except that a private citizen who drove the car that brought Lyons to McAleser witnessed this second confession.

Lyons is married and was twenty-one or two years of age at the time of the arrest. The extent of his education or his occupation does not appear. He signed the second confession. From the transcript of his evidence, there is no indication of a subnormal intelligence. He had served two terms in the penitentiary—one for chicken stealing and one for burglary. Apparently he lived with various relatives.

While petitioner was competently represented before and at the trial, counsel was not supplied him until after his preliminary examination, which was subsequent to the confessions. His wife and family visited him between his arrest and the first confession. There is testimony by Lyons of physical abuse by the police officers at the time of his arrest and first interrogation on January 11th. His sister visited him in jail shortly afterwards and testified as to marks of violence on his body and a blackened eye. Lyons says that this violence was accompanied by threats of further harm unless he confessed. This evidence was denied in toto by officers who were said to have participated.

Eleven days later the second interrogation occurred. Again the evidence of assault is conflicting. Eleven or twelve officials were in and out of the prosecutor's small office during the night. Lyons says that he again suffered assault. Denials of violence were made by all the participants accused by Lyons except the county attorney, his assistant, the jailer and a highway patrolman. Disinterested witnesses testified to statements by an investigator which tended to implicate that officer in the use of force, and the prosecutor in cross-examination used language which gave color to defendant's charge. It is not disputed that the inquiry continued until two-thirty in the morning before an oral confession was obtained and that a pan of the victims' bones was placed in Lyon's lap by his interrogators to bring about his confession. As the confession obtained at this time was not offered in evidence, the only bearing these events have here is their tendency to show that the later confession at McAlester was involuntary.

After the oral confession in the early morning hours of January 23, Lyons was taken to the scene of the crime and subjected to further questioning about the instruments which were used to commit the murders. He was returned to the jail about eight-thirty A.M. and left there until early afternoon. After that the prisoner was taken to a nearby town of Antlers, Oklahoma. Later in the day a deputy sheriff and a private citizen took the petitioner to the penitentiary. There, sometime between eight and eleven o'clock on that same evening, the petitioner signed the second confession.

When the confession which was given at the penitentiary was offered, objection was made on the ground that force was practiced to secure it and that even if no force was then practiced, the fear instilled by the prisoner's former treatment at Hugo on his first and second interrogations continued sufficiently coercive in its effect to require the rejection of the second confession.

The judge in accordance with Oklahoma practice and, after hearing evidence from the prosecution and the defense in the absence of the jury, first passed favorably upon its admissibility as a matter of law, and then, after witnesses testified before the jury as to the voluntary character of the confession, submitted the guilt or innocence of the defendant to the jury under a full instruction, approved by the Criminal Court of Appeals, to the effect that voluntary confessions are admissible against the person making them but are to be 'carefully scrutinized and received with great caution' by the jury and rejected if obtained by punishment, intimidation or threats. It was added that the mere fact that a confession was made in answer to inquiries 'while under arrest or in custody' does not prevent consideration of the evidence if made 'freely and voluntarily.' The instruction did not specifically cover the defendant's contention, embodied in a requested instruction, that the second confession sprang from the fear engendered by the treatment he had received at Hugo.

The mere questioning of a suspect while in the custody of police officers is not prohibited either as a matter of common law or due process. The question of how specific an instruction in a state court must be upon the involuntary character of a confession is, as a matter of procedure or practice, solely for the courts of the state. When the state-approved instruction fairly raises the question of whether or not the challenged confession was voluntary, as this instruction did, the requirements of due process, under the Fourteenth Amendment, are satisfied and this Court will not require a modification of local practice to meet views that it might have as to the advantages of concreteness. The instruction given satisfies the legal requirements of the State of Oklahoma as to the particularity with which issues must be presented to its juries, and in view of the scope of that instruction, it was sufficient to preclude any claim of violation of the Fourteenth Amendment.

The federal question presented is whether the second confession was given under such circumstances that its use as evidence at the trial constitutes a violation of the due process clause of the Fourteenth Amendment, which requires that state criminal proceedings 'shall be consistent with the fundamental principles of liberty and justice.'

No formula to determine this question by its application to the facts of a given case can be devised. *Hopt v. Utah*, 110 U.S. 574. Here improper methods were used to obtain a confession, but that confession was not used at the trial. Later, in another place and with different persons present, the accused again told the facts of the crime. Involuntary confessions, of course, may be given either simultaneously with or subsequently to unlawful pressures, force or threats. The question of whether those confessions subsequently given are themselves voluntary depends on the inferences as to the continuing effect of the coercive practices which may fairly be drawn from the surrounding circumstances. *Lisenba v. California*, 314 U.S. 219. The voluntary or involuntary character of a confession is determined by a conclusion as to whether the accused, at the time he confesses, is in possession of 'mental freedom' to confess to or deny a suspected participation in a crime. *Ashcraft v. State of Tennessee*, 322 U.S. 143.

When conceded facts exist which are irreconcilable with such mental freedom, regardless of the contrary conclusions of the triers of fact, whether judge or jury, this Court cannot avoid responsibility for such injustice by leaving the burden of adjudication solely in other hands. But where there is a dispute as to whether the acts which are charged to be coercive actually occurred, or where different inferences may fairly be drawn from admitted facts, the trial judge and the jury are not only in a better position to appraise the truth or falsity of the defendant's assertions from the demeanor of the witnesses but the legal duty is upon them to make the decision. *Lisenba v. California*, supra, 314 U.S. page 238.

Review here deals with circumstances which require examination into the possibility as to whether the judge and jury in the trial court could reasonably conclude that the McAlester confession was voluntary. The fact that there is evidence which would justify a contrary conclusion is immaterial. To triers of fact is left the determination of the truth or error of the testimony of prisoner and official alike. It is beyond question that if the triers of fact accepted as true the evidence of the immediate events at McAlester, which were detailed by Warden Dunn and the other witnesses, the verdict would be that the confession was voluntary, so that the petitioner's case rests upon the theory that the McAlester confession was the unavoidable outgrowth of the events at Hugo.

The Fourteenth Amendment does not protect one who has admitted his guilt because of forbidden inducements against the use at trial of his subsequent confessions under all possible circumstances. The admissibility of the later confession depends upon the same test—is it voluntary. Of course the fact that the earlier statement was obtained from the prisoner by coercion is to be considered in appraising the character of the later confession. The effect of earlier abuse may be so clear as to forbid any other inference than that it dominated the mind of the accused to such an extent that the later confession is involuntary. If the relation between the earlier and later confession is not so close that one must say the facts of one control the character of the other, the inference is one for the triers of fact and their conclusion, in such an uncertain situation, that the confession should be admitted as voluntary, cannot be a denial of due process. *Canty v. Alabama*, 309 U.S. 629, cannot be said to go further than to hold that the admission of confessions obtained by acts of oppression is sufficient to require a reversal of a state conviction by this Court. Our judgment there relied solely upon *Chambers v. Florida*, 309 U.S. 227. The Oklahoma Criminal Court of Appeals in the present case decided that the evidence would justify a determination that the effect of a prior coercion was dissipated before the second confession and we agree.

Petitioner suggests a presumption that earlier abuses render subsequent confessions involuntary unless there is clear and definite evidence to overcome the presumption. We need not analyze this contention further than to say that in this case there is evidence for the state which, if believed, would make it abundantly clear that the events at Hugo did not bring about the confession at McAlester.

In our view, the earlier events at Hugo do not lead unescapably to the conclusion that the later McAlester confession was brought about by the earlier mistreatments. The McAlester confession was separated from the early morning statement by a full twelve hours. It followed the prisoner's transfer from the control of the sheriff's force to that of the warden. One person who had been present during a part of the time while the Hugo interrogation was in progress was present at McAlester, it is true, but he was not among those charged with abusing Lyons during the questioning at Hugo. There was evidence from others present that Lyons readily confessed without any show of force or threats within a very short time of his surrender to Warden Dunn and after being warned by Dunn that anything he might say would be used against him and that he should not 'make a statement unless he voluntarily wanted to.' Lyons, as a former inmate of the institution, was acquainted with the warden. The petitioner testified to nothing in the past that would indicate any reason for him to fear mistreatment there. The fact that Lyons, a few days later, frankly admitted the killings to a sergeant of the prison guard, a former acquaintance from his own locality, under circumstances free of coercion suggests strongly that the petitioner had concluded that it was wise to make a clean breast of his guilt and that his confession to Dunn was voluntary. The answers to the warden's questions, as transcribed by a prison stenographer, contain statements correcting and supplementing the questioner's information and do not appear to be mere supine attempts to give the desired response to leading questions.

The Fourteenth Amendment is a protection against criminal trials in state courts conducted in such a manner as amounts to a disregard of 'that fundamental fairness essential to the very concept of justice,' and in a way that 'necessarily prevent(s) a fair trial.' *Lisenba v. California*, 314 U.S. 219, 236. A coerced confession is offensive to basic standards of justice, not because the victim has a legal grievance against the police, but because declarations procured by torture are not premises from which a civilized forum will infer guilt. The Fourteenth Amendment does not provide review of mere error in jury verdicts, even though the error concerns the voluntary character of a confession. We cannot say that an inference of guilt based in part upon Lyons' McAlester confession is so illogical and unreasonable as to deny the petitioner a fair trial.

Affirmed.

Note

Justice Black, who authored the *Chambers* opinion, joins in the dissent written by Justice Murphy, regarding the *Lyons* willingness to view the subsequent statements as "cleansed". Murphy notes in language that expressed concern over the future psychologically coercion in confessions:

This flagrant abuse by a state of the rights on an American citizen accused of murder ought not to be approved. The Fifth Amendment prohibits the federal government from convicting a defendant on evidence that he was compelled to give against himself.

. . . .

Even though approximately twelve hours intervened between the two confessions and even assuming that there was no violence surrounding the second confession, it is inconceivable under these circumstances that the second confession was free from the coercive atmosphere that admittedly impregnated the first one. The whole confession technique used here constituted one single, continuing transaction. To conclude that the brutality inflicted at the time of the first confession suddenly lost all of its effect in the short space of twelve hours is to close one's eyes to the realities of human nature. An individual does not that easily forget the type of torture that accompanied petitioner's previous refusal to confess, nor does a person like petitioner so quickly recover from the gruesome effects of having had a pan of human bones placed on his knees in order to force incriminating testimony from him. [citations omitted] Moreover, the trial judge refused petitoner's request that the jury be charged that the second confession was not free and voluntary if it was obtained while petitioner was still suffering from the inhuman treatment he had previously received. Thus it cannot be said that we are confronted with a finding by the trier of facts that the coercive effect of the prior brutality had completely worn off by the time the second confession was signed.

Presumably, therefore, this decision means that state officers are free to force a confession from an individual by ruthless methods, knowing full well that they dare not use such a confession at the trial, and then, as a part of the same continuing transaction and before the effects of the coercion can fairly be said to have completely worn off, procure another confession without any immediate violence being inflicted. The admission of such a tainted confession does not accord with the Fourteenth Amendment's command that a state shall not convict a defendant on evidence that he was compelled to give against himself.

The concern over the treatment of disproportionately non-white suspects, particularly in the South, in the interrogation process continued its shift in focus from physical torture to include psychological coercion. Additionally, the Court expanded its concern regarding the reliability of confessions produced through coercion to include disapproval of police conduct. The cases that formed the basis of the due Process "Coerced Confession" test also expanded to include a closer examination of police practices outside the south as well. See, Rogers v. Richmond, 365 U.S.534 (1961) and Townsend v. Sain, 372 U.S. 293 (1963).

HALEY V. OHIO.

332 U.S. 596 (1948)

Mr. Justice DOUGLAS announced the judgment of the Court and an opinion in which Mr. Justice BLACK, Mr. Justice MURPHY, and Mr. Justice RUTLEDGE join.

Petitioner was convicted in an Ohio court of murder in the first degree and sentenced to life imprisonment. The Court of Appeals of Ohio sustained the judgment of conviction over the objection that the admission of petitioner's confession at the trial violated the Fourteenth Amendment of the Constitution. The Ohio Supreme Court, being of the view that no debatable constitutional question was presented, dismissed the appeal. The case is here on a petition for a writ of certiorari which we granted because we had doubts whether the ruling of the court below could be squared with Chambers v. State of Florida, 309 U.S. 227,; *Malinski v. People of State of New York*, 324 U.S. 401, , and like cases in this Court.

A confectionery store was robbed near midnight on October 14, 1945, and William Karam, its owner, was shot. It was the prosecutor's theory, supported by some evidence which it is unnecessary for us to relate, that petitioner, a Negro boy age 15, and two others, Willie Lowder, age 16, and Al Parks, age 17, committed the crime, petitioner acting as a lookout. Five days later—around midnight October 19, 1945—petitioner was arrested at his home and taken to police headquarters.

There is some contrariety in the testimony as to what then transpired. There is evidence that he was beaten. He took the stand and so testified. His mother testified that the clothes he wore when arrested, which were exchanged two days later for clean ones she brought to the jail, were torn and blood-stained. She also testified that when she first saw him five days after his arrest he was bruised and skinned. The police testified to the contrary on this entire line of testimony. So we put to one side the controverted evidence. Taking only the undisputed testimony (*Malinski v. People of State of New York, supra*, 324 U.S. at page 404, and cases cited), we have the following sequence of events. Beginning shortly after midnight this 15-year old lad was questioned by the police for about five hours. Five or six of the police questioned him in relays of one or two each. During this time no friend or counsel of the boy was present. Around 5 a.m.—after being shown alleged confessions of Lowder and Parks—the boy confessed. A confession was typed in question and answer form by the police. At no time was this boy advised of his right to counsel; but the written confession started off with the following statement: 'we want to inform you of your constitutional rights, the law gives you the right to make this statement or not as you see fit. It is made with the understanding that it may be used at a trial in court either for or against you or anyone else involved in this crime with you, of your own free will and accord, you are under no force or duress or compulsion and no promises are being made to you at this time whatsoever.

'Do you still desire to make this statement and tell the truth after having had the above clause read to you? A. Yes.'

He was put in jail about 6 or 6:30 a.m. on Saturday, the 20th, shortly after the confession was signed. Between then and Tuesday, the 23d, he was held incommunicado. A lawyer retained by his mother tried to see him twice but was refused admission by the police. His mother was not allowed to see him until Thursday, the 25th. But a newspaper photographer was allowed to see him and take his picture in the early morning hours of the 20th, right after he had confessed. He was not taken before a magistrate and formally charged with a crime until the 23d—three days after the confession was signed.

The trial court, after a preliminary hearing on the voluntary character of the confession, allowed it to be admitted in evidence over petitioner's objection that it violated his rights under the Fourteenth Amendment. The court instructed the jury to disregard the confession if it found that he did not make the confession voluntarily and of his free will.

But the ruling of the trial court and the finding of the jury on the voluntary character of the confession do not foreclose the independent examination which it is our duty to make here. *Ashcraft v. State of Tennessee*, 322 U.S. 143, 147, 148. If the undisputed evidence suggests that force or coercion was used to exact the confession, we will not permit the judgment of conviction to stand even though without the confession there might have been sufficient evidence for submission to the jury. *Malinski v. People of State of New York, supra*, 324 U.S. at page 404, and cases cited.

We do not think the methods used in obtaining this confession can be squared with that due process of law which the Fourteenth Amendment commands.

What transpired would make us pause for careful inquiry if a mature man were involved. And when, as here, a mere child —an easy victim of the law—is before us, special care in scrutinizing the record must be used. Age 15 is a tender and difficult age for a boy of any race. He cannot be judged by the more exacting standards of maturity. That which would leave a man cold and unimpressed can overawe and overwhelm a lad in his early teens. This is the period of great instability which the crisis of adolescence produces. A 15-year old lad, questioned through the dead of night by relays of police, is a ready victim of the inquisition. Mature men possibly might stand the ordeal from midnight to 5 a.m. But we cannot believe that a lad of tender years is a match for the police in such a contest. He needs counsel and support if he is not to become the victim first of fear, then of panic. He needs someone on whom to lean lest the overpowering presence of the law, as he knows it, may not crush him. No friend stood at the side of this 15-year old boy as the police, working in relays, questioned him hour after hour, from midnight until dawn. No lawyer stood guard to make sure that the police went so far and no farther, to see to it that they stopped short of the point where he became the victim of coercion. No counsel or friend was called during the critical hours of questioning. A photographer was admitted once this lad broke and confessed. But not even a gesture towards getting a lawyer for him was ever made.

This disregard of the standards of decency is underlined by the fact that he was kept incommunicado for over three days during which the lawyer retained to represent him twice tried to see him and twice was refused admission. A photographer was admitted at once; but his closest friend—his mother—was not allowed to see him for over five days after his arrest. It is said that these events are not germane to the present problem because they happened after the confession was made. But they show such a callous attitude of the police towards the safeguards which respect for ordinary standards of human relationships compels that we take with a grain of salt their present apologia that the five-hour grilling of this boy was conducted in a fair and dispassionate manner. When the police are so unmindful of these basic standards of conduct in their public dealings, their secret treatment of a 15-year old boy behind closed doors in the dead of night becomes darkly suspicious.

The age of petitioner, the hours when he was grilled, the duration of his quizzing, the fact that he had no friend or counsel to advise him, the callous attitude of the police towards his rights combine to convince us that this was a confession wrung from a child by means which the law should not sanction. Neither man nor child can be allowed to stand condemned by methods which flout constitutional requirements of due process of law.

But we are told that this boy was advised of his constitutional rights before he signed the confession and that, knowing them, he nevertheless confessed. That assumes, however, that a boy of fifteen, without aid of counsel, would have a full appreciation of that advice and that on the facts of this record he had a freedom of choice. We cannot indulge those assumptions. Moreover, we cannot give any weight to recitals which merely formalize constitutional requirements. Formulas of respect for constitutional safeguards cannot prevail over the facts of life which contradict them. They may not become a cloak for inquisitorial practices and make an empty form of the due process of law for which free men fought and died to obtain.

The course we followed in *Chambers v. State of Florida, supra, White v. State of Texas*, 310 U.S. 530, *Ashcraft v. State of Tennessee, supra*, and *Malinski v. People of State of New York, supra*, must be followed here. The Fourteenth Amendment prohibits the police from using the private, secret custody of either man or child as a device for wringing confessions from them.

Reversed.

Race and Miranda

Miranda v. Arizona, 384 U.S. 436 (1966) followed on the heels of *Escobedo v. Illinois*, 374 U.S. 478 (1964) in shifting the primary focus of judicial scrutiny regarding custodial interrogation away from reliability and voluntariness and more towards oversight of police conduct. Although both Miranda and Escobedo were non-white suspects interrogated in police custody by predominately white officers, the majority opinion does not comment on the racial aspects of interrogation. As pointed out in the material below the role of race in interrogations both still persists after the "Miranda Revolution" and was on the mind of at least Chief Justice Warren.

....

LeRoy Pernell, *Racial Justice and Federal Habeas Corpus As Postconviction Relief From State Convictions*, 69 MERCER LAW REVIEW 453, 478-480 (2018) (excerpt) (footnotes omitted))(reprint by permission of Mercer Law Review)

....

Miranda is seen as a statement on the relative balance of the position between the police and a criminal suspect in an in-custody interrogation setting. The Court found that the somewhat amorphous totality-of-the-circumstances approach, of the coerced or involuntary confession test, under due process failed to give adequate guidance and control regarding police infringe-ment of the Fifth Amendment right against self-incrimination in the coercive environment of the interrogation room. Less discussed, but nonetheless present, are the racial justice impera-tives still present in police interrogation despite the Inbau-inspired use of psychological manip-ulation. Various scholars have noted that race and Miranda are "inextricably intertwined."

Ernesto Arturo Miranda, of Hispanic descent, was convicted of rape in 1963. "Miranda, by [many] accounts, was a disturbed young man." He was taken into custody for questioning after a vehicle identified in the investigation of the rape and two prior attempted rapes was linked to a residence where he lived with the vehicle's owner. Following a somewhat unreliable line-up identification by the rape victim, Miranda was tricked into giving a confession by the investigat-ing officer using the ploy of telling a "half-truth"—a tactic consistent with the Inbau-developed psychological manipulation technique described earlier.

At no time was Miranda advised of a right to remain silent or to have counsel present during interrogation. The Court had previously determined, in Escobedo v. Illinois, that a suspect cannot be denied access to counsel during interrogation once the investigation has "narrowed" its focus on the accused. The Court then considered questions unanswered in Escobedo, such as what affirmative duty police had to inform the suspect of his or her right to remain silent and to have counsel present in a custodial interrogation setting regardless of whether the investigation has "focused" on the suspect.

The interest in the Court's inquiry went beyond the question of the rights of suspects in general and included racial justice—a matter of great concern in the 1960s. The "reforms" of psychological manipulation, while moderating somewhat the rampant use of physical tor-ture, had not significantly lessened the coercive and racially disproportionate experience of forced confessions. Indeed, Chief Justice Warren, in an early draft of his Miranda majority opinion, stated: "In a series of cases decided by this Court ... Negro defendants were subjected to physical brutality—beatings, hangings, whippings—employed to extort confessions. In 1947, the President's Committee on Civil Rights probed further into police violence upon minority groups." Although this draft language was modified by removing race-specific references, Chief Justice Warren continued to rely on the history of racial injustice and the third degree as support for the landmark reforms announced by the majority. Indeed, the majority opinion concluded that psychological coercion can be mental "torture," even without blood.

The reason for the change from the earlier draft was linked to the need to hold a majority vote together in what was ultimately a 5-4 decision. Justice Brennan objected to turning police tactics in interrogation into a "race problem," as opposed to a broader emphasis on the relative disempowerment of poverty. Warren omitted this passage in a subsequent draft of the opinion in deference to Justice Clark, although Justice Clark ultimately dissented.

The racial-justice significance of Miranda is also borne out considering the broader context of the Civil Rights movement and its recognition of the perceived strong link between crime and race. Although the NAACP Legal Defense Fund did not file an amicus brief in Miranda—perhaps because Thurgood Marshall, the Solicitor General for the United States, had to argue the government's position—its activities in 1968 were well in line with supporting the need for reform of the criminal justice system when it came to interrogations.

Gideon, Mapp, and Miranda were the foundations of not only the criminal justice reform of the Warren Court but also a part of its conscious address of the civil rights struggle. For these cases to have the intended impact, a vehicle needed to exist for addressing decades of injustice that had disproportionately filled the American prison system with persons of color. The prison cell was as much a battle ground for civil rights as a lunch counter, bus, or schoolhouse. The critical tool in this endeavor was habeas corpus, with its ability to go beyond the cold record and provide redress for those victimized by procedural inequality and the politics of race.

....

DAVIS V. NORTH CAROLINA.

384 U.S. 737 (1966)

Opinion of the Court by Mr. Chief Justice WARREN, announced by Mr. Justice BRENNAN.

Petitioner, Elmer Davis, Jr., was tried before a jury in the Superior Court of Mecklenburg County, North Carolina, on a charge of rape-murder. At trial, a written confession and testimony as to an oral confession were offered in evidence. Defense counsel objected on the ground that the confessions were involuntarily given. The trial judge heard testimony on this issue, ruled that the confessions were made voluntarily, and permitted them to be introduced in evidence. The jury returned a verdict of guilty without a recommendation for life imprisonment, and Davis was sentenced to death.

The conviction was affirmed on appeal by the Supreme Court of North Carolina, , and this Court denied certiorari. Davis then sought a writ of habeas corpus in the United States District Court for the Eastern District of North Carolina. The writ was denied without an evidentiary hearing on the basis of the state court record. 196 F.Supp. 488. On appeal, the Court of Appeals for the Fourth Circuit reversed and remanded the case to the District Court for an evidentiary hearing on the issue of the voluntariness of Davis' confessions. 310 F.2d 904. A hearing was held in the District Court, following which the District Judge again held that the confessions were voluntary. 221 F.Supp. 494. The Court of Appeals for the Fourth Circuit, after argument and then resubmission en banc, affirmed with two judges dissenting. 339 F.2d 770. We granted certiorari. 382 U.S. 953, .

We are not called upon in this proceeding to pass on the guilt or innocence of the petitioner of the atrocious crime that was committed. Nor are we called upon to determine whether the confessions obtained are true or false. *Rogers v. Richmond*, 365 U.S. 534(1961). The sole issue presented for review is whether the confessions were voluntarily given or were the result of overbearing by police authorities. Upon thorough review of the record, we have concluded that the confessions were not made freely and voluntarily but rather that Davis' will was overborne by the sustained pressures upon him. Therefore, the confessions are constitutionally inadmissible and the judgment of the court below must be reversed.

Had the trial in this case before us come after our decision in Miranda *v. Arizona*, 384 U.S. 436, 86 S.Ct. 1602, 16 L.Ed.2d 694, we would reverse summarily. Davis was taken into custody by Charlotte police and interrogated repeatedly over a period of 16 days. There is no indication in the record that police advised him of any of his rights until after he had confessed orally on the 16th day. This would be clearly improper under Miranda. Id., 384 U.S. at 478–479. Similarly, no waiver of rights could be inferred from this record since it shows only that Davis was repeatedly interrogated and that he denied the alleged offense prior to the time he finally confessed. Id., at 476, 499.

We have also held today, in *Johnson v. New Jersey*, 384 U.S. 719, 86 S., that our decision in Miranda, delineating procedures to safeguard the Fifth Amendment privilege against self-incrimination during in custody interrogation is to be applied prospectively only. Thus, the present case may not be reversed solely on the ground that warnings were not given and waiver not shown. As we pointed out in Johnson, however, the nonretroactivity of the decision in Miranda does not affect the duty of courts to consider claims that a statement was taken under circumstances which violate the standards of voluntariness which had begun to evolve long prior to our decisions in *Miranda* and Escobedo *v. State of Illinois*, 378 U.S. 478, (1964). This Court has undertaken to review the voluntariness of statements obtained by police in state cases since Brown *v. State of Mississippi*, 297 U.S. 278, (1936). The standard of voluntariness which has evolved in state cases under the Due Process Clause of the Fourteenth Amendment is the same general standard which applied in federal prosecutions—a standard grounded in the policies of the privilege against self-incrimination. Malloy v. Hogan, 378 U.S. 1, 6–8, (1964).

The review of voluntariness in cases in which the trial was held prior to our decisions in Escobedo and Miranda is not limited in any manner by these decisions. On the contrary, that a defendant was not advised of his right to remain silent or of his right respecting counsel at the outset of interrogation, as is now required by Miranda, is a significant factor in considering the voluntariness of statements later made. This factor has been recognized in several of our prior decisions dealing with standards of voluntariness. *Haynes v. State of Washington*, 373 U.S. 503, 510–511, (1963); Culombe *v. Connecticut*, 367 U.S. 568, 610, (1961); Turner *v. Commonwealth of Pennsylvania*, 338 U.S. 62, 64, (1949). See also *Gallegos v. State of Colorado*, 370 U.S. 49, 54, 55, (1962). Thus, the fact that Davis was never effectively advised of his rights gives added weight to the other circumstances described below which made his confessions involuntary.

As is almost invariably so in cases involving confessions obtained through unobserved police interrogation, there is a conflict in the testimony as to the events surrounding the interrogations. Davis alleged that he was beaten, threatened, and cursed by police and that he was told he would get a hot bath and something to eat as soon as he signed a statement. This was flatly denied by each officer who testified. Davis further stated that he had repeatedly asked for a lawyer and that police refused to allow him to obtain one. This was also denied. Davis' sister testified at the habeas corpus hearing that she twice came to the police station and asked to see him, but that each time police officers told her Davis was not having visitors. Police officers testified that, on the contrary, upon learning of Davis' desire to see his sister, they went to her home to tell her Davis wanted to see her, but she informed them she was busy with her children.

These factual allegations were resolved against Davis by the District Court and we need not review these specific findings here.

It is our duty in this case, however, as in all of our prior cases dealing with the question whether a confession was involuntarily given, to examine the entire record and make an independent determination of the ultimate issue of voluntariness. E.g., Haynes v. State of Washington, 373 U.S. 503, 515–516, (1963); Blackburn v. State of Alabama, 361 U.S. 199, 205, (1960); Ashcraft v. State of Tennessee, 322 U.S. 143, 147–148, (1944). Wholly apart from the disputed facts, a statement of the case from facts established in the record, in our view, leads plainly to the conclusion that the confessions were the product of a will overborne.

Elmer Davis is an impoverished Negro with a third or fourth grade education. His level of intelligence is such that it prompted the comment by the court below, even while deciding against him on his claim of involuntariness, that there is a moral question whether a person of Davis' mentality should be executed. Police first came in contact with Davis while he was a child when his mother murdered his father, and thereafter knew him through his long criminal record, beginning with a prison term he served at the age of 15 or 16.

In September 1959, Davis escaped from a state prison camp near Asheville, North Carolina, where he was serving sentences of 17 to 25 years. On September 20, 1959, Mrs. Foy Belle Cooper was raped and murdered in the Elmwood Cemetery in the City of Charlotte, North Carolina. On September 21, police in a neighboring county arrested Davis in Belmont, 12 miles from Charlotte. He was wearing civilian clothes and had in his possession women's undergarments and a billfold with identification papers of one Bishel Buren Hayes. Hayes testified at trial that his billfold and shoes had been taken from him while he lay in a drunken sleep near the Elmwood Cemetery on September 20.

Charlotte police learned of Davis' arrest and contacted the warden of the state prison to get permission to take Davis into their custody in connection with the Cooper murder and other felonies. Having obtained permission, they took Davis from Belmont authorities and brought him to the detective headquarters in Charlotte. From the testimony of the officers, it is beyond dispute that the reason for securing Davis was their suspicion that he had committed the murder.

The second and third floors of the detective headquarters building contain lockup cells used for detention overnight and occasionally for slightly longer periods. It has no kitchen facilities for preparing meals. The cell in which Davis was placed measures 6 by 10 feet and contains a solid steel bunk with mattress, a drinking fountain, and a commode. It is located on the inside of the building with no view of daylight. It is ventilated by two exhaust fans located in the ceiling of the top floor of the building. Despite the fact that a county jail equipped and used for lengthy detention is located directly across the street from detective headquarters, Davis was incarcerated in this cell on an upper floor of the building for the entire period until he confessed. Police Chief Jesse James testified: 'I don't know anybody who has stayed in the city jail as long as this boy.'

When Davis arrived at the detective headquarters, an arrest sheet was prepared giving various statistics concerning him. On this arrest sheet was typed the following illuminating directive: 'HOLD FOR HUCKS & FESPERMAN RE-MRS. COOPER. ESCAPEE FROM HAYWOOD COUNTY STILL HAS 15 YEARS TO PULL. DO NOT ALLOW ANYONE TO SEE DAVIS. OR ALLOW HIM TO USE TELEPHONE.' Both at trial and at the habeas corpus hearing the testimony of police officers on this notation was nearly uniform. Each officer testified that he did not put that directive on the arrest sheet, that he did not know who did, and that he never knew of it. The police captain first testified at trial that there had never been an order issued in the police department that Davis was not to see or talk to anybody. He cited as an example the fact that Davis' sister came to see him (after Davis had confessed). He testified later in the trial, however:

'I don't know, it is possible I could have ordered this boy to be held without privilege of communicating with his friends, relatives and held without the privilege of using the telephone or without the privilege of talking to anybody. * * * No, I did not want him to talk to anybody. For the simple reason he was an escaped convict and it is the rules and regulations of the penal system that if he is a C grade prisoner he is not permitted to see anyone alone or write anyone letters and I was trying to conform to the state regulations.'

The District Court found as a fact that from September 21 until after he confessed on October 6, neither friend nor relative saw Davis. It concluded, however, that Davis was not held incommunicado because he would have been permitted visitors had anyone requested to see him. In so finding, the District Court noted specifically the testimony that police officers contacted Davis' sister for him. But the court made no mention whatever of the notation on the arrest sheet or the testimony of the police captain.

The stark wording of the arrest sheet directive remains, as does Captain McCall's testimony. The denials and evasive testimony of the other officers cannot wipe this evidence from the record. Even accepting that police would have allowed a person to see Davis had anyone actually come, the directive stands unassailably as an indicium of the purpose of the police in holding Davis. As the dissenting judges below stated: 'The instruction not to permit anyone access to Davis and not to allow him to communicate with the outside world can mean only that it was the determination of his custodians to keep him under absolute control where they could subject him to questioning at will in the manner and to the extent they saw fit, until he would confess.' 339 F.2d, at 780. Moreover, the uncontested fact that no one other than the police spoke to Davis during the 16 days of detention and interrogation that preceded his confessions is significant in the determination of voluntariness.

During the time Davis was held by Charlotte police, he was fed two sandwiches, described by one officer as 'thin' and 'dry,' twice a day. This fare was occasionally supplemented with peanuts and other 'stuff' such as cigarettes brought to him by a police officer. The District Court found that the food was the same served prisoners held overnight in the detention jail and that there was no attempt by police to weaken Davis by inadequate feeding. The State contends that 'two sandwiches twice a day supplemented by peanuts 'and other stuff' was not such a poor diet, for an idle person doing no work, as to constitute a violation of due process of law.' Brief for Respondent, p. 7.

We may readily agree that the record does not show any deliberate attempt to starve Davis, compare Payne v. State of Arkansas, 356 U.S. 560, (1958), and that his diet was not below a minimum necessary to sustain him. Nonetheless, the diet was extremely limited and may well have had a significant effect on Davis' physical strength and therefore his ability to resist. There is evidence in the record, not rebutted by the State, that Davis lost 15 pounds during the period of detention.

From the time Davis was first brought to the overnight lockup in Charlotte on September 21, 1959, until he confessed on the 16th day of detention, police officers conducted daily interrogation sessions with him in a special interrogation room in the building. These sessions each lasted 'forty-five minutes or an hour or maybe a little more,' according to one of the interrogating officers. Captain McCall testified that he had assigned his entire force of 26 to 29 men to investigate the case. From this group, Detectives Hucks and Fesperman had primary responsibility for interrogating Davis. These officers testified to interrogating him once or twice each day throughout the 16 days. Three other officers testified that they conducted several interrogation sessions at the request of Hucks and Fesperman. Although the officers denied that Davis was interrogated at night, one testified that the interrogation periods he directed were held some time prior to 11 p.m.8 Captain McCall also interrogated Davis once.

According to each of the officers, no mention of the Cooper murder was made in any of the interrogations between September 21 and October 3. Between these dates they interrogated Davis extensively with respect to the stolen goods in his possession. It is clear from the record, however, that these interrogations were directly related to the murder and were not simply questioning as to unrelated felonies. The express purpose of this line of questioning was to break down Davis' alibis as to where he had obtained the articles. By destroying Davis' contention that he had taken the items from homes some distance from Charlotte, Davis could be placed at the scene of the crime.

In order to put pressure on Davis with respect to these alibis police took him from the lockup on October 1 to have him point out where he had stolen the goods. Davis had told the officers that he took the items from houses along the railroad line between Canton and Asheville. To disprove this story, Davis was aroused at 5 a.m. and driven to Canton. There his leg shackles were removed and he walked on the railroad tracks, handcuffed to an officer, 14 miles to Asheville. When Davis was unable to recognize any landmark along the way or any house that he had burglarized, an officer confronted him with the accusation that his story was a lie. The State points out that Davis was well fed on this day, that he agreed to make the hike, and contends that it was not so physically exhausting as to be coercive. The coercive influence was not, however, simply the physical exertion of the march, but also the avowed purpose of that trek—to break down his alibis to the crime of murder.

On the afternoon of October 3, two officers planned and carried out a ruse to attempt to get Davis to incriminate himself in some manner. They engaged Davis in idle conversation for 10 to 20 minutes and then inquired whether he would like to go out for 'some fresh air.' They then took Davis from the jail and drove him into the cemetery to the scene of the crime in order to observe his reaction.

The purpose of these excursions and of all of the interrogation sessions was known to Davis. On the day of the drive to the cemetery, the interrogators shifted tactics and began questioning Davis specifically about the murder. They asked him if he knew why he was being held. He stated that he believed it was with respect to the Cooper murder. Police then pressed him, asking, 'Well, did you do it?' He denied it. The interrogation sessions continued through the next two days. Davis consistently denied any knowledge of the crime.

On October 6, Detectives Hucks and Fesperman interrogated Davis for the final time. Lieutenant Sykes, who had known Davis' family, but who had not taken part in any of the prior interrogation sessions because he had been away on vacation, asked to sit in. During this interrogation, after repeated earlier denials of guilt, Davis refused to answer questions concerning the crime. At about 12:45 p.m., Lieutenant Sykes inquired of Davis if he would like to talk to any of the officers alone about Mrs. Cooper. Davis said he would like to talk to Sykes. The others left the room. Lieutenant Sykes then asked Davis if he had been reading a testament which he was holding. Davis replied that he had. Sykes asked Davis if he had been praying. Davis replied that he did not know how to pray and agreed he would like Sykes to pray for him. The lieutenant offered a short prayer. At that point, as the dissent below aptly put it, the prayers of the police officer were answered—Davis confessed. He was driven to the cemetery and asked to re-enact the crime. Police then brought him back to the station where he repeated the confession to several of the officers. In the presence of six officers, a two-page statement of the confession Davis had made was transcribed. Although based on the information Davis had given earlier, Captain McCall dictated this statement employing his own choice of format, wording, and content. He paused periodically to ask Davis if he agreed with the statement so far. Each time Davis acquiesced. Davis signed the statement. Captain McCall then contacted the press and stated, 'He finally broke down today.'

The concluding paragraphs of this confession, dictated by the police, contain, along with the standard disclaimer that the confession was free and voluntary, a statement that unwittingly summarizes the coercive effect on Davis of the prolonged period of detention and interrogation. They read:

'In closing, I want to say this. I have known in my own mind that (sic) you people were holding me for, and all the time I have been lying in jail, it has been worrying me, and I knew that sooner or later, I would have to tell you about it.

'I have made this statement freely and voluntarily. Captain McCall has dictated this statement in the presence of Detectives W. F. Hucks, E. F. Fesperman, H. C. Gardner, C. E. Davis, and Detective Lieutenant C. L. Sykes. I am glad it is over, because I have been going thru a big strain.'

The facts established on the record demonstrate that Davis went through a prolonged period in which substantial coercive influences were brought to bear upon him to extort the confessions that marked the culmination of police efforts. Evidence of extended interrogation in such a coercive atmosphere has often resulted in a finding of involuntariness by this Court. E.g., Culombe v. Connecticut, 367 U.S. 568, (1961); Fikes v. State of Alabama, 352 U.S. 191, (1957); Turner v. Commonwealth of Pennsylvania, 338 U.S. 62, (1949). We have never sustained the use of a confession obtained after such a lengthy period of detention and interrogation as was involved in this case.

The fact that each individual interrogation session was of relatively short duration does not mitigate the substantial coercive effect created by repeated interrogation in these surroundings over 16 days. So far as Davis could have known, the interrogation in the overnight lockup might still be going on today had he not confessed. Moreover, as we have noted above, the fact that police did not directly accuse him of the crime until after a substantial period of eroding his will to resist by a tangential line of interrogation did not reduce the coercive influence brought to bear upon him. Similarly, it is irrelevant to the consideration of voluntariness that Davis was an escapee from a prison camp. Of course Davis was not entitled to be released. But this does not alleviate the coercive effect of his extended detention and repeated interrogation while isolated from everyone but the police in the police jail.

In light of all of the factors discussed above, the conclusion is inevitable—Davis' confessions were the involuntary end product of coercive influences and are thus constitutionally inadmissible in evidence. Accordingly, the judgment of the Court of Appeals for the Fourth Circuit must be reversed and the case remanded to the District Court. On remand, the District Court should enter such orders as are appropriate and consistent with this opinion, allowing the State a reasonable time in which to retry petitioner.

Reversed and remanded.

Note

In 1991 Anthony Wright, a 22- year old African American, was charged with the rape and murder of a 77-year-old woman. A significant part of the prosecution's case was a purported confession. Wright was convicted despite the fact that he argued his innocence and indicated that the confession was the result of an interrogation where White officers threatened to rip his eyes out and "skull-fuck" him if he did not confess. Wright spent 18 years fighting his conviction. After an Innocence Project took up his case in 2005 he successfully overcame the efforts of the Philadelphia district Attorney's office to block introduction of exonerating DNA evidence in *Commonwealth v. Pennsylvania*, 609 PA. 22 (2011). In reaching the issue of coerced confession the Court said "a confession is not a per se bar to a convicted individual's ability to seek DNA testing to prove his or her actual innocence", Id. at 55.

A significant part of the court's decision was the amicus brief of the American Psychological Association which addresses, among other things the impact of race on coerced confessions.

SUPREME COURT OF PENNSYLVANIA.
WRIGHT V. PENNSYLVANIA
November 13, 2008.
E.D. Allocatur Docket 2008

BRIEF FOR AMICUS CURIAE
(footnotes omitted)

....

V. ARGUMENT

A. Confessions That Are Voluntary As A Matter of Law Can Be Unreliable in Fact

Over the years, psychologists, other social scientists, and legal scholars have examined the causes, characteristics, and consequences of false confessions. This empirical literature is broadly grounded in three types of research: (1) individual and aggregated case studies of wrongful convictions involving known innocent suspects who had confessed; (2) basic research on core principles of human behavior established across a range of non-forensic domains of psychology; and (3) laboratory and field experiments, naturalistic observation studies, and self-report surveys that specifically focus on the processes of interviewing, interrogation, and the elicitation of confessions. Collectively, this literature provides a strong empirical foundation concerning the phenomenon of false confessions.

1. Innocent People Sometimes Confess To Crimes They Did Not Commit

Although a precise prevalence rate is unknown, it is clear that false confessions occur with some degree of regularity. Within the recent and growing population of post-conviction DNA exonerations reported by the Innocence Project, false confessions were a contributing factor in 20% to 25% of these cases—a sample that may represent the tip of an iceberg. Other less direct sources reinforce these data. In Europe, 12% of prisoners, 3-4% of college students, and 1-2% of older university students report that they have confessed to crimes they did not commit. In the United States and Canada, 631 police investigators recently surveyed estimated that, on average, 4.78% of innocent people confess during interrogation.

Proving conclusively that a confession is, in fact, false requires the existence of verifiable contrary evidence. In one study that analyzed demographic, legal, and case-specific data from 125 cases of proven false confessions, four methods were described by which disputed confessions can be classified as "proven" to be false. First, a proven false confession can occur when it can be objectively established that the confessed crime did not occur. Second, a confession can be classified as false when it is established objectively that it was physically impossible for the confessor to have committed the crime (e.g., the suspect was in custody or was too young to have produced semen). Third, a proven false confession can be identified when the true perpetrator is apprehended and his guilt is objectively established. Fourth, a proven false confession can occur when DNA or other scientific evidence dispositively establishes the confessor's innocence. As a result of these methods, and in contrast to the belief that people do not confess to crimes they did not commit, it is clear that significant numbers of men and women have been wrongfully prosecuted, convicted, and imprisoned because of false confessions. Thus, where the crime actually occurred, impossibility is not a factor, and the true perpetrator has not been identified, the consideration of post-conviction DNA evidence under 42 Pa.C.S. § 9543.1 is the only means in Pennsylvania for an innocent confessor to establish his innocence.

2. Pennsylvania Law Recognizes That Innocent People Have Confessed Only Later To Be Exonerated by DNA Evidence

Two basic propositions cannot reasonably be disputed: (1) innocent people have confessed to crimes they did not commit; and (2) in numerous cases, exculpatory DNA tests and other evidence have undermined the reliability of confessions. Yet, until recently, some courts have been reluctant to grant post-conviction motions for DNA testing. For example, the Superior Court of Pennsylvania denied the request for DNA testing in Commonwealth v. Godschalk because "appellant's conviction rest[ed] largely on his own confession which contains details of the rapes which were not available to the public." But in 2001, a federal court held that Godschalk v. Montgomery County Dist. Attorney's Office, 177 F. Supp. 2d 366, 370 (E.D. Pa. 2001) had a "due process" right to the biological testing of DNA evidence.15 After spending 15 years in prison for a crime he did not commit, Godschalk was exonerated in February 2002 based on the same scientific testing that Anthony Wright urges this Court to allow.

Cases like Godschalk caution against hard and fast rules that would favor potentially unreliable confessions over DNA evidence. Hence, 44 jurisdictions, including Pennsylvania, have recently passed statutes to ensure the right to post-conviction DNA testing. See, e.g., 42 Pa.C.S. § 9543.1. The goal of Section 9543.1 is to determine the truth and to free the innocent. As a result of Section 9543.1, a petitioner may establish his innocence convincingly through DNA testing of evidence.

In contrast, confession evidence does not conclusively establish guilt or innocence and is not, without corroboration, a failsafe predictor of the truth. Therefore, to preclude DNA testing solely because the defendant tendered a confession-even one that is determined to be "voluntary" — contradicts the intent behind Section 9543.1. The "overriding goal of seeking the truth to protect the innocent ...means that all relevant and admissible evidence should be permitted to guide the court in determining the possible significance (or lack of significance) of such evidence." The very purpose of Section 9543.1 is to ensure that if the jury did not have the opportunity to consider the results of DNA testing, the verdict resulting from confession evidence does not bar the examination of such potentially exculpatory evidence.

B. Why Innocent People Confess.

Sometimes, innocent people volunteer confessions without undue pressure from police. For example, when Charles Lindbergh's baby was kidnapped in 1932, approximately 200 people stepped forward to confess. More recently, in 2006, John Mark Karr voluntarily claimed responsibility for the unsolved murder of JonBenet Ramsey. There are several reasons why innocent people might voluntarily confess—such as a pathological need for attention or notoriety; feelings of guilt or delusions of involvement; the perception of tangible gain; or the desire to protect a parent, child, or someone else.

In the vast majority of known cases, however, false confessions are induced by interrogation processes that are designed to elicit confessions from suspects. In addition, there are two categories of factors that increase the risk that an innocent person may confess. First, certain interrogation tactics— especially when used in the extreme—can lead ordinary people to capitulate in order to extricate themselves from a highly aversive situation; second, some people in particular are uniquely vulnerable to influence and malleable in the face of pressure.

1. Police Interrogation Involves a Multi-step Set of Processes

The process of custodial interrogation and the resulting elicitation of self-incriminating statements is a valuable and necessary law enforcement tool. Custodial interrogation helps police solve crimes and enables prosecutors to bring offenders to justice. The surgical objective is to secure admissions and full confessions from suspects who are guilty but not from those, initially misjudged, who are innocent. In theory, interrogation draws confessions from suspects by increasing the anxiety associated with denial and lessening the perceived consequences of confession. Clearly, these objectives can be achieved through unlawful threats, promises, and physical mistreatment the literature on wrongful convictions, however, supported by empirical research, indicates that certain lawful interrogation tactics may also lead not only offenders—but also innocent suspects—to confess.

Typically, the confrontational process of police interrogation is preceded by an information-gathering interview conducted to determine if the police believe a suspect is guilty or innocent. For a person who is falsely accused, this first impression may determine whether he or she is interrogated or sent home. Police interrogation involves a multistep process designed to elicit incriminating statements, admissions and full narrative confessions from suspects who are presumed guilty. In theory, this occurs by increasing the anxiety associated with denial and minimizing the perceived consequences of confession. It is clear that these objectives may be achieved through unlawful threats, promises, and physical mistreatment. However, the literature on wrongful convictions supported by empirical research indicates that certain lawful interrogation tactics may also lead some innocent suspects alike to confess.

To elicit confessions, police investigators isolate the suspect often in a small, bare, windowless private room, without family or friends. These conditions heighten the suspect's anxiety, sense of helplessness, and need for relief. In the process that ensues, trained interrogators employ a combination of positive and negative incentives. First, they confront the suspect in custody with strong accusations of guilt, without opportunity for denial, and they may bolster these assertions by citing either real or manufactured incriminating evidence. During this phase, the suspect's denials are interrupted and challenged. Over time, a suspect may come to feel trapped by the apparent weight of the evidence and fell into a state of hopelessness and despair. Second, interrogators often offer sympathy and understanding, minimize the crime, and provide moral justification. They may suggest that the crime was spontaneous, accidental, provoked, drug-induced, peer pressured, or otherwise justified by extenuating circumstances. Themes that minimize the seriousness of the crime can lead a beleaguered suspect to see confession as an expedient means of relief. Once a suspect is persuaded to admit guilt, interrogators seek to convert that admission into a full narrative confession. Both natural observational studies and self-report surveys of police confirm that these techniques are routinely employed.

2. Certain Police Interrogation Tactics Can Elicit False Confessions from Ordinary, Law Abiding Citizens

Lawful interrogation tactics have elicited false confessions from ordinary and law-abiding adults. In particular, three aspects of custodial interrogation can increase this risk. First, false confessions tend to occur after lengthy interrogations. Most interrogations last between 30 minutes and two hours. In fact, from a law enforcement training perspective, it has been suggested that interrogators will seldom require more than four hours to obtain a confession, even for crimes of a serious nature. Yet in contrast to these parameters, in a large sample of proven false confessions in which time records were available, 34% lasted 6 to 12 hours, 39% lasted 12 to 24 hours, and the average was 16.3 hours.

The effect of custody and interrogation time on the innocent suspect is not surprising. Lengthy sessions are often accompanied by some degree of deprivation. Suspects become desperate to stop the questioning, sleep, eat, make a phone call, go home, or obtain needed medication or drugs to which they are addicted. For example, controlled laboratory experiments have shown that sleep deprivation heightens a person's susceptibility to influence, limits the ability to sustain attention, reduces flexibility in thinking, and impairs decision-making in complex tasks. Similar performance decrements have been observed in medical interns, motorists, and F-117 fighter pilots. Leading researchers have concluded that "sleep deprivation strongly impairs human functioning." Therefore, while true confessions may result from police questioning after sleep deprivation, the risk of false confessions is increased.

A second interrogation tactic that can induce confessions from innocent people involves the presentation of false evidence. Investigators will sometimes confront a suspect with allegedly incontrovertible evidence of guilt such as a fingerprint, blood or hair sample, eyewitness, or failed polygraph, even if that evidence is false. This tactic was employed in numerous proven false confession cases. The presentation of false evidence has been implicated in numerous convictions of innocent people, including those resulting in DNA exonerations.

From a convergence of sources, there is strong support for the proposition that this type of deception, while only sparingly used, puts innocent suspects at risk to confess both by fostering confusion and by leading them to feel trapped by the apparent weight of the case against them. Hence, the National Research Council Committee to Review the Scientific Evidence on the Polygraph recently expressed concern over the risk of false confession that is produced by telling suspects they had failed the polygraph. While it is permissible for police to mislead suspects about evidence supposedly linking them to a crime, the belief that the fictitious evidence exists can drive suspects into a state of despair.

A third interrogation tactic that poses risk if used in the extreme is minimization, whereby a sympathetic interrogator minimizes the crime through "theme development," suggesting to suspects that their actions were spontaneous, accidental, provoked, peer-pressured, or otherwise justifiable by external factors. Analyses of numerous tape recorded interrogations and transcripts has revealed that these techniques are often used to imply promises and threats. Indeed, research confirms that minimization tactics lead people to infer that they would be treated with leniency upon confession even when no explicit promises are made. In one controlled experiment, for example, this tactic led 18% of innocent college students to confess that they cheated on an experimental problem that they were supposed to solve without assistance, a possible violation of the university honor code.

3. Some People Are Highly Vulnerable To Influence During Interrogation

Given certain situational factors, anyone may be at risk of rendering a false confession, but certain individual factors make this outcome even more likely. Some people are characteristically more vulnerable to influence than others, and hence at greater risk to confess during a police interrogation. Statistics show a disproportionate number of juveniles and individuals with mental retardation comprise the population of false confessors. In the earlier described database of 125 proven false confessions, for example, 35% involved juveniles, most of whom had confessed, often in vivid detail, to brutal murder.

Developmental psychology research indicates that adolescents are more vulnerable, more compliant, and suggestible than adults. Their decision-making is characterized by an "immaturity of judgment" a pattern of behavior marked by impulsivity, a focus on immediate gratification, and a diminished capacity for perceptions of risk. To the adolescent who lacks sufficient focus on long-term consequences, confession may thus serve as an expedient way out of a stressful interrogation. To further exacerbate matters, the National Center for Mental Health and Juvenile Justice estimates that the vast majority of justice-involved youth have diagnosable psychological disorders, also a risk factor for false confessions.

The intellectually impaired are also more vulnerable to influence in an interrogation. In the previously cited sample of false confessors, individuals with mental retardation, as measured by conventional intelligence tests, comprised at least 22%. Research shows that most individuals with mental retardation cannot comprehend the Miranda warnings they receive rendering their rights to silence and to counsel as "words without meaning." Controlled experiments have shown that individuals with mental retardation also exhibit a high need for approval, particularly in the presence of authority figures. Furthermore, they display an acquiescence response bias that leads them to answer "yes" to a wide range of questions, even when an affirmative response is incorrect, inappropriate, or absurd. They are also highly suggestible, as measured by their influence to leading and misleading questions. In Atkins v. Virginia [536 U.S. 304, 320 (2002)], the U.S. Supreme Court thus cited the possibility of false confession as a rationale for its decision to exclude individuals with mental retardation from capital punishment.

C. Voluntary False Confessions Are Difficult For Judges, Juries, and Others to Discern.

False confessions rendered by innocent suspects for crimes they did not commit are not readily detected or corrected by prosecutors, courts, and jurors who may mistakenly credit them with truthfulness. The safety net that should protect innocent confessors requires that key decision makers can distinguish with accuracy between true and false confessions and discount the latter in their decision making. Yet, as demonstrated by the convictions of many innocent people who confessed but then retracted their confessions and pled not guilty, this is not the case.

The inability to differentiate between true and false confessions can be attributed to two factors. First, common sense dictates that we trust confessions because they represent statements that go against the suspect's self-interest Because people tend to behave in self-serving ways, it is natural to conclude that confessions must be particularly diagnostic of guilt. Second, numerous scientific experiments have shown that most people—including police investigators, psychologists, customs inspectors, judges, and other "experts" — are not adept at detecting deception and struggle to distinguish truth from-untruth at high levels of accuracy.

1. False Confessions Often Contain Vivid Details And Other Hallmarks of Credibility

Particularly misleading and problematic is that false confessions often contain content cues that are presumed to be associated with truthfulness. Research shows that false confessions made by innocent suspects may appear so similar to those made by their guilty counterparts that people mistakenly credit them with truthfulness. In a study in which male prisoners delivered both videotaped false confessions and confessions to the crimes that they actually committed, neither experienced police investigators nor college students were able to distinguish between the true and false confessions at high levels of accuracy. These study participants scored only 42% to 64% of the confessions accurately, a performance that is not significantly better than mere chance. Examination of proven false confessions reveals that these statements often contain vivid and accurate details about the crime and victim that the innocent confessor learned from leading questions, photographs, visits to the crime scene, and other secondary sources of information. To further confuse matters, many false confessions contain not only a narrative account of what the suspect allegedly did and how he did it, but a motivational statement about why as well as apologies and expressions of remorse. As a result of the failure to appreciate the factors that contribute to this phenomenon, as described above, false confessions are often trusted.

The Commonwealth of Pennsylvania case involving exonerated confessor, Barry Laughman, illustrates the point. In 2004, Laughman was exonerated of a rape-murder conviction after serving more than 16 years in prison. The conviction rested largely on his false confession which contained a number of details about the crime that were verifiable, strikingly accurate, and not in the public domain. Despite his innocence, Laughman's statement revealed where the victim was found and in what position, that a window was open, that she was vaginally raped, that she had suffocated on pills, that she was hit in the head and grabbed by the wrists, and that a handful of cigarette butts had been strewn throughout the house. Particularly troubling is that the confession also contained descriptions of a cover-up, statements of motivation for both the rape and murder that were later disproved, and expressions of shame and remorse—gratuitous aspects of the confession that inevitably misled a judge and jury. However, post-conviction DNA testing pursuant to § 9543.1 resulted in Laughman's exoneration.

2. False Confessions Can Corrupt Other Evidence, Creating an Illusion of Corroboration.

Judges and juries may also struggle to identify false confessions, even in the context of a full trial, because these confessions can taint other evidence. In Laughman's case, the defendant confessed to rape and murder during an unrecorded interrogation. The next day, however, serology tests show that Laughman had Type B blood; yet the semen recovered from the victim was from a Type A secretor. Clearly influenced by the confession, the state forensic chemist went on to propose four theories not grounded in science to explain away the mismatch. Sixteen years later, Laughman was set free.

Grounded in a large body of psychological research on behavioral confirmation biases, recent empirical studies have demonstrated the problem as well. In one experiment, for example, researchers presented five latent fingerprint experts with pairs of prints from a crime scene and suspect in an actual case in which they had previously made a match or exclusion judgment. The prints were accompanied either by no extraneous information, an instruction that the suspect had confessed (suggesting a match), or an instruction that the suspect was in custody while the crime was committed (suggesting an exclusion). Strikingly, the misinformation produced a change in 17% of the original, previously correct judgments. In a second study, research participants witnessed a staged theft and made photographic identification decisions from a photographic lineup. One week later, individual witnesses, depending on the experimental condition to which they were randomly assigned, were told that the person they had identified denied guilt, or that he confessed, or that a specific other lineup member confessed Influenced by this information, many witnesses went on to change their identification decisions. Among those who had made a selection but were told that another lineup member confessed, 61% changed their identifications and did so with confidence. Among those who had not made a previous identification, 50% erroneously went on to select the confessor, again doing so with confidence.

Therefore, taken as a whole, the body of evidence that flows from false confession evidence compounds the problem. Judges and juries group seemingly independent sources of corroborative evidence together rather than appreciate the influence that false confessions wield in creating that evidence

3. Innocent Suspects Are Not Necessarily Protected by Miranda.

Numerous false confessions have been taken from suspects who had voluntarily waived their rights under Miranda v. Arizona, In Miranda, the U.S. Supreme Court provided a means by which those accused can protect themselves from self-incrimination. Over the years, the Miranda warning and waiver requirement have served as a means of inferring the voluntariness of confessions thereafter elicited by police. Some studies have shown, however, that suspects with serious mental disorders or mental retardation, 60 and many young adolescents face substantial impairments in understanding the rights afforded under Miranda. Comprehension notwithstanding, other studies have shown that roughly four out of five suspects waive their rights and submit to questioning. The tendency to waive their rights to silence and to counsel is most evident among individuals without a criminal record. Consistent with the recidivist proposition that first-timers are less likely to offend, controlled experiments and self-report surveys of policesuggest that innocent suspects who believe that they have nothing to fear or hide and seek to prove their innocence are particularly prone to waive their rights. As a consequence, many innocents, including some who ultimately confess, do not avail themselves of the constitutional rights they are afforded.

D. The Presence of a Voluntary Confession Should Neither Preclude a Later Assertion of Innocence Nor Bar A DNA Test Under 42 Pa.C. S § 9543.1.

The availability of post-conviction DNA testing through 42 P.C.S.A. § 9543.1 serves to counterbalance the undue weight that may be given to confessions in the criminal justice system. The United States Supreme Court has noted that:

> A system of criminal law enforcement which comes to depend on the 'confession' will, in the long run, be less reliable and more subject to abuses than a system which depends on extrinsic evidence independently secured through skillful investigation.

But a suspect who confesses, even if that confession is false, will be treated more harshly throughout the process.68 In many cases, once a suspect confesses, investigators tend to "close the investigation, clear the case as solved, and make no effort to pursue other possible leads."

Prosecutors often charge defendants who have confessed with the highest number of offenses and do not accept plea bargains. Moreover, judges rarely suppress confessions and juries typically disbelieve claims of innocence made by defendants who have confessed. When proven false confessors pled not guilty and proceeded to trial, the jury conviction rates ranged from 73% to 81%. If a false confessor is convicted, he is then typically sentenced more harshly than other defendants. In sum, a false confession may "contaminate the perception and treatment of a case as it makes its way through the entire criminal justice process."

Despite its limitations, confession evidence is so powerful that "the introduction of a confession makes the other aspects of a trial in court superfluous, and the real trial, for all practical purposes, occurs when the confession is obtained." An analysis of case outcomes illustrates the point. In a study that examined proven false confession cases in the United States from 1971 to 2002, roughly four out of five innocent confessors who went to trial were convicted. In this study, 93% of the false confessors were men and 81% occurred in murder cases. Forty six percent of exonerations were based on the discovery of new scientific evidence. Four out of the five false confessors in this sample who went to trial were convicted. When compared to the numerous post-conviction exonerations, the influence of confessions is plain. Confession evidence has thus been described as "inherently prejudicial and highly damaging" even when it is unsupported by other evidence or later disproved beyond a reasonable doubt by DNA evidence.

Controlled mock jury research reinforces these case outcome data by showing that confession evidence typically has more impact on jurors than other potent forms of evidence and that people do not fully discount confessions even if it is logically or legally appropriate to do so. In one experiment, participants were significantly prompted to vote guilty by a defendant's confession to police that was indisputably induced by an explicit promise of leniency. In a second experiment, participants were significantly influenced by an indirect or "secondary confession" reported by an accomplice or jailhouse informant—even when told that this cooperating witness had a personal incentive to claim that the defendant had confessed.In a third experiment, the presence of a confession significantly boosted the conviction rate even among jurors who perceived it to be coerced, among those specifically admonished to disregard such confessions, and among those who later reported that the confession did not influence their decisions.

VI. CONCLUSION

"Voluntary" confessions have been shown to be false and unreliable in numerous cases, and psychologists have explained the circumstances that have sometimes led innocent people to confess. Prohibiting DNA testing that may conclusively establish a convicted individual's innocence (or guilt) based solely on the existence of a confession is unsound, particularly when the DNA test results may disprove the trueness of the confession.

For the foregoing reasons, the Amicus urges this Court to decline the Commonwealth's invitation to erode the post-conviction protections in 42 Pa.C.S. §9543.1. Instead, we encourage the Court to reverse the decision of the Superior Court and hold that the existence of a voluntary confession does not preclude a prima facie finding that exculpatory results from DNA testing could establish actual innocence.

Chapter Three: Race and the Fourth Amendment

Race and Probable Cause to Seize or Arrest for Criminal Activity

DAVIS V. MISSISSIPPI.
394 U.S. 721 (1969)

Mr. Justice BRENNAN delivered the opinion of the Court.

Petitioner was convicted of rape and sentenced to life imprisonment by a jury in the Circuit Court of Lauderdale County, Mississippi. The only issue before us is whether fingerprints obtained from petitioner should have been excluded from evidence as the product of a detention which was illegal under the Fourth and Fourteenth Amendments.

The rape occurred on the evening of December 2, 1965, at the victim's home in Meridian, Mississippi. The victim could give no better description of her assailant than that he was a Negro youth. Finger and palm prints found on the sill and borders of the window through which the assailant apparently entered the victim's home constituted the only other lead available at the outset of the police investigation. Beginning on December 3, and for a period of about 10 days, the Meridian police, without warrants, took at least 24 Negro youths to police headquarters where they were questioned briefly, fingerprinted, and then released without charge. The police also interrogated 40 or 50 other Negro youths either at police headquarters, at school, or on the street. Petitioner, a 14-year-old youth who had occasionally worked for the victim as a yardboy, was brought in on December 3 and released after being fingerprinted and routinely questioned. Between December 3 and December 7, he was interrogated by the police on several occasions— sometimes in his home or in a car, other times at police headquarters. This questioning apparently related primarily to investigation of other potential suspects. Several times during this same period petitioner was exhibited to the victim in her hospital room. A police officer testified that these confrontations were for the purpose of sharpening the victim's description of her assailant by providing 'a gauge to go by on size and color.' The victim did not identify petitioner as her assailant at any of these confrontations.

On December 12, the police drove petitioner 90 miles to the city of Jackson and confined him overnight in the Jackson jail. The State conceded on oral argument in this Court that there was neither a warrant nor probable cause for this arrest. The next day, petitioner, who had not yet been afforded counsel, took a lie detector test and signed a statement. He was then returned to and confined in the Meridian jail. On December 14, while so confined, petitioner was fingerprinted a second time. That same day, these December 14 prints, together with the fingerprints of 23 other Negro youths apparently still under suspicion, were sent to the Federal Bureau of Investigation in Washington, D.C., for comparison with the latent prints taken from the window of the victim's house. The FBI reported that petitioner's prints matched those taken from the window. Petitioner was subsequently indicted and tried for the rape, and the fingerprint evidence was admitted in evidence at trial over petitioner's timely objections that the fingerprints should be excluded as the product of an unlawful detention. The Mississippi Supreme Court sustained the admission of the fingerprint evidence and affirmed the conviction. We granted certiorari. We reverse.

At the outset, we find no merit in the suggestion in the Mississippi Supreme Court's opinion that fingerprint evidence, because of its trustworthiness, is not subject to the proscriptions of the Fourth and Fourteenth Amendments. Our decisions recognize no exception to the rule that illegally seized evidence is inadmissible at trial, however relevant and trustworthy the seized evidence may be as an item of proof. The exclusionary rule was fashioned as a sanction to redress and deter overreaching governmental conduct prohibited by the Fourth Amendment. To make an exception for illegally seized evidence which is trustworthy would fatally undermine these purposes. Thus, in *Mapp v. Ohio*, 367 U.S. 643, 655 (1961), we held that 'all evidence obtained by searches and seizures in violation of the Constitution is, by that same authority, inadmissible in a state court.' (Italics supplied.) Fingerprint evidence is no exception to this comprehensive rule. We agree with and adopt the conclusion of the Court of Appeals for the District of Columbia Circuit in *Bynum v. United States*, 262 F.2d 465, 467 (1958):

> 'True, fingerprints can be distinguished from statements given during detention. They can also be distinguished from articles taken from a prisoner's possession. Both similarities and differences of each type of evidence to and from the others are apparent. But all three have the decisive common characteristic of being something of evidentiary value which the public authorities have caused an arrested person to yield to them during illegal detention. If one such product of illegal detention is proscribed, by the same token all should be proscribed.'

We turn then to the question whether the detention of petitioner during which the fingerprints used at trial were taken constituted an unreasonable seizure of his person in violation of the Fourth Amendment. The opinion of the Mississippi Supreme Court proceeded on the mistaken premise that petitioner's prints introduced at trial were taken during his brief detention on December 3. In fact, as both parties before us agree, the fingerprint evidence used at trial was obtained on December 14, while petitioner was still in detention following his December 12 arrest. The legality of his arrest was not determined by the Mississippi Supreme Court. However, on oral argument here, the State conceded that the arrest on December 12 and the ensuing detention through December 14 were based on neither a warrant nor probable cause and were therefore constitutionally invalid. The State argues, nevertheless, that this invalidity should not prevent us from affirming petitioner's conviction. The December 3 prints were validly obtained, it is argued, and 'it should make no difference in the practical or legal sense which (fingerprint) card was sent to the F.B.I. for comparison.'[3] It may be that it does make a difference in light of the objectives of the exclusionary rule, but we need not decide the question since we have concluded that the prints of December 3, were not validly obtained.

The State makes no claim that petitioner voluntarily accompanied the police officers to headquarters on December 3 and willingly submitted to fingerprinting. The State's brief also candidly admits that '(a)ll that the Meridian Police could possibly have known about petitioner at the time * * * would not amount to probable cause for his arrest * * *.' The State argues, however, that the December 3 detention was of a type which does not require probable cause. Two rationales for this position are suggested. First, it is argued that the detention occurred during the investigatory rather than accusatory stage and thus was not a seizure requiring probable cause. The second and related argument is that, at the least, detention for the sole purpose of obtaining fingerprints does not require probable cause.

It is true that at the time of the December 3 detention the police had no intention of charging petitioner with the crime and were far from making him the primary focus of their investigation. But to argue that the Fourth Amendment does not apply to the investigatory stage is fundamentally to misconceive the purposes of the Fourth Amendment. Investigatory seizures would subject unlimited numbers of innocent persons to the harassment and ignominy incident to involuntary detention. Nothing is more clear than that the Fourth Amendment was meant to prevent wholesale intrusions upon the personal security of our citizenry, whether these intrusions be termed 'arrests' or 'investigatory detentions.' We made this explicit only last Term in *Terry v. Ohio*, 392 U.S. 1, 19, 88 S.Ct. 1868, 1878, 1879, 20 L.Ed.2d 889 (1968), when we rejected 'the notions that the Fourth Amendment does not come into play at all as a limitation upon police conduct if the officers stop short of something called a 'technical arrest or a 'full-blown search.''

Detentions for the sole purpose of obtaining fingerprints are no less subject to the constraints of the Fourth Amendment. It is arguable, however, that, because of the unique nature of the fingerprinting process, such detentions might, under narrowly defined circumstances, be found to comply with the Fourth Amendment even though there is no probable cause in the traditional sense. See *Camara v. Municipal Court*, 387 U.S. 523, 87 S.Ct. 1727, 18 L.Ed.2d 930 (1967). Detention for fingerprinting may constitute a much less serious intrusion upon personal security than other types of police searches and detentions. Fingerprinting involves none of the probing into an individual's private life and thoughts that marks an interrogation or search. Nor can fingerprint detention be employed repeatedly to harass any individual, since the police need only one set of each person's prints. Furthermore, fingerprinting is an inherently more reliable and effective crime-solving tool than eyewitness identifications or confessions and is not subject to such abuses as the improper line-up and the 'third degree.' Finally, because there is no danger of destruction of fingerprints, the limited detention need not come unexpectedly or an inconvenient time. For this same reason, the general requirement that the authorization of a judicial officer be obtained in advance of detention would seem not to admit of any exception in the fingerprinting context.

We have no occasion in this case, however, to determine whether the requirements of the Fourth Amendment could be met by narrowly circumscribed procedures for obtaining, during the course of a criminal investigation, the fingerprints of individuals for whom there is no probable cause to arrest. For it is clear that no attempt was made here to employ procedures which might comply with the requirements of the Fourth Amendment: the detention at police headquarters of petitioner and the other young Negroes was not authorized by a judicial officer; petitioner was unnecessarily required to undergo two fingerprinting sessions; and petitioner was not merely fingerprinted during the December 3 detention but also subjected to interrogation. The judgment of the Mississippi Supreme Court is therefore reversed.

Reversed.

WHREN V. UNITED STATES
517 U.S. 806 (1996)

Justice SCALIA delivered the opinion of the Court.

In this case we decide whether the temporary detention of a motorist who the police have probable cause to believe has committed a civil traffic violation is inconsistent with the Fourth Amendment's prohibition against unreasonable seizures unless a reasonable officer would have been motivated to stop the car by a desire to enforce the traffic laws.

I

On the evening of June 10, 1993, plainclothes vice-squad officers of the District of Columbia Metropolitan Police Department were patrolling a "high drug area" of the city in an unmarked car. Their suspicions were aroused when they passed a dark Pathfinder truck with temporary license plates and youthful occupants waiting at a stop sign, the driver looking down into the lap of the passenger at his right. The truck remained stopped at the intersection for what seemed an unusually long time—more than 20 seconds. When the police car executed a U-turn in order to head back toward the truck, the Pathfinder turned suddenly to its right, without signaling, and sped off at an "unreasonable" speed. The policemen followed, and in a short while overtook the Pathfinder when it stopped behind other traffic at a red light. They pulled up alongside, and Officer Ephraim Soto stepped out and approached the driver's door, identifying himself as a police officer and directing the driver, petitioner Brown, to put the vehicle in park. When Soto drew up to the driver's window, he immediately observed two large plastic bags of what appeared to be crack cocaine in petitioner Whren's hands. Petitioners were arrested, and quantities of several types of illegal drugs were retrieved from the vehicle.

Petitioners were charged in a four-count indictment with violating various federal drug laws, including 21 U.S.C. §§ 844(a) and 860(a). At a pretrial suppression hearing, they challenged the legality of the stop and the resulting seizure of the drugs. They argued that the stop had not been justified by probable cause to believe, or even reasonable suspicion, that petitioners were engaged in illegal drug-dealing activity; and that Officer Soto's asserted ground for approaching the vehicle—to give the driver a warning concerning traffic violations—was pretextual. The District Court denied the suppression motion, concluding that "the facts of the stop were not controverted," and "[t]here was nothing to really demonstrate that the actions of the officers were contrary to a normal traffic stop." .

Petitioners were convicted of the counts at issue here. The Court of Appeals affirmed the convictions, holding with respect to the suppression issue that, "regardless of whether a police officer subjectively believes that the occupants of an automobile may be engaging in some other illegal behavior, a traffic stop is permissible as long as a reasonable officer in the same circumstances *could have* stopped the car for the suspected traffic violation." 53 F.3d 371, 374–375 (C.A.D.C.1995). We granted certiorari.

II

The Fourth Amendment guarantees "[t]he right of the people to be secure in their persons, houses, papers, and effects, against unreasonable searches and seizures." Temporary detention of individuals during the stop of an automobile by the police, even if only for a brief period and for a limited purpose, constitutes a "seizure" of "persons" within the meaning of this provision. See *Delaware v. Prouse,* 440 U.S. 648, 653, (1979); *United States v. Martinez–Fuerte,* 428 U.S. 543, 556, 96 (1976); *United States v. Brignoni–Ponce,* 422 U.S. 873, 878, (1975). An automobile stop is thus subject to the constitutional imperative that it not be "unreasonable" under the circumstances. As a general matter, the decision to stop an automobile is reasonable where the police have probable cause to believe that a traffic violation has occurred. See *Prouse*, supra, at 659, *Pennsylvania v. Mimms*, 434 U.S. 106, 109 (1977) *(per curiam)*.

Petitioners accept that Officer Soto had probable cause to believe that various provisions of the District of Columbia traffic code had been violated. See 18 D.C. Mun. Regs. §§ 2213.4 (1995) ("An operator shall ... give full time and attention to the operation of the vehicle"); 2204.3 ("No person shall turn any vehicle... without giving an appropriate signal"); 2200.3 ("No person shall drive a vehicle ... at a speed greater than is reasonable and prudent under the conditions"). They argue, however, that "in the unique context of civil traffic regulations" probable cause is not enough. Since, they contend, the use of automobiles is so heavily and minutely regulated that total compliance with traffic and safety rules is nearly impossible, a police officer will almost invariably be able to catch any given motorist in a technical violation. This creates the temptation to use traffic stops as a means of investigating other law violations, as to which no probable cause or even articulable suspicion exists. Petitioners, who are both black, further contend that police officers might decide which motorists to stop based on decidedly impermissible factors, such as the race of the car's occupants. To avoid this danger, they say, the Fourth Amendment test for traffic stops should be, not the normal one (applied by the Court of Appeals) of whether probable cause existed to justify the stop; but rather, whether a police officer, acting reasonably, would have made the stop for the reason given.

A

Petitioners contend that the standard they propose is consistent with our past cases' disapproval of police attempts to use valid bases of action against citizens as pretexts for pursuing other investigatory agendas. We are reminded that in *Florida v. Wells*, 495 U.S. 1, 4, (1990), we stated that "an inventory search"[1] must not be a ruse for a general rummaging in order to discover incriminating evidence"; that in *Colorado v. Bertine*, 479 U.S. 367, 372, (1987), in approving an inventory search, we apparently thought it significant that there had been "no showing that the police, who were following standardized procedures, acted in bad faith or for the sole purpose of investigation"; and that in *New York v. Burger*, 482 U.S. 691, 716–717, n. 27(1987), we observed, in upholding the constitutionality of a warrantless administrative inspection, that the search did not appear to be "a 'pretext' for obtaining evidence of ... violation of ... penal laws." But only an undiscerning reader would regard these cases as endorsing the principle that ulterior motives can invalidate police conduct that is justifiable on the basis of probable cause to believe that a violation of law has occurred. In each case we were addressing the validity of a search conducted in the *absence* of probable cause. Our quoted statements simply explain that the exemption from the need for probable cause (and warrant), which is accorded to searches made for the purpose of inventory or administrative regulation, is not accorded to searches that are *not* made for those purposes. See *Bertine, supra,* at 371–372,; Burger, supra, at 702–703.

Petitioners also rely upon *Colorado v. Bannister,* 449 U.S. 1, (1980) *(per curiam),* a case which, like this one, involved a traffic stop as the prelude to a plain-view sighting and arrest on charges wholly unrelated to the basis for the stop. Petitioners point to our statement that "[t]here was no evidence whatsoever that the officer's presence to issue a traffic citation was a pretext to confirm any other previous suspicion about the occupants" of the car. Id., at 4, n. 4, That dictum *at most* demonstrates that the Court in Bannister found no need to inquire into the question now under discussion; not that it was certain of the answer. And it may demonstrate even less than that: If by "pretext" the Court meant that the officer really had not seen the car speeding, the statement would mean only that there was no reason to doubt probable cause for the traffic stop.

It would, moreover, be anomalous, to say the least, to treat a statement in a footnote in the *per curiam Bannister* opinion as indicating a reversal of our prior law. Petitioners' difficulty is not simply a lack of affirmative support for their position. Not only have we never held, outside the context of inventory search or administrative inspection (discussed above), that an officer's motive invalidates objectively justifiable behavior under the Fourth Amendment; but we have repeatedly held and asserted the contrary. In *United States v. Villamonte–Marquez,* 462 U.S. 579, 584, n. 3, (1983), we held that an otherwise valid warrantless boarding of a vessel by customs officials was not rendered invalid "because the customs officers were accompanied by a Louisiana state policeman, and were following an informant's tip that a vessel in the ship channel was thought to be carrying marihuana." We flatly dismissed the idea that an ulterior motive might serve to strip the agents of their legal justification. In *United States v. Robinson,* 414 U.S. 218 (1973), we held that a traffic-violation arrest (of the sort here) would not be rendered invalid by the fact that it was "a mere pretext for a narcotics search," id., at 221, n. 1, and that a lawful post arrest search of the person would not be rendered invalid by the fact that it was not motivated by the officer-safety concern that justifies such searches, see id., at 236, See also *Gustafson v. Florida,* 414 U.S. 260, 266, (1973). And in *Scott v. United States,* 436 U.S. 128, 138, (1978), in rejecting the contention that wiretap evidence was subject to exclusion because the agents conducting the tap had failed to make any effort to comply with the statutory requirement that unauthorized acquisitions be minimized, we said that "[s]ubjective intent alone ... does not make otherwise lawful conduct illegal or unconstitutional." We described Robinson as having established that "the fact that the officer does not have the state of mind which is hypothecated by the reasons which provide the legal justification for the officer's action does not invalidate the action taken as long as the circumstances, viewed objectively, justify that action." 436 U.S., at 136, 138.

We think these cases foreclose any argument that the constitutional reasonableness of traffic stops depends on the actual motivations of the individual officers involved. We of course agree with petitioners that the Constitution prohibits selective enforcement of the law based on considerations such as race. But the constitutional basis for objecting to intentionally discriminatory application of laws is the Equal Protection Clause, not the Fourth Amendment. Subjective intentions play no role in ordinary, probable-cause Fourth Amendment analysis.

B

Recognizing that we have been unwilling to entertain Fourth Amendment challenges based on the actual motivations of individual officers, petitioners disavow any intention to make the individual officer's subjective good faith the touchstone of "reasonableness." They insist that the standard they have put forward—whether the officer's conduct deviated materially from usual police practices, so that a reasonable officer in the same circumstances would not have made the stop for the reasons given—is an "objective" one.

But although framed in empirical terms, this approach is plainly and indisputably driven by subjective considerations. Its whole purpose is to prevent the police from doing under the guise of enforcing the traffic code what they would like to do for different reasons. Petitioners' proposed standard may not use the word "pretext," but it is designed to combat nothing other than the perceived "danger" of the pretextual stop, albeit only indirectly and over the run of cases. Instead of asking whether the individual officer had the proper state of mind, the petitioners would have us ask, in effect, whether (based on general police practices) it is plausible to believe that the officer had the proper state of mind.

Why one would frame a test designed to combat pretext in such fashion that the court cannot take into account *actual and admitted pretext* is a curiosity that can only be explained by the fact that our cases have foreclosed the more sensible option. If those cases were based only upon the evidentiary difficulty of establishing subjective intent, petitioners' attempt to root out subjective vices through objective means might make sense. But they were not based only upon that, or indeed even principally upon that. Their principal basis—which applies equally to attempts to reach subjective intent through ostensibly objective means—is simply that the Fourth Amendment's concern with "reasonableness" allows certain actions to be taken in certain circumstances, *whatever* the subjective intent. See, *e.g., Robinson, supra,* at 236 ("Since it is the fact of custodial arrest which gives rise to the authority to search, it is of no moment that [the officer] did not indicate any subjective fear of the [arrestee] or that he did not himself suspect that [the arrestee] was armed") (footnotes omitted); *Gustafson, supra,* at 266, (same). But even if our concern had been only an evidentiary one, petitioners' proposal would by no means assuage it. Indeed, it seems to us somewhat easier to figure out the intent of an individual officer than to plumb the collective consciousness of law enforcement in order to determine whether a "reasonable officer" would have been moved to act upon the traffic violation. While police manuals and standard procedures may sometimes provide objective assistance, ordinarily one would be reduced to speculating about the hypothetical reaction of a hypothetical constable—an exercise that might be called virtual subjectivity.

Moreover, police enforcement practices, even if they could be practicably assessed by a judge, vary from place to place and from time to time. We cannot accept that the search and seizure protections of the Fourth Amendment are so variable, cf. *Gustafson, supra*, at 265, 94 S.Ct., at 491; *United States v. Caceres*, 440 U.S. 741, 755–756, (1979), and can be made to turn upon such trivialities. The difficulty is illustrated by petitioners' arguments in this case. Their claim that a reasonable officer would not have made this stop is based largely on District of Columbia police regulations which permit plainclothes officers in unmarked vehicles to enforce traffic laws "only in the case of a violation that is so grave as to pose an *immediate threat* to the safety of others." Metropolitan Police Department, Washington, D.C., General Order 303.1, pt. 1, Objectives and Policies (A)(2)(4) (Apr. 30, 1992), reprinted as Addendum to Brief for Petitioners. This basis of invalidation would not apply in jurisdictions that had a different practice. And it would not have applied even in the District of Columbia, if Officer Soto had been wearing a uniform or patrolling in a marked police cruiser.

Petitioners argue that our cases support insistence upon police adherence to standard practices as an objective means of rooting out pretext. They cite no holding to that effect, and dicta in only two cases. In *Abel v. United States,* 362 U.S. 217, (1960), the petitioner had been arrested by the Immigration and Naturalization Service (INS), on the basis of an administrative warrant that, he claimed, had been issued on pretextual grounds in order to enable the Federal Bureau of Investigation (FBI) to search his room after his arrest. We regarded this as an allegation of "serious misconduct," but rejected Abel's claims on the ground that "[a] finding of bad faith is ... not open to us on th[e] record" in light of the findings below, including the finding that " 'the proceedings taken by the [INS] differed in no respect from what would have been done in the case of an individual concerning whom [there was no pending FBI investigation],' " id., at 226–227. But it is a long leap from the proposition that following regular procedures is some evidence of lack of pretext to the proposition that failure to follow regular procedures *proves* (or is an operational substitute for) pretext. *Abel,* moreover, did not involve the assertion that pretext could invalidate a search or seizure for which there was probable cause—and even what it said about pretext in other contexts is plainly inconsistent with the views we later stated in *Robinson, Gustafson, Scott,* and *Villamonte–Marquez.* In the other case claimed to contain supportive dicta, United States v. Robinson, 414 U.S. 218 (1973), in approving a search incident to an arrest for driving without a license, we noted that the arrest was "not a departure from established police department practice." Id., at 221, n. 1. That was followed, however, by the statement that "[w]e leave for another day questions which would arise on facts different from these." *Ibid.* This is not even a dictum that purports to provide an answer, but merely one that leaves the question open.

III

In what would appear to be an elaboration on the "reasonable officer" test, petitioners argue that the balancing inherent in any Fourth Amendment inquiry requires us to weigh the governmental and individual interests implicated in a traffic stop such as we have here. That balancing, petitioners claim, does not support investigation of minor traffic infractions by plainclothes police in unmarked vehicles; such investigation only minimally advances the government's interest in traffic safety, and may indeed retard it by producing motorist confusion and alarm—a view said to be supported by the Metropolitan Police Department's own regulations generally prohibiting this practice. And as for the Fourth Amendment interests of the individuals concerned, petitioners point out that our cases acknowledge that even ordinary traffic stops entail "a possibly unsettling show of authority"; that they at best "interfere with freedom of movement, are inconvenient, and consume time" and at worst "may create substantial anxiety," *Prouse*, 440 U.S., at 657. That anxiety is likely to be even more pronounced when the stop is conducted by plainclothes officers in unmarked cars.

It is of course true that in principle every Fourth Amendment case, since it turns upon a "reasonableness" determination, involves a balancing of all relevant factors. With rare exceptions not applicable here, however, the result of that balancing is not in doubt where the search or seizure is based upon probable cause. That is why petitioners must rely upon cases like *Prouse* to provide examples of actual "balancing" analysis. There, the police action in question was a random traffic stop for the purpose of checking a motorist's license and vehicle registration, a practice that—like the practices at issue in the inventory search and administrative inspection cases upon which petitioners rely in making their "pretext" claim—involves police intrusion *without the probable cause that is its traditional justification.* Our opinion in *Prouse* expressly distinguished the case from a stop based on precisely what is at issue here: "probable cause to believe that a driver is violating any one of the multitude of applicable traffic and equipment regulations." Id., at 661. It noted approvingly that "[t]he foremost method of enforcing traffic and vehicle safety regulations ... is acting upon observed violations," id., at 659, which afford the "'quantum of individualized suspicion'" necessary to ensure that police discretion is sufficiently constrained, id., at 654–655, (quoting *United States v. Martinez–Fuerte,* 428 U.S., at 560, What is true of *Prouse* is also true of other cases that engaged in detailed "balancing" to decide the constitutionality of automobile stops, such as *Martinez–Fuerte,* which upheld checkpoint stops, see 428 U.S., at 556–562, and *Brignoni–Ponce,* which disallowed so-called "roving patrol" stops, see 422 U.S., at 882–884: The detailed "balancing" analysis was necessary because they involved seizures without probable cause.

Where probable cause has existed, the only cases in which we have found it necessary actually to perform the "balancing" analysis involved searches or seizures conducted in an extraordinary manner, unusually harmful to an individual's privacy or even physical interests—such as, for example, seizure by means of deadly force, see *Tennessee v. Garner*, 471 U.S. 1, (1985), unannounced entry into a home, see *Wilson v. Arkansas*, 514 U.S. 927 (1995), entry into a home without a warrant, see *Welsh v. Wisconsin*, 466 U.S. 740 (1984), or physical penetration of the body, see Winston v. Lee, 470 U.S. 753 (1985). The making of a traffic stop out of uniform does not remotely qualify as such an extreme practice, and so is governed by the usual rule that probable cause to believe the law has been broken "outbalances" private interest in avoiding police contact.

Petitioners urge as an extraordinary factor in this case that the "multitude of applicable traffic and equipment regulations" is so large and so difficult to obey perfectly that virtually everyone is guilty of violation, permitting the police to single out almost whomever they wish for a stop. But we are aware of no principle that would allow us to decide at what point a code of law becomes so expansive and so commonly violated that infraction itself can no longer be the ordinary measure of the lawfulness of enforcement. And even if we could identify such exorbitant codes, we do not know by what standard (or what right) we would decide, as petitioners would have us do, which particular provisions are sufficiently important to merit enforcement.

For the run-of-the-mine case, which this surely is, we think there is no realistic alternative to the traditional common-law rule that probable cause justifies a search and seizure.

* * *

Here the District Court found that the officers had probable cause to believe that petitioners had violated the traffic code. That rendered the stop reasonable under the Fourth Amendment, the evidence thereby discovered admissible, and the upholding of the convictions by the Court of Appeals for the District of Columbia Circuit correct. The judgment is

Affirmed.

Note

The Court in *Whren* states the following:

> We of course agree with petitioners that the Constitution prohibits selective enforcement
> of the law based on considerations such as race. But the constitutional basis for objecting to
> intentionally discriminatory application of laws is the Equal Protection Clause, not the Fourth
> Amendment. As to the issue of Equal Protection and intentional discrimination, see the next
> following excerpt from Professor Omar Saleem.

Omar Saleem, *Overcoming Environmental Discrimination: The Need for a Disparate Impact Test and Improved Notice Requirements in Facility Siting Decisions*, 19 COLUM. J. ENVTL. L. 211, 225 (1994)

....

The Equal Protection Clause declares that no state shall "deny to any person within its jurisdiction the equal protection of the laws." Courts have construed the clause form an antidiscrimination perspective and from an anti-subjugation perspective. The Supreme Court tends to adopt the antidiscrimination approach in applying the Clause. This approach focuses on the actor or perpetrator. The Court acknowledges a disparate impact on the minority group but goes on to examine the actor's intent – i.e., whether the decision was motivated by race – rather than focus on the impact of the actor's conduct on the victim. Such an approach tends to view racial discrimination as an isolated event by a few deviant individuals. In effect, "[E]qual protection jurisprudence reflects a society that merely rebukes accidental manifestations of prejudice, condemning them as social blunders rather than recognizing them as symptoms of a deeper societal pathology." The approach implicitly assumes that we live in a color-blind society. Racism is perceived as an abnormal growth of a liberal democracy and something we want to abolish, not something that reinforces American society. The antidiscrimination approach ignores the possibility, if not probability, that certain inadvertent or indifferent government conduct – as opposed to purposeful conduct may foster and perpetuate racial subjugation.

The anti-subjugation approach, on the other hand, focuses not on the mental state of the actor but on the impact of conduct or policies on the victim. The fundamental premise of this approach is recognition of the equal worth of all people. Under this approach, the equal protection analysis examines challenged conduct such as sitting hazardous waste facilities in a broader social and historical context and determines whether oppressive conditions persist. This approach has solid legal antecedents and is sensitive to the difficulties of proof inherent in an intent-based inquiry. Using this approach, courts would therefore focus on the community, considering the evidence that a disproportionate number of facilities exist in low-income racial minority communities, and examine siting policies in a broader social and historical context. Such an analysis would critically examine siting practices that harm traditionally disfavored communities.

Race and the Existence of Fourth Amendment Seizure

For Fourth Amendment purposes a seizure of the person occurs "whenever police officer accosts an individual and restrains his freedom to walk away" *Terry v. Ohio*, 392 U.S. 1 at 16 (1968). Actual physical restraint is not necessary as long as the individual is restrained under show of authority from leaving. *Henry v. United States* 361 US 98 (1959). In *United States v. Mendenhall*, 446 U.S. 544 (1980), (included below) the Court declared that a Fourth Amendment seizure occurs when "in view of all the circumstances surrounding the incident, a reasonable person would have believed that he was not free to leave". But given the nature of the historic and antagonistic relationship that often exists between the police and communities of color, should that psychological perception play a role in determining "free to leave"? Professor Tracey Maclin suggests that the dynamics surrounding an encounter between police and African Americans in particular may present a very different perception of free to leave. Tracey Maclin, "*Black and Blue Encounters-Some Preliminary Thoughts About Fourth Amendment Seizures: Should Race Matter?* 26 VAL. U. L. REV. 243, 250 (1991). How "free to leave" where the persons of color in the following cases?

CALIFORNIA V. HODARI D.
499 U.S. 621 (1991)

Justice SCALIA delivered the opinion of the Court.

Late one evening in April 1988, Officers Brian McColgin and Jerry Pertoso were on patrol in a high-crime area of Oakland, California. They were dressed in street clothes but wearing jackets with "Police" embossed on both front and back. Their unmarked car proceeded west on Foothill Boulevard, and turned south onto 63rd Avenue. As they rounded the corner, they saw four or five youths huddled around a small red car parked at the curb. When the youths saw the officers' car approaching they apparently panicked, and took flight. The respondent here, Hodari D., and one companion ran west through an alley; the others fled south. The red car also headed south, at a high rate of speed.

The officers were suspicious and gave chase. McColgin remained in the car and continued south on 63rd Avenue; Pertoso left the car, ran back north along 63rd, then west on Foothill Boulevard, and turned south on 62nd Avenue. Hodari, meanwhile, emerged from the alley onto 62nd and ran north. Looking behind as he ran, he did not turn and see Pertoso until the officer was almost upon him, whereupon he tossed away what appeared to be a small rock. A moment later, Pertoso tackled Hodari, handcuffed him, and radioed for assistance. Hodari was found to be carrying $130 in cash and a pager; and the rock he had discarded was found to be crack cocaine.

In the juvenile proceeding brought against him, Hodari moved to suppress the evidence relating to the cocaine. The court denied the motion without opinion. The California Court of Appeal reversed, holding that Hodari had been "seized" when he saw Officer Pertoso running towards him, that this seizure was unreasonable under the Fourth Amendment, and that the evidence of cocaine had to be suppressed as the fruit of that illegal seizure. The California Supreme Court denied the State's application for review. We granted certiorari

As this case comes to us, the only issue presented is whether, at the time he dropped the drugs, Hodari had been "seized" within the meaning of the Fourth Amendment. If so, respondent argues, the drugs were the fruit of that seizure and the evidence concerning them was properly excluded. If not, the drugs were abandoned by Hodari and lawfully recovered by the police, and the evidence should have been admitted. (In addition, of course, Pertoso's seeing the rock of cocaine, at least if he recognized it as such, would provide reasonable suspicion for the unquestioned seizure that occurred when he tackled Hodari. Cf. Rios v. United States, 364 U.S. 253(1960).)

We have long understood that the Fourth Amendment's protection against "unreasonable ... seizures" includes seizure of the person, see *Henry v. United States*, 361 U.S. 98, 100 (1959). From the time of the founding to the present, the word "seizure" has meant a "taking possession," 2 N. Webster, An American Dictionary of the English Language 67 (1828); 2 J. Bouvier, A Law Dictionary 510 (6th ed. 1856); Webster's Third New International Dictionary 2057 (1981). For most purposes at common law, the word connoted not merely grasping, or applying physical force to, the animate or inanimate object in question, but actually bringing it within physical control. A ship still fleeing, even though under attack, would not be considered to have been seized as a war prize. Cf. *The Josefa Segunda*, 10 Wheat. 312, 325–326, 6 L.Ed. 320 (1825). A res capable of manual delivery was not seized until "tak[en] into custody." *Pelham v. Rose*, 9 Wall. 103, 106, 19 L.Ed. 602 (1870). To constitute an arrest, however—the quintessential "seizure of the person" under our Fourth Amendment jurisprudence—the mere grasping or application of physical force with lawful authority, whether or not it succeeded in subduing the arrestee, was sufficient. See, *e.g.*, *Whitehead v. Keyes*, 85 Mass. 495, 501 (1862) ("[A]n officer effects an arrest of a person whom he has authority to arrest, by laying his hand on him for the purpose of arresting him, though he may not succeed in stopping and holding him"); 1 Restatement of Torts § 41, Comment *h* (1934). As one commentator has described it:

> "There can be constructive detention, which will constitute an arrest, although the party is never
> actually brought within the physical control of the party making an arrest. This is accomplished
> by merely touching, however slightly, the body of the accused, by the party making the arrest
> and for that purpose, although he does not succeed in stopping or holding him even for an
> instant; as where the bailiff had tried to arrest one who fought him off by a fork, the court
> said, 'If the bailiff had touched him, that had been an arrest....' " A. Cornelius, SEARCH AND
> SEIZURE 163–164 (2d ed. 1930) (footnote omitted).

To say that an arrest is effected by the slightest application of physical force, despite the arrestee's escape, is not to say that for Fourth Amendment purposes there is a *continuing* arrest during the period of fugitivity. If, for example, Pertoso had laid his hands upon Hodari to arrest him, but Hodari had broken away and had *then* cast away the cocaine, it would hardly be realistic to say that that disclosure had been made during the course of an arrest. Cf. *Thompson v. Whitman*, 18 Wall. 457, 471, 21 L.Ed. 897 (1874) ("A seizure is a single act, and not a continuous fact"). The present case, however, is even one step further removed. It does not involve the application of any physical force; Hodari was untouched by Officer Pertoso at the time he discarded the cocaine. His defense relies instead upon the proposition that a seizure occurs "when the officer, by means of physical force *or show of authority,* has in some way restrained the liberty of a citizen." *Terry v. Ohio*, 392 U.S. 1, 19, n. 16, 88 S.Ct. 1868, 1879, n. 16, 20 L.Ed.2d 889 (1968) (emphasis added). Hodari contends (and we accept as true for purposes of this decision) that Pertoso's pursuit qualified as a "show of authority" calling upon Hodari to halt. The narrow question before us is whether, with respect to a show of authority as with respect to application of physical force, a seizure occurs even though the subject does not yield. We hold that it does not.

The language of the Fourth Amendment, of course, cannot sustain respondent's contention. The word "seizure" readily bears the meaning of a laying on of hands or application of physical force to restrain movement, even when it is ultimately unsuccessful. ("She seized the purse-snatcher, but he broke out of her grasp.") It does not remotely apply, however, to the prospect of a policeman yelling "Stop, in the name of the law!" at a fleeing form that continues to flee. That is no seizure.[2] Nor can the result respondent wishes to achieve be produced— indirectly, as it were—by suggesting that Pertoso's uncomplied-with show of authority was a common-law arrest, and then appealing to the principle that all common-law arrests are seizures. An arrest requires *either* physical force (as described above) *or,* where that is absent, *submission* to the assertion of authority.

> "Mere words will not constitute an arrest, while, on the other hand, no actual, physical touching is essential. The apparent inconsistency in the two parts of this statement is explained by the fact that an assertion of authority and purpose to arrest followed by submission of the arrestee constitutes an arrest. There can be no arrest without either touching or submission." Perkins, The Law of Arrest, 25 Iowa L.Rev. 201, 206 (1940) (footnotes omitted).

We do not think it desirable, even as a policy matter, to stretch the Fourth Amendment beyond its words and beyond the meaning of arrest, as respondent urges. Street pursuits always place the public at some risk, and compliance with police orders to stop should therefore be encouraged. Only a few of those orders, we must presume, will be without adequate basis, and since the addressee has no ready means of identifying the deficient ones it almost invariably is the responsible course to comply. Unlawful orders will not be deterred, moreover, by sanctioning through the exclusionary rule those of them that are *not* obeyed. Since policemen do not command "Stop!" expecting to be ignored, or give chase hoping to be outrun, it fully suffices to apply the deterrent to their genuine, successful seizures.

Respondent contends that his position is sustained by the so-called *Mendenhall* test, formulated by Justice Stewart's opinion in *United States v. Mendenhall*, 446 U.S. 544, 554, (1980), and adopted by the Court in later cases, see *Michigan v. Chesternut*, 486 U.S. 567, 573 (1988); INS v. Delgado, 466 U.S. 210, 215 (1984): "[A] person has been 'seized' within the meaning of the Fourth Amendment only if, in view of all the circumstances surrounding the incident, a reasonable person would have believed that he was not free to leave." 446 U.S., at 554. See also *Florida v. Royer*, 460 U.S. 491, 502 (1983) (opinion of WHITE, J.). In seeking to rely upon that test here, respondent fails to read it carefully. It says that a person has been seized "only if," not that he has been seized "whenever"; it states a *necessary*, but not a *sufficient*, condition for seizure—or, more precisely, for seizure effected through a "show of authority." *Mendenhall* establishes that the test for existence of a "show of authority" is an objective one: not whether the citizen perceived that he was being ordered to restrict his movement, but whether the officer's words and actions would have conveyed that to a reasonable person. Application of this objective test was the basis for our decision in the other case principally relied upon by respondent, *Chesternut, supra,* where we concluded that the police cruiser's slow following of the defendant did not convey the message that he was not free to disregard the police and go about his business. We did not address in *Chesternut,* however, the question whether, if the *Mendenhall* test was met—if the message that the defendant was not free to leave *had* been conveyed—a Fourth Amendment seizure would have occurred. See 486 U.S., at 577 (KENNEDY, J., concurring).

Quite relevant to the present case, however, was our decision in *Brower v. Inyo County*, 489 U.S. 593, 596, (1989). In that case, police cars with flashing lights had chased the decedent for 20 miles—surely an adequate "show of authority"—but he did not stop until his fatal crash into a police-erected blockade. The issue was whether his death could be held to be the consequence of an unreasonable seizure in violation of the Fourth Amendment. We did not even consider the possibility that a seizure could have occurred during the course of the chase because, as we explained, that "show of authority" did not produce his stop. Id., at 597. And we discussed, ibid., an opinion of Justice Holmes, involving a situation not much different from the present case, where revenue agents had picked up containers dropped by moonshiners whom they were pursuing without adequate warrant. The containers were not excluded as the product of an unlawful seizure because "[t]he defendant's own acts, and those of his associates, disclosed the jug, the jar and the bottle—and there was no seizure in the sense of the law when the officers examined the contents of each after they had been abandoned." *Hester v. United States*, 265 U.S. 57, 58, (1924). The same is true here.

In sum, assuming that Pertoso's pursuit in the present case constituted a "show of authority" enjoining Hodari to halt, since Hodari did not comply with that injunction he was not seized until he was tackled. The cocaine abandoned while he was running was in this case not the fruit of a seizure, and his motion to exclude evidence of it was properly denied. We reverse the decision of the California Court of Appeal, and remand for further proceedings not inconsistent with this opinion.

It is so ordered.

UNITED STATES V. MENDENHALL.

446 U.S. 544 (1980)

Mr. Justice STEWART announced the judgment of the Court and delivered an opinion, in which Mr. Justice REHNQUIST joined.

The respondent was brought to trial in the United States District Court for the Eastern District of Michigan on a charge of possessing heroin with intent to distribute it. She moved to suppress the introduction at trial of the heroin as evidence against her on the ground that it had been acquired from her through an unconstitutional search and seizure by agents of the Drug Enforcement Administration (DEA). The District Court denied the respondent's motion, and she was convicted after a trial upon stipulated facts. The Court of Appeals, reversed, finding the search of the respondent's person to have been unlawful. We granted certiorari to consider whether any right of the respondent guaranteed by the Fourth Amendment was violated in the circumstances presented by this case.

I

At the hearing in the trial court on the respondent's motion to suppress, it was established how the heroin she was charged with possessing had been obtained from her. The respondent arrived at the Detroit Metropolitan Airport on a commercial airline flight from Los Angeles early in the morning on February 10, 1976. As she disembarked from the airplane, she was observed by two agents of the DEA, who were present at the airport for the purpose of detecting unlawful traffic in narcotics. After observing the respondent's conduct, which appeared to the agents to be characteristic of persons unlawfully carrying narcotics, the agents approached her as she was walking through the concourse, identified themselves as federal agents, and asked to see her identification and airline ticket. The respondent produced her driver's license, which was in the name of Sylvia Mendenhall, and, in answer to a question of one of the agents, stated that she resided at the address appearing on the license. The airline ticket was issued in the name of "Annette Ford." When asked why the ticket bore a name different from her own, the respondent stated that she "just felt like using that name." In response to a further question, the respondent indicated that she had been in California only two days. Agent Anderson then specifically identified himself as a federal narcotics agent and, according to his testimony, the respondent "became quite shaken, extremely nervous. She had a hard time speaking."

After returning the airline ticket and driver's license to her, Agent Anderson asked the respondent if she would accompany him to the airport DEA office for further questions. She did so, although the record does not indicate a verbal response to the request. The office, which was located up one flight of stairs about 50 feet from where the respondent had first been approached, consisted of a reception area adjoined by three other rooms. At the office the agent asked the respondent if she would allow a search of her person and handbag and told her that she had the right to decline the search if she desired. She responded: "Go ahead." She then handed Agent Anderson her purse, which contained a receipt for an airline ticket that had been issued to "F. Bush" three days earlier for a flight from Pittsburgh through Chicago to Los Angeles. The agent asked whether this was the ticket that she had used for her flight to California, and the respondent stated that it was.

A female police officer then arrived to conduct the search of the respondent's person. She asked the agents if the respondent had consented to be searched. The agents said that she had, and the respondent followed the policewoman into a private room. There the policewoman again asked the respondent if she consented to the search, and the respondent replied that she did. The policewoman explained that the search would require that the respondent remove her clothing. The respondent stated that she had a plane to catch and was assured by the policewoman that if she were carrying no narcotics, there would be no problem. The respondent then began to disrobe without further comment. As the respondent removed her clothing, she took from her undergarments two small packages, one of which appeared to contain heroin, and handed both to the policewoman. The agents then arrested the respondent for possessing heroin.

It was on the basis of this evidence that the District Court denied the respondent's motion to suppress. The court concluded that the agents' conduct in initially approaching the respondent and asking to see her ticket and identification was a permissible investigative stop under the standards of *Terry v. Ohio*, 392 U.S. 1 and *United States v. Brignoni-Ponce*, 422 U.S. 873 finding that this conduct was based on specific and articulable facts that justified a suspicion of criminal activity. The court also found that the respondent had not been placed under arrest or otherwise detained when she was asked to accompany the agents to the DEA office, but had accompanied the agents "'voluntarily in a spirit of apparent cooperation.'" It was the court's view that no arrest occurred until after the heroin had been found. Finally, the trial court found that the respondent "gave her consent to the search [in the DEA office] and . . . such consent was freely and voluntarily given."

The Court of Appeals reversed the respondent's subsequent conviction, stating only that "the court concludes that this case is indistinguishable from *United States v. McCaleb*," 552 F.2d 717 (CA6 1977). In *McCaleb* the Court of Appeals had suppressed heroin seized by DEA agents at the Detroit Airport in circumstances substantially similar to those in the present case. The Court of Appeals there disapproved the Government's reliance on the so-called "drug courier profile," and held that the agents could not reasonably have suspected criminal activity in that case, for the reason that "the activities of the [persons] observed by DEA agents, were consistent with innocent behavior," id., at 720. The Court of Appeals further concluded in *McCaleb* that, even if the initial approach had been permissible, asking the suspects to accompany the agents to a private room for further questioning constituted an arrest requiring probable cause. Finally, the court in *McCaleb* held that the consent to the search in that case had not been voluntarily given, principally because it was the fruit of what the court believed to have been an unconstitutional detention.

On rehearing en banc of the present case, the Court of Appeals reaffirmed its original decision, stating simply that the respondent had not validly consented to the search "within the meaning of [*McCaleb*]." 596 F.2d 706, 707.

II

The Fourth Amendment provides that "the right of the people to be secure in their persons, houses, papers, and effects, against unreasonable searches and seizures, shall not be violated . . .." There is no question in this case that the respondent possessed this constitutional right of personal security as she walked through the Detroit Airport, for "the Fourth Amendment protects people, not places," *Katz v. United States*, 389 U.S. 347, 351. Here the Government concedes that its agents had neither a warrant nor probable cause to believe that the respondent was carrying narcotics when the agents conducted a search of the respondent's person. It is the Government's position, however, that the search was conducted pursuant to the respondent's consent,[4] and thus was excepted from the requirements of both a warrant and probable cause. See *Schneckloth v. Bustamonte*, 412 U.S. 218. Evidently, the Court of Appeals concluded that the respondent's apparent consent to the search was in fact not voluntarily given and was in any event the product of earlier official conduct violative of the Fourth Amendment. We must first consider, therefore, whether such conduct occurred, either on the concourse or in the DEA office at the airport.

A

The Fourth Amendment's requirement that searches and seizures be founded upon an objective justification, governs all seizures of the person, "including seizures that involve only a brief detention short of traditional arrest. *Terry v. Ohio*, 392 U.S. 1, 16–19 (1968)." *United States v. Brignoni-Ponce, supra*, at 878,. Accordingly, if the respondent was "seized" when the DEA agents approached her on the concourse and asked questions of her, the agents' conduct in doing so was constitutional only if they reasonably suspected the respondent of wrongdoing. But "[o] bviously, not all personal intercourse between policemen and citizens involves 'seizures' of persons. Only when the officer, by means of physical force or show of authority, has in some way restrained the liberty of a citizen may we conclude that a 'seizure' has occurred." *Terry v. Ohio*, 392 U.S., at 19, n. 16 .

The distinction between an intrusion amounting to a "seizure" of the person and an encounter that intrudes upon no constitutionally protected interest is illustrated by the facts of *Terry v. Ohio*, which the Court recounted as follows: "Officer McFadden approached the three men, identified himself as a police officer and asked for their names. . .. When the men 'mumbled something' in response to his inquiries, Officer McFadden grabbed petitioner Terry, spun him around so that they were facing the other two, with Terry between McFadden and the others, and patted down the outside of his clothing." Id., at 6–7. Obviously the officer "seized" Terry and subjected him to a "search" when he took hold of him, spun him around, and patted down the outer surfaces of his clothing, id. What was not determined in that case, however, was that a seizure had taken place before the officer physically restrained Terry for purposes of searching his person for weapons. The Court "assume[d] that up to that point no intrusion upon constitutionally protected rights had occurred." Id., at 19, n. 16. The Court's assumption appears entirely correct in view of the fact, noted in the concurring opinion of Mr. Justice WHITE, that "[t]here is nothing in the Constitution which prevents a policeman from addressing questions to anyone on the streets," id., at 34. Police officers enjoy "the liberty (again, possessed by every citizen) to address questions to other persons," id., at 31 (Harlan, J., concurring), although "ordinarily the person addressed has an equal right to ignore his interrogator and walk away." *Ibid.*

Similarly, the Court in *Sibron v. New York*, 392 U.S. 40, a case decided the same day as *Terry v. Ohio*, indicated that not every encounter between a police officer and a citizen is an intrusion requiring an objective justification. In that case, a police officer, before conducting what was later found to have been an unlawful search, approached Sibron in a restaurant and told him to come outside, which Sibron did. The Court had no occasion to decide whether there was a "seizure" of Sibron inside the restaurant antecedent to the seizure that accompanied the search. The record was "barren of any indication whether Sibron accompanied [the officer] outside in submission to a show of force or authority which left him no choice, or *whether he went voluntarily in a spirit of apparent cooperation* with the officer's investigation." 392 U.S., at 63 (emphasis added). Plainly, in the latter event, there was no seizure until the police officer in some way demonstrably curtailed Sibron's liberty.

We adhere to the view that a person is "seized" only when, by means of physical force or a show of authority, his freedom of movement is restrained. Only when such restraint is imposed is there any foundation whatever for invoking constitutional safeguards. The purpose of the Fourth Amendment is not to eliminate all contact between the police and the citizenry, but "to prevent arbitrary and oppressive interference by enforcement officials with the privacy and personal security of individuals." *United States v. Martinez-Fuerte*, 428 U.S. 543, 554. As long as the person to whom questions are put remains free to disregard the questions and walk away, there has been no intrusion upon that person's liberty or privacy as would under the Constitution require some particularized and objective justification.

Moreover, characterizing every street encounter between a citizen and the police as a "seizure," while not enhancing any interest secured by the Fourth Amendment, would impose wholly unrealistic restrictions upon a wide variety of legitimate law enforcement practices. The Court has on other occasions referred to the acknowledged need for police questioning as a tool in the effective enforcement of the criminal laws. "Without such investigation, those who were innocent might be falsely accused, those who were guilty might wholly escape prosecution, and many crimes would go unsolved. In short, the security of all would be diminished. *Haynes v. Washington*, 373 U.S. 503, 515,." *Schneckloth v. Bustamonte*, 412 U.S., at 225 .

We conclude that a person has been "seized" within the meaning of the Fourth Amendment only if, in view of all of the circumstances surrounding the incident, a reasonable person would have believed that he was not free to leave. Examples of circumstances that might indicate a seizure, even where the person did not attempt to leave, would be the threatening presence of several officers, the display of a weapon by an officer, some physical touching of the person of the citizen, or the use of language or tone of voice indicating that compliance with the officer's request might be compelled. See *Terry v. Ohio*, supra, 392 U.S., at 19, n. 16; *Dunaway v. New York*, 442 U.S. 200, 207; 3 W. LaFave, Search and Seizure 53–55 (1978). In the absence of some such evidence, otherwise inoffensive contact between a member of the public and the police cannot, as a matter of law, amount to a seizure of that person.

On the facts of this case, no "seizure" of the respondent occurred. The events took place in the public concourse. The agents wore no uniforms and displayed no weapons. They did not summon the respondent to their presence, but instead approached her and identified themselves as federal agents. They requested, but did not demand to see the respondent's identification and ticket. Such conduct without more, did not amount to an intrusion upon any constitutionally protected interest. The respondent was not seized simply by reason of the fact that the agents approached her, asked her if she would show them her ticket and identification, and posed to her a few questions. Nor was it enough to establish a seizure that the person asking the questions was a law enforcement official. See (Harlan, J., concurring). See also ALI, Model Code of

Pre-Arraignment Procedure § 110.1(1) and commentary, at 257–261 (1975). In short, nothing in the record suggests that the respondent had any objective reason to believe that she was not free to end the conversation in the concourse and proceed on her way, and for that reason we conclude that the agents' initial approach to her was not a seizure.

Our conclusion that no seizure occurred is not affected by the fact that the respondent was not expressly told by the agents that she was free to decline to cooperate with their inquiry, for the voluntariness of her responses does not depend upon her having been so informed. See *Schneckloth v. Bustamonte, supra.* We also reject the argument that the only inference to be drawn from the fact that the respondent acted in a manner so contrary to her self-interest is that she was compelled to answer the agents' questions. It may happen that a person makes statements to law enforcement officials that he later regrets, but the issue in such cases is not whether the statement was self-protective, but rather whether it was made voluntarily.

The Court's decision last Term in *Brown v. Texas,* 443 U.S. 47, on which the respondent relies, is not apposite. It could not have been plainer under the circumstances there presented that Brown was forcibly detained by the officers. In that case, two police officers approached Brown in an alley, and asked him to identify himself and to explain his reason for being there. Brown "refused to identify himself and angrily asserted that the officers had no right to stop him," *id.,* at 49. Up to this point there was no seizure. But after continuing to protest the officers' power to interrogate him, Brown was first frisked, and then arrested for violation of a state statute making it a criminal offense for a person to refuse to give his name and address to an officer "who has lawfully stopped him and requested the information." The Court simply held in that case that because the officers had no reason to suspect Brown of wrongdoing, there was no basis for detaining him, and therefore no permissible foundation for applying the state statute in the circumstances there presented. Id., at 52–53 .

The Court's decisions involving investigatory stops of automobiles do not point in any different direction. In *United States v. Brignoni-Ponce,* 422 U.S. 873, the Court held that a roving patrol of law enforcement officers could stop motorists in the general area of an international border for brief inquiry into their residence status only if the officers reasonably suspected that the vehicle might contain aliens who were illegally in the country. Id., at 881–882. The Government did not contend in that case that the persons whose automobiles were detained were not seized. Indeed, the Government acknowledged that the occupants of a detained vehicle were required to respond to the officers' questions and on some occasions to produce documents evidencing their eligibility to be in the United States. Id., at 880. Moreover, stopping or diverting an automobile in transit, with the attendant opportunity for a visual inspection of areas of the passenger compartment not otherwise observable, is materially more intrusive than a question put to a passing pedestrian, and the fact that the former amounts to a seizure tells very little about the constitutional status of the latter. See also *Delaware v. Prouse,* 440 U.S. 648, *United States v. Martinez-Fuerte,* 428 U.S., at 556–559, .

B

Although we have concluded that the initial encounter between the DEA agents and the respondent on the concourse at the Detroit Airport did not constitute an unlawful seizure, it is still arguable that the respondent's Fourth Amendment protections were violated when she went from the concourse to the DEA office. Such a violation might in turn infect the subsequent search of the respondent's person.

The District Court specifically found that the respondent accompanied the agents to the office "'voluntarily in a spirit of apparent cooperation,'" quoting *Sibron v. New York*, 392 U.S., at 63, Notwithstanding this determination by the trial court, the Court of Appeals evidently concluded that the agents' request that the respondent accompany them converted the situation into an arrest requiring probable cause in order to be found lawful. But because the trial court's finding was sustained by the record, the Court of Appeals was mistaken in substituting for that finding its view of the evidence. See *Jackson v. United States*, 122 U.S.App.D.C. 324, 353 F.2d 862 (1965).

The question whether the respondent's consent to accompany the agents was in fact voluntary or was the product of duress or coercion, express or implied, is to be determined by the totality of all the circumstances, *Schneckloth v. Bustamonte*, 412 U.S., at 227, and is a matter which the Government has the burden of proving. Id., at 222, citing *Bumper v. North Carolina*, 391 U.S. 543, 548. The respondent herself did not testify at the hearing. The Government's evidence showed that the respondent was not told that she had to go to the office, but was simply asked if she would accompany the officers. There were neither threats nor any show of force. The respondent had been questioned only briefly, and her ticket and identification were returned to her before she was asked to accompany the officers.

On the other hand, it is argued that the incident would reasonably have appeared coercive to the respondent, who was 22 years old and had not been graduated from high school. It is additionally suggested that the respondent, a female and a Negro, may have felt unusually threatened by the officers, who were white males. While these factors were not irrelevant, see *Schneckloth v. Bustamonte, supra,* 412 U.S., at 226, neither were they decisive, and the totality of the evidence in this case was plainly adequate to support the District Court's finding that the respondent voluntarily consented to accompany the officers to the DEA office.

C

Because the search of the respondent's person was not preceded by an impermissible seizure of her person, it cannot be contended that her apparent consent to the subsequent search was infected by an unlawful detention. There remains to be considered whether the respondent's consent to the search was for any other reason invalid. The District Court explicitly credited the officers' testimony and found that the "consent was freely and voluntarily given," citing *Schneckloth v. Bustamonte, supra.* There was more than enough evidence in this case to sustain that view. First, we note that the respondent, who was 22 years old and had an 11th-grade education, was plainly capable of a knowing consent. Second, it is especially significant that the respondent was twice expressly told that she was free to decline to consent to the search, and only thereafter explicitly consented to it. Although the Constitution does not require "proof of knowledge of a right to refuse as the *sine qua non* of an effective consent to a search," id., at 234, (footnote omitted), such knowledge was highly relevant to the determination that there had been consent. And, perhaps more important for present purposes, the fact that the officers themselves informed the respondent that she was free to withhold her consent substantially lessened the probability that their conduct could reasonably have appeared to her to be coercive.

Counsel for the respondent has argued that she did in fact resist the search, relying principally on the testimony that when she was told that the search would require the removal of her clothing, she stated to the female police officer that "she had a plane to catch." But the trial court was entitled to view the statement as simply an expression of concern that the search be conducted quickly. The respondent had twice unequivocally indicated her consent to the search, and when assured by the police officer that there would be no problem if nothing were turned up by the search, she began to undress without further comment.

Counsel for the respondent has also argued that because she was within the DEA office when she consented to the search, her consent may have resulted from the inherently coercive nature of those surroundings. But in view of the District Court's finding that the respondent's presence in the office was voluntary, the fact that she was there is little or no evidence that she was in any way coerced. And in response to the argument that the respondent would not voluntarily have consented to a search that was likely to disclose the narcotics that she carried, we repeat that the question is not whether the respondent acted in her ultimate self-interest, but whether she acted voluntarily.

III

We conclude that the District Court's determination that the respondent consented to the search of her person "freely and voluntarily" was sustained by the evidence and that the Court of Appeals was, therefore, in error in setting it aside. Accordingly, the judgment of the Court of Appeals is reversed, and the case is remanded to that court for further proceedings.

It is so ordered.

Note

Consider also *Florida v. Bostick,* 501 US 429 (1991). Was a young Black man traveling on a bus and confronted by police really free to leave? What about the largely Latino workforce that were subjected to questioning for two hours at work, while Immigration officers blocked doors an exit. *INS v. Delgado,* 466 US 210 (1984). In *Bostick* it was also contended that Bostick consented to the search of his luggage. Given racial dynamics of such confrontation how voluntary was that consent? Consider the *Bumper* case below.

Race and Consent to Search

BUMPER V. STATE OF NORTH CAROLINA
391 U.S. 543 (1968)

Mr. Justice STEWART delivered the opinion of the Court.

....

II.

The petitioner lived with his grandmother, Mrs. Hattie Leath, a 66-year-old Negro widow, in a house located in a rural area at the end of an isolated mile-long dirt road. Two days after the alleged offense but prior to the petitioner's arrest, four white law enforcement officers—the county sheriff, two of his deputies, and a state investigator—went to this house and found Mrs. Leath there with some young children. She met the officers at the front door. One of them announced, 'I have a search warrant to search your house.' Mrs. Leath responded, 'Go ahead,' and opened the door. In the kitchen the officers found the rifle that was later introduced in evidence at the petitioner's trial after a motion to suppress had been denied.

At the hearing on this motion, the prosecutor informed the court that he did not rely upon a warrant to justify the search, but upon the consent of Mrs. Leath.[7] She testified at the hearing, stating, among other things:

'Four of them came. I was busy about my work, and they walked into the house and one of them walked up and said, 'I have a search warrant to search your house,' and I walked out and told them to come on in. He just come on in and said he had a warrant to search the house, and he didn't read it to me or nothing. So, I just told him to come on in and go ahead and search, and I went on about my work. I wasn't concerned what he was about. I was just satisfied. He just told me he had a search warrant, but he didn't read it to me. He did tell me he had a search warrant.

'* * * He said he was the law and had a search warrant to search the house, why I thought he could go ahead. I believed he had a search warrant. I took him at his word. * * * I just seen them out there in the yard. They got through the door when I opened it. At that time, I did not know my grandson had been charged with crime. Nobody told me anything. They didn't tell me anything, just picked it up like that. They didn't tell me nothing about my grandson.'

Upon the basis of Mrs. Leath's testimony, the trial court found that she had given her consent to the search, and denied the motion to suppress. The Supreme Court of North Carolina approved the admission of the evidence on the same basis.

The issue thus presented is whether a search can be justified as lawful on the basis of consent when that 'consent' has been given only after the official conducting the search has asserted that he possesses a warrant. We hold that there can be no consent under such circumstances.

When a prosecutor seeks to rely upon consent to justify the lawfulness of a search, he has the burden of proving that the consent was, in fact, freely and voluntarily given.This burden cannot be discharged by showing no more than acquiescence to a claim of lawful authority. A search conducted in reliance upon a warrant cannot later be justified on the basis of consent if it turns out that the warrant was invalid.[14] The result can be no different when it turns out that the State does not even attempt to rely upon the validity of the warrant, or fails to show that there was, in fact, any warrant at all.

When a law enforcement officer claims authority to search a home under a warrant, he announces in effect that the occupant has no right to resist the search. The situation is instinct with coercion—albeit colorably lawful coercion. Where there is coercion there cannot be consent.

We hold that Mrs. Leath did not consent to the search, and that it was constitutional error to admit the rifle in evidence against the petitioner. Mapp v. Ohio, 367 U.S. 643. Because the rifle was plainly damaging evidence against the petitioner with respect to all three of the charges against him, its admission at the trial was not harmless error. Chapman v. State of California, 386 U.S. 18.

The judgment of the Supreme Court of North Carolina is, accordingly, reversed, and the case is remanded for further proceedings not inconsistent with this opinion. It is so ordered.

Judgment reversed and case remanded

Note

In *Schneckloth v. Bustamonte*, 412 U.S. 218 (1973) the Court found that valid consent for Fourth Amendment purposes would be determined by a totality of the circumstances and not just by the suspect's lack of knowledge that he or she could refuse. But what role does race, a practical matter, play in determining valid, voluntary consent? Bumper was an African American grandmother confronted by White police officers who purported to have authority to search that they did not actually have. But Bustamonte and his companion were Hispanics similarly confronted. Should the racial difference play a role? Justice Marshall, who would have applied *Bumper* differently than the majority, states in dissent in *Bustamonte*, "The proper resolution of this case turns, I believe, on a realistic assessment of the nature of the interchange between citizens and the police, and of the practical import of allocating the burden of proof in one way rather than another." *Id.* at 289

IN RE J.M.

619 A.2d 497 (D.C. Ct. of App.1992)

ON REHEARING EN BANC

FARRELL, Associate Judge:

> On reconsideration by the court en banc, we have decided to remand this case for explicit findings by the trial judge with respect to the key factual issue presented, namely, the bearing of appellant's age—fourteen at the time of his arrest—upon the voluntariness of his consent to the search of his person.
>
> ....

MACK, Senior Judge, dissenting, but concurring in the order of remand:

As a matter of law, I would have concluded that J.M. was seized when cornered by drug interdiction officers on board the bus. Moreover, even accepting the facts as developed at trial, I could not have concluded that J.M. freely consented to an intrusive body search. With the issue of consent still open, however, I want to go on record as agreeing with my colleagues that, on remand, the trial court must consider J.M.'s youth. Moreover, to speak the "unspeakable," the trial court should also consider the fact that J.M. was a fourteen year old *black* youth who had no previous involvement with the criminal justice system and who had not been advised that he could walk away or refuse to answer.

In our preoccupation with standards of review with respect to "two conceptually distinct yet, in practice, often overlapping issues," *i.e.*, whether there has been seizure and/or consent for Fourth Amendment purposes, we must not lose sight of the fact that, regardless of the applicable standards, judges at both the trial and appellate levels must rest any decisions on the "totality of [factual] circumstances." This is true whether those circumstances are objective only, or both objective and subjective. In my view, J.M. was seized when cornered by police in the early morning hours of October 31, 1989. I cannot find that a reasonable person, even an innocent person, (in the circumstances in which J.M. found himself) would feel "free to decline the officers' request or otherwise terminate the encounter" in the physically confining interior of an interstate bus commandeered by armed drug interdiction officers at 2:00 a.m. for the purpose of conducting interviews during a rest stop.

II.

As to the consent issue, I read both *Miller v. Fenton*, 474 U.S. 104, 106 S.Ct. 445, 88 L.Ed.2d 405 (1985) and *Florida v. Jimeno*, 500 U.S. 248, 111 S.Ct. 1801, 114 L.Ed.2d 297 (1991), to hold that consent is a question of law for the appellate court, deferring to the trial court's findings on secondary or subsidiary issues (of fact). I do not belabor the point because I do not rely upon what I perceive here to be an impermissible seizure to question the validity of any subsequent consent to search. The coercive nature of the setting, coupled with other facts established by trial testimony, leads me to conclude that the trial court's finding of J.M.'s free and voluntary consent was at least clearly deficient, and at most clearly erroneous. *See Kelly v. United States*, 580 A.2d 1282 (D.C.1990).

For the average law-abiding citizen, the idea of having police officers conduct a "pat down" body search in public is a disconcerting one. It is safe to surmise, and the Corporation Counsel so argued, that this thought would be even more disconcerting to a person with cocaine strapped to his body. For distinctly different but equally compelling reasons, this court should review with "the most careful scrutiny" all the surrounding circumstances attendant to a finding of consent, especially when the search cannot be justified by probable cause or articulable suspicion. *See Schneckloth v. Bustamonte*, supra, 412 U.S. at 229, 248, 93 S.Ct. at 2048, 2058; *see also United States v. Blake*, 888 F.2d 795 (11th Cir.1989).

The conclusion that J.M. freely consented because he did not want to make the searching officer suspicious, culled from a scenario generated by the prosecutor during J.M.'s cross-examination and reiterated in the trial court's reasoning, fails to comport with the reality of human experience, with the record in this case, and with the law of consent as I see it. In my view, this finding cannot be sustained.

When the government seeks to rely upon consent to justify the lawfulness of a search, the government bears the burden of proving that the consent was, in fact, freely and voluntarily given. *Bumper v. North Carolina*, 391 U.S. 543, 548, 88 S.Ct. 1788, 1791, 20 L.Ed.2d 797 (1968). Voluntariness is a question of fact to be determined from the totality of *all* the circumstances, including the characteristics of the accused, the details of the interrogation, and the failure to advise the accused of his constitutional rights. *See Schneckloth, supra*, 412 U.S. at 226, 227, 93 S.Ct. at 2047, 2048. Only after a careful sifting through the unique facts and circumstances of each case can such a determination be made. If it appears that the consent was not given voluntarily—that it was coerced, or granted only in submission to a claim of lawful authority—the consent is invalid and therefore the search is unreasonable. Id. at 233, 93 S.Ct. at 2050. Voluntariness traditionally has taken into account, *inter alia,* such evidence as a suspect's minimal schooling, low intelligence and lack of effective warnings to a suspect of his rights. Id. at 248, 93 S.Ct. at 2058; *see also Florida v. Bostick, supra*, 501 U.S. at ----, ----, 111 S.Ct. at 2382, 2385 (the fact that the accused had been informed of his right to refuse consent was considered "worth noting"). Moreover, personal characteristics of the accused such as age, sex, race and even widowhood have been worth noting in the assessment of coercion. *See Mendenhall, supra*, 446 U.S. at 558, 100 S.Ct. at 1879; *see also Bumper, supra*, 391 U.S. at 546, 88 S.Ct. at 1790.

In the instant case, there was no evidence of verbal or written consent to a body search. Detective Zattau, a member of the elite "drug interdiction" team described by the trial judge as "well-trained and experienced", conceded his awareness that consent would be a major legal question arising from his drug interdiction duties. The detective also testified that if a subject refused to permit a search of luggage or submit to a "pat-down," the officer could go no farther "at that point." Yet, the detective conceded that he did not share this information with J.M. and the other passengers on the bus. He testified that, after receiving J.M.'s permission to search his luggage and finding no drugs therein, he asked J.M. whether he was carrying any drugs or weapons on his person and J.M. said "no." More significantly, Detective Zattau testified that when he asked J.M. if he would "mind" a "pat-down," *J.M. did not say anything.* J.M. gradually turned his body in the officer's direction and raised his arms. Asked why he raised his hands, J.M. replied "[b]ecause, you know, I had no other choice but to." J.M. said that he "was feeling kind of afraid," that he did not believe that he could walk off the bus, and that he knew the officers were armed even though Zattau did not display his gun (as did Zattau's partner who was then stationed behind J.M.).

It was the government's cross-examination that broached the subject of J.M.'s "cooperation," suggesting that J.M. was making efforts to avoid conduct that would make the police "suspicious." After having tried unsuccessfully to obtain an admission from J.M. that the drugs were taped to a particular location on his body in order to attract less attention, the prosecutor asked J.M.:

[PROSECUTOR]: You had no intention of stopping him from patting you down, did you?

[J.M.]: No, because if I would have tried to, he would have got more suspicious of me.

Whatever J.M. meant by this answer to a series of leading questions, it appears that he was not admitting that he freely consented to the search. Rather, J.M. was explaining why he did not resist an officer who he said was already searching him (his luggage and his person) on a bus where egress was impossible. In this coercive environment, J.M.'s raising of his arms may have been no more than his submission to authority or succumbing to fear of the consequences of refusal. *See Mendenhall, supra*, 446 U.S. at 559, 100 S.Ct. at 1879; Bumper, supra, 391 U.S. at 548–49, 88 S.Ct. at 1792; *United States v. Alexander*, 755 F.Supp. 448, 452 (D.D.C.1991).

It is against this backdrop that the oral findings of the trial court must be measured. After rejecting J.M.'s argument as to seizure primarily on the ground that the detective was not overbearing, the court turned to the issue of consent. Beginning with the question of whether Detective Zattau had asked J.M. if he could pat him down (a fact J.M denied), the court credited the officer in the context of this case and in the context of his training, suggesting that J.M. might have forgotten or not heard the officer, adding:

> Be that as it may, I do credit the detective that he asked to do a pat-down and that [J.M.] consistent with his desire to deflect suspicion from himself turned to the officer and cooperated and raised his hands and I think hoped against hope that by golly, maybe he won't find it.
>
> The court, further noting that the officer "did find it," said that it felt "comfortable finding that [J.M.] consented to everything that went right up and down the line." The court said it believed that J.M. had consented to a pat-down and that it "*would be willing to bet*" that, if the facts were different, J.M. *would have* consented. "It was part of the pattern of his *whole reaction to the situation that was in front of him*."

One defers to the trial court's assessment of credibility. For whatever reason, one might "believe," as the trial court believed, that J.M. consented to an intrusive search of his body. Is this, however, the kind of factual finding of consent to which this court wants to defer for Fourth Amendment purposes? This may well be one of those cases where the inquiries of seizure and consent overlap. Under any standard of review, I see no voluntary consent on these facts and I would opt for reversal for the reasons stated so eloquently by Judge Schwelb at the division level.

Because the majority remands this case so that the trial court can factor J.M.'s youth into the consent equation, I concur in the order of remand. I would hope, however, that a new overall appraisal of the question of consent could be made in view of this record. In this connection, J.M.'s counsel asked the trial court to note that J.M. was fourteen at the time of this encounter, arguing:

He was traveling alone and certainly under the circumstances alone, *black,* barely a teenage
youth, would feel pressure when the police came up to him.

On remand, I would not want to impose upon the able trial court a formidable task of the centuries. It would be helpful to me, however, to have its appraisal of, not only whether the raising of J.M.'s arms in such a setting was in fact a consent, but also what bearing such a setting
might have on any non-verbal consent by a fourteen year old black male who had no previous
involvement with the criminal justice system and who had not been advised that he could walk
away or refuse to answer.

Whether the courts speak of it or not, race is a factor that has for many years engendered
distrust between black males and law enforcement personnel. *See* Tracey Maclin, *"Black and
Blue Encounters"—Some Preliminary Thoughts about Fourth Amendment Seizures: Should Race
Matter?,* 26 VAL.U.L.REV. 243 (1991); *see also* Sheri Lynn Johnson, Race and the Decision to
Detain a Suspect, 93 YALE L.J. 214 (1983). America's history in large measure may be responsible
for this phenomenon; it is painful to remember the era when some local sheriffs, deputies, jailers, policemen and prominent citizens cooperated with purveyors of mob violence to provide
punishment for blacks accused of crime. *See* Walter White, "I Investigate Lynchings," *reprinted in*
THE NEGRO CARAVAN (Sterling A. Brown, et al. eds. 1941). (For enterprising researchers, who
remain in doubt as to numbers, read the Congressional Record detailing unsuccessful attempts
to introduce and pass anti-lynching legislation.) Even today, arrest statistics suggest, whatever
the causes of crime, a litany of fear and distrust. Sadly, in the interest of protecting the public,
these statistics can be used negatively to justify unequal treatment and thus engender hostility. *See generally* Andrew Hacker, TWO NATIONS, BLACK & WHITE, SEPARATE, HOSTILE,
UNEQUAL (1992). To the extent that a "drug courier profile" (alluded to by the dissenting justices in *Florida v. Bostick, supra*) might embrace race, it becomes circular exercise in institutionalized stereotyping. Our very diversity has always produced stereotyping which in turn
has produced statistical data, which in turn has produced stereotyping. This in turn makes it
difficult for our courts to apply meaningful legal standards consistent with our Constitution. I
respectfully venture to suggest that no reasonable innocent black male (with any knowledge of
American history) would feel free to ignore or walk away from a drug interdicting team. I would
also suggest that if this hypothetical man was neither innocent nor reasonable, and armed, the
lives of innocent people might be endangered in the close confines of a bus.

The trial court was right when it suggested that J.M. would have consented to anything. The
issue, however, is whether that consent was voluntary. In determining the voluntariness of J.M.'s
consent, I would factor into the totality of the circumstances the relevant characteristics of age
and race, as well as the fact that appellant was not told that he was free to decline to consent to
the search. *See Mendenhall,* supra, 446 U.S. at 558, 100 S.Ct. at 1879, citing *Schneckloth,* supra, 412
U.S. at 226, 93 S.Ct. at 2046.

SUPREME COURT OF THE UNITED STATES.
SIBRON V. NEW YORK

PETERS V. NEW YORK

TERRY V. OHIO
1967 WL 113672
Brief for the N.A.A.C.P. Legal Defense and Educational Fund, Inc., as
Amicus Curiae

....

The Issues.

These stop and frisk cases present a congeries of issues. May a police officer constitutionally restrain an individual for the sole purpose of investigating him? If so, under what circumstances? Upon probable cause to believe him guilty of a crime? Upon "reasonable suspicion"? What is the permissible extent of the restraint? How long may it last? How much force may be used to effect it? May the police officer constitutionally search the citizen incident to such restraint, or incident to questioning without restraint? If so, under what circumstances? Whenever a citizen is restrained or questioned? When there is probable cause to believe (or when there is "reasonable suspicion") that the citizen is armed? How intrusive may the search be? May some or all objects discovered in the search be admitted into evidence against the citizen in a criminal trial? Weapons? Burglars' tools? Narcotics?

This Court may wish to treat these issues more or less discretely. But their proliferation should not conceal the point that what is fundamentally in question here is the choice, under the Constitution, between two antagonistic models of the police investigative process. This is true conceptually, as study of the burgeoning literature of stop and frisk reveals. It is true historically, because the Court is now asked for the first time to legitimate criminal investigative activity that significantly intrudes upon the privacy of individuals who are undifferentiable from Everyman as the probable perpetrators of a crime. It is true in the practical, day-to-day world of the streets and the lower courts, as we propose to develop more fully in the discussion that follows. Initially it will be helpful, we believe, to identify the two contending models and their attributes.

The Classical Arrest-Search Model

Under classical criminal procedure, the police may accost and question any person for the purpose of criminal investigation. But they may not detain him, restrain or "arrest" his liberty of movement in any significant way, except for the purpose of holding him to answer criminal charges. Any such restraint of an individual is an arrest, and may be made only on probable cause to believe him guilty of an offense. The police may not make a personal search of an individual, without a warrant or effective consent, except that, incidental to a valid arrest, they may make a more or less intensive personal search. The *Classical Arrest-Search Model* thus recognizes two categories of police investigative powers. Powers whose exercise does not significantly invade personal liberty and the right of privacy—the "right to be let alone"___are given the police to use at large, indiscriminately, at their discretion, and without judicial supervision. Powers whose exercise does invade these rights may be used by the police, but not indiscriminately, not against Everyman. They may be used only against persons whom there is probable cause, to believe are criminal actors, and hence distinguishable from Everyman. The "probable cause" determination made by a policeman as the precondition of the exercise of these powers is judicially reviewable. "The rule of probable cause is a practical, nontechnical conception affording the best compromise that has been found for accommodating these often opposing interests [of law enforcement and personal liberty]. Requiring more would unduly hamper law enforcement. To allow less would be to leave law-abiding citizens at the mercy of the officers' whim or caprice."

The Stop-Frisk Model

In theory, the *Stop-Frisk Model* differs from the *Classical Arrest-Search Model* in that it recognizes at least three, perhaps more, categories of police powers. First, police may accost and question any person, so long as they do not restrain or search him. Second, they may arrest him on probable cause and search his person incident to that valid arrest. The third category of powers is lodged between these two. A law enforcement officer lacking probable cause but having some state of mind (or encountering some circumstances) which makes his focus upon a given individual something other than random, something more particularized than whim, may "stop" or detain the individual without an "arrest." The nature of the prerequisite state of mind (or set of circumstances) varies. The Uniform Arrest Act uses the phrase "reasonable ground to suspect." New York Code of Criminal Procedure, § 180-a, employs "reasonably suspects." The A. L. I. Model Code of Pre-Arraignment Procedure uses other formulations. The common theme is something less than probable cause, but something which purports to provide a judicial curb against wholly indiscriminate police action.

The nature of the "stop" that is not an arrest also varies. The Uniform Arrest Act permits an officer, unsatisfied by initial answers to questioning, to detain his suspect for two hours. The A. L. I. Model Code limits the period to twenty minutes, and expressly disallows the use of deadly force in effecting a "stop." The New York statute is silent both on the period of permitted detention and on the amount of force which the officer may employ to enforce it. Specific "stop" authorizations also differ as to whether the "stopping" officer is allowed to remove his detainee from the scene of their first encounter. They differ with regard to the places in which and the circumstances under which the "stop" power is given. The Uniform Arrest Act allows stops of persons "abroad." The A. L. I. Code has no such restriction, but delimits the stop power by providing that it shall not be used "solely to aid in investigation or prevention of" designated offenses. The New York statute uses the term "abroad in a public place" (which the Court of Appeals in *Peters* construed to include the common hallways of apartment buildings, inconsistently with the construction previously put on the phrase in a circular published for police guidance by the New York State Combined Council of Law Enforcement Officials), and also delimits the "reasonable suspicion" to suspicion of felonies and designated misdemeanors.

Under the *Stop-Frisk Model,* persons authorized to be detained may also be "frisked" or searched. (Undoubtedly, a legislature might give the power to "stop" without accompanying power to "frisk," but all of the significant pieces of legislation so far proposed or enacted couple "stop" with "frisk," and the proponents of stop and frisk seem unanimous that "frisk" is necessary if "stop" is to be effective. Frisk may be allowed whenever stop is allowed; or it may be allowed only upon the fulfilment of additional conditions, such as the existence of reasonable grounds to suspect that the officer is in danger. It may be allowed more or less extensively and more or less intrusively. Its object may be limited or unlimited, and the nature of the items discovered in the search which may be seized may also be limited or unlimited. The common characteristic of the "frisk" authorizations is that they seek to delimit in some fashion the personal searches that may be made incident to a "stop," but none apparently include within the limitations any requirement of probable cause (in the classical sense) to believe that the person searched has a weapon.

It is relatively clear that the *Classical Arrest-Search Model* was and is the common law of England, which has never permitted detention for investigation nor on less than probable cause. The same model has also been invariably assumed by this Court to describe the constitutional law of the Fourth Amendment. This is more than historical happenstance. For the root notion of "probable cause" which is mainstay of the model is not simply a long cherished Anglo-American symbol of individual liberty. It is, in view of the practical realities of criminal administration, an inevitable evolutionary product of our system's use of courts to confine police power within reasonable bounds consistent with the conscience of a free people.

II.
The Genius of Probable Cause.

Whatever uncertainties there may be in the pre-Constitutional history and the post-Constitutional evolution of the Fourth Amendment, two core conceptions of the Amendment emerge with indisputable clarity. First, the Amendment's purpose is to restrict the allowance of intrusive police investigative powers to circumstances of *particularized justification,* disallowing police discretion to employ those powers against the citizenry in general. Second, this restriction is enforced by the interposition of *judicial judgment* between the police decision to intrude and the allowability of intrusion.

The first conception is visible upon the face of the Amendment. It is the essential idea that gives meaning both to the requirement of "probable cause" and to the requirement of warrants "particularly describing" the place to be searched, and the things or persons to be seized. Concerning both the occasions and extent of police intrusion upon the individual, "nothing is left to the discretion of the officer...." Berger v. New York, 388U. S. 41, _____, 87 S. Ct. 1873, 1883 (1967), quoting Marron v. United. States, 275 U. S. 192, 196 (1927).

History tells us why. The general warrants and writs of assistance against which the Fourth Amendment was principally aimed were vicious precisely because they "permitted the widest discretion to petty officials." "Armed with their roving commission, they set forth in quest of unknown offenders; and unable to take evidence, listened to rumors, idle tales, and curious guesses. They held in their hands the liberty of every man whom they pleased to suspect." This practice was doubly damnable. In a society profoundly committed to the liberty of the subject, the notion that government should be given the power to intrude indiscriminately and at the mere will of its officers into the affairs of every citizen was wholly unacceptable. Neither the random visitations of the King's messengers nor the practice in its more terrifying forms as an increasingly powerful bureaucracy might develop it-such as the South African "blitz" described in note 11 *supra-were* to be countenanced in this free country. Government could not invade the province of Everyman. To further its important purposes, including criminal investigation, it might invade the provinces of some individual men, but only those whom circumstances sufficiently distinguished from the generality of men so that the invasion could not be broadside. The general warrant infringed this concern and was accordingly denounced as a "'ridiculous warrant against the whole English nation.'"

In addition, the unbounded discretion allowed under the general warrants and writs of assistance left government officers free to heed every urging of personal spite, paltry tyranny, arbitrariness and discrimination. "In effect, complete discretion was given to the executing officials; in the words of James Otis, their use 'placed the liberty of every man in the hands of every petty officer.'" "The right of privacy was deemed too precious to entrust to the discretion of those whose job is the detection of crime and the arrest of criminals. Power is a heady thing, and history shows that the police acting on their own cannot be trusted." So the Fourth Amendment was designed both to delimit the breadth of power and to constrain the possibility of its abuse. Its language sometimes speaks obscurely in the context of twentieth century circumstances, "but this much is certain: there is no authority [in any American government] for the molestation of all those on whom the long shadow of suspicion falls in the hope that something damaging might turn up in the course of the search."

Not surprisingly, these concerns of the Fourth Amendment converge with others that our society has found essential and given enduring constitutional expression. They deserve to be recalled here, because all are threatened by the *Stop-Frisk Model* of criminal investigative process. The Fifth Amendment Privilege also forbids government to treat suspicion as guilt and to throw upon the citizen the obligation to exculpate or explain himself to a government officer. Miranda v. Arizona, 384 U. S. 436 (1966). It denies government power to employ coercive force of any sort (be it brief or extended physical restraint or other means of compulsion) to secure the cooperation of the citizen in pursuing law enforcement efforts that may secure his own criminal conviction. *Ibid.* Lessons to which the First Amendment and the Due Process Clauses of the Fifth and Fourteenth respond have taught us the impermissibility of making law enforcement officers the unconstrained rulers of the streets. Shuttlesworth v. Birmingham, 382 U. S. 87 (1965).And our especial national history has given us the Equal Protection Clause as a bulwark both against arbitrary and discriminatory abuses of our citizens by government officials, and against the dangerous generality of governmental authorizations rife with the potential for such abuses.

But the Fourth Amendment, most specifically addressed to protecting these concerns where they may be threatened by powers exercised in the investigative process, provides its own singular procedural mechanism for the necessary accommodation of individual privacy and investigation. That mechanism is judicial review of the police justification offered to support an investigative intrusion. Time and again this Court has repeated the theme:

"The point of the Fourth Amendment, which often is not grasped by zealous officers, is not that it denies law enforcement the support of the usual inferences which reasonable men draw from evidence. Its protection consists in requiring that those inferences be drawn by a neutral and detached magistrate instead of being judged by the officer engaged in the often competitive enterprise of ferreting out crime. Any assumption that evidence sufficient to support a magistrate's disinterested determination to issue a search warrant will justify the officers in making a search without a warrant would reduce the Amendment to a nullity and leave the people's homes secure only in the discretion of police officers."

The Court has insisted upon procedures which assure that the judicial determination will be rendered as an independent judgment, not a mere routine validation of police discretion. See Aguilar v. Texas, 378 U. S. 108 (1964). Although the requirement of *prior* judicial authorization of police intrusions has sometimes been excused on considerations of history and practicability, the provision of some available and effective judicial review of the police has always been insisted upon. See Henry v. United States, 361 U. S. 98, 104 (1959). Whether the forum be a criminal trial against the individual who claims abuse of the police investigative power, Mapp v. Ohio, 367 U. S. 643 (1961), or a damage action by the individual, Monroe v. Pape, 365 U. S. 167 (1961), a court sits to provide in the last analysis the "neutral and detached" judgment which the Fourth Amendment commands. This is no less true of arrests than of other searches and seizures. Beck v. Ohio, 379 U.S. 89 (1964).

Within this framework, the significance and the unique genius of the "probable cause" concept is apparent. "Probable cause" is not a self-efficient talisman. Nothing depends upon the words themselves. "Probable cause" is not inherently more fit for use than the verbalism "reasonable suspicion" (which the English have long used to serve the same function). But as it has evolved, probable cause has taken on an operative meaning and efficiency that *is* inherently fit-indeed, irreplaceable-as an instrument for mediating the demands of order and liberty in criminal investigation. The particular efficacy assigned to it in the *Beck* opinion, *id.* at 91, bears repeating: "[P]robable cause is a practical, non-technical conception affording the best compromise that has been found for accommodating these often opposing interests."

Probable cause is addressed bluntly to the issue of particularized justification that is the Fourth Amendment's first principle. As it has developed judicially, the phrase connotes exactly that quantum of evidence pointing to likely or probable guilt that serves to single an individual out reasonably persuasively from the mass of men. It is the standard designed to distinguish him from Everyman with sufficient sureness that, if the individual's arrest or search be authorized, Everyman's arrest or search will not be authorized by parity of reasoning.

To serve such a function-to protect the "liberty of every man" from subjection to police discretion-a test must be relatively objective. The probable cause standard seeks precisely to objectify, to regularize, the reasoning process by which the judgment of allowability of police intrusions is made. Of course, no judgmental standard governing an issue of this sort can wholly eliminate the influence of subjective and impressionistic responses-particularly a standard composed for general service in a multitude of varying factual circumstances. And so (as the proponents of the *Stop-Frisk Model* are quick to point out) even the Justices of this Court have from time to time divided in applying "probable cause" to the facts of one case or another. But the probable cause conception does operate-and its essential design makes it operate with peculiar efficiency-to diminish as much as is institutionally possible the impact of subjective factors.

First, probable cause invokes that traditional juridical device for the depersonalization of judgment: the enforced perspective of the "reasonable man" or "ordinary man." Second, it frames very specifically the question which it purports to submit to the ordinary judgment of the "ordinary man." The question is one of objective factual probabilities: is the individual whose arrest is sought to be justified likely guilty on the perceived facts? No debatable issue of values is expressly submitted. Doubtless, policemen and judges do in fact import some normative considerations into the determination. They may conclude "likely *enough* guilty," or "not likely *enough* guilty." But this is a small matter compared to tests (the inevitable instruments of the *Stop-Frisk Model*, as we shall see) which baldly invite consideration of the normative desirability of the particular police practice sought to be justified: "Is the suspect likely enough guilty so that he should be arrested?" "Is he likely enough guilty so that he should not be arrested, but should be detained?" There are no answers to such questions that do not turn almost entirely upon one's personal approval or disapproval of arrest or of detention.

Third, probable cause speaks to policeman's, to the judge's and to the citizen's common thought processes as rational men. Although it may take account of the specialized knowledge and the expert perceptual accuity of the policeman (to the extent that these can be objectified and communicated to a court), it subjects them to review by ordinary judgment operating upon objective facts. It avoids the dangerous mysticism of police professional, and professionally motivated, intuition—what Mr. Justice Jackson recognized as the mobilized mentality of "the officer engaged in the often competitive enterprise of ferreting out crime." (We shall discuss the characteristics of that mentality more fully in the next section of this brief.) Probable cause therefore directs the judge toward an exercise of independent and autonomous judgment, properly responsive to the policeman's expert capacity for observation and induction, but freed from the controlling imposition of police value judgments or from necessary reliance upon the policeman's inexplicable "hunches" which inevitably embody those value judgments.

In short, probable cause is a common denominator for police, judicial and citizen judgment. It permits the judge, after hearing the officer's account of his observations and his inferences from them, to pass a detached, independent and objective judgment on the rationality of those inferences. It permits the judge to express his judgment in terms that are more or less comprehensible to the police, for their future guidance. The same terms are more or less accessible to the citizen who wants to know his rights or to pass political judgment in turn upon a system which functions as the probable cause system does. This is not to say that "probable cause" functions unerringly, or with perfect clarity. Of course, it does not. No standard for the case-by-case determination of the legitimacy of police investigative intrusions could. But the very failings of "probable cause" in this regard, together with its relative successes, caution against its abandonment in favor of more arcane, more impressionistic, less objective, less historically developed standards. It should not be forgotten that probable cause is the *only* standard which this Court has ever developed under the Fourth Amendment for judicial regulation of the police. We think that the nature of the concept and the setting of its use as we have just described them demonstrate the inevitably, as well as the wisdom, of this development. We turn now to the "reasonable suspicion" construct with which the *Stop and Frisk Model* undertakes-for partial but vitally important purposes—to displace probable cause.

III.
The Deceptive Allure of "Reasonable Suspicion."

At first blush, the argument for a *Stop-Frisk Model* of criminal investigation, controlled by the standard of "reasonable suspicion," seems eminently, beguilingly reasonable. Surely, say the proponents of stop and frisk, our inherited notions of "arrest" and "search" and "probable cause" are too dogmatic, too inflexible. Not all police intrusions are equally intrusive. Therefore, the same degree of justification should not be demanded for all. "The attempt to apply a single standard of probable cause to all [police] interferences [with individual privacy and liberty]—i.e., to treat a stop as an arrest and a frisk as a search—produces a standard either so strict that reasonable and necessary police work becomes unlawful or so diluted that the individual is not adequately protected." Far more sensible, far more realistic, is the accommodating approach of "balancing" the extent of each particular police intrusion against the extent of its justification. This "balancing" approach (which seems to have been borrowed from the First Amendment area without carrying along the First Amendment's strong preference for individual freedom) finds its most articulate expression in Dean Edward L. Barrett's often quoted suggestion:

> "Would not the policy of the Fourth Amendment be better served by an approach which determines the reasonableness of each [police] investigative technique by balancing the seriousness of the suspected crime and the degree of reasonable suspicion possessed by the police against the magnitude of the invasion of the personal security and property rights of the individual involved?"

The answer to that provocative question, *amicus curiac* submits, is a flat and unequivocal No. However intellectually reasonable Dean Barrett's balancing approach may be in the corridors of academe, it is a delusive and unworkable proposition on the streets of our cities, and particularly on the streets of our ghettos where stop-frisk logic does its daily work. Closely inspected, we believe, both the "balancing" theory of Fourth Amendment rights and the *Stop-Frisk Model* that is built upon it show themselves to be mere fine, scholastic pretexts for oppression. The "minor interference with personal liberty" that they sanction is a major interference; the protections which they promise are unreal illusions; the "balance" scale which they purport to employ is invariably tipped by the police commissioner's thumb; and their consequence is nothing more or less than a police dictatorship of the streets. We urge this Court to repudiate any such triflings with the vital freedoms secured by the Fourth Amendment, and to respond as it did nearly one hundred years ago when asked to approve another like "minor" invasion of those same freedoms:

> "It may be that it is the obnoxious thing in its mildest and least repulsive form; but illegitimate and unconstitutional practices get their first footing in that way, namely: by silent approaches and slight deviations from legal modes of procedure. This can only be obviated by adhering to the rule that constitutional provisions for the security of person and property should be liberally construed.... It is the duty of courts to be watchful for the constitutional rights of the citizen, and against any stealthy encroachments thereon. Their motto should be *obsta principiis*."

Let us examine first the nature of the "minor" invasion of liberty involved. Proponents of the "stop" like to portray it as though it consisted at worst of a police "Hey, there." Several points should be obvious about this "Hey, there."

(1) "Hey, there" itself, when said by a policeman, is a significant intrusion, except perhaps to those fortunate citizens whose sole image of the police is a vague memory of the friendly face of the school crossing guard. Such citizens are not very often stopped. "Hey, there" to the man likely to be stopped-the man on the street in a "bad" neighborhood, the man in the ghetto-is a challenge, an act of dominion by the Fuzz, a thinly veiled threat of force.

(2) "Hey, there" may or may not be thought unduly intrusive-once. But the man likely to be stopped is not likely to be stopped once. He is likely to be stopped again and again, day in day out, and for the same reasons. The following comment of a "lower income Negro," which the National Crime Commission's Task Force on Police thought worthy of publication, is a perfectly representative picture of ghetto life-and resultant ghetto attitudes:

> "When they stop everybody, they say, well, they haven't seen you around, you know, they want to get to know your name, and all this. I can see them stopping you one time, but the same police stopping you every other day, and asking you the same old question."

(3) "Hey, there" looks better on paper than it sounds on the streets. (We put aside the consideration that it is almost invariably "Hey, there, *boy*" in the ghetto.[61]) "Field interrogation procedure" is thus described (at its mildest) in an instructional article for police:

> "... Meeting head-on. Let the subject get up even with you or slightly beyond you. Then turn toward the subject facing his side. Your hand should either be holding onto the subject's arm at

the elbow or in a ready position so that you will be able to spin him forward and away from you in a defensive move. This is the position of interrogation. You should make a habit of interrogating from this position. Your greatest hazard is the unknown."

(4) The method of police approach just described, the power of the policeman to make "Hey there" sound like a threat, and the inevitable citizen response together make the "stop" power a *de facto* arrest power. The pattern can be observed daily on any ghetto street. The policeman on "aggressive patrol" (as it is coming to be known in police circles) makes his approach; the citizen, touched on the elbow or startled by the voice at his side and the policeman with his hands up, raises an arm slightly in an instinctive defensive gesture; the policeman is now free to arrest him for assaulting an officer, obstructing an officer, etc. Every policeman on the beat knows that the power to make an enforced stop is the power to escalate the episode into a technical "assault" and to make an arrest for the assault. The ghetto resident knows it too—although he is seldom clever and dispassionate enough to avoid the trick.

(5) In any event, the authority which the proponents of "stop" seek to give the police is not the authority to say "Hey, there." It is the authority to *detain* the citizen who does not stop when "Hey, there" is said. It is the power to order him to a stand-still, and to lay hands on him if he moves. It is the power, in the American Law Institute's draft Model Code, to use all force short of deadly force to stop him. We do not know that New York or Ohio law embodies even that humane limitation. Assuming that it does, the "stop" power ranges from a hand on the sleeve to a tackle, a patrol car careening up on the sidewalk, a bullet in the citizen's leg. It must be thus, we are informed, because "it would be frustrating and humiliating to the officer to grant him an authority to order persons to stop, and then ask him to stand by while his order is flouted."

(6) Finally, the "stop" power comports the "frisk" power. The argumentation of the proponents of stop and frisk is, in this regard, wonderfully devious. We are told that "stop" should be allowed without probable cause because it is not very intrusive; and, in support of this proposition, the attributes of "stop" alone are described (or partially described). Invariably, we are later told that the "frisk" power is absolutely indispensable to the safe exercise of the police power to "stop"; hence, that once the power to "stop" is given, the power to "frisk" must follow. We suggest that this is chop-logic. If "frisk" is indeed the necessary accoutrement of "stop," we think it obvious that the rind of intrusion involved in "frisk" must be taken into account in the initial determination whether "stop" is, indeed, not very intrusive. We think that the intrusiveness of "frisk" hardly needs demonstration.

We pass next to the supposed safeguard of stop and frisk—the preventive against its abuse— the prerequisite of "reasonable suspicion." Used as the English use it, the phrase means "probable cause" in the American constitutional sense. But where it is used to mean something less than probable cause, as it is in the *Stop-Frisk Model*, what exactly does it mean? It seems to mean, under Dean Barrett's balancing formula, the degree of suspicion which is sufficient so that the police *ought* to be allowed to do whatever it is they do, in light of its intrusiveness. That is a simply impossible test, depending as it does upon the normative appraisal of the policeman himself in the first instance and (in the few cases that come to court) upon the retrospective, subjective and impressionistic judgment of a lower-court judge who has before him a defendant caught with the goods. It should not be forgotten that this Court does not sit to decide every search-and-seizure case in this country, still less every stop-and-frisk *case*, still less every *instance* of stop and frisk. With all due deference, we suggest that the liberty of the citizen in the street would be a meaningless thing if it were committed almost wholly to *ad hoc* police and criminal court determinations of the normative propriety of particular police intrusions.

One careful student of stop and frisk has offered the conception that "reasonable suspicion" is something more objective. "If probable cause … can be defined as a reasonable belief in the probability that a crime has been committed [and, to justify an arrest, that a particular citizen has committed it],… [reasonable suspicion] means that it must be reasonably possible that the individual has committed some crime." But as to what citizen is it not reasonably possible that he has committed some crime? As to what unknown citizen on the street (even a crowded street) near the scene of a known crime? As to what group of ill-dressed young men on a ghetto street corner? As to what Negro abroad on the streets in a "white" neighborhood late in the day? Surely, it is reasonably possible that each of these has committed a crime (or is about to commit one, as the New York statute and common *Stop-Frisk* logic provide). "The finger of suspicion is a long one. In an individual case it may point to all of a certain race, age group or locale. Commonly it extends to any who have committed similar crimes in the past. Arrest on mere suspicion collides violently with the basic human right of liberty. It can be tolerated only in a society which is willing to concede to its government powers which history and experience teach are the inevitable accoutrements of tyranny."

Speaking for the New York Court of Appeals in *Peters,* Judge Keating assures us that "Where a person's activities are *perfectly normal,* he is fully protected from any detention or search." That is hardly very reassuring. It is still less reassuring when it is announced that "By requiring the reasonable suspicion of a police officer, the statute incorporates the experienced officer's intuitive knowledge and appraisal of the appearances of criminal activity." Yet here, we suggest, Judge Keating has laid his finger precisely on the pulse of "reasonable suspicion" and given the best available sententious description of its character.

For the native quality of "reasonable suspicion"-as opposed to the "probable cause" concept which our constitutional law has heretofore developed-consists precisely in judicial recognition of the trained police "hunch" or "intuition," without more, as the basis for legitimating police action. All of the mysticism of police expertise, of police "feel" for a street situation, is invoked here.Judges are not expected to detach themselves from the reasoning processes of the police. They are not to take an independent view of police logic. They are to assimilate police logic and appraise the officer's work product by its lights. They are to accept the attitudes of police intelligence for the purpose of adjudging the soundness of police guesswork—exclusively in cases, of course, where that guesswork has already proved itself right. Sound police intuition thus becomes the measure of the citizen's protection under the Fourth Amendment.

What exactly is the nature of that intuition? Jerome Skolnick's recent systematic observation of the police confirms the obvious:

> "[T]he policeman's role contains two principal variables, danger and authority, which should be interpreted in light of a 'constant' pressure to appear efficient. The element of danger seems to make the policeman especially attentive to signs indicating a potential for violence and law-breaking. As a result, the policeman is generally a 'suspicious' person.
> "...

> "However complex the motives aroused by the element of danger, its consequences for sustaining police culture are unambiguous. This element requires him, like the combat soldier, the European Jew, the South African (white or black), to live in a world straining toward duality, and suggesting danger when 'they' are perceived. Consequently, it is in the nature of the policeman's situation that his conception of order emphasize regularity and predictability. It is, therefore, a conception shaped by persistent *suspicion* ...

> "Policemen are indeed specifically *traded* to be suspicious, to perceive events or changes in the physical surroundings that indicate the occurrence or probability of disorder...."

This suspicious cast of mind is intensified in the ghetto. The policeman on patrol in the inner city has little understanding of the way of life of the people he observes, and he believes (with considerable justification) that they are hostile to him. The result is inevitable. "The patrolman in Westville, and probably in most communities, has come to identify the black man with danger ...." Little wonder that "field interrogations are sometimes used in a way which discriminates against minority groups, the poor, and the juvenile."

This is not an isolated or ephemeral abuse, nor one that courts can control under the rubric of "reasonable suspicion." Can any court say that the policeman is *not* reasonably suspicious of the group of young men lounging on the ghetto corner? Of the man on parole for narcotics violations who consorts with another? Of the man walking at night with two companions who have records for robbery? Of the interracial couple in the neighborhood frequented by prostitutes? A police authority on field interrogation gives policemen this advice respecting the "selection of subjects":

"A. Be suspicious. This is a healthy police attitude, but it should be controlled and not too obvious. [*Sic.*]

"B. Look for the unusual.
    1. Persons who do not 'belong' where they are observed.
    2. Automobiles which do not 'look right.'
    3. Businesses opened at odd hours, or not according to routine or custom.

"C. Subjects who should be subjected to field interrogations.
...

1. Suspicious persons known to the officer from previous arrests, field interrogations, and observations.
...

4. Any person observed in the immediate vicinity of a crime very recently committed or reported as 'in progress.'

5. Known trouble-makers near large gatherings.

6. Persons who attempt to avoid or evade the officer.

7. Exaggerated unconcern over contact with the officer.

8. Visibly 'rattled' when near the policeman.

9. Unescorted women or young girls in public places, particularly at night in such places as cafes, bars, bus and train depots, or street corners.
...

20. Many others. How about your own personal experiences ?"

Is a judge to say that these bases of suspicion are unreasonable? How, in any meaningful way, is he to review a police "stop" based on any of them?

The answer to this question is evident from the reports. The courts have not in fact imposed any limitations or restrictions upon the stop and frisk power once that power is granted. They have not done so because they could not do so-because the essence of the doctrine of stop and frisk on less than probable cause is judicial abdication to police judgment. The judicial decisions demonstrate trenchantly the practical unworkability of the *Stop-Frisk Model.* New York's cases will serve as an example.

As we shall see, the major failing of the cases is that "reasonable suspicion" has proved to be a broad, all-purpose rubber stamp for validating police intrusions. Before passing to that point, however, we pause to examine the nature of the intrusions which the New York cases allow upon "reasonable suspicion." What appears from such examination is a thorough vindication of the most dire predictions of those commentators who warned that no mere wordplay could make a "stop" something less than an arrest, or "frisk" something less than a search.[83]

"The stopping of the individual to inquire is not an arrest," the New York Court of Appeals announced in its first stop and frisk decision, explaining why "the ground upon which the police may make the inquiry may be less incriminating than the ground for an arrest ...." People v. Rivera, 14 N. Y. 2d 441, 445, 201 N. E. 2d 32 (1964). Yet within two years, in the *Peters* case now before this Court, the Court of Appeals was prepared to sanction as a "stop" something that seems to all appearances a quite conventional arrest. A police officer collared Peters at gunpoint on a stairway between floors of a private apartment building. He tugged Peters down a flight of stairs to the next floor where he questioned him. He then felt his clothing, removed an opaque packet, took it out of Peters' reach, and searched it. About all that is wanting here to exhaust the powers ordinarily given an officer who makes an arrest is a trip to the precinct station. The question of the propriety of such a trip was not reached in *Peters* because the "frisk" had served its purpose. It had disclosed the making of a *de jure* arrest, which followed. In any event, the Court of Appeals had already made clear in People v. Pugach, 15 N. Y. 2d 65, 204 N. E. 2d 176 (1964), that the "stop" power alone included a trip to the precinct station, if the officer found that desirable. *Accord:* People v. Hoffman, 24 App. Div. 2d 497, 261 N. Y. S. 2d 651 (1965).

"The frisk is less ... invasion [of privacy] than an initial full search of the person would be." So held People v. Rivera, supra, 14 N. Y. 2d at 446, reasoning that it "ought to be distinguishable also on pragmatic grounds from the degree of constitutional protection that would surround a full-blown search of the person." *Ibid.* However valid this proposition, its endurance was fleeting. In *Pugach, supra,* the Court of Appeals sustained as a "frisk" the searching of a brief case which police officers had taken from their "stopped" suspect in a squad car en route to the precinct station. *Peters,* we have seen, sustained the search of an opaque packet taken from the suspect and wholly within the control of an armed policeman. *Sibron* sustained a policeman who "without first frisking the defendant, reached into his pocket and pulled out ... narcotics." Lower New York courts have gone further. People v. Reason, 52 Misc. 2d 425, 276 N. Y. S. 2d 196 (Sup. Ct. 1966), authorizes search of a tin box standing atop a pile of other articles on the sidewalk near the suspect. People v. Cassese, 47 Misc. 2d 1031, 263 N. Y. S. 2d 734 (Sup. Ct. 1965) (alternative ground), holds that a frisk may encompass the search of an automobile in which the "stopped" suspect is riding. There is no need to put our own characterization on this New York evolution of the "frisk." The Court of Appeals has recently reviewed its prior decisions and, explicitly recognizing that in *Pugach, Sibron* and *Peters* "the arresting [sic] officers engaged in 'searches' rather than 'frisks' in order to obtain inculpating evidence," nevertheless adhered to those holdings. *People v. Taggart*, C. A. N. Y., App. T. 2, No. 120, decided July 7, 1967.

It is significant that the New York courts have been as unable to restrain police subversion of the purpose of the "frisks" that they have authorized as to contain their extent or intrusiveness. Although the New York statute authorizes only a search for weapons, and the Court of Appeals in sustaining its constitutionality continues to stress that concept, the police ignore it with impunity. The officer in *Sibron,* for example, had no concern with weapons. He suspected Sibron of narcotics dealings, asked him for narcotics, and searched him for narcotics. Indeed, he was so little concerned with his own self-protection, that he let Sibron go into his pocket. This is apparently no rare practice. The National Crime Commission Task Force on Police reports that "In some cities, searches are made in a high proportion of instances not for the purpose of protecting the officer but to obtain drugs or other incriminating evidence. In New York, for example, where searches are permitted only when the officer reasonably believes he is in bodily danger, searches were made in 81.6 percent of stops reported."

Particularly as the scope of permissible "stop" and "frisk" expanded, and as evidence of their use as pretexts to justify plainly illicit searches accumulated, one might have expected the Court of Appeals to tighten up on the standards for "reasonable suspicion." It has not been able to do so. In the first place, the statutory requirement for a "frisk," that the officer "reasonably suspects ... he is in danger of life or limb," has been entirely abrogated by the New York Court. This has been done by recognizing what appears to be a conclusive presumption that officers making a "stop" are always in danger. Such might very well be doubtful as a fact,but surely the Court of Appeals cannot be faulted for believing that an officer may always "reasonably suspect" he is in danger.That is the nature of reasonable suspicion.

As for the reasonable suspicion that is a statutory prerequisite to the initial stop, it is fair to say that police officers in New York State have been left to define that concept pretty much as they go along. In the recent *Taggart* decision of the Court of Appeals, an anonymous telephone tip that a described young man on a designated street corner had a gun was held to justify an officer's accosting him, placing him against a wall, and searching his pockets. In *Sibron,* eight hours' observation of the defendant by a police officer discovered nothing but that he was holding conversations with a number of narcotics addicts; nothing passed hands, and the officer overheard none of the conversations. Reasonable suspicion was found. The procedural history of the case, as we read the record, portrays quite starkly the role of stop and frisk logic in the dialectic of Fourth Amendment evasion. The arresting officer appears at first to have wanted to present the case as an ordinary "dropsie" —one of those wonderfully lucky cases in which the defendant takes occasion to toss away a packet of heroin just as the officer appears on the horizon. (See Complaint, Sibron R. 1.) At the hearing, however, his testimony seemed designed to make out a "consent" case (*id.*, 16). When the judge properly found no consent (*id.*, 19), the prosecutor persuaded him that there was probable cause for an arrest and search (*id.*, 19-20). That, of course, would not stand up on the record, and "reasonable suspicion" stepped into the breach at one or another appellate stage. "Reasonable suspicion" being essentially unreviewable because the officer had a hunch which proved right, the *Stop-Frisk Model* amply served to justify the unjustifiable.

We have found only one New York decision in which any court invalidated a stop for want of reasonable suspicion: People v. Anonymous, 48 Misc. 2d 713, 265 N. Y. S. 2d 705 (Cty. Ct. 1965), where an officer stopped a boy walking on a summer Sunday, in Hicksville, Long Island, with a carton of books. It is enlightening, we think, to compare that decision with *People v. Reason, supra.* In the latter case, reasonable suspicion was found to be made out by an officer's observation that two Negro men got very quickly into a taxi, on a Harlem street, one carrying a portable phonograph and the other a portable T.V., during daylight hours when the streets were full of people. A few days prior to this date, the officer had attended a community meeting at which residents complained of numerous burglaries in the area, but no complaint was made of burglaries in the building before which the two Negro men were seen to hail a cab, nor in the immediate surroundings, nor did the officer have any information relating to any burglaries accomplished or in progress on that date. Harlem is not Hicksville, however; burglaries *do* occur frequently in Harlem; and there, doubtless lies the difference in the cases. Such again is the nature of reasonable suspicion.

One additional point in the New York experience deserves note. Coincidentally with the enactment of the Stop and Frisk statute in that State, a circular was issued by the New York State Combined Council of Law Enforcement Officials setting guidelines for police performance under the stop and frisk authorization. That circular is appended as Appendix A to this brief. *Inter alia,* it provides that the suspect is to be questioned and frisked "in the immediate area in which he was stopped," *but see People v. Pugach, supra; People v. Hoffman, supra;* that for "purposes of practical enforcement procedures," the language of the statute "abroad in a public place" does not include public portions of private buildings, such as hotel lobbies, etc., *but see People v. Peters, supra;* and that if "the suspect is carrying an object such as a handbag, suitcase, sack, etc., which may conceal a weapon, the officer should not open that item, but should see that it is placed out of reach of the suspect so that its presence will not represent any immediate danger to the officer," -but see *People v. Pugach, supra; People v. Peters, supra; People v. Reason, supra;* and *People v. Cassesse, supra.* Obviously, officers have regularly broken these rules, and the New York courts as regularly have ignored them. The rules-flexible and imprecise as they are-appear to be altogether too confining for a volatile conception of the nature of reasonable suspicion.

We submit that what has happened even on the face of the reported judicial decisions in New York fully confirms our description earlier in this brief of the inevitable consequences of the *Stop-Frisk Model.* "Stops" have been sanctioned that are not distinguishable in the extent of their invasion of privacy from arrests; full-blown searches are conducted in the name of "frisks"; and "reasonable suspicion," incapable alike of explanation and judicial supervision, serves only as a sophistical pretext for the wholesale destruction of Fourth Amendment rights.

We do not think that the New York experience is aberrant in this regard, or that other States and other varieties of stop and frisk might succeed where New York and its section 180-a have totally failed. It is the basic *Stop-Frisk Model*, we believe, that is aberrant. The intrusions which it authorizes against the liberty and privacy of the citizen are intolerable in a free society, unless they are hedged about with effective checks and restraints. Such restraints involve, first, the requirement of particularized justification for the use of the intrusions against particular individuals reliably believed to be criminally connected. They require, second, that the justificatory standard be couched in terms sufficiently objective and communicable that the citizen can ascertain some inkling of the nature of his rights and the policeman some conception of his powers and their limitations, so that, if those limitations be oppressively transgressed, the policeman and his superiors can be held accountable legally or politically as the case may be. They require, in this last aspect, some fair opportunity for independent review by the judiciary of the policeman's asserted justification for intrusion upon the citizen. The means of providing these several related safeguards in Anglo-American law has always been the probable cause concept; and this Court has noted that it is a "troublesome line" which separates "mere suspicion" from probable cause. *Brinegar v. United States,* 339 U. S. 160, 176 (1949). The innovation of stop and frisk theory which purports to straddle that line with a turbid, amorphous, unsubstantial conception of some state of police-perceived putative guiltiness that is more than suspicion but less than cause-whether the state be called "reasonable suspicion" or some other euphemism-is inherently, irremediably defective.

The defect is exposed, we suggest, at the point where the *Stop-Frisk Model* meets the real world of streets and courts. There is nothing endemically wrong with the *idea* of stop and frisk. Indeed, the mission of stop and frisk theory to establish some third state of police powers, midway between those that can be exercised wholly arbitrarily (such as the power of non-coercive, non-detentive street questioning) and those available only upon probable cause (such as arrest and search), has the allure of sweet reasonableness and compromise. The rub is simply that, in the real world, there is no third state; the reasonableness of theory is paper thin; there can be no compromise. Probable cause is the objective, solid and efficacious method of reasoning—itself highly approximative and adaptable, but withal tenacious in its insistence that common judgment and detached, autonomous scrutiny fix the limits of police power—which has become, within our system of criminal law administration, the indispensable condition of non-arbitrariness in police conduct. Police power exercised without probable cause *is* arbitrary. To say that the police may accost citizens at their whim and may detain them upon reasonable suspicion is to say, in reality, that the police may both accost and detain citizens at their whim. But against that dangerous doctrine the Fourth Amendment sets its head. We urge that the Court so hold, unequivocally and forcefully, in these cases.

We so urge although we recognize that, in some ways, the issues before the Court in the *Sibron, Peters* and *Terry* cases are framed quite narrowly. The immediate questions are whether, on each record, the respective rights of Sibron, Peters and Terry were violated and, in the New York cases, whether Code of Criminal Procedure, § 180-a is facially unconstitutional, see *Berger v. New York, supra.* Those questions naturally invite attention to the factual circumstances of each case-which show, we think, differing degrees of police intrusiveness and differing degrees of ostensible justification for it-and to the detailed body of legal rules (which might be held separately or in combination offensive to the Fourth Amendment) that emerge from the several provisions of the New York statute as construed. In this situation, we earnestly hope that the Court will not choose to treat the questions before it as isolated and independent matters-perhaps, in the process, giving some color of authority to a "balancing" theory of the Fourth Amendment. Apart from Sibron, Peters and Terry, thousands of our citizens daily are being stopped, detained and searched without probable cause. The extent of the intrusion varies from case to case; but all are unconstitutional, we believe, if there is (a) any restraint, or communicated sense of restraint, of the citizen's liberty of movement; or (b) any physical touching, probing, "frisking" or searching of the citizen, (c) without probable cause in its time-honored Fourth Amendment sense. We urge the Court to so declare.

IV.
Stop-and-Frisk, Law Enforcement and the People.

We have as yet said nothing about the various arguments to necessity and/or efficiency of the proponents of stop and frisk. We think that, on any fair appraisal of the state of present knowledge,those arguments can be dispatched summarily: either as not proved (as the Court viewed similar arguments urged upon it from Chambers v. Florida, 309 U. S. 227 (1940), to Miranda v. Arizona, 384 U. S. 436 (1966)), or as necessarily subordinated by the Constitution of the United States (as the Court viewed the efficiency arguments made in *Berger v. New York, supra).* Particularly where, as here, the argument of police need is advanced to support the allowance of *new* police powers -powers never heretofore given under the Constitution; indeed, powers that erode *pro tanto* the bedrock principle of probable cause which undergirds the settled constitutional doctrine of the Fourth Amendment-we believe that the showing of need required to sustain the argument should be both factually convincing and normatively compelling. The argument of police need for street detention and frisk powers is neither.

Professor Herman Goldstein, a long-time student of the police and police administrator put the matter most succinctly in a recent article:

"It is probably true that a program of preventive patrol does reduce the amount of crime on the street, although there has been no careful effort to measure its effectiveness. It is also apparent, however, that some of the practices included in a preventive patrol program contribute to the antagonism toward the police felt by minority groups whose members are subjected to them. A basic issue, never dealt with explicitly by police, is whether, even from a purely law enforcement point of view, the gain in enforcement outweighs the cost of community alienation."

Others have asked the same or similar questions.

Proponents of stop and frisk are fond of asserting that "aggressive patrol" keeps the crime rate down. We have not seen convincing evidence of this proposition. But even were it established that the *result* of aggressive patrol *was* a decrease in street crime, of course it would not follow that the stop and frisk methods of aggressive patrol were *necessary* to achieve the decrease. Aggressive patrol involves both increased police presence on the streets and increased police intrusion. To say, when a program of aggressive patrol is followed by lower rates of reported crime (if it is) that the increased intrusion, or the combination of increased intrusion and presence is causing the observed effect—rather than that the increased presence alone is causing it—is mere speculation. The South African "blitz" practice described in note 11, *supra,* provides an obvious example. We are told that when a wave of 1000 to 2500 policemen suddenly inundates an area and manhandle all the blacks in sight, the robbery rate falls 50 per cent. That is an impressive figure. But one is led to wonder whether the robbery rate would not be quite as startlingly affected if 1000 to 2500 policemen suddenly appeared on the streets of the same small area, even if they did not stop and search the blacks. Surely, 2500 policemen flooding a neighborhood would have some effect, even if they did nothing but stand on the corners and talk to one another.

However that may be, the point remains, as Professor Goldstein notes, that the evidence of the ill effects of stop and frisk practices, particularly in the ghetto, is as strong at least as any evidence of their good effects "from a purely law enforcement point of view." We have earlier noted the obvious, unhappy fact that the policeman today is the object of widespread and intense hatred in our inner cities. The National Crime Commission's Task Force on Police points to stop and frisk practices as one (obviously, only one) of the causes of this phenomenon.

"Misuse of field interrogations … is causing serious friction with minority groups in many localities. This is becoming particularly true as more police departments adopt 'aggressive patrol' in which officers are encouraged routinely to stop and question persons on the street who are unknown to them, who are suspicious, or whose purpose for being abroad is not readily evident. The Michigan State survey found that both minority group leaders and persons sympathetic to minority groups throughout the country were almost unanimous in labelling field interrogation as a principal problem in police community relations."

The least implication of these observations is that the police assertion of a need for stop and frisk power may itself reflect the same battle psychology that is responsible for over-frequent use of the power—a psychology that is not always conducive to the best judgment, even on the question of what is good for the police. But the observations have other, more troubling implications which, in candor, we cannot pretermit. We are gravely concerned by the dangers of legitimating stop and frisk, and thus encouraging, and increasing the frequency of occasions for, police-citizen aggressions. Speaking bluntly, we believe that what the ghetto does *not* need is more stop and frisk.

It is no accident that many major riots suffered since 1964 have been sparked by a public confrontation between the police and Negroes. Regardless of the underlying factors which set the stage for riot or increase its likelihood, it is plain that police-community encounters have triggered outbreaks of group hostility:

> In Cincinnati a Negro man protesting the death sentence of another Negro is arrested. In Boston, police advance with truncheons on women sitting-in at the welfare department. In Tampa, a cop shoots a Negro burglary suspect in the back after he had refused to halt. Each incident triggered violence. Stores were burned and looted, people injured. Rioting ended in Boston not because the police had dispersed crowds, but because the cops went away.

Or as the *New York Times* put it:

> "Even before Newark the script was familiar. Some minor incident begins it all, often the arrest of a Negro by a policeman."[102]

We do not suggest, we emphasize lest we be misunderstood, that police conduct in any way "causes" riot or is responsible for it. Would it were so; the wrong could then be more readily righted. We will not repeat the "appallingly familiar, statistical litany" of social ills which are responsible. We only observe that the frustration and bitterness of poverty, unemployment, slum housing, ignorance and segregation easily fixes on the police; that in return, and often for quite good reasons, the police view the Negro with fear; and—how apt the word here—suspicion. The bloody turmoils which we have experienced are ignited and intensified by this mutual hostility.

The gap between Negroes and the police is enormous. A study by the National Crime Commission shows that "nonwhites, particularly Negroes, are significantly more negative than whites in evaluating police effectiveness in law enforcement."Negroes and whites have widely different perceptions of police discourtesy, misconduct and honesty and the need for police protection. The Commission's study supports the conclusions of the Director of the Lemberg Center for the Study of Violence, in a letter to counsel, that the police and Negro youth have perceptions of each other which escalate the conflict between them.

You have asked whether the Lemberg Center for the Study of Violence is in a position to make a statement on police-community relations as they affect behavior within the Negro ghetto. We have done a great deal of face-to-face interviewing with Negroes in the ghettos of six different cities and have accumulated observations on some of the psychological aspects of interactions between Negro youth and young adults on the one hand and white police officers on the other.

According to our observation, police attitudes toward working class Negro youths and young adults are often based on the concept of the Negro as a savage, or animal, or some being outside of the human species. Therefore, the police expect behavior from Negroes in accordance with this concept. The young Negroes in cities have complementary attitudes toward police officers. The police are perceived as animal-like, brutal, and sadistic-again, outside the human species.

Because of the police officer's conception of the Negro male, he frequently feels that most Negroes are dangerous and need to be dealt with as an enemy even in the absence of visible criminal behavior. Since he feels that he is dealing with an unreliable and powerful enemy, he has to deal with the threat in drastic ways, namely by suddenly and ruthlessly stripping and disarming any Negro who has aroused his suspicion. Because of the Negro's concept of the police, the young Negro male feels that he has only two alternatives open to him-intense resistance or abject surrender. These complementary attitudes result in a vicious circle of behavior which serves to confirm the image which Negro males and police officers hold of each other. In addition, police practices meant to overpower or cow the suspect before evidence of his offense is obtained have mainly a provocative effect. Such provocation is especially unfortunate in that it tends to produce an impression in the suspect that the police are not only as brutal as assumed, but are also frightened. In the mind of the Negro male, the police officer is over-reacting to the potential offense involved in the usual situation and this over-reaction is probably the result of fear as well as sadism. If the policeman is perceived as either frightened or brutal, the Negro male develops an attitude of contempt for the policeman as for his authority.

It is clear to me that it will be difficult to correct this complex process of interaction. As a start, better guidelines are needed for police behavior in respect to young Negro males. Specifically, it would be helpful if the police were trained to make more careful discriminations, wherever possible, with respect to potential Negro offenders. They should begin by interrogating any suspect as if he were a human being and as if he could be trusted to give responsible answers to the police officer in his mandatory role of investigating possible criminal behavior. It is often said that the police should be asked to show more "respect" for ghetto dwellers. I think this expression oversimplifies the situation as it is difficult to show respect to someone not considered to be a human being. My idea is that police officers should have more familiarity with the psychology of Negro youths so that they could make a more differentiated and appreciated response to their behavior. This would enable the police officer more readily and reliably to distinguish those Negro youths who are actually dangerous from those who would cooperate with police officers if they were treated as responsible human beings.

I realize that these statements are only a beginning and that much more work in this area needs to be done. However, I hope that you will find what I have to say helpful in your own work.

John P. Spiegel, M.D.
Director

The Center's study of recent riots describes how police conduct may function, if perceived as unjust, to ignite violence:

> "... riots tend to break out as a result of the interaction of two factors-the 'grievance level' of people in the ghetto and the inflammatory nature of the event which precipitates the initial disturbance. These two factors are in a reciprocal relation with each other: the higher the grievance level, the slighter the event required to trigger the riot. Low levels of Negro discontent require an event which is highly inflammatory in order that a riot break out. An 'inflammatory event' is usually an incident which is initiated by white people and which is perceived by black people in the ghetto as an act of injustice or as an insult to their community. The greater the injustice is perceived to be, the more 'inflammatory' is the effect of the incident.

There is, therefore, growing dissatisfaction on the part of many Negroes, especially the young, which focuses on the police as the most visible and provocative members of the white community. At the same time, police conduct and capacity is viewed in a dramatically distinct manner by Negroes, the police and other residents of the community.

In such a context, the need for "better guidelines ... for police behavior", as Dr. Spiegel writes, is obvious. The National Crime Commission Task Force on Police felt compelled to repeat again and again the conclusion we have previously noted: that "field interrogations are a major source of friction between the police and minority groups" and that "misuse of field interrogations" causes "serious friction with minority groups in many localities." Arbitrary police conduct epitomizes, and sets off a response to, many grievances.

To legitimate detention and search on "reasonable suspicion"-without probable cause-therefore is to give free reign to police intervention in the most dangerous way (without objective standards) in the most dangerous place (the ghetto street). If the police and the ghetto dweller view each other with fear, suspicion, often hatred, any enforced stop is a potential source of conflict. But when the stop is based on the inarticulate, unregulated judgment of the cop on the beat, the potential is magnified.

We do not suppose that such considerations as these can or should determine the Fourth Amendment question. We have rested our constitutional submission not on them, but on the firm grounds of history, authority and (we respectfully submit) reason, set out in Parts I-III of this Brief. However, we anticipate that the States of New York and Ohio will make the familiar inflated claims for stop and frisk as tools of law and order. If they do, let there be no mistake about this call to practicality. Whatever its conveniences and benefits to a narrow view of law-enforcement, stop and frisk carries with it an intense danger of inciting destructive community conflict. To arm the police with an inherently vague and standardless power to detain and search, especially where that power cannot effectively be regulated, contributes to the belief which many Negroes undeniably have that police suspicion is mainly suspicion of them, and police oppression their main lot in life. Arbitrary police interrogation, street detention, and frisk are nothing less than a major part of that social and psychological constellation which in them produces "untoward counter reactions of violence." Lankford v. Gelston, 364 F. 2d 197, 204, n. 7 (4th Cir. 1966).

CONCLUSION

The Court should hold that neither stops nor frisks may be made without probable cause. In each of these cases, the judgment of conviction should be reversed.

ILLINOIS V. WARDLOW.
528 U.S. 119 (2000)

Chief Justice REHNQUIST delivered the opinion of the Court.

Respondent Wardlow fled upon seeing police officers patrolling an area known for heavy narcotics trafficking. Two of the officers caught up with him, stopped him and conducted a protective patdown search for weapons. Discovering a .38–caliber handgun, the officers arrested Wardlow. We hold that the officers' stop did not violate the Fourth Amendment to the United States Constitution.

On September 9, 1995, Officers Nolan and Harvey were working as uniformed officers in the special operations section of the Chicago Police Department. The officers were driving the last car of a four car caravan converging on an area known for heavy narcotics trafficking in order to investigate drug transactions. The officers were traveling together because they expected to find a crowd of people in the area, including lookouts and customers.

As the caravan passed 4035 West Van Buren, Officer Nolan observed respondent Wardlow standing next to the building holding an opaque bag. Respondent looked in the direction of the officers and fled. Nolan and Harvey turned their car southbound, watched him as he ran through the gangway and an alley, and eventually cornered him on the street. Nolan then exited his car and stopped respondent. He immediately conducted a protective patdown search for weapons because in his experience it was common for there to be weapons in the near vicinity of narcotics transactions. During the frisk, Officer Nolan squeezed the bag respondent was carrying and felt a heavy, hard object similar to the shape of a gun. The officer then opened the bag and discovered a .38–caliber handgun with five live rounds of ammunition. The officers arrested Wardlow.

The Illinois trial court denied respondent's motion to suppress, finding the gun was recovered during a lawful stop and frisk. App. 14. Following a stipulated bench trial, Wardlow was convicted of unlawful use of a weapon by a felon. The Illinois Appellate Court reversed Wardlow's conviction, concluding that the gun should have been suppressed because Officer Nolan did not have reasonable suspicion sufficient to justify an investigative stop pursuant to *Terry v. Ohio*, 392 U.S. 1, 88 S.Ct. 1868, 20 L.Ed.2d 889 (1968). 287 Ill.App.3d 367, 222 Ill.Dec. 658, 678 N.E.2d 65 (1997).

The Illinois Supreme Court agreed. 183 Ill.2d 306, 233 Ill.Dec. 634, 701 N.E.2d 484 (1998). While rejecting the Appellate Court's conclusion that Wardlow was not in a high crime area, the Illinois Supreme Court determined that sudden flight in such an area does not create a reasonable suspicion justifying a *Terry* stop. 183 Ill.2d, at 310, 233 Ill.Dec. 634, 701 N.E.2d, at 486. Relying on *Florida v. Royer*, 460 U.S. 491, 103 S.Ct. 1319, 75 L.Ed.2d 229 (1983), the court explained that although police have the right to approach individuals and ask questions, the individual has no obligation to respond. The person may decline to answer and simply go on his or her way, and the refusal to respond, alone, does not provide a legitimate basis for an investigative stop. 183 Ill.2d, at 311–312, 233 Ill.Dec. 634, 701 N.E.2d, at 486–487. The court then determined that flight may simply be an exercise of this right to "go on one's way," and, thus, could not constitute reasonable suspicion justifying a *Terry* stop. 183 Ill.2d, at 312, 233 Ill.Dec. 634, 701 N.E.2d, at 487.

The Illinois Supreme Court also rejected the argument that flight combined with the fact that it occurred in a high crime area supported a finding of reasonable suspicion because the "high crime area" factor was not sufficient standing alone to justify a *Terry* stop. Finding no independently suspicious circumstances to support an investigatory detention, the court held that the stop and subsequent arrest violated the Fourth Amendment. We granted certiorari, 526 U.S. 1097, 119 S.Ct. 1573, 143 L.Ed.2d 669 (1999), and now reverse.

This case, involving a brief encounter between a citizen and a police officer on a public street, is governed by the analysis we first applied in *Terry*. In *Terry*, we held that an officer may, consistent with the Fourth Amendment, conduct a brief, investigatory stop when the officer has a reasonable, articulable suspicion that criminal activity is afoot. 392 U.S., at 30, 88 S.Ct. 1868. While "reasonable suspicion" is a less demanding standard than probable cause and requires a showing considerably less than preponderance of the evidence, the Fourth

Amendment requires at least a minimal level of objective justification for making the stop. *United States v. Sokolow*, 490 U.S. 1, 7, 109 S.Ct. 1581, 104 L.Ed.2d 1 (1989). The officer must be able to articulate more than an "inchoate and unparticularized suspicion or 'hunch'" of criminal activity. Terry, supra, at 27, 88 S.Ct. 1868.

Nolan and Harvey were among eight officers in a four-car caravan that was converging on an area known for heavy narcotics trafficking, and the officers anticipated encountering a large number of people in the area, including drug customers and individuals serving as lookouts. App. 8. It was in this context that Officer Nolan decided to investigate Wardlow after observing him flee. An individual's presence in an area of expected criminal activity, standing alone, is not enough to support a reasonable, particularized suspicion that the person is committing a crime. *Brown v. Texas*, 443 U.S. 47, 99 S.Ct. 2637, 61 L.Ed.2d 357 (1979). But officers are not required to ignore the relevant characteristics of a location in determining whether the circumstances are sufficiently suspicious to warrant further investigation. Accordingly, we have previously noted the fact that the stop occurred in a "high crime area" among the relevant contextual considerations in a *Terry* analysis. *Adams v. Williams*, 407 U.S. 143, 144, 147–148, 92 S.Ct. 1921, 32 L.Ed.2d 612 (1972).

In this case, moreover, it was not merely respondent's presence in an area of heavy narcotics trafficking that aroused the officers' suspicion, but his unprovoked flight upon noticing the police. Our cases have also recognized that nervous, evasive behavior is a pertinent factor in determining reasonable suspicion. *United States v. Brignoni—Ponce*, 422 U.S. 873, 885, 95 S.Ct. 2574, 45 L.Ed.2d 607 (1975); *Florida v. Rodriguez*, 469 U.S. 1, 6, 105 S.Ct. 308, 83 L.Ed.2d 165 (1984) *(per curiam); United States v. Sokolow, supra*, at 8–9, 109 S.Ct. 1581. Headlong flight—wherever it occurs—is the consummate act of evasion: It is not necessarily indicative of wrongdoing, but it is certainly suggestive of such. In reviewing the propriety of an officer's conduct, courts do not have available empirical studies dealing with inferences drawn from suspicious behavior, and we cannot reasonably demand scientific certainty from judges or law enforcement officers where none exists. Thus, the determination of reasonable suspicion must be based on common-sense judgments and inferences about human behavior. See *United States v. Cortez*, 449 U.S. 411, 418, 101 S.Ct. 690, 66 L.Ed.2d 621 (1981). We conclude Officer Nolan was justified in suspecting that Wardlow was involved in criminal activity, and, therefore, in investigating further.

Such a holding is entirely consistent with our decision in *Florida v. Royer*, 460 U.S. 491, 103 S.Ct. 1319, 75 L.Ed.2d 229 (1983), where we held that when an officer, without reasonable suspicion or probable cause, approaches an individual, the individual has a right to ignore the police and go about his business. Id., at 498, 103 S.Ct. 1319. And any "refusal to cooperate, without more, does not furnish the minimal level of objective justification needed for a detention or seizure." *Florida v. Bostick*, 501 U.S. 429, 437, 111 S.Ct. 2382, 115 L.Ed.2d 389 (1991). But unprovoked flight is simply not a mere refusal to cooperate. Flight, by its very nature, is not "going about one's business"; in fact, it is just the opposite. Allowing officers confronted with such flight to stop the fugitive and investigate further is quite consistent with the individual's right to go about his business or to stay put and remain silent in the face of police questioning.

Respondent and *amici* also argue that there are innocent reasons for flight from police and that, therefore, flight is not necessarily indicative of ongoing criminal activity. This fact is undoubtedly true, but does not establish a violation of the Fourth Amendment. Even in *Terry*, the conduct justifying the stop was ambiguous and susceptible of an innocent explanation. The officer observed two individuals pacing back and forth in front of a store, peering into the window and periodically conferring. 392 U.S., at 5–6, 88 S.Ct. 1868. All of this conduct was by itself lawful, but it also suggested that the individuals were casing the store for a planned robbery. *Terry* recognized that the officers could detain the individuals to resolve the ambiguity. Id., at 30, 88 S.Ct. 1868.

In allowing such detentions, *Terry* accepts the risk that officers may stop innocent people. Indeed, the Fourth Amendment accepts that risk in connection with more drastic police action; persons arrested and detained on probable cause to believe they have committed a crime may turn out to be innocent. The *Terry* stop is a far more minimal intrusion, simply allowing the officer to briefly investigate further. If the officer does not learn facts rising to the level of probable cause, the individual must be allowed to go on his way. But in this case the officers found respondent in possession of a handgun, and arrested him for violation of an Illinois firearms statute. No question of the propriety of the arrest itself is before us.

The judgment of the Supreme Court of Illinois is reversed, and the cause is remanded for further proceedings not inconsistent with this opinion.

It is so ordered.

SUPREME COURT OF THE UNITED STATES
ILLINOIS V. WARDLOW

No. 98-1036.

August 9, 1999.

BRIEF FOR THE NAACP LEGAL DEFENSE & EDUCATIONAL FUND, INC. AS AMICUS CURIAE IN SUPPORT OF RESPONDENT

....

ARGUMENT

Without More, Flight From Police Fails To Establish Likelihood of Criminal Activity.

A. The Terry/Sibron Compromise: Police May Utilize Stop & Frisk Tactics But Only When Circumstances Show Ample Factual Justification That Suggests Criminal Activity Is Afoot.

This Court's decision in Terry was a milestone for both the Fourth Amendment and police-citizen relations. For the first time, the Court gave its blessing to police-initiated encounters in the absence of probable cause. The Court concluded that when an officer possesses objective factors that reasonably suggest a citizen might well be about to commit a crime, the Fourth Amendment allows the officer to stop that person briefly, and if circumstances reasonably suggest the suspect might be armed, to conduct a brief pat-down search for weapons. Such "legitimate and restrained conduct undertaken on the basis of ample factual justification" is not "unreasonable" under the Fourth Amendment, the Court concluded; indeed it exemplifies effective policing. Id. at 15.

At the same time, the Terry Court fully acknowledged the weighty constitutional and community security costs that arise when stop and frisk practices are employed in the absence of such articulable, objective factors. The Fourth Amendment right to be free from unreasonable searches and seizures is an "inestimable right of personal security," Id. at 8-9, and a pat-down search of a citizen's body "is a serious intrusion upon the sanctity of the person, which may inflict great indignity and arouse strong resentment, and it is not to be taken lightly." Id. at 17. "Even a limited search of the outer clothing for weapons constitutes a severe, though brief, intrusion upon cherished personal security, and it must surely be an annoying, frightening and perhaps humiliating experience." Id. at 24-25.

The Court recognized as well the judiciary's important role in securing police compliance with its rule. Because illicit use of stop and frisk tactics can "only serve to exacerbate police-community tensions in the crowded centers of our Nation's cities, ... courts ... retain their traditional responsibility to guard against police conduct which is over-bearing or harassing, or which trenches upon personal security without the objective evidentiary justification which the Constitution requires. When such conduct is identified, it must be condemned by the Judiciary ...." Id. at 12, 15 (emphasis added).

In application, the Court has consistently approved encounters supported by credible indicia of likely criminal activity and rejected ones that lacked adequate factual support. The Terry Court found Officer McFadden's confrontation and search of Terry reasonable because it took place only after attentive study of what first appeared to be innocent behavior, but as time passed strongly suggested that Terry and others were preparing to commit armed robbery. Id. at 27-30. Similarly in United States v. Cortez, 449 U.S. 411 (1980), the Court found reasonable a stop of a truck because border patrol officers had first carefully analyzed a number of factors that, collectively, firmly suggested the track likely contained illegal aliens and their guide. 449 U.S. at 419-420.

On the other hand, the Court has not hesitated to reject as constitutionally impermissible encounters that lack sufficient indicia of wrongdoing. In Terry's companion case, Sibron v. New York, 392 U.S. 40 (1968), an eight-hour surveillance yielded only that Sibron was cavorting with several known drug addicts; the officer's subsequent search based on this information was firmly rejected as unreasonable. In Brown *v. Texas*, 443 U.S. 47 (1979), the Court determined that a citizen's presence in a high-crime area and refusal to identify himself to police lacked adequate indicia of wrongdoing. 443 U.S. at 52. In Reid *v. Georgia*, 448 U.S. 438 (1980), the Court rejected Reid's traveling with another person but walking apart from him and occasionally looking back at his companion, as insufficient suggestion of drug trafficking. 448 U.S. at 441. Thus, unless the circumstances as a whole reasonably suggest criminal behavior is likely afoot, the Fourth Amendment protection against government intrusion requires police to refrain from stop and frisk activities.

B. The Currently Troubled State of Police-Minority Community Relations Is Highly Relevant To Understanding Why Citizens Flee From Police.

Illinois and its amici ask the Court to conclude that the mere fact of flight from police in a high-crime area is sufficiently suggestive of likely involvement in imminent criminal conduct under Terry to justify an otherwise unconstitutional seizure and search. Illinois argues that while some avoidance behavior, such as a citizen's avoiding eye contact with the police, is not necessarily suggestive of suspicious conduct, "running away from a clearly identifiable police officer constitutes an innately suspicious reaction to the presence of police." Illinois Br. at 9. The United States argues that while flight "may be undertaken for innocent reasons, it is not behavior in which innocent persons commonly engage — and it is far more likely to signal a consciousness of wrongdoing and a fear of apprehension." United States Br. at 6 (emphasis in original). Several state Attorneys General assert more boldly that when citizens face unwanted police attention, the innocent walk way, but the guilty flee. Ohio et. al. Br. at 5 ("A potential suspect with a guilty conscience may or may not know the police have independent information tying her to particular crimes; but when the officer shows up, the citizen does not want to stay and find out — she runs. On the other hand, the citizen without the guilty conscience may desire to avoid interacting with police, so she declines to listen to, or to answer, police questions and walks on ...."). The Criminal Justice Legal Foundation (herein CJLF) asserts that a per se rule is appropriate because "flight supports reasonable suspicion because of the close relationship between flight from authority and a guilty mind." CJLF Br. at 3.

As we show below, these views ask too much. There is good reason why the majority of courts that have considered the issue have rejected this position. Simply put, the circumstances under which a citizen will run from the police are too numerous, and too often based in innocence, to justify a per se rule. At most, it can be but one factor among many warranting consideration. Moreover, while Illinois and its amici profess to accept the Terry principle that reviewing courts must examine the totality of the circumstances before adjudging an encounter reasonable as a constitutional matter, see, e.g., Cortez, 449 U.S. at 418, none discuss or consider a factor that has enormous relevance to understanding why inner-city African-American residents would flee from police. That circumstance is fear, the sincere and understandable response that many inner-city minority residents - the law-abiding no less than the criminal - to potential encounters of any type with police.

C. Overwhelming Evidence Shows That Minority Citizens Fear Law Enforcement Officers Because of Systemic Harassment and Abuse.

There is no question the Terry Court was correct in recognizing the subversive effect upon both Fourth Amendment values and constructive law enforcement-community relations that result when police accost citizens in the absence of reasonable suspicion of criminal activity. Yet in many minority communities in contemporary America, youth and adults are to a staggering degree subjected to stops, frisk, beatings, and in some instances, to lethal injuries, in the absence of any wrongdoing on their part. These tragic patterns of pervasive police misconduct have many harmful consequences, not the least of which is that many minority citizens - and especially young men in inner cities - no longer perceive an approaching police officer as a benign force. To the contrary, bitter experience teaches - and empirical research confirms - that officers often initiate such encounters in bad faith, with little regard to these citizens' basic human dignity, let alone their constitutional rights.

Police experts understand the effects of unrestrained police stop and frisk activity upon a subject community. The "real problem with Terry is that police stop and frisk when it isn't as justified as it was in Terry." A highly decorated-former officer believes unauthorized stops poison police-citizen relations because "a Terry stop says terrible things about its subject; it is the officer's way of telling a person you look wrong and I am going to check out my feelings about you even if it embarrasses you." Thus:

> [a] citizen's good or poor opinion may largely be formed by the impression the citizen has of those fleeting contacts with ... [police]. No other state officials have the discretionary power, sometimes exercised within seconds, to consider and apply the law to a citizen, to restrain a citizen's liberty by temporary detention, to invade a citizen's privacy by search or even to injure or kill a citizen in self-defense or in protection of others.

Yet despite the Court's and law enforcement's understanding of the corrosive harm that results from illicit and unwanted police-initiated encounters with citizens, the widespread practice by beat officers in many urban and minority communities is to defy rather than to comply with Terry's admonitions. James Baldwin's haunting declaration from three decades ago - "from the most circumspect church member to the most shiftless adolescent, who does not have a long tale to tell of police incompetence, injustice, or brutality?" - sadly is as apt today as when it was first written. This view is shared not only by police critics but also by some of the most respected voices in law enforcement.

Charles H. Ramsey, Chief of Police in Washington, D.C., noted earlier this year that "despite tremendous gains throughout this century in civil rights, voting rights, fair employment and housing, sizeable percentages of Americans today, especially Americans of color, still view policing in the United States to be discriminatory, if not by policy and definition, certainly in its day to day application." One major reason for these views is stop and frisk. "Field interrogations that are excessive, that are discourteous, and that push people around, generate friction." George Kelling, a Rutgers University criminal justice professor and well known proponent of the "broken windows" theory of crime control, agrees that stop and frisk practices possess "tremendous potential for abuse," and he is deeply critical of police departments which "indiscriminately stop and frisk people." Former Officer Fyfe observes that in his experience, too many officers today are "just making guesses and quite often they are wrong."

One likely explanation for this state of affairs is that a significant minority of line officers believe that no countervailing consideration - be it the respect for personal security embodied in the Fourth Amendment or the equal treatment mandate of the Fourteenth - should constrain the work of ferreting out crime. A Baltimore police officer and president of the Baltimore Fraternal Order of Police openly remarked recently, "of course we do racial profiling at the train station. If 20 people get off a train and 19 are white guys in suits and one is a black female, guess who gets followed? If racial profiling is intuition and experience, I guess we all racial-profile." Another experienced officer in Southern California recently confided "racial profiling is a tool we use, and don't let anyone say otherwise.... Like up in the valley, ... I know who all the crack sellers were — they look like Hispanics who should be cutting your lawn."

Minority police officers who have found the courage to speak on the record complain that in many departments, a number of fellow officers routinely harass minority citizens. Gene Jones, a black police officer in Philadelphia and a staff sergeant in the New Jersey National Guard told of the lengths that he goes to in order to avoid traveling on the New Jersey Turnpike so he will not be stopped by state patrol officers; "Yeah, I go to Jersey for Guard weekend, I take the back roads. I won't get on the turnpike. I won't mess with those troopers."16 Several minority New Jersey State Police officers recently filed suit against that agency, confirming the prevalence of racial prejudice in its operations. In another instance, a black Philadelphia police officer related that he was pulled over in a predominantly white suburb, purportedly because his inspection sticker was placed "abnormally high" on his windshield.

Because these aggressive tactics flout the very law the officers are duty-bound to enforce, police departments throughout the country are seeing increased numbers of complaints of arbitrary and unfair street stops, as well as for use of excessive force, and brutality. Such large numbers of complaints from minority community citizens have prompted the NAACP to announce that ending racial profiling is a top organizational priority. National and local civil rights commissions are increasingly called to investigate harassing police practices. In Omaha, Nebraska, the Human Relations Board recently found that there was little trust between Omaha police and African-American citizens, and that many people of color felt mistreated or harassed by the police because of their race. A task force in Montgomery County, Maryland held similar hearings at which numerous witnesses recounted having been stopped because they were in predominantly white neighborhoods. In Worcester, Massachusetts, the local civil rights commission held a series of hearings at which troubling and substantial allegations of racial profiling and excessive force were aired.25 In Denver, the local newspaper listed a string of clear abuses of authority all arising in a single year: "a patrolman is captured on videotape aiming his gun at a woman in a holding cell; an officer kicks a suspected cop killer as a TV photographer tapes him; a seven year veteran of the police force is arrested for allegedly ramming a man with his police cruiser, then breaking his jaw with three kicks to the face."In New York City, the United States Civil Rights Commission recently held hearings on the stop and frisk practice of the NYPD's Street Crimes Unit.

Emerging data reveals that minority citizens are increasingly unhappy with these aggressive police practices, and that they often are the targets of distasteful encounters that rarely lead to arrest. In May of 1999, the Department of Justice released a twelve-city survey on community perceptions of law enforcement. The survey found that African-American residents were twice as likely to be dissatisfied with police practices than were white residents in the same community. These data nearly mirror findings of 30 years ago. A study by the Joint Center for Political and Economic Studies in April 1996 found that 43% of African Americans consider "police brutality and harassment of African-Americans a serious problem" in their own community. In fact a survey of polls conducted across the nation and reported in the National Institute of Justice's Journal suggests that "many black Americans are disaffected and suspicious. They are not confident that the police will be fair. They are not confident that the police will be professional. They are not confident that the police will 'protect and serve.' DD"

Available data on stop and frisk practices show these misgivings to be well-founded. The data show that a large number of citizens who are stopped and often frisked - disproportionately members of racial and ethnic minority groups -were engaged in no criminal conduct. Over a two-year period starting in 1997, the New York City Police Department Street Crimes Unit stopped and frisked 45,000 citizens focusing on "high crime areas." Only twenty percent of the individuals stopped were arrested. The other 35,500 citizens who lived, worked and traveled in these neighborhoods were subjected to the """annoying, frightening and perhaps humiliating experience," Terry, 392 U.S. at 25, of police detainment despite being innocent of any of the wrongdoing of which they were "suspected." A New York newspaper survey found that 81 out of 100 randomly questioned young black and Hispanic men living in New York City had been stopped and frisked by the police at least once. The survey reported that none of the 81 stops resulted in arrests. In Pittsburgh, young black males were stopped an average of 3.47 times during a five year period compared to white residents who were stopped an average of 1.53 times during the same period. In St. Petersburg, Florida, a study of police field interrogation reports found that police conducted street stops of more than 9,000 people over a period of twenty months, with African-American residents being stopped entirely out of proportion to their share of the City's population. A review of the reasons listed by police officers to justify the stops included standing by a pay phone, standing outside a house smoking a cigarette, and riding a bicycle the wrong way down a one-way street.

A 1991 report on the Boston Police Department conducted by the Massachusetts Attorney General concluded that police officers engaged in improper, and unconstitutional, conduct in the 1989-90 period with respect to stops and searches of minority individuals. The report went on to note that:

> the most disturbing evidence was that the scope [emphasis in original] of a number of Terry searches went far beyond anything authorized by that case and indeed, beyond anything that we believe would be acceptable under the federal and state constitutions even where probable cause existed to conduct a full search incident to an arrest. Forcing young men to lower their trousers or otherwise searching inside their underwear, on public streets or in public hallways, is so demeaning and invasive of fundamental precepts of privacy that it can only be condemned in the strongest terms.

This report also documented numerous incidents of police brutality that occurred during street stops. One sixteen year-old African-American male reported being stopped, strip-searched approximately seven times, and forced to lie face down on the ground. The youth's account, credited by investigators, reported that "the officers often emerged from the cruisers with guns drawn, put the guns right to his face, and said that if he moved, they would shoot him or 'blow [his] flattop off.'DD' A seventeen year old black male reported credibly that in 1990 while standing on a corner, two police officers said "you fucking niggers, get [out]. We don't want you hanging on the street anymore." The police officer, after asking the youth what was in his mouth, hit him and threw him to the ground and then proceeded to conduct a strip search. Neither youth was arrested, let alone charged with any crime.

The Massachusetts Report concluded in no uncertain terms that "the communities hardest hit by crime must not be forced to accept the harassment of their young people as the price for aggressive law enforcement. ... It is hardly an object lesson in respect for the law and for the police to be searched for no other reason than that you are young, black and wearing a baseball cap."

In Philadelphia, when race was recorded on the police department field reports, the overwhelming majority (80.2%) of stops were of African Americans even though the districts in question were racially integrated. A review of these reports for three districts over a week revealed that the police recorded no explanation in over half of the stops. None of these stops resulted in an arrest. Moreover, a number of field reports listed """stopped for investigation" as the primary reason for making the stop. Other justifications recorded by police officers included hanging out on a corner, being homeless, and observing a female in a known prostitution area. In addition to the fact that these stops were based on wholly innocent activities insufficient to constitute reasonable suspicion, nearly twice as many minorities were subject to stops and frisks as compared to white residents.

Recent studies also show that more often than not, minority citizens are subject to harsher treatment than whites during these encounters. The Christopher Commission's examination of police practices in Los Angeles in the wake of the first Rodney King verdict documented how minority residents were more likely to be subjected to excessive force, longer detentions not resulting in a charge, and to invasive and humiliating police tactics.

The Commission further determined that when the Los Angeles Police Department adopted a policing model emphasizing aggressive street patrol, one result was the alienation of the majority of law abiding citizens. The report concluded that these citizens "viewed the police department with mistrust, since they were perceived by the police as potential criminals." In that same report, a survey of 900 police officers in LAPD found that one quarter of the respondents felt that "racial bias (prejudice) on the part of the officers towards minority citizens currently exists and contributes to a negative interaction between police and community."

Increasingly, even citizens who were initially supportive of aggressive stop and frisk efforts in their neighborhoods are expressing second thoughts. As one Upper Manhattan resident recently explained, "in the beginning we all wanted the police to bomb the crack houses. But now it's backfiring at the cost of the community. I think the cops have been given free rein to intimidate people at large."

Others - predominantly African-American and Latino parents - have felt sufficiently fearful of the dangers of contact with the police that they have enrolled themselves and their children in seminars that teach how to decrease the likelihood of harm when encountering the police. Moreover, the Allstate Insurance Company has become so concerned with the state of police relations with youth that it recently undertook to finance a joint project with the NAACP to distribute pamphlets to youngsters on how to act when confronted by a police officer. The pamphlets, entitled "The Law and You," instruct teenagers to "avoid any action or language that might trigger a more volatile situation, possibly endangering your life or personal well-being."

This glimpse of the present status of police-community relations in many areas of the country is sadly similar to the one the Terry/Sibron Court confronted and acknowledged three decades ago. As it informed the Court's holding then that stop and frisk tactics be employed only on the basis of ample factual justification, the stubborn presence of these very same conditions today require the Court to consider, as a circumstance of this case, the fear that minority citizens in inner cities reasonably hold when they see officers of the law.

D. Consideration of All the Relevant Facts Requires A Conclusion That Wardlow's Flight Is Not Sufficiently Suggestive of Likely Imminent Criminal Conduct to Justify a Terry Seizure.

This case contrasts with those in which the Court has been willing to uphold seizures and frisks in the absence of probable cause, and resembles far more closely the ones in which the Court has found the factual showing inadequate. Unlike the careful and deliberate police work described in Terry and Cortez, Officer Nolan's decision to seize and frisk Wardlow was made nearly instantly, upon Wardlow's flight, and without the development of any other fact that might have confirmed the hunch that Wardlow was about to commit a crime. Indeed, prior to seeing Wardlow, Nolan had no information of any reported crime in the area, nor was there any suggestion that Wardlow might be involved in any criminal activity. In appearance, Wardlow was violating no law. He was merely standing on the sidewalk, and like many urban residents, was carrying a bag. And even after he began to run, he broke no law, nor gave Nolan any further articulable reason to believe he was committing, or about to commit a crime, or was armed. At the moment that Nolan seized control of Wardlow and commenced to pat him down, Nolan possessed no additional information that suggested that Wardlow was violating any law. This case is much more like Brown v. Texas in that in both, the police acted quickly on hunches and failed to develop sufficient evidence that criminal conduct was afoot prior to the stop.

CONCLUSION

The issue that divides us from Illinois is not whether flight can be considered as a Terry factor, but whether flight alone satisfies Terry's "ample factual justification" requirement. Given the state of police-community relations, flight from police neither reliably nor sufficiently suggests that criminal activity is afoot. Because Illinois and its amici have failed to show otherwise, the Court should affirm the judgement of the Illinois Supreme Court.

UTAH V. STRIEFF
136 S.Ct. 2056 (2016)

Justice SOTOMAYOR, with whom Justice GINSBURG joins as to Parts I, II, and III, dissenting.

The Court today holds that the discovery of a warrant for an unpaid parking ticket will forgive a police officer's violation of your Fourth Amendment rights. Do not be soothed by the opinion's technical language: This case allows the police to stop you on the street, demand your identification, and check it for outstanding traffic warrants—even if you are doing nothing wrong. If the officer discovers a warrant for a fine you forgot to pay, courts will now excuse his illegal stop and will admit into evidence anything he happens to find by searching you after arresting you on the warrant. Because the Fourth Amendment should prohibit, not permit, such misconduct, I dissent.

....

IV

Writing only for myself, and drawing on my professional experiences, I would add that unlawful "stops" have severe consequences much greater than the inconvenience suggested by the name. This Court has given officers an array of instruments to probe and examine you. When we condone officers' use of these devices without adequate cause, we give them reason to target pedestrians in an arbitrary manner. We also risk treating members of our communities as second-class citizens.

Although many Americans have been stopped for speeding or jaywalking, few may realize how degrading a stop can be when the officer is looking for more. This Court has allowed an officer to stop you for whatever reason he wants—so long as he can point to a pretextual justification after the fact. *Whren v. United States*, 517 U.S. 806, 813, 116 S.Ct. 1769, 135 L.Ed.2d 89 (1996). That justification must provide specific reasons why the officer suspected you were breaking the law, *Terry*, 392 U.S., at 21, 88 S.Ct. 1868 but it may factor in your ethnicity, *United States v. Brignoni–Ponce*, 422 U.S. 873, 886–887, 95 S.Ct. 2574, 45 L.Ed.2d 607 (1975), where you live, *Adams v. Williams*, 407 U.S. 143, 147, 92 S.Ct. 1921, 32 L.Ed.2d 612 (1972), what you were wearing, *United States v. Sokolow*, 490 U.S. 1, 4–5, 109 S.Ct. 1581, 104 L.Ed.2d 1 (1989), and how you behaved, *Illinois v. Wardlow*, 528 U.S. 119, 124–125, 120 S.Ct. 673, 145 L.Ed.2d 570 (2000). The officer does not even need to know which law you might have broken so long as he can later point to any possible infraction—even one that is minor, unrelated, or ambiguous. *Devenpeck v. Alford*, 543 U.S. 146, 154–155, 125 S.Ct. 588, 160 L.Ed.2d 537 (2004); *Heien v. North Carolina*, 574 U.S. ––––, 135 S.Ct. 530, 190 L.Ed.2d 475 (2014).

The indignity of the stop is not limited to an officer telling you that you look like a criminal. See Epp, Pulled Over, at 5. The officer may next ask for your "consent" to inspect your bag or purse without telling you that you can decline. See *Florida v. Bostick*, 501 U.S. 429, 438, 111 S.Ct. 2382, 115 L.Ed.2d 389 (1991). Regardless of your answer, he may order you to stand "helpless, perhaps facing a wall with [your] hands raised." *Terry*, 392 U.S., at 17, 88 S.Ct. 1868. If the officer thinks you might be dangerous, he may then "frisk" you for weapons. This involves more than just a pat down. As onlookers pass by, the officer may "'feel with sensitive fingers every portion of [your] body. A thorough search [may] be made of [your] arms and armpits, waistline and back, the groin and area about the testicles, and entire surface of the legs down to the feet.'" Id., at 17, n. 13, 88 S.Ct. 1868.

The officer's control over you does not end with the stop. If the officer chooses, he may handcuff you and take you to jail for doing nothing more than speeding, jaywalking, or "driving [your] pickup truck … with [your] 3–year–old son and 5–year–old daughter … without [your] seatbelt fastened." *Atwater v. Lago Vista*, 532 U.S. 318, 323–324, 121 S.Ct. 1536, 149 L.Ed.2d 549 (2001). At the jail, he can fingerprint you, swab DNA from the inside of your mouth, and force you to "shower with a delousing agent" while you "lift [your] tongue, hold out [your] arms, turn around, and lift [your] genitals." *Florence v. Board of Chosen Freeholders of County of Burlington*, 566 U.S. ––––, –––– – ––––, 132 S.Ct. 1510, 1514, 182 L.Ed.2d 566 (2012); *Maryland v. King*, 569 U.S. ––––, ––––, 133 S.Ct. 1958, 1980, 186 L.Ed.2d 1 (2013). Even if you are innocent, you will now join the 65 million Americans with an arrest record and experience the "civil death" of discrimination by employers, landlords, and whoever else conducts a background check. Chin, The New Civil Death, 160 U. Pa. L. Rev. 1789, 1805 (2012); see J. Jacobs, The Eternal Criminal Record 33–51 (2015); Young & Petersilia, Keeping Track, 129 Harv. L. Rev. 1318, 1341–1357 (2016). And, of course, if you fail to pay bail or appear for court, a judge will issue a warrant to render you "arrestable on sight" in the future. A. Goffman, On the Run 196 (2014).

This case involves a *suspicionless* stop, one in which the officer initiated this chain of events without justification. As the Justice Department notes, *supra,* at 2068 – 2069, many innocent people are subjected to the humiliations of these unconstitutional searches. The white defendant in this case shows that anyone's dignity can be violated in this manner. See M. Gottschalk, Caught 119–138 (2015). But it is no secret that people of color are disproportionate victims of this type of scrutiny. See M. Alexander, The New Jim Crow 95–136 (2010). For generations, black and brown parents have given their children "the talk"—instructing them never to run down the street; always keep your hands where they can be seen; do not even think of talking back to a stranger—all out of fear of how an officer with a gun will react to them. See, *e.g.,* W.E.B. Du Bois, The Souls of Black Folk (1903); J. Baldwin, The Fire Next Time (1963); T. Coates, Between the World and Me (2015).

By legitimizing the conduct that produces this double consciousness, this case tells everyone, white and black, guilty and innocent, that an officer can verify your legal status at any time. It says that your body is subject to invasion while courts excuse the violation of your rights. It implies that you are not a citizen of a democracy but the subject of a carceral state, just waiting to be cataloged.

We must not pretend that the countless people who are routinely targeted by police are "isolated." They are the canaries in the coal mine whose deaths, civil and literal, warn us that no one can breathe in this atmosphere. See L. Guinier & G. Torres, The Miner's Canary 274–283 (2002). They are the ones who recognize that unlawful police stops corrode all our civil liberties and threaten all our lives. Until their voices matter too, our justice system will continue to be anything but.

* * *

I dissent.

FLOYD V. CITY OF NEW YORK

959 F.Supp.2d 540 (S.D. N.Y 2013)

OPINION AND ORDER

SHIRA A. SCHEINDLIN, District Judge:

INTRODUCTION

New Yorkers are rightly proud of their city and seek to make it as safe as the largest city in America can be. New Yorkers also treasure their liberty. Countless individuals have come to New York in pursuit of that liberty. The goals of liberty and safety may be in tension, but they can coexist—indeed the Constitution mandates it.

This case is about the tension between liberty and public safety in the use of a proactive policing tool called "stop and frisk." The New York City Police Department ("NYPD") made 4.4 million stops between January 2004 and June 2012. Over 80% of these 4.4 million stops were of blacks or Hispanics. In each of these stops a person's life was interrupted. The person was detained and questioned, often on a public street. More than half of the time the police subjected the person to a frisk.

Plaintiffs—blacks and Hispanics who were stopped—argue that the NYPD's use of stop and frisk violated their constitutional rights in two ways: (1) they were stopped without a legal basis in violation of the Fourth Amendment, and (2) they were targeted for stops because of their race in violation of the Fourteenth Amendment. Plaintiffs do not seek to end the use of stop and frisk. Rather, they argue that it must be reformed to comply with constitutional limits. Two such limits are paramount here: *first,* that all stops be based on "reasonable suspicion" as defined by the Supreme Court of the United States; and *second,* that stops be conducted in a racially neutral manner.

I emphasize at the outset, as I have throughout the litigation, that this case is not about the effectiveness of stop and frisk in deterring or combating crime. This Court's mandate is solely to judge the *constitutionality* of police behavior, *not* its effectiveness as a law enforcement tool. Many police practices may be useful for fighting crime—preventive detention or coerced confessions, for example—but because they are unconstitutional they cannot be used, no matter how effective. "The enshrinement of constitutional rights necessarily takes certain policy choices off the table."[3]

This case is also not primarily about the nineteen individual stops that were the subject of testimony at trial Rather, this case is about whether the City has a *policy* or *custom* of violating the Constitution by making unlawful stops and conducting unlawful frisks.

The Supreme Court has recognized that "the degree of community resentment aroused by particular practices is clearly relevant to an assessment of the quality of the intrusion upon reasonable expectations of personal security." In light of the very active and public debate on the issues addressed in this Opinion—and the passionate positions taken by both sides—it is important to recognize the human toll of unconstitutional stops. While it is true that any one stop is a limited intrusion in duration and deprivation of liberty, each stop is also a demeaning and humiliating experience. No one should live in fear of being stopped whenever he leaves his home to go about the activities of daily life. Those who are routinely subjected to stops are overwhelmingly people of color, and they are justifiably troubled to be singled out when many of them have done nothing to attract the unwanted attention. Some plaintiffs testified that stops make them feel unwelcome in some parts of the City, and distrustful of the police. This alienation cannot be good for the police, the community, or its leaders. Fostering trust and confidence between the police and the community would be an improvement for everyone.

Plaintiffs requested that this case be tried to the Court without a jury. Because plaintiffs seek only injunctive relief, not damages, the City had no right to demand a jury. As a result, I must both find the facts and articulate the governing law. I have endeavored to exercise my judgment faithfully and impartially in making my findings of fact and conclusions of law based on the nine-week trial held from March through May of this year.

I begin with an Executive Summary of the most important points in the Opinion. Next, I address the legal standards governing the ability of police to conduct stops and frisks. I provide a statistical overview of the 4.4 million stops made between January 2004 and June 2012, followed by a discussion of the expert analyses of those stops. I then address the question of whether the City had notice of allegations of racial profiling in the conduct of stops and frisks, and the institutional response to that notice in terms of monitoring, supervision, training, and discipline. After addressing these big picture issues, I make findings of fact with respect to each of the nineteen stops of the twelve class members who provided testimony at trial.

Finally, I present my conclusions of law based on my findings of fact. I will address the question of remedies in a separate opinion, because the remedies overlap with a different case involving stop and frisk in which I have already found that preliminary injunctive relief is warranted.

It is important that this Opinion be read synergistically. Each section of the Opinion is only a piece of the overall picture. Some will quarrel with the findings in one section or another. But, when read as a whole, with an understanding of the interplay between each section, I hope that this Opinion will bring more clarity and less disagreement to this complex and sensitive issue.

II. EXECUTIVE SUMMARY

Plaintiffs assert that the City, and its agent the NYPD, violated both the Fourth Amendment and the Equal Protection Clause of the Fourteenth Amendment of the United States Constitution. In order to hold a municipality liable for the violation of a constitutional right, plaintiffs "must prove that 'action pursuant to official municipal policy' caused the alleged constitutional injury." "Official municipal policy includes the decisions of a government's lawmakers, the acts of its policymaking officials, and practices so persistent and widespread as to practically have the force of law."

The Fourth Amendment protects all individuals against unreasonable searches or seizures. The Supreme Court has held that the Fourth Amendment permits the police to "stop and briefly detain a person for investigative purposes if the officer has a reasonable suspicion supported by articulable facts that criminal activity 'may be afoot,' even if the officer lacks probable cause." "Reasonable suspicion is an objective standard; hence, the subjective intentions or motives of the officer making the stop are irrelevant." The test for whether a stop has taken place in the context of a police encounter is whether a reasonable person would have felt free to terminate the encounter." '[T]o proceed from a stop to a frisk, the police officer must reasonably suspect that the person stopped is armed and dangerous.' "

The Equal Protection Clause of the Fourteenth Amendment guarantees to every person the equal protection of the laws. It prohibits intentional discrimination based on race. Intentional discrimination can be proved in several ways, two of which are relevant here. A plaintiff can show: (1) that a facially neutral law or policy has been applied in an intentionally discriminatory manner; or (2) that a law or policy expressly classifies persons on the basis of race, and that the classification does not survive strict scrutiny. Because there is rarely direct proof of discriminatory intent, circumstantial evidence of such intent is permitted. "The impact of the official action—whether it bears more heavily on one race than another—may provide an important starting point."

The following facts, discussed in greater detail below, are uncontested:

- Between January 2004 and June 2012, the NYPD conducted over 4.4 million *Terry* stops.

- The number of stops per year rose sharply from 314,000 in 2004 to a high of 686,000 in 2011.

- 52% of all stops were followed by a protective frisk for weapons. A weapon was found after 1.5% of these frisks. In other words, in 98.5% of the 2.3 million frisks, no weapon was found.

- 8% of all stops led to a search into the stopped person's clothing, ostensibly based on the officer feeling an object during the frisk that he suspected to be a weapon, or immediately perceived to be contraband other than a weapon. In 9% of these searches, the felt object was in fact a weapon. 91% of the time, it was not. In 14% of these searches, the felt object was in fact contraband. 86% of the time it was not.

- 6% of all stops resulted in an arrest, and 6% resulted in a summons. The remaining 88% of the 4.4 million stops resulted in no further law enforcement action.

- In 52% of the 4.4 million stops, the person stopped was black, in 31% the person was Hispanic, and in 10% the person was white.

- In 2010, New York City's resident population was roughly 23% black, 29% Hispanic, and 33% white.

- In 23% of the stops of blacks, and 24% of the stops of Hispanics, the officer recorded using force. The number for whites was 17%.

- Weapons were seized in 1.0% of the stops of blacks, 1.1% of the stops of Hispanics, and 1.4% of the stops of whites.

- Contraband other than weapons was seized in 1.8% of the stops of blacks, 1.7% of the stops of Hispanics, and 2.3% of the stops of whites.

- Between 2004 and 2009, the percentage of stops where the officer failed to state a specific suspected crime rose from 1% to 36%.

Both parties provided extensive expert submissions and testimony that is also discussed in detail below. Based on that testimony and the uncontested facts, I have made the following findings with respect to the expert testimony.

With respect to plaintiffs' Fourth Amendment claim, I begin by noting the inherent difficulty in making findings and conclusions regarding 4.4 million stops. Because it is impossible to *individually* analyze each of those stops, plaintiffs' case was based on the imperfect information contained in the NYPD's database of forms ("UF–250s") that officers are required to prepare after each stop. The central flaws in this database all skew toward underestimating the number of unconstitutional stops that occur: the database is incomplete, in that officers do not prepare a UF–250 for every stop they make; it is one-sided, in that the UF–250 only records the officer's version of the story; the UF–250 permits the officer to merely check a series of boxes, rather than requiring the officer to explain the basis for her suspicion; and many of the boxes on the form are inherently subjective and vague (such as "furtive movements"). Nonetheless, the analysis of the UF–250 database reveals that *at least* 200,000 stops were made without reasonable suspicion.

The actual number of stops lacking reasonable suspicion was likely far higher, based on the reasons stated above, and the following points: (1) Dr. Fagan was unnecessarily conservative in classifying stops as "apparently unjustified." For example, a UF–250 on which the officer checked only Furtive Movements (used on roughly 42% of forms) and High Crime Area (used on roughly 55% of forms) is not classified as "apparently unjustified." The same is true when only Furtive Movements and Suspicious Bulge (used on roughly 10% of forms) are checked. Finally, if an officer checked only the box marked "other" on either side of the form (used on roughly 26% of forms), Dr. Fagan categorized this as "ungeneralizable" rather than "apparently unjustified." (2) Many UF–250s did not identify *any* suspected crime (36% of all UF–250s in 2009). (3) The rate of arrests arising from stops is low (roughly 6%), and the yield of seizures of guns or other contraband is even lower (roughly 0.1% and 1.8% respectively). (4) "Furtive Movements," "High Crime Area," and "Suspicious Bulge" are vague and subjective terms. Without an accompanying narrative explanation for the stop, these checkmarks cannot reliably demonstrate individualized reasonable suspicion.

With respect to plaintiffs' Fourteenth Amendment claim, I reject the testimony of the City's experts that the race of crime suspects is the appropriate benchmark for measuring racial bias in stops. The City and its highest officials believe that blacks and Hispanics should be stopped at the same rate as their proportion of the local criminal suspect population. But this reasoning is flawed because the stopped population is overwhelmingly innocent—not criminal. There is no basis for assuming that an innocent population shares the same characteristics as the criminal suspect population in the same area. Instead, I conclude that the benchmark used by plaintiffs' expert—a combination of local population demographics and local crime rates (to account for police deployment) is the most sensible.

Based on the expert testimony I find the following: (1) The NYPD carries out more stops where there are more black and Hispanic residents, even when other relevant variables are held constant. The racial composition of a precinct or census tract predicts the stop rate *above and beyond* the crime rate. (2) Blacks and Hispanics are more likely than whites to be stopped within precincts and census tracts, even after controlling for other relevant variables. This is so even in areas with low crime rates, racially heterogenous populations, or predominately white populations. (3) For the period 2004 through 2009, when any law enforcement action was taken following a stop, blacks were 30% more likely to be arrested (as opposed to receiving a summons) than whites, for the same suspected crime. (4) For the period 2004 through 2009, after controlling for suspected crime and precinct characteristics, blacks who were stopped were about 14% more likely—and Hispanics 9% more likely—than whites to be subjected to the use of force. (5) For the period 2004 through 2009, all else being equal, the odds of a stop resulting in any further enforcement action were 8% *lower* if the person stopped was black than if the person stopped was white. In addition, the greater the black population in a precinct, the less likely that a stop would result in a sanction. Together, these results show that blacks are likely targeted for stops based on a lesser degree of objectively founded suspicion than whites.

With respect to both the Fourth and Fourteenth Amendment claims, one way to prove that the City has a custom of conducting unconstitutional stops and frisks is to show that it acted with deliberate indifference to constitutional deprivations caused by its employees—here, the NYPD. The evidence at trial revealed significant evidence that the NYPD acted with deliberate indifference.

As early as 1999, a report from New York's Attorney General placed the City on notice that stops and frisks were being conducted in a racially skewed manner. Nothing was done in response. In the years following this report, pressure was placed on supervisors to increase the number of stops. Evidence at trial revealed that officers have been pressured to make a certain number of stops and risk negative consequences if they fail to achieve the goal. Without a system to ensure that stops are justified, such pressure is a predictable formula for producing unconstitutional stops. As one high ranking police official noted in 2010, this pressure, without a comparable emphasis on ensuring that the activities are legally justified, "could result in an officer taking enforcement action for the purpose of meeting a quota rather than because a violation of the law has occurred."

In addition, the evidence at trial revealed that the NYPD has an unwritten policy of targeting "the right people" for stops. In practice, the policy encourages the targeting of young black and Hispanic men based on their prevalence in local crime complaints. This is a form of racial profiling. While a person's race may be important if it fits the description of a particular crime suspect, it is impermissible to subject all members of a racially defined group to heightened police enforcement because some members of that group are criminals. The Equal Protection Clause does not permit race-based suspicion.

Much evidence was introduced regarding inadequate monitoring and supervision of unconstitutional stops. Supervisors routinely review the *productivity* of officers, but do not review the facts of a stop to determine whether it was legally warranted. Nor do supervisors ensure that an officer has made a proper record of a stop so that it can be reviewed for constitutionality. Deficiencies were also shown in the training of officers with respect to stop and frisk and in the disciplining of officers when they were found to have made a bad stop or frisk. Despite the mounting evidence that many bad stops were made, that officers failed to make adequate records of stops, and that discipline was spotty or non-existent, little has been done to improve the situation.

One example of poor training is particularly telling. Two officers testified to their understanding of the term "furtive movements." One explained that "furtive movement is a very broad concept," and could include a person "changing direction," "walking in a certain way," "[a]cting a little suspicious," "making a movement that is not regular," being "very fidgety," "going in and out of his pocket," "going in and out of a location," "looking back and forth constantly," "looking over their shoulder," "adjusting their hip or their belt," "moving in and out of a car too quickly," "[t]urning a part of their body away from you," "[g]rabbing at a certain pocket or something at their waist," "getting a little nervous, maybe shaking," and "*stutter[ing]*." Another officer explained that "usually" a furtive movement is someone "hanging out in front of [a] building, sitting on the benches or something like that" and then making a "quick movement," such as "bending down and quickly standing back up," "going inside the lobby ... and then quickly coming back out," or "all of a sudden becom[ing] very nervous, very aware." If officers believe that the behavior described above constitutes furtive movement that justifies a stop, then it is no surprise that stops so rarely produce evidence of criminal activity.

I now summarize my findings with respect to the individual stops that were the subject of testimony at trial. Twelve plaintiffs testified regarding nineteen stops. In twelve of those stops, both the plaintiffs and the officers testified. In seven stops no officer testified, either because the officers could not be identified or because the officers dispute that the stop ever occurred. I find that nine of the stops and frisks were unconstitutional—that is, they were not based on reasonable suspicion. I also find that while five other stops were constitutional, the frisks following those stops were unconstitutional. Finally, I find that plaintiffs have failed to prove an unconstitutional stop (or frisk) in five of the nineteen stops. The individual stop testimony corroborated much of the evidence about the NYPD's policies and practices with respect to carrying out and monitoring stops and frisks.

In making these decisions I note that evaluating a stop in hindsight is an imperfect procedure. Because there is no contemporaneous recording of the stop (such as could be achieved through the use of a body-worn camera), I am relegated to finding facts based on the often conflicting testimony of eyewitnesses. This task is not easy, as every witness has an interest in the outcome of the case, which may consciously or unconsciously affect the veracity of his or her testimony. Nonetheless, a judge is tasked with making decisions and I judged the evidence of each stop to the best of my ability. I am also aware that a judge deciding whether a stop is constitutional, with the time to reflect and consider all of the evidence, is in a far different position than officers on the street who must make split-second decisions in situations that may pose a danger to themselves or others. I respect that police officers have chosen a profession of public service involving dangers and challenges with few parallels in civilian life.

In conclusion, I find that the City is liable for violating plaintiffs' Fourth and Fourteenth Amendment rights. The City acted with deliberate indifference toward the NYPD's practice of making unconstitutional stops and conducting unconstitutional frisks. Even if the City had not been deliberately indifferent, the NYPD's unconstitutional practices were sufficiently widespread as to have the force of law. In addition, the City adopted a policy of indirect racial profiling by targeting racially defined groups for stops based on local crime suspect data. This has resulted in the disproportionate and discriminatory stopping of blacks and Hispanics in violation of the Equal Protection Clause. Both statistical and anecdotal evidence showed that minorities are indeed treated differently than whites. For example, once a stop is made, blacks and Hispanics are more likely to be subjected to the use of force than whites, despite the fact that whites are more likely to be found with weapons or contraband. I also conclude that the City's highest officials have turned a blind eye to the evidence that officers are conducting stops in a racially discriminatory manner. In their zeal to defend a policy that they believe to be effective, they have willfully ignored overwhelming proof that the policy of targeting "the right people" is racially discriminatory and therefore violates the United States Constitution. One NYPD official has even suggested that it is permissible to stop racially defined groups just to instill fear in them that they are subject to being stopped at any time for any reason—in the hope that this fear will deter them from carrying guns in the streets. The goal of deterring crime is laudable, but this method of doing so is unconstitutional.

I recognize that the police will deploy their limited resources to high crime areas. This benefits the communities where the need for policing is greatest. But the police are not permitted to target people for stops based on their race. Some may worry about the implications of this decision. They may wonder: if the police believe that a particular group of people is disproportionately responsible for crime in one area, why should the police *not* target that group with increased stops? Why should it matter if the group is defined in part by race? Indeed, there are contexts in which the Constitution permits considerations of race in law enforcement operations. What is clear, however, is that the Equal Protection Clause prohibits the practices described in *this* case. A police department may not target a racially defined group for stops *in general*—that is, for stops based on suspicions of general criminal wrongdoing—simply because members of that group appear frequently in the police department's suspect data. The Equal Protection Clause does not permit the police to target a racially defined group as a whole because of the misdeeds of some of its members.

To address the violations that I have found, I shall order various remedies including, but not limited to, an immediate change to certain policies and activities of the NYPD, a trial program requiring the use of body-worn cameras in one precinct per borough, a community-based joint remedial process to be conducted by a court-appointed facilitator, and the appointment of an independent monitor to ensure that the NYPD's conduct of stops and frisks is carried out in accordance with the Constitution and the principles enunciated in this Opinion, and to monitor the NYPD's compliance with the ordered remedies.

....

Targeting "the Right People"

The role of race in stop and frisk has been a source of contention since the Supreme Court first sanctioned the practice in 1968. In *Terry*, the Supreme Court recognized that " '[i]n many communities, field interrogations are a major source of friction between the police and minority groups,' " and that friction " 'increases as more police departments [encourage] officers ... routinely to stop and question persons on the street.' " In 1996, the Ninth Circuit noted that these stops "are humiliating, damaging to the detainees' self-esteem, and reinforce the reality that racism and intolerance are for many African–Americans a regular part of their daily lives."

The NYPD maintains two different policies related to racial profiling in the practice of stop and frisk: a written policy that prohibits racial profiling and requires reasonable suspicion for a stop—and another, unwritten policy that encourages officers to focus their reasonable-suspicion-based stops on "the right people, the right time, the right location."

Based on the evidence summarized below, I find that the NYPD's policy of targeting "the right people" encourages the disproportionate stopping of the members of any racial group that is heavily represented in the NYPD's crime suspect data. This is an indirect form of racial profiling. In practice, it leads NYPD officers to stop blacks and Hispanics who would not have been stopped if they were white. There is no question that a person's race, like a person's height or weight, is a permissible consideration where a stop is based on a specific description of a suspect. But it is equally clear that it is impermissible to subject all members of a racially defined group to heightened police enforcement because some members of that group appear more frequently in criminal complaints. The Equal Protection Clause does not permit race-based suspicion.

Chief Esposito, the highest ranking uniformed member of the NYPD throughout the class period and the chair at Compstat meetings, was especially frank about the NYPD's policy of targeting racially defined groups for stops, provided that reasonable suspicion is also present:

Q. Quality stops are stops that are in the right place at the right time, correct?

A. Yes.

Q. And targeting ... the right people, correct?

A. Among other things.

Q. And the right people would be young black and Hispanic youths 14 to 20, correct?

A. At times. [pause] You failed to mention reasonable suspicion.

Chief Esposito conceded that not all stops are based on a specific suspect description from a crime complaint. In fact, officers check "Fits Description" on only 13% of UF–250s. Nevertheless, Esposito testified, the NYPD uses criminal suspect data to target certain individuals for stops even when there is no suspect description:

Q: Do you believe the disparity in stop, question and frisk among black and Latino men is evidence of racial profiling?

A: No. I don't believe that.... Because the stops are based on complaints that we get from the public.

...

THE COURT: But there are many street stops that have nothing to do with complaints, right?

THE WITNESS: Correct.

THE COURT: It's observed conduct.... It's not based on a complaint of a victim.

THE WITNESS: It's based on the totality of, okay, who is committing the—who is getting shot in a certain area? ... *Well who is doing those shootings? Well, it's young men of color in their late teens, early 20s.*

Thus, within the pool of people that an officer could reasonably suspect of criminal activity, the people who match the general demographics of the local criminal suspect data are "the right people" to be stopped.

Other evidence corroborates this interpretation of Chief Esposito's testimony. On one of the Serrano recordings, Deputy Inspector Christopher McCormack explained to Officer Serrano that stopping "the right people, [at] the right time, [in] the right location" meant not stopping "a 48–year–old lady [who] was walking through St. Mary's Park when it was closed." He continued as follows:

INSPECTOR: This is about stopping the right people, the right place, the right location.

SERRANO: Okay.

INSPECTOR: Again, take Mott Haven where we had the most problems. And the most problems we had, they was robberies and grand larcenies.

SERRANO: And who are those people robbing?

INSPECTOR: The problem was, what, male blacks. And I told you at roll call, and I have no problem telling you this, male blacks 14 to 20, 21. I said this at roll call.

Deputy Inspector McCormack testified that his statements in the recording were based on suspect descriptions from victims. But he also acknowledged that the descriptions of the suspects consisted only of the information stated here: males, black, between 14 and 21.

Earlier in the recording, when challenged by Officer Serrano, Deputy Inspector McCormack clarified that he does not believe "every black and Hispanic" is subject to being stopped based on the crime suspect data. Deputy Inspector McCormack, like Chief Esposito, recognized that reasonable suspicion is required for every stop. But both believe that, within the pool of people displaying reasonably suspicious behavior, those who fit the general race, gender, and age profile of the criminal suspects in the area should be particularly targeted for stops.

The stop of Cornelio McDonald illustrates the NYPD's policy of indirect racial profiling based on crime suspect data. Officer Edward French (now a detective) was aware of crime reports that a black male had been burglarizing residences in Queens, as well as reports of a black male committing armed robberies of commercial establishments in the borough. The only information known about the suspects in these robbery patterns was that they were male and black—a very general description that would not justify a stop based on "fits description." Nevertheless, Officer French stopped McDonald in part because he fit the suspect description. McDonald was a black man crossing the street late on a winter night with his hands in his pockets, and as a *black* man he was treated as more suspicious than an identically situated white man would have been. In other words, because two black males committed crimes in Queens, all black males in that borough were subjected to heightened police attention.

The UF–250s prepared by Officer Gonzalez, one of the most aggressive stoppers in 2009, provide a different illustration of an officer responding to the NYPD's policy of indirect racial profiling based on crime suspect data. Officer Gonzalez checked "Fits Description" on 132 of his

134 UF–250s, although he also indicated that not a single one of those stops was based on an ongoing investigation, a report from a victim, or a radio run. Nonetheless, Gonzalez's supervisor, then-Sergeant Charlton Telford, testified that he was not concerned by this discrepancy. Telford insisted that Officer Gonzalez's stops were based on "the race, the height, [and] the age" of criminal suspects. The following were the suspect descriptions that formed the basis for Officer Gonzalez's 134 stops:

> The burglaries, the description we had was a male Hispanic, between 5′ 8″, 5′9″, in his 30s. The robberies were male blacks, anywhere from four to five [in number], between the ages of 14 to 19. And the shooting was a male black in his 20s.

Perhaps as a result of Officer Gonzalez's reliance on this general suspect data, 128 of the 134 people he stopped were black or Hispanic. This is roughly in line with the percentage of criminal suspects in his precinct who are either black or Hispanic (93%), but far exceeds the percentage of blacks and Hispanics in the local population (60%). Thus, Officer Gonzalez's UF–250s provide a perfect example of how racial profiling leads to a correlation between the racial composition of crime suspects and the racial composition of those who are stopped by the police. By checking "Fits Description" as a basis for nearly every stop, Officer Gonzalez documented what appears to be a common practice among NYPD officers—treating generic crime complaint data specifying little more than race and gender as a basis for heightened suspicion.

New York State Senator Eric Adams' testimony provided further evidence of official acquiescence in racial profiling by NYPD leadership. Senator Adams, a former NYPD captain, testified about a small meeting he attended at the Governor's office in Manhattan in July 2010. Former New York Governor David Paterson, Senator Adams, another state senator, a state assemblyman, and Commissioner Kelly were all present to discuss a bill related to stop and frisk. Senator Adams raised his concern that a disproportionate number of blacks and Hispanics were being targeted for stops. Commissioner Kelly responded that he focused on young blacks and Hispanics "because he wanted to instill fear in them, every time they leave their home, they could be stopped by the police." Senator Adams testified that he was "amazed" that Commissioner Kelly was "comfortable enough to say that in the setting."

I find Senator Adams' testimony credible, especially in light of the Senator's former affiliation with the NYPD, Commissioner Kelly's decision not to appear at trial to rebut the testimony, the City's failure to offer *any* rebuttal evidence regarding Commissioner Kelly's statement at this meeting, and the other evidence of tolerance toward racial profiling at the NYPD. In fact, the substance of Commissioner Kelly's statement is not so distant from the City's publicly announced positions. Mayor Bloomberg stated in April that the NYPD's use of stop and frisk is necessary "to *deter* people from carrying guns.... [I]f you end stops looking for guns, ... there will be more guns in the hands of young people and more people will be getting killed." At the same time, the City emphasized in its opening arguments that "blacks and Hispanics account for a dispro-portionate share of ... crime perpetrators," and that "90 percent of all violent crime suspects are black and Hispanic." When these premises are combined—that the purpose of stop and frisk is to deter people from carrying guns and that blacks and Hispanics are a disproportionate source of violent crime—it is only a short leap to the conclusion that blacks and Hispanics should be targeted for stops in order to deter gun violence, regardless of whether they appear objectively suspicious. Commissioner Kelly simply made explicit what is readily inferrable from the City's public positions.

....

Unconstitutional Stop and Frisk

a. Leroy Downs

i. Findings of Fact

Leroy Downs is a black male resident of Staten Island in his mid-thirties. On the evening of August 20, 2008, Downs arrived home from work and, before entering his house, called a friend on his cell phone while standing in front of a chain link fence in front of his house. Downs used an earpiece connected to the phone by a cord, and held the cell phone in one hand and the black mouthpiece on the cord in the other.

Downs saw a black Crown Victoria drive past and recognized it as an unmarked police car. The car stopped, reversed, and double-parked in front of Downs's house, at which point Downs told his friend he would call back. Two white plainclothes officers, later identified as Officers Scott Giacona and James Mahoney, left the car and approached Downs. One officer said in an aggressive tone that it looked like Downs was smoking weed. They told him to "get the [fuck] against the fence," then pushed him backwards until his back was against the fence. Downs did not feel free to leave.

Downs explained that he was talking on his cell phone, not smoking marijuana, that he is a drug counselor, and that he knows the captain of the 120th Precinct. Without asking permission, the officers patted down the outside of his clothing around his legs and torso, reached into his front and back pants pockets and removed their contents: a wallet, keys, and a bag of cookies from a vending machine. The officers also searched his wallet.

After the officers failed to find any contraband, they started walking back to the car. Downs asked for their badge numbers. The officers "laughed [him] off" and said he was lucky they did not lock him up. Downs said he was going to file a complaint, and one of them responded by saying, "I'm just doing my [fucking] job." Charles Joseph, a friend of Downs who lives on the same block, witnessed the end of the stop. After the officers drove away, Downs walked to the 120th Precinct to file a complaint.

Downs told Officer Anthony Moon at the front desk that he wanted to make a complaint and described what had happened. Officer Moon said that he could not take the complaint because Downs did not have the officers' badge numbers, and that Downs should file a complaint with the CCRB. As Downs left the station he saw the two officers who stopped him driving out of the precinct in their Crown Victoria, and he wrote down its license plate number on his hand.

Downs then returned to the station. He tried to give Officer Moon the license plate information, but Officer Moon said that he should give the information to the CCRB instead. Downs waited at the station until he saw the two officers come through the back door with two young black male suspects.

Downs pointed out the two officers to Officer Moon and asked him, "Can you get their badge numbers?" Officer Moon talked to the officers and then told Downs "maybe you can ask them." At that point, Downs went outside again and took a picture of the license plate on the Crown Victoria, which was the same number he had written on his hand.

Eventually, Downs spoke with a supervisor, who said he would try to get the officers' badge numbers and then call Downs. The call never came. Having spent a few hours at the station, Downs went home.

The next day, Downs submitted a complaint to the CCRB. Five months later, Officers Mahoney and Giacona both testified under oath to the CCRB that they had no memory of stopping and frisking Downs—an assertion that was "not entirely credited" by the CCRB, because it is "unlikely that PO Giacona and PO Mahoney would not recall their actions immediately prior to effecting two arrests." The CCRB substantiated Downs's complaint that Officers Mahoney and Giacona failed to provide their badge numbers. The CCRB found the complaints that the officers stopped Downs without reasonable suspicion, and used profanity unsubstantiated. The CCRB found Downs's allegation of a search into his pants pockets "unfounded," based in part on Joseph's testimony that he did not witness a search. The CCRB substantiated the complaint against Officer Moon for failing to process Downs's complaint.

Neither Officer Mahoney nor Officer Giacona received any discipline as a result of the CCRB's recommendations. Instead, each lost five vacation days for failing to make a memo book entry for the Downs stop. They also failed to prepare a UF–250 for the stop, but received no discipline for this. Officer Mahoney has since been promoted to Sergeant.[443]

Officers Mahoney and Giacona testified that they have no recollection of the Downs stop. Like the CCRB, I do not find their denials of recollection credible.

Downs testified that he has been stopped "[m]any times" other than the stop on August 20, 2008.

ii. Mixed Findings of Fact and Law

Downs was stopped when the officers told him to "get the [fuck] against the fence." The officers lacked reasonable suspicion to stop Downs. The officers seized Downs based on a glimpse of a small object in Downs's hand from the window of their passing car. The officers' hunch, unaided by any effort to confirm that what they glimpsed was contraband, was too unreliable, standing alone, to serve as a basis for a *Terry* stop.

Moreover, whatever legal justification the officers might have had for the stop dissipated shortly after they approached Downs. The absence of any physical evidence, smoke or marijuana smell, and Downs's explanation that he was talking on his mouthpiece, negated any ground for reasonable suspicion. Just as an officer may not reach into the pocket of a suspect after a frisk has negated the possibility that the pocket contains a dangerous weapon or immediately perceptible contraband, so an officer may not persist in stopping a person after the suspicion giving rise to the stop has been negated. Officers Mahoney and Giacona violated Downs's rights under the Fourth Amendment by stopping him based on a hunch, and continuing to detain him after it became clear that he had not been smoking marijuana.

The officers further violated the Fourth Amendment by frisking Downs without any objective basis for suspecting that he was armed and dangerous. Nothing about the suspected infraction—marijuana use—in combination with the facts summarized above provides reasonable suspicion that Downs was armed and dangerous.

The officers further violated Downs's Fourth Amendment rights by searching his pockets and wallet after the frisk. Such a search would only have been justified if the officers' frisk of the outer surfaces of Downs's pockets gave rise to reasonable suspicion that his pockets contained a dangerous weapon, or if the frisk made it *immediately apparent* that an object in his pockets was a form of contraband. Nothing in Downs's pockets could have provided reasonable suspicion that he was armed; nor could it have been immediately apparent from the patdown that Downs's pockets contained contraband.

b. Devin Almonor

i. Findings of Fact

Devin Almonor is a sixteen-year-old black male high school student living in Manhattan. In 2010, Almonor was thirteen years old. He was approximately five foot ten and weighed approximately 150 pounds.

On March 20, 2010, a Saturday, around 8:45 p.m., Almonor left his house to walk his friend Levon Loggins to the bus stop at 145th Street and Amsterdam. After Loggins boarded the bus, Almonor began to walk home along Hamilton Place toward a bodega where he planned to meet his brother Malik. A group of males was standing outside the bodega and, after talking to friends outside, Almonor continued home with another individual.

Around 10:00 p.m., Officer Brian Dennis and Sergeant Jonathan Korabel were driving an unmarked vehicle in the vicinity of Hamilton Place in response to nine 911 calls describing a group of about forty youths fighting, throwing garbage cans, and setting off car alarms. A few calls indicated the possibility that weapons were involved. The calls suggested that the youths were dispersing when marked cars arrived and then returning. When the officers arrived at Hamilton Place there were garbage cans in the middle of the street and car alarms still going off. The only description they had of the individuals was that they were young black males.

The officers briefly observed Almonor and another individual walking on Hamilton Place in the direction from which the calls originated. The individuals crossed 141st Street. The officers—two white males in plainclothes—pulled up alongside Almonor, at which point Almonor retreated onto the sidewalk. After the officers exited the car and approached Almonor, Officer Dennis grabbed Almonor's arm and said: "Police." Almonor pulled away and within moments, Officer Dennis pushed Almonor down on the hood of the police car because he was not "satisfied [that Almonor] did not have something in his waist."

Together the officers handcuffed Almonor Without explanation, Officer Dennis patted Almonor down from his feet to his torso, during which Almonor was saying, "What are you doing? I'm going home. I'm a kid." The officers did not recover anything—Almonor only had a cell phone in his right front pocket and a few dollars.

The officers did not ask Almonor his name until after he was handcuffed. Almonor did not have ID but identified himself as "Devin Al."Almonor told the officers that he was thirteen years old and was going home, which was a few blocks away.At some point, though not initially, Almonor gave the officers his full address The officers did not ask for Almonor's phone number or whether his parents were home—instead the officers put Almonor in the back of the patrol car, took him to the precinct, and placed him in the juvenile room because of the possibility that he was thirteen.

After Almonor was released, Officer Dennis completed a handwritten UF 250 form and a juvenile report. The suspected crime was criminal possession of a weapon, and the circumstances of the stop indicated on the form were "fits description" and "furtive movements." The "suspicious bulge" box was not checked and Officer Dennis testified that he did not see a suspicious bulge that night. No contemporaneous document noted that Almonor was touching his waistband.The juvenile report form indicated that Almonor was "resisting arrest," although Almonor was never arrested. The next morning, Officer Dennis filled out a computerized UF–250 and another juvenile report worksheet, both of which noted a suspicious bulge.

ii. Mixed Findings of Fact and Law

Almonor was stopped when the officers approached him on the sidewalk, and Officer Dennis grabbed Almonor's arm and said: "Police." Even if credited, Almonor's alleged furtive movements—looking over his shoulder and jaywalking—in combination with the generic description of young black male does not establish the requisite individualized suspicion that Almonor was engaged in criminal activity. The officers could have approached Almonor and asked him some questions, but instead chose to physically restrain and handcuff him first, and ask questions later. The circumstances did not justify any restraint of Almonor's liberty, much less immediate physical restraint and the use of handcuffs.

Even if the officers had possessed the requisite basis to stop Almonor—which they did not—they had no basis to frisk him. While some of the 911 calls suggested that some youths involved in the fighting may have had weapons, that alone does not establish individualized suspicion that Almonor was armed and dangerous. No contemporaneous document indicates a suspicious bulge, and Almonor was not in possession of anything that would have created a suspicious bulge. Almonor's actions did not indicate that he was armed.

Finally, not only were Almonor's Fourth Amendment rights violated at the inception of both the stop and the frisk, but the officers made no effort to minimize the intrusion on his liberty. Instead, they used the most intrusive methods at their disposal, thereby exacerbating the violation of his rights.

c. Cornelio McDonald

i. Findings of Fact

Cornelio McDonald is a middle-aged black male who resides on Parsons Boulevard, in a private co-op apartment building in Queens. McDonald often cares for his mother who lives across the street from him in a New York City Housing Authority ("NYCHA") complex called Pomonok Houses.Parsons Boulevard is a wide street with a concrete island dividing two lanes and cars parked on both sides of each lane. The majority of residents on McDonald's side of the block are white, while the majority of residents on his mother's side of the block are black.

On December 18, 2009, a Friday, McDonald spent approximately ten hours at his mother's house and left her building around 1:00 a.m. Because the weather that night was below freezing, McDonald was wearing a zipped-up jacket, with his hands in his pockets the entire time he was crossing the street. He had his cell phone in his left jacket pocket, his keys in his right pants pocket, and his wallet in his back pocket. McDonald turned his body sideways to pass through the cars parked along the divider.

McDonald had crossed the first lane of Parsons Boulevard and was standing between two parked cars on the far side of the island, getting ready to cross the second lane, when he saw an unmarked red van with plainclothes individuals inside make a u-turn and pull up in front of him, trapping him between two parked cars.

The driver rolled down the window and, without identifying himself as police, asked McDonald where he was coming from, to which McDonald responded, "Why you stopping me for?" At that point both officers in the van, one of whom was Officer Edward French, and both of whom were white, stepped out of the car, identified themselves as police, and began to search McDonald without explanation. Officer French told McDonald to remove his hands from his pockets, patted down the outside of McDonald's pockets, asked McDonald to take out his keys—which McDonald did—placed his hand inside McDonald's pocket, and removed a cell phone. When McDonald asked why he was being frisked, the officer said he wanted to be sure McDonald did not have a weapon.

After conducting the frisk, which failed to produce any contraband, Officer French asked McDonald for ID. McDonald obliged and then asked for the officers' identification. Only Officer French identified himself and gave his shield number. McDonald was then permitted to leave. No summons was issued and the entire incident took seven to ten minutes.

On the UF–250, Officer French listed McDonald's suspected crime as criminal possession of a weapon. Officer French did not believe he needed to include the reason he suspected a person of a crime in his memo book—he believed that the reason for stopping a person was enough. At trial, however, Officer French testified that his suspicion was based on crime patterns and a suspicious bulge.

Officer French testified about three crime patterns. *First,* he made an arrest for armed robbery a month earlier in the general vicinity where he stopped McDonald. *Second,* he was aware of a robbery pattern somewhere in Queens on the night he stopped McDonald—specifically, a black male holding up commercial establishments. *Third,* he was aware that a black male had been burglarizing residential establishments in Queens, but could not be more specific about the location of the burglaries. The other explanation Officer French gave for his suspicion was his observation that McDonald had his hands in his pockets and was leaning to one side, and had a "suspicious bulge" in his left front pocket. I do not believe that Officer French saw a *suspicious* bulge.

McDonald believes that he was stopped based on his race because other, non-black individuals—whites or Asians—were coming out of a bowling alley about twenty-five feet from where he was stopped, and none of them were stopped.

ii. Mixed Findings of Fact and Law

McDonald was stopped when two officers pulled up to him in a police van, trapped him between two cars, and proceeded to question him. The officers made a u-turn and specifically targeted him in a manner that would not have made a reasonable person feel free to simply walk away.

The only articulated bases for the stop were the existence of highly generalized crime patterns involving black males—a month-old armed robbery, a robbery pattern *somewhere* in Queens and a burglary pattern *somewhere* in Queens—the fact that McDonald was walking with his hands in his pockets in December and a supposedly suspicious bulge, which turned out to be a cell phone. "[P]resence in an area of expected criminal activity, standing alone, is not enough to support a reasonable, particularized suspicion that the person is committing a crime." Moreover, a crime area defined as the entire borough of Queens is far too broad to contribute to a totality of the circumstances establishing reasonable suspicion, let alone to form the sole basis. This, combined with the vague description of "black males" and the entirely unsuspicious act of putting one's hands in one's pockets in the wintertime, is a far cry from the *individualized* suspicion of wrongdoing that constitutes reasonable suspicion. Absent any other justification, there was no basis for a *Terry* stop, and there was certainly no basis to believe that McDonald was armed and dangerous.

I also find that McDonald was stopped because of his race. The only suspect description was "black male," the street was racially stratified, and other non-black individuals were present and presumably behaving no differently than McDonald—yet only McDonald was stopped. In sum, McDonald was stopped, in violation of the Fourth and Fourteenth Amendments, because he was a black man crossing the street late at night in Queens.

d. Nicholas Peart—August 5, 2006

i. Findings of Fact

Nicholas Peart is a twenty-four-year-old black resident of Harlem. He is the legal guardian of three younger siblings and works for a non-profit organization as an after-school program facilitator. On August 5, 2006, around 5:00 a.m., Peart was with his cousin and a friend, both of whom are also black, after celebrating his eighteenth birthday at his sister's house.It was dark out and Peart was wearing light blue basketball shorts and a white—or black and white—tank top. At least one of the men was wearing a hat.

Peart and his companions were standing in the median at 96th and Broadway when three marked police cars pulled up on 96th Street. Approximately five uniformed officers exited the cars with their guns drawn. Officer White stated: "Police. Don't move. Let me see your hands" and, when the men did not immediately show their hands, ordered them to get down on the ground. Peart and his companions protested but eventually obeyed the order. Once Peart was on the ground, Officer White patted him down over his shorts and in the groin area and buttocks, without consent. Officer White also frisked the other two men

After frisking the men, Officer White told them to stand up and asked for ID. In response to Peart's inquiries about why they were stopped, Officer White played the radio call three times to show that the men fit the description in the radio call. The dispatcher's report described a call coming from a payphone at 96th and Broadway about three black males—one carrying a firearm and wearing blue pants and a black shirt, and two others wearing blue and white tank tops, shorts and red hats—walking uptown on Broadway toward 98th Street.After hearing the radio run, Peart and his companions were free to leave.[514] However, they continued to ask why they had been stopped, and stated their belief that the only reason they were stopped was because they were black.

Following the stop, Peart filed a complaint with the CCRB. He declined to state his race in filing the complaint. Over a year later, Peart received a letter informing him that the officers had been exonerated.

The officers who stopped Peart and his friends were responding to a radio run based on a report from an anonymous caller. The officers stopped the three men because they resembled the description relayed by the dispatcher and were in the same location from which the call had been made only minutes before. Based on the descriptions from the radio run, Officer White believed he had stopped the right people, although no weapons were found.

Officer White completed three UF–250s after the stop. He checked the boxes for "fits description" and "suspicious bulge." As reasons for the frisk, he listed violent crime suspected, suspicious bulge, and refusal to comply with directions (relating to the command that the men show their hands and get on the ground).On each form Officer White noted that the "bulge in pocket" had in fact been a cell phone. As additional circumstances, Officer White noted "report from victim witness" and "proximity to crime location." However, nothing about the radio run suggested that the caller was a victim rather than a mere observer.

ii. Mixed Findings of Fact and Law

Peart and his companions were stopped when the officers exited their car with guns drawn. Although it is a close call, I am constrained by controlling Supreme Court law to find that the officers lacked reasonable suspicion to forcibly stop the men. In *Florida v. J.L.*, the Supreme Court held that "an anonymous caller['s report] that a young black male standing at a particular bus stop and wearing a plaid shirt was carrying a gun" did not establish reasonable suspicion for a stop and frisk. The Court held that "reasonable suspicion ... requires that a tip be reliable in its assertion of illegality, not just in its tendency to identify a determinate person." The Court rejected an exception for reports of firearms, explaining that "[s]uch an exception would enable any person seeking to harass another to set in motion an intrusive, embarrassing police search of the targeted person simply by placing an anonymous call falsely reporting the target's unlawful carriage of a gun." *Florida v. J.L.* makes clear that a suspect description from an anonymous caller cannot by itself justify the forcible stop and frisk of Peart and his companions. Although the Second Circuit held that a 911 call reporting that an assault (or any crime for that matter) was in progress would require less corroboration, the calls here did not indicate that an assault was in progress.

The only additional factor cited as the basis for the stop was the bulges in the men's waistband area. The only items recovered from the frisk were cell phones. Because the men were wearing minimal clothing, it would be difficult to mistake a cell phone for a firearm. Moreover, to conclude that the bulge created by the now ubiquitous cell phone can provide the additional corroboration necessary to justify an invasive stop and frisk would eliminate the corroboration requirement entirely.

I do not find credible the assertion that the officers saw any *suspicious* bulges that would corroborate the anonymous caller's statement that the men stopped were armed. Rather, I find that they stopped the men solely on the basis of the description in the radio run. No other factor establishes reasonable suspicion for the highly intrusive stop. Because there was no legally sufficient justification for the stop, the frisk was also unconstitutional.

e. Nicholas Peart—April 13, 2011 Stop

i. Findings of Fact

On April 13, 2011, around 11:00 p.m., Peart was walking on 144th Street between Lenox and Seventh Avenue—the block on which he resides—on his way to the corner store. Peart was wearing sneakers, jeans and a red hooded sweatshirt. He was sending a text message while walking when two uniformed officers appeared directly in front of him. One officer was white, shorter than Peart, and wore glasses ("Officer A"). The other officer was roughly Peart's height and had salt-and-pepper hair ("Officer B").

One of the officers took Peart's cell phone and instructed Peart to put his hands up against the wall of a church. Officer A patted Peart down outside his clothing over his entire body and put his hands in his pockets. Officer B also put his hands in Peart's pockets, removed Peart's keys and wallet, and searched the wallet for ID. Officer B did not ask permission to search the wallet and Peart did not consent. During the search Peart asked, "why is this happening?" In response to questions about what building he was coming from, he explained that he was coming from his apartment in the Frederick Samuel House, which is a NYCHA building.

Officer A then grabbed Peart's sweatshirt with his fist near Peart's chest area and handcuffed him. Officer B, who had Peart's keys, asked which key opened Peart's door, and Peart identified the key in order to prove that he lived where he said he did. He did not give Officer B permission to enter the apartment, but Officer B entered the building and remained for about five minutes.

While Officer B was in the building, Officer A, who was still holding Peart's sweatshirt, placed Peart, still handcuffed, in the back of an unmarked police vehicle parked in front of the church. Officer A removed Peart's sneakers, patted down his socks and asked Peart if he had weed on him. Peart said he did not. Eventually, Officer B came out of Peart's building. The officers opened the car, let Peart out, removed the handcuffs, and returned his keys, phone and wallet. The officers explained that Peart fit the description of someone who had been ringing a doorbell at the Frederick Samuel House. Peart was then free to go.

ii. Mixed Findings of Fact and Law

Peart was stopped when the officers blocked his path and told him to put his arms against the wall. The stated reason for the stop was that he fit a suspect description of someone who was ringing doorbells in NYCHA housing. While I cannot know from Peart's testimony whether the description he allegedly fit was sufficiently detailed to form the basis for reasonable suspicion, the stop the officers conducted was not justified by the circumstances. The officers had every right to ask Peart whether he lived in the Frederick Samuel House—a question he could have answered easily. Instead, they forced him up against a wall and handcuffed him.

The officers violated Peart's Fourth Amendment rights by frisking him, going into his pockets and searching his wallet. The officers further abused their authority—and Peart's rights—when Officer B took Peart's keys and entered his apartment without permission while Officer A continued to search Peart and question him about drugs.

f. Ian Provost

i. Findings of Fact

Ian Provost is a forty-two-year-old black male who currently resides in North Carolina but lived in Queens from 1978 to 2011. On November 24, 2009, Provost was at his girlfriend's apartment in the Seth Low Houses at 365 Sackman Street in Brooklyn, which is a NYCHA housing project with a high crime rate. Provost had a key to access the apartment and the front door lock was broken. That day Provost had been doing odd jobs around his girlfriend's apartment, which involved tools including a knife with a four-inch blade.

Provost left his girlfriend's apartment around 2:15 p.m. to get food at a restaurant across the street on Belmont Avenue. He was wearing jeans, a hooded sweatshirt and a down jacket, which did not cover his back pockets, and was carrying the knife in his right back pocket. As he reached the corner of Belmont and Sackman, Provost saw two uniformed police officers, since identified as Jonathan Rothenberg and David Furman. After he passed them, Officer Rothenberg said "excuse me," and Provost stopped and turned around. The officers asked if Provost was from around there, where he was going, and where he was coming from. Provost responded that he was from Queens and that he was coming from a friend's house. When Officer Rothenberg asked where he was going, Provost responded that it was not the officer's business which led to an argument about whether the officer had the right to question Provost's comings and goings. Provost said, "you have no reason to stop me. This is harassment." Officer Rothenberg told Provost he was being stopped for criminal trespass.

Provost tried to use his cell phone and Officer Rothenberg commanded him not to. When Provost asked why, Officer Rothenberg said that he did not like people using their cell phones when he was talking to them. When Provost attempted to use his cell phone a second time, Officer Rothenberg grabbed his right hand, which was holding the cell phone, handcuffed him, and pushed him up against the fence.As he was being handcuffed, Provost repeated Officer Rothenberg's name and badge number so he could remember it to file a complaint. Provost also yelled out to his girlfriend in hopes that she would hear him from her apartment.

After Provost was handcuffed, Officer Rothenberg frisked him. Provost informed Officer Rothenberg that he had a knife and told him which pocket it was in. After retrieving the knife from Provost's pocket, Officer Rothenberg called Sergeant Houlahan. Officer Rothenberg then searched Provost's person and looked through Provost's cell phone.

When Sergeant Houlahan arrived, he felt it was unsafe to stay on the street where crowds sometimes gathered and became violent, so he instructed the officers to put Provost in his car and then drove him to the precinct.After the officers determined that the knife was not a gravity knife, Provost was given a summons for carrying a knife with a blade exceeding four inches and a summons for disorderly conduct for being loud and boisterous.

Officer Rothenberg's memo book entry for the stop reflected that he had stopped Provost for possible criminal trespass, but did not include any information about the circumstances leading to the stop. Rothenberg had observed Provost going in and out of the Seth Low Buildings and did not observe him use a key, but Rothenberg acknowledged that he did not have reasonable suspicion to believe that Provost was engaged in criminal trespass. Officer Rothenberg testified that he observed an inch or two of a knife handle sticking out of Provost's pocket when Provost approached the corner where he and another officer were standing, and that this was the reason for his stop.

Provost filed a CCRB complaint after the incident and was interviewed. The complaint was not substantiated. Provost does not believe that the officers saw the knife before he informed them that he was carrying it, which occurred after the stop but before the frisk.

ii. Mixed Findings of Fact and Law

Provost was stopped when Officer Rothenberg informed him that he was being stopped on suspicion of criminal trespass, and possibly earlier. Whether the stop was unlawful turns on whether I credit Officer Rothenberg's testimony that he stopped Provost because he saw the knife in his right back pants pocket. I do not. While it is plausible that an officer would delay handcuffing and frisking an individual suspected of possessing a gravity knife, the testimony suggests that Officer Rothenberg had not, in fact, seen the knife when he first stopped Provost. In particular, the fact that Officer Rothenberg wrote in his memo book—the only contemporaneous record of the stop—that he stopped Provost for possible criminal trespass rather than not possession of a weapon, suggests that the knife was not the original reason for the stop.

In light of this conclusion, there was no basis to stop Provost on suspicion of criminal trespass. Going in and out of his girlfriend's building is not in and of itself suspicious behavior and, without more, does not rise to the level of reasonable suspicion. Handcuffing and then frisking Provost was also unreasonable. Although Officer Rothenberg's actions may have been influenced by the fact that he had been assaulted in the area on a prior occasion, nothing in Provost's actions—arguing about his right not to disclose where he was coming from, reaching for his cell phone while stating that he was reaching for his cell phone—suggested that he presented a sufficient threat to warrant handcuffing him. The frisk was unreasonable for the same reason, particularly in light of the fact that Provost was already handcuffed and could not have harmed Officer Rothenberg or anyone else.

g. David Ourlicht—January 30, 2008 Stop

i. Findings of Fact

David Ourlicht is a twenty-five-year-old male of mixed black and white heritage who grew up and currently lives in Manhattan. At the time of his testimony Ourlicht was applying for admission to law school. On January 30, 2008, Ourlicht was enrolled at St. John's University in Queens. Around 2:00 p.m., he left school and walked his girlfriend to her job. Ourlicht then began walking north on 164th Street to a deli near his dorm. He was wearing a black down Marmot jacket, a sweatshirt, jeans and sneakers. The jacket had six pockets which held Ourlicht's keys, cell phone, wallet, passport, ipod, pens, and a five-subject notebook. Most of the items were in the jacket's interior pockets, but the notebook lay flat in one of the front external pockets, with about twenty-five percent sticking out of the pocket.

As Ourlicht was walking up 164th Street, he saw a uniformed officer, Christopher Moran, on a police scooter drive past him from behind. They made brief eye contact but Ourlicht kept walking. When Ourlicht reached the intersection where Officer Moran's scooter was stopped,

Officer Moran asked what Ourlicht was doing in the area and where he was going. Ourlicht did not feel free to leave.

Officer Moran left the scooter and asked Ourlicht for ID, to which Ourlicht responded, "why are you stopping me?" Officer Moran asked whether Ourlicht went to school around there, and Ourlicht said, "why are you asking me this?" Officer Moran again asked for ID and Ourlicht asked, "why do you need to see ID? What did I do?" in an irritated way. Officer Moran responded that it looked like Ourlicht had a gun on him, and proceeded to pat down his waist area. Officer Moran did not reach into Ourlicht's pockets.

As soon as Officer Moran told Ourlicht he suspected him of having a gun, Ourlicht asked if he could give him his ID, and then reached into the inside breast pocket of his jacket and handed Officer Moran his passport and his St. John's student ID. Officer Moran recorded Ourlicht's information at which point Ourlicht said, "now that you have my information do you mind if I take down yours?" Officer Moran said sure, and Ourlicht made clear that he was going to reach into his pocket to get a pen and paper and began to write down Officer Moran's badge number, nameplate, and scooter number.

Officer Moran had radioed for backup and a patrol car pulled up. Officer Moran then said, "okay now you're going to get the full treatment, get against the wall." Two uniformed police officers got out of the car. Ourlicht faced the wall with his hands behind his head and the officers proceeded to pull everything out of his jacket pockets and reached into his jeans pockets, which were empty. The officers instructed Ourlicht to sit on the ground, which he did, while Officer Moran returned to the scooter with Ourlicht's ID.

Officer Moran returned and asked Ourlicht for his address, which Ourlicht provided, and Officer Moran accused him of lying. Ourlicht then provided his mailing address, which was different from his residence—a college dorm. Moran wrote Ourlicht a ticket for disorderly conduct. When Ourlicht learned what the ticket was for he said "that's fucked up" and "I'm going to fight this." Ourlicht was then free to go. The summons was dismissed. Ourlicht's mother filed a CCRB complaint regarding the stop.

Officer Moran observed Ourlicht for no more than two minutes—as he approached Ourlicht on the scooter and after he passed him, from his rearview mirror. Officer Moran believed Ourlicht was "blading" the right side of his body in order to protect something in his right waist area that was preventing him from taking normal steps. Officer Moran claimed he saw an object running from Ourlicht's hip along his ribs. Based on that and the way Ourlicht was walking, Officer Moran decided to stop him.

Officer Moran completed a UF–250 in connection with the stop of Ourlicht. He checked the "suspicious bulge" box but did not identify what the bulge ultimately was. Officer Moran noted in his memo book that he stopped a male around 2:15 p.m. based on a suspicious bulge, and issued a summons. No other details about the stop were recorded.

ii. Mixed Findings of Fact and Law

Ourlicht was stopped when Officer Moran confronted him on the sidewalk and began questioning him—and certainly when the men began to argue about Officer Moran's authority to demand information about Ourlicht's comings and goings. The only articulated basis for the stop was the "blading." Even if Officer Moran saw Ourlicht walking strangely because he had a five-subject notebook in his pocket, that is insufficient to form a "reasonable, particularized suspicion that the person is committing a crime." Nothing else about the circumstances provided added basis for suspicion. It was daytime and Ourlicht made eye contact with Officer Moran, and did not attempt to evade his presence.

I also do not find that Officer Moran reasonably believed that Ourlicht was armed and dangerous. The five-subject notebook, the only item that could have been the object that supposedly caused Officer Moran to believe Ourlicht was armed, could not be confused for a gun, and, in fact, would be easily identifiable as a notebook. Therefore, I also find that the first frisk was unreasonable.

[72] [73] Even if the first frisk were justified, the search when the other officers arrived was not justified because Moran had already frisked Ourlicht and found nothing. Nothing that Ourlicht did after the initial stop justified Moran's suspicion that Ourlicht was hiding "something," much less that he was hiding a weapon. *Terry*'s authorization of "strictly circumscribed" protective searches contemplated that evidence of criminal conduct might be missed, but concluded that the Constitution did not permit a more intrusive search absent probable cause.

h. Clive Lino—February 5, 2008 Stop

i. Findings of Fact

Clive Lino is a thirty-two-year-old black resident of the Bronx. He works as a social worker at a non-profit faith-based organization. Lino is about five foot ten and weighs about 175 pounds.

On February 5, Officer Brian Kovall, who is white, and Officer Edward Arias, who is black, learned during roll call of a robbery pattern involving two black males, one wearing a beige or yellow coat and the other wearing a blue or black coat, committing gunpoint robberies in the vicinity of a check-cashing location near 103rd Street and Lexington Avenue, a high crime area. The height range for the suspects was five foot six to six foot two, the weight range was 170 to 200 pounds, and the age range was mid-twenties. Officer Kovall watched a video of the two suspects running, which was taken around noon on January 30.

Around 8:00 p.m. on February 5, Lino and his friend James went to pick up takeout from a Chinese restaurant at 103rd Street and Lexington Avenue. At the time, Lino lived just two blocks from the restaurant. Lino and James ordered food and were waiting outside the restaurant facing the street. Lino was wearing a tan State Property-brand jacket and James was wearing the same jacket in a greenish color.

As Lino and James waited outside for their food, Officers Kovall and Arias approached and ordered Lino and James to take their hands out of their pockets, which they did after several requests. The officers asked the men what they were doing on the corner, where they were going, where they were coming from, where they lived, and if they had ID. Lino said he did not have ID because he had just come from his apartment to get food and was going right back there. Lino and James were not free to leave.

The officers informed Lino and James that they were stopped because they fit the description of armed robbery suspects. Officer Arias stated that they had orders to stop anyone on that particular corner whenever they felt like it. Officer Arias frisked Lino's pockets and waist but did not reach inside his pockets. The officers obtained Lino and James's names and addresses.

The officers called their supervising Lieutenant to come down and confirm whether these men were the robbery suspects, which took five to ten minutes. During that time, Officer Kovall permitted Lino to enter the restaurant and get the food because Officer Kovall was "satisfied that there were absolutely no weapons on either individual."

After Lino returned with the food, Lieutenant Gaglio and two other officers arrived in plain-clothes. Lino knew they were officers because "they spoke to the officers who were already there, and they were able to have access to us." After asking the same questions that Officers Kovall and Arias had asked, Lieutenant Gaglio told Officer Kovall and Arias that these were not the men.Lieutenant Gaglio told Officers Kovall and Arias to run the men's names. While they were doing so, one of the plainclothes officers frisked Lino again.

Officers Kovall and Arias returned and reported a summons that Lino and James had received in January. The plainclothes officers left and Lino asked Kovall and Arias for their badge numbers. Officer Kovall provided his name and badge number, while Officer Arias just walked away. Lino was then free to go. He did not receive a summons and was not arrested.

Following the stop, Lino filed a complaint with the CCRB, which was unsubstantiated. Lino believed he and James were stopped because of their race.

The officers stopped the men because their coats matched the description in the robbery pattern—one light coat and one dark coat. In addition, the officers observed Lino and James standing outside on a cold night in the vicinity of the robberies, and they were still there after the officers circled the block and returned. Officer Arias frisked Lino because the suspected crime was armed robbery.

Officer Kovall filled out a UF–250 after stopping Lino. Under circumstances that led to the stop he checked "Fits Description"; "Area Has High Incidence Of Reported Offense Of Type Under Investigation"; and "Time Of Day, Day Of Week, Season Corresponding To Reports Of Criminal Activity" because of "Ongoing Investigations, e.g. Robbery Pattern." As the reason for the frisk, Officer Kovall checked "Violent Crime Suspected" and "Knowledge Of Suspect's Prior

Criminal Violent Behavior/Use of Force/Use of Weapon," to refer to the fact that he was looking for an armed robbery suspect. "Refusal To Comply With Officer's Directions" was also checked, in reference to Officer Kovall's initial instruction to Lino to remove his hands from his pockets.

ii. Mixed Findings of Fact and Law

Lino and James were stopped when the officers approached and told them to remove their hands from their pockets. Although it is a close question, I find that the officers lacked reasonable suspicion to forcibly stop Lino and James. The suspect description alone—two black men, of average height and weight, one wearing a light jacket and one wearing dark—is too generic to form the basis for reasonable suspicion, especially given the passage of time between the commission of the armed robberies and the stop of Lino and James.

The act of standing outside in the cold near the check-cashing location for the amount of time it took the officers to circle the block does not raise the totality of the circumstances to reasonable suspicion justifying a forcible stop of Lino and James. No other circumstances provided additional cause for suspicion. Furthermore, Officer Arias told Lino that the officers had orders to stop anyone on that corner whenever they felt like it. Such an order ignores the requirement of individualized, articulable suspicion, and Officer Arias' reference to it discredits the officers' assertions that they had the requisite suspicion in this instance. Thus, the initial stop of Lino violated his Fourth Amendment rights.

I note that the officers could easily have observed for a few minutes longer to determine whether there was an innocent explanation for this conduct—namely obtaining the food—at no cost to their safety or law enforcement objectives.Moreover, they would have been justified in approaching the men and asking them some questions—the equivalent of a *DeBour* level one stop. But the intrusion here was considerably more severe and included a frisk of the men's persons. The second frisk by the plainclothes officers further violated Lino's rights, as there was clearly no threat at that point that the men were armed and dangerous.

i. Lalit Clarkson

i. Findings of Fact

Lalit Clarkson is a thirty-one-year-old black male who works as a union organizer and lives in New Jersey, but visits New York frequently. When he was stopped in January, 2006, Clarkson worked as a teacher's assistant at Grand Concourse Academy, a school located at 169th Street in the Bronx. Clarkson was returning to the school after picking up lunch at a Subway around 1:00 p.m., wearing slacks, a tie, and a collared shirt. Clarkson entered a bodega on the corner of 169th and Walton, across from the school, holding a clear Subway bag containing a sandwich. He saw two plainclothes officers, one white and one Hispanic, standing in the back of the bodega, and assumed they were police because of the way they were standing and his experience in the neighborhood. Clarkson did not interact with the officers in the bodega. He purchased a food item, put it in his pocket and left the store.

As he was about to cross the street, he heard a voice say, "hey" and he turned around. The white officer said, "come over here, can I talk to you," and Clarkson went over. The officers showed their badges and identified themselves as police. The officers came closer to Clarkson so that eventually his back was against the bodega wall and the officers were standing between Clarkson and the street.

The officers told Clarkson they had seen him walk past a building down the block that they knew to be a drug building. Clarkson had walked past the building because it was on the route he took back to school, but had not stopped or spoken to anyone. The officers asked twice if Clarkson had any contraband on him, and he said he did not. Then they asked: "if I go in your pockets you don't have anything on you?" Again Clarkson said no. He did not consent to a search and the officers did not search him. The officers left after Clarkson said a third time that he had no contraband, and did not consent to be searched. The stop lasted a few minutes. At no point did Clarkson feel free to leave.

ii. Mixed Findings of Fact and Law

Clarkson was stopped when the officers called him over and surrounded him with his back against the wall. Although merely blocking a means of egress may not constitute a seizure where the police do not actually prevent a person from leaving, the act of surrounding an individual on the street against a wall is an intentional "assertion of authority to restrain a person's freedom of movement" sufficient to constitute a seizure.[629] Clarkson was not required to attempt to push past the officers in order to test whether or not he was, in fact, free to leave. Because the officers lacked reasonable suspicion to stop Clarkson where all he did was walk past a building known to be associated with drugs, this stop violated the Fourth Amendment.

2. Unconstitutional Frisk Only

a. Dominique Sindayiganza

i. Findings of Fact

Dominique Sindayiganza is a middle-aged, black male who resides in Queens with his wife and two daughters. In 2010, Sindayiganza worked at a non-profit organization in Manhattan. On February 12, 2010, Sindayiganza left his office at Lexington Avenue and 25th Street around

5:30 p.m. carrying a backpack and wearing dark blue rain pants and a green winter jacket. After running an errand in Union Square, he was walking along Broadway toward the F train at 14th Street and Sixth Avenue to go home. He entered Petco on the corner of Broadway and East 17th Street thinking it was a store that sold children's clothes. He quickly realized it was a pet store, and as he started to exit he heard someone say: "this is the guy." Four young white male uniformed officers, including Luke White and Sean Gillespie, surrounded him and forcibly escorted him out of the store.

Once outside, the officers surrounded Sindayiganza on the sidewalk and aggressively questioned him about what he was doing there, where he came from, and whether he was armed. The officers told him that a lady had identified him as the man who was following her and asking her for money. Sindayiganza replied that he was an educator, that he was buying supplies for a field trip and then going home to Queens, and that he had not followed any lady. He asked to see the woman so he could clear his name and was told he could not. At some point during this initial interaction, Officer White frisked Sindayiganza.

Officer White asked Sindayiganza for ID and then went into Petco to see if the woman could identify Sindayiganza as the harasser. The other officers continued to aggressively question Sindayiganza. The woman identified Sindayiganza and stated that she just wanted him to leave. Officer White went back outside and told Sindayiganza that he could go but that he had to walk north up Broadway. Sindayiganza asked if he could go to the 4 train or the F train, both of which were south, and was told he could not. Sindayiganza asked indignantly why, if he was free to go, he could not go to the train that would take him directly home. He was speaking loudly at this point, but was not yelling.

Officer White went back inside Petco and conferred with the woman who said she wanted Sindayiganza arrested. Officer White then told Sindayiganza that he was going to teach him a lesson and told him to put his hands against the wall, made him take off his backpack, handcuffed him, and forced him to sit down on the sidewalk. Another officer looked through Sindayiganza's backpack and removed items, and opened his jacket and searched his pockets, all without consent. When Sindayiganza asked why he was being arrested, the officers told him it was for "excessive panhandling." Sindayiganza was then taken in a police car to the precinct and given a summons for disorderly conduct, which was never prosecuted. Sindayiganza submitted a CCRB complaint online a day or two after the event and provided a sworn statement seven months later.

Officer White believed he had reasonable suspicion to stop Sindayiganza because he matched the woman's description—tall, light-skinned black male with dark hair, a big backpack, glasses, a green jacket, and green pants—and was in close proximity to the location of the incident. Officer White believed he had probable cause to arrest Sindayiganza for aggravated harassment based on the woman's allegations and identification. He further believed that once he handcuffed Sindayiganza, he had the right to search him incident to arrest. No arrest report was filled out and only a summons for disorderly conduct was issued.

ii. Mixed Findings of Law and Fact

Sindayiganza was stopped when the police surrounded him and escorted him outside. The police had reasonable suspicion to forcibly stop Sindayiganza for suspected harassment because he matched a specific description provided by an identified victim, and was in close proximity to the reported harassment just minutes after it allegedly occurred.

There was, however, no basis to frisk Sindayiganza. His stop was based on a woman's report that a man had been following her and asking her repeatedly for money, which caused her alarm. The woman never said she believed her harasser was armed, or that she had been physically threatened.

The frisk cannot be justified as a search incident to arrest that preceded the arrest. As a preliminary matter, the officers almost certainly lacked probable cause under New York law to arrest Sindayiganza. Based on the woman's allegations, Officer White at most had reasonable suspicion that Sindayiganza had committed harassment in the second degree, a violation under New York law. New York law prohibits arrest based on second-degree harassment that does not occur in the arresting officer's presence.

Even if probable cause for an arrest had existed, when Officer White frisked Sindayiganza he had no intention of arresting him; rather he planned to let Sindayiganza leave, as long as he walked north. A frisk cannot be justified after the fact as a search incident to arrest, where there is no intent to arrest at the time the frisk is conducted.

b. David Floyd—April 20, 2007 Stop

i. Findings of Fact

David Floyd is a thirty-three-year-old black male who lived in the Bronx from 2001 until 2010, when he left to attend medical school. On or around April 20, 2007, a Friday, Floyd was coming from the subway walking towards his home at 1359 Beach Avenue in the Bronx, wearing jeans and sneakers, and carrying his wallet, keys and cell phone in his pocket. As he crossed East 172nd Street, Floyd saw two police officers about a block-and-a-half away interacting with another individual. The officers then got into a van and Floyd continued walking down Beach Avenue toward his home. Shortly thereafter, the van pulled up to Floyd and the officer in the driver's seat said, "Excuse me, may I speak to you, sir?" Floyd immediately stopped walking.

Three uniformed officers, one Latino male, one white male and one female, exited the vehicle and one asked Floyd for ID. Floyd asked whether he had to give ID, but did not feel free to refuse. After he produced the ID, Floyd reached into his pocket to get his cell phone or a pen to write down the officers' identification. The white male officer jumped toward him and Floyd immediately stopped and put his hands up and said, "it's a cellphone." The officer said that it made him nervous when people put their hands in their pockets. The officer asked Floyd if he had a weapon, and Floyd said he did not and that he did not consent to being searched. The officer proceeded to pat down Floyd's entire body including pushing the cell phone, a BlackBerry, up out of Floyd's pocket with his finger.

The frisk lasted about thirty seconds and then the officer holding Floyd's ID told him it was illegal for him not to have a New York City license—Floyd's ID was out-of-state. The officers then got back in the van. Floyd asked for names and badge numbers and two of the officers identified themselves as Rodriguez and Goodman and provided badge numbers. The officers then left. Floyd did not file a CCRB complaint in connection with this stop.

ii. Mixed Finding of Fact and Law

Without testimony from the stopping officers, I have insufficient evidence to determine whether they had reasonable suspicion to approach Floyd and question him. However, I credit Floyd's testimony and find that there was no basis for the frisk. The officers did not appear to believe that Floyd was armed and dangerous when they approached him, because they did not immediately frisk him. Nothing in Floyd's behavior gave the officers reason to reconsider whether Floyd was "armed and dangerous." He reached for his cell phone and promptly identified it as such. The officer asked Floyd if he had a weapon and Floyd said he did not. I find that there was no credible basis for believing Floyd was armed and dangerous. Therefore, the frisk was unconstitutional.

c. David Floyd—February 27, 2008 Stop

i. Findings of Fact

On February 27, 2008, Floyd resided on Beach Avenue in a three-family home with a separate cottage. Floyd's Godmother owned the property and lived on the top floor, and tenants occupied the ground floor and the basement. Floyd lived in the cottage. Around 3:00 p.m., Floyd left the cottage carrying a backpack, with his wallet, cell phone, keys, and some change in his pocket. Before Floyd got to the street, the basement tenant, also a black male, told Floyd that he was locked out of his apartment and asked for Floyd's assistance because Floyd had access to the spare keys.

Floyd retrieved seven to ten keys on separate key rings from his Godmother's apartment and went to the door of the basement apartment with the tenant. Because the keys were not marked, both Floyd and the tenant tried five or six different keys for a minute or two. At that point, three plainclothes officers, since identified as Officers Cormac Joyce and Eric Hernandez, and Sergeant James Kelly, approached and told Floyd and the tenant to stop what they were doing and put their hands up. Floyd obeyed. Officer Joyce patted Floyd down and searched Floyd's pockets without his consent. He did not remove anything from Floyd's pockets.

After frisking the men, the officers remained calm throughout the encounter. The officers asked the men for ID, and Floyd showed his Louisiana drivers' license. The tenant did not have ID on him. After additional inquiries, Floyd produced an electric bill with his name and address on it, and the tenant went inside his apartment and got ID. Floyd asked why he had been stopped and the officers informed him that there had been a pattern of burglaries in the area. Floyd asked for the officers' names and badge numbers and the officers provided them. The officers then left.

Earlier that day the officers had been patrolling Beach Avenue in response to reports of robberies and burglaries of private homes in the area—specifically the area of the 43rd Precinct near the Cross–Bronx Expressway. Proximity to the Cross–Bronx Expressway was significant because it provided easy access for a vehicle to get away from the area quickly. The majority of the burglaries in the pattern identified during trial occurred in January 2008, with the last occurring on February 2.

The officers observed Floyd and the tenant for about two minutes before approaching them. Sergeant Kelly observed them playing with the door knob, and also saw a bag on the ground next to Floyd. When he approached the men, he saw that they were trying numerous keys, which was consistent with his belief that they might be burglars, because burglars sometimes have master keys. The basis for the frisk was the belief that Floyd and the tenant were in the process of committing a violent felony.

Officer Joyce filled out a UF–250 in connection with this stop. He checked the box for Furtive Movements based on the jostling of the doorknob and the keys. He also checked time of day corresponding to criminal activity.

ii. Mixed Findings of Fact and Law

Floyd was stopped when the officers told him to stop what he was doing and raise his hands. The totality of the circumstances established reasonable suspicion to stop Floyd and his neighbor. The officers observed the men jostling the door knob and trying numerous keys in the door, and also observed a backpack on the ground. Beach Avenue is near the Cross Bronx Expressway, which makes it a target for burglary. The officers also had knowledge of a specific burglary pattern in the area of Beach Avenue. Although the last reported burglary was over three weeks before Floyd was stopped, the totality of the circumstances just recounted justified the officers' belief that the men might be in the process of committing a daytime burglary.

Furthermore, because burglary is often a violent crime, the officers were justified in promptly telling the men to put their hands up and frisking their outer garments for weapons before further investigating. The stop was also reasonable in duration because Floyd's ID was out of state and the basement tenant did not have ID on him. Therefore, the officers were justified in continuing to investigate the possibility that the men were burglars. However, Officer Joyce did not testify that he felt anything that might be a weapon or anything that was clearly contraband. Therefore, Officer Joyce violated Floyd's Fourth Amendment rights when he felt inside his pockets.

d. Clive Lino—February 24, 2011 Stop

i. Findings of Fact

On the night of February 24, 2011, Lino was at a party at his mother's apartment at 102nd Street and Third Avenue. He left the apartment to take the subway home, wearing a red leather Pelle Pelle brand jacket and carrying a white plastic grocery bag full of Tupperware containing leftover food.

Lino entered the subway at 103rd Street and Lexington Avenue and noticed two male police officers, since identified as Officer Daniel Leek, who is white, and Officer Edgar Figueroa, who is Hispanic. Lino went down to the uptown platform. As an uptown-bound train was pulling into the station, the officers entered the uptown platform. Lino stepped back on the platform to let them pass but instead the officers surrounded him.

Officer Figueroa immediately put his hand in Lino's right jacket pocket, and Lino pushed it away while stepping aside. Lino asked what the problem was, to which the officers responded that he needed to wait with them. Lino missed the train. Lino asked why he was being stopped and stated his belief that his race was the reason. Officer Leek said, "If you shut the fuck up, we'll tell you why we stopped you."

The officers told Lino to put the bag of food on the platform, which he refused to do because it was filthy. Officer Figueroa said "just put the [fuck]ing bag down" and reached for the bag. Lino placed the bag on the bench. The officers asked for ID, which Lino produced.

Officer Leek asked Lino if he had anything on him that he shouldn't have and Lino said no. Officer Leek then said, "Do you mind if we check?" While Lino may have initially consented, he clearly did not agree to be searched and at one point said, "you can't search me." Yet Officer Leek patted his waist and front pockets, and Officer Figueroa reached into his back pockets. When Lino looked back at what Officer Figueroa was doing, Officer Figueroa asked if Lino had a "fucking problem." Lino said he did have a problem because the officer "was in his pockets." He had not yet been told why he had been stopped. Officer Leek eventually informed Lino that he was being stopped because there were reports of a shooting suspect wearing a jacket similar to Lino's.

After frisking Lino, the officers forced Lino to go upstairs with them without explaining why. At no point was Lino free to walk away. Outside the subway station, Officer Figueroa stayed with Lino while Officer Leek took Lino's ID to the police van where his Sergeant was waiting.

Officer Leek attempted, unsuccessfully, to locate the wanted poster describing the shooting suspect. He did not run Lino's ID because Lino had not, to Officer Leek's knowledge, committed a crime.Officer Leek returned and the officers walked Lino back down to the platform, without his having to pay another fare, and returned his ID.

Lino never received a ticket or summons. The interaction lasted about twenty minutes Following the interaction, Lino filed a complaint with the CCRB. The CCRB complaint was substantiated with respect to the stop and charges were recommended against the officers. The allegations regarding the search and the officers' use of rude or obscene language were unsubstantiated.

The officers stopped Lino because he matched a description of a homicide suspect from a wanted poster given to them by their sergeant at the beginning of their tour that day. The poster stated that the crime occurred on February 10, 2011, two weeks earlier, at 108th Street and Madison Avenue, two avenues and five blocks away from where Lino was stopped. The poster described a black male approximately five foot nine to six feet tall and showed a security photo of the suspect leaving the shooting wearing a red leather Pelle Pelle jacket, and two stock photos of such a jacket.From the photo, Officer Leek discerned the suspect's height, weight, and an age range of eighteen to thirty.

Officer Leek believed that Lino's jacket, height and complexion matched the crime scene photo. In addition, he noticed that the jacket was loose-fitting and bulky. Officer Leek frisked Lino because he matched the description of a murder suspect, had a bulky jacket that could conceal a weapon, and was in a high crime area.

ii. Mixed Findings of Fact and Law

Lino was stopped when the officers surrounded him on the subway platform. Although the murder was two weeks old, the distinctiveness of the red leather Pelle Pelle jacket, along with the three-inch height range—which was verifiable from the suspect photo—and the suspect's race, "afford[ed] a sufficient basis for 'selective investigative procedures' vis-a-vis a universe made up of all [potential suspects] of the crime in question." It was reasonable to assume that the murder suspect might have lived in the neighborhood and remained or returned within an eight-block radius.

Murder is a violent crime that would justify a frisk. Although the crime was two weeks old, it was reasonable to believe that the suspect in a shooting might still be armed and, if approached and questioned about the murder, would pose a danger to the officers. Because the jacket was loose and a train was approaching, the officers could not readily verify whether Lino was the right person or whether he was armed before stopping and frisking him.

Although both the stop and the frisk were justified at their inception, the frisk was not "reasonably related in scope to the justification for [its] initiation." Officer Figueroa immediately put his hands in Lino's pockets without Lino's consent, and the officers later conducted a search, to which they acknowledge Lino did not consent. The frisk, particularly in combination with the abusive manner in which the stop was conducted, violated Lino's Fourth Amendment rights.

e. Deon Dennis

i. Findings of Fact

Deon Dennis was raised in Harlem and resides in South Carolina, but visits New York frequently. Around 8:00 p.m. on January 12, 2008, Dennis arrived at the apartment of his then-girlfriend at 122nd Street and Seventh Avenue to help set up for her birthday party, which was scheduled to begin at 11:00 p.m. While setting up he drank a beer and some brandy in a plastic cup. Later, Dennis went to smoke a cigarette on the sidewalk outside the building on Seventh Avenue, while his girlfriend went to the store. The street was empty. Dennis was wearing a jacket and jeans, and had his cell phone, keys, wallet and cigarettes in his pocket.

After Dennis finished his cigarette, an NYPD van pulled up and two uniformed officers, Angelica Salmeron and Luis Pichardo, both of whom are Hispanic, approached Dennis. Dennis was not free to leave. Officer Salmeron pointed to a cup several feet to the right of Dennis and asked if it was his cup. Dennis said it was not. Officer Pichardo asked if Dennis had been drinking, and Dennis said he had been drinking earlier. The officers claim that Dennis had a cup in his hands and was drinking from it when they approached him, and that there was a bottle of Hennessy on the sidewalk.

The officers asked Dennis for ID and he produced his driver's license from the wallet in his pocket. Officer Salmeron took Dennis's ID to the van while Officer Pichardo stayed and searched Dennis's jacket and pants pockets without consent. During the search, Dennis was standing with his wallet in his hand and his hands raised at chest level.

Officer Salmeron returned from the van having discovered an active warrant against Dennis. The officers then handcuffed Dennis and put him in the back of the van based on the open container violation and the active warrant. Dennis's girlfriend returned and saw Dennis handcuffed. No summons was issued and Dennis was never prosecuted for drinking in public. No alcohol was vouchered or put in evidence. Neither officer recorded the incident in his or her memo book. Dennis's girlfriend filed a CCRB complaint about Dennis's arrest, and Dennis spoke with a CCRB officer about the incident. Dennis believes that he was stopped because of his race, because "only blacks and Hispanics get stopped in Harlem."

ii. Mixed Findings of Fact and Law

Based on the conflicting testimony about what the officers saw when they approached Dennis, and because plaintiffs bear the burden of proof, I cannot find by a preponderance of the evidence that the officers lacked reasonable suspicion that Dennis was violating New York's open container law. However, even if the officers saw Dennis drinking from a plastic cup, they would only have had reasonable suspicion to approach him and investigate further. They did not have reasonable suspicion to frisk or search Dennis.

The officers acknowledge that when they took Dennis's ID to the van, they intended to issue him a summons, not to arrest him. *Even assuming* the officers were justified in issuing Dennis a summons for violating open container laws, and even with knowledge of an active warrant, there was no basis for Officer Pichardo to frisk, let alone search, Dennis. The authority to conduct a protective frisk when issuing a summons for a violation is limited to occasions where officers have reason to believe that the suspect is armed and dangerous. Absent any indication that Dennis posed a threat to the officers' safety, there was no basis to conduct a frisk or search prior to arresting Dennis. Officer Pichardo's search violated Dennis's Fourth Amendment rights.

3. Failure of Proof

a. John Doe Stops of Nicholas Peart in Spring 2008 and February 2010 and David
Ourlicht in February and June 2008

In the John Doe stops discussed below, plaintiffs' testimony did not provide sufficiently detailed credible information for me to find, by a preponderance of the evidence, that the stop and, in some cases, frisk, lacked reasonable suspicion. Nicholas Peart testified that he was stopped and frisked in the Spring of 2008 in Brooklyn, based on a burglary pattern. Although the existence of a burglary pattern alone would not provide reasonable suspicion, I cannot conclude that there was not reasonable suspicion to stop and frisk Peart without knowing what additional information the officers had. Peart also testified that, in September of 2010, he was stopped and frisked at 144th Street, between Seventh and Eighth Avenues. Because I have no information about the basis for this stop, I cannot find that the stop and frisk lacked reasonable suspicion.

David Ourlicht testified that on February 21, 2008, he and a friend were stopped and frisked near the subway station at 168th Street in the Bronx. I do not fully credit Ourlicht's version of the events, and without the officers' version of what occurred, I cannot find that Ourlicht's Fourth or Fourteenth Amendment rights were violated. Ourlicht also testified that in June 2008, he was stopped and frisked at an apartment complex at 115th Street and Park Avenue based on reports of a gun in the area. Without information about the officers' knowledge about the gun in the area, I cannot find that the stop and frisk lacked reasonable suspicion.

b. Kristianna Acevedo Stop

Kristianna Acevedo is a thirty-year-old Hispanic female resident of Staten Island and works as a recruiter of home health aides. In 2007 she lived in Queens. On Tuesday, May 29, 2007, Acevedo was walking on 43rd Street in a desolate area when she noticed two men, since identified as Detectives Louis DeMarco and Damian Vizcarrondo, in a minivan. Detective DeMarco spoke to Acevedo to obtain information about drug activity.Acevedo did not believe the men were police, so she kept walking and then began to run.

Acevedo stopped at a UPS truck parked up the block. The van reversed and stopped, and three officers—Detectives DeMarco, Vizcarrondo, and a female officer, Detective Michele Hawkins—got out, approached Acevedo, and identified themselves as police. The officers wanted to assure Acevedo that she was not in danger because there had been recent media reports of individuals impersonating police officers. The detectives did not stop Acevedo based on reasonable suspicion.After a brief exchange, the officers left.

Acevedo called 911 to report what happened and filed a CCRB complaint. The CCRB substantiated the charges that the detectives abused their authority by stopping Acevedo, and failing to record the incident in their memo books. As discipline, the officers were docked one vacation day. Detective DeMarco was exonerated of the charges relating to his questioning of Acevedo and the other charges were unsubstantiated.

Acevedo clearly felt free to leave when the detectives first spoke to her because she continued walking and eventually ran. What occurred after the detectives exited the van is unclear. Acevedo's version of the events is irreconcilable with the officers' testimony. Although the CCRB found that the officers stopped Acevedo, I did not find her story sufficiently credible to conclude by a preponderance of the evidence that a forcible stop or frisk occurred in violation of her Fourth Amendment rights.

c. Clive Lino—August 3, 2008

Lino testified about an August 3, 2008 interaction with Officers Jose Colon and Mohamed Hassan in the lobby of his apartment, a NYCHA building at 102nd Street and Third Avenue. Lino's testimony about what occurred is incompatible with the officers' testimony. Because I credit the officers' testimony, I do not find that Lino's Fourth or Fourteenth Amendment rights were violated by this interaction.

....

CONCLUSIONS OF LAW

A. The City Is Liable for Violations of Plaintiffs' Fourth Amendment Rights

Plaintiffs established the City's liability for the NYPD's violation of their Fourth Amendment rights under two theories, either of which is adequate under *Monell: first,* plaintiffs showed that senior officials in the City and at the NYPD were deliberately indifferent to officers conducting unconstitutional stops and frisks; and *second,* plaintiffs showed that practices resulting in unconstitutional stops and frisks were sufficiently widespread that they had the force of law.

1. Deliberate Indifference

There is no dispute that the primary concern of a police department can and should be combating crime. At the same time, section 1983 limits the *lack* of concern that any municipal agency may show toward constitutional violations by its employees. The NYPD's senior officials have violated section 1983 through their deliberate indifference to unconstitutional stops, frisks, and searches. They have received both actual and constructive notice since at least 1999 of widespread Fourth Amendment violations occurring as a result of the NYPD's stop and frisk practices. Despite this notice, they deliberately maintained and even escalated policies and practices that predictably resulted in even more widespread Fourth Amendment violations. Moreover, while the NYPD is an acknowledged leader in the use of data collection and analysis to improve the *effectiveness* of policing, it has hindered the collection of accurate data concerning the constitutionality of its stops, and made no effective use of the limited data that is available. The NYPD has repeatedly turned a blind eye to clear evidence of unconstitutional stops and frisks.

Further evidence of deliberate indifference is found in the City's current positions as expressed at trial. The City continues to argue that *no* plaintiff or class member was subjected to an unconstitutional stop or frisk—not Downs, Almonor, McDonald, Sindayiganza, or any of the other plaintiffs.The City defends Officer Dang's stops in the third quarter of 2009 as unproblematic, despite the fact that he stopped 120 black people and 0 white people during that period. Officer Dang relied on a routine set of vague and unreliable stop justifications, and in only 5.5% of his stops made an arrest or summons. The City also defends the contents of the tape recordings quoted above, arguing that they "provide no basis whatsoever from which any reasonable inference can be drawn that ... pressure for activity existed that drove officers to make unconstitutional stops." In addition, the City recognizes the impossibility of tracking unconstitutional stops through UF–250s, but disclaims the need to develop a better, more adequate system of documentation and review. Indeed, the City continues to believe that there is no need to alter the status quo. Confronted with the persuasive statistical evidence that stops frequently lack reasonable suspicion, the City argues that even if "18% ... of the 4.43 million stops" were legally unjustified, that "is not necessarily a widespread pattern," and would not require a remedy.

Throughout the class period, the need for better supervision, monitoring, training, and discipline to protect against constitutional violations was obvious, but senior officials at the NYPD "'fail[ed] to make meaningful efforts to address the risk of harm to plaintiffs.'" Even if "deliberate indifference" were not the standard for liability, it would still perfectly describe the attitude of senior officials at the NYPD toward the risk of officers conducting stops, frisks, and searches in violation of the Fourth Amendment.

2. Widespread Practice

Despite the NYPD's deliberate failure to collect accurate data regarding stops that violate the Fourth Amendment, there is sufficient evidence of such stops to establish *Monell* liability based on "practices so persistent and widespread as to practically have the force of law." As described above, the likely number of stops lacking reasonable suspicion was far higher than the roughly 200,000 "apparently unjustified" stops identified by Dr. Fagan. In particular, this conclusion is supported by the number of UF–250s that do not identify a suspected crime (36% of all forms in 2009), the problems inherent in the two most commonly checked stop factors (Furtive Movements and High Crime Area), and the fact that only 6% of all stops result in an arrest for any crime. The NYPD's practice of making stops that lack individualized reasonable suspicion has been so pervasive and persistent as to become not only a part of the NYPD's standard operating procedure, but a fact of daily life in some New York City neighborhoods.

Likewise, the pervasiveness of unconstitutional frisks was established by the uncontested fact that over half of all people stopped are frisked, while only 1.5% of frisks reveal a weapon, as well as the institutional evidence of inaccurate training regarding when to frisk, testimony by officers who did not know the constitutional standard for a frisk, and anecdotal evidence of routine unconstitutional frisks in this case. "The security of one's privacy against arbitrary intrusion by the police—which is at the core of the Fourth Amendment—is basic to a free society." Far too many people in New York City have been deprived of this basic freedom far too often.

B. The City Is Liable for Violations of Plaintiffs' Fourteenth Amendment Rights

Plaintiffs have established the City's liability for the NYPD's violation of plaintiffs' Fourteenth Amendment rights under two theories, either of which is adequate under *Monell. First,* plaintiffs showed that the City, through the NYPD, has a *policy* of indirect racial profiling based on local criminal suspect data. *Second,* plaintiffs showed that senior officials in the City and at the NYPD have been *deliberately indifferent* to the intentionally discriminatory application of stop and frisk at the managerial and officer levels.

1. Policy of Indirect Racial Profiling

Throughout this litigation the City has acknowledged and defended the NYPD's policy of conducting stops based in part on criminal suspect data, of which race is a primary factor. The NYPD implements this policy by emphasizing to officers the importance of stopping "the right people." In practice, officers are directed, sometimes expressly, to target certain racially defined groups for stops.

"The Constitution prohibits selective enforcement of the law based on considerations such as race." The Second Circuit has admonished that courts should "not condone racially motivated police behavior" and must "take seriously an allegation of racial profiling." Racial profiling constitutes intentional discrimination in violation of the Equal Protection Clause if it involves any of the following: an express classification based on race that does not survive strict scrutiny; the application of facially neutral criminal laws or law enforcement policies "in an intentionally discriminatory manner;" or a facially neutral policy that has an adverse effect and was motivated by discriminatory animus. The City's policy of targeting "the right people" for stops clearly violates the Equal Protection Clause under the second method of proof, and, insofar as the use of race is explicit, the first.

a. Intentionally Discriminatory Application of a Facially Neutral Policy

In order to establish an equal protection violation based on an intentionally discriminatory application of a facially neutral policy, plaintiffs "must prove that the defendants' actions had a discriminatory effect and were motivated by a discriminatory purpose." In this case, plaintiffs' statistical evidence of racial disparities in stops is sufficient to show a discriminatory effect. In particular, plaintiffs showed that: (1) the NYPD carries out more stops where there are more black and Hispanic residents, even when other relevant variables are held constant; (2) NYPD officers are more likely to stop blacks and Hispanics than whites *within* precincts and census tracts, even after controlling for other relevant variables; (3) NYPD officers are more likely to use force against blacks and Hispanics than whites, after controlling for other relevant variables; and (4) NYPD officers stop blacks and Hispanics with less justification than whites.In addition to their statistical evidence of a racially disproportionate impact, plaintiffs provided significant anecdotal evidence, such as the stark racial disparities in the UF–250s prepared by Officers Dang and Gonzalez, and the fact that Officer French chose to stop McDonald, rather than similarly situated non-blacks nearby, based in part on generalized crime complaints about black males.

To establish discriminatory intent, plaintiffs must show that those responsible for the profiling did so "at least in part 'because of,' not merely 'in spite of,' its adverse effects upon" the profiled racial groups. Plaintiffs are not required to prove that race was the sole, predominant, or determinative factor in a police enforcement action. Nor must the discrimination be based on "ill will, enmity, or hostility."

The NYPD has directed officers to target young black and Hispanic men because these groups are heavily represented in criminal suspect data—the reliability of which is questionable—in those areas where the NYPD carries out most of its stops. Under the NYPD's policy, targeting the "right people" means stopping people in part because of their race. Together with Commissioner Kelly's statement that the NYPD focuses stop and frisks on young blacks and Hispanics in order to instill in them a fear of being stopped, and other explicit references to race discussed in the next section, there is a sufficient basis for inferring discriminatory intent.

The fact that the targeted racial groups were identified based on crime victim complaints does not eliminate the discriminatory intent. Just as it would be impermissible for a public housing agency to adopt a facially race-neutral policy of disfavoring applications from any group that is disproportionately subject to tenant complaints, and then apply this policy to disfavor applications from a racially defined group, so it is impermissible for a police department to target its general enforcement practices against racially defined groups based on crime suspect data.

b. Express Classification

Plaintiffs have readily established that the NYPD implements its policies regarding stop and frisk in a manner that intentionally discriminates based on race. While it is a closer call, I also conclude that the use of race is sufficiently integral to the policy of targeting "the right people" that the policy depends on express racial classifications. When an officer is directed to target "male blacks 14 to 21" for stops *in general* based on local crime suspect data—a practice that the City has defended throughout this litigation—the reference to "blacks" is an express racial classification subject to strict scrutiny. Chief Esposito's concession that the NYPD has targeted young blacks and Hispanics for stops confirms that explicit references to race are not limited to a few rogue supervisors. The City has not attempted to defend—nor could it defend—the proposition that the targeting of young black males or any other racially defined group for stops is narrowly tailored to achieve a compelling government interest. Because the use of express racial classifications in the City's policy of indirect racial profiling cannot withstand strict scrutiny, the policy violates the Equal Protection Clause.

This policy far exceeds the permissible use of race in stopping suspects as set forth in *Brown v. City of Oneonta, New York*. [235 F.3d 769, 779–83 (2d Cir.2000)] There, the Second Circuit held that when the police carry out stops as part of a "search[ ] for a particular perpetrator," the use of racial information from the victim's description of the suspect is not an express racial classification subject to strict scrutiny. The court explained that the Oneonta police department's "policy was to investigate crimes by interviewing the victim, getting a description of the assailant, and seeking out persons who matched that description" and, as such, "was race-neutral on its face."

The NYPD's policy of targeting "the right people" for stops, by contrast, is not directed toward the identification of a specific perpetrator. Rather, it is a policy of targeting expressly identified racial groups for stops *in general*. There is no dispute that it would violate equal protection for a police department to adopt an express policy of targeting members of one race for stops or other enforcement activities—such as an express policy of only pulling over speeding drivers who are Hispanic. Similarly, the following hypothetical police department policy would surely be subject to strict scrutiny, despite its failure to mention any *specific* race at the outset: "No one is to be stopped except the members of whatever race participated at the highest rate in violent crime during the previous month, based on suspect descriptions." Such a policy would be especially deserving of strict scrutiny if its drafters knew that the same race would be targeted every month, and managers implementing the policy were responsible for expressly directing officers to stop members of that race. The NYPD's policy of indirect racial profiling is closer to this hypothetical policy than it is to the race-neutral policy in *Brown*.

c. Conclusion

Whether through the use of a facially neutral policy applied in a discriminatory manner, or through express racial profiling, targeting young black and Hispanic men for stops based on the alleged criminal conduct of other young black or Hispanic men violates bedrock principles of equality. Two young men in the 81st Precinct who are similarly situated in every way, except that one is black and the other white, are similarly situated for the purposes of equal protection and must be treated alike. *Brown* establishes the common-sense principle that if a description of a specific criminal suspect includes the fact that the suspect is black, then the police need not focus equal attention on individuals of other races in pursuit of that suspect. But *Brown* specifically rejects the use of racial profiling as a basis for enforcement activity. The Equal Protection Clause does not sanction treating similarly situated members of different racial groups differently based on racial disparities in crime data. Indeed, such treatment would eviscerate the core guarantees of the Equal Protection Clause. If equal protection means anything, it means that individuals may not be punished or rewarded based on the government's views regarding their racial group, regardless of the source of those views.

2. Deliberate Indifference

In a case alleging that a municipality bears *Monell* liability based on senior officials' deliberate indifference to equal protection violations by subordinates, it is not necessary for plaintiffs to provide *direct* evidence that the senior officials were motivated by a discriminatory purpose. Rather, it is sufficient if plaintiffs show that: (1) subordinates followed a course of action in part because of its adverse effects on an identifiable group, and (2) senior officials were deliberately indifferent to those adverse effects in such a way that a reasonable inference can be drawn that those officials *intended* those adverse effects to occur.

Plaintiffs in this case *did* provide direct evidence of discriminatory intent, as discussed above. But plaintiffs also showed that senior officials in the City and at the NYPD have been deliberately indifferent to the discriminatory application of stop and frisk at the managerial and officer level such that a reasonable inference of discriminatory intent can be drawn. Despite frequent and ongoing notice of troubling racial disparities in stops, the NYPD has long shown its lack of concern for racial profiling through the failure of NYPD officials and managers to discuss racial profiling among themselves or at Compstat meetings, and through the numerous failures of supervision, monitoring, training, and discipline discussed above. In addition, senior NYPD officials such as Deputy Commissioner Farrell have adopted an attitude of willful blindness toward statistical evidence of racial disparities in stops and stop outcomes. During trial this indifference was further demonstrated by many officials' apparent belief that racial profiling is a myth created by the media, as well as by the testimony describing and defending the targeting of "the right people" for stops.

The City and the NYPD's highest officials also continue to endorse the unsupportable position that racial profiling cannot exist provided that a stop is based on reasonable suspicion. This position is fundamentally inconsistent with the law of equal protection and represents a particularly disconcerting manifestation of indifference. As I have emphasized throughout this section, the Constitution "prohibits *selective* enforcement of the law based on considerations such as race." Thus, plaintiffs' racial discrimination claim does not depend on proof that stops of blacks and Hispanics are suspicionless. A police department that has a practice of targeting blacks and Hispanics for pedestrian stops cannot defend itself by showing that all the stopped pedestrians were displaying suspicious behavior. Indeed, the targeting of certain races *within* the universe of suspicious individuals is especially insidious, because it will increase the likelihood of further enforcement actions against members of those races as compared to other races, which will then increase their representation in crime statistics. Given the NYPD's policy of basing stops on crime data, these races may then be subjected to even more stops and enforcement, resulting in a self-perpetuating cycle.

The Equal Protection Clause's prohibition on selective enforcement means that suspicious blacks and Hispanics may not be treated differently by the police than equally suspicious whites.

Individuals of all races engage in suspicious behavior and break the law. Equal protection guarantees that similarly situated individuals of these races will be held to account equally.

Note

What impact did the *Floyd* decision have on New York City Stop and Frisk? The American Civil Liberties Union reports the following:

> As was true throughout the Bloomberg administration and despite a record low number of reported stops in recent years, black and Latino people have continued to be overwhelmingly the targets of stop-and-frisk activity. Of the 92,383 recorded stops between 2014 and 2017, 49,362 (53 percent) were of black people, and 26,181 (28 percent) were of Latino people. Only 10,228 (11 percent) of those stopped were white. The proportion of white people stopped has only marginally increased since the height of stop-and-frisk in 2011, when nine percent of those stopped were white. NYCLU, STOP-AND-FRISK IN THE DE BLASIO ERA, (March 2019) p.9

Challenging Racial Profiling – The Use of Race as Justification for Fourth Amendment Intrusion

Note

Issues of race, racism and justice still deeply divide and impact our society. No issue has more currency and widespread application than does racial profiling. There are virtually no African Americans, particularly men, who do not report instances of victimization as a result of differential treatment, accusation or invasive police contact because of race-based perceptions. Latinos/Latinas and Asians also report such instances with occurrences increasing at an alarming rate.

Although racial profiling is a term that is fast becoming a substitute for a wide range of racist conduct and policies, the concept is more properly described as the establishment of policy (usually governmental and most often law enforcement) based on the assignment of behavioral characteristics or conduct expectations to individuals because of perceived statistical correlations or stereotypes based on race

The profiling of supposed characteristics of drug couriers first appeared in the early 1970's as a result of the efforts of Drug Enforcement Agency Agent Paul Markonni. See, Mark J. Kadish, *The Drug Courier Profile: In Planes, Trains, And Automobiles; And Now in the Jury Box*, 46 AMER. L. REV. 747 (1997) Based on the success in profile use by the Federal Aviation Agency in identifying terrorists and hijackers, Markonni and his agents developed a list of characteristics of drug couriers drawn from law enforcement experience. These characteristics although not explicitly including race and ethnicity, tended to include factors and circumstances more readily associated with communities of color. The focus on source cities and those who travel to and from such cities has a particularly disparate impact on minorities because those cities tend to be large urban areas having the highest concentration of people of col

Prior to the development of the drug courier profile and its use of race, the United Supreme Court considered the use of race as a suspicion base in a series of cases involving interdiction on roads and points of transit such as airports.

UNITED STATES V. BRIGNONI-PONCE.
422 U.S. 873 (1975)

Mr. Justice POWELL delivered the opinion of the Court.

This case raises questions as to the United States Border Patrol's authority to stop automobiles in areas near the Mexican border. It differs from our decision in Almeida-*Sanchez v. United States*, 413 U.S. 266, 93 S.Ct. 2535, 37 L.Ed.2d 596 (1973), in that the Border Patrol does not claim authority to search cars, but only to question the occupants about their citizenship and immigration status.

I

As a part of its regular traffic-checking operations in southern California, the Border Patrol operates a fixed checkpoint on Interstate Highway 5 south of San Clemente. On the evening of March 11, 1973, the checkpoint was closed because of inclement weather, but two officers were observing northbound traffic from a patrol car parked at the side of the highway. The road was dark, and they were using the patrol car's headlights to illuminate passing cars. They pursued respondent's car and stopped it, saying later that their only reason for doing so was that its three occupants appeared to be of Mexican descent. The officers questioned respondent and his two passengers about their citizenship and learned that the passengers were aliens who had entered the country illegally. All three were then arrested, and respondent was charged with two counts of knowingly transporting illegal immigrants, a violation of s 274(a)(2) of the Immigration and Nationality Act, 66 Stat. 228, 8 U.S.C. s 1324(a)(2). At trial respondent moved to suppress the testimony of and about the two passengers, claiming that this evidence was the fruit of an illegal seizure. The trial court denied the motion, the aliens testified at trial, and respondent was convicted on both counts.

Respondent's appeal was pending in the Court of Appeals for the Ninth Circuit when we announced our decision in *Almeida-Sanchez v. United States, supra,* holding that the Fourth Amendment prohibits the use of roving patrols to search vehicles, without a warrant or probable cause, at points removed from the border and its functional equivalents. The Court of Appeals, sitting en banc, held that the stop in this case more closely resembled a roving-patrol stop than a stop at a traffic checkpoint, and applied the principles of Almeida-Sanchez. The court held that the Fourth Amendment, as interpreted in Almeida-Sanchez, forbids stopping a vehicle, even for the limited purpose of questioning its occupants, unless the officers have a "founded suspicion" that the occupants are aliens illegally in the country. The court refused to find that Mexican ancestry alone supported such a "founded suspicion" and held that respondent's motion to suppress should have been granted. 499 F.2d 1109 (1974). We granted certiorari and set the case for oral argument with No. 73–2050, *United States v. Ortiz,* 422 U.S. 891, 95 S.Ct. 2585, 45 L.Ed.2d 623, and No. 73–6848, *Bowen v. United States,* 422 U.S. 916, 95 S.Ct. 2569, 45 L.Ed.2d 641. 419 U.S. 824, 95 S.Ct. 40, 42 L.Ed.2d 48 (1974).

The Government does not challenge the Court of Appeals' factual conclusion that the stop of respondent's car was a roving-patrol stop rather than a checkpoint stop. Brief for United States. Nor does it challenge the retroactive application of Almeida-Sanchez, Brief for United States, or contend that the San Clemente checkpoint is the functional equivalent of the border. The only issue presented for decision is whether a roving patrol may stop a vehicle in an area near the border and question its occupants when the only ground for suspicion is that the occupants appear to be of Mexican ancestry. For the reasons that follow, we affirm the decision of the Court of Appeals.

II

The Government claims two sources of statutory authority for stopping cars without warrants in the border areas. Section 287(a)(1) of the Immigration and Nationality Act, 8 U.S.C. s 1357(a) (1), authorizes any officer or employee of the Immigration and Naturalization Service (INS) without a warrant, "to interrogate any alien or person believed to be an alien as to his right to be or to remain in the United States." There is no geographical limitation on this authority. The Government contends that, at least in the areas adjacent to the Mexican border, a person's apparent Mexican ancestry alone justifies belief that he or she is an alien and satisfies the requirement of this statute. Section 287(a)(3) of the Act, 8 U.S.C. s 1357(a)(3), authorizes agents, without a warrant, "within a reasonable distance from any external boundary of the United States, to board and search for aliens any vessel within the territorial waters of the United States and any railway car, aircraft, conveyance, or vehicle . . .."

Under current regulations, this authority may be exercised anywhere within 100 miles of the border. 8 CFR s 287.1(a) (1975). The Border Patrol interprets the statute as granting authority to stop moving vehicles and question the occupants about their citizenship, even when its officers have no reason to believe that the occupants are aliens or that other aliens may be concealed in the vehicle.3 But 'no Act of Congress can authorize a violation of the Constitution,' *Almeida-Sanchez, supra,* 413 U.S. at 272, 93 S.Ct. at 2539, and we must decide whether the Fourth Amendment allows such random vehicle stops in the border areas.

III

The Fourth Amendment applies to all seizures of the person, including seizures that involve only a brief detention short of traditional arrest. *Davis v. Mississippi,* 394 U.S. 721, 89 S.Ct. 1394, 22 L.Ed.2d 676 (1969); Terry *v. Ohio,* 392 U.S. 1, 16—19, 88 S.Ct. 1868, 1877, 20 L.Ed.2d 889 (1968)." (W)henever a police officer accosts an individual and restrains his freedom to walk away, he has 'seized' that person,' id., at 16, 88 S.Ct., at 1877, and the Fourth Amendment requires that the seizure be "reasonable." As with other categories of police action subject to Fourth Amendment constraints, the reasonableness of such seizures depends on a balance between the public interest and the individual's right to personal security free from arbitrary interference by law officers. Id., at 20—21, 88 S.Ct., at 1879; Camara *v. Municipal Court,* 387 U.S. 523, 536—537, 87 S.Ct. 1727, 1734, 18 L.Ed.2d 930 (1967).

The Government makes a convincing demonstration that the public interest demands effective measures to prevent the illegal entry of aliens at the Mexican border. Estimates of the number of illegal immigrants in the United States vary widely. A conservative estimate in 1972 produced a figure of about one million, but the INS now suggests there may be as many as 10 or 12 million aliens illegally in the country. Whatever the number, these aliens create significant economic and social problems, competing with citizens and legal resident aliens for jobs, and generating extra demand for social services. The aliens themselves are vulnerable to exploitation because they cannot complain of substandard working conditions without risking deportation. See generally Hearings on Illegal Aliens before Subcommittee No. 1 of the House Committee on the Judiciary, 92d Cong., 1st and 2d Sess., ser. 13, pts. 1—5 (1971—1972).

The Government has estimated that 85% of the aliens illegally in the country are from Mexico. *United States v. Baca,* 368 F.Supp. 398, 402 (SD Cal.1973).5 The Mexican border is almost 2,000 miles long, and even a vastly reinforced Border Patrol would find it impossible to prevent illegal border crossings. Many aliens cross the Mexican border on foot, miles away from patrolled areas, and then purchase transportation from the border area to inland cities, where they find jobs and elude the immigration authorities. Others gain entry on valid temporary border-crossing permits, but then violate the conditions of their entry. Most of these aliens leave the border area in private vehicles, often assisted by professional 'alien smugglers.' The Border Patrol's traffic-checking operations are designed to prevent this inland movement. They succeed in apprehending some illegal entrants and smugglers, and they deter the movement of others by threatening apprehension and increasing the cost of illegal transportation.

Against this valid public interest we must weigh the interference with individual liberty that results when an officer stops an automobile and questions its occupants. The intrusion is modest. The Government tells us that a stop by a roving patrol "usually consumes no more than a minute." Brief for United States 25. There is no search of the vehicle or its occupants, and the visual inspection is limited to those parts of the vehicle that can be seen by anyone standing alongside. According to the Government, "(a)ll that is required of the vehicle's occupants is a response to a brief question or two and possibly the production of a document evidencing a right to be in the United States." *Ibid.*

Because of the limited nature of the intrusion, stops of this sort may be justified on facts that do not amount to the probable cause required for an arrest. In Terry v. Ohio, supra, the Court declined expressly to decide whether facts not amounting to probable cause could justify an "investigative 'seizure'" short of an arrest, 392 U.S., at 19 n. 16, 88 S.Ct. at 1879, but it approved a limited search—a pat-down for weapons—for the protection of an officer investigating suspicious behavior of persons he reasonably believed to be armed and dangerous. The Court approved such a search on facts that did not constitute probable cause to believe the suspects guilty of a crime, requiring only that "the police officer . . . be able to point to specific and articulable facts which, taken together with rational inferences from those facts, reasonably warrant" a belief that his safety or that of others is in danger. Id., at 21, 88 S.Ct., at 1880; see id., at 27, 88 S.Ct., at 1883.

We elaborated on *Terry* in *Adams v. Williams*, 407 U.S. 143, 92 S.Ct. 1921, 32 L.Ed.2d 612 (1972), holding that a policeman was justified *881 in approaching the respondent to investigate a tip that he was carrying narcotics and a gun.

"The Fourth Amendment does not require a policeman who lacks the precise level of information necessary for probable cause to arrest to simply shrug his shoulders and allow a crime to occur or a criminal to escape. On the contrary, Terry recognizes that it may be the essence of good police work to adopt an intermediate response. . . .. A brief stop of a suspicious individual, in order to determine his identity or to maintain the status quo momentarily while obtaining more information, may be most reasonable in light of the facts known to the officer at the time." Id., at 145–146, 92 S.Ct. at 1923.

These cases together establish that in appropriate circumstances the Fourth Amendment allows a properly limited 'search' or 'seizure' on facts that do not constitute probable cause to arrest or to search for contraband or evidence of crime. In both Terry and Adams v. Williams the investigating officers had reasonable grounds to believe that the suspects were armed and that they might be dangerous. The limited searches and seizures in those cases were a valid method of protecting the public and preventing crime. In this case as well, because of the importance of the governmental interest at stake, the minimal intrusion of a brief stop, and the absence of practical alternatives for policing the border, we hold that when an officer's observations lead him reasonably to suspect that a particular vehicle may contain aliens who are illegally in the country, he may stop the car briefly and investigate the circumstances that provoke suspicion. As in Terry, the stop and inquiry must be 'reasonably related in scope to the justification for their initiation.' 392 U.S., at 29, 88 S.Ct. at 1884. The officer may question the driver and passengers about their citizenship and immigration status, and he may ask them to explain suspicious circumstances, but any further detention or search must be based on consent or probable cause.

We are unwilling to let the Border Patrol dispense entirely with the requirement that officers must have a reasonable suspicion to justify roving-patrol stops. In the context of border area stops, the reasonableness requirement of the Fourth Amendment demands something more than the broad and unlimited discretion sought by the Government. Roads near the border carry not only aliens seeking to enter the country illegally, but a large volume of legitimate traffic as well. San Diego, with a metropolitan population of 1.4 million, is located on the border. Texas has two fairly large metropolitan areas directly on the border: El Paso, with a population of 360,000, and the Brownsville-McAllen area, with a combined population of 320,000. We are confident that substantially all of the traffic in these cities is lawful and that relatively few of their residents have any connection with the illegal entry and transportation of aliens. To approve roving-patrol stops of all vehicles in the border area, without any suspicion that a particular vehicle is carrying illegal immigrants, would subject the residents of these and other areas to potentially unlimited interference with their use of the highways, solely at the discretion of Border Patrol officers. The only formal limitation on that discretion appears to be the administrative regulation defining the term 'reasonable distance' in s 287(a)(3) to mean within 100 air miles from the border. 8 CFR s 287.1(a) (1975). Thus, if we approved the Government's position in this case, Border Patrol officers could stop motorists at random for questioning, day or night, anywhere within 100 air miles of the 2,000-mile border, on a city street, a busy highway, or a desert road, without any reason to suspect that they have violated any law.

We are not convinced that the legitimate needs of law enforcement require this degree of interference with lawful traffic. As we discuss in Part IV, infra, the nature of illegal alien traffic and the characteristics of smuggling operations tend to generate articulable grounds for identifying violators. Consequently, a requirement of reasonable suspicion for stops allows the Government adequate means of guarding the public interest and also protects residents of the border areas from indiscriminate official interference. Under the circumstances, and even though the intrusion incident to a stop is modest, we conclude that it is not 'reasonable' under the Fourth Amendment to make such stops on a random basis.

The Government also contends that the public interest in enforcing conditions on legal alien entry justifies stopping persons who may be aliens for questioning about their citizenship and immigration status. Although we may assume for purposes of this case that the broad congressional power over immigration, see *Kleindienst v. Mandel*, 408 U.S. 753, 765–767, 92 S.Ct. 2576, 2583, 33 L.Ed.2d 683 (1972), authorizes Congress to admit aliens on condition that they will submit to reasonable questioning about their right to be and remain in the country, this power cannot diminish the Fourth Amendment rights of citizens who may be mistaken for aliens. For the same reasons that the Fourth Amendment forbids stopping vehicles at random to inquire if they are carrying aliens who are illegally in the country, it also forbids stopping or detaining persons for questioning about their citizenship on less than a reasonable suspicion that they may be aliens.

IV

The effect of our decision is to limit exercise of the authority granted by both s 287(a)(1) and s 287(a)(3). Except at the border and its functional equivalents, officers on roving patrol may stop vehicles only if they are aware of specific articulable facts, together with rational inferences from those facts, that reasonably warrant suspicion that the vehicles contain aliens who may be illegally in the country

Any number of factors may be taken into account in deciding whether there is reasonable suspicion to stop a car in the border area. Officers may consider the characteristics of the area in which they encounter a vehicle. Its proximity to the border, the usual patterns of traffic on the particular road, and previous experience with alien traffic are all relevant. See Carroll *v. United States*, 267 U.S. 132, 159–161, 45 S.Ct. 280, 69 L.Ed. 543 (1925); United *States v. Jaime-Barrios*, 494 F.2d 455 (CA9), cert. denied, 417 U.S. 972, 94 S.Ct. 3178, 41 L.Ed.2d 1143 (1974).10 They also may consider information about recent illegal border crossings in the area. The driver's behavior may be relevant, as erratic driving or obvious attempts to evade officers can support a reasonable suspicion. See *United States v. Larios-Montes,* 500 F.2d 941 (CA9 1974); *Duprez v. United States,* 435 F.2d 1276 (CA9 1970). Aspects of the vehicle itself may justify suspicion. For instance, officers say that certain station wagons, with large compartments for fold-down seats or spare tires, are frequently used for transporting concealed aliens. See United *States v. Bugarin-Casas*, 484 F.2d 853 (CA9 1973), cert. denied, 414 U.S. 1136, 94 S.Ct. 881, 38 L.Ed.2d 762 (1974); *United States v. Wright,* 476 F.2d 1027 (CA5 1973). The vehicle may appear to be heavily loaded, it may have an extraordinary number of passengers, or the officers may observe persons trying to hide. See *United States v. Larios-Montes, supra.* The Government also points out that trained officers can recognize the characteristic appearance of persons who live in Mexico, relying on such factors as the mode of dress and haircut. Reply Brief for United States 12—13, in United *States v. Ortiz*, 422 U.S. 891, 95 S.Ct. 2585, 45 L.Ed.2d 623. In all situations the officer is entitled to assess the facts in light of his experience in detecting illegal entry and smuggling. *Terry v. Ohio*, 392 U.S., at 27, 88 S.Ct., at 1883.

In this case the officers relied on a single factor to justify stopping respondent's car: the apparent Mexican ancestry of the occupants. We cannot conclude that this furnished reasonable grounds to believe that the three occupants were aliens. At best the officers had only a fleeting glimpse of the persons in the moving car, illuminated by headlights. Even if they saw enough to think that the occupants were of Mexican descent, this factor alone would justify neither a reasonable belief that they were aliens, nor a reasonable belief that the car concealed other aliens who were illegally in the country. Large numbers of native-born and naturalized citizens have the physical characteristics identified with Mexican ancestry, and even in the border area a relatively small proportion of them are aliens. The likelihood that any given person of Mexican ancestry is an alien is high enough to make Mexican appearance a relevant factor, but standing alone it does not justify stopping all Mexican-Americans to ask if they are aliens.

The judgment of the Court of Appeals is affirmed.

Affirmed.

UNITED STATES V. MARTINEZ-FUERTE
428 U.S. 543 (1976)

Mr. Justice POWELL delivered the opinion of the Court.

These cases involve criminal prosecutions for offenses relating to the transportation of illegal Mexican aliens. Each defendant was arrested at a permanent checkpoint operated by the Border Patrol away from the international border with Mexico, and each sought the exclusion of certain evidence on the ground that the operation of the checkpoint was incompatible with the Fourth Amendment. In each instance whether the Fourth Amendment was violated turns primarily on whether a vehicle may be stopped at a fixed checkpoint for brief questioning of its occupants even though there is no reason to believe the particular vehicle contains illegal aliens. We reserved this question last Term in United *States v. Ortiz*, 422 U.S. 891, 897 n. 3, 95 S.Ct. 2585, 2589, 45 L.Ed.2d 623 (1975). We hold today that such stops are consistent with the Fourth Amendment. We also hold that the operation of a fixed checkpoint need not be authorized in advance by a judicial warrant.

I

A

The respondents in No. 74-1560 are defendants in three separate prosecutions resulting from arrests made on three different occasions at the permanent immigration checkpoint on Interstate 5 near San Clemente, Cal. Interstate 5 is the principal highway between San Diego and Los Angeles, and the San Clemente checkpoint is 66 road miles north of the Mexican border. We previously have described the checkpoint as follows:

> " 'Approximately one mile south of the checkpoint is a large black on yellow sign with flashing yellow lights over the highway stating "ALL VEHICLES, STOP AHEAD, 1 MILE." Three-quarters of a mile further north are two black on yellow signs suspended over the highway with flashing lights stating "WATCH FOR BRAKE LIGHTS." At the checkpoint, which is also the location of a State of California weighing station, are two large signs with flashing red lights suspended over the highway. These signs each state" STOP HERE U. S. OFFICERS. "Placed on the highway are a number of orange traffic cones funneling traffic into two lanes where a Border Patrol agent in full dress uniform, standing behind a white on red "STOP"sign checks traffic. Blocking traffic in the unused lanes are official U. S. Border Patrol vehicles with flashing red lights. In addition, there is a permanent building which houses the Border Patrol office and temporary detention facilities. There are also floodlights for nighttime operation.'" *United States v. Ortiz, supra*, at 893, 95 S.Ct., at 2587, quoting United *States v. Baca*, 368 F.Supp. 398, 410-411 (SD Cal.1973).

The "point" agent standing between the two lanes of traffic visually screens all northbound vehicles, which the checkpoint brings to a virtual, if not a complete, halt.1 Most motorists are allowed to resume their progress without any oral inquiry or close visual examination. In a relatively small number of cases the "point" agent will conclude that further inquiry is in order. He directs these cars to a secondary inspection area, where their occupants are asked about their citizenship and immigration status. The Government informs us that at San Clemente the average length of an investigation in the secondary inspection area is three to five minutes. A direction to stop in the secondary inspection area could be based on something suspicious about a particular car passing through the checkpoint, but the Government concedes that none of the three stops at issue in No. 74-1560 was based on any articulable suspicion. During the period when these stops were made, the checkpoint was operating under a magistrate's "warrant of inspection," which authorized the Border Patrol to conduct a routine-stop operation at the San Clemente location.

We turn now to the particulars of the stops involved in No. 74-1560, and the procedural history of the case. Respondent Amado Martinez-Fuerte approached the checkpoint driving a vehicle containing two female passengers. The women were illegal Mexican aliens who had entered the United States at the San Ysidro port of entry by using false papers and rendezvoused with Martinez-Fuerte in San Diego to be transported northward. At the checkpoint their car was directed to the secondary inspection area. Martinez-Fuerte produced documents showing him to be a lawful resident alien, but his passengers admitted being present in the country unlawfully. He was charged, Inter alia, with two counts of illegally transporting aliens in violation of 8 U.S.C. s 1324(a)(2). He moved before trial to suppress all evidence stemming from the stop on the ground that the operation of the checkpoint was in violation of the Fourth Amendment.3 The motion to suppress was denied, and he was convicted on both counts after a jury trial.

Respondent Jose Jiminez-Garcia attempted to pass through the checkpoint while driving a car containing one passenger. He had picked the passenger up by prearrangement in San Ysidro after the latter had been smuggled across the border. Questioning at the secondary inspection area revealed the illegal status of the passenger, and Jiminez-Garcia was charged in two counts with illegally transporting an alien, 8 U.S.C. s 1324(a)(2), and conspiring to commit that offense, 18 U.S.C. s 371. His motion to suppress the evidence derived from the stop was granted.

Respondents Raymond Guillen and Fernando Medrano-Barragan approached the checkpoint with Guillen driving and Medrano-Barragan and his wife as passengers. Questioning at the secondary inspection area revealed that Medrano-Barragan and his wife were illegal aliens. A subsequent search of the car uncovered three other illegal aliens in the trunk. Medrano-Barragan had led the other aliens across the border at the beach near Tijuana, Mexico, where they rendezvoused with Guillen, a United States citizen. Guillen and Medrano-Barragan were jointly indicted on four counts of illegally transporting aliens, 8 U.S.C. s 1324(a)(2), four counts of inducing the illegal entry of aliens, s 1324(a)(4), and one conspiracy count, 18 U.S.C. s 371. The District Court granted the defendants' motion to suppress.

Martinez-Fuerte appealed his conviction, and the Government appealed the granting of the motions to suppress in the respective prosecutions of Jiminez-Garcia and of Guillen and Medrano-Barragan. The Court of Appeals for the Ninth Circuit consolidated the three appeals, which presented the common question whether routine stops and interrogations at checkpoints are consistent with the Fourth Amendment. The Court of Appeals held, with one judge dissenting, that these stops violated the Fourth Amendment, concluding that a stop for inquiry is constitutional only if the Border Patrol reasonably suspects the presence of illegal aliens on the basis of articulable facts. It reversed Martinez-Fuerte's conviction, and affirmed the orders to suppress in the other cases. 514 F.2d 308 (1975). We reverse and remand.

B

Petitioner in No. 75-5387, Rodolfo Sifuentes, was arrested at the permanent immigration checkpoint on U. S. Highway 77 near Sarita, Tex. Highway 77 originates in Brownsville, and it is one of the two major highways running north from the lower Rio Grande valley. The Sarita checkpoint is about 90 miles north of Brownsville, and 65-90 miles from the nearest points of the Mexican border. The physical arrangement of the checkpoint resembles generally that at San Clemente, but the checkpoint is operated differently in that the officers customarily stop all northbound motorists for a brief inquiry. Motorists whom the officers recognize as local inhabitants, however, are waved through the checkpoint without inquiry. Unlike the San Clemente checkpoint the Sarita operation was conducted without a judicial warrant.

Sifuentes drove up to the checkpoint without any visible passengers. When an agent approached the vehicle, however, he observed four passengers, one in the front seat and the other three in the rear, slumped down in the seats. Questioning revealed that each passenger was an illegal alien, although Sifuentes was a United States citizen. The aliens had met Sifuentes in the United States, by prearrangement, after swimming across the Rio Grande.

Sifuentes was indicted on four counts of illegally transporting aliens. 8 U.S.C. s 1324(a)(2). He moved on Fourth Amendment grounds to suppress the evidence derived from the stop. The motion was denied and he was convicted after a jury trial. Sifuentes renewed his Fourth Amendment argument on appeal, contending primarily that stops made without reason to believe a car is transporting aliens illegally are unconstitutional. The United States Court of Appeals for the Fifth Circuit affirmed the conviction, 517 F.2d 1402 (1975), relying on its opinion in *United States v. Santibanez*, 517 F.2d 922 (1975). There the Court of Appeals had ruled that routine checkpoint stops are consistent with the Fourth Amendment. We affirm.

II

The Courts of Appeals for the Ninth and the Fifth Circuits are in conflict on the constitutionality of a law enforcement technique considered important by those charged with policing the Nation's borders. Before turning to the constitutional question, we examine the context in which it arises.

A

It has been national policy for many years to limit immigration into the United States. Since July 1, 1968, the annual quota for immigrants from all independent countries of the Western Hemisphere, including Mexico, has been 120,000 persons. Act of Oct. 3, 1965, s 21(e), 79 Stat. 921. Many more aliens than can be accommodated under the quota want to live and work in the United States. Consequently, large numbers of aliens seek illegally to enter or to remain in the United States. We noted last Term that "(e)stimates of the number of illegal immigrants (already) in the United States vary widely. A conservative estimate in 1972 produced a figure of about one million, but the Immigration and Naturalization Service now suggests there may be as many as 10 or 12 million aliens illegally in the country." *United States v. Brignoni-Ponce*, 422 U.S. 873, 878, 95 S.Ct. 2574, 2578, 45 L.Ed.2d 607 (1975) (footnote omitted). It is estimated that 85% of the illegal immigrants are from Mexico, drawn by the fact that economic opportunities are significantly greater in the United States than they are in Mexico. *United States v. Baca*, 368 F.Supp., at 402.

Interdicting the flow of illegal entrants from Mexico poses formidable law enforcement problems. The principal problem arises from surreptitious entries. Id., at 405. The United States shares a border with Mexico that is almost 2,000 miles long, and much of the border area is uninhabited desert or thinly populated arid land. Although the Border Patrol maintains personnel, electronic equipment, and fences along portions of the border, it remains relatively easy for individuals to enter the United States without detection. It also is possible for an alien to enter unlawfully at a port of entry by the use of falsified papers or to enter lawfully but violate restrictions of entry in an effort to remain in the country unlawfully. Once within the country, the aliens seek to travel inland to areas where employment is believed to be available, frequently meeting by prearrangement with friends or professional smugglers who transport them in private vehicles. *United States v. Brignoni-Ponce*, supra, 422 U.S., at 879, 95 S.Ct., at 2579.

The Border Patrol conducts three kinds of inland traffic-checking operations in an effort to minimize illegal immigration. Permanent checkpoints, such as those at San Clemente and Sarita, are maintained at or near intersections of important roads leading away from the border. They operate on a coordinated basis designed to avoid circumvention by smugglers and others who transport the illegal aliens. Temporary checkpoints, which operate like permanent ones, occasionally are established in other strategic locations. Finally, roving patrols are maintained to supplement the checkpoint system. See *Almeida-Sanchez v. United States*, 413 U.S. 266, 268, 93 S.Ct. 2535, 2537, 37 L.Ed.2d 596 (1973).8 In fiscal 1973, 175,511 deportable aliens were apprehended throughout the Nation by "line watch" agents stationed at the border itself. Traffic-checking operations in the interior apprehended approximately 55,300 more deportable aliens.9 Most of the traffic-checking apprehensions were at checkpoints, though precise figures are not available. *United States v. Baca*, supra, at 405, 407, and n. 2.

B

We are concerned here with permanent checkpoints, the locations of which are chosen on the basis of a number of factors. The Border Patrol believes that to assure effectiveness, a checkpoint must be (i) distant enough from the border to avoid interference with traffic in populated areas near the border, (ii) close to the confluence of two or more significant roads leading away from the border, (iii) situated in terrain that restricts vehicle passage around the checkpoint, (iv) on a stretch of highway compatible with safe operation, and (v) beyond the 25-mile zone in which "border passes," , Supra, are valid. *United States v. Baca, supra*, at 406.

The record in No. 74-1560 provides a rather complete picture of the effectiveness of the San Clemente checkpoint. Approximately 10 million cars pass the checkpoint location each year, although the checkpoint actually is in operation only about 70% of the time.10 In calendar year 1973, approximately 17,000 illegal aliens were apprehended there. During an eight-day period in 1974 that included the arrests involved in No. 74-1560, roughly 146,000 vehicles passed through the checkpoint during 124 1/6 hours of operation. Of these, 820 vehicles were referred to the secondary inspection area, where Border Patrol agents found 725 deportable aliens in 171 vehicles. In all but two cases, the aliens were discovered without a conventional search of the vehicle. A similar rate of apprehensions throughout the year would have resulted in an annual total of over 33,000, although the Government contends that many illegal aliens pass through the checkpoint undetected. The record in No. 75-5387 does not provide comparable statistical information regarding the Sarita checkpoint. While it appears that fewer illegal aliens are apprehended there, it may be assumed that fewer pass by undetected, as every motorist is questioned.

III

The Fourth Amendment imposes limits on search-and-seizure powers in order to prevent arbitrary and oppressive interference by enforcement officials with the privacy and personal security of individuals. See United *States v. Brignoni-Ponce*, 422 U.S., at 878, 95 S.Ct., at 2578; United *States v. Ortiz*, 422 U.S., at 895, 95 S.Ct., at 2588; Camara *v. Municipal Court*, 387 U.S. 523, 528, 87 S.Ct. 1727, 1730, 18 L.Ed.2d 930 (1967). In delineating the constitutional safeguards applicable in particular contexts, the Court has weighed the public interest against the Fourth Amendment interest of the individual, United *States v. Brignoni-Ponce, supra*, 422 U.S., at 878, 95 S.Ct., at 2578; Terry *v. Ohio*, 392 U.S. 1, 20-21, 88 S.Ct. 1868, 1879-1880, 20 L.Ed.2d 889 (1968), a process evident in our previous cases dealing with Border Patrol traffic-checking operations.

In *Almeida-Sanchez v. United States, supra*, the question was whether a roving-patrol unit constitutionally could search a vehicle for illegal aliens simply because it was in the general vicinity of the border. We recognized that important law enforcement interests were at stake but held that searches by roving patrols impinged so significantly on Fourth Amendment privacy interests that a search could be conducted without consent only if there was probable cause to believe that a car contained illegal aliens, at least in the absence of a judicial warrant authorizing random searches by roving patrols in a given area. Compare 413 U.S., at 273, 93 S.Ct., at 2539, with id., at 283-285, 93 S.Ct., at 2544-2546 (Powell, J., concurring), and id., at 288, 93 S.Ct., at 2547 (White, J., dissenting). We held in *United States v. Ortiz, supra*, that the same limitations applied to vehicle searches conducted at a permanent checkpoint.

In *United States v. Brignoni-Ponce, supra*, however, we recognized that other traffic-checking practices involve a different balance of public and private interests and appropriately are subject to less stringent constitutional safeguards. The question was under what circumstances a roving patrol could stop motorists in the general area of the border for brief inquiry into their residence status. We found that the interference with Fourth Amendment interests involved in such a stop was "modest," 422 U.S., at 880, 95 S.Ct., at 2579, while the inquiry served significant law enforcement needs. We therefore held that a roving-patrol stop need not be justified by probable cause and may be undertaken if the stopping officer is "aware of specific articulable facts, together with rational inferences from those facts, that reasonably warrant suspicion" that a vehicle contains illegal aliens. Id., at 884, 95 S.Ct., at 2582.11

IV

It is agreed that checkpoint stops are "seizures" within the meaning of the Fourth Amendment. The defendants contend primarily that the routine stopping of vehicles at a checkpoint is invalid because *Brignoni-Ponce* must be read as proscribing any stops in the absence of reasonable suspicion. Sifuentes alternatively contends in No. 75-5387 that routine checkpoint stops are permissible only when the practice has the advance judicial authorization of a warrant. There was a warrant authorizing the stops at San Clemente but none at Sarita. As we reach the issue of a warrant requirement only if reasonable suspicion is not required, we turn first to whether reasonable suspicion is a prerequisite to a valid stop, a question to be resolved by balancing the interests at stake.

A

Our previous cases have recognized that maintenance of a traffic-checking program in the interior is necessary because the flow of illegal aliens cannot be controlled effectively at the border. We note here only the substantiality of the public interest in the practice of routine stops for inquiry at permanent checkpoints, a practice which the Government identifies as the most important of the traffic-checking operations. Brief for United States in No. 74-1560, pp. 19-20.12 These checkpoints are located on important highways; in their absence such highways would offer illegal aliens a quick and safe route into the interior. Routine checkpoint inquiries apprehend many smugglers and illegal aliens who succumb to the lure of such highways. And the prospect of such inquiries forces others onto less efficient roads that are less heavily traveled, slowing their movement and making them more vulnerable to detection by roving patrols. Cf. *United States v. Brignoni-Ponce*, 422 U.S., at 883-885, 95 S.Ct., at 2581-2582.

A requirement that stops on major routes inland always be based on reasonable suspicion would be impractical because the flow of traffic tends to be too heavy to allow the particularized study of a given car that would enable it to be identified as a possible carrier of illegal aliens. In particular, such a requirement would largely eliminate any deterrent to the conduct of well-disguised smuggling operations, even though smugglers are known to use these highways regularly.

B

While the need to make routine checkpoint stops is great, the consequent intrusion on Fourth Amendment interests is quite limited. The stop does intrude to a limited extent on motorists' right to "free passage without interruption," *Carroll v. United States,* 267 U.S. 132, 154, 45 S.Ct. 280, 285, 69 L.Ed. 543 (1925), and arguably on their right to personal security. But it involves only a brief detention of travelers during which

> "'(a)ll that is required of the vehicle's occupants is a response to a brief question or two and possibly the production of a document evidencing a right to be in the United States.'" *United States v. Brignoni-Ponce, supra,* 422 U.S., at 880, 95 S.Ct., at 2579.

Neither the vehicle nor its occupants are searched, and visual inspection of the vehicle is limited to what can be seen without a search. This objective intrusion the stop itself, the questioning, and the visual inspection also existed in roving-patrol stops. But we view checkpoint stops in a different light because the subjective intrusion the generating of concern or even fright on the part of lawful travelers is appreciably less in the case of a checkpoint stop. In Ortiz, we noted:

> "(T)he circumstances surrounding a checkpoint stop and search are far less intrusive than those attending a roving-patrol stop. Roving patrols often operate at night on seldom-traveled roads, and their approach may frighten motorists. At traffic checkpoints the motorist can see that other vehicles are being stopped, he can see visible signs of the officers' authority, and he is much less likely to be frightened or annoyed by the intrusion." 422 U.S., at 894-895, 95 S.Ct., at 2587.

In *Brignoni-Ponce,* we recognized that Fourth Amendment analysis in this context also must take into account the overall degree of interference with legitimate traffic. 422 U.S., at 882-883, 95 S.Ct., at 2580-2581. We concluded there that random roving-patrol stops could not be tolerated because they "would subject the residents of . . . (border) areas to potentially unlimited interference with their use of the highways, solely at the discretion of Border Patrol officers. . . . (They) could stop motorists at random for questioning, day or night, anywhere within 100 air miles of the 2,000-mile border, on a city street, a busy highway, or a desert road . . .." Ibid. There also was a grave danger that such unreviewable discretion would be abused by some officers in the field. Ibid.

Routine checkpoint stops do not intrude similarly on the motoring public. First, the potential interference with legitimate traffic is minimal. Motorists using these highways are not taken by surprise as they know, or may obtain knowledge of, the location of the checkpoints and will not be stopped elsewhere. Second, checkpoint operations both appear to and actually involve less discretionary enforcement activity. The regularized manner in which established checkpoints are operated is visible evidence, reassuring to law-abiding motorists, that the stops are duly authorized and believed to serve the public interest. The location of a fixed checkpoint is not chosen by officers in the field, but by officials responsible for making overall decisions as to the most effective allocation of limited enforcement resources. We may assume that such officials will be unlikely to locate a checkpoint where it bears arbitrarily or oppressively on motorists as a class. And since field officers may stop only those cars passing the checkpoint, there is less room for abusive or harassing stops of individuals than there was in the case of roving-patrol stops. Moreover, a claim that a particular exercise of discretion in locating or operating a checkpoint is unreasonable is subject to post-stop judicial review.

The defendants arrested at the San Clemente checkpoint suggest that its operation involves a significant extra element of intrusiveness in that only a small percentage of cars are referred to the secondary inspection area, thereby "stigmatizing" those diverted and reducing the assurances provided by equal treatment of all motorists. We think defendants overstate the consequences. Referrals are made for the sole purpose of conducting a routine and limited inquiry into residence status that cannot feasibly be made of every motorist where the traffic is heavy. The objective intrusion of the stop and inquiry thus remains minimal. Selective referral may involve some annoyance, but it remains true that the stops should not be frightening or offensive because of their public and relatively routine nature. Moreover, selective referrals rather than questioning the occupants of every car tend to advance some Fourth Amendment interests by minimizing the intrusion on the general motoring public.

C

The defendants note correctly that to accommodate public and private interests some quantum of individualized suspicion is usually a prerequisite to a constitutional search or seizure. See *Terry v. Ohio*, 392 U.S., at 21, and n. 18, 88 S.Ct., at 1880. But the Fourth Amendment imposes no irreducible requirement of such suspicion. This is clear from Camara *v. Municipal Court*, 387 U.S. 523, 87 S.Ct. 1727, 18 L.Ed.2d 930 (1967). See also Almeida-*Sanchez v. United States*, 413 U.S., at 283-285, 93 S.Ct., at 2544-2546 (Powell, J., concurring); In Camara the Court required an "area" warrant to support the reasonableness of inspecting private residences within a particular area for building code violations, but recognized that "specific knowledge of the condition of the particular dwelling" was not required to enter any given residence. 387 U.S., at 538, 87 S.Ct., at 1736. In so holding, the Court examined the government interests advanced to justify such routine intrusions "upon the constitutionally protected interests of the private citizen," Id., at 534-535, 87 S.Ct., at 1734, and concluded that under the circumstances the government interests outweighed those of the private citizen.

We think the same conclusion is appropriate here, where we deal neither with searches nor with the sanctity of private dwellings, ordinarily afforded the most stringent Fourth Amendment protection. See, e. g., McDonald v. United States, 335 U.S. 451, 69 S.Ct. 191, 93 L.Ed. 153 (1948). As we have noted earlier, one's expectation of privacy in an automobile and of freedom in its operation are significantly different from the traditional expectation of privacy and freedom in one's residence. United States v. Ortiz, 422 U.S., at 896 n. 2, 95 S.Ct., at 2588; see Cardwell v. Lewis, 417 U.S. 583, 590-591, 94 S.Ct. 2464, 2469-2470, 41 L.Ed.2d 325 (1974) (plurality opinion). And the reasonableness of the procedures followed in making these checkpoint stops makes the resulting intrusion on the interests of motorists minimal. On the other hand, the purpose of the stops is legitimate and in the public interest, and the need for this enforcement technique is demonstrated by the records in the cases before us. Accordingly, we hold that the stops and questioning at issue may be made in the absence of any individualized suspicion at reasonably located checkpoints.

We further believe that it is constitutional to refer motorists selectively to the secondary inspection area at the San Clemente checkpoint on the basis of criteria that would not sustain a roving-patrol stop. Thus, even if it be assumed that such referrals are made largely on the basis of apparent Mexican ancestry, we perceive no constitutional violation. Cf. United States v. Brignoni-Ponce, 422 U.S., at 885-887, 95 S.Ct., at 2582-2583. As the intrusion here is sufficiently minimal that no particularized reason need exist to justify it, we think it follows that the Border Patrol officers must have wide discretion in selecting the motorists to be diverted for the brief questioning involved.

V

Fuentes' alternative argument is that routine stops at a checkpoint are permissible only if a warrant has given judicial authorization to the particular checkpoint location and the practice of routine stops. A warrant requirement in these circumstances draws some support from Camara, where the Court held that, absent consent, an "area" warrant was required to make a building code inspection, even though the search could be conducted absent cause to believe that there were violations in the building searched.

We do not think, however, that Camara is an apt model. It involved the search of private residences, for which a warrant traditionally has been required. See, E. g., McDonald v. United States, 335 U.S. 451, 69 S.Ct. 191, 93 L.Ed. 153 (1948). As developed more fully above, the strong Fourth Amendment interests that justify the warrant requirement in that context are absent here. The degree of intrusion upon privacy that may be occasioned by a search of a house hardly can be compared with the minor interference with privacy resulting from the mere stop for questioning as to residence. Moreover, the warrant requirement in Camara served specific Fourth Amendment interests to which a warrant requirement here would make little contribution. The Court there said:

> "(W)hen (an) inspector (without a warrant) demands entry, the occupant has no way of knowing whether enforcement of the municipal code involved requires inspection of his premises, no way of knowing the lawful limits of the inspector's power to search, and no way of knowing whether the inspector himself is acting under proper authorization." 387 U.S., at 532, 87 S.Ct., at 1732.

A warrant provided assurance to the occupant on these scores. We believe that the visible manifestations of the field officers' authority at a checkpoint provide substantially the same assurances in this case.

Other purposes served by the requirement of a warrant also are inapplicable here. One such purpose is to prevent hindsight from coloring the evaluation of the reasonableness of a search or seizure. Cf. *United States v. Watson*, 423 U.S. 411, 455-456, n. 22, 96 S.Ct. 820, 843, 46 L.Ed.2d 598 (1976) (Marshall, J., dissenting). The reasonableness of checkpoint stops, however, turns on factors such as the location and method of operation of the checkpoint, factors that are not susceptible to the distortion of hindsight, and therefore will be open to post-stop review notwithstanding the absence of a warrant. Another purpose for a warrant requirement is to substitute the judgment of the magistrate for that of the searching or seizing officer. *United States v. United States District Court*, 407 U.S. 297, 316-318, 92 S.Ct. 2125, 2136-2137, 32 L.Ed.2d 752 (1972). But the need for this is reduced when the decision to seize "is not entirely in the hands of the officer in the field, and deference is to be given to the administrative decisions of higher ranking officials.

VI

In summary, we hold that stops for brief questioning routinely conducted at permanent checkpoints are consistent with the Fourth Amendment and need not be authorized by warrant. The principal protection of Fourth Amendment rights at checkpoints lies in appropriate limitations on the scope of the stop. See Terry *v. Ohio*, 392 U.S., at 24-27, 88 S.Ct., at 1881-1883; United States *v. Brignoni-Ponce*, 422 U.S., at 881-882, 95 S.Ct., at 2580-2581. We have held that checkpoint searches are constitutional only if justified by consent or probable cause to search. United States v. Ortiz, 422 U.S. 891, 95 S.Ct. 2585, 45 L.Ed.2d 623 (1975). And our holding today is limited to the type of stops described in this opinion. "(A)ny further detention . . . must be based on consent or probable cause." *United States v. Brignoni-Ponce, supra*, at 882, 95 S.Ct., at 2580. None of the defendants in these cases argues that the stopping officers exceeded these limitations. Consequently, we affirm the judgment of the Court of Appeals for the Fifth Circuit, which had affirmed the conviction of Sifuentes. We reverse the judgment of the Court of Appeals for the Ninth Circuit and remand the case with directions to affirm the conviction of Martinez-Fuerte and to remand the other cases to the District Court for further proceedings.

It is so ordered.

GUIDANCE FOR FEDERAL LAW ENFORCEMENT AGENCIES REGARDING THE USE OF RACE, ETHNICITY, GENDER, NATIONAL ORIGIN, RELIGION, SEXUAL ORIENTATION, OR GENDER IDENTITY

U.S. Department of Justice
December 2014

INTRODUCTION AND EXECUTIVE SUMMARY

This Guidance supersedes the Department of Justice's 2003 Guidance Regarding the Use of Race by Federal Law Enforcement Agencies. It builds upon and expands the framework of the 2003 Guidance, and it reaffirms the Federal government's deep commitment to ensuring that its law enforcement agencies conduct their activities in an unbiased manner. Biased practices, as the Federal government has long recognized, are unfair, promote mistrust of law enforcement, and perpetuate negative and harmful stereotypes. Moreover—and vitally important—biased practices are ineffective. As Attorney General Eric Holder has stated, such practices are "simply not good law enforcement."

Law enforcement practices free from inappropriate considerations, by contrast, strengthen trust in law enforcement agencies and foster collaborative efforts between law enforcement and communities to fight crime and keep the Nation safe. In other words, fair law enforcement practices are smart and effective law enforcement practices.

Even-handed law enforcement is therefore central to the integrity, legitimacy, and efficacy of all Federal law enforcement activities. The highest standards can—and should—be met across all such activities. Doing so will not hinder—and, indeed, will bolster—the performance of Federal law enforcement agencies' core responsibilities.

This new Guidance applies to Federal law enforcement officers performing Federal law enforcement activities, including those related to national security and intelligence, and defines not only the circumstances in which Federal law enforcement officers may take into account a person's race and ethnicity—as the 2003 Guidance did—but also when gender, national origin, religion, sexual orientation, or gender identity may be taken into account. This new Guidance also applies to state and local law enforcement officers while participating in Federal law enforcement task forces. Finally, this Guidance promotes training and accountability, to ensure that its contents are understood and implemented appropriately.

Biased law enforcement practices, as the 2003 Guidance recognized with regard to racial profiling, have a terrible cost, not only for individuals but also for the Nation as a whole. This new Guidance reflects the Federal government's ongoing commitment to keeping the Nation safe while upholding our dedication to the ideal of equal justice under the law.

Two standards in combination should guide use by Federal law enforcement officers of race, ethnicity, gender, national origin, religion, sexual orientation, or gender identity in law enforcement or intelligence activities:

- In making routine or spontaneous law enforcement decisions, such as ordinary traffic stops, Federal law enforcement officers may not use race, ethnicity, gender, national origin, religion, sexual orientation, or gender identity to any degree, except that officers may rely on the listed characteristics in a specific suspect description. This prohibition applies even where the use of a listed characteristic might otherwise be lawful.

- In conducting all activities other than routine or spontaneous law enforcement activities, Federal law enforcement officers may consider race, ethnicity, gender, national origin, religion, sexual orientation, or gender identity only to the extent that there is trustworthy information, relevant to the locality or time frame, that links persons possessing a particular listed characteristic to an identified criminal incident, scheme, or organization, a threat to national or homeland security, a violation of Federal immigration law, or an authorized intelligence activity. In order to rely on a listed characteristic, law enforcement officers must also reasonably believe that the law enforcement, security, or intelligence activity to be undertaken is merited under the totality of the circumstances, such as any temporal exigency and the nature of any potential harm to be averted. This standard applies even where the use of a listed characteristic might otherwise be lawful.

....

The Constitution protects individuals against the invidious use of irrelevant individual characteristics. See Whren v. United States, 517 U.S. 806, 813 (1996). Such characteristics should never be the sole basis for a law enforcement action. This Guidance sets out requirements beyond the Constitutional minimum that shall apply to the use of race, ethnicity, gender, national origin, religion, sexual orientation, and gender identity by Federal law enforcement officers. This Guidance applies to such officers at all times, including when they are operating in partnership with non-Federal law enforcement agencies.

I. GUIDANCE FOR FEDERAL LAW ENFORCEMENT OFFICERS

A. Routine or Spontaneous Activities in Domestic Law Enforcement

In making routine or spontaneous law enforcement decisions, such as ordinary traffic stops, Federal law enforcement officers may not use race, ethnicity, gender, national origin, religion, sexual orientation, or gender identity to any degree, except that officers may rely on the listed characteristics in a specific suspect description. This prohibition applies even where the use of a listed characteristic might otherwise be lawful.

....

Law enforcement agencies and officers sometimes engage in law enforcement activities, such as traffic and foot patrols, that generally do not involve either the ongoing investigation of specific criminal activities or the prevention of catastrophic events or harm to national or homeland security. Rather, their activities are typified by spontaneous action in response to the activities of individuals whom they happen to encounter in the course of their patrols and about whom they have no information other than their observations. These general enforcement responsibilities should be carried out without any consideration of race, ethnicity, gender, national origin, religion, sexual orientation, or gender identity.

....

Some have argued that overall discrepancies in certain crime rates among certain groups could justify using a listed characteristic as a factor in general traffic enforcement activities and would produce a greater number of arrests for non-traffic offenses (e.g., narcotics trafficking).

We emphatically reject this view. Profiling by law enforcement based on a listed characteristic is morally wrong and inconsistent with our core values and principles of fairness and justice. Even if there were overall statistical evidence of differential rates of commission of certain offenses among individuals possessing particular characteristics, the affirmative use of such generalized notions by law enforcement officers in routine, spontaneous law enforcement activities are tantamount to stereotyping. It casts a pall of suspicion over every member of certain groups without regard to the specific circumstances of a particular law enforcement activity, and it offends the dignity of the individual improperly targeted. Whatever the motivation, it is patently unacceptable and thus prohibited under this Guidance for law enforcement officers to act on the belief that possession of a listed characteristic signals a higher risk of criminality. This is the core of invidious profiling, and it must not occur.

The situation is different when an officer has specific information, based on trustworthy sources, to "be on the lookout" for specific individuals identified at least in part by a specific listed characteristic. In such circumstances, the officer is not acting based on a generalized assumption about individuals possessing certain characteristics; rather, the officer is helping locate specific individuals previously identified as involved in crime.

- Example: While parked by the side of the George Washington Parkway, a Park Police Officer receives an "All Points Bulletin" to be on the lookout for a fleeing bank robbery suspect, a man of a particular race and particular hair color in his 30s driving a blue automobile. The officer may use this description, including the race and gender of the particular suspect, in deciding which speeding motorists to pull over.

B. All Activities Other Than Routine or Spontaneous Law Enforcement Activities

In conducting all activities other than routine or spontaneous law enforcement activities, Federal law enforcement officers may consider race, ethnicity, gender, national origin, religion, sexual orientation, or gender identity only to the extent that there is trustworthy information, relevant to the locality or time frame, that links persons possessing a particular listed characteristic to an identified criminal incident, scheme, or organization, a threat to national or homeland security, a violation of Federal immigration law, or an authorized intelligence activity. In order to rely on a listed characteristic, law enforcement officers must also reasonably believe that the law enforcement, security, or intelligence activity to be undertaken is merited under the totality of the circumstances, such as any temporal exigency and the nature of any potential harm to be averted. This standard applies even where the use of a listed characteristic might otherwise be lawful.

....

Combatting the Use of Racial Profiling as Motivation for Intrusion

Note

In instances where reliance on racial profiling is not the asserted justification for law enforcement intervention, it still can play a role regarding selective scrutiny and police action. Racial Profiling has become an everyday fact of life for many Americans. Professor David A. Harris reports, in David A. Harris, *The Stories, The Statistics, And the Law: Why "Driving While Black" Matters*, 84 MINN. L. REV. 265 (1999) that in a study of motorist traveling along the New Jersey Turnpike, African Americans made up 36 percent of those stopped for traffic violations and 73 percent of those arrested. These statistics are all the more significant when it is considered that African Americans made up only 14 percent of the turnpike motorists.

MARYLAND STATE CONFERENCE OF NAACP BRANCHES V. MARYLAND DEPARTMENT OF STATE POLICE,

72 F.Supp.2d 560 (D. Maryland.)

MEMORANDUM
BLAKE, District Judge.

On April 10, 1998, plaintiffs Maryland State Conference of NAACP Branches and several named individuals filed a class action lawsuit against the Maryland State Police, Col. David Mitchell, and several supervisory and individual members of the Maryland State Police ("MSP") alleging constitutional and statutory violations in connection with an alleged pattern of racially discriminatory stops, detentions and searches of minority motorists traveling on I-95 in the state of Maryland. After an initial stay was lifted in June 1998, an amended complaint was filed and preliminary discovery began, which was consolidated with discovery in the related case of Wilkins v. Maryland State Police, Civil Case No. CCB-93-468.

On August 14, 1998, the defendants filed a motion to dismiss or for summary judgment. In October, the plaintiffs filed a four-count second amended complaint and an opposition to the motion to dismiss. In December, the defendants filed a reply and a motion to strike portions of the second amended complaint. Briefing was completed in January 1999, and the parties have continued to engage in discovery, primarily directed at the issue of class certification. No hearing is necessary to resolve the pending motions.

I. Eleventh Amendment Immunity

As both parties recognize, claims for monetary relief against state officials in their official capacity are barred by the Eleventh Amendment; claims for prospective injunctive relief are not. The plaintiffs have clarified that they seek monetary damages against state officials in their individual capacities only. Accordingly, there is no Eleventh Amendment bar to Counts II–IV.3

....

III. Supervisory Liability

[Supervisory state officials may not be held liable for the unconstitutional actions of individual employees on the basis of respondeat superior; they may, however, be liable where their own conduct amounts to deliberate indifference or tacit authorization of their subordinates' activity. Slakan v. Porter, 737 F.2d 368, 372–73 (4th Cir.1984). As explained by the Fourth Circuit, a plaintiff must prove the following three elements:

> (1) that the supervisor had actual or constructive knowledge that his subordinate was engaged in conduct that posed "a pervasive and unreasonable risk" of constitutional injury to citizens like the plaintiff; (2) that the supervisor's response to that knowledge was so inadequate as to show "deliberate indifference to or tacit authorization of the alleged offensive practices,"; and (3) that there was an "affirmative causal link" between the supervisor's inaction and the particular constitutional injury suffered by the plaintiff.

Shaw v. Stroud, 13 F.3d 791, 799 (4th Cir.1994).

The plaintiffs have alleged in the second amended complaint, supplemented by information obtained in the Wilkins case, a sufficient basis to support a claim for supervisory liability. MSP officials were on notice not only through statistics but also through internal memoranda and through the course of the Wilkins case of the need to take corrective action. Whether the actions taken were adequate to absolve these officials of liability under § 1983 is not appropriate for determination on the present record.

Further, as to supervisory liability, the plaintiffs allege that the discretion given to troopers to detain motorists until a drug-detecting dog can "sniff" the vehicle, in the absence of articulable suspicion, is a matter of official policy that violates the Fourth Amendment. While defendants certainly may dispute this, if the plaintiffs are correct they have stated a basis for supervisory liability that requires further development.6

V. Qualified Immunity

Government officials performing discretionary functions are entitled to qualified immunity from liability for civil damages to the extent that "their conduct does not violate clearly established statutory or constitutional rights of which a reasonable person would have known." Harlow v. Fitzgerald, 457 U.S. 800, 818, 102 S.Ct. 2727, 73 L.Ed.2d 396 (1982). As the Fourth Circuit has explained:

> although the exact conduct at issue need not have been held to be unlawful in order for the law governing an officer's actions to be clearly established, the existing authority must be such that the unlawfulness of the conduct is manifest. See Anderson v. Creighton, 483 U.S. 635, 640, 107 S.Ct. 3034, 97 L.Ed.2d 523 (1987); Pritchett v. Alford, 973 F.2d 307, 314 (4th Cir.1992).

Wilson v. Layne, 141 F.3d 111, 114 (4th Cir.1998) (en banc). "In determining whether the specific right allegedly violated was 'clearly established,' the proper focus is not upon the right at its most general or abstract level, but at the level of its application to the specific conduct being challenged." Gould v. Davis, 165 F.3d 265, 269 (4th Cir.1998), quoting Pritchett, 973 F.2d at 312. "The contours of the right must be sufficiently clear that a reasonable official would understand that what he is doing violates that right." Anderson, 483 U.S. at 640, 107 S.Ct. 3034.

It is clearly established, according to both plaintiffs and defendants, that stopping, detaining, or searching motorists on the basis of race violates the Constitution. Whether it would have been clear to an individual trooper at the appropriate level of particularity that his conduct violated the Constitution depends on the resolution of disputed facts or at least on the further development of those facts, in the course of discovery. The same is true as to the issue of supervisory liability. Mere adoption of a non-discriminatory policy that is not adequately implemented and enforced cannot be said to satisfy the Constitution. Whether the supervisory defendants' response to the apparent discriminatory practices of some individual troopers was constitutionally adequate remains to be determined at the close of discovery, or after trial.

Defendants misinterpret the significance of the statistical showing in this case. While it is not dispositive on the issue of discrimination, it is relevant evidence that minority motorists were treated differently from whites, at least for a period of time on a portion of I–95. In regard to qualified immunity, the plaintiffs do not suggest there was a clearly established right to have "balanced" statistics (see Def'ts. Reply at 36); rather, the "unbalanced" statistics were notice to supervisors of an apparent violation of the clearly established right not to be stopped, detained or searched on the basis of race.

VI.

In Count I, the plaintiffs allege that the MSP, which received federal financial assistance from the Department of Justice, has violated Title VI of the Civil Rights Act of 1964, 42 U.S.C. § 2000d, which provides:

> No person in the United States shall, on the ground of race, color, or national origin, be excluded from participation in, be denied the benefits of, or be subjected to discrimination under any program or activity receiving Federal financial assistance.

They also contend that the MSP has violated federal regulations promulgated under Title VI which provide that no program receiving financial assistance through the Department of Justice shall utilize criteria or methods of administration which have the effect of subjecting individuals to discrimination because of their race, color, or national origin, or have the effect of defeating or substantially impairing accomplishment of the objectives of the program as respects individuals of a particular race, color, or national origin.

28 C.F.R. § 42.104(b)(2).

Title VI implies a private right of action under the statute for victims of intentional discrimination. See Franklin v. Gwinnett County Pub. Sch., 503 U.S. 60, 112 S.Ct. 1028, 1035, 117 L.Ed.2d 208 (1992)("a clear majority [in Guardians Ass'n v. City of New York, 463 U.S. 582, 103 S.Ct. 3221, 77 L.Ed.2d 866 (1983)] expressed the view that damages were available under Title VI in an action seeking remedies for an intentional violation"); Cannon v. University of Chicago, 441 U.S. 677, 702–03, 99 S.Ct. 1946, 60 L.Ed.2d 560 (1979). The plaintiffs state detailed allegations of intentional discrimination in their second amended complaint. On the record associated with this early round of motions, granting summary judgment would be premature.

Whether a private right of action exists under the Title VI regulation prohibiting disparate-impact discrimination is less well settled. The United States requested and received permission to file an amicus brief in this case supporting the recognition of such a right. Upon review, I agree with the district court in Sandoval v. Hagan, 7 F.Supp.2d 1234 (M.D.Ala.1998) (holding that a private right of action is available to enforce the disparate impact regulation), based on the persuasive reasoning stated by the Third Circuit in Chester Residents Concerned for Quality Living v. Seif, 132 F.3d 925 (3d Cir.1997), judgment vacated as moot, 524 U.S. 974, 119 S.Ct. 22, 141 L.Ed.2d 783 (Aug. 17, 1998). I note also that another district court in this Circuit has approved (in dictum) the test used by the Third Circuit for determining when a private right of action to enforce a federal regulation properly may be implied. See CSX Transportation Inc. v. PKV Limited Partnership, 906 F.Supp. 339, 343, n. 2 (S.D.W.Va.1995); citing Angelastro v. Prudential–Bache Sec., Inc., 764 F.2d 939, 947 (3d Cir.1985). The Seif court in turn relied on this test.

Like the court in Sandoval, I also find that the plaintiffs satisfy the prudential standing requirements for a suit under Title VI. See also Bryant v. New Jersey Dep't of Transp., 998 F.Supp. 438, 443–46 (D.N.J.1998). The two goals of Title VI are to avoid the use of federal resources to support discriminatory practices and to provide individual citizens effective protection against those practices. See Cannon, 99 S.Ct. at 1961. Thus, the interests to be protected by the statute are those of persons against whom federally funded programs discriminate. See Bryant, 998 F.Supp. at 445. Since the I–95 plaintiffs are asserting that federal funding is being used to stop minority motorists in a discriminatory fashion, these plaintiffs fall within the "zone of interests" sought to be protected by Title VI. In National Credit Union Admin. v. First Nat'l Bank and Trust Co., 522 U.S. 479, 118 S.Ct. 927, 140 L.Ed.2d 1 (1998), the Supreme Court explicitly rejected the "intended beneficiary" test, at least for claims brought under the APA, instead holding that a plaintiff has standing if the plaintiff is "arguably within the zone of interests to be protected or regulated by the statute ... in question." Id. at 933, 118 S.Ct. 927 (quoting Ass'n of Data Processing Serv. Orgs., Inc. v. Camp, 397 U.S. 150, 90 S.Ct. 827, 829, 25 L.Ed.2d 184 (1970)). The Court stated: "Although our prior cases have not stated a clear rule for determining when a plaintiff's interest is 'arguably within the zone of interests' to be protected by a statute, they nonetheless establish that we should not inquire whether there has been a congressional intent to benefit the would-be plaintiff." National Credit Union, 118 S.Ct. at 933. Accordingly, in the absence of any controlling Fourth Circuit or Supreme Court precedent to the *568 contrary, the defendants' motion to dismiss Count I will be denied.

Right to Travel

In Count IV, the plaintiffs claim a violation of the federal guarantee of interstate travel. According to the Supreme Court's recent decision in Saenz v. Roe, 526 U.S. 489, 119 S.Ct. 1518, 143 L.Ed.2d 689 (1999), the right to travel "embraces at least three different components." Id. at 1525. According to the Court, the right to travel:

> protects the right of a citizen of one State to enter and to leave another State, the right to be treated as a welcome visitor rather than an unfriendly alien when temporarily present in the second State, and, for those travelers who elect to become permanent residents, the right to be treated like other citizens of that State.
>
> ....

Neither the second nor the third components cited in Saenz are implicated in this case. Unlike Saenz, the defendants here are not treating "new" residents differently from "old" residents and, therefore, the third component has no relevance to this case. As for the second component, while the plaintiffs do make an allegation in the second amended complaint that the out-of-state license plates of some of the plaintiffs "made harassment more likely," this is insufficient to support a right to travel claim. The essence of the plaintiffs' complaint remains that they, both Maryland residents and non-residents alike, have experienced the same unlawful treatment by the defendants based on race. Accordingly, the defendants are not discriminating on the basis of residency, and the second Saenz component is not implicated.

Thus, the real issue in addressing the plaintiffs' right to travel claim is whether their right to enter and leave the State of Maryland is being abridged. See id. Since this component was not at issue in Saenz, the Court did not give extensive guidance as to what actions it encompassed. Cases prior to Saenz, however, spoke in terms of "actual barriers" to interstate movement. See Bray v. Alexandria Women's Health Clinic, 506 U.S. 263, 113 S.Ct. 753, 763, 122 L.Ed.2d 34 (1993); Zobel v. Williams, 457 U.S. 55, 102 S.Ct. 2309, 2313 n. 6, 72 L.Ed.2d 672 (1982). Here, the plaintiffs assert that they continue to travel along I–95 and, therefore, do not face an "actual barrier" to interstate travel.

Furthermore, the two cases cited by Saenz in discussing the first component of the right to travel both involved a greater restriction on the right to travel then the I–95 plaintiffs face. The first case cited in Saenz, Edwards v. California, 314 U.S. 160, 62 S.Ct. 164, 86 L.Ed. 119 (1941), involved a Texas law making it a misdemeanor to bring an indigent person into the state. Id. at 165–66. The other case cited by the Saenz Court in describing this first component was United States v. Guest, 383 U.S. 745, 86 S.Ct. 1170, 16 L.Ed.2d 239 (1966). Guest involved a conspiracy by whites to deprive African–American citizens of full and equal use of the public streets and highways in the vicinity of Athens, Georgia. Id. at 1172–73. While the first component as stated in Saenz may be broader then the "actual barrier" language of Bray and Zobel, and may encompass some actions which are less egregious than those in Edwards and *569 Guest, in order to establish a constitutional violation, more of an impediment to travel is needed than the stops alleged by the I–95 plaintiffs.9 Accordingly, the defendants' motion will be granted as to Count IV.
....

KOLENDER V. LAWSON
461 Us 352 (1983)

I

Appellee Edward Lawson was detained or arrested on approximately 15 occasions between March 1975 and January 1977 pursuant to Cal.Penal Code § 647(e). Lawson was prosecuted only twice, and was convicted once. The second charge was dismissed.

Lawson then brought a civil action in the District Court for the Southern District of California seeking a declaratory judgment that § 647(e) is unconstitutional, a mandatory injunction seeking to restrain enforcement of the statute, and compensatory and punitive damages against the various officers who detained him. The District Court found that § 647(e) was overbroad because "a person who is stopped on less than probable cause cannot be punished for failing to identify himself." Juris. Statement, at A–78. The District Court enjoined enforcement of the statute, but held that Lawson could not recover damages because the officers involved acted in the good faith belief that each detention or arrest was lawful.

Appellant H.A. Porazzo, Deputy Chief Commander of the California Highway Patrol, appealed the District Court decision to the Court of Appeals for the Ninth Circuit. Lawson cross-appealed, arguing that he was entitled to a jury trial on the issue of damages against the officers. The Court of Appeals affirmed the District Court determination as to the unconstitutionality of § 647(e). The appellate court determined that the statute was unconstitutional in that it violates the Fourth Amendment's proscription against unreasonable searches and seizures, it contains a vague enforcement standard that is susceptible to arbitrary enforcement, and it fails to give fair and adequate notice of the type of conduct prohibited. Finally, the Court of Appeals reversed the District Court as to its holding that Lawson was not entitled to a jury trial to determine the good faith of the officers in his damages action against them, and remanded the case to the District Court for trial.

The officers appealed to this Court from that portion of the judgment of the Court of Appeals which declared § 647(e) unconstitutional and which enjoined its enforcement. We noted probable jurisdiction pursuant to 28 U.S.C. § 1254(2). 455 U.S. 999, 102 S.Ct. 1629, 71 L.Ed.2d 865 (1982).

II

In the courts below, Lawson mounted an attack on the facial validity of § 647(e).3 "In evaluating a facial challenge to a state law, a federal court must, of course, consider any limiting construction that a state court or enforcement agency has proffered." *Village of Hoffman Estates v. Flipside, Hoffman Estates*, 455 U.S. 489, 494, 102 S.Ct. 1186, 1191, 71 L.Ed.2d 362 (1982). As construed by the California Court of Appeal,4 § 647(e) requires that an individual provide "credible and reliable" identification when requested by a police officer who has reasonable suspicion of criminal activity sufficient to justify a Terry detention. People v. *Solomon*, 33 Cal.App.3d 429, 108 Cal. Rptr. 867 (1973). "Credible and reliable" identification is defined by the state Court of Appeal as identification "carrying reasonable assurance that the identification is authentic and providing means for later getting in touch with the person who has identified himself." Id., at 438, 108 Cal. Rptr. 867. In addition, a suspect may be required to "account for his presence ... to the extent that it assists in producing credible and reliable identification ...." Ibid. Under the terms of the statute, failure of the individual to provide "credible and reliable" identification permits the arrest.

III

Our Constitution is designed to maximize individual freedoms within a framework of ordered liberty. Statutory limitations on those freedoms are examined for substantive authority and content as well as for definiteness or certainty of expression. See generally M. Bassiouni, Substantive Criminal Law 53 (1978).

As generally stated, the void-for-vagueness doctrine requires that a penal statute define the criminal offense with sufficient definiteness that ordinary people can understand what conduct is prohibited and in a manner that does not encourage arbitrary and discriminatory enforcement. *Village of Hoffman Estates v. Flipside,* 455 U.S. 489, 102 S.Ct. 1186, 71 L.Ed.2d 362 (1982); *Smith v. Goguen,* 415 U.S. 566, 94 S.Ct. 1242, 39 L.Ed.2d 605 (1974); *Grayned v. City of Rockford,* 408 U.S. 104, 92 S.Ct. 2294, 33 L.Ed.2d 222 (1972); *Papachristou v. City of Jacksonville,* 405 U.S. 156, 92 S.Ct. 839, 31 L.Ed.2d 110 (1972); *Connally v. General Construction Co.,* 269 U.S. 385, 46 S.Ct. 126, 70 L.Ed. 322 (1926). Although the doctrine focuses both on actual notice to citizens and arbitrary enforcement, we have recognized recently that the more important aspect of vagueness doctrine "is not actual notice, but the other principal element of the doctrine—the requirement that a legislature establish minimal guidelines to govern law enforcement." *Smith, supra,* 415 U.S. at 574, 94 S.Ct., at 1247–1248. Where the legislature fails to provide such minimal guidelines, a criminal statute may permit "a standardless sweep [that] allows policemen, prosecutors, and juries to pursue their personal predilections." Id., at 575, 94 S.Ct., at 1248.7

[4] Section 647(e), as presently drafted and construed by the state courts, contains no standard for determining what a suspect has to do in order to satisfy the requirement to provide a "credible and reliable" identification. As such, the statute vests virtually complete discretion in the hands of the police to determine whether the suspect has satisfied the statute and must be permitted to go on his way in the absence of probable cause to arrest. An individual, whom police may think is suspicious but do not have probable cause to believe has committed a crime, is entitled to continue to walk the public streets "only at the whim of any police officer" who happens to stop that individual under § 647(e). *Shuttlesworth v. City of Birmingham,* 382 U.S. 87, 90, 86 S.Ct. 211, 213, 15 L.Ed.2d 176 (1965). Our concern here is based upon the "potential for arbitrarily suppressing First Amendment liberties ...." Id., at 91, 86 S.Ct., at 213. In addition, § 647(e) implicates consideration of the constitutional right to freedom of movement. See Kent v. Dulles, 357 U.S. 116, 126, 78 S.Ct. 1113, 1118, 2 L.Ed.2d 1204 (1958); Aptheker v. Secretary of State, 378 U.S. 500, 505–506, 84 S.Ct. 1659, 1663–1664, 12 L.Ed.2d 992 (1964).

Section 647(e) is not simply a "stop-and-identify" statute. Rather, the statute requires that the individual provide a "credible and reliable" identification that carries a "reasonable assurance" of its authenticity, and that provides "means for later getting in touch with the person who has identified himself." *Solomon, supra*, 33 Cal.App.3d 438, 108 Cal.Rptr. 867. In addition, the suspect may also have to account for his presence "to the extent it assists in producing credible and reliable identification." Ibid.

At oral argument, the appellants confirmed that a suspect violates § 647(e) unless "the officer [is] satisfied that the identification is reliable." Tr. of Oral Arg. 6. In giving examples of how suspects would satisfy the requirement, appellants explained that a jogger, who was not carrying identification, could, depending on the particular officer, be required to answer a series of questions concerning the route that he followed to arrive at the place where the officers detained him,9 or could satisfy the identification requirement simply by reciting his name and address. See id., at 6–10.

It is clear that the full discretion accorded to the police to determine whether the suspect has provided a "credible and reliable" identification necessarily "entrust[s] lawmaking 'to the moment-to-moment judgment of the policeman on his beat.'" *Smith, supra*, 415 U.S., at 575, 94 S.Ct., at 1248 (quoting Gregory *v. City of Chicago*, 394 U.S. 111, 120, 89 S.Ct. 946, 951, 22 L.Ed.2d 134 (1969) (Black, J., concurring)). Section 647(e) "furnishes a convenient tool for 'harsh and discriminatory enforcement by local prosecuting officials, against particular groups deemed to merit their displeasure,'" *Papachristou, supra,* 405 U.S., at 170, 92 S.Ct., at 847–848 (quoting *Thornhill v. Alabama*, 310 U.S. 88, 97–98, 60 S.Ct. 736, 741–742, 84 L.Ed. 1093 (1940)), and "confers on police a virtually unrestrained power to arrest and charge persons with a violation." *Lewis v. City of New Orleans,* 415 U.S. 130, 135, 94 S.Ct. 970, 973, 39 L.Ed.2d 214 (1974) (POWELL, J., concurring). In providing that a detention under § 647(e) may occur only where there is the level of suspicion sufficient to justify a Terry stop, the State ensures the existence of "neutral limitations on the conduct of individual officers." *Brown v. Texas*, 443 U.S. 47, 51, 99 S.Ct. 2637, 2640, 61 L.Ed.2d 357 (1979). Although the initial detention is justified, the State fails to establish standards by which the officers may determine whether the suspect has complied with the subsequent identification requirement.

Appellants stress the need for strengthened law enforcement tools to combat the epidemic of crime that plagues our Nation. The concern of our citizens with curbing criminal activity is certainly a matter requiring the attention of all branches of government. As weighty as this concern is, however, it cannot justify legislation that would otherwise fail to meet constitutional standards for definiteness and clarity. See Lanzetta *v. New Jersey*, 306 U.S. 451, 59 S.Ct. 618, 83 L.Ed. 888 (1939). Section 647(e), as presently construed, requires that "suspicious" persons satisfy some undefined identification requirement, or face criminal punishment. Although due process does not require "impossible standards" of clarity, see United *States v. Petrillo*, 332 U.S. 1, 7–8, 67 S.Ct. 1538, 1541–1542, 91 L.Ed. 1877 (1947), this is not a case where further precision in the statutory language is either impossible or impractical.

IV

We conclude § 647(e) is unconstitutionally vague on its face because it encourages arbitrary enforcement by failing to describe with sufficient particularity what a suspect must do in order to satisfy the statute.10 Accordingly, the judgment of the Court of Appeals is affirmed, and the case is remanded for further proceedings consistent with this opinion.

It is so ordered.

Race and Unreasonable Seizure – The Use of Deadly Force

TENNESSEE V. GARNER
471 U.S. 1 (1985)

Justice WHITE delivered the opinion of the Court.

This case requires us to determine the constitutionality of the use of deadly force to prevent the escape of an apparently unarmed suspected felon. We conclude that such force may not be used unless it is necessary to prevent the escape and the officer has probable cause to believe that the suspect poses a significant threat of death or serious physical injury to the officer or others.

I

At about 10:45 p.m. on October 3, 1974, Memphis Police Officers Elton Hymon and Leslie Wright were dispatched to answer a "prowler inside call." Upon arriving at the scene they saw a woman standing on her porch and gesturing toward the adjacent house. She told them she had heard glass breaking and that "they" or "someone" was breaking in next door. While Wright radioed the dispatcher to say that they were on the scene, Hymon went behind the house. He heard a door slam and saw someone run across the backyard. The fleeing suspect, who was appellee-respondent's decedent, Edward Garner, stopped at a 6-feet-high chain link fence at the edge of the yard. With the aid of a flashlight, Hymon was able to see Garner's face and hands. He saw no sign of a weapon, and, though not certain, was "reasonably sure" and "figured" that Garner was unarmed. App. 41, 56; Record 219. He thought Garner was 17 or 18 years old and about 5′5″ or 5′7″ tall. While Garner was crouched at the base of the fence, Hymon called out "police, halt" and took a few steps toward him. Garner then began to climb over the fence. Convinced that if Garner made it over the fence he would elude capture, Hymon shot him. The bullet hit Garner in the back of the head. Garner was taken by ambulance to a hospital, where he died on the operating table. Ten dollars and a purse taken from the house were found on his body.

In using deadly force to prevent the escape, Hymon was acting under the authority of a Tennessee statute and pursuant to Police Department policy. The statute provides that "[i]f, after notice of the intention to arrest the defendant, he either flee or forcibly resist, the officer may use all the necessary means to effect the arrest." Tenn.Code Ann. § 40–7–108 (1982). The Department policy was slightly more restrictive than the statute, but still allowed the use of deadly force in cases of burglary. App. 140–144. The incident was reviewed by the Memphis Police Firearm's Review Board and presented to a grand jury. Neither took any action. *Id.,* at 57.

Garner's father then brought this action in the Federal District Court for the Western District of Tennessee, seeking damages under 42 U.S.C. § 1983 for asserted violations of Garner's constitutional rights. The complaint alleged that the shooting violated the Fourth, Fifth, Sixth, Eighth, and Fourteenth Amendments of the United States Constitution. It named as defendants Officer Hymon, the Police Department, its Director, and the Mayor and city of Memphis. After a 3-day bench trial, the District Court entered judgment for all defendants. It dismissed the claims against the Mayor and the Director for lack of evidence. It then concluded that Hymon's actions were authorized by the Tennessee statute, which in turn was constitutional. Hymon had employed the only reasonable and practicable means of preventing Garner's escape. Garner had "recklessly and heedlessly attempted to vault over the fence to escape, thereby assuming the risk of being fired upon." App. to Pet. for Cert. A10.

The Court of Appeals for the Sixth Circuit affirmed with regard to Hymon, finding that he had acted in good-faith reliance on the Tennessee statute and was therefore within the scope of his qualified immunity. It remanded for reconsideration of the possible liability of the city, however, in light of *Monell v. New York City Dept. of Social Services,* 436 U.S. 658, 98 S.Ct. 2018, 56 L.Ed.2d 611 (1978), which had come down after the District Court's decision. The District Court was directed to consider whether a city enjoyed a qualified immunity, whether the use of deadly force and hollow point bullets in these circumstances was constitutional, and whether any unconstitutional municipal conduct flowed from a "policy or custom" as required for liability under *Monell.*

The District Court concluded that *Monell* did not affect its decision. While acknowledging some doubt as to the possible immunity of the city, it found that the statute, and Hymon's actions, were constitutional. Given this conclusion, it declined to consider the "policy or custom" question. App. to Pet. for Cert. A37–A39.

The Court of Appeals reversed and remanded. It reasoned that the killing of a fleeing suspect is a "seizure" under the Fourth Amendment, and is therefore constitutional only if "reasonable."

The Tennessee statute failed as applied to this case because it did not adequately limit the use of deadly force by distinguishing between felonies of different magnitudes—"the facts, as found, did not justify the use of deadly force under the Fourth Amendment." Officers cannot resort to deadly force unless they "have probable cause ... to believe that the suspect [has committed a felony and] poses a threat to the safety of the officers or a danger to the community if left at large."

The State of Tennessee, which had intervened to defend the statute, see 28 U.S.C. § 2403(b), appealed to this Court. The city filed a petition for certiorari. We noted probable jurisdiction in the appeal and granted the petition.

II

Whenever an officer restrains the freedom of a person to walk away, he has seized that person. *United States v. Brignoni-Ponce*, 422 U.S. 873, 878, 95 S.Ct. 2574, 2578, 45 L.Ed.2d 607 (1975). While it is not always clear just when minimal police interference becomes a seizure, see *United States v. Mendenhall*, 446 U.S. 544, 100 S.Ct. 1870, 64 L.Ed.2d 497 (1980), there can be no question that apprehension by the use of deadly force is a seizure subject to the reasonableness requirement of the Fourth Amendment.

A

A police officer may arrest a person if he has probable cause to believe that person committed a crime. *E.g., United States v. Watson*, 423 U.S. 411, 96 S.Ct. 820, 46 L.Ed.2d 598 (1976). Petitioners and appellant argue that if this requirement is satisfied the Fourth Amendment has nothing to say about *how* that seizure is made. This submission ignores the many cases in which this Court, by balancing the extent of the intrusion against the need for it, has examined the reasonableness of the manner in which a search or seizure is conducted. To determine the constitutionality of a seizure "[w]e must balance the nature and quality of the intrusion on the individual's Fourth Amendment interests against the importance of the governmental interests alleged to justify the intrusion." *United States v. Place*, 462 U.S. 696, 703, 103 S.Ct. 2637, 2642, 77 L.Ed.2d 110 (1983); We have described "the balancing of competing interests" as "the key principle of the Fourth Amendment." *Michigan v. Summers*, 452 U.S. 692, 700, n. 12, 101 S.Ct. 2587, 2593, n. 12, 69 L.Ed.2d 340 (1981). See also *Camara v. Municipal Court*, 387 U.S. 523, 536–537, 87 S.Ct. 1727, 1734–1735, 18 L.Ed.2d 930 (1967). Because one of the factors is the extent of the intrusion, it is plain that reasonableness depends on not only when a seizure is made, but also how it is carried out. *United States v. Ortiz*, 422 U.S. 891, 895, 95 S.Ct. 2585, 2588, 45 L.Ed.2d 623 (1975); *Terry v. Ohio*, 392 U.S. 1, 28–29, 88 S.Ct. 1868, 1883–1884, 20 L.Ed.2d 889 (1968).

Applying these principles to particular facts, the Court has held that governmental interests did not support a lengthy detention of luggage, *United States v. Place, supra,* an airport seizure not "carefully tailored to its underlying justification," *Florida v. Royer,* 460 U.S. 491, 500, 103 S.Ct. 1319, 1325, 75 L.Ed.2d 229 (1983) (plurality opinion), surgery under general anesthesia to obtain evidence, *Winston v. Lee,* 470 U.S. 753, 105 S.Ct. 1611, 84 L.Ed.2d 662 (1985), or detention for fingerprinting without probable cause, *Davis v. Mississippi,* 394 U.S. 721, 89 S.Ct. 1394, 22 L.Ed.2d 676 (1969); *Hayes v. Florida,* 470 U.S. 811, 105 S.Ct. 1643, 84 L.Ed.2d 705 (1985). On the other hand, under the same approach it has upheld the taking of fingernail scrapings from a suspect, *Cupp v. Murphy,* 412 U.S. 291, 93 S.Ct. 2000, 36 L.Ed.2d 900 (1973), an unannounced entry into a home to prevent the destruction of evidence, *Ker v. California,* 374 U.S. 23, 83 S.Ct. 1623, 10 L.Ed.2d 726 (1963), administrative housing inspections without probable cause to believe that a code violation will be found, *Camara v. Municipal Court, supra,* and a blood test of a drunken-driving suspect, *Schmerber v. California,* 384 U.S. 757, 86 S.Ct. 1826, 16 L.Ed.2d 908 (1966). In each of these cases, the question was whether the totality of the circumstances justified a particular sort of search or seizure.

B

The same balancing process applied in the cases cited above demonstrates that, notwithstanding probable cause to seize a suspect, an officer may not always do so by killing him. The intrusiveness of a seizure by means of deadly force is unmatched. The suspect's fundamental interest in his own life need not be elaborated upon. The use of deadly force also frustrates the interest of the individual, and of society, in judicial determination of guilt and punishment. Against these interests are ranged governmental interests in effective law enforcement. It is argued that overall violence will be reduced by encouraging the peaceful submission of suspects who know that they may be shot if they flee. Effectiveness in making arrests requires the resort to deadly force, or at least the meaningful threat thereof. "Being able to arrest such individuals is a condition precedent to the state's entire system of law enforcement." Brief for Petitioners 14.

Without in any way disparaging the importance of these goals, we are not convinced that the use of deadly force is a sufficiently productive means of accomplishing them to justify the killing of nonviolent suspects. Cf. *Delaware v. Prouse, supra,* 440 U.S., at 659, 99 S.Ct., at 1399. The use of deadly force is a self-defeating way of apprehending a suspect and so setting the criminal justice mechanism in motion. If successful, it guarantees that that mechanism will not be set in motion. And while the meaningful threat of deadly force might be thought to lead to the arrest of more live suspects by discouraging escape attempts, the presently available evidence does not support this thesis. The fact is that a majority of police departments in this country have forbidden the use of deadly force against nonviolent suspects. See *infra,* at 1704–1705. If those charged with the enforcement of the criminal law have abjured the use of deadly force in arresting nondangerous felons, there is a substantial basis for doubting that the use of such force is an essential attribute of the arrest power in all felony cases. See *Schumann v. McGinn*, 307 Minn. 446, 472, 240 N.W.2d 525, 540 (1976) (Rogosheske, J., dissenting in part). Petitioners and appellant have not persuaded us that shooting nondangerous fleeing suspects is so vital as to outweigh the suspect's interest in his own life.

The use of deadly force to prevent the escape of all felony suspects, whatever the circumstances, is constitutionally unreasonable. It is not better that all felony suspects die than that they escape. Where the suspect poses no immediate threat to the officer and no threat to others, the harm resulting from failing to apprehend him does not justify the use of deadly force to do so. It is no doubt unfortunate when a suspect who is in sight escapes, but the fact that the police arrive a little late or are a little slower afoot does not always justify killing the suspect. A police officer may not seize an unarmed, nondangerous suspect by shooting him dead. The Tennessee statute is unconstitutional insofar as it authorizes the use of deadly force against such fleeing suspects.

It is not, however, unconstitutional on its face. Where the officer has probable cause to believe that the suspect poses a threat of serious physical harm, either to the officer or to others, it is not constitutionally unreasonable to prevent escape by using deadly force. Thus, if the suspect threatens the officer with a weapon or there is probable cause to believe that he has committed a crime involving the infliction or threatened infliction of serious physical harm, deadly force may be used if necessary to prevent escape, and if, where feasible, some warning has been given. As applied in such circumstances, the Tennessee statute would pass constitutional muster.

III

A

It is insisted that the Fourth Amendment must be construed in light of the common-law rule, which allowed the use of whatever force was necessary to effect the arrest of a fleeing felon, though not a misdemeanant. As stated in Hale's posthumously published Pleas of the Crown:

> "[I]f persons that are pursued by these officers for felony or the just suspicion thereof ... shall
> not yield themselves to these officers, but shall either resist or fly before they are apprehended
> or being apprehended shall rescue themselves and resist or fly, so that they cannot be otherwise
> apprehended, and are upon necessity slain therein, because they cannot be otherwise taken, it is
> no felony." 2 M. Hale, Historia Placitorum Coronae 85 (1736).

See also 4 W. Blackstone, Commentaries. Most American jurisdictions also imposed a flat prohibition against the use of deadly force to stop a fleeing misdemeanant, coupled with a general privilege to use such force to stop a fleeing felon. *E.g., Holloway v. Moser*, 193 N.C. 185, 136 S.E. 375 (1927); *State v. Smith*, 127 Iowa 534, 535, 103 N.W. 944, 945 (1905); *Reneau v. State*, 70 Tenn. 720 (1879); *Brooks v. Commonwealth*, 61 Pa. 352 (1869); *Roberts v. State*, 14 Mo. 138 (1851); see generally R. Perkins & R. Boyce, Criminal Law 1098–1102 (3d ed. 1982); Day, Shooting the Fleeing Felon: State of the Law, 14 Crim.L.Bull. 285, 286–287 (1978); Wilgus, Arrest Without a Warrant, 22 Mich.L.Rev. 798, 807–816 (1924). But see *Storey v. State*, 71 Ala. 329 (1882); *State v. Bryant*, 65 N.C. 327, 328 (1871); *Caldwell v. State*, 41 Tex. 86 (1874).

The State and city argue that because this was the prevailing rule at the time of the adoption of the Fourth Amendment and for some time thereafter, and is still in force in some States, use of deadly force against a fleeing felon must be "reasonable." It is true that this Court has often looked to the common law in evaluating the reasonableness, for Fourth Amendment purposes, of police activity. See, *e.g., United States v. Watson*, 423 U.S. 411, 418–419, 96 S.Ct. 820, 825–826, 46 L.Ed.2d 598 (1976); *Gerstein v. Pugh*, 420 U.S. 103, 111, 114, 95 S.Ct. 854, 861, 863, 43 L.Ed.2d 54 (1975); *Carroll v. United States*, 267 U.S. 132, 149–153, 45 S.Ct. 280, 283–285, 69 L.Ed. 543 (1925). On the other hand, it "has not simply frozen into constitutional law those law enforcement practices that existed at the time of the Fourth Amendment's passage." *Payton v. New York*, 445 U.S. 573, 591, n. 33, 100 S.Ct. 1371, 1382, n. 33, 63 L.Ed.2d 639 (1980). Because of sweeping change in the legal and technological context, reliance on the common-law rule in this case would be a mistaken literalism that ignores the purposes of a historical inquiry.

B

It has been pointed out many times that the common-law rule is best understood in light of the fact that it arose at a time when virtually all felonies were punishable by death. "Though effected without the protections and formalities of an orderly trial and conviction, the killing of a resisting or fleeing felon resulted in no greater consequences than those authorized for punishment of the felony of which the individual was charged or suspected." American Law Institute, Model Penal Code § 3.07, Comment 3, p. 56 (Tentative Draft No. 8, 1958) (hereinafter Model Penal Code Comment). Courts have also justified the common-law rule by emphasizing the relative dangerousness of felons. See, *e.g., Schumann v. McGinn*, 307 Minn., at 458, 240 N.W.2d, at 533; *Holloway v. Moser, supra*, 193 N.C., at 187, 136 S.E., at 376 (1927).

Neither of these justifications makes sense today. Almost all crimes formerly punishable by death no longer are or can be. See, *e.g., Enmund v. Florida*, 458 U.S. 782, 102 S.Ct. 3368, 73 L.Ed.2d 1140 (1982); *Coker v. Georgia*, 433 U.S. 584, 97 S.Ct. 2861, 53 L.Ed.2d 982 (1977). And while in earlier times "the gulf between the felonies and the minor offences was broad and deep," 2 Pollock & Maitland 467, n. 3; *Carroll v. United States, supra*, 267 U.S., at 158, 45 S.Ct., at 287, today the distinction is minor and often arbitrary. Many crimes classified as misdemeanors, or nonexistent, at common law are now felonies. Wilgus, 22 Mich.L.Rev., at 572–573. These changes have undermined the concept, which was questionable to begin with, that use of deadly force against a fleeing felon is merely a speedier execution of someone who has already forfeited his life. They have also made the assumption that a "felon" is more dangerous than a misdemeanant untenable. Indeed, numerous misdemeanors involve conduct more dangerous than many felonies.

There is an additional reason why the common-law rule cannot be directly translated to the present day. The common-law rule developed at a time when weapons were rudimentary. Deadly force could be inflicted almost solely in a hand-to-hand struggle during which, necessarily, the safety of the arresting officer was at risk. Handguns were not carried by police officers until the latter half of the last century. L. Kennett & J. Anderson, The Gun in America 150–151 (1975). Only then did it become possible to use deadly force from a distance as a means of apprehension. As a practical matter, the use of deadly force under the standard articulation of the common-law rule has an altogether different meaning—and harsher consequences—now than in past centuries. See Wechsler & Michael, A Rationale for the Law of Homicide: I, 37 Colum.L.Rev. 701, 741 (1937).

One other aspect of the common-law rule bears emphasis. It forbids the use of deadly force to apprehend a misdemeanant, condemning such action as disproportionately severe. See *Holloway v. Moser*, 193 N.C., at 187, 136 S.E., at 376; *State v. Smith*, 127 Iowa, at 535, 103 N.W., at 945. See generally Annot., 83 A.L.R.3d 238 (1978).

In short, though the common-law pedigree of Tennessee's rule is pure on its face, changes in the legal and technological context mean the rule is distorted almost beyond recognition when literally applied.

C

In evaluating the reasonableness of police procedures under the Fourth Amendment, we have also looked to prevailing rules in individual jurisdictions. See, *e.g., United States v. Watson*, 423 U.S., at 421–422, 96 S.Ct., at 826–827. The rules in the States are varied. See generally Comment, 18 Ga.L.Rev. 137, 140–144 (1983). Some 19 States have codified the common-law rule, though in two of these the courts have significantly limited the statute. Four States, though without a relevant statute, apparently retain the common-law rule. Two States have adopted the Model Penal Code's provision verbatim. Eighteen others allow, in slightly varying language, the use of deadly force only if the suspect has committed a felony involving the use or threat of physical or deadly force, or is escaping with a deadly weapon, or is likely to endanger life or inflict serious physical injury if not arrested. Louisiana and Vermont, though without statutes or case law on point, do forbid the use of deadly force to prevent any but violent felonies. The remaining States either have no relevant statute or case law, or have positions that are unclear.

It cannot be said that there is a constant or overwhelming trend away from the common-law rule. In recent years, some States have reviewed their laws and expressly rejected abandonment of the common-law rule. Nonetheless, the long-term movement has been away from the rule that deadly force may be used against any fleeing felon, and that remains the rule in less than half the States.

This trend is more evident and impressive when viewed in light of the policies adopted by the police departments themselves. Overwhelmingly, these are more restrictive than the common-law rule. C. Milton, J. Halleck, J. Lardner, & G. Abrecht, Police Use of Deadly Force 45–46 (1977). The Federal Bureau of Investigation and the New York City Police Department, for example, both forbid the use of firearms except when necessary to prevent death or grievous bodily harm. *Id.,* at 40–41; App. 83. For accreditation by the Commission on Accreditation for Law Enforcement Agencies, a department must restrict the use of deadly force to situations where "the officer reasonably believes that the action is in defense of human life ... or in defense of any person in immediate danger of serious physical injury." Commission on Accreditation for Law Enforcement Agencies, Inc., Standards for Law Enforcement Agencies 1–2 (1983) (italics deleted). A 1974 study reported that the police department regulations in a majority of the large cities of the United States allowed the firing of a weapon only when a felon presented a threat of death or serious bodily harm. Boston Police Department, Planning & Research Division, The Use of Deadly Force by Boston Police Personnel (1974), cited in *Mattis v. Schnarr,* 547 F.2d 1007, 1016, n. 19 (CA8 1976), vacated as moot *sub nom. Ashcroft v. Mattis,* 431 U.S. 171, 97 S.Ct. 1739, 52 L.Ed.2d 219 (1977). Overall, only 7.5% of departmental and municipal policies explicitly permit the use of deadly force against any felon; 86.8% explicitly do not. K. Matulia, A Balance of Forces: A Report of the International Association of Chiefs of Police 161 (1982) (table). See also Record 1108–1368 (written policies of 44 departments). See generally W. Geller & K. Karales, Split-Second Decisions 33–42 (1981); Brief for Police Foundation et al. as *Amici Curiae.* In light of the rules adopted by those who must actually administer them, the older and fading common-law view is a dubious indicium of the constitutionality of the Tennessee statute now before us.

D

Actual departmental policies are important for an additional reason. We would hesitate to declare a police practice of long standing "unreasonable" if doing so would severely hamper effective law enforcement. But the indications are to the contrary. There has been no suggestion that crime has worsened in any way in jurisdictions that have adopted, by legislation or departmental policy, rules similar to that announced today. *Amici* noted that "[a]fter extensive research and consideration, [they] have concluded that laws permitting police officers to use deadly force to apprehend unarmed, non-violent fleeing felony suspects actually do not protect citizens or law enforcement officers, do not deter crime or alleviate problems caused by crime, and do not improve the crime-fighting ability of law enforcement agencies." *Id.,* at 11. The submission is that the obvious state interests in apprehension are not sufficiently served to warrant the use of lethal weapons against all fleeing felons. See *supra,* at 1700–1701, and n. 10.

Nor do we agree with petitioners and appellant that the rule we have adopted requires the police to make impossible, split-second evaluations of unknowable facts. See Brief for Petitioners 25; Brief for Appellant 11. We do not deny the practical difficulties of attempting to assess the suspect's dangerousness. However, similarly difficult judgments must be made by the police in equally uncertain circumstances. See, *e.g., Terry v. Ohio,* 392 U.S., at 20, 27, 88 S.Ct., at 1879, 1883. Nor is there any indication that in States that allow the use of deadly force only against dangerous suspects, see nn. 15, 17–19, *supra,* the standard has been difficult to apply or has led to a rash of litigation involving inappropriate second-guessing of police officers' split-second decisions. Moreover, the highly technical felony/misdemeanor distinction is equally, if not more, difficult to apply in the field. An officer is in no position to know, for example, the precise value of property stolen, or whether the crime was a first or second offense. Finally, as noted above, this claim must be viewed with suspicion in light of the similar self-imposed limitations of so many police departments.

IV

The District Court concluded that Hymon was justified in shooting Garner because state law allows, and the Federal Constitution does not forbid, the use of deadly force to prevent the escape of a fleeing felony suspect if no alternative means of apprehension is available. See App. to Pet. for Cert. A9–A11, A38. This conclusion made a determination of Garner's apparent dangerousness unnecessary. The court did find, however, that Garner appeared to be unarmed, though Hymon could not be certain that was the case. *Id.,* at A4, A23. See also App. 41, 56; Record 219. Restated in Fourth Amendment terms, this means Hymon had no articulable basis to think Garner was armed.

In reversing, the Court of Appeals accepted the District Court's factual conclusions and held that "the facts, as found, did not justify the use of deadly force." 710 F.2d, at 246. We agree. Officer Hymon could not reasonably have believed that Garner—young, slight, and unarmed—posed any threat. Indeed, Hymon never attempted to justify his actions on any basis other than the need to prevent an escape. The District Court stated in passing that "[t]he facts of this case did not indicate to Officer Hymon that Garner was 'non-dangerous.'" App. to Pet. for Cert. A34. This conclusion is not explained, and seems to be based solely on the fact that Garner had broken into a house at night. However, the fact that Garner was a suspected burglar could not, without regard to the other circumstances, automatically justify the use of deadly force. Hymon did not have probable cause to believe that Garner, whom he correctly believed to be unarmed, posed any physical danger to himself or others.

The dissent argues that the shooting was justified by the fact that Officer Hymon had probable cause to believe that Garner had committed a nighttime burglary. *Post,* at 1711, 1712. While we agree that burglary is a serious crime, we cannot agree that it is so dangerous as automatically to justify the use of deadly force. The FBI classifies burglary as a "property" rather than a "violent" crime. See Federal Bureau of Investigation, Uniform Crime Reports, Crime in the United States 1 (1984). Although the armed burglar would present a different situation, the fact that an unarmed suspect has broken into a dwelling at night does not automatically mean he is physically dangerous. This case demonstrates as much. See also *Solem v. Helm,* 463 U.S. 277, 296–297, and nn. 22–23, 103 S.Ct. 3001, 3012–3013, and nn. 22–23, 77 L.Ed.2d 637 (1983). In fact, the available statistics demonstrate that burglaries only rarely involve physical violence. During the 10-year period from 1973–1982, only 3.8% of all burglaries involved violent crime. Bureau of Justice Statistics, Household Burglary 4 (1985). See also T. Reppetto, Residential Crime 17, 105 (1974); Conklin & Bittner, Burglary in a Suburb, 11 Criminology 208, 214 (1973).

V

We wish to make clear what our holding means in the context of this case. The complaint has been dismissed as to all the individual defendants. The State is a party only by virtue of 28 U.S.C. § 2403(b) and is not subject to liability. The possible liability of the remaining defendants—the Police Department and the city of Memphis—hinges on *Monell v. New York City Dept. of Social Services,* 436 U.S. 658, 98 S.Ct. 2018, 56 L.Ed.2d 611 (1978), and is left for remand. We hold that the statute is invalid insofar as it purported to give Hymon the authority to act as he did. As for the policy of the Police Department, the absence of any discussion of this issue by the courts below, and the uncertain state of the record, preclude any consideration of its validity.

The judgment of the Court of Appeals is affirmed, and the case is remanded for further proceedings consistent with this opinion.

So ordered.

THE STATE OF TENNESSEE
V.
CLEAMTEE GARNER, AS FATHER AND NEXT OF KIN OF EDWARD EUGENE GARNER, A DECEASED MINOR, RESPONDENT-APPELLEE.

October, 1984.

BRIEF OF AMICUS CURIAE FOR THE RESPONDENT-APPELLEE

Florida Chapter of the National Bar Association, on behalf of The National Bar Association,

ARGUMENT I

The Racially Neutral Common Law Fleeing Felon Statute Which Confers Unlimited Discretion on Police Officers in Determining When a Non-Dangerous, Fleeing Felon Should Be Shot Is Racially Discriminatory as Applied.

One of the grounds upon which appellee-respondent maintains the Court should affirm the decision of the Sixth Circuit Court of Appeals is that the Memphis Police Department policy authorizing the discretionary shooting of non-dangerous fleeing property crime suspects violates the Equal Protection Clause of the Fourteenth Amendment because it discriminates against people because of their race.

Statistics recorded for the City of Memphis substantially show that a disproportionate number of blacks and other minorities will be victims at the hands of police officers under the common "fleeing felon" or "deadly force" statute than whites. The record is replete with statistics that when appropriately analyzed dictates the abolition of the common law deadly force statute in Tennessee. App. 1460-1469.[1]

From October 10th, 1966, to October 3rd, 1974, the Memphis Police Department recorded approximately 225 instances of firearm discharges to attempt to stop fleeing felony suspects. Approximately 31 instances of police firearm discharges resulted in death. *Id.* Non-violent property crime suspects accounted for 114 of those shot at by the police. Of the 114 shot, 96 were black (21 juveniles, 37 adults, and 37 of unknown age) and 16 were white (one juvenile, ten adults and five unknown). Two were of unknown race or age. Of the 17 victims suspected of burglary, while only four were white, 13 were black (five juveniles and eight adults). *Id.* Amazingly, only 24 victims were killed in the commission of violent crimes or because the police were acting in self defense or in the defense of others.

A detailed analysis of use of deadly force by the Memphis Police Department is found in Appellee's Brief at 27-29. Analysis of the data reveals that although black citizens were found to account for 70.6 percent of the arrest population for property crime offenses, they accounted for 88.4 percent of the shooting victims in property crimes. *Id.* at 27. Thus, in a city where the white population was greater than that of the black, the death rate for black property crime suspects was substantially higher at .63 per 1000 black property crime arrests, than white citizens at .45 per 1000 white property crime arrests.

The disparities increase tremendously for property crime suspects who are shot at by police. Black citizens have the highest rate of 4.33 per 1000 black property crime arrests compared with a white rate of 1.81 per 1000.

Finally, the statistics reveal that blacks are four times more likely to be wounded by police than whites, .586 per 1000 blacks and .113 per 1000 whites. These figures undoubtedly show that the use of deadly force by the City of Memphis police department had a disproportionate impact on black citizens. More devestatingly, a close look at the evidence shows that black juveniles are the victims of police shootings far more often than white juveniles.

In each separate category of criminal offenses, police officers more readily discharged their firearms at black youths, killing more of them than white adults and white juvenile? combined. Just as in *Garner,* the majority of these black youths are killed in situations involving nonviolent property crimes.

Data collected from major cities throughout the United States demonstrate that a significantly higher percentage of blacks are victims of police use of deadly force. For example, from 1950-1960, blacks comprised 22 percent of the total population in Philadelphia, yet they accounted for 87.5 percent of the deaths by police officers. R.1083. Taking into account the differential racial representation in the arrest population, black suspects were approximately twenty-two times more likely to be killed than whites. Analysis of these shooting incidents also revealed that more than half of the victims were under 24 years old.

Similarly in Chicago, from 1969-1970, although blacks constituted only 33 percent of the population, they accounted for 55.4 percent of the arrest population and 70.9 percent of the fatalities. This is especially significant in light of the fact that the fatality rate of whites is approximately one/sixth that of blacks, and whites only constitute 35.7 percent of the arrest population. R.1084. In a study performed in Chicago during the same period, statistics revealed that Spanish-Americans had the highest death rate for the entire population at 4.5 per 100,000; black deaths accounted for 2.67 per 100,000; and whites, 0.34 per 100,000. R.1085. This study also indicated that blacks accounted for 73.3 percent of the arrest population for felony offenses and 74.7 percent of the fatality victims, a conclusion consistent with the prior Chicago study.

The fatality rate was greatest for suspects under 25 years old. This observation is consistent with the evidence for Philadelphia. Although 85.5 percent of the cases were designated justifiable homicides by the coroner, the researchers accounted for the interdependence of the coroner's office with the police department, state attorney, and internal affairs division, and adjusted this rate downward. An objective review of the evidence indicated 36.8 percent of the investigated incidents exhibited evidence of police misconduct. R.1084. The reasons attributed to this disproportionate percentage of justifiable homicides are the "lack of independent examinations within the system," *id.*, and closed investigative proceedings shielded from the public's view.

All of the Chicago data was collected during a period when the State of Illinois had a common law fleeing felon statute in effect. In a recent decision, *Simmons v. City of Chicago*, 118 Ill. App.3d 676, 455 N.E.2d 232, (1983), interpreting Ill. Rev. Stat., ch. 38, §7-5(a) (1977) the court recognized that the common law authority of police officers to use deadly force was curtailed to use only against offenders engaged in a "forcible felony". States proscribing this common law rule have not been challenged on constitutional grounds.

A study conducted in New York for the years 1970 to 1973 show that 73 percent of the individuals killed by police were minorities: 52 percent black and 21 percent Hispanic, in comparison to 10 percent white. R.1086.

The report also revealed that there are significant disparities based on the race of the policeman/offender, and that this disparity occurs as the result of racial discrimination on the part of indivdual officers. During this period white officers fatally shot 96 black and 4 Hispanic criminal suspects. *Id.* In contrast, the number of white suspects killed by black and Hispanic police officers combined, was only two. Hispanic officers accounted for one percent of the police force, yet killed two percent of the black victims, and six percent of all Hispanic victims. R.1086. Yet, these figures do not preclude a finding of racial discrimination against minorities.

In the aggregate sample of 320 shootings from seven large cities in the United States, it was determined that 30 percent were fatal shootings and 79 percent of the shooting victims were black. R.1093.

At the time of this study three other cities that codified the common law statute permitting the use of deadly force to arrest a felony suspect were Kansas City, Miami and Milwaukee. Based on the data provided for Kansas City, black citizens were 7.5 times more likely to be victims of police use of deadly force, than their white counterparts. Similarly, in Miami the ratio of blacks killed in comparison with whites was 8.8 to one. However, Milwaukee exhibited the most disproportionate rate of all three cities. Blacks were victimized by police use of deadly force at a rate 29.5 times more than their white counterparts. Although the authors concluded Kansas City and Miami exhibited high rates of justifiable homicides, 4.50 per 1,000,000 and 7.06 per 1,000,000, respectively, these figures are questionable. The discretion permitted police officers in the use of deadly force to effect arrests under common law statutes are subject to different interpretations statewide throughout various law enforcement departments. This lack of specific guidelines for the use of deadly weapons under this common law statute means that the killing of a non-violent property crime suspect may be considered justifiable in one part of the state and not another. Thus, it is inevitable that these disparities in perception are bound to exist among officers within the same department.

One study reveals that approximately 89 percent of all police nationwide who killed civilians were white, 7 percent of the police were black and 4 percent were Spanish American. R.1080.

Nationwide data also show that a larger number of blacks become civilian fatalities at the hands of police than whites. Non-whites constituted between 47 and 50 percent of the fatally injured. Although blacks constituted approximately 10-11 percent of the total American population in 1964 and 1968, one study shows blacks constituted 28 percent of total arrests and 51 percent of total civilian deaths. Thus, the disproportionate number of blacks fatally wounded by police use of force justifies an assessment of whether there has been a violation of the equal protection clause of the Fourteenth Amendment.

The Court has long recognized that the discriminatory application of a state statute on the basis of race is prohibited under the equal protection clause of the Fourteenth Amendment. *See Yick Wo v. Hopkins*, 118 U.S. 356, (1886). A state law neutral on its face, yet reserving arbitrary discretion in the law enforcement officers to determine whether a suspect should live or die, opens the door for unending discrimination against any race or class of people, thus, nullifying the right to equal protection under the law. *See id.* at 362. The common law fleeing felon statutes impose no guidelines or standards on police officers discretion in using deadly force to effect an arrest. *See* Tenn. Code Ann. §40-7-108; Accord, Florida Stat. Ann. §776.05 (1983):

> A law enforcement officer, or any person whom he has summoned or directed to assist him, need not retreat or desist from efforts to make a lawful arrest because of resistance or threatened resistance to the arrest. He is justified in the use of force which he reasonably believes to be necessary to defend himself or another from bodily harm while making the arrest or when necessarily committed in retaking felons who have escaped *or when necessarily committed in arresting felons fleeing from justice.* (emphasis added)

These statutes and others which codify the common law allow law enforcement officers to use diverse methods, including deadly force, to effect an arrest. Lack of standards permit a host of factors, including race, to play a part in which suspects are shot and which are arrested by some less destructive alternative. Statistics bear out the fact that left to their own discretion, a significantly disproportionate number of black suspects will be fatally shot by police.

Prevailing case law clearly embraces the proposition that racial discrimination can be inferred from the historical background underlying the decision. *Arlington Heights v. Metropolitan Housing Corp.*, 429 U.S. 252, 266-267 (1977). Historical discrimination within the Memphis Police Department is a fact. The number of blacks and minorities employed within the department at the time of Garner's death was less than 6 percent. This number was significantly lower than the racial distribution of the entire population of Memphis: 61 percent white, 39 percent black. As late as 1968, "recruitment, selection and promotion in the department was essentially political." Discrimination was recognized by the public, police officials and sociologists. The tension that existed between white officers and black citizens had led to the creation of programs to improve police-community relations. However, in Memphis, police liaisons with the black community rarely relayed these citizens concerns about police brutality and shoddy police service. Even local politicians dared not "give in" to the numerous requests of the black community because it would be detrimental to their political careers

Sociologists recognized that most major urban cities are torn along racial lines over the administration of the law and the enforcement of order. Policemen are seen as products of a white environment. They experience fear, anger, confusion and frustration when patrolling black communities.

This consistent pattern of racial discrimination on the part of Memphis police officials, politicians, and street-level officers clearly shows a violation of the Equal Protection Clause.

In addition, the highly discretionary policy in effect at the time Garner was killed contributes to the pattern of racial discrimination on the part of police officers. The policies are subject to the individual's perception of the circumstances at the time he apprehends a fleeing felon. Individual interpretations lead to the application of the common law in a non-systematic manner within one single police department. These interpretations are influenced by the values of the department and the society that supports them. Thus, use of deadly force in apprehending fleeing felony suspects will vary considerably among the numerous departments despite the similarities codified in the state statutes.

The common law policy does not preclude invidious discrimination of any racial classification. Thus, because the statute is not applied in the same manner, some officers are apt to discriminate on the basis of race, in violation of the equal protection clause of the Fourteenth Amendment.

As in jury selection cases, where disproportionate impact on a specific racial class is coupled with a system of selection that is discretionary or easily subject to abuse, discriminatory intent may be inferred. *See Castaneda v. Partida*, 430 U.S. 482, (1977); *Hernandez v. Texas*, 347 U.S. 478 (1945), *Atkins v. Texas*, 325 U.S. 398 (1945).

A similar analysis can be employed to show a violation of equal protection has occurred in the context of fleeing felon cases. In Memphis blacks accounted for 70.6 percent of those arrested for property crimes between 1969 and 1976, and 88.4 percent of these suspects were shot by the Memphis police. Appellee's Brief, *supra*, at 27. Of those suspects fatally wounded 50 percent were unarmed and nonassaultive. *Id.* at 28. "Memphis police killed 2.6 unarmed, non-assaultive blacks for each armed, assaultive white" *Id.* (citation omitted). These differences are as great as those deemed significant in the jury selection cases. The discretionary aspect of the common law statutes result in an unreasonable and totally disproportionate number of blacks and minorities being killed by police officers. These results clearly question whether police officers treat all similarly situated non-violent fleeing felons in the same manner. Murdering a significantly disproportional number of blacks bears no rational relationship to a state objective to preserve the peace within a community and apprehend all felony suspects.

In the instant case, appellee provided the United States District Court for the Sixth Circuit with enough evidence to prove the City of Memphis policy on deadly force was motivated by racial animosity. This evidence was erroneously deemed insufficient to set forth a prima facie case to prove the existence of racial discrimination in police homicides. However, the equal protection claim in *Garner,* buttressed by City and Nationwide data serve to show that the Tennessee policy was racially motivated.

ARGUMENT II

A State Statute Allowing Law Enforcement Officers to Shoot Fleeing Felon Suspects, Whom the Officers Reasonably Assume to Be Unarmed and Engaged in Non-Violent Property Crimes, Violate the Suspects' Due Process of Law.

Appellee correctly asserted that the Due Process Clause of the Fourth Amendment prohibits police officers from using deadly force to arrest an unarmed person suspected of committing a non-violent property crime.Relying on *Terry v. Ohio,* 392 U.S. 1 (1968) and *Jenkins v. Averett,* 424 F.2d 1228 (4th Cir. 1970), the Sixth Circuit Court of Appeals found that the method of applying deadly force to secure the arrest and seizure of a nonviolent fleeing felon by police constituted an unreasonable seizure of young Garner.

Unlike in the case at bar, the defendant in *Terry v. Ohio* had a concealed weapon and sought to have the same suppressed. Terry argued that since he was not engaged in any criminal activity the police had no reason to arrest and search him on the suspicion of being an armed and dangerous character. *Id.* at 9. Yet, although confirming Terry's conviction, this Court still maintained the proposition that the Constitution forbids unreasonable searches and seizures.

When the arresting officer proceeded to apprehend young Garner to effect an arrest, it was incumbent upon the officer to act in a reasonable manner. An arrest is no less than a "seizure" of the person, *United States v. Watson,* 423 U.S. 408 (1976); therefore, arrestees are entitled to the protection of the Fourth Amendment against unreasonable seizures of their persons. *See Terry v. Ohio, supra; Cupp v. Murphy,* 412 U.S. 216 (1973). To kill an apparently unarmed person just to insure that he does not walk away is a method "unique in its severity and irrevocability." *Garner v. Memphis Police Dept.,* 710 F.2d at 243, quoting *Gregg v. Georgia,* 428 U.S. 153, 187 (1976). In the case at bar, the police officer, by his own testimony, confessed that he believed young Garner not to be armed, yet he shot Garner in the head because Garner was running to climb a fence in an attempt to get away. Surely, the police officer and his companion officer could have used a reasonable manner of apprehending young Garner short of seizing the boy's life.

The Tennessee Fleeing Felon Statute, Tenn. Code Ann §40-7-108, which the Sixth Circuit ruled unconstitutional, clearly gave police officers complete discretion to use deadly force against any and all felons to effect an arrest. Ruling that Tennessee's Fleeing Felon Statute is unconstitutional was not something done blindly by the Sixth Circuit, nor was it the first time the statute came before that Court or any other Court.

In *Wiley v. Memphis Police Dept.*, 548 F.2d 1247, 1253 (6th Cir. 1977), based in part on the fact that guns were found nearby, the court found the use of deadly force reasonable under the circumstances concluding the act of fleeing from the scene of the burglary constituted a continuous commission of the burglary. *See also* the concurring opinion of Judge McCree in *Wiley, supra,* at 1256.

During 15th Century England and 18th Century America, law enforcement officers were widely permitted to use deadly force in arresting a felony suspect because all felonies were punishable by death; therefore, "the use of deadly force was seen as merely accelerating the penal process" without the inconvenience of a trial.

The 18th Century American view of the common law rule was weakened in the second half of the 19th Century because although the number of crimes classified as felonies increased, the number of capital punishment crimes decreased. Thus, as of 1976, in the twenty odd states who codified the common law deadly force rule, police officers, were authorized to use deadly force in many more situations than was authorized at common law. Consequently, boys like Garner who may have ordinarily received a minimum sentence term or probation are facing the maximum sentence of death without a judge or jury. More than thirty states have already recognized the injustices of the common law deadly force rule, and the Sixth Circuit should be applauded for doing the same in Tennessee.

In *Rochin v. People of California*, 342 U.S. 165 (1951), this Court was faced with whether the sheriffs violated the accused's right to due process when the sheriffs, having souse information that the accused was selling ?? narcotics, entered an open door to the dwelling, forced open the door to the accused's bedroom and forcibly attempted to extract capsules from the accused's mouth; and when that didn't work, directed a doctor to pump the accused's stomach against the accused's will and therefrom extracted two capsules containing morphine. *Id.* at 206. In looking at the Due Process question, this Court acknowledged that the administration of criminal justice is predominantly committed to the care of the States. *Id.* at 168. However, this Court further went on to say that

"the requirements of the Due Process Clause" inescapably imposes upon the Court an exercise

of judgment upon the whole course of the proceedings [resulting in a conviction] in order to

ascertain whether they offend those canons of decency and fairness which express the notions of

justice of English-speaking peoples even toward those charged with the most heinous offenses.

Id. at 169, citing *Malinsky v. New York*, 324 U.S. 401, 416-417 (1945).

In the case at bar, to uphold the constitutionality of the common law deadly force statute would be sanctioning questionable police policies and tactics that not only result in honest mistakes, but deliberate violations of the right to human life. Chief Justice Burger's dissent in *Bivens v. Six Unknown Named Agents of Federal Bureau of Narcotics,* was well taken when he said

> I wonder what would be the judicial response to a police order authorizing "shoot to kill" with respect to every fugitive. It is easy to predict our collective wrath and outrage. We, in common with all rational minds, would say that the police response must relate to the gravity and need; that a "shoot" order might conceivably be tolerated to prevent the escape of a convicted killer but surely not for a car thief, a pickpocket or a shoplifter. 403 U.S. 388, 411 (1971).

The Court has stated that "it would be a stultification of the responsibility which the Court of constitutional history has cast upon this Court to hold that in order to convict a man the police cannot extract by force what is in his mind, but can extract what is in his stomach. *Rochin, supra,* at 173. Yet, would it not be a greater stultification for this Court to say an unarmed person cannot be sentenced to death for committing a nonviolent property crime by a judge or jury, but that same person can be killed, and in effect sentenced to death, for running from the scene of a nonviolent property crime by a police officer even though the fleeing victim was not placing anyone's life in danger, but, apparently, his own.

Therefore, justice dictates that this Court affirm the Sixth Circuit Court of Appeals holding that the Tennessee Statute as well as other state common law statutes on deadly force, violates the Due Process Clause of the Constitution, and is, therefore, unconstitutional.

GRAHAM V. CONNOR
490 U.S. 386 (1989)

Chief Justice REHNQUIST delivered the opinion of the Court.

This case requires us to decide what constitutional standard governs a free citizen's claim that law enforcement officials used excessive force in the course of making an arrest, investigatory stop, or other "seizure" of his person. We hold that such claims are properly analyzed under the Fourth Amendment's "objective reasonableness" standard, rather than under a substantive due process standard.

In this action under 42 U.S.C. § 1983, petitioner Dethorne Graham seeks to recover damages for injuries allegedly sustained when law enforcement officers used physical force against him during the course of an investigatory stop. Because the case comes to us from a decision of the Court of Appeals affirming the entry of a directed verdict for respondents, we take the evidence hereafter noted in the light most favorable to petitioner. On November 12, 1984, Graham, a diabetic, felt the onset of an insulin reaction. He asked a friend, William Berry, to drive him to a nearby convenience store so he could purchase some orange juice to counteract the reaction. Berry agreed, but when Graham entered the store, he saw a number of people ahead of him in the check outline. Concerned about the delay, he hurried out of the store and asked Berry to drive him to a friend's house instead.

Respondent Connor, an officer of the Charlotte, North Carolina, Police Department, saw Graham hastily enter and leave the store. The officer became suspicious that something was amiss and followed Berry's car. About one-half mile from the store, he made an investigative stop. Although Berry told Connor that Graham was simply suffering from a "sugar reaction," the officer ordered Berry and Graham to wait while he found out what, if anything, had happened at the convenience store. When Officer Connor returned to his patrol car to call for backup assistance, Graham got out of the car, ran around it twice, and finally sat down on the curb, where he passed out briefly.

In the ensuing confusion, a number of other Charlotte police officers arrived on the scene in response to Officer Connor's request for backup. One of the officers rolled Graham over on the sidewalk and cuffed his hands tightly behind his back, ignoring Berry's pleas to get him some sugar. Another officer said: "I've seen a lot of people with sugar diabetes that never acted like this. Ain't nothing wrong with the M.F. but drunk. Lock the S.B. up." App. 42. Several officers then lifted Graham up from behind, carried him over to Berry's car, and placed him face down on its hood. Regaining consciousness, Graham asked the officers to check in his wallet for a diabetic decal that he carried. In response, one of the officers told him to "shut up" and shoved his face down against the hood of the car. Four officers grabbed Graham and threw him headfirst into the police car. A friend of Graham's brought some orange juice to the car, but the officers refused to let him have it. Finally, Officer Connor received a report that Graham had done nothing wrong at the convenience store, and the officers drove him home and released him.

At some point during his encounter with the police, Graham sustained a broken foot, cuts on his wrists, a bruised forehead, and an injured shoulder; he also claims to have developed a loud ringing in his right ear that continues to this day. He commenced this action under 42 U.S.C. § 1983 against the individual officers involved in the incident, all of whom are respondents here, alleging that they had used excessive force in making the investigatory stop, in violation of "rights secured to him under the Fourteenth Amendment to the United States Constitution and 42 U.S.C. § 1983." Complaint ¶ 10, App. 5. The case was tried before a jury. At the close of petitioner's evidence, respondents moved for a directed verdict. In ruling on that motion, the District Court considered the following four factors, which it identified as "[t]he factors to be considered in determining when the excessive use of force gives rise to a cause of action under

§ 1983": (1) the need for the application of force; (2) the relationship between that need and the amount of force that was used; (3) the extent of the injury inflicted; and (4) "[w]hether the force was applied in a good faith effort to maintain and restore discipline or maliciously and sadistically for the very purpose of causing harm." 644 F.Supp. 246, 248 (WDNC 1986). Finding that the amount of force used by the officers was "appropriate under the circumstances," that "[t]here was no discernable injury inflicted," and that the force used "was not applied maliciously or sadistically for the very purpose of causing harm," but in "a good faith effort to maintain or restore order in the face of a potentially explosive situation," id., at 248–249, the District Court granted respondents' motion for a directed verdict.

A divided panel of the Court of Appeals for the Fourth Circuit affirmed. 827 F.2d 945 (1987). The majority ruled first that the District Court had applied the correct legal standard in assessing petitioner's excessive force claim. Id., at 948–949. Without attempting to identify the specific constitutional provision under which that claim arose,the majority endorsed the four-factor test applied by the District Court as generally applicable to all claims of "constitutionally excessive force" brought against governmental officials. Id., at 948. The majority rejected petitioner's argument, based on Circuit precedent, that it was error to require him to prove that the allegedly excessive force used against him was applied "maliciously and sadistically for the very purpose of causing harm." Ibid. Finally, the majority held that a reasonable jury applying the four-part test it had just endorsed to petitioner's evidence "could not find that the force applied was constitutionally excessive." Id., at 949–950. The dissenting judge argued that this Court's decisions in Terry v. Ohio, 392 U.S. 1, 88 S.Ct. 1868, 20 L.Ed.2d 889 (1968), and Tennessee v. Garner, 471 U.S. 1, 105 S.Ct. 1694, 85 L.Ed.2d 1 (1985), required that excessive force claims arising out of investigatory stops be analyzed under the Fourth Amendment's "objective reasonableness" standard. 827 F.2d, at 950–952. We granted certiorari, and now reverse.

Fifteen years ago, in Johnson v. Glick, 481 F.2d 1028, cert. denied, 414 U.S. 1033, 94 S.Ct. 462, 38 L.Ed.2d 324 (1973), the Court of Appeals for the Second Circuit addressed a § 1983 damages claim filed by a pretrial detainee who claimed that a guard had assaulted him without justification. In evaluating the detainee's claim, Judge Friendly applied neither the Fourth Amendment nor the Eighth, the two most textually obvious sources of constitutional protection against physically abusive governmental conduct.Instead, he looked to "substantive due process," holding that "quite apart from any 'specific' of the Bill of Rights, application of undue force by law enforcement officers deprives a suspect of liberty without due process of law." 481 F.2d, at 1032. As support for this proposition, he relied upon our decision in Rochin v. California, 342 U.S. 165, 72 S.Ct. 205, 96 L.Ed. 183 (1952), which used the Due Process Clause to void a state criminal conviction based on evidence obtained by pumping the defendant's stomach. 481 F.2d, at 1032–1033. If a police officer's use of force which "shocks the conscience" could justify setting aside a criminal conviction, Judge Friendly reasoned, a correctional officer's use of similarly excessive force must give rise to a due process violation actionable under § 1983. Ibid. Judge Friendly went on to set forth four factors to guide courts in determining "whether the constitutional line has been crossed" by a particular use of force—the same four factors relied upon by the courts below in this case. Id., at 1033.

In the years following *Johnson v. Glick*, the vast majority of lower federal courts have applied its four-part "substantive due process" test indiscriminately to all excessive force claims lodged against law enforcement and prison officials under § 1983, without considering whether the particular application of force might implicate a more specific constitutional right governed by a different standard. Indeed, many courts have seemed to assume, as did the courts below in this case, that there is a generic "right" to be free from excessive force, grounded not in any particular constitutional provision but rather in "basic principles of § 1983 jurisprudence."

We reject this notion that all excessive force claims brought under § 1983 are governed by a single generic standard. As we have said many times, § 1983 "is not itself a source of substantive rights," but merely provides "a method for vindicating federal rights elsewhere conferred." *Baker v. McCollan*, 443 U.S. 137, 144, n. 3, 99 S.Ct. 2689, 2694, n. 3, 61 L.Ed.2d 433 (1979). In addressing an excessive force claim brought under § 1983, analysis begins by identifying the specific constitutional right allegedly infringed by the challenged application of force. See id., at 140, 99 S.Ct., at 2692 ("The first inquiry in any § 1983 suit" is "to isolate the precise constitutional violation with which [the defendant] is charged"). In most instances, that will be either the Fourth Amendment's prohibition against unreasonable seizures of the person, or the Eighth Amendment's ban on cruel and unusual punishments, which are the two primary sources of constitutional protection against physically abusive governmental conduct. The validity of the claim must then be judged by reference to the specific constitutional standard which governs that right, rather than to some generalized "excessive force" standard. See *Tennessee v. Garner, supra*, 471 U.S., at 7–22, 105 S.Ct., at 1699–1707 (claim of excessive force to effect arrest analyzed under a Fourth Amendment standard); *Whitley v. Albers*, 475 U.S. 312, 318–326, 106 S.Ct. 1078, 1083–1088, 89 L.Ed.2d 251 (1986) (claim of excessive force to subdue convicted prisoner analyzed under an Eighth Amendment standard).

Where, as here, the excessive force claim arises in the context of an arrest or investigatory stop of a free citizen, it is most properly characterized as one invoking the protections of the Fourth Amendment, which guarantees citizens the right "to be secure in their persons ... against unreasonable ... seizures" of the person. This much is clear from our decision in *Tennessee v. Garner, supra*. In *Garner*, we addressed a claim that the use of deadly force to apprehend a fleeing suspect who did not appear to be armed or otherwise dangerous violated the suspect's constitutional rights, notwithstanding the existence of probable cause to arrest. Though the complaint alleged violations of both the Fourth Amendment and the Due Process Clause, see 471 U.S., at 5, 105 S.Ct., at 1698, we analyzed the constitutionality of the challenged application of force solely by reference to the Fourth Amendment's prohibition against unreasonable seizures of the person, holding that the "reasonableness" of a particular seizure depends not only on *when* it is made, but also on *how* it is carried out. *Id.*, at 7–8, 105 S.Ct., at 1699–1700. Today we make explicit what was implicit in *Garner* 's analysis, and hold that *all* claims that law enforcement officers have used excessive force—deadly or not—in the course of an arrest, investigatory stop, or other "seizure" of a free citizen should be analyzed under the Fourth Amendment and its "reasonableness" standard, rather than under a "substantive due process" approach. Because the Fourth Amendment provides an explicit textual source of constitutional protection against this sort of physically intrusive governmental conduct, that Amendment, not the more generalized notion of "substantive due process," must be the guide for analyzing these claims.

Determining whether the force used to effect a particular seizure is "reasonable" under the Fourth Amendment requires a careful balancing of " 'the nature and quality of the intrusion on the individual's Fourth Amendment interests' " against the countervailing governmental interests at stake. *Id.*, at 8, 105 S.Ct., at 1699, quoting *United States v. Place*, 462 U.S. 696, 703, 103 S.Ct. 2637, 2642, 77 L.Ed.2d 110 (1983). Our Fourth Amendment jurisprudence has long recognized that the right to make an arrest or investigatory stop necessarily carries with it the right to use some degree of physical coercion or threat thereof to effect it. See Terry v. Ohio, 392 U.S., at 22–27, 88 S.Ct., at 1880–1883. Because "[t]he test of reasonableness under the Fourth Amendment is not capable of precise definition or mechanical application," *Bell v. Wolfish*, 441 U.S. 520, 559, 99 S.Ct. 1861, 1884, 60 L.Ed.2d 447 (1979), however, its proper application requires careful attention to the facts and circumstances of each particular case, including the severity of the crime at issue, whether the suspect poses an immediate threat to the safety of the officers or others, and whether he is actively resisting arrest or attempting to evade arrest by flight. See *Tennessee v. Garner*, 471 U.S., at 8–9, 105 S.Ct., at 1699–1700 (the question is "whether the totality of the circumstances justifie[s] a particular sort of ... seizure").

The "reasonableness" of a particular use of force must be judged from the perspective of a reasonable officer on the scene, rather than with the 20/20 vision of hindsight. See *Terry v. Ohio*, supra, 392 U.S., at 20–22, 88 S.Ct., at 1879–1881. The Fourth Amendment is not violated by an arrest based on probable cause, even though the wrong person is arrested, *Hill v. California*, 401 U.S. 797, 91 S.Ct. 1106, 28 L.Ed.2d 484 (1971), nor by the mistaken execution of a valid search warrant on the wrong premises, *Maryland v. Garrison*, 480 U.S. 79, 107 S.Ct. 1013, 94 L.Ed.2d 72 (1987). With respect to a claim of excessive force, the same standard of reasonableness at the moment applies: "Not every push or shove, even if it may later seem unnecessary in the peace of a judge's chambers," *Johnson v. Glick*, 481 F.2d, at 1033, violates the Fourth Amendment. The calculus of reasonableness must embody allowance for the fact that police officers are often forced to make split-second judgments—in circumstances that are tense, uncertain, and rapidly evolving—about the amount of force that is necessary in a particular situation.

As in other Fourth Amendment contexts, however, the "reasonableness" inquiry in an excessive force case is an objective one: the question is whether the officers' actions are "objectively reasonable" in light of the facts and circumstances confronting them, without regard to their underlying intent or motivation. See *Scott v. United States*, 436 U.S. 128, 137–139, 98 S.Ct. 1717, 1723–1724, 56 L.Ed.2d 168 (1978); see also *Terry v. Ohio*, supra, 392 U.S., at 21, 88 S.Ct., at 1879 (in analyzing the reasonableness of a particular search or seizure, "it is imperative that the facts be judged against an objective standard"). An officer's evil intentions will not make a Fourth Amendment violation out of an objectively reasonable use of force; nor will an officer's good intentions make an objectively unreasonable use of force constitutional. See *Scott v. United States*, supra, 436 U.S., at 138, 98 S.Ct., at 1723, citing *United States v. Robinson*, 414 U.S. 218, 94 S.Ct. 467, 38 L.Ed.2d 427 (1973).

Because petitioner's excessive force claim is one arising under the Fourth Amendment, the Court of Appeals erred in analyzing it under the four-part *Johnson v. Glick* test. That test, which requires consideration of whether the individual officers acted in "good faith" or "maliciously and sadistically for the very purpose of causing harm," is incompatible with a proper Fourth Amendment analysis. We do not agree with the Court of Appeals' suggestion, see 827 F.2d, at 948, that the "malicious and sadistic" inquiry is merely another way of describing conduct that is objectively unreasonable under the circumstances. Whatever the empirical correlations between "malicious and sadistic" behavior and objective unreasonableness may be, the fact remains that the "malicious and sadistic" factor puts in issue the subjective motivations of the individual officers, which our prior cases make clear has no bearing on whether a particular seizure is "unreasonable" under the Fourth Amendment. Nor do we agree with the Court of Appeals' conclusion, see *id.*, at 948, n. 3, that because the subjective motivations of the individual officers are of central importance in deciding whether force used against a convicted prisoner violates the Eighth Amendment, see *Whitley v. Albers*, 475 U.S., at 320–321, 106 S.Ct., at 1084–1085, it cannot be reversible error to inquire into them in deciding whether force used against a suspect or arrestee violates the Fourth Amendment. Differing standards under the Fourth and Eighth Amendments are hardly surprising: the terms "cruel" and "punishments" clearly suggest some inquiry into subjective state of mind, whereas the term "unreasonable" does not. Moreover, the less protective Eighth Amendment standard applies "only after the State has complied with the constitutional guarantees traditionally associated with criminal prosecutions." *Ingraham v. Wright*, 430 U.S. 651, 671, n. 40, 97 S.Ct. 1401, 1412, n. 40, 51 L.Ed.2d 711 (1977). The Fourth Amendment inquiry is one of "objective reasonableness" under the circumstances, and subjective concepts like "malice" and "sadism" have no proper place in that inquiry.

Because the Court of Appeals reviewed the District Court's ruling on the motion for directed verdict under an erroneous view of the governing substantive law, its judgment must be vacated and the case remanded to that court for reconsideration of that issue under the proper Fourth Amendment standard.

It is so ordered.

Race and "No Knock" Warrants

Note

Law enforcement execution of "no knock" warrants has also been a cause of Fourth Amendment concern, particularly in communities of color. The concept of "no knock" warrants centers around a law enforcement perceived need to execute a validly-issued warrant by force-entry into a residence without first announcing to an intent to enter or the presence of law enforcement. The United States Supreme Court debated the issue of reasonableness in a series of cases. Noting that the need to preserve evidence from destruction and to protect officers from harm would sometimes justify a "no knock" entry, *Wilson v. Arkansas*, 514 U.S. 927 (1995), if such risks were supported by reasonable suspicion, *Richards v. Wisconsin*, 420 U.S. 385 (1997) recognized broad discretion on the part of law enforcement to "on the scene" determinations of circumstances demonstrating reasonable suspicion. (in fact, in *Richards* the warrant-issuing magistrate struck out of the warrant specific language authorizing "no knock" entry.) In the absence of reasonable suspicion, the common law standard requiring "knock and announce" has been held to be embodied in the Reasonableness Clause of the Fourth Amendment. (*Wilson*) However evidence seized in violation of "knock and announce" is not required to be suppressed under the Fourth Amendment, *Hudson v. Michigan*, 547 U.S. 586 (2006), leaving in question what penalties, if any, can be placed against police officers who unconstitutionally invade a home in this manner.

Of particular significance in this section is the violent and often deadly consequences that can befall residents in their own home – including persons who have not engaged in criminal activity. While "No Knock" entries are typically used in drugs cases (although the Supreme Court in *Richards* rejects the notion that such entries can be based on a blanket approach to any crime category), there is some indication that communities of color have been particularly vulnerable to such raids – with deadly consequences.

In the early morning hours of December 5, 2017 92-year old Natalio Conde was awakened by "intruders' who burst into his Bronx apartment. When his 69-year-old brother-in-law, Mario Sanabria, sought to investigate, he was shot dead. Mario was shot by police officers who had entered the apartment without knocking or announcing to execute a search warrant. Neither the person the police were seeking (Mr. Conde's son) nor any incriminating evidence were in the apartment. James C. McKinley Jr., *After Police Raid Kills Man, 69, Family Asks Why Trigger Was Pulled* https://www.nytimes.com/2017/12/13/nyregion/nypd-police-shooting-bronx-mario-sanabria-lawsuit.html

More recently, attention has been drawn to the death of Breonna Taylor. On March 13, 2020, in Louisville Kentucky, Breonna Taylor, a 26-year-old African America emergency medical technician, was shot in her own apartment eight times by police who entered without announcing or knocking. Police were looking for possible packages belonging to a friend who did not live in the apartment but was suspected of selling controlled substances. When Ms. Taylor's boyfriend, a licensed firearm owner responded to the unknown intruders by firing his weapon, police responded by firing more than twenty shots throughout the apartment – some passing through walls and entering the dwellings of other residents in the apartment building, and some fired from outside the apartment through closed blinds and curtains.

Public reactions of outrage at the police actions were heightened following the national attention focused on the death of George Young in Minneapolis, killed while in police custody on May 25, 2020.

The deaths of Breonna Taylor and George Young, together with the numerous deaths of other African Americans, Latinos and person of color by law enforcement, has led in 2020 to a national and international civil rights outcry perhaps not seen since the death of Emmet Till in 1955.

Breonna Taylor's death has led Louisville City Council to adopt what has become known as "Breonna's Law". This ordinance provides, in part:

> No LMPD officer shall seek a no-knock search warrant unless the warrant application includes:
> (1) All documentation and materials the issuing court requires; and (2) A completed Warrant
> Application Form as provided in Section 36. XX. (B). No-knock warrants may only be sought in
> cases involving imminent threat of harm or death to law enforcement and/or to civilians, which
> shall be limited to the following offenses: murder, hostage taking, kidnapping, terrorism, human
> trafficking and sexual trafficking. (ORDINANCE NO. ___, SERIES 2020, Section 36.XX (A) and
> (B)

Federal legislation to ban or restrict "No Knock" warrants has also been proposed in the House of Representatives as part of the Justice in Policing Act of 2020 and by Senator Rand Paul in the Justice for Breonna Taylor Act.

"Black Lives Matter", Police Violence and Proposals for Reform

History of Police Racial Violence

The Amicus Brief of the NAACP Legal Defense Fund in *Tennessee v. Garner*, included above, documents a long history of concern regarding the disproportionate use of deadly force by law enforcement in the apprehension, seizure and searching of African Americans and persons of color. Looking at police shootings, as just one form of police violence, The Washington Post began collecting comprehensive date from 2015 to present on all fatal shootings by on-duty police officers.

The Washington Post determined aspart of its database entitled "Fatal Force" https://www. washingtonpost.com/graphics/investigations/police-shootings-database/ that more than 5,000 persons, since 2015, have been killed by police shootings.

While half of the 5,000 persons fatally shot by the police have been White, African Americans are shot at a rate more than twice that of Caucasians. (shooting of Blacks 31 per million, shooting of Whites 13 per million). Hispanics/Latinos are also disproportionately shot (23 per million). Perhaps no shooting of an unarmed African American by police during a stop received more attention than that concerning the 2014 death of Michael Brown Jr in Ferguson, Missouri. The Michael Brown death led to civil unrest and attempts at reform of policing. See, The Ferguson Commission, FORWARD through FERGUSON: A PATH TOWARD RACIAL EQUITY, https:// forwardthroughferguson.org/report/executive-summary/

National concern has also begun to focus on police use deadly force other than shooting. Specifically, the death of Eric Garner at the hands of New York City police in 2014, caused by the use of a "choke hold "and Elijah McClain, Aurora, Colorado, also involving a "choke hold" led to national concern as to the appropriateness of such tactics and the prevalence of such use, against individuals of color. Ironically, the "choke hold" as a martial arts device, introduced in Judo in 1882, was not intended as a fatal tactic and should not produce fatality if properly used. E. Karl Koiwai, M.D., *Deaths Allegedly Caused by The Use Of "Choke Holds" (Shime-Waza)*, https://judoinfo.com/chokes6/ Unlike the Washington Post database, few statistics if any are kept regarding police-caused death by means other than shooting. However, it was the death of George Floyd, in Minneapolis, caused by a knee pressed into Floyd's throat, for more than 12 minutes, by a police officer caught on camera, that sparked a society-wide outrage and questioning of police use of deadly force against persons of color and gave further voice to the "Black Lives Matter" movement.

The Rise of "Black Lives Matter"

Note, The Early History of The Black Lives Matter Movement, And the Implications Thereof, 18 NEV. L.J. 1091(2018) (excerpt)(reprint by permission of Nevada Law Journal, William S. Boyd School of Law, UNLV)

....

I. THE CATALYST: TRAYVON MARTIN AND GEORGE ZIMMERMAN

A. *The Killing of Trayvon Martin*

BLM began as a response to a court case—much like the direct-action campaign that followed *Brown v. Board of Education*, and other civil rights movements throughout American history -specifically, the verdict in *State of Florida v. George Michael Zimmerman*. George Zimmerman's killing of Trayvon Martin and the jury's verdict in Zimmerman's criminal trial sparked outrage among many and brought light to what would become a disturbing trend ...

On February 26, 2012, George Zimmerman, a local resident and member of the neighborhood watch shot Trayvon Martin, a seventeen-year-old African American man who was visiting his father in Sanford, Florida to death. Before the shooting, Zimmerman called 911 to report a suspicious person— Martin. Despite the 911 operator instructing him to stay in his vehicle, Zimmerman confronted Martin. What followed would become the centerpiece of a media frenzy for the next year and a half. Recordings from the 911 call painted a vague, yet disturbing picture of the confrontation between Zimmerman and Martin. A cry for help, and the gunshot that followed, were the only evidence of what happened between the two.

On March 19, 2012, the Justice Department and FBI announced the launch of an investigation into Martin's death. A petition on Change.org calling for the arrest of Zimmerman surpassed 1.3 million signatures three days later. The next day, less than one month after Martin's death, President Obama made a public statement regarding the shooting, saying that the incident required "soul-searching." On March 26, 2012, one month after Martin's death, rallies were held across the country. Finally, on April 11, 2012, Zimmerman was formally charged with second-degree murder.

B. *The Trial of George Zimmerman*

The media attention building up to George Zimmerman's trial raised tensions even further. At the end of April, Zimmerman entered a written plea of not guilty to the charge of second-degree murder. In July, Zimmerman fought to get the Judge to recuse himself for making disparaging remarks during the bail order, and also made a television appearance on Fox News in which Zimmerman said that he would not have done anything differently during the incident. In December, Zimmerman sued NBC Universal for allegedly editing the 911 recordings to make Zimmerman appear to be racist. In February of 2013, the Justice for Trayvon Martin Foundation held a "Day of Remembrance Community Peace Walk and Forum" in Miami.

The trial finally began on June 24, 2013. Inside the courtroom, the discussion focused on whether Zimmerman's actions constituted self-defense. Outside, the nation watched with a sense of urgency because the discussion involved racial violence. News outlets focused on

Zimmerman and the allegations of racism, on Martin's family, and on the community at large. Finally, on July 13, 2013, after deliberating for more than sixteen hours, the jury returned its verdict: George Zimmerman was not guilty.

....

E. Civil Rights Sentiment

The importance and significance of the early BLM social media posts reveal much of why the movement became a center-point of traditional and social media coverage in America. The combination of love and anger, and the feeling that racial tensions had reached a breaking point, was shared by people throughout the nation. In the week following the Zimmerman verdict, many communities responded by holding public prayers, protests, and other demonstrations. In Atlanta, more than two thousand people gathered in front of CNN Center. In Sanford, Florida, where the trial was held, pastors held a prayer service. In Washington, D.C. demonstrators outside the Justice Department called for civil rights charges against Zimmerman (though these requests would ultimately be formally denied in February, 2015).Similar demonstrations took place in Times Square. The Black community particularly echoed feelings that have reverberated throughout each generation's civil rights struggle, yet the community lacked a cohesive rallying cry.

The acquittal of George Zimmerman inspired feelings of anger and disillusionment throughout the Black community, which, in turn, inspired action and activism outside of the courtroom, in much the same way that the Supreme Court's decision in *Brown v. Board of Education* inspired the direct-action campaign of the early 1960s. Following *Brown*, many young African Americans felt that the legal system could not supply the large-scale reform that more direct, non-legal action could. This feeling led to the sit-ins and large-scale public demonstrations that are commonly associated with the civil rights movement in the 1960s. As discussed in greater detail below, these same feelings are inherent in Garza and Cullors's social media posts, as well as many others, following the Zimmerman verdict. And, as they did in the 1960s after *Brown*, these feelings ultimately inspired the activism outside of the courtroom.

....

A. Starting the Discussion

Black Lives Matter spread rapidly, using social media and the internet to facilitate widespread awareness. However, #BlackLivesMatter remained an article of social media. In terms of the Black Lives Matter movement, 2013 generated little in the way of action or reform. However, the issue of racial violence and inequality had been exposed, and had again become part of the national conversation. In November of 2013, *The Daily Show*, hosted by Jon Stewart, showed a satirical video containing tips on how to avoid racial profiling while shopping, called "Black Friday Profiling." While the video was parodic, it shone light on the increasing racial tension in post-Zimmerman America.

By the end of 2013 #BlackLivesMatter had not yet become a civil rights movement in the traditional sense, despite its frequent social-media presence and the backlash to the Zimmerman verdict. But #BlackLivesMatter had become a conversation point, more and more frequently seen in social media posts, as well as occasionally receiving traditional media attention, because it touched on the growing discontent with racial inequality in the legal system. And in 2014, America would witness the transition from social media discussion to rallying cry, as Black Lives Matter, the movement, came into existence.

B. Ferguson, Staten Island, and the Disease of Racial Police Violence

On August 9, 2014, Michael Brown, a black teenager, was shot and killed by a white police officer, Darren Wilson, in Ferguson, Missouri. What followed were demonstrations that devolved into full-blown rioting, and which went on for weeks The rioting became so intense that Governor Jay Nixon eventually declared a state of emergency and deployed the Missouri National Guard to deal with the riots. Just weeks before, in Staten Island, New York, Eric Garner, a forty-three-year-old black man, died after being placed in a chokehold by a white police officer, while in police custody. With these deaths, and their aftermath, the issue of racial violence in America reached its boiling point.

Again, the nation, and particularly the Black community, was horrified by the violence that had occurred in Staten Island and Ferguson, and the racial undertones that plagued each death. And again, the utter lack of legal consequences for the deaths made them all the more disturbing. On September 16, in Ferguson, Officer Wilson testified before a St. Louis County grand jury tasked with deciding whether Wilson should be indicted on criminal charges. On November 24, the grand jury announced that it would not indict Officer Wilson in the shooting of Michael Brown. In Staten Island, though continuing investigations are allegedly being conducted, the only official inquiry was a similar grand-jury proceeding. In spite of the chokehold being explicitly banned by police policies, the grand jury found that Officer Pantaleo committed no crime when he killed Eric Garner. Where the Zimmerman verdict had jump-started the feelings of racial inequality, and Black Lives Matter with them, the egregious deaths in Ferguson and Staten Island dramatically intensified the tension. What happened in Ferguson and Staten Island were merely instances of systemic, institutionalized racism that had become a way of life in many communities, without drawing national attention. These deaths brought light to a dark and disturbing problem in America.
....

Proposals for Police Reform

Holding Police Civilly Accountable

TORRES V. MADRID
769 Fed.Appx. 654 (10th Cir. 2019)

ORDER AND JUDGMENT[*]

Monroe G. McKay, Circuit Judge

In this excessive-force case, Roxanne Torres appeals from a district court order that granted the defendants' motion for summary judgment on the basis of qualified immunity. Exercising jurisdiction under 28 U.S.C. § 1291, we affirm.

BACKGROUND

Early in the morning on July 15, 2014, New Mexico State Police officers went to an apartment complex in Albuquerque to arrest a woman, Kayenta Jackson, who was "involved with an organized crime ring." Aplt. App. at 120. The officers saw two individuals standing in front of the woman's apartment next to a Toyota FJ Cruiser. The Cruiser was backed into a parking spot, with cars parked on both sides of it. The officers, who were wearing tactical vests with police markings, decided to make contact with the two individuals in case one was the subject of their arrest warrant.

As the officers approached the Cruiser, one of the individuals ran into the apartment, while the other individual, Torres, got inside the Cruiser and started the engine. At the time, Torres was "trip[ping] ... out" from having used meth "[f]or a couple of days." *Id.* at 108.

Officer Richard Williamson approached the Cruiser's closed driver-side window and told Torres several times, "Show me your hands," as he perceived Torres was making "furtive movements ... that [he] couldn't really see because of the [Cruiser's] tint[ed]" windows. *Id.* at 124 (internal quotation marks omitted). Officer Janice Madrid took up a position near the Cruiser's driver-side front tire. She could not see who the driver was, but she perceived the driver was making "aggressive movements inside the vehicle." *Id.* at 115.

According to Torres, she did not know that Williamson and Madrid were police officers, and she could not hear anything they said. But when she "heard the flicker of the car door" handle, she "freak[ed] out" and "put the car into drive," thinking she was being carjacked. *Id.* at 205.

When Torres put the car in drive, Officer Williamson brandished his firearm. At some point, Officer Madrid drew her firearm as well. Torres testified that she "stepped on the gas ... to get away," and the officers "shot as soon as the [Cruiser] creeped a little inch or two." *Id.* at 206. Officer Madrid testified that the Cruiser "drove at [her]" and she fired "at the driver through the windshield" "to stop the driver from running [her] over." *Id.* at 114. Officer Williamson testified that he shot at the driver because he feared being "crush[ed]" between the Cruiser and the neighboring car, as well as "to stop the action of [the Cruiser] going towards [Officer] Madrid." *Id.* at 125.

Two bullets struck Torres. She continued forward, however, driving over a curb, through some landscaping, and onto a street. After colliding with another vehicle, she stopped in a parking lot, exited the Cruiser, laid down on the ground, and attempted to "surrender" to the "carjackers" (who she believed might be in pursuit). *Id.* at 208.

Torres "was [still] tripping out bad." *Id.* She asked a bystander to call police, but she did not want to wait around because she had an outstanding arrest warrant. So, she stole a Kia Soul that was left running while its driver loaded material into the trunk. Torres drove approximately 75 miles to Grants, New Mexico, and went to a hospital, where she identified herself as "Johanna rae C. Olguin." *Id.* at 255. She was airlifted to a hospital in Albuquerque, properly identified, and arrested by police on July 16, 2014. She ultimately pled no contest to three crimes: (1) aggravated fleeing from a law-enforcement officer (Officer Williamson); (2) assault upon a police officer (Officer Madrid); and (3) unlawfully taking a motor vehicle.

In October 2016, Torres filed a civil-rights complaint in federal court against Officers Williamson and Madrid. She asserted one excessive-force claim against each officer, alleging that the "intentional discharge of a fire arm [sic] ... exceeded the degree of force which a reasonable, prudent law enforcement officer would have applied." *Id.* at 15, 16. She also asserted a claim against each officer for conspiracy to engage in excessive force, alleging that the officers had "formed a single plan through non-verbal communication ... to use excessive force." *Id.* at 15, 16.

The district court construed Torres's complaint as asserting the excessive-force claims under the Fourth Amendment, and the court concluded that the officers were entitled to qualified immunity. It reasoned that the officers had not seized Torres at the time of the shooting, and without a seizure, there could be no Fourth Amendment violation.

DISCUSSION

I. Standards of Review

"We review the district court's summary judgment decision de novo, applying the same standards as the district court." *Punt v. Kelly Servs.*, 862 F.3d 1040, 1046 (10th Cir. 2017). Summary judgment is required when "there is no genuine dispute as to any material fact and the movant is entitled to judgment as a matter of law." Fed. R. Civ. P. 56(a).

Ordinarily, once the moving party meets its initial burden of demonstrating the absence of a genuine issue of material fact, the burden shifts to the nonmoving party to set forth specific facts showing that there is a genuine triable issue. *See Schneider v. City of Grand Junction Police Dep't*, 717 F.3d 760, 767 (10th Cir. 2013). But where, as here, a defendant seeks summary judgment on the basis of qualified immunity, our review is somewhat different.

"When a defendant asserts qualified immunity at summary judgment, the burden shifts to the plaintiff, who must clear two hurdles in order to defeat the defendant's motion." *Riggins v. Goodman*, 572 F.3d 1101, 1107 (10th Cir. 2009). First, "[t]he plaintiff must demonstrate on the facts alleged ... that the defendant violated [her] constitutional or statutory rights." *Id.* While "we ordinarily accept the plaintiff's version of the facts," we do not do so if that version "is blatantly contradicted by the record, so that no reasonable jury could believe it." *Halley v. Huckaby*, 902 F.3d 1136, 1144 (10th Cir. 2018) (internal quotation marks omitted). Second, the plaintiff must show "that the right was clearly established at the time of the alleged unlawful activity." *Riggins*, 572 F.3d at 1107. "If, and only if, the plaintiff meets this two-part test does a defendant then bear the traditional burden of the movant for summary judgment—showing that there are no genuine issues of material fact and that he or she is entitled to judgment as a matter of law." *Nelson v. McMullen*, 207 F.3d 1202, 1206 (10th Cir. 2000) (internal quotation marks omitted).

As explained below, Torres's claims fail under the first prong of the qualified-immunity analysis.

II. Excessive Force

"We treat claims of excessive force as seizures subject to the Fourth Amendment's objective requirement for reasonableness." *Lindsey v. Hyler*, 918 F.3d 1109, 1113 (10th Cir. 2019) (internal quotation marks omitted). Thus, "[t]o establish [her] claim, [Torres] ... must show both that a seizure occurred and that the seizure was unreasonable." *Farrell v. Montoya*, 878 F.3d 933, 937 (10th Cir. 2017) (internal quotation marks omitted). Consequently, "[w]ithout a seizure, there can be no claim for excessive use of force" under the Fourth Amendment. *Id.* (internal quotation marks omitted).

We agree with the district court that Torres failed to show she was seized by the officers' use of force. Specifically, the officers fired their guns in response to Torres's movement of her vehicle. Despite being shot, Torres did not stop or otherwise submit to the officers' authority. Although she exited her vehicle in a parking lot some distance away and attempted to surrender, her intent was to give herself up to "carjackers." Indeed, she testified that she did not want to wait around for police to arrive because she had an outstanding warrant for her arrest. She then stole a car and resumed her flight. She was not taken into custody until after she was airlifted back to a hospital in Albuquerque and identified by police.

These circumstances are governed by *Brooks v. Gaenzle*, 614 F.3d 1213, 1223-24 (10th Cir. 2010), where this court held that a suspect's continued flight after being shot by police negates a Fourth Amendment excessive-force claim. This is so, because "a seizure requires restraint of one's freedom of movement." *Id.* at 1219 (internal quotation marks omitted). Thus, an officer's intentional shooting of a suspect does not effect a seizure unless the "gunshot ... terminate[s] [the suspect's] movement or otherwise cause[s] the government to have physical control over him." *Id.* at 1224.

Here, the officers' use of deadly force against Torres failed to "control [her] ability to evade capture or control." *Id.* at 1223 (internal quotation marks omitted). Because Torres managed to elude police for at least a full day after being shot, there is no genuine issue of material fact as to whether she was seized when Officers Williamson and Madrid fired their weapons into her vehicle. *See id.* (rejecting plaintiff's contention that "his shooting alone constitute[d] a seizure," given that "he continued to flee without the deputies' acquisition of physical control" and "remained at large for days"); *see also Farrell*, 878 F.3d at 939 (concluding that plaintiffs were not seized when an officer fired his gun at them, because they continued fleeing for several minutes). Without a seizure, Torres's excessive-force claims (and the derivative conspiracy claims) fail as a matter of law.[1]

We, therefore, determine that the district court properly entered summary judgment in favor of Officers Williamson and Madrid on the basis of qualified immunity.

BAXTER V. BRACEY
590 U.S. ___ (2020)

Justice THOMAS, dissenting from the denial of certiorari.

Petitioner Alexander Baxter was caught in the act of burgling a house. It is undisputed that police officers released a dog to apprehend him and that the dog bit him. Petitioner alleged that he had already surrendered when the dog was released. He sought damages from two officers under Rev. Stat. § 1979, 42 U. S. C. § 1983, alleging excessive force and failure to intervene, in violation of the Fourth Amendment. Applying our qualified immunity precedents, the Sixth Circuit held that even if the officers' conduct violated the Constitution, they were not liable because their conduct did not violate a clearly established right. Petitioner asked this Court to reconsider the precedents that the Sixth Circuit applied.

I have previously expressed my doubts about our qualified immunity jurisprudence. See *Ziglar v. Abbasi*, 582 U. S. ----, ---- – ----, 137 S.Ct. 1843, 1869–1872, 198 L.Ed.2d 290 (2017) (THOMAS, J., concurring in part and concurring in judgment). Because our § 1983 qualified immunity doctrine appears to stray from the statutory text, I would grant this petition.

I

A

In the wake of the Civil War, Republicans set out to secure certain individual rights against abuse by the States. Between 1865 and 1870, Congress proposed, and the States ratified, the Thirteenth, Fourteenth, and Fifteenth Amendments. These Amendments protect certain rights and gave Congress the power to enforce those rights against the States.

Armed with its new enforcement powers, Congress sought to respond to "the reign of terror imposed by the Klan upon black citizens and their white sympathizers in the Southern States." *Briscoe v. LaHue*, 460 U.S. 325, 337, 103 S.Ct. 1108, 75 L.Ed.2d 96 (1983). Congress passed a statute variously known as the Ku Klux Act of 1871, the Civil Rights Act of 1871, and the Enforcement Act of 1871. Section 1, now codified, as amended, at 42 U. S. C. § 1983, provided that

> "any person who, under color of any law, statute, ordinance, regulation, custom, or usage of any
> State, shall subject, or cause to be subjected, any person within the jurisdiction of the United
> States to the deprivation of any rights, privileges, or immunities secured by the Constitution
> of the United States, shall ... be liable to the party injured in any action at law, suit in equity, or
> other proper proceeding for redress ...." Act of Apr. 20, 1871, § 1, 17 Stat. 13.

Put in simpler terms, § 1 gave individuals a right to sue state officers for damages to remedy certain violations of their constitutional rights.

B

The text of § 1983 "ma[kes] no mention of defenses or immunities." *Ziglar*, supra, at ----, 137 S.Ct., at 1870 (opinion of THOMAS, J.). Instead, it applies categorically to the deprivation of constitutional rights under color of state law.

For the first century of the law's existence, the Court did not recognize an immunity under § 1983 for good-faith official conduct. Although the Court did not squarely deny the availability of a good-faith defense, it did reject an argument that plaintiffs must prove malice to recover. *Myers v. Anderson*, 238 U.S. 368, 378–379, 35 S.Ct. 932, 59 L.Ed. 1349 (1915) (imposing liability); *id.*, at 371, 35 S.Ct. 932 (argument by counsel that malice was an essential element). No other case appears to have established a good-faith immunity.

In the 1950s, this Court began to "as[k] whether the common law in 1871 would have accorded immunity to an officer for a tort analogous to the plaintiff's claim under § 1983." *Ziglar*, supra, at ----, 137 S.Ct., at 1871 (opinion of THOMAS, J.). The Court, for example, recognized absolute immunity for legislators because it concluded Congress had not "impinge[d] on a tradition [of legislative immunity] so well grounded in history and reason by covert inclusion in the general language" of § 1983. *Tenney v. Brandhove*, 341 U.S. 367, 376, 71 S.Ct. 783, 95 L.Ed. 1019 (1951). The Court also extended a qualified defense of good faith and probable cause to police officers sued for unconstitutional arrest and detention. *Pierson v. Ray*, 386 U.S. 547, 557, 87 S.Ct. 1213, 18 L.Ed.2d 288 (1967). The Court derived this defense from "the background of tort liabilit[y] in the case of police officers making an arrest." Id., at 556–557, 87 S.Ct. 1213. These decisions were confined to certain circumstances based on specific analogies to the common law.

Almost immediately, the Court abandoned this approach. In *Scheuer v. Rhodes*, 416 U.S. 232, 94 S.Ct. 1683, 40 L.Ed.2d 90 (1974), without considering the common law, the Court remanded for the application of qualified immunity doctrine to state executive officials, National Guard members, and a university president, *id.*, at 234–235, 94 S.Ct. 1683. It based the availability of immunity on practical considerations about "the scope of discretion and responsibilities of the office and all the circumstances as they reasonably appeared at the time of the action on which liability is sought to be based," *id.*, at 247, 94 S.Ct. 1683, rather than the liability of officers for analogous common-law torts in 1871. The Court soon dispensed entirely with context-specific analysis, extending qualified immunity to a hospital superintendent sued for deprivation of the right to liberty. *O'Connor v. Donaldson*, 422 U.S. 563, 577, 95 S.Ct. 2486, 45 L.Ed.2d 396 (1975); see also *Procunier v. Navarette*, 434 U.S. 555, 561, 98 S.Ct. 855, 55 L.Ed.2d 24 (1978) (prison officials and officers).

Then, in *Harlow v. Fitzgerald*, 457 U.S. 800, 102 S.Ct. 2727, 73 L.Ed.2d 396 (1982), the Court eliminated from the qualified immunity inquiry any subjective analysis of good faith to facilitate summary judgment and avoid the "substantial costs [that] attend the litigation of" subjective intent, *id.*, at 816, 102 S.Ct. 2727. Although *Harlow* involved an implied constitutional cause of action against federal officials, not a § 1983 action, the Court extended its holding to § 1983 without pausing to consider the statute's text because "it would be 'untenable to draw a distinction for purposes of immunity law.' " *Id.*, at 818, n. 30, 102 S.Ct. 2727 (quoting *Butz v. Economou*, 438 U.S. 478, 504, 98 S.Ct. 2894, 57 L.Ed.2d 895 (1978)). The Court has subsequently applied this objective test in § 1983 cases. See, *e.g., Ziglar*, 582 U. S., at ––––, 137 S.Ct., at 1866–1867 (majority opinion).

II

In several different respects, it appears that "our analysis is no longer grounded in the common-law backdrop against which Congress enacted the 1871 Act." *Id.*, at ––––, 137 S.Ct., at 1871 (opinion of THOMAS, J.).

There likely is no basis for the objective inquiry into clearly established law that our modern cases prescribe. Leading treatises from the second half of the 19th century and case law until the 1980s contain no support for this "clearly established law" test. Indeed, the Court adopted the test not because of " 'general principles of tort immunities and defenses,' " *Malley v. Briggs*, 475 U.S. 335, 339, 106 S.Ct. 1092, 89 L.Ed.2d 271 (1986), but because of a "balancing of competing values" about litigation costs and efficiency, *Harlow*, supra, at 816, 102 S.Ct. 2727.

There also may be no justification for a one-size-fits-all, subjective immunity based on good faith. Nineteenth-century officials sometimes avoided liability because they exercised their discretion in good faith. See, *e.g., Wilkes v. Dinsman*, 7 How. 89, 130–131, 12 L.Ed. 618 (1849); see also Nielson & Walker, *A Qualified Defense of Qualified Immunity*, 93 Notre Dame L. Rev. 1853, 1864–1868 (2018); Baude, *Is Qualified Immunity Unlawful?* 106 Cal. L. Rev. 45, 57 (2018); Engdahl, *Immunity and Accountability for Positive Governmental Wrongs*, 44 U. Colo. L. Rev. 1, 48–55 (1972). But officials were not *always* immune from liability for their good-faith conduct. See, *e.g., Little v. Barreme*, 2 Cranch 170, 179, 2 L.Ed. 243 (1804) (Marshall, C. J.); *Miller v. Horton*, 152 Mass. 540, 548, 26 N.E. 100, 103 (1891) (Holmes, J.); see also Baude, *supra*, at 55–58; Woolhandler, *Patterns of Official Immunity and Accountability*, 37 Case W. Res. L. Rev. 396, 414–422 (1986); Engdahl, *supra*, at 14–21.

Although I express no definitive view on this question, the defense for good-faith official conduct appears to have been limited to authorized actions within the officer's jurisdiction. See, *e.g., Wilkes*, supra, at 130; T. Cooley, Law of Torts 688–689 (1880); J. Bishop, Commentaries on Non-Contract Law § 773, p. 360 (1889). An officer who acts unconstitutionally might therefore fall within the exception to a common-law good-faith defense.

Regardless of what the outcome would be, we at least ought to return to the approach of asking whether immunity "was 'historically accorded the relevant official' in an analogous situation 'at common law.' " *Ziglar*, supra, at ––––, 137 S.Ct., at 1870 (opinion of THOMAS, J.) (quoting *Imbler v. Pachtman*, 424 U.S. 409, 421, 96 S.Ct. 984, 47 L.Ed.2d 128 (1976)). The Court has continued to conduct this inquiry in absolute immunity cases, even after the sea change in qualified immunity doctrine. See *Burns v. Reed*, 500 U.S. 478, 489–492, 111 S.Ct. 1934, 114 L.Ed.2d 547 (1991). We should do so in qualified immunity cases as well.

* * *

I continue to have strong doubts about our § 1983 qualified immunity doctrine. Given the importance of this question, I would grant the petition for certiorari

Note

Following the 2020 death of George Floyd, while being arrested by Minneapolis police, large scale demonstrations and outcry, combined with some local and state reaction, raised the possibility of "defunding the police" as a method of addressing disproportionate death and injury to non-white suspects during arrest procedures. Initial questions existed, however, as to what is meant by "defunding the police" and how would it work as a practical matter.

Over 114 billion dollars are spent annually by state and local governments on policing. Much of the discussion regarding defunding the police actually takes the form of reallocation of some of that money to other programs that provide services that if successful would reduce the need for standard law enforcement intervention. These programs include quality of life efforts in area such as homelessness, drug usage, housing and domestic violence. As an example, the mayor of New York City has proposed shifting of some of New York's 6 billion annual police budget to other "substantial" areas such as youth programs. Similarly Los Angeles Mayor Garcetti sought to direct 250 million dollars from the annual police budget to youth jobs and health programs. For a discussion of these approaches see *"What Does It Mean to Defund the Police or Disband the Police?"* Lisa Hagen, U.S. NEWS & WORLD REPORT, June 9, 2020. A more cautious approach than that of many police reform advocates is suggested by Stephen Rushin, Roger Michalsk, *Police Funding*, 72 FLA. L. REV. 277 (2020).

Past efforts at addressing police misconduct through police supervisory and disciplinary efforts have sometimes resulted mixed and often disappointing results. See, Craig B. Futterman, H. Melissa Mather, Melanie Miles, *The Use of Statistical Evidence to Address Police Supervisory And Disciplinary Practices: The Chicago Police Department's Broken System*, 1 DePaul J. for Soc. Just. 251 (2008).

The lack of reliable, national data on race and police practices has also called for recommendations of aggressive fact-gathering by the Department of Justice. See, Michael C. McKeown, *Police Misconduct: Ineffective Police Department Complaint-Review Procedures and The Proposition of Corrective Federal Oversight*, 51 SUFFOLK U. L. REV. 309 (2018).

KOREMATSU V. UNITED STATES

323 U.S. 214 (1944)

Mr. Justice BLACK delivered the opinion of the Court.

The petitioner, an American citizen of Japanese descent, was convicted in a federal district court for remaining in San Leandro, California, a 'Military Area', contrary to Civilian Exclusion Order No. 34 of the Commanding General of the Western Command, U.S. Army, which directed that after May 9, 1942, all persons of Japanese ancestry should be excluded from that area. No question was raised as to petitioner's loyalty to the United States. The Circuit Court of Appeals affirmed, and the importance of the constitutional question involved caused us to grant certiorari.

It should be noted, to begin with, that all legal restrictions which curtail the civil rights of a single racial group are immediately suspect. That is not to say that all such restrictions are unconstitutional. It is to say that courts must subject them to the most rigid scrutiny. Pressing public necessity may sometimes justify the existence of such restrictions; racial antagonism never can.

In the instant case prosecution of the petitioner was begun by information charging violation of an Act of Congress, of March 21, 1942, 56 Stat. 173, 18 U.S.C.A. s 97a, which provides that

> " * * * whoever shall enter, remain in, leave, or commit any act in any military area or military zone prescribed, under the authority of an Executive order of the President, by the Secretary of War, or by any military commander designated by the Secretary of War, contrary to the restrictions applicable to any such area or zone or contrary to the order of the Secretary of War or any such military commander, shall, if it appears that he knew or should have known of the existence and extent of the restrictions or order and that his act was in violation thereof, be guilty of a misdemeanor and upon conviction shall be liable to a fine of not to exceed $5,000 or to imprisonment for not more than one year, or both, for each offense."

Exclusion Order No. 34, which the petitioner knowingly and admittedly violated was one of a number of military orders and proclamations, all of which were substantially based upon Executive Order No. 9066, 7 Fed.Reg. 1407. That order, issued after we were at war with Japan, declared that "the successful prosecution of the war requires every possible protection against espionage and against sabotage to national-defense material, national-defense premises, and national-defense utilities. * * *"

One of the series of orders and proclamations, a curfew order, which like the exclusion order here was promulgated pursuant to Executive Order 9066, subjected all persons of Japanese ancestry in prescribed West Coast military areas to remain in their residences from 8 p.m. to 6 a.m. As is the case with the exclusion order here, that prior curfew order was designed as a "protection against espionage and against sabotage." In *Kiyoshi Hirabayashi v. United States,* 320 U.S. 81, 63 S.Ct. 1375, 87 L.Ed. 1774, we sustained a conviction obtained for violation of the curfew order. The Hirabayashi conviction and this one thus rest on the same 1942 Congressional Act and the same basic executive and military orders, all of which orders were aimed at the twin dangers of espionage and sabotage.

The 1942 Act was attacked in the Hirabayashi case as an unconstitutional delegation of power; it was contended that the curfew order and other orders on which it rested were beyond the war powers of the Congress, the military authorities and of the President, as Commander in Chief of the Army; and finally that to apply the curfew order against none but citizens of Japanese ancestry amounted to a constitutionally prohibited discrimination solely on account of race. To these questions, we gave the serious consideration which their importance justified. We upheld the curfew order as an exercise of the power of the government to take steps necessary to prevent espionage and sabotage in an area threatened by Japanese attack.

In the light of the principles we announced in the Hirabayashi case, we are unable to conclude that it was beyond the war power of Congress and the Executive to exclude those of Japanese ancestry from the West Coast war area at the time they did. True, exclusion from the area in which one's home is located is a far greater deprivation than constant confinement to the home from 8 p.m. to 6 a.m. Nothing short of apprehension by the proper military authorities of the gravest imminent danger to the public safety can constitutionally justify either. But exclusion from a threatened area, no less than curfew, has a definite and close relationship to the prevention of espionage and sabotage. The military authorities, charged with the primary responsibility of defending our shores, concluded that curfew provided inadequate protection and ordered exclusion. They did so, as pointed out in our Hirabayashi opinion, in accordance with Congressional authority to the military to say who should, and who should not, remain in the threatened areas.

In this case the petitioner challenges the assumptions upon which we rested our conclusions in the H*irabayashi* case. He also urges that by May 1942, when Order No. 34 was promulgated, all danger of Japanese invasion of the West Coast had disappeared. After careful consideration of these contentions we are compelled to reject them.

Here, as in the *Hirabayashi* case, supra, 320 U.S. at page 99, 63 S.Ct. at page 1385, 87 L.Ed. 1774, "* * * we cannot reject as unfounded the judgment of the military authorities and of Congress that there were disloyal members of that population, whose number and strength could not be precisely and quickly ascertained. We cannot say that the war-making branches of the Government did not have ground for believing that in a critical hour such persons could not readily be isolated and separately dealt with, and constituted a menace to the national defense and safety, which demanded that prompt and adequate measures be taken to guard against it."

Like curfew, exclusion of those of Japanese origin was deemed necessary because of the presence of an unascertained number of disloyal members of the group, most of whom we have no doubt were loyal to this country. It was because we could not reject the finding of the military authorities that it was impossible to bring about an immediate segregation of the disloyal from the loyal that we sustained the validity of the curfew order as applying to the whole group. In the instant case, temporary exclusion of the entire group was rested by the military on the same ground. The judgment that exclusion of the whole group was for the same reason a military imperative answers the contention that the exclusion was in the nature of group punishment based on antagonism to those of Japanese origin. That there were members of the group who retained loyalties to Japan has been confirmed by investigations made subsequent to the exclusion. Approximately five thousand American citizens of Japanese ancestry refused to swear unqualified allegiance to the United States and to renounce allegiance to the Japanese Emperor, and several thousand evacuees requested repatriation to Japan.

We uphold the exclusion order as of the time it was made and when the petitioner violated it. Cf. *Chastleton Corporation v. Sinclair*, 264 U.S. 543, 547, 44 S.Ct. 405, 406, 68 L.Ed. 841; *Block v. Hirsh*, 256 U.S. 135, 154, 155, 41 S.Ct. 458, 459, 65 L.Ed. 865, 16 A.L.R. 165. In doing so, we are not unmindful of the hardships imposed by it upon a large group of American citizens. Cf. *Ex parte Kumezo Kawato*, 317 U.S. 69, 73, 63 S.Ct. 115, 117, 87 L.Ed. 58. But hardships are part of war, and war is an aggregation of hardships. All citizens alike, both in and out of uniform, feel the impact of war in greater or lesser measure. Citizenship has its responsibilities as well as its privileges, and in time of war the burden is always heavier. Compulsory exclusion of large groups of citizens from their homes, except under circumstances of direst emergency and peril, is inconsistent with our basic governmental institutions. But when under conditions of modern warfare our shores are threatened by hostile forces, the power to protect must be commensurate with the threatened danger.

It is argued that on May 30, 1942, the date the petitioner was charged with remaining in the prohibited area, there were conflicting orders outstanding, forbidding him both to leave the area and to remain there. Of course, a person cannot be convicted for doing the very thing which it is a crime to fail to do. But the outstanding orders here contained no such contradictory commands.

There was an order issued March 27, 1942, which prohibited petitioner and others of Japanese ancestry from leaving the area, but its effect was specifically limited in time "until and to the extent that a future proclamation or order should so permit or direct." 7 Fed.Reg. 2601. That 'future order', the one for violation of which petitioner was convicted, was issued May 3, 1942, and it did 'direct' exclusion from the area of all persons of Japanese ancestry, before 12 o'clock noon, May 9; furthermore, it contained a warning that all such persons found in the prohibited area would be liable to punishment under the March 21, 1942 Act of Congress. Consequently, the only order in effect touching the petitioner's being in the area on May 30, 1942, the date specified in the information against him, was the May 3 order which prohibited his remaining there, and it was that same order, which he stipulated in his trial that he had violated, knowing of its existence. There is therefore no basis for the argument that on May 30, 1942, he was subject to punishment, under the March 27 and May 3rd orders, whether he remained in or left the area.

It does appear, however, that on May 9, the effective date of the exclusion order, the military authorities had already determined that the evacuation should be effected by assembling together and placing under guard all those of Japanese ancestry, at central points, designated as 'assembly centers', in order "to insure the orderly evacuation and resettlement of Japanese voluntarily migrating from military area No. 1 to restrict and regulate such migration." Public Proclamation No. 4, 7 Fed.Reg. 2601. And on May 19, 1942, eleven days before the time petitioner was charged with unlawfully remaining in the area, Civilian Restrictive Order No. 1, 8 Fed.Reg. 982, provided for detention of those of Japanese ancestry in assembly or relocation centers. It is now argued that the validity of the exclusion order cannot be considered apart from the orders requiring him, after departure from the area, to report and to remain in an assembly or relocation center. The contention is that we must treat these separate orders as one and inseparable; that, for this reason, if detention in the assembly or relocation center would have illegally deprived the petitioner of his liberty, the exclusion order and his conviction under it cannot stand.

We are thus being asked to pass at this time upon the whole subsequent detention program in both assembly and relocation centers, although the only issues framed at the trial related to petitioner's remaining in the prohibited area in violation of the exclusion order. Had petitioner here left the prohibited area and gone to an assembly center we cannot say either as a matter of fact or law, that his presence in that center would have resulted in his detention in a relocation center. Some who did report to the assembly center were not sent to relocation centers, but were released upon condition that they remain outside the prohibited zone until the military orders were modified or lifted. This illustrates that they pose different problems and may be governed by different principles. The lawfulness of one does not necessarily determine the lawfulness of the others. This is made clear when we analyze the requirements of the separate provisions of the separate orders. These separate requirements were that those of Japanese ancestry (1) depart from the area; (2) report to and temporarily remain in an assembly center; (3) go under military control to a relocation center there to remain for an indeterminate period until released conditionally or unconditionally by the military authorities. Each of these requirements, it will be noted, imposed distinct duties in connection with the separate steps in a complete evacuation program. Had Congress directly incorporated into one Act the language of these separate orders, and provided sanctions for their violations, disobedience of any one would have constituted a separate offense. Cf. *Blockburger v. United States*, 284 U.S. 299, 304, 52 S.Ct. 180, 182, 76 L.Ed. 306. There is no reason why violations of these orders, insofar as they were promulgated pursuant to congressional enactment, should not be treated as separate offenses.

The *Endo case (Ex parte Mitsuye Endo)* 323 U.S. 283, 65 S.Ct. 208, graphically illustrates the difference between the validity of an order to exclude and the validity of a detention order after exclusion has been effected.

Since the petitioner has not been convicted of failing to report or to remain in an assembly or relocation center, we cannot in this case determine the validity of those separate provisions of the order. It is sufficient here for us to pass upon the order which petitioner violated. To do more would be to go beyond the issues raised, and to decide momentous questions not contained within the framework of the pleadings or the evidence in this case. It will be time enough to decide the serious constitutional issues which petitioner seeks to raise when an assembly or relocation order is applied or is certain to be applied to him, and we have its terms before us.

Some of the members of the Court are of the view that evacuation and detention in an Assembly Center were inseparable. After May 3, 1942, the date of Exclusion Order No. 34, Korematsu was under compulsion to leave the area not as he would choose but via an Assembly Center. The Assembly Center was conceived as a part of the machinery for group evacuation. The power to exclude includes the power to do it by force if necessary. And any forcible measure must necessarily entail some degree of detention or restraint whatever method of removal is selected. But whichever view is taken, it results in holding that the order under which petitioner was convicted was valid.

It is said that we are dealing here with the case of imprisonment of a citizen in a concentration camp solely because of his ancestry, without evidence or inquiry concerning his loyalty and good disposition towards the United States. Our task would be simple, our duty clear, were this a case involving the imprisonment of a loyal citizen in a concentration camp because of racial prejudice. Regardless of the true nature of the assembly and relocation centers—and we deem it unjustifiable to call them concentration camps with all the ugly connotations that term implies—we are dealing specifically with nothing but an exclusion order. To cast this case into outlines of racial prejudice, without reference to the real military dangers which were presented, merely confuses the issue. Korematsu was not excluded from the Military Area because of hostility to him or his race. He was excluded because we are at war with the Japanese Empire, because the properly constituted military authorities feared an invasion of our West Coast and felt constrained to take proper security measures, because they decided that the military urgency of the situation demanded that all citizens of Japanese ancestry be segregated from the West Coast temporarily, and finally, because Congress, reposing its confidence in this time of war in our military leaders—as inevitably it must—determined that they should have the power to do just this. There was evidence of disloyalty on the part of some, the military authorities considered that the need for action was great, and time was short. We cannot—by availing ourselves of the calm perspective of hindsight—now say that at that time these actions were unjustified.

Affirmed.

RASUL V. BUSH
542 U.S. 466 (2004)

Justice STEVENS delivered the opinion of the Court.

These two cases present the narrow but important question whether United States courts lack jurisdiction to consider challenges to the legality of the detention of foreign nationals captured abroad in connection with hostilities and incarcerated at the Guantanamo Bay Naval Base, Cuba.

I

On September 11, 2001, agents of the al Qaeda terrorist network hijacked four commercial airliners and used them as missiles to attack American targets. While one of the four attacks was foiled by the heroism of the plane's passengers, the other three killed approximately 3,000 innocent civilians, destroyed hundreds of millions of dollars of property, and severely damaged the U.S. economy. In response to the attacks, Congress passed a joint resolution authorizing the President to use "all necessary and appropriate force against those nations, organizations, or persons he determines planned, authorized, committed, or aided the terrorist attacks ... or harbored such organizations or persons." Authorization for Use of Military Force, Pub.L. 107–40, §§ 1–2, 115 Stat. 224. Acting pursuant to that authorization, the President sent U.S. Armed Forces into Afghanistan to wage a military campaign against al Qaeda and the Taliban regime that had supported it.

Petitioners in these cases are 2 Australian citizens and 12 Kuwaiti citizens who were captured abroad during hostilities between the United States and the Taliban. Since early 2002, the U.S. military has held them—along with, according to the Government's estimate, approximately 640 other non-Americans captured abroad—at the naval base at Guantanamo Bay. Brief for Respondents 6. The United States occupies the base, which comprises 45 square miles of land and water along the southeast coast of Cuba, pursuant to a 1903 Lease Agreement executed with the newly independent Republic of Cuba in the aftermath of the Spanish–American War. Under the agreement, "the United States recognizes the continuance of the ultimate sovereignty of the Republic of Cuba over the [leased areas]," while "the Republic of Cuba consents that during the period of the occupation by the United States ... the United States shall exercise complete jurisdiction and control over and within said areas."In 1934, the parties entered into a treaty providing that, absent an agreement to modify or abrogate the lease, the lease would remain in effect "[s]o long as the United States of America shall not abandon the ... naval station of Guantanamo."

In 2002, petitioners, through relatives acting as their next friends, filed various actions in the U.S. District Court for the District of Columbia challenging the legality of their detention at the base. All alleged that none of the petitioners has ever been a combatant against the United States or has ever engaged in any terrorist acts. They also alleged that none has been charged with any wrongdoing, permitted to consult with counsel, or provided access to the courts or any other tribunal. App. 29, 77, 108.

The two Australians, Mamdouh Habib and David Hicks, each filed a petition for writ of habeas corpus, seeking release from custody, access to counsel, freedom from interrogations, and other relief. *Id.*, at 98–99, 124–126. Fawzi Khalid Abdullah Fahad Al Odah and the 11 other Kuwaiti detainees filed a complaint seeking to be informed of the charges against them, to be allowed to meet with their families and with counsel, and to have access to the courts or some other impartial tribunal. *Id.*, at 34. They claimed that denial of these rights violates the Constitution, international law, and treaties of the United States. Invoking the court's jurisdiction under 28 U.S.C. §§ 1331 and 1350, among other statutory bases, they asserted causes of action under the Administrative Procedure Act, 5 U.S.C. §§ 555, 702, 706; the Alien Tort Statute, 28 U.S.C. § 1350; and the general federal habeas corpus statute, §§ 2241–2243. App. 19.

Construing all three actions as petitions for writs of habeas corpus, the District Court dismissed them for want of jurisdiction. The court held, in reliance on our opinion in Johnson v. Eisentrager, 339 U.S. 763, 70 S.Ct. 936, 94 L.Ed. 1255 (1950), that "aliens detained outside the sovereign territory of the United States [may not] invok[e] a petition for a writ of habeas corpus." 215 F.Supp.2d 55, 68 (D.D.C.2002). The Court of Appeals affirmed. Reading *Eisentrager* to hold that " 'the privilege of litigation' does not extend to aliens in military custody who have no presence in 'any territory over which the United States is sovereign,' " 321 F.3d 1134, 1144 (C.A.D.C.2003) (quoting *Eisentrager*, 339 U.S., at 777–778, 70 S.Ct. 936), it held that the District Court lacked jurisdiction over petitioners' habeas actions, as well as their remaining federal statutory claims that do not sound in habeas. We granted certiorari, and now reverse.

II

Congress has granted federal district courts, "within their respective jurisdictions," the authority to hear applications for habeas corpus by any person who claims to be held "in custody in violation of the Constitution or laws or treaties of the United States." 28 U.S.C. §§ 2241(a), (c)(3). The statute traces its ancestry to the first grant of federal-court jurisdiction: Section 14 of the Judiciary Act of 1789 authorized federal courts to issue the writ of habeas corpus to prisoners who are "in custody, under or by colour of the authority of the United States, or are committed for trial before some court of the same." Act of Sept. 24, 1789, ch. 20, § 14, 1 Stat. 82. In 1867, Congress extended the protections of the writ to "all cases where any person may be restrained of his or her liberty in violation of the constitution, or of any treaty or law of the United States." Act of Feb. 5, 1867, ch. 28, 14 Stat. 385. See *Felker v. Turpin*, 518 U.S. 651, 659–660, 116 S.Ct. 2333, 135 L.Ed.2d 827 (1996).

Habeas corpus is, however, "a writ antecedent to statute, ... throwing its root deep into the genius of our common law." *Williams v. Kaiser*, 323 U.S. 471, 484, n. 2, 65 S.Ct. 363, 89 L.Ed. 398 (1945) (internal quotation marks omitted). The writ appeared in English law several centuries ago, became "an integral part of our common-law heritage" by the time the Colonies achieved independence, *Preiser v. Rodriguez*, 411 U.S. 475, 485, 93 S.Ct. 1827, 36 L.Ed.2d 439 (1973), and received explicit recognition in the Constitution, which forbids suspension of "[t]he Privilege of the Writ of Habeas Corpus ... unless when in Cases of Rebellion or Invasion the public Safety may require it," Art. I, § 9, cl. 2.

As it has evolved over the past two centuries, the habeas statute clearly has expanded habeas corpus "beyond the limits that obtained during the 17th and 18th centuries." *Swain v. Pressley*, 430 U.S. 372, 380, n. 13, 97 S.Ct. 1224, 51 L.Ed.2d 411 (1977). But "[a]t its historical core, the writ of habeas corpus has served as a means of reviewing the legality of Executive detention, and it is in that context that its protections have been strongest." *INS v. St. Cyr*, 533 U.S. 289, 301, 121 S.Ct. 2271, 150 L.Ed.2d 347 (2001). See also *Brown v. Allen*, 344 U.S. 443, 533, 73 S.Ct. 397, 97 L.Ed. 469 (1953) (Jackson, J., concurring in result) ("The historic purpose of the writ has been to relieve detention by executive authorities without judicial trial"). As Justice Jackson wrote in an opinion respecting the availability of habeas corpus to aliens held in U.S. custody:

> "Executive imprisonment has been considered oppressive and lawless since John, at Runnymede, pledged that no free man should be imprisoned, dispossessed, outlawed, or exiled save by the judgment of his peers or by the law of the land. The judges of England developed the writ of habeas corpus largely to preserve these immunities from executive restraint." *Shaughnessy v. United States ex rel. Mezei*, 345 U.S. 206, 218–219, 73 S.Ct. 625, 97 L.Ed. 956 (1953) (dissenting opinion).

Consistent with the historic purpose of the writ, this Court has recognized the federal courts' power to review applications for habeas relief in a wide variety of cases involving executive detention, in wartime as well as in times of peace. The Court has, for example, entertained the habeas petitions of an American citizen who plotted an attack on military installations during the Civil War, *Ex parte Milligan*, 4 Wall. 2, 18 L.Ed. 281 (1866), and of admitted enemy aliens convicted of war crimes during a declared war and held in the United States, *Ex parte Quirin*, 317 U.S. 1, 63 S.Ct. 2, 87 L.Ed. 3 (1942), and its insular possessions, *In re Yamashita*, 327 U.S. 1, 66 S.Ct. 340, 90 L.Ed. 499 (1946).

The question now before us is whether the habeas statute confers a right to judicial review of the legality of executive detention of aliens in a territory over which the United States exercises plenary and exclusive jurisdiction, but not "ultimate sovereignty."

III

Respondents' primary submission is that the answer to the jurisdictional question is controlled by our decision in *Eisentrager*. In that case, we held that a Federal District Court lacked authority to issue a writ of habeas corpus to 21 German citizens who had been captured by U.S. forces in China, tried and convicted of war crimes by an American military commission headquartered in Nanking, and incarcerated in the Landsberg Prison in occupied Germany. The Court of Appeals in *Eisentrager* had found jurisdiction, reasoning that "any person who is deprived of his liberty by officials of the United States, acting under purported authority of that Government, and who can show that his confinement is in violation of a prohibition of the Constitution, has a right to the writ." *Eisentrager v. Forrestal*, 174 F.2d 961, 963 (C.A.D.C.1949). In reversing that determination, this Court summarized the six critical facts in the case:

> "We are here confronted with a decision whose basic premise is that these prisoners are entitled, as a constitutional right, to sue in some court of the United States for a writ of *habeas corpus*. To support that assumption we must hold that a prisoner of our military authorities is constitutionally entitled to the writ, even though he (a) is an enemy alien; (b) has never been or resided in the United States; (c) was captured outside of our territory and there held in military custody as a prisoner of war; (d) was tried and convicted by a Military Commission sitting outside the United States; (e) for offenses against laws of war committed outside the United States; (f) and is at all times imprisoned outside the United States." 339 U.S., at 777, 70 S.Ct. 936.

On this set of facts, the Court concluded, "no right to the writ of *habeas corpus* appears." *Id.*, at 781, 70 S.Ct. 936.

Petitioners in these cases differ from the *Eisentrager* detainees in important respects: They are not nationals of countries at war with the United States, and they deny that they have engaged in or plotted acts of aggression against the United States; they have never been afforded access to any tribunal, much less charged with and convicted of wrongdoing; and for more than two years they have been imprisoned in territory over which the United States exercises exclusive jurisdiction and control.

Not only are petitioners differently situated from the *Eisentrager* detainees, but the Court in *Eisentrager* made quite clear that all six of the facts critical to its disposition were relevant only to the question of the prisoners' *constitutional* entitlement to habeas corpus. *Id.*, at 777, 70 S.Ct. 936. The Court had far less to say on the question of the petitioners' *statutory* entitlement to habeas review. Its only statement on the subject was a passing reference to the absence of statutory authorization: "Nothing in the text of the Constitution extends such a right, nor does anything in our statutes." Id., at 768, 70 S.Ct. 936.

Reference to the historical context in which *Eisentrager* was decided explains why the opinion devoted so little attention to the question of statutory jurisdiction. In 1948, just two months after the *Eisentrager* petitioners filed their petition for habeas corpus in the U.S. District Court for the District of Columbia, this Court issued its decision in *Ahrens v. Clark*, 335 U.S. 188, 68 S.Ct. 1443, 92 L.Ed. 1898, a case concerning the application of the habeas statute to the petitions of 120 Germans who were then being detained at Ellis Island, New York, for deportation to Germany. The *Ahrens* detainees had also filed their petitions in the U.S. District Court for the District of Columbia, naming the Attorney General as the respondent. Reading the phrase "within their respective jurisdictions" as used in the habeas statute to require the petitioners' presence within the district court's territorial jurisdiction, the Court held that the District of Columbia court lacked jurisdiction to entertain the detainees' claims. *Id.*, at 192, 68 S.Ct. 1443. *Ahrens* expressly reserved the question "of what process, if any, a person confined in an area not subject to the jurisdiction of any district court may employ to assert federal rights." Id., at 192, n. 4, 68 S.Ct. 1443. But as the dissent noted, if the presence of the petitioner in the territorial jurisdiction of a federal district court were truly a jurisdictional requirement, there could be only one response to that question. *Id.*, at 209, 68 S.Ct. 1443 (opinion of Rutledge, J.).[7]

When the District Court for the District of Columbia reviewed the German prisoners' habeas application in *Eisentrager,* it thus dismissed their action on the authority of *Ahrens.* See *Eisentrager*, 339 U.S., at 767, 790, 70 S.Ct. 936. Although the Court of Appeals reversed the District Court, it implicitly conceded that the District Court lacked jurisdiction under the habeas statute as it had been interpreted in *Ahrens.* The Court of Appeals instead held that petitioners had a constitutional right to habeas corpus secured by the Suspension Clause, U.S. Const., Art. I, § 9, cl. 2, reasoning that "if a person has a right to a writ of habeas corpus, he cannot be deprived of the privilege by an omission in a federal jurisdictional statute." *Eisentrager v. Forrestal*, 174 F.2d, at 965. In essence, the Court of Appeals concluded that the habeas statute, as construed in *Ahrens,* had created an unconstitutional gap that had to be filled by reference to "fundamentals." 174 F.2d, at 963. In its review of that decision, this Court, like the Court of Appeals, proceeded from the premise that "nothing in our statutes" conferred federal-court jurisdiction, and accordingly evaluated the Court of Appeals' resort to "fundamentals" on its own terms. 339 U.S., at 768, 70 S.Ct. 936.

Because subsequent decisions of this Court have filled the statutory gap that had occasioned *Eisentrager's* resort to "fundamentals," persons detained outside the territorial jurisdiction of any federal district court no longer need rely on the Constitution as the source of their right to federal habeas review. In *Braden v. 30th Judicial Circuit Court of Ky.*, 410 U.S. 484, 495, 93 S.Ct. 1123, 35 L.Ed.2d 443 (1973), this Court held, contrary to *Ahrens,* that the prisoner's presence within the territorial jurisdiction of the district court is not "an invariable prerequisite" to the exercise of district court jurisdiction under the federal habeas statute. Rather, because "the writ of habeas corpus does not act upon the prisoner who seeks relief, but upon the person who holds him in what is alleged to be unlawful custody," a district court acts "within [its] respective jurisdiction" within the meaning of § 2241 as long as "the custodian can be reached by service of process." 410 U.S., at 494–495, 93 S.Ct. 1123. *Braden* reasoned that its departure from the rule of *Ahrens* was warranted in light of developments that "had a profound impact on the continuing vitality of that decision." 410 U.S., at 497, 93 S.Ct. 1123. These developments included, notably, decisions of this Court in cases involving habeas petitioners "confined overseas (and thus outside the territory of any district court)," in which the Court "held, if only implicitly, that the petitioners' absence from the district does not present a jurisdictional obstacle to the consideration of the claim." *Id.,* at 498, 93 S.Ct. 1123 (citing *Burns v. Wilson,* 346 U.S. 137, 73 S.Ct. 1045, 97 L.Ed. 1508 (1953), rehearing denied, 346 U.S. 844, 851–852, 74 S.Ct. 3, 98 L.Ed. 363 (opinion of Frankfurter, J.); *United States ex rel. Toth v. Quarles,* 350 U.S. 11, 76 S.Ct. 1, 100 L.Ed. 8 (1955); *Hirota v. MacArthur,* 338 U.S. 197, 199, 69 S.Ct. 197, 93 L.Ed. 1902 (1948) (Douglas, J., concurring (1949))). *Braden* thus established that *Ahrens* can no longer be viewed as establishing "an inflexible jurisdictional rule," and is strictly relevant only to the question of the appropriate forum, not to whether the claim can be heard at all. 410 U.S., at 499–500, 93 S.Ct. 1123.

Because *Braden* overruled the statutory predicate to *Eisentrager's* holding, *Eisentrager* plainly does not preclude the exercise of § 2241 jurisdiction over petitioners' claims.

IV

Putting *Eisentrager* and *Ahrens* to one side, respondents contend that we can discern a limit on § 2241 through application of the "longstanding principle of American law" that congressional legislation is presumed not to have extraterritorial application unless such intent is clearly manifested. *EEOC v. Arabian American Oil Co.,* 499 U.S. 244, 248, 111 S.Ct. 1227, 113 L.Ed.2d 274 (1991). Whatever traction the presumption against extraterritoriality might have in other contexts, it certainly has no application to the operation of the habeas statute with respect to persons detained within "the territorial jurisdiction" of the United States. *Foley Bros., Inc. v. Filardo,*

336 U.S. 281, 285, 69 S.Ct. 575, 93 L.Ed. 680 (1949). By the express terms of its agreements with Cuba, the United States exercises "complete jurisdiction and control" over the Guantanamo Bay Naval Base, and may continue to exercise such control permanently if it so chooses. 1903 Lease Agreement, Art. III; 1934 Treaty, Art. III. Respondents themselves concede that the habeas statute would create federal-court jurisdiction over the claims of an American citizen held at the base. Tr. of Oral Arg. 27. Considering that the statute draws no distinction between Americans and aliens held in federal custody, there is little reason to think that Congress intended the geographical coverage of the statute to vary depending on the detainee's citizenship. Aliens held at the base, no less than American citizens, are entitled to invoke the federal courts' authority under § 2241.

Application of the habeas statute to persons detained at the base is consistent with the historical reach of the writ of habeas corpus. At common law, courts exercised habeas jurisdiction over the claims of aliens detained within sovereign territory of the realm, as well as the claims of persons detained in the so-called "exempt jurisdictions," where ordinary writs did not run, and all other dominions under the sovereign's control. As Lord Mansfield wrote in 1759, even if a territory was "no part of the realm," there was "no doubt" as to the court's power to issue writs of habeas corpus if the territory was "under the subjection of the Crown." *King v. Cowle*, 2 Burr. 834, 854–855, 97 Eng. Rep. 587, 598–599 (K.B.). Later cases confirmed that the reach of the writ depended not on formal notions of territorial sovereignty, but rather on the practical question of "the exact extent and nature of the jurisdiction or dominion exercised in fact by the Crown." *Ex parte Mwenya*, [1960] 1 Q.B. 241, 303 (C.A.) (Lord Evershed, M. R.).

In the end, the answer to the question presented is clear. Petitioners contend that they are being held in federal custody in violation of the laws of the United States. No party questions the District Court's jurisdiction over petitioners' custodians. Cf. *Braden*, 410 U.S., at 495, 93 S.Ct. 1123. Section 2241, by its terms, requires nothing more. We therefore hold that § 2241 confers on the District Court jurisdiction to hear petitioners' habeas corpus challenges to the legality of their detention at the Guantanamo Bay Naval Base.

V

In addition to invoking the District Court's jurisdiction under § 2241, the Al Odah petitioners' complaint invoked the court's jurisdiction under 28 U.S.C. § 1331, the federal-question statute, as well as § 1350, the Alien Tort Statute. The Court of Appeals, again relying on *Eisentrager*, held that the District Court correctly dismissed the claims founded on § 1331 and § 1350 for lack of jurisdiction, even to the extent that these claims "deal only with conditions of confinement and do not sound in habeas," because petitioners lack the "privilege of litigation" in U.S. courts. 321 F.3d, at 1144 (internal quotation marks omitted). Specifically, the court held that because petitioners' § 1331 and § 1350 claims "necessarily rest on alleged violations of the same category of laws listed in the habeas corpus statute," they, like claims founded on the habeas statute itself, must be "beyond the jurisdiction of the federal courts." *Id.*, at 1144–1145.

As explained above, *Eisentrager* itself erects no bar to the exercise of federal-court jurisdiction over the petitioners' habeas corpus claims. It therefore certainly does not bar the exercise of federal-court jurisdiction over claims that merely implicate the "same category of laws listed in the habeas corpus statute." But in any event, nothing in *Eisentrager* or in any of our other cases categorically excludes aliens detained in military custody outside the United States from the " 'privilege of litigation' " in U.S. courts. 321 F.3d, at 1139. The courts of the United States have traditionally been open to nonresident aliens. Cf. *Disconto Gesellschaft v. Umbreit*, 208 U.S. 570, 578, 28 S.Ct. 337, 52 L.Ed. 625 (1908) ("Alien citizens, by the policy and practice of the courts of this country, are ordinarily permitted to resort to the courts for the redress of wrongs and the protection of their rights"). And indeed, 28 U.S.C. § 1350 explicitly confers the privilege of suing for an actionable "tort ... committed in violation of the law of nations or a treaty of the United States" on aliens alone. The fact that petitioners in these cases are being held in military custody is immaterial to the question of the District Court's jurisdiction over their nonhabeas statutory claims.

VI

Whether and what further proceedings may become necessary after respondents make their response to the merits of petitioners' claims are matters that we need not address now. What is presently at stake is only whether the federal courts have jurisdiction to determine the legality of the Executive's potentially indefinite detention of individuals who claim to be wholly innocent of wrongdoing. Answering that question in the affirmative, we reverse the judgment of the Court of Appeals and remand these cases for the District Court to consider in the first instance the merits of petitioners' claims.

It is so ordered.

CHAPTER FOUR: RACE AND THE CHARGING DECISION

The Decision Not to Prosecute

INMATES OF ATTICA CORRECTIONAL FACILITY V. ROCKEFELLER

477 F.2d 375 (2d Cir. 1973)

MANSFIELD, Circuit Judge:

This appeal raises the question of whether the federal judiciary should, at the instance of victims, compel federal and state officials to investigate and prosecute persons who allegedly have violated certain federal and state criminal statutes. Plaintiffs in the purported class suit, which was commenced in the Southern District of New York against various state and federal officers, are certain present and former inmates of New York State's Attica Correctional Facility ("Attica"), the mother of an inmate who was killed when Attica was retaken after the inmate uprising in September 1971, and Arthur O. Eve, a New York State Assemblyman and member of the Subcommittee on Prisons. They appeal from an order of the district court, Lloyd F. MacMahon, Judge, dismissing their complaint. We affirm.

The complaint alleges that before, during, and after the prisoner revolt at and subsequent recapture of Attica in September 1971, which resulted in the killing of 32 inmates and the wounding of many others, the defendants, including the Governor of New York, the State Commissioner of Correctional Services, the Executive Deputy Commissioner of the State Department of Correctional Services, the Superintendent at Attica, and certain State Police, Corrections Officers, and other officials, either committed, conspired to commit, or aided and abetted in the commission of various crimes against the complaining inmates and members of the class they seek to represent. It is charged that the inmates were intentionally subjected to cruel and inhuman treatment prior to the inmate riot, that State Police, Troopers, and Correction Officers (one of whom is named) intentionally killed some of the inmate victims without provocation during the recovery of Attica, that state officers (several of whom are named and whom the inmates claim they can identify) assaulted and beat prisoners after the prison had been successfully retaken and the prisoners had surrendered, see Inmates of Attica Correctional Facility v.

Rockefeller, 453 F.2d 12 (2d Cir. 1971), that personal property of the inmates was thereafter stolen or destroyed, and that medical assistance was maliciously denied to over 400 inmates wounded during the recovery of the prison.

The complaint further alleges that Robert E. Fischer, a Deputy State Attorney General specially appointed by the Governor to supersede the District Attorney of Wyoming County and, with a specially convened grand jury, to investigate crimes relating to the inmates' takeover of Attica and the resumption of control by the state authorities, see Inmates, supra at 16 and n. 3, "has not investigated, nor does he intend to investigate, any crimes committed by state officers." Plaintiffs claim, moreover, that because Fischer was appointed by the Governor he cannot neutrally investigate the responsibility of the Governor and other state officers said to have conspired to commit the crimes alleged. It is also asserted that since Fischer is the sole state official currently authorized under state law to prosecute the offenses allegedly committed by the state officers, no one in the State of New York is investigating or prosecuting them.

With respect to the sole federal defendant, the United States Attorney for the Western District of New York, the complaint simply alleges that he has not arrested, investigated, or instituted prosecutions against any of the state officers accused of criminal violation of plaintiffs' federal civil rights, 18 U.S.C. §§ 241, 242, and he has thereby failed to carry out the duty placed upon him by 42 U.S.C. § 1987, discussed below.

As a remedy for the asserted failure of the defendants to prosecute violations of state and federal criminal laws, plaintiffs request relief in the nature of mandamus (1) against state officials, requiring the State of New York to submit a plan for the independent and impartial investigation and prosecution of the offenses charged against the named and unknown state officers, and insuring the appointment of an impartial state prosecutor and state judge to "prosecute the defendants forthwith," and (2) against the United States Attorney, requiring him to investigate, arrest and prosecute the same state officers for having committed the federal offenses defined by 18 U.S.C. §§ 241 and 242. The latter statutes punish, respectively, conspiracies against a citizen's free exercise or enjoyment of rights secured by the Constitution and laws of the United States, see United States v. Guest, 383 U.S. 745, 86 S.Ct. 1170, 16 L.Ed.2d 239 (1966), and the willful subjection of any inhabitant, under color of law, to the deprivation of such rights or to different punishment or penalties on account of alienage, color, or race than are prescribed for the punishment of citizens, see *Screws v. United States*, 325 U.S. 91, 65 S.Ct. 1031, 89 L.Ed. 1495 (1945); *United States v. Classic*, 313 U.S. 299, 61 S.Ct. 1031, 85 L.Ed. 1368 (1941).3

Federal jurisdiction over the claim against the state defendants was based on 42 U.S.C. § 1983 and 28 U.S.C. § 1343(3) and over the claim against the United States Attorney on the mandamus statute. 28 U.S.C. § 1361. Venue in the Southern District of New York was predicated on 28 U.S.C. §§ 1391(b), 1392(a). The motions of the federal and state defendants to dismiss the complaint for failure to state claims upon which relief can be granted, Rule 12(b)(6), F.R.Civ.P., were granted by Judge MacMahon without opinion. We agree that the extraordinary relief sought cannot be granted in the situation here presented.

STANDING

At the outset, we must note that the Supreme Court's recent decision in *Linda R.S. v. Richard D.*, 410 U.S. 614, 93 S.Ct. 1146, 35 L.Ed.2d 536 (1973), to which the attention of the parties in this case was not drawn prior to argument, raises the preliminary question of whether plaintiffs have a sufficient "personal stake in the outcome of the controversy," *Baker v. Carr*, 369 U.S. 186, 204, 82 S.Ct. 691, 703, 7 L.Ed.2d 663 (1962), to confer standing upon them to invoke the judicial process. In Linda R.S. the mother of an illegitimate child sought to attack as unconstitutionally discriminatory the application of a Texas criminal statute prohibiting the willful refusal of "any parent" to support his or her child on the ground that it was enforced by the state, as a result of state court interpretation of the statute, against married but not unmarried fathers. Holding that she lacked standing, the Supreme Court, in a majority opinion by Justice Marshall, observed:

"The Court's prior decisions consistently hold that a citizen lacks standing to contest the policies of the prosecuting authority when he himself is neither prosecuted nor threatened with prosecution. See *Younger v. Harris*, 401 U.S. 37, 42, 91 S.Ct. 746, 27 L. Ed.2d 669 (1971); *Bailey v. Patterson*, 369 U.S. 31, 33, 82 S.Ct. 549, 7 L.Ed.2d 512 (1962); *Poe v. Ullman*, 367 U.S. 497, 501, 81 S.Ct. 752, 6 L. Ed.2d 989 (1961). Although these cases arose in a somewhat different context, they demonstrate that, in American jurisprudence at least, a private citizen lacks a judicially cognizable interest in the prosecution or nonprosecution of another." 410 U.S. at 619, 93 S.Ct. at 1149.

The broad reach of this language would, at first blush, appear to preclude the plaintiffs here from seeking to contest the nonprosecution of third parties they accuse of criminal conduct. However, the present case is in some respects distinguishable from Linda R.S. Unlike the mother there the inmates here might be said to have sustained or be immediately in danger of sustaining direct personal injury as the result of nonenforcement of the criminal laws against the accused state officers. See 410 U.S. at 619, 93 S.Ct. 1146; *Massachusetts v. Mellon*, 262 U.S. 447, 488, 43 S.Ct. 597, 67 L.Ed. 1078 (1923). They allege that at least some of them suffered direct physical injury at the hands of those they seek to have prosecuted and that if the state officers accused of criminal conduct are not prosecuted, such conduct will continue.

Thus a more immediate and direct danger of injury resulting from nonenforcement is presented here than in Linda R.S., where the Court stressed that the only result of the relief sought by the illegitimate child's mother would be the jailing of the child's father, not the support of the child. Where a successful prosecution, however, would serve to deter the accused from harming the complainant rather than merely supply a penal inducement to perform a duty to provide assistance, the complaining person does show a more direct nexus between his personal interest in protection from harm and the prosecution. But in the present case this rationale in support of standing assumes that injunctive relief, which we conditionally authorized in *Inmates of Attica Correctional Facility v. Rockefeller*, supra, 453 F.2d at 22-25, restraining physical abuse, torture, beatings or other forms of brutality, or threats of such conduct, is ineffective to protect the plaintiffs from harm.

It may also be argued that since 37 inmates have been indicted for crimes relating to the events at Attica in September 1971, without any indictment having been filed against any of the accused state officials, the complaint alleges a sufficient threat of selective and discriminatory prosecution of the plaintiff inmates to meet the standing requirements discussed in Linda R.S. v. Richard D., supra. On the other hand, the challenge in the present case is not to any criminal statute, as construed, but to the failure of the prosecuting authorities to enforce the criminal laws against a particular group of individuals.

Thus in order to determine whether plaintiffs have standing to sue we would be required to resolve troublesome questions. However, we need not decide the issue of standing because we believe that even if they may properly present their claims for judicial resolution, they seek relief which cannot, in this case at least, be granted either against the state or federal prosecuting authorities.

THE INSUFFICIENCY OF THE COMPLAINT

(1) CLAIM AGAINST THE UNITED STATES ATTORNEY

With respect to the defendant United States Attorney, plaintiffs seek mandamus to compel him to investigate and institute prosecutions against state officers, most of whom are not identified, for alleged violations of 18 U.S.C. §§ 241 and 242. Federal mandamus is, of course, available only "to compel an officer or employee of the United States . . . to perform a duty owed to the plaintiff." 28 U.S.C. § 1361. And the legislative history of § 1361 makes it clear that ordinarily the courts are "'not to direct or influence the exercise of discretion of the officer or agency in the making of the decision,'" United *States ex rel. Schonbrun v. Commanding Officer*, 403 F.2d 371, 374 (2d Cir. 1968), cert. denied, 394 U.S. 929, 89 S. Ct. 1195, 22 L.Ed.2d 460 (1969). More particularly, federal courts have traditionally and, to our knowledge, uniformly refrained from overturning, at the instance of a private person, discretionary decisions of federal prosecuting authorities not to prosecute persons regarding whom a complaint of criminal conduct is made. E. g., *Milliken v. Stone*, 16 F.2d 981 (2d Cir.), cert. denied, 274 U.S. 748, 47 S.Ct. 764, 71 L.Ed. 1331 (1927); *Pugach v. Klein*, 193 F.Supp. 630 (S.D.N.Y.1961); *Powell v. Katzenbach*, 123 U. S.App.D.C. 250, 359 F.2d 234 (1965), cert. denied, 384 U.S. 906, 86 S.Ct. 1341, 16 L.Ed.2d 359, rehearing denied, 384 U.S. 967, 86 S.Ct. 1584, 16 L.Ed.2d 679 (1966); *Smith v. United States,* 375 F. 2d 243 (5th Cir.), cert. denied, 389

U.S. 841, 88 S.Ct. 76, 19 L.Ed.2d 106 (1967). See also *Confiscation Cases*, 74 U.S. (7 Wall.) 454, 19 L.Ed. 196 (1868); *Goldberg v. Hoffman*, 225 F.2d 463 (7th Cir. 1955); *United States v. Cox*, 342 F.2d 167 (5th Cir.), cert. denied sub nom., *Cox v. Hauberg*, 381 U.S. 935, 85 S.Ct. 1767, 14 L.Ed.2d 700 (1965); *Newman v. United States*, 127 U.S.App.D.C. 263, 382 F.2d 479 (1967).

This judicial reluctance to direct federal prosecutions at the instance of a private party asserting the failure of United States officials to prosecute alleged criminal violations has been applied even in cases such as the present one where, according to the allegations of the complaint, which we must accept as true for purposes of this appeal, see *Inmates of Attica Correctional Facility v. Rockefeller*, supra, 453 F.2d at 24 (and cases there cited), serious questions are raised as to the protection of the civil rights and physical security of a definable class of victims of crime and as to the fair administration of the criminal justice system. *Moses v. Kennedy*, 219 F.Supp. 762 (D.D.C.1963), affd. sub nom., Moses *v. Katzenbach*, 119 U.S.App.D.C. 352, 342 F.2d 931 (1965); Peek *v. Mitchell*, 419 F.2d 575 (6th Cir. 1970).

The primary ground upon which this traditional judicial aversion to compelling prosecutions has been based is the separation of powers doctrine.

"Although as a member of the bar, the attorney for the United States is an officer of the court, he is nevertheless an executive official of the Government, and it is as an officer of the executive department that he exercises a discretion as to whether or not there shall be a prosecution in a particular case. It follows, as an incident of the constitutional separation of powers, that the courts are not to interfere with the free exercise of the discretionary powers of the attorneys of the United States in their control over criminal prosecutions." *United States v. Cox, supra* 342 F.2d at 171.

Accord, Pugach *v. Klein*, supra 193 F. Supp. at 634; Moses *v. Kennedy*, 219 F. Supp. at 764-765; Peek *v. Mitchell*, supra 419 F.2d at 577-578.

Although a leading commentator has criticized this broad view as unsound and incompatible with the normal function of the judiciary in reviewing for abuse or arbitrariness administrative acts that fall within the discretion of executive officers, K. C. Davis, Administrative Law Treatise § 28.16(4) at 982-990 (1970 Supp.), he has also recognized, as have most of the cases cited above, that the manifold imponderables which enter into the prosecutor's decision to prosecute or not to prosecute make the choice not readily amenable to judicial supervision.

In the absence of statutorily defined standards governing reviewability, or regulatory or statutory policies of prosecution, the problems inherent in the task of supervising prosecutorial decisions do not lend themselves to resolution by the judiciary. The reviewing courts would be placed in the undesirable and injudicious posture of becoming "superprosecutors." In the normal case of review of executive acts of discretion, the administrative record is open, public and reviewable on the basis of what it contains. The decision not to prosecute, on the other hand, may be based upon the insufficiency of the available evidence, in which event the secrecy of the grand jury and of the prosecutor's file may serve to protect the accused's reputation from public damage based upon insufficient, improper, or even malicious charges. In camera review would not be meaningful without access by the complaining party to the evidence before the grand jury or U.S. Attorney. Such interference with the normal operations of criminal investigations, in turn, based solely upon allegations of criminal conduct, raises serious questions of potential abuse by persons seeking to have other persons prosecuted. Any person, merely by filing a complaint containing allegations in general terms (permitted by the Federal Rules) of unlawful failure to prosecute, could gain access to the prosecutor's file and the grand jury's minutes, notwithstanding the secrecy normally attaching to the latter by law. See Rule 6(e), F.R.Cr.P.

Nor is it clear what the judiciary's role of supervision should be were it to undertake such a review. At what point would the prosecutor be entitled to call a halt to further investigation as unlikely to be productive? What evidentiary standard would be used to decide whether prosecution should be compelled? How much judgment would the United States Attorney be allowed? Would he be permitted to limit himself to a strong "test" case rather than pursue weaker cases? What collateral factors would be permissible bases for a decision not to prosecute, e. g., the pendency of another criminal proceeding elsewhere against the same parties? What sort of review should be available in cases like the present one where the conduct complained of allegedly violates state as well as federal laws? See generally, Schwartz, Federal Criminal Jurisdiction and Prosecutors' Discretion, 13 Law & Contemp.Prob. 64 (1948). With limited personnel and facilities at his disposal, what priority would the prosecutor be required to give to cases in which investigation or prosecution was directed by the court?

These difficult questions engender serious doubts as to the judiciary's capacity to review and as to the problem of arbitrariness inherent in any judicial decision to order prosecution. On balance, we believe that substitution of a court's decision to compel prosecution for the U.S. Attorney's decision not to prosecute, even upon an abuse of discretion standard of review and even if limited to directing that a prosecution be undertaken in good faith, see Note, Discretion to Prosecute Federal Civil Rights Crimes, 74 Yale L.J. 1297, 1310-12 (1965), would be unwise.

Plaintiffs urge, however, that Congress withdrew the normal prosecutorial discretion for the kind of conduct alleged here by providing in 42 U.S.C. § 19874 that the United States Attorneys are "authorized and required . . . to institute prosecutions against all persons violating any of the provisions of [18 U.S.C. §§ 241, 242]" (emphasis supplied), and, therefore, that no barrier to a judicial directive to institute prosecutions remains. This contention must be rejected. The mandatory nature of the word "required" as it appears in § 1987 is insufficient to evince a broad Congressional purpose to bar the exercise of executive discretion in the prosecution of federal civil rights crimes. Similar mandatory language is contained in the general direction in 28 U.S.C. § 547(1) ("each United States attorney, . . . shall–(1) prosecute for all offenses against the United States; . . ." (emphasis supplied)) and in other statutes in particular areas of concern, e. g., 33 U.S.C. § 413 ("it shall be the duty of United States attorneys to vigorously prosecute all offenders" of certain provisions of the Rivers and Harbors Act when requested to do so by the appropriate officials). See also 45 U.S.C. § 152 (Tenth).

Such language has never been thought to preclude the exercise of prosecutorial discretion. See *Bass Angler's Sportsman's Society v. Scholze Tannery, Inc.*, 329 F.Supp. 339, 345-346 (E.D.Tenn. 1971). Indeed the same contention made here was specifically rejected in *Moses v. Kennedy*, 219 F.Supp. 762, 765 (D.D.C.1963), aff'd. 119 U.S.App.D.C. 352, 342 F.2d 931 (1965), where seven black residents and one white resident of Mississippi sought mandamus to compel the Attorney General of the United States and the Director of the F.B.I. to investigate, arrest, and prosecute certain individuals, including state and local law enforcement officers, for willfully depriving the plaintiffs of their civil rights. There the Court noted that "considerations of judgment and discretion apply with special strength to the area of civil rights, where the Executive Department must be largely free to exercise its considered judgment on questions of whether to proceed by means of prosecution, injunction, varying forms of persuasion, or other types of action." See also *Peek v. Mitchell*, supra.

Nor do we find the legislative history of § 1987 persuasive of an intent by Congress to depart so significantly from the normal assumption of executive discretion. *In re Upchurch*, 38 F. 25, 27 (C.C.N.C.1889), relied upon by plaintiffs, held only that a United States commissioner had the power under § 1987 to appoint a person other than the marshal, or one of his deputies, to execute process. It may well be that the legislative background of § 1987 would compel a reading that Congress intended that federal marshals have no choice but to execute warrants issued pursuant to that section, since it also provided for criminal penalties for those who refused to do so and for the appointment of other persons to execute warrants and make arrests. No such conclusion can persuasively be drawn with respect to the exercise by United States Attorneys of prosecutorial discretion, especially in the absence of any similar statutory deterrent against their failure or refusal to prosecute. See Note, Discretion to Prosecute Federal Civil Rights Crimes, 74 Yale L. J. 1297, 1306-07 and n. 46 (1965). Thus, we do not read § 1987 as stripping the United States Attorneys of their normal prosecutorial discretion for the civil rights crimes specified.

It therefore becomes unnecessary to decide whether, if Congress were by explicit direction and guidelines to remove all prosecutorial discretion with respect to certain crimes or in certain circumstances we would properly direct that a prosecution be undertaken. Cf. *Powell v. Katzenbach*, supra, 359 F.2d at 235; Note, *supra* at 1305.

(2) Claims Against the State Officials

With respect to the state defendants, plaintiffs also seek prosecution of named and unknown persons for the violation of state crimes. However, they have pointed to no statutory language even arguably creating any mandatory duty upon the state officials to bring such prosecutions. To the contrary, New York law reposes in its prosecutors a discretion to decide whether or not to prosecute in a given case, which is not subject to review in the state courts. *Hassan v. Magistrates Court*, 20 Misc.2d 509, 191 N.Y.S.2d 238 (1959), appeal dismissed, 10 A.D.2d 908, 202 N.Y.S.2d 1002 (2d Dept.), leave to appeal denied, 8 N.Y.2d 750, 201 N.Y.S.2d 765, cert. denied, 364 U.S. 844, 81 S.Ct. 86, 5 L.Ed. 2d 68 (1960). Yet the federal district court is asked to compel state prosecutions and appoint an "impartial" state prosecutor and state judge to conduct them, as well as to require the submission of a plan for impartial investigation and prosecution of the alleged offenses, on the basis of 42 U.S.C. § 1983, in the context of a continuing grand jury investigation into criminal conduct connected with the Attica uprising, supra n. 1, and where the state itself on September 30, 1971, appointed a Special Commission on Attica which has now published its findings.5 The very elaborateness of the relief believed by plaintiffs to be required indicates the difficulties inherent in judicial supervision of prosecutions, federal or state, which render such a course inadvisable.

Plaintiffs point to language in our earlier opinion, *Inmates of Attica Correctional Facility v. Rockefeller*, 453 F.2d 12, 20 (2d Cir. 1971), to the effect that "the State has the duty to investigate and prosecute all persons, including inmates, who may have engaged in criminal conduct before, during and after the uprising." But the statement does not support their present demands. The existence of such a duty does not define its dimensions or imply that an alleged failure to perform the duty completely or equally, as between inmates and state officials, will support federal judicial supervision of state criminal prosecutions. The serious charge that the state's investigation is proceeding against inmates but not against state officers, if shown to be accurate, might lead the Governor to supplement or replace those presently in charge of the investigation or the state legislature to act. But the gravity of the allegation does not reduce the inherent judicial incapacity to supervise.

The only authority supporting the extraordinary relief requested here is the Seventh Circuit's recent decision in Littleton *v. Berbling*, 468 F.2d 389 (1972), cert. granted, 411 U.S. 915, 93 S.Ct. 1544, 36 L.Ed.2d 306 (1973). There a class of black citizens of Cairo, Illinois, brought suit for damages and injunctive relief against a state prosecutor, an investigator for him, a magistrate and a state judge, charging that the defendants had "systematically applied the state criminal laws so as to discriminate against plaintiffs and their class on the basis of race, interfering thereby with the free exercise of their constitutional rights." *Id.* at 392. They alleged a long history indicating a concerted pattern of officially sponsored racial discrimination. In reversing the district court's dismissal of the complaint, a divided panel concluded that a state judge, while not subject to suit for damages under § 1983, *Pierson v. Ray*, 386 U.S. 547, 87 S.Ct. 1213, 18 L.Ed.2d 288 (1967), may be enjoined from unconstitutionally fixing bails and imposing sentences that discriminated sharply against black persons, and that the State Attorney's quasi-judicial immunity from suit for damages when performing his prosecutorial function, id. 468 F.2d at 410, "does not extend to complete freedom from injunction," id. at 411. Finding other possible remedies either unavailable or ineffective, the Court approved the possibility of some type of injunctive relief, not fully specified, but which might include a requirement of "periodic reports of various types of aggregate data on actions on bail and sentencing and dispositions of complaints." Id. at 415.

However, the decision in *Littleton* is clearly distinguishable. There the claim, unlike that here, alleged a systematic and lengthy course of egregious racial discrimination in which black persons were denied equal access to and treatment by the state criminal justice system. Furthermore, the Court's decision does not appear to have compelled the institution of criminal prosecutions, which is the principal relief sought here. In short, we believe that Littleton should be strictly limited to its peculiar facts, as apparently did the Court itself. See id. at 415. To the extent that it may be construed as approving federal judicial review and supervision of the exercise of prosecutorial discretion and as compelling the institution of criminal proceedings, we do not share such an extension of its views.

The order of the district court is affirmed.

UNITED STATES V. COX
342 F.2d 167 (5th Cir. 1965)

JONES, Circuit Judge:

On October 22, 1964, an order of the United States District Court for the Southern District of Mississippi, signed by Harold Cox, a judge of that Court, was entered. The order, with caption and formal closing omitted, is as follows:

'THE GRAND JURY, duly elected, impaneled and organized, for the Southern District of Mississippi, reconvened on order of the Court at 9:00 A.M., October 21, 1964, in Court Room Number 2 in Jackson, Mississippi, for the general dispatch of its business. The grand jury was fully instructed as to their duties, powers and responsibilities and retired to the grand jury room number 538 in the Federal Building at Jackson to do its work. The United States Attorney (and one of his assistants) sat with the grand jury throughout the day on October 21 and explained in detail to the grand jury the perjury laws and the Court's construction of such laws for their information. The grand jury heard witnesses throughout the day on October 21, 1964. On the morning of October 22, 1964, the grand jury, through its foreman, made known to the Court in open court that they had requested Robert E. Hauberg, United States Attorney, to prepare certain indictments which they desired to bring against some of the persons under consideration and about which they had heard testimony, and the United States Attorney refused to draft or sign any such indictments on instructions of the Acting Attorney General of the United States;

whereupon the Court ordered and directed said United States Attorney to draft such true bills or no bills as the grand jury may have duly voted and desired to report and to sign such instruments as required by law under penalty of contempt. The United States Attorney was afforded one hour within which to decide as to whether or not he would abide by the instructions and order of the Court in such respect. At the end of such time, the Court re-convened and the United States Attorney was specifically asked in open court as to whether or not he intended to conform with the order and direction of the Court in said respects whereupon the United States Attorney answered that he respectfully declined to do so on instructions from Nicholas Katzenbach, Acting Attorney General. He was thereupon duly adjudged by the Court to be in civil contempt of the Court and was afforded an opportunity to make any statement which he desired to make to the Court before sentence; whereupon the United States Attorney reiterated his inability to comply with the order of the Court upon express and direct instructions from Nicholas Katzenbach, Acting Attorney General of the United States.

'WHEREFORE, IT IS ORDERED AND ADJUDGED by the Court that Robert E. Hauberg, United States Attorney, is guilty of civil contempt of this Court and in the presence of the Court for his said refusal to obey its said order and he is ordered into custody of the United States Marshal to be confined by him in the Hinds County, Mississippi, jail, there to remain until he purges himself of this contempt by agreeing to conform to said order by performing his official duty for the grand jury as requested in the several (about five) pending cases before them on October 21 and October 22, 1964.

'IT IS FURTHER ORDERED by the Court that a citation issue to Nicholas Katzenbach, Acting Attorney General of the United States, directing him to appear before this Court and show cause why he should not be adjudged guilty of contempt of this Court for his instructions and directions to the United States Attorney to disregard and disobey the orders of this Court in the respects stated.

'The United States Attorney requested a stay of enforcement of this order and further proceedings herein for five days after this date to enable him to apply to the United States Court of Appeals for the Fifth Circuit for a writ of prohibition and such request is granted; and these proceedings and enforcement of this order in its entirety is stayed for five days, subject to the further orders of the United States Court of Appeals on said application; and for the enforcement of all of which, let proper process issue.'

The United States Attorney, Robert E. Hauberg, and the Acting Attorney General, Nicholas Katzenbach, have appealed from the order and they, joined by the United States, seek a writ of prohibition against the District Judge from enforcing the Court's order, and from asserting jurisdiction to require the Attorney General or the United States Attorney 'to institute criminal prosecutions or to take any steps in regard thereto.' The facts recited in the order are uncontroverted. No further facts are essential to a decision of the issues before this Court. Although the issues here presented arose, in part at least, as an incident of a civil rights matter, no civil rights questions are involved in the rather broad inquiry which we are called upon to make.

The constitutional requirement of an indictment or presentment as a predicate to a prosecution for capital or infamous crimes has for its primary purpose the protection of the individual from jeopardy except on a finding of probable cause by a group of his fellow citizens, and is designed to afford a safeguard against oppressive actions of the prosecutor or a court. The constitutional provision is not to be read as conferring on or preserving to the grand jury, as such, any rights or prerogatives. The constitutional provision is, as has been said, for the benefit of the accused. The constitutional provision is not to be read as precluding, as essential to the validity of an indictment, the inclusion of requisites which did not exist at common law.

Traditionally, the Attorney for the United States had the power to enter a nolle prosequi of a criminal charge at any time after indictment and before trial, and this he could have done without the approval of the court or the consent of the accused. It may be doubted whether, before the adoption of the Federal Rules of Criminal Procedure, he had any authority to prevent the return of an indictment by a grand jury. There would be no constitutional barrier to a requirement that the signature of a United States Attorney upon an indictment is essential to its validity.

It is now provided by the Federal Rules of Criminal Procedure that the Attorney General or the United States Attorney may by leave of court file a dismissal of an indictment. Rule 48(a) Fed.Rules Crim.Proc. 18 U.S.C.A. In the absence of the Rule, leave of court would not have been required. The purpose of the Rule is to prevent harassment of a defendant by charging, dismissing and re-charging without placing a defendant in jeopardy. *Woodring v. United States*, 8th Cir. 1963, 311 F.2d 417. Rule 7 eliminates the necessity for the inclusion in an indictment of many of the technical and prolix averments which were required at common law, by providing that the indictment shall be a plain, concise and definite written statement of the essential facts constituting the offense charged. The Rule also provides that 'It shall be signed by the attorney for the government.' Rule 7(c) Fed.Rules Crim.Proc. 18 U.S.C.A.

The judicial power of the United States is vested in the federal courts, and extends to prosecutions for violations of the criminal laws of the United States. The executive power is vested in the President of the United States, who is required to take care that the laws be faithfully executed. The Attorney General is the hand of the President in taking care that the laws of the United States in legal proceedings and in the prosecution of offenses, be faithfully executed. The role of the grand jury is restricted to a finding as to whether or not there is probable cause to believe that an offense has been committed. The discretionary power of the attorney for the United States in determining whether a prosecution shall be commenced or maintained may well depend upon matters of policy wholly apart from any question of probable cause. Although as a member of the bar, the attorney for the United States is an officer of the court, he is nevertheless an executive official of the Government, and it is as an officer of the executive department that he exercises a discretion as to whether or not there shall be a prosecution in a particular case. It follows, as an incident of the constitutional separation of powers, that the courts are not to interfere with the free exercise of the discretionary powers of the attorneys of the United States in their control over criminal prosecutions. The provision of Rule 7, requiring the signing of the indictment by the attorney for the Government, is a recognition of the power of Government counsel to permit or not to permit the bringing of an indictment. If the attorney refuses to sign, as he has the discretionary power of doing, we conclude that there is no valid indictment. It is not to be supposed that the signature of counsel is merely an attestation of the act of the grand jury. The signature of the foreman performs that function. It is not to be supposed that the signature of counsel is a certificate that the indictment is in proper form to charge an offense. The sufficiency of the indictment may be tested before the court. Rather, we think, the requirement of the signature is for the purpose of evidencing the joinder of the attorney for the United States with the grand jury in instituting a criminal proceeding in the court. Without the signature there can be no criminal proceeding brought upon an indictment. Substantial compliance rather than technical exactness meets the requirement of the rule. There seems to be no authority for the statement that the absence of a signature is not fatal. 4 Barron & Holtzoff Federal Practice & Procedure 61, § 1913.

If it were not for the discretionary power given to the United States Attorney to prevent an indictment by withholding his signature, there might be doubt as to the constitutionality of the requirement of Rule 48 for leave of court for a dismissal of a pending prosecution.

Because, as we conclude, the signature of the Government attorney is necessary to the validity of the indictment and the affixing or withholding of the signature is a matter of executive discretion which cannot be coerced or reviewed by the courts, the contempt order must be reversed. It seems that, since the United States Attorney cannot be required to give validity to an indictment by affixing his signature, he should not be required to indulge in an exercise of futility by the preparation of the form of an indictment which he is unwilling to vitalize with his signature. Therefore he should not be required to prepare indictments which he is unwilling and under no duty to sign.

Judges Tuttle, Jones, Brown and Wisdom join in the conclusion that the signature of the United States Attorney is essential to the validity of an indictment. Judge Brown, as appears in his separate opinion, is of the view that the United States Attorney is required, upon the request of the grand jury, to draft forms of indictments in accordance with its desires. The order before us for review is in the conjunctive; it requires the United States Attorney to prepare and sign. A majority of the court, having decided that the direction to sign is erroneous, the order on appeal will be reversed.

So much of the order of the district court as adjudges the United States Attorney for the Southern District of Mississippi to be in contempt is a final order, appealable as such, and for the reasons here assigned, is reversed. That part of the order of the district court as would require the Acting Attorney General to show cause why he should not be held in contempt is interlocutory and not appealable, and the appeal of the Acting Attorney General will be dismissed.

There remains for our consideration and disposition the petition of the United States, the Acting Attorney General and the United States, for a Writ of Prohibition to prohibit the Respondent District Judge from enforcing the order. The reversal of the order as to the United States Attorney makes unnecessary, so far as he is concerned, any consideration of the application for a Writ of Prohibition. There has been no citation issued for service on the Attorney General requiring him to show cause. He has not yet been put in jeopardy. Our disposition of the appeal makes it improbable that such citation will be issued and served. It does not appear that there is any necessity at this time for the issuance of the discretionary Writ of Prohibition. The petition will be denied.

We are of the opinion that whenever a United States Attorney is under a legal duty which he has been directed to perform by a valid order of court, his refusal to perform such duty and comply with such order will not be justified or excused by instructions from the Attorney General to disregard his duty and disobey the order. Thus the way is open for relief if a further order is entered with respect to the rendering of assistance to the grand jury by the United States Attorney in the preparation of indictments.

The respondent-appellee has challenged the right of the United States to join in the petition for a Writ of Prohibition. We find it unnecessary to pass on this question.

The Court's mandate will issue forthwith. Appeal dismissed as to Katzenbach, Acting Attorney General. Order on appeal reversed as to Hauberg, United States Attorney. Petition for writ of prohibition denied.

NATIONAL ASSOCIATION FOR THE ADVANCEMENT OF COLORED PEOPLE V. LEVI

418 F.Supp. 1109 (D.C. 1976)

MEMORANDUM OPINION

PARKER, District Judge:

This proceeding presents troublesome questions of standing and prosecutorial discretion. They arise in connection with a citizen's death from gunshot wounds while in custody of Arkansas law enforcement officers. The plaintiffs allege that Federal officials failed to conduct an affirmative and exhaustive investigation of the incident and that they acted arbitrarily, capriciously and in a racially discriminatory manner to determine if the citizen's constitutionally guaranteed and other rights provided by Federal law had been violated.

At this point the defendants present two challenges to the litigation: a motion for change of venue and a motion to dismiss. For the reasons detailed below, the Court concludes that these initial challenges should be denied and that this proceeding should advance to trial.

The plaintiffs are the National Association for the Advancement of Colored People (NAACP), Mrs. Clementine Russ, widow of Carnell Russ and the Russ minor children. The defendants are Edward Levi, the Attorney General of the United States, Clarence Kelley, the Director of the Federal Bureau of Investigation (FBI or Bureau) and certain FBI agents assigned to the Little Rock, Arkansas, office.

Jurisdiction is asserted under 28 U.S.C. s 1343(4) together with the Fifth, Thirteenth and Fourteenth Amendments and the Civil Rights Acts (42 U.S.C. ss 1981 and 1985). Also, 28 U.S.C. s 1361 in conjunction with 18 U.S.C. s 242, 28 U.S.C. s 509 and the Civil Rights Acts (42 U.S.C. s 1981) are invoked as grounds for jurisdiction.

In an amended complaint seeking declaratory, injunctive and other equitable relief, plaintiffs assert violations of the constitutional and civil rights of Carnell Russ, deceased, a citizen of Arkansas. They seek this Court's aid compelling the defendants to undertake a thorough and meaningful investigation into his fatal shooting. The shooting took place at the Lincoln County Courthouse, Star City, Arkansas, while Russ was in the custody of Arkansas law enforcement officers.

A motion to transfer the proceedings to the Eastern District of Arkansas has been filed by the defendants. They also move to dismiss the complaint and assert: that the plaintiffs lack standing to bring this suit; that they have failed to state a claim upon which relief can be granted; that the Court lacks jurisdiction over the subject matter of the complaint; and, that the doctrine of sovereign immunity shields the defendants from this litigation.

FACTUAL BACKGROUND

On May 31, 1971, Carnell Russ, a 24 year old black, while operating his motor vehicle on an Arkansas highway, was arrested for an alleged speeding violation by Jerry Mac Green, a white state trooper. Russ was accompanied by his wife, their minor children and an adult cousin. The trooper directed him to the County Courthouse. Russ complied and upon arrival, parked his vehicle and was escorted into the Courthouse by the arresting trooper and two other white law enforcement officers, Charles Ratliff and Norman Draper.3 Minutes later, Russ returned to the vehicle where his family awaited. He requested and received from his wife sufficient money to post the necessary collateral. He then joined the three officers who were close by observing his actions. The four retraced their steps with Russ again in custody.

A short time thereafter, Mrs. Russ first observed two of the officers leave and minutes later an ambulance depart from the rear of the Courthouse area where her husband had just entered in the officers' custody. She later learned that Mr. Russ, while under detention, had been shot in the center of his forehead by Ratliff and then transported to a hospital. Green and Draper were the sole witnesses to the shooting. Her husband died from the gunshot wound within hours.

The Governor of Arkansas ordered an immediate investigation of the incident by the State Police. In less than one week Ratliff was indicted for voluntary manslaughter. Plaintiffs allege that minutes or transcripts of the grand jury proceedings were not maintained. Ratliff was tried in January, 1972. The jurors' deliberations consumed less than 15 minutes and in that period they selected a foreperson, reviewed and considered the evidence and returned a verdict of "not guilty". Ratliff's weapon was not offered in evidence during his criminal trial. There was no evidence or testimony that Carnell Russ possessed or had access to a weapon while in custody. Indeed, the testimony was to the contrary.

The shooting triggered the attention of both the national and Arkansas branches of the NAACP. Immediately, those organizations embarked upon a campaign importuning the Justice Department to undertake an independent investigation to determine whether Federal laws had been violated in any manner. Several months following the acquittal of the state trooper, Assistant Attorney General David L. Norman of the Civil Rights Division of the Justice Department wrote to the General Counsel of the NAACP:

After careful examination of the (Ratliff trial) transcript, as well as materials previously submitted by the Federal Bureau of Investigation, this Division has determined that this incident lacks prosecutive merit under federal criminal civil rights statutes. Therefore, we are closing our file.

The plaintiffs allege that subsequent events and disclosures led them to believe that the Department's investigation was superficial, less than thorough and meaningless. The substance of their claim is that the FBI abdicated its responsibility and in effect applied a "whitewash" to the incident; that the Bureau deferred to and relied principally upon a report of the Criminal Investigation Division of the Arkansas State Police; and that the policy to rely solely on the state and local criminal justice system for vindication of a citizen's rights was unreasonable, improper, arbitrary and without a rational basis. Fairly read, the complaint alleges that the defendants acted in an arbitrary, capricious and discriminatory manner by failing to investigate the Russ shooting to determine if his constitutional rights and Federal statutes had been violated by Arkansas law enforcement authorities.

....

THE MOTION TO DISMISS

The Question of Standing

For more than the last 50 years the NAACP has participated as party plaintiff, as intervenor and as amicus curiae in a variety and ever increasing amount of civil rights litigation. On behalf of its membership and black minorities it has achieved a reputation in both state and Federal courts as an organization with a special interest in the preservation and protection of their civil and constitutional rights. In 1963, Justice William J. Brennan recognized the standing of the NAACP to assert the rights of its members and remarked that the organization engages in litigation

> . . . (as) a means for achieving the lawful objectives of equality of treatment by all government, federal, state and local, for the members of the Negro community in this country.

> . . . the litigation it assists, while serving to vindicate the legal rights of members of the American Negro community, at the same time and perhaps more importantly, makes possible the distinctive contribution of a minority group to the ideas and beliefs of our society.

That same observation is true today and as the plaintiffs have pointed out, the standing of this organization to sue and represent its members and nonmembers in the context of its objectives has never been denied in any reported judicial opinion.

The NAACP's interest in the issues presented in this litigation is not abstract or general but rather it is real and direct. In their pleadings and affidavits the plaintiffs point to the past and continuing efforts of the organization to secure the civil rights of its memberships and others under Federal law against the arbitrary and discriminatory acts of government officials. Likewise, the Russ widow and children have a direct, significant and substantial interest. Accepting as true, as we must, the plaintiffs' allegations detailing the highly suspect circumstances of Mr. Russ' death, the government's investigation of the incident to determine if there had been a violation of Federal laws, was half-hearted at best. The family seeks a vindication of the deceased's rights and requests equitable relief against named Federal officials.

The plaintiffs have an interest in free access to and an even-handed application of the legal and criminal justice procedures of the Federal Government. They allege that they were injured because of the defendants' failure to undertake a sincere and meaningful investigation of Carnell Russ' death. This failure, they claim, was racially discriminatory and had the effect of denying to him, his family and to black Americans equal application of the laws in violation of their rights under the Constitution and the Civil Rights Acts. The Court concludes that the plaintiffs have shown that they satisfy the injury in fact element of the standing requirement.

The Constitutional and statutory enactments which the plaintiffs invoke are for the protection of persons against discriminatory treatment by government officials. Thus, the plaintiffs have shown that they are within the zone of interest protected by such enactments. Since the NAACP has long been committed to the civil rights struggle and because the Russ plaintiffs have an obvious desire to vindicate the rights of their deceased husband and father, the "logical nexus" between the plaintiffs' status and the government action from which they seek relief is also present.

The government contends that plaintiffs lack standing since they have not shown that they have a sufficient "personal stake in the outcome of the controversy," *Baker v. Carr*, 369 U.S. 186, 204, 82 S.Ct. 691, 703, 7 L.Ed.2d 663 (1962); have not shown that injuries have been or will be sustained by them; and, because the "logical nexus" between any injury to the NAACP and the Russ family on the one hand and the government action complained of is insufficient or absent. In adopting this stance, they rely principally on Linda *R. S. v. Richard D.*, 410 U.S. 614, 93 S.Ct. 1146, 35 L.Ed.2d 536 (1973). There, the mother of an illegitimate child challenged as unconstitutionally discriminatory the application of a Texas criminal statute prohibiting the willful refusal of a parent to support his child on the ground that it was enforced by the state, as a result of state court interpretation of the statute, against married but not unmarried fathers. In holding that she lacked standing the majority court observed:

> . . . we hold that, in the unique context of a challenge to a criminal statute, appellant has failed
> to allege a sufficient nexus between her injury and the government action which she attacks to
> justify judicial intervention. To be sure, appellant no doubt suffered an injury stemming from the
> failure of her child's father to contribute support payments. But the bare existence of an abstract
> injury meets only the first half of the standing requirement. 'The party who invokes (judicial)
> power must be able to show . . . that he has sustained or is immediately in danger of sustaining
> some direct injury as the result of (a statute's) enforcement,' (citations omitted). As this Court
> made plain in *Flast v. Cohen*, supra, a plaintiff must show 'a logical nexus between the status
> asserted and the claim sought to be adjudicated. . . . Such inquiries into the nexus between the
> status asserted by the litigant and the claim he presents are essential to assure that he is a proper
> and appropriate party to invoke federal judicial power. . . .' 410 U.S. at 617, 618, 93 S.Ct. at 1149.

The majority opinion of Justice Thurgood Marshall further stated ". . . that, in American jurisprudence at least, a private citizen lacks a judicially cognizable interest in the prosecution or nonprosecution of another." Id. at 619, 93 S.Ct. at 1149.

This historic role of the NAACP in its efforts to secure for its members and others through litigation, the guaranteed civil rights which have been denied, cannot be ignored. Had Carnell Russ survived his encounter with the Arkansas law enforcement officers, there would be no question of his standing. Before this Court in his stead is the Russ family, seeking a vindication of his rights under law. The allegations of the complaint support the conclusion that they too have standing.

Failure to State a Claim and Prosecutorial Discretion

A prosecutor's chief responsibility is to see that the laws are faithfully executed and enforced in order to maintain the rule of law. He has an affirmative responsibility to investigate prudently suspected illegal activity when it is not adequately pursued by other agencies. In Linda, supra, the question of standing focused on whether or not the plaintiff was an appropriate person to request judicial intervention and more specifically, whether the victim of criminal acts may sue to correct allegedly unlawful prosecutorial conduct. Federal courts have traditionally acquiesced in discretionary decisions of the United States Attorney not to prosecute persons against whom a complaint of criminal conduct is made. The rule in this circuit is not otherwise. *United States v. Gainey*, 142 U.S.App.D.C. 262, 440 F.2d 290 (1971); *Newman v. United States*, 127 U.S.App.D.C. 263, 382 F.2d 479 (1967); *Powell v. Katzenbach*, 123 U.S.App.D.C. 250, 359 F.2d 234 (1965); *Moses v. Katzenbach*, 119 U.S.App.D.C. 352, 342 F.2d 931 (1965); *Moses v. Kennedy*, 219 F.Supp. 762 (D.D.C.1963). Even though judicial restraint is generally observed, an unfettered discretion is questionable when it fails to promote the ends of justice and denies rights conferred upon a citizen by the Constitution and by Federal law.

In *Nader v. Saxbe* our Court of Appeals was concerned with an application for a mandatory injunction against the Attorney General and others to exercise their discretion to initiate prosecutions against violators of the Federal Corrupt Practices Act. The plaintiffs were an individual citizen and a nonprofit corporation. The Act was enacted in 1925. While many violations had been committed, only one prosecution, a test case, had been brought. The Attorney General had exercised his prosecutorial discretion of nonenforcement.

The case was mooted by the repeal of the statute during the course of the litigation. However, Circuit Judge J. Skelly Wright suggested that prosecutorial discretion was not totally free from judicial review

The instant complaint does not ask the court to assume the essentially Executive function of deciding whether a particular alleged violator should be prosecuted. Rather, the complaint seeks a conventionally judicial determination of whether certain fixed policies allegedly followed by the Justice Department and the United States Attorney's office lie outside the constitutional and statutory limits of 'prosecutorial discretion.' 497 F.2d at 679.

....

The Executive's constitutional duty to 'take Care that the Laws be faithfully executed,' Art. II, s 3, applies to all laws, not merely to criminal statutes, see In *re Neagle*, 135 U.S. 1, 63-64, 10 S.Ct. 658, 34 L.Ed. 55 (1890). It would seem to follow that the exercise of prosecutorial discretion, like the exercise of Executive discretion generally, is subject to statutory and constitutional limits enforceable through judicial review (citations omitted). The law has long recognized the distinction between judicial usurpation of discretionary authority and judicial review of the statutory and constitutional limits to that authority (citations omitted). Judicial review of the latter sort is normally available unless Congress has expressly withdrawn it (citations omitted) 497 F.2d at 679, 680, fn. 19.

The judiciary has the responsibility of assuring that the purpose and intent of congressional enactments are not negated and frustrated by arbitrary conduct of government officials. *In Medical Committee for Human Rights v. S. E. C.*, 139 U.S.App.D.C. 226, 432 F.2d 659 (1970), Circuit Judge Edward A. Tamm noted

> (T)he decisions of this court have never allowed the phrase 'prosecutorial discretion' to be treated as a magical incantation which automatically provides a shield for arbitrariness. 432 F.2d at 673.

The amended complaint, together with supporting affidavits and memoranda show: that named defendants undertook a token investigation to determine if a citizen's rights had been violated by Arkansas law enforcement personnel; that the Department of Justice adhered to a general policy when there were alleged violations of an individual's constitutional and civil rights by state officials, namely deferring to state criminal investigation rather than its own affirmative and objective investigation; that this policy was followed by the Attorney General in the Russ investigation; that the Federal Bureau of Investigation at the time was less than vigorous and diligent in investigating charges of unlawful conduct of state law enforcement officers against black individuals. This, the plaintiffs claim, was arbitrary and racially discriminatory conduct by Federal officials. They should be afforded an opportunity to support these allegations.

Lack of Subject Matter Jurisdiction and Sovereign Immunity

The amended complaint invokes jurisdiction primarily under 28 U.S.C. s 1343(4) and s 1361 in conjunction with the Fifth, Thirteenth and Fourteenth Amendments, the Civil Rights Acts (42 U.S.C. ss 1981 and 1985), and 18 U.S.C. s 242. Section 1343(4) confers jurisdiction in a district court to grant equitable or other relief under any Act of Congress providing for the protection of civil rights. Section 1361 authorizes mandamus actions.

The defendants question the applicability of s 1981 and suggest that it does not generally support a cause of action charging discrimination by Federal officials or the Federal government. There is, however, persuasive authority to the contrary which this Court recognizes. *Penn v. Schlesinger*, 400 F.2d 700 (5th Cir. 1973); *Baker v. F & F Investment Co.*, 489 F.2d 829 (7th Cir. 1973). Further, Congress has explicitly given district courts power to consider cases in the nature of mandamus against Federal officials. When it is claimed that Federal officials are acting contrary to law, abusing their discretion and acting outside the limits of their permissible discretion, and when official conduct extends beyond any rational exercise of discretion, even though it is within the letter of the authority granted, mandamus affords the appropriate judicial relief.

Nor does the defense of sovereign immunity, as defendants urge, serve as an absolute jurisdictional bar to the maintenance of this action against the named defendants. See: *Scheuer v. Rhodes*, 416 U.S. 232, 94 S.Ct. 1683, 40 L.Ed.2d 90 (1974); Economou *v. Department of Agriculture*, 535 F.2d 688 (1976). If they have engaged in racially discriminatory practices proscribed by ss 1981 or 1985, the plaintiffs should not be stopped at the threshold. Where the manner in which public officials exercise their authority is challenged as contrary to constitutional and statutory mandates, the doctrine of sovereign immunity may not prevail. *Larson v. Domestic & Foreign Commerce Corp.*, 337 U.S. 682, 702, 69 S.Ct. 1457, 93 L.Ed. 1628 (1949). While the plaintiffs may be limited as to the extent of the relief afforded by the Court, a consideration of that aspect at this time is speculative and premature. There is no sound basis for this Court to deny subject matter jurisdiction and sovereign immunity may not be asserted to avoid a hearing on the merits.

In *Scheuer v. Rhodes*, Mr. Chief Justice Burger, in delivering the opinion for the court remarked

When a federal court reviews the sufficiency of a complaint, before the reception of any evidence either by affidavit or admissions, its task is necessarily a limited one. The issue is not whether a plaintiff will ultimately prevail but whether the claimant is entitled to offer evidence to support the claims. Indeed it may appear on the face of the pleadings that a recovery is very remote and unlikely but that is not the test. Moreover, it is well established that, in passing on a motion to dismiss, whether on the ground of lack of jurisdiction over the subject matter or for failure to state a cause of action, the allegations of the complaint should be construed favorably to the pleader. 416 U.S. 232 at 236, 94 S.Ct. at 1686 (1974).

....

The Decision to Prosecute: Selective Prosecution Defense

UNITED STATES V. ARMSTRONG
517 U.S. 456 (1996)

Chief Justice REHNQUIST delivered the opinion of the Court.

In this case, we consider the showing necessary for a defendant to be entitled to discovery on a claim that the prosecuting attorney singled him out for prosecution on the basis of his race. We conclude that respondents failed to satisfy the threshold showing: They failed to show that the Government declined to prosecute similarly situated suspects of other races.

In April 1992, respondents were indicted in the United States District Court for the Central District of California on charges of conspiring to possess with intent to distribute more than 50 grams of cocaine base (crack) and conspiring to distribute the same, in violation of 21 U.S.C. §§ 841 and 846 (1988 ed. and Supp. IV), and federal firearms offenses. For three months prior to the indictment, agents of the Federal Bureau of Alcohol, Tobacco, and Firearms and the Narcotics Division of the Inglewood, California, Police Department had infiltrated a suspected crack distribution ring by using three confidential informants. On seven separate occasions during this period, the informants had bought a total of 124.3 grams of crack from respondents and witnessed respondents carrying firearms during the sales. The agents searched the hotel room in which the sales were transacted, arrested respondents Armstrong and Hampton in the room, and found more crack and a loaded gun. The agents later arrested the other respondents as part of the ring.

In response to the indictment, respondents filed a motion for discovery or for dismissal of the indictment, alleging that they were selected for federal prosecution because they are black. In support of their motion, they offered only an affidavit by a "Paralegal Specialist," employed by the Office of the Federal Public Defender representing one of the respondents. The only allegation in the affidavit was that, in every one of the 24 § 841 or § 846 cases closed by the office during 1991, the defendant was black. Accompanying the affidavit was a "study" listing the 24 defendants, their race, whether they were prosecuted for dealing cocaine as well as crack, and the status of each case.

The Government opposed the discovery motion, arguing, among other things, that there was no evidence or allegation "that the Government has acted unfairly or has prosecuted non-black defendants or failed to prosecute them." App. 150. The District Court granted the motion. It ordered the Government (1) to provide a list of all cases from the last three years in which the Government charged both cocaine and firearms offenses, (2) to identify the race of the defendants in those cases, (3) to identify what levels of law enforcement were involved in the investigations of those cases, and (4) to explain its criteria for deciding to prosecute those defendants for federal cocaine offenses. Id., at 161–162.

The Government moved for reconsideration of the District Court's discovery order. With this motion it submitted affidavits and other evidence to explain why it had chosen to prosecute respondents and why respondents' study did not support the inference that the Government was singling out blacks for cocaine prosecution. The federal and local agents participating in the case alleged in affidavits that race played no role in their investigation. An Assistant United States Attorney explained in an affidavit that the decision to prosecute met the general criteria for prosecution, because "there was over 100 grams of cocaine base involved, over twice the threshold necessary for a ten year mandatory minimum sentence; there were multiple sales involving multiple defendants, thereby indicating a fairly substantial crack cocaine ring; ... there were multiple federal firearms violations intertwined with the narcotics trafficking; the overall evidence in the case was extremely strong, including audio and videotapes of defendants; ... and several of the defendants had criminal histories including narcotics and firearms violations." Id., at 81.

The Government also submitted sections of a published 1989 Drug Enforcement Administration report which concluded that "[l]arge-scale, interstate trafficking networks controlled by Jamaicans, Haitians and Black street gangs dominate the manufacture and distribution of crack." J. Featherly & E. Hill, Crack Cocaine Overview 1989; App. 103.

In response, one of respondents' attorneys submitted an affidavit alleging that an intake coordinator at a drug treatment center had told her that there are "an equal number of caucasian users and dealers to minority users and dealers." Id., at 138. Respondents also submitted an affidavit from a criminal defense attorney alleging that in his experience many nonblacks are prosecuted in state court for crack offenses, id., at 141, and a newspaper article reporting that federal "crack criminals ... are being punished far more severely than if they had been caught with powder cocaine, and almost every single one of them is black," Newton, Harsher Crack Sentences Criticized as Racial Inequity, Los Angeles Times, Nov. 23, 1992, p. 1; App. 208–210.

The District Court denied the motion for reconsideration. When the Government indicated it would not comply with the court's discovery order, the court dismissed the case.

A divided three-judge panel of the Court of Appeals for the Ninth Circuit reversed, holding that, because of the proof requirements for a selective-prosecution claim, defendants must "provide a colorable basis for believing that 'others similarly situated have not been prosecuted'" to obtain discovery. 21 F.3d 1431, 1436 (1994) (quoting United States v. Wayte, 710 F.2d 1385, 1387 (C.A.9 1983), aff'd, 470 U.S. 598, 105 S.Ct. 1524, 84 L.Ed.2d 547 (1985)). The Court of Appeals voted to rehear the case en banc, and the en banc panel affirmed the District Court's order of dismissal, holding that "a defendant is not required to demonstrate that the government **1485 has failed to prosecute others who are similarly situated." 48 F.3d 1508, 1516 (1995) (emphasis deleted). We granted certiorari to determine the appropriate standard for discovery for a selective-prosecution claim. 516 U.S. 942, 116 S.Ct. 377, 133 L.Ed.2d 301 (1995).

Neither the District Court nor the Court of Appeals mentioned Federal Rule of Criminal Procedure 16, which by its terms governs discovery in criminal cases. Both parties now discuss the Rule in their briefs, and respondents contend that it supports the result reached by the Court of Appeals. Rule 16 provides, in pertinent part:

"Upon request of the defendant the government shall permit the defendant to inspect and copy or photograph books, papers, documents, photographs, tangible objects, buildings or places, or copies or portions thereof, which are within the possession, custody or control of the government, and which are material to the preparation of the defendant's defense or are intended for use by the government as evidence in chief at the trial, or were obtained from or belong to the defendant." Fed. Rule Crim. Proc. 16(a)(1)(C).

Respondents argue that documents "within the possession ... of the government" that discuss the Government's prosecution strategy for cocaine cases are "material" to respondents' selective-prosecution claim. Respondents argue that the Rule applies because any claim that "results in nonconviction" if successful is a "defense" for the Rule's purposes, and a successful selective-prosecution claim has that effect. Tr. of Oral Arg. 30.

We reject this argument, because we conclude that in the context of Rule 16 "the defendant's defense" means the defendant's response to the Government's case in chief. While it might be argued that as a general matter, the concept of a "defense" includes any claim that is a "sword," challenging the prosecution's conduct of the case, the term may encompass only the narrower class of "shield" claims, which refute the Government's arguments that the defendant committed the crime charged. Rule 16(a)(1)(C) tends to support the "shield-only" reading. If "defense" means an argument in response to the prosecution's case in chief, there is a perceptible symmetry between documents "material to the preparation of the defendant's defense," and, in the very next phrase, documents "intended for use by the government as evidence in chief at the trial."

If this symmetry were not persuasive enough, subdivision (a)(2) of Rule 16 establishes beyond peradventure that "defense" in subdivision (a)(1)(C) can refer only to defenses in response to the Government's case in chief. Rule 16(a)(2), as relevant here, exempts from defense inspection "reports, memoranda, or other internal government documents made by the attorney for the government or other government agents in connection with the investigation or prosecution of the case."

Under Rule 16(a)(1)(C), a defendant may examine documents material to his defense, but, under Rule 16(a)(2), he may not examine Government work product in connection with his case. If a selective-prosecution claim is a "defense," Rule 16(a)(1)(C) gives the defendant the right to examine Government work product in every prosecution except his own. Because respondents' construction of "defense" creates the anomaly of a defendant's being able to examine all Government work product except the most pertinent, we find their construction implausible. We hold that Rule 16(a)(1)(C) authorizes defendants to examine Government documents material to the preparation of their defense against the Government's case in chief, but not to the preparation of selective-prosecution claims.

In Wade v. United States, 504 U.S. 181, 112 S.Ct. 1840, 118 L.Ed.2d 524 (1992), we considered whether a federal court may review a Government decision not to file a motion to reduce a defendant's sentence for substantial assistance to the prosecution, to determine whether the Government based its decision on the defendant's race or religion. In holding that such a decision was reviewable, we assumed that discovery would be available if the defendant could make the appropriate threshold showing, although we concluded that the defendant in that case did not make such a showing. See *id.*, at 186, 112 S.Ct., at 1844. We proceed on a like assumption here.

A selective-prosecution claim is not a defense on the merits to the criminal charge itself, but an independent assertion that the prosecutor has brought the charge for reasons forbidden by the Constitution. Our cases delineating the necessary elements to prove a claim of selective prosecution have taken great pains to explain that the standard is a demanding one. These cases afford a "background presumption," cf. *United States v. Mezzanatto*, 513 U.S. 196, 203, 115 S.Ct. 797, 803, 130 L.Ed.2d 697 1995) that the showing necessary to obtain discovery should itself be a significant barrier to the litigation of insubstantial claims.

A selective-prosecution claim asks a court to exercise judicial power over a "special province" of the Executive. *Heckler v. Chaney*, 470 U.S. 821, 832, 105 S.Ct. 1649, 1656, 84 L.Ed.2d 714 (1985). The Attorney General and United States Attorneys retain "'broad discretion'" to enforce the Nation's criminal laws. *Wayte v. United States*, 470 U.S. 598, 607, 105 S.Ct. 1524, 1530–1531, 84 L.Ed.2d 547 (1985) (quoting United *States v. Goodwin*, 457 U.S. 368, 380, n. 11, 102 S.Ct. 2485, 2492, n. 11, 73 L.Ed.2d 74 (1982)). They have this latitude because they are designated by statute as the President's delegates to help him discharge his constitutional responsibility to "take Care that the Laws be faithfully executed." U.S. Const., Art. II, § 3; see 28 U.S.C. §§ 516, 547. As a result, "[t]he presumption of regularity supports" their prosecutorial decisions and, "in the absence of clear evidence to the contrary, courts presume that they have properly discharged their official duties." *United States v. Chemical Foundation, Inc.*, 272 U.S. 1, 14–15, 47 S.Ct. 1, 6, 71 L.Ed. 131 (1926). In the ordinary case, "so long as the prosecutor has probable cause to believe that the accused committed an offense defined by statute, the decision whether or not to prosecute, and what charge to file or bring before a grand jury, generally rests entirely in his discretion." *Bordenkircher v. Hayes*, 434 U.S. 357, 364, 98 S.Ct. 663, 668, 54 L.Ed.2d 604 (1978).

Of course, a prosecutor's discretion is "subject to constitutional constraints." *United States v. Batchelder*, 442 U.S. 114, 125, 99 S.Ct. 2198, 2204–2205, 60 L.Ed.2d 755 (1979). One of these constraints, imposed by the equal protection component of the Due Process Clause of the Fifth Amendment, *Bolling v. Sharpe*, 347 U.S. 497, 500, 74 S.Ct. 693, 694–695, 98 L.Ed. 884 (1954), is that the decision whether to prosecute may not be based on "an unjustifiable standard such as race, religion, or other arbitrary classification," *Oyler v. Boles*, 368 U.S. 448, 456, 82 S.Ct. 501, 506, 7 L.Ed.2d 446 (1962). A defendant may demonstrate that the administration of a criminal law is "directed so exclusively against a particular class of persons ... with a mind so unequal and oppressive" that the system of prosecution amounts to "a practical denial" of equal protection of the law. *Yick Wo v. Hopkins*, 118 U.S. 356, 373, 6 S.Ct. 1064, 1073, 30 L.Ed. 220 (1886).

In order to dispel the presumption that a prosecutor has not violated equal protection, a criminal defendant must present "clear evidence to the contrary." Chemical Foundation, supra, at 14–15, 47 S.Ct., at 6. We explained in Wayte why courts are "properly hesitant to examine the decision whether to prosecute." 470 U.S., at 608, 105 S.Ct., at 1531. Judicial deference to the decisions of these executive officers rests in part on an assessment of the relative competence of prosecutors and courts. "Such factors as the strength of the case, the prosecution's general deterrence value, the Government's enforcement priorities, and the case's relationship to the Government's overall enforcement plan are not readily susceptible to the kind of analysis the courts are competent to undertake." Id., at 607, 105 S.Ct., at 1530. It also stems from a concern not to unnecessarily impair the performance of a core executive constitutional function. "Examining the basis of a prosecution delays the criminal proceeding, threatens to chill law enforcement by subjecting the prosecutor's motives and decisionmaking to outside inquiry, and may undermine prosecutorial effectiveness by revealing the Government's enforcement policy." *Ibid.*

The requirements for a selective-prosecution claim draw on "ordinary equal protection standards." Id., at 608, 105 S.Ct., at 1531. The claimant must demonstrate that the federal prosecutorial policy "had a discriminatory effect and that it was motivated by a discriminatory purpose." *Ibid.; accord, Oyler*, supra, at 456, 82 S.Ct., at 506. To establish a discriminatory effect in a race case, the claimant must show that similarly situated individuals of a different race were not prosecuted. This requirement has been established in our case law since Ah *Sin v. Wittman*, 198 U.S. 500, 25 S.Ct. 756, 49 L.Ed. 1142 (1905). Ah Sin, a subject of China, petitioned a California state court for a writ of habeas corpus, seeking discharge from imprisonment under a San Francisco County *466 ordinance prohibiting persons from setting up gambling tables in rooms barricaded to stop police from entering. Id., at 503, 25 S.Ct., at 757. He alleged in his habeas petition "that the ordinance is enforced 'solely and exclusively against persons of the Chinese race and not otherwise.'" Id., at 507, 25 S.Ct., at 758–759. We rejected his contention that this averment made out a claim under the Equal Protection Clause, because it did not allege "that the conditions and practices to which the ordinance was directed did not exist exclusively among the Chinese, or that there were other offenders against the ordinance than the Chinese as to whom it was not enforced." Id., at 507–508, 25 S.Ct., at 758–759.

The similarly situated requirement does not make a selective-prosecution claim impossible to prove. Twenty years before Ah *Sin*, we invalidated an ordinance, also adopted by San Francisco, that prohibited the operation of laundries in wooden buildings. *Yick Wo*, 118 U.S., at 374, 6 S.Ct., at 1073. The plaintiff in error successfully demonstrated that the ordinance was applied against Chinese nationals but not against other laundry-shop operators. The authorities had denied the applications of 200 Chinese subjects for permits to operate shops in wooden buildings, but granted the applications of 80 individuals who were not Chinese subjects to operate laundries in wooden buildings "under similar conditions." Ibid. We explained in Ah Sin why the similarly situated requirement is necessary:

"No latitude of intention should be indulged in a case like this. There should be certainty to every intent. Plaintiff in error seeks to set aside a criminal law of the State, not on the ground that it is unconstitutional on its face, not that it is discriminatory in tendency and ultimate actual operation as the ordinance was which was passed on in the Yick *Wo* case, but that it was made so by the manner of its administration. This is a matter of proof, and no fact should be omitted to make it out completely, when the power of a Federal court is invoked to interfere with the course of criminal justice of a State." 198 U.S., at 508, 25 S.Ct., at 759 (emphasis added).

Although Ah *Sin* involved federal review of a state conviction, we think a similar rule applies where the power of a federal court is invoked to challenge an exercise of one of the core powers of the Executive Branch of the Federal Government, the power to prosecute.

Respondents urge that cases such as Batson *v. Kentucky,* 476 U.S. 79, 106 S.Ct. 1712, 90 L.Ed.2d 69 (1986), and Hunter *v. Underwood,* 471 U.S. 222, 105 S.Ct. 1916, 85 L.Ed.2d 222 (1985), cut against any absolute requirement that there be a showing of failure to prosecute similarly situated individuals. We disagree. In Hunter, we invalidated a state law disenfranchising persons convicted of crimes involving moral turpitude. Id., at 233, 105 S.Ct., at 1922–1923. Our holding was consistent with ordinary equal protection principles, including the similarly situated requirement. There was convincing direct evidence that the State had enacted the provision for the purpose of disfranchising blacks, id., at 229–231, 105 S.Ct., at 1920–1922, and indisputable evidence that the state law had a discriminatory effect on blacks as compared to similarly situated whites: Blacks were " 'by even the most modest estimates at least 1.7 times as likely as whites to suffer disfranchisement under' " the law in question, id., at 227, 105 S.Ct., at 1919–1920 (quoting *Underwood v. Hunter,* 730 F.2d 614, 620 (C.A.11 1984)). Hunter thus affords no support for respondents' position.

In Batson, we considered "[t]he standards for assessing a prima facie case in the context of discriminatory selection of the venire" in a criminal trial. 476 U.S., at 96, 106 S.Ct., at 1723. We required a criminal defendant to show "that the prosecutor has exercised peremptory challenges to remove from the venire members of the defendant's race" and that this fact, the potential for abuse inherent in a peremptory strike, and "any other relevant circumstances raise an inference that the prosecutor used that practice to exclude the veniremen from the petit jury on account of their race." Ibid. During jury selection, the entire res gestae take place in front of the trial judge. Because the judge has before him the entire venire, he is well situated to detect whether a challenge to the seating of one juror is part of a "pattern" of singling out members of a single race for peremptory challenges. See id., at 97, 106 S.Ct., at 1723. He is in a position to discern whether a challenge to a black juror has evidentiary significance; the significance may differ if the venire consists mostly of blacks or of whites. Similarly, if the defendant makes out a prima facie case, the prosecutor is called upon to justify only decisions made in the very case then before the court. See id., at 97–98, 106 S.Ct., at 1723–1724. The trial judge need not review prosecutorial conduct in relation to other venires in other cases.

Having reviewed the requirements to prove a selective-prosecution claim, we turn to the showing necessary to obtain discovery in support of such a claim. If discovery is ordered, the Government must assemble from its own files documents which might corroborate or refute the defendant's claim. Discovery thus imposes many of the costs present when the Government must respond to a prima facie case of selective prosecution. It will divert prosecutors' resources and may disclose the Government's prosecutorial strategy. The justifications for a rigorous standard for the elements of a selective-prosecution claim thus require a correspondingly rigorous standard for discovery in aid of such a claim.

The parties, and the Courts of Appeals which have considered the requisite showing to establish entitlement to discovery, describe this showing with a variety of phrases, like "colorable basis," "substantial threshold showing," Tr. of Oral Arg. 5, "substantial and concrete basis," or "reasonable likelihood," Brief for Respondents Martin et al. 30. However, the many labels for this showing conceal the degree of consensus about the evidence necessary to meet it. The Courts of Appeals "require some evidence tending to show the existence of the essential elements of the defense," discriminatory effect and discriminatory intent. *United States v. Berrios*, 501 F.2d 1207, 1211 (C.A.2 1974).

In this case we consider what evidence constitutes "some evidence tending to show the existence" of the discriminatory effect element. The Court of Appeals held that a defendant may establish a colorable basis for discriminatory effect without evidence that the Government has failed to prosecute others who are similarly situated to the defendant. 48 F.3d, at 1516. We think it was mistaken in this view. The vast majority of the Courts of Appeals require the defendant to produce some evidence that similarly situated defendants of other races could have been prosecuted, but were not, and this requirement is consistent with our equal protection case law. *United States v. Parham*, 16 F.3d 844, 846–847 (C.A.8 1994); *United States v. Fares*, 978 F.2d 52, 59–60 (C.A.2 1992); *United States v. Peete*, 919 F.2d 1168, 1176 (C.A.6 1990); *C.E. Carlson, Inc. v. SEC*, 859 F.2d 1429, 1437–1438 (C.A.10 1988); *United States v. Greenwood*, 796 F.2d 49, 52–53 (C.A.4 1986); *United States v. Mitchell*, 778 F.2d 1271, 1277 (C.A.7 1985). As the three-judge panel explained, "'[s]elective prosecution' implies that a selection has taken place." 21 F.3d, at 1436.3

The Court of Appeals reached its decision in part because it started "with the presumption that people of all races commit all types of crimes—not with the premise that any type of crime is the exclusive province of any particular racial or ethnic group." 48 F.3d, at 1516–1517. It cited no authority for this proposition, which seems contradicted by the most recent statistics of the United States Sentencing Commission. Those statistics show: More than 90% of the persons sentenced in 1994 for crack cocaine trafficking were black, United States Sentencing Comm'n, 1994 Annual Report 107 (Table 45); 93.4% of convicted LSD dealers were white, ibid.; and 91% of those convicted for pornography or prostitution were white, id., at 41 (Table 13). Presumptions at war with presumably reliable statistics have no proper place in the analysis of this issue.

The Court of Appeals also expressed concern about the "evidentiary obstacles defendants face." 48 F.3d, at 1514. But all of its sister Circuits that have confronted the issue have required that defendants produce some evidence of differential treatment of similarly situated members of other races or protected classes. In the present case, if the claim of selective prosecution were well founded, it should not have been an insuperable task to prove that persons of other races were being treated differently than respondents. For instance, respondents could have investigated whether similarly situated persons of other races were prosecuted by the State of California and were known to federal law enforcement officers, but were not prosecuted in federal court. We think the required threshold—a credible showing of different treatment of similarly situated persons—adequately balances the Government's interest in vigorous prosecution and the defendant's interest in avoiding selective prosecution.

In the case before us, respondents' "study" did not constitute "some evidence tending to show the existence of the essential elements of" a selective-prosecution claim. *Berrios*, supra, at 1211. The study failed to identify individuals who were not black and could have been prosecuted for the offenses for which respondents were charged, but were not so prosecuted. This omission was not remedied by respondents' evidence in opposition to the Government's motion for reconsideration. The newspaper article, which discussed the discriminatory effect of federal drug sentencing laws, was not relevant to an allegation of discrimination in decisions to prosecute. Respondents' affidavits, which recounted one attorney's conversation with a drug treatment center employee and the experience of another attorney defending drug prosecutions in state court, recounted hearsay and reported personal conclusions based on anecdotal evidence. The judgment of the Court of Appeals is therefore reversed, and the case is remanded for proceedings consistent with this opinion.

It is so ordered.

UNITED STATES V. JACKSON
2018 WL 748372 (D. NM 2018)

MEMORANDUM OPINION AND ORDER

M. CHRISTINA ARMIJO, Chief United States District Judge

THIS MATTER is before the Court on Defendants' Motion to Compel Discovery pertaining to Claim of Selective Enforcement. [Doc. 2362:29; Doc. 2363:28] The Government responded [Doc.32], and Defendants replied. [Doc.35] After the Government provided some of the materials sought in Defendants' Motion, Defendants submitted a supplemental brief [Doc. 45], in which they outlined the remaining items sought, and the Government responded to the supplement. [Doc.47] Defendants filed a reply as well. [Doc.52] An evidentiary hearing was held on October 30, 2017 and December 13, 2017.

The Court has considered the parties' submissions, the evidence presented at the hearings, and the relevant law, and is otherwise fully informed. For the following reasons, the Court GRANTS IN PART Defendants' Motion.

I. Background and Summary of Requested Information

Lonnie Jackson was indicted for distribution of methamphetamine in violation of 21 U.S.C. §§ 841(a)(1) and (b)(1)(A). [Doc. 2] Diamond Coleman was indicted for distribution of methamphetamine, using and carrying a firearm during and in relation to a drug trafficking crime, and being a felon in possession of a firearm and ammunition. [Doc. 2363:2] Both Defendants were arrested during a "surge" operation in Albuquerque by the Bureau of Alcohol, Tobacco, and Firearms (ATF) in 2016. During the surge, the ATF was aided by five confidential informants, who were recruited from throughout the country. Three of the confidential informants were black and two were described as Hispanic. [12/13/17, 44:5-11] One hundred and four people were arrested as a result of the surge. Twenty-eight of those arrested are black, twelve are white, and sixty-four are Hispanic. [Def. Exh. O; Doc. 28-5; 10/13/17, 78:6-10]

Defendants seek discovery of a wide range of materials relating to the surge and to a possible claim of selective enforcement. Defendants, who are black, argue that they are entitled to these materials because they have shown sufficient evidence of discriminatory intent behind and discriminatory effect of the ATF sting. [Doc. 29]

In their original Motion to Compel Discovery, Defendants sought disclosure of fourteen types of information. [Doc. 29] A hearing on Defendants' Motion to Compel Discovery was originally scheduled for June 27, 2017. That hearing was continued on Defendants' motion so that the parties could meet and work out discovery without intervention. [Doc. 39; Doc. 40] The Government subsequently provided some of the information requested and objected to other requests. [Doc. 45-2] On September 21, 2017, Defendants filed a supplement to their motion requesting types of information which had not been provided. [Doc. 45] The Government responded. [Doc. 47]

The current information sought by Defendants is:

1. The [National Crime Information Center (NCIC)] criminal history report relied on by the ATF during the investigation of the member of the Albuquerque ATF surge defendant class, in each of the 103 Albuquerque ATF surge cases. [Doc. 45, pg. 7]

The Government argues that it has already provided pretrial services reports to the defense and that those reports should be sufficient. [Doc. 47, pg. 5] Defendants counter that they need to know what the agents knew at the time they made the decision to arrest (or not arrest) people encountered during the surge. [Doc. 52, pg. 8] The defense wants to use this information to show whether the criminal history that the ATF claims to have relied on was the deciding factor in arrest decisions, or not. [Doc. 45, pg. 10] Because Defendants already have NCIC reports for cases represented by the Federal Public Defender's office, they are requesting only the NCIC reports for defendants not represented by that office. [Doc. 45, pg. 9]

2. The address of the location where a confidential informant approached the initial target that ultimately led to the arrest of a member of the Albuquerque ATF Surge defendant class, in each of the 103 Albuquerque ATF surge cases. [Doc. 45, pg. 10]

   The Government argues that this information is immaterial and irrelevant. [Doc. 47, pg. 7] Defendants counter that the information is material because they want to know whether the location of first contact is consistent with the target area for the surge as described by the ATF. [Doc. 45, pg. 11; Doc. 52, pg. 10]

3. All NCIC criminal history reports requested or generated, related to the Albuquerque ATF Surge, by any law enforcement officer working on the Albuquerque ATF Surge, between March 1, 2016 and September 30, 2016. [Doc. 45, pg. 11-12]

   Defendants argue that this information is necessary so that they can see if, for example, white individuals with criminal histories within the target criteria were identified by the ATF but not pursued. [Doc. 45, pg. 12] The Government relies on its objection to #1 above. [Doc. 45-2] It also argued at the hearing that this request is overly burdensome, presented issues with privacy, and could lead to similar requests by other defendants. [10/30/17, 15:4–20:9]

4. Any grant proposals and funding requests, as well as any other documents or communication, delineating the purpose and intended effect of the Albuquerque ATF Surge operation. [Doc. 45, pg. 13]

   Defendants argue that they need this information to understand what ATF had in mind as the effect of the Surge and to see if ATF had instituted measures to avoid racial profiling in its operations. [Doc. 45, pg. 13] The Government argues that it did not receive any grant funding for the operation in Albuquerque in 2016, and further objects to providing funding requests as irrelevant. It asserts that it has provided any documentation it has regarding the purpose of the ATF Surge operation. [Doc. 45-2, pg. 3]

5. All documents and communications reflecting what, if anything, any confidential informant involved in the Albuquerque ATF Surge was told about which individuals or class of individuals to target/not to target. [Doc. 45, pg. 14]

    Defendants argue that, although the ATF maintains that the confidential informants were only told which geographic area to target, it does not make sense that they were not also told which individuals to target. [Doc. 45, pg. 14] Thus, they seek any information about what the confidential informants were told about whom to target within the specified geographic area. The Government argues that it did not use individual target selection criteria, but rather focused on a geographic area. It further asserts that information about the target geographic area was disclosed already. [Doc. 47, pg. 7-8; Doc. 45-2, pg. 3]

6. All communications between any confidential informant involved in the Albuquerque ATF Surge and any target of the Albuquerque ATF Surge, whether the target was ultimately arrested and charged or not, to include all communications from any and all phones utilized by the confidential informant, business or personal, official or unofficial, as well as all emails, text messages, voicemail messages, audio and video recordings, recorded phone calls, and social media communications. [Doc. 45, pg. 15]

    Again, Defendants want to be able to compare the communications with defendants to those who were not arrested, to see if race was the deciding factor in the arrest decision. [Doc. 45, pg. 15] The Government objects to this request as overbroad and irrelevant. [Doc. 45-2, pg. 4]

7. All documents and communications ... between any persons employed or contracted by the ATF, related to: the area of town to target, the decision to target (or not to target) anyone pursuant to the ATF Surge, the decision to pursue (or not to pursue) any target of the ATF Surge, the decision to arrest (or not to arrest) anyone pursuant to the ATF Surge; the charging criteria for the ATF Surge; the decision to charge (or not to charge) anyone as a result of the ATF Surge; and the race of any target, potential target, and/or defendant in the ATF Surge.... [Doc. 45, pg. 17]

The Government objects to this request as overbroad and irrelevant. [Doc. 45-2, pg. 4]

8. All training manuals utilized in or influencing the manner of execution of the Albuquerque ATF Surge. [Doc. 45, pg. 17]

   The Government objects to this request as overbroad and irrelevant. [Doc. 45-2, pg. 4]

9. All documents, communications, meeting notes, data, studies, and reports relied upon in selecting the so-called SE quadrant of Albuquerque as the target area. [Doc. 45, pg. 17-18]

   The Government maintains that, to the extent such materials exist, they have been provided already. [Doc. 45-2, pg. 5]

10. All TLOxp reports requested or generated, related to the Albuquerque ATF Surge, by any law enforcement officer working on the Albuquerque ATF Surge, between March 21, 2016, and September 30, 2016. [Doc. 45, pg. 18]

    Defendants argue that this information is relevant to determining whether there were some non-black individuals who fit the target criteria but who were not pursued. [Doc. 45, pg. 19] The Government maintains that this information does not exist. [Doc. 45-2, pg. 5]

11. Any and all contemporaneous reports created or generated during the investigation into Yusef Casanova's white male methamphetamine supplier, to include vehicle registration reports, driver's license information, and NCIC reports. [Doc. 45, pg. 19]

    The parties differ on the facts of the encounter with Mr. Casanova, and thus on what materials were generated during the investigation. [Doc. 45-2, pg. 5; Doc. 45, pg. 19]

12. All documents and communications reflecting what, if anything, any confidential informant involved in the Albuquerque ATF Surge was told about which areas of the city to target/not to target. [Doc. 45, pg. 20]

    The Government maintains that this information does not exist. [Doc. 45-2, pg. 5]

II. Discussion

1. The Discovery Standard

"Racially selective law enforcement violates this nation's constitutional values at the most fundamental level; indeed, unequal application of criminal law to white and Black persons was one of the central evils addressed by the framers of the Fourteenth Amendment." *Marshall v. Columbia Lea Regional Hosp.*, 345 F.3d 1157, 1167 (10th Cir. 2003). Our Tenth Circuit Court of Appeals has outlined what a plaintiff alleging selective enforcement must prove:

> The requirements for a claim of racially selective law enforcement draw on what the Supreme Court has called "ordinary equal protection standards." The plaintiff must demonstrate that the defendant's actions [1] had a discriminatory effect and [2] were motivated by a discriminatory purpose.... The discriminatory purpose need not be the only purpose, but it must be a motivating factor in the decision ...

Id. at 1168 (citations omitted).

Here, of course, Defendants seek not to prove selective enforcement, but to obtain discovery by which they might use to make a selective enforcement claim. A defendant is not required to prove selective enforcement in order to obtain discovery related to it. *United States v. James*, 257 F.3d 1173, 1178 (10th Cir. 2001). ("[T]he defendants need not establish a prima facie case of selective prosecution to obtain discovery on these issues."). In *United States v. Armstrong*, the Supreme Court addressed the showing necessary to receive discovery related to a selective prosecution claim and held that the courts "require some evidence tending to show the existence of the essential elements of the defense, discriminatory effect and discriminatory intent." 517 U.S. 456, 468 (1996) (internal quotation marks and citation omitted). The Court equated this "some evidence" standard with a "colorable basis," "substantial threshold showing," "substantial and concrete basis," or "reasonable likelihood." Id. (citations omitted).

The *Armstrong* Court began its analysis by noting that "[t]he Attorney General and United States Attorneys retain broad discretion to enforce the Nation's criminal laws" and that "[a]s a result, the presumption of regularity supports their prosecutorial decisions and, in the absence of clear evidence to the contrary, courts presume that they have properly discharged their official duties." Id. at 465 (internal quotation marks and citations omitted).

Another part of the rationale in *Armstrong* was based on the burden discovery can place on the Government and the costs of disclosure of certain types of information. Id. ("If discovery is ordered, the Government must assemble from its own files documents which might corroborate or refute the defendant's claim. Discovery thus imposes many of the costs present when the Government must respond to a prima facie case of selective prosecution. It will divert prosecutors' resources and may disclose the Government's prosecutorial strategy."). Judicial deference to prosecutor's decisions hence also "stems from a concern not to unnecessarily impair the performance of a core executive constitutional function." Id. "'Examining the basis of a prosecution delays the criminal proceeding, threatens to chill law enforcement by subjecting the prosecutor's motives and decisionmaking to outside inquiry, and may undermine prosecutorial effectiveness by revealing the Government's enforcement policy.'" Id. (quoting Wayte *v. United States*, 470 U.S. 598, 607 (1985)). Because of the presumption of regularity and these concerns, the standard for discovery related to selective prosecution is heightened. Id.

The parties diverge on whether the *Armstrong* standard for obtaining discovery related to selective prosecution claims applies to selective enforcement claims. [Doc. 35, pgs. 3-5; Doc. 32, pgs. 5-6] Defendants argue that "with a claim of selective prosecution, movant must contend with the presumption of regularity afforded to prosecutors [but] with a selective enforcement claim, ... there is no presumption of regularity afforded to law enforcement officers." [Doc. 35] Defendants point to *United States v. Davis*, in which the Seventh Circuit held that [a]gents of the ATF and FBI are not protected by a powerful privilege or covered by a presumption of constitutional behavior. Unlike prosecutors, agents regularly testify in criminal cases, and their credibility may be relentlessly attacked by defense counsel. They also may have to testify in pretrial proceedings, such as hearings on motions to suppress evidence, and again their honesty is open to challenge. Statements that agents make in affidavits for search or arrest warrants may be contested, and the court may need their testimony to decide whether if shorn of untruthful statements the affidavits would have established probable cause. Agents may be personally liable for withholding evidence from prosecutors and thus causing violations of the constitutional requirement that defendants have access to material, exculpatory evidence. Before holding hearings (or civil trials) district judges regularly, and properly, allow discovery into nonprivileged aspects of what agents have said or done.

793 F.3d 712, 720–21 (7th Cir. 2015) (citations omitted). The Court concluded that the concerns animating "Armstrong do not apply to a contention that agents of the FBI or ATF engaged in racial discrimination when selecting targets for sting operations, or when deciding which suspects to refer for prosecution." *Id.* at 721.

Several courts have noted the *Davis* holding approvingly. See, e.g., United *States v. Hare*, 820 F.3d 93, 101 (4th Cir.), cert. denied, 137 S. Ct. 224 (2016), reh'g denied, 137 S. Ct. 460 (2016); United *States v. Mumphrey*, 193 F. Supp. 3d 1040, 1048 (N.D. Cal. 2016). The Third Circuit recently stated that we find ourselves in agreement with the core rationale of *Davis*: the special solicitude shown to prosecutorial discretion, which animated the Supreme Court's reasoning in *Armstrong* and *Bass*—and our own reasoning in our pre-*Armstrong/Bass* case law on the same subject—does not inevitably flow to the actions of law enforcement, or even to prosecutors acting in an investigative capacity. Prosecutors are ordinarily shielded by absolute immunity for their prosecutorial acts, but police officers and federal agents enjoy no such categorical protection. *United States v. Washington*, 869 F.3d 193, 219 (3d Cir. 2017) (footnotes omitted), cert. denied, No. 17-6986, 2018 WL 311803 (U.S. Jan. 8, 2018).

Other courts have criticized the Armstrong requirements, noting their seeming impossibility. The District Court of Kansas held that, in selective prosecution claims, "making a showing of a similarly situated individual is possible [because] [t]he claimant is dealing with a defined universe of individuals with whom to compare; individuals who were arrested and prosecuted for the same offenses in that jurisdiction or some other jurisdiction." *United States v. Mesa-Roche*, 288 F. Supp. 2d 1172, 1185 (D. Kan. 2003). In contrast, "[i]n the context of a challenged traffic stop ... imposing the similarly situated requirement makes the selective enforcement claim impossible to prove. It would require the defendant to make a credible showing that a similarly situated individual was not stopped by the law enforcement. How could a defendant, without discovery, ever make such a showing?" Id. at 1186; see also United *States v. Paxton*, No. 13 CR 103, 2014 WL 1648746, at (N.D. Ill. Apr. 17, 2014) (stating that "in selective prosecution claims, there should exist records of individuals who were charged and then subsequently treated in a different manner than the defendant. In selective enforcement cases, however, identifying the class of individuals is a much more burdensome endeavor, and one that may prove insurmountable" and holding that the defendants had met their burden in that case).

In *Alcaraz-Arellano*, our Tenth Circuit Court of Appeals noted that the standard for discovery related to selective prosecution claims is a "demanding" one, because "a claimant is requesting the judiciary to exercise power over a special province of the executive branch" and then noted that this standard was applied to a selective enforcement discovery request in United *States v. James*, 257 F.3d 1173, 1177 (10th Cir. 2001). *United States v. Alcaraz-Arellano*, 441 F.3d 1252, 1264 (10th Cir. 2006) (internal quotation marks and citation omitted). The Court echoed the concerns in Armstrong, stating that:

> caution is required in reviewing a claim of selective law enforcement. "[C]harges of racial discrimination ... may be easy to make and difficult to disprove." *Marshall*, 345 F.3d at 1167. Executive-branch officials possess broad discretion in determining when to make a traffic stop or an arrest. See id. Judicial interference with law-enforcement discretion might "induce police officers to protect themselves against false accusations in ways that are counterproductive to fair and effective enforcement of the laws," such as by directing law-enforcement resources away from minority neighborhoods. Id. Accordingly, the standard for proving a selective-enforcement claim should be, as with selective-prosecution claims, "a demanding one." [*Id.*]

Alcaraz-Arellano, 441 F.3d at 1264. Thus, the Tenth Circuit concluded that the showing necessary to obtain discovery for a selective [enforcement] defense must itself be a significant barrier to the litigation of insubstantial claims. Although defendants seeking discovery need not establish a prima facie case of selective [enforcement], they must satisfy a rigorous standard[.] They must produce some evidence of both discriminatory effect and discriminatory intent.

2. Discriminatory Intent

"Discriminatory intent can be shown by either direct or circumstantial evidence." Id. Defendants argue that they have shown sufficient circumstantial evidence of discriminatory intent, and that they seek direct evidence of discriminatory intent through discovery. [Doc. 29, pg. 23]

a. Homophily

First, Defendants argue that the ATF's selection of black confidential informants (CIs) "prefigures the selection of defendants and, in this foreshadowing, manifests the existence of selective enforcement." [Doc. 29, pg. 23] They point to the idea of "homophily," which "is the principle that a contact between similar people occurs at a higher rate than among dissimilar people." Miller McPherson, Lynn Smith-Lovin, and James M Cook, BIRDS OF A FEATHER: Homophily in Social Networks, Annu. Rev. Sociol. 2001. 27:415–44, available at http://aris. ss.uci.edu/~lin/52.pdf. Defendants maintain that, because of homophily, "for every Black 'principal' a confidential informant targeted, a web of several Black codefendants was often spun." [Doc. 29, pg. 24] The Government argues that this position is "ridiculous" because "[a]n argument that Black confidential informants will only interact with other Black confidential informants is an assumption that is itself racist." [Doc. 32, pg. 7] While it does not "deny that the ATF uses [confidential informants] that are similar in background to the criminals it tries to stop," it maintains that "the key characteristic of the selected confidential informants in the Albuquerque operation was not their race: it was their background of dealing or selling controlled substances." [Doc. 32, pg. 7]

Essentially, Defendants' argument is that ATF recruited black confidential informants when they knew or should have known that black confidential informants would interact with more black drug or firearms dealers than with dealers of other races. At the hearing, Agent Johnson and Agent Zayas testified as to how the confidential informants were selected for the operation in Albuquerque. Agent Johnson testified that the confidential informants were "confidential informants that [the ATF had] worked with in the past, and they come from all over the country." [Tr. 10/30/17, 28:25–29:1; see also 12/13/17 43:19–44:25 (stating that the ATF selected "guys that have worked these kinds of operations before")] He also stated that there were no white confidential informants available at the time. [12/13/17, 44:12-15 ("Q. You did not choose to use one White confidential informant? A. I don't have any White confidential informants—or I didn't at the time.")] At the end of Agent Zayas' testimony, the Court asked him how the confidential informants were selected. [12/13/17, 108:2-3] Agent Zayas stated in response,

> I do the selection of the agents, so while I'm selecting the agents and I'm talking to individuals around the country, I'm trying to determine what confidential informants are available and then the reliability of those confidential informants. So as I'm seeking agents and I'm trying to obtain different agents to come to Albuquerque based upon their experience and their ability to work with others and all that type of thing, I'm also questioning the agents throughout the country as to their confidential informants and if those confidential informants are reliable.

[12/13/17, 108:4-14] The Court also asked whether the ATF has access to any white confidential informants. Agent Zayas stated that there are white confidential informants working for the ATF, but that selection is "just whoever happens to be available at that time that I'm able to vet, that the information comes back to me that these people are reliable." [12/13/17, 110:2-8] He went on, "For the most part, I don't even ask what their race is. It doesn't matter." [Id.] He also testified that he was not given any information about the composition of the Albuquerque community with respect to ethnicity or race while recruiting agents and confidential informants. [12/13/17, 109:14-22] He stated that "[e]ach particular city has their own idiosyncrasies, but at the end of the day, firearms trafficking and narcotics trafficking is basically the same throughout the country" and that the "idiosyncrasies" of Albuquerque were its "proximity to Mexico" and the amount and quality of drugs available here as a result. [12/13/17, 111:4-17] He did not discuss how the ATF recruits confidential informants to work in particularly homogenous or insular communities.

However, Agent Johnson also testified about how some of the suspects identified during the Albuquerque operation were introduced to the ATF by other suspects. He stated that there were twenty-six instances which he called "conspiracies," which he defined as "two or more people engaged in criminal activity together that we ultimately charged" but which did not necessarily lead to conspiracy charges. [10/30/17, 31:17-19; Gov't Exh. 57] Seventy-five of the 104 surge defendants were associated with one of these "conspiracies." [Gov't Exh. 57] Agent Johnson testified about several instances in which the confidential informant met one person, who then introduced the confidential informant to another person, who ultimately provided the confidential informant with drugs or weapons. For example, he described one such transaction this way:

> A. ... This one involves an individual named [W.G.]. [W.G.] met one of our CIs. They discussed methamphetamine. [W.G.] took the confidential informant to [G.R.]'s residence. [W.G.] acquired the methamphetamine from Mr. R and provided it to us for a finder's fee. And that occurred on two occasions.
>
> Q. Okay. And was Mr. R also charged in connection with the surge?

A. Yes. Both individuals have been charged.

[10/30/17, 34:16-24] He went on to describe several other transactions.

A. This case involves [N.U], [A.S], and [P.Z]. It began with [N.U]—the case began with [N.U.] selling methamphetamine to an ATF undercover. [N.U] then took the undercover to [A.S.]. And then later, [A.S.] took the undercover to [P.Z.] for the purchase of meth.

So all three were involved in the methamphetamine trade.

Q. And connected with each other?

A. That is correct.

[B.M.] reported himself a methamphetamine dealer. We purchased some smaller amounts of methamphetamine. Then he brought [R.L.] to meet the undercover, who in turn sold ounce quantities of meth to the undercover.

[10/30/17, 35:1-15] Agent Johnson testified similarly as to twenty-three other instances in which multiple defendants were involved. In each case, initial contact by a confidential informant or an undercover agent led to introductions by the contact with others, often (but not always) previously unknown to the confidential informant or the undercover agent. [10/30/17, 34:16–43:15] He went on to state that once the confidential informants and/or undercover agents met with a contact, they would had no influence over the people to whom the contact would introduce them next. He stated,

A. ... when we meet with somebody, we don't choose who they bring. We don't choose who their source of supply is. We don't choose who they're associated with. You know, they make that decision. They associate with whoever they want to associate with. We have no control over that.

Q. And did you take the conspiracies as you found them?

A. Yes.

Q. So, again, if a conspiracy exists which is either multi-racial or homogenous in terms of race, and you found that conspiracy, what control would ATF have over the racial composition?

A. None.

[10/30/17, 50:17–51:4; see 10/30/17, 52:13-20]

Of the twenty-six cases involving multiple suspects, fifteen involved a black confidential informant. [Gov't Exh. 57] Of these fifteen instances, seven involved one or more black suspects. [Id.] At the same time, only two of the eleven multiple suspect cases involving non-black confidential informants involved black suspects. [Gov't Exh. 57] Similar figures (i.e., the number of cases involving a black confidential informant that also involved a black suspect) was not presented for the twenty-seven other cases.

Taken together, both Agent Johnson's testimony and the figures in Government's Exhibit 57 support Defendants' homophily theory. Nevertheless, even if the ATF knew of the potential impact of such preferences, this evidence is insufficient on its own to show that the ATF purposefully selected black confidential informants so as to target black people in Albuquerque. See Wayte v. United States, 470 U.S. 598, 610 (1985) (stating, '[D]iscriminatory purpose' ... implies more than ... intent as awareness of consequences. It implies that the decisionmaker ... selected or reaffirmed a particular course of action at least in part 'because of,' not merely 'in spite of,' its adverse effects upon an identifiable group." (quoting Pers. Adm'r of Massachusetts v. Feeney, 442 U.S. 256 (1979)).

b. Prior Misconduct

Defendants next argue that ATF's prior "misconduct" is evidence of discriminatory intent. [Doc. 35, pg. 5] They maintain that "[e]vidence of ATF's past behavior is highly relevant circumstantial evidence that may be used to infer intent, particularly when many of the agents involved in prior sullied operations were also involved in the Albuquerque ATF sting that led to [Defendants'] arrest." [Doc. 35, pg. 5] As evidence of "past misconduct," Defendants rely on articles about ATF operations in the past and on cases discussing the "dubious" nature of those operations. [Doc. pgs. 6-14] The Government argues that these past operations are irrelevant to the operation at issue here. [Doc. 32, pg. 9]

Defendants' argument is unavailing. Defendants' request for discovery in this case must be based on evidence related to the ATF's Albuquerque operation, not on actions in other operations. In addition, the surge in Albuquerque differs from the operations addressed by Defendants, which involved undercover storefronts, phony stash houses, and "Operation Fast and Furious." [Doc. 29] The primary tactic that was castigated in the stash house cases as "tawdry" was the dangling of large amounts of money in front of "unsophisticated, and perhaps desperate," defendants. See, e.g., United States v. Lewis, 641 F.3d 773, 777 (7th Cir. 2011). This tactic was not used here.

c. Targeted Areas

Defendants argue that the ATF's confidential informants sought out suspects "in locations that would virtually guarantee netting an inordinate number of minorities—and specifically,

Blacks." [Doc. 29] Other than asserting that the neighborhood known as "the Kirk" is a "historically Black neighborhood," Defendants provide no evidence that this is true, or that the area targeted by the ATF includes a higher population of minority residents than other areas. [Doc. 45, pg. 18 (describing the target area as a "minority-concentrated corner of Albuquerque")] Although the Government stated in its Response to Defendants' Motion that "as many as 19.2 percent of the residents [of zip code 87108, which the Government states includes the target area] identify as [B]lack," no evidence was submitted to support this figure and the Court was unable to confirm it on the Census Bureau website cited by the Government. [Doc. 32, n. 6; see also Doc. 35, n.7] The Court notes that, contrary to both parties' arguments, the population of black residents of the "Southeast/Primary" "crime cluster" identified in the ABQ i-team report admitted by the Government was 5.12% as of August 2017.3 [Gov't Exh. 58, pg. 38] The "Southeast/Primary" area overlaps with the area targeted by the ATF as stated by Agent Johnson. Defendants' showing as to discriminatory intent based on selection of the target area is insufficient at this time.

3. Discriminatory Effect

"To prove discriminatory effect in a race-based selective [enforcement] claim, a defendant must make a credible showing that a ... similarly-situated individual of another race could have been, but was not, arrested or referred for federal prosecution for the offense for which the defendant was arrested and referred." *James*, 257 F.3d at 1179. "The defendant may satisfy [this] requirement by identifying a similarly-situated individual or through the use of statistical evidence." Id.

a. Similarly-Situated Individual

Although the circuits differ in some respects as to how they define a "similarly situated individual," the Tenth Circuit has adopted the Fourth Circuit's formulation: "[D]efendants are similarly situated when their circumstances present no distinguishable legitimate prosecutorial factors that might justify making different prosecutorial decisions with respect to them." *United States v. Deberry*, 430 F.3d 1294, 1301 (10th Cir. 2005) citing United *States v. Olvis*, 97 F.3d 739, 744 (4th Cir. 1996). The strictness of this standard is part of what makes selective enforcement claims so difficult to demonstrate, as it "seems to require that defendants be virtually identical (not merely similar) with other unprosecuted individuals. Under [this test], defendants must show that the prosecutor could not have differentiated the defendants from other unprosecuted individuals by using legitimate prosecutorial factors." Thomas P. McCarty, *United States v. Khan*, 461 F.3d 477 (4th Cir. 2006): Discovering Whether "Similarly Situated" Individuals and the Selective Prosecution Defense Still Exist, 87 Neb. L. Rev. 538, 562 (2008); id. (stating that "the Fourth Circuit's definition of 'similarly situated' may make it easier for prosecutors to selectively prosecute defendants for invidious purposes."); *United States v. Venable*, 666 F.3d 893, 901 (4th Cir. 2012), as amended (Feb. 15, 2012) (stating that the Fourth Circuit has "rejected a narrow approach to relevant factors to be considered when deciding whether persons are similarly situated for prosecutorial decisions." (internal quotation marks and citation omitted)).

At the hearing, Defendants elicited testimony from Agent Johnson regarding a specific investigation in which a confidential informant reported meeting with a white male. [10/31/17, 175:10–178:3] After informing the ATF about the white male, Agent Johnson identified the white male and obtained an NCIC report about him. The NCIC report indicated that "he had prior convictions for battery, domestic assault, robbery, assault with serious physical injury, felon in possession of a firearm, and two other assault convictions." [10/30/17, 176:17-21; Gov't Exh. 30] The white male also had tattoos on his face that ATF agents identified as being associated with two specific street gangs. [Gov't Exh. 30] After the ATF obtained this information, the confidential informant arranged to buy methamphetamine from the white male, but on the day of the sale, the white male did not show up. Although the confidential informant spoke to the suspect again about a purchase, subsequent calls by the confidential informant went unanswered. In a meeting a few weeks later, the confidential informant related to Agent Johnson that he/she had run into the white male and that the suspect had discussed breaking into homes and a robbery in which he beat up a woman. The suspect then told the confidential informant to let him know when the informant had spoken with his/her associate who also committed robberies. [10/31/17, 175:10–178:3; Gov't Exh. 30] Agent Johnson testified that the white male was not one of the defendants from the surge. [10/31/17, 178:3]

Agent Johnson also testified about two investigations involving a suspect and a source of supply. In one instance, an ATF agent purchased methamphetamine from a suspect, who identified her source of supply as one of two white males seated in a nearby car. [Def. Exh. I; 10/30/17, 169:6-173:9] Agent Johnson testified that the license plate of the car in which the white males were seated "would have been queried." [10/30/17, 172:18-23] No NCIC report was attached to the Report of Investigation for this transaction and Agent Johnson testified that he did not know if one was obtained. [Id.] Agent Johnson stated that neither of the white males in the car was pursued "[b]ecause they didn't do anything wrong, other than her saying that. There's no evidence that they possessed any meth." [10/30/17, 173:7-9]

In contrast, in another investigation, the black source of supply was arrested even though agents did not observe any transaction between the seller and the source. Agent Johnson testified that an agent met twice with a suspect to purchase methamphetamine. In the first transaction, the suspect directed the agent to an apartment, where an "unidentified black male" was standing outside. Both the suspect and the unidentified black male went into an apartment and the suspect returned and sold methamphetamine to the agent. [Def. Exh. K] On another date, after meeting the agent at a restaurant, the suspect instructed the agent to follow him to the same apartment. Once at the apartment building, the suspect and entered one apartment and shortly came out again. [10/30/17, 193:12-195:22; Def. Exh. K] Agent Johnson testified that a person (later determined to be the same "unidentified black male" as seen in the first transaction) stepped out of the apartment. The "unidentified black male" was later identified through the license plate of the car in front of the apartment, and agents obtained an NCIC report about him. [Def. Exh. K; 10/30/17, 195:11-22] The black male was subsequently arrested and is a surge defendant.4 [10/30/17, 195:22] Defendants point to the contrast between these two cases as evidence that the ATF agents made decisions to pursue suspects differently based on race. [Doc. 52]

b. Statistical Evidence

Defendant maintains that he has provided sufficient statistical support for his contention that similarly-situated persons of a different race could have been investigated but were not. [Doc. 29] "[A] defendant cannot satisfy the discriminatory effect prong by providing statistical evidence which simply shows that the challenged government action tends to affect one particular group. Rather, the proffered statistics must address the critical issue of whether that particular group was treated differently than a similarly-situated group." *James*, 257 F.3d at 1179. For statistics to be meaningful, they must include "a reliable measure of the demographics of the relevant population, a means of telling whether the data represent similarly situated individuals, and a point of comparison to the actual incidence of crime among different racial or ethnic segments of the population." *Marshall*, 345 F.3d at 1168 (citations omitted). A comparison of the percentage of black defendants arrested for a certain crime with the percentage of non-black defendants arrested is significant only if non-black defendants commit that crime at a proportional rate. In other words, the fact that the percentage of black defendants facing crack possession charges is higher than the percentage of black people in Albuquerque is significant only if it is true that all populations in Albuquerque possess crack at rates proportionate to their population. For instance, in United *States v. Venable*, the Fourth Circuit rejected the defendant's evidence "showing that for the three years preceding his prosecution—2005, 2006, and 2007—approximately 87 percent of the firearms prosecutions under Project Exile were brought by Black defendants" because it "contain[ed] no appropriate basis for comparison. It provide[d] no statistical evidence about the number of blacks who were actually committing firearms offenses or whether a greater percentage of whites could have been prosecuted for such crimes" and did "not even provide any evidence regarding the proportion of blacks residing within the relevant geographical area." 666 F.3d at 903.

Here, Defendants point to two statistics. First, the general population of black people in Bernalillo County as of July 1, 2016 was 3.4%. See United States Census Bureau, QuickFacts, available at https://www.census.gov/quickfacts/fact/table/bernalillocountynewmexico,US/PST045216 (last visited 02/02/2018). [Doc. 29, pg. 5] The Government does not contest this assertion. [Doc. 32, pg. 12] Based on an assumption that the proportion of black defendants caught in the surge should be the same as the proportion of black people in the general population, Defendants argue that the fact that 27.2% of the defendants were caught in the surge demonstrates discriminatory effect. [Doc. 29, pg. 5-6] However, the Albuquerque operation did not target all of Bernalillo County, or even all of Albuquerque. Rather, Agent Johnson testified that the ATF targeted "the southeast quadrant" of Albuquerque, which he described as an area stretching from Eubank Boulevard west to San Mateo Boulevard and from Interstate 40 south to Gibson Boulevard. [10/30/17, 27:8-13] In addition, this simplistic analysis has been rejected by several courts because there is no evidence for the assumption that all races commit this crime at proportional rates. See, e.g., Mesa-Roche, 288 F. Supp. 2d at 1190 (stating that "the courts have rejected a number of Equal Protection and Fourth Amendment challenges based on assumptions that discrete racial or ethnic groups violate particular laws at the same rate as other groups" (citing Armstrong, 517 U.S. at 469 and James, 257 F.3d at 1179–80)).

Defendants also point to statistics from the United States Sentencing Commission on the percentage of black defendants sentenced for drug trafficking and firearms crimes in the District of New Mexico. [Doc. 29, pg. 5; Doc. 29-4 Exh. D] See United States Sentencing Bureau Interactive Sourcebook, Primary Offense and Offender Characteristics/Race of Offenders in Each Primary Offense Category, available at https://isb.ussc.gov/USSC?userid=USSC_Guest&password=USSC_Guest&toc-section=2 (last visited Feb. 2, 2018). That data shows that black defendants make up 5.4% of drug trafficking defendants and 5.9% of firearms defendants,5 less than the 27.2% found here. [Id.] Defendants argue based on these figures that the percentage of black defendants arrested during the surge should be between 5 and 6 percent. [Id.] While this comparison is more specific, it is still problematic for several reasons. First, the District of New Mexico encompasses the entire state of New Mexico. These statistics do not break down or indicate the percentage of black defendants from Albuquerque and more importantly, the area targeted by the ATF. In other words, the statistics cited by Defendants do not indicate whether the persons represented are "similarly situated" to those targeted by the ATF, which were people dealing in drugs or firearms who have violent criminal histories. See Hare, 820 F.3d at 99 (rejecting similar statistics); Olvis, 97 F.3d at 745 (stating that where the defendants presented a study showing that of "all the federal crack cocaine trafficking prosecutions in federal court since 1992 in which the defendant's race was apparent, over 90% involved black defendants," the study was inadequate because it "provide[d] no statistical evidence on the number of blacks who were actually committing crack cocaine offenses or whether a greater percentage of whites could have been prosecuted for such crimes"); Blackwell v. Strain, 496 Fed. Appx. 836 (10th Cir. 2012) (rejecting similar statistics offered to show discriminatory intent).

4. Analysis

The Court will order the Government to disclose to Defendants at this time only the NCIC reports requested in items 1 and 3 above. See United *States v. Alexander*, No. 11 CR 148-1, 2013 WL 6491476, (N.D. Ill. Dec. 10, 2013) (allowing "limited discovery of the ATF'a policies and procedures regarding the selection criteria for targets of phony stash-house robbery cases in place at the time of [the defendant's] arrest"). Those requests include 1) NCIC reports generated by ATF for each of the 104 surge defendants, and 2) NCIC reports generated by ATF between March 1, 2016 and September 30, 2016. As Defendants acknowledge [Doc. 45], their showing is insufficient to meet the Alcaraz-Arellano standard. However, Defendants maintain that "to ensure a precisely-crafted similarly situated comparison group the defense needs reliable and complete information which currently lies in the hands of the United States." [Doc. 45] They further argue that, with the information known to the ATF at the time of the decision to arrest, a statistician "will be able to run a regression analysis between the defendant class and the [similarly situated comparison group], which can isolate the independent variable (i.e., race, age, sex, criminal history) having the greatest effect on the dependent variable (i.e., the likelihood of being charged in the ATF Surge cases)." [Doc. 45] They argue that the results of analysis of the NCIC reports will go to both discriminatory intent and discriminatory effect. [Id.] See Alcaraz-*Arellano*, 441 F.3d at 1265 (stating that "[i]n some circumstances, '[s]tatistics showing racial or ethnic imbalance are probative ... because such imbalance is often a telltale sign of purposeful discrimination.'" (quoting Int'l *Bhd. of Teamsters v. United States*, 431 U.S. 324, 339 n. 20 (1977)).

The Court agrees that Defendants' burden to demonstrate disparate treatment in the face of ATF's criteria for arrest is essentially insurmountable without access to the information ATF had when it made those decisions. As the *Hare* Court observed,

[e]ven if a defendant could, for example, use state or federal prosecutions to identify white individuals involved in drug offenses or armed robberies, without discovery into what ATF knew about these individuals, the defendant would be hard pressed to demonstrate that there were no distinguishing factors that would justify different enforcement treatment.

In its objection to release of the NCIC reports, the Government acknowledged that

"[t]he ATF agent [in a related case] testified that decisions to charge or not charge defendant were made based on criminal history, when it was available. Thus, if ATF were intending to discriminate against a particular group of people based on race, they would have arrested individuals of that race who had less criminal history than the criminal history of those defendants whom were not being discriminated against based on race. In other words, ATF would have lowered the arrest threshold for black defendants."

[Doc. 47; *see U.S. v. Casanova*, No. CR 16-2917 JAP, Transcript (taken April 5, 2017), Doc. 51, 78:2-5 (stating that criminal history was key to identifying the "worst of the worst," which were the ATF's targets)]

At the hearing in this matter, Agent Johnson testified that the Albuquerque surge was a "120-day detail where myself and other undercover agents and case agents, along with confidential informants, came into Albuquerque, New Mexico, to help ATF and other law enforcement combat violent crime in the area." [10/30/17, 23:1-5] He also testified that the ATF made decisions to pursue a given target based on a number of factors, including criminal history. He stated,

> There was not an official decision-making process. We'd look at the information that the [confidential informants] would provide. What is this particular individual involved in? Is it firearms? Is it narcotics? We'd look at criminal history; outside factors; talk to local police officers that we worked with as a part of the operation. So there wasn't a hard set, okay, this is the criteria, you've got to check these boxes. It was all on a case-by-case basis, depending on the information we received.

[10/30/17, 29:2-15] Review of the NCIC reports relied on by the ATF in making arrest decisions may allow Defendants to identify whether those not arrested had distinguishing characteristics other than race.

Moreover, the Government's objections to disclosure of the NCIC reports to Defendants boil down to the threat of a breach of privacy and the burden of disclosure. Yet the Government acknowledges that they disclosed to Defendants the Pretrial Services Reports and argues that they contain "contain the known criminal history for the [s]urge defendants of all races." [Doc. 47, pg. 5] Hence, any privacy issues related to disclosure of the criminal history information in those reports is moot. Privacy concerns related to the other NCIC reports can be addressed through a confidentiality agreement.

Finally, the Court notes that the NCIC reports requested have been ordered to be disclosed to a surge defendant in another case. See *U.S. v. Casanova*, No. CR 16-2917 JAP, Doc. 83 (filed 12/13/17).

If, after receipt of the NCIC reports, Defendants can make a showing of discriminatory intent and discriminatory effect that meets the Alcaraz-Arellano standard, the Court will consider a renewed motion regarding the remainder of their discovery requests.

III. Conclusion

FOR THE FOREGOING REASONS, the Court GRANTS in PART Defendants' Motion to Compel Discovery pertaining to Claim of Selective Enforcement. [Doc. 2362:29; Doc. 2363:28]

FURTHERMORE, the parties are ordered to confer regarding the necessity of a confidentiality agreement and, if such an agreement is necessary, to submit a proposed agreement to the Court.

FINALLY, the Court and the parties are aware of the requests by members of the press for access to the exhibits admitted at the various hearings in this matter. The Court understands the parties to agree to the release of exhibits, not previously released, upon this Court's ruling on this pending motion. The parties are directed to meet and confer regarding which, if any, as yet unreleased exhibits should be redacted prior to release. Once redacted, the exhibits shall be released. Further concerns relating to this matter should be directed to the Court.

UNITED STATES V. DAVIS
793 F.3d 712 (7th Cir. 2015)

EASTERBROOK, Circuit Judge.

The United States has appealed from a district court's order dismissing an indictment, but without prejudice to a new indictment (should one be returned within the statute of limitations). The district judge took this step to permit appellate review of his discovery order, with which the prosecutor had declined to comply. Once the indictment had been dismissed, the Solicitor General authorized an appeal under the Criminal Appeals Act, 18 U.S.C. § 3731. But a panel of this court dismissed the appeal for lack of jurisdiction, 766 F.3d 722 (7th Cir.2014), ruling that the Act authorizes appeal only if the dismissal of an indictment would be final within the meaning of 28 U.S.C. § 1291. The possibility of reindictment and recurrence of the discovery dispute made this dismissal non-final, the panel held. We granted the United States' petition for rehearing en banc.

I

The indictment charges Paul Davis and six confederates—Alfred Withers, Julius Morris, Jayvon Byrd, Vernon Smith, Corey Barbee, and Dante Jeffries—with several federal offenses arising from a plan to rob a stash house, where the defendants believed they would find drugs and money. We need not set out the plan's details or the precise statutes involved, because proceedings on the merits of the charges never got under way in the district court. What matters now is that the stash house the defendants thought they would rob did not exist. They were caught in a sting.

According to the prosecutor, Davis repeatedly approached someone he thought to be a potential partner in crime and asked whether he knew of any opportunities to conduct robberies. Davis did not know that his interlocutor was cooperating with the FBI. Acting on the informant's reports, agents bought drugs from Davis three times; this gave some credibility to the informant's report that Davis was interested in robbing stash houses to get drugs to sell. The FBI passed the information to the Bureau of Alcohol, Tobacco, Firearms and Explosives (ATF), which sent an undercover agent to conduct a sting. Posing as a disgruntled drug courier, the agent told Davis about an opportunity to rob a stash house, supposedly containing 50 kilograms of cocaine. Davis recruited assistants (the other six defendants). They discussed the possibility of killing the stash houses' guards and the undercover agent too in order to eliminate witnesses and avoid sharing the loot. When arrested at the assembly point for the planned robbery, three of the seven defendants carried firearms.

They maintain that the prosecutor, the FBI, and the ATF engaged in racial discrimination, in violation of the Due Process Clause's equal-protection component. The defendants told the district court that since 2006 the United States Attorney for the Northern District of Illinois has prosecuted 20 stash-house stings, and that of the defendants in these cases 75 were black and 19 white. According to defendants, 13 of the 19 white defendants were Hispanic. All seven defendants in this prosecution are black. Defendants asserted that these figures "present a picture of stark discriminatory practices by the ATF and FBI who target, through the use of informants and undercover agents, select persons to present with the opportunity to commit a hypothetical … lucrative crime."

Defendants asked the judge to direct the prosecutor to provide extensive information about who is prosecuted, how they (and others) were selected for attention by the FBI and ATF, and how the United States Attorney's office makes decisions after receiving reports from investigators. The prosecutor opposed this motion, contending that United States v. Armstrong, 517 U.S. 456, 116 S.Ct. 1480, 134 L.Ed.2d 687 (1996), forbids discovery into prosecutorial selectivity unless the defense first shows that similarly situated persons have not been prosecuted. The defense's data about who had been prosecuted did not include any information about who could have been prosecuted, but was not.

The district court entered a discovery order substantially as the defense had proposed it, writing in a short explanation that "the prosecution in this District has brought at least twenty purported phony stash house cases, with the overwhelming majority of the defendants named being individuals of color. In light of this information, it is necessary to permit Defendants discovery on the following issues...." The district court did not identify any similarly situated person who had not been prosecuted or explain why Armstrong allows a court to compel disclosures by the prosecutor in the absence of that information.

Coupled with the breadth of the discovery order (which we discuss in Part III of this opinion), this led the United States to decline to comply. The Criminal Appeals Act does not authorize appeals from discovery orders, but it does authorize appeals from orders dismissing indictments. The district judge agreed to facilitate appellate review by dismissing the indictment without prejudice, and the United States appealed. That brings us to the jurisdictional question.

II

If this were a civil case, and a complaint had been dismissed without prejudice in an attempt to permit immediate review of a discovery order, an appeal would not be possible. See, e.g., Doctor's *Associates, Inc. v. Duree*, 375 F.3d 618 (7th Cir.2004) (dismissing an appeal where the parties reserved the right to reactivate the litigation later); Furnace *v. Board of Trustees*, 218 F.3d 666 (7th Cir.2000) (same). For 28 U.S.C. § 1291, which governs most civil appeals, requires a "final decision," and to be final the dismissal of a complaint generally must be with prejudice. Some statutes, such as 28 U.S.C. § 1292, authorize interlocutory appeals; so do some rules, such as Fed.R.Civ.P. 23(f); but in the main a final decision is essential—and the Supreme Court insists that the exceptions to the final-decision rule be applied sparingly, to avoid dragging litigation out. See, e.g., Mohawk *Industries, Inc. v. Carpenter*, 558 U.S. 100, 130 S.Ct. 599, 175 L.Ed.2d 458 (2009). The Justices have said that this is likewise true for appeals by defendants in pending criminal cases, which also are covered by § 1291. See, e.g., Flanagan *v. United States*, 465 U.S. 259, 104 S.Ct. 1051, 79 L.Ed.2d 288 (1984). Compare *Abney v. United States*, 431 U.S. 651, 97 S.Ct. 2034, 52 L.Ed.2d 651 (1977), with United *States v. MacDonald*, 435 U.S. 850, 98 S.Ct. 1547, 56 L.Ed.2d 18 (1978).

But the United States relies on the Criminal Appeals Act, 18 U.S.C. § 3731, which applies exclusively to the prosecutor's appeals in criminal cases. This statute provides:

In a criminal case an appeal by the United States shall lie to a court of appeals from a decision, judgment, or order of a district court dismissing an indictment or information or granting a new trial after verdict or judgment, as to any one or more counts, or any part thereof, except that no appeal shall lie where the double jeopardy clause of the United States Constitution prohibits further prosecution.

An appeal by the United States shall lie to a court of appeals from a decision or order of a district court suppressing or excluding evidence or requiring the return of seized property in a criminal proceeding, not made after the defendant has been put in jeopardy and before the verdict or finding on an indictment or information, if the United States attorney certifies to the district court that the appeal is not taken for purpose of delay and that the evidence is a substantial proof of a fact material in the proceeding.

An appeal by the United States shall lie to a court of appeals from a decision or order, entered by a district court of the United States, granting the release of a person charged with or convicted of an offense, or denying a motion for revocation of, or modification of the conditions of, a decision or order granting release.

The appeal in all such cases shall be taken within thirty days after the decision, judgment or order has been rendered and shall be diligently prosecuted.

The provisions of this section shall be liberally construed to effectuate its purposes.

Defendants maintain, and the panel held, that the first clause of § 3731's first paragraph, referring to "a decision, judgment, or order of a district court dismissing an indictment", covers only the sort of dismissal that would be "final" for the purpose of an appeal under § 1291.

The rest of § 3731 provides context for evaluating this position—as does a comparison with § 1291, which permits appeals from "final" decisions. The word "final" does not appear in § 3731, nor does any similar word.

Context begins with the first paragraph of § 3731, which after mentioning an indictment or information adds "or granting a new trial after verdict or judgment, as to any one or more counts, or any part thereof". An order setting a case for a new trial is not a final decision. Nor is an order setting one count for a new trial, or a "part" of one count for a new trial. And if we read the "count" language as modifying both indictments and new trials—so that we get "dismissing an indictment or information ... as to any one or more counts"—again § 3731 ¶ 1 authorizes appeals from non-final decisions, for in ordinary civil litigation a decision dismissing one count of a complaint cannot be appealed unless the requirements of Fed.R.Civ.P. 54(b) are met.

Paragraph 2 of § 3731 authorizes appeals from orders suppressing or excluding evidence, or ordering the return of property (though the rest of the case continues). Orders excluding evidence and disposing of some property while the litigation continues are not final decisions under § 1291.

The third paragraph continues the pattern by authorizing an appeal from an order granting a person's release on bail (while the case proceeds), or denying a motion to modify conditions of release, or to revoke release on bail. None of these orders is a final decision that ends the litigation and leaves nothing but execution of the judgment, the standard definition of "final" under § 1291. See, e.g., *Gelboim v. Bank of America Corp.*, –––U.S. ––––, 135 S.Ct. 897, 902, 190 L.Ed.2d 789 (2015); Catlin *v. United States*, 324 U.S. 229, 233, 65 S.Ct. 631, 89 L.Ed. 911 (1945).

It seems apt to say that all of § 3731 is an exception to the final-decision rule. And so the Supreme Court has described it. In the course of distinguishing appeals under § 1291 from those under § 3731, the Court called § 3731 "a statutory exception to the final judgment rule". *Flanagan*, 465 U.S. at 265 n. 3, 104 S.Ct. 1051. If finality were essential then, when responding to the holding of United *States v. Sanges*, 144 U.S. 310, 12 S.Ct. 609, 36 L.Ed. 445 (1892), that the United States needs express authority to appeal, Congress could have amended § 1291 so that a prosecutor, like other litigants, may use it plus interlocutory appeals by permission under § 1292(b). (Defendant and prosecutor alike also could use 18 U.S.C. § 3742, which authorizes appeals of sentences in criminal cases.) Instead Congress created a separate Criminal Appeals Act and has amended it over the years to include the many categories of non-final orders that we have mentioned. *United States v. Wilson*, 420 U.S. 332, 336–39, 95 S.Ct. 1013, 43 L.Ed.2d 232 (1975), traces this history.

Defendants want us to hold that the first clause of § 3731 ¶ 1 alone has an atextual finality requirement, which not only would divorce orders dismissing indictments from every other kind of order under § 3731 but also would create the anomaly that a dismissal of one count would be immediately appealable (though non-final in civil practice) while the dismissal of all counts would not be appealable. Neither the text nor the structure of § 3731 permits such an approach.

Section 3731 authorizes interlocutory appeals in part because the Double Jeopardy Clause of the Fifth Amendment creates special obstacles for a prosecutor who contends that a district court's order is erroneous. The Supreme Court stressed in decisions such as Mohawk Industries that, if a district court errs, an appeal from the final decision usually allows the mistake to be corrected, if necessary by holding a new trial. But errors in favor of the defense in a criminal prosecution may lead to acquittal, and the prosecution cannot appeal from a mid-trial acquittal by the judge, or an end-of-trial acquittal by the jury, no matter how erroneous the ruling that led to this outcome—even though in parallel civil litigation the losing litigant would have a full appellate remedy. See, e.g., Fong *Foo v. United States*, 369 U.S. 141, 82 S.Ct. 671, 7 L.Ed.2d 629 (1962); Sanabria *v. United States*, 437 U.S. 54, 98 S.Ct. 2170, 57 L.Ed.2d 43 (1978). That's why § 3731 departs from § 1291 and why it is inappropriate to read into § 3731 a "finality" requirement that it lacks (but § 1291 contains).

Congress has not taken the final-decision rule as far as it might go. The books are full of exceptions thought helpful to facilitate accurate or prompt decision. We have mentioned § 1292, which permits appeals from orders granting, denying, or modifying injunctions (interlocutory or final) plus orders certified by district judges and accepted by courts of appeals. Another statute, 28 U.S.C. § 1453(c), permits immediate appellate review of orders remanding suits that had been removed on the authority of the Class Action Fairness Act. And § 1447(d) permits appeals of remands in civil-rights cases or those removed by federal officers. Rule 23(f) permits appeals from orders certifying or declining to certify class actions. Section 3731 is just another in the complement of exceptions to § 1291's final-decision rule.

Even if we were disposed to fight against the language of § 3731 (which lacks the word "final"), and its structure, and its objective of accommodating the prosecution's need to obtain appellate review in a way consistent with the Double Jeopardy Clause, we would still respect the Supreme Court's description of § 3731 as "remov[ing] all statutory barriers to Government appeals". *Wilson*, 420 U.S. at 337, 95 S.Ct. 1013. *Ditto, United States v. Martin Linen Supply Co.*, 430 U.S. 564, 568, 577, 97 S.Ct. 1349, 51 L.Ed.2d 642 (1977). Perhaps this is an overstatement; after all, § 3731 contains a list of appealable orders, which does not include discovery orders. That's why the prosecutor asked the district court to choose a remedy on the statutory list. But the minimum meaning of the statement in Wilson is that if the district court enters a listed order, there are no further barriers to appeal. A final-decision rule imported from § 1291 would be such a further barrier.

Because discovery orders are not on the § 3731 list, appellate review depended on the district court's cooperation. The judge chose a response that was listed; if the judge had decided to exclude vital evidence as a sanction for the prosecutor's stance, that too would have authorized an appeal. It is hard to see why this appeal should be foreclosed because the judge chose what seemed to be the cleanest way to proceed. But if in the future a district judge believes than an interlocutory appeal would be unduly disruptive, the court has only to avoid issuing one of the sorts of orders that fall within the scope of § 3731. The prosecutor cannot dismiss an indictment on his own but requires the court's approval. Fed.R.Crim.P. 48(a). (The prosecutor may of course decline to proceed with a case, whether or not a judge dismisses the indictment, but a prosecutor can't appeal from his own decision.) If the judge chooses a response not on the § 3731 list, then to obtain review the prosecutor would need to meet the stringent requirements of a writ of mandamus, a discretionary remedy limited to the clearest errors and usurpations of power.

Although, as we have mentioned, Wilson may be thought to slight the fact that § 3731 contains a specific list of appealable orders, the Justices themselves seem willing to take the language of Wilson and Flanagan at face value.

United States v. Bass, 536 U.S. 862, 122 S.Ct. 2389, 153 L.Ed.2d 769 (2002), offers an illustration. In the wake of Armstrong, which held that discovery relating to a claim of selective prosecution depends on proof that eligible persons of a different race have not been prosecuted, a defendant contended that the Attorney General took race into account when deciding when to authorize a prosecutor to seek capital punishment. The defense offered the same sort of evidence that had been deemed inadequate in Armstrong: that black defendants were charged with capital crimes out of proportion to the general population. The district court ordered discovery into the exercise of prosecutorial discretion and, when the United States declined to provide the information, dismissed the prosecutor's notice of intent to seek the death penalty. The United States appealed, the court of appeals affirmed, and the Supreme Court summarily reversed, holding the discovery order incompatible with Armstrong. Yet the district court's order dismissing the notice of intent to seek the death penalty not only was interlocutory (the criminal prosecution remained pending) but also is not on the list in § 3731. Still, the court of appeals and the Supreme Court did not see a jurisdictional problem. We recognize that an opinion disregarding an issue, even a jurisdictional one, does not establish a holding. See, e.g., Steel *Co. v. Citizens for Better Environment*, 523 U.S. 83, 91–92, 118 S.Ct. 1003, 140 L.Ed.2d 210 (1998). But the Court may have let the issue pass precisely because it sees no need to retreat from the statements made about § 3731 in *Flanagan, Wilson*, and *Martin Linen*.

Other courts of appeals take the Justices at their word. Several have entertained appeals from orders dismissing indictments without prejudice. See, e.g., United *States v. Lester*, 992 F.2d 174, 176 (8th Cir.1993), and United *States v. Woodruff*, 50 F.3d 673, 675 (9th Cir.1995). As far as we know, no court of appeals has added a finality requirement to § 3731 ¶ 1 and thus forbidden the appeal from an order dismissing an indictment without prejudice—or for that matter required "finality" for the appeal of any order covered by § 3731.

Defendants insist that United *States v. Clay*, 481 F.2d 133 (7th Cir.1973) (Stevens, J.), commits this court to a different path. Yet in Clay the court held that § 3731 allows an appeal from an order dismissing an indictment without prejudice. Along the way, Clay remarked that, despite the district court's choice of label, the order was "final" in the sense that the dispute would not recur. Defendants read that as a holding that if a dispute can recur—as this discovery dispute could recur if another grand jury returned another indictment—then an appeal is forbidden. This reads too much into Clay. Saying "if conclusive, then appealable" (as Clay did) differs from saying "only if conclusive, then appealable." Clay did not have a non-final order and could not announce a holding about that subject—nor did it purport to do so.

But suppose this is wrong and Clay did think that finality is essential. Since then, the Supreme Court has said repeatedly that barriers (other than the Double Jeopardy Clause) not stated in § 3731 itself do not foreclose appeals. Section 3731 does not contain a final-decision rule. The language in Clay, though not its holding, has been overtaken by developments in the Supreme Court, and this court, sitting en banc in 2015, is not bound by what one panel believed about § 3731 in 1973.

We hold that § 3731 authorizes an appeal when a district court dismisses an indictment, or a count of an indictment, or a part of a count of an indictment, without prejudice to the possibility of a successive indictment containing the same charge. The court therefore has jurisdiction to decide whether the indictment was properly dismissed, which depends on whether the discovery order was itself proper. (Armstrong reached the Supreme Court in the same way, as the United States used the dismissal of an indictment to present a question about the propriety of a discovery order.)

III

Before entering the discovery order, the district court said only that "the prosecution in this District has brought at least twenty purported phony stash house cases, with the overwhelming majority of the defendants named being individuals of color. In light of this information, it is necessary to permit Defendants discovery" about prosecutorial practices and criteria. That decision is inconsistent with Armstrong. The record in Armstrong showed that every defendant in every crack-cocaine prosecution filed by a particular United States Attorney's office and assigned to the public defender was black. If, as the Supreme Court held, that evidence did not justify discovery into the way the prosecutor selected cases, then proof that in the Northern District of Illinois three-quarters of the defendants in stash-house cases have been black does not suffice.

The United States believes that we should stop here and reverse. But things are not that simple. Armstrong was about prosecutorial discretion. The defendants assumed that state and federal law-enforcement agents arrested all those they found dealing in crack cocaine, and they suspected that the federal prosecutor was charging the black suspects while letting the white suspects go. The Supreme Court replied that federal prosecutors deserve a strong presumption of honest and constitutional behavior, which cannot be overcome simply by a racial disproportion in the outcome, for disparate impact differs from discriminatory intent. See Personnel *Administrator of Massachusetts v. Feeney*, 442 U.S. 256, 99 S.Ct. 2282, 60 L.Ed.2d 870 (1979). The Justices also noted that there are good reasons why the Judicial Branch should not attempt to supervise how the Executive Branch exercises prosecutorial discretion. In order to give a measure of protection (and confidentiality) to the Executive Branch's deliberative processes, which are covered by strong privileges, see *Cheney v. United States District Court*, 542 U.S. 367, 124 S.Ct. 2576, 159 L.Ed.2d 459 (2004); In re United States, 503 F.3d 638 (7th Cir.2007); *In re United States*, 398 F.3d 615 (7th Cir.2005); *United States v. Zingsheim*, 384 F.3d 867 (7th Cir.2004), the Court in Armstrong insisted that the defendant produce evidence that persons of a different race, but otherwise comparable in criminal behavior, were presented to the United States Attorney for prosecution, but that prosecution was declined. Bass held the same about the selection of capital prosecutions, and for the same reasons.

To the extent that Davis and the other six defendants want information about how the United States Attorney has exercised prosecutorial discretion, Armstrong is an insuperable obstacle (at least on this record). But the defendants' principal targets are the ATF and the FBI. They maintain that these agencies offer lucrative-seeming opportunities to black and Hispanic suspects, yet not to those similarly situated in criminal background and interests but of other ethnicity. If the agencies do that, they have violated the Constitution—and the fact that the United States Attorney may have prosecuted every case the agencies presented, or chosen 25% of them in a race-blind lottery, would not matter, since the constitutional problem would have preceded the prosecutor's role and could not be eliminated by the fact that things didn't get worse at a later step. Cf. *Connecticut v. Teal*, 457 U.S. 440, 102 S.Ct. 2525, 73 L.Ed.2d 130 (1982) (rejecting a "bottom-line defense" in an employment-discrimination suit).

Agents of the ATF and FBI are not protected by a powerful privilege or covered by a presumption of constitutional behavior. Unlike prosecutors, agents regularly testify in criminal cases, and their credibility may be relentlessly attacked by defense counsel. They also may have to testify in pretrial proceedings, such as hearings on motions to suppress evidence, and again their honesty is open to challenge. Statements that agents make in affidavits for search or arrest warrants may be contested, and the court may need their testimony to decide whether if shorn of untruthful statements the affidavits would have established probable cause. See Franks *v. Delaware*, 438 U.S. 154, 98 S.Ct. 2674, 57 L.Ed.2d 667 (1978). Agents may be personally liable for withholding evidence from prosecutors and thus causing violations of the constitutional requirement that defendants have access to material, exculpatory evidence. See, e.g., Armstrong *v. Daily*, 786 F.3d 529 (7th Cir.2015); Newsome v. McCabe, 256 F.3d 747, 752 (7th Cir.2001). Before holding hearings (or civil trials) district judges regularly, and properly, allow discovery into nonprivileged aspects of what agents have said or done. In sum, the sort of considerations that led to the outcome in Armstrong do not apply to a contention that agents of the FBI or ATF engaged in racial discrimination when selecting targets for sting operations, or when deciding which suspects to refer for prosecution.

How does the district court's order hold up by these standards? Here is its full text, which requires the United States to produce:

(1) A list by case name and number of each phony stash house rip off case brought by the U.S. Attorney's Office for the Northern District of Illinois in which ATF alone or in conjunction with the FBI was the federal investigatory agency from 2006 to the present. With respect to each case, the Government shall provide the race of each defendant investigated and prosecuted.

(2) For each case identified in response to (1) above, a statement regarding prior criminal contact that the federal agency responsible for the investigation had with each defendant prior to initiating the operation. If all such information for a particular case is contained in the criminal complaint, a reference to the complaint is sufficient.

(3) The statutory or regulatory authority for the ATF and the FBI to instigate and/or pursue phony staff [sic] house ripoff cases involving illegal drugs or any decision by any federal agency, the Justice Department or the White House to authorize ATF and the FBI to pursue such cases in the Northern District of Illinois.

(4) All national and Chicago Field Office ATF and FBI manuals, circulars, field notes, correspondence or any other material which discuss phony stash house ripoffs, including protocols and/or directions to agents and to confidential informants regarding how to conduct such operations, how to determine which persons to pursue as potential targets or ultimate defendants, how to ensure that the targets do not seek to quit or leave before an arrest can be made and how to ensure that agents are not targeting persons for such operations on the basis of their race, color, ancestry or national origin.

(5) All documents that contain information on how supervisors and managers of the Chicago area ATF and FBI were to ensure and/or did ensure or check that its agents did not target persons on the basis of their race, color, ancestry, or national origin for the phony stash house ripoffs and what actions the Chicago area ATF and FBI supervisors and managers operating in the Northern District of Illinois took to determine whether agents were not

targeting persons for such operations on the basis of their race, color, ancestry, or national origin.

(6) The factual basis for the decision to pursue or initiate an investigation against each of the individuals listed as defendants in each case cited in Paragraph 7 of Defendants' Motion for Discovery and in response to each case produced pursuant to the request contained in Paragraph (1) above.

(7) All documents containing instructions given during the tenure of Patrick Fitzgerald or Gary Shapiro as the U.S. Attorney for the Northern District of Illinois about the responsibilities of prosecutors to ensure that defendants in cases brought by the Office of the U.S. Attorney for the Northern District of Illinois are not targeted due to their race, color, ancestry, or national origin. Specifically, materials that demonstrate that the individuals charged as defendants in phony stash house cases in which ATF alone or in conjunction with the FBI was the investigatory agency have not been targeted due to their race, color, ancestry, or national origin, and that such prosecutions have not been brought with any discriminatory intent on the basis of the defendant's race, color, ancestry, or national origin.

(8) All documents that contain information about all actions taken during the tenure of Patrick Fitzgerald or Gary Shapiro as the U.S. Attorney for the Northern District of Illinois about the responsibilities of prosecutors to ensure that defendants in cases brought by the Office of the U.S. Attorney for the Northern District of Illinois have not been targeted due to their race, color, ancestry, or national origin and, specifically, that those persons who are defendants in phony stash house cases in which ATF alone or in conjunction with the FBI was the investigatory agency have not been targeted due to their race, color, ancestry or national origin and that such prosecutions have not been brought with any discriminatory intent on the basis of the defendant's race, color, ancestry, or national origin.

This order is vastly overbroad. A good deal of the discovery it requires is blocked by Armstrong (on the current record) because it concerns the exercise of prosecutorial discretion. Other discovery is blocked by executive privilege independent of Armstrong; a district court is not entitled to require "the White House" (which is to say, the President) to reveal confidential orders given to criminal investigators. But some of the discovery asks for information from supervisors or case agents of the FBI and ATF, and this is outside the scope of Armstrong, the executive privilege, and the deliberative-process privilege.

To say that some of the information is potentially discoverable is not to vindicate any part of this particular order, however. Consider ¶ 5, which requires the United States to produce "all documents" that contain any "information" about how the FBI and ATF manage stings (pejoratively called "phony stash house ripoffs"), plus all details concerning how these agencies curtail discrimination. This demands the disclosure of thousands (if not millions) of documents generated by hundreds (if not thousands) of law-enforcement personnel. It would bog down this case (and perhaps the agencies) for years.

Or consider ¶ 4, which requires the public disclosure of all criteria the agencies employ to decide when and how to conduct sting operations. Agencies understandably want to keep such information out of the hands of persons who could use it to reduce the chance that their own criminal conduct will come to light. For the same reason that the IRS does not want to reveal its audit criteria, the FBI and ATF do not want to reveal their investigative criteria. Perhaps the FBI and ATF might be able to improve the public's understanding and acceptance of their selection criteria by releasing more information, but that's not a legal obligation.

Similar things could be said about other paragraphs, but the point has been made. This order is an abuse of discretion.

The racial disproportion in stash-house prosecutions remains troubling, however, and it is a legitimate reason for discovery provided that the district court does not transgress Armstrong or an applicable privilege.

Instead of starting with a blunderbuss order, a district court should proceed in measured steps. Logically the first question is whether there is any reason to believe that race played a role in the investigation of these seven defendants. The prosecutor says that it cannot have done, because Davis himself initiated matters by pestering the informant for robbery opportunities and then chose his own comrades. Still, it remains possible that the FBI and the ATF would not have pursued this investigation had Davis been white. Defendants contend that they have additional evidence (beyond that presented to the district court) that could support such a conclusion. The judge should receive this evidence and then decide whether to make limited inquiries, perhaps including affidavits or testimony of the case agents, to determine whether forbidden selectivity occurred or plausibly could have occurred. If not, there would not be a basis to attribute this prosecution to the defendants' race, and the district court could turn to the substance of the charges.

If the initial inquiry gives the judge reason to think that suspects of another race, and otherwise similarly situated, would not have been offered the opportunity for a stash-house robbery, it might be appropriate to require the FBI and ATF to disclose, in confidence, their criteria for stash-house stings. Analysis of the targeting criteria (and whether agents followed those rules in practice) could shed light on whether an initial suspicion of race discrimination in this case is justified. Keeping that part of the investigation in camera would respect the legitimate interest of law enforcement in preventing suspects (and potential suspects) from learning how to avoid being investigated or prosecuted. If after that inquiry the judge continues to think that racial discrimination may have led to this prosecution, more information could be gathered.

We do not want to tie the judge's hands, but we do think it essential, lest this and other prosecutions be sidetracked (both defendants and the public have a right to speedy resolution of criminal cases), to start with limited inquiries that can be conducted in a few weeks, and to enlarge the probe only if evidence discovered in the initial phase justifies a wider discovery program. Only if information learned during these limited inquiries satisfies the Armstrong criteria may discovery be extended to the prosecutor's office, and even then the judge should ensure that required disclosures make no more inroads on prosecutorial discretion than are vital to ensuring vindication of the defendants' constitutional right to be free of race discrimination.

The judgment dismissing the indictment is reversed, and the case is remanded for proceedings consistent with this opinion.

Note

In *Wayte v. United States*, cited by the Court in *Armstrong*, the Petitioner claimed that he was prosecuted for having exercised his First Amendment right to protest the military draft. The Supreme Court, per Justice Powell, held that the Government's passive enforcement policy, under which the Government prosecuted only those who reported themselves as having violated the law, or who were reported by others, did not violate the First or Fifth Amendments. The Court did note, however, that decisions to prosecute may not be deliberately based upon unjustifiable standards such as race, religion or other arbitrary classification, including exercise of protected statutory and constitutional rights. As noted above in Armstrong, in order for a defendant to prevail on a claim of selective prosecution "the claimant must demonstrate that the federal prosecutorial policy "had a discriminatory effect and that it was motivated by a discriminatory purpose." Given the restrictions on discovery in Armstrong how can a defendant prevail? How much evidence is enough? Consider the following case.

UNITED STATES V. BASS
266 F.3d 532 (6th Cir. 2001)

OPINION
BOYCE F. MARTIN, Jr., Chief Judge.

On December 8, 1998, a federal grand jury returned a second superseding indictment charging defendant John Bass with the intentional firearm killing of two individuals. Shortly thereafter, the United States filed its notice of intent to seek the death penalty on those charges. Bass moved to dismiss the death penalty notice and, in the alternative, requested discovery pertaining to the United States's capital charging practices. The district court granted Bass's discovery request and, after the United States refused to comply with the order, dismissed the death penalty notice. We now affirm the district court's discovery order, and remand to allow the United States to submit the requested materials for an *in camera* review.

I.

According to a Department of Justice report, "The Federal Death Penalty System: A Statistical Survey" (September 12, 2000), all death-eligible charges brought by the United States since 1995 are subjected to the Department's death penalty decision-making procedures. Under the protocol, the individual United States Attorneys offices retain discretion in only three areas: whether to bring federal charges or defer to state prosecutions, whether to charge defendants with a capital-eligible offense, and whether to enter into a plea agreement. Otherwise, the sole power to authorize seeking the death penalty lies with the Attorney General. Once the Attorney General authorizes seeking the death penalty, the United States must file a notice of its intent to do so. See 18 U.S.C. § 3593(a). Each time the United States charges a defendant with a death-eligible crime, it must submit specific forms, including a recommendation on whether to seek the death penalty, a "Death Penalty Evaluation Form," and a memorandum outlining the theory of liability, the facts and evidence, including any evidence relating to any aggravating or mitigating factors, the defendant's background and criminal history, the basis for federal prosecution and other relevant information. See U.S. Attys. Man. § 9–10.040.

Bass requested from the Michigan United States Attorney's office all such materials relating to his prosecution, all policies or manuals used in the Eastern District of Michigan to determine whether to charge defendants federally, and a list of all death-eligible defendants in that district since January 1, 1995, including each defendant's race, and the ultimate disposition of each case. Bass also requested all materials submitted to the Attorney General for death-eligible prosecutions between January 1, 1995 and September 1, 2000, as well as captions and case numbers of such cases, a description of the offense charged, and the ultimate disposition of the case. Finally, Bass requested all standards, policies, practices, or criteria employed by the Department of Justice to guard against the influence of race in the death penalty protocol, any correspondence between the Department of Justice and the United States Attorneys regarding such policies or requesting identification of death-eligible defendants, and a list of all nonnegligent homicide cases throughout the United States since January 1, 1995, in which one or more offenders were arrested and charged and in which the facts would have rendered the offender eligible for the death penalty. As evidence in support of his discovery motion,

Bass introduced, among other studies, the Department of Justice's Survey. Bass also introduced public comments regarding the Survey made on the day of its release by then-Attorney General Janet Reno and then-Deputy Attorney General Eric Holder, as well as comments by the current Attorney General, John Ashcroft. The United States opposed Bass's motion on the grounds that the requested information was protected by both the work-product and deliberative process privileges, that Bass had failed to make the evidentiary showing necessary to obtain further discovery, and that the requested materials were either non-existent or already in Bass's possession.

On October 24, 2000, following a hearing on Bass's motion, the district court found that he had presented sufficient evidence of racial bias in the death-penalty decision process to justify further discovery. The district court, noting that the United States did not offer any of the allegedly privileged materials for in camera review, further found that any privileges that may have attached to the materials were outweighed by the constitutional interests implicated by Bass's allegations and the death penalty context. Finally, it cited 18 U.S.C. § 3593(f), "Special precaution to ensure against discrimination," which requires a jury to determine that its individual members would have imposed a death sentence regardless of the defendant's race as a prerequisite to imposing such a sentence under Section 3593(e). The district court noted that for Section 3593(f) to have its intended effect of ensuring that a defendant's race plays no role in his death sentence, discovery of the sort requested by Bass must be allowed.

The United States refused to comply with the discovery order. On January 10, 2001, the district court sanctioned the United States by dismissing its notice of intent to seek the death penalty. The United States timely appealed.

II.

As an initial matter, we agree with the United States that we have jurisdiction to review the district court's pre-trial discovery order because that court's dismissal of the death penalty notice constitutes a final, appealable order under 18 U.S.C. § 3731. Under Section 3731, "an appeal by the United States shall lie to a court of appeals from a decision, judgment, or order of a district court dismissing an indictment or information...." We have previously allowed the United States to appeal, under Section 3731, pre-trial discovery rulings. See, e.g., *United States v. Presser*, 844 F.2d 1275, 1280 (6th Cir.1988). In *Presser*, we exercised jurisdiction over the United States's appeal from an order granting a defendant's discovery request because the district court indicated that if the United States failed to comply, it would suppress the relevant evidence, which would likely result in dismissal of the indictment. Here, the United States's failure to comply with the district court's discovery order resulted in dismissal of the death penalty notice—in effect, a partial dismissal of the charge. Accordingly, we find that, as in Presser, we have jurisdiction to hear the

United States's appeal from the district court's pre-trial discovery order, and will now proceed to the merits of its argument.

III.

"It is well established that the scope of discovery is within the sound discretion of the trial court." *United States v. One Tract of Real Property*, 95 F.3d 422, 427 (6th Cir.1996) (citations and internal punctuation omitted). We thus review a district court's discovery order in a criminal case for an abuse of discretion. See *United States v. Kincaide*, 145 F.3d 771, 780 (6th Cir.1998). Under this standard, "the relevant inquiry is not how the reviewing judges would have ruled if they had been considering the case in the first place, but rather, whether any reasonable person could agree with the district court." *Morales v. American Honda Motor Co., Inc.*, 151 F.3d 500, 511 (6th Cir.1998).

The United States argues that Bass's evidence in support of his discovery request, including the Department of Justice's Survey and the Department officials' statements, did not constitute sufficient evidence of selective prosecution to warrant discovery. Accordingly, it contends that the district court abused its discretion in ordering the United States to produce the relevant documents. Bass does not dispute that the evidence he presented to the district court was insufficient to constitute a prima facie case of selective prosecution. He does, however, argue that the evidence was sufficient to warrant further investigation through discovery.

To make out a claim of selective prosecution, a defendant must show both a discriminatory effect and a discriminatory purpose or intent. See *United States v. Armstrong*, 517 U.S. 456, 465, 116 S.Ct. 1480, 134 L.Ed.2d 687 (1996). In *Armstrong*, the Supreme Court discussed the threshold showing a criminal defendant must make in order to obtain discovery on a selective prosecution claim. See id. at 463, 116 S.Ct. 1480. The Supreme Court noted that "in the absence of clear evidence to the contrary, courts presume that [prosecutors] have properly discharged their official duties." *Armstrong*, 517 U.S. at 464, 116 S.Ct. 1480 (citations omitted). Accordingly, "the showing necessary to obtain discovery [in a selective prosecution case] should itself be a significant barrier to the litigation of insubstantial claims." Id. *Armstrong* 's plain language requires only that a defendant must present "some evidence tending to show the existence of the discriminatory effect element." Id. at 469, 116 S.Ct. 1480 (citations and internal punctuations omitted). Nonetheless, we have read Armstrong to require some evidence of the discriminatory intent element as well. See *United States v. Jones*, 159 F.3d 969, 978 (6th Cir.1998). To establish discriminatory effect, a defendant "must show that similarly situated individuals of a different race were not prosecuted." *Armstrong*, 517 U.S. at 465, 116 S.Ct. 1480. As an example of "some evidence" showing a "discriminatory effect on blacks as compared to similarly situated whites," Armstrong cited a statistic showing that blacks were "at least 1.7 times as likely as whites" to have a state's disenfranchisement law applied to them. Id. at 467, 116 S.Ct. 1480 (citing *Hunter v. Underwood*, 471 U.S. 222, 105 S.Ct. 1916, 85 L.Ed.2d 222 (1985)). To establish discriminatory intent, a defendant must show that the prosecutorial policy "was motivated by racial animus." Jones, 159 F.3d at 976–77.

A. Bass's Evidence

Through the Department of Justice's Survey and other statistical evidence, Bass presented the following evidence tending to show that selective prosecution taints the death penalty protocol. First, the Survey showed a significant difference between the percentage of white and black prisoners in the general federal prison population (white: fifty-seven percent; black: thirty-eight percent) and those charged by the United States with death-eligible crimes (white: twenty percent; black: forty-eight percent). Of the seventeen defendants charged with a death-eligible crime in the Eastern District of Michigan, none were white and fourteen were black (the other three were Hispanic).

Second, the Survey showed that the United States entered into a plea bargain with forty-eight percent of the white defendants against whom it sought the death penalty, compared with twenty-five percent of similarly situated black defendants. The United States entered into plea agreements with twenty-eight percent of Hispanics, and twenty-five percent of other non-white defendants.

Third, the Survey showed that two of the three death-eligible offenses charged most frequently against whites and blacks were the same, but that the percentages by race of those charged with each crime were vastly different. Sixteen percent of death-eligible whites were charged with firearms murder, compared with thirty-two percent of death-eligible blacks. Fifteen percent of death-eligible whites were charged with racketeering murder, compared with twenty-two percent of death-eligible blacks. The Survey noted that firearms murder, racketeering murder, and continuing criminal enterprise murder (the three charges brought most frequently against death-eligible blacks) "can be charged in a wide array of circumstances, and [are] therefore more likely to be available as a charging option in a given case than more narrowly defined offenses such as kidnaping-related murder." However, death-eligible whites were most often charged with murder within a federal jurisdiction (twenty-one percent of all death-eligible whites).

Bass also introduced other statistics indicating that blacks are no more likely to commit violent federal offenses than whites. For instance, the United States Sentencing Commission's statistics for 1999 (the most recent statistics currently available) show that twenty-eight percent of people sentenced for federal murder were white, while eighteen percent were black. See 1999 Sourcebook of Federal Sentencing Statistics. In fact, there were only four federal offense categories where whites comprised twenty percent or less of the total defendants sentenced.

The Commission's 1999 sentencing statistics reflect three of them: manslaughter (whites: seventeen percent; blacks: eleven percent), sexual abuse (whites: eighteen percent; blacks: seven percent), and immigration (whites: four percent; blacks: four percent). The Survey reflects the fourth: death-eligible defendants (whites: twenty percent; blacks: forty-eight percent). In contrast, the only federal offense reflected in the 1999 sentencing statistics where blacks represented forty-eight percent or more of the total defendants sentenced was robbery (blacks: forty-eight percent; whites: forty-one percent). In the few non-death-eligible offense categories in which blacks actually constituted a higher percentage of total offenders sentenced than whites, none reflected a statistical racial disparity comparable to the disparity reflected by the Survey for death-eligible charges.

In addition to the statistical evidence, Bass introduced public comments made on the Survey's release date by then-Attorney General Reno and then-Deputy Attorney General Holder who expressed concern over the significant racial disparities uncovered by the Survey. For instance, Holder commented:

> I can't help but be both personally and professionally disturbed by the numbers that we discuss today. To be sure, many factors have led to the disproportionate representation of racial and ethnic minorities throughout the federal death penalty process. Nevertheless, no one reading this report can help but be disturbed, troubled, by this disparity.

In response to another question, Holder tacitly recognized that the Survey's results implicate the very concerns forming the basis of Bass's selective prosecution claim: "I'm particularly struck by the facts that African–Americans and Hispanics are over-represented in those cases presented for consideration of the death penalty, and those cases where the defendant is actually sentenced to death." (emphasis added). Reno also expressed concern over the Survey's results, even while acknowledging the various non-racial factors that could affect them: "So in some respects I'm not surprised [by the racial disparities], but I continue to be sorely troubled."[1] While cautioning that intentional racial bias could not fairly be inferred simply as a result of the numbers, Reno emphatically endorsed future studies to determine whether the disparities were shaped, in part, by racial animus: "More information is needed to better understand the many factors that affect how homicide cases make their way into the federal system and, once in the federal system, why they follow different paths. An even broader analysis must therefore be undertaken to determine if bias does in fact play any role in the federal death penalty system" (emphasis added). Therefore, the top Department of Justice officials have taken the position that, although the Survey's results do not conclusively show intentional racial bias, neither do they conclusively show the lack of bias. Rather, in Reno's and Holder's view, the results demonstrate a clear racial disparity and raise questions warranting further study to determine whether that disparity is caused by intentional racial discrimination.

B. Discriminatory Effect

Bass's evidence shows the same type of statistical disparity the Supreme Court previously approved of in both Hunter and Armstrong as "indisputable evidence" of a law's discriminatory effect. For example, the evidence shows that although whites make up the majority of all federal prisoners, they are only one-fifth of those charged by the United States with death-eligible offenses. The United States charges blacks with a death-eligible offense more than twice as often as it charges whites. Cf. *Armstrong*, 517 U.S. at 467, 116 S.Ct. 1480 (citing evidence in Hunter as example of type of proof needed to obtain discovery in selective prosecution claim); *Hunter*, 471 U.S. at 227, 105 S.Ct. 1916 (citing single statistic showing blacks at least 1.7 times as likely as whites to have challenged state law applied to them). In addition, the United States charges blacks with racketeering murder one-and-a-half times as often as it charges whites, and with firearms murder (Bass's charge) more than twice as often as it charges blacks. Among death penalty defendants, the United States enters plea bargains with whites almost twice as often as it does with blacks. Under the "1.7 times" standard approved of in Armstrong, then, the statistics presented by Bass constitute sufficient evidence of a discriminatory effect to warrant further discovery as a matter of law.

The United States concedes that the Survey shows a statistical disparity at the charging stage, but argues that Bass's evidence does not satisfy the "similarly situated" requirement because Bass has failed to identify white defendants who could have been charged with death-eligible crimes but were not. We find, however, that with the plea bargaining statistics, Bass has identified a pool of similarly situated defendants—those whose crimes shared sufficient aggravating factors that the United States chose to pursue the death penalty against each of them. Of those defendants, the United States enters plea bargains with one in two whites; it enters plea bargains with one in four blacks. Therefore, the United States's assertion that Bass has failed to show a discriminatory effect on similarly situated whites and blacks is simply wrong.

Of course non-discriminatory reasons may explain such glaring discrepancies, but Bass need not address any of them at this pre-discovery stage. The current death penalty protocol leaves only three areas where the United States Attorneys can exercise discretion (and, of course, it is the manner in which that discretion is exercised that forms the basis of Bass's claim): bringing federal charges, bringing death-eligible charges, and plea bargaining. In the two areas addressed by the Survey—bringing death-eligible charges and plea bargaining—the racial disparities are clear. Viewing the totality of Bass's evidence, the district court did not abuse its discretion in finding that the statistical disparities are, at the least, some evidence tending to show the death penalty protocol's discriminatory effect warranting discovery.

C. Discriminatory Intent

With regard to the discriminatory intent element, we again find that Bass presented some evidence tending to show that the United States considers the defendant's race when determining whether to charge him or her with a death-eligible offense. The racial disparities identified by Bass in the death penalty charging phase do not occur in any non-death-eligible federal offenses. Therefore, they suggest that a defendant's race does play a role during the death penalty protocol. The Department of Justice's officials' comments bear this out. As Bass states in his brief, "[t]he precise point made by the Attorneys General and the former Deputy Attorney General is that they are deeply troubled because race may be systemically biasing federal capital charging, and that they need more information to know for sure" (emphasis added). If the Department of Justice's official position is that these statistics, standing alone, show sufficient evidence of the possibility of racial animus to warrant further study, we cannot fairly deny Bass the same opportunity to investigate when he has introduced not only the Survey, but several other statistics showing that the grave racial disparities identified by the Survey are unique to the death penalty protocol.

The United States attempts to preclude us from drawing any inference of intentional race discrimination from Bass's statistics by arguing that *McCleskey v. Kemp*, 481 U.S. 279, 107 S.Ct. 1756, 95 L.Ed.2d 262 (1987), prohibits such inferences. McCleskey held that statistics showing the discriminatory effect of a state's death penalty procedure do not, without more, constitute proof of a discriminatory intent. See id. at 294–95, 107 S.Ct. 1756. In *McCleskey*, however, the Supreme Court, sitting in federal habeas review, was addressing whether the defendant had carried his burden of proof on the merits of his selective prosecution claim. In contrast, we must determine only whether Bass has shown "some evidence tending to show the existence of ... discriminatory intent" sufficient to warrant discovery. Jones, 159 F.3d at 978 ("Obviously, a defendant need not prove his case in order to justify discovery on an issue."). *McCleskey* will certainly preclude Bass's selective prosecution claim if, at the end of discovery, he fails to show any additional evidence that the United States intentionally discriminates against blacks through the death penalty protocol. It does not, however, pose any bar to Bass at this preliminary stage. Here as well, the United States has failed to show that the district court abused its discretion in ordering discovery on the grounds that the stark discriminatory effect of the federal death penalty protocol, coupled with the Department of Justice's official statements recognizing the possibility of intentional discrimination in light of the protocol's discriminatory effect, presents some evidence tending to show that race in fact plays a role in the United States's decision-making process.

IV.

We can dispose of both parties' remaining arguments relatively easily. The United States argues that the district court abused its discretion by citing 18 U.S.C. § 3593(f) as an alternative ground for its discovery order. The United States is correct. That statute, by its plain language, requires only that each jury member swear that he or she voted to impose the death penalty without regard to improper considerations, including the defendant's race. Jury members are simply not responsible for also asserting that the defendant was not prosecuted because of his or her race. Questions regarding the prosecution's motivation are more properly addressed in the type of selective prosecution claim Bass presents. Section 3593(f) does nothing to grant him a right to either obtain discovery or present evidence to a jury regarding alleged discrimination in the prosecution, and the district court abused its discretion in holding otherwise. Nonetheless, because we affirm the district court's discovery order on other grounds, our decision to reverse the district court on this issue does not effect the outcome of this appeal.

Second, the United States argues that the requested items are either not relevant, non-existent, or already in Bass's possession. The district court indicated that it would hear from the United States as to the unavailability or irrelevancy of particular documents, but the United States chose instead to refuse to comply with the entire order. That refusal also prohibited the district court from reviewing the requested documents to determine whether the United States' claimed privileges applied to any of them. Therefore, we find the record insufficiently developed to allow us to assess the merits of the United States's arguments relating to the content of the requested documents. Because of this, and because we think the district court should have the opportunity to review each requested item's relevancy and privileged status in the first instance, we remand to the district court with instructions to allow the United States to produce the documents for an in camera review. If the United States again fails to comply, the district court remains free to impose whatever sanction it deems appropriate under the circumstances.

V.

For the foregoing reasons, we AFFIRM the district court's discovery order, and REMAND for further proceedings consistent with this opinion.

Note

The United Supreme Court reversed in a Per Curiam opinion, *United States v. Bass*, 536 U.S. 862 (2002) stating:

Even assuming that the Armstrong requirement can be satisfied by a nationwide showing (as opposed to a showing regarding the record of the decisionmakers in respondent's case), raw statistics regarding overall charges say nothing about charges brought against similarly situated defendants. And the statistics regarding plea bargains are even less relevant, since respondent was offered a plea bargain but declined it. Under Armstrong, therefore, because respondent failed to submit relevant evidence that similarly situated persons were treated differently, he was not entitled to discovery.

The use of nationwide statistics in Bass was put forth in support of the Armstrong requirement of proof of discriminatory impact. But what of discriminatory intent? Earlier the Sixth Circuit decided United States v. Jones, 159 F.3d 969 (6th Cir. 1998), cited in Bass, which found that the defendant had established discriminatory intent. In that case Tennessee law enforcement referred the defendant and another African American for federal prosecution regarding various drug and weapons charges while not referring White defendants similarly situated. Additionally evidence produced during an earlier motion to dismiss, revealed bizarre behavior by the state police officers. Evidence showed an officer sent to Jones, while his case was pending trial, a postcard of an African–American woman with bananas on her head, and did not choose any other available postcards such as the sunset or the beach. Jones testified at his sentencing hearing that to him the postcard meant "nigger, you're a monkey with bananas.". Prior to the planned arrest of Jones and his wife, the two officers had t-shirts made with Jones's picture emblazoned on the front accompanied by the printed words, "See ya, wouldn't want to be ya" above the picture, and below, "going back to prison." On the back of the t-shirts appeared a picture of Jones's wife, a co-defendant, with the words, "wait on me, Slow, I am coming, too." The two officers were wearing the t-shirts when they arrested Jones in August of 1995.

This police conduct, which district court referred to as childish and highly unprofessional, also established a prima facie case of discriminatory intent. The district court concluded that ven though a prima facie case of intent was established, the second prong of Wayte, discriminatory impact was not. However, the existence of a prima facie case of intent was, in the Sixth Circuit's view enough to order compliance with the defendant's discovery request in accordance with Armstrong. The United States Supreme Court refused to grant certiorari, but conceivably its decision in Bass places Jones in question.

What then is the remedy, if any, where it is established that the underlying motivation of a criminal prosecution is racial bias? In *Armstrong* the Court states "In the ordinary case, so long as prosecutor has probable cause to believe that accused committed offense defined by statute, decision whether to prosecute, and what charge to file or bring before a grand jury, generally rests entirely in his discretion." (517 U.S. at 464). An option that has not been considered much in recent years, might address racial bias-based prosecutions that rise to the level of bad faith prosecutions.

Over forty years ago it was decided in *Younger v. Harris* 401 U.S. 37 (1971) that bad faith state prosecutions might be enjoined. Although the court denied injunctive relief in Younger it did that bad faith and harassment are extraordinary circumstances that would justify federal intervention. This approach has lain largely dormant except in instances in which both harassment and unconstitutional legislation are thought to exist. Cf. *Samuels v. Mackell*, 401 U.S. 66 (1971).

Attempts to address race discrimination through civil actions, as opposed to challenging a criminal conviction, in the criminal justice process itself, has been difficult at best. Note the traditional position taken by the Supreme Court in *O'Shea v. Littleton*, 414 U.S. 488 (1974). There the Court found that a civil action brought by seventeen African Americans, for injunctive relief could not be maintained because the none of the named plaintiffs were identified as themselves having suffered any injury in the manner specified, and there were no allegations that any relevant state criminal statute was unconstitutional on its face or as applied or that plaintiffs.

Are there race biased offenses? Offenses that are prosecuted solely or disproportionately against persons of color? The Court in *Armstrong* indicates that there are such possibilities and cited to *Yick Wo v. Hopkins*, 118 U.S. 356.

YICK WO V. HOPKINS
118 U.S. 356 (1886)

Opinion
MATTHEWS, J.

In the case of the petitioner, brought here by writ of error to the supreme court of California, our jurisdiction is limited to the question whether the plaintiff in error has been denied a right in violation of the constitution, laws, or treaties of the United States. The question whether his imprisonment is illegal, under the constitution and laws of the state, is not open to us. And although that question might have been considered in the circuit court in the application made to it, and by this court on appeal from its order, yet judicial propriety is best consulted by accepting the judgment of the state court upon the points involved in that inquiry. That, however, does not preclude this court from putting upon the ordinances of the supervisors of the county and city of San Francisco an independent construction; for the determination of the question whether the proceedings under these ordinances, and in enforcement of them, are in conflict with the constitution and laws of the United States, necessarily involves the meaning of the ordinances, which, for that purpose, we are required to ascertain and adjudge.

We are consequently constrained, at the outset, to differ from the supreme court of California upon the real meaning of the ordinances in question. That court considered these ordinances as vesting in the board of supervisors a not unusual discretion in granting or withholding their assent to the use of wooden buildings as laundries, to be exercised in reference to the circumstances of each case, with a view to the protection of the public against the dangers of fire. We are not able to concur in that interpretation of the power conferred upon the supervisors. There is nothing in the ordinances which points to such a regulation of the business of keeping and conducting laundries. They seem intended to confer, and actually to confer, not a discretion to be exercised upon a consideration of the circumstances of each case, but a naked and arbitrary power to give or withhold consent, not only as to places, but as to persons; so that, if an applicant for such consent, being in every way a competent and qualified person, and having complied with every reasonable condition demanded by any public interest, should, failing to obtain the requisite consent of the supervisors to the prosecution of his business, apply for redress by the judicial process of mandamus to require the supervisors to consider and act upon his case, it would be a sufficient answer for them to say that the law had conferred upon them authority to withhold their assent, without reason and without responsibility. The power given to them is not confided to their discretion in the legal sense of that term, but is granted to their mere will. It is purely arbitrary and acknowledges neither guidance nor restraint.

This erroneous view of the ordinances in question led the supreme court of California into the further error of holding that they were justified by the decisions of this court in the cases of *Barbier v. Connelly*, 113 U. S. 27, S. C. 5 Sup. Ct. Rep. 357, and *Soon Hing v. Crowley*, 113 U. S. 703, S. C. 5 Sup. Ct. Rep. 730. In both of these cases the ordinance involved was simply a prohibition to carry on the washing and ironing of clothes in public laundries and wash houses, within certain prescribed limits of the city and county of San Francisco, from 10 o'clock at night until 6 o'clock in the morning of the following day. This provision was held to be purely a police regulation, within the competency of any municipality possessed of the ordinary powers belonging to such bodies,-a necessary measure of precaution in a city composed largely of wooden buildings, like San Francisco, in the application of which there was no invidious discrimination against any one within the prescribed limits; all persons engaged in the same business being treated alike, and subject to the same restrictions, and entitled to the same privileges, under similar conditions. For these reasons that ordinance was adjudged not to be within the prohibitions of the fourteenth amendment to the constitution of the United States, which, it was said in the first case cited, 'undoubtedly intended, not only that there should be no arbitrary deprivation of life or liberty, or arbitrary spoliation of property, but that equal protection and security should be given to all under like circumstances in the enjoyment of their personal and civil rights; that all persons should be equally entitled to pursue their happiness, and acquire and enjoy property; that they should have like access to the courts of the country for the protection of their persons and property, the prevention and redress of wrongs, and the enforcement of contracts; that no impediment should be interposed to the pursuits of any one, except as applied to the same pursuits by others under like circumstances; that no greater burdens should be laid upon one than are laid upon others in the same calling and condition; and that, in the administration of criminal justice, no different or higher punishment should be imposed upon one than such as is prescribed to all for like offenses. Class legislation, discriminating against some and favoring others, is prohibited; but legislation which, in carrying out a public purpose, is limited in its application, if, within the sphere of its operation, it affects alike all persons similarly situated, is not within the amendment.'

The ordinance drawn in question in the present case is of a very different character. It does not prescribe a rule and conditions, for the regulation of the use of property for laundry purposes, to which all similarly situated may conform. It allows, without restriction, the use for such purposes of buildings of brick or stone; but, as to wooden buildings, constituting nearly all those in previous use, it divides the owners or occupiers into two classes, not having respect to their personal character and qualifications for the business, nor the situation and nature and adaptation of the buildings themselves, but merely by an arbitrary line, on one side of which are those who are permitted to pursue their industry by the mere will and consent of the supervisors, and on the other those from whom that consent is withheld, at their mere will and pleasure. And both classes are alike only in this: that they are tenants at will, under the supervisors, of their means of living. The ordinance, therefore, also differs from the not unusual case where discretion is lodged by law in public officers or bodies to grant or withhold licenses to keep taverns, or places for the sale of spirituous liquors, and the like, when one of the conditions is that the applicant shall be a fit person for the exercise of the privilege, because in such cases the fact of fitness is submitted to the judgment of the officer, and calls for the exercise of a discretion of a judicial nature.

The rights of the petitioners, as affected by the proceedings of which they complain, are not less because they are aliens and subjects of the emperor of China. By the third article of the treaty between this government and that of China, concluded November 17, 1880, (22 St. 827), it is stipulated: 'If Chinese laborers, or Chinese of any other class, now either permanently or temporarily residing in the territory of the United States, meet with ill treatment at the hands of any other persons, the government of the United States will exert all its powers to devise measures for their protection, and to secure to them the same rights, privileges, immunities, and exemptions as may be enjoyed by the citizens or subjects of the most favored nation, and to which they are entitled by treaty.' The fourteenth amendment to the constitution is not confined to the protection of citizens. It says: 'Nor shall any state deprive any person of life, liberty, or property without due process of law; nor deny to any person within its jurisdiction the equal protection of the laws.' These provisions are universal in their application, to all persons within the territorial jurisdiction, without regard to any differences of race, of color, or of nationality; and the equal protection of the laws is a pledge of the protection of equal laws. It is accordingly enacted by section 1977 of the Revised Statutes that 'all persons within the jurisdiction of the United States shall have the same right, in every state and territory, to make and enforce contracts, to sue, be parties, give evidence, and to the full and equal benefit of all laws and proceedings for the security of persons and property as is enjoyed by white citizens, and shall be subject to like punishment, pains, penalties, taxes, licenses, and exactions of every kind, and to no other.' The questions we have to consider and decide in these cases, therefore, are to be treated as involving the rights of every citizen of the United States equally with those of the strangers and aliens who now invoke the jurisdiction of the court.

It is contended on the part of the petitioners that the ordinances for violations of which they are severally sentenced to imprisonment are void on their face, as being within the prohibitions of the fourteenth amendment, and, in the alternative, if not so, that they are void by reason of their administration, operating unequally, so as to punish in the present petitioners what is permitted to others as lawful, without any distinction of circumstances,-an unjust and illegal discrimination, it is claimed, which, though not made expressly by the ordinances, is made possible by them.

When we consider the nature and the theory of our institutions of government, the principles upon which they are supposed to rest, and review the history of their development, we are constrained to conclude that they do not mean to leave room for the play and action of purely personal and arbitrary power. Sovereignty itself is, of course, not subject to law, for it is the author and source of law; but in our system, while sovereign powers are delegated to the agencies of government, sovereignty itself remains with the people, by whom and for whom all government exists and acts. And the law is the definition and limitation of power. It is, indeed, quite true that there must always be lodged somewhere, and in some person or body, the authority of final decision; and in many cases of mere administration, the responsibility is purely political, no appeal lying except to the ultimate tribunal of the public judgment, exercised either in the pressure of opinion, or by means of the suffrage. But the fundamental rights to life, liberty, and the pursuit of happiness, considered as individual possessions, are secured by those maxims of constitutional law which are the monuments showing the victorious progress of the race in securing to men the blessings of civilization under the reign of just and equal laws, so that, in the famous language of the Massachusetts bill of rights, the government of the commonwealth 'may be a government of laws and not of men.' For the very idea that one man may be compelled to hold his life, or the means of living, or any material right essential to the enjoyment of life, at the mere will of another, seems to be intolerable in any country where freedom prevails, as being the essence of slavery itself.

There are many illustrations that might be given of this truth, which would make manifest that it was self-evident in the light of our system of jurisprudence. The case of the political franchise of voting is one. Though not regarded strictly as a natural right, but as a privilege merely conceded by society, according to its will, under certain conditions, nevertheless it is regarded as a fundamental political right, because preservative of all rights. In reference to that right, it was declared by the supreme judicial court of Massachusetts, in *Capen v. Foster*, 12 Pick. 485, 488, in the words of Chief Justice SHAW, 'that in all cases where the constitution has conferred a political right or privilege, and where the constitution has not particularly designated the manner in which that right is to be exercised, it is clearly within the just and constitutional limits of the legislative power to adopt any reasonable and uniform regulations, in regard to the time and mode of exercising that right, which are designed to secure and facilitate the exercise of such right in a prompt, orderly, and convenient manner;' nevertheless, 'such a construction would afford no warrant for such an exercise of legislative power as, under the pretense and color of regulating, should subvert or injuriously restrain, the right itself.' It has accordingly been held generally in the states that whether the particular provisions of an act of legislation establishing means for ascertaining the qualifications of those entitled to vote, and making previous registration in lists of such, a condition precedent to the exercise of the right, were or were not reasonable regulations, and accordingly valid or void, was always open to inquiry, as a judicial question. See *Daggett v. Hudson*, 3 N. E. Rep. 538, decided by the supreme court of Ohio, where many of the cases are collected; *Monroe v. Collins*, 17 Ohio St. 666.

The same principle has been more freely extended to the quasi legislative acts of inferior municipal bodies, in respect to which it is an ancient jurisdiction of judicial tribunals to pronounce upon the reasonableness and consequent validity of their by-laws. In respect to these it was the doctrine that every by-law must be reasonable, not inconsistent with the charter of the corporation, nor with any statute of parliament, nor with the general principles of the common law of the land, particularly those having relation to the liberty of the subject, or the rights of private property. Dill. Mun. Corp. (3d Ed.) § 319, and cases cited in notes. Accordingly, in the case of *State v. Cincinnati Gas-light & Coke Co.*, 18 Ohio St. 262, 300, an ordinance of the city council purporting to fix the price to be charged for gas, under an authority of law giving discretionary power to do so, was held to be bad, if passed in bad faith, fixing an unreasonable price, for the fraudulent purpose of compelling the gas company to submit to an unfair appraisement of their works. And a similar question, very pertinent to the one in the present cases, was decided by the court of appeals of Maryland in the case of *City of Baltimore v. Radecke*, 49 Md. 217. In that case the defendant had erected and used a steam-engine, in the prosecution of his business as a carpenter and box-maker in the city of Baltimore, under a permit from the mayor and city council, which contained a condition that the engine was 'to be removed after six months' notice to that effect from the mayor.' After such notice, and refusal to conform to it, a suit was instituted to recover the penalty provided by the ordinance, to restrain the prosecution of which a bill in equity was filed. The court holding the opinion that 'there may be a case in which an ordinance, passed under grants of power like those we have cited, is so clearly unreasonable, so arbitrary, oppressive, or partial, as to raise the presumption that the legislature never intended to confer the power to pass it, and to justify the courts in interfering and setting it aside as a plain abuse of authority,' it proceeds to speak, with regard to the ordinance in question, in relation to the use of steam-engines, as follows: 'It does not profess to prescribe regulations for their construction, location, or use; nor require such precautions and safeguards to be provided by those who own and use them as are best calculated to render them less dangerous to life and property; nor does it restrain their use in box factories and other similar establishments within certain defined limits; not in any other way attempt to promote their safety and security without destroying their usefulness. But it commits to the unrestrained will of a single public officer the power to notify every person who now employs a steam-engine in the prosecution of any business in the city of Baltimore to cease to do so, and, by providing compulsory fines for every day's disobedience of such notice and order of removal, renders his power over the use of steam in that city practically absolute, so that he may prohibit its use altogether. But if he should not choose to do this, but only to act in particular cases, there is nothing in the ordinance to guide or control his action. It lays down no rules by which its impartial execution can be secured, or partiality and oppression prevented. It is clear that giving and enforcing these notices may, and quite likely will, bring ruin to the business of those against whom they are directed, while others, from whom they are withheld, may be actually benefited by what is thus done to their neighbors; and, when we remember that this action of non-action may proceed from enmity or prejudice, from partisan zeal or animosity, from favoritism and other improper influences and motives easy of concealment, and difficult to be detected and exposed, it becomes unnecessary to suggest or comment upon the injustice capable of being wrought under cover of such a power, for that becomes apparent to every one who gives to the subject a moment's consideration. In fact, an ordinance which clothes a single individual with such power hardly falls within the domain of law, and we are constrained to pronounce it inoperative and void.' This conclusion, and the reasoning on which it is based, are deductions from the face of the ordinance, as to its necessary pendency and ultimate actual operation.

In the present cases, we are not obliged to reason from the probable to the actual, and pass upon the validity of the ordinances complained of, as tried merely by the opportunities which their terms afford, of unequal and unjust discrimination in their administration; for the cases present the ordinances in actual operation, and the facts shown establish an administration directed so exclusively against a particular class of persons as to warrant and require the conclusion that, whatever may have been the intent of the ordinances as adopted, they are applied by the public authorities charged with their administration, and thus representing the state itself, with a mind so unequal and oppressive as to amount to a practical denial by the state of that equal protection of the laws which is secured to the petitioners, as to all other persons, by the broad and benign provisions of the fourteenth amendment to the constitution of the United States. Though the law itself be fair on its face, and impartial in appearance, yet, if it is applied and administered by public authority with an evil eye and an unequal hand, so as practically to make unjust and illegal discriminations between persons in similar circumstances, material to their rights, the denial of equal justice is still within the prohibition of the constitution. This principle of interpretation has been sanctioned by this court in *Henderson v. Mayor of New York,* 92 U. S. 259; *Chy Luny v. Freeman,* 92 U. S. 275; *Ex parte Virginia,* 100 U. S. 339; *Neal v. Delaware,* 103 U.S. 370; and *Soon Hing v. Crowley,* 113 U. S. 703; S. C. 5 Sup. Ct. Rep. 730.

The present cases, as shown by the facts disclosed in the record, are within this class. It appears that both petitioners have complied with every requisite deemed by the law, or by the public officers charged with its administration, necessary for the protection of neighboring property from fire, or as a precaution against injury to the public health. No reason whatever, except the will of the supervisors, is assigned why they should not be permitted to carry on, in the accustomed manner, their harmless and useful occupation, on which they depend for a livelihood; and while this consent of the supervisors is withheld from them, and from 200 others who have also petitioned, all of whom happen to be Chinese subjects, 80 others, not Chinese subjects, are permitted to carry on the same business under similar conditions. The fact of this discrimination is admitted. No reason for it is shown, and the conclusion cannot be resisted that no reason for it exists except hostility to the race and nationality to which the petitioners belong, and which, in the eye of the law, is not justified. The discrimination is therefore illegal, and the public administration which enforces it is a denial of the equal protection of the laws, and a violation of the fourteenth amendment of the constitution. The imprisonment of the petitioners is therefore illegal, and they must be discharged. To this end the judgment of the supreme court of California in the Case of *Yick Wo,* and that of the circuit court of the United States for the district of California in the Case of Wo Lee, are severally reversed, and the cases remanded, each to the proper court, with directions to discharge the petitioners from custody and imprisonment.

UNITED STATES V. CLARY
34 F.3d 709 (8th Cir. 1994)

Opinion
JOHN R. GIBSON, Senior Circuit Judge.

The United States appeals from the sentence imposed upon Edward James Clary for possession with intent to distribute cocaine base in violation of 21 U.S.C. § 841(b)(1)(A)(iii). Clary entered a guilty plea to the charge which called for a ten-year mandatory minimum sentence. After conducting a four-day hearing, the district court sentenced Clary to four years. The court held that the 100 to 1 ratio for crack cocaine to powder cocaine was disproportionate and in violation of the Equal Protection Clause both generally and as applied, and that the selective prosecution of crack cases on the basis of race was constitutionally impermissible as applied to Clary. The United States essentially argues that these issues have been repeatedly decided and there was no equal protection violation or selective prosecution of Clary. We reverse and remand for resentencing in accord with the applicable statutes and guidelines.

After Clary's guilty plea but before sentencing, he filed a motion arguing that the ten-year mandatory minimum sentence contained in the crack cocaine statute, 21 U.S.C. § 841(b)(A)(iii), and United States Sentencing Guideline section 2D1.1, violated his Equal Protection rights guaranteed by the Fifth Amendment.1 Clary presented eleven witnesses who testified about the profound impact of the crack statute and its ten year mandatory minimum sentence on African Americans. The district court determined that in spite of earlier decisions from this court stating that the differentiation between the treatment of powder cocaine and crack cocaine was constitutional and did not violate the Equal Protection Clause, we invited arguments presenting new facts and legal analysis in *United States v. Marshall*, 998 F.2d 634, 635 n. 2 (8th Cir.1993).

The district court began its factual analysis by examining the role that racism has played in criminal punishment in this country since the late seventeenth century. *United States v. Clary*, 846 F.Supp. 768, 774-782 (E.D.Mo.1994). The district court touched on such recent events as the turmoil of the 1960's and the "cataclysmic economic change" in the 1980's. Id. at 777-78. The court also examined unemployment levels, which the court concluded impacted African Americans more than the general population. Id. at 777. According to the court, African Americans' anger and frustration led to increased drug traffic and associated violence. Id. at 777-78.

The district court also discussed the unconscious predisposition of legislators, and reasoned that although overt racial animus may not have led to Congress' enactment of the crack statute, its failure to account for a substantial and foreseeable disparate impact would violate the spirit and letter of equal protection. Id. at 782. Accordingly, it concluded that the statute should be reviewed under strict scrutiny and the rules announced in *Arlington Heights v. Metropolitan Housing Development Corp.*, 429 U.S. 252, 266, 97 S.Ct. 555, 564, 50 L.Ed.2d 450 (1977). The court listed the seven factors outlined by Arlington as circumstantial evidence of a racially-discriminatory legislative purpose. The factors are: (1) adverse racial impact, (2) historical background, (3) specific sequence of events leading up to the decision, (4) departure from normal procedure sequence, (5) substantive departure from routine decision, (6) contemporary statements made by decisionmakers, and (7) the inevitability or foreseeability of the consequence of the law. 846 F.Supp. at 783.

The court outlined the events leading up to passage of the crack statute. The court cited several news articles submitted by members of Congress for publication in the Congressional Record which portrayed crack dealers as unemployed, gang-affiliated, gun-toting, young black males. Id. at 783-84. Legislators, the court reasoned, used these media accounts as informational support for the statute. The district court also pointed to perceived procedural irregularities surrounding Congress' approval of the crack sentencing provisions. Id. at 784-85. For instance, few hearings were held in the House on the enhanced penalties for crack. Id. at 785. While many Senators called for a more measured response, the Senate committee conducted a single morning hearing. Id. at 784-85. Finally, although the penalties were originally set at 50 to 1, they were arbitrarily doubled. Id. at 784.

The district court also observed that 98.2 percent of defendants convicted of crack cocaine charges in the Eastern District of Missouri between the years 1988 and 1992 were African American. Id. at 786. Nationally, 92.6 percent of those convicted of crack cocaine charges were African American, as opposed to 4.7 percent who were white. With respect to powder cocaine, the percentages were largely reversed. Id. The court found that this statistical evidence demonstrated both the disparate impact of the 100 to 1 ratio and the probability that "the subliminal influence of unconscious racism ha[d] permeated federal prosecution throughout the nation." Id. at 791.

While the government directed the court to evidence that Congress considered crack to be more dangerous because of its potency, addictiveness, affordability and prevalence, the court found evidence in the record contradicting many of the legislators' beliefs. Id. at 781-92. In particular, the court questioned Congress' conclusion that crack was 100 times more potent or dangerous than powder cocaine, referring to testimony that there is no reliable medical evidence that crack cocaine is more addictive than powder cocaine. Id. In light of these factors, the court found the punishment of crack at 100 times greater than powder cocaine to be a "frenzied, irrational response." Id. at 792. The court repeatedly stressed that "cocaine is cocaine." Id. at 793.

The district court held the portions of 21 U.S.C. section 841 mandating punishment 100 times greater for crack than powder cocaine to be constitutionally invalid generally and as applied in this case.

We believe that this case could well be decided on the basis of past decisions by this court. See *United States v. Maxwell*, 25 F.3d 1389, 1396-97 (8th Cir.1994); *United States v. Simms*, 18 F.3d 588, 595 (8th Cir.1994); *United States v. Parris*, 17 F.3d 227, 230 (8th Cir.), cert. denied, 511 U.S. 1077, 114 S.Ct. 1662, 128 L.Ed.2d 378 (1994); *United States v. Johnson*, 12 F.3d 760, 763-64 (8th Cir.1993), cert. denied, 512 U.S. 1211, 114 S.Ct. 2689, 129 L.Ed.2d 821 (1994); United *States v. Echols*, 2 F.3d 849, 850 (8th Cir.1993); *United States v. Womack*, 985 F.2d 395, 400 (8th Cir.), cert. denied, 510 U.S. 902, 114 S.Ct. 276, 126 L.Ed.2d 227 (1993); *United States v. Williams*, 982 F.2d 1209, 1213 (8th Cir.1992); United *States v. Lattimore*, 974 F.2d 971, 974-76 (8th Cir.1992), cert. denied, 507 U.S. 1020, 113 S.Ct. 1819, 123 L.Ed.2d 449 (1993); *United States v. Willis*, 967 F.2d 1220, 1225 (8th Cir.1992); *United States v. Simmons*, 964 F.2d 763, 767 (8th Cir.), cert. denied, 506 U.S. 1011, 113 S.Ct. 632, 121 L.Ed.2d 563 (1992); *United States v. Hechavarria*, 960 F.2d 736, 738 (8th Cir.1992) (per curiam); *United States v. McDile*, 946 F.2d 1330, 1331 (8th Cir.1991); *United States v. Johnson*, 944 F.2d 396, 409 (8th Cir.), cert. denied, 502 U.S. 1008, 112 S.Ct. 646, 116 L.Ed.2d 663 (1991); *United States v. House*, 939 F.2d 659, 664 (8th Cir.1991); *United States v. Winfrey*, 900 F.2d 1225, 1226-27 (8th Cir.1990); *United States v. Reed*, 897 F.2d 351, 352-53 (8th Cir.1990) (per curiam); *United States v. Buckner*, 894 F.2d 975, 978-80 (8th Cir.1990).

In *Lattimore*, Chief Judge Arnold carefully examined earlier authority holding that Congress clearly had rational motives for creating the distinction between crack and powder cocaine. 974 F.2d at 974-75. Among the reasons were "the potency of the drug, the ease with which drug dealers can carry and conceal it, the highly addictive nature of the drug, and the violence which often accompanies trade in it." Id. at 975. Lattimore squarely rejects the argument that crack cocaine sentences disparately impact on African Americans. Id. *Citing Personnel Administrator of Massachusetts v. Feeney*, 442 U.S. 256, 99 S.Ct. 2282, 60 L.Ed.2d 870 (1979), we observed that even if a neutral law has a disproportionate adverse impact on a racial minority, it is unconstitutional only if that effect can be traced to a discriminatory purpose. *Lattimore*, 974 F.2d at 975. Discriminatory purpose "implies that the decisionmaker, in this case [Congress], selected or reaffirmed a particular course of action at least in part 'because of' not merely 'in spite of,' its adverse effects upon an identifiable group." Id. (quoting *Feeney*, 442 U.S. at 279, 99 S.Ct. at 2296). We concluded that there was no evidence that Congress or the Sentencing Commission had a racially discriminatory motive when it crafted the Guidelines with extended sentences for crack cocaine felonies. *Lattimore*, 974 F.2d at 975.

Lattimore also referred to *Buckner*, 894 F.2d 975, a case dealing with a substantive due process challenge to the 100 to 1 ratio. In *Buckner*, we held that requiring more severe penalties for crack than cocaine powder was not arbitrary or irrational. Id. at 980. We referred to the Senate hearing on crack, citing statements by five Senators on the dangers of crack cocaine. Id. at 978-79 n. 9 (citing "Crack" Cocaine: Hearing Before the Permanent Subcomm. on Investigations of the Senate Comm. on Government Affairs, 99th Cong., 2d. Sess. 20 (1986)). *Buckner* also discussed the testimony before Congress of Dr. Robert Byck, Professor of Psychiatry and Pharmacology at Yale University, who contrasted inhaling crack vapor to packing a nose with cocaine powder (the most common form of using cocaine powder). *Id.* Byck stated that crack is more dangerous than cocaine powder because as a person breathes crack vapor, an almost unlimited amount of the drug can enter the body. Id. "Moreover, the speed of the material going to the brain is very rapid." Id. He also commented on the marketability of crack cocaine, stating that "[h]ere suddenly, we have cocaine available in a little package, in unit dosage, available at a price that kids can pay initially." *Id.*

Similarly, in *Maxwell*, we rejected a strict scrutiny argument that was based on the continued enforcement of the statute rather than its enactment. 25 F.3d at 1396-97. We referred to Lattimore and Feeney, and held that the defendants had presented no evidence that Congress or the Sentencing Commission had "permitted the challenged provisions to remain in effect 'at least in part because of, not merely in spite of, their adverse effects upon' a racial minority." *Maxwell*, 25 F.3d at 1397 (quoting Johnson, 12 F.3d at 763-64).

The district court's painstakingly-crafted opinion demonstrates the careful consideration it gave not only to the testimony before it, but also to the voluminous documents introduced by

Clary, including both law review and text materials. This case undoubtedly presents the most complete record on this issue to come before this court. Nevertheless, we are satisfied that both the record before the district court and the district court's findings fall short of establishing that Congress acted with a discriminatory purpose in enacting the statute, and that Congress selected or reaffirmed a particular course of action "at least in part 'because of,' not merely 'in spite of' its adverse effects upon an identifiable group." *Lattimore*, 974 F.2d at 975 (quoting *Feeney*), 442 U.S. at 279, 99 S.Ct. at 2296. While impact is an important starting point, *Arlington Heights* made clear that impact alone is not determinative absent a pattern as stark as that in *Gomillion v. Lightfoot*, 364 U.S. 339, 81 S.Ct. 125, 5 L.Ed.2d 110 (1960), or *Yick Wo v. Hopkins*, 118 U.S. 356, 6 S.Ct. 1064, 30 L.Ed. 220 (1886). 429 U.S. at 266, 97 S.Ct. at 564.

We first question the district court's reliance on "unconscious racism." 846 F.Supp. at 778-782. The court reasoned that a focus on purposeful discrimination will not show more subtle and deeply-buried forms of racism. Id. at 781. The court's reasoning, however, simply does not address the question whether Congress acted with a discriminatory purpose. Similar failings affect the court's statement that although intent per se may not have entered into Congress' enactment of the crack statutes, Congress' failure to account for a substantial and foreseeable disparate impact on African Americans nonetheless violates the spirit and letter of equal protection.

We also question the court's reliance on media-created stereotypes of crack dealers and its conclusion that this information "undoubtedly served as the touchstone that influenced racial perceptions held by legislators and the public as related to the 'crack epidemic.' " *Id.* at 784. Although the placement of newspaper and magazine articles in the Congressional Record indicates that this information may have affected at least some legislators, these articles hardly demonstrate that the stereotypical images "undoubtedly" influenced the legislators' racial perceptions. It is too long a leap from newspaper and magazine articles to an inference that Congress enacted the crack statute because of its adverse effect on African American males, instead of the stated purpose of responding to the serious impact of a rapidly-developing and particularly-dangerous form of drug use. Similarly, the evidence of the haste with which Congress acted and the action it took is as easily explained by the seriousness of the perceived problem as by racial animus.

The district court's final conclusion that objective evidence supports the belief that racial animus was a motivating factor in enacting the crack statute further belies the weakness of its position. A belief that racial animus was a motivating factor, based on disproportionate impact, is simply not enough since the Equal Protection Clause is violated "only if that impact can be traced to a discriminatory purpose." *Feeney*, 442 U.S. at 272, 99 S.Ct. at 2293. The chain of reasoning of the district court simply will not support a conclusion or a finding that the crack statutes were passed "because of, not merely in spite of" the adverse effect upon an identifiable group. Id. at 279, 99 S.Ct. at 2296.

Other testimony before the district court demonstrates the particular lack of support for the court's conclusion about Congress' motivation in passing the statute. The testimony of Eric E. Sterling, Counsel to the Subcommittee of Criminal Justice of the House of Representatives at the time the statutes in question were passed, is the most pertinent. Sterling stated that the members of Congress did not have racial animus, but rather "racial consciousness," an awareness that the "problem in the inner cities ... was about to explode into the white part of the country." Sterling believed that Congress wanted the penalties to be applied wherever crack was being trafficked, although Congress was aware that crack was used primarily by minorities. He further described the seriousness of the problem as reported by the popular press, and stated his view that the creation and promulgation of the law was based on "crass political interest." His opinion was that the motivating factor for the legislation was a perception that crack cocaine posed a unique and unprecedented problem for American narcotics enforcement. Similarly, David Courtwright, who described himself as an historian of drug laws, stated that he did not know if racial considerations led to the passage of the crack laws, and that he had no special or expert knowledge as to the motives of the legislators voting for the 1986 law.

For the most part, the other witnesses that testified before the district court were medical witnesses, several of whom contested the medical information before the Senate that showed differences between crack and powder cocaine. Scientific disagreement with testimony in congressional hearings, offered at a later time and after additional research, simply does not establish discriminatory purpose, or for that matter, a lack of scientific support for Congress' action.

The district court also found it "likely ... that the subliminal influence of unconscious racism has permeated federal prosecution throughout the nation." 846 F.Supp. at 791. Clary concedes he "did not claim below that he was selectively prosecuted because of his race ... [because he] was mindful of the even more difficult burden of proof he would have had to carry." Appellees's Brief at 43. To prevail on such a claim, a defendant "must establish that the decision to bring the federal charges against him, and not against others who committed federal crack violations and thus were similarly situated, itself had a racially discriminatory effect." *United States v. Brown*, 9 F.3d 1374, 1376 (8th Cir.1993), cert. denied, 511 U.S. 1043, 114 S.Ct. 1568, 128 L.Ed.2d 213 (1994). Even more to the point, Clary presented only statistical evidence and offered nothing else to show selective prosecution. As we held in Brown, this is simply not enough. Id.

We reverse and remand to the district court for resentencing consistent with this opinion.

Note

Is the *Armstrong* standard impossible for a defendant to meet? In *Bass* there appears to be no question and the lower court concluded that discriminatory bias existed, but the Supreme Court found lack of establishment that similarly situated White individuals were treated differently.

In *Clary* there seems to be acceptance of the fact that evidence existed that similarly situated non-African Americans were prosecuted differently but there was not proof of discriminatory intent. Consider the suggestion in Yoav Sapir, *Neither Intent nor Impact: A Critique of the Racially Based Selective Prosecution Jurisprudence and a Reform Proposal*, 19 HARV. BLACKLETTER L. J. 127 (2003). The author suggests that the uniqueness of criminal prosecution and the pervasiveness of the problem should mandate a different equal protection approach. He suggests that proof of intent be replaced by a requirement that the defendant prove that a single, similarly non-minority, situated person was prosecuted or not prosecuted differently. Once the defendant established a prima facie case of different treatment, the burden would shift to the prosecution to present statistical evidence that such differential treatment was not motivated by race.

Challenging the Racial Composition of the Grand Jury

Note

The right to an indictment, unless waived, as a prerequisite to felony prosecution within the federal system, is guaranteed by the Fifth Amendment to The United States Constitution which states that "[n]o person shall be held to answer for a capital, or otherwise infamous crime, unless on a presentment or indictment of a Grand Jury." See, *Ex Parte Wilson*, 114 U.S. 417 (1885). The grand jury serves what has been described as a "sword and shield" function. *United States v. Cox*, 342 F.2d 167 (5th Cir. 1965). In particular, its shield function serves "as a primary security to the innocent against hasty, malicious and oppressive persecution: it serves the invaluable function in our society of standing between the accuser and the accused, whether the latter be an individual, minority group or other..." *Wood v. Georgia*, 370 U.S. 375 (1962). While this protection of the Fifth Amendment has not been incorporated and made applicable to the states through the Due Process Clause of the Fourteenth Amendment, *Hurtado v. California*, 110 U.S. 516 (1884), where extended to state citizens through state constitutions or statute, constitutional questions and protections against racial discriminations have long been included amongst the protections for defendants.

STRAUDER V. WEST VIRGINIA.
100 U.S. 303 (1879)

MR. JUSTICE STRONG delivered the opinion of the court.

The plaintiff in error, a colored man, was indicated for murder in the Circuit Court of Ohio County, in West Virginia, on the 20th of October, 1874, and upon trial was convicted and sentenced. The record was then removed to the Supreme Court of the State, and there the judgment of the Circuit Court was affirmed. The present case is a writ of error to that court, and it is now, in substance, averred that at the trial in the State court the defendant (now plaintiff in error) was denied rights to which he was entitled under the Constitution and laws of the United States.

In the Circuit Court of the State, before the trial of the indictment was commenced, the defendant presented his petition, verified by his oath, praying for a removal of the cause into the Circuit Court of the United States, assigning, as ground for the removal, that 'by virtue of the laws of the State of West Virginia no colored man was eligible to be a member of the grand jury or to serve on a petit jury in the State; that white men are so eligible, and that by reason of his being a colored man and having been a slave, he had reason to believe, and did believe, he could not have the full and equal benefit of all laws and proceedings in the State of West Virginia for the security of his person as is enjoyed by white citizens, and that he had less chance of enforcing in the courts of the State his rights on the prosecution, as a citizen of the United States, and that the probabilities of a denial of them to him as such citizen on every trial which might take place on the indictment in the courts of the State were much more enhanced than if he was a white man.' This petition was denied by the State court, and the cause was forced to trial.

Motions to quash the venire, 'because the law under which it was issued was unconstitutional, null, and void,' and successive motions to challenge the array of the panel, for a new trial, and in arrest of judgment were then made, all of which were overruled and made by exceptions parts of the record.

The law of the State to which reference was made in the petition for removal and in the several motions was enacted on the 12th of March, 1873 (Acts of 1872–73, p. 102), and it is as follows: 'All white male persons who are twenty-one years of age and who are citizens of this State shall be liable to serve as jurors, except as herein provided.' The persons excepted are State officials.

In this court, several errors have been assigned, and the controlling questions underlying them all are, first, whether, by the Constitution and laws of the United States, every citizen of the United States has a right to a trial of an indictment against him by a jury selected and impanelled without discrimination against his race or color, because of race or color; and, second, if he has such a right, and is denied its enjoyment by the State in which he is indicted, may he cause the case to be removed into the Circuit Court of the United States?

It is to be observed that the first of these questions is not whether a colored man, when an indictment has been preferred against him, has a right to a grand or a petit jury composed in whole or in part of persons of his own race or color, but it is whether, in the composition or selection of jurors by whom he is to be indicted or tried, all persons of his race or color may be excluded by law, solely because of their race or color, so that by no possibility can any colored man sit upon the jury.

The questions are important, for they demand a construction of the recent amendments of the Constitution. If the defendant has a right to have a jury selected for the trial of his case without discrimination against all persons of his race or color, because of their race or color, the right, if not created, is protected by those amendments, and the legislation of Congress under them. The Fourteenth Amendment ordains that 'all persons born or naturalized in the United States and subject to the jurisdiction thereof are citizens of the United States and of the State wherein they reside. No State shall make or enforce any laws which shall abridge the privileges or immunities of citizens of the United States, nor shall any State deprive any person of life, liberty, or property, without due process of law, nor deny to any person within its jurisdiction the equal protection of the laws.'

This is one of a series of constitutional provisions having a common purpose; namely, securing to a race recently emancipated, a race that through many generations had been held in slavery, all the civil rights that the superior race enjoy. The true spirit and meaning of the amendments, as we said in the Slaughter-House Cases (16 Wall. 36), cannot be understood without keeping in view the history of the times when they were adopted, and the general objects they plainly sought to accomplish. At the time when they were incorporated into the Constitution, it required little knowledge of human nature to anticipate that those who had long been regarded as an inferior and subject race would, when suddenly raised to the rank of citizenship, be looked upon with jealousy and positive dislike, and that State laws might be enacted or enforced to perpetuate the distinctions that had before existed. Discriminations against them had been habitual. It was well known that in some States laws making such discriminations then existed, and others might well be expected. The colored race, as a race, was abject and ignorant, and in that condition was unfitted to command the respect of those who had superior intelligence. Their training had left them mere children, and as such they needed the protection which a wise government extends to those who are unable to protect themselves. They especially needed protection against unfriendly action in the States where they were resident. It was in view of these considerations the Fourteenth Amendment was framed and adopted. It was designed to assure to the colored race the enjoyment of all the civil rights that under the law are enjoyed by white persons, and to give to that race the protection of the general government, in that enjoyment, whenever it should be denied by the States. It not only gave citizenship and the privileges of citizenship to persons of color, but it denied to any State the power to withhold from them the equal protection of the laws, and authorized Congress to enforce its provisions by appropriate legislation. To quote the language used by us in the Slaughter-House Cases, 'No one can fail to be impressed with the one pervading purpose found in all the amendments, lying at the foundation of each, and without which none of them would have been suggested,—we mean the freedom of the slave race, the security and firm establishment of that freedom, and the protection of the newly made freeman and citizen from the oppressions of those who had formerly exercised unlimited dominion over them.' So again: 'The existence of laws in the States where the newly emancipated negroes resided, which discriminated with gross injustice and hardship against them as a class, was the evil to be remedied, and by it [the Fourteenth Amendment] such laws were forbidden. If, however, the States did not conform their laws to its requirements, then, by the fifth section of the article of amendment, Congress was authorized to enforce it by suitable legislation.' And it was added, 'We doubt very much whether any action of a State, not directed by way of discrimination against the negroes, as a class, will ever be held to come within the purview of this provision.'

If this is the spirit and meaning of the amendment, whether it means more or not, it is to be construed liberally, to carry out the purposes of its framers. It ordains that no State shall make or enforce any laws which shall abridge the privileges or immunities of citizens of the United States (evidently referring to the newly made citizens, who, being citizens of the United States, are declared to be also citizens of the State in which they reside). It ordains that no State shall deprive any person of life, liberty, or property, without due process of law, or deny to any person within its jurisdiction the equal protection of the laws. What is this but declaring that the law in the States shall be the same for the black as for the white; that all persons, whether colored or white, shall stand equal before the laws of the States, and, in regard to the colored race, for whose protection the amendment was primarily designed, that no discrimination shall be made against them by law because of their color? The words of the amendment, it is true, are prohibitory, but they contain a necessary implication of a positive immunity, or right, most valuable to the colored race,—the right to exemption from unfriendly legislation against them distinctively as colored,—exemption from legal discriminations, implying inferiority in civil society, lessening the security of their enjoyment of the rights which others enjoy, and discriminations which are steps towards reducing them to the condition of a subject race.

That the West Virginia statute respecting juries—the statute that controlled the selection of the grand and petit jury in the case of the plaintiff in error—is such a discrimination ought not to be doubted. Nor would it be if the persons excluded by it were white men. If in those States where the colored people constitute a majority of the entire population a law should be enacted excluding all white men from jury service, thus denying to them the privilege of participating equally with the blacks in the administration of justice, we apprehend no one would be heard to claim that it would not be a denial to white men of the equal protection of the laws. Nor if a law should be passed excluding all naturalized Celtic Irishmen, would there by any doubt of its inconsistency with the spirit of the amendment. The very fact that colored people are singled out and expressly denied by a statute all right to participate in the administration of the law, as jurors, because of their color, though they are citizens, and may be in other respects fully qualified, is practically a brand upon them, affixed by the law, an assertion of their inferiority, and a stimulant to that race prejudice which is an impediment to securing to individuals of the race that equal justice which the law aims to secure to all others.

The right to a trial by jury is guaranteed to every citizen of West Virginia by the Constitution of that State, and the constitution of juries is a very essential part of the protection such a mode of trial is intended to secure. The very idea of a jury is a body of men composed of the peers or equals of the person whose rights it is selected or summoned to determine; that is, of his neighbors, fellows, associates, persons having the same legal status in society as that which he holds. Blackstone, in his Commentaries, says, 'The right of trial by jury, or the country, is a trial by the peers of every Englishman, and is the grand bulwark of his liberties, and is secured to him by the Great Charter.' It is also guarded by statutory enactments intended to make impossible what Mr. Bentham called 'packing juries.' It is well known that prejudices often exist against particular classes in the community, which sway the judgment of jurors, and which, therefore, operate in some cases to deny to persons of those classes the full enjoyment of that protection which others enjoy. Prejudice in a local community is held to be a reason for a change of venue. The framers of the constitutional amendment must have known full well the existence of such prejudice and its likelihood to continue against the manumitted slaves and their race, and that knowledge was doubtless a motive that led to the amendment. By their manumission and citizenship the colored race became entitled to the equal protection of the laws of the States in which they resided; and the apprehension that through prejudice they might be denied that equal protection, that is, that there might be discrimination against them, was the inducement to bestow upon the national government the power to enforce the provision that no State shall deny to them the equal protection of the laws. Without the apprehended existence of prejudice that portion of the amendment would have been unnecessary, and it might have been left to the States to extend equality of protection.

In view of these considerations, it is hard to see why the statute of West Virginia should not be regarded as discriminating against a colored man when he is put upon trial for an alleged criminal offence against the State. It is not easy to comprehend how it can be said that while every white man is entitled to a trial by a jury selected from persons of his own race or color, or, rather, selected without discrimination against his color, and a negro is not, the latter is equally protected by the law with the former. Is not protection of life and liberty against race or color prejudice, a right, a legal right, under the constitutional amendment? And how can it be maintained that compelling a colored man to submit to a trial for his life by a jury drawn from a panel from which the State has expressly excluded every man of his race, because of color alone, however well qualified in other respects, is not a denial to him of equal legal protection?

We do not say that within the limits from which it is not excluded by the amendment a State may not prescribe the qualifications of its jurors, and in so doing make discriminations. It may confine the selection to males, to freeholders, to citizens, to persons within certain ages, or to persons having educational qualifications. We do not believe the Fourteenth Amendment was ever intended to prohibit this. Looking at its history, it is clear it had no such purpose. Its aim was against discrimination because of race or color. As we have said more than once, its design was to protect an emancipated race, and to strike down all possible legal discriminations against those who belong to it. To quote further from 16 Wall., supra: 'In giving construction to any of these articles [amendments], it is necessary to keep the main purpose steadily in view.' 'It is so clearly a provision for that race and that emergency, that a strong case would be necessary for its application to any other.' We are not now called upon to affirm or deny that it had other purposes.

The Fourteenth Amendment makes no attempt to enumerate the rights it designed to protect. It speaks in general terms, and those are as comprehensive as possible. Its language is prohibitory; but every prohibition implies the existence of rights and immunities, prominent among which is an immunity from inequality of legal protection, either for life, liberty, or property. Any State action that denies this immunity to a colored man is in conflict with the Constitution.

Concluding, therefore, that the statute of West Virginia, discriminating in the selection of jurors, as it does, against negroes because of their color, amounts to a denial of the equal protection of the laws to a colored man when he is put upon trial for an alleged offence against the State, it remains only to be considered whether the power of Congress to enforce the provisions of the Fourteenth Amendment by appropriate legislation is sufficient to justify the enactment of sect. 641 of the Revised Statutes.

A right or an immunity, whether created by the Constitution or only guaranteed by it, even without any express delegation of power, may be protected by Congress. Prigg v. The Commonwealth of Pennsylvania, 16 Pet. 539. So in United States v. Reese (92 (U. S. 214), it was said by the Chief Justice of this court: 'Rights and immunities created by or dependent upon the Constitution of the United States can be protected by Congress. The form and manner of the protection may be such as Congress in the legitimate exercise of its legislative discretion shall provide. These may be varied to meet the necessities of the particular right to be protected.' But there is express authority to protect the rights and immunities referred to in the Fourteenth Amendment, and to enforce observance of them by appropriate congressional legislation. And one very efficient and appropriate mode of extending such protection and securing to a party the enjoyment of the right or immunity, is a law providing for the removal of his case from a State court, in which the right is denied by the State law, into a Federal court, where it will be upheld. This is an ordinary mode of protecting rights and immunities conferred by the Federal Constitution and laws. Sect. 641 is such a provision. It enacts that 'when any civil suit or criminal prosecution is commenced in any State court for any cause whatsoever against any person who is denied, or cannot enforce, in the judicial tribunals of the State, or in the part of the State where such prosecution is pending, any right secured to him by any law providing for the equal civil rights of citizens of the United States, or of all persons within the jurisdiction of the United States, such suit or prosecution may, upon the petition of such defendant, filed in said State court at any time before the trial, or final hearing of the case, stating the facts, and verified by oath, be removed before trial into the next Circuit Court of the United States to be held in the district where it is pending.'

This act plainly has reference to sects. 1977 and 1978 of the statutes which partially enumerate the rights and immunities intended to be guaranteed by the Constitution, the first of which declares that 'all persons within the jurisdiction of the United States shall have the same right in every State and Territory to make and enforce contracts, to sue, be parties, give evidence, and to the full and equal benefit of all laws and proceedings for the security of persons and property, as is enjoyed by white citizens, and shall be subject to like punishment, pains, penalties, taxes, licenses, and exactions of every kind, and to no other.' This act puts in the form of a statute what had been substantially ordained by the constitutional amendment. It was a step towards enforcing the constitutional provisions. Sect. 641 was an advanced step, fully warranted, we think, by the fifth section of the Fourteenth Amendment.

We have heretofore considered and affirmed the constitutional power of Congress to authorize the removal from State courts into the circuit courts of the United States, before trial, of criminal prosecutions for alleged offences against the laws of the State, when the defence presents a Federal question, or when a right under the Federal Constitution or laws is involved. Tennessee v. Davis, supra, p. 257. It is unnecessary now to repeat what we there said.

That the petition of the plaintiff in error, filed by him in the State court before the trial of his case, made a case for removal into the Federal Circuit Court, under sect. 641, is very plain, if, by the constitutional amendment and sect. 1977 of the Revised Statutes, he was entitled to immunity from discrimination against him in the selection of jurors, because of their color, as we have endeavored to show that he was. It set forth sufficient facts to exhibit a denial of that immunity, and a denial by the statute law of the State.

There was error, therefore, in proceeding to the trial of the indictment against him after his petition was filed, as also in overruling his challenge to the array of the jury, and in refusing to quash the panel.

The judgment of the Supreme Court of West Virginia will be reversed, and the case remitted with instructions to reverse the judgment of the Circuit Court of Ohio county; and it is

So ordered.

CASSELL V. TEXAS.
339 U.S. 282 (1950)

Justice BLACK and Mr. Justice CLARK concurred.

Review was sought in this case to determine whether there had been a violation by Texas of petitioner's federal constitutional right to a fair and impartial grand jury. The federal question was raised by a motion to quash the indictment on the ground that petitioner, a Negro, suffered unconstitutional discrimination through the selection of white men only for the grand jury that indicted him. After full hearing, the trial court denied the motion, and this action was sustained by the Court of Criminal Appeals of Texas in affirming petitioner's conviction. Cassell v. State, 216 S.W.2d 813.

The Court of Criminal Appeals accepted the federal rule that a Negro is denied the equal protection of the laws when he is indicted by a grand jury from which Negroes as a race have been intentionally excluded. *Cassell v. State*, supra, 216 S.W.2d 819; *Neal v. State of Delaware*, 103 U.S. 370, 394, 26 L.Ed. 567; *Smith v. State of Texas*, 311 U.S. 128, 130, 61 S.Ct. 164, 165, 85 L.Ed. 84; *Hill v. State of Texas*, 316 U.S. 400, 404, 62 S.Ct. 1159, 1161, 86 L.Ed. 1559; *Akins v. State of Texas*, 325 U.S. 398, 403, 65 S.Ct. 1276, 1279, 89 L.Ed. 1692. It was from an examination of facts that the court deduced its conclusion that racial discrimination had not been practiced. Since the result reached may deny a federal right, we may reexamine the facts to determine whether petitioner has sustained by proof his allegation of discrimination. Certiorari was granted, 336 U.S. 943, 69 S.Ct. 805, to consider petitioner's claim that in this case Negroes were omitted from the list of grand jurymen either because of deliberate limitation by the Dallas County jury commissioners, or because of failure by the commissioners to acquaint themselves with available Negroes.

Acting under the Texas statutes, the Dallas County grand-jury commissioners chose a list of sixteen males for this September 1947 grand jury from citizens eligible under the statute. The judge chose twelve of these for the panel. No challenge is now made to the fairness of this statutory system. We have approved it.

Petitioner's attack is upon the way the statutory method of grand-jury selection has been administered by the jury commissioners. One charge is that discrimination must have been practiced because the Negro proportion of grand jurors is less than the Negro proportion of the county's population. Under the 1940 census the total population of Dallas County was 398,564, of whom 61,605 were Negroes. This is about 15.5%. In weighing this matter of custom, we limit ourselves, as do the parties, to the period between June 1, 1942, when Hill v. Texas, supra, was decided, and November 1947, when petitioner was indicted. There were 21 grand juries in this period; of the 252 members of the panels,9 17, or 6.7% were Negroes. But this apparent discrepancy may be explained by the fact that Texas grand jurors must possess certain statutory qualifications. Grand jurors must ordinarily be eligible to vote; eligibility requires payment of a poll tax; and the validity of the poll-tax requirement is not challenged. The record shows 5,500 current Negro poll-tax payers in Dallas County in 1947, and nothing indicates that this number varied substantially from year to year. The corresponding figure for all poll-tax payers, male and female, is 83,667. These figures would indicate that as a proportional matter 6.5% of grand jurors would be Negroes, a percentage approximating the ratio of Negroes actually sitting on the 21 grand jury panels. Without more it cannot be said that Negroes had been left off grand-jury panels to such a degree as to establish a prima facie case of discrimination.

A different question is presented by petitioner's next charge that subsequent to the Hill case the Dallas County grand-jury commissioners for 21 consecutive lists had consistently limited Negroes selected for grand-jury service to not more than one on each grand jury. The contention is that the Akins case has been interpreted in Dallas County to allow a limitation of the number of Negroes on each grand jury, provided the limitation is approximately proportional to the number of Negroes eligible for grand-jury service. Since the Hill case the judges of the trial court have been careful to instruct their jury commissioners that discrimination on grounds of race or color is forbidden. The judge did so here. If, notwithstanding this caution by the trial court judges, commissioners should limit proportionally the number of Negroes selected for grand-jury service, such limitation would violate our Constitution. Jurymen should be selected as individuals, on the basis of individual qualifications, and not as members of a race.

We have recently written why proportional representation of races on a jury is not a constitutional requisite. Succinctly stated, our reason was that the Constitution requires only a fair jury selected without regard to race. Obviously the number of races and nationalities appearing in the ancestry of our citizens would make it impossible to meet a requirement of proportional representation. Similarly, since there can be no exclusion of Negroes as a race and no discrimination because of color, proportional limitation is not permissible. That conclusion is compelled by the United States Code, Title 18, s 243, 18 U.S.C.A. s 243,[20] based on s 4 of the Civil Rights Act of 1875. While the language of the section directs attention to the right to serve as a juror, its command has long been recognized also to assure rights to an accused. Prohibiting racial disqualification of Negroes for jury service, this congressional enactment under the Fourteenth Amendment, s 5,[21] has been consistently sustained and its violation held to deny a proper trial to a Negro accused. Proportional racial limitation is therefore forbidden. An accused is entitled to have charges against him considered by a jury in the selection of which there has been neither inclusion nor exclusion because of race.

Our holding that there was discrimination in the selection of grand jurors in this case, however, is based on another ground. In explaining the fact that no Negroes appeared on this grand-jury list, the commissioners said that they knew none available who qualified; at the same time they said they chose jurymen only from those people with whom they were personally acquainted. It may be assumed that in ordinary activities in Dallas County, acquaintanceship between the races is not on a sufficiently familiar basis to give citizens eligible for appointment as jury commissioners an opportunity to know the qualifications for grand-jury service of many members of another race. An individual's qualifications for grand-jury service, however, are not hard to ascertain, and with no evidence to the contrary, we must assume that a large proportion of the Negroes of Dallas County met the statutory requirements for jury service. When the commissioners were appointed as judicial administrative officials, it was their duty to familiarize themselves fairly with the qualifications of the eligible jurors of the county without regard to race and color. They did not do so here, and the result has been racial discrimination. We repeat the recent statement of Chief Justice Stone in *Hill v. Texas*, 316 U.S. 400, 404, 62 S.Ct. 1159, 1161, 86 L.Ed. 1559: 'Discrimination can arise from the action of commissioners who exclude all negroes whom they do not know to be qualified and who neither know nor seek to learn whether there are in fact any qualified to serve. In such a case discrimination necessarily results where there are qualified negroes available for jury service. With the large number of colored male residents of the county who are literate, and in the absence of any countervailing testimony, there is no room for inference that there are not among them householders of good moral character, who can read and write, qualified and available for grand jury service.'

The existence of the kind of discrimination described in the Hill case does not depend upon systematic exclusion continuing over a long period and practiced by a succession of jury commissioners. Since the issue must be whether there has been discrimination in the selection of the jury that has indicted petitioner, it is enough to have direct evidence based on the statements of the jury commissioners in the very case. Discrimination may be proved in other ways than by evidence of long continued unexplained absence of Negroes from many panels. The statements of the jury commissioners that they chose only whom they knew, and that they knew no eligible Negroes in an area where Negroes made up so large a proportion of the population, prove the intentional exclusion that is discrimination in violation of petitioner's constitutional rights.

The judgment of the Court of Criminal Appeals of Texas is reversed.

Reversed.

Note

An associated issue with racial discrimination in the selection of grand jurors is the question of discrimination in the selection of the grand jury foreperson. The foreperson has a unique and important set of responsibilities. It is through the foreperson that the grand jury's findings are reported to the court. Unlike the foreperson of the petit jury, the foreperson of the grand jury is often chosen by the court as opposed to being elected by the jury. See Rule 6 (c) Federal Rules of Criminal Procedure. In *Rose v. Mitchell*, 443 U.S. 545 (1979) the United States Supreme Court determined that racial discrimination in the selection of the foreperson violated equal protection and furthermore, if the defendant satisfies the requirements for an equal protection claim under the Fourteenth Amendment, he or she would be entitled to reversal of a subsequent conviction. The defendant in *Rose* was Black and alleged that Blacks were systematically excluded from consideration or appointment as forepersons. The Court however, in Hobby v. United States, 468 U.S. 339 (1984), indicated that it was not inclined to extend the relief to a White defendant, asserting that Blacks were systematically excluded from foreperson consideration in his case.

Justice KENNEDY delivered the opinion of the Court.

We must decide whether a white criminal defendant has standing to object to discrimination against black persons in the selection of grand jurors. Finding he has the requisite standing to raise equal protection and due process claims, we reverse and remand.

I

A grand jury in Evangeline Parish, Louisiana, indicted petitioner Terry Campbell on one count of second-degree murder. Campbell, who is white, filed a timely pretrial motion to quash the indictment on the grounds the grand jury was constituted in violation of his equal protection and due process rights under the Fourteenth Amendment and in violation of the Sixth Amendment's fair-cross-section requirement. Campbell alleged a longstanding practice of racial discrimination in the selection of grand jury forepersons in the parish. His sole piece of evidence is that, between January 1976 and August 1993, no black person served as a grand jury foreperson in the parish, even though more than 20 percent of the registered voters were black persons. See Brief for Petitioner 16. The State does not dispute this evidence. The trial judge refused to quash the indictment because "Campbell, being a white man accused of killing another white man," lacked standing to complain "where all of the forepersons were white." App. to Pet. for Cert. G–33.

After Campbell's first trial resulted in a mistrial, he was retried, convicted of second-degree murder, and sentenced to life in prison without possibility of parole. Campbell renewed his challenge to the grand jury foreperson selection procedures in a motion for new trial, which was denied. See id., at 1–2. The Louisiana Court of Appeal reversed, because, under our decision in *Powers v. Ohio*, 499 U.S. 400, 111 S.Ct. 1364, 113 L.Ed.2d 411 (1991), Campbell had standing to object to the alleged discrimination even though he is white. 651 So.2d 412 (1995). The Court of Appeal remanded the case for an evidentiary hearing because it found Campbell's evidence of discrimination inadequate. Id., at 413.

The Louisiana Supreme Court reversed. It distinguished *Powers* as turning on the "considerable and substantial impact" that a prosecutor's discriminatory use of peremptory challenges has on a defendant's trial as well as on the integrity of the judicial system. See 661 So.2d 1321, 1324 (1995). The court declined to extend *Powers* to a claim of discrimination in the selection of a grand jury foreperson. It also found *Hobby v. United States*, 468 U.S. 339, 104 S.Ct. 3093,

82 L.Ed.2d 260 (1984), did not afford Campbell standing to raise a due process objection. In *Hobby*, this Court held no relief could be granted to a white defendant even if his due process rights were violated by discrimination in the selection of a federal grand jury foreperson. Noting that *Hobby* turned on the ministerial nature of the federal grand jury foreperson's duties, the Louisiana Supreme Court held "[t]he role of the grand jury foreman in Louisiana appears to be similarly ministerial" such that any discrimination "has little, if any, effect on the defendant's due process right of fundamental fairness." 661 So.2d, at 1324. Because the Court of Appeal had not addressed Campbell's other asserted points of error, the Louisiana Supreme Court remanded the case. After the Court of Appeal rejected Campbell's remaining claims, 673 So.2d 1061 (1996), the Louisiana Supreme Court refused to reconsider its ruling on the grand jury issue, 685 So.2d 140 (1997). We granted certiorari to address the narrow question of Campbell's standing to raise equal protection, due process, and fair-cross-section claims.

II

As an initial matter, we note Campbell complains about more than discrimination in the selection of his grand jury foreperson; he alleges that discrimination shaped the composition of the grand jury itself. In the federal system and in most States which use grand juries, the foreperson is selected from the ranks of the already seated grand jurors. See 1 S. Beale, W. Bryson, J. Felman, & M. Elston, Grand Jury Law and Practice § 4:6, pp. 4–20 to 4–21 (2d ed.1997) (either the judge selects the foreperson or fellow grand jurors elect him or her). Under those systems, the title "foreperson" is bestowed on one of the existing grand jurors without any change in the grand jury's composition. In Louisiana, by contrast, the judge selects the foreperson from the grand jury venire before the remaining members of the grand jury have been chosen by lot. La.Code Crim. Proc. Ann., Art. 413(B) (West Supp.1997); see also 1 Beale, supra, at 4–22, n. 11 (Ohio, Oklahoma, Tennessee, and Virginia use procedures similar to Louisiana's). In addition to his other duties, the foreperson of the Louisiana grand jury has the same full voting powers as other grand jury members. As a result, when the Louisiana judge selected the foreperson, he also selected one member of the grand jury outside of the drawing system used to compose the balance of that body. These considerations require us to treat the case as one alleging discriminatory selection of grand jurors.

III

Standing to litigate often turns on imprecise distinctions and requires difficult line-drawing. On occasion, however, we can ascertain standing with relative ease by applying rules established in prior cases. See *Allen v. Wright*, 468 U.S. 737, 751, 104 S.Ct. 3315, 3324–3325, 82 L.Ed.2d 556 (1984). Campbell's equal protection claim is such an instance.

In *Powers v. Ohio*, supra, we found a white defendant had standing to challenge racial discrimination against black persons in the use of peremptory challenges. We determined the defendant himself could raise the equal protection rights of the excluded jurors. Recognizing our general reluctance to permit a litigant to assert the rights of a third party, we found three preconditions had been satisfied: (1) the defendant suffered an "injury in fact"; (2) he had a "close relationship" to the excluded jurors; and (3) there was some hindrance to the excluded jurors asserting their own rights. *Powers, supra*, at 411, 111 S.Ct., at 1370–1371 (citing *Singleton v. Wulff*, 428 U.S. 106, 96 S.Ct. 2868, 49 L.Ed.2d 826 (1976)). We concluded a white defendant suffers a serious injury in fact because discrimination at the voir dire stage " 'casts doubt on the integrity of the judicial process' ... and places the fairness of a criminal proceeding in doubt." 499 U.S., at 411, 111 S.Ct., at 1371. This cloud of doubt deprives the defendant of the certainty that a verdict in his case "is given in accordance with the law by persons who are fair." Id., at 413, 111 S.Ct., at 1372. Second, the excluded juror and criminal defendant have a close relationship: They share a common interest in eliminating discrimination, and the criminal defendant has an incentive to serve as an effective advocate because a victory may result in overturning his conviction. *Id.*, at 413–414, 111 S.Ct., at 1372–1373. Third, given the economic burdens of litigation and the small financial reward available, "a juror dismissed because of race probably will leave the courtroom possessing little incentive to set in motion the arduous process needed to vindicate his own rights." *Id.*, at 415, 111 S.Ct., at 1373. Upon consideration of these factors, we concluded a white defendant had standing to bring an equal protection challenge to racial discrimination against black persons in the petit jury selection process.

Although Campbell challenges discriminatory selection of grand jurors, rather than petit jurors, *Powers'* reasoning applies to this case on the question of standing. Our prior cases have not decided whether a white defendant's own equal protection rights are violated when the composition of his grand jury is tainted by discrimination against black persons. We do not need to address this issue because Campbell seeks to assert the well-established equal protection rights of black persons not to be excluded from grand jury service on the basis of their race. See Tr. 9 (Dec. 2, 1993); see also *Carter v. Jury Comm'n of Greene Cty.*, 396 U.S. 320, 329–330, 90 S.Ct. 518, 523–524, 24 L.Ed.2d 549 (1970) (racial exclusion of prospective grand and petit jurors violates their constitutional rights). Campbell satisfies the three preconditions for third-party standing outlined in *Powers*.

Regardless of his or her skin color, the accused suffers a significant injury in fact when the composition of the grand jury is tainted by racial discrimination. "[D]iscrimination on the basis of race in the selection of members of a grand jury ... strikes at the fundamental values of our judicial system" because the grand jury is a central component of the criminal justice process. *Rose v. Mitchell*, 443 U.S. 545, 556, 99 S.Ct. 2993, 3000, 61 L.Ed.2d 739 (1979). The Fifth

Amendment requires the Federal Government to use a grand jury to initiate a prosecution, and 22 States adopt a similar rule as a matter of state law. See 1 Beale, supra, § 1:2, at 1–3; see also *Hurtado v. California*, 110 U.S. 516, 4 S.Ct. 111, 28 L.Ed. 232 (1884) (Fifth Amendment's grand jury requirement is not binding on the States). The grand jury, like the petit jury, "acts as a vital check against the wrongful exercise of power by the State and its prosecutors." Powers, supra, at 411, 111 S.Ct., at 1371. It controls not only the initial decision to indict, but also significant decisions such as how many counts to charge and whether to charge a greater or lesser offense, including the important decision to charge a capital crime. See *Vasquez v. Hillery*, 474 U.S. 254, 263, 106 S.Ct. 617, 623–624, 88 L.Ed.2d 598 (1986). The integrity of these decisions depends on the integrity of the process used to select the grand jurors. If that process is infected with racial discrimination, doubt is cast over the fairness of all subsequent decisions. See Rose, supra, at 555–556, 99 S.Ct., at 2999–3000 ("Selection of members of a grand jury because they are of one race and not another destroys the appearance of justice and thereby casts doubt on the integrity of the judicial process").

Powers emphasized the harm inflicted when a prosecutor discriminates by striking racial minorities in open court and in front of the entire jury pool. The Court expressed concern that this tactic might encourage the jury to be lawless in its own actions. See 499 U.S., at 412–413, 111 S.Ct., at 1371–1372. The State suggests this sort of harm is not inflicted when a single grand juror is selected based on racial prejudice because the discrimination is invisible to the grand jurors on that panel; it only becomes apparent when a pattern emerges over the course of years. See Brief for Respondent 16. This argument, however, underestimates the seriousness of the allegations. In *Powers*, even if the prosecutor had been motivated by racial prejudice, those responsible for the defendant's fate, the judge and the jury, had shown no actual bias. If, by contrast, the allegations here are true, the impartiality and discretion of the judge himself would be called into question.

The remaining two preconditions to establish third-party standing are satisfied with little trouble. We find no reason why a white defendant would be any less effective as an advocate for excluded grand jurors than for excluded petit jurors. See *Powers, supra*, at 413–414, 111 S.Ct., at 1372–1373. The defendant and the excluded grand juror share a common interest in eradicating discrimination from the grand jury selection process, and the defendant has a vital interest in asserting the excluded juror's rights because his conviction may be overturned as a result. See *Vasquez, supra*, at 264, 106 S.Ct., at 623–624; *Rose,* supra, at 551, 99 S.Ct., at 2997–2998; *Cassell v. Texas*, 339 U.S. 282, 70 S.Ct. 629, 94 L.Ed. 839 (1950). The State contends Campbell's connection to "the excluded class of … jurors … who were not called to serve … for the prior 16 ½ years is tenuous, at best." Brief for Respondent 22. This argument confuses Campbell's underlying claim with the evidence needed to prove it. To assert the rights of those venirepersons who were excluded from serving on the grand jury in his case, Campbell must prove their exclusion was on account of intentional discrimination. He seeks to do so based on past treatment of similarly situated venirepersons in other cases, see *Castaneda v. Partida*, 430 U.S. 482, 494, 97 S.Ct. 1272, 1280, 51 L.Ed.2d 498 (1977), but this does not mean he seeks to assert those venirepersons' rights. As a final matter, excluded grand jurors have the same economic disincentives to assert their own rights as do excluded petit jurors. See *Powers, supra*, at 415, 111 S.Ct., at 1373. We find Campbell, like any other white defendant, has standing to raise an equal protection challenge to discrimination against black persons in the selection of his grand jury.

IV

It is axiomatic that one has standing to litigate his or her own due process rights. We need not explore the nature and extent of a defendant's due process rights when he alleges discriminatory selection of grand jurors, and confine our holding to his standing to raise the issue. Our decision in *Peters v. Kiff* addressed the due process question, although a majority of Justices could not agree on a comprehensive statement of the rule or an appropriate remedy for any violation. See 407 U.S. 493, 504, 92 S.Ct. 2163, 2169, 33 L.Ed.2d 83 (1972) (opinion of Marshall, J.) ("[W]hatever his race, a criminal defendant has standing to challenge the system used to select his grand ... jury, on the ground that it arbitrarily excludes ... members of any race, and thereby denies him due process of law"); id., at 507, 92 S.Ct., at 2170 (White, J., joined by Brennan and Powell, JJ., concurring in judgment) ("[T]he strong statutory policy of [18 U.S.C.] § 243, which reflects the central concern of the Fourteenth Amendment" permits a white defendant to challenge discrimination in grand jury selection). Our more recent decision in *Hobby v. United States* proceeded on the implied assumption that a white defendant had standing to raise a due process objection to discriminatory appointment of a federal grand jury foreperson and skipped ahead to the question whether a remedy was available. 468 U.S., at 350, 104 S.Ct., at 3099. It is unnecessary here to discuss the nature and full extent of due process protection in the context of grand jury selection. That issue, to the extent it is still open based upon our earlier precedents, should be determined on the merits, assuming a court finds it necessary to reach the point in light of the concomitant equal protection claim. The relevant assumption of *Hobby*, and our holding here, is that a defendant has standing to litigate whether his conviction was procured by means or procedures which contravene due process.

The Louisiana Supreme Court erred in reading *Hobby* to foreclose Campbell's standing to bring a due process challenge. 661 So.2d, at 1324. In *Hobby*, we held discrimination in the selection of a federal grand jury foreperson did not infringe principles of fundamental fairness because the foreperson's duties were "ministerial." See *Hobby, supra*, at 345–346, 104 S.Ct., at 3096–3097. In this case, the Louisiana Supreme Court decided a Louisiana grand jury foreperson's duties were ministerial too, but then couched its decision in terms of Campbell's lack of standing to litigate a due process claim. 661 So.2d, at 1324.

The Louisiana Supreme Court was wrong on both counts. Its interpretation of *Hobby* is inconsistent with the implicit assumption of standing we have just noted and with our explicit reasoning in that case. In *Hobby*, a federal grand jury foreperson was selected from the existing grand jurors, so the decision to pick one grand juror over another, at least arguably, affected the defendant only if the foreperson was given some significant duties that he would not have had as a regular grand juror. See supra, at 1422. Against this background, the Court rejected the defendant's claim because the ministerial role of a federal grand jury foreperson "is not such a vital one that discrimination in the appointment of an individual to that post significantly invades" due process. *Hobby*, supra, at 346, 104 S.Ct., at 3097. Campbell's challenge is different in kind and degree because it implicates the impermissible appointment of a member of the grand jury. See *supra*, at 1422. What concerns Campbell is not the foreperson's performance of his duty to preside, but performance as a grand juror, namely voting to charge Campbell with second-degree murder.

The significance of this distinction was acknowledged by *Hobby*'s discussion of a previous case, *Rose v. Mitchell*, 443 U.S. 545, 99 S.Ct. 2993, 61 L.Ed.2d 739 (1979). In *Rose*, we assumed relief could be granted for a constitutional challenge to discrimination in the appointment of a state grand jury foreperson. See id., at 556, 99 S.Ct., at 3000. Hobby distinguished Rose in part because it involved Tennessee's grand jury system. Under the Tennessee law then in effect, 12 members of the grand jury were selected at random, and then the judge appointed a 13th member who also served as foreperson. See *Hobby*, 468 U.S., at 347, 104 S.Ct., at 3097–3098. As a result, Hobby pointed out discrimination in selection of the foreperson in Tennessee was much more serious than in the federal system because the former can affect the composition of the grand jury whereas the latter cannot: "So long as the grand jury itself is properly constituted, there is no risk that the appointment of any one of its members as foreman will distort the overall composition of the array or otherwise taint the operation of the judicial process." Id., at 348, 104 S.Ct., at 3098. By its own terms, then, *Hobby* does not address a claim like Campbell's.

V

One of the questions raised on certiorari is whether Campbell also has standing to raise a fair-cross-section claim. It appears neither the Louisiana Supreme Court nor the Louisiana Court of Appeal discussed this contention. "With 'very rare exceptions,' ... we will not consider a petitioner's federal claim unless it was either addressed by or properly presented to the state court that rendered the decision we have been asked to review." *Adams v. Robertson*, 520 U.S. 83, 86, 117 S.Ct. 1028, 1029, 137 L.Ed.2d 203 (1997) (per curiam). Campbell has made no effort to meet his burden of showing this issue was properly presented to the Louisiana appellate courts, even after the State pointed out this omission before this Court. See Brief for Respondent 29–30. In fact, Campbell devotes no more than one page of text in his brief to his fair-cross-section claim. See Brief for Petitioner 31–32. We decline to address the issue.

The judgment of the Louisiana Supreme Court is reversed. The case is remanded for further proceedings not inconsistent with this opinion.

It is so ordered.

Note

Did the Court in *Campbell* in essence overrule *Hobby*? *Campbell* is often referred to as a "third-party standing" case. Why would the interest of a defendant not a member of the discriminated-against class be granted status to assert a claim? Whose interest are protected here and why?

What does "race" mean for purposes of determining improper exclusion from grand jury service. Consider the following.

SANCHEZ V. STATE.
147 Tex.Crim. 436 (Tex. Ct. App.1944)

KRUEGER, Judge.

The offense is murder. The punishment assessed is confinement in the state penitentiary for a term of forty years.

Appellant's first contention is that the trial court erred in declining to sustain his motion to quash the indictment based on the ground of alleged race discrimination in the selection of the grand jury which returned the indictment in this case. He alleged that he was of Mexican descent and belonged to the Mexican race; that the jury commissioners, in the selection of grand jurors, deliberately and designedly discriminated against the members of his race in that they intentionally declined to select any Mexicans as members of the grand jury notwithstanding there were numerous American citizens of Mexican or Spanish descent in Hudspeth County qualified to serve as grand jurors; that this practice of intentionally excluding American citizens of Mexican or Spanish descent from grand jury service has existed and continued from the year 1922 up to the present time (1943); that the act of the jury commissioners as aforesaid was a denial of the equal protection of the law guaranteed to him by the Fourteenth amendment to the Constitution of the United States, etc.

The testimony relative to the action of the jury commissioners in selecting the grand jury which returned the indictment against him shows that they did not intentionally or designedly fail or refuse to select any member of Mexican or Spanish descent; that they selected men whom they considered best qualified for grand jury service; that there were a great number of persons of Mexican or Spanish descent in Hudspeth County who were not citizens, quite a number who could not read, write or speak English, and only a few had paid a poll tax; that approximately forty or fifty per cent of the population of Hudspeth County were of Mexican or Spanish descent. There were a few who could read, write and speak English, who had paid a poll tax but some of them were in the Army. The poll tax list for the year 1942 of Precinct No. 1 showed 28 persons of Mexican or Spanish descent, some of whom were women. The list of Precinct No. 2 disclosed the names of 23 persons. Precinct No. 3 showed none, and the same is true of Precinct No. 4. This showed a sum total of 51, some of whom were women.

Article 339, C.C.P., provides as follows:

'No person shall be selected or serve as a grand juror who does not possess the following qualifications:

'1. He must be a citizen of the State, and of the county in which he is to serve, and qualified under the Constitution and laws to vote in said county; but, whenever it shall be made to appear to the court that the requisite number of jurors who have paid their poll taxes can not be found within the county, the court shall not regard the payment of poll taxes as a qualification for service as a juror.

'2. He must be a freeholder within the State, or a householder within the county.

'3. He must be of sound mind and good moral character.

'4. He must be able to read and write.

'5. He must not have been convicted of any felony.

'6. He must not be under indictment or other legal accusation for theft or of any felony.'

These mandatory provisions of the statute, which are not deemed to be unfair, must be observed by the jury commission in the selection of the prospective grand jurors, and unless a person possesses the required qualifications he is not a competent and qualified grand juror.

In filing his motion to quash the indictment, appellant assumed the burden of sustaining his allegations therein by proof. The trial court patiently heard all the testimony relative to the question presented and decided it adversely to the appellant's contention. We do not feel that under the evidence adduced upon the hearing thereof that we would be authorized or justified in setting aside the conclusion reached by the court on the facts as presented by the record.

Appellant's next complaint relates to the trial court's action in overruling his motion for a change of venue. It was alleged in the motion that there existed such prejudice against American citizens of Mexican or Spanish descent that a person of such nationality could not get a fair and impartial trial in Hudspeth County; that he was a member of the Mexican race; and that American citizens of Mexican or Spanish descent are not called to serve as grand and petit jurors; that no person of Mexican or Spanish descent had been called to serve as jurors for a period of more than six years. It will be noted that there is no allegation in the application that there were citizens of Mexican or Spanish descent who were qualified under the law to serve either as grand or petit jurors. However, the allegation of the existence of prejudice is sufficient, if supported by proof, to have authorized a change of venue. The evidence relative to this issue was pro and con. Three witnesses testified for the appellant that there existed in Hudspeth County prejudice against the appellant; that by some members of the jury panel the defendant could get a fair and impartial trial but that by others he could not; that they heard the case discussed and that the discussion had not all been on one side; that part of them had been favorable to the defendant and part had been unfavorable to him. Two witnesses for the State testified that in their opinion there was no such prejudice existing against American citizens of Mexican or Spanish descent as to prevent appellant from getting a fair and impartial trial; that in their opinion he could get such a trial in Hudspeth County. The bill relating to this matter is qualified by the trial court who states that in the selection of the jury appellant only exhausted ten of his fifteen peremptory challenges.

It will thus be noted that the testimony adduced on the motion presented conflicting theories. It is the rule in this state that if conflicting theories as to prejudice arise from the evidence, the trial court has the discretion of adopting either theory, it being his duty to weigh the evidence. A judgment denying the application will not be disturbed unless it be made to appear that the trial court abused his discretion with respect thereto. See *Davis v. State*, 120 Tex.Cr.R. 114, 28 S.W.2d 794; *Willis v. State*, 128 Tex.Cr.R. 504, 81 S.W.2d 693; Garza v. State, 135 Tex.Cr.R. 138, 117 S.W.2d 429. We are unable to reach the conclusion that the record reflects an abuse of discretion on the part of the trial court. We therefore overrule his contention.

Appellant next complains of the court's action in declining to peremptorily instruct the jury to acquit him on the ground that the evidence showed that appellant acted in defense of himself and his father. We are unable to agree with him. The evidence introduced by the State, briefly stated, shows that Mariano Sanchez, the father of appellant, was employed by Bill Hargrove as a farm hand and appellant was also in the employ of Hargrove. On Sunday afternoon Hargrove drove out to his farm and learned that the father of appellant was not there to go to irrigating the crop. Hargrove drove to the town of Acala and saw Mariano leaning against the wall of a store. He approached Mariano and said to him: 'Come on, and let's go to work.' Mariano replied that he did not want to work. Hargrove then got out of his car and slapped him. At this juncture appellant stepped in between his father and Hargrove and asked Hargrove not to hit his father any more. Hargrove complied with the request of appellant and advised him to take his father home as he was drunk and get him away from town. Hargrove then returned to his automobile, and as he was in the act of driving away, the deceased (George A. Cox) came from a cafe and inquired of Hargrove if he needed any help. While this conversation was going on, Mariano walked back and forth with an empty beer bottle in his hand, and when he reached a point near the automobile the deceased struck Mariano and knocked him down. Thereupon appellant struck deceased with a knife. The deceased, in turn, struck appellant and knocked him down with his fist. Appellant immediately arose and stabbed the deceased again. At this juncture, other parties interfered, and the deceased returned to the cafe, where he fell to the floor and died about the time they arrived with him at the hospital. Some of the State's witnesses described the knife used by appellant as a dirk with a blade about five or six inches in length, with a sharp double edge.

Appellant's evidence does not materially differ from that of the State except that the knife which he used had a blade of about two inches long with a little chain at one end thereof. He testified that he stabbed the deceased in his own self-defense and in the defense of his father, Mariano. He also proved that he was nineteen years of age; that he was practically blind and had been discharged from the military service on the ground of mental deficiency.

It will be noted from the foregoing brief statement of the evidence that it raised an issue of fact as to whether or not appellant immediately resorted to the use of a deadly weapon or an instrument calculated to produce death or serious bodily injury without first resorting to other means at hand to repel the aggression. Article 1224, P.C., provides as follows:

> 'Homicide is justifiable also in the protection of the person or property against any other unlawful and violent attack besides those mentioned, and in such cases all other means must be resorted to for the prevention of the injury, and the killing must take place while the person killed is in the very act of making such unlawful and violent attack, and the person interfering in such case in behalf of the party about to be injured is not justified in killing the aggressor unless the life or person of the injured party is in peril by reason of such attack upon his property.'

It is to be observed that the nature of the assault against which the defense is made, and the means used, as well as the character of the resistance made, are matters to be considered by the jury in determining the grade of the offense, if any, and the extent of the punishment to be meted out. See *Schutz v. State*, 96 Tex.Cr.R. 287, 257 S.W. 880; *Fambro v. State*, 142 Tex.Cr.R. 473, 154 S.W.2d 840; *Hathcock v. State*, 103 Tex.Cr.R. 518, 281 S.W. 859; *Prater v. State*, 142 Tex.Cr.R. 626, 155 S.W.2d 934.

By a bill of exception appellant complains because the court declined to peremptorily instruct the jury to acquit him on the plea of insanity. There is no merit in this contention. It is true that one doctor testified that appellant had the mind of a five-year-old child, but another doctor testified that while he was discharged from army service by reason of mental deficiency, still he did know the right from the wrong, etc. Under such state of facts it was entirely a question for the jury to determine.

There are two bills of exception in the record complaining of certain remarks by the District Attorney in his argument to the jury. These bills are deficient in that they fail to show that such argument was not provoked or invited by appellant's counsel. See *Richardson v. State*, 99 Tex. Cr.R. 514, 270 S.W. 854; *Winslow v. State*, 50 Tex.Cr.R. 465, 98 S.W. 866; *Gonzales v. State*, 88 Tex. Cr.R. 248, 226 S.W. 405; *Fowler v. State*, 89 Tex.Cr.R. 623, 232 S.W. 515; *Clowers v. State*, Tex.Crim. App., 171 S.W.2d 143; and *Fuller v. State*, Tex.Crim.App., 180 S.W.2d 361, not yet reported [in State Reports]. We think, however, that the argument was a reasonable deduction from the evidence.

All other matters complained of have been examined by us and are deemed to be without merit.

From what we have said it follows that the judgment of the trial court should be affirmed, and it is so ordered.

PER CURIAM.

The foregoing opinion of the Commission of Appeals has been examined by the Judges of the Court of Criminal Appeals and approved by the Court.

On Appellant's Motion for Rehearing.

DAVIDSON, Judge.

Appellant, a Mexican, insists that the long, continued, and uninterrupted failure to call members of the Mexican or Spanish nationalities for jury service in Hudspeth County constitutes a denial to him of equal protection under the 14th Amendment to the Federal Constitution, and that we erred in reaching a contrary conclusion. In support of his contention, appellant relies upon *Norris v. State of Alabama*, 294 U.S. 587, 55 S.Ct. 579, 79 L.Ed. 1074; Smith v. State of Texas, 311 U.S. 128, 61 S.Ct. 164, 85 L.Ed. 84; and *Hill v. State of Texas,* 316 U.S. 400, 62 S.Ct. 1159, 86 L.Ed. 1559, and authorities therein cited.

In the case of *Norris v. State of Alabama*, supra, said court announced the rule contended by appellant as being applicable to and controlling members of the Negro race. We have discovered no case wherein that court has applied the same rule to members of different nationalities.

In the absence of a holding by the Supreme Court of the United States that nationality and race bear the same relation, within the meaning of the constitutional provision mentioned, we shall continue to hold that the statute law of this State furnishes the guide for the selection of juries in this State, and that, in the absence of proof showing express discrimination by administrators of the law, a jury so selected in accordance therewith is valid.

We remain convinced of the correctness of our original conclusion, and the appellant's motion for rehearing is overruled.

Note

What is the consequence of racial discrimination in the selection of grand jurors or the foreperson of the grand jury? The United States Supreme Court has traditionally maintained that "[a]n indictment returned by a legally constituted and unbiased grand jury, ... is enough, if valid on its face, to call for trial of the charge on the merits" *Costello v. United States*, 350 U.S 359,409 (1956). Justice Stewart in the following case of *Rose v. Mitchell* 443 U.S. 545 (1979) notes in dissent that "[a]ny possible prejudice to the defendant resulting from an indictment returned by an invalid grand jury thus disappears when a constitutionally valid trial jury later finds him guilty beyond a reasonable doubt" 443 U.S. at 575. Stewart's position has been particularly rejected when it comes to race discrimination as pointed out by the majority below.

VASQUEZ V. HILLERY
474 U.S. 254 (1986)

Justice MARSHALL delivered the opinion of the Court.

The Warden of San Quentin State Prison asks this Court to retire a doctrine of equal protection jurisprudence first announced in 1880. The time has come, he urges, for us to abandon the rule requiring reversal of the conviction of any defendant indicted by a grand jury from which members of his own race were systematically excluded.

I

In 1962, the grand jury of Kings County, California, indicted respondent, Booker T. Hillery, for a brutal murder. Before trial in Superior Court, respondent moved to quash the indictment on the ground that it had been issued by a grand jury from which blacks had been systematically excluded. A hearing on respondent's motion was held by Judge Meredith Wingrove, who was the sole Superior Court Judge in the county and had personally selected all grand juries, including the one that indicted respondent, for the previous seven years. Absolving himself of any discriminatory intent, Judge Wingrove refused to quash the indictment. Respondent was subsequently convicted of first-degree murder.

For the next 16 years, respondent pursued appeals and collateral relief in the state courts, raising at every opportunity his equal protection challenge to the grand jury that indicted him. Less than one month after the California Supreme Court foreclosed his final avenue of state relief in 1978, respondent filed a petition for a writ of habeas corpus in federal court, raising that same challenge. The District Court concluded that respondent had established discrimination in the grand jury, and granted the writ. See *Hillery v. Pulley*, 563 F.Supp. 1228 (ED Cal.1983). The Court of Appeals affirmed, 733 F.2d 644 (CA9 1984), and we granted certiorari,

II

As a threshold matter, we turn to petitioner's contention that respondent has circumvented his obligation to exhaust state remedies before seeking collateral relief in federal court. 28 U.S.C. § 2254(b). The exhaustion issue had its genesis in this case when the Federal District Judge saw a need to "supplement and clarify" the state-court record presented for review. Record, Doc. No. 8, p. 2. Upon authority of 28 U.S.C. § 2254 Rule 7, the judge directed the State to provide more figures "demonstrating what portion of the Black population in Kings County was eligible for grand jury service." Record, Doc. No. 8, p. 3. He also directed the parties to present their views regarding the application of statistical probability analysis to the facts of this case, to assist him in "focus[ing] on the likelihood that chance or accident alone could account for the exclusion of a group from grand jury service." Ibid. Petitioner objects that the submissions made in response to the judge's order "drastically" altered respondent's claim and rendered it unsuitable for federal habeas review without prior consideration by the state courts. Brief for Petitioner 81.

The exhaustion doctrine seeks to afford the state courts a meaningful opportunity to consider allegations of legal error without interference from the federal judiciary. *Rose v. Lundy*, 455 U.S. 509, 515, 102 S.Ct. 1198, 1201, 71 L.Ed.2d 379 (1982). Under standards established by this Court, a state prisoner may initiate a federal habeas petition "[o]nly if the state courts have had the first opportunity to hear the claim sought to be vindicated...." *Picard v. Connor*, 404 U.S. 270, 276, 92 S.Ct. 509, 512, 30 L.Ed.2d 438 (1971). "It follows, of course, that once the federal claim has been fairly presented to the state courts, the exhaustion requirement is satisfied." Id., at 275, 92 S.Ct., at 512; see also *Humphrey v. Cady*, 405 U.S. 504, 516–517, n. 18, 92 S.Ct. 1048, 1055–56 n. 18, 31 L.Ed.2d 394 (1972). We have never held that presentation *258 of additional facts to the district court, pursuant to that court's directions, evades the exhaustion requirement when the prisoner has presented the substance of his claim to the state courts. See Picard, supra, 404 U.S. at 278, 92 S.Ct. at 513.

Rule 7(b) permits a federal district court in a habeas proceeding to expand the existing record to "include, without limitation, ... documents, exhibits, and answers under oath, if so directed, to written interrogatories propounded by the judge. Affidavits may be submitted and considered as a part of the record." In this case, the District Court sought to clarify the relevant facts, an endeavor wholly consistent with Rule 7 and the purpose of the writ. See *Townsend v. Sain*, 372 U.S. 293, 313, 83 S.Ct. 745, 757, 9 L.Ed.2d 770 (1963). The sole question here is whether this valid exercise of the court's power to expand the record had the effect of undermining the policies of the exhaustion requirement.

Several affidavits challenged here as "new" evidence supported respondent's allegations that no black had ever served on the grand jury in Kings County and that qualified blacks in the county were available to serve, which he had pressed in his pretrial motion to quash in Superior Court, App. 28–30, and throughout the state proceedings. The California Supreme Court found that the total absence of blacks from the grand jury in the history of Kings County was an undisputed fact. *People v. Hillery*, 62 Cal.2d 692, 709, 44 Cal.Rptr. 30, 42, 401 P.2d 382, 392 (1965), cert. denied, 386 U.S. 938 (1967). That fact was entitled, therefore, to a presumption of correctness on federal review. *Sumner v. Mata*, 449 U.S. 539, 545–546, 101 S.Ct. 764, 768, 66 L.Ed.2d 722 (1981); see *Hillery v. Pulley*, 533 F.Supp. 1189, 1201, n. 25 (ED Cal.1982). The California Supreme Court also discussed Judge Wingrove's consideration of blacks' qualifications, and found that blacks had served as petit jurors, 62 Cal.2d, at 710, 44 Cal.Rptr., at 42–43, 401 P.2d, at 392–393, minimum eligibility requirements for which were substantially the same as for grand jurors, see 563 F.Supp., at 1245; Mar, The California Grand Jury: Vestige of Aristocracy, 1 Pac.L.J. 36, 40 1970). Consequently, the additional affidavits introduced no claim upon which the state courts had not passed.

The remaining "new" evidence under attack, a computer analysis submitted in response to the District Court's request, assessed the mathematical probability that chance or accident could have accounted for the exclusion of blacks from the Kings County grand jury over the years at issue. Petitioner would have us conclude that the "sophisticated computer techniques" rendered respondent's claim a "wholly different animal." Brief for Petitioner 80–81. These statistical estimates, however, added nothing to the case that this Court has not considered intrinsic to the consideration of any grand jury discrimination claim. As early as 1942, this Court rejected a contention that absence of blacks on the grand jury was insufficient to support an inference of discrimination, summarily asserting that "chance or accident could hardly have accounted for the continuous omission of negroes from the grand jury lists for so long a period as sixteen years or more." *Hill v. Texas*, 316 U.S. 400, 404, 62 S.Ct. 1159, 1161, 86 L.Ed. 1559 (1942). This proposition, which the Court derived solely on the basis of judicial intuition, is precisely what respondent sought to establish by methods now considered somewhat more reliable.

More recently, in reviewing a habeas corpus proceeding, this Court independently applied general statistical principles to the evidence on the record in order to assess the role of chance in the exclusion of Mexican-Americans from a grand jury in Texas. *Castaneda v. Partida*, 430 U.S. 482, 496–497, n. 17, 97 S.Ct. 1272, 1281 n. 17, 51 L.Ed.2d 498 (1977). Form would indeed triumph over substance were we to allow the question of exhaustion to turn on whether a federal judge has relied on educated conjecture or has sought out a more sophisticated interpretative aid to accomplish the same objective.

We emphasize that the District Court's request for further information was evidently motivated by a responsible concern that it provide the meaningful federal review of constitutional claims that the writ of habeas corpus has contemplated throughout its history. 533 F.Supp., at 1202–1203; see *Townsend v. Sain, supra,* 372 U.S., at 311–312, 83 S.Ct., at 756. Respondent had initially submitted only the evidence that had been considered in state court, and subsequently complied with the court's request by furnishing materials no broader than necessary to meet the needs of the court. Accordingly, the circumstances present no occasion for the Court to consider a case in which the prisoner has attempted to expedite federal review by deliberately withholding essential facts from the state courts. We hold merely that the supplemental evidence presented by respondent did not fundamentally alter the legal claim already considered by the state courts, and, therefore, did not require that respondent be remitted to state court for consideration of that evidence.

III

On the merits, petitioner urges this Court to find that discrimination in the grand jury amounted to harmless error in this case, claiming that the evidence against respondent was overwhelming and that discrimination no longer infects the selection of grand juries in Kings County. Respondent's conviction after a fair trial, we are told, purged any taint attributable to the indictment process. Our acceptance of this theory would require abandonment of more than a century of consistent precedent.

In 1880, this Court reversed a state conviction on the ground that the indictment charging the offense had been issued by a grand jury from which blacks had been excluded. We reasoned that deliberate exclusion of blacks "is practically a brand upon them, affixed by the law, an assertion of their inferiority, and a stimulant to that race prejudice which is an impediment to securing to individuals of the race that equal justice which the law aims to secure to all others." *Strauder v. West Virginia,* 10 Otto 303, 308, 100 U.S. 303, 308, 25 L.Ed. 664 (1880).

Thereafter, the Court has repeatedly rejected all arguments that a conviction may stand despite racial discrimination in the selection of the grand jury. See, e.g., *Neal v. Delaware,* 13 Otto 370, 396, 103 U.S. 370, 396, 26 L.Ed. 567 (1881); *Bush v. Kentucky,* 17 Otto 110, 107 U.S. 110, 1 S.Ct. 625, 27 L.Ed. 354 (1883); *Gibson v. Mississippi,* 162 U.S. 565, 16 S.Ct. 904, 40 L.Ed. 1075 (1896); *Carter v. Texas,* 177 U.S. 442, 20 S.Ct. 687, 44 L.Ed. 839 (1900); *Rogers v. Alabama,* 192 U.S. 226, 24 S.Ct.

257, 48 L.Ed. 417 (1904); *Pierre v. Louisiana*, 306 U.S. 354, 59 S.Ct. 536, 83 L.Ed. 757 (1939); *Smith v. Texas*, 311 U.S. 128, 61 S.Ct. 164, 85 L.Ed. 84 (1940); *Hill v. Texas*, supra; *Cassell v. Texas*, 339 U.S. 282, 70 S.Ct. 629, 94 L.Ed. 839 (1950); *Reece v. Georgia*, 350 U.S. 85, 76 S.Ct. 167, 100 L.Ed. 77 (1955); *Eubanks v. Louisiana*, 356 U.S. 584, 78 S.Ct. 970, 2 L.Ed.2d 991 (1958); *Arnold v. North Carolina*, 376 U.S. 773, 84 S.Ct. 1032, 12 L.Ed.2d 77 (1964); *Alexander v. Louisiana*, 405 U.S. 625, 92 S.Ct. 1221, 31 L.Ed.2d 536 (1972). Only six years ago, the Court explicitly addressed the question whether this unbroken line of case law should be reconsidered in favor of a harmless-error standard, and determined that it should not. *Rose v. Mitchell*, 443 U.S. 545, 99 S.Ct. 2993, 61 L.Ed.2d 739 (1979).[4] We reaffirmed our conviction that discrimination on the basis of race in the selection of grand jurors "strikes at the fundamental values of our judicial system and our society as a whole," and that the criminal defendant's right to equal protection of the laws has been denied when he is indicted by a grand jury from which members of a racial group purposefully have been excluded. Id., at 556, 99 S.Ct. at 3000.

Petitioner argues here that requiring a State to retry a defendant, sometimes years later, imposes on it an unduly harsh penalty for a constitutional defect bearing no relation to the fundamental fairness of the trial. Yet intentional discrimination in the selection of grand jurors is a grave constitutional trespass, possible only under color of state authority, and wholly within the power of the State to prevent. Thus, the remedy we have embraced for over a century—the only effective remedy for this violation[5] —is not disproportionate to the evil that it seeks to deter. If grand jury discrimination becomes a thing of the past, no conviction will ever again be lost on account of it.

Nor are we persuaded that discrimination in the grand jury has no effect on the fairness of the criminal trials that result from that grand jury's actions. The grand jury does not determine only that probable cause exists to believe that a defendant committed a crime, or that it does not. In the hands of the grand jury lies the power to charge a greater offense or a lesser offense; numerous counts or a single count; and perhaps most significant of all, a capital offense or a noncapital offense—all on the basis of the same facts. Moreover, "[t]he grand jury is not bound to indict in every case where a conviction can be obtained." *United States v. Ciambrone*, 601 F.2d 616, 629 (CA2 1979) (Friendly, J., dissenting). Thus, even if a grand jury's determination of probable cause is confirmed in hindsight by a conviction on the indicted offense, that confirmation in no way suggests that the discrimination did not impermissibly infect the framing of the indictment and, consequently, the nature or very existence of the proceedings to come.

When constitutional error calls into question the objectivity of those charged with bringing a defendant to judgment, a reviewing court can neither indulge a presumption of regularity nor evaluate the resulting harm. Accordingly, when the trial judge is discovered to have had some basis for rendering a biased judgment, his actual motivations are hidden from review, and we must presume that the process was impaired. See *Tumey v. Ohio*, 273 U.S. 510, 535, 47 S.Ct. 437, 445, 71 L.Ed. 749 (1927) (reversal required when judge has financial interest in conviction, despite lack of indication that bias influenced decisions). Similarly, when a petit jury has been selected upon improper criteria or has been exposed to prejudicial publicity, we have required reversal of the conviction because the effect of the violation cannot be ascertained. See *Davis v. Georgia*, 429 U.S. 122, 97 S.Ct. 399, 50 L.Ed.2d 339 (1976) (per curiam); *Sheppard v. Maxwell*, 384 U.S. 333, 351–352, 86 S.Ct. 1507, 1516, 16 L.Ed.2d 600 (1966). Like these fundamental flaws, which never have been thought harmless, discrimination in the grand jury undermines the structural integrity of the criminal tribunal itself, and is not amenable to harmless-error review.

Just as a conviction is void under the Equal Protection Clause if the prosecutor deliberately charged the defendant on account of his race, see *United States v. Batchelder*, 442 U.S. 114, 125, and n. 9, 99 S.Ct. 2198, 2205, n. 9, 60 L.Ed.2d 755 (1979), a conviction cannot be understood to cure the taint attributable to a charging body selected on the basis of race. Once having found discrimination in the selection of a grand jury, we simply cannot know that the need to indict would have been assessed in the same way by a grand jury properly constituted. The overriding imperative to eliminate this systemic flaw in the charging process, as well as the difficulty of assessing its effect on any given defendant, requires our continued adherence to a rule of mandatory reversal.

The opinion of the Court in Mitchell ably presented other justifications, based on the necessity for vindicating Fourteenth Amendment rights, supporting a policy of automatic reversal in cases of grand jury discrimination. That analysis persuasively demonstrated that the justifications retain their validity in modern times, for "114 years after the close of the War Between the States and nearly 100 years after Strauder, racial and other forms of discrimination still remain a fact of life, in the administration of justice as in our society as a whole." 443 U.S., at 558–559, 99 S.Ct. at 3001. The six years since Mitchell have given us no reason to doubt the continuing truth of that observation.

IV

The dissent propounds a theory, not advanced by any party, which would condition the grant of relief upon the passage of time between a conviction and the filing of a petition for federal habeas corpus, depending upon the ability of a State to obtain a second conviction. Sound jurisprudence *265 counsels against our adoption of that approach to habeas corpus claims.

The Habeas Corpus Rules permit a State to move for dismissal of a habeas petition when it "has been prejudiced in its ability to respond to the petition by delay in its filing." 28 U.S.C. § 2254 Rule 9(a). Indeed, petitioner filed such a motion in this case, and it was denied because the District Court found that no prejudicial delay had been caused by respondent. *Hillery v. Sumner*, 496 F.Supp. 632, 637 (ED Cal.1980). Congress has not seen fit, however, to provide the State with an additional defense to habeas corpus petitions based on the difficulties that it will face if forced to retry the defendant. The Judicial Conference Advisory Committee on Criminal Rules has drafted a proposed amendment to Rule 9(a), which would permit dismissal of a habeas corpus petition upon a demonstration that the State has been prejudiced, either in defending against the prisoner's federal claim or in bringing the prisoner to trial again should the federal claim prove meritorious. 52 U.S.L.W. 2145 (1983). That proposal has not been adopted. And, despite many attempts in recent years, Congress has yet to create a statute of limitations for federal habeas corpus actions. See L. Yackle, Post-conviction Remedies § 19 (Supp.1985) (describing relevant bills introduced in past several Congresses). We should not lightly create a new judicial rule, in the guise of constitutional interpretation, to achieve the same end.

V

Today's decision is supported, though not compelled, by the important doctrine of stare decisis, the means by which we ensure that the law will not merely change erratically, but will develop in a principled and intelligible fashion. That doctrine permits society to presume that bedrock principles are founded in the law rather than in the proclivities of individuals, and thereby contributes to the integrity of our constitutional system of government, both in appearance and in fact. While stare decisis is not an inexorable command, the careful observer will discern that any detours from the straight path of stare decisis in our past have occurred for articulable reasons, and only when the Court has felt obliged "to bring its opinions into agreement with experience and with facts newly ascertained." Burnet v. Coronado Oil & Gas Co., 285 U.S. 393, 412, 52 S.Ct. 443, 449, 76 L.Ed. 815 (1932) (Brandeis, J., dissenting).

Our history does not impose any rigid formula to constrain the Court in the disposition of cases. Rather, its lesson is that every successful proponent of overruling precedent has borne the heavy burden of persuading the Court that changes in society or in the law dictate that the values served by stare decisis yield in favor of a greater objective. In the case of grand jury discrimination, we have been offered no reason to believe that any such metamorphosis has rendered the Court's long commitment to a rule of reversal outdated, ill-founded, unworkable, or otherwise legitimately vulnerable to serious reconsideration. On the contrary, the need for such a rule is as compelling today as it was at its inception.

The judgment of the Court of Appeals, accordingly, is affirmed.

Note

In *Rose v. Mitchell,* 443 U.S. 545 (1979), the defendants challenged the indictment by way of a pretrial Plea in Abatement which was treated as a motion to dismiss. In *Vasquez* the defendant moved to quash the indictment prior to trial. Both motions were denied. Most jurisdictions require that challenges to an indictment be raised as a pretrial motion or risk waiver. A typical provision is found in Federal Rules of Criminal Procedure 6 (b) which provides:

Objection to the Grand Jury or to a Grand Juror.

(1) Challenges. Either the government or a defendant may challenge the grand jury on the ground that it was not lawfully drawn, summoned, or selected, and may challenge an individual juror on the ground that the juror is not legally qualified.

(2) Motion to Dismiss an Indictment. A party may move to dismiss the indictment based on an objection to the grand jury or on an individual juror's lack of legal qualification, unless the court has previously ruled on the same objection under Rule 6(b)(1). The motion to dismiss is governed by 28 U.S.C. §1867 (e). The court must not dismiss the indictment on the ground that a grand juror was not legally qualified if the record shows that at least 12 qualified jurors concurred in the indictment.

The Jury Selection and Service Act, 28 U.S.C.A. Sec. 1862, specifically prohibits racial discrimination in the selection of grand jurors:

No citizen shall be excluded from service as a grand or petit juror in the district courts of the United States or in the Court of International Trade on account of race, color, religion, sex, national origin, or economic status.

28 U.S.C.A. 1867 (a) and (b) provide that any objection or motion to dismiss an indictment on the grounds of discrimination must be made within seven days after the defendant or Attorney General of the United States " discovered or could have discovered, by the exercise of diligence," the grounds for the motion.

Florida, like several jurisdiction, require that any challenge to the grand jury composition be made before the jury is impaneled and sworn. West's F.S.A. § 905.05. Because of the short time frame for raising objections based on racial discrimination in the selection of grand jurors, a defendant might have a "particularized need" (See *United States v. Broyles,* 37 F.3d at 1318; *U.S. v. Warren,* 16 F.3d 247, 253 (8th Cir. 1994)) to gain discovery access to the grand jury proceedings, such as the Voir Dire questions used by the judge in screening potential grade jurors.

In establishing an equal protection violation claim regarding racial exclusion from the grand jury, is it enough in order to establish a prima facie case, to show statistical pattern without evidence of intent?

CASTANEDA V. PARTIDA.

430 U.S. 482 (1977)

Mr. Justice BLACKMUN delivered the opinion of the Court.

The sole issue presented in this case is whether the State of Texas, in the person of petitioner, the Sheriff of Hidalgo County, successfully rebutted respondent prisoner's prima facie showing of discrimination against Mexican-Americans in the state grand jury selection process. In his brief, petitioner, in claiming effective rebuttal, asserts:

'This list (of the grand jurors that indicted respondent) indicates that 50 percent of the names appearing thereon were Spanish. The record indicates that 3 of the 5 jury commissioners, 5 of the grand jurors who returned the indictment, 7 of the petit jurors, the judge presiding at the trial, and the Sheriff who served notice on the grand jurors to appear had Spanish surnames.' Brief for Petitioner 6.

I

This Court on prior occasions has considered the workings of the Texas system of grand jury selection. See *Hernandez v. Texas*, 347 U.S. 475, 74 S.Ct. 667, 98 L.Ed. 866 (1954); *Cassell v. Texas*, 339 U.S. 282, 70 S.Ct. 629, 94 L.Ed. 839 (1950); *Akins v. Texas*, 325 U.S. 398, 65 S.Ct. 1276, 89 L.Ed. 1692 (1945); *Hill v. Texas*, 316 U.S. 400, 62 S.Ct. 1159, 86 L.Ed. 1559 (1942); *Smith v. Texas*, 311 U.S. 128, 61 S.Ct. 164, 85 L.Ed. 84 (1940). Texas employs the 'key man' system, which relies on jury commissioners to select prospective grand jurors from the community at large. The procedure begins with the state district judge's appointment of from three to five persons to serve as jury commissioners. Tex.Code Crim.Proc., Art. 19.01 (1966). The commissioners then 'shall select not less than 15 nor more than 20 persons from the citizens of different portions of the county' to compose the list from which the actual grand jury will be drawn. Art. 19.06 (Supp.1976-1977). When at least 12 of the persons on the list appear in court pursuant to summons, the district judge proceeds to 'test their qualifications.' Art. 19.21. The qualifications themselves are set out in Art. 19.08: A grand juror must be a citizen of Texas and of the county, be a qualified voter in the county, be 'of sound mind and good moral character,' be literate, have no prior felony conviction, and be under no pending indictment 'or other legal accusation for theft or of any felony.' Interrogation under oath is the method specified for testing the prospective juror's qualifications. Art. 19.22. The precise questions to be asked are set out in Art. 19.23, which, for the most part, tracks the language of Art. 19.08. After the court finds 12 jurors who meet the statutory qualifications, they are impaneled as the grand jury. Art. 19.26.

II

Respondent, Rodrigo Partida, was indicted in March 1972 by the grand jury of the 92d District Court of Hidalgo County for the crime of burglary of a private residence at night with intent to rape. Hidalgo is one of the border counties of southern Texas. After a trial before a petit jury, respondent was convicted and sentenced to eight years in the custody of the Texas Department of Corrections. He first raised his claim of discrimination in the grand jury selection process on a motion for new trial in the State District Court. In support of his motion, respondent testified about the general existence of discrimination against Mexican-Americans in that area of Texas and introduced statistics from the 1970 census and the Hidalgo County grand jury records. The census figures show that in 1970, the population of Hidalgo County was 181,535. United States Bureau of the Census, 1970 Census of Population, Characteristics of the Population, vol. 1, pt. 45, s 1, Table 119, p. 914. Persons of Spanish language or Spanish surname totaled 143,611. Ibid., and id., Table 129, p. 1092. On the assumption that all the persons of Spanish language or Spanish surname were Mexican-Americans, these figures show that 79.1% of the county's population was Mexican-American.

Respondent's data compiled from the Hidalgo County grand jury records from 1962 to 1972 showed that over that period, the average percentage of Spanish-surnamed grand jurors was 39%. In the 2 ½-year period during which the District Judge who impaneled the jury that indicted respondent was in charge, the average percentage was 45.5%. On the list from which the grand jury that indicted respondent was selected, 50% were Spanish surnamed. The last set of data that respondent introduced, again from the 1970 census, illustrated a number of ways in which Mexican-Americans tend to be underprivileged, including poverty-level incomes, less desirable jobs, substandard housing, and lower levels of education. The State offered no evidence at all either attacking respondent's allegations of discrimination or demonstrating that his statistics were unreliable in any way. The State District Court, nevertheless, denied the motion for a new trial.

On appeal, the Texas Court of Criminal Appeals affirmed the conviction. *Partida v. State*, 506 S.W.2d 209 (1974). Reaching the merits of the claim of grand jury discrimination, the court held that respondent had failed to make out a prima facie case. In the court's view, he should have shown how many of the females who served on the grand juries were Mexican-Americans married to men with Anglo-American surnames, how many Mexican-Americans were excused for reasons of age or health, or other legal reasons, and how many of those listed by the census would not have met the statutory qualifications of citizenship, literacy, sound mind, moral character, and lack of criminal record or accusation. Id., at 210-211. Quite beyond the uncertainties in the statistics, the court found it impossible to believe that discrimination could have been directed against a Mexican-American, in light of the many elective positions held by Mexican-Americans in the county and the substantial representation of Mexican-Americans on recent grand juries. Id., at 211. In essence, the court refused to presume that Mexican-Americans would discriminate against their own kind.

After exhausting his state remedies, respondent filed his petition for habeas corpus in the Federal District Court, alleging a denial of due process and equal protection, quaranteed by the Fourteenth Amendment, because of gross under-representation of Mexican-Americans on the Hidalgo County grand juries. At a hearing at which the state transcript was introduced, petitioner presented the testimony of the state judge who selected the jury commissioners who had compiled the list from which respondent's grand jury was taken. The judge first reviewed the State's grand jury selection process. In selecting the jury commissioners, the judge stated that he tried to appoint a greater number of Mexican-Americans than members of other ethnic groups. He testified that he instructed the commissioners about the qualifications of a grand juror and the exemptions provided by law. The record is silent, however, with regard to instructions dealing with the potential problem of discrimination directed against any identifiable group. The judge admitted that the actual results of the selection process had not produced grand jury lists that were 'representative of the ethnic balance in the community.' App. 84. The jury commissioners themselves, who were the only ones in a position to explain the apparent substantial underrepresentation of Mexican-Americans and to provide information on the actual operation of the selection process, were never called.

On the basis of the evidence before it, the court concluded that respondent had made out a 'bare prima facie case' of invidious discrimination with his proof of 'a long continued disproportion in the composition of the grand juries in Hidalgo County.' 384 F.Supp. 79, 90 (S.D.Tex.1974) (emphasis in original). Based on an examination of the reliability of the statistics offered by respondent, however, despite the lack of evidence in the record justifying such an inquiry, the court stated that the prima facie case was weak. The court believed that the census statistics did not reflect the true situation accurately, because of recent changes in the Hidalgo County area and the court's own impression of the demographic characteristics of the Mexican-American community. On the other hand, the court recognized that the Texas key-man system of grand jury selection was highly subjective, and was 'archaic and inefficient,' id., at 91, and that this was a factor arguing for less tolerance in the percentage differences. On balance, the court's doubts about the reliability of the statistics, coupled with its opinion that Mexican-Americans constituted a 'governing majority' in the county, caused it to conclude that the prima facie case was rebutted. The 'governing majority' theory distinguished respondent's case from all preceding cases involving similar disparities. On the basis of those findings, the court dismissed the petition.

The United States Court of Appeals for the Fifth Circuit reversed. 524 F.2d 481 (1975). It agreed with the District Court that respondent had succeeded in making out a prima facie case. It found, however, that the State had failed to rebut that showing. The 'governing majority' theory contributed little to the State's case in the absence of specific proof to explain the disparity. In light of the State's abdication of its responsibility to introduce controverting evidence, the court held that respondent was entitled to prevail.

We granted certiorari to consider whether the existence of a 'governing majority' in itself can rebut a prima facie case of discrimination in grand jury selection, and, if not, whether the State otherwise met its burden of proof.

III

A. This Court has long recognized that 'it is a denial of the equal protection of the laws to try a defendant of a particular race or color under an indictment issued by a grand jury . . . from which all persons of his race or color have, solely because of that race or color, been excluded by the State . . .'12 Hernandez v. Texas, 347 U.S., at 477, 74 S.Ct., at 670. See *Alexander v. Louisiana*, 405 U.S. 625, 628, 92 S.Ct. 1221, 1224, 31 L.Ed.2d 536 (1972); *Carter v. Jury Comm'n*, 396 U.S. 320, 330, 90 S.Ct. 518, 523, 24 L.Ed.2d 549 (1970). See also *Peters v. Kiff*, 407 U.S. 493, 497, 92 S.Ct. 2163, 2165, 33 L.Ed.2d 83 (1972) (plurality opinion); Id., at 507, 92 S.Ct., at 2170 (dissenting opinion). While the earlier cases involved absolute exclusion of an identifiable group, later cases established the principle that substantial underrepresentation of the group constitutes a constitutional violation as well, if it results from purposeful discrimination. See *Turner v. Fouche*, 396 U.S. 346, 90 S.Ct. 532, 24 L.Ed.2d 567 (1970); *Carter v. Jury Comm'n, supra; Whitus v. Georgia*, 385 U.S. 545, 552, 87 S.Ct. 643, 647, 17 L.Ed.2d 599 (1967); *Swain v. Alabama*, 380 U.S. 202, 85 S.Ct. 824, 13 L.Ed.2d 759 (1965); *Cassell v. Texas*, 339 U.S. 282, 70 S.Ct. 629, 94 L.Ed. 839 (1950). Recent cases have established the fact that an official act is not unconstitutional solely because it has a racially disproportionate impact. *Washington v. Davis*, 426 U.S. 229, 239, 96 S.Ct. 2040, 2047, 48 L.Ed.2d 597 (1976); see *Arlington Heights v. Metropolitan Housing Dev. Corp.*, 429 U.S. 252, 264-265, 97 S.Ct. 555, 563, 50 L.Ed.2d 450 (1977). Nevertheless, as the Court recognized in Arlington Heights, '(s)ometimes a clear pattern, unexplainable on grounds other than race, emerges from the effect of the state action even when the governing legislation appears neutral on its face.' Id., at 266, 97 S.Ct., at 564. In *Washington v. Davis*, the application of these principles to the jury cases was considered:

> 'It is also clear from the cases dealing with racial discrimination in the selection of juries that the systematic exclusion of Negroes is itself such an 'unequal application of the law . . . as to show intentional discrimination.' . . . A prima facie case of discriminatory purpose may be proved as well by the absence of Negroes on a particular jury combined with the failure of the jury commissioners to be informed of eligible Negro jurors in a community, . . . or with racially non-neutral selection procedures . . .. With a prima facie case made out, 'the burden of proof shifts to the State to rebut the presumption of unconstitutional action by showing that permissible racially

neutral selection criteria and procedures have produced the monochromatic result.' *Alexander v. Louisiana*, 405 U.S.,) at 632, 92 S.Ct. 1221.' 426 U.S., at 241, 96 S.Ct., at 2048.

See *Arlington Heights, supra*, at 266 n. 13, 97 S.Ct., at 564.

Thus, in order to show that an equal protection violation has occurred in the context of grand jury selection, the defendant must show that the procedure employed resulted in substantial underrepresentation of his race or of the identifiable group to which he belongs. The first step is to establish that the group is one that is a recognizable, distinct class, singled out for different treatment under the laws, as written or as applied. *Hernandez v. Texas*, 347 U.S., at 478-479, 74 S.Ct., at 670-671. Next, the degree of underrepresentation must be proved, by comparing the proportion of the group in the total population to the proportion called to serve as grand jurors, over a significant period of time. Id., at 480, 74 S.Ct., at 671. See *Norris v. Alabama*, 294 U.S. 587, 55 S.Ct. 579, 79 L.Ed. 1074 (1935). This method of proof, sometimes called the 'rule of exclusion,' has been held to be available as a method of proving discrimination in jury selection against a delineated class. *Hernandez v. Texas*, 347 U.S., at 480, 74 S.Ct., at 671. Finally, as noted above, a selection procedure that is susceptible of abuse or is not racially neutral supports the presumption of discrimination raised by the statistical showing. *Washington v. Davis*, 426 U.S., at 241, 96 S.Ct., at 2048; *Alexander v. Louisiana*, 405 U.S., at 630, 92 S.Ct., at 1225. Once the defendant has shown substantial underrepresentation of his group, he has made out a prima facie case of discriminatory purpose, and the burden then shifts to the State to rebut that case.

B. In this case, it is no longer open to dispute that Mexican-Americans are a clearly identifiable class. See, e. g., *Hernandez v. Texas*, supra. Cf. *White v. Regester*, 412 U.S. 755, 767, 93 S.Ct. 2332, 2340, 37 L.Ed.2d 314 (1973). The statistics introduced by respondent from the 1970 census illustrate disadvantages to which the group has been subject. Additionally, as in Alexander v. Louisiana, the selection procedure is not racially neutral with respect to Mexican-Americans; Spanish surnames are just as easily identifiable as race was from the questionnaires in Alexander or the notations and card colors in *Whitus v. Georgia*, supra, and in *Avery v. Georgia*, 345 U.S. 559, 73 S.Ct. 891, 97 L.Ed. 1244 (1953).

The disparity proved by the 1970 census statistics showed that the population of the county was 79.1% Mexican-American, but that, over an 11-year period, only 39% of the persons summoned for grand jury service were Mexican-American.This difference of 40% is greater than that found significant in *Turner v. Fouche*, 396 U.S. 346, 90 S.Ct. 532, 24 L.Ed.2d 567 (1970) (60% Negroes in the general population, 37% on the grand jury lists). Since the State presented no evidence showing why the 11-year period was not reliable, we take it as the relevant base for comparison.16 The mathematical disparities that have been accepted by this Court as adequate for a prima facie case have all been within the range presented here. For example, in *Whitus v. Georgia*, 385 U.S. 545, 87 S.Ct. 643, 17 L.Ed.2d 599 (1967), the number of Negroes listed on the tax digest amounted to 27.1% of the taxpayers, but only 9.1% of those on the grand jury venire. The disparity was held to be sufficient to make out a prima facie case of discrimination. See *Sims v. Georgia*, 389 U.S. 404, 88 S.Ct. 523, 19 L.Ed.2d 634 (1967) (24.4% of tax lists, 4.7% of grand jury lists); *Jones v. Georgia*, 389 U.S. 24, 88 S.Ct. 4, 19 L.Ed.2d 25 (1967) (19.7% of tax lists, 5% of jury list). We agree with the District Court and the Court of Appeals that the proof in this case was enough to establish a prima facie case of discrimination against the Mexican-Americans in the Hidalgo County grand jury selection.

Supporting this conclusion is the fact that the Texas system of selecting grand jurors is highly subjective. The facial constitutionality of the key-man system, of course, has been accepted by this Court. See, e. g., *Carter v. Jury Comm'n*, 396 U.S. 320, 90 S.Ct. 518, 24 L.Ed.2d 549 (1970); *Akins v. Texas*, 325 U.S. 398, 65 S.Ct. 1276, 89 L.Ed. 1692 (1945); *Smith v. Texas*, 311 U.S. 128, 61 S.Ct. 164, 85 L.Ed. 84 (1940). Nevertheless, the Court has noted that the system is susceptible of abuse as applied. See *Hernandez v. Texas*, 347 U.S., at 479, 74 S.Ct., at 671. Additionally, as noted, persons with Spanish surnames are readily identifiable.

The showing made by respondent therefore shifted the burden of proof to the State to dispel the inference of intentional discrimination. Inexplicably, the State introduced practically no evidence. The testimony of the State District Judge dealt principally with the selection of the jury commissioners and the instructions given to them. The commissioners themselves were not called to testify. A case such as *Swain v. Alabama*, 380 U.S., at 207, n. 4, 209, 85 S.Ct., at 828, 829, illustrates the potential usefulness of such testimony, when it sets out in detail the procedures followed by the commissioners. The opinion of the Texas Court of Criminal Appeals is particularly revealing as to the lack of rebuttal evidence in the record:

> 'How many of those listed in the census figures with Mexican-American names were not citizens of the state, but were so-called 'wet-backs' from the south side of the Rio Grande; how many were migrant workers and not residents of Hidalgo County; how many were illiterate and could not read and write; how many. were not of sound mind and good moral character, how many had been convicted of a felony or were under indictment or legal accusation for theft or a felony; none of these facts appear in the record.' 506 S.W.2d, at 211 (emphasis added).

In fact, the census figures showed that only a small part of the population reported for Hidalgo County was not native born. See n. 6, supra. Without some testimony from the grand jury commissioners about the method by which they determined the other qualifications for grand jurors prior to the statutory time for testing qualifications, it is impossible to draw any inference about literacy, sound mind and moral character, and criminal record from the statistics about the population as a whole. See n. 8, supra. These are questions of disputed fact that present problems not amenable to resolution by an appellate court. We emphasize, however, that we are not saying that the statistical disparities proved here could never be explained in another case; we are simply saying that the State did not do so in this case. See *Turner v. Fouche*, 396 U.S., at 361, 90 S.Ct., at 540.

C. In light of our holding that respondent proved a prima facie case of discrimination that was not rebutted by any of the evidence presently in the record, we have only to consider whether the District Court's 'governing majority' theory filled the evidentiary gap. In our view, it did not dispel the presumption of purposeful discrimination in the circumstances of this case. Because of the many facets of human motivation, it would be unwise to presume as a matter of law that human beings of one definable group will not discriminate against other members of their group. Indeed, even the dissent of Mr. Justice POWELL does not suggest that such a presumption would be appropriate. See Post, at 1290-1291, n. 6, 1291 n. 7. The problem is a complex one, about which widely differing views can be held, and, as such, it would be somewhat precipitate to take judicial notice of one view over another on the basis of a record as barren as this.

Furthermore, the relevance of a governing majority of elected officials to the grand jury selection process is questionable. The fact that certain elected officials are Mexican-American demonstrates nothing about the motivations and methods of the grand jury commissioners who select persons for grand jury lists. The only arguably relevant fact in this record on the issue is that three of the five jury commissioners in respondent's case were Mexican-American. Knowing only this, we would be forced to rely on the reasoning that we have rejected that human beings would not discriminate against their own kind in order to find that the presumption of purposeful discrimination was rebutted. Without the benefit of this simple behavioral presumption, discriminatory intent can be rebutted only with evidence in the record about the way in which the commissioners operated and their reasons for doing so. It was the State's burden to supply such evidence, once respondent established his prima facie case. The State's failure in this regard leaves unchallenged respondent's proof of purposeful discrimination.

Finally, even if a 'governing majority' theory has general applicability in cases of this kind, the inadequacy of the record in this case does not permit such an approach. Among the evidentiary deficiencies are the lack of any indication of how long the Mexican-Americans have enjoyed 'governing majority' status, the absence of information about the relative power inherent in the elective offices held by Mexican-Americans, and the uncertain relevance of the general political power to the specific issue in this case. Even for the most recent time period, when presumably the political power of Mexican-Americans was at its greatest, the discrepancy between the number of Mexican-Americans in the total population and the number on the grand jury lists was substantial. Thus, under the facts presented in this case, the 'governing majority' theory is not developed fully enough to satisfy the State's burden of rebuttal.

IV

Rather than relying on an approach to the jury discrimination question that is as faintly defined as the 'governing majority' theory is on this record, we prefer to look at all the facts that bear on the issue, such as the statistical disparities, the method of selection, and any other relevant testimony as to the manner in which the selection process was implemented. Under this standard, the proof offered by respondent was sufficient to demonstrate a prima facie case of discrimination in grand jury selection. Since the State failed to rebut the presumption of purposeful discrimination by competent testimony, despite two opportunities to do so, we affirm the Court of Appeals' holding of a denial of equal protection of the law in the grand jury selection process in respondent's case.

It is so ordered.

Race and the Selection of the Foreperson of the Grand Jury

ROSE V. MITCHELL
443 U.S. 545 (1979)

Mr. Justice BLACKMUN delivered the opinion of the Court.

In this federal habeas corpus case, respondents claim they were the victims of racial discrimination, in violation of the Equal Protection Clause of the Fourteenth Amendment, in the selection of the foreman of the Tennessee grand jury that indicted them for murders in the first degree. As the case comes to this Court, no issue of discrimination in the selection of the venire is presented; we are concerned only with the selection of the foreman.

I

In November 1972 respondents James E. Mitchell and James Nichols, Jr., and two other men were jointly indicted by the grand jury of Tipton County, Tenn. The four were charged in two counts of first-degree murder in connection with the shooting deaths of patrons during the robbery of a place known as White's Cafe. Prior to trial, respondents filed with the county court a written pro se motion in the nature of a plea in abatement. App. 1. They sought thereby, together with other relief, the dismissal of the indictment on the grounds that the grand jury array, and the foreman, had been selected in a racially discriminatory fashion. Each respondent is a Negro.

The court appointed counsel to represent respondents and in due course conducted an evidentiary hearing on the plea in abatement. At that hearing, testimony on behalf of the respondents was taken from the 3 Tipton County jury commissioners; from 2 former Tipton County grand jury foremen; from the foreman of the grand jury serving at the time respondents were indicted; and from 11 of the 12 other members of that grand jury. The court clerk was a witness on behalf of the State. Id., at 3-35.

At the close of this evidence, the court denied the plea in abatement, first orally, and then by written order, without comment. Id., at 35 and 36.

Respondents were then tried jointly to a jury. A verdict of guilty of first-degree murder on each count was returned. Respondents received sentences of 60 years on each count, the sentences to run consecutively with credit allowed for time spent in jail awaiting trial.

On appeal, the Court of Criminal Appeals of Tennessee affirmed the convictions, finding, with respect to an assignment of error relating to the plea in abatement, that the "facts here do not demonstrate a systematic exclusion of Negroes upon racial grounds." Id., at 38-39. The Supreme Court of Tennessee denied certiorari. Id., at 42.

Respondents each then filed a pro se petition for a writ of habeas corpus in the United States District Court for the Western District of Tennessee, id., at 43-52, 62-73, renewing, among other things, the allegation of discrimination in the selection of the Tipton County grand jury and its foreman. The District Court referred the petitions to a magistrate who, after reviewing the evidence introduced in the state court at the hearing on the plea in abatement and studying the method of selection, recommended that the court hold an evidentiary hearing on the grand jury and jury foreman selection issues. Specifically, the magistrate concluded that respondents had presented an unrebutted prima facie case with respect to the selection of the foreman. Id., at 84, 90, 97. The District Court disagreed with the magistrate as to the grand jury, and concluded that the state judge had ruled correctly on that issue. On the foreman question, the District Court went along with the magistrate, and ordered the State to make further response. Id., at 98. The State then submitted affidavits from the acting foreman of the grand jury that indicted respondents and from the state trial judge who appointed the foreman. Id., at 102-106, 108-113. On the basis of these affidavits, the petitions were ordered dismissed. Id., at 121-122.

The District Judge, however, granted the certificate of probable cause required by Fed.Rule App.Proc. 22(b), App. 126-127, and respondents appealed to the United States Court of Appeals for the Sixth Circuit.

The Court of Appeals reversed. 570 F.2d 129 (1978). That court deemed it unnecessary to resolve respondents' contentions concerning discrimination in the selection of the grand jury venire, id., at 134, since it found sufficient grounds to reverse with respect to the selection of the foreman. It remanded the case with instructions for the entry of an order that respondents' murder convictions be set aside and that respondents be reindicted within 60 days or be released. Id., at 137.

We granted certiorari to consider the foreman issue. 439 U.S. 816, 99 S.Ct. 76, 58 L.Ed.2d 107 (1978).

II

We initially address two arguments that, aside from the specific facts of this particular case, go to the question whether a federal court, as a matter of policy, should hear claims of racial discrimination in the selection of a grand jury when reviewing a state conviction. First, we consider whether claims of grand jury discrimination should be considered harmless error when raised, on direct review or in a habeas corpus proceeding, by a defendant who has been found guilty beyond a reasonable doubt by a properly constituted petit jury at a trial on the merits that was free from other constitutional error. Second, we consider the related question whether such claims should be cognizable any longer on federal habeas corpus in light of the decision in *Stone v. Powell*, 428 U.S. 465, 96 S.Ct. 3037, 49 L.Ed.2d 1067 (1976).

A

For nearly a century, this Court in an unbroken line of cases has held that "a criminal conviction of a Negro cannot stand under the Equal Protection Clause of the Fourteenth Amendment if it is based on an indictment of a grand jury from which Negroes were excluded by reason of their race." *Alexander v. Louisiana*, 405 U.S. 625, 628, 92 S.Ct. 1221, 1224, 31 L.Ed.2d 536 (1972); *Bush v. Kentucky*, 107 U.S. 110, 119, 1 S.Ct. 625, 633, 27 L.Ed. 354 (1883); *Neal v. Delaware*, 103 U.S. 370, 394, 26 L.Ed. 567 (1881). See *Castaneda v. Partida*, 430 U.S. 482, 492-495, and n. 12, 97 S.Ct. 1272, 1278-1281, and n. 12, 51 L.Ed.2d 498 (1977). A criminal defendant "is entitled to require that the State not deliberately and systematically deny to members of his race the right to participate as jurors in the administration of justice." *Alexander v. Louisiana*, 405 U.S., at 628-629, 92 S.Ct., at 1224. Accordingly, where sufficient proof of discrimination in violation of the Fourteenth Amendment has been made out and not rebutted, this Court uniformly has required that the conviction be set aside and the indictment returned by the unconstitutionally constituted grand jury be quashed. E. g., *Hill v. Texas*, 316 U.S. 400, 406, 62 S.Ct. 1159, 1162, 86 L.Ed. 1559 (1942).

Until today, only one Justice among those who have served on this Court in the 100 years since *Strauder v. West Virginia*, 100 U.S. 303, 25 L.Ed. 664 (1880), has departed from this line of decisions. In his dissent in *Cassell v. Texas*, 339 U.S. 282, 298, 70 S.Ct. 629, 637, 94 L.Ed. 839 (1950), Mr. Justice Jackson voiced this lone objection by arguing that federal courts should not set aside criminal convictions solely on the ground that discrimination occurred in the selection of the grand jury, so long as no constitutional impropriety tainted the selection of the petit jury, and guilt was established beyond a reasonable doubt at a trial free from constitutional error. The Cassell dissent noted that discrimination in the selection of the grand jury had nothing to do with the fairness of the trial or the guilt or innocence of the defendant, and that reversals based on such discrimination conflicted "with another principle important to our law, viz., that no conviction should be set aside for errors not affecting substantial rights of the accused." Id., at 299, 70 S.Ct., at 637.

Mr. Justice Jackson could discern no reason to permit this conflict. In the first place, he noted, the convicted defendant suffered no possible prejudice. Unlike the petit jury, the grand jury sat only to determine probable cause to hold the defendant for trial. It did not consider the ultimate issue of guilt or innocence. Once a trial court heard all the evidence and determined it was sufficient to submit the case to the trier of fact, and once that trier determined that the defendant was guilty beyond a reasonable doubt, Mr. Justice Jackson believed that it "hardly lies in the mouth of a defendant . . . to say that his indictment is attributable to prejudice." Id., at 302, 70 S.Ct., at 639. "Under such circumstances," he concluded, "it is frivolous to contend that any grand jury, however constituted, could have done its duty in any way other than to indict." Ibid.

Nor did Mr. Justice Jackson believe the Strauder line of cases to be justified by a need to enforce the rights of those discriminated against to sit on grand juries without regard to their race. He pointed out that Congress had made it a crime to discriminate in this manner, 18 U.S.C. § 243, and that civil remedies at law and equity were available to members of the class discriminated against. Accordingly, Mr. Justice Jackson would have held that "discrimination in selection of the grand jury . . ., however great the wrong toward qualified Negroes of the community, was harmless to this defendant," 339 U.S., at 304, 70 S.Ct., at 640, and would have left enforcement of Fourteenth Amendment interests to criminal prosecutions under § 243 and civil actions instituted by such "qualified Negroes."

This position for the first time has attracted the support of additional Members of the Court, as expressed in the separate opinion of Mr. Justice STEWART in this case. Echoing the Cassell dissent, this separate opinion asserts that "the time has come to acknowledge that Mr. Justice Jackson's [position] is unanswerable, and to hold that a defendant may not rely on a claim of grand jury discrimination to overturn an otherwise valid conviction." Post, at 3010. It argues that the conviction of the defendant should be a break in the chain of events that preceded it, and notes that where Fourth or Fifth Amendment rights are violated, the evidence illegally obtained is suppressed, but "the prosecution is not barred altogether." Post, at 3011 n. 4. The separate opinion believes that any other interests that are harmed by grand jury discrimination may be protected adequately by prosecutions, civil actions, or pretrial remedies available to defendants. In such circumstances, it finds the heavy social cost entailed in a reversal unjustified, especially in light of the fact the defendant himself has suffered no prejudice. Accordingly, the separate opinion would not recognize, either on direct review or on an application for a writ of habeas corpus, a claim of grand jury discrimination as a valid ground for setting aside a criminal conviction.

This Court, of course, consistently has rejected this argument. It has done so implicitly in those cases in which it has reaffirmed the Strauder principle in the context of grand jury discrimination. E. g., *Reece v. Georgia*, 350 U.S. 85, 87, 76 S.Ct. 167, 169, 100 L.Ed. 77 (1955); *Alexander v. Louisiana*, 405 U.S., at 628, 92 S.Ct., at 1224. And it has done so expressly, where the argument was pressed in the guise of the claim that the constitutional rights of the defendant are not violated by grand jury discrimination since an indictment only brings that defendant before the petit jury for trial. *Pierre v. Louisiana*, 306 U.S. 354, 356-358, 59 S.Ct. 536, 537-539, 83 L.Ed. 757 (1939). See *Cassell v. Texas*, 339 U.S., at 290, 70 S.Ct., at 633 (Frankfurter, J., concurring); id., at 296, 70 S.Ct. at 636 (Clark, J., concurring). We decline now to depart from this longstanding consistent practice, and we adhere to the Court's previous decisions.

Discrimination on account of race was the primary evil at which the Amendments adopted after the War Between the States, including the Fourteenth Amendment, were aimed. The Equal Protection Clause was central to the Fourteenth Amendment's prohibition of discriminatory action by the State: it banned most types of purposeful discrimination by the State on the basis of race in an attempt to lift the burdens placed on Negroes by our society. It is clear from the earliest cases applying the Equal Protection Clause in the context of racial discrimination in the selection of a grand jury, that the Court from the first was concerned with the broad aspects of racial discrimination that the Equal Protection Clause was designed to eradicate, and with the fundamental social values the Fourteenth Amendment was adopted to protect, even though it addressed the issue in the context of reviewing an individual criminal conviction. Thus, in the first case establishing the principles that have guided the Court's decisions these 100 years, the Court framed the issue in terms of the larger concerns with racial discrimination in general that it understood as being at the core of the Fourteenth Amendment:

> "The very fact that colored people are singled out and expressly denied by a statute all right to participate in the administration of the law, as jurors, because of their color, though they are citizens, and may be in other respects fully qualified, is practically a brand upon them, affixed by the law, an assertion of their inferiority, and a stimulant to that race prejudice which is an impediment to securing to individuals of the race that equal justice which the law aims to secure to all others. ... [T]he apprehension that through prejudice [such persons] might be denied that equal protection, that is, that there might be discrimination against them, was the inducement to bestow upon the national government the power to enforce the provision that no State shall deny to them the equal protection of the laws." Strauder v. West Virginia, 100 U.S., at 308, 309.

Discrimination on the basis of race, odious in all aspects, is especially pernicious in the administration of justice. Selection of members of a grand jury because they are of one race and not another destroys the appearance of justice and *556 thereby casts doubt on the integrity of the judicial process. The exclusion from grand jury service of Negroes, or any group otherwise qualified to serve, impairs the confidence of the public in the administration of justice. As this Court repeatedly has emphasized, such discrimination "not only violates our Constitution and the laws enacted under it but is at war with our basic concepts of a democratic society and a representative government." *Smith v. Texas*, 311 U.S. 128, 130, 61 S.Ct. 164, 165, 85 L.Ed. 84 (1940) (footnote omitted). The harm is not only to the accused, indicted as he is by a jury from which a segment of the community has been excluded. It is to society as a whole. "The injury is not limited to the defendant-there is injury to the jury system, to the law as an institution, to the community at large, and to the democratic ideal reflected in the processes of our courts." *Ballard v. United States*, 329 U.S. 187, 195, 67 S.Ct. 261, 265, 91 L.Ed. 181 (1946).

Because discrimination on the basis of race in the selection of members of a grand jury thus strikes at the fundamental values of our judicial system and our society as a whole, the Court has recognized that a criminal defendant's right to equal protection of the laws has been denied when he is indicted by a grand jury from which members of a racial group purposefully have been excluded. E. g., *Neal v. Delaware*, 103 U.S., at 394; *Reece v. Georgia*, 350 U.S., at 87, 76 S.Ct., at 169. For this same reason, the Court also has reversed the conviction and ordered the indictment quashed in such cases without inquiry into whether the defendant was prejudiced in fact by the discrimination at the grand jury stage. Since the beginning, the Court has held that where discrimination in violation of the Fourteenth Amendment is proved, " '[t]he court will correct the wrong, will quash the indictment[,] or the panel[;] or, if not, the error will be corrected in a superior court,' and ultimately in this court upon review," and all without regard to prejudice. *Neal v. Delaware*, 103 U.S., at 394, quoting *Virginia v. Rives*, 100 U.S. 313, 322, 25 L.Ed. 667 (1880). See *Bush v. Kentucky*, i 107 U.S., at 119, 1 S.Ct., at 633. The Court in *Hill v. Texas*, 316 U.S., at 406, 62 S.Ct., at 1162, stated:

> "[N]o state is at liberty to impose upon one charged with crime a discrimination in its trial
> procedure which the Constitution, and an Act of Congress passed pursuant to the Constitution,
> alike forbid. Nor is this Court at liberty to grant or withhold the benefits of equal protection,
> which the Constitution commands for all, merely as we may deem the defendant innocent or
> guilty. *Tumey v. Ohio*, 273 U.S. 510, 535, 47 S.Ct. 437, 445, 71 L.Ed. 749, 50 A.L.R. 1243. It is the
> state's function, not ours, to assess the evidence against a defendant. But it is our duty as well as
> the state's to see to it that throughout the procedure for bringing him to justice he shall enjoy
> the protection which the Constitution guarantees. Where, as in this case, timely objection has
> laid bare a discrimination in the selection of grand jurors, the conviction cannot stand, because
> the Constitution prohibits the procedure by which it was obtained. Equal protection of the laws
> is something more than an abstract right. It is a command which the state must respect, the ben-
> efits of which every person may demand. Not the least merit of our constitutional system is that
> its safeguards extend to all-the least deserving as well as the most virtuous."

We do not deny that there are costs associated with this approach. But the remedy here is in many ways less drastic than in situations where other constitutional rights have been violated. In the case of a Fourth or Fifth Amendment violation, the violation often results in the suppression of evidence that is highly probative on the issue of guilt. Here, however, reversal does not render a defendant "immune from prosecution," nor is a subsequent reindictment and reprosecution "barred altogether," as Mr. Justice STEWART's opinion suggests. Post, at 3011 n. 4. "A prisoner whose conviction is reversed by this Court need not go free if he is in fact guilty, for [the State] may indict and try him again by the procedure which conforms to constitutional requirements." Hill v. Texas, 316 U.S., at 406, 62 S.Ct., at 1162. And in that subsequent prosecution, the State remains free to use all the proof it introduced to obtain the conviction in the first trial.

In any event, we believe such costs as do exist are outweighed by the strong policy the Court consistently has recognized of combating racial discrimination in the administration of justice. And regardless of the fact that alternative remedies remain to vindicate the rights of those members of the class denied the chance to serve on grand juries, the fact is that permitting challenges to unconstitutional state action by defendants has been, and is, the main avenue by which Fourteenth Amendment rights are vindicated in this context. Prosecutions under 18 U.S.C. § 243 have been rare, and they are not under the control of the class members and the courts. Civil actions, expensive to maintain and lengthy, have not often been used. And even assuming that some type of pretrial procedure would be open to a defendant, e. g., petitioning for a writ of habeas corpus in federal court, under such a procedure the vindication of federal constitutional rights would turn on a race to obtain a writ before the State could commence the trial.

We think the better view is to leave open the route that over time has been the main one by which Fourteenth Amendment rights in the context of grand jury discrimination have been vindicated. For we also cannot deny that, 114 years after the close of the War Between the States and nearly 100 years after Strauder, racial and other forms of discrimination still remain a fact of life, in the administration of justice as in our society as a whole. Perhaps today that discrimination takes a form more subtle than before. But it is not less real or pernicious. We therefore decline "to reverse a course of decisions of long standing directed against racial discrimination in the administration of justice," Cassell v. Texas, 339 U.S., at 290, 70 S.Ct., at 633 (Frankfurter, J., concurring), and we adhere to our position that discrimination in the selection of the grand jury remains a valid ground for setting aside a criminal conviction.

B

The State makes the additional argument that the decision in Stone v. Powell, 428 U.S. 465, 96 S.Ct. 3037, 49 L.Ed.2d 1067 (1976), should be extended so as to foreclose a grant of federal habeas corpus relief to a state prisoner on the ground of discrimination in the selection of the grand jury. Mr. Justice POWELL, dissenting in *Castaneda v. Partida*, 430 U.S., at 508 n. 1, 97 S.Ct., at 1287 n. 1, joined by THE CHIEF JUSTICE and Mr. Justice REHNQUIST, and at least inferentially by Mr. Justice STEWART, id., at 507, 97 S.Ct., at 1286, specifically observed that a "strong case may be made that claims of grand jury discrimination are not cognizable on federal habeas corpus after Stone v. Powell." In this connection, Mr. Justice POWELL noted that a claim by a convicted prisoner of grand jury discrimination goes only to the "moot determination by the grand jury that there was sufficient cause to proceed to trial [and not to any] flaw in the trial itself." *Id.*, at 508 n. 1, 97 S.Ct., at 1287. He concluded that, as in Stone, "the incremental benefit of extending habeas corpus as a means of correcting unconstitutional grand jury selection procedures might be viewed as 'outweighed by the acknowledged costs to other values vital to a rational system of criminal justice.' " 430 U.S., at 508 n. 1, 97 S.Ct., at 1287 n. 1, quoting Stone, 428 U.S., at 494, 96 S.Ct., at 3052.

The State echoes these arguments. It contends that habeas corpus relief should be granted only where the error alleged in support of that relief affected the determination of guilt. In this case, as in Stone v. Powell, it argues, no error affected the trial on the merits. Moreover, only a relatively minor error, involving the nonvoting foreman of the grand jury and not the entire venire, is at issue. Accordingly, following its interpretation of Stone, the State contends that the benefits derived from extending habeas relief in this case are outweighed by the costs associated with reversing a state conviction entered upon a finding of guilt beyond a reasonable doubt at a trial free from constitutional error.

In *Stone v. Powell*, however, the Court carefully limited the reach of its opinion. It stressed that its decision to limit review was "not concerned with the scope of the habeas corpus statute as authority for litigating constitutional claims generally." 428 U.S., at 495 n. 37, 96 S.Ct., at 3052-3053 (emphasis in original). Rather, the Court made it clear that it was confining its ruling to cases involving the judicially created exclusionary rule, which had minimal utility when applied in a habeas corpus proceeding. "In sum," the Court concluded, it was holding "only that a federal court need not apply the exclusionary rule on habeas review of a Fourth Amendment claim absent a showing that the state prisoner was denied an opportunity for a full and fair litigation of that claim at trial and on direct review." Ibid.

Mindful of this limited reach of Stone, we conclude that a claim of discrimination in the selection of the grand jury differs so fundamentally from application on habeas of the Fourth Amendment exclusionary rule that the reasoning of *Stone v. Powell* should not be extended to foreclose habeas review of such claims in federal court.

In the first place, claims such as those pressed by respondents in this case concern allegations that the trial court itself violated the Fourteenth Amendment in the operation of the grand jury system. In most such cases, as in this one, this same trial court will be the court that initially must decide the merits of such a claim, finding facts and applying the law to those facts. This leads us to doubt that claims that the operation of the grand jury system violates the Fourteenth

Amendment in general will receive the type of full and fair hearing deemed essential to the holding of Stone. See, e. g., 428 U.S., at 494, 495 n. 37, 96 S.Ct., at 3052, 3053 n. 37. In Fourth Amendment cases, courts are called upon to evaluate the actions of the police in seizing evidence, and this Court believed that state courts were as capable of performing this task as federal habeas courts. Id., at 493-494, n. 35, 96 S.Ct., at 3052 n. 35. But claims that the state judiciary itself has purposely violated the Equal Protection Clause are different. There is a need in such cases to ensure that an independent means of obtaining review by a federal court is available on a broader basis than review only by this Court will permit. A federal forum must be available if a full and fair hearing of such claims is to be had.

Beyond this, there are fundamental differences between the claim here at issue and the claim at issue in *Stone v. Powell*. Allegations of grand jury discrimination involve charges that state officials are violating the direct command of the Fourteenth Amendment, and federal statutes passed under that Amendment, that "[n]o State shall . . . deny to any person within its jurisdiction the equal protection of the laws." Since the first days after adoption of the Amendment, the Court has recognized that by its direct operation the Equal Protection Clause forbids the States to discriminate in the selection of members of a grand jury. This contrasts with the situation in Stone, where the Court considered application of "a judicially created remedy rather than a personal constitutional right." 428 U.S., at 495 n. 37, 96 S.Ct., at 3053. Indeed, whereas the Fourteenth Amendment by its terms always has been directly applicable to the States, the Fourth Amendment and its attendant exclusionary rule only recently have been applied fully to the States.

In this context, the federalism concerns that motivated the Court to adopt the rule of Stone v. Powell are not present. Federal courts have granted relief to state prisoners upon proof of the proscribed discrimination for nearly a century. See, e. g., *Virginia v. Rives*, 100 U.S., at 322, 25 L.Ed. 667. The confirmation that habeas corpus remains an appropriate vehicle by which federal courts are to exercise their Fourteenth Amendment responsibilities is not likely further to increase " 'friction between our federal and state systems of justice, [or impair] the maintenance of the constitutional balance upon which the doctrine of federalism is founded.' " *Stone v. Powell*, 428 U.S., at 491 n. 31, 96 S.Ct., at 3051, quoting *Schneckloth v. Bustamonte*, 412 U.S. 218, 259, 93 S.Ct. 2041, 2064, 36 L.Ed.2d 854 (1973) (POWELL, J., concurring).

Further, Stone rested to a large extent on the Court's perception that the exclusionary rule is of minimal value when applied in a federal habeas proceeding. The Court there found that the deterrent value of the exclusionary rule was not enhanced by the possibility that a "conviction obtained in state court and affirmed on direct review might be overturned in collateral proceedings often occurring years after the incarceration of the defendant." 428 U.S., at 493, 96 S.Ct., at 3052. Nor did the Court believe that the "overall educative effect of the exclusionary rule would be appreciably diminished if search-and-seizure claims could not be raised in federal habeas corpus review of state convictions." Ibid. And it could not find any basis to say that federal review would reveal flaws in the search or seizure that had gone undetected at trial or on appeal. Ibid. In these circumstances, the Court concluded that the benefits of applying the Fourth Amendment exclusionary rule on federal habeas did not outweigh the costs associated with it.

None of this reasoning has force here. Federal habeas review is necessary to ensure that constitutional defects in the state judiciary's grand jury selection procedure are not overlooked by the very state judges who operate that system. There is strong reason to believe that federal review would indeed reveal flaws not appreciated by state judges perhaps too close to the day-to-day operation of their system to be able properly to evaluate claims that the system is defective. The educative and deterrent effect of federal review is likely to be great, since the state officials who operate the system, judges or employees of the judiciary, may be expected to take note of a federal court's determination that their procedures are unconstitutional and must be changed.

We note also that Stone rested to an extent on the Court's feeling that state courts were as capable of adjudicating Fourth Amendment claims as were federal courts. But where the allegation is that the state judiciary itself engages in discrimination in violation of the Fourteenth Amendment, there is a need to preserve independent federal habeas review of the allegation that federal rights have been transgressed. As noted above, in this case, the very judge whose conduct respondents challenged decided the validity of that challenge.

It is also true that the concern with judicial integrity, deprecated by the Court in Stone in the context of habeas review of exclusionary rule issues, is of much greater concern in grand jury discrimination cases. The claim that the court has discriminated on the basis of race in a given case brings the integrity of the judicial system into direct question. The force of this justification for extending federal habeas review cannot be said to be minimal where allegations of improper judicial conduct are made.

As pointed out in our discussion of the Cassell dissent, it is tempted to exaggerate the costs associated with quashing an indictment returned by an improperly constituted grand jury. In fact, the costs associated with quashing an indictment are significantly less than those associated with suppressing evidence. Evidence suppressed under the Fourth Amendment may not be used by the State in any new trial, though it be highly probative on the issue of guilt. In contrast, after a federal court quashes an indictment, the State remains free to use at a second trial any and all evidence it employed at the first proceeding. A prisoner who is guilty in fact is less likely to go free, therefore, than in cases involving the exclusionary rule. *Hill v. Texas*, 316 U.S., at 406, 62 S.Ct., at 1162. Providing federal habeas corpus relief is, as a consequence, less of an intrusion on the State's system of criminal justice than was the case in Stone.

Finally, we note that the constitutional interests that a federal court adjudicating a claim on habeas of grand jury discrimination seeks to vindicate are substantially more compelling than those at issue in Stone. As noted above, discrimination on account of race in the administration of justice strikes at the core concerns of the Fourteenth Amendment and at fundamental values of our society and our legal system. Where discrimination that is "at war with our basic concepts of a democratic society and a representative government," *Smith v. Texas*, 311 U.S., at 130, 61 S.Ct., at 165, infects the legal system, the strong interest in making available federal habeas corpus relief outweighs the costs associated with such relief.

We therefore decline to extend the rationale of *Stone v. Powell* to a claim of discrimination in the selection of the grand jury that indicts the habeas petitioner. And we hold that federal habeas corpus relief remains available to provide a federal forum for such claims.

III

Notwithstanding these holdings that claims of discrimination in the selection of members of the grand jury are cognizable *565 on federal habeas corpus, and will support issuance of a writ setting aside a state conviction and ordering the indictment quashed, it remains true that to be entitled to habeas relief the present respondents were required to prove discrimination under the standards set out in this Court's cases. That is, "in order to show that an equal protection violation has occurred in the context of grand jury [foreman] selection, the defendant must show that the procedure employed resulted in substantial underrepresentation of his race or of the identifiable group to which he belongs." *Castaneda v. Partida*, 430 U.S., at 494, 97 S.Ct., at 1280. Specifically, respondents were required to prove their prima facie case with regard to the foreman as follows:

> "The first step is to establish that the group is one that is a recognizable, distinct class, singled out for different treatment under the laws, as written or as applied. . . . Next, the degree of underrepresentation must be proved, by comparing the proportion of the group in the total population to the proportion called to serve as [foreman], over a significant period of time. . . . This method of proof, sometimes called the 'rule of exclusion,' has been held to be available as a method of proving discrimination in jury selection against a delineated class. . . . Finally . . . a selection procedure that is susceptible of abuse or is not racially neutral supports the presumption of discrimination raised by the statistical showing." Ibid.

Only if respondents established a prima facie case of discrimination in the selection of the foreman in accord with this approach, did the burden shift to the State to rebut that prima facie case. Id., at 495, 97 S.Ct., at 1280.

There is no question, of course, that respondents, as Negroes, are members of a group recognizable as a distinct class capable of being singled out for different treatment under the laws. Id., at 494, 97 S.Ct., at 1280; *566 *Hernandez v. Texas*, 347 U.S. 475, 478-479, 74 S.Ct. 667, 670-671,

98 L.Ed. 866 (1954). And one may assume for purposes of this case that the Tennessee method of selecting a grand jury foreman is susceptible of abuse. Accordingly, we turn to a consideration of the evidence offered by respondents in their attempt to prove sufficient underrepresentation to make out a prima facie case.

Respondents' case at the hearing on the plea in abatement consisted in its entirety of the following:

Respondents first called as witnesses the three Tipton County jury commissioners. These commissioners, all white, testified only as to the selection of the grand jury venire. In view of the Tennessee method of foreman selection, n. 2, supra, they did not testify, and could hardly be expected to have testified, as to the method of selection of foremen; neither did any of them refer to the race of any past foremen.

Respondents next called two former foremen and the current foreman of the Tipton County grand jury. The first, Frank McBride, testified that he was a lifelong resident of the county, but there was no evidence as to his age and thus as to the years he lived in the county. McBride stated that he had served as foreman, "ten or twelve years ago . . . for five or six years . . . and then about two or three times since then, just for one session of Court." App. 17. In answer to respondents' inquiry whether he had "ever known of any foreman that was a black man," McBride said "No, sir." Id., at 18. The second past foreman, Peyton J. Smith, stated that he had resided in Tipton County all his life but, again, no inquiry was made to as to how long that had been. Smith testified that he had served as foreman "for several years back in the early '50's, and . . . several times since then on occasion of the illness of the foreman at that time." Id., at 20. Like McBride, Smith answered "No" when asked whether he had ever known of a Negro foreman. Ibid. Jimmy Neifeh, the current foreman, testified that he had served for approximately two years and that he did not know "if there was or if there wasn't" ever a Negro foreman of the county grand jury. Id., at 25. No inquiry was made of Naifeh as to **3006 the length of time he had lived in the county.

Respondents then called 11 of the 12 grand jurors10 (other than the foreman) who were serving when respondents were indicted. Not one testified relative to the selection of the foreman or the race of past foremen. Their testimony, individually and collectively, was to the effect that one among their number was a Negro; that they had heard only one witness, a deputy sheriff, on respondents' case; that no one voiced any prejudice or hostility toward respondents because of their race; and that there was no consideration of the fact that respondents were Negroes. Indeed, when some were asked whether they knew whether respondents were Negroes, they answered in the negative. Id., at 26-32.

This was all the evidence respondents presented in support of their case. In rebuttal, the State called only the clerk of the trial court. He was asked no question relating to grand jury foremen, and respondents made no inquiry of him on cross-examination on that or on any other topic. Id., at 34-35.

Two additional facts were stressed by the State at the later federal habeas proceeding. The first was the recruitment, at the 1972 term, of temporary (and former) foreman Smith in place of regular foreman Naifeh. Smith had testified at the hearing on the plea in abatement that Naifeh "could not be here and I was asked to come and appear before this Court and the judge asked me to serve." Id., at 21. The State argued that Smith had been selected only because the judge believed Smith, in view of his experience, would be a capable temporary replacement for the regular foreman. This proper motive, the State said, negated any claim that racial discrimination played a role in the selection of Smith to be temporary foreman. The second fact was that the temporary foreman did not vote on the indictment returned against respondents, see id., at 105; this was because the other 12 had all voted to indict and the temporary foreman's vote therefore was unnecessary. Thus, the State argued, any possible error in the selection of the foreman was harmless and of no consequence to respondents.

In support of its argument to the federal habeas court, the State submitted the affidavit of the judge who had selected the temporary foreman and the permanent foreman, and who had presided at the hearing on the plea in abatement as well as at respondents' trial. The judge, who had served since 1966, id., at 5, a period of seven years, stated that Naifeh "was unable to serve because he was going to be out of the County at the November 1972 term." Id., at 112. The judge went on to say that he had appointed Smith temporary foreman because Smith had had experience "and does a good job as such foreman." The affidavit concluded:

> "In my five counties, I do not have a black grand jury foreman, although I have a black member of my Jury Commission in one county. Most all of my Grand Juries and Petit Juries have sizeable numbers of blacks on them, both men and women. I don't appoint Grand Jury Foreman very often because when their two year term expires, I usually reappoint them, thus they serve a long time and the problem doesn't come up very often. I don't think that I have really given any thought to appointing a black foreman but I have no feeling against doing so." Id., at 113.

It was on the basis of this material in rebuttal that the District Court declined to issue the writs of habeas corpus. It found that no racial discrimination had been proved, since the foreman had been "selected for other than racial reasons, and . . . did not vote at the time the indictment was rendered." Id., at 122.

The Court of Appeals, in reversing, conceded: "The facts elicited at the pretrial hearing were meager." 570 F.2d, at 132. It went on, however, to note: "There has never been a black foreman or forewoman of a grand jury in Tipton County according to the recollections of the trial judge, three jury commissioners, and three former foremen." Id., at 134-135. This fact, the court concluded, coupled with the opportunity for discrimination found to be inherent in the selection system, was sufficient to make out a prima facie case of discrimination in the selection of the foreman. And the Court of Appeals held that the State had failed to rebut that case. The exculpatory affidavit of the judge asserting a benign reason for the selection of the foreman, in the court's view, could not serve to rebut respondents' case in the absence of proof that there were no qualified Negroes to serve as foreman. The fact the foreman did not vote, the court held, similarly did not support the District Court's judgment, since the broad powers exercised by the foreman in conducting the grand jury's proceedings meant that respondents could have been prejudiced even though the foreman had not cast a vote against them.

IV

In reaching our conclusion in disagreement with the Court of Appeals, we note first that that court seems to have overemphasized and exaggerated the evidence in support of its conclusion that there had "never been a black foreman or forewoman of a grand jury in Tipton County." The Court of Appeals believed this conclusion had been proved by the recollections of the trial judge, the testimony of three jury commissioners, and the testimony of three former foremen. *Ibid.* But recollections of the trial judge-by which the Court of Appeals presumably meant the affidavit filed in Federal District Court by the trial judge-formed no part of the case put on by respondents. (Indeed, the Court of Appeals seems to have recognized this in another portion of its opinion, where it considered the state trial judge's affidavit to have been offered in rebuttal of the respondents' asserted prima facie case.) And the jury commissioners gave no testimony whatsoever relating to foremen of the grand jury, to the method of selecting foremen, or to the race of past foremen. Thus, respondents' prima facie case as to discrimination in the selection of grand jury foremen rested entirely and only on the testimony of the three foremen. On the record of this case, it is that testimony alone upon which respondents' allegations of discrimination must stand or fall.

The testimony of the three foremen, however, did not establish respondents' case. First, it cannot be said that the testimony covered any significant period of time. Smith testified that he served in the early 1950's and occasionally thereafter, but except for the fact that Smith was resident in the county, and for his negative answer to the question whether he had "known of any foreman that has been black," there is nothing in the record to show that Smith knew who had served as foremen in the interim years when he was not serving. Similarly, McBride testified that he had served for 5 or 6 years some 10 or 12 years prior to the 1973 hearing, and on two or three occasions since then, and had not known of any Negro's having acted as foreman of the grand jury, but he gave no indication that he was knowledgeable as to the years not covered by this service. Naifeh's testimony was the weakest from respondents' point of view. He had served as foreman for only two years prior to the hearing, and he did not know one way or the other whether a Negro had served as foreman of the county grand jury. Thus, even assuming that the period 1951-1973 is the significant one for purposes of this case, respondents' evidence covered only portions of that time and left a number of years during that period about which no evidence whatsoever was offered.

Moreover, such evidence as was provided by the testifying foremen was of little force. McBride and Smith simply said "No" in response to the question whether either had ever known of any Negro foreman. Naifeh could give no information on the point. There thus was no positive testimony that no Negro had ever served during the critical period of time; the only testimony was that three foremen who served for parts of that period had no knowledge of any. And there is no indication in the record that Smith, McBride, and Naifeh necessarily would have been aware had a Negro ever served as foreman.

Most important, there was no evidence as to the total number of foremen appointed by the judges in Tipton County during the critical period of time. Absent such evidence, it is difficult to say that the number of Negroes appointed foreman, even if zero, is statistically so significant as to make out a case of discrimination under the "rule of exclusion." The only testimony in the record concerning Negro population of the county was to the effect that it was approximately 30%. App. 11. Given the fact that any foreman was not limited in the number of 2-year terms he could serve, and given the inclination on the part of the judge to reappoint, it is likely that during the period in question only a few persons in actual number served as foremen of the grand jury. If the number was small enough, the disparity between the ratio of Negroes chosen to be foreman to the total number of foremen, and the ratio of Negroes to the total population of the county, might not be "sufficiently large [that] it is unlikely that [this disparity] is due solely to chance or accident." *Castaneda v. Partida*, 430 U.S., at 494, n. 13, 97 S.Ct., at 1280. Inasmuch as there is no evidence in the record of the number of foremen appointed, it is not possible to perform the calculations and comparisons needed to permit a court to conclude that a statistical case of discrimination had been made out, id., at 496-497, n. 17, 97 S.Ct., at 1281-1282, n. 17, and proof under the "rule of exclusion" fails. *Id.*, at 494, n. 13, 97 S.Ct., at 1280, n. 13; see *Hernandez v. Texas*, 347 U.S., at 480, 74 S.Ct., at 671.

Comparison of the proof introduced by respondents in this case with the proof offered by defendants in cases where this Court has found that a prima facie case was made out is most instructive. In *Norris v. Alabama*, 294 U.S. 587, 55 S.Ct. 579, 79 L.Ed. 1074 (1935), for example, the defendant proved his case by witnesses who testified as to the number of Negroes called for jury duty. The evidence in support of the prima facie case was summarized by the Court:

> "It appeared that no negro had served on any grand or petit jury in that county within the
> memory of witnesses who had lived there all their lives. Testimony to that effect was given by
> men whose ages ran from fifty to seventy-six years. Their testimony was uncontradicted. It was
> supported by the testimony of officials. The clerk of the jury commission and the clerk of the
> circuit court had never known of a negro serving on a grand jury in Jackson County. The court

reporter, who had not missed a session in that county in twenty-four years, and two jury commissioners testified to the same effect. One of the latter, who was a member of the commission which made up the jury roll for the grand jury which found the indictment, testified that he had 'never known of a single instance where any negro sat on any grand or petit jury in the entire history of that county.' " Id., at 591, 55 S.Ct., at 581.

See *Castaneda v. Partida*, 430 U.S., at 495-496, 97 S.Ct., at 1280-1281; *Eubanks v. Louisiana*, 356 U.S. 584, 586-587, 78 S.Ct. 970, 972-973, 2 L.Ed.2d 991 (1958); *Reece v. Georgia*, 350 U.S., at 87-88, 76 S.Ct., at 169-170; *Hill v. Texas*, 316 U.S., at 402-404, 62 S.Ct., at 1160-1161.

The comparison of the evidence in Norris and in the other cited cases stands in stark contrast with the evidence in the present case. All that we have here to establish the prima facie case is testimony from two former foremen and from a briefly serving present foreman that they had no knowledge of a Negro's having served. There is no evidence that these foremen were knowledgeable about years other than the ones in which they themselves served. And there is no evidence to fill in the gaps for the years they did not serve. In contrast to Norris, there is no direct assertion that for long periods of time no Negro had ever served, or that officials with access to county records could state that none had ever served. And there is no basis in the record upon which to determine that, even assuming no Negro had ever served as foreman, that fact statistically was so significant as to support an inference that the disparity between the Negroes serving and the Negro population in the county was the result of discrimination in violation of the Fourteenth Amendment.

It thus was error for the District Court to have concluded initially that respondents made out a prima facie case. And it was error, as well, for the Court of Appeals to have reached the same final conclusion. The State, however, under questioning at oral argument, tended to concede that the finding that a prima facie case had been established was correct ("we did not contest that"), Tr. of Oral Arg. 6-7, and did the same in its brief, although there it described the proof as "very questionable." Brief for Petitioner 26.

Normally, a flat concession by the State might be given effect. But the inadequacy of respondents' proof is plain. And the error of the Court of Appeals in exaggerating the extent of that proof is equally plain. We decline to overlook so fundamental a defect in respondents' case.

Accordingly, we hold that, as a matter of law, respondents failed to make out a prima facie case of discrimination in violation of the Equal Protection Clause of the Fourteenth Amendment with regard to the selection of the grand jury foreman. The judgment of the Court of Appeals is therefore reversed, and the case is remanded for further proceedings consistent with this opinion.

It is so ordered.

HOBBY V. UNITED STATES.

468 U.S. 339 (1984)

Opinion

Chief Justice BURGER delivered the opinion of the Court.

We granted certiorari to resolve a conflict among the Circuits as to whether discrimination in the selection of federal grand jury foremen, resulting in the underrepresentation of Negroes and women in that position, requires reversal of the conviction of a white male defendant and dismissal of the indictment against him.

I

Petitioner, a white male, was indicted on one count of conspiring to defraud the United States of funds appropriated under the Comprehensive Employment and Training Act of 1973, 29 U.S.C. § 801 et seq. (CETA), in violation of 18 U.S.C. §§ 371 and 665, and three counts of fraudulently obtaining and misapplying CETA grant funds, in violation of 18 U.S.C. § 665. Prior to trial in the United States District Court for the Eastern District of North Carolina, petitioner moved for dismissal of the indictment against him "due to improper selection of grand jurors." App. 32. In particular, he alleged that the grand jury selection plan "exclude[d] citizens from service ... on account of race, color, economic status and occupation, in violation of ... the Fifth and Sixth Amendments of the United States Constitution." Id., at 33.

At an evidentiary hearing on the motion to dismiss, petitioner introduced the testimony of a statistical social science consultant regarding the characteristics of the persons selected as grand jury foremen or deputy foremen in the Eastern District of North Carolina between 1974 and 1981. The expert witness reported that none of the 15 grand juries empaneled during this 7–year period had had a Negro or female foreman. Of the 15 deputies appointed during this interval, so this expert testified, 3 had been Negroes and 6 had been women. From these data the expert witness concluded that Negroes and women were underrepresented among grand jury foremen and deputy foremen serving in the Eastern District of North Carolina. Rejecting petitioner's claim of discrimination in the selection process, the District Court denied petitioner's motion to dismiss the indictment, and petitioner was convicted after a jury trial.

The United States Court of Appeals for the Fourth Circuit affirmed. 702 F.2d 466 (1983). Reasoning that the foreman of a federal grand jury performs a strictly ministerial function, the Court of Appeals viewed the foreman's impact upon the justice system and the rights of criminal defendants as minimal and incidental at most. In response to petitioner's contention that appointment as foreman may enlarge an individual's capacity to influence the other grand jurors, the Court of Appeals concluded that this likelihood was too vague and speculative to warrant dismissals of indictments and reversals of convictions.

The Court of Appeals recognized that in *Rose v. Mitchell*, 443 U.S. 545, 551–552, n. 4, 99 S.Ct. 2993, 2997–2998, n. 4, 61 L.Ed.2d 739 (1979), this Court assumed without deciding that discrimination in the selection of the foreman of a state grand jury would require that a subsequent conviction be set aside. The Court of Appeals noted, however, that the function of the grand jury foreman in the federal system differs substantially from the role of the grand jury foreman in the states. The court concluded that the rights of defendants are fully protected by assuring that the composition of the federal grand jury as a whole is not the product of discriminatory selection.

We granted certiorari to resolve a conflict among the Circuits on this issue, and we affirm.

II

A

It is well settled, of course, that purposeful discrimination against Negroes or women in the selection of federal grand jury foremen is forbidden by the Fifth Amendment to the Constitution. The question presented here, however, is the narrow one of the appropriate remedy for such a violation. It is only the narrow question of the remedy that we consider. No factual evidence was presented to the District Court on the issue of discrimination; instead, petitioner relied upon inferences to be drawn from the failure to select a woman or Negro as foreman of the grand jury for the seven years studied. As did the Court of Appeals, we proceed on the assumption that discrimination occurred in order to treat the constitutional issue presented by the motion to dismiss.

Invoking the Due Process Clause of the Fifth Amendment, petitioner argues that discrimination in the selection of grand jury foremen requires the reversal of his conviction and dismissal of the indictment against him. In *Peters v. Kiff*, 407 U.S. 493, 92 S.Ct. 2163, 33 L.Ed.2d 83 (1972), the opinion announcing the judgment discussed the due process concerns implicated by racial discrimination in the composition of grand and petit juries as a whole. Emphasizing the defendant's due process right to be fairly tried by a competent and impartial tribunal, see *In re Murchison*, 349 U.S. 133, 136, 75 S.Ct. 623, 625, 99 L.Ed. 942 (1955), the opinion reasoned that unconstitutionally discriminatory jury selection procedures create the appearance of institutional bias, because they "cast doubt on the integrity of the whole judicial process." 407 U.S., at 502, 92 S.Ct., at 2168. Moreover, the opinion perceived an important societal value in assuring diversity of representation on grand and petit juries:

"When any large and identifiable segment of the community is excluded from jury service, the effect is to remove from the jury room qualities of human nature and varieties of human experience, the range of which is unknown and perhaps unknowable. It is not necessary to assume that the excluded group will consistently vote as a class in order to conclude, as we do, that its exclusion deprives the jury of a perspective on human events that may have unsuspected importance in any case that may be presented." Id., at 503–504, 92 S.Ct., at 2168–2169 (footnote omitted).

Discrimination in the selection of grand jury foremen—as distinguished from discrimination in the selection of the grand jury itself—does not in any sense threaten the interests of the defendant protected by the Due Process Clause. Unlike the grand jury itself, the office of grand jury foreman is not a creature of the Constitution; instead, the post of foreman was originally instituted by statute for the convenience of the court. See 28 U.S.C. § 420 (1934 ed.); Rev.Stat. § 809 (1878). Today, authority for the appointment of a grand jury foreman is found in Federal Rule of Criminal Procedure 6(c), which provides:

"The court shall appoint one of the jurors to be foreman and another to be deputy foreman. The foreman shall have power to administer oaths and affirmations and shall sign all indictments. He or another juror designated by him shall keep a record of the number of jurors concurring in the finding of every indictment and shall file the record with the clerk of the court, but the record shall not be made public except on order of the court. During the absence of the foreman, the deputy foreman shall act as foreman."

Rule 6(c) has somewhat ancient roots, cast as it is in what are now obsolete terms: foreman and deputy foreman. Centuries of usage, relating back to a day when women did not serve on juries, have embedded such terms in the law as in our daily vocabulary. However, it is not for us to amend the Rule outside the processes fixed by Congress for rulemaking; that is a task for the appropriate committees and the Judicial Conference of the United States.

As Rule 6(c) illustrates, the responsibilities of a federal grand jury foreman are essentially clerical in nature: administering oaths, maintaining records, and signing indictments. The secrecy imperative in grand jury proceedings demands that someone "mind the store," just as a secretary or clerk would keep records of other sorts of proceedings. But the ministerial trappings of the post carry with them no special powers or duties that meaningfully affect the rights of persons that the grand jury charges with a crime, beyond those possessed by every member of that body. The foreman has no authority apart from that of the grand jury as a whole to act in a manner that determines or influences whether an individual is to be prosecuted. Even the foreman's duty to sign the indictment is a formality, for the absence of the foreman's signature is a mere technical irregularity that is not necessarily fatal to the indictment. *Frisbie v. United States*, 157 U.S. 160, 163–165, 15 S.Ct. 586, 587–588, 39 L.Ed. 657 (1895).

As the Court of Appeals noted, the impact of a federal grand jury foreman upon the criminal justice system and the rights of persons charged with crime is "minimal and incidental at best." 702 F.2d, at 471. Given the ministerial nature of the position, discrimination in the selection of one person from among the members of a properly constituted grand jury can have little, if indeed any, appreciable effect upon the defendant's due process right to fundamental fairness. Simply stated, the role of the foreman of a federal grand jury is not so significant to the administration of justice that discrimination in the appointment of that office impugns the fundamental fairness of the process itself so as to undermine the integrity of the indictment.

Nor does discrimination in the appointment of grand jury foremen impair the defendant's due process interest in assuring that the grand jury includes persons with a range of experiences and perspectives. The due process concern that no "large and identifiable segment of the community [be] excluded from jury service," *Peters v. Kiff*, 407 U.S., at 503, 92 S.Ct., at 2168, does not arise when the alleged discrimination pertains only to the selection of a foreman from among the members of a properly constituted federal grand jury. That the grand jury in this case was so properly constituted is not questioned. No one person can possibly represent all the "qualities of human nature and varieties of human experience," ibid., that may be present in a given community. So long as the composition of the federal grand jury as a whole serves the representational due process values expressed in Peters, discrimination in the appointment of one member of the grand jury to serve as its foreman does not conflict with those interests.

The ministerial role of the office of federal grand jury foreman is not such a vital one that discrimination in the appointment of an individual to that post significantly invades the distinctive interests of the defendant protected by the Due Process Clause. Absent an infringement of the fundamental right to fairness that violates due process, there is no basis upon which to reverse petitioner's conviction or dismiss the indictment.

B

Petitioner argues that the Court's decision in *Rose v. Mitchell*, 443 U.S. 545, 99 S.Ct. 2993, 61 L.Ed.2d 739 (1979), supports his position that discrimination in the selection of federal grand jury foremen warrants the reversal of his conviction and dismissal of the indictment against him. In Rose, two Negro defendants brought an equal protection challenge to the selection of grand jury foremen in Tennessee. The Court rejected the view that claims of grand jury discrimination should be considered harmless error when raised by a defendant who had been convicted by a properly constituted petit jury at an error-free trial on the merits, and adhered to the position that discrimination in the selection of the grand jury was a valid ground for setting aside a criminal conviction. Id., at 551–559, 99 S.Ct., at 2997–3002. The Court then assumed "without deciding that discrimination with regard to the selection of only the foreman requires that a subsequent conviction be set aside, just as if the discrimination proved had tainted the selection of the entire grand jury venire." Id., at 551–552, n. 4, 99 S.Ct., at 2997–2998, n. 4 (emphasis added). The Court concluded, however, that the defendants were not entitled to have their convictions set aside because they had failed to make out a prima facie case of discrimination in violation of the Equal Protection Clause with regard to the selection of grand jury foremen. Id., at 564–574, 99 S.Ct., at 3004–3009.

Petitioner's reliance upon Rose is misplaced. Rose involved a claim brought by two Negro defendants under the Equal Protection Clause. As members of the class allegedly excluded from service as grand jury foremen, the Rose defendants had suffered the injuries of stigmatization and prejudice associated with racial discrimination. The Equal Protection Clause has long been held to provide a mechanism for the vindication of such claims in the context of challenges to grand and petit juries. See, e.g., *Castaneda v. Partida*, 430 U.S. 482, 97 S.Ct. 1272, 51 L.Ed.2d 498 (1977); *Hernandez v. Texas*, 347 U.S. 475, 74 S.Ct. 667, 98 L.Ed. 866 (1954); *Strauder v. West Virginia*, 100 U.S. 303, 25 L.Ed. 664 (1880). Petitioner, however, has alleged only that the exclusion of women and Negroes from the position of grand jury foreman violates his right to fundamental fairness under the Due Process Clause. As we have noted, discrimination in the selection of federal grand jury foremen cannot be said to have a significant impact upon the due process interests of criminal defendants. Thus, the nature of petitioner's alleged injury and the constitutional basis of his claim distinguish his circumstances from those of the defendants in *Rose*.

Moreover, *Rose* must be read in light of the method used in Tennessee to select a grand jury and its foreman. Under that system, 12 members of the grand jury were selected at random by the jury commissioners from a list of qualified potential jurors. The foreman, however, was separately appointed by a judge from the general eligible population at large. The foreman then served as " 'the thirteenth member of each grand jury organized during his term of office, having equal power and authority in all matters coming before the grand jury with the other members thereof.' " *Rose v. Mitchell*, supra, at 548, n. 2, 99 S.Ct., at 2996, n. 2 (quoting Tenn.Code Ann. § 40–1506 (Supp.1978)). The foreman selection process in Rose therefore determined not only who would serve as presiding officer, but also who would serve as the 13th voting member of the grand jury. The result of discrimination in foreman selection under the Tennessee system was that 1 of the 13 grand jurors had been selected as a voting member in an impermissible fashion. Under the federal system, by contrast, the foreman is chosen from among the members of the grand jury after they have been empaneled, see Fed.Rule Crim.Proc. 6(c); the federal foreman, unlike the foreman in Rose, cannot be viewed as the surrogate of the judge. So long as the grand jury itself is properly constituted, there is no risk that the appointment of any one of its members as foreman will distort the overall composition of the array or otherwise taint the operation of the judicial process.

Finally, the role of the Tennessee grand jury foreman differs substantially from that of the foreman in the federal system. The Tennessee foreman had the following duties:

> "He or she is charged with the duty of assisting the district attorney in investigating crime, may order the issuance of subpoenas for witnesses before the grand jury, may administer oaths to grand jury witnesses, must endorse every bill returned by the grand jury, and must present any indictment to the court in the presence of the grand jury.... The absence of the foreman's endorsement makes an indictment 'fatally defective.' Bird v. State, 103 Tenn. 343, 344, 52 S.W. 1076 (1899)." Rose v. Mitchell, supra, at 548, n. 2, 99 S.Ct., at 2996, n. 2.

The investigative and administrative powers and responsibilities conferred upon the grand jury foreman in Tennessee, who possessed virtual veto power over the indictment process, stand in sharp contrast to the ministerial powers of the federal counterpart, who performs strictly clerical tasks and whose signature on an indictment is a mere formality. *Frisbie v. United States*, 157 U.S. 160, 15 S.Ct. 586, 39 L.Ed. 657 (1895); see supra, at 3096–3097.

Given the nature of the constitutional injury alleged in Rose, the peculiar manner in which the Tennessee grand jury selection operated, and the authority granted to the one who served as foreman, the Court assumed in Rose that discrimination with regard to the foreman's selection would require the setting aside of a subsequent conviction, "just as if the discrimination proved had tainted the selection of the entire grand jury venire." *Rose v. Mitchell*, 443 U.S., at 551–552, n. 4, 99 S.Ct., at 2997–2998, n. 4. No such assumption is appropriate here, however, in the very different context of a due process challenge by a white male to the selection of foremen of federal grand juries.

III

At oral argument, petitioner eschewed primary reliance upon any particular constitutional provision and instead invoked this Court's supervisory power over the federal courts as a basis for the relief he seeks. Tr. of Oral Arg. 4–5, 7, 13–14. Only by setting aside his conviction and dismissing the indictment against him, petitioner urges, will this Court deter future purposeful exclusion of minorities and women from the post of federal grand jury foreman. It is true that this Court's "supervision of the administration of criminal justice in the federal courts implies the duty of establishing and maintaining civilized standards of procedure and evidence." *McNabb v. United States*, 318 U.S. 332, 340, 63 S.Ct. 608, 612, 87 L.Ed. 819 (1943). See *United States v. Hasting*, 461 U.S. 499, 103 S.Ct. 1974, 76 L.Ed.2d 96 (1983). However, we decline petitioner's invitation to embark upon the course of vacating criminal convictions because of discrimination in the selection of foremen. Less Draconian measures will suffice to rectify the problem.

In no sense do we countenance a purposeful exclusion of minorities or women from appointment as foremen of federal grand juries. We are fully satisfied that the district judges charged with the appointment of federal grand jury foremen will see to it that no citizen is excluded from consideration for service in that position on account of race, color, religion, sex, national origin, or economic status. Cf. 28 U.S.C. § 1862.

IV

We hold that, assuming discrimination entered into the selection of federal grand jury foremen, such discrimination does not warrant the reversal of the conviction of, and dismissal of the indictment against, a white male bringing a claim under the Due Process Clause. Accordingly, the judgment of the United States Court of Appeals for the Fourth Circuit is

Affirmed.

Race and Prosecutorial Conduct Before the Grand Jury

Note

Prosecutors exercise tremendous influence on grand juries and do so largely in secret. What then of prosecutorial misconduct by way of improper race discriminatory comment? In *United States v. Seburo*, 604 F 2d 807 (3rd Cir. 1979), the court found prosecutorial misconduct sufficient to justify dismissal of the indictment where the prosecutor claimed the defendant was part of an undesirable class (Italian Costa Nostra). In doing so the court said:

The fact that grand jury proceedings are secret, Ex parte and largely under the control of the federal prosecutor, magnifies this concern. Aware of the potential for abuse inherent in grand jury proceedings, this court and others have increasingly exercised our supervisory power over the administration of justice to regulate the manner in which grand jury investigations are conducted.

The American Bar Association, *Criminal Justice Standards for the Prosecution Function* provides:

c) The prosecutor should not make statements or arguments to a grand jury in an effort to influence grand jury action in a manner that would be impermissible in a trial.

[Standard 3-4.5 Relationship with a Grand Jury]

Comments in which the prosecutor referred to African Americans as "bad people", *Moore v. Morton* 255 F. 3d 95 (3rd Cir. 2001); repeated reference to the Black defendant's race in a prosecution for sexual battery of white woman, *Reynolds v. State*, 580 So. 2d 254 (1st D.C. A. Fla. 1991); and asserting to the jury that African Americans as a whole were not really part of the same community as the jury, *United States ex. Rel. Haynes v. McKendrick*, 350 F. Supp. 990 (S.D.N.Y. 1972), where all determined to be improper and to dent the defendant fair trial.

The grand jury has had a mixed history regarding the civil rights movement. Prosecution of individuals, including member of the Ku Klux Klan for crimes up to and including murder were often frustrated by grand jury nullification. See, Blanche Davis Blank, THE NOT SO GRAND JURY, University Press of America, (1993).

Note

Pretrial detention poses one of the most severe challenges regarding racial disparity in the criminal justice system. Of the more than 405 thousand people in American jails held without trial, over 51 percent are African American or Hispanic. See Todd D. Minton & Zhen Zeng, BUREAU OF JUSTICE STATISTICS, U.S. DEP'T OF JUSTICE, JAIL INMATES IN 2015 (December 2016), *https://www.bjs.gov/content/pub/pdf/ji15.pdf.* *[http://perma.cc/TW6K-UZ6X]*. African Americans are particularly more likely to have bail denied than similarly situated Whites (33 percent). (Minton and Zeng). The consequences of detention before trial are significant. Data indicates that pretrial detention increases the odds of conviction and the odds of receiving less favorable sentences and plea offers. See, *Bellamy v. Judges and Justices*, 342 N.Y.S. 2d 137 (1973) *Report to the United Nations on Racial Disparities in the United States Criminal Justice System https://www. sentencingproject.org/publications/un-report-on-racial-disparities/*.

Combatting the influence of race on pretrial detention is particularly difficult and seldom successfully attempted as part of criminal litigation, for several reasons. The issue and role of race is closely intertwined with issues of poverty. Largely money-oriented bail systems impact an arrestee population the majority of whom fall within the poorest third of society. *Detaining the Poor: How money bail Perpetuates an Endless Cycle of Poverty and Jail Time*, https://www.prisonpolicy.org/reports/incomejails.html. Amongst this income-poor population Black men have a 64 percent lower income differential between their median income and that of non-incarcerated Whites as opposed to a 58 percent differential between incarcerated and non-incarcerated Whites. Similar differences exist regarding Hispanic detainees. *Ibid.*

The few constitutional challenges to bail, other than the implied Eighth Amendment application in *Stack v. Boyle*, 342 U.S. 1 (1951) have largely focused on the equal protection and due process consequences of decisions that have a disparate impact on the poor. *Pugh v. Rainwater*, 557 F.2d 1189 (5th Cir. 1977), *United States v. Madoff*, 586 F. Supp. 2d 240 (S.D.N.Y. 2009). The Court in *Stack* determined that bail set in an amount greater that is reasonably calculated to assure the defendant's reappearance is "excessive" under the Eighth Amendment. It was not clear from the opinion if this Eighth Amendment restriction was incorporated by way of the Due Process Clause of the Fourteenth Amendment and made applicable to the states. That question may have been more clearly resolved in *Timbs v. Inidiana*, __ U.S. __, 138 S.Ct. 265 (2018) where the Court held that The Eighth Amendment's Excessive Fines Clause, which protects against excessive punitive economic sanctions," is fundamental to the scheme of ordered liberty, with deep roots in the Nation's history and tradition, and thus the Clause is an incorporated protection applicable to the States under the Fourteenth Amendment's Due Process Clause."

In *Bandy v. United States*, 82 S. Ct. 11 (1961) Justice Douglas considered the application of the petitioner for release on personal recognizance because he could not afford a money bail. Although denying the application because of an unresolved question as to whether a single Supreme Court justice or Court of Appeals judge had the power to grant such a request, Justice Douglas did note "Further reflection has led me to conclude that no man should be denied release because of indigence" Id. at 13. In doing so Douglas cites to *Griffin v. Illinois,* 351 U.S. 12, the first of a series of cases that have established the equal protection-due process principle that justice cannot 'depends on the amount of money he has" (Id. at 13).

Raising the significance of racial discrimination regarding pretrial release, within the criminal prosecution, is also made difficult because pretrial release decisions are typically not considered final appealable orders and are generally made moot by a subsequent criminal conviction. [Cf. *Bandy v. United States,* Supra,.] Additionally, and, in part, because of the difficulty in reviewing such decisions, constitutional questions regarding the impact of pretrial detention have been approached under the Fourth Amendment "reasonableness" standard. *Gerstein v. Pugh*, 420 U.S. 103 (1975) holds that the Fourth Amendment requires that a Fourth Amendment based determination of probable cause be made by a neutral magistrate regarding anyone held in pretrial detention. However, as we will see later in *Whren v. United States* [infra. __] reasonableness for Fourth Amendment purposes may be determined without regard to racial motivation as long as "objective" probable cause also exist.

But what if race combines with pretrial detention to impact the fairness of the trial itself? Consider the following case.

KINNEY V. LENON
425 F.2d 209 (9th Cir. 1970)

Opinion
EUGENE A. WRIGHT, Circuit Judge.

Appellant is a minor child of seventeen years now detained in the Juvenile Detention Home in Multnomah County, Oregon, pending trial in Juvenile Court on charges arising out of a schoolyard fight.

Appellant alleges that there were many potential witnesses to the fight, that he cannot identify them by name but would recognize them by sight, that appellant's attorneys are white though he and the potential witnesses are black, that his attorneys would consequently have great practical difficulty in interviewing and lining up the witnesses, and that appellant is the sole person who can do so. His request to be released into the custody of his parents was denied by the Juvenile Court. Relief was sought and denied in the United States District Court for the District of Oregon, and application for an order restraining appellant's continued detention has been made to this court.

1 We do not need to decide in this case, as appellant urges us to do, the constitutionality of Ore. Rev.Stat. 419.583, which prohibits the granting of bail in juvenile cases, though the question is not insubstantial. *Trimble v. Stone*, 187 F.Supp. 483 (D.D.C.1960); cf. In re Gault, 387 U.S. 1, 87 S.Ct. 1428, 18 L.Ed.2d 527 (1967). Nor need we delimit the circumstances under which a statutory provision that juveniles be released in the custody of their parents may be a constitutionally adequate substitute for bail. *Fulwood v. Stone*, 129 U.S.App.D.C. 314, 394 F.2d 939 (1967); *Baldwin v. Lewis*, 300 F.Supp. 1220 (D.Wis.1969). For appellant here was granted release neither on bond nor into the custody of his parents. And we are of the opinion that, in the peculiar circumstances of this case, failure to permit appellant's release for the purpose of aiding the preparation of his defense unconstitutionally interfered with his due-process right to a fair trial.

The ability of an accused to prepare his defense by lining up witnesses is fundamental, in our adversary system, to his chances of obtaining a fair trial. Recognition of this fact of course underlies the bail system. *Stack v. Boyle*, 342 U.S. 1, 4, 72 S.Ct. 1, 96 L.Ed. 3 (1951). But it is equally implicit in the requirements that trial occur near in time, *Klopfer v. North Carolina*, 386 U.S. 213, 87 S.Ct. 988, 18 L.Ed.2d 1 (1967), and place (U.S.Const. Amend. VI) to the offense, and that the accused have compulsory process to obtain witnesses in his behalf. *Washington v. Texas*, 388 U.S. 14, 87 S.Ct. 1920, 18 L.Ed.2d 1019 (1967). Indeed, compulsory process as a practical matter would be of little value without an opportunity to contact and screen potential witnesses before trial.

This is not a case where release from detention is sought simply for the convenience of the appellant. There is here a strong showing that the appellant is the only person who can effectively prepare his own defense. We may take notice, as judges and lawyers, of the difficulties often encountered, even by able and conscientious counsel, in overcoming the apathy and reluctance of potential witnesses to testify. It would require blindness to social reality not to understand that these difficulties may be exacerbated by the barriers of age and race. Yet the alternative to some sort of release for appellant is to cast the entire burden of assembling witnesses onto his attorneys, with almost certain prejudice to appellant's case.

3 The appellee suggests that appellant is properly detained in view of what are claimed to be previous instances of harassment of the state's witnesses. But the Juvenile Court is not without

power to take appropriate measures to prevent any such misconduct, and our order so provides. Cf. 18 U.S.C. 3146(a).

ORDER

Appellants' motion for temporary restraining order and release from custody has been considered and it is

Ordered that defendants be directed forthwith to release appellant minor to the custody of his parents if they are suitable and available custodians; and otherwise to the custody of his counsel or other suitable person, and it is

Further ordered that such release be made upon appropriate conditions to permit appellant to aid his counsel in seeking witnesses to testify on his behalf, but protecting any such witnesses from harassment.

Preventive Detention: Race and Predictions of Dangerousness

Note

Despite the Eighth Amendment contra-indications of *Stack v. Boyle* the issue of danger to the community as a factor of bail decision making has consistently presented itself as a permissible factor in bail setting. See, Sandra G. Mayson, DANGEROUS DEFENDANTS, 127 Yale L.J. 490 (2018).

Professor Mayson points out that by 1984 thirty-four states had adopted some form of pre-trial detention without bail for individuals who are determined to be a danger to the community pending resolution of the criminal charges against them. [Mayson at 502].

Most notably the federal system enacted the Bail Reform Act of 1984, 18 U.S.C. Secs 3141-3150. Pursuant to this act and like similar provisions at various state levels, a defendant may be held without bail, even if otherwise eligible, if no condition or combination of conditions, will reasonably assure the safety of another person and the community. The determination of dangerousness is made upon finding after hearing, after consideration among other things, the nature of the offense charged, the prior record of the defendant, the weight of the evidence against the person, personal characteristics such as employment resources and prior drug or alcohol use.

The United States Supreme Court upheld the Act in *Salerno v. United States*, 481 U.S. 739 (1987) against the challenge that preventive detention is punishment without trial and in violation of the Eighth Amendment proscription against excessive bail. The Court concluded that the Act is regulatory and not punishment because congress did not intent otherwise and that there is no implicit right to bail in the Eighth Amendment's guarantee against excessive bail.

The *Salerno* Court did not consider the claim that due process is not consistent with detention based on the predictions of future dangerous based on factors such as prior record. The precursor to the Bail Reform Act of 1984; the District of Columbia Court Reform and Criminal Procedures Act of 1970, Pub. L. No. 91-358, 84 Stat. 473 (codified at D.C. Code Ann. §§ 23-1321 to -1323 (West 2017), was challenged in *Blunt v. United States*, 322 A.2d 579 (App. D.C. 1974). The Court there concluded that based primarily on the defendant's extensive prior criminal record, he was a "dangerous person" within the meaning of the statute.

A conclusion of future dangerousness based on past conduct has begun to raise significant questions regarding the impact of racial disproportionality. While no preventive detention statute would openly state race as a consideration in determining dangerousness, the use and reliance on allegedly race-neutral factors, such as prior convictions and arrests may indirectly have the effect of disproportionately impacting non-whites and incorrectly imply that non-whites are more dangerous than whites in terms of predictive behavior.

As noted by Professor Eaglin, while African American men often interact with the criminal justice system more frequently and at an earlier age, such does not necessarily mean greater "criminality". The African American community receives greater scrutiny, particularly in the area of drug enforcement, despite a lack of evidence of disproportionate drug usage. See, Jessica M. Eaglin, Constructing Recidivism Risk, 67 EMORY L.J. 59 (2017) at 95. See also, Bernard E. Harcourt, Risk As A Proxy For Race: The Dangers of Risk Assessment, 27 Federal Sentencing Reporter 237 (2015).

Challenging preventive detention because of racial bias has not been largely successful. See *United States v. Perry*, 788 F.2d 100 (3rd Cir. 1986). Perry claimed that his Equal Protection rights were violated because the preventive detention under the Bail Reform Act was more likely to be applied against minorities. The Court rejected that claim finding that the Act is facially neutral in respect to race and therefore does not create a suspect class. Without a suspect class the legislature action in creating the statute has a rational basis sufficient to satisfy equal protection concerns.

What about racial fears regarding threats that often are particularly associated with racial fears and stereotype? Consider the following case in the context of fear of Muslims – particularly non-white Muslims.

UNITED STATES V. ZARRAB

2016 WL 3681423(S.D.N.Y. 2016)

DECISION & ORDER
RICHARD M. BERMAN, U.S.D.J.

I. Background

Having reviewed the record herein, including, without limitation, (i) the defense bail application, including submissions dated May 18, 2016, May 31, 2016, June 1, 2016, and June 7, 2016 (collectively, "Defense Motion"); (ii) the Government's opposition to bail, including submissions dated May 25, 2016, June 1, 2016, and June 3, 2016 (collectively, "Government Opposition"); (iii) the Pretrial Services Report (Florida), dated March 21, 2016; (iv) the transcript of the bail hearing conducted on June 2, 2016, and (v) Defendant Reza Zarrab's Turkish, Iranian, and Macedonian passports, the Court respectfully denies Mr. Zarrab's application for bail after finding both that Defendant is a flight risk and that there are no conditions or combination of conditions of release that will reasonably assure the appearance of the Defendant.

In a four count Superseding Indictment, filed on March 30, 2016, the Government charges Mr. Zarrab with the following crimes: 1) conspiracy to defraud the United States and to impede the lawful functions of the United States Department of Treasury, Office of Foreign Assets Control ("OFAC"), under 18 U.S.C. § 371; 2) conspiracy to violate the International Emergency Economic Powers Act ("IEEPA"), 50 U.S.C. §§ 1701- 1706, and the Iranian Transactions and Sanctions Regulations ("ITSR"), 31 C.F.R. §§ 560.202-205; 3) conspiracy to commit bank fraud, under 18 U.S.C. § 1349; and 4) conspiracy to commit money laundering, in violation of 18 U.S.C. §§ 1956- 1957. (See Superseding Indictment ¶¶ 13, 15, 16, 17, 19, 20, 22, 23.) As summarized by the Government at the June 2, 2016 bail hearing: "What the Defendant is charged with is orchestrating and conducting a scheme to allow sanctioned entities, and the government of Iran, to access the international financial networks, and especially the United States financial networks ... specifically for the purpose of evading sanctions." (See Transcript, dated June 2, 2016 ("Tr."), at 44:17-21.)

Mr. Zarrab is, at 33 years of age, a wealthy and successful international businessman and an experienced international traveler. He is a dual national of Turkey and Iran, and has no ties to New York or to the United States. Mr. Zarrab, who travels on (separate) Turkish, Iranian, and Macedonian passports, has been detained since his arrest in Miami, Florida on March 21, 2016 while enroute with his wife and five year old daughter to Disneyworld.

The Defense Motion proposes the following bail conditions: 1) a $50 million personal recognizance bond secured by $10 million in cash; 2) travel restricted to the Southern District of New

York; 3) surrender of all travel documents with no new applications; 4) strict Pretrial Services supervision; 5) home detention with GPS monitoring at Mr. Zarrab's recently leased apartment in Manhattan. Mr. Zarrab proposes to leave this apartment only for medical treatment, legal counsel meetings, religious services, and court appearances, all with prior notification to Pretrial Services; and 6) Mr. Zarrab's presence at his apartment is to be secured by Guidepost Solutions LLC ("Guidepost"), a security company, with these additional restrictions: i) two or more armed (former or off duty) law enforcement officers at all times; ii) one supervisory security professional overseeing and scheduling Mr. Zarrab's security detail; iii) security at both the apartment and whenever (and to wherever) Mr. Zarrab leaves the apartment building; iv) a security vehicle with driver when Mr. Zarrab travels to counsel's office, court, religious services, or medical treatment; and v) regular Guidepost communication with the Court, Pretrial Services, and the U.S. Attorney's Office. (See Def.'s Mot. at 3-4.)

In support of its bail application, the defense argues: "Because Mr. Zarrab is not charged with a violent crime, is not facing any mandatory minimum prison sentence and is otherwise eligible for bail, we urge this Court not to detain him simply because he is wealthy and lacks ties to the United States. Our bail proposal removes any possible concern of flight." (Id. at 22.)

The Government opposes Mr. Zarrab's bail proposal, arguing that "[t]here are no conditions that can reasonably assure the defendant's appearance." (See Gov.'s Opp'n at 1.) The Government contends that the proposed bail conditions "do not mitigate the risk of flight created by the nature of the charges, weight of evidence, Mr. Zarrab's personal background, and his duplicity to date." (Id. at 2.)

The U.S. Pretrial Services Department (Southern District of Miami) issued a Pretrial Services Report, dated March 21, 2016, in which it concluded that there are no conditions or combination of conditions to reasonably assure the Defendant's appearance in court. (See Pretrial Services Report, dated March 21, 2016, at 3.) This conclusion was based upon Mr. Zarrab's: 1) offenses charged; 2) extensive foreign travel; 3) no family ties to the United States; 4) Turkish citizenship; and 5) unknown immigration status. The Pretrial Services Report also concluded that "the defendant may pose a financial danger to the community based on ... the offense charged." (Id.)

II. Legal Standard

Under 18 U.S.C. § 3142(b) the court shall order the pretrial release of the person unless the judicial officer determines that such release will not reasonably assure the appearance of the person as required or will endanger the safety of any other person or the community. The government bears the burden of showing by a preponderance of the evidence that the defendant poses a flight risk and/or by clear and convincing evidence that the defendant poses a danger to the community. See *U.S. v. Ferranti*, 66 F.3d 540, 542 (2d Cir 1995); *U.S. v. Gebro*, 948 F.2d 1118 (9th

Cir. 1991). "[T]he government carries a dual burden in seeking pre-trial detention. First, it must establish by a preponderance of the evidence that the defendant, if released, presents an actual risk of flight ... Assuming it satisfies this burden, the government must then demonstrate by a preponderance of the evidence that no condition or combination of conditions could be imposed on the defendant that would reasonably assure his presence in court." *United States v. Sabhnani,* 493 F.3d 63, 75 (2d Cir. 2007).

"The court evaluating risk of flight is to consider the nature of the offense, the weight of the evidence against the suspect, the history and character of the person charged, and the nature and seriousness of the risk to the community." See *United States v. Dreier,* 596 F. Supp. 2d 831, 833 (S.D.N.Y. 2009); see also 18 U.S.C. § 3142(g).

In *United States v. Banki,* a panel of the Second Circuit Court of Appeals determined that it is "not legal error for a district court to decline to accept ... as a substitute for detention" hiring private security guards to monitor the defendant while he is on home confinement. 369 Fed. Appx. 152, 153 (2d Cir. 2010) (summary order). "Indeed, such conditions might be best seen not as specific conditions of release, but simply as a less onerous form of detention available only to the wealthy." Id. The Court in *Banki* was "troubled" by the idea that wealthy defendants may be allowed to buy their way out of prison by constructing their own private jail. Id. at 153. The Court noted that "because the only issue actually decided in [*United States v. Sabhnani,* 493 F.3d 63 (2d Cir. 2007)] was the adequacy of the particular terms of the proposed monitoring arrangement, we did not there hold that district courts routinely must consider the retention of self-paid private security guards as an acceptable condition of release before ordering detention." Id. at 153-154.

III. Analysis

In the Court's view, the four bail factors support continued detention rather than release of Mr. Zarrab by a preponderance of the evidence.

1) The nature and circumstances of the offenses charged

   The defense concedes that the Indictment sets forth "serious felony charges" but also points out that Mr. Zarrab "has not been charged with any crime involving violence, sex trafficking, terrorism, minor children, narcotics or weapons." (See Def.'s Mot. at 5, 12.) According to the defense, "there is nothing about the nature and circumstance of the charged offenses to suggest that pretrial detention is necessary to achieve the purposes of the Bail Reform Act." Id.

   The Government, on the other hand, emphasizes the national security nature of the crimes charged. (See, e.g., Gov.'s Opp'n at 16-20.) "The IEEPA authorizes the President to deal with 'unusual and extraordinary threat[s]... to the national security, foreign policy, or economy of the United States' by declaring a national emergency with respect to such threats ... The President has repeatedly declared such a national emergency with respect to the Government of Iran." (Id. at 3.) The Government also points out that as recently as March 9, 2016, the President stated that, notwithstanding the Joint Comprehensive Plan of Action ("JCPOA") entered into between the United States, Iran, and other nations concerning Iran's nuclear program, "certain actions and policies of the Government of Iran [including those charged in this case] continue to pose an unusual and extraordinary threat to the national security, foreign policy, and economy of the United States." (Id. at 4.)

The Government contends that "Zarrab facilitated millions of dollars worth of transactions on behalf of Iran and sanctioned entities that were designed to evade the U.S. sanctions." (Id. at 5.) "The entities aided by Zarrab include entities that, at the time, were arms of the IRGC [Iran's Islamic Revolutionary Guard], which is notorious for its facilitation of terrorism ... Zarrab's conduct ... was not limited to any specific banned set of products, but rather, enabled Iran to engage in the full course of conduct that threatens the United States." (Id. at 16, n.7.)

The Government states the four felonies with which Defendant is charged "carry a statutory maximum term of imprisonment of 75 years and a likely sentencing range under the United States Sentencing Guidelines of decades." (Id. at 1.)

The Court concludes that the charges against the Defendant are indeed serious and that the Defendant, if he were to be convicted, may well face a substantial term of imprisonment.4 The United States has imposed economic sanctions and regulations to help ensure that the Government of Iran and Iranian companies do no harm the United States. "Every President since President Clinton has continued the national emergency with respect to Iran and Executive Orders 13059, 12959, and 12957, given that the actions and policies of Iran continue to threaten the national security, foreign policy, and economy of the United States." (Id. at 4.) This factor weighs in favor of continued detention.

2) The weight of evidence against the person

The defense argues that the "charges are ill-founded and that the Government will not prevail at trial." (See Def.'s Mot. at 12.) According to defense counsel, this case "hang[s] by a jurisdictional thread," and "the only basis upon which the alleged conduct in this case could be subject to the jurisdiction of the United States is that the non-U.S. banks that Mr. Zarrab used to send the U.S. dollar payments to the non-U.S. recipients elected to do so by involving U.S. banks in the payment chain." (See Def.'s Reply at 11, 17.)

During the June 2, 2016 bail hearing, defense counsel also argued that the Defendant "didn't intend to defraud the bank, because he had no idea that those transactions were going to pass through a United States Federal Reserve, because they were sent by non-U.S. banks to other non-U.S. banks." (Tr. at 38:14-18.) Defense counsel also commented that Adam Szubin, the U.S. Acting Under Secretary of Treasury and former Director of OFAC made statements which suggest that the "assertion of jurisdiction in this matter is entirely inappropriate." (See Def.'s Reply at 11; see also discussion at pp. 8-9.) The Defense asserts: "There is no incentive to flee a case that is defensible and Mr. Zarrab is intent on remaining in the Southern District of New York to fight these charges and clear his name." (Id. at 17.)

The Government counters that "the evidence of Zarrab's participation in the charged offenses is overwhelming: his culpability is captured in voluminous and unimpeachable email communications among Zarrab and his subordinates and coconspirators, business records, and financial evidence that document his orchestration of the charged schemes." (See Gov.'s Opp'n at 1.) There is, according to the Government, a clear "paper trail that shows Zarrab engaging in millions of dollars worth of sanctioned financial transactions." (Id. at 19.) The Indictment alleges, as an example, that on or about June 1, 2011 an email was sent to Zarrab from an individual with Iran's Mellat Exchange which had "very urgent" written in Farsi in the subject line and which attached several additional documents, including letters and messages that certain payments had been "blocked" by United States banks pursuant to the sanctions imposed by OFAC. (See Superseding Indictment at 9-10.) "Zarrab was warned explicitly that financial transactions in which he engaged were banned by U.S. banks because they ran afoul of OFAC regulations." (See Gov.'s Opp'n at 19.) "Zarrab himself direct[ed] transactions that were not for the benefit of the company in whose name they were executed, but rather, for NIOC [National Iranian Oil Company], which was at the time, designated as an arm of the IRGC [Islamic Revolutionary Guard]." (Id.)

The Government asserts that jurisdiction in the U.S. courts is entirely proper. (See Gov.'s Surreply at 4.) The charged offenses "apply to foreign nationals operating in foreign countries when they conspire to evade or avoid the IEEPA and the ITSR or to cause a violation of those provisions," and Congress has the authority to enforce its laws beyond the territorial boundaries of the United States. (Id.) The Government also contends that the IEEPA and ITSR prohibit "any transaction ... that evades or avoids, has the purpose of evading or avoiding, causes a violation of, or attempts to violate any of the prohibitions in the ITSR and any conspiracy formed to violate any of the prohibitions in the ITSR – without regard to the nationality or location of the individuals involved in the prohibited transaction or conspiracy". (Id. at 5.) "[T]he evidence is overwhelming that Zarrab and his coconspirators knew about the existence of U.S. and international sanctions against Iran; that Zarrab and his co-conspirators knew that these U.S. dollar transactions on behalf of and for the benefit of Iranian entities and the Government of

Iran would be processed by U.S. financial institutions; and that Zarrab and his cocon-spirators knew that the transactions would be blocked whenever the connection to Iran was apparent." (Id. at 8.)

Jurisdictional and evidentiary (and other) issues may well be the subject of pretrial motion practice. And, the ultimate merit or strength of the Government's case will be tested at or before trial. These matters are not being determined conclusively at this time. See *United States v. Bellomo*, 944 F. Supp. 1160, 1163 (S.D.N.Y. 1996) ("The issue now before the Court is whether there is a risk that [Defendant] will flee the jurisdiction or endanger others before the trial can be held, not whether he is guilty or innocent of the charges in the indictment."); *United States v. Fama*, 2013 WL 2467985, (S.D.N.Y. June 7, 2013) ("The Court recognizes the difficulty inherent in assessing the Government's case before trial, and is mindful not to reach any conclusions about [Defendant's] guilt or innocence."). But, the Court is persuaded for purposes of setting bail that the evidence against the Defendant appears strong, including, without limitation, the exhibits attached to the Government's Opposition, as well as the emails and allegations described in the Superseding Indictment (at pp. 6-12). This factor weighs in favor of continued detention.

3) The history and characteristics of the defendant

It is conceded by the defense that Mr. Zarrab has no ties to the United States. (Tr. at 8:17-22.) As noted, he is a 33 year old successful international businessman who was born in Iran and lives in Turkey. He is a dual national of Turkey and Iran. Mr. Zarrab is, not-withstanding his relatively young age, an experienced world traveler. He holds Iranian, Turkish and Macedonian passports. Mr. Zarrab is married and has a young daughter.

Among Defendant's business enterprises are the following: a Turkish gold brokerage and currency exchange; a shipbuilding company in Istanbul named Royal Shipping; a real estate construction company; a furniture manufacturing operation in Istanbul named Royal Mobilya; and a tea brokerage business trading Sri Lankan tea destined for Turkey. (See Def.'s Mot. at 13, 14, 18.) According to defense counsel, Mr. Zarrab was listed as "the 56th largest taxpayer in Turkey" in 2015. (Id. at 17.)

Defense counsel also states that Mr. Zarrab suffers from a "series of medical issues," including intestinal polyps, a stomach ulcer, and tumor located near his kidney. Defendant "requires a special diet and medical supervision properly to maintain his health ..." (Id. at 21.) The Pretrial Services Report states: "The Defendant suffers from Irritable Bowel Syndrome (IBS), tumor on his kidney, kidney issues, and stomach prob-lems." (Pretrial Services Report at 2.)

Defense counsel presents charts and other documentation showing that Mr. Zarrab has made numerous charitable contributions to worthy causes in Turkey, including medical care for the needy, assistance to mentally disadvantaged children, and access to quality schooling for residents of low income Turkish communities. (Def.'s Mot. at 15.)

The Government contends that Mr. Zarrab is an "extraordinary flight risk" and bases this assertion principally upon the absence of any ties of the Defendant to the United States, Defendant's significant wealth and resources, and Defendant's relationships to several foreign countries, including countries that seemingly would not extradite him (back) to the United States to face the pending charges. (See Gov.'s Opp'n at 21.) The Government also contends that Mr. Zarrab was not truthful (forthcoming) to Pretrial Services. (Id.) "When asked to truthfully quantify his wealth, Zarrab minimized his business income from several billion dollars to less than a million dollars, and omitted millions of dollars worth of assets. Similarly, when asked about his travel over the past decade, Zarrab chose to mention a few countries that he visited purportedly for vacation, but failed to disclose his travel to countries like Lebanon, Russia, and Saudi Arabia." (Id.) "[T]here are no bail conditions that will assure his presence in Court." (Id. at 1.)

According to the Government, the Defendant's "commercial ventures generate a tremendous amount of revenue – more than \$11 billion annually – in foreign countries." (Id. at 22.). An exhibit to the Government's Opposition appears to quote the Defendant as saying that for some time in 2014 he was exporting a ton of gold a day and was responsible for "approximately 25 billion Turkish lira in exports, or more than \$11 billion." (Id. at 8 and Exhibit B.). The Government describes one of Defendant's businesses as a money exchange house that "sold and bought \$3,452,919,870 and \$3.452,928,229, respectively, in 2011." (Id. at 8.) The Government also lists assets of the Defendant, including a private airplane; "approximately 20 properties"; "approximately 24 firearms"; horses; luxury automobiles; and "artwork valued at more than \$10 million." (Id. at 10.) The Government also emphasizes the facts that Defendant holds Iranian and Macedonian passports (in addition to his Turkish passport) and that those two countries do not have extradition treaties with the United States.

The Government also contends that the Defendant regularly travels to other countries that do not have extradition treaties with the United States, including Russia, Lebanon, and Saudi Arabia. (Id. at 21.) It states that while Turkey does have an extradition treaty with the United States, Turkey does not extradite its citizens. (Id.)

Defendant's Forthrightness and His English and Farsi Language Skills

In making its case for continued detention rather than release on bail, the Government argues that Defendant was untruthful with Pretrial Services and did not, for example, fully disclose the extent of his wealth or the extent of his prior foreign travel. (See Gov.'s Opp'n at 7.) This is contested by the defense, which explains that there was an English language problem or barrier which affected Mr. Zarrab's interview with Pretrial

Services. According to the defense, what may appear as misinformation or partial disclosure by Mr. Zarrab is explained by the fact there was no Turkish interpreter present at the Pretrial Services interview in Miami on March 21, 2016. Defense counsel asks that the Court "view the Miami Pretrial Services Report in two ways: first, as a minimally probative document given the language barrier, and second, as a minor part of what has been a [subsequent] full, thorough examination and disclosure of defendant's assets and overall wealth" by counsel. (See Def.'s Reply at 8-9.)

Mr. Zarrab's language skills were fully debated at the June 2, 2016 bail hearing (and in subsequent submissions). AUSA Lockard contended that: "Mr. Zarrab saying he doesn't understand English well enough to participate at a pretrial services interview is ... flatly contradicted by the evidence." (See Tr. at 50:13-15.) Lockard pointed to "voluminous e-mail and electronic communications in which Mr. Zarrab communicates with others in English. And that is both on his telephone, on his Bureau of Prisons e-mail account, he receives documents, including business documents, in English. He receives texts and e-mails in English and responds in English." (Id. at 51:1-6.) Defense counsel countered that "the government's suggestion that this defendant was not honest with the pretrial services interview in Miami ... is somewhat offensive. I think that what you only need to do is actually look at the first section of the pretrial services report, where the author of the report says 'Although the interview was conducted in English, the defendant is in need of a Turkish interpreter and none was provided.' " (Id. at 10:12-21.)

During the bail hearing, AUSA Lockard also addressed Mr. Zarrab's Farsi language skills, which he claims are more sophisticated than the defense suggests: "Mr. Zarrab acknowledges that he can speak and hear Farsi. His family members are Iranian. He has business interests in Iran. He has friends in Iran. And the electronic communications on his telephone and in his e-mail account show that he repeatedly receives communications and documents written in Farsi, and that he understands and responds to these communications." (See Tr. at 49:21-25, 50:1-2.)

Following the bail hearing, the Government provided, by letter dated June 3, 2016, examples of Defendant's proficiency in the English language, including emails and images obtained from the Defendant's cellphone. For example, there is an email, dated May 30, 2015, from Mr. Zarrab to "Sama Petrol" to which Mr. Zarrab attaches a written letter in English on the letterhead of one of his companies which discusses a recent business deal: "Although the agreement has been realized between our company and the esteemed company Sama Petrol, all the mutual understandings were obtained through direct negotiations with NICO [Naftiran Intertrade Company] and henceforth any correspondence with our company regarding the subject of this agreement will be realized, only if it is issued by NICO." (Gov.'s Letter, Exhibit J.). In another email, written in English and dated March 20, 2013, Mr. Zarrab appears to respond to certain banking/

regulatory questions, including questions regarding economic sanctions and the ability of a company to wire money. (Gov.'s Letter, Exhibit K.) Another illustration of Mr. Zarrab's English language skill appears to be reflected in a lengthy series of recorded chats from in or about November 2015 through March 2016 between the Defendant and a business associate discussing diverse business and personal topics. (Gov.'s Letter, Exhibit I.)

The Government also submitted numerous documents and emails that reflect Defendant's proficiency in communicating in Farsi. These exhibits include Farsi text message screenshots, emails, and typed and handwritten contracts in Farsi. (See Gov.'s Letter, Exhibits O-Q.) The Government asserts that one of the documents is a handwritten Farsi contract signed by the Defendant. (Id., Exhibit Q.)

The Defense, as noted, disputes any deception by Mr. Zarrab. The defense counters by stating that "[i]t is undisputed that Mr. Zarrab can understand and speak basic English but requires an interpreter for complex conversation involving legal or technical terms, phrases or words" and that the Government's submission "sheds no new light on this issue." (See Def.'s Letter at 3-4.)

According to the defense, the Government exhibits do not, for example, show that "Zarrab ever looked at the images ... [or] understood them"; or that "Mr. Zarrab has English-speaking employees who might assist him in drafting English– language communications." (Id. at 4.) The defense contends, with respect to Mr. Zarrab's prison emails, that "you can have help from other inmates in how you compose your e-mail ... [and] there is a self-correcting feature on the CorrLinks e-mail [that] fixes any of your grammatical errors, any of your spelling errors." (Tr. at 62:22-25.)

And, with regard to Defendant's proficiency in Farsi, defense counsel argues that although Mr. Zarrab speaks and understands Farsi, he cannot read or write it. (See Tr. at 22:21 (MR. BRAFMAN: "[T]he defendant does not read Farsi ... he speaks Farsi.").) According to the defense, the Government's exhibits "show nothing of value," and "as a general matter, Mr. Zarrab works with people who do in fact speak Farsi and who can assist him when necessary." (See Def.'s Letter at 5.) And, "the government needs to understand that you will find that there are Farsi e-mails that were sent to him that he forwarded to others. Others forwarded to him. And the problem with an e-mail ... is once you hit the send button, you have no idea where that e-mail ends up, and you have no control over what e-mail comes to you." (Tr. at 63:10-16.)

The precise extent and level of sophistication of Mr. Zarrab's English or Farsi language skills or the full extent of his wealth and resources are not conclusive of the bail issue currently before the Court. These matters may well be discussed again at subsequent proceedings, including trial. Based upon the record, the Court is convinced that Mr. Zarrab has a good grasp of English and Farsi – himself and perhaps with the assistance of others – sufficient to engage in complex international, financial, and business transactions. The Court also concludes that in these legal proceedings, it is appropriate that Mr. Zarrab continue to have the benefit of a Turkish interpreter. See Pagan v. Berbary, 2007 WL 2932775, (N.D.N.Y. Oct. 5, 2007). The Court is also grateful to defense counsel for submitting a fuller picture of Mr. Zarrab's businesses, wealth, assets, and resources.

For purposes of deciding bail or remand, the Court finds most persuasive the following: Defendant's lack of ties to the United States; his significant wealth and his substantial resources; his extensive international travel; and his strong ties to foreign countries, including countries without extradition. These factors, among others stated, provide Mr. Zarrab with the incentive and the wherewithal to flee and render him a flight risk. See, e.g., *United States v. Epstein*, 155 F. Supp. 2d 323, 326 (E.D. Penn. 2001) ("The crucial factor, however, is defendant's lack of ties to the United States and his extensive ties to Brazil with which no extradition treaty exists. In our view, his forfeiture of $1 million worth of assets in the United States would not deter him from flight when in Brazil he has significant wealth, a lucrative job, the presence of his family, and insulation from ever being forced to stand trial."); *United States v. Abdullahu*, 488 F. Supp. 2d 433, 445 (D.N.J. 2007) ("After reviewing the totality of the evidence, the Court has reached the inescapable conclusion that the government has proved by a preponderance of the evidence that no condition or combination of conditions exist that will reasonably assure the defendant's appearance at trial. The defendant faces serious criminal charges ... The defendant faces a potential ten year prison sentence and involuntary deportation. The defendant does not have permanent and longstanding ties to this area, he has the means and incentive to flee and he has family ties and a place to live in an overseas country that will not extradite him to the United States."); *United States v. Seif*, 2001 WL 1415034, (D. Arizona Nov. 8, 2001) (Where defendant, a foreign national, had no family ties to United States, and was an experienced international traveler with substantial connections in countries that do not have extradition treaties.) These factors weigh in favor of continued detention.

4) The nature and seriousness of the danger to any person or the community that would be posed by the person's release

The Defense argues that "there is very little authority supporting the argument that a court should consider a defendant's propensity to commit further economic crimes as 'danger to the community' contemplated by the Bail Reform Act." (See Def.'s Mot. at 18.) "Furthermore, as a practical matter, Mr. Zarrab could not engage in the conduct alleged in the Indictment if he is under house arrest in the United States." (Id. at 19.)

Although its principal focus is upon risk of flight, the Government points out that the Defendant "has aided sanctioned Iranian financial institutions, such as Bank Mellat, the Mellat Exchange, and Bank Karafarin, by giving them access to the very financial markets that the sanctions scheme was designed to cut them off from. He has helped the IRGC [Islamic Revolutionary Guard] earn millions of dollars that could be used to finance its weapons proliferation and support for terrorism by facilitating shipping and petroleum transactions for IRGC-controlled entities, like NIOC [National Iranian Oil Company]. In doing so, the Defendant eased the pressure on Iran and the IRGC created by the sanctions, and worked to diminish their deterrent effect. Zarrab's actions, in a very real sense, compromised the well-being and security of the United States." (See Gov.'s Opp'n at 18.)

As noted, the Pretrial Services Report concluded that the Defendant "may pose a financial danger to the community." See supra p. 4.

The Court concludes that undermining U.S. sanctions against Iran may well pose a threat to the United States and that Mr. Zarrab's release may exacerbate that threat by, for example, enabling him to communicate with business associates or others at or from his New York City apartment. The Court also notes that U.S. Under Secretary Szubin has stated the following: "Iran continues to be the world's leading state sponsor of terrorism, and to play a significant role in destabilizing the [Middle East] region. It supplies funding and weapons to Hizballah, to the Assad regime, and to the Houthis in Yemen. It continues to develop its ballistic missile program, in contravention of UN Security Council provisions. And it continues to violate human rights." (See Testimony of Acting Under-Secretary for Terrorism and Financial Intelligence Adam J. Szubin before the House Committee on Foreign Affairs (May 25, 2016); see also United States v. Kuvumcu, No. 16-cr-00308 (E.D.N.Y. June 14, 2016).) This factor also weighs in favor of continued detention.

Privately Funded Armed Guards: "The Elephant in the Room"

Having determined by a preponderance of the evidence that Mr. Zarrab is a flight risk, the Court next determines whether there are bail conditions which will "reasonably assure the appearance of the person as required." 18 U.S.C. §§ 3142(b)- (f)(2); see also Banki. 369 Fed.Appx. at 153. Bail conditions approved by the court in such circumstances must be "reasonable." See United States v. Madoff, 586 F. Supp. 2d 240, 247 (S.D.N.Y. 2009) ("The Court must determine whether there are reasonable conditions of release that can be set or whether detention is appropriate.").

The defense argues – in support of the "24/7" privately funded armed guard feature of its bail application – that "the unblemished professional reputation of Guidepost [the proposed private security agency] ... will ensure Mr. Zarrab's return to court whenever required." (Def.'s Reply at 29.) The defense also states that "[t]he inequities in the criminal justice system on the state and federal level between people of means and people of not means is not something that is Mr. Zarrab's fault, and it is nothing we are going to remedy in this case. It is sad, but it's true.... But that does not mean that you claim someone is very rich and, therefore … say [that] you can't use your wealth to create a prison." (Tr. at 18:15-24.)

The Government argues, relying in part upon *United States v. Banki*, that the Court need not (even) consider the Defendant's private armed guard proposal. (Gov.'s Opp'n at 23). In *Banki*. the Court stated: "we did not hold [in *Sabhnani*] that district courts routinely must consider the retention of self-paid private security guards as an acceptable condition of release before ordering detention." *Banki*, 369 Fed.Appx. at 154; see also *Sabhnani*. 493 F.3d at 78 n. 18 ("The government has not argued and, therefore, we have no occasion to consider whether it would be contrary to principles of detention and release on bail to allow wealthy defendants to buy their way out by constructing a private jail.") The Government also contends that "Zarrab's proposed private security arrangement does not mitigate the risk of flight" because, among other reasons, Guidepost is "put in a position where they suffer a conflict of interest because they are jailers being paid by the inmate," (Tr. 58 at 12-14), and because "a private security firm simply cannot replicate the controlled environment of a federal correctional facility." (Gov.'s Opp'n at 24.)

On the facts of this case, and having thoroughly considered Defendant's entire bail application, the Court concludes that Mr. Zarrab's continued detention is warranted. The bail package, including the privately funded armed guard regime proposed by the Defendant, does not reasonably assure the appearance of Mr. Zarrab in future proceedings. The Court's analysis is as follows:

1. It is reasonable to consider Mr. Zarrab's bail proposal as detailing a form of continued detention, and not "release." During the bail hearing on June 2, 2016, the Government pointed out that: "There is [ ] in the case law a debate … about whether conditions that put the defendant in confinement in a private apartment under armed security, whether this is any longer a question about conditions of release, or whether it is now about conditions of detention." (See Tr. at 55:21-56:2.) Given the very severe restrictions sought to be imposed upon Mr. Zarrab, the Defendant's proposal does not appear to contemplate "release" so much as it describes a very expensive form of private jail or detention. See 18 U.S.C. § 3142. The Defendant's proposal includes, among its other elements, the following: travel restricted to the Southern District of New York; surrender of all travel documents with no new applications; home detention with GPS-monitoring of Mr. Zarrab's residence; two or more armed (former or off-duty) law enforcement officers residing with Mr. Zarrab around-the-clock; one additional supervisory security professional continuously overseeing Mr. Zarrab's whereabouts; an enhanced security detail – including car and driver – whenever and wherever Mr. Zarrab travels; meetings with defense counsel limited to Mr. Zarrab's

apartment and not counsel's office; and Mr. Zarrab signing a waiver of liability for the use of reasonable force in the event of an attempted escape.17 See also *Banki*, 369 Fed. Appx. at 154 ("Indeed, such conditions might be best seen not as specific conditions of release, but simply as a less onerous form of detention available only to the wealthy.") (emphasis added); *United States v. Valerio*, 9 F. Supp. 3d 283, 293-94 (E.D.N.Y. 2014) ("There is nothing in the Bail Reform Act that would suggest that a defendant ... has a statutory right to replicate or construct a private jail in a home or some other location. The Bail Reform Act address conditions of release, not conditions of detention. Of course, the Act clearly allows for forms of home detention less restrictive than jail. However, once the home detention becomes so restrictive (including with the use of private security guards) that it simply replicates a jail, it is highly questionable whether the Bail Reform Act contemplates 'release' in that context.").)

2. The privately funded armed guard regime proposed by the defense is not reasonable because, in too many respects, it substitutes judicial oversight and management for (more appropriate) reliance upon trained, experienced, and qualified professionals from the U.S. Bureau of Prisons and the U.S. Marshals Service. The Affirmation, dated May 26, 2016, of Joseph Jaffe, Guidepost's Chief Compliance Officer and Deputy General Counsel, is instructive as to the Court's projected role in overseeing Mr. Zarrab's detention. Mr. Jaffe states: "In pretrial release cases ... we follow the directions and orders of the Judge ordering pretrial release, to secure and oversee the individual releasee according to the Judge's orders, and report to and interface with the Court." (Jaffe Aff. at ¶ 6.) Mr. Jaffe further states: "Similarly, in all of our monitoring assignments, the order or agreement establishing and governing our retention, the Court, oversight, regulatory, enforcement or prosecuting authority sets the parameters of our actions." (Id. at ¶ 6 n.1.)

During the June 2, 2016 bail hearing, the following colloquy about to the Court's role took place:

THE COURT: If you'd look at Mr. Jaffe's affirmation ... it says "In pretrial release cases, as in all of our monitoring assignments, we follow the directions and orders of the judge, ordering pretrial release to secure and oversee the individual release according to the judge's orders ... So, I don't quite understand what that means ... I'm not going to be on the phone to Guidepost to say [ ] that sounds like a dangerous situation, you should act or not act ... What's that about? ...

MR. BRAFMAN: [Rhetorically, to be sure, counsel stated:] This is not a situation where Guidepost bothers the Court with 'we think we should hit him over the head with a hammer because he is being obnoxious.' This will not bother the Court at all. To the contrary. Once the Court sets the conditions of release ... then the Court isn't bothered.

See Tr. at 66:13-67:17.

But judicial involvement is inherent in the proposed privately funded armed guard regime. Here are some examples:

- The Court may be asked to decide whether the private security guards should be armed or unarmed. (See Jaffe Aff. at 3 ("Guidepost is prepared and has agreed that, should the Court approve the pretrial release of Mr. Zarrab, we will provide an appropriate number of experienced, armed (if required by the Court) security professionals (all former, or off-duty, law enforcement officers), 24-hours per day, seven days per week, as oversight of Mr. Zarrab ...") (emphasis added); see also Tr. at 68:14-20 (THE COURT: "I do think that actually there's some suggestion there that whether or not they have a gun [ ] is a function of whether the Court determines they should or shouldn't." MR. BRAFMAN: "Yes, but Judge, once you set that in place, they only use arm[ed] guards. And if you say that it doesn't matter, that's up to their discretion.").)

- The Court may be asked to determine the appropriate level of force that may be used to secure Mr. Zarrab. (See Tr. at 68:22-69:15 (THE COURT: "If I say have a gun, that is suggesting that you use the gun." MR BRAFMAN: "No. Judge, these are trained – everyone is a trained law enforcement person." THE COURT: "Just hear me out. There's obviously a distinction between an armed guard and an unarmed guard ... [and] if the judge says they should be armed, then there is some suggestion at least that if something happens, you use that gun ..." MR. BRAFMAN: "I understand your Honor's concern. I don't want the issue of whether the officer chooses to use a weapon to be brought back to your direction that it has to be armed.").) The Government raised a related (pertinent) issue during the June 2, 2016 bail hearing regarding the use of force: "Another fundamental problem with the defendant's private armed guard proposal is that it does put the private armed guards in a situation that is unlike the situation faced by federal officers, federal correctional officers, and federal marshals. These are private individuals, notwithstanding their law enforcement background, they are still private individuals. Their conduct is not governed or supervised by federal law or federal agencies. They are neither supervised nor disciplined by federal agencies. [And, in fact, they are paid by the person they are guarding]. The scope of their ability to use force is different, the potential consequences to them of using force, frankly, I don't know." (Tr. at 58:1-11.) E.D.N.Y. District Judge Joseph F. Bianco's observation in United States v. Valerio is relevant here. "The questions about the legal authorization for the private security firm to use force against defendant should he violate the terms of his release, and the questions over whether the guards can or should be armed, underscore the legal and practical uncertainties—indeed, the imperfections—of the private jail-like concept envisioned by defendant, as compared to the more secure option of an actual jail." 9 F. Supp. 3d at 295.18

- The Court may also be asked to make attorney/client determinations for Mr. Zarrab, i.e., to decide whether the Defendant may travel to his attorneys' offices for consultation or whether, as in Dreier, the attorneys must travel to him. See Dreier, 596 F. Supp. at 833. The Jaffe Affirmation provides in 10 that: "Additional security and monitoring personnel also shall be provided whenever Mr. Zarrab leaves the premises, if he is permitted to do so pursuant to the bail conditions ... [w]e will also provide, as needed, a security vehicle with driver, whenever such travel is required and authorized by the court."

And, at the bail hearing, the following colloquy took place:

THE COURT: I imagine you are aware [ ] even ... in the Dreier case, I don't even think Mr. Dreier was able to go to his lawyer's office, I think the lawyer [ ] had to come to his apartment."

MR. BRAFMAN: That's correct.... We will agree to whatever conditions you deem appropriate, and if it requires us to come to his apartment, we have secured an apartment that is big enough to have a meeting room so the lawyers can work so that's easy .... If that's part of the mix, Judge, we won't fight you on any of those conditions."

Tr. at 70:3-20.

3. The Defendant's private guard proposal is unreasonable because, as noted, it raises serious issues of liability surrounding the use of force against the Defendant and persons who may interact with him. In several other cases, courts have required waivers from defendants permitting the "future use of reasonable force" against them. This "unusual" practice was invoked in Dreier, where the defendant was required expressly to "consent in writing to the use, by the armed security guards, of 'temporary preventive detention and the use of reasonable force' to thwart any attempt to flee." Dreier, 596 F. Supp. at 834. Similarly, in United States v. Ng Lap

Seng, the court required that "Defendant consents to members of the Guidepost security detail's use of reasonable, legal force as they deem appropriate to prevent Defendant from fleeing the Southern District of New York or otherwise violating the terms of release." 15-cr-706, (S.D.N.Y. Oct. 23, 2015). In this case, the defense has stipulated that Mr. Zarrab "will sign a waiver ... that agrees they [i.e., the armed guards] are permitted to use reasonable force to detain him if he attempts to flee." (See Tr. at 69:16-18.) But the Court questions whether such waivers are valid and/or enforceable or if they are reasonable. The Court shares the concern expressed in *Jaffe v. Pallotta Team Works*, that "[a]s with the proscription against prospective waiver of tort liability for intentional torts or for strict liability, such [waiver] agreements interfere with the ability of the state to ensure that persons do not put each other at risk of bodily harm, a policy that often serves goals beyond the protection of the immediate contracting party." 374 F.3d 1223, 1226 (D.C. Cir. 2004); see also *Am. Auto. Ins. Co. v. Rest Assured Alarm Sys., Inc.*, 786 F. Supp. 2d 798, 807 (S.D.N.Y. 2011) ("[T]o the extent that such agreements purport to grant exemption for liability for willful or grossly negligent acts, they have been viewed as wholly void."); Restatement (Second) of Contracts § 195 ("A term exempting a party from tort liability for harm caused intentionally or recklessly is unenforceable."). The Court appreciates the observation in Valerio, where, quoting *United States v. Colorado-Cebado*, Judge Bianco stated: "What more compelling case for an order of detention is there than a case in which only an armed guard and the threat of deadly force is sufficient to assure the defendant's appearance? There are some conditions that are simply not appropriate to be contracted out, and detention under armed guard would seem to be one of those." 9 F. Supp. 3d at 295 (quoting 2013 WL 5852621, at *6 (W.D. Tex. Oct. 30, 2013)).

Most importantly, the Defendant's privately funded armed guard proposal is unreasonable because it helps to foster inequity and unequal treatment in favor of a very small cohort of criminal defendants who are extremely wealthy, such as Mr. Zarrab. As was eloquently stated by then Chief Justice Earl Warren, "[t]he quality of a nation's civilization can be largely measured by the method it uses in the enforcement of its criminal law. When those methods result in arbitrary inequality because of race, indigence or otherwise, the nation as a whole suffers as well as those who are victims of inequality." (See Attorney General Kennedy's National Conference on Bail and Criminal Justice (1964).) And, in a case concerning an indigent defendant's right of access to trial transcripts, the U.S. Supreme Court wisely found that "differences in access to the instruments needed to vindicate legal rights, when based upon the financial situation of the defendant, are repugnant to the Constitution." *Roberts v. LaVallee*, 389 U.S. 40, 42 (1967). With respect to a bail package similar to the Defendant's proposal, the court in United States v. Cilins observed that "[f]ederal judges swear an oath ... to 'administer justice without respect to persons, and do equal right to the poor and to the rich.' That pledge is violated if a defendant, who is a serious risk of flight with every incentive to flee and the means to do so, is permitted to buy his way out of detention." 2013 WL 3802012, (S.D.N.Y. July 19, 2013).19 Former E.D.N.Y. District Judge

Eugene H. Nickerson tellingly found in Borodin v. Ashcroft, that "[i]t is contrary to underlying principles of detention and release on bail that individuals otherwise ineligible for release should be able to buy their way out by constructing a private jail, policed by security guards not trained or ultimately accountable to the government, even if carefully selected." 136 F. Supp. 2d 125, 134 (E.D.N.Y. 2001). And, while the court in *Banki* found that it had "no occasion to consider whether it would be contrary to principles of detention and release on bail to allow wealthy defendants to buy their way out by constructing a private jail," it, nonetheless, explained that "[w]e remain troubled by that possibility." 369 Fed.Appx. at 153-54 (internal citations omitted).

IV. Conclusion & Order

Based upon the facts presented here, and after having reviewed carefully the parties' submissions and applicable authorities, and for the reasons stated above, the Court concludes that the Government has shown by a preponderance of the evidence that Mr. Zarrab poses a risk of flight and that no condition or combination of conditions, including privately funded armed guards, will reasonably assure his appearance at trial. The Court respectfully denies Mr. Zarrab's application for bail [#16].

Note

In the *Awadallah* case below the court approves the use of detention *via* Material Witness designation without any showing that a deposition as an alternative was not available.

UNITED STATES V. AWADALLAH
349 F.3d 42 (2nd Cir. 2003)

Opinion
Judge STRAUB concurs in the opinion except as to Part II.C.3, and has filed a separate concurrence.
JACOBS, Circuit Judge.

This appeal, which arises from the government's investigation of the September 11, 2001 terrorist attacks, presents questions about the scope of the federal material witness statute and the government's powers of arrest and detention thereunder. See 18 U.S.C. § 3144. The district court (Scheindlin, J.) ruled that the statute cannot be applied constitutionally to a grand jury witness such as the defendant-appellee, Osama Awadallah, and dismissed the perjury indictment against him as fruit of an illegal detention. The court also suppressed his grand jury testimony as fruit of an illegal detention on the alternative ground that the affidavit in support of the arrest warrant included material misrepresentations.

We conclude that these rulings must be reversed and the indictment reinstated. We also reverse the district court's independent ruling that the FBI's unreasonable searches and seizures on September 20 and 21, 2001, before Awadallah was arrested as a material witness, require suppression at trial of certain statements and physical evidence.

BACKGROUND

In the days immediately following September 11, 2001, the United States Attorney for the Southern District of New York initiated a grand jury investigation into the terrorist attacks. Investigators quickly identified Nawaf Al–Hazmi and Khalid Al–Mihdhar as two of the hijackers on American Airlines Flight 77, which crashed into the Pentagon. The Justice Department released the identities of all nineteen hijackers on Friday, September 14, 2001, and news media around the country publicized their names and photographs the following day.

A search of the car Al–Hazmi abandoned at Dulles Airport in Virginia produced a piece of paper with the notation, "Osama 589–5316." Federal agents tracked this number to a San Diego address at which the defendant, Osama Awadallah, had lived approximately eighteen months earlier. Al–Hazmi and Al–Mihdhar also had lived in the San Diego vicinity around that time.

The district court made extensive factual findings concerning the ensuing events of September 20 and 21, 2001. See United States v. Awadallah, 202 F.Supp.2d 82, 85–96 (S.D.N.Y.2002) ("Awadallah IV "). With two minor exceptions, the court credited Awadallah's testimony over that of the FBI agents. See id. at 88 n. 9. The government states that it "strongly disagrees with the account of events accepted by the District Judge, and believes the agents testified truthfully and acted entirely properly in their dealings with Awadallah." (Appellant's Br. at 8.) However, the government "has elected not to appeal Judge Scheindlin's credibility findings and does not contest them here." (Id.) For purposes of this appeal, then, the government accepts and relies on the facts found by the district court, as does Awadallah. (Appellee's Br. at 1–2.) Our recitation of the facts conforms to the district court's findings.

On the morning of September 20, 2001, federal agents went to Awadallah's current residence in San Diego. When the agents arrived at the apartment, Awadallah was attending a course in English as a second language at nearby Grossmont College, where he was enrolled. The agents interviewed Awadallah's roommate in their apartment for several hours.

When Awadallah came home at around 2:00 p.m. that afternoon, several agents approached him as he entered the parking lot and got out of his car (a gray Honda). They questioned him in the parking lot for a few minutes and then told him that he had to accompany them to the FBI office for questioning. Awadallah insisted on returning to his apartment first to observe the afternoon Muslim prayer, which he did as the agents watched. When Awadallah went into the bathroom, the agents insisted that the bathroom door be left open.

Before leaving for the FBI office, an agent asked Awadallah to sign a consent form allowing them to search his apartment and car. Otherwise, the agent told him, they would get a warrant and "tear up" his home. Believing he had no choice, Awadallah signed the form without reading it. See Awadallah IV, 202 F.Supp.2d at 89 & n. 13. The agents then put him in their car and drove him to the FBI office. Awadallah told them that he had to return in time for a 6:00 p.m. computer class; they told him that would be no problem.

At the FBI office, agents offered Awadallah a drink, but he declined because he was fasting. They asked him to sign another consent form for the search of his second car, an inoperative white Honda in the parking lot of his apartment building. This time, Awadallah read the form and learned that he had a right to refuse consent; and though he signed the consent form for his second car, he explicitly revoked his consent for the search of the first car. An agent tried to reach the agents at the apartment building by cell phone, but did not reach them until fifteen minutes later, after the search of the first car had been completed. The agents at the scene then searched the apartment and the second car. The search of Awadallah's home produced several computer-generated photographs of Osama bin Laden; the searches of his cars produced two videotapes on Bosnia and one on Islam and a retractable razor which could be described as a box-cutter or a carpet knife.

Awadallah was alone in a locked interview room for a while, until agents arrived to question him. They did not advise him of his rights or tell him that he could leave. They asked him about the September 11 hijackers and about his life and acquaintances. He told the agents that he knew Al–Hazmi, and that he had frequently seen another man with him, whose name he did not know.

The district court found that Awadallah was "cooperative" throughout this questioning. See Awadallah IV, 202 F.Supp.2d at 92. We construe this finding to mean that he responded to questions, not that he necessarily responded truthfully or completely.

When 6:00 p.m. approached, the agents told Awadallah that they had called his school and that it was alright for him to miss class. They told him he would "have to stay" with them until they were finished. The entire interview lasted approximately six hours, ending at nearly 11:00 p.m. Before allowing Awadallah to leave, the agents scheduled a polygraph examination for the next morning. The record does not show whether an agent was posted at Awadallah's apartment building overnight, but the district court stated that "[h]e was not guarded or surveilled overnight." Awadallah IV, 202 F.Supp.2d at 99.

At 6:30 a.m. the following day, September 21, 2001, Awadallah called the FBI and refused to come in for the polygraph test until he had a lawyer. The agent told him they would get an arrest warrant. Believing he had no choice, Awadallah went with two agents who picked him up at his apartment at 7:00 a.m.

At the FBI office, agents advised Awadallah of his rights and he signed an advice-of-rights acknowledgment form. The polygraph exam lasted one-and-a-half to two hours. Afterward, the agents told Awadallah that the polygraph registered lies in response to two questions: whether he had advance knowledge of the September 11 attacks and whether he had participated in them in any way. It is unclear whether these were in fact the results. The conversation became heated as the agents accused Awadallah of being a terrorist. They refused Awadallah's requests to call a lawyer and his brother, and did not release him in time for Friday prayer.

Throughout the questioning that day, the FBI agents in San Diego had been in contact with an Assistant United States Attorney ("AUSA") in New York. At approximately 2:00 p.m. Eastern time, the AUSA instructed the agents to arrest Awadallah as a material witness. The agents handcuffed Awadallah and took him to the San Diego correctional center for booking.

Meanwhile, prosecutors and agents in New York prepared an application for a material witness warrant. In the supporting affidavit, FBI Special Agent Ryan Plunkett recounted how the FBI found the phone number in Al–Hazmi's car, Awadallah's admission that he knew Al–Hazmi, and the results of the agents' searches, including the "box-cutter" and the photographs of bin Laden. Agent Plunkett stated that it might become difficult to secure Awadallah's grand jury testimony because he had extensive family ties in Jordan and might be a flight risk. The affidavit did not say when Awadallah said he had last seen Al–Hazmi (over a year earlier); that Awadallah had moved eighteen months earlier from the address associated with the phone number; that Awadallah had used the "box-cutter" recently to install a new carpet in his apartment; that Awadallah had been (ostensibly) cooperative with the FBI agents in San Diego; or that Awadallah had three brothers who lived in San Diego, one of whom was an American citizen. Also, the affidavit stated that the "box-cutter" had been found in Awadallah's apartment when, in fact, it had been found in his inoperative second car. See Awadallah IV, 202 F.Supp.2d at 96.

Shortly before 6:00 p.m. Eastern time, Agent Plunkett and an AUSA presented the material witness warrant application to Chief Judge Mukasey of the United States District Court for the Southern District of New York. Based solely on the contents of Agent Plunkett's affidavit, Chief Judge Mukasey issued a warrant to arrest Awadallah as a material witness pursuant to 18 U.S.C. § 3144. The court was unaware that Awadallah had already been arrested as a material witness three hours earlier. See Awadallah IV, 202 F.Supp.2d at 95.

On September 25, 2001, Awadallah appeared before a Magistrate Judge Ruben B. Brooks in the Southern District of California, who declined to release him on bail and ordered that he be removed to New York. On October 2, 2001, the day after he arrived in New York, Awadallah appeared before Chief Judge Mukasey for a second bail hearing. Chief Judge Mukasey also declined to release Awadallah on bail, finding his continued detention to be "reasonable under the circumstances."

During the period of his detention, Awadallah spent time in four prisons as he was transferred to the New York correctional center by way of Oklahoma City. He alleges that he received harsh and improper treatment during this period. Because these allegations of abuse and mistreatment were immaterial to the issues before the district court, Judge Scheindlin expressly declined to make "findings of fact on disputed issues regarding the conditions of confinement." See *United States v. Awadallah*, 202 F.Supp.2d 55, 59 n. 4 (S.D.N.Y.2002) ("*Awadallah III* "). Nonetheless, Judge Scheindlin noted that Awadallah spent most of his time in solitary confinement; at times lacked access to his family, his lawyer, or a phone; and was repeatedly strip-searched. See id. at 60–61 & n. 5. The government did not dispute that, by October 4, 2001, "Awadallah had bruises on his upper arms," and an agent's report indicated several other injuries on his shoulder, ankles, hand, and face. See id. at 61. Awadallah sometimes refrained from eating because the meals provided did not comply with his religious dietary restrictions.

On October 10, 2001, twenty days after his arrest as a material witness, Awadallah testified before the grand jury in the Southern District of New York. The prosecutor questioned him for most of the day. In the course of his testimony, Awadallah denied knowing anyone named Khalid Al–Mihdhar or Khalid. The government then showed him an examination booklet he had written in September, which the government obtained from his English teacher in San Diego. The booklet contained the following handwritten sentence: "One of the qui[e] test people I have met is Nawaf. Another one his name Khalid. They have stayed in S.D. [San Diego] for 6 months." Awadallah acknowledged that it was his examination booklet, and that most of the writing in it was his own, but he denied that the name Khalid and a few other words on the page were written in his handwriting. On October 15, 2001, when Awadallah again appeared before the grand jury, he stated that his recollection of Khalid's name had been refreshed by his October 10 testimony and that the disputed writing in the exam booklet was in fact his own. However, he did not admit to making false statements in his first grand jury appearance.

The United States Attorney for the Southern District of New York filed charges against Awadallah on two counts of making false statements to the grand jury in violation of 18 U.S.C. § 1623: falsely denying that he knew Khalid Al–Mihdhar (Count One); and falsely denying that the handwriting in the exam booklet was his own (Count Two).

On November 27, 2001, the district court (Scheindlin, J.) granted Awadallah's bail application. See United States v. Awadallah, 173 F.Supp.2d 186, 192–93 (S.D.N.Y.2001) ("*Awadallah I* "). He satisfied the bail conditions and was released approximately two weeks later.

In December 2001, Awadallah moved to dismiss the indictment on four grounds: (1) recantation; (2) mistreatment in violation of his due process rights; (3) interference with his right to counsel; and (4) violation of the Vienna Convention on Consular Relations. He also moved to suppress the statements and search evidence obtained by the FBI on September 20 and 21, on the grounds that he had been seized illegally and that his consent to the searches was involuntary.

On January 31, 2002, the district court rejected the grounds cited by Awadallah for dismissal. See United States v. Awadallah, 202 F.Supp.2d 17 (S.D.N.Y.2002) ("Awadallah II "). In the same order, however, the court sua sponte raised two other possible grounds for dismissal: (1) the possibility that Awadallah was the victim of a "perjury trap," id. at 43–44, and (2) the court's supervisory power to suppress his grand jury testimony if suppression *49 is warranted by the circumstances of his arrest and treatment, id. at 52–53. The court ordered that these issues, in addition to Awadallah's Fourth Amendment claims, be taken up at an evidentiary hearing.

On April 30, 2002, after an evidentiary hearing and further briefing, the district court issued two orders dismissing the indictment against Awadallah. In Awadallah III, the court ruled that the federal material witness statute, 18 U.S.C. § 3144, did not apply to grand jury witnesses. 202 F.Supp.2d at 61–79. This ruling evidently was made without briefing or argument.4 The court held that Awadallah's arrest and detention were therefore unlawful. Applying reasoning developed in the Awadallah II decision, Judge Scheindlin ruled that Awadallah's perjured grand jury testimony had to be suppressed as fruit of this illegal arrest and detention. Id. at 79–82.

In Awadallah IV, the district court held in the alternative that the indictment also had to be dismissed because the government's affidavit in support of the material witness warrant contained material omissions and misrepresentations. Id. at 96–100. Once again, the court held that the grand jury testimony was fruit of the illegal arrest and detention. Id. As a separate matter, the district court also ruled that Awadallah had been seized in violation of the Fourth Amendment and that he had given no voluntary consent to the searches. Id. at 101–07. Accordingly, the court suppressed statements and physical evidence obtained by the FBI on September 20 and 21, 2001 before Awadallah's arrest as a material witness. Id. at 100–07.

The government filed a timely notice of appeal from the Awadallah III and Awadallah IV decisions on May 2, 2002. In this same notice, the government appealed the Awadallah II decision, which had been issued over three months earlier. Awadallah remains free on bail at this time.

DISCUSSION

We consider the issues presented on appeal in the order in which the district court developed them: (1) whether the federal material witness statute, 18 U.S.C. § 3144, may be applied to grand jury witnesses like Awadallah; (2) whether material misrepresentations in the government's affidavit in support of the material witness warrant require the suppression of Awadallah's grand jury testimony and the dismissal of the indictment against him; and (3) whether evidence obtained by the government on September 20 and 21 before Awadallah was formally detained as a material witness must be suppressed as the fruit of illegal searches and seizures.

I. Applicability of 18 U.S.C. § 3144

1 The first issue presented is whether the federal material witness statute, 18 U.S.C. § 3144, allows the arrest and detention of grand jury witnesses. In Awadallah III, the district court determined that it did not. Shortly thereafter, however, on July 11, 2002, Chief Judge Mukasey issued an opinion in an unrelated case that declined to follow the reasoning and holding of Awadallah III. Specifically, Judge Mukasey held that 18 U.S.C. § 3144 applies to grand jury witnesses. See *In re Material Witness Warrant*, 213 F.Supp.2d 287, 288 (S.D.N.Y.2002). Thus there is now a split of authority within the Circuit on this question.

As discussed at oral argument, we might evade this issue by holding that Awadallah's allegedly false testimony should not have been suppressed as fruit of the poisonous tree even if his detention under § 3144 was improper, and that the indictment therefore should not have been dismissed. We reach the issue, however, because the present split within our Circuit on the scope of § 3144 affects the liberty interests of persons identified as material witnesses, the security and law enforcement interests of the government, and the ability of courts to make prompt and fair rulings on present and future detentions. It is true that "at times courts are well advised to avoid an issue presented in litigation by relying on an alternative ground." *United States v. Tomasi*, 313 F.3d 653, 659 n. 4 (2d Cir.2002). "But there is no principle of law or jurisprudence to the effect that such avoidance is required. In some circumstances it is the better course to decide, rather than avoid, a question presented." Id. Both parties to this appeal, as well as the amici, persuasively urge us to decide whether § 3144 may properly be applied to grand jury witnesses. The issue is squarely presented, has been fully briefed, and will tend to evade review in future cases where the detention is brief or matters take a different procedural course.

Section 3144, titled "[r]elease or detention of a material witness," provides in its entirety:

> If it appears from an affidavit filed by a party that the testimony of a person is material in a criminal proceeding, and if it is shown that it may become impracticable to secure the presence of the person by subpoena, a judicial officer may order the arrest of the person and treat the person in accordance with the provisions of section 3142 of this title. No material witness may be detained because of inability to comply with any condition of release if the testimony of such witness can adequately be secured by deposition, and if further detention is not necessary to prevent a failure of justice. Release of a material witness may be delayed for a reasonable period of time until the deposition of the witness can be taken pursuant to the Federal Rules of Criminal Procedure.

18 U.S.C. § 3144. The statute is cast in terms of a material witness in "a criminal proceeding." The decisive question here is whether that term encompasses proceedings before a grand jury.

Based on its study of the statutory wording, context, legislative history, and case law, the district court held that "Section 3144 only allows the detention of material witnesses in the pre-trial (as opposed to the grand jury) context." *Awadallah III*, 202 F.Supp.2d at 76. We have found no other decision that has arrived at this conclusion.

The only prior case that squarely considered the issue held that 18 U.S.C. § 3149, the precursor to today's material witness statute, allowed detention of grand jury witnesses. See *Bacon v. United States*, 449 F.2d 933, 936–41 (9th Cir.1971). The Ninth Circuit conceded that "[t]he term 'criminal proceeding,' absent a clear context, [was] ambiguous," id. at 939, but held that the relevant statutes and Federal Rules of Criminal Procedure, "[t]aken as a whole," were "clearly broad enough in scope to encompass grand jury investigations," id. at 941.

Other courts, including this one, have assumed that the material witness statute authorizes detention of grand jury witnesses. See *In re Grand Jury Subpoena (United States v. Koecher)*, 755 F.2d 1022, 1024 & n. 2 (2d Cir.1985) (noting prior unpublished order which required that defendant "remain subject to the warrant of arrest as a material witness" during remand to determine proper scope of grand jury investigation), vacated as moot, 475 U.S. 133, 106 S.Ct. 1253, 89 L.Ed.2d 103 (1986); see also *In re De Jesus Berrios*, 706 F.2d 355, 356–58 (1st Cir.1983) (upholding on other grounds the arrest of a material witness in a grand jury investigation); *United States v. Oliver*, 683 F.2d 224, 230–31 (7th Cir.1982) (same); *United States v. McVeigh*, 940 F.Supp. 1541, 1562 (D.Colo.1996) (finding government affidavit sufficient to justify arrest of defendant Terry Nichols under § 3144 to testify as material witness before grand jury investigating the Oklahoma City bombing); *In re Thornton*, 560 F.Supp. 183, 184 (S.D.N.Y.1983) (denying motion for relief from civil contempt order by witness who had been "arrested on a material witness warrant issued ... pursuant to 18 U.S.C. § 3149 ... to appear and testify before a federal grand jury"); cf. *Arnsberg v. United States*, 757 F.2d 971, 981–82 (9th Cir.1985) (finding federal agents immune from false imprisonment suit after they arrested a grand jury witness pursuant to a warrant issued under § 3149).

Two judges have also declined to follow the district court's ruling in this case. In *In re Material Witness Warrant*, 213 F.Supp.2d 287 (S.D.N.Y.2002), Chief Judge Mukasey "decline[d] to follow the reasoning and holding in Awadallah," id. at 288, holding instead:

> Given the broad language of the statute, its legislative history ..., the substantial body of case law indicating that there is no constitutional impediment to detention of grand jury witnesses, and the unquestioned application of the statute to grand jury witnesses over a period of decades before Awadallah, to perceive a Congressional intention that grand jury witnesses be excluded from the reach of section 3144 is to perceive something that is not there.

Id. at 300; see also *In re Grand Jury Material Witness Detention*, 271 F.Supp.2d 1266, 1268 (D.Or.2003) (concluding that "a grand jury proceeding constitutes a 'criminal proceeding,' as the term is used in § 3144"). Having the benefit of thorough opinions on both sides of the question, we conclude that the district court's ruling in this case must be reversed.

A. Standard of Review

2 When "[t]he district court's dismissal of [an] indictment raises questions of constitutional interpretation, ... we review the district court's decision de novo." *United States v. King*, 276 F.3d 109, 111 (2d Cir.2002) (reversing dismissal of indictment because statute in question was "a permissible exercise of Congressional authority under the Commerce Clause"). This standard of review comports with our customary approach to questions of statutory interpretation and constitutionality. See *United States v. Pettus*, 303 F.3d 480, 483 (2d Cir.2002) (reviewing a "question of statutory interpretation and of the constitutionality of [a statute] de novo "); *Muller v. Costello*, 187 F.3d 298, 307 (2d Cir.1999).

In construing a statute, we begin with its language and plain meaning. See *United States v. Koh*, 199 F.3d 632, 636 (2d Cir.1999); *United States v. Figueroa*, 165 F.3d 111, 114 (2d Cir.1998); *United States v. Proyect*, 989 F.2d 84, 87 (2d Cir.1993) ("[W]hen the language of the statute is clear, its plain meaning ordinarily controls its construction."). "However, where statutory language is ambiguous a court may resort to the canons of statutory interpretation and to the statute's legislative history to resolve the ambiguity." *Canada Life Assurance Co. v. Converium Ruckversicherung* (Deutschland) AG, 335 F.3d 52, 57 (2d Cir.2003).

B. Language of the Statute

As noted above, § 3144 applies to witnesses whose testimony is material in "a criminal proceeding." 18 U.S.C. § 3144. "Criminal proceeding" is a broad and capacious term, and there is good reason to conclude that it includes a grand jury proceeding. First, it has long been recognized that "[t]he word 'proceeding' is not a technical one, and is aptly used by courts to designate an inquiry before a grand jury." *Hale v. Henkel*, 201 U.S. 43, 66, 26 S.Ct. 370, 50 L.Ed. 652 (1906); cf. *Cobbledick v. United States*, 309 U.S. 323, 327, 60 S.Ct. 540, 84 L.Ed. 783 (1940) ("The proceeding before a grand jury constitutes 'a judicial inquiry' of the most ancient lineage.") (citation omitted).

Second, the term "criminal proceeding" has been construed in other statutes to encompass grand jury proceedings. For example, the statute authorizing the government to appeal from "a decision or order of a district court suppressing or excluding evidence ... in a criminal proceeding," 18 U.S.C. § 3731 (emphasis added), has been construed to authorize appeal of such an order from a grand jury proceeding. See, e.g., *In re Grand Jury Subpoena Duces Tecum* Dated Jan. 2, 1985, 775 F.2d 499, 502 (2d Cir.1985) ("It has been held that a grand jury proceeding is 'a criminal proceeding' within the portion of the Criminal Appeals Act, 18 U.S.C. § 3731, that entitles the Government to appeal from a decision or order of a district court suppressing or excluding evidence."); In re Grand Jury Empanelled Feb. 14, 1978, 597 F.2d 851, 857 (3d Cir.1979) (observing that, "[i]n deciding questions pertaining to appellate jurisdiction, this circuit and others have adopted the view that the grand jury is a criminal proceeding"). At least one court has reached the same conclusion under a statute that punishes interstate flight "to avoid giving testimony in any criminal proceedings," 18 U.S.C. § 1073 (emphasis added). See *Hemans v. United States*, 163 F.2d 228, 235–37 (6th Cir.1947) (construing former version of statute codified at 18 U.S.C. § 408e).

Notwithstanding this support for the general view that "criminal proceedings" encompass grand jury proceedings, however, we cannot say that the statutory wording alone compels that conclusion. Black's Law Dictionary defines a "criminal proceeding" as "[a] proceeding instituted to determine a person's guilt or innocence or to set a convicted person's punishment; a criminal hearing or trial." Black's Law Dictionary 1221 (7th ed.1999). It defines a "grand jury" as "[a] body of ... people ... who, in ex parte proceedings, decide whether to issue indictments. If the grand jury decides that evidence is strong enough to hold a suspect for trial, it returns a bill of indict-ment ... charging the suspect with a specific crime." Id. at 706. Defined this way, a grand jury proceeding is not a "proceeding instituted to determine a person's guilt or innocence or to set a convicted person's punishment," but rather a proceeding to "decide whether to issue indict-ments." Cf. *United States v. Mandujano*, 425 U.S. 564, 573, 96 S.Ct. 1768, 48 L.Ed.2d 212 (1976) ("[T]he grand jury's mission is ... to determine whether to make a presentment or return an indict-ment."). A grand jury proceeding is certainly a stage of criminal justice; and it is certainly a proceeding. As a proceeding, it is certainly not civil, administrative, arbitral, commercial, social, or any type of proceeding other than (or as much as) criminal. Even so, the dictionary entries could suggest that grand jury proceedings lie outside the scope of § 3144.

As the district court observed, this Court applied such a view in United States v. Thompson, 319 F.2d 665 (2d Cir.1963). In *Thompson*, a divided panel held that the meaning of the term "crimi-nal proceeding" was ambiguous as used in the Walsh Act, 28 U.S.C. § 1783 et seq., which con-fers power upon district courts to issue subpoenas to witnesses outside the United States. The panel ultimately concluded that the term did not encompass grand jury proceedings. 319 F.2d at 668–70. In dissent, Judge Kaufman observed that the majority's conclusion was "tortured" and argued that the plain meaning of "criminal proceeding" encompassed grand jury proceedings. Id. at 671–73. Congress agreed with Judge Kaufman the following year.5 But the split in a panel of this Court runs counter to the view that a "criminal proceeding" plainly encompasses a grand jury proceeding.

The statutory context does not allay all uncertainty. Under § 3144, a judge "may order the arrest of the person and treat the person in accordance with the provisions of section 3142 of this title." 18 U.S.C. § 3144. Section 3142, which sets conditions for the "[r]elease or detention of a defendant pending trial," uses terms not normally associated with grand juries. It provides:

> Upon the appearance before a judicial officer of a person charged with an offense, the judicial
> officer shall issue an order that, pending trial, the person be—(1) released on personal recog-
> nizance or upon execution of an unsecured appearance bond ...; (2) released on a condition
> or combination of conditions ...; (3) temporarily detained to permit revocation of conditional
> release, deportation, or exclusion ...; or (4) detained ....

18 U.S.C. § 3142(a) (emphasis added). By its own terms, § 3142 applies during the post-indictment ("a person charged with an offense") and pretrial ("pending trial") phase of criminal prosecution. The section also goes on to identify factors to be considered "in determining whether there are conditions of release that will reasonably assure the appearance of the person as required and the safety of any other person and the community." 18 U.S.C. § 3142(g). Two of the four listed considerations have little bearing on the situation of an individual detained as a material witness in a grand jury proceeding. See 18 U.S.C. § 3142(g)(1) ("[t]he nature and circumstances of the offense charged"); id. § 3142(g)(2) ("the weight of the evidence against the person"). For these reasons, we must look beyond the text of § 3144 to discern the meaning of "criminal proceeding."

C. Legislative History

The legislative history of § 3144 makes clear Congress's intent to include grand jury proceedings within the definition of "criminal proceeding." Congress enacted § 3144 in its current form as part of the Bail Reform Act of 1984. See Pub.L. No. 98–473, 98 Stat. 1837, 1976–81 (1984). Its language is nearly identical to the text of its predecessor statute, 18 U.S.C. § 1349 (1966),6 which the Ninth Circuit construed to encompass grand juries. See Bacon, 449 F.2d at 939–41.

The most telling piece of legislative history appears in the Senate Judiciary Committee Report that accompanied the 1984 enactment of § 3144. The Report stated that, "[i]f a person's testimony is material in any criminal proceeding, and if it is shown that it may become impracticable to secure his presence by subpoena, the government is authorized to take such person into custody." S.Rep. No. 98–225, at 28 (1983), reprinted in 1984 U.S.C.C.A.N. 3182, 3211. A footnote to this statement advised categorically that "[a] grand jury investigation is a 'criminal proceeding' within the meaning of this section. Bacon v. United States, 449 F.2d 933 (9th Cir.1971)." Id. at 25 n. 88, 1984 U.S.C.C.A.N. at 3208. The approving citation to Bacon by the Senate Committee with responsibility for this bill is as indicative as the text of the footnote.

Committee reports are not always reliable interpretive tools, see *Shannon v. United States*, 512 U.S. 573, 583, 114 S.Ct. 2419, 129 L.Ed.2d 459 (1994) (noting that "a single passage of legislative history" should not be given "authoritative weight" when it "is in no way anchored in the text of the statute"), but we may look to them in discerning Congressional intent:

> In surveying legislative history we have repeatedly stated that the authoritative source for finding the Legislature's intent lies in the Committee Reports on the bill, which "represen[t] the considered and collective understanding of those Congressmen involved in drafting and studying proposed legislation."

Garcia v. United States, 469 U.S. 70, 76, 105 S.Ct. 479, 83 L.Ed.2d 472 (1984) (citation omitted); see also *Eldred v. Ashcroft*, 537 U.S. 186, 210 n. 16, 123 S.Ct. 769, 154 L.Ed.2d 683 (2003); *Thornburg v. Gingles*, 478 U.S. 30, 44 n. 7, 106 S.Ct. 2752, 92 L.Ed.2d 25 (1986). Here, the Senate committee report states in so many words the intent to include grand jury proceedings within the ambit of the statute—an intent that is consistent with the statute's language, even if not compelled by it.

This statement of congressional intent is particularly telling, because the Bail Reform Act of 1984 reenacted the provisions of the former § 3149 in nearly identical language. "Congress is presumed to be aware of an administrative or judicial interpretation of a statute and to adopt that interpretation when it re-enacts a statute without change." See *Lorillard v. Pons*, 434 U.S. 575, 580, 98 S.Ct. 866, 55 L.Ed.2d 40 (1978). In Lorillard, as here, there was clear evidence that Congress had considered the specific judicial interpretation in question. See id. at 581, 98 S.Ct. 866; see also *Holder v. Hall*, 512 U.S. 874, 961, 114 S.Ct. 2581, 129 L.Ed.2d 687 (1994) (separate opinion of Stevens, J.) (noting that, "[w]hen a Congress that re-enacts a statute voices its approval of an administrative or other interpretation thereof, Congress is treated as having adopted that interpretation, and [the courts are] bound thereby"); *In re Material Witness Warrant*, 213 F.Supp.2d at 297.

Awadallah and an amicus party supporting his position argue that this principle of ratification by reenactment is inapplicable because there was no "settled judicial interpretation" of the term "criminal proceeding" when § 3144 was enacted in 1984. (Amicus Br. of NYCDL at 23 (quoting Holder, 512 U.S. at 920, 114 S.Ct. 2581).) We disagree. The Senate report stated that "[a] grand jury investigation is a 'criminal proceeding' within the meaning of this section." S.Rep. No. 98–225, at 25 n. 88 (1983), 1984 U.S.C.C.A.N. at 3208 (emphasis added). As of 1984, a single court had expressly considered whether the term "criminal proceeding" within the meaning of the federal material witness statute included grand jury proceedings—and it had held that it did. See *Bacon*, 449 F.2d at 939–41. This Court had reached a different conclusion in *Thompson*, but only in connection with an unrelated statute, 319 F.2d at 668–70, and that interpretation was legislatively overruled the following year, see supra note 5. When Congress enacted § 3144—and until the district court ruled otherwise in this case—there was a settled view that a grand jury proceeding is a "criminal proceeding" for purposes of the material witness statute. We therefore conclude that a grand jury proceeding is a "criminal proceeding" for purposes of § 3144.

D. Constitutional Considerations

In concluding that § 3144 does not apply to grand jury witnesses, the district court invoked the canon of constitutional avoidance, under which a court should construe an ambiguous statute to avoid constitutional problems if a viable alternative interpretation exists. See *Awadallah III*, 202 F.Supp.2d at 76–77 (citing INS v. St. Cyr, 533 U.S. 289, 299–300, 121 S.Ct. 2271, 150 L.Ed.2d 347 (2001); *Edward J. DeBartolo Corp. v. Florida Gulf Coast Bldg. & Constr. Trades Council*, 485 U.S. 568, 575, 108 S.Ct. 1392, 99 L.Ed.2d 645 (1988)). This rule, which facilitates a choice between alternative interpretations of an ambiguous statute, has no bearing if the meaning of the statute is known. See *Dep't of Hous. & Urban Dev. v. Rucker*, 535 U.S. 125, 134, 122 S.Ct. 1230, 152 L.Ed.2d 258 (2002) (noting that "the canon of constitutional avoidance ... 'has no application in the absence of statutory ambiguity' ") (*quoting United States v. Oakland Cannabis Buyers' Coop.*, 532 U.S. 483, 494, 121 S.Ct. 1711, 149 L.Ed.2d 722 (2001)). Here, we have determined that Congress intended to place grand jury proceedings within the scope of § 3144. The canon of constitutional avoidance therefore does not come into play. Cf. St. Cyr, 533 U.S. at 299, 121 S.Ct. 2271 (noting the corollary rule that, "when a particular interpretation of a statute invokes the outer limits of Congress' power, we expect a clear indication that Congress intended that result").

Assuming arguendo that there are two viable interpretations of § 3144, "the canon ... applies only when there are serious concerns about the statute's constitutionality." *Harris v. United States*, 536 U.S. 545, 555, 122 S.Ct. 2406, 153 L.Ed.2d 524 (2002) (citation omitted). The district court determined that "[i]mprisoning a material witness for a grand jury investigation raises a serious constitutional question" under the Fourth Amendment's prohibition against unreasonable search and seizure.8 Awadallah III, 202 F.Supp.2d at 77. We respectfully disagree.

As a threshold matter, the detention of material witnesses for the purpose of securing grand jury testimony has withstood constitutional challenge. In *New York v. O'Neill*, 359 U.S. 1, 79 S.Ct. 564, 3 L.Ed.2d 585 (1959), the Supreme Court considered "the constitutionality of a Florida statute entitled 'Uniform Law to Secure the Attendance of Witnesses from Within or Without a State in Criminal Proceedings.' " Id. at 3, 79 S.Ct. 564. This statute—which had been adopted in 42 states and the Commonwealth of Puerto Rico—enabled a judge of one state to certify "the necessity of the appearance of [a] witness in a criminal prosecution or grand jury investigation," and concomitantly enabled the state where that witness could be found to "take the witness into immediate custody" and "deliver the witness to an officer of the requesting State." Id. at 4–5, 79 S.Ct. 564. The Court held that this statute did not violate the Privileges and Immunities Clause of the Fourteenth Amendment. Id. at 6–7, 79 S.Ct. 564. In doing so, it observed that "Florida undoubtedly could have held respondent within Florida if he had been a material witness in a criminal proceeding within that State." Id. at 7, 79 S.Ct. 564. The Court observed that "[a] citizen cannot shirk his duty, no matter how inconvenienced thereby, to testify in criminal proceedings and grand jury investigations in a State where he is found. There is no constitutional provision granting him relief from this obligation to testify even though he must travel to another State to do so." Id. at 11, 79 S.Ct. 564.

The Supreme Court has made similar pronouncements in other cases. In *Stein v. New York,* 346 U.S. 156, 73 S.Ct. 1077, 97 L.Ed. 1522 (1953), overruled in part on other grounds by Jackson v. Denno, 378 U.S. 368, 84 S.Ct. 1774, 12 L.Ed.2d 908 (1964), the petitioners claimed that confessions were coerced by custodial interrogation and that their admission into evidence was unconstitutional. Id. at 159–60, 73 S.Ct. 1077. Even in the less august context of a police investigation (no grand jury had been convened), the Supreme Court observed that "[t]he duty to disclose knowledge of crime rests upon all citizens," and that this duty "is so vital that one known to be innocent may be detained, in the absence of bail, as a material witness. This Court never has held that the Fourteenth Amendment prohibits a state from such detention and interrogation of a suspect as under the circumstances appears reasonable and not coercive." Id. at 184, 73 S.Ct. 1077 (citing N.Y.Code Crim. Proc. § 618–b; Fed.R.Crim.P. 46(b)); cf. *Allen v. Nix,* 55 F.3d 414, 415–17 (8th Cir.1995) (affirming denial of habeas relief to petitioner who claimed, among other things, that his detention on a state material witness warrant during a murder investigation violated the Fourth Amendment).

Similarly, the Court has observed that the Senate has "the power in some cases to issue a warrant of arrest to compel" the "attendance of witnesses," and that this power was "a necessary incident of the power to adjudge, in no wise inferior under like circumstances to that exercised by a court of justice." *Barry v. United States ex rel. Cunningham,* 279 U.S. 597, 616, 49 S.Ct. 452, 73 L.Ed. 867 (1929). "[A] court has power in the exercise of a sound discretion to issue a warrant of arrest without a previous subpoena, when there is good reason to believe that otherwise the witness will not be forthcoming." *Id.* at 616, 49 S.Ct. 452 (citing former 28 U.S.C. § 659).9 The *Barry* case made clear that it was saying nothing new: "The constitutionality of [28 U.S.C. § 659] apparently has never been doubted. Similar statutes exist in many of the states and have been enforced without question." Id. at 617, 49 S.Ct. 452.

This Court has likewise upheld the constitutionality of detaining grand jury witnesses under a New York material witness statute, former § 618–b of the New York Code of Criminal Procedure. In *United States ex rel. Allen v. LaVallee,* 411 F.2d 241 (2d Cir.1969), we upheld the admissibility of a confession obtained during the detention of a state grand jury witness under § 618–b. Id. at 244. We rejected the petitioner's argument that "he was illegally detained as a material witness, because there was no criminal action or proceeding then pending, as required by § 618–b;" the grand jury proceeding and the ongoing police investigation were enough.10 Id. at 243.

We reached a similar conclusion in *United States ex rel. Glinton v. Denno,* 309 F.2d 543 (2d Cir.1962) ("Glinton I "), which rejected a constitutional challenge to the admission of statements obtained while the petitioner was detained as a material witness for a state grand jury investigation. Although the New York material witness statute "require[d] a criminal action or proceeding to be pending in some New York court," we held that this requirement was satisfied by the grand jury investigation under way at the time of Glinton's arrest, id. at 544, observing that such statutes "appear to be fairly common and to have been enforced without question." Id.

Glinton's Fourth Amendment claim, based on his detention for two weeks after the grand jury was discharged, was procedurally untenable in *Glinton I*, but was fully considered in *United States ex rel. Glinton v. Denno*, 339 F.2d 872 (2d Cir.1964) *("Glinton II ")*. In *Glinton II*, we saw "no reason to reverse our earlier holding that ... [*Glinton's*] initial commitment, in lieu of bail, on November 13 as a material witness was lawful .... There cannot be any doubt that *Glinton* was validly committed as a material witness." Id. at 874–75 (citation omitted). We continued:

> [T]he district attorney easily could have preserved the legality of Glinton's detention by keeping
> the grand jury proceeding alive or by commencing a new one.... Assuming that Glinton's pres-
> ence as a material witness was still necessary, this continued detention would not have violated
> the Fourth Amendment. It cannot seriously be urged, therefore, that a detention which has
> been proper in all respects becomes violative of the Constitution merely upon a technicality, the
> discharging of the grand jury.

Id. at 876.12

The district court failed to account for these cases in detecting a constitutional problem in the detention of a material witness, and focused instead on developing its own Fourth Amendment analysis. Even meeting the district court decision on those terms, we see no serious constitutional problem that would warrant the exclusion of grand jury proceedings from the scope of § 3144.

The Fourth Amendment prohibits "unreasonable searches and seizures." U.S. Const. amend. IV. Determining the reasonableness of a seizure involves a balancing of competing interests:

> The essential purpose of the proscriptions in the Fourth Amendment is to impose a standard of
> "reasonableness" upon the exercise of discretion by government officials, including law enforce-
> ment agents, in order "to safeguard the privacy and security of individuals against arbitrary
> invasions ...." Thus, the permissibility of a particular law enforcement practice is judged by
> balancing its intrusion on the individual's Fourth Amendment interests against its promotion of
> legitimate governmental interests.

Delaware v. Prouse, 440 U.S. 648, 653–54, 99 S.Ct. 1391, 59 L.Ed.2d 660 (1979) (citations and footnotes omitted); see also *Michigan v. Summers*, 452 U.S. 692, 700 n. 12, 101 S.Ct. 2587, 69 L.Ed.2d 340 (1981) (" '[T]he key principle of the Fourth Amendment is reasonableness—the balancing of competing interests.' ") (quoting Dunaway, 442 U.S. at 219, 99 S.Ct. 2248 (White, J., concurring)). Thus we must consider both "the nature and quality of the intrusion on the individual's Fourth

Amendment interests" and "the importance of the governmental interests alleged to justify the intrusion." *Tennessee v. Garner*, 471 U.S. 1, 8, 105 S.Ct. 1694, 85 L.Ed.2d 1 (1985) (citing *United States v. Place*, 462 U.S. 696, 703, 103 S.Ct. 2637, 77 L.Ed.2d 110 (1983)).

In its balancing analysis, the district court found that "[t]he only legitimate reason to detain a grand jury witness is to aid in 'an ex parte investigation to determine whether a crime has been committed and whether criminal proceedings should be instituted against any person.' " *Awadallah III*, 202 F.Supp.2d at 77 (emphasis omitted) (quoting United States v. Calandra, 414 U.S. 338, 343–44, 94 S.Ct. 613, 38 L.Ed.2d 561 (1974)). This is no small interest. In *United States v. Mandujano*, 425 U.S. 564, 96 S.Ct. 1768, 48 L.Ed.2d 212 (1976), the Supreme Court explained:

> The grand jury is an integral part of our constitutional heritage which was brought to this country with the common law.... Indispensable to the exercise of its power is the authority to compel the attendance and the testimony of witnesses .... When called by the grand jury, witnesses are thus legally bound to give testimony. This principle has long been recognized.

Id. at 571–72, 96 S.Ct. 1768 (citations omitted). "[I]t is clearly recognized that the giving of testimony and the attendance upon court or grand jury in order to testify are public duties which every person within the jurisdiction of the Government is bound to perform upon being properly summoned." *Blair v. United States*, 250 U.S. 273, 281, 39 S.Ct. 468, 63 L.Ed. 979 (1919) (emphasis added).

The district court noted (and we agree) that it would be improper for the government to use § 3144 for other ends, such as the detention of persons suspected of criminal activity for which probable cause has not yet been established. See *Awadallah IV*, 202 F.Supp.2d at 77 n. 28. However, the district court made no finding (and we see no evidence to suggest) that the government arrested *Awadallah* for any purpose other than to secure information material to a grand jury investigation. Moreover, that grand jury was investigating the September 11 terrorist attacks. The particular governmental interests at stake therefore were the indictment and successful prosecution of terrorists whose attack, if committed by a sovereign, would have been tantamount to war, and the discovery of the conspirators' means, contacts, and operations in order to forestall future attacks.

On the other side of the balance, the district court found in essence that § 3144 was not calibrated to minimize the intrusion on the liberty of a grand jury witness. See *Awadallah III*, 202 F.Supp.2d at 78–79. According to the district court, several procedural safeguards available to trial witnesses are not afforded in the grand jury context. See id. at 62–67, 78–79. We agree with the district court, of course, that arrest and detention are significant infringements on liberty, but we conclude that § 3144 sufficiently limits that infringement and reasonably balances it against the government's countervailing interests.

The first procedural safeguard to be considered is § 3144's provision that "[n]o material witness may be detained because of inability to comply with any condition of release if the testimony of such witness can adequately be secured by deposition, and if further detention is not necessary to prevent a failure of justice." 18 U.S.C. § 3144 (emphasis added). The district court agreed with the government that this deposition provision does not apply to grand jury witnesses. See *Awadallah III*, 202 F.Supp.2d at 78. The government's altered position on appeal is that "Congress intended depositions to be available as a less restrictive alternative to detaining a grand jury witness." (Appellant's Reply Br. at 18.) Such a pivot by the government on appeal is awkward, but we accept the government's explanation that it was persuaded by Chief Judge Mukasey's view in *In re Material Witness Warrant*, 213 F.Supp.2d at 296. (Appellant's Br. at 67–69; Appellant's Reply Br. at 18–19.)

We conclude that the deposition mechanism is available for grand jury witnesses detained under § 3144. At the time of Awadallah's detention, the Federal Rule of Criminal Procedure that governs depositions provided:

> If a witness is detained pursuant to [§ 3144], the court on written motion of the witness and upon notice to the parties may direct that the witness' deposition be taken. After the deposition has been subscribed the court may discharge the witness.

Fed.R.Crim.P. 15(a) (1987).13 The district court is thereby authorized to order a deposition and to release the witness once it has been taken. Awadallah and the NYCDL argue that this provision cannot apply to grand jury witnesses because there can be no "party" or "trial" prior to indictment. (Appellee's Br. at 43–46; NYCDL Br. at 10, 34–36.) The prosecutor and the witness may broadly be deemed parties, however, in the sense that each has interests to advance or protect before the grand jury. Thus, the rule governing the issuance of subpoenas—which indisputably applies during grand jury proceedings (Appellee's Br. at 28)—refers to "the party requesting" a subpoena. Fed.R.Crim.P. 17(a).

The district court found the deposition provision inapplicable in the grand jury context in part because a conventional deposition is inconsistent with the procedural and evidentiary rules of a grand jury hearing. See *Awadallah III*, 202 F.Supp.2d at 78. However, the district court may set additional conditions for the conduct of a deposition. Compare Fed.R.Crim.P. 15(d) (1987) ("[s]ubject to such additional conditions as the court shall provide"), with Fed.R.Crim.P. 15(e) (2003) ("[u]nless these rules or a court order provides otherwise"). The court thus can limit the deposition according to grand jury protocol, for example by limiting the witness's right to have counsel present during the deposition or by permitting the use of hearsay.

Rule 46 of the Federal Rules of Criminal Procedure, which governs detention and release, further supports the view that depositions are available to grand jury witnesses detained under § 3144. The version of Rule 46 in effect at the time of Awadallah's detention provided that "[t] he attorney for the government shall make a biweekly report to the court listing each defendant and witness who has been held in custody pending indictment, arraignment or trial for a period in excess of ten days," and as to "each witness so listed," state "the reasons why such witness should not be released with or without the taking of a deposition pursuant to Rule 15(a)." Fed.R.Crim.P. 46(g) (1993) (emphasis added). The new version of the rule, which omits the reference to defendants, is even more explicit:

> An attorney for the government must report biweekly to the court, listing each material witness held in custody for more than 10 days pending indictment, arraignment, or trial. For each material witness listed in the report, an attorney for the government must state why the witness should not be released with or without a deposition being taken under Rule 15(a).

Fed.R.Crim.P. 46(h)(2) (2003) (emphasis added). Both versions of the rule expressly contemplate the deposition of a "witness held in custody ... pending indictment." Id. It follows that the deposition mechanism of § 3144 is a safeguard available to grand jury witnesses.

The second procedural safeguard at issue is § 3144's express invocation of the bail and release provisions set forth in 18 U.S.C. § 3142. Section 3144 directs that "a judicial officer may ... treat the [detained] person in accordance with the provisions of section 3142 of this title." 18 U.S.C. § 3144. As noted above, § 3142 sets conditions for the "[r]elease or detention of a defendant pending trial," as follows:

> Upon the appearance before a judicial officer of a person charged with an offense, the judicial officer shall issue an order that, pending trial, the person be—(1) released on personal recognizance or upon execution of an unsecured appearance bond ...; (2) released on a condition or combination of conditions ...; (3) temporarily detained to permit revocation of conditional release, deportation, or exclusion ...; or (4) detained ....

18 U.S.C. § 3142(a).

As the district court observed, some of the terms used in § 3142—namely, "a person charged with an offense" and "pending trial"—do not comport with the structure of grand jury proceedings. However, we do not deduce (as the district court did) that "it is plain that section 3142 cannot apply to grand jury proceedings." Awadallah III, 202 F.Supp.2d at 63. We agree with Chief Judge Mukasey that the provisions of § 3142 govern insofar as they are applicable in the grand jury setting:

> [T]he common sense reading of section 3144 is that it refers to section 3142 only insofar as that section is applicable to witnesses, in making available such alternatives to incarceration as release on bail or on conditions, in suggesting standards such as risk of flight, likelihood that the

person will appear, and danger to the community, and in providing for a detention hearing. Not every provision of section 3142 applies to witnesses, but some do, and those govern.

In re Material Witness Warrant, 213 F.Supp.2d at 295. Thus, a person detained as a material witness in a grand jury investigation may obtain a hearing on the propriety of his continued detention and the conditions, if any, which will allow his release.

The district court also observed that the closed nature of a grand jury investigation limits the court's ability to assess the materiality of a witness's testimony. See Awadallah III, 202 F.Supp.2d at 63. This may be true at the margins, because the materiality of the testimony given by a trial witness can be assessed on the basis of the indictment, discovery materials, and trial evidence, whereas grand jury secrecy requires the judge to rely largely on the prosecutor's representations about the scope of the investigation and the materiality of the witness's testimony. However, as Chief Judge Mukasey observed, "courts make similar determinations all the time, based on sealed submissions, when deciding whether a subpoena calls for relevant information, whether such information is privileged, and the like." In re Material Witness Warrant, 213 F.Supp.2d at 294 (noting that "I've done it myself"). Moreover, "the hypothesized difficulty of the materiality decision can be just as great, or greater, when a court must determine if a trial witness must be detained, because the decision likely will have to be made before the trial begins and thus before it is possible to fit the witness's testimony into the grid of other evidence." Id. at 294–95. The materiality determination called for by § 3144 lies within the district court's competence.

Finally, Awadallah and the NYCDL argue that § 3144 provides no limit on how long a grand jury witness may be detained, whereas the detention of a trial witness is implicitly limited (or speeded) by the time limits on prosecution contained in the Speedy Trial Act, 18 U.S.C. § 3161 et seq. (Appellee's Br. at 55; NYCDL Br. at 27–31.) However, the Speedy Trial Act permits delay for various reasons, see 18 U.S.C. § 3161(h), which may have the collateral effect of extending the detention of a material witness; and nothing in the Speedy Trial Act requires a court to consider the effect of a continuance or delay on a detained witness. The Act therefore provides cold comfort to a detained trial witness.

While § 3144 contains no express time limit, the statute and related rules require close institutional attention to the propriety and duration of detentions: "[n]o material witness may be detained because of inability to comply with any condition of release if the testimony of such witness can adequately be secured by deposition, and if further detention is not necessary to prevent a failure of justice." 18 U.S.C. § 3144. The court must "treat the person in accordance with the provisions of section 3142," which provides a mechanism for release. Id. And release may be delayed only "for a reasonable period of time until the deposition of the witness can be taken pursuant to the Federal Rules of Criminal Procedure." Id. Perhaps most important, Rule 46 requires the government to make a "biweekly report" to the court listing each material witness held in custody for more than ten days and justifying the continued detention of each witness.

Fed.R.Crim.P. 46(g) (1993); see also Fed.R.Crim.P. 46(h)(2) (2003). These measures tend to ensure that material witnesses are detained no longer than necessary.

In light of the foregoing analysis, we must ask whether Awadallah was properly detained when he was held for several weeks without being allowed to give his deposition and obtain release. Such a detention constitutes a significant intrusion on liberty, since a material witness can be arrested with little or no notice, transported across the country, and detained for several days or weeks. Under the circumstances of this case, however, we are satisfied that Awadallah's detention was not unreasonably prolonged.

As indicated above, the deposition mechanism invoked in § 3144 is available to grand jury witnesses, but it is not required in every instance. Section 3144 requires release after deposition only if "the testimony of such witness can adequately be secured by deposition" and "further detention is not necessary to prevent a failure of justice." 18 U.S.C. § 3144 (emphasis added). Similarly, § 3142 provides that a person may be detained if, "after a hearing ..., the judicial officer finds that no condition or combination of conditions will reasonably assure the appearance of the person as required and the safety of any other person and the community." 18 U.S.C. § 3142(e).

The procedural history demonstrates that Awadallah received adequate process to ensure that the duration of his detention was reasonable. Awadallah was arrested on Friday, September 21, 2001. He first appeared before a magistrate judge in San Diego for a bail hearing on Monday, September 24. That hearing was adjourned until the following day in order for Awadallah's counsel to obtain a translator. When Awadallah appeared before the magistrate judge the next day, the court received testimony from his witnesses and heard argument from counsel. Awadallah's attorney argued, among other things, that a deposition should be taken pursuant to § 3144. The court found that, under § 3142, there were no conditions of release that would reasonably assure Awadallah's appearance before the grand jury.15 The court denied bail and ordered that Awadallah be removed to New York.

The government transported Awadallah across the country, and he arrived in New York on Monday, October 1. The next day, he appeared for a second bail hearing before Chief Judge Mukasey in the Southern District of New York. Chief Judge Mukasey also declined to release Awadallah from detention, finding that, "given the facts alleged in the application[,] he may well have incentive to leave," and that "[t]here is no way to prevent him from leaving, no effective way, unless he is detained." The court found that his continued detention was "reasonable under the circumstances." During this hearing, the government informed the court that the grand jury met only on Mondays and Wednesdays, that the following Monday was a holiday, and that the next opportunity to present Awadallah to the grand jury would be Wednesday, October 10. The court therefore set October 11 as a control date for further hearings.

When Awadallah appeared before the grand jury on Wednesday, October 10, he made statements that resulted in perjury charges being filed against him. He testified before the grand jury a second time on Monday, October 15, and he was arrested on the perjury charges on Friday, October 19.16

All told, Awadallah spent 20 days in detention as a material witness before testifying before the grand jury and uttering the allegedly perjurious statements. The undisputed facts establish that he received two bail hearings pursuant to § 3142 within days of his arrest, and that the judges in both hearings found his continued detention to be both reasonable and necessary. Under these circumstances, Awadallah's detention as a material witness was a scrupulous and constitutional use of the federal material witness statute.

II. Validity of the Material Witness Warrant

Having concluded that Awadallah was properly detained under § 3144 as a material grand jury witness, we now consider the district court's alternative basis for suppressing his grand jury testimony and dismissing the indictment. In Awadallah IV, the court assumed § 3144's applicability and asked "whether Awadallah was appropriately detained in accordance with the requirements of that statute." 202 F.Supp.2d at 96. The court ruled, in essence, that "the indictment must be dismissed because of material omissions and misrepresentations in the application for the arrest warrant." Id. at 85.

A. Legal Framework

As explained in Part I, § 3144 permits the detention of a material witness "[i]f it appears from an affidavit filed by a party that the testimony of a person is material in a criminal proceeding, and if it is shown that it may become impracticable to secure the presence of the person by subpoena." 18 U.S.C. § 3144. Under the Warrant Clause of the Fourth Amendment, "no Warrants shall issue, but upon probable cause, supported by Oath or affirmation, and particularly describing the place to be searched, and the persons or things to be seized." U.S. Const. amend. IV. Therefore, an application for a material witness warrant under § 3144 must establish probable cause to believe that (1) the witness's testimony is material, and (2) it may become impracticable to secure the presence of the witness by subpoena. See Bacon, 449 F.2d at 942–43 (holding that probable cause is the appropriate standard for § 3144 material witness warrants).

1011 Ordinarily, a search or seizure pursuant to a warrant is presumed valid. In certain circumstances, however, a defendant may challenge the truthfulness of factual statements made in the affidavit, and thereby undermine the validity of the warrant and the resulting search or seizure.17 See *Franks v. Delaware*, 438 U.S. 154, 164–72, 98 S.Ct. 2674, 57 L.Ed.2d 667 (1978); *United States v. Canfield*, 212 F.3d 713, 717 (2d Cir.2000). In order to invoke the *Franks* doctrine, Awadallah must show that there were intentional and material misrepresentations or omissions in Agent Plunkett's warrant affidavit. A misrepresentation or omission is intentional when "the claimed inaccuracies or omissions are the result of the affiant's deliberate falsehood or reckless disregard for the truth." Canfield, 212 F.3d at 717–18 (quoting United States v. Salameh, 152 F.3d 88, 113 (2d Cir.1998)). It is material when "the alleged falsehoods or omissions were necessary to the [issuing] judge's probable cause finding." Id. at 718. We gauge materiality by a process of subtraction:

> To determine if the false information was necessary to the issuing judge's probable cause determination, i.e., material, "a court should disregard the allegedly false statements and determine whether the remaining portions of the affidavit would support probable cause to issue the warrant." If the corrected affidavit supports probable cause, the inaccuracies were not material to the probable cause determination and suppression is inappropriate.

Id. at 718 (citation omitted). "The ultimate inquiry is whether, after putting aside erroneous information and material omissions, 'there remains a residue of independent and lawful information sufficient to support probable cause.' " Id. (citation omitted); see also United States v. Trzaska, 111 F.3d 1019, 1027–28 (2d Cir.1997).

B. Standard of Review

12 On appeal, we review de novo the legal question of "[w]hether the untainted portions [of the affidavit] suffice to support a probable cause finding." Canfield, 212 F.3d at 717 (citation omitted); see also *United States v. Reeves*, 210 F.3d 1041, 1044 (9th Cir.2000) ("Whether probable cause is lacking because of alleged misstatements or omissions in the supporting affidavit is ... reviewed de novo."). "The issue of materiality may be characterized as a mixed question of law and fact, or as a pure question of law," but "[w]e are not bound by the findings of the district court under either characterization." *United States v. Marin–Buitrago*, 734 F.2d 889, 894 (2d Cir.1984) (citations omitted). However, "[w]hether a person acted deliberately or recklessly is a factual question of intent" that we review only for clear error. *Trzaska*, 111 F.3d at 1028 (citing *United States v. Moore*, 968 F.2d 216, 220–21 (2d Cir.1992), for the proposition that a "district court's factual determinations during [a] Franks hearing are reviewed for clear error").

C. Analysis

Within this framework, the district court saw two principal problems in Agent Plunkett's affidavit. First, the court ruled that Agent Plunkett "could not have made an informed judgment about the materiality of Awadallah's testimony to the grand jury's investigation as he was never present in the grand jury." Awadallah IV, 202 F.Supp.2d at 97. Second, the court ruled that there were material misrepresentations and omissions in the affidavit such that, "[i]f the misleading information had been removed and the omitted information disclosed, it is overwhelmingly likely that the court would have found that Awadallah's presence at the grand jury could have been secured by a subpoena." Id. at 98. For the reasons that follow, we disagree.

1. Knowledge

As a threshold matter, we reject the idea that only a prosecutor, and not an FBI agent, may assess the materiality of a grand jury witness's testimony. See Awadallah IV, 202 F.Supp.2d at 97 (invalidating the warrant in part because the affidavit "was submitted by Agent Plunkett based solely upon his personal knowledge" and he "could not have made an informed judgment about the materiality of Awadallah's testimony to the grand jury's investigation" since "he was never present in the grand jury"). As the government observes (Appellant's Reply Br. at 43), Awadallah does not press this argument on appeal; and we have found no case prohibiting an FBI agent from signing an affidavit for a material witness warrant. True, a panel of the Ninth Circuit held in Bacon that, "[i]n the case of a grand jury proceeding, we think that a mere statement by a responsible official, such as the United States Attorney, is sufficient to satisfy [materiality]," 449 F.2d at 943 (emphasis added), but the panel did not say that only the United States Attorney could attest to materiality.

Under § 3144, a material witness warrant may issue only if "it appears from an affidavit filed by a party that the testimony of a person is material in a criminal proceeding." 18 U.S.C. § 3144. In *Trzaska*, we stated that "the person preparing the affidavit" for a search warrant "should have had at least some personal knowledge of what had transpired." 111 F.3d at 1028. Applying this notion in the context of a material witness warrant, we believe that an FBI agent who works closely with a prosecutor in a grand jury investigation may satisfy the "personal knowledge" requirement.

Agent Plunkett stated in his affidavit that he had "participated in the investigation of Usama Bin Laden and the al Qaeda terrorist group." He described previous indictments and recent convictions obtained in the Southern District of New York as part of the same overarching investigation. "Based on information developed to date, including interviews with witnesses and analyses of other evidence," he described the focus of the ongoing grand jury investigation as "a series of terrorist attacks that were carried out, apparently in coordinated fashion, on September 11, 2001." He stated that he had "debriefed other agents and law enforcement officers who [had] been involved in this investigation," and that he "reviewed relevant reports, documents and records in this investigation." The record shows that he worked closely with an AUSA in the Southern District of New York and was in close contact with the agents who were dealing with Awadallah in San Diego. Under these circumstances, we conclude that Agent Plunkett had personal knowledge sufficient to file an affidavit from which "it appears ... that the testimony of [Awadallah was] material in a criminal proceeding." 18 U.S.C. § 3144.

2. Intention

14 The district court identified five statements in Agent Plunkett's affidavit that it deemed misleading. First, the court believed the affidavit misled by stating that Awadallah had "substantial family ties in Jordan and elsewhere overseas," but omitting that Awadallah had three brothers in San Diego, one of them a citizen. Awadallah IV, 202 F.Supp.2d at 97. Second, the court believed the affidavit misled by stating that Awadallah's phone number had been found in the car at Dulles Airport, but omitting that the phone number belonged to Awadallah at a prior residence eighteen months earlier. Id. at 98. Third, the court believed the affidavit misled by omitting that Awadallah had been "cooperative" with FBI agents on September 20 and 21.19 Id. at 97–98. Fourth, the court believed the affidavit misled by stating that a "box-cutter" had been found in Awadallah's apartment, but omitting that it was really a carpet knife; that it had actually been found in his inoperative second car; and that witnesses had seen him install a carpet recently. Id. at 98 n. 27. Finally, the court believed the affidavit misled by referring to "prior conduct" for which Awadallah might have feared being investigated, when no such conduct was known. Id. at 97.

We do not see how the final statement can be regarded as misleading when read in context. The affidavit stated that "Awadallah may also be concerned that his prior conduct, as set out above, may provide a basis for law enforcement authorities to investigate and possibly prosecute him." The district court failed to appreciate the limitation in the phrase "as set out above," which makes clear that the statement references the preceding paragraphs of the affidavit itself and does not describe or suggest any additional conduct for which Awadallah could have been prosecuted. It does not matter that the conduct described in the affidavit was not prosecutable: the affidavit stated only that Awadallah "may ... be concerned" about prosecution and that he therefore had considerable "incentive to flee."

It is a stretch to say that any of the four other statements identified by the district court were in fact misleading, but assuming that they are misleading for purposes of our *Franks* analysis, we find no basis to conclude that these misrepresentations and omissions were intentional. Awadallah must establish that the misleading statements were the result of "deliberate falsehood or reckless disregard for the truth." Canfield, 212 F.3d at 717–18. The district court did not find that the statements were intentionally or recklessly misleading; it said they were "not a result of mistake or accident." *Awadallah IV*, 202 F.Supp.2d at 98–99. Although we review factual findings on intent only for clear error, see *Trzaska*, 111 F.3d at 1028, this finding is insufficient as a matter of law under the *Franks* doctrine.

Our review of the record reveals no basis for a finding that Agent Plunkett intentionally misled the court or recklessly disregarded the truth. The evidentiary hearing held by the district court was limited in scope. See generally *Awadallah II*, 202 F.Supp.2d at 21 (discussing issues that required hearing). Agent Plunkett testified only with regard to (1) whether any information had been presented orally to Chief Judge Mukasey to supplement the warrant application; and (2) Awadallah's October 4 proffer to the government. The AUSA who helped Agent Plunkett prepare the affidavit did not testify. There was no examination of Agent Plunkett's intent or of additional knowledge that might have been imputed to him.

The affidavit itself disclaims any pretense of completeness: "Because the limited purpose of this affidavit is to support the issuance of the requested warrant, I have not set forth all the facts known to me, or to other agents or law enforcement personnel concerning this nationwide investigation." The finding that omissions were not made by "mistake or accident" is compatible with this express disclaimer. But the mere intent to exclude information is insufficient, as the Fourth Circuit has observed:

> An affiant cannot be expected to include in an affidavit every piece of information gathered in the course of an investigation. However, every decision not to include certain information in the affidavit is 'intentional' insofar as it is made knowingly. If ... this type of 'intentional' omission is all that Franks requires, the Franks intent prerequisite would be satisfied in almost every case.... [Rather,] Franks protects against omissions that are designed to mislead, or that are made in reckless disregard of whether they would mislead, the magistrate.

United States v. Colkley, 899 F.2d 297, 300–01 (4th Cir.1990) (emphasis in original). The district court, which was cognizant of this standard, made no finding of recklessness or bad intent. And the nature of the omissions does not itself suggest concealment.20 Therefore, even assuming that four of the statements identified by the district court were misleading, there is no basis to conclude that they were intentionally or recklessly so.

3. Materiality

We also conclude that the material witness warrant was valid because Agent Plunkett's affidavit, even with any necessary emendations, established probable cause to believe that Awadallah's testimony was material to the grand jury investigation and that it might become impracticable to secure his presence by subpoena. Before proceeding with this materiality analysis, we must first consider an additional category of information that the district court could (and probably should) have excised from the affidavit.

We have held that "[e]vidence seized during an illegal search should not be included in a [search] warrant affidavit."21 *Trzaska*, 111 F.3d at 1026. While "[t]he mere inclusion of tainted evidence in an affidavit does not, by itself, taint the warrant or the evidence seized pursuant to the warrant," the court "should excise the tainted evidence and determine whether the remaining, untainted evidence would provide a neutral magistrate with probable cause to issue a warrant." Id. (citations omitted).

As further discussed in Part III below, the district court held that FBI agents subjected Awadallah to unreasonable searches and seizures on September 20 and 21, 2001, before obtaining the warrant for his arrest. The court ruled that, if the prosecution proceeds, statements and physical evidence obtained by the FBI during these searches and seizures must be suppressed as fruit of the poisonous tree. See Awadallah IV, 202 F.Supp.2d at 100–07. The government assumes for purposes of this appeal (or at least does not contest) that "Awadallah was illegally seized on September 20 and again on September 21, as Judge Scheindlin found," focusing instead on the district court's application of the exclusionary rule. (Appellant's Br. at 122.)

Based on this Fourth Amendment ruling, the district court probably should have excised the fruits of the improper searches and seizures from Agent Plunkett's affidavit. First, the affidavit should not have referenced at all the three videotapes, the "box-cutter," and the bin Laden photographs seized from Awadallah's apartment and cars. Second, the affidavit should not have stated that Awadallah entered the United States on a student visa in 1999, that he admitted knowing Al–Hazmi, that he admitted being associated with the phone number, or that he has family overseas, since all of this information was gleaned from interviewing Awadallah.

The district court did not consider excising these fruits of the improper searches and seizures from the affidavit, no doubt because it found sufficient reason to invalidate the warrant without them. Awadallah does not appeal from the district court's failure to make these additional excisions, and he addresses the issue only in passing. (Appellee's Br. at 101.) In the interest of completeness, however, we exercise our discretion to incorporate the additional excisions into our analysis. Because the FBI obtained the videotapes, the "box-cutter," the photographs, and Awadallah's admissions during their searches and seizures on September 20 and 21, we assume that this information, like the misleading statements, should not have been used in the government's warrant application.

Nonetheless, even after excising the information obtained in violation of the Fourth Amendment and emending the four misleading statements discussed above, "there remains a residue of independent and lawful information sufficient to support probable cause." Canfield, 212 F.3d at 718 (citation omitted); see also Trzaska, 111 F.3d at 1027–28. The corrected affidavit includes the following undisputed facts:

- Nawaf Al–Hazmi was a passenger on American Airlines Flight 77, which crashed into the Pentagon;

- Al–Hazmi entered the United States at the Port of Los Angeles, California, in January 2000;

- A car registered to Al–Hazmi and discovered at Dulles Airport on September 11 contained documents belonging to Khalid Al–Mihdhar, another passenger on Flight 77, documents that linked Al–Mihdhar to San Diego, California;

- The car also contained "a piece of paper, on which the following name and number were written: 'Osama 589–5316;' "

- An FBI search of telephone databases revealed that the phone number belonged to Awadallah approximately eighteen months earlier at an address in La Mesa, California;

- "On September 20, 2001, Agents of the FBI located and interviewed Osama Awadallah in La Mesa, California;"

- Awadallah's connection to the hijackers was under investigation;

- Awadallah was "cooperative" with the FBI agents in the sense that he responded to questions;

- "Given Awadallah's connections to one or more of the hijackers who committed the terrorist attacks that are the subject of the grand jury's investigation, Awadallah may have an incentive to avoid appearing before the grand jury and/or deprive the investigation of relevant information;"

- "Awadallah may also be concerned that his prior conduct, as set out *70 above, may provide a basis for law enforcement authorities to investigate and possibly prosecute him;" and

- "[T]here is no assurance that [Awadallah] would appear in the grand jury as directed."

(Affidavit of Agent Ryan Plunkett, dated Sept. 21, 2001, at 5–7.) This information makes clear that at least one of the September 11 hijackers possessed Awadallah's home phone number and lived in the same vicinity as Awadallah for some length of time. The same piece of paper supports the inference that Awadallah knew one or more of the hijackers. These facts alone establish probable cause to believe that Awadallah's testimony would be material to the grand jury investigating the September 11 attacks.

With regard to the impracticability of securing Awadallah's presence by subpoena, it is telling that the FBI agents "located" Awadallah on September 20. This means that, in the wake of a mass atrocity and in the midst of an investigation that galvanized the nation, Awadallah did not step forward to share information he had about one or more of the hijackers, whose names and faces had been widely publicized across the country.

It is of course possible, even plausible, that Awadallah feared what might happen to him if he presented himself to the FBI in the days following September 11. It is also possible he did not remember Al–Hazmi or Al–Mihdhar until FBI agents asked him about them, or that he did not see their names in the newspapers and on television. But the relevant inquiry is not whether Awadallah has some explanation for avoiding the FBI. The question is whether his failure to come forward, in combination with the other facts listed above, establishes probable cause to believe that he had information material to the grand jury and that it might become impracticable to secure his presence by subpoena. In the circumstances presented in this case—in which the totality of the circumstances known to the court included the terrorist attacks known to everyone else on the planet, and the implicit threat of further attacks—we hold that it does.

For these reasons, we conclude that the material witness warrant was valid, that Awadallah's grand jury testimony should not have been suppressed, and that the indictment must therefore be reinstated.

III. Applicability of the Fourth Amendment Exclusionary Rule to Evidence Obtained on September 20 and 21

Although the district court dismissed the indictment, it applied and extended its analysis to rule that, in a trial, certain evidence would be excluded as the fruit of Fourth Amendment violations. The court expressly did this to obviate an interlocutory appeal that might otherwise result if the dismissal of the indictment were reversed. See *Awadallah IV*, 202 F.Supp.2d at 85. We have reversed the dismissal of the indictment, and we now consider the application of the Fourth Amendment exclusionary rule.

The district court ruled that statements and evidence obtained from Awadallah by the FBI on September 20 and 21, 2001 had to be suppressed as fruit of the poisonous tree because the FBI violated Awadallah's Fourth Amendment right against unreasonable search and seizure. See Awadallah IV, 202 F.Supp.2d at 100. The court ruled that the FBI agents seized Awadallah illegally on September 20 when they confronted him at his home and took him to their office, and that they did so again the next day after his polygraph test. It also ruled that Awadallah's consent to the September 20 searches was involuntary and tainted by that day's illegal seizure. Id. at 101–07.

As noted above, the government does not dispute in this appeal that "Awadallah was illegally seized on September 20 and again on September 21, as Judge Scheindlin found." (Appellant's Br. at 122, 128.) Rather, the government challenges the district court's application of the Fourth Amendment exclusionary rule, arguing that this Court's decision in *United States v. Varela*, 968 F.2d 259 (2d Cir.1992), prohibits the suppression of evidence when the perjury alleged in the indictment was committed after the constitutional violation. We conclude that the district court erred by ordering suppression of the evidence obtained on September 20 and 21.

A. Standard of Review

When examining a ruling on a motion to suppress, "we review the district court's factual findings for clear error and its conclusions of law de novo," viewing the evidence "in the light most favorable to the prevailing party." *United States v. Harrell*, 268 F.3d 141, 145 (2d Cir.2001); see also *United States v. Dhinsa*, 171 F.3d 721, 724 (2d Cir.1998). The applicability of the fruit of the poisonous tree doctrine is "a question of law reviewed de novo." *Howard v. Moore*, 131 F.3d 399, 409 (4th Cir.1997) (citing *United States v. Elie*, 111 F.3d 1135, 1140 (4th Cir.1997)); see also *United States v. Ienco*, 182 F.3d 517, 526 (7th Cir.1999).

B. Analysis

The Fourth Amendment provides that "[t]he right of the people to be secure in their persons, houses, papers, and effects, against unreasonable searches and seizures, shall not be violated." U.S. Const. amend. IV. The Supreme Court has "recognized, however, that the Fourth Amendment contains no provision expressly precluding the use of evidence obtained in violation of its commands." *Arizona v. Evans*, 514 U.S. 1, 10, 115 S.Ct. 1185, 131 L.Ed.2d 34 (1995) (citing *United States v. Leon*, 468 U.S. 897, 906, 104 S.Ct. 3405, 82 L.Ed.2d 677 (1984)). "The wrong condemned by the [Fourth] Amendment is fully accomplished by the unlawful search or seizure itself, and the use of the fruits of a past unlawful search or seizure work[s] no new Fourth Amendment wrong." Id. (internal quotation marks and citations omitted).

In order to discourage or prevent such violations, however, the courts have fashioned an "exclusionary rule [that] operates as a judicially created remedy designed to safeguard against future violations of Fourth Amendment rights through the rule's general deterrent effect." Id. (citations omitted). "As with any remedial device, the rule's application has been restricted to those instances where its remedial objectives are thought most efficaciously served. Where 'the exclusionary rule does not result in appreciable deterrence, then, clearly, its use ... is unwarranted.' " Id. at 11, 115 S.Ct. 1185 (quoting *United States v. Janis*, 428 U.S. 433, 454, 96 S.Ct. 3021, 49 L.Ed.2d 1046 (1976)). Moreover, "[i]ndiscriminate application of the exclusionary rule ... may well 'generat[e] disrespect for the law and administration of justice.' " *Leon*, 468 U.S. at 908, 104 S.Ct. 3405 (quoting *Stone v. Powell*, 428 U.S. 465, 491, 96 S.Ct. 3037, 49 L.Ed.2d 1067 (1976)).

We are therefore appropriately cautious about any extension of the exclusionary rule:

> [A]ny extension of the rule beyond its core application—normally, barring use of illegally seized items as affirmative evidence in the trial of the matter for which the search was conducted—must be justified by balancing the 'additional marginal deterrence' of the extension against the cost to the public interest of further impairing the pursuit of truth.

Tirado v. Commissioner, 689 F.2d 307, 310 (2d Cir.1982) (citations omitted). In determining whether exclusion will have the requisite deterrent effect, "the key question is whether the particular challenged use of the evidence is one that the seizing officials were likely to have had an interest in at the time," that is, "whether it was within their predictable contemplation and, if so, whether it was likely to have motivated them." *Id.* at 311. "[I]f law enforcement officers are already deterred from Fourth Amendment violations by a prohibition against using illegally seized evidence to secure convictions for the offenses they are investigating, the further question is whether some significant incremental deterrence is achieved by prohibiting use of the evidence for additional purposes." *Id.*

The present case lies outside the "core application" of the exclusionary rule. Federal agents seized Awadallah and searched his property in the course of determining whether he had information material to the grand jury investigation; they had no probable cause to believe he had committed any crime. Having detained Awadallah as a material witness and presented him to the grand jury, the government now prosecutes him for making allegedly false statements during his testimony. The charged crime was thus committed twenty days after the improper searches and seizures.

Applying the test described above to these facts, we ask whether excluding the fruits of the improper searches and seizures from Awadallah's perjury trial would have sufficient deterrence value to justify application of the exclusionary rule. We have confronted analogous circumstances in two cases. In *United States v. Ceccolini*, 542 F.2d 136 (2d Cir.1976), rev'd in part, 435 U.S. 268, 98 S.Ct. 1054, 55 L.Ed.2d 268 (1978), an illegal search led police to question an employee in a store owned by Ceccolini. Based on the information thus obtained, the government subpoenaed Ceccolini to testify before a grand jury about illegal gambling. 542 F.2d at 138. In his testimony, Ceccolini denied taking bets at his store. Id. The employee contradicted this statement, and the government indicted and prosecuted Ceccolini for perjury. Id. After the illegal search came to light, the district court suppressed the employee's testimony as fruit of the illegal search and set aside Ceccolini's guilty verdict. Id. at 139.

As here, the prosecutor in the Ceccolini appeal did not dispute that the search in question was illegal, but challenged the suppression. See id. at 140 & n. 5. A divided panel rejected the prosecutor's argument that "the rule excluding the fruit of an illegal search is inappropriate in a perjury prosecution, especially when the perjury occurred after the illegal intrusion." Id. at 142. We saw "no sufficient basis for distinguishing trials of perjury charges from trials on charges of other serious crimes to which the exclusionary rule would apply in the Government's direct case at trial." Id. Without elaboration, we "disagree[d] with the Government's contention that the exclusionary rule serve[d] no purpose" in the case. Id. at 143.

That assessment was one of two grounds for affirming the suppression of the employee's testimony and the district court's decision to set aside the guilty verdict. We also rejected the government's argument that the employee's testimony was an act of free will sufficiently removed from the illegal search as to purge any taint: "the road to [the employee's] testimony from [the officer's] concededly unconstitutional search [was] both straight and uninterrupted ...." Id. at 142. The Supreme Court reversed, concluding that we "erred in holding that the degree of attenuation was not sufficient to dissipate the connection between the illegality and the testimony." *United States v. Ceccolini*, 435 U.S. 268, 279, 98 S.Ct. 1054, 55 L.Ed.2d 268 (1978). The Supreme Court therefore "[did] not reach the Government's contention that the exclusionary rule should not be applied when the evidence derived from the search is being used to prove a subsequent crime such as perjury." Id. at 273, 98 S.Ct. 1054.

The district court here cited Ceccolini in support of its decision to suppress the evidence obtained illegally on September 20 and 21. See *Awadallah II*, 202 F.Supp.2d at 48–49. Like the district court, we think that what remains of *Ceccolini* supports the view that the exclusionary rule may be applied in perjury prosecutions even though the charged perjury occurred after the illegal search or seizure. But *Ceccolini* does not require application of the exclusionary rule in such cases. Rather, as in other situations, we must determine whether "the exclusionary rule serves [a] purpose here." *Ceccolini*, 542 F.2d at 143.

Would exclusion of the evidence obtained by the FBI on September 20 and 21 yield significant deterrence value? On this question, we are guided by *United States v. Varela*, 968 F.2d 259 (2d Cir.1992), the second case in which we confronted a similar factual scenario. In Varela, the defendant made incriminating statements regarding cocaine trafficking after police arrested him without probable cause. Id. at 260. By reason of the Fourth Amendment violation, a district court suppressed his statements and dismissed the drug charges against him. Id. Several months later, Varela appeared before a grand jury to testify about cocaine trafficking by his alleged co-conspirators, and he made false statements that contradicted his previously suppressed statements. *Id.* at 261. The previously suppressed statements were then used to prosecute and convict him for perjury. Id.

We affirmed Varela's conviction. Balancing "the deterrence value of a particular application of the exclusionary rule" against "society's interest in bringing all probative evidence to bear on the questions before the court," *id.* at 261, we held that "statements obtained as fruit of an illegal arrest may be introduced in a perjury trial, if the alleged perjury occurred after the illegal arrest and there is no actual evidence of collusion between the proponents of the evidence and the arresting officers," *id.* at 263. Since the "law enforcement officials already [were] prohibited from using unlawfully seized evidence to convict [the] defendant of the offenses under investigation," we asked whether "any incremental deterrence [would] result [ ] from excluding the same evidence in a subsequent proceeding." *Id.* at 262. We found that any incremental deterrence failed to outweigh society's interest in using the evidence, because we "would have [had] to make the unlikely assumption that when the ... agents arrested Varela unlawfully and solicited his cooperation, they were motivated in part by the belief that Varela would later choose to lie to a grand jury." Id. That possibility was "too remote to serve as a motivating factor." *Id.* We therefore "join [ed] the First, Fifth, and Ninth Circuits in concluding that the exclusionary rule does not apply in such a case." Id. at 260 (citing *United States v. Finucan*, 708 F.2d 838, 845 (1st Cir.1983); *United States v. Raftery*, 534 F.2d 854, 857 (9th Cir.1976); and *United States v. Turk*, 526 F.2d 654, 667 (5th Cir.1976)).26

As the district court observed, there are distinctions between *Varela* and Awadallah's case. First, Varela's statements had already been suppressed once in the prior prosecution for which they were initially obtained, whereas the evidence obtained by the FBI while questioning Awadallah as a possible material witness would first be used in his forthcoming perjury prosecution. See Awadallah II, 202 F.Supp.2d at 52. Second, a court had already determined that Varela's prior statements were obtained unlawfully by the time he uttered false statements to a grand jury, whereas no court had yet found the seizure of Awadallah to be unlawful when he appeared before the grand jury. See *id.*

Thus our case differs from Varela insofar as the Fourth Amendment violations have not yet caused the government to suffer a disadvantage in prosecuting Awadallah. However, Fourth Amendment exclusionary rule jurisprudence does not require that law enforcement officials and the public be penalized by an actual exclusion of evidence—and a frustrated prosecution—before one may conclude that the circumstances of the case require no further exclusion of evidence or exaction of penalty. So long as the deterrent force created by exclusion has already been brought to bear, there is no significant need to suppress the evidence in a subsequent prosecution for criminal conduct (here, perjury) that post-dates the Fourth Amendment violation.

On the facts of this case, we think the incentive to avoid exclusion was sufficiently strong at the time of the search and seizure. The FBI agents detained and questioned Awadallah as a possible material witness, but they must have had a lively sense that their investigation could potentially evolve into a criminal prosecution. Awadallah's telephone number was in the possession of one of the September 11 hijackers, and he was therefore one of the few people known, at that time, to have some connection to them; he lived in the vicinity of the hijackers for some length of time; and he had not come forward to assist an investigation that galvanized the rest of the country.

The district court looked at these circumstances and thought that perjury was a foreseeable consequence of the FBI agents' conduct. See *Awadallah II*, 202 F.Supp.2d at 52. As a matter of law, however, we must ask not just "whether the particular challenged use of the evidence ... was within [the seizing officials'] predictable contemplation," but also "whether it was likely to have motivated them." *Tirado*, 689 F.2d at 311. Here, the government's motivation may have evolved as the investigation proceeded in ensuing days, but viewing this case (as we must) in light of all the circumstances, we think it is untenable to say that the FBI agents, just ten days after the September 11 attacks, sought to elicit perjury rather than truthful information. Cf. *United States v. Turk*, 526 F.2d 654, 667 (5th Cir.1976) (refusing to assume "that the police could be so confident that an immunized search victim would prevaricate before a grand jury that they would be willing to seize evidence of a crime illegally, and thus to forego the possibility of direct prosecution").

We therefore conclude that the "law enforcement officers [were] already deterred from Fourth Amendment violations," and that no "significant incremental deterrence is achieved by prohibiting use of the evidence" in Awadallah's perjury prosecution. *Tirado*, 689 F.2d at 311. The information and evidence obtained by the FBI on September 20 and 21, twenty days before Awadallah appeared before the grand jury, is not excludable as fruit of the improper searches and seizures.

CONCLUSION

For the foregoing reasons, we reverse the decisions of the district court and remand for reinstatement of the indictment and further proceedings consistent with this opinion.

CHAPTER SEVEN: RACE AND THE EFFECTIVE ASSISTANCE OF COUNSEL

LeRoy Pernell, Racial Justice and Federal Habeas Corpus as Postconviction Relief from State Convictions, 69 MERCER LAW REVIEW 453, 459-467 (2018) (excerpt)) (reprint by permission of Mercer Law Review)

A. The Sixth Amendment Right to Counsel

Cases such as [*Brown v. Mississippi, Supra*] show that the basic tenets of due process were not always available for African-American defendants. This was no truer than in the events that occurred in the year prior to Brown, in Scottsboro, Alabama. In the battle for civil rights, which particularly consumed the nation for the remainder of the twentieth century, the case of the "Scottsboro Boys" was a major social and legal battleground. Out of these events, the Supreme Court ultimately issued three significant decisions. The first, *Powell v. Alabama*, was perhaps the most important for criminal procedure reform. Although not a habeas corpus case, its progeny expanded into the Sixth Amendment of the United States Constitution through the use of federal habeas corpus.

The basic facts, riveting as any in Brown, have fueled books, movies, and documentaries. On March 25, 1931, following an altercation on a train bound from Chattanooga to Memphis, Tennessee, several hoboing white men were ejected from a train by what was described as several black youths. The station master in Stevenson, Alabama discovered these white males and, after hearing of their ejection from the train by the black youths, telephoned ahead for the train to be stopped in Scottsboro, Alabama. The train, having already passed through Scottsboro, was halted in Paint Rock, Alabama by a sheriff's posse, which discovered not only the nine black youths but two white women as well. The two women, Ruby Bates and Victoria Price, alleged they had been raped,35 although a later dispassionate review of the evidence showed no rape had occurred. However, the accusation was enough to stir a lynch mob so set on hanging these black teenagers that the local sheriff sought and received the assistance of the Alabama National Guard. Against this backdrop, the defendants were indicted, arraigned, and brought to trial within twelve days of the alleged offense. An additional defendant was added for a total of nine, and the defendants were divided into three groups for trial. Each trial was what could most charitably be referred to as a mockery of justice.

At arraignment, the Scottsboro defendants appeared without counsel. At the trial itself, a mere six days after indictment, no one answered for the defendants or appeared to represent them except for the curious appearance of a "Mr. Roddy." Roddy, a Tennessee lawyer, was not a member of the local bar, but was there because "people who were interested had spoken to him about the case." Roddy was very careful not to agree to representation of the defendants and suggested that he would be willing to assist if local counsel appeared. A "Mr. Moody," who later commentators suggested may have lacked the competency to handle this capital case, referred vaguely to the trial court's prior appointment of the "entire bar" and suggested that all had been done that could be done to prepare for trial.43 As stated by the Court, "[a]nd in this casual fashion the matter of counsel in a capital case was disposed of."

The issue of race dominated the setting and the issues in this case. Adding to the racially-hostile climate was the fact that the Scottsboro defendants were tried before juries from which qualified African-Americans were systematically excluded because of race. This was one of the denials of due process and equal protection complained of before the Court in *Powell*. However, the only issue that the Court chose to address was that of denial of counsel. Rather than addressing directly what mistreatment the Scottsboro defendants suffered constitutionally because of race, the Court turned instead to the basic tenets of procedural due process under the Fourteenth Amendment.

The landmark decision in *Powell* is the fountainhead for much of what we know today as procedural due process in criminal procedure. It is certainly the beginning of what ultimately became the Sixth Amendment right to appointed counsel as well as the Sixth Amendment concept of effective assistance of counsel. Basing its analysis on the Due Process Clause of the Fourteenth Amendment, the Court determined that procedural Due Process at a minimum always requires reasonable notice and an opportunity to be heard prior to judgment.

Regarding the "opportunity to be heard," the Court linked such a right to the need to be effectively heard through counsel. Although tempted, the Court, through its discussion, avoided directly holding that appointed counsel is necessary for those who cannot afford counsel, and avoided applying the Sixth Amendment to the states via the Fourteenth Amendment. Instead, the Court stressed that the right to be heard "would be, in many cases, of little avail if it did not comprehend the right to be heard by counsel."

For counsel to be effective it must be more than in name only. Appointed counsel must be assigned "at such a time or under such circumstances as to [not] preclude the giving of effective aid in the preparation and trial of the case." This bedrock principle of due process was stated in terms many perceived to have universal application for indigents facing criminal prosecution without counsel.53 As such, it appeared to take on a meaning devoid of its racial justice history. This perception was drastically altered by the habeas corpus decision in *Betts v. Brady* ten years later.

Betts concerned an unemployed forty-three-year-old white farmhand accused of robbery. Unemployed and minimally educated, Betts sought appointed counsel. His request was denied, and he was found guilty at trial and sentenced to eight years. Relying on the Court's holding in Powell, Betts asserted that due process required the appointment of counsel for an indigent accused of crime as a fundamental protective right. The Court in *Betts* both declined to recognize a right to appointed counsel as an "incorporated" right of the Sixth Amendment made applicable to the State via the Due Process Clause of the Fourteenth Amendment and declined to hold that Due Process directly required appointed counsel for indigents as a result of its opinion in Powell.

Finding that Powell required "special circumstances" to be decided on a case-by-case basis in order for a defendant to be constitutionally entitled to appointed counsel, the Court noted that the racial tension, poverty, and perceived intellect of the Scottsboro defendants were key to the finding of a due process violation. Although Betts was also indigent and possessed a limited education, his situation did not have the climate of racial injustice present in Powell. The Court's path of expansion of "circumstances" beyond the racially charged climate of Powell and towards a generalized concept of appointed counsel via the Sixth Amendment ran through a growing list of key situations dependent less on correcting racial injustice and more on the significance of counsel to the trustworthiness of the adjudication system.

Gideon v. Wainwright, a federal habeas corpus original action, firmly resolved the right to appointed counsel for indigent defendants. Under the incorporated Sixth Amendment, a "flat" right applies to all indigents regardless of special circumstances. However, while Clarence Earl Gideon was not a poor African-American, the significance of this decision should be considered in the context of both the emerging national struggle over civil rights for African-Americans and in the specific context of the Court's own activity incorporating Bill of Rights protections for criminal defendants.

The Court agreed to hear the handwritten petition of Gideon on June 4, 1962. That year marked a key point in the Civil Rights movement timeline. James Meredith became the first African-American student to enroll at the University of Mississippi. Just a few months earlier, during the spring and summer of 1961, "Freedom Rides"67 to end segregation in transportation and travel began throughout the South. By the time of the Court's decision in 1963, Dr. Martin Luther King's Letters from Birmingham Jail68 was just weeks away, and Medgar Evers would be murdered in approximately ninety days. Most importantly, perhaps, the historic March on Washington, D.C., was already announced to take place in August.

Despite the seminal role that *Gideon* played in establishing rights for all criminal defendants, it was, at its heart, a case concerned with racial justice. Professor Chin states, "Gideon was a race case, in that Gideon and the Court's other criminal procedure cases of the era were concerned with institutional racism." Citing back to *Powell*, Chin sees Gideon as an "outgrowth of Jim Crow ideology" where the Court resolved injustice against African-Americans by accepting racial stereotypes of African-Americans as ignorant, incompetent, and requiring special scrutiny by providing the "guiding hand of counsel" throughout adjudication.

The connection between the right to appointed counsel and race is at least as strong as the connection between the right to counsel and poverty. The challenge for the Warren Court in

Gideon, however, was to move away from the race-oriented conception of the importance of a right to appointed counsel and towards a right with broad and uniform application through incorporation of the Sixth Amendment.

The goal of a broader application, less dependent on race, as a special circumstance, was aided by the fact that the NAACP Legal Defense and Education Fund did not file an amicus brief as it did in two other cases. Two amici mention race only in passing, though in the context of the aforementioned questionable link of being black to ignorance.

Perhaps the most significant link of the right to counsel to race— African-Americans in particular—can be found in recognizing the importance of counsel to the African-American prisoner. The African-American prisoner, greatly overrepresented in the prison population, has particular need for the guiding hand of counsel. The need for counsel to challenge unjust convictions and sentences has been a source for challenging the extent of Gideon's application.

It was in the federal habeas corpus case of *Mempa v. Rhay* that the Court first addressed whether Gideon applied to post-adjudication of guilt. The Court in *Mempa* concluded that Gideon applied to sentencing, even where that sentencing is on a date separate from adjudication of guilt. Applying its "critical stage" rationale, which dates back to Powell, the Court found that appointment of counsel for an indigent defendant is required at every stage of the criminal proceeding where substantial rights of a criminal accused may be won or lost.

This critical issue of legal representation for prisoners who, after imprisonment, have even fewer resources for hiring counsel is important to any sense of justice for the incarcerated. In *Johnson v. Avery*, the Court addressed this issue. Once again, habeas corpus was the tool of choice. The Court considered whether practical access to assistance from a "jailhouse lawyer" could be barred where such a bar meant the realistic denial of an illiterate and poor-access inmate to federal habeas corpus relief. Significantly, and perhaps ironically, the opinion in Johnson is authored by Abe Fortas, the then lawyer who successfully argued Gideon just seven years earlier. While declining sub silentio to extend Gideon to postconviction relief attempts, Justice Fortas wrote, presumably as a matter of Due Process: "[U]nless and until the State provides some reasonable alternative to assist inmates in the preparation of petitions for postconviction relief, it may not validly enforce a regulation such as that here in issue, barring inmates from furnishing such assistance to other prisoners."

In *Bounds v. Smith*, the court again considered the need of poor and often illiterate prisoners for assistance in perfecting postconviction claims absent a right to appointed counsel. In Bounds, North Carolina inmates sought, via a civil action, to require the state to provide adequate libraries or adequate persons trained in the law to help provide inmates meaningful access to the courts to pursue federal habeas corpus or postconviction relief.

Absent the availability of a Sixth Amendment rationale for requiring appointed counsel in a post-sentencing context, the Court, relying on *Avery*, nonetheless recognized some of the same values associated with effective assistance of counsel. The Court, relying on Avery and Griffin

v. Illinois, recognized that a constitutional right to access to the courts for habeas corpus review requires that access be meaningful. Consistent with the Court's past application of the Griffin analysis, the Court in Bounds held that the Constitution mandated prisoners be provided access to an adequate law library or adequate assistance from persons trained in the law.

[footnotes omitted]

Note

As noted above, *Powell* based its Due Process rationale on whether special circumstances required timely appointment of counsel. The Court emphasized that such circumstances included recognizing that the defendants were "poor, illiterate negros". This denigrating characterization, although perhaps intending to be supportive of defendants, and perhaps even accurate in that instance, reflected the stereotypic view of African Americans often expressed in court decisions of the time. [In *Walton v. State*,163 S.W.2d 203 (Tex. Crim. App.1942 the court set aside a defendant's guilty plea because he was an ignorant, illiterate negro..."; *Henry v. State*, 119 P. 278 (Okla Crim App. 1911) " appellant is only a poor, ignorant negro, and is dependent upon the charity of his attorneys for his defense...". And even in the United States Supreme Court; *Moore v. Dempsey*, 261 U.S. 86, 102 (1923) (McReynolds, J., dissenting)"... petitioners are poor and ignorant and black naturally arous[ing] sympathy..."; *Chambers v. Florida*, 309 U.S. 227,238 (1940) describes the interrogation of "ignorant young colored tenant farmers..."; *Reece v. Georgia*, 350 U.S. 85,89 (1955) "semi-illiterate negro of low mentality"...]

Given the disproportionate representation of African Americans and Hispanic Americans in the criminal justice system, even in the first half of the twentieth century. is race really a special circumstance?

If *Gideon* with its focus on the importance of fair trial and innocence was nonetheless a civil rights case, as suggested in Gabriel Chin, Race and the Disappointing Right to Counsel, 122 YALE LAW JOURNAL 2236 (2013) then it would presuppose that the appointment of counsel for the indigent would be a significant part of the answer to racism in the criminal justice system. If that is so, how successful has it been considering that Chin reports that over thirty-two percent of those admitted to state or federal prison in 1960 were African American.? 122 YALE LAW JOURNAL, at 2251

Issues of race and the right to counsel may not be a question just for African American and Latino defendants. See, Barbara Creel, *The Right to Counsel for Indians Accused of Crime: A Tribal and Congressional Imperative*, 18 MICHIGAN JOURNAL OF RACE AND LAW, 317 (2013)

Powell v. Alabama, made it clear in 1932 that any right to counsel meant more than just a warm body. It meant counsel who had the opportunity to be effective counsel – counsel who had the realistic opportunity to apply legal training as an advocate for his or her client. This concept was incorporated in the Sixth Amendment right to counsel as expressed in *Gideon*. In the fifty plus years since *Gideon* question has been raised by many as to whether *Gideon* has ultimately failed because the lack of resources provided by way of funding for appointed counsel is so lacking as to make the promise of Gideon lacking. See, Eric H. Holder, Jr., *Reflections on Gideon – A Watershed Moment*, THE CHAMPION, June 2012; National Association of Criminal Defense Lawyers, *Gideon at 50: A Three-Part Examination of Indigent Defense in America, Part I – Rationing Justice: The Underfunding of Assigned Counsel Systems*, March 2013; Note, *Gideon's Promise Unfulfilled: The Need for Litigated Reform of Indigent Defense*, 113 HARV. L. REV. 2062 (2000). The underfunding of appointed counsel has been linked to racial disparity and over-incarceration. See, Rebecca Marcus, *Racism in Our Courts: The Underfunding of Public Defenders and Its Disproportionate Impact Upon Racial Minorities*, 22 HASTNGS CONST. L. Q. 219 (1994); Richard Klein, Civil Rights in Crisis: *The Racial Impact of the Denial of the Sixth Amendment Right to Counsel*, 14 U. MD. L. J. RACE RELIG. GENDER & CLASS 163 (2015)

Given the significance of the connection between adequate funding of appointed counsel and racial disparity in the criminal justice system consider the response of Florida in the following case.

PUBLIC DEFENDER, ELEVENTH JUDICIAL CIRCUIT OF FLORIDA V. ELEVENTH JUDICIAL CIRCUIT OF FLORIDA

115 So.3d 261(Fla. 2013)

QUINCE, J.

This matter is before the Court for review of the decisions of the Third District Court of Appeal in *State v. Public Defender, Eleventh Judicial Circuit*, 12 So.3d 798 (Fla. 3d DCA 2009), and *State v. Bowens*, 39 So.3d 479 (Fla. 3d DCA 2010). We accepted review in Public Defender because the decision directly affects a class of constitutional officers, namely public defenders. In Bowens, the district court ruled upon the following question, which the court certified to be of great public importance:

Whether section 27.5303(1)(d), Florida Statutes (2007), which prohibits a trial court from granting a motion for withdrawal by a public defender based on "conflicts arising from underfunding, excessive caseload or the prospective inability to adequately represent a client," is unconstitutional as a violation of an indigent client's right to effective assistance of counsel and access to the courts, and a violation of the separation of powers mandated by Article II, section 3 of the

Florida Constitution as legislative interference with the judiciary's inherent authority to provide counsel and the Supreme Court's exclusive control over the ethical rules governing lawyer conflicts of interest?

Bowens, 39 So.3d at 482. We have jurisdiction in both cases. See art. V, § 3(b)(3), (4), Fla. Const. For the reasons stated below, we quash the decision of the Third District in Public Defender and quash in part and affirm in part the decision in Bowens. We also remand to the trial court for a determination of whether the circumstances still warrant granting the Public Defender's motion to decline appointments in future third-degree felony cases under the standards approved in this decision.

I. FACTS AND PROCEDURAL HISTORY

The Public Defender for the Eleventh Judicial Circuit (the Public Defender) filed motions in twenty-one criminal cases seeking to be relieved of the obligations to represent indigent defendants in non-capital felony cases. The Public Defender certified a conflict of interest in each case, claiming that excessive caseloads caused by underfunding meant the office could not carry out its legal and ethical obligations to the defendants. The trial court consolidated all of the motions and denied the State Attorney's Office (the State) standing to oppose the Public Defender's motions. The trial court did allow the State to participate in the proceedings as amicus curiae. The trial court determined that the Public Defender's caseload was excessive by any reasonable standard and that this excessive caseload only allowed the Public Defender to provide minimally competent representation. The trial court issued an order permitting the Public Defender to decline appointments in future third-degree felony cases, although the Public Defender was still required to represent those defendants through arraignment. See Public Defender, 12 So.3d at 804.

The State appealed to the Third District Court of Appeal, which stayed the trial court's order and certified the order on appeal as having a great effect on the proper administration of justice throughout the state and requiring immediate resolution by this Court. See art. V, § 3(b)(5), Fla. Const. This Court dismissed the case for lack of jurisdiction. See *State v. Public Defender, Eleventh Judicial Circuit*, 996 So.2d 213 (Fla.2008) (table). The Third District then entered its decision in the instant case, in which it reversed the trial court's order. Public Defender, 12 So.3d at 805–06. The Third District made a number of legal conclusions in its decision. First, the district court concluded that the State did have standing to oppose the motion in the trial court, based on section 27.02(1), Florida Statutes (2007), which gives the State standing to oppose all motions in cases in which it is a party. Id. at 801. Second, the Third District concluded that the Public Defender's withdrawal from a case based on conflict must be determined on a case-by-case basis, and not in the aggregate. Id. at 802–03. Third, the Third District dismissed the Public Defender's argument that the Rules Regulating the Florida Bar should be the governing standard to determine whether withdrawal is appropriate. The Third District determined that the rules did not apply to the Public Defender's Office as a whole, but rather to individual attorneys. Id. at 803. Fourth, the Third District concluded that excessive caseloads do not constitute a conflict of interest under section 27.5303, Florida Statutes (2007), because the Legislature had not included excessive caseload as part of the its definition of conflicts of interest. Contrary to the trial court's ruling, the Third District concluded that section 27.5303 was applicable in this case because there is no distinction between withdrawing from cases and declining new appointments under the clear meaning of the statute and the structure of the Public Defender's Office. *Id.* at 803–05. Finally, in considering the issue of underfunding, the Third District noted that the Public Defender had failed to hire new attorneys since 2005, despite receiving funding from the Legislature for such positions. The Third District found insufficient evidence to conclude that a small budget decrease would require a dramatic decrease in the Public Defender's caseload. Id. at 805. This Court accepted review of the Third District's decision on the basis that it expressly affects a class of constitutional officers.

In *Bowens*, 39 So.3d at 480, assistant public defender Jay Kolsky filed a motion to withdraw from representing defendant Antoine Bowens. The motion alleged that the excessive caseload of the assigned public defender created a conflict of interest. The Public Defender also challenged the constitutionality of section 27.5303(1)(d), Florida Statutes (2007), the statute that excludes excessive caseload as a ground for withdrawal. After an evidentiary hearing, the circuit court granted the motion to withdraw, finding that the public defender had demonstrated adequate, individualized proof of prejudice to Bowens as a direct result of Kolsky's workload. However, the circuit court denied the constitutional challenge. On certiorari review, the Third District quashed the trial court's order granting the attorney's motion to withdraw. The Third District held that prejudice or harm to a client must be made on a case-by-case basis with individualized proof, which does not include excessive caseload. The Third District also upheld the constitutionality of the statute. However, because this Court had granted review in Public Defender, SC09–1181, the Third District certified the question of great public importance to this Court. Bowens, 39 So.3d at 482. This Court voted to grant review and granted the Public Defender's motion to consolidate the two cases for all purposes.

II. ANALYSIS

In order to address the various issues raised in this case, we first review the history and law regarding indigent criminal defense. Criminal defendants are guaranteed the right to effective assistance of counsel under the Sixth Amendment to the United States Constitution, see *Gideon*

v. *Wainwright*, 372 U.S. 335, 83 S.Ct. 792, 9 L.Ed.2d 799 (1963), and article I, section 16 of the Florida Constitution. In addition, "the right to effective assistance of counsel encompasses the right to representation free from actual conflict." Hunter v. State, 817 So.2d 786, 791 (Fla.2002). Conflict of interest cases usually arise at the trial level, but can arise at any level of the judicial process where one attorney represents two or more clients. See *Barclay v. Wainwright*, 444 So.2d 956, 958 (Fla.1984) (granting habeas relief based on appellate counsel's conflict of interest in representing two codefendants). Generally, an attorney has an ethical obligation to avoid conflicts of interest and should advise the court when one arises. See *Cuyler v. Sullivan*, 446 U.S. 335, 346, 100 S.Ct. 1708, 64 L.Ed.2d 333 (1980). An actual conflict of interest that adversely affects a lawyer's performance violates a defendant's Sixth Amendment right to effective assistance of counsel. Id. at 348, 100 S.Ct. 1708.

In an effort to meet its responsibility to provide counsel to indigent defendants, as guaranteed under the Sixth Amendment and applied to the states in *Gideon v. Wainwright*, the Florida Legislature first established the office of the Public Defender in 1963. See ch. 63–409, § 1, Laws of Fla. (enacting section 27.50, Florida Statutes (1963), which created the office of the Public Defender). The Legislature subsequently approved a proposal to amend the Florida Constitution and elevate the Office of the Public Defender to the level of a constitutional officer, which was approved by the electorate and adopted in 1972. See art. V, § 18, Fla. Const.; see also Summary of Amendment Revising Florida Court Structure, Senate Joint Res. No. 52D (noting that "[t]he position of public defender gains constitutional status" in article V in the 1972 amendment).

The public defender in each circuit is primarily responsible for representing indigent defendants who have been charged or arrested for an enumerated list of criminal offenses and in a limited number of civil proceedings. See § 27.51(1), Fla. Stat. (2007). However, in those cases where the public defender has a conflict of interest, the Legislature provided for the appointment of the Office of Criminal Conflict and Civil Regional Counsel (RCC). See § 27.511(5), Fla. Stat. (2007).

The statutory provision governing withdrawal by the public defender based on conflicts of interest was originally contained in section 27.53(3). Until its amendment in 1999, section 27.53 required a trial court to grant a public defender's motion to withdraw based on conflict without conducting any factual inquiry. In *Guzman v. State*, 644 So.2d 996 (Fla.1994), we reversed a defendant's conviction for first-degree murder and his death sentence because the trial court erroneously denied the public defender's motion to withdraw based on conflicts of interest between Guzman and other clients of the public defender's office. *Id.* at 997. We concluded that once a public defender moves to withdraw under section 27.53(3), based on a conflict due to adverse or hostile interests between two clients, the trial court must grant separate representation. Id. at 999.

Following our decision in Guzman, the Legislature amended section 27.53(3) to provide that under such circumstances the public defender shall file a motion to withdraw and the court shall review and may inquire or conduct a hearing into the adequacy of the public defender's representations regarding a conflict of interest without requiring the disclosure of any confidential communications. The court shall permit withdrawal unless the court determines that the asserted conflict is not prejudicial to the indigent client. If the court grants the motion to withdraw, it may appoint [a member of the Bar] ... to represent those accused.

Ch. 99–282, § 1, at 3084–85, Laws of Fla. (emphasis added). The staff analysis of the bill specifically references this Court's opinion in Guzman, noting that "[a]lthough the statute uses permissive language, according to the Florida Supreme Court, when a public defender certifies that there is conflict of interest, the trial court must grant the motion to withdraw ... [and] may not reweigh the facts that gave rise to the public defender's determination that a conflict exists." Fla. H.R. Comm. on Crime & Pun., CS for HB 327 (1999) Staff Analysis 2 (final June 14, 1999). The amended statute provided for a court to review the adequacy of the public defender's representations as to conflict and to inquire further, if necessary. Thus, the amendment was intended to change this Court's previous interpretation of how motions to withdraw should be handled. Under the amended statute, a court was no longer required to automatically grant a public defender's motion to withdraw based upon an assertion of conflict. In fact, the court is specifically charged with reviewing the motion and making a determination of whether the asserted conflict is prejudicial to the client.

Effective July 2004, this provision was moved to section 27.5303 as part of a comprehensive bill dealing with the implementation of Revision 7 to Article V of the Florida Constitution. See ch.2003–402, § 19, at 3668–70, Laws of Fla. The staff analysis dealing with "Conflict motions" states that the bill "expressly directs judges to look into the adequacy of the motion to withdraw due to an ethical conflict." Fla. H.R. Comm. on Approp., HB 113A (2003), Staff Analysis 7 (May 14, 2003). The analysis also notes that "[c]urrently, there appears to be some difference of opinion concerning the extent to which the court can inquire into the sufficiency of a motion filed by a public defender to withdraw from representation due to an ethical conflict of interest." Id. Additionally, the new provision contained a subsection providing that "[i]n no case shall the court approve a withdrawal by the public defender based solely upon inadequacy of funding or excess workload of the public defender." Ch.2003–402, § 19, at 3669, Laws of Fla. This prohibition was originally codified in section 27.5303(1)(c), Florida Statutes (2003), but was subsequently moved to subsection (1)(d) in the 2007 amendment to the statute. See ch.2007–62, § 10, at 446, Laws of Fla.

Section 27.5303(1)(d) is the primary provision at issue in this case. The parties have raised several issues relating to this subsection, including whether the statutory prohibition usurps the courts' inherent authority to protect the constitutional rights of indigent defendants to effective counsel and whether the statute conflicts with a lawyer's professional obligation to provide effective assistance and to inform the court of obstacles to that obligation. The parties also disagree on the standard for assessing whether the grounds asserted for withdrawal are sufficient, whether aggregate relief can be granted or must be handled on a case-by-case basis, what constitutes sufficient proof under the statute, and whether motions seeking to decline future appointments constitute withdrawals under the statute.

Applicability of Section 27.5303(1)(d)

The initial issue that we must address is whether section 27.5303(1)(d) is even applicable in this case. This subsection of the statute provides that "[i]n no case shall the court approve a withdrawal by the public defender or criminal conflict and civil regional counsel based solely upon inadequacy of funding or excess workload of the public defender or regional counsel." § 27.5303(1)(d), Fla. Stat. (2007) (emphasis added). The Public Defender contends that this subsection is not applicable to this case because the motion he filed was not a motion to withdraw, but rather a motion to decline future appointments. The State responds that this is an "exercise in semantics" that circumvents the intent of the statute and cites the reasoning of the Third District in this regard. See Public Defender, 12 So.3d at 804.

The Public Defender's motion in the trial court was styled as "Motion to Appoint Other Counsel in Unappointed Noncapital Cases Due to Conflict of Interest." In its memorandum of law in support of the motion, the Public Defender argued that because the plain language of section 27.5303(1)(d) governed motions to withdraw and his office was not moving to withdraw from any case to which it was currently assigned, the statute was not applicable to this situation. The trial court's order granting in part and denying in part the Public Defender's motion does not acknowledge section 27.5303 at all. The Third District found the withdraw/decline distinction to be unpersuasive for two reasons. First, permitting the Public Defender "to withdraw by merely couching its requests as motions to decline future appointments, would circumvent the plain language of section 27.5303(1)(d)." Public Defender, 12 So.3d at 804. The Third District stated that such an "exercise in semantics" would "undo the clear intent of the statute" and render section 27.5303(1)(d) meaningless. Id. Second, because the trial court's order required the Public Defender to accept appointments at first appearances and continue to represent those defendants until arraignment, it was "fanciful to suggest that the subsequent appointment of alternate counsel is anything other than a withdrawal." Id. (footnote omitted). As mentioned above, the Eleventh Circuit Public Defender's Office has created a system whereby one set of attorneys, the Early Representation Unit (ERU), represents clients from first appearance until arraignment and then representation shifts to another set of attorneys. Under normal circumstances, the representation of a defendant passes at arraignment from an ERU attorney to another attorney in the public defender's office. Thus, under normal circumstances there is no withdrawal because representation remains at all times with the Public Defender. Under the trial court's order here, the ERU representation would remain intact, but representation would transfer to a non-public defender attorney at arraignment. Thus, the Third District concluded, the public defender attorney from the ERU would have to withdraw in all of these cases. Public Defender, 12 So.3d at 804 n. 6.

The statutes governing the public defenders and their duties support the Third District's conclusion that motions to decline future appointments are in essence motions to withdraw, which are governed by section 27.5303. Section 27.40(1) mandates that "the court shall appoint a public defender to represent indigent persons." § 27.40(1), Fla. Stat. (2007) (emphasis added). Section 27.51(1) provides that the public defender "shall represent ... any person determined to be indigent" who is under arrest or charged with various criminal offenses that could result in imprisonment. § 27.51(1), Fla. Stat. (2007). To be relieved of these duties, even as to future cases, the public defender would have to seek court approval to be removed.

In In re Certification of Conflict in Motions to Withdraw Filed by Public Defender of the Tenth Judicial Circuit, 636 So.2d 18 (Fla.1994), we considered the report and recommendations of a Special Commissioner appointed to consider a motion of the Public Defender to withdraw from a large number of overdue appeals. Among the commissioner's recommendations was the "[a]doption of a prospective withdrawal procedure ... to allow the Public Defender to withdraw early based on a recognition that the cases cannot be timely handled in the future." Id. at 21. This Court declined to take action on the "adoption of a prospective withdrawal system" and instead referred the commissioner's suggestions to the appropriate committees of The Florida Bar for study. Id. at 22. However, we clearly labeled the motion to decline future appointments as a motion for "prospective withdrawal," id., which would subject such motions to the dictates of section 27.5303.

However, as discussed in more detail below, section 27.5303 should not be interpreted to proscribe courts from considering or granting motions for "prospective withdrawal" when necessary to safeguard the constitutional rights of indigent defendants to have competent representation. "[W]hen understaffing creates a situation where indigent [defendants] are not afforded effective assistance of counsel, the public defender may be allowed to withdraw." Day v. State, 570 So.2d 1003, 1004 (Fla. 1st DCA 1990). See also In Re Order on Prosecution of Criminal Appeals by the Tenth Judicial Circuit Public Defender, 561 So.2d 1130, 1135 (Fla.1990) ("When excessive caseload forces the public defender to choose between the rights of the various indigent criminal defendants he represents, a conflict of interest is inevitably created.") (emphasis added); Escambia Cnty. v. Behr, 384 So.2d 147, 150 (Fla.1980) (England, C.J., concurring) ("The problem of excessive caseload in the public defender's office should be resolved at the outset of representation, rather than at some later point in a trial proceeding.") (emphasis added).

Scope of Relief

Each of the parties in this case has taken a diametrically opposed position as to the scope of relief that may be addressed in a motion to withdraw under section 27.5303. The State argues that aggregate relief cannot be afforded and such motions are not intended to address systemic relief. Instead, the State argues that each incidence of conflict must be addressed on a case-by-case basis. The Third District specifically concluded that "[t]he office-wide solution to the problem ... lies with the legislature or the internal administration of [the Eleventh Circuit Public Defender], not with the courts." Public Defender, 12 So.3d at 806. Additionally, the Third District noted that the Legislature provided guidance within section 27.5303(1)(e) as to what constitutes a conflict of interest for purposes of withdrawal by the public defender. Subsection (1)(e) directs that in "determining whether or not there is a conflict of interest, the public defender or regional counsel shall apply the standards contained in the Uniform Standards for Use in Conflict of Interest Cases found in appendix C to the Final Report of the Article V Indigent Services Advisory Board dated January 6, 2004." § 27.5303(1)(e), Fla. Stat. (2007). The Third District noted that the only conflicts addressed in the appendix are "conflicts involving codefendants and certain kinds of witnesses or parties. Conspicuously absent are conflicts arising from underfunding, excessive caseload, or the prospective inability to adequately represent a client." Public Defender, 12 So.3d at 804. Thus, the Third District concluded that the only conflicts of interest contemplated by section 27.5303 are "traditional conflicts arising from the representation of codefendants." Id.

The Public Defender, and many of the amicus curiae who have filed briefs in these cases, contend that systemic or aggregate prospective relief is required by the Florida Rules of Professional Conduct and by the Sixth Amendment rights of indigent defendants. Additionally, they argue that the courts have inherent authority to issue such relief when necessary to fulfill their constitutional obligations.

The Public Defender also contends that a number of Rules of Professional Conduct are implicated in this case and are at odds with the Third District's interpretation of section 27.5303(1)(d). "The Rules provide no exception for lawyers who represent indigent persons charged with crimes." ABA, "Ethical Obligations of Lawyers Who Represent Indigent Criminal Defendants When Excessive Caseloads Interfere with Competent & Diligent Representation," Formal Opinion 06–441, at 3. Furthermore, "the public defender is an advocate, who once appointed owes a duty only to his client, the indigent defendant. His role does not differ from that of privately retained counsel." *Crist v. Florida Ass'n of Criminal Defense Lawyers, Inc.*, 978 So.2d 134, 147 (Fla.2008) (quoting *Schreiber v. Rowe*, 814 So.2d 396, 398 (Fla.2002)). "All attorneys, whether state-supplied or privately retained, are under the professional duty not to neglect any legal matters entrusted to them." *State v. Meyer*, 430 So.2d 440, 443 (Fla.1983) (citing Rule 4–1.3, Rules Regulating Fla. Bar (Diligence) formerly Fla. Bar Code Prof. Resp. D.R. 6–101(A)(3)). Whether an indigent defendant is represented by an elected public defender, the appointed regional counsel, or a private attorney appointed by the court, the attorney has an independent professional duty to "effectively" and "zealously" represent his or her client. Crist, 978 So.2d at 147. See also *Wilson v. Wainwright*, 474 So.2d 1162, 1164 (Fla.1985) ("[T]he basic requirement of due process in our adversarial legal system is that a defendant be represented in court, at every level, by an advocate who represents his client zealously within the bounds of the law. Every attorney in Florida has taken an oath to do so and we will not lightly forgive a breach of this professional duty in any case.").

The parties also contend that "[the] courts have authority to do things that are absolutely essential to the performance of their judicial functions." *Rose v. Palm Beach Cnty.*, 361 So.2d 135, 137 (Fla.1978). This authority emanates from the courts' constitutional powers set forth in the Florida Constitution. See art. II, § 3, Fla. Const. ("The powers of the state government shall be divided into legislative, executive and judicial branches. No person belonging to one branch shall exercise any powers appertaining to either of the other branches unless expressly provided therein."); art. V, § 1, Fla. Const. ("The judicial power shall be vested in a supreme court, district courts of appeal, circuit courts and county courts."). This doctrine of inherent judicial power "exists because it is crucial to the survival of the judiciary as an independent, functioning and co-equal branch of government. The invocation of the doctrine is most compelling when the judicial function at issue is the safe-guarding of fundamental rights." *Maas v. Olive*, 992 So.2d 196, 204 (Fla.2008) (Olive II) (quoting Rose, 361 So.2d at 137).

We cited the doctrine of inherent judicial authority in considering the statutory scheme in sections 27.710 and 27.711 of the Florida Statutes (2007), which governs the statewide registry of attorneys who are qualified to represent defendants in capital collateral proceedings. See *Olive v. Maas*, 811 So.2d 644 (Fla.2002) (Olive I). Section 27.711(4) limits the compensable hours available to registry attorneys and sets a maximum amount payable for each stage of postconviction representation. Additionally, section 27.711(3) provides that this fee and payment schedule is "the exclusive means of compensating a court-appointed attorney who represents a capital defendant." We concluded that trial courts are authorized to grant attorney's fees in excess of the statutory schedule where extraordinary or unusual circumstances exist in a case. Olive I, 811 So.2d at 654.

Only weeks after we issued our decision in Olive I, the Legislature added section 27.7002 to the Florida statutes, providing that compensation above the statutory schedule was not authorized and requiring any attorney who sought fees in excess of the cap to be permanently removed from the registry. *Olive II*, 992 So.2d at 199–200 (citing ch.2002–31, § 2, at 74–75, Laws of Fla.). Once again we invoked the doctrine of inherent judicial authority. "[W]e have consistently held that statutory limits for compensation of counsel may not constitutionally be applied in a manner that would curtail the trial court's inherent authority to ensure adequate representation." Id. at 202.

This Court has also cited the doctrine in a long line of cases involving attorney compensation as it relates to safeguarding a defendant's right to effective representation. See, e.g., *Remeta v. State*, 559 So.2d 1132, 1135 (Fla.1990) (holding that "courts have the authority to exceed statutory fee caps to compensate court-appointed counsel for the representation of indigent, death-sentenced prisoners in executive clemency proceedings when necessary to ensure effective representation"); *White v. Bd. of Cnty. Comm'rs*, 537 So.2d 1376, 1379 (Fla.1989) (concluding that the statute setting a cap on attorney's fees in a first-degree murder case "is unconstitutional when applied in such a manner that curtails the court's inherent power to secure effective, experienced counsel for the representation of indigent defendants in capital cases"); *Makemson v. Martin Cnty.*, 491 So.2d 1109, 1112 (Fla.1986) (concluding that statute setting fee caps on compensation provided to attorneys who represented defendants at trial and first appeal would be unconstitutional "when applied in such a manner as to curtail the court's inherent power to ensure the adequate representation of the criminally accused").

The Third District's conclusion that the courts cannot fashion an "office-wide solution" to the public defender's excessive caseload does not comport with Florida case law. We have approved aggregate or systemic relief in a number of cases where public defenders were experiencing excessive caseloads or where the offices were underfunded. In *In re Public Defender's Certification of Conflict & Motion to Withdraw Due to Excessive Caseload & Motion for Writ of Mandamus*, 709 So.2d 101, 104 (Fla.1998), we approved the Second District Court of Appeal's order providing that the Public Defender of the Tenth Judicial Circuit would accept no new appellate cases until further order of the district court. In In Re Certification of Conflict in Motions to Withdraw Filed by Public Defender of the Tenth Judicial Circuit, 636 So.2d 18, 19 (Fla.1994), we considered the district court's actions in appointing a Special Commissioner to conduct fact-finding related to the public defender's motion to withdraw from 382 overdue appeals "because of conflict caused by an excessive caseload." We also approved the district court's determination to grant withdrawal in all of those cases. In *In Re Order on Prosecution of Criminal Appeals by the Tenth Judicial Circuit Public Defender*, 561 So.2d 1130, 1132, 1138 (Fla.1990), we recognized that the backlog of cases in the public defender's office was due to "the woefully inadequate funding" of the office and that such an excessive caseload can create a conflict. In Behr, 384 So.2d at 148–49, we considered the proper course of action when the public defender's excessive caseload created a problem regarding effective representation. In Hatten v. State, 561 So.2d 562, 563 (Fla.1990), we described the public defender's failure to prepare and timely file Hatten's appellate brief as "not merely an isolated incident, but ... symptomatic of a larger problem" and recognized that excessive caseload in the public defender's office "precludes effective representation of indigent clients."

The Third District found the instant cases to be distinguishable from these other cases in which aggregate or "office-wide" relief has been afforded because of the method by which the public defender sought relief and the type of harm claimed. It is true that almost all of the aggregate relief cases have involved appellate cases where appeals and briefs have not been filed in a timely fashion. In some instances, the defendants had served their prison sentences or completed their probation before their appellate briefs were even filed by the public defender's office. See *Certification of Conflict*, 709 So.2d at 102. The instant cases involved representation of defendants at trial and the Public Defender sought to withdraw en masse rather than seeking "individualized withdrawal" on a case-by-case basis. Public Defender, 12 So.3d at 802.

However, we find the Third District's characterization that the instant cases involved "excessive caseload and no more," id., to be a gross over simplification of the evidence presented here and the situation existing at the time the Public Defender sought relief. While we cannot succinctly recount the lengthy records in these two cases, we are struck by the breadth and depth of the evidence of how the excessive caseload has impacted the Public Defender's representation of indigent defendants. For example, the number of criminal cases assigned to the Public Defender has increased by 29% since 2004, while his trial budget was reduced by 12.6% through budget cuts and holdbacks over the fiscal years 2007–2008 and 2008–2009. After the implementation of Article V revisions in July 2004, the Legislature only funded 32 of the 82 overload attorneys that Miami–Dade County had been funding. The noncapital felony caseload has been in the range of 400 cases per attorney for a number of years. Yet, even the highest caseload standard recommended by professional legal organizations is 200 to 300 less. At the time the motions were filed in these cases, there were 105 attorneys to represent clients in 45,055 new and reopened cases. While the Public Defender has utilized a number of procedures to reduce the excessive caseloads (such as applying for grants in order to hire more attorneys; creating special units to handle bond hearings and early representation; and assigning third-degree felony caseloads to supervising attorneys, capital case attorneys, and first and second-degree felony attorneys), it has not alleviated the overall problem. Third-degree felony attorneys often have as many as fifty cases set for trial in one week because of the excessive caseload. Clients who are not in custody are essentially unrepresented for long periods between arraignment and trial. Attorneys are routinely unable to interview clients, conduct investigations, take depositions, prepare mitigation, or counsel clients about pleas offered at arraignment.8 Instead, the office engages in "triage" with the clients who are in custody or who face the most serious charges getting priority to the detriment of the other clients.

While this evidence is different from the deficiencies presented in the appellate cases where aggregate relief has been afforded in the past, it is still a damning indictment of the poor quality of trial representation that is being afforded indigent defendants by the Public Defender in the Eleventh Circuit. Additionally, the public defender's lack of adequate resources or excessive caseload is likely to affect each client's case differently in the pretrial context as the attorney "juggles" the cases against each other in "triage."

In extreme circumstances where a problem is system-wide, the courts should not address the problem on a piecemeal case-by-case basis. This approach wastes judicial resources on redundant inquiries. If this Court had not approved systemic aggregate relief in the appellate cases cited above, the courts would have been clogged with hundreds of individual motions to withdraw. This is tantamount to applying a band aid to an open head wound.

Thus, we reaffirm that aggregate/systemic motions to withdraw are appropriate in circumstances where there is an office-wide or wide-spread problem as to effective representation.

Standard Applicable under Section 27.5303

We next address the standard for reviewing motions to withdraw under section 27.5303. In Public Defender, the Third District held that the public defender was required to prove prejudice or conflict, separate from excessive caseload, and must prove the prejudice or conflict on an individual basis in order to be permitted to withdraw from representing an indigent client. 12 So.3d at 805, 806. The district court also explained "[t]hat is not to say that an individual attorney cannot move for withdrawal when a client is, or will be, prejudiced or harmed by the attorney's ineffective representation." Id. at 805. In *Bowens*, the trial court concluded that the Third District's use of the disjunctive phrase "or will be" clearly indicated that a trial court may properly consider possible future harm. State v. Bowens, Case No. F09–019364, at 9 (Fla. 11th Cir. Oct. 25, 2009) (order denying public defender motion to declare statute unconstitutional and granting motion to withdraw).

The trial court also looked to Rule 4–1.7(a)(2) of the Rules Regulating The Florida Bar, which prohibits representation if there is a substantial risk that representation of one or more clients will be materially limited by the lawyer's responsibilities to another client. The trial court concluded that the phrase "substantial risk" in the rule also contemplates future harm. Id. The trial court accordingly determined that in order to permit withdrawal based on excessive caseload, there "must be an individualized showing of substantial risk that representation of one or more clients will be materially limited by the lawyer's responsibilities to another client." Id. (emphasis added). The trial court concluded that assistant public defender Kolsky had demonstrated the requisite prejudice to Bowens based on uncontroverted evidence that Kolsky had been able to do virtually nothing in preparation of Bowens' defense, had not obtained a list of defense witnesses from Bowens, had not taken any depositions, had not visited the scene of the alleged crime, had not looked for defense witnesses or interviewed any, had not prepared a mitigation package, had not filed any motions, and had to request a continuance at the calendar call.

Additionally, expert witnesses presented credible testimony and evidence that the prejudice was a direct result of Kolsky's excessive workload, is not an intentional effort to avoid representing Bowens, and is not the result of a lack of skills or knowledge.11 Id. at 10. Accordingly, the trial court determined that Bowens' constitutional rights were prejudiced by Kolsky's inability to properly represent him and granted Kolsky's motion to withdraw.

On appeal, the Third District concluded that there was no evidence of "actual or imminent prejudice to Bowens' constitutional rights." *Bowens*, 39 So.3d at 481. The Third District explained that prejudice "means there must be a real potential for damage to a constitutional right, such as effective assistance of counsel or the right to call a witness, or that a witness might be lost if not immediately investigated." *Id.* The Third District found the public defender's failure to show "individualized prejudice or conflict separate from that which arises out of an excessive caseload" to be "the critical fact." *Id.* The Third District deemed the prejudice to be "merely possible or speculative" and concluded that "the plain language of the statute" defeated the claim. Id. at 482.

The Public Defender argues that even though the Third District did not cite any authority for the "actual or imminent prejudice" standard, this is the Strickland standard that applies to post-conviction claims of ineffective assistance of counsel. See *Strickland v. Washington*, 466 U.S. 668, 104 S.Ct. 2052, 80 L.Ed.2d 674 (1984). The State contends that there are adequate remedies available through the appellate process and postconviction proceedings to remedy any violations of the indigent defendant's right to effective counsel that may ensue from the conflict of an excessive caseload. The State's position is that we cannot know if a particular deficiency is harmless until viewed in the context of the whole trial. See *Platt v. State*, 664 N.E.2d 357, 363 (Ind.App. Ct.1996) ("[A]ny violation of the Sixth Amendment must be reviewed in the context of the whole trial process, as the determination of the effectiveness of counsel is whether the defendant had the assistance necessary to justify reliance on the outcome of the proceeding.") (rejecting indigent defendant's claim that the public defender system violated his Sixth Amendment right to effective pretrial assistance of counsel). But see *New York Cnty. Lawyers' Ass'n v. N.Y.*, 294 A.D.2d 69, 76, 742 N.Y.S.2d 16 (N.Y.App.Div.2002) (rejecting the state's argument that indigent clients who receive ineffective assistance because of inadequate compensation in the assigned counsel system have other postjudgment remedies to vindicate their rights such as an appeal of the conviction on grounds of ineffective assistance).

The Strickland standard has been criticized as "inappropriate" for suits seeking prospective relief. See *Luckey v. Harris*, 860 F.2d 1012, 1017 (11th Cir.1988). As the Eleventh Circuit explained,

> The sixth amendment protects rights that do not affect the outcome of a trial. Thus, deficiencies that do not meet the "ineffectiveness" standard may nonetheless violate a defendant's rights under the sixth amendment. In the post-trial context, such errors may be deemed harmless because they did not affect the outcome of the trial. Whether an accused has been prejudiced by the denial of a right is an issue that relates to relief—whether the defendant is entitled to have his or her conviction overturned—rather than to the question of whether such a right exists and can be protected prospectively.

Luckey, 860 F.2d at 1017. Additionally, there are powerful considerations in the postconviction context that warrant the deferential prejudice standard. These include: concerns for finality, concern that extensive post-trial burdens would discourage counsel from accepting cases, and concern for the independence of counsel. *Strickland*, 466 U.S. at 690, 104 S.Ct. 2052. These considerations do not apply when only prospective relief is sought. "Prospective relief is designed to avoid future harm. Therefore, it can protect constitutional rights, even if the violation of these rights would not affect the outcome of a trial." *Luckey*, 860 F.2d at 1017 (citation omitted). See also Rodger Citron, Note, (Un)Luckey v. Miller: The Case for a Structural Injunction to Improve Indigent Defense Services, 101 Yale L.J. 481, 493–94 (1991) ("[T]he right to counsel is more than just the right to an outcome.").

Luckey involved a civil rights action brought on behalf of indigent defendants seeking injunctive relief in order to remedy alleged deficiencies in the provision of indigent services in Georgia. The federal district court had dismissed the action on several grounds, including that the suit failed to state a claim for which relief could be granted. The district court ruled that the indigent defendants had to prove "an across-the-board future inevitability of ineffective assistance" under the standard set forth in *Strickland. Luckey*, 860 F.2d at 1016. On appeal, the Eleventh Circuit reversed the district court's order and explained that the defendants' burden was to show "the likelihood of substantial and immediate irreparable injury, and the inadequacy of remedies at law." *Id.* at 1017 (quoting *O'Shea v. Littleton*, 414 U.S. 488, 502, 94 S.Ct. 669, 38 L.Ed.2d 674 (1974)). The Eleventh Circuit concluded that the defendants' allegations stated a sufficient claim upon which relief could be granted. These allegations included that:

> systemic delays in the appointment of counsel deny them their sixth amendment right to the representation of counsel at critical stages in the criminal process, hamper the ability of their counsel to defend them, and effectively deny them their eighth and fourteenth amendment right to bail, that their attorneys are denied investigative and expert resources necessary to defend them effectively, that their attorneys are pressured by courts to hurry their case to trial or to enter a guilty plea, and that they are denied equal protection of the laws.

Id. at 1018.

The Louisiana Supreme Court considered a similar issue in *Peart*, 621 So.2d at 784, in which an indigent defendant filed a "Motion for Relief to Provide Constitutionally Mandated Protection and Resources." The defendant Peart was assigned an attorney from the Orleans Indigent Defender Program (which is based on the public defender model) to represent him on a number of criminal charges. Id. at 784. At a hearing regarding the defense services being provided to Peart and other indigent defendants, the trial court learned that the attorney was handling seventy active felony cases; clients were routinely incarcerated for thirty to seventy days before the attorney met with them; the attorney had represented 418 defendants in an eight-month period that year; the attorney had entered guilty pleas at arraignment for 130 of these defendants; the attorney had at least one serious case set for trial on every trial date of that eight-month period; the attorney received no investigative support in most of his cases; and there were no funds for expert witnesses. *Id.*

One of the questions that the Louisiana Supreme Court considered was whether a trial court could address a claim of ineffective assistance of counsel before trial. The Louisiana Supreme

Court concluded that "[i]f the trial court has sufficient information before trial, the judge can most efficiently inquire into any inadequacy and attempt to remedy it." *Id.* at 787. The court explained that this approach furthers judicial economy, protects defendants' constitutional rights, and preserves the integrity of the trial process. "It matters not that the ineffective assistance rendered may or may not affect the outcome of the trial to the defendant's detriment." *Id.* Moreover, as legal commentators have noted, the application of the Strickland standard to systemic deficiencies

> provides no guarantee that indigent defendants will receive adequate assistance of counsel. By requiring the defendant to demonstrate that the ineffectiveness of counsel was prejudicial, the Strickland criteria tend to focus on errors of commission; however, especially with overworked defense attorneys, ineffective assistance more often results from an attorney's errors of omission.

(Un)Luckey, 101 Yale L.J. at 487.

The New York Court of Appeals has characterized very similar circumstances to those presented in the instant cases as nonrepresentation rather than ineffective representation. *Hurrell–Harring v. New York*, 15 N.Y.3d 8, 904 N.Y.S.2d 296, 930 N.E.2d 217 (2010). In *Hurrell–Harring*, a group of indigent criminal defendants brought a class action alleging that the public defender system was deficient and presented an unacceptable risk that indigent defendants were being denied the constitutional right to counsel. The action had been dismissed by a lower court, holding that there was no cognizable claim for ineffective assistance of counsel other than in a claim for postconviction relief. Id. 904 N.Y.S.2d 296, 930 N.E.2d at 220. The Court of Appeals described the following circumstances after counsel was nominally appointed: counsel was uncommunicative with the clients, made very little or no efforts on the clients' behalf subsequent to arraignment, waived important rights without consulting the client, acted as mere conduits for plea offers, and were often unprepared to proceed when they made court appearances. *Id.* 904 N.Y.S.2d 296, 930 N.E.2d at 222, 224. The Court of Appeals explained that "[a]ctual representation assumes a certain basic representational relationship" and that the allegations by the indigent defendants raised the "distinct possibility that merely nominal attorney-client pairings" were occurring with regularity. *Id.* 904 N.Y.S.2d 296, 930 N.E.2d at 224.

The instant case involves similar circumstances to *Hurrell–Harring*. Witnesses from the Public Defender's office described "meet and greet pleas" as being routine procedure. The assistant public defender meets the defendant for the first time at arraignment during a few minutes in the courtroom or hallway and knows nothing about the case except for the arrest form provided by the state attorney, yet is expected to counsel the defendant about the State's plea offer. In this regard, the public defenders serve "as mere conduits for plea offers." The witnesses also described engaging in "triage" with their cases—giving priority to the cases of defendants in custody, leaving out-of-custody defendants effectively without representation for lengthy periods subsequent to arraignment. The witnesses also testified that the attorneys almost never visited the crime scenes, were unable to properly investigate or interview witnesses themselves, often had other attorneys conduct their depositions, and were often unprepared to proceed to trial when the case was called. Thus, the circumstances presented here involve some measure of nonrepresentation and therefore a denial of the actual assistance of counsel guaranteed by Gideon and the Sixth Amendment.

The United States Supreme Court recently addressed two postconviction claims of ineffective assistance of counsel involving pleas. See *Lafler v. Cooper*, --- U.S. ----, 132 S.Ct. 1376, 182 L.Ed.2d 398 (2012); *Missouri v. Frye*, --- U.S. ----, 132 S.Ct. 1399, 182 L.Ed.2d 379, cert. denied, --- U.S. ----, 132 S.Ct. 1789, 182 L.Ed.2d 615 (2012). The Supreme Court recognized "the reality that criminal justice today is for the most part a system of pleas, not a system of trials," noting that ninety-seven percent of federal convictions and ninety-four percent of state convictions are the result of guilty pleas. *Lafler*, 132 S.Ct. at 1388; *Frye*, 132 S.Ct. at 1407. Thus, the Supreme Court explained, "it is insufficient simply to point to the guarantee of a fair trial as a backstop that inoculates any errors in the pretrial process." *Lafler*, 132 S.Ct. at 1388; *Frye*, 132 S.Ct. at 1407. In *Frye*, the Supreme Court held that an attorney's failure to timely communicate a plea offer to a defendant resulting in the offer expiring could deny the defendant the effective assistance of counsel, even where the defendant subsequently entered a knowing and voluntary plea on less favorable terms. *Frye*, 132 S.Ct. at 1408. In *Lafler*, the Supreme Court held that an attorney's incorrect legal advice regarding a plea offer which resulted in the offer being turned down could deny the defendant effective assistance of counsel, even where the defendant was subsequently convicted following a full and fair trial before a jury. *Lafler*, 132 S.Ct. at 1386. In both cases, the Supreme Court rejected the State's argument that there was no *Strickland* prejudice because the defendant was later convicted or entered a guilty plea on less favorable terms. *Lafler*, 132 S.Ct. at 1386; *Frye*, 132 S.Ct. at 1406.

Based on the cases and analysis above, we conclude that the prejudice required for withdrawal under section 27.5303 when it is based on an excessive caseload is a showing of "a substantial risk that the representation of [one] or more clients will be materially limited by the lawyer's responsibilities to another client." R. Regulating Fla. Bar 4–1.7(a)(2). The records in the instant cases show competent, substantial evidence to support the trial courts' findings and conclusions of law to that effect.

The trial court concluded that the caseload of felony public defenders in the Eleventh Judicial Circuit "far exceeds any recognized standard for the maximum number of felony cases a criminal defense attorney should handle annually." In re: Reassignment & Consolidation of Public Defender's Motions to Appoint Other Counsel in Unappointed Noncapital Felony Cases, Case No. 08–1, at 4 (Fla. 11th Jud.Cir.Ct. Sept. 3, 2008). Additionally, third-degree felony cases, which comprise approximately sixty percent of all felony filings in the Eleventh Circuit, are "clogging the system and negatively impacting the [Public Defender's] felony attorneys' caseload." Id. at 4–5. Supervising attorneys are handling third-degree felony cases to the detriment of their ability to handle capital cases and first and second-degree felony cases. Id. at 4. The reduced budget of the Public Defender and the excessive workload have contributed to a decrease in the number of assistant public defenders at the same time that the number of noncapital felony cases assigned to the office has increased by twenty-nine percent. Id. at 5. See also State v. Bowens, Case No. F09–019364, at 2–5 (Fla. 11th Cir.Ct. Oct. 25, 2009) (findings of fact regarding detrimental effect of attorney Kolsky's caseload on ability to represent clients).

Therefore, we agree that the Public Defender has demonstrated cause for withdrawal pursuant to section 27.5303. However, we remand these cases to the trial court to determine if the same conditions still exist at this time.

Constitutionality of Section 27.5303(1)(d)

The Third District also certified a question regarding the constitutionality of section 27.5303(1)(d), which provides that "[i]n no case shall the court approve a withdrawal by the public defender ... based solely on the inadequacy of funding or excess workload." See *Bowens*, 39 So.3d at 481.12 The Third District stated that it agreed with the trial court's analysis of the constitutionality of the statute and denied the Public Defender's cross-petition for certiorari on that issue. Id. The certified question raises four possible constitutional challenges, asking whether the statute violates an indigent client's (1) right to effective assistance of counsel and (2) right of access to courts and (3) whether it violates the separation of powers as a legislative interference with the judiciary's inherent power to provide counsel and (4) the Supreme Court's exclusive control over the ethical rules governing lawyer conflicts of interest.

The constitutionality of a statute is a question of law subject to de novo review by this Court. *Crist v. Fla. Ass'n of Criminal Def. Lawyers*, 978 So.2d at 139; *Fla. Dep't of Revenue v. City of Gainesville*, 918 So.2d 250, 256 (Fla.2005); *Zingale v. Powell*, 885 So.2d 277, 280 (Fla.2004). Although our review is de novo, statutes come clothed with a presumption of constitutionality and must be construed whenever possible to effect a constitutional outcome. See *City of Gainesville*, 918 So.2d at 256 (quoting *Fla. Dep't of Revenue v. Howard*, 916 So.2d 640, 642 (Fla.2005)). "[S]hould any doubt exist that an act is in violation ... of any constitutional provision, the presumption is in favor of constitutionality. To overcome the presumption, the invalidity must appear beyond reasonable doubt, for it must be assumed the legislature intended to enact a valid law." *Franklin v. State*, 887 So.2d 1063, 1071 (Fla.2004) (quoting State ex rel. *Flink v. Canova*, 94 So.2d 181, 184 (Fla.1957)). It is a "settled principle of constitutional law that courts should not pass upon the constitutionality of statutes if the case in which the question arises may be effectively disposed of on other grounds." *Singletary v. State*, 322 So.2d 551, 552 (Fla.1975). Additionally, a determination that a statute is facially unconstitutional means that no set of circumstances exists under which the statute would be valid. *Lewis v. Leon Cnty.*, 73 So.3d 151, 153 (Fla.2011); City of Gainesville, 918 So.2d at 256.

The language currently contained in section 27.5303(1)(d) was added when this statute was created in 2003 and became effective July 1, 2004. See ch.2003–402, § 19, at 3668–70, Laws of Fla. This provision states that "[i] n no case shall the court approve a withdrawal by the public defender or criminal conflict and civil regional counsel based solely upon inadequacy of funding or excess workload of the public defender or regional counsel." § 27.5303(1)(d), Fla. Stat. (2007) (emphasis added.)

In addressing the constitutionality, we read the challenged subsection in pari materia with subsections (1)(a) and (1)(e). These subsections provide, in pertinent part:

> (1)(a) If, at any time during the representation of two or more defendants, a public defender determines that the interests of those accused are so adverse or hostile that they cannot all be counseled by the public defender or his or her staff without conflict of interest, or that none can be counseled by the public defender or his or her staff because of a conflict of interest, then the public defender shall file a motion to withdraw and move the court to appoint other counsel. The court shall review and may inquire or conduct a hearing into the adequacy of the public defender's representations regarding a conflict of interest without requiring the disclosure of any confidential communications. The court shall deny the motion to withdraw if the court finds the grounds for withdrawal are insufficient or the asserted conflict is not prejudicial to the indigent client.
>
> ....
>
> (e) In determining whether or not there is a conflict of interest, the public defender or regional counsel shall apply the standards contained in the Uniform Standards for Use in Conflict of Interest Cases found in appendix C to the Final Report of the Article V Indigent Services Advisory Board dated January 6, 2004.

The only conflicts addressed in the Uniform Standards for Use in Conflict of Interest Cases are conflicts involving codefendants and certain kinds of witnesses or parties. There is no discussion of "conflicts arising from underfunding, excessive caseload, or the prospective inability to adequately represent a client." Public Defender, 12 So.3d at 804. The Third District concluded that the Legislature's promulgation of this law "which prohibited withdrawal based on excessive caseload and which stated that the 'conflict of interest' contemplated by section 27.5303 included only the traditional conflicts arising from the representation of codefendants" prevents the courts from considering other conflicts of interest as a basis for a motion to withdraw. Id.

However, we rejected a similar argument regarding the same statutory language when it was previously contained in section 27.53(3). In Behr, 384 So.2d at 148, the County argued that the only circumstance under which the public defender could withdraw was a conflict of interest between the clients of the office and did not include the circumstance of excessive caseload. We rejected this argument, as well as the argument that excessive caseload was a special circumstance that provided a lawful ground for the appointment of substitute counsel for the public defender.13 Id. at 149–50. Instead, we adopted the dissenting opinion from the court below as our rationale, concluding that the trial court's discretion to appoint a special assistant public defender was "virtually unfettered" and "not dependent" on a showing of lawful ground or special circumstances. Id. at 149.

The State argues that the issue is moot because assistant public defender Kolsky was replaced as counsel on Bowens' case after the Court accepted it for review. Thus, the State argues, the Court should not consider the constitutionality of the statute. However, the mootness doctrine does not destroy this Court's jurisdiction in a case where the question before it is of great public importance and is likely to recur. See *State v. Matthews*, 891 So.2d 479, 484 (Fla.2004); *Holly v. Auld*, 450 So.2d 217, 218 n. 1 (Fla.1984) ("It is well settled that mootness does not destroy an appellate court's jurisdiction ... when the questions raised are of great public importance or are likely to recur.").

The trial court concluded that the used of the word "solely" in section 27.5303(1)(d) is not a prohibition on considering excessive caseload as a factor in an attorney's motion to withdraw, just that other considerations must also be present. *State v. Bowens*, Case No. F09–019364, at 7 (Fla. 11th Cir.Ct. Oct. 25, 2009) (order denying public defender's motion to declare section 27.5303(1)(d) unconstitutional and granting public defender's motion to withdraw). The trial court concluded that there "exists a cognizable difference between a withdrawal based solely on workload, and a withdrawal where an individualized showing is made that there is a substantial risk that a defendant's constitutional rights may be prejudiced as a result of the workload." *Id.* at 8. Because the trial court found that this distinction "allows judicial relief where prejudice to constitutional rights is adequately demonstrated," it found the statute not to be constitutionally infirm. *Id.*

The cases dealing with the statutory caps on attorney's fees guide our resolution of this issue. See *Maas*, 992 So.2d at 196; *White*, 537 So.2d at 1376; *Makemson*, 491 So.2d at 1109. In each instance, we did not find the statutes unconstitutional on their face, but concluded that they "could be unconstitutional when applied to curtail the [trial] court's inherent authority to ensure adequate representation of the criminally accused." Olive, 992 So.2d at 203. The same applies in the instant case. If section 27.5303(1)(d) is interpreted as prohibiting any motions to withdraw based on excessive caseloads or underfunding, then it would violate the courts' inherent authority to ensure adequate representation of indigent defendants.

Moreover, this Court has repeatedly recognized that excessive caseload in the public defender's office creates a problem regarding effective representation. See *Certification of Conflict*, 636 So.2d at 23 n. 1 (Harding, J., concurring) (recognizing that public defender had demonstrated sufficient grounds for withdrawal in nearly 400 appeals "because of conflict caused by an excessive caseload"); *Order on Prosecution*, 561 So.2d at 1135 ("When excessive caseload forces the public defender to choose between the rights of the various indigent criminal defendants he represents, a conflict of interest is inevitably created."); *Behr,* 384 So.2d at 147 (Fla.1980) ("[T]he Public Defender for the First Judicial Circuit filed motions to withdraw as counsel in a number of felony cases on the ground that his excessive case load would preclude the performance of effective representation on behalf of the indigent defendants."). "[W]here the backlog of cases in the public defender's office is so excessive that there is no possible way he can timely handle those cases, it is his responsibility to move the court to withdraw." Order on Prosecution, 561 So.2d at 1138.

Thus, we find the statute to be facially constitutional and answer the certified question in the negative. However, the statute should not be applied to preclude a public defender from filing a motion to withdraw based on excessive caseload or underfunding that would result in ineffective representation of indigent defendants nor to preclude a trial court from granting a motion to withdraw under those circumstances.

Standing of State Attorney's Office

Finally, we address whether the State Attorney's Office has standing to oppose a public defender's certification of conflict. The trial court denied standing, but allowed the State Attorney's Office to participate in the proceedings as amicus curiae. Public Defender, 12 So.3d at 800. On appeal, the Third District cited the state attorney's statutory obligation under section 27.02(1) to "appear in the circuit and county courts within his or her judicial circuit and prosecute or defend on behalf of the state all suits, applications, or motions, civil or criminal, in which the state is a party." Public Defender, 12 So.3d at 801. The Third District concluded that this statutory obligation and the State's status as a party to criminal cases conferred standing on the state attorney to challenge the motions filed by the Public Defender. *Id.*

"Determining whether a party has standing is a pure question of law to be reviewed de novo." *Sanchez v. Century Everglades, LLC,* 946 So.2d 563, 564 (Fla. 3d DCA 2006) (quoting *Alachua Cnty. v. Scharps,* 855 So.2d 195, 198 (Fla. 1st DCA 2003)). Generally, standing "requires a would-be litigant to demonstrate that he or she reasonably expects to be affected by the outcome of the proceedings, either directly or indirectly." *Hayes v. Guardianship of Thompson,* 952 So.2d 498, 505 (Fla.2006); see generally *Brown v. Firestone,* 382 So.2d 654, 662 (Fla.1980) ("[T]his Court has long been committed to the rule that a party does not possess standing to sue unless he or she can demonstrate a direct and articulable stake in the outcome of a controversy."); *Weiss v. Johansen,* 898 So.2d 1009, 1011 (Fla. 4th DCA 2005) ("Standing depends on whether a party has a sufficient stake in a justiciable controversy, with a legally cognizable interest which would be affected by the outcome of the litigation."). Thus, standing to bring or participate in a particular legal proceeding often depends on the nature of the interest asserted.

This issue was disposed of in our recent decision in *Johnson v. State,* 78 So.3d 1305, 1314–15 (Fla.2012), which addressed the standing of the Office of Criminal Conflict and Civil Regional

Counsel (RCC) to object to a public defender's motion to withdraw. We concluded that RCC did not have standing because it was not a party to the proceedings, even though it has an "articulable stake in the outcome of the proceedings" because it has a statutory duty of representation should the public defender be permitted to withdraw. RCC's interest was similar to that of the counties who sought standing to be heard on public defenders' motions to withdraw based on the counties' financial responsibilities of compensating appointed private counsel. See *In re Order on Prosecution of Criminal Appeals by Tenth Judicial Circuit Public Defender*, 561 So.2d 1130 (Fla.1990); Behr, 384 So.2d at 150.

We explained that an articulable stake in the outcome of the proceedings (such as the counties' financial obligations to pay the appointed counsel or the possibility that RCC would be appointed as counsel if a motion to withdraw was granted) was not the same as the State's role as a party to the proceedings. *Johnson*, 78 So.3d at 1314. Additionally, we cited with approval the ruling in Public Defender that the State had standing to oppose a motion to withdraw by the public defender because the State is a party to criminal cases and the state attorney has a statutory obligation to prosecute or defend on behalf of the State. Id. Thus, we approve the Third District's conclusion that "the State had standing to challenge the motions filed by [the public defender]." Public Defender, 12 So.3d at 801.

III. CONCLUSION

Consistent with the analysis above, we quash the Third District's decision in Public Defender and quash in part and affirm in part its decision in Bowens. We also remand for the trial court to determine if the circumstances still warrant granting the Public Defender's motion to decline appointments in future third-degree felony cases under the standards approved in this decision.

It is so ordered.

Note

The ability of appointed counsel to withdraw, rather than provide ineffective assistance of counsel due to lack of resources, even if consistent with the Sixth Amendment and the ethical responsibility of the public defender, does not answer the question – "what then for minority, indigent defendant"? Nor is the challenge of quality of legal services rendered by the appointed counsel, who does not withdraw, answered. Given the defendant-borne burden of meeting the two-pronged test of *Strickland v. Washington*, 466 U.S. 668 (1984) (defendant must show that counsel failed to act as a reasonably competent attorney and show that there is a reasonable probability that but for counsel's unprofessional errors, the results of the proceeding would have been different) what role should race, and racial attitudes play in determining if there is ineffective assistance of counsel?

Race and Effective Assistance of Counsel

BUCK V. DAVIS,
137 S.Ct. 759 (2017)

Chief Justice ROBERTS delivered the opinion of the Court.

A Texas jury convicted petitioner Duane Buck of capital murder. Under state law, the jury could impose a death sentence only if it found that Buck was likely to commit acts of violence in the future. Buck's attorney called a psychologist to offer his opinion on that issue. The psychologist testified that Buck probably would not engage in violent conduct. But he also stated that one of the factors pertinent in assessing a person's propensity for violence was his race, and that Buck was statistically more likely to act violently because he is black. The jury sentenced Buck to death.

Buck contends that his attorney's introduction of this evidence violated his Sixth Amendment right to the effective assistance of counsel. This claim has never been heard on the merits in any court, because the attorney who represented Buck in his first state postconviction proceeding failed to raise it. In 2006, a Federal District Court relied on that failure—properly, under then-governing law—to hold that Buck's claim was procedurally defaulted and unreviewable.

In 2014, Buck sought to reopen that 2006 judgment by filing a motion under Federal Rule of Civil Procedure 60(b)(6). He argued that this Court's decisions in *Martinez v. Ryan*, 566 U.S. 1, 132 S.Ct. 1309, 182 L.Ed.2d 272 (2012), and *Trevino v. Thaler*, 569 U.S. ----, 133 S.Ct. 1911, 185 L.Ed.2d 1044 (2013), had changed the law in a way that provided an excuse for his procedural default, permitting him to litigate his claim on the merits. In addition to this change in the law, Buck's motion identified ten other factors that, he said, constituted the "extraordinary circumstances" required to justify reopening the 2006 judgment under the Rule. See *Gonzalez v. Crosby*, 545 U.S. 524, 535, 125 S.Ct. 2641, 162 L.Ed.2d 480 (2005).

The District Court below denied the motion, and the Fifth Circuit declined to issue the certificate of appealability (COA) requested by Buck to appeal that decision. We granted certiorari, and now reverse.

I

A

On the morning of July 30, 1995, Duane Buck arrived at the home of his former girlfriend, Debra Gardner. He was carrying a rifle and a shotgun. Buck entered the home, shot Phyllis Taylor, his stepsister, and then shot Gardner's friend Kenneth Butler. Gardner fled the house, and Buck followed. So did Gardner's young children. While Gardner's son and daughter begged for their mother's life, Buck shot Gardner in the chest. Gardner and Butler died of their wounds. Taylor survived.

Police officers arrived soon after the shooting and placed Buck under arrest. An officer would later testify that Buck was laughing at the scene. He remained "happy" and "upbeat" as he was driven to the police station, "[s]miling and laughing" in the back of the patrol car. App. 134a–135a, 252a.

Buck was tried for capital murder, and the jury convicted. During the penalty phase of the trial, the jury was charged with deciding two issues. The first was what the parties term the "future dangerousness" question. At the time of Buck's trial, a Texas jury could impose the death penalty only if it found—unanimously and beyond a reasonable doubt—"a probability that the defendant would commit criminal acts of violence that would constitute a continuing threat to society." Tex.Code Crim. Proc. Ann., Art. 37.071, § 2(b)(1) (Vernon 1998). The second issue, to be reached only if the jury found Buck likely to be a future danger, was whether mitigating circumstances nevertheless warranted a sentence of life imprisonment instead of death. See § 2(e).

The parties focused principally on the first question. The State called witnesses who emphasized the brutality of Buck's crime and his evident lack of remorse in its aftermath. The State also called another former girlfriend, Vivian Jackson. She testified that, during their relationship, Buck had routinely hit her and had twice pointed a gun at her. Finally, the State introduced evidence of Buck's criminal history, including convictions for delivery of cocaine and unlawfully carrying a weapon. App. 125a–127a, 185a.

Defense counsel answered with a series of lay witnesses, including Buck's father and stepmother, who testified that they had never known him to be violent. Counsel also called two psychologists to testify as experts. The first, Dr. Patrick Lawrence, observed that Buck had previously served time in prison and had been held in minimum custody. From this he concluded that Buck "did not present any problems in the prison setting." Record in No. 4:04–cv–03965 (SD Tex.), Doc. 5–116, pp. 12–13. Dr. Lawrence further testified that murders within the Texas penal system tend to be gang related (there was no evidence Buck had ever been a member of a gang) and that Buck's offense had been a "crime of passion" occurring within the context of a romantic relationship. Id., at 4, 19, 21. Based on these considerations, Dr. Lawrence determined that Buck was unlikely to be a danger if he were sentenced to life in prison. Id., at 20–21.

Buck's second expert, Dr. Walter Quijano, had been appointed by the presiding judge to conduct a psychological evaluation. Dr. Quijano had met with Buck in prison prior to trial and shared a report of his findings with defense counsel.

Like Dr. Lawrence, Dr. Quijano thought it significant that Buck's prior acts of violence had arisen from romantic relationships with women; Buck, of course, would not form any such relationships while incarcerated. And Dr. Quijano likewise considered Buck's behavioral record in prison a good indicator that future violence was unlikely. App. 36a, 39a–40a.

But there was more to the report. In determining whether Buck was likely to pose a danger in the future, Dr. Quijano considered seven "statistical factors." The fourth factor was "race." His report read, in relevant part: "4. Race. Black: Increased probability. There is an over-representation of Blacks among the violent offenders." Id., at 19a.

Despite knowing Dr. Quijano's view that Buck's race was competent evidence of an increased probability of future violence, defense counsel called Dr. Quijano to the stand and asked him to discuss the "statistical factors" he had "looked at in regard to this case." Id., at 145a–146a. Dr. Quijano responded that certain factors were "know[n] to predict future dangerousness" and, consistent with his report, identified race as one of them. Id., at 146a. "It's a sad commentary," he testified, "that minorities, Hispanics and black people, are over represented in the Criminal Justice System." Ibid. Through further questioning, counsel elicited testimony concerning factors Dr. Quijano thought favorable to Buck, as well as his ultimate opinion that Buck was unlikely to pose a danger in the future. At the close of Dr. Quijano's testimony, his report was admitted into evidence. Id., at 150a–152a.

After opening cross-examination with a series of general questions, the prosecutor likewise turned to the report. She asked first about the statistical factors of past crimes and age, then questioned Dr. Quijano about the roles of sex and race: "You have determined that the sex factor, that a male is more violent than a female because that's just the way it is, and that the race factor, black, increases the future dangerousness for various complicated reasons; is that correct?" Id., at 170a. Dr. Quijano replied, "Yes." Ibid.

During closing arguments, defense counsel emphasized that Buck had proved to be "controllable in the prison population," and that his crime was one of "jealousy, ... passion and emotion" unlikely to be repeated in jail. Id., at 189a–191a. The State stressed the crime's brutal nature and Buck's lack of remorse, along with the inability of Buck's own experts to guarantee that he would not act violently in the future—a point it supported by reference to Dr. Quijano's testimony. See id., at 198a–199a ("You heard from Dr. Quijano, ... who told you that ... the probability did exist that [Buck] would be a continuing threat to society.").

The jury deliberated over the course of two days. During that time it sent out four notes, one of which requested the "psychology reports" that had been admitted into evidence. Id., at

209a. These reports—including Dr. Quijano's—were provided. The jury returned a sentence of death.

B

Buck's conviction and sentence were affirmed on direct appeal. Buck v. State, No. 72,810 (Tex.Crim.App., Apr. 28, 1999). His case then entered a labyrinth of state and federal collateral review, where it has wandered for the better part of two decades.

Buck filed his first petition for a writ of habeas corpus in Texas state court in 1999. The four claims advanced in his petition, however, were all frivolous or noncognizable. See *Ex parte Buck*, No. 699684–A (Dist. Ct. Harris Cty., Tex., July 11, 2003), pp. 6–7. The petition failed to mention defense counsel's introduction of expert testimony that Buck's race increased his propensity for violence.

But Dr. Quijano had testified in other cases, too, and in 1999, while Buck's first habeas petition was pending, one of those cases reached this Court. The petitioner, Victor Hugo Saldano, argued that his death sentence had been tainted by Dr. Quijano's testimony that Saldano's Hispanic heritage "was a factor weighing in the favor of future dangerousness." App. 302a. Texas confessed error on that ground and asked this Court to grant Saldano's petition for certiorari, vacate the state court judgment, and remand the case. In June 2000, the Court did so. *Saldano v. Texas*, 530 U.S. 1212, 120 S.Ct. 2214, 147 L.Ed.2d 246.

Within days, the Texas Attorney General, John Cornyn, issued a public statement concerning the cases in which Dr. Quijano had testified. The statement affirmed that "it is inappropriate to allow race to be considered as a factor in our criminal justice system." App. 213a. In keeping with that principle, the Attorney General explained that his office had conducted a "thorough audit" and "identified eight more cases in which testimony was offered by Dr. Quijano that race should be a factor for the jury to consider in making its determination about the sentence in a capital murder trial." Ibid. Six of those cases were "similar to that of Victor Hugo Saldano"; in those cases, letters had been sent to counsel apprising them of the Attorney General's findings. Id., at 213a–214a. The statement closed by identifying the defendants in those six cases. Buck was one of them. Id., at 215a–217a. By the close of 2002, the Attorney General had confessed error, waived any available procedural defenses, and consented to resentencing in the cases of five of those six defendants. See Alba v. Johnson, 232 F.3d 208 (C.A.5 2000) (Table); Memorandum and Order in Blue v. Johnson, No. 4:99–cv–00350 (SD Tex.), pp. 15–17; Order in Garcia v. Johnson, No. 1:99–cv–00134 (ED Tex.), p. 1; Order in Broxton v. Johnson, No. 4:00–cv–01034 (SD Tex.), pp. 10–11; Final Judgment in Gonzales v. Cockrell, No. 7:99–cv–00072 (WD Tex.), p. 1.

Not, however, in Buck's. In 2002, Buck's attorney filed a new state habeas petition alleging that trial counsel had rendered ineffective assistance by introducing Dr. Quijano's testimony. The State was not represented by the Attorney General in this proceeding—the Texas Attorney

General represents state respondents in federal habeas cases, but not state habeas cases—and it did not confess error. Because Buck's petition was successive, the Texas Court of Criminal Appeals dismissed it as an abuse of the writ. *Ex parte Buck*, Nos. 57,004–01, 57,004–02 (Tex. Crim.App., Oct. 15, 2003) (per curiam).

Buck turned to the federal courts. He filed a petition for habeas corpus under 28 U.S.C. § 2254 in October 2004, by which time Attorney General Cornyn had left office. See *Buck v. Dretke*, 2006 WL 8411481, (S.D.Tex., July 24, 2006). Buck sought relief on the ground that trial counsel's introduction of Dr. Quijano's testimony was constitutionally ineffective. The State responded that the state court had dismissed Buck's ineffective assistance claim because Buck had failed to press it in his first petition, raising it for the first time in a procedurally improper second petition. The State argued that such reliance on an established state rule of procedure was an adequate and independent state ground precluding federal review. Texas acknowledged that it had waived similar procedural defenses in Saldano's case. But it argued that Buck's case was different because "[i]n Saldano's case Dr. Quijano testified for the State "; in Buck's, "it was Buck who called Dr. Quijano to testify." Answer and Motion for Summary Judgment in No. 4:04–cv–03965 (SD Tex.), p. 20.

Buck countered that, notwithstanding his procedural default, the District Court should reach the merits of his claim because a failure to do so would result in a miscarriage of justice. Buck did not argue that his default should be excused on a showing of "cause" and "prejudice"—that is, cause for the default, and prejudice from the denial of a federal right. And for good reason: At the time Buck filed his § 2254 petition, our decision in *Coleman v. Thompson*, 501 U.S. 722, 752–753, 111 S.Ct. 2546, 115 L.Ed.2d 640 (1991), made clear that an attorney's failure to raise an ineffective assistance claim during state postconviction review could not constitute cause. The District Court rejected Buck's miscarriage of justice argument and held that, because of his procedural default, his ineffective assistance claim was unreviewable. *Buck v. Dretke*, 2006 WL 8411481, . Buck unsuccessfully sought review of the District Court's ruling. See *Buck v. Thaler*, 345 Fed.Appx. 923 (C.A.5 2009) (per curiam) (denying application for a COA), cert. denied, 559 U.S. 1072, 130 S.Ct. 2096, 176 L.Ed.2d 730 (2010).

In 2011, Buck sought to reopen his case, arguing that the prosecution had violated the Equal Protection and Due Process Clauses by asking Dr. Quijano about the relationship between race and future violence on cross-examination and referring to his testimony during summation. Buck also argued that the State's decision to treat him differently from the other defendants affected by Dr. Quijano's testimony justified relieving him of the District Court's adverse judgment. The Fifth Circuit disagreed, see *Buck v. Thaler*, 452 Fed.Appx. 423, 427–428 (C.A.5 2011) (per curiam), and we denied certiorari, *Buck v. Thaler*, 565 U.S. 1022, 132 S.Ct. 32, 181 L.Ed.2d 411 (2011). Buck, still barred by Coleman from avoiding the consequences of his procedural default, did not pursue his ineffective assistance claim.

C

In 2012, this Court "modif[ied] the unqualified statement in Coleman that an attorney's ignorance or inadvertence in a postconviction proceeding does not qualify as cause to excuse a procedural default." *Martinez*, 566 U.S., at 9, 132 S.Ct. 1309. We held that when a state formally limits the adjudication of claims of ineffective assistance of trial counsel to collateral review, a prisoner may establish cause for procedural default if (1) "the state courts did not appoint counsel in the initial-review collateral proceeding," or "appointed counsel in [that] proceeding ... was ineffective under the standards of *Strickland v. Washington*, 466 U.S. 668 [104 S.Ct. 2052, 80 L.Ed.2d 674] (1984)"; and (2) "the underlying ... claim is a substantial one, which is to say that ... the claim has some merit." Id., at 14, 132 S.Ct. 1309.

By its terms, *Martinez* did not bear on Buck's ineffective assistance claim. At the time of Buck's conviction and appeal, Texas did not formally require criminal defendants to reserve such claims for collateral review. In *Trevino*, however, the Court concluded that the exception announced in *Martinez* extended to state systems that, as a practical matter, deny criminal defendants "a meaningful opportunity" to press ineffective assistance claims on direct appeal. 569 U.S., at ----, 133 S.Ct., at 1921. The Court further concluded that the system in Texas, where petitioner had been convicted, was such a system. Ibid. The upshot: Had *Martinez* and *Trevino* been decided before Buck filed his § 2254 petition, a federal court could have reviewed Buck's ineffective assistance claim if he demonstrated that (1) state postconviction counsel had been constitutionally ineffective in failing to raise it, and (2) the claim had "some merit." *Martinez*, 566 U.S., at 14, 132 S.Ct. 1309.

D

When *Trevino* was decided, Buck's third state habeas petition was pending in Texas court. That petition was denied in November 2013. *Ex parte Buck*, 418 S.W.3d 98 (Tex.Crim.App.2013) (per curiam). Two months later, Buck returned to federal court, where he filed a motion to reopen his § 2254 case under Federal Rule of Civil Procedure 60(b)(6). Rule 60(b) enumerates specific circumstances in which a party may be relieved of the effect of a judgment, such as mistake, newly discovered evidence, fraud, and the like. The Rule concludes with a catchall category—subdivision (b)(6)—providing that a court may lift a judgment for "any other reason that justifies relief." Relief is available under subdivision (b)(6), however, only in "extraordinary circumstances," and the Court has explained that "[s]uch circumstances will rarely occur in the habeas context." *Gonzalez*, 545 U.S., at 535, 125 S.Ct. 2641.

In his motion, Buck identified 11 factors that, in his view, justified reopening the judgment. These included his attorney's introduction of expert testimony linking Buck's race to violence, the central issue at sentencing; the prosecution's questions about race and violence on cross-examination and reliance on Dr. Quijano's testimony in summation; the State's confession of error in other cases in which Dr. Quijano testified, but its refusal to concede error in Buck's case; and the change in law effected by Martinez and Trevino, which, if they had been decided earlier, would have permitted federal review of Buck's defaulted claim. App. 283a–285a.

The District Court denied relief on two grounds. First, the court concluded that Buck had failed to demonstrate extraordinary circumstances. To that end, the court observed that a change in decisional law is rarely extraordinary by itself. *Buck v. Stephens*, 2014 WL 11310152, (S.D.Tex., Aug. 29, 2014). It further determined that the State's "promise" not to oppose resentencing did not count for much, reasoning that "Buck's case is different in critical respects from the cases in which Texas confessed error" in that Buck's lawyer, not the prosecutor, had first elicited the objectionable testimony. The court also dismissed the contention that the nature of Dr. Quijano's testimony argued for reopening the case. Although "the introduction of any mention of race was," in the court's view, "ill[ ]advised at best and repugnant at worst," it was also "de minimis ": Dr. Quijano had discussed the connection between race and violence only twice. The court accordingly concluded that Buck had failed to make out the predicate for Rule 60(b)(6) relief.

Second, the court determined that—even if the circumstances were extraordinary—Buck's claim would fail on the merits. The court noted that under Strickland, Buck was obliged to show that counsel's performance was both deficient and prejudicial. The court held that Buck's lawyer had indeed performed deficiently in calling Dr. Quijano to give testimony that "len[t] credence to any potential latent racial prejudice held by the jury." 2014 WL 11310152. But, the court concluded, Buck had failed to demonstrate prejudice. It observed that Buck's crime had been "horrific." Ibid. And the court had already concluded that "the introduction of any mention of race was … de minimis." Id. For those reasons, it held, Buck had failed to show a reasonable probability that he would not have been sentenced to death but for Dr. Quijano's testimony about race and violence.

Buck sought to appeal the denial of his Rule 60(b)(6) motion. He accordingly filed an application for a COA with the Fifth Circuit. To obtain a COA, Buck was required to make "a substantial showing of the denial of a constitutional right." 28 U.S.C. § 2253(c)(2).

The Fifth Circuit denied a COA, concluding that Buck's case was "not extraordinary at all in the habeas context." *Buck v. Stephens*, 623 Fed.Appx. 668, 673 (2015). The panel agreed with the District Court that Martinez and Trevino were not significant factors in the analysis. It characterized most of the other factors Buck had identified as "variations on the merits" of his claim, which was "at least unremarkable as far as [ineffective assistance] claims go." 623 Fed.Appx., at 673. The panel likewise rejected Buck's argument that he was entitled to relief because the State had issued a press release indicating that his case would be treated like Saldano's, and then had confessed error in the other cases identified as similar in the statement, but not in Buck's. *Id.*, at 674. Because Buck had "not shown extraordinary circumstances that would permit relief under

Federal Rule of Civil Procedure 6o(b)(6)," the panel "den[ied] the application for a COA." *Id.*, at 669.

Buck's motion for rehearing en banc was denied over two dissenting votes. *Buck v. Stephens,* 630 Fed.Appx. 251 (C.A.5 2015) (per curiam). We granted certiorari.

II

A state prisoner whose petition for a writ of habeas corpus is denied by a federal district court does not enjoy an absolute right to appeal. Federal law requires that he first obtain a COA from a circuit justice or judge. 28 U.S.C. § 2253(c)(1). A COA may issue "only if the applicant has made a substantial showing of the denial of a constitutional right." § 2253(c)(2). Until the prisoner secures a COA, the Court of Appeals may not rule on the merits of his case. *Miller–El v. Cockrell,* 537 U.S. 322, 336, 123 S.Ct. 1029, 154 L.Ed.2d 931 (2003).

The COA inquiry, we have emphasized, is not coextensive with a merits analysis. At the COA stage, the only question is whether the applicant has shown that "jurists of reason could disagree with the district court's resolution of his constitutional claims or that jurists could conclude the issues presented are adequate to deserve encouragement to proceed further." *Id.*, at 327, 123 S.Ct. 1029. This threshold question should be decided without "full consideration of the factual or legal bases adduced in support of the claims." *Id.*, at 336, 123 S.Ct. 1029. "When a court of appeals sidesteps [the COA] process by first deciding the merits of an appeal, and then justifying its denial of a COA based on its adjudication of the actual merits, it is in essence deciding an appeal without jurisdiction." *Id.*, at 336–337, 123 S.Ct. 1029.

The court below phrased its determination in proper terms—that jurists of reason would not debate that Buck should be denied relief, 623 Fed.Appx., at 674—but it reached that conclusion only after essentially deciding the case on the merits. As the court put it in the second sentence of its opinion: "Because [Buck] has not shown extraordinary circumstances that would permit relief under Federal Rule of Civil Procedure 6o(b)(6), we deny the application for a COA." *Id.*, at 669. The balance of the Fifth Circuit's opinion reflects the same approach. The change in law effected by *Martinez* and *Trevino*, the panel wrote, was "not an extraordinary circumstance." 623 Fed.Appx., at 674. Even if Texas initially indicated to Buck that he would be resentenced, its "decision not to follow through" was "not extraordinary." *Ibid.* Buck "ha[d] not shown why" the State's alleged broken promise "would justify relief from the judgment." *Ibid.*

But the question for the Fifth Circuit was not whether Buck had "shown extraordinary circumstances" or "shown why [Texas's broken promise] would justify relief from the judgment." *Id.*, at 669, 674. Those are ultimate merits determinations the panel should not have reached. We reiterate what we have said before: A "court of appeals should limit its examination [at the COA stage] to a threshold inquiry into the underlying merit of [the] claims," and ask "only if the District Court's decision was debatable." *Miller–El*, 537 U.S., at 327, 348, 123 S.Ct. 1029.

The dissent does not accept this established rule, arguing that a reviewing court that deems a claim nondebatable "must necessarily conclude that the claim is meritless." Post, at 781 (opinion of THOMAS, J.). Of course when a court of appeals properly applies the COA standard and determines that a prisoner's claim is not even debatable, that necessarily means the prisoner has failed to show that his claim is meritorious. But the converse is not true. That a prisoner has failed to make the ultimate showing that his claim is meritorious does not logically mean he failed to make a preliminary showing that his claim was debatable. Thus, when a reviewing court (like the Fifth Circuit here) inverts the statutory order of operations and "first decid[es] the merits of an appeal, ... then justif[ies] its denial of a COA based on its adjudication of the actual merits," it has placed too heavy a burden on the prisoner at the COA stage. *Miller–El*, 537 U.S., at 336–337, 123 S.Ct. 1029. Miller–El flatly prohibits such a departure from the procedure prescribed by § 2253. Ibid.

The State defends the Fifth Circuit's approach by arguing that the court's consideration of an application for a COA is often quite thorough. The court "occasionally hears oral argument when considering whether to grant a COA in a capital case." Brief for Respondent 50. Indeed, in one recent case, it "received nearly 200 pages of initial briefing, permitted a reply brief, considered the parties' supplemental authorities, invited supplemental letter briefs from both sides, and heard oral argument before denying the request for a COA." *Id.*, at 50–51.

But this hurts rather than helps the State's case. "[A] claim can be debatable even though every jurist of reason might agree, after the COA has been granted and the case has received full consideration, that petitioner will not prevail." *Miller–El*, 537 U.S., at 338, 123 S.Ct. 1029. The statute sets forth a two-step process: an initial determination whether a claim is reasonably debatable, and then—if it is—an appeal in the normal course. We do not mean to specify what procedures may be appropriate in every case. But whatever procedures are employed at the COA stage should be consonant with the limited nature of the inquiry.

Given the approach of the court below, it is perhaps understandable that the parties have essentially briefed and argued the underlying merits at length. See, e.g., Brief for Petitioner 32 ("[T]rial counsel rendered deficient performance under Strickland."); id., at 39 ("[T]here is a reasonable probability that Dr. Quijano's race-as-dangerousness opinion swayed the judgment of jurors in favor of death." (internal quotation marks and alteration omitted)); id., at 59 (Buck "has demonstrated his entitlement to relief under Rule 60(b)(6)"); Brief for Respondent 40 ("The particular facts of petitioner's case do not establish extraordinary circumstances justifying relief from the judgment." (boldface type deleted)). With respect to this Court's review, § 2253 does not limit the scope of our consideration of the underlying merits, and at this juncture we think it proper to meet the decision below and the arguments of the parties on their own terms.

III

Buck's request for a COA raised two separate questions for the Fifth Circuit, one substantive and one procedural: first, whether reasonable jurists could debate the District Court's conclusion that Buck was not denied his right to effective assistance of counsel under *Strickland* ; and second, whether reasonable jurists could debate the District Court's procedural holding that Buck had not made the necessary showing to reopen his case under Rule 60(b)(6).

A

We begin with the District Court's determination (not specifically addressed by the Fifth Circuit) that Buck's constitutional claim failed on the merits. The Sixth Amendment right to counsel "is the right to the effective assistance of counsel." *Strickland*, 466 U.S., at 686, 104 S.Ct. 2052 (quoting *McMann v. Richardson*, 397 U.S. 759, 771, n. 14, 90 S.Ct. 1441, 25 L.Ed.2d 763 (1970)). A defendant who claims to have been denied effective assistance must show both that counsel performed deficiently and that counsel's deficient performance caused him prejudice. 466 U.S., at 687, 104 S.Ct. 2052.

1

Strickland 's first prong sets a high bar. A defense lawyer navigating a criminal proceeding faces any number of choices about how best to make a client's case. The lawyer has discharged his constitutional responsibility so long as his decisions fall within the "wide range of professionally competent assistance." *Id.*, at 690, 104 S.Ct. 2052. It is only when the lawyer's errors were "so serious that counsel was not functioning as the 'counsel' guaranteed ... by the Sixth Amendment" that *Strickland* 's first prong is satisfied. *Id.*, at 687, 104 S.Ct. 2052.

The District Court determined that, in this case, counsel's performance fell outside the bounds of competent representation. We agree. Counsel knew that Dr. Quijano's report reflected the view that Buck's race disproportionately predisposed him to violent conduct; he also knew that the principal point of dispute during the trial's penalty phase was whether Buck was likely to act violently in the future. Counsel nevertheless (1) called Dr. Quijano to the stand; (2) specifically elicited testimony about the connection between Buck's race and the likelihood of future violence; and (3) put into evidence Dr. Quijano's expert report that stated, in reference to factors bearing on future dangerousness, "Race. Black: Increased probability." App. 19a, 145a–146a.

Given that the jury had to make a finding of future dangerousness before it could impose a death sentence, Dr. Quijano's report said, in effect, that the color of Buck's skin made him more deserving of execution. It would be patently unconstitutional for a state to argue that a defendant is liable to be a future danger because of his race. See *Zant v. Stephens*, 462 U.S. 862, 885, 103 S.Ct. 2733, 77 L.Ed.2d 235 (1983) (identifying race among factors that are "constitutionally impermissible or totally irrelevant to the sentencing process"). No competent defense attorney would introduce such evidence about his own client. See *Buck v. Thaler*, 565 U.S., at 1022, 132 S.Ct. 32 (statement of ALITO, J., joined by Scalia and BREYER, JJ., respecting denial of certiorari) (Buck's case "concerns bizarre and objectionable testimony").

2

To satisfy *Strickland*, a litigant must also demonstrate prejudice—"a reasonable probability that, but for counsel's unprofessional errors, the result of the proceeding would have been different." 466 U.S., at 694, 104 S.Ct. 2052. Accordingly, the question before the District Court was whether Buck had demonstrated a reasonable probability that, without Dr. Quijano's testimony on race, at least one juror would have harbored a reasonable doubt about whether Buck was likely to be violent in the future. The District Court concluded that Buck had not made such a showing. We disagree.

In arguing that the jury would have imposed a death sentence even if Dr. Quijano had not offered race-based testimony, the State primarily emphasizes the brutality of Buck's crime and his lack of remorse. A jury may conclude that a crime's vicious nature calls for a sentence of death. See *Wong v. Belmontes*, 558 U.S. 15, 130 S.Ct. 383, 175 L.Ed.2d 328 (2009) (per curiam). In this case, however, several considerations convince us that it is reasonably probable—notwithstanding the nature of Buck's crime and his behavior in its aftermath—that the proceeding would have ended differently had counsel rendered competent representation.

Dr. Quijano testified on the key point at issue in Buck's sentencing. True, the jury was asked to decide two issues—whether Buck was likely to be a future danger, and, if so, whether mitigating circumstances nevertheless justified a sentence of life imprisonment. But the focus of the proceeding was on the first question. Much of the penalty phase testimony was directed to future dangerousness, as were the summations for both sides. The jury, consistent with the focus of the parties, asked during deliberations to see the expert reports on dangerousness. See App. 187a–196a, 198a–203a, 209a.

Deciding the key issue of Buck's dangerousness involved an unusual inquiry. The jurors were not asked to determine a historical fact concerning Buck's conduct, but to render a predictive judgment inevitably entailing a degree of speculation. Buck, all agreed, had committed acts of terrible violence. Would he do so again?

Buck's prior violent acts had occurred outside of prison, and within the context of romantic relationships with women. If the jury did not impose a death sentence, Buck would be sentenced to life in prison, and no such romantic relationship would be likely to arise. A jury could conclude that those changes would minimize the prospect of future dangerousness.

But one thing would never change: the color of Buck's skin. Buck would always be black. And according to Dr. Quijano, that immutable characteristic carried with it an "[i]ncreased probability" of future violence. Id., at 19a. Here was hard statistical evidence—from an expert—to guide an otherwise speculative inquiry.

And it was potent evidence. Dr. Quijano's testimony appealed to a powerful racial stereotype—that of black men as "violence prone." *Turner v. Murray*, 476 U.S. 28, 35, 106 S.Ct. 1683, 90 L.Ed.2d 27 (1986) (plurality opinion). In combination with the substance of the jury's inquiry, this created something of a perfect storm. Dr. Quijano's opinion coincided precisely with a particularly noxious strain of racial prejudice, which itself coincided precisely with the central question at sentencing. The effect of this unusual confluence of factors was to provide support for making a decision on life or death on the basis of race.

This effect was heightened due to the source of the testimony. Dr. Quijano took the stand as a medical expert bearing the court's imprimatur. The jury learned at the outset of his testimony that he held a doctorate in clinical psychology, had conducted evaluations in some 70 capital murder cases, and had been appointed by the trial judge (at public expense) to evaluate Buck. App. 138a–141a. Reasonable jurors might well have valued his opinion concerning the central question before them. See *Satterwhite v. Texas*, 486 U.S. 249, 259, 108 S.Ct. 1792, 100 L.Ed.2d 284 (1988) (testimony from "a medical doctor specializing in psychiatry" on the question of future dangerousness may have influenced the sentencing jury).

For these reasons, we cannot accept the District Court's conclusion that "the introduction of any mention of race" during the penalty phase was "de minimis." 2014 WL 11310152. There were only "two references to race in Dr. Quijano's testimony"—one during direct examination, the other on cross. Ibid. But when a jury hears expert testimony that expressly makes a defendant's race directly pertinent on the question of life or death, the impact of that evidence cannot be measured simply by how much air time it received at trial or how many pages it occupies in the record. Some toxins can be deadly in small doses.

The State acknowledges, as it must, that introducing "race or ethnicity as evidence of criminality" can in some cases prejudice a defendant. Brief for Respondent 31. But it insists that this is not such a case, because Buck's own counsel, not the prosecution, elicited the offending testimony. We are not convinced. In fact, the distinction could well cut the other way. A prosecutor is seeking a conviction. Jurors understand this and may reasonably be expected to evaluate the government's evidence and arguments in light of its motivations. When a defendant's own lawyer puts in the offending evidence, it is in the nature of an admission against interest, more likely to be taken at face value.

The effect of Dr. Quijano's testimony on Buck's sentencing cannot be dismissed as "de minimis." Buck has demonstrated prejudice.

B

1

We now turn to the lower courts' procedural holding: that Buck failed to demonstrate that he was entitled to have the judgment against him reopened under Rule 60(b)(6). We have held that a litigant seeking a COA must demonstrate that a procedural ruling barring relief is itself debatable among jurists of reason; otherwise, the appeal would not "deserve encouragement to proceed further." *Slack v. McDaniel*, 529 U.S. 473, 484, 120 S.Ct. 1595, 146 L.Ed.2d 542 (2000) (quoting *Barefoot v. Estelle*, 463 U.S. 880, 893, n. 4, 103 S.Ct. 3383, 77 L.Ed.2d 1090 (1983)).

The Rule 60(b)(6) holding Buck challenges would be reviewed for abuse of discretion during a merits appeal, see 11 C. Wright, A. Miller, & M. Kane, Federal Practice and Procedure § 2857 (3d ed. 2012), and the parties agree that the COA question is therefore whether a reasonable jurist could conclude that the District Court abused its discretion in declining to reopen the judgment. See Brief for Petitioner 54–57; Brief for Respondent 34.

Buck brought his Rule 60(b) motion under the Rule's catchall category, subdivision (b)(6), which permits a court to reopen a judgment for "any other reason that justifies relief." Rule 60(b) vests wide discretion in courts, but we have held that relief under Rule 60(b)(6) is available only in "extraordinary circumstances." *Gonzalez*, 545 U.S., at 535, 125 S.Ct. 2641. In determining whether extraordinary circumstances are present, a court may consider a wide range of factors. These may include, in an appropriate case, "the risk of injustice to the parties" and "the risk of undermining the public's confidence in the judicial process." *Liljeberg v. Health Services Acquisition Corp.*, 486 U.S. 847, 863–864, 108 S.Ct. 2194, 100 L.Ed.2d 855 (1988).

In the circumstances of this case, the District Court abused its discretion in denying Buck's Rule 60(b)(6) motion. The District Court's conclusion that Buck "ha[d] failed to demonstrate that this case presents extraordinary circumstances" rested in large measure on its determination that "the introduction of any mention of race"—though "ill[ ]advised at best and repugnant at worst"—played only a "de minimis " role in the proceeding. 2014 WL 11310152. The Fifth Circuit, for its part, failed even to mention the racial evidence in concluding that Buck's claim was "at least unremarkable as far as [ineffective assistance] claims go." 623 Fed.Appx., at 673. But our holding on prejudice makes clear that Buck may have been sentenced to death in part because of his race. As an initial matter, this is a disturbing departure from a basic premise of our criminal justice system: Our law punishes people for what they do, not who they are. Dispensing punishment on the basis of an immutable characteristic flatly contravenes this guiding principle. As petitioner correctly puts it, "[i]t stretches credulity to characterize Mr. Buck's [ineffective assistance of counsel] claim as run-of-the-mill." Brief for Petitioner 57.

This departure from basic principle was exacerbated because it concerned race. "Discrimination on the basis of race, odious in all aspects, is especially pernicious in the administration of justice."

Rose v. Mitchell, 443 U.S. 545, 555, 99 S.Ct. 2993, 61 L.Ed.2d 739 (1979). Relying on race to impose a criminal sanction "poisons public confidence" in the judicial process. *Davis v. Ayala*, 576 U.S. ----, ----, 135 S.Ct. 2187, 2208, 192 L.Ed.2d 323 (2015). It thus injures not just the defendant, but "the law as an institution, ... the community at large, and ... the democratic ideal reflected in the processes of our courts." *Rose*, 443 U.S., at 556, 99 S.Ct. 2993 (internal quotation marks omitted). Such concerns are precisely among those we have identified as supporting relief under Rule 60(b)(6). See Liljeberg, 486 U.S., at 864, 108 S.Ct. 2194.

The extraordinary nature of this case is confirmed by what the State itself did in response to Dr. Quijano's testimony. When the case of Victor Hugo Saldano came before this Court, Texas confessed error and consented to resentencing. The State's response to Saldano's petition for certiorari succinctly expressed the injustice Saldano had suffered: "the infusion of race as a factor for the jury to weigh in making its determination violated his constitutional right to be sentenced without regard to the color of his skin." App. 306a.

The Attorney General's public statement, issued shortly after we vacated the judgment in Saldano's case, reflected this sentiment. It explained that the State had responded to Saldano's troubling petition by conducting a "thorough audit" of criminal cases, finding six similar to Saldano's "in which testimony was offered by Dr. Quijano that race should be a factor for the jury to consider." Id., at 213a. The statement affirmed that "it is inappropriate to allow race to be considered as a factor in our criminal justice system." Ibid. Consistent with this position—and to its credit—the State confessed error in the cases of five of the six defendants identified in the Attorney General's statement, waiving all available procedural defenses and consenting to resentencing.

These were remarkable steps. It is not every day that a State seeks to vacate the sentences of five defendants found guilty of capital murder. But then again, these were—as the State itself put it at oral argument here—"extraordinary" cases. Tr. of Oral Arg. 41; *see Buck v. Thaler*, 565 U.S., at 1030, 132 S.Ct. 32 (SOTOMAYOR, J., joined by KAGAN, J., dissenting from denial of certiorari) ("Especially in light of the capital nature of this case and the express recognition by a Texas attorney general that the relevant testimony was inappropriately race charged, Buck has presented issues that 'deserve encouragement to proceed further.'" (quoting *Miller–El*, 537 U.S., at 327, 123 S.Ct. 1029)).

To be sure, the State has repeatedly attempted to justify its decision to treat Buck differently from the other five defendants identified in the Attorney General's statement, including on asserted factual grounds that the State has been required to abjure. See Brief for Respondent 46, n. 10 (the State's initial opposition to Buck's habeas petition "erroneously" argued that Buck was treated differently because defense counsel, not the State, called Dr. Quijano as a witness; that was also true of two of the other defendants). The State continues its efforts before this Court, arguing that Buck's was the only one of the six cases in which defense counsel, not the prosecution, first elicited Dr. Quijano's opinion on race. See also post, at 784 (opinion of THOMAS, J.).

But this is beside the point. The State's various explanations for distinguishing Buck's case have nothing to do with the Attorney General's stated reasons for confessing error in Saldano and the cases acknowledged as similar. Regardless of which party first broached the subject, race was in all these cases put to the jury "as a factor ... to weigh in making its determination." App. 306a. The statement that "it is inappropriate to allow race to be considered as a factor in our criminal justice system" is equally applicable whether the prosecution or ineffective defense counsel initially injected race into the proceeding. Id., at 213a. The terms of the State's announcement provide every reason for originally including Buck on the list of defendants situated similarly to Saldano, and no reason for later taking him off.

In opposition, the State reminds us of the importance of preserving the finality of judgments. Brief for Respondent 34. But the "whole purpose" of Rule 60(b) "is to make an exception to finality." *Gonzalez*, 545 U.S., at 529, 125 S.Ct. 2641. And in this case, the State's interest in finality deserves little weight. When Texas recognized that the infusion of race into proceedings similar to Saldano's warranted confession of error, it effectively acknowledged that the people of Texas lack an interest in enforcing a capital sentence obtained on so flawed a basis. In concluding that the value of finality does not demand that we leave the District Court's judgment in place, we do no more than acknowledge what Texas itself recognized 17 years ago.

2

Our Rule 60(b)(6) analysis has thus far omitted one significant element. When Buck first sought federal habeas relief in 2004, Coleman barred the District Court from hearing his claim. Today, however, a claim of ineffective assistance of trial counsel defaulted in a Texas postconviction proceeding may be reviewed in federal court if state habeas counsel was constitutionally ineffective in failing to *780 raise it, and the claim has "some merit." *Martinez*, 566 U.S., at 14, 132 S.Ct. 1309; see *Trevino*, 569 U.S., at ----, 133 S.Ct., at 1920–1921. Buck cannot obtain relief unless he is entitled to the benefit of this rule—that is, unless *Martinez* and *Trevino*, not *Coleman*, would govern his case were it reopened. If they would not, his claim would remain unreviewable, and Rule 60(b)(6) relief would be inappropriate. See 11 Wright & Miller, Federal Practice and Procedure § 2857 (showing "a good claim or defense" is a precondition of Rule 60(b)(6) relief).

Until merits briefing in this Court, both parties litigated this matter on the assumption that Martinez and Trevino would apply if Buck reopened his case. See Pet. for Cert. 27–28; Brief in Opposition 11–13; Amended Application for Certificate of Appealability and Brief in Support 26, Respondent–Appellee's Opposition to Pet. for En Banc Rehearing 9–11, and Respondent's Opposition to Application for Certificate of Appealability 15–17 in No. 14–70030(CA5); Amended Response to Motion for Relief from Judgment in No. 4:04–cv–03965 (SD Tex.), pp. 11–13. But the State's brief adopts a new position on this issue. The State now argues that those cases announced a "new rule" that, under *Teague v. Lane,* 489 U.S. 288, 109 S.Ct. 1060, 103 L.Ed.2d

334 (1989) (plurality opinion), does not apply retroactively to cases (like Buck's) on collateral review. Brief for Respondent 38–40. Buck responds that Teague analysis applies only to new rules of criminal procedure that govern trial proceedings—not new rules of habeas procedure that govern collateral proceedings—and that the State has in any event waived its Teague argument. Reply Brief 20.

We agree that the argument has been waived. See *Danforth v. Minnesota*, 552 U.S. 264, 289, 128 S.Ct. 1029, 169 L.Ed.2d 859 (2008) ("States can waive a Teague defense ... by failing to raise it in a timely manner...."). It was not advanced in District Court, before the Fifth Circuit, or in the State's brief in opposition to Buck's petition for certiorari. Although we may reach the issue in our discretion, we have observed before that a State's failure to raise a Teague argument at the petition stage is particularly "significant" in deciding whether such an exercise of discretion is appropriate. *Schiro v. Farley*, 510 U.S. 222, 228–229, 114 S.Ct. 783, 127 L.Ed.2d 47 (1994). When "a legal issue appears to warrant review, we grant certiorari in the expectation of being able to decide that issue." Id., at 229, 114 S.Ct. 783. If we were to entertain the State's eleventh-hour *Teague* argument and find it persuasive, Buck's Strickland and Rule 60(b)(6) contentions—the issues we thought worthy of review—would be insulated from our consideration. We therefore decline to reach the Teague question and conclude that Martinez and Trevino apply to Buck's claim. We reach no broader determination concerning the application of these cases.

C

For the foregoing reasons, we conclude that Buck has demonstrated both ineffective assistance of counsel under Strickland and an entitlement to relief under Rule 60(b)(6). It follows that the Fifth Circuit erred in denying Buck the COA required to pursue these claims on appeal.

The judgment of the United States Court of Appeals for the Fifth Circuit is reversed, and the case is remanded for further proceedings consistent with this opinion.

It is so ordered.

OPINION

PER CURIAM:

Ezzard Ellis, a California inmate, appeals the district court's denial of his petition for writ of habeas corpus. He contends that he was denied his Sixth Amendment right to effective counsel because his trial attorney held deeply racist beliefs about African Americans in general and him in particular. Our precedent involving the same attorney and mostly the same evidence requires us to reject this contention. When defense counsel does not express his racist views to his client, no conflict will be presumed, and the defendant must show both deficient performance and prejudice to establish a Sixth Amendment violation. Since Ellis fails to do so here, we affirm the district court.

I.

Ellis and his co-defendant were charged with the November 1989 murder, attempted murder, and robbery of two men who were waiting in their car at a McDonald's drive-through window. Several witnesses who observed the crime to varying extents testified with corresponding certainty that Ellis looked like the shooter. Although the surviving victim repeatedly failed to identify Ellis in live and photographic lineups, a McDonald's employee who knew Ellis from school testified that he was the shooter.

Attorney Donald Ames, now deceased, was appointed to represent Ellis. Ellis's first two trials ended in mistrials due to witnesses being unavailable. His third and fourth trials resulted in hung juries. At the conclusion of his fifth trial in June 1991, Ellis was convicted of special circumstance murder, attempted murder, and two counts of robbery. He received a sentence of life without the possibility of parole. His conviction became final on May 29, 1996.

In March or April 2003, Ellis's friend sent him a newspaper article about Ames's "lousy" performance as a capital defense attorney. The article described Ames as "deceptive, untrustworthy, and disloyal to his capital clients" (quoting *Anderson v. Calderon*, 276 F.3d 483, 484 (9th Cir. 2001) (Reinhardt, J., dissenting from denial of rehearing en banc)). It recounted the testimony of Ames's adult daughters regarding his "frequent use of deprecating remarks and racial slurs about his clients."

Ellis obtained declarations from two of Ames's daughters in which they described their father's racism. According to one, Ames harbored "contempt for people of other races and ethnic groups" and "especially ridiculed black people, referring to them with racial invectives." The other daughter recalled a May 1990 conversation in which Ames referred to his client Melvin Wade as a "nigger" who "got what he deserved."

Ellis also obtained declarations from individuals who worked with Ames. A fiscal clerk at the San Bernardino Superior Court stated in a declaration that Ames employed "racist terms to characterize court personnel, his employees, and his clients." A legal secretary who worked for Ames from September 1990 to January 1991 heard Ames talking about a client: "because his client was black," Ames said, "he did not trust him and did not care what happened to him." A secretary in Ames's office from January to June 1991 stated that Ames "consistently refer[red] to his African American employees as 'niggers' " and "his African-American co-counsel as 'a big black nigger trying to be a white man.' " In the fifth trial, which took place during the first half of 1991, Ellis's co-defendant was represented by an African American attorney.

Ellis sought habeas relief in the state courts, arguing that he received constitutionally ineffective assistance of counsel because his counsel's "racial prejudice against African-Americans" created an actual conflict of interest. When that proved unsuccessful, Ellis filed a federal habeas petition pursuant to 28 U.S.C. § 2254. The district court initially denied relief on the ground that Ellis's petition was untimely. We reversed, holding that the petition could be timely if Ellis were entitled to equitable tolling. Ellis v. Harrison, 270 Fed. Appx. 721 (9th Cir. 2008). On remand, the district court determined that Ellis was not entitled to equitable tolling and again denied relief. We disagreed and once more remanded for further proceedings. Ellis v. Harrison, 563 Fed.Appx. 531 (9th Cir. 2014). Ellis now appeals the district court's denial of his Sixth Amendment claim on the merits.

II.

We have jurisdiction under 28 U.S.C. § § 1291 and 2253. Because Ellis's habeas petition is subject to the Antiterrorism and Effective Death Penalty Act of 1996 ("AEDPA"), we cannot grant relief unless he meets its "demanding standard." *Virginia v. LeBlanc,* --- U.S. ----, 137 S.Ct. 1726, 1727, 198 L.Ed.2d 186 (2017) (per curiam). As applicable here, Ellis must show that "the underlying state court merits ruling was 'contrary to, or involved an unreasonable application of, clearly established Federal law' as determined by [the Supreme] Court." Id. (quoting 28 U.S.C. § 2254(d)(1)). In making this determination, we look to the last reasoned state court decision, see *Wilson v. Sellers,* --- U.S. ----, 138 S.Ct. 1188, 1192, 200 L.Ed.2d 530 (2018), which is the state superior court's order denying Ellis's habeas petition.

Whether the Sixth Amendment's guarantee of effective counsel was satisfied is generally analyzed under the standard of *Strickland v. Washington,* 466 U.S. 668, 104 S.Ct. 2052, 80 L.Ed.2d 674 (1984). *Strickland* requires a showing of both deficient performance by counsel and consequent prejudice. Id. at 687, 104 S.Ct. 2052. In this context, "prejudice" means "a reasonable probability that, but for counsel's unprofessional errors, the result of the proceeding would have been different." Id. at 694, 104 S.Ct. 2052. A "reasonable probability" is less than a preponderance of the evidence. See id. at 693, 104 S.Ct. 2052 ("[A] defendant need not show that counsel's deficient conduct more likely than not altered the outcome in the case.").

Not every Sixth Amendment claim requires the same showing of prejudice. When the assistance of counsel is actually or constructively denied altogether, "prejudice is presumed." Id. at 692, 104 S.Ct. 2052 (citing *United States v. Cronic*, 466 U.S. 648, 659 & n.25, 104 S.Ct. 2039, 80 L.Ed.2d 657 (1984)). A similar but more limited presumption of prejudice arises "when counsel is burdened by an actual conflict of interest." Id. (citing *Cuyler v. Sullivan*, 446 U.S. 335, 345–50, 100 S.Ct. 1708, 64 L.Ed.2d 333 (1980)). Prejudice is presumed in such cases only if counsel "actively represented conflicting interests" and "an actual conflict of interest adversely affected [the] lawyer's performance." Id. (quoting Sullivan, 446 U.S. at 350, 348, 100 S.Ct. 1708).

The Supreme Court has not established the applicable standard of prejudice— *Strickland, Cronic,* or *Sullivan*—when counsel is alleged to have performed deficiently on account of racial animus towards a client. The superior court, evidently applying Strickland, concluded that Ellis was not prejudiced because "[h]e has not reasonably shown by competent evidence that, absent any or all of [Ames's] acts, the outcome of the trial would have been more favorable to him." However, the superior court required "proof of this prejudice" to be "by a preponderance of the evidence," a standard more stringent than and therefore "contrary to" *Strickland, Cronic,* and *Sullivan.* 28 U.S.C. § 2254(d)(1); see *Williams v. Taylor*, 529 U.S. 362, 405–06, 120 S.Ct. 1495, 146 L.Ed.2d 389 (2000) ("If a state court were to reject a prisoner's claim of ineffective assistance of counsel on the grounds that the prisoner had not established by a preponderance of the evidence that the result of his criminal proceeding would have been different, that decision would be [contrary] to our clearly established precedent [under] Strickland...."). Consequently, the state court decision is not entitled to AEDPA deference, and we review Ellis's claim de novo. See *Lafler v. Cooper*, 566 U.S. 156, 173, 132 S.Ct. 1376, 182 L.Ed.2d 398 (2012); *Frantz v. Hazey*, 533 F.3d 724, 735 (9th Cir. 2008) (en banc).

III.

Even under de novo review, any relief for Ellis must be based on a rule that was clearly established at the time his conviction was final. See *Teague v. Lane*, 489 U.S. 288, 310, 109 S.Ct. 1060, 103 L.Ed.2d 334 (1989) ("[N]ew constitutional rules of criminal procedure will not be applicable to those cases which have become final before the new rules are announced."). This differs from AEDPA review in that we may consider our own as well as Supreme Court precedent in determining which rules are clearly established. See *Williams*, 529 U.S. at 412, 120 S.Ct. 1495; *Burton v. Davis*, 816 F.3d 1132, 1142 (9th Cir. 2016).

Before Ellis's conviction was final, we decided a case concerning "an appointed lawyer who calls [the defendant] to his face a 'stupid nigger son of a bitch' and who threatens to provide substandard performance for him if he chooses to exercise his right to go to trial." *Frazer v. United States*, 18 F.3d 778, 783 (9th Cir. 1994). We held that these facts "would render so defective the relationship inherent in the right to trial counsel guaranteed by the Sixth Amendment that [the defendant] would be entitled to a new trial with a different attorney," id. at 784, and that the constitutional defect was "so egregious ... that 'a presumption of prejudice [would be] appropriate without inquiry into the actual conduct of the trial,' " id. at 785 (quoting *Cronic*, 466 U.S. at 660, 104 S.Ct. 2039).

Frazer's rule of prejudice per se relied in part on the outburst itself. The racial slur combined with the extortionate statement "completely destroy[ed] and negate[d] the channels of open communication needed for the [attorney-client] relationship to function as contemplated in the Constitution." Id. at 785. At the same time, *Frazer* also relied on the attorney's racial animus, regardless of the defendant's awareness of it. See id. at 782 ("[A]n attorney who adopts and acts upon a belief that his client should be convicted 'fail[s] to function in any meaningful sense as the Government's adversary.' " (quoting *Osborn v. Shillinger*, 861 F.2d 612, 625 (10th Cir. 1988))); id. at 784 ("Discrimination within the judicial system is most pernicious because it is 'a stimulant to that race prejudice which is an impediment to securing to [black citizens] that equal justice which the law aims to secure to all others.' " (quoting *Batson v. Kentucky*, 476 U.S. 79, 87–88, 106 S.Ct. 1712, 90 L.Ed.2d 69 (1986))).

Seven years later, however, we rejected a claim that "Ames' racism and his concern that he not be perceived by the San Bernardino bar or bench as requesting too much funding prevented [him] from effectively representing [the defendant]." *Mayfield v. Woodford*, 270 F.3d 915, 924 (9th Cir. 2001) (en banc). The habeas petitioner submitted the same declarations from Ames's daughters and colleagues upon which Ellis now relies. Analyzing the claim under *Sullivan*, we held that the petitioner "ha[d] not demonstrated that Ames performed poorly because of the alleged conflicts" and therefore was not entitled to relief. Id. at 925. To the extent *Frazer* held that defense counsel's extreme animus towards the persons of the defendant's race violates the Sixth Amendment without need to show prejudice, Mayfield implicitly overruled that holding.

IV.

In order to demonstrate that Ames's racist views prejudiced him, Ellis must show either that he knew of these views during a critical phase of the proceedings, leading to a complete breakdown in communication as in *Frazer*, or that Ames's racism otherwise adversely affected his performance as counsel. Ellis concedes that he was unaware of Ames's racism until several years after his conviction was final. And while the relationship between counsel's bigotry and his performance at Ellis's trial is much less attenuated than in *Mayfield*—here, the representation occurred contemporaneously with the statements at issue whereas Mayfield's trial was held approximately a decade earlier—Ellis fails to identify any acts or omissions by Ames that "fell below an objective standard of reasonableness." *Strickland*, 466 U.S. at 688, 104 S.Ct. 2052 (1984). We are therefore bound under *Mayfield* to reject his claim.

AFFIRMED.

NGUYEN, Circuit Judge, with whom HAWKINS and TASHIMA, Circuit Judges, join, concurring:

If we were writing on a blank slate, I would vote to grant relief. Of the constitutional rights given to a criminal defendant, none is more important than the Sixth Amendment right to counsel. By allowing Ellis's conviction to stand, we make a mockery of that right.

Ellis's lawyer, Donald Ames, openly and repeatedly expressed contempt for people who look like Ellis based on the ugliest of racial stereotypes. This was not just the depressingly common assumption that criminal defendants of certain races are more likely to be guilty, but something far more sinister: a belief in the inferiority of all people of color—be they support staff, co-counsel, or judge. Most damning of all, Ames made it clear that he did not care what happened to his black clients. It would be impossible for anyone with such views to adequately represent a non-white defendant.

I do not suggest that a conviction should be overturned whenever a racially tinged comment by defense counsel comes to light. Racism has as many shades as race, and we generally assume that counsel can set aside any personal distaste for a client, whatever its motivation, to zealously advocate on his behalf. But when an attorney expresses such utter contempt and indifference about the fate of his minority clients as Ames did here, he has ceased providing the reasonably competent representation that the Sixth Amendment demands. A defendant in such an untenable position may be better off with no counsel at all.

Lawyers today look very different than they did in 1991, when Ellis was tried. Within a generation, diversity among legal practitioners has markedly increased. On appeal in our court, of the three judges and two advocates at oral argument, four were people of color. These changes matter. Minority lawyers' greater representation on the bar has led to a growing acknowledgment and intolerance of racial bias in the practice of law. But it has not ended racism, both subtle and overt. People of color are still underrepresented in the legal profession but overrepresented among criminal defendants and face greater odds of conviction and higher average sentences. See, e.g., Robert J. Smith et al., Implicit White Favoritism in the Criminal Justice System, 66 Ala. L. Rev. 871, 877–90 (2015).

When examining the reasonableness of counsel's performance, we extend considerable deference to strategic choices. This deference is predicated on the assumption that counsel is acting in the client's best interest. For an attorney as deeply racist as Ames, that assumption is unfounded. It makes no difference that Ellis was unaware of his counsel's beliefs. The deleterious effect of such racism on the outcome is usually impossible to prove and, under these circumstances, we should presume prejudice.

Because I cannot in good faith distinguish Ellis's case from *Mayfield*, I reluctantly concur in the opinion. Had we not been bound by *Mayfield*, I would have granted Ellis's petition.

Note

Given the limitations expressed in *Morris v. Slappy*, 461 U.S. 1, 23, 103 S .Ct. 1610, 1622, 75 L.Ed.2d 610 (1983), regarding the inability of a defendant to insist upon appointed counsel with whom he or she had or can form a positive report, what are the options for the defendant? See, Kenneth Troccoli, *I Want a Black Lawyer to Represent Me: Addressing a Black Defendant's Concerns with Being Assigned a White Court-Appointed Lawyer*, 20 LAW & INEQ. 1 (2002). If the defendant asks for self-representation rather than proceed with a lawyer with whom there is not report, is that really a request for self-representation? Recall the case of Bobby Seale, the Chairman of the Black Panther Party during the trial of the Chicago Seven, which produced the iconic image of a Black man bound and gagged at his own trial.

UNITED STATES V. SEALE

461 F.2d 345 (7th Cir. 1972)

Opinion
CUMMINGS, Circuit Judge.

Defendant Seale and seven other persons were indicted for violating the Federal Anti-riot Statute and for conspiracy to violate it (18 U.S.C. §§ 2101 and 371). When Seale and his co-defendants were arraigned on April 9, 1969, Charles R. Garry of the California Bar informed the district judge that he would represent Seale and defendants Hoffman, Weiner, and Froines at the trial. September 24, 1969, was fixed as the trial date.

At pretrial proceedings on August 27, 1969, co-counsel William Kunstler advised the judge that the defendants would be represented "by a trial team," and that Mr. Garry was chief counsel and "essentially will be representing [Seale] assuming that he [Garry] gets back in time from [a] gall bladder operation." A continuance of the trial date, requested on the grounds of pretrial publicity and conflicting litigation schedules of counselors Kunstler and Garry, was denied.

On September 9, 1969, Garry requested a postponement of the trial date until November 15 because of the necessity of his undergoing a gall bladder operation at the conclusion of a California trial in which he was then engaged. This postponement was also denied. The court noted that Messrs. Michael Tigar, Irving Birnbaum, and Stanley Bass had also entered appearances for Seale, and therefore concluded that it was unnecessary to give Seale an opportunity to secure other counsel in place of Garry. In response to the complaint that these attorneys were engaged solely for special pretrial work or were only local counsel and were never intended to function as trial counsel, the trial judge stated there was no such thing as a limited appearance in a criminal case.

At the commencement of the trial proceedings, Mr. Kunstler filed a written appearance on behalf of Seale and three other defendants. He qualified his statement of representation to the court by saying that all defendants took the position they were not fully represented in Mr. Garry's absence and asked that each defendant be permitted to make a statement to that effect. The court disallowed the request. Co-counsel, Mr. Weinglass, informed the court that Seale was in fact without counsel but, relying on the appearances filed in Seale's behalf, the court stated that was not a fact and refused to hear argument on that point. When Seale was introduced to the group of prospective jurors, the court informed them that Seale was represented by Messrs. Garry, Tigar, Birnbaum, and Bass. Asked if there was additional counsel for Seale, Mr. Kunstler stated he had filed an appearance, and the court included Mr. Kunstler in the list of Seale's counsel.

On September 26, after the jury had been impanelled but prior to hearing the evidence, the court denied Seale's motion requesting a continuance until Garry could be present to represent him and requesting dismissal of his attorneys of record in the event no continuance was allowed. On the same day, after the opening statements of defense counsel, Seale unsuccessfully attempted to make his own opening statement, and Kunstler refused to make an opening statement on Seale's behalf on the ground that Kunstler was not Seale's attorney. The court announced:

> "If any defendant here has any rights which he perceives to have been violated by going ahead with this trial with lawyers that have appearances on file, without the attendance of Mr. Garry, their rights are there."

Thereafter the trial judge relied completely on Kunstler's written appearance as counsel for Seale as being dispositive of Seale's claim he was not represented and of Kunstler's protestations that he did not in fact represent Seale. On this basis the court refused to permit Seale to represent himself. Accordingly, Seale's October 20 pro se motion to represent himself was denied, as was Kunstler's October 22 motion to withdraw as counsel for Seale.

On subsequent occasions Seale vehemently complained that his Sixth Amendment right to counsel of his choice and his right to represent himself were being denied. Several times Seale attempted to represent himself. He was bound and gagged on the afternoon of October 29 in an effort to maintain courtroom decorum. This was a measure deemed permissible in *Illinois v. Allen*, 397 U.S. 337, 90 S.Ct. 1057, 25 L.Ed.2d 353. However, his restraints were removed on November 3.

On November 5, after six weeks of trial, the court *sua sponte* declared a mistrial as to Seale, and his trial was severed from that of his co-defendants. Acting under Rule 42(a) of the Federal Rules of Criminal Procedure, the court simultaneously adjudged Seale guilty of sixteen acts of contempt, resulting in a sentence of three-month terms apiece, or a total of four years' imprisonment. Seale claims that nearly all sixteen acts arose out of his objections to Garry's absence and his attempts to represent himself at the trial.

In the certificate of contempt, the trial judge found that each of the 16 specified acts of contempt

> "constituted a deliberate and wilful attack upon the administration of justice in an attempt to sabotage the functioning of the Federal judicial system; that the misconduct was of so grave a character as to continually disrupt the orderly administration of justice."

....

Necessity to Inquire of Seale Why He Objected to Counsel

During argument on the August 27, 1969, motion for a continuance, defense counsel Weinglass advised the district judge that Seale was represented only by Mr. Garry. Responding to the prosecutor's argument that Messrs. Tigar, Birnbaum, and Bass were also counsel for Seale, Weinglass stated that Birnbaum and Bass were merely local counsel and were never intended as trial counsel, and Tigar was only engaged as a specialist to argue defense motions on wiretapping. Mr. Birnbaum, speaking for himself and Mr. Bass, corroborated Weinglass' assertion that they were acting only as local counsel in accordance with the court rule requiring local counsel.20 The trial court simply stated it was of "the opinion that either Mr. Bass or Mr. Birnbaum could represent any one of their clients and do a good professional job" and so found. No inquiry was addressed to the desires of Seale, who was then incarcerated in California; the court relied exclusively on the appearances filed by Bass and Birnbaum in Seale's behalf.

At the September 9, 1969, hearing on the renewed motion for a continuance based on Garry's impending operation, the trial court found that although normally the inability of retained counsel to serve would entail allowing his client to secure other counsel, that was unnecessary since other counsel were of record. Again the court noted that attorneys Birnbaum, Bass and Tigar had entered appearances for Seale. The court dismissed Garry's assertion that these attorneys had been engaged exclusively for pretrial work with the statement that they had entered general appearances, for there was no such thing as a limited appearance in a criminal case. Again the court did not advert to Seale's desires. Garry then told the court that Seale would be without counsel at the time he was brought to Chicago for trial from his San Francisco incarceration.

On September 24, when the trial commenced, Mr. Kunstler entered an appearance for Seale and defendants Hoffman, Froines, and Weiner. At the same time, Kunstler told the court that all defendants took the position that they were not fully represented because of Garry's absence. He asked that all defendants be allowed to speak to that point, but the court refused. Weinglass then stated that Seale did not have counsel but the court silenced him with the response, "That is not a fact, as it appears from the record." Thereafter the court told the jury that Seale was represented by Messrs. Kunstler, Garry, Tigar, Birnbaum, and Bass. Two days later, after the jury was impanelled but prior to the opening statements, Seale presented pro se his hand-written motion requesting postponement until Garry could be present to represent him. The motion, which was denied, also dismissed all counsel of record except Garry. Later that morning, Seale attempted pro se to make an opening statement and reiterated that his lawyer was Garry. Upon being interrogated by the court, Mr. Kunstler replied that he did not represent Seale, but the court concluded otherwise because Kunstler had filed an appearance in Seale's behalf, although Kunstler explained that his appearance for Seale had been limited to giving him access from jail to the outside world.

Thereafter the trial judge consistently adhered to his view that Kunstler's appearance was conclusive on the question of his representation of Seale. When on October 20 Seale presented a formal motion to proceed pro se, the trial court denied it on the grounds that Seale's self-representation would produce a "disruptive effect," would be inappropriate in view of the complexity of the case, and would be more prejudicial to his defense than a denial of the motion. To this position the trial judge likewise consistently adhered.

We note the trial judge's earlier reliance on the appearances of attorneys Tigar, Birnbaum, and Bass in view of his felt need to begin the trial on schedule and the difficulty of immediately confronting the absent Seale. Moreover, we sympathize with his later dependence on Kunstler's appearance in view of Kunstler's previous statement that the defendants had agreed to be represented by a trial team consisting of himself and attorneys Garry and Weinglass and in view of the progressing time. However, nothing in the appearance rule negates a limited appearance. (See note 1, supra.) Even if limited appearances were precluded, the trial judge would be justified in relying on the appearance rule only to control the relationship between the court and counsel or between counsel and clients desirous of their representation. He would not be justified in using any such rule to determine summarily the attorney-client relationship at least where, as here, there was protestation that the appearances did not in fact reflect the true consensual relationship between the defendant and the attorneys of record for him. Certainly Seale could not be bound by the appearances of counsel engaged only for pretrial work when, perhaps, their specialized employ was only the delegation of chosen trial counsel. Neither could Seale be bound by Kunstler's action in filing an unauthorized appearance. In sum, the right to counsel of choice could not be denied by exclusive recourse to appearances on record where Seale did not actually agree to the trial reresentation of the appearing attorneys or where he was not shown to be engaging in unwarranted dilatory tactics.

The Government argues that the grant of a continuance is a matter left solely to the sound discretion of the trial judge. The denial of a continuance below is said to have been proper, inter alia, in view of the fact that Seale had other counsel of record. The point is, however, that the trial judge was confronted from the very beginning with objections that these attorneys of record were not in fact counsel chosen by the defendant to represent him at trial.

The Government has cited no authority to show that a trial judge may eschew inquiry into the objections of a defendant who unexpectedly finds himself without chosen trial counsel. If the Sixth Amendment right to the effective assistance of counsel means anything, it certainly means that it is the actual choice of the defendant which deserves consideration. This is not to say that Seale was unequivocally entitled to a continuance until Garry could be present. But if an inquiry disclosed that this defendant had never consented to be represented at trial by the other record attorneys in Garry's absence, was unwilling to proceed with any counsel except Garry and was sincere in his position, other alternatives were available to the trial court. The grant of severance and a reasonable continuance to secure substitute counsel or leave to Seale to represent himself would have permitted the trial to continue promptly and may well have obviated many of the difficulties that later occurred.

The Govenment argues that the trial court was not obligated to inquire of Seale whether he desired to represent himself until he unequivocally asked to proceed pro se and points to the fact that Seale did not formally file a motion to act in his own defense until October 20, the seventeenth day of trial. By that time, the Government contends the trial was well under way, and accordingly Seale's right to proceed pro se was strictly limited, exercisable only in the trial court's sound discretion.

We agree with then Circuit Judge Burger, concurring in *Brown v. United States*, 105 U.S.App.D.C. 77, 264 F.2d 363, 368 (D.C.Cir.) (en banc), certiorari denied, 360 U.S. 911, 79 S.Ct. 1299, 3 L.Ed.2d 1262 (1958), that "[t]he issue here is not whether an accused has a right to try his own case in proper person; nor is the issue whether an accused must in all circumstances be informed explicitly by the court that he had a right to proceed as his own counsel. The heart of the matter is the scope of discretion of the trial court when an objection to counsel is made known." Here the trial court was put on notice when hearing the continuance motions on August 27 and September 9, and when conducting the pretrial procedings on September 24, that Seale was dissatisfied with any counsel except Garry. Moreover, on September 26, at the earliest opportunity after the impanelling of the jury,26 Seale's pro se motion advised the court that he had relieved all other counsel of record for him in Garry's absence. Soon thereafter he attempted pro se to make an opening statement to the jury, thus reiterating his non-acceptance of these attorneys of record. Since Seale had amply indicated dissatisfaction with counsel, the trial court was under a duty to inquire into the subject. As then Circuit Judge Burger explained in his concurring opinion in Brown v. United States, supra at 369, the entire court there agreed on the following proposition which he espoused:

> "[W]hen, for the first time, an accused makes known to the court in some way that he has a complaint about his counsel, the court must rule on the matter. If the reasons are made known to the court, the court may rule without more. If no reasons are stated, the court then has a duty to inquire into the basis for the client's objection to counsel and should withhold a ruling until reasons are made known."

See *United States v. Mitchell*, 138 F.2d 831 (2d Cir. 1943), certiorari denied, 321 U.S. 794, 64 S.Ct. 785, 88 L.Ed. 1083 (1944); *United States v. Birrell*, 286 F. Supp. 885 (S.D.N.Y.1968). We are in accord. Since the trial judge was bound to look into the basis of Seale's dissatisfaction with his lawyers of record apart from the hospitalized Mr. Garry, failure to do so was an abuse of discretion.

It is immaterial whether Seale had a right to a continuance until Mr. Garry could represent him or had a right to appear pro se. What is crucial is that in the circumstances of this case, the trial judge had a duty to inquire of Seale as early as August 27 and no later than September 26 as to his objections to counsel of record and to take appropriate action to make sure that his Sixth Amendment right to the assistance of counsel and his right to represent himself were appropriately honored.

As shown in a November 4 colloquy between the trial court and Seale, if there had been an inquiry of Seale about the authorization of Kunstler's appearance, Seale apparently would have told the court that he never had a pretrial conference with Kunstler (but see note 2 supra), that Garry was the only lawyer to whom he talked regarding his case, that he was never asked regarding Kunstler's filing of an appearance, and that Kunstler had appeared on his own accord without any request by or consultation with Seale. Judging from Seale's September 26 motion and his attempt to make an opening statement in his own behalf as well as from his subsequent demands for and attempts at self-representation, it is only realistic to assume that during the requisite inquiry Seale would have expressly voiced his desire to proceed pro se in the event a continuance was disallowed. We note only that if the above facts regarding Kunstler's attorney-ship were found true and Seale was found to be free of ulterior motivation, it would have been error for the trial court to force Kunstler's services upon Seale over his insistence on defending himself.

The Government relies on this Court's opinion in *United States v. Cozzi*, 354 F.2d 637 (1965), certiorari denied, 383 U.S. 911, 86 S.Ct. 896, 15 L.Ed.2d 666. When that cause was called for trial, John Cogan, attorney for Cozzi, explained that because of a prosecution subpoena served on Anthony Butera, Jr., whom he had also represented, there appeared to be a conflict of interest. However, the prosecutor assured the court Butera would not be called as a witness, so that the court quite properly refused to allow Cogan to withdraw as Cozzi's counsel. There the defendant was not complaining that any counsel was being imposed upon him instead of counsel of choice. As we said,

> "Cozzi does not question the competency of Cogan, counsel of his own selection, nor the quality of Cogan's representation. There is no suggestion that Cogan's original undertaking to represent both Cozzi and Butera [who had previously been convicted upon a guilty plea] involved any conflict of interest-or possible prejudice to either defendant." 354 F.2d at 639.

Cozzi was a case where a single reason-conflict of interest-was inquired into, assessed and correctly found insufficient to warrant substitution of counsel. Since *Cozzi's* position was simply an adoption of Cogan's conflict of interest objection, we of course held that the trial court did not err in declining personally to interrogate the defendant concerning Cogan's request for substitution. Cozzi is not inconsistent with our present holding that in this case it was error not to interrogate Seale about his objection to counsel other than Garry.

....

Note

No area of race and criminal procedure has received more recent attention than jury selection. This is due in large part to the attention paid to the Supreme Court's decision in *Batson v. Kentucky* 476 U.S. 79 (1986). The right to a jury free of racial bias and exclusion, like public trial, is fundamental and represents interests beyond just that of the accused. See *Johnson v. Virginia*, 373 U.S. 61 (1963). *Norris v. Alabama*, 294 U.S. 587 (1935) and *Patterson v. Alabama*, 294 U.S. 600 (1935), both cases arising from the infamous case of the Scottsboro defendants, declared that the Equal Protection Clause and Due Process Clause of the Fourteenth Amendment to the United States Constitution forbade the deliberate exclusion of African Americans from the jury pool. Subsequent to the incorporation of the Sixth Amendment protections, the Court in the *Taylor* case below has extended the Sixth Amendment protection to include defendant's protected right to a jury venire that represents a "fair cross section" of the relevant community.

Race and the Fair Cross-Section Requirement

TAYLOR V. LOUISIANA
419 U.S. 522 (1974)

Mr. Justice WHITE delivered the opinion of the Court.

When this cases was tried, Art. VII, s 41,1 of the Louisiana Constitution, and Art. 402 of the Louisiana Code of Criminal Procedure provided that a woman should not be selected for jury service unless she had previously filed a written declaration of her desire to be subject to jury service. The constitutionality of these provisions is the issue in this case.

I

Appellant, Billy J. Taylor, was indicted by the grand jury of St. Tammany Parish, in the Twenty-second Judicial District of Louisiana, for aggravated kidnaping. On April 12, 1972, appellant moved the trial court to quash the petit jury venire drawn for the special criminal term beginning with his trial the following day. Appellant alleged that women were systematically excluded from the venire and that he would therefore be deprived of what he claimed to be his federal constitutional right to 'a fair trial by jury of a representative segment of the community . . . .'

The Twenty-second Judicial District comprises the parishes of St. Tammany and Washington. The appellee has stipulated that 53% of the persons eligible for jury service in these parishes were female, and that no more than 10% of the persons on the jury wheel in St. Tammany Parish were women. During the period from December 8, 1971, to November 3, 1972, 12 females were among the 1,800 persons drawn to fill petit jury venires in St. Tammany Parish. It was also stipulated that the discrepancy between females eligible for jury service and those actually included in the venire was the result of the operation of La.Const., Art. VII, s 41, and La.Code Crim.Proc., Art. 402. In the present case, a venire totaling 175 persons was drawn for jury service beginning April 13, 1972. There were no females on the venire.

Appellant's motion to quash the venire was denied that same day. After being tried, convicted, and sentenced to death, appellant sought review in the Supreme Court of Louisiana, where he renewed his claim that the petit jury venire should have been quashed. The Supreme Court of Louisiana, recognizing that this claim drew into question the constitutionality of the provisions of the Louisiana Constitution and Code of Criminal Procedure dealing with the service of women on juries, squarely held, one justice dissenting, that these provisions were valid and not unconstitutional under federal law. 282 So.2d 491, 497 (1973).

Appellant appealed from that decision to this Court. We noted probable jurisdiction, to consider whether the Louisiana jury-selection system deprived appellant of his Sixth and Fourteenth Amendment right to an impartial jury trial. We hold that it did and that these Amendments were violated in this case by the operation of La.Const., Art. VII, s 41, and La.Code Crim.Proc., Art. 402. In consequence, appellant's conviction must be reversed.

II

The Louisiana jury-selection system does not disqualify women from jury service, but in operation its conceded systematic impact is that only a very few women, grossly disproportionate to the number of eligible women in the community, are called for jury service. In this case, no women were on the venire from which the petit jury was drawn. The issue we have, therefore, is whether a jury-selection system which operates to exclude from jury service an identifiable class of citizens constituting 53% of eligible jurors n the community comports with the Sixth and Fourteenth Amendments.

The State first insists that Taylor, a male, has no standing to object to the exclusion of women from his jury. But Taylor's claim is that he was constitutionally entitled to a jury drawn from a venire constituting a fair cross section of the community and that the jury that tried him was not such a jury by reason of the exclusion of women. Taylor was not a member of the excluded class; but there is no rule that claims such as Taylor presents may be made only by those defendants who are members of the group excluded from jury service. In *Peters v. Kiff*, 407 U.S. 493, 92 S.Ct. 2163, 33 L.Ed.2d 83 (1972), the defendant, a white man, challenged his conviction on the ground that Negroes had been systematically excluded from jury service. Six Members of the Court agreed that petitioner was entitled to present the issue and concluded that he had been deprived of his federal rights. Taylor, in the case before us, was similarly entitled to tender and have adjudicated the claim that the exclusion of women from jury service deprived him of the kind of factfinder to which he was constitutionally entitled.

III

The background against which this case must be decided includes our holding in *Duncan v. Louisiana*, 391 U.S. 145, 88 S.Ct. 1444, 20 L.Ed.2d 491 (1968), that the Sixth Amendment's provision for jury trial is made binding on the States by virtue of the Fourteenth Amendment. Our inquiry is whether the presence of a fair cross section of the community on venires, panels, of lists from which petit juries are drawn is essential to the fulfillment of the Sixth Amendment's guarantee of an impartial jury trial in criminal prosecutions.

The Court's prior cases are instructive. Both in the course of exercising its supervisory powers over trials in federal courts and in the constitutional context, the Court has unambiguously declared that the American concept of the jury trial contemplates a jury drawn from a fair cross section of the community. A unanimous Court stated in Smith *v. Texas*, 311 U.S. 128, 130, 61 S.Ct. 164, 165, 85 L.Ed. 84 (1940), that '(i)t is part of the established tradition in the use of juries as instruments of public justice that the jury be a body truly representative of the community.' To exclude racial groups from jury service was said to be 'at war with our basic concepts of a democratic society and a representative government.' A state jury system that resulted in systematic exclusion of Negroes as jurors was therefore held to violate the Equal Protection Clause of the Fourteenth Amendment. *Glasser v. United States*, 315 U.S. 60, 85–86, 62 S.Ct. 457, 472, 86 L.Ed. 680 (1942), in the context of a federal criminal case and the Sixth Amendment's jury trial requirement, stated that '(o)ur notions of what a proper jury is have developed in harmony with our basic concepts of a democratic system and representative government,' and repeated the

Court's understanding that the jury "be a body truly representative of the community' . . . and not the organ of any special group or class.'

A federal conviction by a jury from which women had been excluded, although eligible for service under state law, was reviewed in *Ballard v. United States*, 329 U.S. 187, 67 S.Ct. 261, 91 L.Ed. 181 (1946). Noting the federal statutory 'design to make the jury 'a cross-section of the community" and the fact that women had been excluded, the Court exercised its supervisory powers over the federal courts and reversed the conviction. In *Brown v. Allen*, 344 U.S. 443, 474, 73 S.Ct. 397, 416, 97 L.Ed. 469 (1953), the Court declared that '(o)ur duty to protect the federal constitutional rights of all does not mean we must or should impose on states our conception of the proper source of jury lists, so long as the source reasonably reflects a cross-section of the population suitable in character and intelligence for that civic duty.'

Some years later in *Carter v. Jury Comm'n*, 396 U.S. 320, 330, 90 S.Ct. 518, 524, 24 L.Ed.2d 549 (1970), the Court observed that the exclusion of Negroes from jury service because of their race 'contravenes the very idea of a jury—' a body truly representative of the community' . . ..' (Quoting from Smith v. Texas, supra.) At about the same time it was contended that the use of six-man juries in noncapital criminal cases violated the Sixth Amendment for failure to provide juries drawn from a cross section of the community, *Williams v. Florida*, 399 U.S. 78, 90 S.Ct. 1893, 26 L.Ed.2d 446 (1970). In the course of rejecting that challenge, we said that the number of persons on the jury should 'be large enough to promote group deliberation, free from outside attempts at intimidation, and to provide a fair possibility for obtaining a representative cross-section of the community.' Id., at 100, 90 S.Ct. at 1906. In like vein, in *Apodaca v. Oregon*, 406 U.S. 404, 410–411, 92 S.Ct. 1628, 1633, 32 L.Ed.2d 184 (1972) (plurality opinion), it was said that 'a jury will come to such a (commonsense) judgment as long as it consists of a group of laymen representative of a cross section of the community who have the duty and the opportunity to deliberate . . . on the question of a defendant's guilt.' Similarly, three Justices in *Peters v. Kiff*, 407 U.S., at 500, 92 S.Ct., at 2167, observed that the Sixth Amendment comprehended a fair possibility for obtaining a jury constituting a representative cross section of the community.

The unmistakable import of this Court's opinions, at least since 1940, Smith v. Texas, supra, and not repudiated by intervening decisions, is that the selection of a petit jury from a representative cross section of the community is an essential component of the Sixth Amendment right to a jury trial. Recent federal legislation governing jury selection within the federal court system has a similar thrust. Shortly prior to this Court's decision in Duncan v. Louisiana, supra, the Federal Jury Selection and Service Act of 19686 was enacted. In that Act, Congress stated 'the policy of the United States that all litigants in Federal courts entitled to trial by jury shall have the right to grand and petit juries selected at random from a fair cross section of the community in the district or division wherein the court convenes.' 28 U.S.C. s 1861. In that Act, Congress also established the machinery by which the stated policy was to be implemented. 28 U.S.C. ss 1862—1866. In passing this legislation, the Committee Reports of both the House and the Senate recognized that the jury plays a political function in the administration of the law and that the requirement of a jury's being chosen from a fair cross section of the community is fundamental to the American system of justice. Debate on the floors of the House and Senate on the Act invoked the Sixth Amendment, the Constitution generally, and prior decisions of this Court in support of the Act.

We accept the fair-cross-section requirement as fundamental to the jury trial guaranteed by the Sixth Amendment and are convinced that the requirement has solid foundation. The purpose of a jury is to guard against the exercise of arbitrary power—to make available the commonsense judgment of the community as a hedge against the overzealous or mistaken prosecutor and in preference to the professional or perhaps overconditioned or biased response of a judge. *Duncan v. Louisiana*, 391 U.S., at 155–156, 88 S.Ct., at 1450–1451. This prophylactic vehicle is not provided if the jury pool is made up of only special segments of the populace or if large, distinctive groups are excluded from the pool. Community participation in the administration of the criminal law, moreover, is not only consistent with our democratic heritage but is also critical to public confidence in the fairness of the criminal justice system. Restricting jury service to only special groups or excluding identifiable segments playing major roles in the community cannot be squared with the constitutional concept of jury trial. 'Trial by jury presupposes a jury drawn from a pool broadly representative of the community as well as impartial in a specific case. . . . (T)he broad representative character of the jury should be maintained, partly as assurance of a diffused impartiality and partly because sharing in the administration of justice is a phase of civic responsibility.' Thiel v. Southern Pacific Co., 328 U.S. 217, 227, 66 S.Ct. 984, 90 L.Ed. 1181 (1946) (Frankfurter, J., dissenting).

IV

We are also persuaded that the fair-cross-section requirement is violated by the systematic exclusion of women, who in the judicial district involved here amounted to 53% of the citizens eligible for jury service. This conclusion necessarily entails the judgment that women are sufficiently numerous and distinct from men and that if they are systematically eliminated from jury panels, the Sixth Amendment's fair-cross-section requirement cannot be satisfied. This very matter was debated in Ballard v. United States, supra. Positing the fair-cross-section rule— there said to be a statutory one—the Court concluded that the systematic exclusion of women was unacceptable. The dissenting view that an all-male panel drawn from various groups in the community would be as truly representative as if women were included, was firmly rejected:

'The thought is that the factors which tend to influence the action of women are the same as those which influence the action of men—personality, background, economic status—and not sex. Yet it is not enough to say that women when sitting as jurors neither act nor tend to act as a class. Men likewise do not act as a class. But, if the shoe were on the other foot, who would claim that a jury was truly representative of the community if all men were intentionally and systematically excluded from the panel? The truth is that the two sexes are not fungible; a community made up exclusively of one is different from a community composed of both; the subtle interplay of influence one on the other is among the imponderables. To insulate the courtroom from either may not in a given case make an iota of difference. Yet a flavor, a distinct quality is lost if either sex is excluded. The exclusion of one may indeed make the jury less representative of the community than would be true if an economic or racial group were excluded.' 329 U.S., at 193–194, 67 S.Ct., at 264.12

In this respect, we agree with the Court in Ballard: If the fair-cross-section rule is to govern the selection of juries, as we have concluded it must, women cannot be systemactically excluded from jury panels from which petit juries are drawn. This conclusion is consistent with the current judgment of the country, now evidenced by legislative or constitutional provisions in every State and at the federal level qualifying women for jury service.

V

There remains the argument that women as a class serve a distinctive role in society and that jury service would so substantially interfere with that function that the State has ample justification for excluding women from service unless they volunteer, even though the result is that almost all jurors are men. It is true that *Hoyt v. Florida*, 368 U.S. 57, 82 S.Ct. 159, 7 L.Ed.2d 118 (1961), held that such a system14 did not deny due process of law or equal protection of the laws because there was a sufficiently rational basis for such an exemption. But Hoyt did not involve a defendant's Sixth Amendment right to a jury drawn from a fair cross section of the community and the prospect of depriving him of that right if women as a class are systematically excluded. The right to a proper jury cannot be overcome on merely rational grounds. There must be weightier reasons if a distinctive class representing 53% of the eligible jurors is for all practical purposes to be excluded from jury service. No such basis has been tendered here.

The States are free to grant exemptions from jury service to individuals in case of special hardship or incapacity and to those engaged in particular occupations the uninterrupted performance of which is critical to the community's welfare. *Rawlins v. Georgia*, 201 U.S. 638, 26 S.Ct. 560, 50 L.Ed. 899 (1906). It would not appear that such exemptions would pose substantial threats that the remaining pool of jurors would not be representative of the community. A system excluding all women, however, is a wholly different matter. It is untenable to suggest these days that it would be a special hardship for each and every woman to perform jury service or that society cannot spare any women from their present duties. This may be the case with many, and it may be burdensome to sort out those who should be exempted from those who should serve. But that task is performed in the case of men, and the administrative convenience in dealing with women as a class is insufficient justification for diluting the quality of community judgment represented by the jury in criminal trials.

VI

Although this judgment may appear a foregone conclusion from the pattern of some of the Court's cases over the past 30 years, as well as from legislative developments at both federal and state levels, it is nevertheless true that until today no case had squarely held that the exclusion of women from jury venires deprives a criminal defendant of his Sixth Amendment right to trial by an impartial jury drawn from a fair cross section of the community. It is apparent that the first Congress did not perceive the Sixth Amendment as requiring women on criminal jury panels; for the direction of the First Judiciary Act of 1789 was that federal jurors were to have the qualifications required by the States in which the federal court was sitting and at the time women were disqualified under state law in every State. Necessarily, then, federal juries in criminal cases were all male, and it was not until the Civil Rights Act of 1957, 71 Stat. 638, 28 U.S.C. s 1861 (1964 ed.), that Congress itself provided that all citizens, with limited exceptions, were competent to sit on federal juries. Until that time, federal courts were required by statute to exclude women from jury duty in those States where women were disqualified. Utah was the first State to qualify women for juries; it did so in 1898, n. 13, supra. Moreover, *Hoyt v. Florida* was decided and has stood for the proposition that, even if women as a group could not be constitutionally disqualified from jury service, there was ample reason to treat all women differently from men for the purpose of jury service and to exclude them unless they volunteered.

Accepting as we do, however, the view that the Sixth Amendment affords the defendant in a criminal trial the opportunity to have the jury drawn from venires representative of the community, we think it is no longer tenable to hold that women as a class may be excluded to given automatic exemptions based solely on sex if the consequence is that criminal jury venires are almost totally male. To this extent we cannot follow the contrary implications of the prior cases, including *Hoyt v. Florida*. If it was ever the case that women were unqualified to sit on juries or were so situated that none of them should be required to perform jury service, that time has long since passed. If at one time it could be held that Sixth Amendment juries must be drawn from a fair cross section of the community but that this requirement permitted the almost total exclusion of women, this is not the case today. Communities differ at different times and places. What is a fair cross section at one time or place is not necessarily a fair cross section at another time or a different place. Nothing persuasive has been presented to us in this case suggesting that all-male venires in the parishes involved here are fairly representative of the local population otherwise eligible for jury service.

VII

Our holding does not augur or authorize the fashioning of detailed jury selection codes by federal courts. The fair-cross-section principle must have much leeway in application. The States remain free to prescribe relevant qualifications for their jurors and to provide reasonable exemptions so long as it may be fairly said that the jury lists or panels are representative of the community. Carter v. Jury Comm'n, supra, as did Brown v. Allen, supra; Rawlins v. Georgia, supra, and other cases, recognized broad discretion in the States in this respect. We do not depart from the principles enunciated in Carter. But, as we have said, Louisiana's special exemption for women operates to exclude them from petit juries, which in our view is contrary to the command of the Sixth and Fourteenth Amendments.

It should also be emphasized that in holding that petit juries must be drawn from a source fairly representative of the community we impose no requirement that petit juries actually chosen must mirror the community and reflect the various distinctive groups in the population. Defendants are not entitled to a jury of any particular composition, *Fay v. New York*, 332 U.S. 261, 284, 67 S.Ct. 1613, 1625, 91 L.Ed. 2043 (1947); Apodaca v. Oregon, 406 U.S., at 413, 92 S.Ct., at 1634 (plurality opinion); but the jury wheels, pools of names, panels, or venires from which juries are drawn must not systematically exclude distinctive groups in the community and thereby fail to be reasonably representative thereof.

The judgment of the Louisiana Supreme Court is reversed and the case remanded to that court for further proceedings not inconsistent with this opinion.

So ordered.

Reversed and remanded.

Note

It is worth noting that *Taylor* was not a case of alleged racial discrimination but rather a question of gender discrimination. It is equally significant, however, that the defendant, for Sixth Amendment purposes, need not be a member of the class discriminated against. (Taylor was male). The discussion in *Taylor* makes it clear, however, that the concept of "fair cross-section" includes race and ethnicity.

In *Duren v. Missouri* 439 U.S. 357 (1979), a case in which Missouri allowed women to voluntarily excuse themselves from jury service, the Court reiterated that a defendant, in order to successfully assert a claim that the venire from which the jury was selected, did not represent a "fair cross-section", must establish a prima facie case that satisfies a three-prong test; 1) the group alleged to be excluded is a distinctive group in the community, 2) the representation of this group in the venire is not fair and reasonable in relation to the numbers of such persons in the community, and 3) the underrepresentation is due to systematic exclusion of the group in the jury-selection process. The defendant may use statistical data to establish a prima facie case. *Duren* makes clear that once the defendant establishes a prima facie case the burden shifts to the state to demonstrate that a significant state interest exists to justify infringing upon the right to a fair cross section.

BERGHUIS V. SMITH.
559 U.S. 314 (2010)

Justice GINSBURG delivered the opinion of the Court.

The Sixth Amendment secures to criminal defendants the right to be tried by an impartial jury drawn from sources reflecting a fair cross section of the community. See *Taylor v. Louisiana*, 419 U.S. 522, 95 S.Ct. 692, 42 L.Ed.2d 690 (1975). The question presented in this case is whether that right was accorded to respondent Diapolis Smith, an African–American convicted of second-degree murder by an all-white jury in Kent County, Michigan in 1993. At the time of Smith's trial, African–Americans constituted 7.28% of Kent County's jury-eligible population, and 6% of the pool from which potential jurors were drawn.

In *Duren v. Missouri*, 439 U.S. 357, 99 S.Ct. 664, 58 L.Ed.2d 579 (1979), this Court described three showings a criminal defendant must make to establish a prima facie violation of the Sixth Amendment's fair-cross-section requirement. He or she must show: "(1) that the group alleged to be excluded is a 'distinctive' group in the community; (2) that the representation of this group in venires from which juries are selected is not fair and reasonable in relation to the number of such persons in the community; and (3) that this underrepresentation is due to systematic exclusion of the group in the jury-selection process." Id., at 364, 99 S.Ct. 664. The first showing is, in most cases, easily made; the second and third are more likely to generate controversy.

The defendant in Duren readily met all three measures. He complained of the dearth of women in the Jackson County, Missouri, jury pool. To establish underrepresentation, he proved that women were 54% of the jury-eligible population, but accounted for only 26.7% of the persons summoned for jury service, and only 14.5% of the persons on the postsummons weekly venires from which jurors were drawn. To show the "systematic" cause of the underrepresentation, Duren pointed to Missouri's law exempting women from jury service, and to the manner in which Jackson County administered the exemption. Concluding that no significant state interest could justify Missouri's explicitly gender-based exemption, this Court held the law, as implemented in Jackson County, violative of the Sixth Amendment's fair-cross-section requirement.

We here review the decision of the United States Court of Appeals for the Sixth Circuit holding that Smith "satisf[ied] the prima facie test established by *Duren*," and granting him habeas corpus relief, i.e., release from imprisonment absent a new trial commenced within 180 days of the Court of Appeals' order. 543 F.3d 326, 336 (2008). Despite marked differences between Smith's case and Duren's, and a cogent Michigan Supreme Court decision holding that Smith "ha[d] not shown ... systematic exclusion," *People v. Smith*, 463 Mich. 199, 205, 615 N.W.2d 1, 3 (2000), the Sixth Circuit found the matter settled. Cognizant of the restrictions Congress placed on federal habeas review of state-court convictions, the Court of Appeals considered that a decision contrary to its own would "involv[e] an unreasonable application o [f] clearly established Federal law, as determined by the Supreme Court of the United States," 28 U.S.C. § 2254(d)(1). 543 F.3d, at 335.

The Sixth Circuit erred in so ruling. No decision of this Court "clearly establishe[s]" Smith's entitlement to federal-court relief. According to the Sixth Circuit, Smith had demonstrated that a Kent County prospective-juror-assignment procedure, which Smith calls "siphoning," "systematic[ally] exclu[ded]" African–Americans. Under this procedure, Kent County assigned prospective jurors first to local district courts, and, only after filling local needs, made remaining persons available to the countywide Circuit Court, which heard felony cases like Smith's. The Michigan Supreme Court, however, had rejected Smith's "siphoning" plea for lack of proof that the assignment procedure caused underrepresentation. Smith, 463 Mich., at 205, 615 N.W.2d, at 3. As that determination was not at all unreasonable, the Sixth Circuit had no warrant to disturb it. See § 2254(d)(2).

In addition to renewal of his "siphoning" argument, Smith here urges that a host of factors combined to reduce systematically the number of African– Americans appearing on Kent County jury lists, for example, the Kent County court's practice of excusing people without adequate proof of alleged hardship, and the refusal of Kent County police to enforce orders for prospective jurors to appear. Brief for Respondent 53–54. Our decisions do not address factors of the kind Smith urges. We have cautioned, however, that "[t]he fair-cross-section principle must have much leeway in application." *Taylor*, 419 U.S., at 537–538, 95 S.Ct. 692; see id., at 537, 95 S.Ct. 692 (Court's holding that Sixth Amendment is violated by systematic exclusion of women from jury service "does not augur or authorize the fashioning of detailed jury-selection codes by federal courts.").

A

On November 7, 1991, Christopher Rumbley was shot and killed during a bar brawl in Grand Rapids, Michigan. The bar was crowded at the time of the brawl, with 200-to-300 people on the premises. All patrons of the bar were African–American. The State charged Smith with the murder in Kent County Circuit Court.

Voir dire for Smith's trial took place in September 1993. The venire panel included between 60 and 100 individuals. The parties agree that, at most, three venire members were African–American. Smith unsuccessfully objected to the composition of the venire panel.

Smith's case proceeded to trial before an all-white jury. The case for the prosecution turned on the identity of the man who shot Rumbley. Thirty-seven witnesses from the bar, including Smith, testified at the trial. Of those, two testified that Smith fired the gun. Five testified that the shooter was not Smith, and the remainder made no identifications of the shooter. The jury convicted Smith of second- degree murder and possession of a firearm during a felony, and the court sentenced him to life imprisonment with the possibility of parole.

B

On first appeal, the Michigan Court of Appeals ordered the trial court to conduct an evidentiary hearing on Smith's fair-cross-section claim. The hearing occurred in early 1998. Smith's evidence showed that Grand Rapids, the largest city in Kent County, was home to roughly 37% of Kent County's population, and to 85% of its African–American residents. Felony charges in Kent County were tried in a sole Circuit Court. Misdemeanors were prosecuted in 12 district courts, each covering a discrete geographical area. To fill the courts' venires, Kent County sent questionnaires to prospective jurors. The Circuit Court Administrator testified that about 5% of the forms were returned as undeliverable, and another 15 to 20% were not answered. App. 13a. From the pool of prospective jurors who completed questionnaires, the County granted requests for hardship exemptions, e.g., for lack of transportation or child care. Id., at 21a. Kent County then assigned nonexempt prospective jurors to their local district courts' venires. After filling the district courts' needs, the County assigned the remaining prospective jurors to the Circuit Court's panels. Id., at 20a, 22a.

The month after voir dire for Smith's trial, Kent County reversed the assignment order. It did so, according to the Circuit Court Administrator, based on "[t]he belief ... that the respective districts essentially swallowed up most of the minority jurors," leaving the Circuit Court with a jury pool that "did not represent the entire county." Id., at 22a. The Jury Minority Representation Committee, its co-chair testified, held the same view concerning the impact of choosing district court jurors first and not returning unused persons to the pool available for Circuit Court selections. Id., at 64a–65a.

The trial court considered two means of measuring the extent of underrepresentation of African–Americans on Circuit Court venires: " absolute disparity" and "comparative disparity." "Absolute disparity" is determined by subtracting the percentage of African–Americans in the jury pool (here, 6% in the six months leading up to Smith's trial) from the percentage of African–Americans in the local, jury-eligible population (here, 7.28%). By an absolute disparity measure, therefore, African–Americans were underrepresented by 1.28%. "Comparative disparity" is determined by dividing the absolute disparity (here, 1.28%) by the group's representation in the jury-eligible population (here, 7.28%). The quotient (here, 18%), showed that, in the six months prior to Smith's trial, African–Americans were, on average, 18% less likely, when compared to the overall jury-eligible population, to be on the jury-service list. App. to Pet. for Cert. 215a.

Isolating the month Smith's jury was selected, Smith's statistics expert estimated that the comparative disparity was 34.8%.App. 181a. In the 11 months after Kent County discontinued the district-court-first assignment policy, the comparative disparity, on average, dropped from 18% to 15.1%. Id., at 102a–103a, 113a.

Smith also introduced the testimony of an expert in demographics and economics, who tied the underrepresentation to social and economic factors. In Kent County, the expert explained, these forces made African–Americans less likely than whites to receive or return juror-eligibility questionnaires, and more likely to assert a hardship excuse. Id., at 79a–80a.

The hearing convinced the trial court that African–Americans were underrepresented in Circuit Court venires. App. to Pet. for Cert. 210a. But Smith's evidence was insufficient, that court held, to prove that the juror-assignment order, or any other part of the jury-selection process, had systematically excluded African–Americans. Id., at 210a–212a. The court therefore rejected Smith's fair-cross-section claim.

C

The Michigan Court of Appeals concluded that the juror-allocation system in place at the relevant time did result in the underrepresentation of African–Americans. Id., at 182a–183a. Reversing the trial court's judgment, the intermediate appellate court ordered a new trial, with jurors selected under the Circuit–Court–first assignment order installed shortly after the voir dire in Smith's case. Ibid.; see supra, at 1389–1390.

The Michigan Supreme Court, in turn, reversed the Court of Appeals' judgment, concluding that Smith "ha[d] not established a prima facie violation of the Sixth Amendment fair-cross-section requirement." Smith, 463 Mich., at 207, 615 N.W.2d, at 4. The Michigan High Court observed, first, that this Court has specified "[no] preferred method for measuring whether representation of a distinctive group in the jury pool is fair and reasonable." Id., at 203, 615 N.W.2d, at 2. The court then noted that lower federal courts had applied three different methods to measure fair and reasonable representation: the absolute and comparative disparity tests, described supra, at 1390, and "the standard deviation test."

Recognizing that no single test was entirely satisfactory, the Michigan Supreme Court adopted a case-by-case approach allowing consideration of all three means of measuring under-representation. Smith, 463 Mich., at 204, 615 N.W.2d, at 3. Smith's statistical evidence, the court found, "failed to establish a legally significant disparity under either the absolute or comparative disparity tests." *Id.*, at 204–205, 615 N.W.2d, at 3. (The parties had presented no expert testimony regarding application of the standard deviation test. Id., at 204, n. 1, 615 N.W.2d, at 3, n. 1; supra, at 1390.)

Nevertheless "grant[ing] [Smith] the benefit of the doubt on unfair and unreasonable under-representation," the Michigan Supreme Court ultimately determined that "he ha[d] not shown systematic exclusion." Smith, 463 Mich., at 203, 205, 615 N.W.2d, at 2, 3. Smith's evidence, the court said, did not show "how the alleged siphoning of African American jurors to district courts affected the circuit court jury pool." Id., at 205, 615 N.W.2d, at 3. In particular, the court observed, "[t]he record does not disclose whether the district court jury pools contained more, fewer, or approximately the same percentage of minority jurors as the circuit court jury pool." Ibid. The court also ruled that "the influence of social and economic factors on juror participation does not demonstrate a systematic exclusion." Id., at 206, 615 N.W.2d, at 3.

D

In February 2003, Smith filed a habeas corpus petition in the United States District Court for the Western District of Michigan, reasserting his fair-cross-section claim. Because Smith is "in custody pursuant to the judgment of a State court," the Antiterrorism and Effective Death Penalty Act of 1996 (AEDPA), § 2254, governed the District Court's review of his application for federal habeas corpus relief. Under the controlling provision of AEDPA, codified in § 2254(d), a state prisoner's application may not be granted as to "any claim … adjudicated … in State court" unless the state court's adjudication

"(1) resulted in a decision that was contrary to, or involved an unreasonable application of, clearly established Federal law, as determined by the Supreme Court of the United States; or

"(2) resulted in a decision that was based on an unreasonable determination of the facts in light of the evidence presented in the State court proceeding."

Applying these standards, the District Court dismissed Smith's habeas petition. App. to Pet. for Cert. 40a–42a.

The Court of Appeals reversed. Where, as here, the allegedly excluded group is small, the Sixth Circuit ruled, courts should use the comparative disparity test to measure underrepresentation. 543 F.3d, at 338. In that court's view, Smith's comparative disparity statistics sufficed "to demonstrate that the representation of African American veniremen in Kent County ... was unfair and unreasonable." Ibid. As to systematic exclusion, the Sixth Circuit, in accord with the Michigan intermediate appellate court, believed that the juror-assignment order in effect when Smith's jury was empaneled significantly reduced the number of African–Americans available for Circuit Court venires. Id., at 342. Smith was entitled to relief, the court concluded, because no important state interest supported that allocation system. Id., at 345.

The State petitioned for certiorari attacking the Sixth Circuit's decision on two principal grounds: First, the State charged that the federal appellate court erred in adopting the comparative disparity test to determine whether a distinctive group was underrepresented in the jury pool. Pet. for Cert. ii. Second, the State urged that, in any event, "there was no ... systematic exclusion of African Americans from juries in Kent County, Michigan," id., at 25, and no warrant for the Sixth Circuit's contrary determination. We granted review, and now reverse the Sixth Circuit's judgment.

According to the Sixth Circuit, the Michigan Supreme Court's rejection of Smith's Sixth Amendment plea "involved an unreasonable application o[f] clearly established Federal law, as determined by [this Court in *Duren*]." § 2254(d)(1); see 543 F.3d, at 345. We disagree. As explained below, our *Duren* decision hardly establishes—no less "clearly" so—that Smith was denied his Sixth Amendment right to an impartial jury drawn from a fair cross section of the community.

II

To establish a prima facie violation of the fair-cross-section requirement, this Court's pathmarking decision in Duren instructs, a defendant must prove that: (1) a group qualifying as "distinctive" (2) is not fairly and reasonably represented in jury venires, and (3) "systematic exclusion" in the jury-selection process accounts for the underrepresentation. 439 U.S., at 364, 99 S.Ct. 664; see supra, at 1387–1388.

The defendant in Duren successfully challenged Jackson County's administration of a Missouri exemption permitting any woman to opt out of jury service. 439 U.S., at 360, 99 S.Ct. 664. The Court explained why it was plain that defendant Duren had established a prima facie case. First, women in Jackson County were both "numerous and distinct from men." *Id.*, at 364, 99 S.Ct. 664 (quoting *Taylor*, 419 U.S., at 531, 95 S.Ct. 692). Second, *Duren*'s "statistical presentation" showed gross underrepresentation: Women were over half the jury-eligible population; in stark contrast, they accounted for less than 15% of jury venires. 439 U.S., at 364–366, 99 S.Ct. 664.

Duren also demonstrated systematic exclusion with particularity. He proved that women's underrepresentation was persistent —occurring in every weekly venire for almost a year—and he identified the two stages of the jury-selection process "when ... the systematic exclusion took place." *Id.*, at 366, 99 S.Ct. 664. First, questionnaires for prospective jurors stated conspicuously that women could opt out of jury service. Less than 30% of those summoned were female, suggesting that women in large numbers claimed the exemption at the questionnaire stage. Ibid. "Moreover, at the summons stage women were ... given another opportunity to [opt out]." *Id.*, at 366–367, 99 S.Ct. 664. And if a woman ignored the summons, she was deemed to have opted out; no further inquiry was made. *Id.*, at 367, 99 S.Ct. 664. At this "final, venire, stage," women's representation plummeted to 14.5%. Ibid. In the Federal District Court serving the same territory, the Court noted, despite a women-only childcare exemption, women accounted for nearly 40% of those actually serving on juries. See ibid., n. 25.

The "disproportionate and consistent exclusion of women from the [Jackson County] jury wheel and at the venire stage," the Court concluded, "was quite obviously due to the system by which juries were selected." Id., at 367, 99 S.Ct. 664. "[A]ppropriately tailored" hardship exemptions, the Court added, would likely survive a fair-cross-section challenge if justified by an important state interest. *Id.*, at 370, 99 S.Ct. 664. But no such interest, the Court held, could justify Missouri's exemption for each and every woman—the altogether evident explanation for the underrepresentation. Id., at 369–370, 99 S.Ct. 664.

III

A

As the Michigan Supreme Court correctly observed, see supra, at 1390, neither Duren nor any other decision of this Court specifies the method or test courts must use to measure the representation of distinctive groups in jury pools. The courts below and the parties noted three methods employed or identified in lower federal court decisions: absolute disparity, comparative disparity, and standard deviation. See Smith, 463 Mich., at 204–205, 615 N.W.2d, at 2–3; Brief for Petitioner 3; Brief for Respondent 26; supra, at 1390–1391.

Each test is imperfect. Absolute disparity and comparative disparity measurements, courts have recognized, can be misleading when, as here, "members of the distinctive group comp[ose] [only] a small percentage of those eligible for jury service." Smith, 463 Mich., at 203–204, 615 N.W.2d, at 2–3. And to our knowledge, "[n]o court ... has accepted [a standard deviation analysis] alone as determinative in Sixth Amendment challenges to jury selection systems." *United States v. Rioux*, 97 F.3d 648, 655 (C.A.2 1996).

On direct review, as earlier stated, the Michigan Supreme Court chose no single method "to measur[e] whether representation was fair and reasonable." *Smith*, 463 Mich., at 204, 615 N.W.2d, at 3; see supra, at 1390–1391. Instead, it "adopt[ed] a case-by-case approach." *Smith*, 463 Mich., at 204, 615 N.W.2d, at 3. "Provided that the parties proffer sufficient evidence," that court said, "the results of all of the tests [should be considered]." Ibid. In contrast, the Sixth Circuit declared that "[w]here the distinctive group alleged to have been underrepresented is small, as is the case here, the comparative disparity test is the more appropriate measure of underrepresentation." 543 F.3d, at 338.

Even in the absence of AEDPA's constraint, see supra, at 1391, we would have no cause to take sides today on the method or methods by which underrepresentation is appropriately measured.4 Although the Michigan Supreme Court concluded that "[*Smith*'s] statistical evidence failed to establish a legally significant disparity under either the absolute or comparative disparity tests," *Smith*, 463 Mich., at 204–205, 615 N.W.2d, at 3,5 that court nevertheless gave Smith "the benefit of the doubt on underrepresentation," id., at 205, 615 N.W.2d, at 3. It did so in order to reach the issue ultimately dispositive in *Duren* : To the extent underrepresentation existed, was it due to "systematic exclusion"? Ibid.; see *Duren*, 439 U.S., at 364, 99 S.Ct. 664.

B

Addressing the ground on which the Sixth Circuit rested its decision, Smith submits that the district-court-first assignment order systematically excluded African–Americans from Kent County Circuit Court venires. Brief for Respondent 46–48. But as the Michigan Supreme Court not at all unreasonably concluded, *Smith*, 463 Mich., at 205, 615 N.W.2d, at 3, Smith's evidence scarcely shows that the assignment order he targets caused underrepresentation. Although the record established that some officials and others in Kent County believed that the assignment order created racial disparities, and the County reversed the order in response, supra, at 1389–1390, the belief was not substantiated by Smith's evidence.

Evidence that African–Americans were underrepresented on the Circuit Court's venires in significantly higher percentages than on the Grand Rapids District Court's could have indicated that the assignment order made a critical difference. But, as the Michigan Supreme Court noted, Smith adduced no evidence to that effect. See *Smith*, 463 Mich., at 205, 615 N.W.2d, at 3. Nor did Smith address whether Grand Rapids, which had the County's largest African–American population, "ha[d] more need for jurors per capita than [any other district in Kent County]." Tr. of Oral Arg. 26; id., at 18, 37. Furthermore, Smith did not endeavor to compare the African–American representation levels in Circuit Court venires with those in the Federal District Court venires for the same region. See id., at 46–47; Duren, 439 U.S., at 367, n. 25, 99 S.Ct. 664.

Smith's best evidence of systematic exclusion was offered by his statistics expert, who reported a decline in comparative underrepresentation, from 18 to 15.1%, after Kent County reversed the assignment order. See supra, at 1389–1390. This evidence—particularly in view of AEDPA's instruction, § 2254(d)(2)—is insufficient to support Smith's claim that the assignment order caused the underrepresentation. As Smith's counsel recognized at oral argument, this decrease could not fairly be described as "a big change." Tr. of Oral Arg. 51; see ibid. (the drop was "a step in the right direction"). In short, Smith's evidence gave the Michigan Supreme Court little reason to conclude that the district-court-first assignment order had a significantly adverse impact on the representation of African–Americans on Circuit Court venires.

C

To establish systematic exclusion, Smith contends, the defendant must show only that the underrepresentation is persistent and "produced by the method or 'system' used to select [jurors]," rather than by chance. Brief for Respondent 38, 40. In this regard, Smith catalogs a laundry list of factors in addition to the alleged "siphoning" that, he urges, rank as "systematic" causes of underrepresentation of African–Americans in Kent County's jury pool. Id., at 53–54. Smith's list includes the County's practice of excusing people who merely alleged hardship or simply failed to show up for jury service, its reliance on mail notices, its failure to follow up on nonresponses, its use of residential addresses at least 15 months old, and the refusal of Kent County police to enforce court orders for the appearance of prospective jurors. *Ibid.*

No "clearly established" precedent of this Court supports Smith's claim that he can make out a prima facie case merely by pointing to a host of factors that, individually or in combination, might contribute to a group's underrepresentation. Smith recites a sentence in our Duren opinion that, he says, placed the burden of proving causation on the State. See Tr. of Oral Arg. 33, 35. The sentence reads: "Assuming, arguendo, that the exemptions mentioned by the court below [those for persons over 65, teachers, and government workers] would justify failure to achieve a fair community cross section on jury venires, the State must demonstrate that these exemptions [rather than the women's exemption] caused the underrepresentation complained of." 439 U.S., at 368–369, 99 S.Ct. 664. That sentence appears after the Court had already assigned to Duren—and found he had carried—the burden of proving that the underrepresentation "was due to [women's] systematic exclusion in the jury-selection process." Id., at 366, 99 S.Ct. 664. The Court's comment, which Smith clipped from its context, does not concern the demonstration of a prima face case. Instead, it addresses what the State might show to rebut the defendant's prima facie case. The Michigan Supreme Court was therefore far from "unreasonable," § 2254(d)(1), in concluding that Duren first and foremost required Smith himself to show that the underrepresentation complained of was "due to systematic exclusion." Id., at 364, 99 S.Ct. 664; see *Smith*, 463 Mich., at 205, 615 N.W.2d, at 3.

This Court, furthermore, has never "clearly established" that jury-selection-process features of the kind on Smith's list can give rise to a fair-cross-section claim. In Taylor, we "recognized broad discretion in the States" to "prescribe relevant qualifications for their jurors and to provide reasonable exemptions." 419 U.S., at 537–538, 95 S.Ct. 692. And in *Duren*, the Court understood that hardship exemptions resembling those Smith assails might well "survive a fair-cross-section challenge," 439 U.S., at 370, 99 S.Ct. 664.6 In sum, the Michigan Supreme Court's decision rejecting Smith's fair-cross-section claim is consistent with Duren and "involved [no] unreasonable application o[f] clearly established Federal law," § 2254(d)(1).

* * *

For the reasons stated, the judgment of the Court of Appeals for the Sixth Circuit is reversed, and the case is remanded for further proceedings consistent with this opinion.

It is so ordered.

Note

While the dual constitutional concerns of Sixth Amendment-based Fair-Cross-Section requirement and the Equal Protection approach of the early cases of *Norris* and *Patterson* have significance in protecting against racial bias in jury venires(pools), the Court has now made clear that as to the selection of the petit jury itself, the Fair Cross-Section requirement of the Sixth Amendment does not entitle the defendant to proportional representation, as indicated below in *Holland v. Illinois.*

Race and the Fair Cross-section Requirement: Petit Juries

HOLLAND V. ILLINOIS.
493 U.S. 474 (1990)

Justice SCALIA delivered the opinion of the Court.

The questions presented by this case are (1) whether a white defendant has standing to raise a Sixth Amendment challenge to the prosecutor's exercise of peremptory challenges to exclude all black potential jurors from his petit jury, and (2) whether such exclusion violates his Sixth Amendment right to trial by an impartial jury.

I

Petitioner Daniel Holland was charged in the Circuit Court of Cook County, Illinois, with aggravated kidnaping, rape, deviate sexual assault, armed robbery, and aggravated battery. According to his allegations, a venire of 30 potential jurors was assembled, 2 of whom were black. Petitioner's counsel objected to those of the State's peremptory challenges that struck the two black venire members from the petit jury, on the ground that petitioner had a Sixth Amendment right to "be tried by a representative cross section of the community." App. 7–8. The trial judge overruled the objection, and petitioner was subsequently convicted of all except the aggravated battery charge. The convictions were reversed by the Illinois Appellate Court, First District, 147 Ill.App.3d 323, 100 Ill.Dec. 868, 497 N.E.2d 1230 (1986), on grounds that are irrelevant here, but on further appeal by the State were reinstated by the Illinois Supreme Court, which rejected petitioner's Equal Protection Clause and Sixth Amendment challenges to the exclusion of the black jurors. 121 Ill.2d 136, 117 Ill.Dec. 109, 520 N.E.2d 270 (1987). We granted Holland's petition for certiorari asserting that the Sixth Amendment holding was error.

II

The threshold question is whether petitioner, who is white, has standing to raise a Sixth Amendment challenge to the exclusion of blacks from his jury. We hold that he does.

In *Batson v. Kentucky*, 476 U.S. 79, 96, 106 S.Ct. 1712, 1723, 90 L.Ed.2d 69 (1986), we said that to establish a prima facie Equal Protection Clause violation in the discriminatory exclusion of petit jurors, the defendant "must show that he is a member of a cognizable racial group ... and that the prosecutor has exercised peremptory challenges to remove from the venire members of the defendant's race." (Emphasis added.) We have never suggested, however, that such a requirement of correlation between the group identification of the defendant and the group identification of excluded venire members is necessary for Sixth Amendment standing. To the contrary, our cases hold that the Sixth Amendment entitles every defendant to object to a venire that is not designed to represent a fair cross section of the community, whether or not the systematically excluded groups are groups to which he himself belongs. See, e.g., *Duren v. Missouri*, 439 U.S. 357, 99 S.Ct. 664, 58 L.Ed.2d 579 (1979); *Taylor v. Louisiana*, 419 U.S. 522, 95 S.Ct. 692, 42 L.Ed.2d 690 (1975). Thus, in *Taylor*, we found standing in circumstances analogous to petitioner's:

> "The State first insists that Taylor, a male, has no standing to object to the exclusion of women from his jury. But Taylor's claim is that he was constitutionally entitled to a jury drawn from a venire constituting a fair cross section of the community and that the jury that tried him was not such a jury by reason of the exclusion of women. Taylor was not a member of the excluded class;

but there is no rule that claims such as Taylor presents may be made only by those defendants who are members of the group excluded from jury service." Id., at 526, 95 S.Ct. at 695.

Of course, in this case petitioner seeks an extension of the fair-cross-section requirement from the venire to the petit jury—but that variation calls into question the scope of the Sixth Amendment guarantee, not his standing to assert it. We proceed, then, to the merits of the claim.

III

Petitioner asserts that the prosecutor intentionally used his peremptory challenges to strike all black prospective jurors solely on the basis of their race, thereby preventing a distinctive group in the community from being represented on his jury. This, he contends, violated the Sixth Amendment by denying him a "fair possibility" of a petit jury representing a cross section of the community. Petitioner invites us to remedy the perceived violation by incorporating into the Sixth Amendment the test we devised in Batson to permit black defendants to establish a prima facie violation of the Equal Protection Clause. Under petitioner's approach, a defendant of any race could establish a prima facie violation of the Sixth Amendment by objecting to the use of peremptory challenges to exclude all blacks from the jury. The burden would then shift to the prosecutor to show that the exercise of his peremptory challenges was not based on intentional discrimination against the black potential jurors solely because of their race. Only if the prosecutor could then show nonracial grounds for the strikes would no Sixth Amendment violation be found.

We reject petitioner's fundamental thesis that a prosecutor's use of peremptory challenges to eliminate a distinctive group in the community deprives the defendant of a Sixth Amendment right to the "fair possibility" of a representative jury. While statements in our prior cases have alluded to such a "fair possibility" requirement, satisfying it has not been held to require anything beyond the inclusion of all cognizable groups in the venire, see *Lockhart v. McCree*, 476 U.S. 162, 106 S.Ct. 1758, 90 L.Ed.2d 137 (1986); *Duren*, supra; Taylor, supra, and the use of a jury numbering at least six persons, see *Ballew v. Georgia*, 435 U.S. 223, 98 S.Ct. 1029, 55 L.Ed.2d 234 (1978); *Williams v. Florida*, 399 U.S. 78, 90 S.Ct. 1893, 26 L.Ed.2d 446 (1970). A prohibition upon the exclusion of cognizable groups through peremptory challenges has no conceivable basis in the text of the Sixth Amendment, is without support in our prior decisions, and would undermine rather than further the constitutional guarantee of an impartial jury.

It has long been established that racial groups cannot be excluded from the venire from which a jury is selected. That constitutional principle was first set forth not under the Sixth Amendment but under the Equal Protection Clause. *Strauder v. West Virginia*, 100 U.S. 303, 25

L.Ed. 664 (1880). In that context, the object of the principle and the reach of its logic are not established by our common-law traditions of jury trial, but by the Fourteenth Amendment's prohibition of unequal treatment in general and racial discrimination in particular. That prohibition therefore has equal application at the petit jury and the venire stages, as our cases have long recognized. Thus, in a decision rendered only 12 years after the Fourteenth Amendment was enacted, striking down a West Virginia law that excluded blacks from jury service, we said:

> "[I]t is hard to see why the statute of West Virginia should not be regarded as discriminating against a colored man when he is put upon trial for an alleged criminal offence against the State. It is not easy to comprehend how it can be said that while every white man is entitled to a trial by a jury selected from persons of his own race or color, or, rather, selected without discrimination against his color, and a negro is not, the latter is equally protected by the law with the former. Is not protection of life and liberty against race or color prejudice, a right, a legal right, under the constitutional amendment? And how can it be maintained that compelling a colored man to submit to a trial for his life by a jury drawn from a panel from which the State has expressly excluded every man of his race, because of color alone, however well qualified in other respects, is not a denial to him of equal legal protection?" Strauder, supra, at 309.

Four Terms ago, in Batson, we squarely held that race-based exclusion is no more permissible at the individual petit jury stage than at the venire stage—not because the two stages are inseparably linked, but because the intransigent prohibition of racial discrimination contained in the Fourteenth Amendment applies to both of them.

Our relatively recent cases, beginning with *Taylor v. Louisiana*, hold that a fair-cross-section venire requirement is imposed by the Sixth Amendment, which provides in pertinent part: "In all criminal prosecutions, the accused shall enjoy the right to a speedy and public trial, by an impartial jury of the State and district wherein the crime shall have been committed...." The fair-cross-section venire requirement is obviously not explicit in this text, but is derived from the traditional understanding of how an "impartial jury" is assembled. That traditional understanding includes a representative venire, so that the jury will be, as we have said, "drawn from a fair cross section of the community," *Taylor*, 419 U.S., at 527, 95 S.Ct., at 696 (emphasis added). But it has never included the notion that, in the process of drawing the jury, that initial representativeness cannot be diminished by allowing both the accused and the State to eliminate persons thought to be inclined against their interests—which is precisely how the traditional peremptory-challenge system operates. As we described that system in *Swain v. Alabama*, 380 U.S. 202, 85 S.Ct. 824, 13 L.Ed.2d 759 (1965):

> "[The peremptory challenge] is often exercised ... on grounds normally thought irrelevant to legal proceedings or official action, namely, the race, religion, nationality, occupation or

affiliations of people summoned for jury duty. For the question a prosecutor or defense counsel must decide is not whether a juror of a particular race or nationality is in fact partial, but whether one from a different group is less likely to be." Id., at 220–221, 85 S.Ct., at 836 (citation and footnote omitted).

The Sixth Amendment requirement of a fair cross section on the venire is a means of assuring, not a representative jury (which the Constitution does not demand), but an impartial one (which it does). Without that requirement, the State could draw up jury lists in such manner as to produce a pool of prospective jurors disproportionately ill disposed towards one or all classes of defendants, and thus more likely to yield petit juries with similar disposition. The State would have, in effect, unlimited peremptory challenges to compose the pool in its favor. The fair-cross-section venire requirement assures, in other words, that in the process of selecting the petit jury the prosecution and defense will compete on an equal basis.

But to say that the Sixth Amendment deprives the State of the ability to "stack the deck" in its favor is not to say that each side may not, once a fair hand is dealt, use peremptory challenges to eliminate prospective jurors belonging to groups it believes would unduly favor the other side. Any theory of the Sixth Amendment leading to that result is implausible. The tradition of peremptory challenges for both the prosecution and the accused was already venerable at the time of Blackstone, see 4 W. Blackstone, Commentaries 346–348 (1769), was reflected in a federal statute enacted by the same Congress that proposed the Bill of Rights, see Act of Apr. 30, 1790, ch. 9, § 30, 1 Stat. 112, 119, was recognized in an opinion by Justice Story to be part of the common law of the United States, see *United States v. Marchant*, 12 Wheat. 480, 483–484, 6 L.Ed. 700 (1827), and has endured through two centuries in all the States, see *Swain*, supra, 380 U.S., at 215–217, 85 S.Ct., at 833–834. The constitutional phrase "impartial jury" must surely take its content from this unbroken tradition.1 One could plausibly argue (though we have said the contrary, see *Stilson v. United States*, 250 U.S. 583, 586, 40 S.Ct. 28, 29–30, 63 L.Ed. 1154 (1919)) that the requirement of an "impartial jury" impliedly compels peremptory challenges, but in no way could it be interpreted directly or indirectly to prohibit them. We have gone out of our way to make this clear in our opinions. In Lockhart, we said: "We have never invoked the fair-cross-section principle to invalidate the use of either for-cause or peremptory challenges to prospective jurors, or to require petit juries, as opposed to jury panels or venires, to reflect the composition of the community at large." 476 U.S., at 173, 106 S.Ct., at 1765. In Taylor, we "emphasized that in holding that petit juries must be drawn from a source fairly representative of the community we impose no requirement that petit juries actually chosen must mirror the community and reflect the various distinctive groups in the population. Defendants are not entitled to a jury of any particular composition." 419 U.S., at 538, 95 S.Ct., at 702. *Accord, Duren v. Missouri*, 439 U.S., at 363–364, and n. 20, 99 S.Ct., at 668, and n. 20.

The fundamental principle underlying today's decision is the same principle that underlay Lockhart, which rejected the claim that allowing challenge for cause, in the guilt phase of a capital trial, to jurors unalterably opposed to the death penalty (so-called "Witherspoon-excludables") violates the fair-cross-section requirement. It does not violate that requirement, we said, to disqualify a group for a reason that is related "to the ability of members of the group to serve as jurors in a particular case." 476 U.S., at 175, 106 S.Ct., at 1766 (emphasis added). The "representativeness" constitutionally required at the venire stage can be disrupted at the jury-panel stage to serve a State's "legitimate interest." *Ibid.* In Lockhart the legitimate interest was "obtaining a single jury that can properly and impartially apply the law to the facts of the case at both the guilt and sentencing phases of a capital trial." Id., at 175–176, 106 S.Ct., at 1766. Here the legitimate interest is the assurance of impartiality that the system of peremptory challenges has traditionally provided.

The rule we announce today is not only the only plausible reading of the text of the Sixth Amendment, but we think it best furthers the Amendment's central purpose as well. Although the constitutional guarantee runs only to the individual and not to the State, the goal it expresses is jury impartiality with respect to both contestants: neither the defendant nor the State should be favored. This goal, it seems to us, would positively be obstructed by a petit jury cross section requirement which, as we have described, would cripple the device of peremptory challenge. We have acknowledged that that device occupies "an important position in our trial procedures," *Batson*, 476 U.S., at 98, 106 S.Ct., at 1724, and has indeed been considered "a necessary part of trial by jury," *Swain v. Alabama*, 380 U.S., at 219, 85 S.Ct., at 835. Peremptory challenges, by enabling each side to exclude those jurors it believes will be most partial toward the other side, are a means of "eliminat [ing] extremes of partiality on both sides," ibid., thereby "assuring the selection of a qualified and unbiased jury," *Batson, supra,* 476 U.S., at 91, 106 S.Ct., at 1720 (emphasis added).

Petitioner seeks to minimize the harm that recognition of his claim would cause to the peremptory challenge system by assuring us that the striking of identifiable community groups other than blacks need not be accorded similar treatment. That is a comforting assurance, but the theory of petitioner's case is not compatible with it. If the goal of the Sixth Amendment is representation of a fair cross section of the community on the petit jury, then intentionally using peremptory challenges to exclude any identifiable group should be impermissible—which would, as we said in Lockhart, "likely require the elimination of peremptory challenges." 476 U.S., at 178, 106 S.Ct., at 1767.

Justice MARSHALL argues that prohibiting purposeful peremptory challenge of members of distinctive groups "would leave the peremptory challenge system almost entirely untouched" because the Court is unlikely to recognize many groups as "distinctive." Post, at 819. Misplaced optimism on this subject is cost free to those who in any event "would ... eliminat[e] peremptory challenges entirely in criminal cases," *Batson*, supra 476 U.S., at 107, 106 S.Ct., at 1729

(MARSHALL, J., concurring), but we see no justification for indulging it. To support his prediction, Justice MARSHALL states that the only groups the Court has recognized as distinctive thus far have been women and certain racial groups, post, at 819 (citing Lockhart, 476 U.S., at 175, 106 S.Ct., at 1766). That is true enough, but inasmuch as those groups happen to constitute all the groups we have considered in the venire context, what it demonstrates is not how difficult it is to meet our standards for distinctiveness, but how few groups are systematically excluded from the venire. As we have discussed, however, many groups are regularly excluded from the petit jury through peremptory challenge. *Lockhart* itself suggests, quite rightly, that even so exotic a group as "Witherspoon-excludables" would be a distinctive group whose rejection at the venire stage would violate the Sixth Amendment. 476 U.S., at 176, 106 S.Ct., at 1766–67. If, as Justice MARSHALL would have it, rejection at the venire stage and rejection at the panel stage are one and the same, there is every reason to believe that many commonly exercised bases for peremptory challenge would be rendered unavailable.

Dispassionate analysis does not bear out Justice MARSHALL's contentions that we have "ignor[ed] precedent after precedent," post, at 819, "reject [ed] ... the principles underlying a whole line of cases," ibid., and suffer from "selective amnesia with respect to our cases in this area," post, at 818. His dissent acknowledges that the fair-cross-section decisions it discusses—Taylor, Duren, and Lockhart—"referr[ed] to exclusion of prospective jurors from venires, not their exclusion from petit juries by means of peremptory challenges," post, at 816. It nonetheless counts those cases as "well-grounded precedents," post, at 812, because "the particular context does not affect the analysis," post, at 816. That may be the dissent's view, but it was assuredly not the view expressed in the cases themselves. As noted earlier, all three of those opinions specifically disclaimed application of their analysis to the petit jury. See supra, at 808–809. Last Term, in *Teague v. Lane*, 489 U.S. 288, 109 S.Ct. 1060, 103 L.Ed.2d 334 (1989), we were asked to decide the very same question we decide today—"whether," as Justice O'CONNOR's plurality opinion put it, "the Sixth Amendment's fair cross section requirement should now be extended to the petit jury." *Id.*, at 292, 109 S.Ct., at 1065. We did not reach that question because the four-Justice plurality, with Justice WHITE agreeing as to the result, held that "new constitutional rules of criminal procedure will not be applicable to those cases which have become final before the new rules are announced," *id.*, at 310, 109 S.Ct., at 1075, and found that in asserting a fair-cross-section requirement at the petit jury stage petitioner was urging adoption of such a "new rule," *id.*, at 301, 109 S.Ct., at 1070 that is, a rule producing a result "not dictated by [prior] precedent," *ibid.* (emphasis in original). Though there were four Justices in dissent, only two of them expressed the view that a petit jury fair-cross-section requirement was compelled by prior precedent. See *id.*, at 340–344, 109 S.Ct., at 1091–1094 (BRENNAN, J., dissenting). In short, there is no substance to the contention that what we hold today "ignor[es] precedent after precedent."

Justice MARSHALL's dissent rolls out the ultimate weapon, the accusation of insensitivity to racial discrimination—which will lose its intimidating effect if it continues to be fired so randomly. It is not remotely true that our opinion today "lightly ... set[s] aside" the constitutional goal of "eliminat [ing] racial discrimination in our system of criminal justice." Post, at 819. The defendant in this case is not a black man, but a convicted white rapist who seeks to use the striking of blacks from his jury to overturn his conviction. His Sixth Amendment claim would be just as strong if the object of the exclusion had been, not blacks, but postmen, or lawyers, or clergymen, or any number of other identifiable groups. Race as such has nothing to do with the legal issue in this case. We do not hold that the systematic exclusion of blacks from the jury system through peremptory challenges is lawful; it obviously is not, see Batson, supra. We do not even hold that the exclusion of blacks through peremptory challenges in this particular trial was lawful. Nor do we even hold that this particular (white) defendant does not have a valid constitutional challenge to such racial exclusion. All we hold is that he does not have a valid constitutional challenge based on the Sixth Amendment—which no more forbids the prosecutor to strike jurors on the basis of race than it forbids him to strike them on the basis of innumerable other generalized characteristics.

To be sure, as Justice MARSHALL says, the Sixth Amendment sometimes operates "as a weapon to combat racial discrimination," post, at 820, n. 2—just as statutes against murder sometimes operate that way. But it is no more reasonable to portray this as a civil rights case than it is to characterize a proposal for increased murder penalties as an antidiscrimination law. Since only the Sixth Amendment claim, and not the equal protection claim, is at issue, the question before us is not whether the defendant has been unlawfully discriminated against because he was white, or whether the excluded jurors have been unlawfully discriminated against because they were black, but whether the defendant has been denied the right to "trial ... by an impartial jury." The earnestness of this Court's commitment to racial justice is not to be measured by its willingness to expand constitutional provisions designed for other purposes beyond their proper bounds.

The judgment of the Illinois Supreme Court is Affirmed.

Note

Determining a Basis for a Fair Cross-Section Challenge – The courts have favored systems that compile complete list of eligible jurors and impartially draw a venire from such a list or "pool". Thus, in *Truesdale v. Moore*, 142 F. 3d 749 (4th Cir. 1998), the Court held against the defendant where the venire was selected in such a manner.

> Truesdale also argues that the composition of the jury pool violated the equal protection guarantees of the Fourteenth Amendment as applied in Castaneda v. Partida, 430 U.S. 482, 97 S.Ct. 1272, 51 L.Ed.2d 498 (1977). He acknowledges that to prevail on this claim he must show some

evidence that the selection procedure "is susceptible of abuse or is not racially neutral." Id. at 494, 97 S.Ct. at 1280. Truesdale advances no claim that South Carolina's system of selecting veniremen was manipulable or was otherwise racially biased. On the contrary, the only evidence in the record about how South Carolina's jury system worked suggests that it was safe from racially-motivated abuse—veniremen were drawn at random from a locked jury box containing identical numbered capsules; numbers were assigned alphabetically to names on the unaltered voter registration list; and the Jury Commissioners responsible for jury selection exercised no discretion in selecting from the jury box and did not consider the race or qualifications of potential jurors. Thus Truesdale has not carried his burden of proving discriminatory purpose. See Duren, 439 U.S. at 368

Access to Jury Pool Records – In the somewhat unusual case, *State v. Moore*, 395 S.E.2d 434 (N.C. Ct. of App. 1990), the trial court, although denying the defendant relief regarding a claim of race discrimination in the selection of the foremen of the grand jury, nonetheless said

> Thus a defendant who seeks evidence in support of a motion to quash an indictment on the ground of race discrimination must be given a reasonable opportunity to investigate and produce evidence. Id. (quoting State v. Perry, 248 N.C. 334, 339, 103 S.E.2d 404, 407–08 (1958)). What is "reasonable" depends on the facts of the particular case. Id. To establish a prima facie case of systematic racial discrimination, a defendant generally must produce statistical evidence establishing that blacks were underrepresented on the jury and evidence that the selection procedure was not racially neutral or that, for a substantial period in the past, relatively few blacks...
>
> The initial motion for an appointment of a statistical expert to analyze race discrimination in both the grand and petit jury selection was thus granted. Although the Court of Appeals failed to grant relief to the defendant, the North Carolina Supreme Court reversed and ruled in the defendant's favor where it was shown that because the defendant complained that Blacks were systematically excluded, the prosecutor made a special request that a Black grand jury foremen be deliberately appointed and a new indictment obtained, such was not a satisfactory solution to a statistically-supported Fair Cross Section claim.

Access to Court-Appointed Expert for Venire Pool Analysis in Order to Make Fair Cross-Section Claim – As a general matter the type of statistical data necessary to make the type of *prima facie* case of discrimination in a Fair Cross-Section claim, required by *Duren v. Missouri* and *Berghuis v. Smith*, the defendant must rely on statistical analysis. If the defendant cannot afford his or her own statistics expert, such as the one used by Berghuis, is the defendant entitled to appointment of one? In general, the courts have not been very receptive to such a claim, usually requiring that "particularized need" and/or likely success. See, *United States v. Pritt*, 458 Fed. Appx. 795 (11th Cir. 2012), *State v. Hester*, 324 S.W. 3d 1 (2010), *People v. Pike*, 63

A.D.3d 1692 (S.Ct. App. Div. N.Y. 2009). But note *United States v. Rodriguez-Lara*, 421 F. 3d 932 (9th Cir. 2005):

> Defendant did not have to complete his prima facie case to be entitled to expert assistance in making his underlying fair-cross section claim, since further inquiry was warranted by showing that Hispanics were substantially underrepresented in jury pool, allegation of systematic underrepresentation of Hispanics due to use of voter registration records as sole source of names for jury pool was plausible theory, and expert would have been able to investigate whether Hispanics had been systematically excluded and potentially provided necessary information to complete defendant's prima facie case.

Challenging Juror Selection for Cause and Peremptory Challenges

Challenging Potential Jurors for Cause Based on Racial Attitudes

Note

The Sixth Amendment right to a trial by jury includes the right that such a jury be impartial.:

> [T]he right to jury trial guarantees to the criminally accused a fair trial by a panel of impartial, 'indifferent' jurors. The failure to accord an accused a fair hearing violates even the minimal standards of due process. *Irvin v. Dowd*, 366 U.S. 717, 721 (1961)

A racially bias juror is not an impartial juror and it is incumbent on the trial court to remove such a juror for cause. However, the general rule has been that a potential juror who expresses racial bias during voir dire can remain on the jury if rehabilitated. As the Supreme Court of Minnesota stated in *State v. Logan*, 535 N.W. 2d 320 at 323 (1995); "A juror with an actual bias must be excused from jury service unless the juror is "rehabilitated." While questions of actual bias i.e. statements from the potential juror that she or he will not be impartial as to the specific defendant, give rise to a for cause removal unless rehabilitated, statements of racial animosity create an implied bias that may also mandate a "for cause" removal. Implied bias refers to instances where " a prospective juror is connected to the litigation at issue in such a way that [it] is highly unlikely that he or she could act impartially during deliberations" *State v. Holt*, 772 N.W. 2d 470 at 477 (Minn. 2009).

Expressions of racial bias from a potential juror have also been found to not disqualify "for cause" if the potential juror can provide "unequivocal assurance" that such bias can be set aside and a verdict entered solely on the evidence. *In People v. Benet*, 846 N.Y.S.2d 544 (2007), a prospective juror admitted during voir dire that he had referred to Hispanic persons as "Spics", a racially derogatory term. The trial court thereafter did not discuss further with the prospective juror his racial attitudes and subsequently denied the defendant's motion to have the prospective struck for cause. As a result the defendant was forced to use one of his peremptory challenges to remove the prospective juror. The appellate court, while recognizing that an expression of racial bias raises serious doubt regarding the ability of that prospective juror to be impartial, nonetheless determined that the potential juror offered "unequivocal" assurance that any bias could be set aside, based on the whole record of the prospective juror's response which included a statement that he would find the defendant not guilty prior to hearing any evidence, thus recognizing the presumption of innocence and the prosecution's duty to present evidence of guilt beyond a reasonable doubt.

But when is an assurance of impartiality enough after a prospective juror has indicated racial bias? In *State v. Logan*, 535 N.W. 2d 320 (Minn. 1995), the Court, citing to *Patton v. Young*, 467 U.S. 1025 (1984), that the rehabilitation of a biased potential juror is a two-part inquiry. First, is obtaining an assurance from the prospective juror that his or her bias can be set aside and the case be decided on the evidence presented, Second, it must be determined if that potential juror's "protestation of impartiality (should) have been believed." While a determination of credibility by the trial court is to afforded special deference because the issue is one credibility and demeanor, this standard may imply a duty of the trial court to make further and specific inquiry. In that regard, consider the following case.

HAM V. SOUTH CAROLINA.
409 U.S. 524 (1973)

Mr. Justice REHNQUIST delivered the opinion of the Court.

Petitioner was convicted in the South Carolina trial court of the possession of marihuana in violation of state law. He was sentenced to 18 months' confinement, and on appeal his conviction was affirmed by a divided South Carolina Supreme Court. 256 S.C. 1, 180 S.E.2d 628 (1971). We granted certiorari limited to the question of whether the trial judge's refusal to examine jurors on voir dire as to possible prejudice against petitioner violated the latter's federal constitutional rights.

Petitioner is a young, bearded Negro who has lived most of his life in Florence County, South Carolina. He appears to have been well known locally for his work in such civil rights activities as the Southern Christian Leadership Conference and the Bi-racial Committee of the City of Florence. He has never previously been convicted of a crime. His basic defense at the trial was that law enforcement officers were 'out to get him' because of his civil rights activities, and that he had been framed on the drug charge.

Prior to the trial judge's voir dire examination of prospective jurors, petitioner's counsel requested the judge to ask jurors four questions relating to possible prejudice against petitioner. The first two questions sought to elicit any possible racial prejudice against Negroes; the third question related to possible prejudice against beards; and the fourth dealt with pretrial publicity relating to the drug problem. The trial judge, while putting to the prospective jurors three general questions as to bias, prejudice, or partiality that are specified in the South Carolina statutes, declined to ask any of the four questions posed by petitioner.

The dissenting justices in the Supreme Court of South Carolina thought that this Court's decision in *Aldridge v. United States*, 283 U.S. 308, 51 S.Ct. 470, 75 L.Ed. 1054 (1931), was binding on the State. There a Negro who was being tried for the murder of a white policeman requested that prospective jurors be asked whether they entertained any racial prejudice. This Court reversed the judgment of conviction because of the trial judge's refusal to make such an inquiry. Mr. Chief Justice Hughes, writing for the Court, stated that the 'essential demands of fairness' required the trial judge under the circumstances of that case to interrogate the veniremen with respect to racial prejudice upon the request of counsel for a Negro criminal defendant. *Id.*, at 310, 51 S.Ct., at 471.

The Court's opinion relied upon a number of state court holdings throughout the country to the same effect, but it was not expressly grounded upon any constitutional requirement. Since one of the purposes of the Due Process Clause of the Fourteenth Amendment is to insure these 'essential demands of fairness,' e.g., *Lisenba v. California*, 314 U.S. 219, 236, 62 S.Ct. 280, 289, 86 L.Ed. 166 (1941), and since a principal purpose of the adoption of the Fourteenth Amendment was to prohibit the States from invidiously discriminating on the basis of race, *Slaughter-House Cases*, 16 Wall. 36, 81, 21 L.Ed. 394 (1873), we think that the Fourteenth Amendment required the judge in this case to interrogate the jurors upon the subject of racial prejudice. South Carolina law permits challenges for cause, and authorizes the trial judge to conduct voir dire examination of potential jurors. The State having created this statutory framework for the selection of juries, the essential fairness required by the Due Process Clause of the Fourteenth Amendment requires that under the facts shown by this record the petitioner be permitted to have the jurors interrogated on the issue of racial bias. Cf. *Groppi v. Wisconsin*, 400 U.S. 505, 508, 91 S.Ct. 490, 492, 27 L.Ed.2d 571 (1971); *Bell v. Burson*, 402 U.S. 535, 541, 91 S.Ct. 1586, 1590, 29 L.Ed.2d 90 (1971).

We agree with the dissenting justices of the Supreme Court of South Carolina that the trial judge was not required to put the question in any particular form, or to ask any particular number of questions on the subject, simply because requested to do so by petitioner. The Court in Aldridge was at pains to point out, in a context where its authority within the federal system of courts allows a good deal closer supervision than does the Fourteenth Amendment, that the trial court 'had a broad discretion as to the questions to be asked,' 283 U.S., at 310, 51 S.Ct., at 471. The discretion as to form and number of questions permitted by the Due Process Clause of the Fourteenth Amendment is at least as broad. In this context, either of the brief, general questions urged by the petitioner would appear sufficient to focus the attention of prospective jurors on any racial prejudice they might entertain.

The third of petitioner's proposed questions was addressed to the fact that he wore a beard. While we cannot say that prejudice against people with beards might not have been harbored by one or more of the potential jurors in this case, this is the beginning and not the end of the inquiry as to whether the Fourteenth Amendment required the trial judge to interrogate the prospective jurors about such possible prejudice. Given the traditionally broad discretion accorded to the trial judge in conducting voir dire, *Aldridge v. United States, supra*, and our inability to constitutionally distinguish possible prejudice against beards from a host of other possible similar prejudices, we do not believe the petitioner's constitutional rights were violated when the trial judge refused to put this question. The inquiry as to racial prejudice derives its constitutional stature from the firmly established precedent of Aldridge and the numerous state cases upon which it relied, and from a principal purpose as well as from the language of those who adopted the Fourteenth Amendment. The trial judge's refusal to inquire as to particular bias against beards, after his inquiries as to bias in general, does not reach the level of a constitutional violation.

Petitioner's final question related to allegedly prejudicial pretrial publicity. But the record before us contains neither the newspaper articles nor any description of the television program in question. Because of this lack of material in the record substantiating any pretrial publicity prejudicial to this petitioner, we have no occasion to determine the merits of his request to have this question posed on voir dire.

Because of the trial court's refusal to make any inquiry as to racial bias of the prospective jurors after petitioner's timely request therefor, the judgment of the Supreme Court of South Carolina is reversed.

Judgment reversed.

....

Mr. Justice MARSHALL, concurring in part and dissenting in part.

I, too, concur in that portion of the majority's opinion which holds that the trial judge was constitutionally compelled to inquire into the possibility of racial prejudice on voir dire. I also agree that, on this record, we cannot say that the judge was required to ask questions about pretrial publicity. I cannot agree, however, that the judge acted properly in totally foreclosing other reasonable and relevant avenues of inquiry as to possible prejudice.

Long before the Sixth Amendment was made applicable to the States through the Due Process Clause of the Fourteenth Amendment, see *Duncan v. Louisiana*, 391 U.S. 145, 88 S.Ct. 1444, 20 L.Ed.2d 491 (1948), this Court held that the right to an 'impartial' jury was basic to our system of justice.

> 'In essence, the right to jury trial guarantees to the criminally accused a fair trial by a panel of impartial, 'indifferent' jurors. The failure to accord an accused a fair hearing violates even the minimal standards of due process. . . . In the language of Lord Coke, a juror must be as 'indifferent as he stands unsworne.' Co. Litt. 155b. His verdict must be based upon the evidence developed at the trial. Cf. *Thompson v. City of Louisville*, 362 U.S. 199, 80 S.Ct. 624, 4 L.Ed.2d 654. This is true, regardless of the heinousness of the crime charged, the apparent guilt of the offender or the station in life which he occupies. It was so written into our law as early as 1807 by Chief Justice Mashall in 1 Burr's Trial 416 (1807). 'The theory of the law is that a juror who has formed an opinion cannot be impartial.' *Reynolds v. United States*, 98 U.S. 145, 155, 25 L.Ed. 244.' *Irvin v. Dowd*, 366 U.S. 717, 722, 81 S.Ct. 1639, 1642, 6 L.Ed.2d 751 (1961) (footnote omitted).

See also *Turner v. Louisiana*, 379 U.S. 466, 471–473, 85 S.Ct. 546, 548–550, 13 L.Ed.2d 424 (1965); *Glasser v. United States*, 315 U.S. 60, 84–86, 62 S.Ct. 457, 471–472, 86 L.Ed. 680 (1942).

We have never suggested that this right to impartiality and fairness protects against only certain classes of prejudice or extends to only certain groups in the population. It makes little difference to a criminal defendant whether the jury has prejudged him because of the color of his skin or because of the length of his hair. In either event, he has been deprived of the right to present his case to neutral and detached observers capable of rendering a fair and impartial verdict. It is unsurprising, then, that this Court has invalidated decisions reached by juries with a wide variety of different prejudices. See, e.g., *Witherspoon v. Illinois*, 391 U.S. 510, 88 S.Ct. 1770, 20 L.Ed.2d 776 (1968); *Irvin v. Dowd, supra; Morford v. United States*, 339 U.S. 258, 70 S.Ct. 586, 94 L.Ed. 815 (1950).

Moreover, the Court has also held that the right to an impartial jury carries with it the concomitant right to take reasonable steps designed to insure that the jury is impartial. A variety of techniques is available to serve this end, see *Groppi v. Wisconsin*, 400 U.S. 505, 509–511, 91 S.Ct. 490, 492–494, 27 L.Ed.2d 571 (1971); *Sheppard v. Maxwell*, 384 U.S. 333, 357–363, 86 S.Ct. 1507, 1519–1523, 16 L.Ed.2d 600 (1966), but perhaps the most important of these is the jury challenge. See e.g., *Johnson v. Louisiana*, 406 U.S. 356, 379, 92 S.Ct. 1620, 1642, 32 L.Ed.2d 152 (1972) (opinion of Powell, J.); *Swain v. Alabama*, 380 U.S. 202, 209–222, 85 S.Ct. 824, 829–837, 13 L.Ed.2d 759 (1965). Indeed, the first Mr. Justice Harlan, speaking for a unanimous Court, thought that the right to challenge was 'one of the most important of the rights secured to the accused' and that '(a)ny system for the impaneling of a jury that prevents or embarrasses the full, unrestricted exercise by the accused of that right must be condemned.' *Pointer v. United States*, 151 U.S. 396,

408, 14 S.Ct. 410, 414, 38 L.Ed. 208 (1894). See also *Lewis v. United States*, 146 U.S. 370, 376, 13 S.Ct. 136, 138, 36 L.Ed. 1011 (1892).

Of course, the right to challenge has little meaning if it is unaccompanied by the right to ask relevant questions on voir dire upon which the challenge for cause can be predicated. See *Swain v. Alabama*, supra, 380 U.S., at 221, 85 S.Ct., at 836. It is for this reason that the Court has held that '(p) reservation of the opportunity to prove actual bias is a guarantee of a defendant's right to an impartial jury,' *Dennis v. United States*, 339 U.S. 162, 171–172, 70 S.Ct. 519, 523, 94 L.Ed. 734 (1950), and that the Court has reversed criminal convictions when the right to query on voir dire has been unreasonably infringed. See, e.g., *Aldridge v. United States*, 283 U.S. 308, 51 S.Ct. 470, 75 L.Ed. 1054 (1931). Contrary to the majority's suggestion, these reversals have not been confined to cases where the defendant was prevented from asking about racial prejudice. See, e.g., Morford v. United States, supra. Cf. Dennis v. *United States, supra.*

I do not mean to suggest that a defendant must be permitted to propound any question or that limitless time must be devoted to preliminary voir dire. Although the defendant's interest in a jury free of prejudice is strong, there are countervailing state interests in the expeditious conduct of criminal trials and the avoidance of jury intimidation. These interests bulk larger as the possibility of uncovering prejudice becomes more attenuated. The trial judge has broad discretion to refuse to ask questions that are irrelevant or vexatious. Thus, where the claimed prejudice is of a novel character, the judge might require a preliminary showing of relevance or of possible prejudice before allowing the questions.

But broad as the judge's discretion is in these matters, I think it clear that it was abused in this case. The defense attorney wished to ask no more than four questions, which would have required a scant 15 additional minutes of the court's time. The inquiries, directed inter alia to possible prejudice against people with beards, were obviously relevant, since the defendant was in fact bearded. Moreover, the judge afforded petitioner no opportunity to show that there were a significant number of potential jurors who might be prejudiced against people with beards. At minimum, I think such an opportunity should have been provided. I cannot believe that in these circumstances an absolute ban on questions designed to uncover such prejudice represents a proper balance between the competing demands of fairness and expedition.

It may be that permitting slightly more extensive voir dire examination will put an additional burden on the administration of justice. But, as Mr. Chief Justice Hughes argued 40 years ago, 'it would be far more injurious to permit it to be thought that persons entertaining a disqualifying prejudice were allowed to serve as jurors and that inquiries designed to elicit the fact of disqualification were barred. No surer way could be devised to bring the processes of justice into disrepute.' *Aldridge v. United States*, 283 U.S., at 315, 51 S.Ct., at 473.

I would therefore hold that the defendant in this case, and subject to the limitations set out above, had a constitutionally protected interest in having the judge propound the additional question, in some form, to the jury.

Mr. Justice POWELL delivered the opinion of the Court.

Respondent is a Negro convicted in a state court of violent crimes against a white security guard. The trial judge denied respondent's motion that a question specifically directed to racial prejudice be asked during voir dire in addition to customary questions directed to general bias or prejudice. The narrow issue is whether, under our recent decision in *Ham v. South Carolina*, 409 U.S. 524, 93 S.Ct. 848, 35 L.Ed.2d 46 (1973), respondent was constitutionally entitled to require the asking of a question specifically directed to racial prejudice. The broader issue presented is whether Ham announced a requirement applicable whenever there may be a confrontation in a criminal trial between persons of different races or different ethnic origins. We answer both of these questions in the negative.

I

Respondent, James Ross, Jr., was tried in a Massachusetts court with two other Negroes for armed robbery, assault and battery by means of a dangerous weapon, and assault and battery with intent to murder. The victim of the alleged crimes was a white man employed by Boston University as a uniformed security guard. The Voir dire of prospective jurors was to be conducted by the court, which was required by statute to inquire generally into prejudice. See n. 3, Infra. Each defendant, represented by separate counsel, made a written motion that the prospective jurors also be questioned specifically about racial prejudice. Each defendant also moved that the veniremen be asked about affiliations with law enforcement agencies.

The trial judge consulted counsel for the defendants about their motions. After tentatively indicating that he "(felt) that no purpose would be accomplished by asking such questions in this instance," the judge invited e views of counsel:

> "THE COURT: . . . I thought from something Mr. Donnelly (counsel for a codefendant) said, he might have wanted on the record something which was peculiar to this case, or peculiar to the circumstances which we are operating under here which perhaps he didn't want to say in open court.
>
> "Is there anything peculiar about it, Mr. Donnelly?

"MR. DONNELLY: No, just the fact that the victim is white, and the defendants are black.

"THE COURT: This, unfortunately, is a problem with us, and all we can hope and pray for is that the jurors and all of them take their oaths seriously and understand the spirit of their oath and understand the spirit of what the Court says to them this Judge anyway and I am sure all Judges of this Court would take the time to impress upon them before, during, and after the trial, and before their verdict, that their oath means just what it says, that they are to decide the case on the evidence, with no extraneous considerations.

"I believe that that is the best that can be done with respect to the problems which as I said, I regard as extremely important . . . ." App. 29-30.

Further discussion persuaded the judge that a question about law enforcement affiliations should be asked because of the victim's status as a security guard. But he adhered to his decision not to pose a question directed specifically to racial prejudice.

The Voir dire of five panels of prospective jurors then commenced. The trial judge briefly familiarized each panel with the facts of the case, omitting any reference to racial matters. He then explained to the panel that the clerk would ask a general question about impartiality and a question about affiliations with law enforcement agencies. Consistently with his announced intention to "impress upon (the jurors) . . . that they are to decide the case on the evidence, with no extraneous considerations," the judge preceded the questioning of the panel with an extended discussion of the obligations of jurors. After these remarks the clerk posed the questions indicated to the panel. Panelists answering a question affirmatively were questioned individually at the bench by the judge, in the presence of counsel. This procedure led to the excusing of 18 veniremen for cause on grounds of prejudice, including one panelist who admitted a racial bias.

The jury eventually impaneled convicted each defendant of all counts. On direct appeal Ross contended that his federal constitutional rights were violated by the denial of his request that prospective jurors be questioned specifically about racial prejudice. This contention was rejected by the Supreme Judicial Court of Massachusetts, *Commonwealth v. Ross*, 361 Mass. 665, 282 N.E.2d 70 (1972), and Ross sought a writ of certiorari. While his petition was pending, we held in Ham that a trial court's failure on request to question veniremen specifically about racial prejudice had denied Ham due process of law. We granted Ross' petition for certiorari and remanded for reconsideration in light of *Ham*, 410 U.S. 901, 93 S.Ct. 968, 35 L.Ed.2d 265 (1973); the Supreme Judicial Court again affirmed Ross' conviction. *Commonwealth v. Ross*, 363 Mass. 665, 296 N.E.2d 810 (1973). The court reasoned that Ham turned on the need for questions about racial prejudice presented by its facts and did not announce "a new broad constitutional principle requiring that (such) questions . . . be put to prospective jurors in all State criminal trials when the defendant is black . . .." *Id.*, at 671, 296 N.E.2d, at 815. Ross again sought certiorari, but the writ was denied. 414 U.S. 1080, 94 S.Ct. 599, 38 L.Ed.2d 486 (1973).

In the present case Ross renewed his contention on collateral attack in federal habeas corpus. Relying on Ham, the District Court granted a writ of habeas corpus, and the Court of Appeals for the First Circuit affirmed. 508 F.2d 754 (1974). The Court of Appeals assumed that Ham turned on its facts. But it held that the facts of Ross' case, involving "violence against a white" with "a status close to that of a police officer," presented a need for specific questioning about racial prejudice similar to that in Ham. *Id.*, at 756. We think the Court of Appeals read Ham too broadly.

II

The Constitution does not always entitle a defendant to have questions posed during Voir dire specifically directed to matters that conceivably might prejudice veniremen against him. *Ham, supra*, 409 U.S., at 527-528, 93 S.Ct., at 850. Voir dire "is conducted under the supervision of the court, and a great deal must, of necessity, be left to its sound discretion." *Connors v. United States*, 158 U.S. 408, 413, 15 S.Ct. 951, 953, 39 L.Ed. 1033 (1895); see *Ham, supra*, 409 U.S., at 527-528, 93 S.Ct., at 850; *Aldridge v. United States*, 283 U.S. 308, 310, 51 S.Ct. 470, 471, 75 L.Ed. 1054 (1931). This is so because the "determination of impartiality, in which demeanor plays such an important part, is particularly within the province of the trial judge." *Rideau v. Louisiana*, 373 U.S. 723, 733, 83 S.Ct. 1417, 1423, 10 L.Ed.2d 663 (1963) (Clark, J., dissenting). Thus, the State's obligation to the defendant to impanel an impartial jury6 generally can be satisfied by less than an inquiry into a specific prejudice feared by the defendant. Ham, supra, 409 U.S., at 527-528, 93 S.Ct., at 850.

In Ham, however, we recognized that some cases may present circumstances in which an impermissible threat to the fair trial guaranteed by due process is posed by a trial court's refusal to question prospective jurors specifically about racial prejudice during Voir dire. Ham involved a Negro tried in South Carolina courts for possession of marihuana. He was well known in the locale of his trial as a civil rights activist, and his defense was that law enforcement officials had framed him on the narcotics charge to "get him" for those activities. Despite the circumstances, the trial judge denied Ham's request that the court-conducted Voir dire include questions specifically directed to racial prejudice. We reversed the judgment of conviction because "the essential fairness required by the Due Process Clause of the Fourteenth Amendment requires that under the facts shown by this record the (defendant) be permitted to have the jurors interrogated (during voir dire) on the issue of racial bias." 409 U.S., at 527, 93 S.Ct., at 850.

By its terms *Ham* did not announce a requirement of universal applicability. Rather, it reflected an assessment of whether under all of the circumstances presented there was a constitutionally significant likelihood that, absent questioning about racial prejudice, the jurors would not be as "indifferent as (they stand) unsworn." Coke on Littleton 155b (19th ed. 1832). In this approach Ham was consistent with other determinations by this Court that a State had denied a defendant due process by failing to impanel an impartial jury. See *Irvin v. Dowd*, 366 U.S. 717, 81 S.Ct. 1639, 6 L.Ed.2d 751 (1961); *Rideau v. Louisiana, supra; Turner v. Louisiana*, 379 U.S. 466, 85 S.Ct. 546, 13 L.Ed.2d 424 (1965); cf. *Avery v. Georgia*, 345 U.S. 559, 73 S.Ct. 891, 97 L.Ed. 1244 (1953).

The circumstances in Ham strongly suggested the need for Voir dire to include specific questioning about racial prejudice. Ham's defense was that he had been framed because of his civil rights activities. His prominence in the community as a civil rights activist, if not already known to veniremen, inevitably would have been revealed to the members of the jury in the course of his presentation of that defense. Racial issues therefore were inextricably bound up with the conduct of the trial. Further, Ham's reputation as a civil rights activist and the defense he interposed were likely to intensify any prejudice that individual members of the jury might harbor. In such circumstances we deemed a Voir dire that included questioning specifically directed to racial prejudice, when sought by *Ham*, necessary to meet the constitutional requirement that an impartial jury be impaneled.

We do not agree with the Court of Appeals that the need to question veniremen specifically about racial prejudice also rose to constitutional dimensions in this case. The mere fact that the victim of the crimes alleged was a white man and the defendants were Negroes was less likely to distort the trial than were the special factors involved in Ham. The victim's status as a security officer, also relied upon by the Court of Appeals, was cited by respective defense counsel primarily as a separate source of prejudice, not as an aggravating racial factor, see n. 2, supra, and the trial judge dealt with it by his question about law-enforcement affiliations. The circumstances thus did not suggest a significant likelihood that racial prejudice might infect Ross' trial. This was made clear to the trial judge when Ross was unable to support his motion concerning Voir dire by pointing to racial factors such as existed in Ham or others of comparable significance. In these circumstances, the trial judge acted within the Constitution in determining that the demands of due process could be satisfied by his more generalized but thorough inquiry into the impartiality of the veniremen. Accordingly, the judgment is

Reversed.

TURNER V. MURRAY
476 U.S. 28 (1986)

Justice WHITE announced the judgment of the Court and delivered the opinion of the Court with respect to Parts I and III, and an opinion with respect to Parts II and IV, in which Justice BLACKMUN, Justice STEVENS, and Justice O'CONNOR join.

Petitioner is a black man sentenced to death for the murder of a white storekeeper. The question presented is whether the trial judge committed reversible error at voir dire by refusing petitioner's request to question prospective jurors on racial prejudice.

I

On July 12, 1978, petitioner entered a jewelry store in Franklin, Virginia, armed with a sawed-off shotgun. He demanded that the proprietor, W. Jack Smith, Jr., put jewelry and money from the cash register into some jewelry bags. Smith complied with petitioner's demand, but triggered a silent alarm, alerting the Police Department. When Alan Bain, a police officer, arrived to inquire about the alarm, petitioner surprised him and forced him to surrender his revolver.

Having learned that Smith had triggered a silent alarm, petitioner became agitated. He fired toward the rear wall of the store and stated that if he saw or heard any more police officers, he was going to start killing those in the store. When a police siren sounded, petitioner walked to where Smith was stationed behind a counter and without warning shot him in the head with Bain's pistol, wounding Smith and causing him to slump incapacitated to the floor.

Officer Bain attempted to calm petitioner, promising to take him anywhere he wanted to go and asking him not to shoot again. Petitioner angrily replied that he was going to kill Smith for "snitching," and fired two pistol shots into Smith's chest, fatally wounding him. As petitioner turned away from shooting Smith, Bain was able to disarm him and place him under arrest.

A Southampton County, Virginia, grand jury indicted petitioner on charges of capital murder, use of a firearm in the commission of a murder, and possession of a sawed-off shotgun in the commission of a robbery. Petitioner requested and was granted a change of venue to Northampton County, Virginia, a rural county some 80 miles from the location of the murder.

Prior to the commencement of voir dire, petitioner's counsel submitted to the trial judge a list of proposed questions, including the following:

> "'The defendant, Willie Lloyd Turner, is a member of the Negro race. The victim, W. Jack Smith,
> Jr., was a white Caucasian. Will these facts prejudice you against Willie Lloyd Turner or affect
> your ability to render a fair and impartial verdict based solely on the evidence?'" *Turner v.*
> *Commonwealth*, 221 Va. 513, 522, n. 8, 273 S.E.2d 36, 42, n. 8 (1980).

The judge declined to ask this question, stating that it "has been ruled on by the Supreme Court." App. 15. The judge did ask the venire, who were questioned in groups of five in petitioner's presence, whether any person was aware of any reason why he could not render a fair and impartial verdict, to which all answered "no." *Id.*, at 17, 78. At the time the question was asked, the prospective jurors had no way of knowing that the murder victim was white.

The jury that was empaneled, which consisted of eight whites and four blacks, convicted petitioner on all of the charges against him. Id., at 97 and Addendum. After a separate sentencing hearing on the capital charge, the jury recommended that petitioner be sentenced to death, a recommendation the trial judge accepted. Id., at 18, 19.

Petitioner appealed his death sentence to the Virginia Supreme Court. Among other points, he argued that the trial judge deprived him of his constitutional right to a fair and impartial jury by refusing to question prospective jurors on racial prejudice. The Virginia Supreme Court rejected this argument. Relying on our decision in *Ristaino v. Ross*, 424 U.S. 589, 96 S.Ct. 1017, 47 L.Ed.2d 258 (1976), the court stated that a trial judge's refusal to ask prospective jurors about their racial attitudes, while perhaps not the wisest decision as a matter of policy, is not constitutionally objectionable in the absence of factors akin to those in *Ham v. South Carolina*, 409 U.S. 524, 93 S.Ct. 848, 35 L.Ed.2d 46 (1973).3 *Turner v. Commonwealth, supra,* 221 Va., at 523, 273 S.E.2d, at 42. The court held that "[t]he mere fact that a defendant is black and that a victim is white does not constitutionally mandate ... an inquiry [into racial prejudice]." Ibid.

Having failed in his direct appeal, petitioner sought habeas corpus relief in the Federal District Court for the Eastern District of Virginia. App. 97. Again he argued without success that the trial judge's refusal to ask prospective jurors about their racial attitudes deprived him of his right to a fair trial. Id., at 102-104. The District Court noted that in Ristaino, supra, which involved a crime of interracial violence, we held that inquiry into racial prejudice at voir dire was not constitutionally required because the facts of the case "'did not suggest a significant likelihood that racial prejudice might infect [the defendant's] trial.'" App. 103 (quoting 424 U.S., at 598, 96 S.Ct., at 1022). The court found the present case like Ristaino and unlike Ham in that "racial issues [are] not 'inextricably bound up with the facts at trial.'" App. 103.

The United States Court of Appeals for the Fourth Circuit affirmed the District Court's denial of habeas corpus relief for petitioner. *Turner v. Bass*, 753 F.2d 342 (1985). Like the Virginia Supreme Court and the District Court, the Fourth Circuit found no "special circumstances" in this case analogous to those in Ham. The court rejected the idea that "the nature of the crime or punishment itself is ... a special circumstance." 753 F.2d, at 345. Relying on Ristaino, the court likewise found no special circumstance in the fact that petitioner is black and his victim white.

We granted certiorari to review the Fourth Circuit's decision that petitioner was not constitutionally entitled to have potential jurors questioned concerning racial prejudice. We reverse.

II

The Fourth Circuit's opinion correctly states the analytical framework for evaluating petitioner's argument: "The broad inquiry in each case must be ... whether under all of the circumstances presented there was a constitutionally significant likelihood that, absent questioning about racial prejudice, the jurors would not be indifferent as [they stand] unsworn". 753 F.2d, at 345-346 (internal quotation omitted). The Fourth Circuit was correct, too, in holding that under *Ristaino* the mere fact that petitioner is black and his victim white does not constitute a "special circumstance" of constitutional proportions. What sets this case apart from *Ristaino*, however, is that in addition to petitioner's being accused of a crime against a white victim, the crime charged was a capital offense.

In a capital sentencing proceeding before a jury, the jury is called upon to make a "highly subjective, 'unique, individualized judgment regarding the punishment that a particular person deserves.' " *Caldwell v. Mississippi*, 472 U.S. 320, 340, n. 7, 105 S.Ct. 2633, 2645-2646, n. 7, 86 L.Ed.2d 231 (1985) (quoting *Zant v. Stephens*, 462 U.S. 862, 900, 103 S.Ct. 2733, 2755, 77 L.Ed.2d 235 (1983) (REHNQUIST, J., concurring in judgment)). The Virginia statute under which petitioner was sentenced is instructive of the kinds of judgments a capital sentencing jury must make. First, in order to consider the death penalty, a Virginia jury must find either that the defendant is likely to commit future violent crimes or that his crime was "outrageously or wantonly vile, horrible or inhuman in that it involved torture, depravity of mind or an aggravated battery to the victim." Va.Code § 19.2-264.2 (1983). Second, the jury must consider any mitigating evidence offered by the defendant. Mitigating evidence may include, but is not limited to, facts tending to show that the defendant acted under the influence of extreme emotional or mental disturbance, or that at the time of the crime the defendant's capacity "to appreciate the criminality of his conduct or to conform his conduct to the requirements of law was significantly impaired." § 19.2-264.4(B). Finally, even if the jury has found an aggravating factor, and irrespective of whether mitigating evidence has been offered, the jury has discretion not to recommend the death sentence, in which case it may not be imposed. § 19.2-264.2.

Virginia's death-penalty statute gives the jury greater discretion than other systems which we have upheld against constitutional challenge. See, e.g., *Jurek v. Texas*, 428 U.S. 262, 96 S.Ct. 2950, 49 L.Ed.2d 929 (1976). However, our cases establish that every capital sentencer must be free to weigh relevant mitigating evidence before deciding whether to impose the death penalty, see, e.g., *Eddings v. Oklahoma*, 455 U.S. 104, 102 S.Ct. 869, 71 L.Ed.2d 1 (1982); *Lockett v. Ohio*, 438 U.S. 586, 597-609, 98 S.Ct. 2954, 2960-2967, 57 L.Ed.2d 973 (1978) (plurality opinion), and that in the end it is the jury that must make the difficult, individualized judgment as to whether the defendant deserves the sentence of death.

Because of the range of discretion entrusted to a jury in a capital sentencing hearing, there is a unique opportunity for racial prejudice to operate but remain undetected. On the facts of this case, a juror who believes that blacks are violence prone or morally inferior might well be influenced by that belief in deciding whether petitioner's crime involved the aggravating factors specified under Virginia law. Such a juror might also be less favorably inclined toward petitioner's evidence of mental disturbance as a mitigating circumstance. More subtle, less consciously held racial attitudes could also influence a juror's decision in this case. Fear of blacks, which could easily be stirred up by the violent facts of petitioner's crime, might incline a juror to favor the death penalty.

The risk of racial prejudice infecting a capital sentencing proceeding is especially serious in light of the complete finality of the death sentence. "The Court, as well as the separate opinions of a majority of the individual Justices, has recognized that the qualitative difference of death from all other punishments requires a correspondingly greater degree of scrutiny of the capital sentencing determination." *California v. Ramos,* 463 U.S. 992, 998-999, 103 S.Ct. 3446, 77 L.Ed.2d 1171 (1983). We have struck down capital sentences when we found that the circumstances under which they were imposed "created an unacceptable risk that 'the death penalty [may have been] meted out arbitrarily or capriciously' or through 'whim ... or mistake.' " Caldwell, supra, at 343, 105 S.Ct., at 2647 (O'CONNOR, J., concurring in part and concurring in judgment) (citation omitted). In the present case, we find the risk that racial prejudice may have infected petitioner's capital sentencing unacceptable in light of the ease with which that risk could have been minimized.8 By refusing to question prospective jurors on racial prejudice, the trial judge failed to adequately protect petitioner's constitutional right to an impartial jury.

III

We hold that a capital defendant accused of an interracial crime is entitled to have prospective jurors informed of the race of the victim and questioned on the issue of racial bias.10 The rule we propose is minimally intrusive; as in other cases involving "special circumstances," the trial judge retains discretion as to the form and number of questions on the subject, including the decision whether to question the venire individually or collectively. See *Ham v. South Carolina,* 409 U.S., at 527, 93 S.Ct., at 850-51. Also, a defendant cannot complain of a judge's failure to question the venire on racial prejudice unless the defendant has specifically requested such an inquiry.

IV

The inadequacy of voir dire in this case requires that petitioner's death sentence be vacated. It is not necessary, however, that he be retried on the issue of guilt. Our judgment in this case is that there was an unacceptable risk of racial prejudice infecting the capital sentencing proceeding. This judgment is based on a conjunction of three factors: the fact that the crime charged involved interracial violence, the broad discretion given the jury at the death-penalty hearing, and the special seriousness of the risk of improper sentencing in a capital case. At the guilt phase of petitioner's trial, the jury had no greater discretion than it would have had if the crime charged had been noncapital murder. Thus, with respect to the guilt phase of petitioner's trial, we find this case to be indistinguishable from *Ristaino*, to which we continue to adhere. See n. 5, supra.

The judgment of the Court of Appeals is reversed, and the case is remanded for further proceedings consistent with this opinion.

It is so ordered.

ROSALES-LOPEZ V. UNITED STATES

451 U.S. 182 (1981)

Opinion

Justice WHITE announced the judgment of the Court and delivered an opinion, in which Justice STEWART, Justice BLACKMUN, and Justice POWELL joined.

The question here is whether it was reversible error for a federal trial court in a criminal case to reject the defendant's request that the court's voir dire of prospective jurors inquire further into the possibility of racial or ethnic prejudice against the defendant.

I

Petitioner is of Mexican descent. In February 1979, he was tried before a jury in the United States District Court for the Southern District of California for his alleged participation in a plan by which three Mexican aliens were illegally brought into the country.

The Government's evidence at trial described the following events. On the night of December 10, 1978, three aliens were led across the Mexican-American border and taken to a car, previously left for them on the American side. They drove to Imperial Beach, Cal., a town about eight miles inside the border. Early in the morning of December 11, they reached the home of Virginia Hendricks Bowling, where they were admitted into the garage of the house by petitioner. Bowling was an American citizen, apparently Caucasian, living in Imperial Beach with her 19-year-old daughter. Petitioner had been living with Bowling's daughter in her mother's house since July 1978.

Later in the morning, petitioner hid the three aliens and their guide in the trunk of a green Oldsmobile. Bowling drove the Oldsmobile north, through the San Clemente check-point, while petitioner followed in a grey Ford. After passing through the checkpoint, Bowling and petitioner exchanged cars. Petitioner proceeded to Los Angeles in the Oldsmobile and Bowling returned to Imperial Beach in the Ford. In Los Angeles, petitioner went to an apartment which agents of the Immigration and Naturalization Service had had under surveillance for several weeks because they suspected that it was a drop site for illegal aliens. Upon arrival, the aliens were let out of the trunk and told to go into the apartment by petitioner. Shortly thereafter, petitioner was arrested when he left the apartment with one of the aliens.

At trial, the INS agents, Bowling, the three illegal aliens, and David Falcon-Zavala, another named principal in the smuggling arrangement who was arrested with petitioner, testified for the Government. Petitioner did not testify; his defense was principally to challenge the credibility of the Government witnesses. The jury convicted him of all the charges and the Court of Appeals for the Ninth Circuit affirmed. 617 F.2d 1349 (1980).

Prior to trial, petitioner's counsel formally requested that he be allowed personally to voir dire the prospective members of the jury. At the same time, he filed a list of 26 questions that he requested the trial judge to ask, if the court denied his first motion. Among the questions submitted was one directed toward possible prejudice toward Mexicans:

> "Would you consider the race or Mexican descent of Humberto Rosales-Lopez in your evaluation of this case? How would it affect you?

As permitted by Rule 24 of the Federal Rules of Criminal Procedure and pursuant to the practice in the Southern District of California, the trial judge conducted the voir dire himself. He asked about half of the questions submitted by petitioner. Although he did not ask any question directed specifically to possible racial or ethnic prejudice, he did ask a question directed to attitudes toward the substantive charges involved: "Do any of you have any feelings about the alien problem at all?" He subsequently rephrased this: "Do any of you have any particular feelings one way or the other about aliens or could you sit as a fair and impartial juror if you are called upon to do so?" App. 17-18.3 The judge began the voir dire with the following general statement to the panel:

> "In order that this defendant shall have a fair and impartial jury to try the charges against him, it is necessary that we address certain questions to the panel to make sure that there are no underlying prejudices, there are no underlying reasons why you can't sit as a fair and impartial juror if chosen to do so in this case." Id., at 14.

He ended his general questioning with the following:

> "Does any reason occur to anyone of you why you could not sit in this case as a fair and impartial juror, any reason whatsoever?" Id., at 21.

Following the voir dire, defense counsel restated his request with respect to six of the submitted questions, including the one directed toward racial or ethnic prejudice. He argued at side bar that under *Aldridge v. United States*, 283 U.S. 308, 51 S.Ct. 470, 75 L.Ed. 1054 (1931), a federal court "must explore all racial antagonism against my client because he happens to be of Mexican descent." App. 25. The judge declined to ask any further questions of the jury panel. Peremptory challenges were then exercised and the jury was sworn.

Petitioner appealed, unsuccessfully challenging the refusal of the trial judge to question the jurors about possible racial or ethic bias. The Court of Appeals for the Ninth Circuit noted that there is

> "[a] longstanding rule of criminal justice in the federal courts ... that questions regarding possible racial prejudice should be put to the venire in prosecutions of minority defendants, at least where 'special circumstances' indicate that the defendant's race may be a factor in the trial." 617 F.2d, at 1354.

The court noted that "[t]he extent of the federal rule is unclear." Ibid. It concluded, however, that this case did not contain such "special circumstances."

The Courts of Appeals have adopted conflicting rules as to when the failure to ask such questions will constitute reversible error. Some Circuits have adopted a per se rule, requiring reversal whenever the trial judge fails to ask a question on racial or ethnic prejudice requested by a defendant who is a member of a minority group. See *United States v. Bowles* 574 F.2d 970 (CA8 1978); *United States v. Robinson*, 485 F.2d 1157 (CA3 1973); *United States v. Carter*, 440 F.2d 1132 (CA6 1971); *United States v. Gore*, 435 F.2d 1110 (CA4 1970); *Fraiser v. United States*, 267 F.2d 62 (CA1 1959). Other Circuits, including the Ninth, have rejected such a per se rule, holding that a trial judge is required to pose such a question only where there is some indication that the particular case is likely to have racial overtones or involve racial prejudice. See *United States v. Polk*, 550 F.2d 1265 (CA10 1977); *United States v. Perez-Martinez* 525 F.2d 365 (CA9 1975). In light of this diversity of views, we granted certiorari. 449 U.S. 819, 101 S.Ct. 71, 66 L.Ed.2d 21.

II

Voir dire plays a critical function in assuring the criminal defendant that his Sixth Amendment right to an impartial jury will be honored. Without an adequate voir dire the trial judge's responsibility to remove prospective jurors who will not be able impartially to follow the court's instructions and evaluate the evidence cannot be fulfilled. See *Connors v. United States*, 158 U.S. 408, 413, 15 S.Ct. 951, 953, 39 L.Ed. 1033 (1895). Similarly, lack of adequate voir dire impairs the defendant's right to exercise peremptory challenges where provided by statute or rule, as it is in the federal courts.

Despite its importance, the adequacy of voir dire is not easily subject to appellate review. The trial judge's function at this point in the trial is not unlike that of the jurors later on in the trial. Both must reach conclusions as to impartiality and credibility by relying on their own evaluations of demeanor evidence and of responses to questions. See *Ristaino v. Ross*, 424 U.S. 589, 595, 96 S.Ct. 1017, 1020, 47 L.Ed.2d 258 (1976), quoting *Rideau v. Louisiana*, 373 U.S. 723, 733, 83 S.Ct. 1417, 1422, 10 L.Ed.2d 663 (1963) (Clark, J., dissenting). In neither instance can an appellate court easily second-guess the conclusions of the decision-maker who heard and observed the witnesses.

Because the obligation to impanel an impartial jury lies in the first instance with the trial judge, and because he must rely largely on his immediate perceptions, federal judges have been accorded ample discretion in determining how best to conduct the voir dire. In *Aldridge v. United States*, 283 U.S. 308, 51 S.Ct. 470, 75 L.Ed. 1054 (1931), the Court recognized the broad role of the trial court: "[T]he questions to the prospective jurors were put by the court, and the court had a broad discretion as to the questions to be asked." Id., at 310, 51 S.Ct., at 471. See also *Ham v. South Carolina*, 409 U.S. 524, 528, 93 S.Ct. 848, 851, 35 L.Ed.2d 46 (1973) (recognizing "the traditionally broad discretion accorded to the trial judge in conducting voir dire...."). Furthermore, Rule 24(a), Federal Rules of Criminal Procedure, provides that the trial court may decide to conduct the voir dire itself or may allow the parties to conduct it. If the court conducts it, the parties may "supplement the examination by such further inquiry as [the court] deems proper"; alternatively, the court may limit participation to the submission of additional questions, which the court must ask only "as it deems proper."

There are, however, constitutional requirements with respect to questioning prospective jurors about racial or ethnic bias. The "special circumstances" under which the Constitution requires a question on racial prejudice were described in *Ristaino v. Ross*, supra, by contrasting the facts of that case with those in Ham v. South Carolina, supra, in which we held it reversible error for a state court to fail to ask such a question.

Ham involved a black defendant charged with a drug offense. His defense was that the law enforcement officers had "framed" him in retaliation for his active, and widely known, participation in civil rights activities. The critical factor present in Ham, but not present in *Ristaino*, was that racial issues were "inextricably bound up with the conduct of the trial," and the consequent need, under all the circumstances, specifically to inquire into possible racial prejudice in order to assure an impartial jury. *Ristaino, supra*, 424 U.S., at 596, 597, 96 S.Ct., at 1021. Although *Ristaino* involved an alleged criminal confrontation between a black assailant and a white victim, that fact pattern alone did not create a need of "constitutional dimensions" to question the jury concerning racial prejudice. 424 U.S., at 596, 597, 96 S.Ct., at 1021, 1022. There is no constitutional presumption of juror bias for or against members of any particular racial or ethnic groups. As Ristaino demonstrates, there is no per se constitutional rule in such circumstances requiring inquiry as to racial prejudice. Id., at 596, n. 8, 96 S.Ct., at 1021, n. 8. Only when there are more substantial indications of the likelihood of racial or ethnic prejudice affecting the jurors in a particular case does the trial court's denial of a defendant's request to examine the jurors' ability to deal impartially with this subject amount to an unconstitutional abuse of discretion.

Absent such circumstances, the Constitution leaves it to the trial court, and the judicial system within which that court operates, to determine the need for such questions. In the federal court system, we have indicated that under our supervisory authority over the federal courts, we would require that questions directed to the discovery of racial prejudice be asked in certain circumstances in which such an inquiry is not constitutionally mandated. *Ristaino*, supra, at 597, n. 9, 96 S.Ct., at 1021, n. 9.

Determination of an appropriate nonconstitutional standard for the federal courts does not depend upon a comparison of the concrete costs and benefits that its application is likely to entail. These are likely to be slight: some delay in the trial versus the occasional discovery of an unqualified juror who would not otherwise be discovered. There is, however, a more significant conflict at issue here-one involving the appearance of justice in the federal courts. On the one hand, requiring an inquiry in every case is likely to create the impression "that justice in a court of law may turn upon the pigmentation of skin [or] the accident of birth." *Ristaino*, supra, 424 U.S., at 596, n. 8, 96 S.Ct., at 1021, n. 8. Trial judges are understandably hesitant to introduce such a suggestion into their courtrooms. *See Aldridge, supra*, 283 U.S., at 310, 51 S.Ct., at 471; *Ristaino*, supra, 424 U.S., at 591, 96 S.Ct., at 1018. Balanced against this, however, is the criminal defendant's perception that avoiding the inquiry does not eliminate the problem, and that his trial is not the place in which to elevate appearance over reality.

We first confronted this conflict in Aldridge, supra, and what we said there remains true today:

> "The argument is advanced on behalf of the Government that it would be detrimental to the administration of the law in the courts of the United States to allow questions to jurors as to racial or religious prejudices. We think that it would be far more injurious to permit it to be thought that persons entertaining a disqualifying prejudice were allowed to serve as jurors and that inquiries designed to elicit the fact of disqualification were barred. No surer way could be devised to bring the processes of justice into disrepute." 283 U.S., at 314-315, 51 S.Ct., at 473.

In our judgment, it is usually best to allow the defendant to resolve this conflict by making the determination of whether or not he would prefer to have the inquiry into racial or ethnic prejudice pursued. Failure to honor his request, however, will be reversible error only where the circumstances of the case indicate that there is a reasonable possibility that racial or ethnic prejudice might have influenced the jury.

In *Ristaino*, the Court indicated that under the circumstances of that case, a federal trial court would have been required to "propound appropriate questions designed to identify racial prejudice if requested by the defendant." 424 U.S., at 597, n. 9, 96 S.Ct., at 1022, n. 9. In *Ristaino*, the Court also made clear that the result reached in Aldridge, was based on this Court's supervisory power over the federal courts. 424 U.S., at 598, n. 10, 96 S.Ct., at 1022, n. 10. In *Aldridge*, which *Ristaino* embraced, the Court held that it was reversible error for a federal trial court to fail to inquire into racial prejudice in a case involving a black defendant accused of murdering a white policeman. The circumstances of both cases indicated that there was a "reasonable possibility" that racial prejudice would influence the jury.

Aldridge and *Ristaino* together, fairly imply that federal trial courts must make such an inquiry when requested by a defendant accused of a violent crime and where the defendant and the victim are members of different racial or ethnic groups. This supervisory rule is based upon and consistent with the "reasonable possibility standard" articulated above. It remains an unfortunate fact in our society that violent crimes perpetrated against members of other racial or ethnic groups often raise such a possibility. There may be other circumstances that suggest the need for such an inquiry, but the decision as to whether the total circumstances suggest a reasonable possibility that racial or ethnic prejudice will affect the jury remains primarily with the trial court, subject to case-by-case review by the appellate courts.

III

Evaluated against these standards, there was no reversible error in the voir dire afforded petitioner. At no point has petitioner argued that the matters at issue in his trial involved allegations of racial or ethnic prejudice: neither the Government's case nor his defense involved any such allegations. There were, then, no "special circumstances" of constitutional dimension in this case. Neither did the circumstances of the case reveal a violent criminal act with a victim of a different racial or ethnic group. In fact, petitioner was accused of a victimless crime: aiding members of his own ethnic group to gain illegal entry into the United States. Petitioner, therefore, falls within that category of cases in which the trial court must determine if the external circumstances of the case indicate a reasonable possibility that racial or ethnic prejudice will influence the jury's evaluation of the evidence. For two reasons, we do not believe that such a reasonable possibility has been demonstrated in this case.

First, the trial court reasonably determined that a juror's prejudice toward aliens might affect his or her ability to serve impartially in this case. The court, therefore, questioned the prospective jurors as to their attitudes toward aliens. There can be no doubt that the jurors would have understood a question about aliens to at least include Mexican aliens. The trial court excused two jurors for cause, based on their responses to this question. Removing these jurors eliminated, we believe, any reasonable possibility that the remaining jurors would be influenced by an undisclosed racial prejudice toward Mexicans that would have been disclosed by further questioning.

Second, petitioner contends that "any latent racial antagonism" of the jurors toward Mexicans was likely to be exacerbated by Bowling's testimony concerning the relationship between petitioner and her daughter. Petitioner, however, failed to make this argument to the trial court in support of his requested question. Even if he had, however, it would not create a reasonable possibility that the jury's determination would be influenced by racial prejudice. Bowling's testimony as to petitioner's role in the particular smuggling operation involved in this trial was substantially corroborated by the other witnesses presented by the Government, including Falcon-Zavala and the three illegal aliens. Under the circumstances of this case, the racial or ethnic differences between the defendant and a key Government witness did not create a situation meeting the standard set out above. The judge was not, therefore, required to inquire further than he did.

Under these circumstances, we cannot hold that there was a reasonable possibility that racial or ethnic prejudice would affect the jury. Therefore, the trial court did not abuse its discretion in denying petitioner's request, and the judgment of the Court of Appeals is affirmed.

So ordered.

Race and Peremptory Challenging Jurors During Voir Dire

Note

The promise of *Norris* and *Patterson,* which recognized that Fourteenth Amendment Equal Protection guarantees that Americans cannot be excluded from juries based on race, has been severely tested by the historical practice of allowing the prosecution to make use of the peremptory challenge to remove any juror it wished without a stated reason. Although the peremptory challenge has a common-law history dating back at least prior to 1305, its roots in legal history have a different path for the prosecution as opposed to the criminal defendant. While there is ample precedent for the defendant's right to peremptory challenges to be considered an important part of assuring the constitutional right of a defendant to a fair and impartial trial, *Frazier v. United States*, 335 U.S. 497 (1948), the right of the prosecution in a criminal case to dismiss a potential juror without explanation existed in an unlimited form in English history as a prerogative of the Crown, until 1305 when it was completely abolished by statute under Edward I. *See, United States v. Marchant* 12 Wheat. 480, 6 L. Ed. 700 (1827) and was not again recognized until sometime after the American Revolution. During the mid-1800's it was proposed in the United States that the prosecution be given access to peremptory challenges in order to mitigate "the difficulties of getting convictions where public sentiment was against them". MINIMIZING RACISM IN JURY TRIALS (Ann Fagan Ginger, ed., The National Lawyers Guild 1969), p.241.

The prosecution's use of peremptory challenges to deliberately eliminate potential jurors, based on race, was challenged and struck down in *Swain v. Alabama*, 380 U.S. 202 (1965). The Court's rationale, unlike the Sixth Amendment application used regarding fair cross section, was based on the Equal Protection Clause of the Fourteenth Amendment. As such the Court's action was seen as a vindication of the rights of citizens in general (African Americans in particular) to serve on juries as determined in *Norris* and *Patterson*, and not just the individual right of the defendant. By relying on Equal Protection, the Court also invoked the classic analysis requirement of proof of intent to discriminate. The Court held that a defendant could make a *prima facie* case that the prosecution was violating equal protection by showing that " in case after case, whatever the circumstances, whatever the crime and whoever the defendant or the victim may be, [the prosecution] is responsible for the removal of Negroes who have been selected as qualified jurors by the jury commissioners and who have survived challenges for cause, with the result that no Negroes ever serve on petit juries." 380 U.S. at 223. This result, which required that a defendant have access to and prove the history of prosecutorial actions beyond that of his or her own case, in order to make a prima facie case of equal protection violation, was a crippling burden far beyond the resources of most defendants. The practical impossibility of showing all prosecutorial actions in all prior cases caused the United States Supreme Court to reconsider the matter in *Batson v. Kentucky* below.

BATSON V. KENTUCKY.
476 U.S. 79 (1986)

Opinion

Justice POWELL delivered the opinion of the Court.

This case requires us to reexamine that portion of *Swain v. Alabama*, 380 U.S. 202, 85 S.Ct. 824, 13 L.Ed.2d 759 (1965), concerning the evidentiary burden placed on a criminal defendant who claims that he has been denied equal protection through the State's use of peremptory challenges to exclude members of his race from the petit jury.

I

Petitioner, a black man, was indicted in Kentucky on charges of second-degree burglary and receipt of stolen goods. On the first day of trial in Jefferson Circuit Court, the judge conducted voir dire examination of the venire, excused certain jurors for cause, and permitted the parties to exercise peremptory challenges. The prosecutor used his peremptory challenges to strike all four black persons on the venire, and a jury composed only of white persons was selected. Defense counsel moved to discharge the jury before it was sworn on the ground that the prosecutor's removal of the black veniremen violated petitioner's rights under the Sixth and Fourteenth Amendments to a jury drawn from a cross section of the community, and under the Fourteenth Amendment to equal protection of the laws. Counsel requested a hearing on his motion. Without expressly ruling on the request for a hearing, the trial judge observed that the parties were entitled to use their peremptory challenges to "strike anybody they want to." The judge then denied petitioner's motion, reasoning that the cross-section requirement applies only to selection of the venire and not to selection of the petit jury itself.

The jury convicted petitioner on both counts. On appeal to the Supreme Court of Kentucky, petitioner pressed, among other claims, the argument concerning the prosecutor's use of peremptory challenges. Conceding that *Swain v. Alabama, supra*, apparently foreclosed an equal protection claim based solely on the prosecutor's conduct in this case, petitioner urged the court to follow decisions of other States, *People v. Wheeler*, 22 Cal.3d 258, 148 Cal.Rptr. 890, 583 P.2d 748 (1978); *Commonwealth v. Soares*, 377 Mass. 461, 387 N.E.2d 499, cert. denied, 444 U.S. 881, 100 S.Ct. 170, 62 L.Ed.2d 110 (1979), and to hold that such conduct violated his rights under the Sixth Amendment and § 11 of the Kentucky Constitution to a jury drawn from a cross section of the community. Petitioner also contended that the facts showed that the prosecutor had engaged in a "pattern" of discriminatory challenges in this case and established an equal protection violation under Swain.

The Supreme Court of Kentucky affirmed. In a single paragraph, the court declined petitioner's invitation to adopt the reasoning of *People v. Wheeler, supra*, and *Commonwealth v. Soares, supra*. The court observed that it recently had reaffirmed its reliance on Swain, and had held that a defendant alleging lack of a fair cross section must demonstrate systematic exclusion of a group of jurors from the venire. See *Commonwealth v. McFerron*, 680 S.W.2d 924 (1984). We granted certiorari, 471 U.S. 1052, 105 S.Ct. 2111, 85 L.Ed.2d 476 (1985), and now reverse.

II

In *Swain v. Alabama*, this Court recognized that a "State's purposeful or deliberate denial to Negroes on account of race of participation as jurors in the administration of justice violates the Equal Protection Clause." 380 U.S., at 203-204, 85 S.Ct., at 826-27. This principle has been "consistently and repeatedly" reaffirmed, id., at 204, 85 S.Ct., at 827, in numerous decisions of this Court both preceding and following Swain. We reaffirm the principle today.

A

More than a century ago, the Court decided that the State denies a black defendant equal protection of the laws when it puts him on trial before a jury from which members of his race have been purposefully excluded. *Strauder v. West Virginia*, 10 Otto 303, 100 U.S. 303, 25 L.Ed. 664 (1880). That decision laid the foundation for the Court's unceasing efforts to eradicate racial discrimination in the procedures used to select the venire from which individual jurors are drawn. In *Strauder*, the Court explained that the central concern of the recently ratified Fourteenth Amendment was to put an end to governmental discrimination on account of race. Id., at 306-307. Exclusion of black citizens from service as jurors constitutes a primary example of the evil the Fourteenth Amendment was designed to cure.

In holding that racial discrimination in jury selection offends the Equal Protection Clause, the Court in Strauder recognized, however, that a defendant has no right to a "petit jury composed in whole or in part of persons of his own race." Id., at 305. "The number of our races and nationalities stands in the way of evolution of such a conception" of the demand of equal protection. *Akins v. Texas*, 325 U.S. 398, 403, 65 S.Ct. 1276, 1279, 89 L.Ed. 1692 (1945).6 But the defendant does have the right to be tried by a jury whose members are selected pursuant to nondiscriminatory criteria. *Martin v. Texas*, 200 U.S. 316, 321, 26 S.Ct. 338, 339, 50 L.Ed. 497 (1906); *Ex parte Virginia*, 10 Otto 339, 100 U.S. 339, 345, 25 L.Ed. 676 345 (1880). The Equal Protection Clause guarantees the defendant that the State will not exclude members of his race from the jury venire on account of race, *Strauder*, supra, 100 U.S., at 305,7 or on the false assumption that members of his race as a group are not qualified to serve as jurors, see *Norris v. Alabama*, 294 U.S. 587, 599, 55 S.Ct. 579, 584, 79 L.Ed. 1074 (1935); *Neal v. Delaware*, 13 Otto 370, 397, 103 U.S. 370, 397, 26 L.Ed. 567 (1881).

Purposeful racial discrimination in selection of the venire violates a defendant's right to equal protection because it denies him the protection that a trial by jury is intended to secure. "The very idea of a jury is a body ... composed of the peers or equals of the person whose rights it is selected or summoned to determine; that is, of his neighbors, fellows, associates, persons having the same legal status in society as that which he holds." Strauder, supra, 100 U.S., at 308; see *Carter v. Jury Comm'n of Greene County*, 396 U.S. 320, 330, 90 S.Ct. 518, 524, 24 L.Ed.2d 549 (1970). The petit jury has occupied a central position in our system of justice by safeguarding a person accused of crime against the arbitrary exercise of power by prosecutor or judge. *Duncan v. Louisiana*, 391 U.S. 145, 156, 88 S.Ct. 1444, 1451, 20 L.Ed.2d 491 (1968). Those on the venire must be "indifferently chosen," to secure the defendant's right under the Fourteenth Amendment to "protection of life and liberty against race or color prejudice." *Strauder*, supra, 100 U.S., at 309.

Racial discrimination in selection of jurors harms not only the accused whose life or liberty they are summoned to try. Competence to serve as a juror ultimately depends on an assessment of individual qualifications and ability impartially to consider evidence presented at a trial. See

Thiel v. Southern Pacific Co., 328 U.S. 217, 223-224, 66 S.Ct. 984, 987-88, 90 L.Ed. 1181 (1946). A person's race simply "is unrelated to his fitness as a juror." Id., at 227, 66 S.Ct., at 989 (Frankfurter, J., dissenting). As long ago as Strauder, therefore, the Court recognized that by denying a person participation in jury service on account of his race, the State unconstitutionally discriminated against the excluded juror. 100 U.S., at 308; see *Carter v. Jury Comm'n of Greene County, supra*, 396 U.S., at 329-330, 90 S.Ct., at 523-524; *Neal v. Delaware*, supra, 103 U.S., at 386.

The harm from discriminatory jury selection extends beyond that inflicted on the defendant and the excluded juror to touch the entire community. Selection procedures that purposefully exclude black persons from juries undermine public confidence in the fairness of our system of justice. See *Ballard v. United States*, 329 U.S. 187, 195, 67 S.Ct. 261, 265, 91 L.Ed. 181 (1946); *McCray v. New York*, 461 U.S. 961, 968, 103 S.Ct. 2438, 2443, 77 L.Ed.2d 1322 (1983) (MARSHALL, J., dissenting from denial of certiorari). Discrimination within the judicial system is most pernicious because it is "a stimulant to that race prejudice which is an impediment to securing to [black citizens] that equal justice which the law aims to secure to all others." Strauder, 100 U.S., at 308.

B

In Strauder, the Court invalidated a state statute that provided that only white men could serve as jurors. *Id.*, at 305. We can be confident that no State now has such a law. The Constitution requires, however, that we look beyond the face of the statute defining juror qualifications and also consider challenged selection practices to afford "protection against action of the State through its administrative officers in effecting the prohibited discrimination." *Norris v. Alabama*, supra, 294 U.S., at 589, 55 S.Ct. 579, 580, 79 L.Ed. 1074; see *Hernandez v. Texas*, 347 U.S. 475, 478-479, 74 S.Ct. 667, 670-71, 98 L.Ed. 866 (1954); *Ex parte Virginia*, supra, 100 U.S., at 346-347. Thus, the Court has found a denial of equal protection where the procedures implementing a neutral statute operated to exclude persons from the venire on racial grounds, and has made clear that the Constitution prohibits all forms of purposeful racial discrimination in selection of jurors. While decisions of this Court have been concerned largely with discrimination during selection of the venire, the principles announced there also forbid discrimination on account of race in selection of the petit jury. Since the Fourteenth Amendment protects an accused throughout the proceedings bringing him to justice, *Hill v. Texas*, 316 U.S. 400, 406, 62 S.Ct. 1159, 1162, 86 L.Ed. 1559 (1942), the State may not draw up its jury lists pursuant to neutral procedures but then resort to discrimination at "other stages in the selection process," *Avery v. Georgia*, 345 U.S. 559, 562, 73 S.Ct. 891, 893, 97 L.Ed. 1244 (1953); see *McCray v. New York*, supra, 461 U.S., at 965, 968, 103 S.Ct., at 2440, 2443 (MARSHALL, J., dissenting from denial of certiorari); see also *Alexander v. Louisiana*, 405 U.S. 625, 632, 92 S.Ct. 1221, 1226, 31 L.Ed.2d 536 (1972).

Accordingly, the component of the jury selection process at issue here, the State's privilege to strike individual jurors through peremptory challenges, is subject to the commands of the Equal Protection Clause. Although a prosecutor ordinarily is entitled to exercise permitted peremptory challenges "for any reason at all, as long as that reason is related to his view concerning the outcome" of the case to be tried, *United States v. Robinson*, 421 F.Supp. 467, 473 (Conn.1976), mandamus granted sub nom. *United States v. Newman*, 549 F.2d 240 (CA2 1977), the Equal Protection Clause forbids the prosecutor to challenge potential jurors solely on account of their race or on the assumption that black jurors as a group will be unable impartially to consider the State's case against a black defendant.

III

The principles announced in Strauder never have been questioned in any subsequent decision of this Court. Rather, the Court has been called upon repeatedly to review the application of those principles to particular facts. A recurring question in these cases, as in any case alleging a violation of the Equal Protection Clause, was whether the defendant had met his burden of proving purposeful discrimination on the part of the State. *Whitus v. Georgia*, 385 U.S. 545, 550, 87 S.Ct. 643, 646-647, 17 L.Ed.2d 599 (1967); *Hernandez v. Texas, supra*, 347 U.S., at 478-481, 74 S.Ct., at 670-672; *Akins v. Texas*, 325 U.S., at 403-404, 65 S.Ct., at 1279; *Martin v. Texas*, 200 U.S. 316, 26 S.Ct. 338, 50 L.Ed. 497 (1906). That question also was at the heart of the portion of Swain v. Alabama we reexamine today.

A

Swain required the Court to decide, among other issues, whether a black defendant was denied equal protection by the State's exercise of peremptory challenges to exclude members of his race from the petit jury. 380 U.S., at 209-210, 85 S.Ct., at 830. The record in *Swain* showed that the prosecutor had used the State's peremptory challenges to strike the six black persons included on the petit jury venire. Id., at 210, 85 S.Ct., at 830. While rejecting the defendant's claim for failure to prove purposeful discrimination, the Court nonetheless indicated that the Equal Protection Clause placed some limits on the State's exercise of peremptory challenges. Id., at 222-224, 85 S.Ct., at 837-838.

The Court sought to accommodate the prosecutor's historical privilege of peremptory challenge free of judicial control, id., at 214-220, 85 S.Ct., at 832-836, and the constitutional prohibition on exclusion of persons from jury service on account of race, *id.*, at 222-224, 85 S.Ct., at 837-838. While the Constitution does not confer a right to peremptory challenges, id., at 219, 85 S.Ct., at 835 (citing *Stilson v. United States*, 250 U.S. 583, 586, 40 S.Ct. 28, 29-30, 63 L.Ed. 1154 (1919)), those challenges traditionally have been viewed as one means of assuring the selection of a qualified and unbiased jury, 380 U.S., at 219, 85 S.Ct., at 835.[15] To preserve the peremptory nature of the prosecutor's challenge, the Court in Swain declined to scrutinize his actions in a particular case by relying on a presumption that he properly exercised the State's challenges. Id., at 221-222, 85 S.Ct., at 836-837.

The Court went on to observe, however, that a State may not exercise its challenges in contravention of the Equal Protection Clause. It was impermissible for a prosecutor to use his challenges to exclude blacks from the jury "for reasons wholly unrelated to the outcome of the particular case on trial" or to deny to blacks "the same right and opportunity to participate in the administration of justice enjoyed by the white population." Id., at 224, 85 S.Ct., at 838. Accordingly, a black defendant could make out a prima facie case of purposeful discrimination on proof that the peremptory challenge system was "being perverted" in that manner. Ibid. For example, an inference of purposeful discrimination would be raised on evidence that a prosecutor, "in case after case, whatever the circumstances, whatever the crime and whoever the defendant or the victim may be, is responsible for the removal of Negroes who have been selected as qualified jurors by the jury commissioners and who have survived challenges for cause, with the result that no Negroes ever serve on petit juries." Id., at 223, 85 S.Ct., at 837. Evidence offered by the defendant in Swain did not meet that standard. While the defendant showed that prosecutors in the jurisdiction had exercised their strikes to exclude blacks from the jury, he offered no proof of the circumstances under which prosecutors were responsible for striking black jurors beyond the facts of his own case. Id., at 224-228, 85 S.Ct., at 838-840.

A number of lower courts following the teaching of Swain reasoned that proof of repeated striking of blacks over a number of cases was necessary to establish a violation of the Equal Protection Clause. Since this interpretation of Swain has placed on defendants a crippling burden of proof,prosecutors' peremptory challenges are now largely immune from constitutional scrutiny. For reasons that follow, we reject this evidentiary formulation as inconsistent with standards that have been developed since Swain for assessing a prima facie case under the Equal Protection Clause.

B

Since the decision in Swain, we have explained that our cases concerning selection of the venire reflect the general equal protection principle that the "invidious quality" of governmental action claimed to be racially discriminatory "must ultimately be traced to a racially discriminatory purpose." Washington v. Davis, 426 U.S. 229, 240, 96 S.Ct. 2040, 2048, 48 L.Ed.2d 597 (1976). As in any equal protection case, the "burden is, of course," on the defendant who alleges discriminatory selection of the venire "to prove the existence of purposeful discrimination." Whitus v. Georgia, 385 U.S., at 550, 87 S.Ct., at 646-47 (citing Tarrance v. Florida, 188 U.S. 519, 23 S.Ct. 402, 47 L.Ed. 572 (1903)). In deciding if the defendant has carried his burden of persuasion, a court must undertake "a sensitive inquiry into such circumstantial and direct evidence of intent as may be available." *Arlington Heights v. Metropolitan Housing Development Corp.*, 429 U.S. 252, 266, 97 S.Ct. 555, 564, 50 L.Ed.2d 450 (1977). Circumstantial evidence of invidious intent may include proof of disproportionate impact. *Washington v. Davis*, 426 U.S., at 242, 96 S.Ct., at 2049. We have observed that under some circumstances proof of discriminatory impact "may for all practical purposes demonstrate unconstitutionality because in various circumstances the discrimination is very difficult to explain on nonracial grounds." Ibid. For example, "total or seriously dispro-portionate exclusion of Negroes from jury venires," ibid., "is itself such an 'unequal application of the law ... as to show intentional discrimination,' " id., at 241, 96 S.Ct., at 2048 (quoting *Akins v. Texas*, 325 U.S., at 404, 65 S.Ct., at 1279).

Moreover, since Swain, we have recognized that a black defendant alleging that members of his race have been impermissibly excluded from the venire may make out a prima facie case of purposeful discrimination by showing that the totality of the relevant facts gives rise to an inference of discriminatory purpose. *Washington v. Davis*, supra, 426 U.S., at 239-242, 96 S.Ct., at 2047-49. Once the defendant makes the requisite showing, the burden shifts to the State to explain adequately the racial exclusion. *Alexander v. Louisiana*, 405 U.S., at 632, 92 S.Ct., at 1226. The State cannot meet this burden on mere general assertions that its officials did not discrimi-nate or that they properly performed their official duties. See *Alexander v. Louisiana*, supra, 405 U.S., at 632, 92 S.Ct., at 1226; *Jones v. Georgia*, 389 U.S. 24, 25, 88 S.Ct. 4, 5, 19 L.Ed.2d 25 (1967). Rather, the State must demonstrate that "permissible racially neutral selection criteria and pro-cedures have produced the monochromatic result." *Alexander v. Louisiana, supra*, at 632, 92 S.Ct., at 1226; see *Washington v. Davis, supra*, 426 U.S., at 241, 96 S.Ct., at 2048.18

The showing necessary to establish a prima facie case of purposeful discrimination in selec-tion of the venire may be discerned in this Court's decisions. E.g., *Castaneda v. Partida*, 430 U.S. 482, 494-495, 97 S.Ct. 1272, 1280, 51 L.Ed.2d 498 (1977); *Alexander v. Louisiana, supra*, 405 U.S., at 631-632, 92 S.Ct., at 1225-1226. The defendant initially must show that he is a member of a racial group capable of being singled out for differential treatment. *Castaneda v. Partida*, supra, 430 U.S., at 494, 97 S.Ct., at 1280. In combination with that evidence, a defendant may then make a prima facie case by proving that in the particular jurisdiction members of his race have not been summoned for jury service over an extended period of time. *Id.*, at 494, 97 S.Ct., at 1280. Proof of systematic exclusion from the venire raises an inference of purposeful discrimination because the "result bespeaks discrimination." *Hernandez v. Texas*, 347 U.S., at 482, 74 S.Ct., at 672-73; see *Arlington Heights v. Metropolitan Housing Development Corp., supra*, 429 U.S., at 266, 97 S.Ct., at 564.

Since the ultimate issue is whether the State has discriminated in selecting the defendant's venire, however, the defendant may establish a prima facie case "in other ways than by evidence of long-continued unexplained absence" of members of his race "from many panels." *Cassell v. Texas*, 339 U.S. 282, 290, 70 S.Ct. 629, 633, 94 L.Ed. 839 (1950) (plurality opinion). In cases involv-ing the venire, this Court has found a prima facie case on proof that members of the defendant's race were substantially underrepresented on the venire from which his jury was drawn, and that the venire was selected under a practice providing "the opportunity for discrimination." *Whitus v. Georgia, supra,* 385 U.S., at 552, 87 S.Ct., at 647; see *Castaneda v. Partida, supra,* 430 U.S., at 494, 97 S.Ct., at 1280; *Washington v. Davis, supra,* 426 U.S., at 241, 96 S.Ct., at 2048; *Alexander v. Louisiana, supra,* 405 U.S., at 629-631, 92 S.Ct., at 1224-26. This combination of factors raises the necessary inference of purposeful discrimination because the Court has declined to attribute to chance the absence of black citizens on a particular jury array where the selection mechanism is subject to abuse. When circumstances suggest the need, the trial court must undertake a "factual inquiry" that "takes into account all possible explanatory factors" in the particular case. *Alexander v. Louisiana, supra,* at 630, 92 S.Ct., at 1225.

Thus, since the decision in *Swain,* this Court has recognized that a defendant may make a prima facie showing of purposeful racial discrimination in selection of the venire by relying solely on the facts concerning its selection in his case. These decisions are in accordance with the proposition, articulated in *Arlington Heights v. Metropolitan Housing Department Corp.,* that "a consistent pattern of official racial discrimination" is not "a necessary predicate to a violation of the Equal Protection Clause. A single invidiously discriminatory governmental act" is not "immunized by the absence of such discrimination in the making of other comparable decisions." 429 U.S., at 266, n. 14, 97 S.Ct., at 564, n. 14. For evidentiary requirements to dictate that "several must suffer discrimination" before one could object, *McCray v. New York,* 461 U.S., at 965, 103 S.Ct., at 2440 (MARSHALL, J., dissenting from denial of certiorari), would be inconsistent with the promise of equal protection to all.

C

The standards for assessing a prima facie case in the context of discriminatory selection of the venire have been fully articulated since *Swain.* See *Castaneda v. Partida, supra,* 430 U.S., at 494-495, 97 S.Ct., at 1280; *Washington v. Davis,* 426 U.S., at 241-242, 96 S.Ct., at 2048-2049; *Alexander v. Louisiana, supra,* 405 U.S., at 629-631, 92 S.Ct., at 1224-1226. These principles support our conclusion that a defendant may establish a prima facie case of purposeful discrimination in selection of the petit jury solely on evidence concerning the prosecutor's exercise of peremptory challenges at the defendant's trial. To establish such a case, the defendant first must show that he is a member of a cognizable racial group, *Castaneda v. Partida,* supra, 430 U.S., at 494, 97 S.Ct., at 1280, and that the prosecutor has exercised peremptory challenges to remove from the venire members of the defendant's race. Second, the defendant is entitled to rely on the fact, as to which there can be no dispute, that peremptory challenges constitute a jury selection practice that permits "those to discriminate who are of a mind to discriminate." *Avery v. Georgia,* 345 U.S., at 562, 73 S.Ct., at 892. Finally, the defendant must show that these facts and any other relevant circumstances raise an inference that the prosecutor used that practice to exclude the veniremen from the petit jury on account of their race. This combination of factors in the empaneling of the petit jury, as in the selection of the venire, raises the necessary inference of purposeful discrimination.

In deciding whether the defendant has made the requisite showing, the trial court should consider all relevant circumstances. For example, a "pattern" of strikes against black jurors included in the particular venire might give rise to an inference of discrimination. Similarly, the prosecutor's questions and statements during voir dire examination and in exercising his challenges may support or refute an inference of discriminatory purpose. These examples are merely illustrative. We have confidence that trial judges, experienced in supervising voir dire, will be able to decide if the circumstances concerning the prosecutor's use of peremptory challenges creates a prima facie case of discrimination against black jurors.

Once the defendant makes a prima facie showing, the burden shifts to the State to come forward with a neutral explanation for challenging black jurors. Though this requirement imposes a limitation in some cases on the full peremptory character of the historic challenge, we emphasize that the prosecutor's explanation need not rise to the level justifying exercise of a challenge for cause. See *McCray v. Abrams*, 750 F.2d, at 1132; *Booker v. Jabe*, 775 F.2d 762, 773 (CA6 1985), cert. pending, No. 85-1028. But the prosecutor may not rebut the defendant's prima facie case of discrimination by stating merely that he challenged jurors of the defendant's race on the assumption-or his intuitive judgment-that they would be partial to the defendant because of their shared race. Cf. *Norris v. Alabama*, 294 U.S., at 598-599, 55 S.Ct., at 583-84; see *Thompson v. United States*, 469 U.S. 1024, 1026, 105 S.Ct. 443, 445, 83 L.Ed.2d 369 (1984) (BRENNAN, J., dissenting from denial of certiorari). Just as the Equal Protection Clause forbids the States to exclude black persons from the venire on the assumption that blacks as a group are unqualified to serve as jurors, supra, at 1716, so it forbids the States to strike black veniremen on the assumption that they will be biased in a particular case simply because the defendant is black. The core guarantee of equal protection, ensuring citizens that their State will not discriminate on account of race, would be meaningless were we to approve the exclusion of jurors on the basis of such assumptions, which arise solely from the jurors' race. Nor may the prosecutor rebut the defendant's case merely by denying that he had a discriminatory motive or "affirm[ing] [his] good faith in making individual selections." *Alexander v. Louisiana*, 405 U.S., at 632, 92 S.Ct., at 1226. If these general assertions were accepted as rebutting a defendant's prima facie case, the Equal Protection Clause "would be but a vain and illusory requirement." *Norris v. Alabama*, *supra*, 294 U.S. at 598, 55 S.Ct., at 583-84. The prosecutor therefore must articulate a neutral explanation related to the particular case to be tried. The trial court then will have the duty to determine if the defendant has established purposeful discrimination.

IV

The State contends that our holding will eviscerate the fair trial values served by the peremptory challenge. Conceding that the Constitution does not guarantee a right to peremptory challenges and that Swain did state that their use ultimately is subject to the strictures of equal protection, the State argues that the privilege of unfettered exercise of the challenge is of vital importance to the criminal justice system.

While we recognize, of course, that the peremptory challenge occupies an important position in our trial procedures, we do not agree that our decision today will undermine the contribution the challenge generally makes to the administration of justice. The reality of practice, amply reflected in many state- and federal-court opinions, shows that the challenge may be, and unfortunately at times has been, used to discriminate against black jurors. By requiring trial courts to be sensitive to the racially discriminatory use of peremptory challenges, our decision enforces the mandate of equal protection and furthers the ends of justice. In view of the heterogeneous population of our Nation, public respect for our criminal justice system and the rule of law will be strengthened if we ensure that no citizen is disqualified from jury service because of his race.

Nor are we persuaded by the State's suggestion that our holding will create serious administrative difficulties. In those States applying a version of the evidentiary standard we recognize today, courts have not experienced serious administrative burdens, and the peremptory challenge system has survived. We decline, however, to formulate particular procedures to be followed upon a defendant's timely objection to a prosecutor's challenges.

V

In this case, petitioner made a timely objection to the prosecutor's removal of all black persons on the venire. Because the trial court flatly rejected the objection without requiring the prosecutor to give an explanation for his action, we remand this case for further proceedings. If the trial court decides that the facts establish, prima facie, purposeful discrimination and the prosecutor does not come forward with a neutral explanation for his action, our precedents require that petitioner's conviction be reversed. E.g., *Whitus v. Georgia*, 385 U.S., at 549-550, 87 S.Ct., at 646-47; *Hernandez v. Texas*, 347 U.S., at 482, 74 S.Ct., at 672-673; *Patton v. Mississippi*, 332 U.S., at 469, 68 S.Ct., at 187.25

It is so ordered.

POWERS V. OHIO.

499 U.S. 400 (1991)

Justice KENNEDY delivered the opinion of the Court.

Jury service is an exercise of responsible citizenship by all members of the community, including those who otherwise might not have the opportunity to contribute to our civic life. Congress recognized this over a century ago in the Civil Rights Act of 1875, which made it a criminal offense to exclude persons from jury service on account of their race. See 18 U.S.C. § 243. In a trilogy of cases decided soon after enactment of this prohibition, our Court confirmed the validity of the statute, as well as the broader constitutional imperative of race neutrality in jury selection. See *Strauder v. West Virginia*, 100 U.S. 303, 25 L.Ed. 664 (1880); *Virginia v. Rives*, 100 U.S. 313, 25 L.Ed. 667 (1880); *Ex parte Virginia*, 100 U.S. 339, 25 L.Ed. 676 (1880). In the many times we have confronted the issue since those cases, we have not questioned the premise that racial discrimination in the qualification or selection of jurors offends the dignity of persons and the integrity of the courts. Despite the clarity of these commands to eliminate the taint of racial discrimination in the administration of justice, allegations of bias in the jury selection process persist. In this case, petitioner alleges race discrimination in the prosecution's use of peremptory challenges. Invoking the Equal Protection Clause and federal statutory law, and relying upon well-established principles of standing, we hold that a criminal defendant may object to race-based exclusions of jurors effected through peremptory challenges whether or not the defendant and the excluded juror share the same races.

I

Petitioner Larry Joe Powers, a white man, was indicted in Franklin County, Ohio, on two counts of aggravated murder and one count of attempted aggravated murder. Each count also included a separate allegation that petitioner had a firearm while committing the offense. Powers pleaded not guilty and invoked his right to a jury trial.

In the jury selection process, Powers objected when the prosecutor exercised his first peremptory challenge to remove a black venireperson. Powers requested the trial court to compel the prosecutor to explain, on the record, his reasons for excluding a black person. The trial court denied the request and excused the juror. The State proceeded to use nine more peremptory challenges, six of which removed black venirepersons from the jury. Each time the prosecution challenged a black prospective juror, Powers renewed his objections, citing our decision in *Batson v. Kentucky*, 476 U.S. 79, 106 S.Ct. 1712, 90 L.Ed.2d 69 (1986). His objections were overruled. The record does not indicate that race was somehow implicated in the crime or the trial; nor does it reveal whether any black persons sat on petitioner's petit jury or if any of the nine jurors petitioner excused by peremptory challenges were black persons.

The empaneled jury convicted Powers on counts of murder, aggravated murder, and attempted aggravated murder, each with the firearm specifications, and the trial court sentenced him to a term of imprisonment of 53 years to life. Powers appealed his conviction to the Ohio Court of Appeals, contending that the prosecutor's discriminatory use of peremptories violated the Sixth Amendment's guarantee of a fair cross section in his petit jury, the Fourteenth Amendment's Equal Protection Clause, and Article I, §§ 10 and 16, of the Ohio Constitution. Powers contended that his own race was irrelevant to the right to object to the prosecution's peremptory challenges. The Court of Appeals affirmed the conviction, and the Supreme Court of Ohio dismissed Powers' appeal on the ground that it presented no substantial constitutional question.

Petitioner sought review before us, renewing his Sixth Amendment fair cross section and Fourteenth Amendment equal protection claims. While the petition for certiorari was pending, we decided *Holland v. Illinois*, 493 U.S. 474, 110 S.Ct. 803, 107 L.Ed.2d 905 (1990). In *Holland* it was alleged the prosecution had used its peremptory challenges to exclude from the jury members of a race other than the defendant's. We held the Sixth Amendment did not restrict the exclusion of a racial group at the peremptory challenge stage. Five members of the Court there said a defendant might be able to make the objection on equal protection grounds. See *id.*, at 488, 110 S.Ct., at 811 (KENNEDY, J., concurring); id., at 490, 110 S.Ct., at 812 (MARSHALL, J., joined by Brennan and BLACKMUN, JJ., dissenting); *id.*, at 504, 110 S.Ct., at 820 (STEVENS, J., dissenting). After our decision in *Holland*, we granted Powers' petition for certiorari limited to the question whether, based on the Equal Protection Clause, a white defendant may object to the prosecution's peremptory challenges of black venirepersons. 493 U.S. 1068, 110 S.Ct. 1109, 107 L.Ed.2d 1017 (1990). We now reverse and remand.

II

For over a century, this Court has been unyielding in its position that a defendant is denied equal protection of the laws when tried before a jury from which members of his or her race have been excluded by the State's purposeful conduct. "The Equal Protection Clause guarantees the defendant that the State will not exclude members of his race from the jury venire on account of race, *Strauder*, [100 U.S.,] at 305 [25 L.Ed. 664], or on the false assumption that members of his race as a group are not qualified to serve as jurors, see *Norris v. Alabama*, 294 U.S. 587, 599 [55 S.Ct. 579, 584, 79 L.Ed. 1074] (1935); *Neal v. Delaware*, 103 U.S. 370, 397 [26 L.Ed. 567] (1881)." *Batson, supra,* 476 U.S., at 86, 106 S.Ct., at 1717 (footnote omitted). Although a defendant has no right to a "petit jury composed in whole or in part of persons of [the defendant's] own race," *Strauder*, 100 U.S., at 305, 25 L.Ed. 664, he or she does have the right to be tried by a jury whose members are selected by nondiscriminatory criteria.

We confronted the use of peremptory challenges as a device to exclude jurors because of their race for the first time in *Swain v. Alabama*, 380 U.S. 202, 85 S.Ct. 824, 13 L.Ed.2d 759 (1965). Swain involved a challenge to the so-called struck jury system, a procedure designed to allow both the prosecution and the defense a maximum number of peremptory challenges. The venire in noncapital cases started with about 35 potential jurors, from which the defense and the prosecution alternated with strikes until a petit panel of 12 jurors remained. The defendant in *Swain*, who was himself black, alleged that the prosecutor had used the struck jury system and its numerous peremptory challenges for the purpose of excluding black persons from his petit jury. In finding that no constitutional harm was alleged, the Court in Swain sought to reconcile the command of racial neutrality in jury selection with the utility, and the tradition, of peremptory challenges. The Court declined to permit an equal protection claim premised on a pattern of jury strikes in a particular case, but acknowledged that proof of systematic exclusion of black persons through the use of peremptories over a period of time might establish an equal protection violation. Id., at 222-228, 85 S.Ct., at 836-840.

We returned to the problem of a prosecutor's discriminatory use of peremptory challenges in *Batson v. Kentucky*. There, we considered a situation similar to the one before us today, but with one exception: Batson, the defendant who complained that black persons were being excluded from his petit jury, was himself black. During the voir dire examination of the venire for Batson's trial, the prosecutor used his peremptory challenges to strike all four black persons on the venire, resulting in a petit jury composed only of white persons. Batson's counsel moved without success to discharge the jury before it was empaneled on the ground that the prosecutor's removal of black venirepersons violated his rights under the Sixth and Fourteenth Amendments. Relying upon the Equal Protection Clause alone, we overruled Swain to the extent it foreclosed objections to the discriminatory use of peremptories in the course of a specific trial. 476 U.S., at 90-93, 106 S.Ct., at 1719-1721. In *Batson* we held that a defendant can raise an equal protection challenge to the use of peremptories at his own trial by showing that the prosecutor used them for the purpose of excluding members of the defendant's race. Id., at 96, 106 S.Ct., at 1722.

The State contends that our holding in the case now before us must be limited to the circumstances prevailing in *Batson* and that in equal protection analysis the race of the objecting defendant constitutes a relevant precondition for a Batson challenge. Because Powers is white, the State argues, he cannot object to the exclusion of black prospective jurors. This limitation on a defendant's right to object conforms neither with our accepted rules of standing to raise a constitutional claim nor with the substantive guarantees of the Equal Protection Clause and the policies underlying federal statutory law.

In *Batson*, we spoke of the harm caused when a defendant is tried by a tribunal from which members of his own race have been excluded. But we did not limit our discussion in *Batson* to that one aspect of the harm caused by the violation. *Batson* "was designed 'to serve multiple ends,'" only one of which was to protect individual defendants from discrimination in the selection of jurors. *Allen v. Hardy*, 478 U.S. 255, 259, 106 S.Ct. 2878, 2880, 92 L.Ed.2d 199 (1986) (per curiam) (quoting *Brown v. Louisiana*, 447 U.S. 323, 329, 100 S.Ct. 2214, 2220, 65 L.Ed.2d 159 (1980)). *Batson* recognized that a prosecutor's discriminatory use of peremptory challenges harms the excluded jurors and the community at large. 476 U.S., at 87, 106 S.Ct., at 1718.

The opportunity for ordinary citizens to participate in the administration of justice has long been recognized as one of the principal justifications for retaining the jury system. See *Duncan v. Louisiana*, 391 U.S. 145, 147-158, 88 S.Ct. 1444, 1446-1452, 20 L.Ed.2d 491 (1968). In *Balzac v. Porto Rico*, 258 U.S. 298, 42 S.Ct. 343, 66 L.Ed. 627 (1922), Chief Justice Taft wrote for the Court:

> "The jury system postulates a conscious duty of participation in the machinery of justice.... One of its greatest benefits is in the security it gives the people that they, as jurors actual or possible, being part of the judicial system of the country can prevent its arbitrary use or abuse." *Id.*, at 310, 42 S.Ct., at 347.

And, over 150 years ago, Alexis de Tocqueville remarked:

> "[T]he institution of the jury raises the people itself, or at least a class of citizens, to the bench of judicial authority [and] invests the people, or that class of citizens, with the direction of society.
> . . . . .

> "... The jury ... invests each citizen with a kind of magistracy; it makes them all feel the duties which they are bound to discharge towards society; and the part which they take in the Government. By obliging men to turn their attention to affairs which are not exclusively their own, it rubs off that individual egotism which is the rust of society.
> . . . . .

> "I do not know whether the jury is useful to those who are in litigation; but I am certain it is highly beneficial to those who decide the litigation; and I look upon it as one of the most efficacious means for the education of the people which society can employ." 1 Democracy in America 334-337 (Schocken 1st ed. 1961).

Jury service preserves the democratic element of the law, as it guards the rights of the parties and ensures continued acceptance of the laws by all of the people. See *Green v. United States*, 356 U.S. 165, 215, 78 S.Ct. 632, 659, 2 L.Ed.2d 672 (1958) (Black, J., dissenting). It "affords ordinary citizens a valuable opportunity to participate in a process of government, an experience foster-ing, one hopes, a respect for law." *Duncan, supra,* 391 U.S., at 187, 88 S.Ct., at 1469 (Harlan, J., dissenting). Indeed, with the exception of voting, for most citizens the honor and privilege of jury duty is their most significant opportunity to participate in the democratic process.

[2] While States may prescribe relevant qualifications for their jurors, see *Carter v. Jury Comm'n of Greene County,* 396 U.S. 320, 332, 90 S.Ct. 518, 524, 24 L.Ed.2d 549 (1970), a member of the community may not be excluded from jury service on account of his or her race. See *Batson, supra,* 476 U.S., at 84, 106 S.Ct., at 1716; *Swain,* 380 U.S., at 203-204, 85 S.Ct., at 826-827; *Carter, supra,* 396 U.S., at 329-330, 90 S.Ct., at 523; *Thiel v. Southern Pacific Co.,* 328 U.S. 217, 220-221, 66 S.Ct. 984, 985-986, 90 L.Ed. 1181 (1946); *Neal v. Delaware,* 103 U.S. 370, 386, 26 L.Ed. 567 (1881); *Strauder,* 100 U.S., at 308. "Whether jury service be deemed a right, a privilege, or a duty, the State may no more extend it to some of its citizens and deny it to others on racial grounds than it may invidiously discriminate in the offering and withholding of the elective franchise." Carter, supra, 396 U.S., at 330, 90 S.Ct., at 523. Over a century ago, we recognized that:

> "The very fact that [members of a particular race] are singled out and expressly denied ... all
> right to participate in the administration of the law, as jurors, because of their color, though they
> are citizens, and may be in other respects fully qualified, is practically a brand upon them, affixed
> by the law, an assertion of their inferiority, and a stimulant to that race prejudice which is an
> impediment to securing to individuals of the race that equal justice which the law aims to secure
> to all others." Strauder, supra, 100 U.S., at 308.

Discrimination in the jury selection process is the subject of a federal criminal prohibition, and has been since Congress enacted the Civil Rights Act of 1875. The prohibition has been codified at 18 U.S.C. § 243, which provides:

> "No citizen possessing all other qualifications which are or may be prescribed by law shall be
> disqualified for service as grand or petit juror in any court of the United States, or of any State
> on account of race, color, or previous condition of servitude; and whoever, being an officer or
> other person charged with any duty in the selection or summoning of jurors, excludes or fails to
> summon any citizen for such cause, shall be fined not more than $5,000."

In *Peters v. Kiff,* 407 U.S. 493, 92 S.Ct. 2163, 33 L.Ed.2d 83 (1972), Justice WHITE spoke of "the strong statutory policy of § 243, which reflects the central concern of the Fourteenth Amendment." Id., at 507, 92 S.Ct., at 2170 (opinion concurring in judgment). The Court permit-ted a white defendant to challenge the systematic exclusion of black persons from grand and petit juries. While Peters did not produce a single majority opinion, six of the Justices agreed that racial discrimination in the jury selection process cannot be tolerated and that the race of the defendant has no relevance to his or her standing to raise the claim. See *id.*, at 504-505, 92 S.Ct., at 2169-2170 (opinion of MARSHALL, J.); id., at 506-507, 92 S.Ct., at 2170-2171 (WHITE, J., concurring in judgment).

Racial discrimination in the selection of jurors in the context of an individual trial violates these same prohibitions. A State "may not draw up its jury lists pursuant to neutral procedures but then resort to discrimination at 'other stages in the selection process.' " *Batson*, 476 U.S., at 88, 106 S.Ct., at 1718 (quoting *Avery v. Georgia*, 345 U.S. 559, 562, 73 S.Ct. 891, 892, 97 L.Ed. 1244 (1953)). We so held in *Batson*, and reaffirmed that holding in *Holland*. See 493 U.S., at 479, 110 S.Ct., at 806-807. In *Holland*, the Court held that a defendant could not rely on the Sixth Amendment to object to the exclusion of members of any distinctive group at the peremptory challenge stage. We noted that the peremptory challenge procedure has acceptance in our legal tradition. See id., at 481, 110 S.Ct., at 808. On this reasoning we declined to permit an objection to the peremptory challenge of a juror on racial grounds as a Sixth Amendment matter. As the Holland Court made explicit, however, racial exclusion of prospective jurors violates the over-riding command of the Equal Protection Clause, and "race-based exclusion is no more permissible at the individual petit jury stage than at the venire stage." Id., at 479, 110 S.Ct., at 807.

We hold that the Equal Protection Clause prohibits a prosecutor from using the State's peremptory challenges to exclude otherwise qualified and unbiased persons from the petit jury solely by reason of their race, a practice that forecloses a significant opportunity to participate in civic life. An individual juror does not have a right to sit on any particular petit jury, but he or she does possess the right not to be excluded from one on account of race.

It is suggested that no particular stigma or dishonor results if a prosecutor uses the raw fact of skin color to determine the objectivity or qualifications of a juror. We do not believe a victim of the classification would endorse this view; the assumption that no stigma or dishonor attaches contravenes accepted equal protection principles. Race cannot be a proxy for determining juror bias or competence. "A person's race simply 'is unrelated to his fitness as a juror.' " *Batson, supra*, 476 U.S., at 87, 106 S.Ct., at 1718 (quoting *Thiel v. Southern Pacific Co., supra*, 328 U.S., at 227, 66 S.Ct., at 989 (Frankfurter, J., dissenting)). We may not accept as a defense to racial discrimination the very stereotype the law condemns.

We reject as well the view that race-based peremptory challenges survive equal protection scrutiny because members of all races are subject to like treatment, which is to say that white jurors are subject to the same risk of peremptory challenges based on race as are all other jurors. The suggestion that racial classifications may survive when visited upon all persons is no more authoritative today than the case which advanced the theorem, *Plessy v. Ferguson*, 163 U.S. 537, 16 S.Ct. 1138, 41 L.Ed. 256 (1896). This idea has no place in our modern equal protection jurisprudence. It is axiomatic that racial classifications do not become legitimate on the assumption that all persons suffer them in equal degree. *Loving v. Virginia*, 388 U.S. 1, 87 S.Ct. 1817, 18 L.Ed.2d 1010 (1967).

III

We must consider whether a criminal defendant has standing to raise the equal protection rights of a juror excluded from service in violation of these principles. In the ordinary course, a litigant must assert his or her own legal rights and interests, and cannot rest a claim to relief on the legal rights or interests of third parties. *Department of Labor v. Triplett*, 494 U.S. 715, 720, 110 S.Ct. 1428, 1431, 108 L.Ed.2d 701 (1990); *Singleton v. Wulff*, 428 U.S. 106, 96 S.Ct. 2868, 49 L.Ed.2d 826 (1976). This fundamental restriction on our authority admits of certain, limited exceptions. We have recognized the right of litigants to bring actions on behalf of third parties, provided three important criteria are satisfied: The litigant must have suffered an "injury in fact," thus giving him or her a "sufficiently concrete interest" in the outcome of the issue in dispute, id., at 112, 96 S.Ct., at 2873; the litigant must have a close relation to the third party, id., at 113-114, 96 S.Ct., at 2873-2874; and there must exist some hindrance to the third party's ability to protect his or her own interests. Id., at 115-116, 96 S.Ct., at 2874-2875. See also *Craig v. Boren*, 429 U.S. 190, 97 S.Ct. 451, 50 L.Ed.2d 397 (1976). These criteria have been satisfied in cases where we have permitted criminal defendants to challenge their convictions by raising the rights of third parties. See, e.g., *Eisenstadt v. Baird*, 405 U.S. 438, 92 S.Ct. 1029, 31 L.Ed.2d 349 (1972); *Griswold v. Connecticut*, 381 U.S. 479, 85 S.Ct. 1678, 14 L.Ed.2d 510 (1965); see also *McGowan v. Maryland*, 366 U.S. 420, 81 S.Ct. 1101, 6 L.Ed.2d 393 (1961). By similar reasoning, we have permitted litigants to raise third-party rights in order to prevent possible future prosecution. See, e.g., *Doe v. Bolton*, 410 U.S. 179, 93 S.Ct. 739, 35 L.Ed.2d 201 (1973).

The discriminatory use of peremptory challenges by the prosecution causes a criminal defendant cognizable injury, and the defendant has a concrete interest in challenging the practice. See *Allen v. Hardy*, 478 U.S., at 259, 106 S.Ct., at 2880 (recognizing a defendant's interest in "neutral jury selection procedures"). This is not because the individual jurors dismissed by the prosecution may have been predisposed to favor the defendant; if that were true, the jurors might have been excused for cause. Rather, it is because racial discrimination in the selection of jurors "casts doubt on the integrity of the judicial process," *Rose v. Mitchell*, 443 U.S. 545, 556, 99 S.Ct. 2993, 3000, 61 L.Ed.2d 739 (1979), and places the fairness of a criminal proceeding in doubt.

The jury acts as a vital check against the wrongful exercise of power by the State and its prosecutors. *Batson*, 476 U.S., at 86, 106 S.Ct., at 1717. The intrusion of racial discrimination into the jury selection process damages both the fact and the perception of this guarantee. "Jury selection is the primary means by which a court may enforce a defendant's right to be tried by a jury free from ethnic, racial, or political prejudice, *Rosales-Lopez v. United States*, 451 U.S. 182, 188 [101 S.Ct. 1629, 1634, 68 L.Ed.2d 22] (1981); *Ham v. South Carolina*, 409 U.S. 524 [93 S.Ct. 848, 35 L.Ed.2d 46] (1973); *Dennis v. United States*, 339 U.S. 162 [70 S.Ct. 519, 94 L.Ed. 734] (1950), or predisposition about the defendant's culpability, *Irvin v. Dowd*, 366 U.S. 717 [81 S.Ct. 1639, 6 L.Ed.2d 751] (1961)." *Gomez v. United States,* 490 U.S. 858, 873, 109 S.Ct. 2237, 2246-2247, 104 L.Ed.2d 923

(1989). Active discrimination by a prosecutor during this process condones violations of the United States Constitution within the very institution entrusted with its enforcement, and so invites cynicism respecting the jury's neutrality and its obligation to adhere to the law. The cynicism may be aggravated if race is implicated in the trial, either in a direct way as with an alleged racial motivation of the defendant or a victim, or in some more subtle manner as by casting doubt upon the credibility or dignity of a witness, or even upon the standing or due regard of an attorney who appears in the cause.

Unlike the instances where a defendant seeks to object to the introduction of evidence obtained illegally from a third party, see, e.g., *United States v. Payner*, 447 U.S. 727, 100 S.Ct. 2439, 65 L.Ed.2d 468 (1980), here petitioner alleges that the primary constitutional violation occurred during the trial itself. A prosecutor's wrongful exclusion of a juror by a race-based peremptory challenge is a constitutional violation committed in open court at the outset of the proceedings. The overt wrong, often apparent to the entire jury panel, casts doubt over the obligation of the parties, the jury, and indeed the court to adhere to the law throughout the trial of the cause. The voir dire phase of the trial represents the "jurors' first introduction to the substantive factual and legal issues in a case." *Gomez, supra*, 490 U.S., at 874, 109 S.Ct., at 2247. The influence of the voir dire process may persist through the whole course of the trial proceedings. Ibid. If the defendant has no right to object to the prosecutor's improper exclusion of jurors, and if the trial court has no duty to make a prompt inquiry when the defendant shows, by adequate grounds, a likelihood of impropriety in the exercise of a challenge, there arise legitimate doubts that the jury has been chosen by proper means. The composition of the trier of fact itself is called in question, and the irregularity may pervade all the proceedings that follow.

The purpose of the jury system is to impress upon the criminal defendant and the community as a whole that a verdict of conviction or acquittal is given in accordance with the law by persons who are fair. The verdict will not be accepted or understood in these terms if the jury is chosen by unlawful means at the outset. Upon these considerations, we find that a criminal defendant suffers a real injury when the prosecutor excludes jurors at his or her own trial on account of race.

We noted in Singleton that in certain circumstances "the relationship between the litigant and the third party may be such that the former is fully, or very nearly, as effective a proponent of the right as the latter." 428 U.S., at 115, 96 S.Ct., at 2874. Here, the relation between petitioner and the excluded jurors is as close as, if not closer than, those we have recognized to convey third-party standing in our prior cases. See, e.g., *Griswold v. Connecticut, supra* (Planned Parenthood official and a licensed physician can raise the constitutional rights of contraceptive users with whom they had professional relationships); Craig, supra (licensed beer vendor has standing to raise the equal protection claim of a male customer challenging a statutory scheme prohibiting the sale of beer to males under the age of 21 and to females under the age of 18); *Department of Labor v. Triplett*, 494 U.S. 715, 110 S.Ct. 1428, 108 L.Ed.2d 701 (1990) (attorney may challenge an attorney's fees restriction by asserting the due process rights of the client). Voir dire permits a party to establish a relation, if not a bond of trust, with the jurors. This relation continues throughout the entire trial and may in some cases extend to the sentencing as well.

Both the excluded juror and the criminal defendant have a common interest in eliminating racial discrimination from the courtroom. A venireperson excluded from jury service because of race suffers a profound personal humiliation heightened by its public character. The rejected juror may lose confidence in the court and its verdicts, as may the defendant if his or her objections cannot be heard. This congruence of interests makes it necessary and appropriate for the defendant to raise the rights of the juror. And, there can be no doubt that petitioner will be a motivated, effective advocate for the excluded venirepersons' rights. Petitioner has much at stake in proving that his jury was improperly constituted due to an equal protection violation, for we have recognized that discrimination in the jury selection process may lead to the reversal of a conviction. See *Batson*, 476 U.S., at 100, 106 S.Ct., at 1725; *Vasquez v. Hillery*, 474 U.S. 254, 264, 106 S.Ct. 617, 623, 88 L.Ed.2d 598 (1986); *Rose v. Mitchell*, 443 U.S., at 551, 99 S.Ct., at 2997-2998; *Cassell v. Texas*, 339 U.S. 282, 70 S.Ct. 629, 94 L.Ed. 839 (1950). Thus, "'there seems little loss in terms of effective advocacy from allowing [the assertion of this claim] by' the present jus tertii champion." Craig, supra, 429 U.S., at 194, 97 S.Ct., at 455 (quoting Singleton, 428 U.S., at 118, 96 S.Ct., at 2876).

The final inquiry in our third-party standing analysis involves the likelihood and ability of the third parties, the excluded venirepersons, to assert their own rights. See *Singleton, supra*, at 115-116, 96 S.Ct., at 2874-2875. We have held that individual jurors subjected to racial exclusion have the legal right to bring suit on their own behalf. Carter, 396 U.S., at 329-330, 90 S.Ct., at 523-524. As a practical matter, however, these challenges are rare. See Alschuler, The Supreme Court and the Jury: Voir Dire, Peremptory Challenges, and the Review of Jury Verdicts, 56 U.Chi.L.Rev. 153, 193-195 (1989). Indeed, it took nearly a century after the Fourteenth Amendment and the Civil Rights Act of 1875 came into being for the first such case to reach this Court. See Carter, supra, at 320, 90 S.Ct., at 518.

The barriers to a suit by an excluded juror are daunting. Potential jurors are not parties to the jury selection process and have no opportunity to be heard at the time of their exclusion. Nor can excluded jurors easily obtain declaratory or injunctive relief when discrimination occurs through an individual prosecutor's exercise of peremptory challenges. Unlike a challenge to systematic practices of the jury clerk and commissioners such as we considered in Carter, it would be difficult for an individual juror to show a likelihood that discrimination against him at the voir dire stage will recur. See *Los Angeles v. Lyons*, 461 U.S. 95, 105-110, 103 S.Ct. 1660, 1666-1670, 75 L.Ed.2d 675 (1983). And, there exist considerable practical barriers to suit by the excluded juror because of the small financial stake involved and the economic burdens of litigation. See *Vasquez, supra*, 474 U.S., at 262, n. 5, 106 S.Ct., at 623, n. 5; *Rose v. Mitchell*, supra, 443 U.S., at 558, 99 S.Ct., at 3001. The reality is that a juror dismissed because of race probably will leave the courtroom possessing little incentive to set in motion the arduous process needed to vindicate his own rights. See *Barrows v. Jackson*, 346 U.S. 249, 257, 73 S.Ct. 1031, 1035, 97 L.Ed. 1586 (1953).

We conclude that a defendant in a criminal case can raise the third-party equal protection claims of jurors excluded by the prosecution because of their race. In so doing, we once again decline "to reverse a course of decisions of long standing directed against racial discrimination in the administration of justice." *Cassell v. Texas*, supra, 339 U.S., at 290, 70 S.Ct., at 633 (Frankfurter, J., concurring in judgment). To bar petitioner's claim because his race differs from that of the excluded jurors would be to condone the arbitrary exclusion of citizens from the duty, honor, and privilege of jury service. In Holland and Batson, we spoke of the significant role peremptory challenges play in our trial procedures, but we noted also that the utility of the peremptory challenge system must be accommodated to the command of racial neutrality. *Holland*, 493 U.S., at 486-487, 110 S.Ct., at 810-811; *Batson*, supra, 476 U.S., at 98-99, 106 S.Ct., at 1723-1724.

The Fourteenth Amendment's mandate that race discrimination be eliminated from all official acts and proceedings of the State is most compelling in the judicial system. *Rose v. Mitchell, supra*, 443 U.S., at 555, 99 S.Ct., at 2999-3000. We have held, for example, that prosecutorial discretion cannot be exercised on the basis of race, *Wayte v. United States*, 470 U.S. 598, 608, 105 S.Ct. 1524, 1531, 84 L.Ed.2d 547 (1985), and that, where racial bias is likely to influence a jury, an inquiry must be made into such bias. *Ristaino v. Ross*, 424 U.S. 589, 596, 96 S.Ct. 1017, 1021, 47 L.Ed.2d 258 (1976); see also *Turner v. Murray*, 476 U.S. 28, 106 S.Ct. 1683, 90 L.Ed.2d 27 (1986). The statutory prohibition on discrimination in the selection of jurors, 18 U.S.C. § 243, enacted pursuant to the Fourteenth Amendment's Enabling Clause, makes race neutrality in jury selection a visible, and inevitable, measure of the judicial system's own commitment to the commands of the Constitution. The courts are under an affirmative duty to enforce the strong statutory and constitutional policies embodied in that prohibition. See *Peters v. Kiff*, 407 U.S., at 507, 92 S.Ct., at 2170-2171 (WHITE, J., concurring in judgment); see also id., at 505, 92 S.Ct., at 2169-2170 (opinion of MARSHALL, J.).

The emphasis in *Batson* on racial identity between the defendant and the excused prospective juror is not inconsistent with our holding today that race is irrelevant to a defendant's standing to object to the discriminatory use of peremptory challenges. Racial identity between the defendant and the excused person might in some cases be the explanation for the prosecution's adoption of the forbidden stereotype, and if the alleged race bias takes this form, it may provide one of the easier cases to establish both a prima facie case and a conclusive showing that wrongful discrimination has occurred. But to say that the race of the defendant may be relevant to discerning bias in some cases does not mean that it will be a factor in others, for race prejudice stems from various causes and may manifest itself in different forms.

It remains for the trial courts to develop rules, without unnecessary disruption of the jury selection process, to permit legitimate and well-founded objections to the use of peremptory challenges as a mask for race prejudice. In this case, the State concedes that, if we find the petitioner has standing to object to the prosecution's use of the peremptory challenges, the case should be remanded. We find that petitioner does have standing. The judgment is reversed, and the case is remanded for further proceedings not inconsistent with our opinion.

It is so ordered.

Note

The ability to challenge the discriminatory use of peremptory challenges has been expanded to include not only non-racial minority defendants having standing to challenge exclusion of racial minorities, as in *Powers*, but also to the exclusion of women in *J.E.B. v. Alabama ex. Rel. T.B.*, 511 *U.S. 127 (1994)* and the Ninth Circuit has applied *Batson* to the use of peremptory challenges to exclude on the basis of sexual orientation, *SmithKline Beecham Corp. Abbott Laboratories, 740 F. 3d 471 (9th Cir. 2014)*. Although *SmithKline* was a civil matter (see *Edmonson v. Leesville Concrete Co.*, 500 U.S. 614 (1991) discussed below), At least one state supreme court has applied its rationale in a criminal case. *Morgan v. State*, 134 Nev. 200, 416 P.3d 212 (Nevada 2018).

As noted above the concept of equal protection disapproval of excluding a member of a cognizable group from jury service by use of peremptory challenges was expanded to include civil litigation in *Edmonson v. Leesville Concrete Co.*. In that case Black construction workers sued a private company in negligence for injuries suffered at a federal enclave job site. Plaintiffs challenged the defendants' exclusion of two out of three potential Black jurors. The plaintiffs request that under *Batson* the defendants must present a race-neutral rationale for such exclusion was denied by the federal district trial court. The United States Supreme Court concluded that Batson applied even though this was a civil matter and even though the parties were private litigants. The Court reasoned that "discrimination on the basis of race in selecting a jury in a civil proceeding harms the excluded juror no less than discrimination in a criminal trial. [citation omitted] In either case, race is the sole reason for denying the excluded venireperson the honor and privilege of participating in our system of justice." 500 U.S. at 619.

The Court in *Edmonson* also recognized the extension of *Batson* to include the actions of private litigants reasoning that state/governmental action existed because peremptory challenges only exist in the court system and are the creation of state law. That same rationale, which also recognizes that it is the right of the potential juror that is violated, supports the Court's decision in *Georgia v. McCollum*, 505 U.S. 42 (1992) finding that defendants, who were White, could not exclude potential Black jurors by use of peremptory challenges without compliance with *Batson*.

The struggle to apply *Batson* has centered primarily on the role of the trial court in determining if the proffered race-neutral rationale for exclusion of a cognizable group through peremptory challenges is valid or merely pretextual. The trial court must determine if the defendant has shown purposeful discrimination in light of all the circumstances. While deference is given to the trial court's review and its determination can be considered binding such finding can, and has been rejected if such were an unreasonable determination in light of evidence presented. In *Miller-El v. Dretke*, 545 U.S. 231 (2005), the Supreme Court found the trial court determination that the prosecution use of peremptory challenges to eliminate 10 of 11 black potential jurors as justified and non-pretextual to be wrong by clear and convincing evidence, warranting federal habeas corpus relief, where there was evidence that the prosecution failed to strike similarly situated White jurors and where the prosecutor used two "jury shuffles" (Texas law permitted either side to shuffle the cards bearing panel member names to rearrange the order in which they are questioned.) After a defense shuffle produced four potential jurors in the front row – the row to be voir dired first, the prosecution sought to shuffle the cards again for no apparent reason other than to move the Black potential jurors off the front row) which together with disparate questioning of Black and white venirepersons otherwise similarly situated. Similarly, in *Snyder v. Louisiana*, 552 U.S. 472 (2008) the Court found that the trial court's failure to find discriminatory intent to be clearly erroneous. In that case the prosecution's reason for striking all 5 prospective black jurors suggested discriminatory intent where the defendant centered his prima facie showing of discrimination on the showing that the removal of two Black venirepersons for reasons of their purported expression of conflicting obligations occurred despite the fact that White venirepersons with more compelling conflicts were accepted. *Foster v. Chatman*, 136 S. Ct. 1737 (2016) represents yet another instance where the Supreme Court found the trial court's determination of no substantiation of purposeful discrimination to be clearly erroneous. In this instance, the defendant found through the state's open records act, documentation from state investigators, and used by the prosecution, which identified prospective jurors by race and contained notations next to the names of Black jurors as to whether he or she would be acceptable (in fact "NO" was written in on all but one potential juror).

In *Flowers v. Mississippi* below the Court summarizes the various approaches taken in reviewing the trial court determination and indicates that the entire course of conduct, including state action in the five previous trials of the defendant, as well as a comparison of questioning of Black and White venirepersons.

FLOWERS V. MISSISSIPPI

588 U. S. ____ (2019) |

Justice KAVANAUGH delivered the opinion of the Court.

In Batson v. Kentucky, 476 U.S. 79, 106 S.Ct. 1712, 90 L.Ed.2d 69 (1986), this Court ruled that a State may not discriminate on the basis of race when exercising peremptory challenges against prospective jurors in a criminal trial.

In 1996, Curtis Flowers allegedly murdered four people in Winona, Mississippi. Flowers is black. He has been tried six separate times before a jury for murder. The same lead prosecutor represented the State in all six trials.

In the initial three trials, Flowers was convicted, but the Mississippi Supreme Court reversed each conviction. In the first trial, Flowers was convicted, but the Mississippi Supreme Court reversed the conviction due to "numerous instances of prosecutorial misconduct." Flowers v. State, 773 So.2d 309, 327 (2000). In the second trial, the trial court found that the prosecutor discriminated on the basis of race in the peremptory challenge of a black juror. The trial court seated the black juror. Flowers was then convicted, but the Mississippi Supreme Court again reversed the conviction because of prosecutorial misconduct at trial. In the third trial, Flowers was convicted, but the Mississippi Supreme Court yet again reversed the conviction, this time because the court concluded that the prosecutor had again discriminated against black prospective jurors in the jury selection process. The court's lead opinion stated: "The instant case presents us with as strong a prima facie case of racial discrimination as we have ever seen in the context of a Batson challenge." Flowers v. State, 947 So.2d 910, 935 (2007). The opinion further stated that the "State engaged in racially discriminatory practices during the jury selection process" and that the "case evinces an effort by the State to exclude African-Americans from jury service." Id., at 937, 939.

The fourth and fifth trials of Flowers ended in mistrials due to hung juries.

In his sixth trial, which is the one at issue here, Flowers was convicted. The State struck five of the six black prospective jurors. On appeal, Flowers argued that the State again violated Batson in exercising peremptory strikes against black prospective jurors. In a divided 5-to-4 decision, the Mississippi Supreme Court affirmed the conviction. We granted certiorari on the Batson question and now reverse. See 586 U. S. \-\-\-\-, 139 S.Ct. 451, 202 L.Ed.2d 346 (2018).

Four critical facts, taken together, require reversal. First, in the six trials combined, the State employed its peremptory challenges to strike 41 of the 42 black prospective jurors that it could have struck—a statistic that the State acknowledged at oral argument in this Court. Tr. of Oral Arg. 32. Second, in the most recent trial, the sixth trial, the State exercised peremptory strikes against five of the six black prospective jurors. Third, at the sixth trial, in an apparent effort to find pretextual reasons to strike black prospective jurors, the State engaged in dramatically disparate questioning of black and white prospective jurors. Fourth, the State then struck at least one black prospective juror, Carolyn Wright, who was similarly situated to white prospective jurors who were not struck by the State.

We need not and do not decide that any one of those four facts alone would require reversal. All that we need to decide, and all that we do decide, is that all of the relevant facts and circumstances taken together establish that the trial court committed clear error in concluding that the State's peremptory strike of black prospective juror Carolyn Wright was not "motivated in substantial part by discriminatory intent." Foster v. Chatman, 578 U. S. ----, ----, 136 S.Ct. 1737, 1754, 195 L.Ed.2d 1 (2016) (internal quotation marks omitted). In reaching that conclusion, we break no new legal ground. We simply enforce and reinforce Batson by applying it to the extraordinary facts of this case.

We reverse the judgment of the Supreme Court of Mississippi, and we remand the case for further proceedings not inconsistent with this opinion.

I

The underlying events that gave rise to this case took place in Winona, Mississippi. Winona is a small town in northern Mississippi, just off I–55 almost halfway between Jackson and Memphis. The total population of Winona is about 5,000. The town is about 53 percent black and about 46 percent white.

In 1996, Bertha Tardy, Robert Golden, Derrick Stewart, and Carmen Rigby were murdered at the Tardy Furniture store in Winona. All four victims worked at the Tardy Furniture store. Three of the four victims were white; one was black. In 1997, the State charged Curtis Flowers with murder. Flowers is black. Since then, Flowers has been tried six separate times for the murders. In each of the first two trials, Flowers was tried for one individual murder. In each subsequent trial, Flowers was tried for all four of the murders together. The same state prosecutor tried Flowers each time. The prosecutor is white.

At Flowers' first trial, 36 prospective jurors—5 black and 31 white—were presented to potentially serve on the jury. The State exercised a total of 12 peremptory strikes, and it used 5 of them to strike the five qualified black prospective jurors. Flowers objected, arguing under Batson that the State had exercised its peremptory strikes in a racially discriminatory manner. The trial court rejected the Batson challenge. Because the trial court allowed the State's peremptory strikes, Flowers was tried in front of an all-white jury. The jury convicted Flowers and sentenced him to death.

On appeal, the Mississippi Supreme Court reversed the conviction, concluding that the State had committed prosecutorial misconduct in front of the jury by, among other things, expressing baseless grounds for doubting the credibility of witnesses and mentioning facts that had not been allowed into evidence by the trial judge. Flowers, 773 So.2d at 317, 334. In its opinion, the Mississippi Supreme Court described "numerous instances of prosecutorial misconduct" at the trial. Id., at 327. Because the Mississippi Supreme Court reversed based on prosecutorial misconduct at trial, the court did not reach Flowers' Batson argument. See Flowers, 773 So.2d at 327.

At the second trial, 30 prospective jurors—5 black and 25 white—were presented to potentially serve on the jury. As in Flowers' first trial, the State again used its strikes against all five black prospective jurors. But this time, the trial court determined that the State's asserted reason for one of the strikes was a pretext for discrimination. Specifically, the trial court determined that one of the State's proffered reasons—that the juror had been inattentive and was nodding off during jury selection—for striking that juror was false, and the trial court therefore sustained Flowers' Batson challenge. The trial court disallowed the strike and sat that black juror on the jury. The jury at Flowers' second trial consisted of 11 white jurors and 1 black juror. The jury convicted Flowers and sentenced him to death.

On appeal, the Mississippi Supreme Court again reversed. The court ruled that the prosecutor had again engaged in prosecutorial misconduct in front of the jury by, among other things, impermissibly referencing evidence and attempting to undermine witness credibility without a factual basis. See Flowers v. State, 842 So.2d 531, 538, 553 (2003).

At Flowers' third trial, 45 prospective jurors—17 black and 28 white—were presented to potentially serve on the jury. One of the black prospective jurors was struck for cause, leaving 16. The State exercised a total of 15 peremptory strikes, and it used all 15 against black prospective jurors. Flowers again argued that the State had used its peremptory strikes in a racially discriminatory manner. The trial court found that the State had not discriminated on the basis of race. See Flowers, 947 So.2d at 916. The jury in Flowers' third trial consisted of 11 white jurors and 1 black juror. The lone black juror who served on the jury was seated after the State ran out of peremptory strikes. The jury convicted Flowers and sentenced him to death.

On appeal, the Mississippi Supreme Court yet again reversed, concluding that the State had again violated Batson by discriminating on the basis of race in exercising all 15 of its peremptory strikes against 15 black prospective jurors. See Flowers, 947 So.2d at 939. The court's lead opinion stated: "The instant case presents us with as strong a prima facie case of racial discrimination as we have ever seen in the context of a Batson challenge." Id., at 935. The opinion explained that although "each individual strike may have justifiably appeared to the trial court to be sufficiently race neutral, the trial court also has a duty to look at the State's use of peremptory challenges in toto." Id., at 937. The opinion emphasized that "trial judges should not blindly accept any and every reason put forth by the State, especially" when "the State continues to exercise challenge after challenge only upon members of a particular race." Ibid. The opinion added that the "State engaged in racially discriminatory practices" and that the "case evinces an effort by the State to exclude African-Americans from jury service." Id., at 937, 939.

At Flowers' fourth trial, 36 prospective jurors—16 black and 20 white—were presented to potentially serve on the jury. The State exercised a total of 11 peremptory strikes, and it used all 11 against black prospective jurors. But because of the relatively large number of prospective jurors who were black, the State did not have enough peremptory challenges to eliminate all of the black prospective jurors. The seated jury consisted of seven white jurors and five black jurors. That jury could not reach a verdict, and the proceeding ended in a mistrial.

As to the fifth trial, there is no available racial information about the prospective jurors, as distinct from the jurors who ultimately sat on the jury. The jury was composed of nine white jurors and three black jurors. The jury could not reach a verdict, and the trial again ended in a mistrial.

At the sixth trial, which we consider here, 26 prospective jurors—6 black and 20 white—were presented to potentially serve on the jury. The State exercised a total of six peremptory strikes, and it used five of the six against black prospective jurors, leaving one black juror to sit on the jury. Flowers again argued that the State had exercised its peremptory strikes in a racially discriminatory manner. The trial court concluded that the State had offered race-neutral reasons for each of the five peremptory strikes against the five black prospective jurors. The jury at Flowers' sixth trial consisted of 11 white jurors and 1 black juror. That jury convicted Flowers of murder and sentenced him to death.

In a divided decision, the Mississippi Supreme Court agreed with the trial court on the Batson issue and stated that the State's "race-neutral reasons were valid and not merely pretextual." *Flowers v. State*, 158 So.3d 1009, 1058 (2014). Flowers then sought review in this Court. This Court granted Flowers' petition for a writ of certiorari, vacated the judgment of the Mississippi Supreme Court, and remanded for further consideration in light of the decision in Foster, 578 U. S. ––––, 136 S.Ct. 1737, 195 L.Ed.2d 1. *Flowers v. Mississippi*, 579 U. S. ––––, 136 S.Ct. 2157, 195 L.Ed.2d 817 (2016). In *Foster*, this Court held that the defendant Foster had established a *Batson* violation. 578 U. S., at ––––, 136 S.Ct., at 1755.

On remand, the Mississippi Supreme Court by a 5-to-4 vote again upheld Flowers' conviction. See 240 So.3d 1082 (2017). Justice King wrote a dissent for three justices. He stated: "I cannot conclude that Flowers received a fair trial, nor can I conclude that prospective jurors were not subjected to impermissible discrimination." Id., at 1172. According to Justice King, both the trial court and the Mississippi Supreme Court "completely disregard[ed] the constitutional right of prospective jurors to be free from a racially discriminatory selection process." Id., at 1171. We granted certiorari.

II

A

Other than voting, serving on a jury is the most substantial opportunity that most citizens have to participate in the democratic process. See *Powers v. Ohio*, 499 U.S. 400, 407, 111 S.Ct. 1364, 113 L.Ed.2d 411 (1991).

Jury selection in criminal cases varies significantly based on state and local rules and practices, but ordinarily consists of three phases, which we describe here in general terms. First, a group of citizens in the community is randomly summoned to the courthouse on a particular day for potential jury service. Second, a subgroup of those prospective jurors is called into a particular courtroom for a specific case. The prospective jurors are often questioned by the judge, as well as by the prosecutor and defense attorney. During that second phase, the judge may excuse certain prospective jurors based on their answers. Third, the prosecutor and defense attorney may challenge certain prospective jurors. The attorneys may challenge prospective jurors for cause, which usually stems from a potential juror's conflicts of interest or inability to be impartial. In addition to challenges for cause, each side is typically afforded a set number of peremptory challenges or strikes. Peremptory strikes have very old credentials and can be traced back to the common law. Those peremptory strikes traditionally may be used to remove any potential juror for any reason—no questions asked.

That blanket discretion to peremptorily strike prospective jurors for any reason can clash with the dictates of the Equal Protection Clause of the Fourteenth Amendment to the United States Constitution. This case arises at the intersection of the peremptory challenge and the Equal Protection Clause. And to understand how equal protection law applies to peremptory challenges, it helps to begin at the beginning.

Ratified in 1868 in the wake of the Civil War, the Equal Protection Clause of the Fourteenth Amendment provides that no State shall "deny to any person within its jurisdiction the equal protection of the laws." A primary objective of the Equal Protection Clause, this Court stated just five years after ratification, was "the freedom of the slave race, the security and firm establishment of that freedom, and the protection of the newly-made freeman and citizen from the oppressions of those who had formerly exercised unlimited dominion over him." *Slaughter-House Cases,* 16 Wall. 36, 71, 21 L.Ed. 394 (1873).

In 1875, to help enforce the Fourteenth Amendment, Congress passed and President Ulysses S. Grant signed the Civil Rights Act of 1875. Ch. 114, 18 Stat. 335. Among other things, that law made it a criminal offense for state officials to exclude individuals from jury service on account of their race. 18 U. S. C. § 243. The Act provides: "No citizen possessing all other qualifications which are or may be prescribed by law shall be disqualified for service as grand or petit juror in any court of the United States, or of any State on account of race, color, or previous condition of servitude."

In 1880, just 12 years after ratification of the Fourteenth Amendment, the Court decided *Strauder v. West Virginia*, 100 U.S. 303, 25 L.Ed. 664. That case concerned a West Virginia statute that allowed whites only to serve as jurors. The Court held the law unconstitutional.

In reaching its conclusion, the Court explained that the Fourteenth Amendment required "that the law in the States shall be the same for the black as for the white; that all persons, whether colored or white, shall stand equal before the laws of the States, and, in regard to the colored race, for whose protection the amendment was primarily designed, that no discrimination shall be made against them by law because of their color." Id., at 307. In the words of the *Strauder* Court: "The very fact that colored people are singled out and expressly denied by a statute all right to participate in the administration of the law, as jurors, because of their color, though they are citizens, and may be in other respects fully qualified, is practically a brand upon them, affixed by the law, an assertion of their inferiority, and a stimulant to that race prejudice which is an impediment to securing to individuals of the race that equal justice which the law aims to secure to all others." Id., at 308. For those reasons, the Court ruled that the West Virginia statute excluding blacks from jury service violated the Fourteenth Amendment.

As the Court later explained in *Brown v. Board of Education*, 347 U.S. 483, 74 S.Ct. 686, 98 L.Ed. 873 (1954), the Court's decisions in the Slaughter-House Cases and Strauder interpreted the Fourteenth Amendment "as proscribing all state-imposed discriminations against the Negro race," including in jury service. Brown, 347 U.S. at 490, 74 S.Ct. 686.

In the decades after *Strauder*, the Court reiterated that States may not discriminate on the basis of race in jury selection. See, e.g., *Neal v. Delaware*, 103 U.S. 370, 397, 26 L.Ed. 567 (1881); *Carter v. Texas*, 177 U.S. 442, 447, 20 S.Ct. 687, 44 L.Ed. 839 (1900); *Norris v. Alabama*, 294 U.S. 587, 597–599, 55 S.Ct. 579, 79 L.Ed. 1074 (1935); *Hale v. Kentucky*, 303 U.S. 613, 616, 58 S.Ct. 753, 82 L.Ed. 1050 (1938) (per curiam); *Pierre v. Louisiana*, 306 U.S. 354, 362, 59 S.Ct. 536, 83 L.Ed. 757 (1939); *Smith v. Texas*, 311 U.S. 128, 130–131, 61 S.Ct. 164, 85 L.Ed. 84 (1940); *Avery v. Georgia*, 345 U.S. 559, 562, 73 S.Ct. 891, 97 L.Ed. 1244 (1953); *Hernandez v. Texas*, 347 U.S. 475, 477–478, 482, 74 S.Ct. 667, 98 L.Ed. 866 (1954); *Coleman v. Alabama*, 377 U.S. 129, 133, 84 S.Ct. 1152, 12 L.Ed.2d 190 (1964).

But critical problems persisted. Even though laws barring blacks from serving on juries were unconstitutional after Strauder, many jurisdictions employed various discriminatory tools to prevent black persons from being called for jury service. And when those tactics failed, or were invalidated, prosecutors could still exercise peremptory strikes in individual cases to remove most or all black prospective jurors.

In the century after Strauder, the freedom to exercise peremptory strikes for any reason meant that "the problem of racial exclusion from jury service" remained "widespread" and "deeply entrenched." 5 U. S. Commission on Civil Rights Report 90 (1961). Simple math shows how that happened. Given that blacks were a minority of the population, in many jurisdictions the number of peremptory strikes available to the prosecutor exceeded the number of black prospective jurors. So prosecutors could routinely exercise peremptories to strike all the black prospective jurors and thereby ensure all-white juries. The exclusion of black prospective jurors was almost total in certain jurisdictions, especially in cases involving black defendants. Similarly, defense counsel could use—and routinely did use—peremptory challenges to strike all the black prospective jurors in cases involving white defendants and black victims.

In the aftermath of *Strauder*, the exclusion of black jurors became more covert and less overt—often accomplished through peremptory challenges in individual courtrooms rather than by blanket operation of law. But as this Court later noted, the results were the same for black jurors and black defendants, as well as for the black community's confidence in the fairness of the American criminal justice system. See Batson, 476 U.S. at 98–99, 106 S.Ct. 1712.

Eighty-five years after *Strauder*, the Court decided *Swain v. Alabama*, 380 U.S. 202, 85 S.Ct. 824, 13 L.Ed.2d 759 (1965). The defendant Swain was black. Swain was convicted of a capital offense in Talladega County, Alabama, and sentenced to death. Swain presented evidence that no black juror had served on a jury in Talladega County in more than a decade. See *id.*, at 226, 85 S.Ct. 824. And in Swain's case, the prosecutor struck all six qualified black prospective jurors, ensuring that Swain was tried before an all-white jury. Swain invoked *Strauder* to argue that the prosecutor in his case had impermissibly discriminated on the basis of race by using peremptory challenges to strike the six black prospective jurors. See 380 U.S. at 203, 210, 85 S.Ct. 824.

This Court ruled that Swain had not established unconstitutional discrimination. Most importantly, the Court held that a defendant could not object to the State's use of peremptory strikes in an individual case. In the Court's words: "[W]e cannot hold that the striking of Negroes in a particular case is a denial of equal protection of the laws." *Id.*, at 221, 85 S.Ct. 824. The Swain Court reasoned that prosecutors do not always judge prospective jurors individually when exercising peremptory strikes. Instead, prosecutors choose which prospective jurors to strike "in light of the limited knowledge counsel has of them, which may include their group affiliations, in the context of the case to be tried." Ibid. In the Court's view, the prosecutor could strike prospective jurors on the basis of their group affiliations, including race. In other words, a prosecutor could permissibly strike a prospective juror for any reason, including the assumption or belief that a black prospective juror, because of race, would be favorable to a black defendant or unfavorable to the State. See *id.*, at 220–221, 85 S.Ct. 824.

To be sure, the *Swain* Court held that a defendant could make out a case of racial discrimination by showing that the State "in case after case, whatever the circumstances, whatever the crime and whoever the defendant or the victim may be," had been responsible for the removal of qualified black prospective jurors so that no black jurors "ever serve on petit juries." Id., at 223, 85 S.Ct. 824. But Swain's high bar for establishing a constitutional violation was almost impossible for any defendant to surmount, as the aftermath of Swain amply demonstrated.

Twenty-one years later, in its 1986 decision in *Batson*, the Court revisited several critical aspects of Swain and in essence overruled them. In so doing, the Batson Court emphasized that "the central concern" of the Fourteenth Amendment "was to put an end to governmental discrimination on account of race." 476 U.S. at 85, 106 S.Ct. 1712. The *Batson* Court noted that Swain had left prosecutors' peremptory challenges "largely immune from constitutional scrutiny." 476 U.S. at 92–93, 106 S.Ct. 1712. In his concurrence in *Batson*, Justice Byron White (the author of Swain) agreed that Swain should be overruled. He stated: "[T]he practice of peremptorily eliminating blacks from petit juries in cases with black defendants remains widespread, so much so" that "I agree with the Court that the time has come to rule as it has." 476 U.S. at 101–102, 106 S.Ct. 1712.

Under *Batson*, once a prima facie case of discrimination has been shown by a defendant, the State must provide race-neutral reasons for its peremptory strikes. The trial judge must determine whether the prosecutor's stated reasons were the actual reasons or instead were a pretext for discrimination. Id., at 97–98, 106 S.Ct. 1712.

Four parts of *Batson* warrant particular emphasis here.

First, the *Batson* Court rejected Swain's insistence that a defendant demonstrate a history of racially discriminatory strikes in order to make out a claim of race discrimination. See 476 U.S. at 95, 106 S.Ct. 1712. According to the *Batson* Court, defendants had run into "practical difficulties" in trying to prove that a State had systematically "exercised peremptory challenges to exclude blacks from the jury on account of race." Id., at 92, n. 17, 106 S.Ct. 1712. The *Batson* Court explained that, in some jurisdictions, requiring a defendant to "investigate, over a number of cases, the race of persons tried in the particular jurisdiction, the racial composition of the venire and petit jury, and the manner in which both parties exercised their peremptory challenges" posed an "insurmountable" burden. *Ibid.*

In addition to that practical point, the Court stressed a basic equal protection point: In the eyes of the Constitution, one racially discriminatory peremptory strike is one too many.

For those reasons, the *Batson* Court held that a criminal defendant could show "purposeful discrimination in selection of the petit jury solely on evidence concerning the prosecutor's exercise of peremptory challenges at the defendant's trial." Id., at 96, 106 S.Ct. 1712 (emphasis added).

Second, the *Batson* Court rejected Swain's statement that a prosecutor could strike a black juror based on an assumption or belief that the black juror would favor a black defendant. In some of the most critical sentences in the *Batson* opinion, the Court emphasized that a prosecutor may not rebut a claim of discrimination "by stating merely that he challenged jurors of the defendant's race on the assumption—or his intuitive judgment—that they would be partial to the defendant because of their shared race." 476 U.S. at 97, 106 S.Ct. 1712. The Court elaborated: The Equal Protection Clause "forbids the States to strike black veniremen on the assumption that they will be biased in a particular case simply because the defendant is black. The core guarantee of equal protection, ensuring citizens that their State will not discriminate on account of race, would be meaningless were we to approve the exclusion of jurors on the basis of such assumptions, which arise solely from the jurors' race." Id., at 97–98, 106 S.Ct. 1712. In his concurrence, Justice Thurgood Marshall drove the point home: "Exclusion of blacks from a jury, solely because of race, can no more be justified by a belief that blacks are less likely than whites to consider fairly or sympathetically the State's case against a black defendant than it can be justified by the notion that blacks lack the intelligence, experience, or moral integrity to be entrusted with that role." *Id.*, at 104–105, 106 S.Ct. 1712 (internal quotation marks and citations omitted).

Third, the *Batson* Court did not accept the argument that race-based peremptories should be permissible because black, white, Asian, and Hispanic defendants and jurors were all "equally" subject to race-based discrimination. The Court stated that each removal of an individual juror because of his or her race is a constitutional violation. Discrimination against one defendant or juror on account of race is not remedied or cured by discrimination against other defendants or jurors on account of race. As the Court later explained: Some say that there is no equal protection violation if individuals "of all races are subject to like treatment, which is to say that white jurors are subject to the same risk of peremptory challenges based on race as are all other jurors. The suggestion that racial classifications may survive when visited upon all persons is no more authoritative today than the case which advanced the theorem, *Plessy v. Ferguson*, 163 U.S. 537, 16 S.Ct. 1138, 41 L.Ed. 256 (1896). This idea has no place in our modern equal protection jurisprudence. It is axiomatic that racial classifications do not become legitimate on the assumption that all persons suffer them in equal degree." *Powers*, 499 U.S. at 410, 111 S.Ct. 1364 (citing *Loving v. Virginia*, 388 U.S. 1, 87 S.Ct. 1817, 18 L.Ed.2d 1010 (1967)).

Fourth, the *Batson* Court did not accept the argument that race-based peremptories are permissible because both the prosecution and defense could employ them in any individual case and in essence balance things out. Under the Equal Protection Clause, the Court stressed, even a single instance of race discrimination against a prospective juror is impermissible. Moreover, in criminal cases involving black defendants, the both-sides-can-do-it argument overlooks the percentage of the United States population that is black (about 12 percent) and the cold reality of jury selection in most jurisdictions. Because blacks are a minority in most jurisdictions, prosecutors often have more peremptory strikes than there are black prospective jurors on a particular panel. In the pre- Batson era, therefore, allowing each side in a case involving a black defendant to strike prospective jurors on the basis of race meant that a prosecutor could eliminate all of the black jurors, but a black defendant could not eliminate all of the white jurors. So in the real world of criminal trials against black defendants, both history and math tell us that a system of race-based peremptories does not treat black defendants and black prospective jurors equally with prosecutors and white prospective jurors. Cf. *Batson*, 476 U.S. at 99, 106 S.Ct. 1712.

B

Equal justice under law requires a criminal trial free of racial discrimination in the jury selection process. Enforcing that constitutional principle, *Batson* ended the widespread practice in which prosecutors could (and often would) routinely strike all black prospective jurors in cases involving black defendants. By taking steps to eradicate racial discrimination from the jury selection process, *Batson* sought to protect the rights of defendants and jurors, and to enhance public confidence in the fairness of the criminal justice system. *Batson* immediately revolutionized the jury selection process that takes place every day in federal and state criminal courtrooms throughout the United States.

In the decades since *Batson*, this Court's cases have vigorously enforced and reinforced the decision, and guarded against any backsliding. See *Foster*, 578 U. S. ----, 136 S.Ct. 1737, 195 L.Ed.2d 1; *Snyder v. Louisiana*, 552 U.S. 472, 128 S.Ct. 1203, 170 L.Ed.2d 175 (2008); *Miller-El v. Dretke*, 545 U.S. 231, 125 S.Ct. 2317, 162 L.Ed.2d 196 (2005) (*Miller-El II*). Moreover, the Court has extended *Batson* in certain ways. A defendant of any race may raise a *Batson* claim, and a defendant may raise a *Batson* claim even if the defendant and the excluded juror are of different races. See *Hernandez*, 347 U.S. at 477–478, 74 S.Ct. 667; *Powers*, 499 U.S. at 406, 111 S.Ct. 1364. Moreover, *Batson* now applies to gender discrimination, to a criminal defendant's peremptory strikes, and to civil cases. See J. E. B. v. Alabama ex rel. T. B., 511 U.S. 127, 129, 114 S.Ct. 1419, 128 L.Ed.2d 89 (1994); *Georgia v. McCollum*, 505 U.S. 42, 59, 112 S.Ct. 2348, 120 L.Ed.2d 33 (1992); *Edmonson v. Leesville Concrete Co.*, 500 U.S. 614, 616, 111 S.Ct. 2077, 114 L.Ed.2d 660 (1991).

Of particular relevance here, *Batson*'s holding raised several important evidentiary and procedural issues, three of which we underscore.

First, what factors does the trial judge consider in evaluating whether racial discrimination occurred? Our precedents allow criminal defendants raising Batson challenges to present a variety of evidence to support a claim that a prosecutor's peremptory strikes were made on the basis of race. For example, defendants may present:

- statistical evidence about the prosecutor's use of peremptory strikes against black prospective jurors as compared to white prospective jurors in the case;

- evidence of a prosecutor's disparate questioning and investigation of black and white prospective jurors in the case;

- side-by-side comparisons of black prospective jurors who were struck and white prospective jurors who were not struck in the case;

- a prosecutor's misrepresentations of the record when defending the strikes during the Batson hearing;

- relevant history of the State's peremptory strikes in past cases; or

- other relevant circumstances that bear upon the issue of racial discrimination.

See *Foster*, 578 U. S. ----, 136 S.Ct. 1737, 195 L.Ed.2d 1; *Snyder*, 552 U.S. 472, 128 S.Ct. 1203, 170 L.Ed.2d 175; *Miller-El II*, 545 U.S. 231, 125 S.Ct. 2317, 162 L.Ed.2d 196; *Batson*, 476 U.S. 79, 106 S.Ct. 1712, 90 L.Ed.2d 69.

Second, who enforces *Batson*? As the *Batson* Court itself recognized, the job of enforcing *Batson* rests first and foremost with trial judges. See id., at 97, 99, n. 22, 106 S.Ct. 1712. America's trial judges operate at the front lines of American justice. In criminal trials, trial judges possess the primary responsibility to enforce *Batson* and prevent racial discrimination from seeping into the jury selection process.

As the *Batson* Court explained and as the Court later reiterated, once a prima facie case of racial discrimination has been established, the prosecutor must provide race-neutral reasons for the strikes. The trial court must consider the prosecutor's race-neutral explanations in light of all of the relevant facts and circumstances, and in light of the arguments of the parties. The trial judge's assessment of the prosecutor's credibility is often important. The Court has explained that "the best evidence of discriminatory intent often will be the demeanor of the attorney who exercises the challenge." *Snyder*, 552 U.S. at 477, 128 S.Ct. 1203 (quotation altered). "We have recognized that these determinations of credibility and demeanor lie peculiarly within a trial judge's province." Ibid. (internal quotation marks omitted). The trial judge must determine whether the prosecutor's proffered reasons are the actual reasons, or whether the proffered reasons are pretextual and the prosecutor instead exercised peremptory strikes on the basis of race. The ultimate inquiry is whether the State was "motivated in substantial part by discriminatory intent." *Foster*, 578 U. S., at ----, 136 S.Ct., at 1754 (internal quotation marks omitted).

Third, what is the role of appellate review? An appeals court looks at the same factors as the trial judge, but is necessarily doing so on a paper record. "Since the trial judge's findings in the context under consideration here largely will turn on evaluation of credibility, a reviewing court ordinarily should give those findings great deference." *Batson*, 476 U.S. at 98, n. 21, 106 S.Ct. 1712. The Court has described the appellate standard of review of the trial court's factual determinations in a *Batson* hearing as "highly deferential." *Snyder*, 552 U.S. at 479, 128 S.Ct. 1203. "On appeal, a trial court's ruling on the issue of discriminatory intent must be sustained unless it is clearly erroneous." Id., at 477, 128 S.Ct. 1203.

III

In accord with the principles set forth in *Batson*, we now address Flowers' case.

The Constitution forbids striking even a single prospective juror for a discriminatory purpose. See *Foster*, 578 U. S., at ----, 136 S.Ct., at 1747. The question for this Court is whether the Mississippi trial court clearly erred in concluding that the State was not "motivated in substantial part by discriminatory intent" when exercising peremptory strikes at Flowers' sixth trial. *Id.*, at ----, 136 S.Ct., at 1754 (internal quotation marks omitted); see also *Snyder*, 552 U.S. at 477, 128 S.Ct. 1203. Because this case arises on direct review, we owe no deference to the Mississippi Supreme Court, as distinct from deference to the Mississippi trial court.

Four categories of evidence loom large in assessing the *Batson* issue in Flowers' case: (1) the history from Flowers' six trials, (2) the prosecutor's striking of five of six black prospective jurors at the sixth trial, (3) the prosecutor's dramatically disparate questioning of black and white prospective jurors at the sixth trial, and (4) the prosecutor's proffered reasons for striking one black juror (Carolyn Wright) while allowing other similarly situated white jurors to serve on the jury at the sixth trial. We address each in turn.

A

First, we consider the relevant history of the case. Recall that in *Swain*, the Court held that a defendant may prove racial discrimination by establishing a historical pattern of racial exclusion of jurors in the jurisdiction in question. Indeed, under Swain, that was the only way that a defendant could make out a claim that the State discriminated on the basis of race in the use of peremptory challenges.

In *Batson*, the Court ruled that Swain had imposed too heavy a burden on defendants seeking to prove that a prosecutor had used peremptory strikes in a racially discriminatory manner. Batson lowered the evidentiary burden for defendants to contest prosecutors' use of peremptory *2245 strikes and made clear that demonstrating a history of discriminatory strikes in past cases was not necessary.

In doing so, however, *Batson* did not preclude defendants from still using the same kinds of historical evidence that Swain had allowed defendants to use to support a claim of racial discrimination. Most importantly for present purposes, after *Batson*, the trial judge may still consider historical evidence of the State's discriminatory peremptory strikes from past trials in the jurisdiction, just as Swain had allowed. After Batson, the defendant may still cast *Swain's* "wide net" to gather "'relevant'" evidence. *Miller-El II*, 545 U.S. at 239–240, 125 S.Ct. 2317. A defendant may rely on "all relevant circumstances." Batson, 476 U.S. at 96–97, 106 S.Ct. 1712.

Here, our review of the history of the prosecutor's peremptory strikes in Flowers' first four trials strongly supports the conclusion that his use of peremptory strikes in Flowers' sixth trial was motivated in substantial part by discriminatory intent. (Recall that there is no record evidence from the fifth trial regarding the race of the prospective jurors.)

The numbers speak loudly. Over the course of the first four trials, there were 36 black prospective jurors against whom the State could have exercised a peremptory strike. The State tried to strike all 36. The State used its avail-able peremptory strikes to attempt to strike every single black prospective juror that it could have struck. (At oral argument in this Court, the

State acknowledged that statistic. Tr. of Oral Arg. 32.) Not only did the State's use of peremptory strikes in Flowers' first four trials reveal a blatant pattern of striking black prospective jurors, the Mississippi courts themselves concluded on two separate occasions that the State violated *Batson*. In Flowers' second trial, the trial court concluded that the State discriminated against a black juror. Specifically, the trial court determined that one of the State's proffered reasons—that the juror had been inattentive and was nodding off during jury selection—for striking that juror was false, and the trial court therefore sustained Flowers' *Batson* challenge. In Flowers' next trial—his third trial—the prosecutor used all 15 of its peremptories to strike 15 black prospective jurors. The lead opinion of the Mississippi Supreme Court stated: "The instant case presents us with as strong a prima facie case of racial discrimination as we have ever seen in the context of a *Batson* challenge." Flowers, 947 So.2d at 935. The opinion further stated that "the State engaged in racially discriminatory practices during the jury selection process" and that the "case evinces an effort by the State to exclude African-Americans from jury service." Id., at 937, 939.

To summarize the most relevant history: In Flowers' first trial, the prosecutor successfully used peremptory strikes against all of the black prospective jurors. Flowers faced an all-white jury. In Flowers' second trial, the prosecutor tried again to strike all of the black prospective jurors, but the trial court decided that the State could not strike one of those jurors. The jury consisted of 11 white jurors and 1 black juror. In Flowers' third trial, there were 17 black prospective jurors. The prosecutor used 15 out of 15 peremptory strikes against black prospective jurors. After one black juror was struck for cause and the prosecutor ran out of strikes, one black juror remained. The jury again consisted of 11 white jurors and 1 black juror. In Flowers' fourth trial, the prosecutor again used 11 out of 11 peremptory strikes against black prospective jurors. Because of the large number of black prospective jurors at the trial, the prosecutor ran out of peremptory strikes before it could strike all of the black prospective jurors. The jury for that trial consisted of seven white jurors and five black jurors, and the jury was unable to reach a verdict. To reiterate, there is no available information about the race of prospective jurors in the fifth trial. The jury for that trial consisted of nine white jurors and three black jurors, and the jury was unable to reach a verdict.

Stretching across Flowers' first four trials, the State employed its peremptory strikes to remove as many black prospective jurors as possible. The State appeared to proceed as if Batson had never been decided. The State's relentless, determined effort to rid the jury of black individuals strongly suggests that the State wanted to try Flowers before a jury with as few black jurors as possible, and ideally before an all-white jury. The trial judge was aware of the history. But the judge did not sufficiently account for the history when considering Flowers' Batson claim.

The State's actions in the first four trials necessarily inform our assessment of the State's intent going into Flowers' sixth trial. We cannot ignore that history. We cannot take that history out of the case.

B

We turn now to the State's strikes of five of the six black prospective jurors at Flowers' sixth trial, the trial at issue here. As *Batson* noted, a "'pattern' of strikes against black jurors included in the particular venire might give rise to an inference of discrimination." 476 U.S. at 97, 106 S.Ct. 1712.

Flowers' sixth trial occurred in June 2010. At trial, 26 prospective jurors were presented to potentially serve on the jury. Six of the prospective jurors were black. The State accepted one black prospective juror—Alexander Robinson. The State struck the other five black prospective jurors—Carolyn Wright, Tashia Cunningham, Edith Burnside, Flancie Jones, and Dianne Copper. The resulting jury consisted of 11 white jurors and 1 black juror.

The State's use of peremptory strikes in Flowers' sixth trial followed the same pattern as the first four trials, with one modest exception: It is true that the State accepted one black juror for Flowers' sixth trial. But especially given the history of the case, that fact alone cannot insulate the State from a *Batson* challenge. In *Miller-El II*, this Court skeptically viewed the State's decision to accept one black juror, explaining that a prosecutor might do so in an attempt "to obscure the otherwise consistent pattern of opposition to" seating black jurors. 545 U.S. at 250, 125 S.Ct. 2317. The overall record of this case suggests that the same tactic may have been employed here. In light of all of the circumstances here, the State's decision to strike five of the six black prospective jurors is further evidence suggesting that the State was motivated in substantial part by discriminatory intent.

C

We next consider the State's dramatically disparate questioning of black and white prospective jurors in the jury selection process for Flowers' sixth trial. As *Batson* explained, "the prosecutor's questions and statements during voir dire examination and in exercising his challenges may support or refute an inference of discriminatory purpose." 476 U.S. at 97, 106 S.Ct. 1712.

The questioning process occurred through an initial group voir dire and then more in-depth follow-up questioning by the prosecutor and defense counsel of individual prospective jurors. The State asked the five black prospective jurors who were struck a total of 145 questions. By contrast, the State asked the 11 seated white jurors a total of 12 questions. On average, therefore, the State asked 29 questions to each struck black prospective juror. The State asked an average of one question to each seated white juror.

One can slice and dice the statistics and come up with all sorts of ways to compare the State's questioning of excluded black jurors with the State's questioning of the accepted white jurors. But any meaningful comparison yields the same basic assessment: The State spent far more time questioning the black prospective jurors than the accepted white jurors.

The State acknowledges, as it must under our precedents, that disparate questioning can be probative of discriminatory intent. See *Miller-El v. Cockrell*, 537 U.S. 322, 331–332, 344–345, 123 S.Ct. 1029, 154 L.Ed.2d 931 (2003) (*Miller-El I*). As *Miller-El I* stated, "if the use of disparate questioning is determined by race at the outset, it is likely [that] a justification for a strike based on the resulting divergent views would be pretextual. In this context the differences in the questions posed by the prosecutors are some evidence of purposeful discrimination." Id., at 344, 123 S.Ct. 1029.

But the State here argues that it questioned black and white prospective jurors differently only because of differences in the jurors' characteristics. The record refutes that explanation.

For example, Dianne Copper was a black prospective juror who was struck. The State asked her 18 follow-up questions about her relationships with Flowers' family and with witnesses in the case. App. 188–190. Pamela Chesteen was a white juror whom the State accepted for the jury. Although the State asked questions of Chesteen during group voir dire, the State asked her no individual follow-up questions about her relationships with Flowers' family, even though the State was aware that Chesteen knew several members of Flowers' family. Compare id., at 83, with id., at 111. Similarly, the State asked no individual follow-up questions to four other white prospective jurors who, like Dianne Copper, had relationships with defense witnesses, even though the State was aware of those relationships. Those white prospective jurors were Larry Blaylock, Harold Waller, Marcus Fielder, and Bobby Lester.

Likewise, the State conducted disparate investigations of certain prospective jurors. Tashia Cunningham, who is black, stated that she worked with Flowers' sister, but that the two did not work closely together. To try to disprove that statement, the State summoned a witness to challenge Cunningham's testimony. Id., at 148–150. The State apparently did not conduct similar investigations of white prospective jurors.

It is certainly reasonable for the State to ask follow-up questions or to investigate the relationships of jurors to the victims, potential witnesses, and the like. But white prospective jurors who were acquainted with the Flowers' family or defense witnesses were not questioned extensively by the State or investigated. White prospective jurors who admitted that they or a relative had been convicted of a crime were accepted without apparent further inquiry by the State. The difference in the State's approaches to black and white prospective jurors was stark.

Why did the State ask so many more questions—and conduct more vigorous inquiry—of black prospective jurors than it did of white prospective jurors? No one can know for certain. But this Court's cases explain that disparate questioning and investigation of prospective jurors on the basis of race can arm a prosecutor with seemingly race-neutral reasons to strike the prospective jurors of a particular race. See *Miller-El I*, 537 U.S. at 331–332, 344–345, 123 S.Ct. 1029. In other words, by asking a lot of questions of the black prospective jurors or conducting additional inquiry into their backgrounds, a prosecutor can try to find some pretextual reason—any reason—that the prosecutor can later articulate to justify what is in reality a racially motivated strike. And by not doing the same for white prospective jurors, by not asking white prospective jurors those same questions, the prosecutor can try to distort the record so as to thereby avoid being accused of treating black and white jurors differently. Disparity in questioning and investigation can produce a record that says little about white prospective jurors and is therefore resistant to characteristic-by-characteristic comparisons of struck black prospective jurors and seated white jurors. Prosecutors can decline to seek what they do not want to find about white prospective jurors.

A court confronting that kind of pattern cannot ignore it. The lopsidedness of the prosecutor's questioning and inquiry can itself be evidence of the prosecutor's objective as much as it is of the actual qualifications of the black and white prospective jurors who are struck or seated. The prosecutor's dramatically disparate questioning of black and white prospective jurors—at least if it rises to a certain level of disparity—can supply a clue that the prosecutor may have been seeking to paper the record and disguise a discriminatory intent. See *ibid.*

To be clear, disparate questioning or investigation alone does not constitute a *Batson* violation. The disparate questioning or investigation of black and white prospective jurors may reflect ordinary race-neutral considerations. But the disparate questioning or investigation can also, along with other evidence, inform the trial court's evaluation of whether discrimination occurred.

Here, along with the historical evidence we described above from the earlier trials, as well as the State's striking of five of six black prospective jurors at the sixth trial, the dramatically disparate questioning and investigation of black prospective jurors and white prospective jurors at the sixth trial strongly suggests that the State was motivated in substantial part by a discriminatory intent. We agree with the observation of the dissenting justices of the Mississippi Supreme Court: The "numbers described above are too disparate to be explained away or categorized as mere happenstance." 240 So.3d at 1161 (opinion of King, J.).

D

Finally, in combination with the other facts and circumstances in this case, the record of jury selection at the sixth trial shows that the peremptory strike of at least one of the black prospective jurors (Carolyn Wright) was motivated in substantial part by discriminatory intent. As this Court has stated, the Constitution forbids striking even a single prospective juror for a discriminatory purpose. See *Foster,* 578 U. S., at ––––, 136 S.Ct., at 1747.

Comparing prospective jurors who were struck and not struck can be an important step in determining whether a Batson violation occurred. See *Snyder,* 552 U.S. at 483–484, 128 S.Ct. 1203; *Miller-El II,* 545 U.S. at 241, 125 S.Ct. 2317. The comparison can suggest that the prosecutor's proffered explanations for striking black prospective jurors were a pretext for discrimination. When a prosecutor's "proffered reason for striking a black panelist applies just as well to an otherwise-similar nonblack panelist who is permitted to serve, that is evidence tending to prove purposeful discrimination." *Foster*, 578 U. S., at – – – –, 136 S.Ct., at 1754 (quotation altered). Although a defendant ordinarily will try to identify a similar white prospective juror whom the State did not strike, a defendant is not required to identify an identical white juror for the side-by-side comparison to be suggestive of discriminatory intent. *Miller-El II*, 545 U.S. at 247, n. 6, 125 S.Ct. 2317.

In this case, Carolyn Wright was a black prospective juror who said she was strongly in favor of the death penalty as a general matter. And she had a family member who was a prison security guard. Yet the State exercised a peremptory strike against Wright. The State said it struck Wright in part because she knew several defense witnesses and had worked at Wal-Mart where Flowers' father also worked.

Winona is a small town. Wright had some sort of connection to 34 people involved in Flowers' case, both on the prosecution witness side and the defense witness side. See, 240 So.3d at 1126. But three white prospective jurors—Pamela Chesteen, Harold Waller, and Bobby Lester—also knew many individuals involved in the case. Chesteen knew 31 people, Waller knew 18 people, and Lester knew 27 people. See ibid. Yet as we explained above, the State did not ask Chesteen, Waller, and Lester individual follow-up questions about their connections to witnesses. That is a telling statistic. If the State were concerned about prospective jurors' connections to witnesses in the case, the State presumably would have used individual questioning to ask those potential white jurors whether they could remain impartial despite their relationships. A "State's failure to engage in any meaningful voir dire examination on a subject the State alleges it is concerned about is evidence suggesting that the explanation is a sham and a pretext for discrimination." *Miller-El II*, 545 U.S. at 246, 125 S.Ct. 2317 (internal quotation marks omitted).

Both Carolyn Wright and Archie Flowers, who is the defendant's father, had worked at the local Wal-Mart. But there was no evidence that they worked together or were close in any way. Importantly, the State did not ask individual follow-up questions to determine the nature of their relationship. And during group questioning, Wright said she did not know whether Flowers' father still worked at Wal-Mart, which "supports an inference that Wright and Flowers did not have a close working relationship." 240 So.3d at 1163 (King, J., dissenting). And white prospective jurors also had relationships with members of Flowers' family. Indeed, white prospective juror Pamela Chesteen stated that she had provided service to Flowers' family members at the bank and that she knew several members of the Flowers family. App. 83. Likewise, white prospective juror Bobby Lester worked at the same bank and also encountered Flowers' family members. Id., at 86. Although Chesteen and Lester were questioned during group voir dire, the State did not ask Chesteen or Lester individual follow-up questions in order to explore the depth of their relationships with Flowers' family. And instead of striking those jurors, the State accepted them for the jury. To be sure, both Chesteen and Lester were later struck by the defense. But the State's acceptance of Chesteen and Lester necessarily informs our assessment of the State's intent in striking similarly situated black prospective jurors such as Wright.

The State also noted that Wright had once been sued by Tardy Furniture for collection of a debt 13 years earlier. Id., at 209. Wright said that the debt was paid off and that it would not affect her evaluation of the case. Id., at 71, 90–91. The victims in this case worked at Tardy Furniture. But the State did not explain how Wright's 13-year-old, paid-off debt to Tardy Furniture could affect her ability to serve impartially as a juror in this quadruple murder case. The "State's unsupported characterization of the lawsuit is problematic." 240 So.3d at 1163 (King, J., dissenting). In any event, the State did not purport to rely on that reason alone as the basis for the Wright strike, and the State in this Court does not rely on that reason alone in defending the Wright strike.

The State also explained that it exercised a peremptory strike against Wright because she had worked with one of Flowers' sisters. App. 209. That was incorrect. The trial judge immediately stated as much. Id., at 218–219. But incorrect statements of that sort may show the State's intent: When a prosecutor misstates the record in explaining a strike, that misstatement can be another clue showing discriminatory intent.

That incorrect statement was not the only one made by the prosecutor. The State made apparently incorrect statements to justify the strikes of black prospective jurors Tashia Cunningham, Edith Burnside, and Flancie Jones. The State contradicted Cunningham's earlier statement that she had only a working relationship with Flowers' sister by inaccurately asserting that Cunningham and Flowers' sister were close friends. See id., at 84, 220. The State asserted that Burnside had tried to cover up a Tardy Furniture suit. See id., at 226. She had not. See id., 70–71. And the State explained that it struck Jones in part because Jones was Flowers' aunt. See id., at 229. That, too, was not true. See id., at 86–88. The State's pattern of factually inaccurate statements about black prospective jurors suggests that the State intended to keep black prospective jurors off the jury. See *Foster*, 578 U. S., at –––––, 136 S.Ct., at 1754; *Miller-El II*, 545 U.S. at 240, 245, 125 S.Ct. 2317.

To be sure, the back and forth of a Batson hearing can be hurried, and prosecutors can make mistakes when providing explanations. That is entirely understandable, and mistaken explanations should not be confused with racial discrimination. But when considered with other evidence of discrimination, a series of factually inaccurate explanations for striking black prospective jurors can be telling. So it is here.

The side-by-side comparison of Wright to white prospective jurors whom the State accepted for the jury cannot be considered in isolation in this case. In a different context, the Wright strike might be deemed permissible. But we must examine the whole picture. Our disagreement with the Mississippi courts (and our agreement with Justice King's dissent in the Mississippi Supreme Court) largely comes down to whether we look at the Wright strike in isolation or instead look at the Wright strike in the context of all the facts and circumstances. Our precedents require that we do the latter. As Justice King explained in his dissent in the Mississippi

Supreme Court, the Mississippi courts appeared to do the former. 240 So.3d at 1163–1164. As we see it, the overall context here requires skepticism of the State's strike of Carolyn Wright. We must examine the Wright strike in light of the history of the State's use of peremptory strikes in the prior trials, the State's decision to strike five out of six black prospective jurors at Flowers' sixth trial, and the State's vastly disparate questioning of black and white prospective jurors during jury selection at the sixth trial. We cannot just look away. Nor can we focus on the Wright strike in isolation. In light of all the facts and circumstances, we conclude that the trial court clearly erred in ruling that the State's peremptory strike of Wright was not motivated in substantial part by discriminatory intent.

* * *

In sum, the State's pattern of striking black prospective jurors persisted from Flowers' first trial through Flowers' sixth trial. In the six trials combined, the State struck 41 of the 42 black prospective jurors it could have struck. At the sixth trial, the State struck five of six. At the sixth trial, moreover, the State engaged in dramatically disparate questioning of black and white prospective jurors. And it engaged in disparate treatment of black and white prospective jurors, in particular by striking black prospective juror Carolyn Wright.

To reiterate, we need not and do not decide that any one of those four facts alone would require reversal. All that we need to decide, and all that we do decide, is that all of the relevant facts and circumstances taken together establish that the trial court at Flowers' sixth trial committed clear error in concluding that the State's peremptory strike of black prospective juror Carolyn Wright was not motivated in substantial part by discriminatory intent. In reaching that conclusion, we break no new legal ground. We simply enforce and reinforce Batson by applying it to the extraordinary facts of this case.

We reverse the judgment of the Supreme Court of Mississippi, and we remand the case for further proceedings not inconsistent with this opinion.

It is so ordered.

Conducting Voir Dire of Potential Jurors as to Racial Attitudes

UNITED STATES V. BARBER

80 F.3d 964 (4th Cir. 2019)

NIEMEYER, Circuit Judge:

Norwood W. Barber and his wife, Linda K. Barber, were convicted of laundering cash proceeds from the sale of marijuana, in violation of 18 U.S.C. § 1956. On appeal they challenge mainly the district court's rejection of their request that voir dire of prospective jurors inquire into possible juror prejudice against interracial marriage. Norwood Barber is black, and Linda Barber is white. .....

For the reasons that follow, we affirm.

I

For years, Norwood Barber was a confessed marijuana dealer in the Harrisonburg, Virginia, area. In conversations with Harrisonburg police officers, he has mused that the only thing that he can do in life is to sell marijuana. Linda Barber worked for the local chapter of the Society for the Prevention of Cruelty to Animals.

Over a five-year period beginning in 1984, the Barbers opened five joint accounts in various banks and, as often as two or three times a week, deposited large amounts of cash into them, usually in small bills. Typically, a few days later, they withdrew the cash in larger bills. On one occasion, a bank teller asked Linda Barber whether she wanted her withdrawal in the form of a cashier's check, and she replied that she wanted it in large bills. On several occasions, the Barbers made deposits and withdrawals at various banks on the same day. A number of bank tellers became suspicious of the Barbers' banking activity and reported their observations to law enforcement officials.

At various times, Norwood Barber misrepresented his employment to bank officials and others, stating that he was self-employed in the egg delivery or truck driving business. On their federal income tax returns, however, the Barbers represented that Norwood Barber had no income and was unemployed. When later questioned by law enforcement officers about the source of the cash involved in their banking activity, the Barbers stated that they had saved the money over the past ten years under their bed.

The Barbers were indicted in one count for conspiracy to launder drug proceeds and, in six counts, for laundering money from drug sales in violation of 18 U.S.C. §§ 1956(a)(1)(B)(i) and (2) (B)(i). A jury convicted them on all counts, and the district court sentenced Norwood Barber to 70 months imprisonment and Linda to 57 months. This appeal followed.

II

We turn first to the Barbers' contention that the district court committed reversible error in rejecting their request to inquire during voir dire into prospective jurors' prejudice against interracial marriage.

At the beginning of trial, counsel for the Barbers requested that the trial court ask whether any member of the venire would prejudge the defendants because they were partners in an interracial marriage. The government objected to the request, arguing that posing such a question to the venire would "bring in a race issue that really is irrelevant." While asserting that an affirmative answer to his question would not provide a basis for disqualifying a potential juror, Norwood Barber's counsel stated that it would assist him in exercising his peremptory challenges in an informed manner. He maintained that "race is already injected by the fact that the defendants are sitting there as an interracial couple." Linda Barber's counsel added, "The only reason I like [the question] there is that it literally lets [the jury] know race is not an issue, and we go ahead and we admit the obvious. It is see, look, this is an interracial couple. We all agree race is not an issue." He went on to conclude, "It clears the air.... I'd like to clear [the jurors'] subconscious and agree that it is not an issue, a non-issue."

The district court rejected the Barbers' proposed voir dire question, explaining that it "simply injects race into this trial, and I do not want to see that happen." Responding to the argument made by Linda Barber's counsel, the court stated, "If we want to clear the subconscious in this venire, we will be in there for two weeks in voir dire."

The Barbers contend that the district court's ruling was legal error which should be reviewed de novo. They maintain that they had "serious concerns and outright apprehension that there might be jurors on the panel who had serious, if not, principled opposition to interracial marriage." And they argue that "[t]he rights of the Barbers to direct their concerns in the form of voir dire clearly should have overridden the expressed concerns by the Court that such an inquiry would 'inject race' into the case."

While voir dire serves an important role in furthering the defendant's Sixth Amendment right to trial by an impartial jury, its conduct must be committed to the good judgment of the trial judge whose "immediate perceptions" determine what questions are appropriate for ferreting out relevant prejudices. *Rosales–Lopez v. United States*, 451 U.S. 182, 189, 101 S.Ct. 1629, 1634–35, 68 L.Ed.2d 22 (1981) (plurality opinion). The trial judge is in the best position to make judgments about the "impartiality and credibility" of potential jurors based on the judge's "own evaluations of demeanor evidence and of responses to questions." Id. at 188, 101 S.Ct. at 1634. For that reason trial courts are given "broad discretion as to the questions to be asked." Id. at 189, 101 S.Ct. at 1634 (quoting *Aldridge v. United States*, 283 U.S. 308, 310, 51 S.Ct. 470, 471, 75 L.Ed. 1054 (1931)); see also Fed.R.Crim.P. 24(a). Accordingly, we review a district court's refusal to ask requested voir dire questions for abuse of discretion. See *United States v. Brooks*, 957 F.2d 1138, 1144 (4th Cir.), cert. denied, 505 U.S. 1228, 112 S.Ct. 3051, 120 L.Ed.2d 917 (1992).

[We cannot ignore continuing incidents of racial prejudice that infect the dispensation of justice. Racial prejudice is a persisting malady with deep and complicated historical roots. But every criminal trial cannot be conducted as though race is an issue simply because the trial participants are of different races. If racial prejudice is ever to be eliminated, society's general concerns about such prejudice must not be permitted to erode the courts' efforts to provide impartial trials for the resolution of disputes. Because "[t]here is no constitutional presumption of juror bias for or against members of any particular racial or ethnic groups," *Rosales–Lopez*, 451 U.S. at 190, 101 S.Ct. at 1635, the courts must begin every trial with the idea of not focusing jurors' attention on the participants' membership in those particular groups. Particularly because we are a heterogenous society, courts should not indulge in "the divisive assumption ... that justice in a court of law may turn upon the pigmentation of skin, the accident of birth, or the choice of religion." *Ristaino v. Ross*, 424 U.S. 589, 596 n. 8, 96 S.Ct. 1017, 1021 n. 8, 47 L.Ed.2d 258 (1976).

Moreover, to seek out generalized prejudices during the voir dire would quickly divert the trial's focus from the guilt or innocence of the defendant to peripheral factors, such as the defendant's race or religious beliefs, which are usually irrelevant to the merits of the case. The very process of exploring such factors would heighten their role in the decisionmaking process and tend to subvert the court's express admonition to jurors to convict or acquit only on the evidence before them without partiality to any party.

Even though generalized prejudices should therefore not routinely be made a subject of inquiry during voir dire, it is also clear that when prejudice threatens the fairness of the process or the result, such an inquiry is required to eliminate that prejudice. When racial issues are "inextricably bound up with the conduct of the trial," the constitutional guarantee of a trial by an impartial jury requires that a court not refuse a request for voir dire directed to racial prejudice. *Rosales–Lopez*, 451 U.S. at 189, 101 S.Ct. at 1635 (quoting *Ristaino*, 424 U.S. at 597, 96 S.Ct. at 1021). This circumstance may occur when race is an issue to be tried either as an element of the offense or a defense or where racial issues are connected with the resolution of relevant facts.

Even if racial issues are not "inextricably bound up with the conduct of the trial"—the standard underpinning the constitutional mandate—a federal court may abuse its discretion in refusing to inquire into racial prejudice if there is a "reasonable possibility" that racial prejudice will influence the jury. *Rosales–Lopez*, 451 U.S. at 191, 101 S.Ct. at 1635–36. Under this non-constitutional standard, courts should exercise their discretion on a case-by-case basis, taking into account the totality of the circumstances. Id. at 192, 101 S.Ct. at 1636. See, e.g., *United States v. Okoronkwo*, 46 F.3d 426, 433–35 (5th Cir.) (no error in refusing to question prospective jurors about racial and national origin bias where Nigerian participated in a conspiracy to file false income tax returns and defendant was concerned that Nigerians had a reputation in Texas for fraud), cert. denied, 516 U.S. 833, 116 S.Ct. 107, 133 L.Ed.2d 60 (1995); *United States v. Kyles*, 40 F.3d 519, 524–26 (2d Cir.1994) (no error in refusing to question prospective jurors about racial prejudice where black defendant committed armed robbery against whites because the level of violence was insufficient to "ignite a jury's potential prejudices"), cert. denied, --- U.S. ----, 115 S.Ct. 1419, 131 L.Ed.2d 302 (1995).

In sum, absent special circumstances of a constitutional dimension—where racial issues are "inextricably bound up with the conduct of a trial"—the conduct of voir dire is left to the trial court's broad discretion, and we may find an abuse of discretion in a federal court's refusal to ask prospective jurors about racial prejudice only when (1) such a request has been made and (2) there is a "reasonable possibility" that racial prejudice might influence the jury.

In the case before us, the charges against the Barbers did not involve any element relating to race. Nor was the race of any participant an element of a legitimate defense. Moreover, the proof of facts at trial did not introduce race as an issue in the case. All seven counts of the indictment related to the financial question of whether defendants laundered money. The record is replete with evidence concerning the nature and complexity of the Barbers' financial transactions at five different financial institutions and concerning whether, in carrying out those transactions, the Barbers laundered the proceeds of drug sales in violation of 18 U.S.C. § 1956. The only reference to race in the record is the Barbers' argument to the court during voir dire that jurors could see that Norwood Barber is black and Linda Barber is white. We cannot conclude solely on this basis that racial issues were "inextricably bound up with the conduct of the trial."

While the record presents no indication that the constitutional guarantee of a fair trial required voir dire into racial prejudice in this case, we must still determine whether the district court abused its discretion under the non-constitutional standard. While the Barbers did make a request for voir dire into racial prejudice, they failed to establish a "reasonable possibility" that racial prejudice might influence the jury. The only fact the Barbers relied on was that the jury could see them sitting there as an interracial couple. While counsel for Linda Barber agreed that "race [was] not an issue," he requested voir dire into racial prejudice because it would "clear the air." The desire to "clear the air," however, does not establish a "reasonable possibility" that racial prejudice might influence the jury. The Supreme Court rejected similar arguments in Rosales–Lopez, holding that voir dire on racial prejudice was not required even though the defendant, a Mexican American charged with illegally bringing Mexican aliens into the country, cohabitated with the daughter of a white woman who served as a government witness. 451 U.S. at 193–94, 101 S.Ct. at 1636–37.

The dissent observes that antimiscegenation laws, which were held unconstitutional roughly 30 years ago, reflected a "prevalent social view" that mixed-race marriages were wrong and notes that "deep-seated sexual taboos ... take time to dissipate." While acknowledging that "without doubt attitudes have changed over time," the dissent notes, "The fact remains, no matter how much we dislike it, that we do not live in a color blind world." The dissent concludes, therefore, that the district court committed reversible error by refusing to inquire about prospective jurors' feelings about mixed-race marriages.

As unjust as our history of racial discrimination has been and as serious as the problem of racial prejudice continues to be, we do not believe that such problems are ameliorated by elevating jurors' views about miscegenation into relevant issues in routine money laundering cases, absent some particularized need. Just as "the raw fact of skin color" is not relevant in determining "the objectivity or qualifications of jurors," *Powers v. Ohio*, 499 U.S. 400, 410, 111 S.Ct. 1364, 1370, 113 L.Ed.2d 411 (1991), skin color of defendants is not an appropriate subject about which to inquire of prospective jurors when the sole issue for the jury is whether defendants are guilty of a financial crime.

To effectively ensure impartial juries and, indeed, equal protection generally, courts must focus remedies on specific racial prejudice, rather than on the effects of "past societal discrimination." See *City of Richmond v. J.A. Croson Co.*, 488 U.S. 469, 505, 109 S.Ct. 706, 728, 102 L.Ed.2d 854 (1989). In *Croson*, the Court cautioned that basing particularized remedies on "past societal discrimination" would "open the door to competing claims for 'remedial relief' for every disadvantaged group" and, thereby, undermine the very aspirations of the Equal Protection Clause. "The dream of a Nation of equal citizens in a society where race is irrelevant ... would be lost in a mosaic of shifting preferences based on inherently unmeasurable claims of past wrongs." Id. at 505–06, 109 S.Ct. at 728; see also *Podberesky v. Kirwan*, 38 F.3d 147, 155 (4th Cir.1994), cert. denied, --- U.S. ----, 115 S.Ct. 2001, 131 L.Ed.2d 1002 (1995). Analogously, conducting voir dire based on historical views about miscegenation in a case that does not present racial issues unnecessarily risks introducing such issues and, moreover, could open the door to voir dire demands relating to every societal prejudice. We decline to force courts down that road by requiring them to conduct such voir dire.

Moreover, we believe that the district court soundly decided in this case that voir dire questions about interracial marriage were inappropriate. The court expressed concern that to ask such questions would "inject[ ] race into this trial" and explained that it did "not want to see that happen." We agree with the court that a line of questioning about interracial marriage would have created the greater risk of injustice, or its appearance, by suggesting that even in a case where race is not an issue, justice turns upon the "pigmentation of skin [or] the accident of birth." *Ristaino*, 424 U.S. at 596 n. 8, 96 S.Ct. at 1021 n. 8.

Rather than highlight any one of many generalized prejudices that people may hold, the district court in this case elected—in the absence of any suggestion that a particular prejudice was inextricably bound up with the Barbers' case or posed a reasonable possibility of harmful influence—to avoid the risk of creating issues about those prejudices by pursuing a more neutral approach. The first question directed to the prospective jurors was whether they knew of any reason why they could not "hear the facts of this case fairly and impartially and render a just verdict." And the court asked in various contexts throughout the voir dire whether the jury could "hear the facts fairly and render a just verdict." Finally, the court asked the entire venire toward the end of voir dire whether they were able to render a verdict "solely on the evidence presented at this trial, testimony from the witness stand, the exhibits and in the context of the law as I will give it to you in my instructions, disregarding any other ideas, notions or beliefs about the law that you may have encountered in reaching your verdict." The jurors that were selected thus had stated under oath that they could render a fair and impartial verdict, based solely on the evidence.

In sum, we hold that the fact that the defendants in this money laundering case were partners in an interracial marriage did not, by itself, require the district court to grant their request to ask prospective jurors during voir dire about their views on interracial marriage. Moreover, we believe the district court better served the needs of justice in this instance by avoiding particularized inquiries into racial prejudice to minimize the possibility that race would play a role in the jury's decision. Accordingly, we cannot conclude that the court's refusal to inquire on voir dire about interracial marriage amounted to an unconstitutional abuse or other abuse of the court's discretion in conducting voir dire

....

Note

Perhaps the most famous example of using the voir dire process to both inquire into prospective jurors' attitudes regarding race, and to sensitize the juror on the issue of race, occurred in *People of California v. Huey P. Newton.* Huey P. Newton was tried in 1968 for the murder of John Frey, the assault with a deadly weapon upon Herbert Hearnes, both Oakland, California police officers, and the kidnapping of Dell Ross, also an Oakland police officer. The kidnapping charge was dismissed on a motion for acquittal, and the jury ultimately returned a verdict of not guilty as to the assault charge. The conviction of voluntary manslaughter regarding the Hearnes' death was ultimately reversed. *People v. Newton,* 8 Cal.App.3d 359 (1970).

Huey P. Newton was the co-founder and Minister of Defense of the Black Panther Party (BPP). A great deal of controversy and publicity surrounded the trial, in which no weapon was ever recovered, because of what was perceived as a confrontational relationship between the Black Panther Party and police. Among the activities of the BPP was a program in which party members would patrol Black neighborhoods and when coming upon an arrest in progress the

Party member would observe and from a distance advise the arrestee of his or her legal rights. See, Ralph R. Smith, Larry T. Watts, *Minimizing Racism in Jury Trials: The Voir Dire Conducted by Charles R. Garry in People of California v. Huey P. Newton; Book Review*, 1 NATIONAL BLACK LAW JOURNAL 281 (1971).

Famed criminal defense lawyer Charles R. Garry, in an effort to eliminate "from the *Newton* jury everyone infected with white racism, either objective or subjective", conducted a voir dire that took over two weeks and consumed 1500 pages of trial transcript. See, MINIMIZING RACISM IN JURY TRIALS: The Voir Dire Conducted by Charles R. Garry in People of California v. Huey P. Newton (A.F. Ginger ed., The National Lawyers Guild, 1969) at xxi

Below are some excerpts from that transcript, drawn from the Ginger edited text, that address some of the issues relating to racial attitudes and impartiality.

[excerpt]

Q Have you heard of the Black Panther Party?

Q Do you believe in your opinion . . . are they a good or bad group of men and women?

A Well, I don't know too much about them,

Q Well, what you do know about them, what 's your opinion about them?

A I have no opinion of them.

Q Have you ever expressed an opinion?

A No.

Q Do you believe that they are a threat to the coming society of white people?

A No. I don't think they are.

Q Do you know anything —- have you ever heard the term called black power?

A Yes. I have heard of it. I don't know anything —

Q (Interrupting) And what is your —— do you think that's good or bad?

A Well, I don't think it's too good.

Q What's wrong with it?

A I don't think —— the other term you called, white power, is too good either.

Q Do you believe that there has been nothing but white power for three or four hundred years in this country?

A Well, I couldn't say.

Q -well, do you believe there is white racism In Alameda County?

A I don't know.

Q Do you believe there Is white racism right where you are living In Hayward?

A Not that I know of

Q Do you think there is such a thing called white power?

A I have never heard of it until the last couple of days here at court.

Q Do you believe that the white people are the ones that control the destiny of the black people In Alameda County?

A I wouldn't know.

Q Is this because you have never given the matter any thought or you have just never observed It?

A Well, I haven't given it thought and I haven't observed It either.

Q You have seen those signs that say that, impeach Earl Warren, haven 't you?

A I have saw a few of them.

Q Do you agree or disagree with that?

A I have no opinion on it.

Q You have no opinion as to whether the Chief Justice of the United States is the type of a person who should be retained in his. role as an Independent body of the judiciary?

A Well, as far as I know he is, a nice man, a fine man.

Q Well, then, you do have an opinion?

A I don't know him. I have no opinion.

Q Do you own your own home, sir?

A I am buying it.

Q Now, do you believe that a law that says no person who owns a piece of property shall discriminate against any owner I mean shall discriminate against any tenant or any person that they are selling the property to because of race, color, or creed or national origin? Do you believe —— do you favor such a law?

A No. I don't favor a law.

Q In other words, you feel that a person who owns his property should be able to sell it to any-body he wants to and discriminate against any— body irrespective of whether they are white, black, or green?

A I wouldn't say discriminate, but I think a man should be able to sell his property or anything to anybody he wants to.

Q And you firmly believe that, don't you, that a person who owns his property can sell it to whomever, or rent it to whomever he pleases , and if he wants to discriminate against anybody, no law can say he can't do that, isn't that right?

A That's right.

Q Do you think that is compatible with the Constitution and the Bill of Rights and the question of equality of all men and women irrespective of their race or color?

MR. JENSEN: Objection

THE COURT: You are asking him to be a constitutional lawyer. Objection sustained. You may ask him how he feels about it but —

Mr. GARRY: How do you feel about this business of a person discriminating against another person because he happens to be black, and not rent his property to him?

A I don't think anything of that. I don 't go for that.

Q You don't go for that, yet you don't want any law to extend that?

THE COURT: The juror did not use the word, discriminate. He said he did not discriminate. He has his ideas about sale of property. You may proceed further.

Mr. GARRY: You said you didn't go for that. You didn't approve of that, is that what you said?

THE COURT: If you will make your answer so that the reporter can hear you

THE JUROR: Yes, sir.

Mr. GARRY: Yet you don't approve of any law that prevents a person from doing that very thing you don't approve of?

A No, I don't.

Q Why not?

A Well, as I said, I think anybody should be able to sell to whoever he wants to no matter black or any other color, That has nothing to do with It.

Q And you don't want a law that says that a person cannot discriminate against a person because of his race or color when it comes to renting or selling his property?

A No.

Q Why not?

THE COURT: I think he has already answered that.

MR. GARRY: No, he hasn 't answered that one, Your Honor.

THE JUROR: I just don't believe in it. That is all.

Mr. GARRY: You don't believe In It because you believe in racial segregation and you believe in the right of a property owner to keep a particular area completely white, Isn't that your position, sir?

A No, no.

Q The very fact that you live in an area where It Is predominately white, you want to keep It that way, don't you, sir?

A No, no, I don't.

Q You don't want to keep it that way?

A No, it doesn't make any difference.

Q What organizations do you belong to, Mr. Hall?

A I don 't belong to any.

Q None at all?

....

[Excerpt]

[QUESTIONING PROSPECTIVE JURORS ON PRO-POLICE, ANTI-BLACK PANTHER ATTITUDES]

[Prospective juror Mr. S compared Panther demonstrators to Nazis, liked "Support Your Local Police" bumper strips. Garry used a peremptory challenge on him.]

BY MR. GARRY: And have you had any military service?

A 21 years.

Q What was your rank when you left the service?

A Chief hospital corpsman.

Q And in the course of your duties as a member of the Armed Forces did you ever have occasion to be on any court martials?

A No, I was a witness in a court martial once.

Q Were you a witness for the prosecution or for the accused?

A I was a witness for the defense, for the accused.

Q Have you ever heard of white racism?

A Yes.

Q What is your views about white racism?

A Well, it is a pretty broad term. I have attempted to determine what the meaning was actually and according to the dictionary it Is supposedly a feeling of superiority because of the white race, I don't know what your interpretation is.

Q Well, that is a pretty good interpretation. Do you have any elements of white racism within you?

A Well, again it depends upon what you would refer to as white racism. I suppose that I do have some latent feeling identified with the Caucasian race as a colored person would with the Negro race. Other than that I don't have any animosity to a race particularly.

Q Then what you are really saying when you are talking about latent feeling, you are referring in the area of

subjective feelings you may have ?

A (Nods affirmatively.)

Q But they are not in the open where you can see it, is that right?

A I suppose so.

Q Did you ever hear of black power?

A Yes

Q How do you feel about that?

A Well, again there has been a lot of different discussions on black power.

THE COURT: Do you know what black power is?

THE JUROR: No, sir there has been too many –

THE COURT: Any question you don't know, you say so.

MR. GARRY: Have you any idea what it is?

A I have a number of ideas. Different ideas have been presented to me.

Q What do you know about it? Do you think it is good or bad?

A I would say myself It is a black power and I don't subscribe to the burn baby, burn ... black power ... that has been referred to.

Q You have mentioned the terminology burn baby, burn. What do you understand that means?

A I saw a newscast on television at one of the riots where there were a lot of fires, et cetera, and this was one of the comments that was made at that time. This sort of thing I don't believe In, destroying other people's property and rioting in the streets and total disregard for the law. It just goes against my grain.

Q Do you believe that the black people are responsible for this so— called burn baby, burn?

A I am afraid that I am not in a position to judge who is responsible. If I knew that, I could solve a lot of problems .

Q Well, apparently you have shown some interest in this. Have you read the President 's Commission Report on the so—called riots of the east?

THE COURT: It is the Kerner Report. Have you read that?

THE JUROR: No, sir, I didn't read that.

MR. GARRY: Have you read any of the excerpts or digests that were in the newspaper?

A No, I have read various articles that refer to it briefly but I couldn't begin to tell you any of the contents of it.

Q You have heard of the Black Panthers, have you not?

A Yes.

Q What is your view about them?

JENSEN: Object to that, ambiguous, Your Honor.

THE COURT: Do you know what the Black Panthers stand for?

THE JUROR: Not totally, no.

MR. GARRY: Well, excluding totally, what do you understand about them? Do you think they are good or bad, what do you understand?

MR. JENSEN: Object to that as ambiguous.

GARRY: That is not ambiguous. I want to know whether he has any fixed opinion.

THE COURT: Have you got an opinion on that subject?

THE JUROR: I have mixed emotions on that subject. I suppose, Your Honor, originally, I thought it was another organization similar to the NAACP which were trying to better the Negro popu-lation. I was a bit disturbed in seeing the things that were around the courthouse and the first thing that came to my mind was on the demonstrators in front of the courthouse was that Nazi storm troopers when they were standing with their flags out and at parade rest. So I really don't know that much about it.

THE COURT: Well, whatever you do know, do you think that could make It so you couldn't be completely fair and impartial in this case?

JUROR: No, sir.

GARRY: In other words, Mr. Striplin, you equate the Black Panthers with the Nazi storm troopers?

MR. JENSEN: Object to that, that is not a correct statement of the testimony.

THE COURT: Go ahead. Reframe your question. Do you equate them?

THE JUROR: As I stated when I saw them on the steps, this is the first thing that came to my mind. They were on the steps of the courthouse standing at parade rest all dressed in black with the banners and this is the first thing that came to my mind. I don't equate the organization with the Nazi storm troopers. This particular incident was the only thing.

MR. GARRY: Has there been anything about what you have seen subsequently or later that would change your mind that the first impression was that the Black Panthers reminded you of the Nazi storm troopers?

A As far as I am concerned the Black Panther Party was an organization assisting the colored people. That was my first Impression.

A That wasn't on a voluntary basis. I stood at parade rest; it was because I was ordered to do so.

....

CHAPTER NINE: RACE AND CORPOREAL IDENTIFICATION

Note

There are few aspects of the criminal justice system more frightening or of greater concern, than the wrongful conviction of the innocent. It is conservatively estimated that as many as 10,000 persons may be wrongfully convicted of serious crimes each year. See, C. RONALD HUFF, CONVICTED BUT INNOCENT: WRONGFUL CONVICTION AND PUBLIC POLICY (1996). The "most common cause ... is eyewitness misidentification." Samuel R. Gross et al., Exonerations in the United States 1989 through 2003, 95 J. CRIM. L. & CRIMINOLOGY 523, 542 (2005). Forty percent or more of wrongful eyewitness identifications involve attempts at cross-racial identification. See, Innocence Project, Leading Causes of Wrongful Convictions, NAACP, http://www.naacp.org (2017). See also, Andrew E. Taslitz, *"Curing" Own Race Bias: What Cognitive Science and The Henderson Case Teach About Improving Jurors' Ability to Identify Race-Tainted Eyewitness Error*, 16 N.Y.U. JOURNAL OF LEGISLATIVE & PUB. POLICY, 1049 (2013). Attempts at combatting wrongful eyewitness identification – particularly the dangers of cross-racial identification have centered on three areas. First, the constitutional considerations surrounding mis-identification as a violation of the Due Process Clause of the Fourteenth Amendment and the importance of the Sixth Amendment right to appointed counsel and pre-trial identifications, Second, special instructions to the jury as to the dangers and likelihood of cross-racial misidentification and third, educating the trier of fact of the human fallibility of cross-racial identification through the use of expert testimony. The following explores these three approaches in greater detail.

Race and Constitutional Challenges to Lineup, Show-up and Photographic Identifications

Note

In a series of cases, beginning with *Stovall v. Denno*, 388 U.S. 293 (1967) the United States Supreme Court has considered if and when a pretrial identification, along with a subsequent, but possibly dependent, in-court identification, can be so unreliable as to violate Due Process when the results of such procedures are introduced as evidence against the defendant. In *Manson v.*

Braithwaite, 432 U.S. 98 (1977), the court reiterated its position that as determined by a totality of the circumstances, a pretrial identification violates Due Process where there exists an unduly suggestive identification that creates a substantial likelihood of irreparable misidentification. In determination whether there is a substantial likelihood of irreparable misidentification the Court lists the factors to be considered to include; the opportunity of the witness to view the crime at the time of the crime, the witness' degree of attention, the accuracy of any prior description of the criminal, the level of certainty demonstrated at the confrontation, and the time between the crime and confrontation. The role and degree of difficulty of cross-racial identification is not specifically addressed, but what role if any, should it play in the Due Process analysis?

UNITED STATES V. JONES
762 F.Supp.2d 270 (D. Mass 2010)

....

This case turns on the identification of Jones as the person who set up the drug transaction in question. In the constitutional sense, the identification of Jones could hardly have been more suggestive, but even a suggestive identification does not ipso facto require suppression. See *Manson v. Brathwaite,* 432 U.S. 98, 104, 97 S.Ct. 2243, 53 L.Ed.2d 140 (1977); *Neil v. Biggers,* 409 U.S. 188, 199, 93 S.Ct. 375, 34 L.Ed.2d 401 (1972); *Simmons v. United States,* 390 U.S. 377, 385–86, 88 S.Ct. 967, 19 L.Ed.2d 1247 (1968); *Stovall v. Denno,* 388 U.S. 293, 301–02, 87 S.Ct. 1967, 18 L.Ed.2d 1199 (1967).

Here, defense counsel timely moved for suppression. After a thorough evidentiary hearing, the Court found that, following his standard operating procedure, Massachusetts State Trooper David Patterson ("Patterson"), a white male acting in an undercover capacity and posing as a retail drug purchaser, was roving selected areas of Brockton seeking to engage in modest drug transactions. Patterson was driving a pick-up truck specially equipped with a hidden video camera to record individuals (such as drug sellers) approaching his open driver's side window. In order for this scam to work, Patterson naturally did not know the individuals with whom he dealt nor did they know him. On a good day, Patterson could make a number of buys in this fashion. At the end of the day, Patterson turned a copy of the videotape over to Brockton police officers who patrolled the area through which he had driven to see whether, given their familiarity with the area and its inhabitants as well as local law enforcement intelligence, they could identify anyone on the videotape. Thereafter, such officers would show Patterson a single photo and ask him if he could identify the individual as a person he'd seen selling drugs at the specific time and place. Not surprisingly, using this procedure Patterson made affirmative identifications over 90% of the time.

So it was here. On June 19, 2008, Patterson was trolling for prospective drug sellers in Brockton. He set up such a transaction through a discussion with a black male who he observed across a residential street. This individual then entered the passenger side of a nearby sedan that promptly drove away, and a second individual, later identified as Johnny Richmond, approached Patterson's truck and exchanged .62 grams of crack cocaine for cash through the driver's side window. What took this transaction out of the routine was the fact that, as the first individual was approaching Patterson's truck to set up the transaction, Patterson observed another vehicle evidently patrolling this area. Reasoning that this strange vehicle could be that of a citizen vigilante or a rival gang setting him up for robbery of the cash or drugs, Patterson went on high alert. Having completed this transaction, he sped from the area. When the strange vehicle followed him, he became apprehensive and called for police back-up.

The videotape vividly captures Johnny Richmond approaching Patterson's driver's side window and completing the exchange. Earlier, it displays a most fleeting and out of focus image of another black male. By pausing the tape, one can discern the clothing of this individual and, based upon all the surrounding circumstances, this Court concluded a knowledgeable local police officer could make an identification of that individual. Trooper Erik Telford ("Telford"), a member of a State Police gang unit surveilling this area of Brockton, identified this individual as Daquawn Jones and later showed a single photo of Jones to Patterson, who likewise identified Jones as the individual who had set up the drug transaction in question.

At the conclusion of the hearing of the motion to suppress, after hearing the arguments of counsel and considering all the evidence, this Court, although disapproving the procedure followed here, nevertheless, "unsupported by any literature or social science findings," reasoned that Patterson's heightened awareness of his surroundings due to the presence of the strange vehicle, his concentration on the suspects given his mission, his proximity to the black male across the street, the well lit area, and the short time that elapsed between the observation and the identification rendered his identification of Jones reliable and not the product of the suggestive procedures followed here. Accordingly, the Court denied the motion to suppress, and at trial both Patterson and Telford testified to their observations.

[In addition to denying the defendant's motion to suppress the trial court also upheld it's denial of the admission of expert testimony before the jury on cross-racial identification regarding the credibility of the prosecution's eye-witnesses. The question of expert testimony is discussed in detail below.]

....

Finally, if the court determines that an out-of-court identification has occurred under conditions that are unnecessarily suggestive and unreliable, the burden at trial is on the state to establish by clear and convincing evidence under the totality of the circumstances that the in-court identification is based upon the witness' independent recollection, untainted by the faulty pretrial identification process. See *United States v. Wade*, 388 U.S. 218, 240, 87 S.Ct. 1926, 18 L.Ed.2d 1149 1967); see also *Moore v. Illinois*, 434 U.S. 220, 225–26, 98 S.Ct. 458, 54 L.Ed.2d 424 (1977); *State v. Mitchell*, 204 Conn. 187, 204, 527 A.2d 1168, cert. denied, 484 U.S. 927, 108 S.Ct. 293, 98 L.Ed.2d 252 (1987); *State v. Guertin*, 190 Conn. 440, 458–59, 461 A.2d 963 (1983); *State v. Gordon*, 185 Conn. 402, 418, 441 A.2d 119 (1981), cert. denied, 455 U.S. 989, 102 S.Ct. 1612, 71 L.Ed.2d 848 (1982). In making this assessment, the task of the trial court is to determine whether an in-court identification that follows an impermissibly suggestive out-of-court identification has been tainted so as to render its admission a violation of a defendant's due process rights. *State v. Manson*, 118 Conn.App. 538, 548, 984 A.2d 1099 (2009), cert. denied, 295 Conn. 902, 988 A.2d 878 (2010). In short, an in-court identification after an unnecessarily suggestive and unreliable out-of-court identification procedure should be allowed only "if it is purged of the taint of the defective pretrial procedure by establishment of the fact that it is based upon disassociated and independent observation." (Internal quotation marks omitted.) *State v. Piskorski*, 177 Conn. 677, 741–42, 419 A.2d 866 (superseded by statute on other grounds as stated in *State v. Canady*, 187 Conn. 281, 283–84, 445 A.2d 895 [1982]), cert. denied, 444 U.S. 935, 100 S.Ct. 283, 62 L.Ed.2d 194 (1979).

The court's first task, to determine whether the pretrial identification procedure was unnecessarily suggestive, requires the court to consider first whether the procedure was suggestive and then, if so, whether the suggestive identification was nevertheless justified under the particular circumstances. *State v. Reddick*, supra, 224 Conn. at 465, 619 A.2d 453. If the court finds that the procedure was unduly suggestive, the court's assessment of whether the unduly suggestive identification and any subsequent in-court identification are nonetheless reliable must be based on an examination of the totality of the circumstances. *Id.* The United States Supreme Court in *Manson v. Brathwaite*, 432 U.S. 98, 97 S.Ct. 2243, 53 L.Ed.2d 140 (1977), provided guidance for trial courts in assessing whether an unnecessarily suggestive pretrial identification may nonetheless be admitted at trial. The court enumerated a nonexclusive list of factors to be considered in assessing admissibility. Id., at 114–16, 97 S.Ct. 2243. Those factors include the opportunity of the witness to view the criminal at the time of the crime, the witness' degree of attention, the accuracy of his or her prior description of the criminal, the level of certainty demonstrated at the confrontation and the time between the crime and the confrontation. Id.; see also *State v.*

Gordon, supra, 185 Conn. at 415, 441 A.2d 119. These factors, however, must be weighed against the corrupting effect of the suggestive identification itself, for "[w]here the 'indicators of [a witness'] ability to make an accurate identification' are 'outweighed by the corrupting effect' of law enforcement suggestion, the identification should be suppressed." *Perry v. New Hampshire*, --- U.S. ----, 132 S.Ct. 716, 719, 181 L.Ed.2d 694 (2012); *Manson v. Brathwaite*, supra, at 116, 97 S.Ct. 2243; *State v. Gordon*, supra, at 415, 441 A.2d 119.

The issue of whether an out-of-court identification was unnecessarily suggestive involves a mixed question of law and fact. *State v. Marquez*, 291 Conn. 122, 136, 967 A.2d 56, cert. denied, --- U.S. ----, 130 S.Ct. 237, 175 L.Ed.2d 163 (2009). Accordingly, our review is plenary. Id. Additionally, "because the issue of the suggestiveness of a photographic array implicates the defendant's constitutional right to due process, we undertake a scrupulous examination of the record to ascertain whether the findings are supported by substantial evidence." (Internal quotation marks omitted.) Id., at 137, 967 A.2d 56; see *State v. Mullins*, 288 Conn. 345, 364, 952 A.2d 784 (2008). In conducting our review of the issue of reliability, "we examine the legal question of reliability with exceptionally close scrutiny and defer less than we normally do to the related fact finding of the trial court." (Internal quotation marks omitted.) *State v. Wooten*, 227 Conn. 677, 688, 631 A.2d 271 (1993), quoting *State v. Gordon*, supra, 185 Conn. at 416, 441 A.2d 119; see also *State v. Marquez*, supra, at 137, 967 A.2d 56; *State v. Figueroa*, 235 Conn. 145, 155, 665 A.2d 63 (1995).

Finally, if we find that the court incorrectly permitted, as reliable, evidence flowing from an unreliable and unduly suggestive identification procedure, there remains the further issue of whether the ensuing judgment of conviction may be affirmed on the ground that the due process violation was, nevertheless, harmless in light of all the evidence correctly adduced at trial and untainted by the admission of an unreliable identification. This question requires, in part, that we discuss whether the harmless error doctrine is applicable in this legal context and, if so, the parameters of a harmless error analysis in the context of a constitutional error.

Having set forth an overview of the applicable law regarding the admissibility of identification evidence, we now turn to an analysis of the issue at hand, that is, whether the defendant's due process rights were violated by the admission of unnecessarily suggestive and unreliable eyewitness identifications and, if so, whether the judgment must be reversed.

We first examine the question of whether the identification was unnecessarily suggestive. The following supplemental facts are relevant to a discussion of this issue. At trial, Hartford police Officer Jose Rivera testified that he spoke with Otero at the scene shortly after the assault and that Otero told him that he had initially been struck by a light-skinned black male, approximately five feet, eight inches tall and weighing 180 pounds, who had been the operator of an automobile that almost struck him and that the operator had been the first one to get out of the car. On cross-examination, Rivera confirmed that Otero had made no mention of any of the perpetrators having facial freckles. On direct examination, Otero indicated that he had not seen the initial perpetrator before and that he did not know his name. Rivera further testified that Otero indicated to him that he could not positively identify anyone else involved.

Following Rivera, Otero testified and made an in-court identification of the defendant. He also testified that he had made an out-of-court identification. Otero stated that in the weeks following the incident he received secondhand and thirdhand reports, giving him names of people who might have been involved, including the name "Hershey," which he was told was the defendant's street name. Otero stated that in May, 2008, while at the Hartford police station, he was shown a photographic array of eight individuals from which he was not able to make a positive identification. The defendant's photograph was not part of this array. Otero testified that after he had been told by others, secondhand and thirdhand, that the defendant had been involved in the attack on him, he looked the defendant up on the department of correction website and discovered that the defendant was incarcerated. He stated that on the day he gave Hartford Detective Jeremy Bilbo the defendant's name, Bilbo then brought up the defendant's photograph on his computer. Otero testified that while he expected to see several photographs on the computer screen, there was only one photograph, that of the defendant, and that upon seeing the defendant's photograph, he immediately identified him as the initial assailant.

Bilbo testified that in May, 2008, he showed Otero a photographic array with eight photographs that did not include the defendant. From this array, Otero was not able to make any positive identifications, although he did indicate that two of the photographs were similar to the person who attacked him. One of the photographs tentatively selected by Otero was that of Robert Acevedo. Bilbo indicated, as well, that in June, 2008, he prepared a photographic array for Otero and that this array included the defendant's photograph. However, he did not show this array to Otero because he did not believe that Otero could identify any of his attackers. Nevertheless, Bilbo testified that six or seven months later he did show Otero a booking photograph of the defendant, with the name "Artis" printed across the front of the shirt of the person depicted, while telling Otero that it was a photograph of the defendant, that the defendant was a suspect in the case, and that he was seeking an arrest warrant for him. Contrary to Otero's testimony, Bilbo claimed that Otero was not able to identify the defendant from this one photograph even though he told Otero that it was a photograph of the defendant. Bilbo stated, as well, that when shown the photograph of the defendant, Otero responded that he did not know who his attackers were and acknowledged that he could not identify them. Bilbo did not, at any time before or after he showed Otero the single booking photograph, display the photographic array to him that included the defendant's photograph.

Confronted with the inconsistency between Otero's testimony that he positively identified the defendant from the one photograph shown to him and Bilbo's testimony that Otero did not make an identification, the court concluded, after hearing a motion to suppress, that Otero's testimony was more credible in this regard than Bilbo's. The court, therefore, concluded that Otero had made an out-of-court pretrial identification of the defendant as the initial assailant.

While in a claim of a wrongfully admitted photographic identification, our review of the record is more scrupulous than the norm, it is not our function to make our own credibility determination from the bare record. In this instance, the record provides ample basis for the court to have concluded, as it did, that Otero identified the defendant as his assailant from the one photograph shown to him by Bilbo.

On the basis of these facts, there can be no question that this identification procedure was improper and that it was clearly not made necessary by any extenuating circumstances. Indeed, to characterize the process as merely suggestive belies the facts found by the court. It is undisputed that after Otero had told Bilbo of his belief in the defendant's involvement in the assault that Bilbo then showed the defendant's photograph to Otero while identifying the person in the photograph as the defendant and simultaneously telling Otero that the defendant was a suspect whose arrest he would be seeking. It would be difficult to conceive of a less neutral or more preemptive identification process than the one that occurred in this instance. It was against the backdrop of this dramatically improper identification process that the court was required to assess the identification's reliability.

Our Supreme Court has stated that "almost any one-to-one confrontation between a victim of a crime and a person whom the police present as a suspect is presumptively suggestive ... because it conveys the message to the victim that the police believe the suspect is guilty." (Citation omitted; internal quotation marks omitted.) *State v. Wooten*, supra, 227 Conn. at 686, 631 A.2d 271; see also *State v. Randolph*, 284 Conn. 328, 385–86, 933 A.2d 1158 (2007) (danger of misidentification "will be increased if the police display to the witness only the picture of a single individual who generally resembles the person he saw" [internal quotation marks omitted]); *State v. Crosby*, 36 Conn.App. 805, 819, 654 A.2d 371 ("[w]ithout question, almost any one-to-one confrontation between a victim and a suspect must convey the message that the police have reason to believe him guilty, and is therefore unnecessarily suggestive"), cert. denied, 232 Conn. 921, 656 A.2d 669 (1995). In this instance, there was no implied message. To the contrary, Bilbo was clear and explicit in stating that the photograph was of the defendant, and that he was a suspect in the case whose arrest he was seeking. The process was not merely suggestive; it was preemptory and conclusive.

As to whether an overly suggestive identification procedure is necessary, the court will look to whether exigent circumstances existed, such as a show-up shortly after a crime while the victim's memory is fresh and to quickly eliminate any innocent persons. *State v. Wooten*, supra, 227 Conn. at 686, 631 A.2d 271. Our Supreme Court has stated that an immediate viewing of the suspect may be justified where "it [is] important for the police to separate the prime suspect gold from the suspicious glitter, so as to enable them ... to continue their investigations with a minimum of delay." (Internal quotation marks omitted.) *State v. Collette*, 199 Conn. 308, 311, 507 A.2d 99 (1986). In this instance, in which the one photograph was shown to Otero months following the incident, the state properly makes no argument that exigent circumstances existed.

As noted, Bilbo testified that by June, 2008, he had prepared a photographic array that included the defendant's photograph but that he did not show it to Otero because he had said he could not identify his attackers. Then, months later, for reasons he is unable to fully explain, he stated that he showed Otero a photograph of the defendant while simultaneously identifying him by name and characterizing him as a suspect whose arrest he was seeking. The state makes no claim, nor do we find any basis for concluding, that this identification procedure was necessary.

Having reached the conclusion that the out-of-court identification procedure was constitutionally flawed, we turn next to a consideration of whether, despite the failings of the process, Otero's out-of-court and in-court identifications were reliable under all the circumstances. In making this assessment, we track the factors outlined in *Manson v. Brathwaite*, supra, 432 U.S. at 114–16, 97 S.Ct. 2243, and we weigh those factors against the corrupting influence of the improper identification.

A
The Opportunity of the Witness to View the Defendant at the Time of the Assault

This consideration implicates factors that relate to the victim's condition at the time as well as the external environment. As to the former, and contrary to the trial court's finding that Otero consumed a "couple of beers" in the hour and one-half before the incident, Otero acknowledged that between 11:30 p.m. and 1 a.m., moments before the altercation, he consumed "[a]t least four" beers, which he described as twelve ounce bottles of Heineken beer. One's level of intoxication, we know from the reported research, plays a significant role in one's powers of observation and concentration. See G. Gaulkin, Report of the Special Master, *State v. Henderson*, New Jersey Supreme Court, Docket No. A–8–08 (June 18, 2010) p. 47, (the court noted, as undisputed, a finding that "the effects of alcohol on identification accuracy show that high levels of alcohol promote false identifications" and that "low alcohol intake produces fewer misidentifications than high alcohol intake").

As to external influences on Otero's opportunity to see his assailant during the altercation, Otero testified that shortly after he left Club NV, and while he was en route to Club Blu, he was nearly run over by an automobile. With respect to the lighting, although it is clear that at 1 a.m. on an early February morning it was dark, Rivera testified that, in his experience, the area is well lit. Nevertheless, the record is not explicit regarding the lighting at the exact location of the assault or the distance of any artificial lighting from the site of the altercation. We recognize, however, that the assault took place on an urban street and that, as observed by the court, the lighting was sufficient for Otero to have described the make and model of the car that almost struck him.

Another factor relating to the victim's opportunity to observe his attacker is the amount of time involved in the incident. In this regard, Otero's testimony was inconsistent as to how long the altercation lasted. According to Otero, during the brief duration of the incident, the passenger emerged from the automobile, approached him, struck him in the face and shoulder, and he punched back; each landed approximately two punches before Otero was struck from behind and landed on all fours. At one point during his testimony, Otero was unequivocal in stating that the verbal exchange between himself and his assailant lasted "less than two seconds" before the physical fight began. Otero further acknowledged that the physical altercation started with the assailant landing a punch to his face. At another point in his testimony, Otero stated that he had been face-to-face with the initial assailant for "five, ten" seconds. Elsewhere in his testimony, Otero stated, as to the incident, "I mean, it was fast. Everything happened so fast."

In its analysis of this factor, the court concluded that Otero had an adequate opportunity to see the assailant, and the court made reference to Otero's testimony that he was face-to-face with the assailant for five to ten seconds. The court, however, made no explicit determination of the length of time Otero and his assailant were face-to-face, other than stating it was only a few seconds. Rather, the court based its conclusion on its view that "a good hard look will pass muster, even if it occurs during a fleeting glance"; (internal quotation marks omitted); quoting *State v. Cubano*, 203 Conn. 81, 95, 523 A.2d 495 (1987), and citing *State v. Ledbetter*, 185 Conn. 607, 615, 441 A.2d 595 (1981). Interestingly, the "fleeting glance" referred to in Cubano was a period of several minutes when the witness was within two or three feet of the defendant; *State v. Cubano*, supra, at 95, 523 A.2d 495; and the "fleeting glance" in *Ledbetter* consisted of the witness viewing the robber's face for approximately "fifteen or twenty seconds...." *State v. Ledbetter*, supra, at 615, 441 A.2d 595. Apparently finding comfort in the "fleeting glance" references of these earlier decisions, the court substantially compressed the time period in which a victim may be found to have had a "good hard look."

B
The Witness' Degree of Attention

To buttress its conclusion regarding Otero's opportunity to observe the defendant, the court noted not only that Otero gave an apt description of the defendant's physical appearance but that he had been concentrating on his attacker. In this regard, the court noted, "[Otero's] observation of and description of such [a] facial feature [as freckles] is not merely indicative of [a] perfectly adequate opportunity to observe but also confirms that his concentration was on the perpetrator's face, unlike moments later when he was struck from behind and unable to see or identify his other attackers...." This characterization, however, is inaccurate as, during the trial, Rousseau testified that when he met with Otero at the hospital shortly after the assault, Otero gave him descriptions of three people, one light-skinned black male, twenty-seven to twenty-eight years old, five feet, eight inches to five feet, nine inches tall, and 180 pounds, a light-skinned black male with freckles, twenty-seven to twenty-eight years old, five feet, nine inches, 200 pounds and stocky as the front seat passenger, and a black female, twenty-three to twenty-four years old, five feet, three inches, 120 pounds, whom he did not think was involved in the assault. Furthermore, in this regard, Bilbo testified that when he showed Otero an array of eight photographs, including a photograph of Robert Acevedo, Otero picked out Robert Acevedo and another person as similar to the person who had attacked him. This uncontra-dicted testimony of Otero's detailed descriptions of three individuals allegedly at the scene of the attack and his successful selection of the photograph of Robert Acevedo as looking similar to his attacker contradict the court's conclusion regarding the level of Otero's concentration on his attacker.

Also relevant to Otero's opportunity to view the defendant as his initial assailant is the conflicting testimony regarding the location of the assailant immediately before the incident. Although Rivera testified that Otero told him at the scene that his initial assailant had been the driver of the Infiniti automobile, Otero testified that the assailant had alighted from the front passenger seat of the automobile. Miano, however, testified that she had been the front right side passenger and that the defendant had been either in the vehicle's backseat or in the pro-cess of getting into or out of the car. This conflicting evidence not only speaks to the confused circumstances regarding the fast-moving events that resulted in Otero's injuries but also erodes confidence in the accuracy of his observations at the moment. Finally, it is noteworthy that Otero was not, at any time, able to provide a description, in any manner, of the clothes worn by his assailant.

Thus, although Otero testified that he and the defendant were face-to-face as they exchanged punches, the undisputed testimony from the record reveals that their confrontation in this melee of a few seconds took place in the context of a heated verbal exchange during which Otero was struck twice by his assailant, in the shoulder and facial area, and during which Otero struck the assailant two times. Although there was no direct evidence regarding Otero's emotional condi-tion at the time, it is reasonable to infer that, just having nearly been struck by an automobile and in the midst of a heated physical and verbal exchange, he was agitated and under stress. The notion that a person's level of stress has a correlation to that person's accuracy of observation and recall is not novel and has support in decisional law as well as in social science. In 1976, the United States Court of Appeals for the Sixth Circuit, in *United States v. Russell*, 532 F.2d 1063 (6th Cir.1976), observed, "[t]here is a great potential for misidentification when a witness identi-fies a stranger based solely upon a single brief observation, and this risk is increased when the observation was made at a time of stress or excitement.... This problem is important because of all the evidence that may be presented to a jury, a witness' in-court statement that 'he is the one' is probably the most dramatic and persuasive." (Citations omitted.) Id., at 1066–67. In a similar vein, the Utah Supreme Court observed, "[c]ontrary to much accepted lore, when an observer is experiencing a marked degree of stress, perceptual abilities are known to decrease significantly." *State v. Long*, 721 P.2d 483, 489 (Utah 1986); see also *State v. Henderson*, 208 N.J. 208, 262, 27 A.3d 872 (2011) ("[w]e find that high levels of stress are likely to affect the reliability of eyewitness identifications"); *State v. Cromedy*, 158 N.J. 112, 124, 727 A.2d 457 (1999) ("[t]here is a great potential for misidentification when a witness identifies a stranger based solely upon a single brief observation, and this risk is increased when the observation was made at a time of stress or excitement" [internal quotation marks omitted]); *State v. Dubose*, 285 Wis.2d 143, 166 n. 10, 699 N.W.2d 582 (2005).

C
The Accuracy of the Witness' Prior Description of the Defendant

As noted by the trial court, Otero's identification of the defendant was accurate except with respect to his age. Rivera testified that Otero described his assailant as a light-skinned black male, approximately five feet, eight inches tall and weighing approximately 180 pounds. Bilbo testified that Otero had described his assailant to another officer as the front right seat passenger of the automobile that almost struck him and that this person was a light-skinned black male with freckles on his face. Rousseau testified that he had gone to the hospital after the incident and obtained from Otero descriptions of three individuals. Otero told Rousseau that the front seat passenger was a light-skinned black male with freckles, twenty-seven to twenty-eight years old, approximately five feet, nine inches, 200 pounds and stocky. Otero described another assailant as a light-skinned black male, approximately twenty-seven to twenty-eight years old, five feet, eight inches to five feet, nine inches tall, and weighing approximately 180 pounds. The similarities between these two descriptions weigh against their singularity. Otero described a third person, who he did believe was directly involved, as a black female, age twenty-three to twenty-four years old, five feet, three inches tall and approximately 120 pounds.

Rousseau testified that, at the hospital, Otero told him that he did not think that he could identify any of his attackers. We know from the record that, at the time of the attack Otero was thirty-six years old, and so he was describing the two males who attacked him as eight to nine years younger than he was. We know, as well, from the record, that, on February 15, 2008, the defendant was thirty-seven years old, or nine to ten years older than the assailant initially described by Otero on the day of the incident. While, in other respects, Otero's description of his initial assailant appears to be consistent with the defendant (as well as with the other male who is described), we do not have, from the record, any reference data with which to draw any conclusions regarding the relative distinctiveness of the assailant's description.

D

The Level of Certainty Demonstrated at the Confrontation

This factor warrants little discussion because, at the time of the confrontation, Otero was told, and not asked, by Bilbo that the photograph he was being shown was that of the defendant and that the defendant was a suspect in the case whose arrest Bilbo was seeking. We know, as well, that before this procedure, Otero had heard from "[s]econd, thirdhand" sources that the defendant had been involved in the altercation and that Otero, in fact, had relayed the defendant's name to the police. Therefore, Otero went to the police department with the defendant in his mind as one of the assailants, a belief that immediately was buttressed by Bilbo's confirming to him that the defendant was a suspect whose arrest he was in the process of seeking. Thus, while the record is clear that Otero testified in court that, upon seeing the photograph of the defendant he identified him, with certainty, as his initial assailant, little weight should be accorded to Otero's level of certainty, given the prelude to the photographic identification. The trial court, however, appears to have given great weight to this factor. In placing on the record its reasons for denying the motion to suppress, the court stated: "Most significantly and as is apparent from much of the foregoing, the level of certainty of Mr. Otero's identification of the accused was exceedingly high." Similarly, with regard to the in-court identification, the court observed: "With respect to his in-court identification of the defendant at the evidentiary hearing on this motion, [Otero] expressed or displayed absolutely no uncertainty, hesitation, or equivocation. In my view, Mr. Otero's level of certainty was, as stated, very high." That the court relied considerably on this factor is self-evident from the record. Equally evident from the volumes of social science research on this factor is the lack of any correlation between a victim's level of confidence in his or her identification and its accuracy.

E

The Time Between the Crime and the Confrontation

The next consideration relates to the timing of the identification. As noted, by June, 2008, following the February, 2008 incident, Bilbo was in possession of a photographic array that included a photograph of the defendant. Otero, however, was not shown the array, and instead, he was shown a single photograph of the defendant months later. In *Neil v. Biggers*, supra, 409 U.S. at 188, 93 S.Ct. 375, while not finding that the lapse of time between a criminal event and a subsequent identification procedure required exclusion of the identification evidence, the United States Supreme Court nevertheless expressed the view that a lapse of seven months between the date of a crime and a subsequent confrontation "would be a seriously negative factor in most cases." *Id.*, at 201, 93 S.Ct. 375.

The New Jersey Supreme Court, in a recent opinion, fashioned a protocol for police identification procedures. The court observed: "Memories fade with time. And as the [s]pecial [m]aster observed, memory decay 'is irreversible'; memories never improve. As a result, delays between the commission of a crime and the time an identification is made can affect reliability. That basic principle is not in dispute." *State v. Henderson*, supra, 208 N.J. at 267, 27 A.3d 872. The court continued: "A meta-analysis of fifty-three 'facial memory studies' confirmed that memory strength will be weaker at longer retention intervals [the amount of time that passes] than at briefer ones.... In other words, the more time that passes, the greater the possibility that a witness' memory of a perpetrator will weaken.... However, researchers cannot pinpoint precisely when a person's recall becomes unreliable." (Citations omitted.) *Id.* Suffice to say, a delay of months between the date of the offense and the presentation of the defendant's photograph to Otero is not an indicator of reliability. Finally, because the court did not make a factual finding as to when the defendant's photograph was shown to Otero, it was not in a position to assess this factor fairly. Rather, the court appears to have dismissed this factor as unimportant in light of other indicia of reliability it found.

At trial, the court's assessment of reliability required a balancing analysis. Now, we, too, must do so on review of this mixed question of law and fact. Our review of the record suggests, however, that although the court assessed some of the factors listed in *Manson v. Brathwaite*, supra, 432 U.S. at 114–16, 97 S.Ct. 2243, in its reliability determination, it failed to give proper weight to the corrupting effect of this most inappropriate identification confirmation procedure. In weighing those factors, the trial court gave inappropriate weight to Otero's level of certainty while dismissing, as insignificant, the internal and external circumstances of the assault regarding Otero's condition during the melee and the impact Otero's own investigation of the assault may have had on his readiness to confirm that the photograph shown to him by Bilbo was that of the defendant. Additionally, by not establishing the date or month on which the identification was made, the court failed to consider the impact of such a delay on Otero's ability to identify his initial assailant accurately.

Contrary to the finding by the trial court, our application of the factors listed in *Manson v. Brathwaite*, supra, 432 U.S. at 114–16, 97 S.Ct. 2243, considered against the backdrop of the extraordinarily overbearing manner of the identification procedure, leads us to the conclusion that the pretrial identification of the defendant by Otero was not reliable and that Otero's subsequent in-court identification was not sufficiently removed from the taint of the earlier out-of-court identification to be independently reliable. We conclude, therefore, that both identifications should have been suppressed as unreliable.

We turn now to the question of harm. At the outset, we note that our Supreme Court has, as a matter of policy, emphatically rejected the notion that the doctrine of harmless error is available to uphold a conviction in which the trial court admitted unnecessarily suggestive and unreliable witness identification testimony. *State v. Gordon*, supra, 185 Conn. at 419–20, 441 A.2d

119, In *Gordon*, the court opined: "The state urges that even if the trial court erred in admitting both the station house and the in-court identifications of the defendant by the victim, such error would be harmless because of other overwhelming evidence that the defendant was the assailant." *Id.*, at 419, 441 A.2d 119. Rejecting this argument, the court stated: "Ordinarily the burden of establishing that harm resulted from a trial court error rests on the appellant.... However, there are some constitutional rights so basic to a fair trial that their infraction can never be treated as harmless error.... If error touches a less basic constitutional right, we sometimes apply the harmless error exception, but only sparingly, in a few, discrete circumstances.... Thus, we refuse to expand our harmless constitutional error doctrine to the discrete circumstances of unnecessarily suggestive and unreliable identifications, the admission of which significantly impairs the truth finding function of the jury.... Were we to do so we would fail to correct negligent infractions of constitutional rights and tempt some public officials to overstep the law in their zeal to convict the guilty. Some would yield to such temptation. The devastating nature of both negligently and deliberately obtained, unreliable eyewitness identifications would inevitably lead to the conviction of innocent persons. Hence sound judicial policy requires reversal whenever the erroneous admission of an unnecessarily suggestive and unreliable identification has violated a defendant's constitutional rights." (Citations omitted; internal quotation marks omitted.) *Id.*, at 419–20, 441 A.2d 119.

Our Supreme Court recently has stated: "When an [evidentiary] impropriety is of constitutional proportions, the state bears the burden of proving that the error was harmless beyond a reasonable doubt.... [W]e must examine the impact of the evidence on the trier of fact and the result of the trial.... If the evidence may have had a tendency to influence the judgment of the jury, it cannot be considered harmless.... That determination must be made in light of the entire record [including the strength of the state's case without the evidence admitted in error]." (Internal quotation marks omitted.) *State v. Gonzalez*, 302 Conn. 287, 307, 25 A.3d 648 (2011).

In analyzing harm in other constitutional contexts, our Supreme Court has also opined: "Whether such error is harmless in a particular case depends upon a number of factors, such as the importance of the witness' testimony in the prosecution's case, whether the testimony was cumulative, the presence or absence of evidence corroborating or contradicting the testimony of the witness on material points, the extent of cross-examination otherwise permitted, and, of course, the overall strength of the prosecution's case.... Most importantly, we must examine the impact of the evidence on the trier of fact and the result of the trial.... If the evidence may have had a tendency to influence the judgment of the jury, it cannot be considered harmless." (Emphasis added; internal quotation marks omitted.) *State v. Rolon*, 257 Conn. 156, 174, 777 A.2d 604 (2001).38

The relationship between properly admitted evidence and improperly admitted evidence implicating a constitutional right is significant to our analysis. While consideration of both the good and bad evidence is appropriate, the properly admitted evidence has to be beyond strong in order to uphold a conviction. In *State v. Angel T.*, 292 Conn. 262, 277 n. 10, 973 A.2d 1207 (2009), our Supreme Court described the nexus between the proper and improper trial evidence in this manner: "This is not a situation where the case against the defendant was otherwise 'so overwhelming' that the constitutional error did not, beyond a reasonable doubt, contribute to the conviction." In a similar vein, in *State v. Gerardi*, 237 Conn. 348, 677 A.2d 937 (1996), a case involving a constitutional error unrelated to identification, our Supreme Court stated: "[W]e cannot conclude with any degree of certainty that the evidence adduced at trial was so overwhelming that it foreclosed the possibility that the jury may have relied upon the improper mandatory presumption regarding possession rather than upon that evidence." *Id.*, at 363, 677 A.2d 937. Additionally, in *State v. Gonzalez*, supra, 302 Conn. at 310, 25 A.3d 648, our Supreme Court, adjudicating a claim of improper admission of a statement by the defendant, concluded that the evidence against the defendant was "not so overwhelming that we are convinced beyond a reasonable doubt that the admission of his improperly obtained narration was harmless." Thus, the state can not prevail in a harmless error analysis simply by demonstrating that the properly admitted evidence, absent the tainted evidence, was merely adequate for a conviction. Id., at 306–307, 25 A.3d 648.

Even though we are persuaded that the legal posture of the case at hand is indistinguishable from Gordon, we conduct a harmless error analysis. At the outset, we note that the state's case against the defendant was not overwhelming. To the contrary, there was no physical evidence at the scene, nor was there any forensic evidence. No knife or any dangerous instrumentality was found at the crime scene or connected to this incident, and there were no statements from the defendant. Rather, the state's evidence consisted, mainly, of the testimony of Otero and Miano. The state's additional witnesses, with one exception, were all police officers whose information, in large measure secondhand, came from Otero and Miano. The one witness for the state who was not a police officer, Rego, an employee of Club Blu, testified regarding the physical layout of the scene and the injury to Otero's thumb and stomach, evidence that did not, in any manner, implicate the defendant.

As to Miano, a fair review of her testimony reveals that she stated that the defendant traveled with her and others to and from the area of the altercation on the night in question. She placed the defendant at the scene of the altercation and as a participant. However, her testimony regarding the circumstances of the altercation was confused and imprecise, her ability to observe the events accurately was unclear, and her familiarity with Otero together with her relationship with Robert Acevedo reasonably could have put her objectivity in doubt for the fact finders.

Furthermore, Miano testified that she, together with the defendant and two others, Robert Acevedo and Anna Acevedo, arrived at Club NV at approximately 11 p.m. While at Club NV, Miano did not see the defendant although she did spend time with Otero, giving him a hug, having him take a photograph of her with her camera and later exchanging contact information with him while leaving. Significantly, Miano acknowledged that, by the time she left the club, she was "tipsy" after having consumed two to three "[s]ex on the beach" mixed drinks containing vodka.

As to the altercation itself, Miano acknowledged that when she, Robert Acevedo and Anna Acevedo got into the automobile, she was uncertain of the defendant's whereabouts and was unsure as to whether the defendant had gotten into the automobile before the altercation took place. Although Miano asserted that the defendant was present during the altercation and that she saw one of the two men push the other, she also acknowledged that she did not see the argument that she claimed occurred between the defendant and Otero, or the physical altercation that she claimed took place between them. Additionally, although Miano testified on direct examination that she saw blood on the defendant's shirt after the altercation, she admitted on cross-examination that she had not, in fact, seen any blood on the defendant. We acknowledge that Miano testified that earlier in the evening the defendant had indicated that he had wanted to leave his knife in the automobile before going into Club NV and that, although Miano's testimony regarding the actual altercation was confused and inconsistent, she placed the defendant at the site of the altercation as a participant. From this testimony, the jury reasonably could have concluded that the defendant was a participant in the assault that resulted in Otero's injuries.

Additionally, from our review of Miano's testimony, we acknowledge that the jury could have resolved any credibility and impartiality issues in favor of believing her testimony and could have drawn reasonable inferences from it, and, on that basis alone, the evidence may have been sufficient to sustain the jury's guilty verdict. Our conclusion that the jury could have found the defendant guilty on the basis of Miano's and other properly admitted testimony should not, however, be equated with a finding that the properly admitted evidence of the defendant's guilt was so overwhelming that we can determine, beyond a reasonable doubt, that it was not a factor in the jury's verdict. Indeed, the state's evidence was far from overwhelming.

As noted, harmlessness must be analyzed in context. Thus, in order to affirm the judgment, we must be able to declare that, in light of the properly admitted evidence, the improperly admitted evidence could not have affected the jury verdict. *State v. Gonzalez*, supra, 302 Conn. at 306–307, 25 A.3d 648. This is particularly true in a situation involving eyewitness identification. As Justice William J. Brennan, Jr., of the United States Supreme Court observed: "[D]espite its inherent unreliability, much eyewitness identification evidence has a powerful impact on juries. Juries seem most receptive to, and not inclined to discredit, testimony of a witness who states that he saw the defendant commit the crime. [E]yewitness testimony is likely to be believed by jurors, especially when it is offered with a high level of confidence, even though the accuracy of an eyewitness and the confidence of that witness may not be related to one another at all. All the evidence points rather strikingly to the conclusion that there is almost nothing more convincing than a live human being who takes the stand, points a finger at the defendant, and says That's the one!" (Internal quotation marks omitted.) *Watkins v. Sowders*, 449 U.S. 341, 352, 101

S.Ct. 654, 66 L.Ed.2d 549 (1981) (Brennan, J., dissenting). With implicit agreement, our Supreme Court has noted: "Common sense suggests, and research confirms, that eyewitness identification is an important form of evidence." *State v. Ledbetter*, supra, 275 Conn. at 575, 881 A.2d 290. Additionally, the court observed: "Eyewitness identification evidence is particularly persuasive when the witness exhibits confidence in the identification." *Id.*

The point made by Justice Brennan and echoed by Justice Richard N. Palmer in his concurrence in *State v. Outing*, supra, 298 Conn. at 105, 3 A.3d 1; see footnote 29 of this opinion; was surely not lost on the prosecutor in the case at hand. A review of closing arguments reveals that the prosecutor began his argument to the jury by emphasizing Otero's identification of the defendant, going to the extent of asking the jury to accept, as credible, Otero's identification testimony against the testimony of Bilbo that Otero had not made a pretrial identification. Indeed, in urging the jury to accept Otero's identification of the defendant as accurate, the prosecutor argued: "Don't blame Mr. Otero for the indifference and the incompetence of the Hartford police department." The prosecutor's argument to the jury regarding Otero's identification was neither brief nor incidental. Furthermore, despite Bilbo's claim that Otero had not identified the defendant when shown his photograph in December, 2008, and in light of Otero's testimony to the contrary, the court charged the jury that the state had presented both out-of-court and in-court identification testimony and gave a lengthy charge on the topic of eyewitness identification. Thus, it cannot reasonably be said that Otero's identification testimony was insignificant to the state's presentation or to the court's instructions to the jury. Indeed, from a fair reading of the transcript, it appears that Otero's out-of-court and in-court identifications of the defendant were key elements, if not the centerpiece, of the state's case.

On the basis of our review of this record, we are persuaded that there is no reasonable basis to conclude that the jury was not likely influenced by Otero's improperly admitted out-of-court and in-court identifications of the defendant. We conclude, therefore, that, to the extent the improper admission of unreliable identification evidence is subject to harmless error analysis on appeal, the state has not met its burden of demonstrating beyond a reasonable doubt that the court's incorrect admission of Otero's identifications of the defendant constituted harmless error.

The judgment is reversed and the case is remanded for a new trial.

Note

As noted by the Court in *Artis*, New Jersey has also addressed the application of *Manson v. Brathwaite* to the issue of cross-racial identification. In an exhaustive opinion, which also considers the use of special instructions to the jury on cross-racial misidentification, the Court considers whether *Manson* sets forth adequate standards for determining the admissibility of potentially unduly suggestive pretrial identifications where the issue involves cross-racial identification.

STATE V. HENDERSON
27 A.3d 872 (N.J. 2011)

Introduction

In the thirty-four years since the United States Supreme Court announced a test for the admission of eyewitness identification evidence, which New Jersey adopted soon after, a vast body of scientific research about human memory has emerged. That body of work casts doubt on some commonly held views relating to memory. It also calls into question the vitality of the current legal framework for analyzing the reliability of eyewitness identifications. See *Manson v. Brathwaite*, 432 U.S. 98, 97 S.Ct. 2243, 53 L.Ed.2d 140 (1977); *State v. Madison*, 109 N.J. 223, 536 A.2d 254 (1988).

In this case, defendant claims that an eyewitness mistakenly identified him as an accomplice to a murder. Defendant argues that the identification was not reliable because the officers investigating the case intervened during the identification process and unduly influenced the eyewitness. After a pretrial hearing, the trial court found that the officers' behavior was not impermissibly suggestive and admitted the evidence. The Appellate Division reversed. It held that the officers' actions were presumptively suggestive because they violated guidelines issued by the Attorney General in 2001 for conducting identification procedures.

After granting certification and hearing oral argument, we remanded the case and appointed a Special Master to evaluate scientific and other evidence about eyewitness identifications. The Special Master presided over a hearing that probed testimony by seven experts and produced more than 2,000 pages of transcripts along with hundreds of scientific studies. He later issued an extensive and very fine report, much of which we adopt.

We find that the scientific evidence considered at the remand hearing is reliable. That evidence offers convincing proof that the current test for evaluating the trustworthiness of eyewitness identifications should be revised. Study after study revealed a troubling lack of reliability in eyewitness identifications. From social science research to the review of actual police lineups, from laboratory experiments to DNA exonerations, the record proves that the possibility of mistaken identification is real. Indeed, it is now widely known that eyewitness misidentification is the leading cause of wrongful convictions across the country.

We are convinced from the scientific evidence in the record that memory is malleable, and that an array of variables can affect and dilute memory and lead to misidentifications. Those factors include system variables like lineup procedures, which are within the control of the criminal justice system, and estimator variables like lighting conditions or the presence of a weapon, over which the legal system has no control. To its credit, the Attorney General's Office incorporated scientific research on system variables into the guidelines it issued in 2001 to improve eyewitness identification procedures. We now review both sets of variables in detail to evaluate the current *Manson/ Madison* test.

....

A. Facts

In the early morning hours of January 1, 2003, Rodney Harper was shot to death in an apartment in Camden. James Womble witnessed the murder but did not speak with the police until they approached him ten days later.

Womble and Harper were acquaintances who occasionally socialized at the apartment of Womble's girlfriend, Vivian Williams. On the night of the murder, Womble and Williams brought in the New Year in Williams' apartment by drinking wine and champagne and smoking crack cocaine. Harper had started the evening with them but left at around 10:15 p.m. Williams also left roughly three hours later, leaving Womble alone in the apartment until Harper rejoined him at 2:00 to 2:30 a.m.

Soon after Harper returned, two men forcefully entered the apartment. Womble knew one of them, co-defendant George Clark, who had come to collect $160 from Harper. The other man was a stranger to Womble.

While Harper and Clark went to a different room, the stranger pointed a gun at Womble and told him, "Don't move, stay right here, you're not involved in this." He remained with the stranger in a small, narrow, dark hallway. Womble testified that he "got a look at" the stranger, but not "a real good look." Womble also described the gun pointed at his torso as a dark semiautomatic.

Meanwhile, Womble overheard Clark and Harper argue over money in the other room. At one point, Harper said, "do what you got to do," after which Womble heard a gunshot. Womble then walked into the room, saw Clark holding a handgun, offered to get Clark the $160, and urged him not to shoot Harper again. As Clark left, he warned Womble, "Don't rat me out, I know where you live."

Harper died from the gunshot wound to his chest on January 10, 2003. Camden County Detective Luis Ruiz and Investigator Randall MacNair were assigned to investigate the homicide, and they interviewed Womble the next day. Initially, Womble told the police that he was in the apartment when he heard two gunshots outside, that he left to look for Harper, and that he found Harper slumped over in his car in a nearby parking lot, where Harper said he had been shot by two men he did not know.

The next day, the officers confronted Womble about inconsistencies in his story. Womble claimed that they also threatened to charge him in connection with the murder. Womble then decided to "come clean." He admitted that he lied at first because he did not want to "rat" out anyone and "didn't want to get involved" out of fear of retaliation against his elderly father. Womble led the investigators to Clark, who eventually gave a statement about his involvement and identified the person who accompanied him as defendant Larry Henderson.

The officers had Womble view a photographic array on January 14, 2003. That event lies at the heart of this decision and is discussed in greater detail below. Ultimately, Womble identified defendant from the array, and Investigator MacNair prepared a warrant for his arrest. Upon arrest, defendant admitted to the police that he had accompanied Clark to the apartment where Harper was killed, and heard a gunshot while waiting in the hallway. But defendant denied witnessing or participating in the shooting.

A grand jury in Camden County returned an indictment charging Henderson and Clark with the following offenses: first-degree murder, N.J.S.A. 2C:11–3(a)(1) or (2); second-degree possession of a firearm for an unlawful purpose, N.J.S.A. 2C:39–4(a); fourth-degree aggravated assault, N.J.S.A. 2C:12–1(b)(4); third-degree unlawful possession of a weapon, N.J.S.A. 2C:39–5(b); and possession of a weapon having been convicted of a prior offense, N.J.S.A. 2C:39–7(a) (Henderson) and –7(b) (Clark).

B. Photo Identification and Wade Hearing

As noted above, Womble reviewed a photo array at the Prosecutor's Office on January 14, 2003, and identified defendant as his assailant. The trial court conducted a pretrial Wade1 hearing to determine the admissibility of that identification. Investigator MacNair, Detective Ruiz, and Womble all testified at the hearing. Cherry Hill Detective Thomas Weber also testified.

Detective Weber conducted the identification procedure because, consistent with guidelines issued by the Attorney General, he was not a primary investigator in the case. See Office of the Attorney Gen., N.J. Dep't of Law and Pub. Safety, Attorney General Guidelines for Preparing and Conducting Photo and Live Lineup Identification Procedures 1 (2001) (Attorney General Guidelines or Guidelines). According to the Guidelines, discussed in detail below, primary investigators should not administer photo or live lineup identification procedures "to ensure that inadvertent verbal cues or body language do not impact on a witness." *Ibid.*

Ruiz and MacNair gave Weber an array consisting of seven "filler" photos and one photo of defendant Henderson. The eight photos all depicted headshots of African–American men between the ages of twenty-eight and thirty-five, with short hair, goatees, and, according to Weber, similar facial features. At the hearing, Weber was not asked whether he knew which photograph depicted the suspect. (Later at trial, he said he did not know.)

The identification procedure took place in an interview room in the Prosecutor's Office. At first, Weber and Womble were alone in the room. Weber began by reading the following instructions off a standard form:

In a moment, I will show you a number of photographs one at a time. You may take as much time as you need to look at each one of them. You should not conclude that the person who committed the crime is in the group merely because a group of photographs is being shown to you. The person who committed the crime may or may not be in the group, and the mere display of the photographs is not meant to suggest that our office believes the person who committed the crime is in one of the photographs. You are absolutely not required to choose any of the photographs, and you should feel not obligated to choose any one. The photographs will be shown to you in random order. I am not in any way trying to influence your decision by the order of the pictures presented. Tell me immediately if you recognize the person that committed the crime in one of the photographs. All of the photographs will be shown to you even if you select a photograph.

Please keep in mind that hairstyles, beards, and mustaches are easily changed. People gain and lose weight. Also, photographs do not always show the true complexion of a person. It may be lighter or darker than shown in the photograph. If you select a photograph, please do not ask me whether I agree with or support your selection. It is your choice alone that counts. Please do not discuss whether you selected a photograph with any other witness who may be asked to look at these photographs.

To acknowledge that he understood the instructions, Womble signed the form.

Detective Weber pre-numbered the eight photos, shuffled them, and showed them to Womble one at a time. Womble quickly eliminated five of the photos. He then reviewed the remaining three, discounted one more, and said he "wasn't 100 percent sure of the final two pictures." At the Wade hearing, Detective Weber recalled that Womble "just shook his head a lot. He seemed indecisive." But he did not express any fear to Weber.

Weber left the room with the photos and informed MacNair and Ruiz that the witness had narrowed the pictures to two but could not make a final identification. MacNair and Ruiz testified at the hearing that they did not know whether defendant's picture was among the remaining two photos.

MacNair and Ruiz entered the interview room to speak with Womble. According to MacNair's testimony at the Wade hearing, he and Ruiz believed that Womble was holding back—as he had earlier in the investigation—based on fear. Ruiz said Womble was "nervous, upset about his father."

In an effort to calm Womble, MacNair testified that he "just told him to focus, to calm down, to relax and that any type of protection that [he] would need, any threats against [him] would be put to rest by the Police Department." Ruiz added, "just do what you have to do, and we'll be out of here." In response, according to MacNair, Womble said he "could make [an] identification."

MacNair and Ruiz then left the interview room. Ruiz testified that the entire exchange lasted less than one minute; Weber believed it took about five minutes. When Weber returned to the room, he reshuffled the eight photos and again displayed them to Womble sequentially. This time, when Womble saw defendant's photo, he slammed his hand on the table and exclaimed, "[t]hat's the mother [- - - - - -] there." From start to finish, the entire process took fifteen minutes.

Womble did not recant his identification, but during the Wade hearing he testified that he felt as though Detective Weber was "nudging" him to choose defendant's photo, and "that there was pressure" to make a choice.

After hearing the testimony, the trial court applied the two-part Manson/ Madison test to evaluate the admissibility of the eyewitness identification. See *Manson, supra*, 432 U.S. at 114, 97 S.Ct. at 2253, 53 L.Ed.2d at 154; *Madison, supra*, 109 N.J. at 232–33, 536 A.2d 254. The test requires courts to determine first if police identification procedures were impermissibly suggestive; if so, courts then weigh five reliability factors to decide if the identification evidence is nonetheless admissible. See *Manson, supra*, 432 U.S. at 114, 97 S.Ct. at 2253, 53 L.Ed.2d at 154; *Madison, supra*, 109 N.J. at 232–33, 536 A.2d 254.

The trial court first found that the photo display itself was "a fair makeup." Under the totality of the circumstances, the judge concluded that the photo identification was reliable. The court found that there was "nothing in this case that was improper, and certainly nothing that was so suggestive as to result in a substantial likelihood of misidentification at all." The court also noted that Womble displayed no doubts about identifying defendant Henderson, that he had the opportunity to view defendant at the crime scene, and that Womble fixed his attention on defendant "because he had a gun on him."

C. Trial

The following facts—relevant to Womble's identification of defendant—were adduced at trial after the court determined that the identification was admissible: Womble smoked two bags of crack cocaine with his girlfriend in the hours before the shooting; the two also consumed one bottle of champagne and one bottle of wine; the lighting was "pretty dark" in the hallway where Womble and defendant interacted; defendant shoved Womble during the incident; and Womble remembered looking at the gun pointed at his chest. Womble also admitted smoking about two bags of crack cocaine each day from the time of the shooting until speaking with police ten days later.

At trial, Womble elaborated on his state of mind during the identification procedure. He testified that when he first looked at the photo array, he did not see anyone he recognized. As he explained, "[m]y mind was drawing a blank ... so I just started eliminating photos." To make a final identification, Womble said that he "really had to search deep." He was nonetheless "sure" of the identification.

Womble had no difficulty identifying defendant at trial eighteen months later. From the witness stand, Womble agreed that he had no doubt that defendant—the man in the courtroom wearing "the white dress shirt"—"is the man who held [him] at bay with a gun to [his] chest."

Womble also testified that he discarded a shell casing from the shooting at an intersection five or six blocks from the apartment; he helped the police retrieve the casing ten days later. No guns or other physical evidence were introduced linking defendant to the casing or the crime scene.

Neither Clark nor defendant testified at trial. The primary evidence against defendant, thus, was Womble's identification and Detective MacNair's testimony about defendant's post-arrest statement.

....

The Appellate Division presumed that the identification procedure in this case was impermissibly suggestive under the first prong of the *Manson/ Madison* test. *State v. Henderson*, 397 N.J.Super. 398, 414, 937 A.2d 988 (App.Div.2008). The court reversed and remanded for a new Wade hearing to determine whether the identification was nonetheless reliable under the test's second prong. Id. at 400, 414–15, 937 A.2d 988.

The panel anchored its finding to what it considered to be a material breach of the Attorney General Guidelines. Id. at 412, 937 A.2d 988. Among other things, the Guidelines require that " 'whenever practical' the person conducting the photographic identification procedure 'should be someone other than the primary investigator assigned to the case.' " Id. at 411, 937 A.2d 988 (citing *State v. Herrera*, 187 N.J. 493, 516, 902 A.2d 177 (2006)). The panel specifically found that the investigating officers, MacNair and Ruiz, "consciously and deliberately intruded into the process for the purpose of assisting or influencing Womble's identification of defendant." Id. at 414, 937 A.2d 988. The officers' behavior, the court explained, "certainly violate [d] the spirit of the Guidelines." Id. at 412, 937 A.2d 988. In such circumstances, the panel "conclude[d] that a presumption of impermissible suggestiveness must be imposed, and a new Wade hearing conducted." Id. at 400, 937 A.2d 988.

....

[after noting that cross-racial recognition continues to be a factor that can affect the reliability of an identification, the Court then goes on to fashion a remedy determining unduly suggestive identifications that give rise to substantial probability of misidentification that goes beyond *Manson*]

The Manson/Madison Test Needs to Be Revised

When this Court adopted the framework outlined in *Manson*, it recognized that suggestive police procedures may "so irreparably 'taint[ ]' the out-of-court and in-court identifications" that a defendant is denied due process. Madison, supra, 109 N.J. at 239, 536 A.2d 254. To protect due process concerns, the *Manson* Court's two-part test rested on three assumptions: (1) that it would adequately measure the reliability of eyewitness testimony; (2) that the test's focus on suggestive police procedure would deter improper practices; and (3) that jurors would recognize and discount untrustworthy eyewitness testimony. See *Manson, supra,* 432 U.S. at 112–16, 97 S.Ct. at 2252–54, 53 L.Ed.2d at 152–55.

We remanded this case to determine whether those assumptions and other factors reflected in the two-part *Manson/ Madison* test are still valid. We conclude from the hearing that they are not.

The hearing revealed that *Manson/ Madison* does not adequately meet its stated goals: it does not provide a sufficient measure for reliability, it does not deter, and it overstates the jury's innate ability to evaluate eyewitness testimony.

First, under *Manson/ Madison*, defendants must show that police procedures were "impermissibly suggestive" before courts can consider estimator variables that also bear on reliability. See *Madison*, supra, 109 N.J. at 232, 536 A.2d 254. As a result, although evidence of relevant estimator variables tied to the *Neil v. Biggers* factors is routinely introduced at pretrial hearings, their effect is ignored unless there is a finding of impermissibly suggestive police conduct. In this case, for example, the testimony at the *Wade* hearing related principally to the lineup procedure. Because the court found that the procedure was not "impermissibly suggestive," details about the witness' use of drugs and alcohol, the dark lighting conditions, the presence of a weapon pointed at the witness' chest, and other estimator variables that affect reliability were not considered at the hearing. (They were explored later at trial.)

Second, under *Manson/ Madison*, if a court finds that the police used impermissibly suggestive identification procedures, the trial judge then weighs the corrupting effect of the process against five "reliability" factors. Id. at 239–40, 536 A.2d 254. But three of those factors—the opportunity to view the crime, the witness' degree of attention, and the level of certainty at the time of the identification—rely on self-reporting by eyewitnesses; and research has shown that those reports can be skewed by the suggestive procedures themselves and thus may not be reliable. Self-reporting by eyewitnesses is an essential part of any investigation, but when reports are tainted by a suggestive process, they become poor measures in a balancing test designed to bar unreliable evidence.

Third, rather than act as a deterrent, the *Manson/ Madison* test may unintentionally reward suggestive police practices. The irony of the current test is that the more suggestive the procedure, the greater the chance eyewitnesses will seem confident and report better viewing conditions. Courts in turn are encouraged to admit identifications based on criteria that have been tainted by the very suggestive practices the test aims to deter.

Fourth, the *Manson/ Madison* test addresses only one option for questionable eyewitness identification evidence: suppression. Yet few judges choose that ultimate sanction. An all-or-nothing approach does not account for the complexities of eyewitness identification evidence.

Finally, *Manson/ Madison* instructs courts that "the reliability determination is to be made from the totality of the circumstances in the particular case." Id. at 239, 536 A.2d 254. In practice, trial judges routinely use the test's five reliability factors as a checklist. The State maintains that courts may consider additional estimator variables. Even if that is correct, there is little guidance about which factors to consider, and courts and juries are often left to their own intuition to decide which estimator variables may be important and how they matter.

As a result of those concerns, we now revise the State's framework for evaluating eyewitness identification evidence.

C. Revised Framework

Remedying the problems with the current *Manson/ Madison* test requires an approach that addresses its shortcomings: one that allows judges to consider all relevant factors that affect reliability in deciding whether an identification is admissible; that is not heavily weighted by factors that can be corrupted by suggestiveness; that promotes deterrence in a meaningful way; and that focuses on helping jurors both understand and evaluate the effects that various factors have on memory—because we recognize that most identifications will be admitted in evidence.

Two principal changes to the current system are needed to accomplish that: first, the revised framework should allow all relevant system and estimator variables to be explored and weighed at pretrial hearings when there is some actual evidence of suggestiveness; and second, courts should develop and use enhanced jury charges to help jurors evaluate eyewitness identification evidence.

The new framework also needs to be flexible enough to serve twin aims: to guarantee fair trials to defendants, who must have the tools necessary to defend themselves, and to protect the State's interest in presenting critical evidence at trial. With that in mind, we first outline the revised approach for evaluating identification evidence and then explain its details and the reasoning behind it.

First, to obtain a pretrial hearing, a defendant has the initial burden of showing some evidence of suggestiveness that could lead to a mistaken identification. See *State v. Rodriquez*, supra, 264 N.J.Super. at 269, 624 A.2d 605; *State v. Ortiz*, supra, 203 N.J.Super. at 522, 497 A.2d 552; cf. *State v. Michaels*, 136 N.J. 299, 320, 642 A.2d 1372 (1994) (using same standard to trigger pretrial hearing to determine if child-victim's statements resulted from suggestive or coercive interview techniques). That evidence, in general, must be tied to a system—and not an estimator—variable. But see *Chen*, supra (extending right to hearing for suggestive conduct by private actors).

Second, the State must then offer proof to show that the proffered eyewitness identification is reliable—accounting for system and estimator variables—subject to the following: the court can end the hearing at any time if it finds from the testimony that defendant's threshold allegation of suggestiveness is groundless. We discuss this further below. See infra at 290–91, 27 A.3d at 920–21).

Third, the ultimate burden remains on the defendant to prove a very substantial likelihood of irreparable misidentification. See *Manson, supra*, 432 U.S. at 116, 97 S.Ct. at 2254, 53 L.Ed.2d at 155 (citing *Simmons, supra*, 390 U.S. at 384, 88 S.Ct. at 971, 19 L.Ed.2d at 1253); *Madison, supra*, 109 N.J. at 239, 536 A.2d 254 (same). To do so, a defendant can cross-examine eyewitnesses and police officials and present witnesses and other relevant evidence linked to system and estimator variables.

Fourth, if after weighing the evidence presented a court finds from the totality of the circumstances that defendant has demonstrated a very substantial likelihood of irreparable misidentification, the court should suppress the identification evidence. If the evidence is admitted, the court should provide appropriate, tailored jury instructions, as discussed further below.

To evaluate whether there is evidence of suggestiveness to trigger a hearing, courts should consider the following non-exhaustive list of system variables:

1. Blind Administration. Was the lineup procedure performed double-blind? If double-blind testing was impractical, did the police use a technique like the "envelope method" described above, to ensure that the administrator had no knowledge of where the suspect appeared in the photo array or lineup?

2. Pre-identification Instructions. Did the administrator provide neutral, pre-identification instructions warning that the suspect may not be present in the lineup and that the witness should not feel compelled to make an identification?

3. Lineup Construction. Did the array or lineup contain only one suspect embedded among at least five innocent fillers? Did the suspect stand out from other members of the lineup?

4. Feedback. Did the witness receive any information or feedback, about the suspect or the crime, before, during, or after the identification procedure?

5. Recording Confidence. Did the administrator record the witness' statement of confidence immediately after the identification, before the possibility of any confirmatory feedback?

6. Multiple Viewings. Did the witness view the suspect more than once as part of multiple identification procedures? Did police use the same fillers more than once?

7. Showups. Did the police perform a showup more than two hours after an event? Did the police warn the witness that the suspect may not be the perpetrator and that the witness should not feel compelled to make an identification?

8. Private Actors. Did law enforcement elicit from the eyewitness whether he or she had spoken with anyone about the identification and, if so, what was discussed?

9. Other Identifications Made. Did the eyewitness initially make no choice or choose a different suspect or filler?

The court should conduct a *Wade* hearing only if defendant offers some evidence of suggestiveness. If, however, at any time during the hearing the trial court concludes from the testimony that defendant's initial claim of suggestiveness is baseless, and if no other evidence of suggestiveness has been demonstrated by the evidence, the court may exercise its discretion to end the *291 hearing. Under those circumstances, the court need not permit the defendant or require the State to elicit more evidence about estimator variables; that evidence would be reserved for the jury.

By way of example, assume that a defendant claims an administrator confirmed an eyewitness' identification by telling the witness she did a "good job." That proffer would warrant a Wade hearing. Assume further that the administrator credibly denied any feedback, and the eyewitness did the same. If the trial court finds that the initial allegation is completely hollow, the judge can end the hearing absent any other evidence of suggestiveness. In other words, if no evidence of suggestiveness is left in the case, there is no need to explore estimator variables at the pretrial hearing. Also, trial courts always have the authority to direct the mode and order of proofs, and they may exercise that discretion to focus pretrial hearings as needed.

If some actual proof of suggestiveness remains, courts should consider the above system variables as well as the following non-exhaustive list of estimator variables to evaluate the overall reliability of an identification and determine its admissibility:

1. Stress. Did the event involve a high level of stress?

2. Weapon focus. Was a visible weapon used during a crime of short duration?

3. Duration. How much time did the witness have to observe the event?

4. Distance and Lighting. How close were the witness and perpetrator? What were the lighting conditions at the time?

5. Witness Characteristics. Was the witness under the influence of alcohol or drugs? Was age a relevant factor under the circumstances of the case?

6. Characteristics of Perpetrator. Was the culprit wearing a disguise? Did the suspect have different facial features at the time of the identification?

7. Memory decay. How much time elapsed between the crime and the identification?

8. Race-bias. Does the case involve a cross-racial identification?

Some of the above estimator variables overlap with the five reliability factors outlined in *Neil v. Biggers, supra*, 409 U.S. at 199–200, 93 S.Ct. at 382, 34 L.Ed.2d at 411, which we nonetheless repeat:

9. Opportunity to view the criminal at the time of the crime.

10. Degree of attention.

11. Accuracy of prior description of the criminal.

12. Level of certainty demonstrated at the confrontation.

Did the witness express high confidence at the time of the identification before receiving any feedback or other information?

13. The time between the crime and the confrontation. (Encompassed fully by "memory decay" above.)

The above factors are not exclusive. Nor are they intended to be frozen in time. We recognize that scientific research relating to the reliability of eyewitness evidence is dynamic; the field is very different today than it was in 1977, and it will likely be quite different thirty years from now. By providing the above lists, we do not intend to hamstring police departments or limit them from improving practices. Likewise, we do not limit trial courts from reviewing evolving, substantial, and generally accepted scientific research. But to the extent the police undertake new practices, or courts either consider variables differently or entertain new ones, they must rely on reliable scientific evidence that is generally accepted by experts in the community. See *Chun, supra*, 194 N.J. at 91, 943 A.2d 114; Moore, supra, 188 N.J. at 206, 902 A.2d 1212; Rubanick, supra, 125 N.J. at 432, 593 A.2d 733.

We adopt this approach over the initial recommendation of defendant and the ACDL that any violation of the Attorney General Guidelines should require per se exclusion of the resulting eyewitness identification. Although that approach might yield greater deterrence, it could also lead to the loss of a substantial amount of reliable evidence. We believe that the more flexible framework outlined above protects defendants' right to a fair trial at the same time it enables the State to meet its responsibility to ensure public safety.

D. Pretrial Hearing

As stated above, to obtain a pretrial hearing, a defendant must present some evidence of suggestiveness. Pretrial discovery, which this opinion has enhanced in certain areas, would reveal, for example, if a line-up did not include enough fillers, if those fillers did not resemble the suspect, or if a private actor spoke with the witness about the identification. Armed with that and similar information, defendants could request and receive a hearing.

The hearing would encompass system and estimator variables upon a showing of some suggestiveness that defendant can support. For various reasons, estimator variables would no longer be ignored in the court's analysis until it found that an identification procedure was impermissibly suggestive. First, broader hearings will provide more meaningful deterrence. To the extent officers wish to avoid a pretrial hearing, they must avoid acting in a suggestive manner. Second, more extensive hearings will address reliability with greater care and better reflect how memory works. Suggestiveness can certainly taint an identification, which justifies examining system variables. The same is true for estimator variables like high stress, weapon-focus, and own-race bias. Because both sets of factors can alter memory and affect eyewitness identifications, both should be explored pretrial in appropriate cases to reflect what Manson acknowledged: that "reliability is the linchpin in determining the admissibility of identification testimony." *Manson, supra*, 432 U.S. at 114, 97 S.Ct. at 2253, 53 L.Ed.2d at 154.

But concerns about estimator variables alone cannot trigger a pretrial hearing; only system variables would. This approach differs from the procedure endorsed by the Special Master and proposed by defendant and amici, which would essentially require pretrial hearings in every case involving eyewitness identification evidence. Several reasons favor the approach we outline today.

First, we anticipate that eyewitness identification evidence will likely not be ruled inadmissible at pretrial hearings solely on account of estimator variables. For example, it is difficult to imagine that a trial judge would preclude a witness from testifying because the lighting was "too dark," the witness was "too distracted" by the presence of a weapon, or he or she was under "too much" stress while making an observation. How dark is too dark as a matter of law? How much is too much? What guideposts would a trial judge use in making those judgment calls? In all likelihood, the witness would be allowed to testify before a jury and face cross-examination designed to probe the weaknesses of her identification. Jurors would also have the benefit of enhanced instructions to evaluate that testimony—even when there is no evidence of suggestiveness in the case. As a result, a pretrial hearing triggered by, and focused on, estimator variables would likely not screen out identification evidence and would largely be duplicated at trial.

Second, courts cannot affect estimator variables; by definition, they relate to matters outside the control of law enforcement. More probing pretrial hearings about suggestive police procedures, though, can deter inappropriate police practices.

Third, as demonstrated above, suggestive behavior can distort various other factors that are weighed in assessing reliability. That warrants a greater pretrial focus on system variables.

Fourth, we are mindful of the practical impact of today's ruling. Because defendants will now be free to explore a broader range of estimator variables at pretrial hearings to assess the reliability of an identification, those hearings will become more intricate. They will routinely involve testimony from both the police and eyewitnesses, and that testimony will likely expand as more substantive areas are explored. Also, trial courts will retain discretion to allow expert testimony at pretrial hearings.

In 2009, trial courts in New Jersey conducted roughly 200 Wade hearings, according to the Administrative Office of the Courts. If estimator variables alone could trigger a hearing, that number might increase to nearly all cases in which eyewitness identification evidence plays a part. We have to measure that outcome in light of the following reality that the Special Master observed: judges rarely suppress eyewitness evidence at pretrial hearings. Therefore, to allow hearings in the majority of identification cases might overwhelm the system with little resulting benefit.

We do not suggest that it is acceptable to sacrifice a defendant's right to a fair trial for the sake of saving court resources, but when the likely outcome of a hearing is a more focused set of jury charges about estimator variables, not suppression, we question the need for hearings initiated only by estimator variables.

Appellate review does remain as a backstop to correct errors that may not be caught at or before trial, and the enhanced framework may provide a greater role in that regard in certain cases. If a reviewing court determines that identification evidence should not have been admitted in accordance with the above standards, it can reverse a conviction.

Note

There is no guidance, to date, from the United States Supreme Court as to the constitutional significance of the increased likelihood of misidentification caused the challenges of cross-racial identification. See, Laura Connelly, Cross-Racial Identifications: Solutions to the "They All Look Alike" Effect, 21 MICHIGAN JOURNAL OF RACE AND LAW 125(2015)

The United States Supreme Court has also addressed the question of whether and when a criminal defendant has a right under the Sixth Amendment to have counsel present and appointed if necessary, at a pretrial corporeal identification. As a result of *Gilbert v. California,* 388 U.S. 263 (1967) and *United States v. Wade,* 388 U.S. 218 (1967), an indigent defendant has a Sixth Amendment right to appointed counsel at a pretrial corporeal identification that takes place after the initiation of formal charges (*Moore v. Illinois,* 434 U.S. 220 (1977) because such is considered a critical stage for constitutional purposes. As the Court explains in *Wade,* defense counsel's presence at the confrontation occasioned by a lineup or showup, is critical to the attorney's ability to effectively cross-examine at trial. Observing intricacies and complexities or the identification procedure cannot easily be duplicated outside the pretrial confrontation and cross-examination can have greatly reduced efficacy without that knowledge. But how well the right to counsel will provide for effective cross-examination regarding racially compromised pretrial identification procedures is directly linked to how effective is cross-examination as a tool in combatting the challenges of identifications influenced by issues such as cross-racial identification. As has been noted; "Cross-examination does not help a jury distinguish between a reliable and an unreliable cross-racial identification because a witness's credibility has nothing to do with the degree of own-race bias that has infected an identification. A witness can be— and, this Note assumes, often is— telling what she believes is the truth but still be wrong. More significantly, a witness's certainty or positive racial *1843 attitude may mislead jurors when these have no relevance to the accuracy of the identification" See, Radha Natarajan, *Racialized Memory and Reliability: Due Process Applied to Cross-Racial Eyewitness Identifications,* 78 New York Univ. L.Rev. 1821 (2003) at 1842-1843.

See Also, *Eyewitness Testimony and Cross- Racial Identification,* 35 New Eng. L. Rev. 835 (2001), Sheri Lynn Johnson, *Cross-Racial Identification Errors In Criminal Cases,* 69 CORNELL L. REV. 934 (1984)

STATE V. CROMEDY
727 A.2d 457 (N.J. 1999)

The opinion of the Court was delivered by

COLEMAN, J.

This appeal involves a rape and robbery in which a cross-racial identification was made of defendant as the perpetrator seven months after the offenses occurred. The identification of the perpetrator was the critical issue throughout the trial. The trial court denied defendant's request to have the jury instructed concerning the cross-racial nature of the identification. A majority in the Appellate Division agreed with the trial court. Judge Shebell dissented, concluding that a reversal was warranted because the trial court should have given such a charge.

The novel issue presented is whether a cross-racial identification jury instruction should be required in certain cases before it is established that there is substantial agreement in the scientific community that cross-racial recognition impairment of eyewitnesses is significant enough to warrant a special jury instruction. Our study of the recommendations of a Court-appointed Task Force, judicial literature, and decisional law from other jurisdictions persuades us that there exists a reliable basis for a cross-racial identification charge. We hold that the trial court's failure to submit to the jury an instruction similar to the one requested by defendant requires a reversal of defendant's convictions.

I

On the night of August 28, 1992, D.S., a white female student then enrolled at Rutgers University in New Brunswick, was watching television in her basement apartment. While she was relaxing on the couch, an African-American male entered the brightly-lit apartment and demanded money from D.S., claiming that he was wanted for murder and that he needed funds to get to New York. After D.S. told the intruder that she had no money, he spotted her purse, rifled through it, and removed money and credit cards.

The intruder then placed his hand on D.S.'s leg, demanded that she be quiet and closed the window blinds. He led her by the arm into the brightly-lit kitchen and ordered her to remove her shorts. The intruder then vaginally penetrated D.S. from behind. Throughout the sexual assault,

D.S. was facing the kitchen door with her eyes closed and hand over her mouth to avoid crying loudly.

Once the assault was over, D.S. faced her attacker who, after threatening her again, turned around and left the apartment. At the time of the second threat, D.S. was standing approximately two feet away from her assailant. The attacker made no attempt to conceal his face at any time. D.S. immediately called the New Brunswick Police Department after the intruder left the apartment.

The police dusted for fingerprints and took D.S.'s initial statement. D.S. described her assailant as an African-American male in his late 20's to early 30's, full-faced, about five feet five inches tall, with a medium build, mustache, and unkempt hair. She stated that the intruder was wearing a dirty gray button-down short-sleeved shirt, blue warm-up pants with white and red stripes, and a Giants logo on the left leg. D.S. was then taken to Roosevelt Hospital where rape samples were taken.

The next day, D.S. made a formal statement to the police in which she again described the intruder. Three days later, a composite sketch was drawn by an artist with her assistance. The following day at police headquarters, D.S. was shown many slides and photographs, including a photograph of defendant, in an unsuccessful attempt to identify her assailant.

On April 7, 1993, almost eight months after the crimes were committed, D.S. saw an African-American male across the street from her who she thought was her attacker. She spotted the man while she was standing on the corner of a street in New Brunswick waiting for the light to change. As the two passed on the street, D.S. studied the individual's face and gait. Believing that the man was her attacker, D.S. ran home and telephoned the police, giving them a description of the man she had just seen. Defendant was picked up by the New Brunswick police and taken to headquarters almost immediately.

Within fifteen minutes after seeing defendant on the street, D.S. viewed defendant in a "show-up" from behind a one-way mirror and immediately identified him as the man she had just seen on the street and as her attacker. Defendant was then arrested and, with his consent, saliva and blood samples were taken for scientific analysis.

No forensic evidence linking defendant to the offenses was presented during the trial. The police did not lift any fingerprints belonging to defendant from the apartment. D.S.'s Rape Crisis Intervention Kit, processed by the Middlesex County Rape Crisis Center at Roosevelt Hospital, was submitted to the New Jersey State Police Chemistry Biology Laboratory in Sea Girt for analysis. Testing of the victim's blood revealed that she was a secretor, meaning that she falls within the eighty percent of the population that secretes their blood type in all of their bodily fluids. When defendant's blood and saliva were tested by the same laboratory, it was determined that both the victim and defendant have type "A" blood, but defendant was found to be a non-secretor. That meant that although the rape kit revealed the presence of seminal fluid and spermatozoa, the specimens received from defendant could not be compared with the semen and spermatozoa found on the victim. In other words, the genetic markers found in the semen and spermatozoa could not be said to have come from defendant because he is a non-secretor. On the other hand, the genetic markers were consistent with the victim, who is a secretor.

Because of the nature of the crimes, the races of the victim and defendant, and the inability of the victim to identify defendant from his photograph, and because defendant was not positively identified until almost eight months after the date of the offenses, defense counsel sought a cross-racial identification jury charge. The following language was proposed:

> [Y]ou know that the identifying witness is of a different race than the defendant. When a witness who is a member of one race identifies a member who is of another race we say there has been a cross-racial identification. You may consider, if you think it is appropriate to do so, whether the cross-racial nature of the identification has affected the accuracy of the witness's original perception and/or accuracy of a subsequent identification.

In support of that request, defendant cited the June 1992 New Jersey Supreme Court Task Force on Minority Concerns Final Report, 131 N.J.L.J. 1145 (1992) (Task Force Report).

The trial court denied the request because this Court had not yet adopted the Task Force Report and because there had been no expert testimony with respect to the issue of cross-racial identification. The trial court instead provided the jury with the Model Jury Charge on Identification. The jury convicted defendant of first-degree aggravated sexual assault, second-degree robbery, second-degree burglary, and third-degree terroristic threats.

In the Appellate Division, defendant argued that the case hinged entirely upon D.S.'s identification of him as her assailant and therefore, given the importance of the identification evidence, the trial court was obligated to provide the jury with explicit, fact-specific instructions on identification to guide it in its deliberations.

A majority of the panel believed that there was no error in the trial court's refusal to include an instruction on cross-racial identification. The majority noted that a review of cases from other jurisdictions supports the position that the charge either should not, or need not, be given. The majority was disinclined to require a cross-racial identification charge in view of the fact that the admissibility of expert testimony concerning cross-racial identification has not yet been endorsed in *New Jersey. See State v. Gunter*, 231 N.J.Super. 34, 40-48, 554 A.2d 1356 (App.Div.) (requiring trial court to conduct Rule 8 hearing on reliability of expert testimony respecting factors that affect reliability of eyewitness perception and memory), certif. denied, 117 N.J. 81, 563 A.2d 841 (1989).

Judge Shebell dissented, observing:

> A jury instruction that contains no direct reference to the hidden fires of prejudice and bias which may be stoked by an incident such as the sexual assault in question and fails to call the

jury's attention to the problems of cross-racial identification, so well documented by the [New Jersey Supreme Court Task Force on Minority Concerns], denies minority defendants, such as McKinley Cromedy, their constitutional right to a fair trial.

The issue of a cross-racial identification jury charge is before us as of right. R. 2:2-1(a)(2). The Court also granted certification "limited solely to the identification issues not covered by the dissenting opinion below." 153 N.J. 52, 707 A.2d 156 (1998).

II

Defendant argues that the trial court committed reversible error in denying his request for a cross-racial identification charge. He maintains that cross-racial impairment of eyewitnesses "is a scientifically accepted fact," and that the courts of this State can take judicial notice of the fallibility of trans-racial identifications and approve the report of the Task Force that recommended adoption of a cross-racial identification jury charge. Defendant argues that expert testimony is not a necessary factual predicate for such a jury charge. Alternatively, defendant argues that if the Court should require an expert to testify regarding factors that affect the reliability of eyewitness identification, and cross-racial identification specifically, we should remand the case to the trial court to afford him an opportunity to present that evidence.

The State argues that the trial court properly rejected defendant's request for a cross-racial identification charge. The State maintains that there is no consensus within the scientific community that an "own-race" bias exists. The State argues that because some researchers do not know whether cross-racial impairment affects "real life" identifications, and because even some of the scientists who believe that cross-racial impairment does affect identification cannot say what factors influence a person's ability to identify correctly a member of another race, the Court should reject a cross-racial identification charge. Alternatively, the State argues that this Court should not adopt a cross-racial charge until there is general acceptance that cross-racial impairment exists and general agreement on what factors influence a person's ability to correctly identify a member of another race.

-A-

A cross-racial identification occurs when an eyewitness is asked to identify a person of another race. The reliability of such an identification, though discussed in many cases throughout the country, is an issue of first impression in New Jersey. Because defendant requested a cross-racial identification jury charge, he bore the burden of showing that a reliable basis existed to support the requested charge. Defendant relied on common knowledge, the Task

Force Report, and judicial notice to support his request. Rather than calling an expert to testify regarding the factors that may make some cross-racial eyewitness identifications unreliable, defendant maintained that an expert would not aid the jury. In this context, we must decide whether a cross-racial jury instruction should be required where scientific evidence demonstrating the need for a specific instruction has not been presented.

-B-

For more than forty years, empirical studies concerning the psychological factors affecting eyewitness cross-racial or cross-ethnic identifications have appeared with increasing frequency in professional literature of the behavioral and social sciences. *People v. McDonald*, 37 Cal.3d 351, 208 Cal.Rptr. 236, 690 P.2d 709, 717-18 (1984). One study finds that jurors tend to place great weight on eyewitness identifications, often ignoring other exculpatory evidence. See R.C.L. Lindsay et al., Can People Detect Eyewitness-Identification Accuracy Within and Across Situations?, 66 J. Applied Psychol. 79, 79-89 (1981) (finding that jurors believe eyewitnesses despite poor witnessing conditions). Others have concluded that eyewitnesses are superior at identifying persons of their own race and have difficulty identifying members of another race. See generally Gary L. Wells & Elizabeth F. Loftus, Eyewitness Testimony: Psychological Perspectives 1 (1984); Elizabeth F. Loftus, Eyewitness Testimony (1979). See also Sheri Lynn Johnson, Cross-Racial Identification Errors in Criminal Cases, 69 Cornell L.Rev. 934 (1984); Stephanie J. Platz & Harmon M. Hosch, Cross-Racial/Ethnic Eyewitness Identification: A Field Study, 18 J. Applied Soc. Psychol. 972 (1988). But see R.C.L. Lindsay & Gary L. Wells, What Do We Really Know About Cross-Race Eyewitness Identification?, in Evaluating Witness Evidence: Recent Psychological Research and New Perspectives 219 (Sally M.A. Lloyd-Bostock & Brian R. Clifford eds., 1983) (failing to find cross-racial impairment). This phenomenon has been dubbed the "own-race" effect or "own-race" bias. Its corollary is that eyewitnesses experience a "cross-racial impairment" when identifying members of another race. Studies have consistently shown that the "own-race effect" is "strongest when white witnesses attempt to recognize black subjects." McDonald, supra, 208 Cal.Rptr. 236, 690 P.2d at 720.

Although researchers generally agree that some eyewitnesses exhibit an own-race bias, they disagree about the degree to which own-race bias affects identification. In one study, African-American and white "customers" browsed in a convenience store for a few minutes and then went to the register to pay. Researchers asked the convenience store clerks to identify the "customers" from a photo array. The white clerks were able to identify 53.2% of the white customers but only 40.4% of the African-American subjects. Platz & Hosch, supra, 18 J. Applied Soc. Psychol. at 977-78. The overall accuracy rate for all participants was only 44.2%. Id. at 981. Similar studies have found that own-race bias exists to a lesser degree. See John C. Brigham et al., Accuracy of Eyewitness Identifications in a Field Setting, 42 J. Personality & Soc. Psychol. 673, 681 (1982) (finding white clerks misidentified white "customers" 45% of the time and African-American "customers" 50% of the time). But see Roy S. Malpass & Jerome Kravitz, Recognition for Faces of Own and Other Race, 13 J. Personality & Soc. Psychol. 330, 330-34 (1969) (finding white subjects misidentified black faces two to three times more often than they misidentified white ones). A snap-shot of the literature reveals that although many scientists agree that witnesses are better at identifying suspects of their own race, they cannot agree on the extent to which cross-racial impairment affects identification. See *McDonald, supra*, 208 Cal.Rptr. 236, 690 P.2d at 720; see also *United States v. Nguyen*, 793 F.Supp. 497, 513-14 (D.N.J.1992) (rejecting testimony on cross-racial identification where expert's proffer could not quantify degree to which it is "more difficult" to make accurate cross-racial identifications).

The research also indicates disagreement about whether cross-racial impairment affects all racial groups. Four studies have found that African-American eyewitnesses do not experience cross-racial impairment at all. Johnson, supra, 69 Cornell L.Rev. at 939 (citing studies finding African-American eyewitnesses identified both white and black subjects with same degree of accuracy). Other studies have concluded that white eyewitnesses experience cross-racial impairment more often than African-American eyewitnesses. Ibid. (citing five studies concluding black subjects experience some degree of cross-racial impairment); cf. John C. Brigham, The Influence of Race on Face Recognition, in Aspects of Face Processing 170-77 (Hadyn D. Ellis et al. eds., 1986) (finding cross-race effects were comparable for both races). One study has found that African Americans make better eyewitnesses in general. Platz & Hosch, supra, 18 J. Applied Soc. Psychol. at 978 (finding, overall, eyewitnesses made correct identifications only 44.2% of the time, but that the African-American clerks correctly identified 54.6% of the white "customers" and 63.6% of the black "customers").

Many studies on cross-racial impairment involve subjects observing photographs for a few seconds. Because the subjects remembered the white faces more often than they recalled the African-American faces, researchers concluded that they were biased towards their own-race. See Paul Barkowitz & John C. Brigham, Recognition of Faces: Own-Race Bias, Incentive, and Time Delay, 12 J. Applied Soc. Psychol. 255 (1982). Yet, there is disagreement over whether the results of some of the tests can be generalized to real-world situations in which a victim or witness confronts an assailant face-to-face and experiences the full range of emotions that accompany such a traumatic event.

-C-

The debate among researchers did not prevent the Supreme Court of the United States, in the famous school desegregation case of *Brown v. Board of Education* of Topeka, 347 U.S. 483, 494 n. 11, 74 S.Ct. 686, 692 n. 11, 98 L.Ed. 873 (1954), from using behavioral and social sciences to support legal conclusions without requiring that the methodology employed by those scientists have general acceptance in the scientific community. The ultimate holding in Brown that segregation is harmful "was not only a nomological statement but a sociological observation as well." Paul L. Rosen, The Supreme Court and Social Science ix (1972). The Court's finding that segregation was harmful "was not based simply on [intuition] or common-sense, ... [but] was attributed to ... seven social science studies." Id. at x. The extralegal facts contained in the social science studies conducted by Dr. Kenneth B. Clark and others were presented to the Court in the form of a "Brandeis Brief." That characterization is derived from a brief first submitted by Louis D. Brandeis (later Justice Brandeis) in the case of *Muller v. Oregon*, 208 U.S. 412, 419-20, 28 S.Ct. 324, 325-26, 52 L.Ed. 551 (1908). Thus, Brown v. Board of Education is the prototypical example of an appellate court using modern social and behavioral sciences as legislative evidence to support its choice of a rule of law. John Monahan & Laurens Walker, Social Authority: Obtaining, Evaluating and Establishing Social Science in Law, 134 U. Pa. L.Rev. 477, 484 (1986).

In *United States v. Telfaire*, 469 F.2d 552 (D.C.Cir.1972), Chief Judge Bazelon urged in his concurring opinion that juries be charged on the pitfalls of cross-racial identification. He believed that the cross-racial nature of an identification could affect accuracy in the same way as proximity to the perpetrator and poor lighting conditions. Id. at 559. He felt that a meaningful jury instruction would have to apprise jurors of that fact. To achieve that objective, Judge Bazelon proposed the following instruction:

> In this case the identifying witness is of a different race than the defendant. In the experience
> of many it is more difficult to identify members of a different race than members of one's own.
> If this is also your own experience, you may consider it in evaluating the witness's testimony.
> You must also consider, of course, whether there are other factors present in this case which
> overcome any such difficulty of identification. For example, you may conclude that the witness
> has had sufficient contacts with members of the defendant's race that he would not have greater
> difficulty in making a reliable identification.

[Id. at 561 (Bazelon, C.J., concurring).]

Judge Bazelon rejected the notion that instructions on interracial identifications "appeal to racial prejudice." Id. at 560. Rather, he believed that an explicit jury instruction would safeguard against improper uses of race by the jury and would delineate the narrow context in which it is appropriate to consider racial differences. Id. at 559-61.

Four years later, Judge McCree, who later became Solicitor General, in *United States v. Russell*, 532 F.2d 1063, 1066 (6th Cir.1976), also acknowledged the existence of problems related to eyewitness identification. He observed:

> There is a great potential for misidentification when a witness identifies a stranger based solely
> upon a single brief observation, and this risk is increased when the observation was made at a

time of stress or excitement.... This problem is important because of all the evidence that may be presented to a jury, a witness' [sic] in-court statement that "he is the one" is probably the most dramatic and persuasive.

[*Id.* at 1066-67.]

A year later in *United States v. Smith*, 563 F.2d 1361 (9th Cir.1977), Judge Hufstedler stated that the reliability of a single eyewitness identification is "at best, highly dubious, given the extensive empirical evidence that eyewitness identifications are not reliable." Id. at 1365 (Hufstedler, J., concurring). Judge Hufstedler drew support from Judge Bazelon's suggestion in *United States v. Brown*, 461 F.2d 134 (D.C.Cir.1972), that courts inform themselves of the results of scientific studies relative to the reliability problems of eyewitness identifications. Id. at 145-46 & n. 1 (Bazelon, C.J., concurring and dissenting); see also David L. Bazelon, Eyewitless News, Psychology Today, March 1980, at 102.

One year after Smith was decided, the Second Circuit observed that "[c]enturies of experience in the administration of criminal justice have shown that convictions based solely on testimony that identifies a defendant previously unknown to the witness is highly suspect. Of all the various kinds of evidence it is the least reliable, especially where unsupported by corroborating evidence." *Jackson v. Fogg*, 589 F.2d 108, 112 (2d Cir.1978).

The Supreme Court of the United States has acknowledged that problems exist with eyewitness identifications in general and cross-racial identifications in particular. The Court has stated that "[t]he vagaries of eyewitness identification are well-known; the annals of criminal law are rife with instances of mistaken identification." *United States v. Wade*, 388 U.S. 218, 228, 87 S.Ct. 1926, 1933, 18 L.Ed.2d 1149 (1967). The Court has also noted "the high incidence of miscarriage[s] of justice" caused by such misidentifications and that even uncontradicted

> "identification of strangers [by eyewitnesses] is proverbially untrustworthy. The hazards of such testimony are established by a formidable number of instances in the records of English and American trials. These instances are recent-not due to the brutalities of ancient criminal procedure."

[Ibid. (quoting Felix Frankfurter, The Case of Sacco and Vanzetti 30 (1927)).]

Ten years after Wade was decided, the Supreme Court suggested that an eyewitness identification was more reliable when made by a member of the defendant's own race. *Manson v. Brathwaite*, 432 U.S. 98, 115, 97 S.Ct. 2243, 2253, 53 L.Ed.2d 140 (1977).

-D-

Although there have been no reported decisions in our own State addressing the propriety of requiring a cross-racial identification jury instruction, decisions have been rendered by courts in other jurisdictions. The majority of courts allowing cross-racial identification charges hold that the decision to provide the instruction is a matter within the trial judge's discretion. Omission of such a cautionary instruction has been held to be prejudicial error where identification is the critical or central issue in the case, there is no corroborating evidence, and the circumstances of the case raise doubts concerning the reliability of the identification. See *United States v. Thompson*, 31 M.J. 125 (C.M.A.1990) (calling for cross-racial identification instruction when requested by counsel and when cross-racial identification is a "primary issue"); *People v. Wright*, 45 Cal.3d 1126, 248 Cal. Rptr. 600, 755 P.2d 1049 (1988); *People v. West*, 139 Cal.App.3d 606, 189 Cal.Rptr. 36, 38-39 (1983); *Commonwealth v. Hyatt*, 419 Mass. 815, 647 N.E.2d 1168 (1995); *State v. Long*, 721 P.2d 483 (Utah 1986).

In *People v. Palmer*, 154 Cal.App.3d 79, 203 Cal.Rptr. 474 (1984), for example, the defendant was convicted of robbery based solely on the robbery victims' testimony. *Id.* at 476. There was no physical or circumstantial corroborating evidence, the victims' contacts were brief, some of the victims could not identify defendant at a line-up, and none told police that the robber wore braces. Ibid. The court held that the defendant was entitled to a specific instruction on the inaccuracies of cross-racial identification because the only evidence against the defendant consisted of the victims' identifications, the accuracy of which was the sole issue in the case, and the evidence was conflicting. Ibid. Cf. *People v. Harris*, 47 Cal.3d 1047, 255 Cal.Rptr. 352, 767 P.2d 619 (1989) (finding harmless error in excluding special instruction on cross-racial identification where there was substantial evidence to corroborate the identifications, including eyewitness testimony and extrajudicial admissions by defendant himself).

Courts typically have refused the instruction where the eyewitness or victim had an adequate opportunity to observe the defendant, there was corroborating evidence bolstering the identification, and/or there was no evidence that race affected the identification. See *Hyatt*, *supra*, 647 N.E.2d at 1171 (declining instruction in rape and robbery case where victim was terrorized for fifteen to twenty minutes in broad daylight and could see the attacker's face); see also *Commonwealth v. Engram*, 43 Mass.App.Ct. 804, 686 N.E.2d 1080 (1997) (declining instruction where numerous eyewitnesses saw defendant at close range and positively identified him from a line-up and photo array).

A number of courts have concluded that cross-racial identification simply is not an appropriate topic for jury instruction. See *State v. Willis*, 240 Kan. 580, 731 P.2d 287, 292-93 (1987); *Hyatt*, *supra*, 647 N.E.2d at 1171; *People v. McDaniel*, 217 A.D.2d 859, 630 N.Y.S.2d 112, 113, appeal denied, 87 N.Y.2d 848, 638 N.Y.S.2d 607, 661 N.E.2d 1389 (1995). Those courts have determined that the cross-racial instruction requires expert guidance, and that cross-examination and summation are adequate safeguards to highlight unreliable identifications.

Other jurisdictions have denied the instruction, finding that the results of empirical studies on cross-racial identification are questionable. See *Telfaire,* supra, 469 F.2d at 561-62 (Leventhal, J., concurring) (rejecting cross-racial instruction because data supporting hypothesis is "meager"); *People v. Bias,* 131 Ill.App.3d 98, 86 Ill.Dec. 256, 475 N.E.2d 253, 257 (1985) (rejecting instruction in robbery case where eyewitness failed to describe key distinguishing facial features and gave inconsistent descriptions because empirical studies are not unanimous). One jurisdiction has even rejected cross-racial identification instructions as improper commentary on "the nature and quality" of the evidence. See *State v. Hadrick,* 523 A.2d 441, 444 (R.I.1987) (rejecting such instruction in robbery case where victim viewed perpetrator for two to three minutes at close range during robbery and identified him from a line-up).

-E-

The defense in the present case did not question whether the victim had been sexually assaulted. Rather, the defense asserted that the victim's identification of defendant as the perpetrator was mistaken. It is well-established in this State that when identification is a critical issue in the case, the trial court is obligated to give the jury a discrete and specific instruction that provides appropriate guidelines to focus the jury's attention on how to analyze and consider the trustworthiness of eyewitness identification. *State v. Green,* 86 N.J. 281, 292, 430 A.2d 914 (1981); State v. Melvin, 65 N.J. 1, 18, 319 A.2d 450 (1974); *State v. Middleton,* 299 N.J.Super. 22, 32, 690 A.2d 623 (App.Div.1997); *State v. Frey,* 194 N.J.Super. 326, 329-30, 476 A.2d 884 (App.Div.1984).

Green requires that as a part of an identification charge a trial court inform the jury that the State's case relies on an eyewitness identification of the defendant as the perpetrator, and that in weighing the reliability of that identification the jury should consider, among other things, "the capacity or the ability of the witness to make observations or perceptions ... at the time and under all of the attendant circumstances for seeing that which he says he saw or that which he says he perceived with regard to his identification." 86 N.J. at 293-94, 430 A.2d 914. What defendant sought through the requested charge in the present case was an instruction that informed the jury that it could consider the fact that the victim made a cross-racial identification as part of the "attendant circumstances" when evaluating the reliability of the eyewitness identification.

The Court-appointed Task Force discussed and debated the issue of the need for a cross-racial and cross-ethnic identification jury instruction for more than five years. That Task Force was comprised of an appellate judge, trial judges, lawyers representing both the prosecution and defense, social scientists, and ordinary citizens. Professional consultants to the Task Force included Dr. Howard F. Taylor, Professor, Princeton University; Dr. William J. Chambliss, Professor, George Washington University; and Dr. Kenneth B. Clark, Distinguished Professor of Psychology Emeritus, City University of New York, who was prominently associated with the behavioral science studies submitted to the Supreme Court in Brown v. Board of Education.

Task Force sessions were conducted in much the same way as legislative committees conduct hearings on proposed legislation. The Task Force consulted a substantial body of professional literature in the behavioral and social sciences concerning the reliability of cross-racial identifications. Except for the view expressed by a county prosecutor, the Task Force was unanimously convinced that a problem exists respecting cross-racial identifications and that the Court should take corrective action. Ultimately, in 1992 the Task Force submitted its final report to the Court in which it recommended, among other things, that the Court develop a special jury charge regarding the unreliability of cross-racial identifications.

The Court referred that recommendation to the Criminal Practice Committee. The Criminal Practice Committee reviewed the recommendation and created a subcommittee to draft a cross-racial identification charge for consideration by the full Committee. The subcommittee drafted and submitted to the Criminal Practice Committee the following proposed charge:

You know that the identifying witness is of a different race than the defendant. When a witness, who is a member of one race, identifies a defendant, who is a member of another race, we say that there has been a cross-racial identification. You may consider, if you think it is appropriate to do so, whether the cross-racial nature of the identification has affected the accuracy of the witness' [sic] original perception and/or the accuracy of the subsequent identification(s).

The Criminal Practice Committee, however, decided against recommending a charge to the Court. Development of a cross-racial charge was deemed to be premature because the issue of admissibility of evidence to support the charge had not been decided by case law. Thereafter, the Committee on Minority Concerns submitted to the Model Criminal Jury Charge Committee for its consideration a revised model jury charge on identification that included cross-racial eyewitness identification as a factor to be considered by the jury. As revised, the proposed cross-racial factor reads: "The fact that the witness is not of the same race as the perpetrator and/or defendant and whether that fact might have had an impact on the witness' [sic] ability to make an accurate identification." The Model Criminal Jury Charge Committee is withholding further consideration of a cross-racial identification charge pending the Court's decision in the present case.

-F-

We reject the State's contention that we should not require a cross-racial identification charge before it has been demonstrated that there is substantial agreement in the relevant scientific community that cross-racial recognition impairment is significant enough to support the need for such a charge. This case does not concern the introduction of scientific evidence to attack the reliability of the eyewitness's identification. Defendant's requested jury instruction was not based upon any "scientific, technical, or other specialized knowledge" to assist the jury. N.J.R.E. 702. He relied instead on ordinary human experience and the legislative-type findings of the Task Force because the basis for his request did not involve a matter that was beyond the ken of the average juror.

This case requires us to focus on the well-established differences between adjudicative or hard evidence, argument, and jury instructions. The hard evidence revealed a cross-racial identification and the circumstances under which that identification was made. The State argued to the jury that the identification was credible based on the evidence. Counsel for defendant, on the other hand, argued that there was a mistaken identification based on the totality of the circumstances. Defendant requested a cross-racial identification jury instruction that would treat the racial character of the eyewitness identification as one of the factors bearing on its reliability in much the same way as lighting and proximity to the perpetrator at the time of the offense.

A national review of the use of cross-racial identification jury instructions reveals that only a small minority of jurisdictions have declined such an instruction because studies finding unreliability in cross-racial identifications lack general acceptance in the relevant scientific community. The majority of jurisdictions that have rejected the instruction did so based on judicial discretion. Those discretionary rulings were influenced by factors such as the nature and quality of the eyewitness identification, the existence of strong corroborating evidence, the fact that the eyewitness had an adequate opportunity to observe the perpetrator, or a combination of those reasons.

Consistent with Brown, Wade and Manson; the admonitions expressed by Justice Frankfurter, Judge Bazelon in Telfaire and Brown, Judge McCree in Russell, and Judge Hufstedler in Smith; the California cases of McDonald, Wright and West; our own requirement in Green that a proper identification jury instruction be given when that issue is critical in the case; the Task Force Report; and our review of the professional literature of the behavioral and social sciences, we hold that a cross-racial identification, as a subset of eyewitness identification, requires a special jury instruction in an appropriate case.

Indeed, some courtroom observers have commented that the ordinary person's difficulty of "cross-racial recognition is so commonplace as to be the subject of both cliche and joke: 'they all look alike.' " Johnson, supra, 69 Cornell L.Rev. at 942. Although laboratory studies concerning the reliability of cross-racial identifications have not been validated in actual courtroom atmospheres, the results of many of those experiments suggest that "decreased accuracy in the recognition of other-race faces is not within the observer's conscious control, and that seriousness of criminal proceedings would not improve accuracy." Ibid. Moreover, the stress associated with the courtroom atmosphere, based on human experience, is likely to diminish rather than enhance recognition accuracy.

We embrace the California rule requiring a cross-racial identification charge under the circumstances of this case despite some differences of opinion among the researchers. Notwithstanding those differences, there is an impressive consistency in results showing that problems exist with cross-racial eyewitness identification. *McDonald, supra,* 208 Cal.Rptr. 236,

690 P.2d at 718. We conclude that the empirical data encapsulate much of the ordinary human experience and provide an appropriate frame of reference for requiring a cross-racial identification jury instruction. Under the jurisprudence of this Court, in a prosecution "in which race by definition is a patent factor[, race] must be taken into account to assure a fair trial." *State v. Harris*, 156 N.J. 122, 235, 716 A.2d 458 (1998) (Handler, J., dissenting).

At the same time, we recognize that unrestricted use of cross-racial identification instructions could be counter-productive. Consequently, care must be taken to insulate criminal trials from base appeals to racial prejudice. An appropriate jury instruction should carefully delineate the context in which the jury is permitted to consider racial differences. The simple fact pattern of a white victim of a violent crime at the hands of a black assailant would not automatically give rise to the need for a cross-racial identification charge. More is required.

A cross-racial instruction should be given only when, as in the present case, identification is a critical issue in the case, and an eyewitness's cross-racial identification is not corroborated by other evidence giving it independent reliability. Here, the eyewitness identification was critical; yet it was not corroborated by any forensic evidence or other eyewitness account. The circumstances of the case raise some doubt concerning the reliability of the victim's identification in that no positive identification was made for nearly eight months despite attempts within the first five days following the commission of the offenses. Under those circumstances, turning over to the jury the vital question of the reliability of that identification without acquainting the jury with the potential risks associated with such identifications could have affected the jurors' ability to evaluate the reliability of the identification. We conclude, therefore, that it was reversible error not to have given an instruction that informed the jury about the possible significance of the cross-racial identification factor, a factor the jury can observe in many cases with its own eyes, in determining the critical issue-the accuracy of the identification.

For the sake of clarity, we repeat that the purpose of a cross-racial instruction is to alert the jury through a cautionary instruction that it should pay close attention to a possible influence of race. Because of the "widely held commonsense view that members of one race have greater difficulty in accurately identifying members of a different race," *Telfaire*, supra, 469 F.2d at 559 (Bazelon, C.J., concurring); Brown, supra, 461 F.2d at 134, expert testimony on this issue would not assist a jury, N.J.R.E. 702, and for that reason would be inadmissible. We request the Criminal Practice Committee and the Model Jury Charge Committee to revise the current charge on identification to include an appropriate statement on cross-racial eyewitness identification that is consistent with this opinion.

The judgment of the Appellate Division is reversed. The case is remanded to the Law Division for a new trial.

For reversal and remandment-Chief Justice PORITZ and Justices POLLOCK, O'HERN, GARIBALDI, STEIN and COLEMAN-6.

Opposed-None.

Note

In the *Henderson* decision above, the New Jersey Supreme Court noted its decision in *Cromedy* as to the propriety of special jury instructions on cross-racial eyewitness identification. While maintaining that such an instruction should be given whenever cross-racial identification is in issue, the Court abrogated its earlier conclusion, reflected above in the *Cromedy* decision, which additionally required such instruction only in instances where the eyewitness identification was critical and not corroborated by independent evidence.The Court stated " Since [*Cromedy*] , the additional research on own-race bias ... and the more complete record about eyewitness identification in general, justify giving the charge whenever cross-racial identification is in issue at trial. 208 N.J. at 926.

Despite the extensive discussion and social science research reflected in both *Cromedy* and *Henderson* national and federal recognition of a right to a special jury instruction on cross-race eyewitness identification have been mixed. In *Smith v. State*, 158 Md. App. 673 (2004), Maryland reference to the alleged difficulties of cross-racial identification was not required where pattern jury instructions advised the jury to examine eyewitness testimony with "great care". See also, *Wallace v. State*, 306 Ga.App. 118 (2010).

At least one federal court has considered whether the issue of a special jury instruction on cross-racial eyewitness identification is of United States Constitutional significance:

PEREZ V. GLOVER
2012 Wl 481122 (D. Nj 2012)

Petitioner, Jose Perez ("Perez"), was indicted by a Essex County grand jury, Indictment No. 2005–7–1699, on the following charges: (Count 1) first degree robbery in violation of N.J.S.A. 2C:15–1; (Count 2) third degree unlawful possession of a weapon (handgun) in violation of N.J.S.A. 2C:39–5b; and (Count 3) second degree possession of a weapon for an unlawful purpose in violation of N.J.S.A. 2C:39–4a. (RE–A, Indictment).12 A hearing was held on March 7, 2006, and the out-of-court and in-court identification was ruled admissible.

This matter is before the court pursuant to a petition for a writ of habeas corpus under 28 U.S.C. § 2254, filed by petitioner Jose Perez, challenging his 2006 New Jersey state court conviction. For the reasons stated below, this Court will deny the habeas petition for lack of merit.

Perez next asserts that his Fourteenth Amendment right to a fair trial and due process was denied when the trial court refused to give an instruction to the jury on cross-racial identification, as requested pursuant *State v. Cromedy*, 158 N.J. 112, 727 A.2d 457 (1999).7 Perez noted that he is Hispanic, the two eyewitnesses, Kyung and Min, are Korean, and the police officers, Gilbert and Glover are African–American. Perez raised this claim on direct appeal.

The Appellate Division found no merit to petitioner's claim. Specifically, the court held:

"A cross racial instruction should be given only when ... identification is a critical issue in the case, and an eyewitness's cross-racial identification is not corroborated by other evidence giving it independent reliability." *State v. Cromedy*, 158 N.J. 112, 132, 727 A.2d 457 (1999). The cross-racial instruction is not required where other independent corroborating evidence exists from which the jury may evaluate the reliability of he [sic] identification, such as other eyewitness accounts. Id. at 132–33, 727 A.2d 457.

Here, there was substantial independent evidence corroborating the witnesses' identification of defendant. Both Kyung and Min saw defendant in close proximity in the store and the two officers saw defendant leave the store. Glover chased defendant and never lost sight of him. All of the witnesses gave similar descriptions of defendant and his clothing. This evidence permitted the jury to evaluate the reliability of the identification without a cross-racial identification instruction.

(RE–D, pp. 15–16).

Generally, a jury instruction that is inconsistent with state law does not merit federal habeas relief. Where a federal habeas petitioner challenges jury instructions given in a state criminal proceeding,

[t]he only question for us is "whether the ailing instruction by itself so infected the entire trial that the resulting conviction violates due process." It is well established that the instruction "may not be judged in artificial isolation," but must be considered in the context of the instructions as a whole and the trial record. In addition, in reviewing an ambiguous instruction ..., we inquire "whether there is a reasonable likelihood that the jury has applied the challenged instruction in a way" that violates the Constitution. And we also bear in mind our previous admonition that we "have defined the category of infractions that violate 'fundamental fairness' very narrowly." "Beyond the specific guarantees enumerated in the Bill of Rights, the Due Process Clause has limited operation."

Estelle v. McGuire, 502 U.S. 62, 72–73, 112 S.Ct. 475, 116 L.Ed.2d 385 (1991) (citations omitted); see also *Smith v. Spisak*, ––– U.S. ––––, ––––, 130 S.Ct. 676, 684, 175 L.Ed.2d 595 (2010) (no right to habeas relief if Supreme Court has not previously held jury instruction unconstitutional for same reason); *Waddington v. Sauausad*, 555 U.S. 179, 129 S.Ct. 823, 172 L.Ed.2d 532 (2009).

The United States Court of Appeals for the Third Circuit has observed that a habeas petitioner who challenges state jury instructions must "point to a federal requirement that jury instructions ... must include particular provisions," or demonstrate that the jury "instructions deprived him of a defense which federal law provided to him." *Johnson v. Rosemeyer*, 117 F.3d 104, 110 (3d Cir.1997). This is because district courts do not "sit as super state supreme courts for the purpose of determining whether jury instructions were correct under state law with respect to the elements of an offense and defenses to it." Id. As the Third Circuit explained,

> In considering whether this case involves a claim of error under the Constitution, laws, or trea-
> ties of the United States, it is critical to remember that the Supreme Court has made it clear that
> the states define the elements of state offenses. Accordingly, while there may be constitutionally
> required minimum criteria which must be met for conduct to constitute a state criminal offense,
> in general there is no constitutional reason why a state offense must include particular elements.
> See *McMillan v. Pennsylvania*, 477 U.S. 79, 84–86, 106 S.Ct. 2411, 2415–16, 91 L.Ed.2d 67 (1986).

Johnson, 117 F.3d at 110.

However, a jury instruction that "reduce[s] the level of proof necessary for the Government to carry its burden [of proof beyond a reasonable doubt] is plainly inconsistent with the constitutionally rooted presumption of innocence." *Cool v. United States*, 409 U.S. 100, 104, 93 S.Ct. 354, 34 L.Ed.2d 335 (1972). See also *In re Winship*, 397 U.S. 358, 364, 90 S.Ct. 1068, 25 L.Ed.2d 368 (1970) ("the Due Process Clause protects the accused against conviction except upon proof beyond a reasonable doubt of every fact necessary to constitute the crime with which he is charged"); *Sandstrom v. Montana*, 442 U.S. 510, 523, 99 S.Ct. 2450, 61 L.Ed.2d 39 (1979) (jury instructions that suggest a jury may convict without proving each element of a crime beyond a reasonable doubt violate the constitutional rights of the accused); *Smith v. Horn*, 120 F.3d 400, 416 (1997), cert. denied, 522 U.S. 1109, 118 S.Ct. 1037, 140 L.Ed.2d 103 (1998) (the Due Process Clause is violated only where "the erroneous instructions have operated to lift the burden of proof on an essential element of an offense as defined by state law.").

Additionally, "[a]n omission, or an incomplete instruction, is less likely to be prejudicial than a misstatement of the law." *Henderson v. Kibbe*, 431 U.S. 145, 155, 97 S.Ct. 1730, 52 L.Ed.2d 203 (1977). Specifically, in this case, the Appellate Division determined that the trial court's failure to instruct the jury on cross-racial identification was not in error because there was substantial independent evidence corroborating the witness' identification of Perez that enabled the jury to evaluate the reliability of the identification. Further, the failure to give identification instructions on the issue of cross-racial identification did nothing "to lift the burden of proof on an essential element of an offense." Moreover, there was substantial identification evidence other than the testimony of Kyung and Kim, namely, the testimony of the police officers who pursued Perez and apprehended him without losing sight of Perez when he exited the jewelry store, their observance of petitioner with a handgun during that time, and the fact that all witnesses gave similar descriptions of Perez and his clothing. Finally, having carefully reviewed the jury charges as a whole, and in particular, the trial judge's lengthy and thorough charge on identification testimony, this Court finds that Petitioner was not deprived of a fair trial by those instructions on identification, and any error as asserted by Perez regarding the exclusion of a cross-racial identification instruction was, at the very most, plainly harmless in light of the overall record.

Thus, this Court finds no error of constitutional dimension. The absence of the requested jury instruction did not have the capacity to produce an unjust result. The state court ruling on this issue is neither contrary to nor an unreasonable application of the applicable federal law, nor is the decision based upon an unreasonable determination of the facts. Accordingly, petitioner is not entitled to relief on this claim.

Note

The traditional view that such instructions are an unnecessary departure from standard instructions can be seen in the earlier *Ingram* decision below.

UNITED STATES V. INGRAM
600 F.2d 260 (10th Cir. 1979)

Opinion

McWILLIAMS, Circuit Judge.

In separate indictments Kendal Ingram and his older brother, Keith Ingram, were charged with the robbery of the Key Savings and Loan Association, a federally insured corporation maintaining a branch office at 2400 West Alameda Avenue in Denver, Colorado, in violation of 18 U.S.C. s 2113(a) and (d). In separate trials both defendants were convicted and Kendal Ingram appeals his conviction.

The Government's case-in-chief established that Kendal Ingram and his brother Keith had robbed the Key Savings and Loan Association of some $1,740 in money and approximately $4,800 in travelers cheques on December 29, 1976. Keith Ingram was armed with a gun. The two fled the scene, and Kendal Ingram was arrested some six months later, in St. Louis, Missouri.

One of the two tellers in the office of the Key Savings and Loan Association identified Kendal Ingram at trial as being one of the two robbers. The other teller could not identify Kendal Ingram. A surveillance camera located in the Savings and Loan office took photographs of the robbery in progress, and twenty-four of these exhibits were introduced into evidence and viewed by the jury.

Two Government witnesses who were acquainted with Kendal Ingram had been shown, prior to trial, certain of these surveillance photographs and each admitted in a pre-trial identification statement that she had at that time identified Kendal and Keith Ingram as being the two robbers depicted therein. At trial, however, neither witness would identify Kendal Ingram as being one of the robbers shown in the photographs, though one did identify Kendal's brother, Keith Ingram.

Kendal Ingram testified in his own behalf and denied that he had participated in the robbery. He admitted being in Denver, Colorado on December 29, 1976, the day of the robbery, but said that at the time of the robbery he was several miles away from the Savings and Loan office in the home of a friend playing cards. He testified that he was not one of the two robbers depicted in the surveillance pictures, and other persons who were acquainted with him offered similar testimony.

....

The only issue in the trial of this case was the one of identification. There is no dispute that the Key Savings and Loan Association was robbed at about two o'clock p. m. on December 29, 1976, by two young blacks, one of whom carried a gun. The only issue is whether Kendal Ingram was one of the robbers. Under the circumstances, any instruction concerning identification of the defendant took on added significance. The instruction now in question was given in the language of E. Devitt & C. Blackmar, Federal Jury Practice and Instructions, s 15.19 (3d ed. 1977). According to defense counsel, however, this instruction did not go far enough. Counsel had asked for an additional instruction which would have pointed out to the jury that the teller who identified Ingram was a white person, whereas Ingram was a black person, and then would have gone on to state that "in the experience of many it is more difficult to identify members of a different race than members of one's own." The trial court refused to give such additional instruction, and such refusal is now assigned as reversible error.

In arguing for an additional instruction on inter-racial identification, the defendant relies primarily on a concurring opinion by the then Chief Judge Bazelon in United *States v. Telfaire*, 152 U.S.App.D.C. 146, 469 F.2d 552 (1972). A so-called model instruction on identification was set forth as an appendix to that opinion. The instruction on identification given in the instant case is comparable to the model instruction approved in *Telfaire*, and, as indicated, is virtually verbatim to that appearing in Devitt & Blackmar.

In *Telfaire*, Judge Bazelon, however, would have gone beyond the model instruction there approved and would have included in the model instruction language to the effect that members of one race have greater difficulty in accurately identifying members of a different race. Judge Bazelon's suggestion was not concurred in by the other members of the panel in *Telfaire*, nor do we concur in such suggestion. A jury is to be instructed on the law of the case, and an instruction on inter-racial identification along the lines indicated is more in the realm of argument than law. The instruction given here on identification was, under the circumstances, more than adequate. The refusal to give an inter-racial instruction was not error.

STATE V. ALLEN
76 Wash.2d 611 (2013)

C. JOHNSON, J.

Petitioner Bryan Allen challenges his felony harassment conviction, raising three issues. The primary issue involves whether the trial court erred by not instructing the jury on the potential fallibility of cross-racial eyewitness identification. Based on the facts of this case, Allen cannot show the trial court violated his constitutional rights by refusing to give the cautionary instruction. A second issue involves whether the "true threat" requirement is an essential element of a harassment statute that must be pleaded in the information and included in the "to-convict" instruction. A third issue involves prosecutorial misconduct. The Court of Appeals rejected the arguments raised. We affirm the Court of Appeals.

FACTS

Gerald Kovacs, who is white, was walking near the University of Washington at dusk when he was approached by two young African American men who offered to sell Kovacs marijuana. Irritated, he told them to "F[uck] off." Verbatim Report of Proceedings (VRP) (Oct. 21, 2009) at 8. The men screamed and cursed Kovacs, and then followed him. One of the men told Kovacs, "I'm going to kill you, you B[itch]," and lifted up his shirt to display what Kovacs believed to be a gun. VRP (Oct. 21, 2009) at 11. Kovacs ran to the nearest gas station and called the police.

During the 911 call, Kovacs described the man with the gun as an African American in his mid-20s, wearing a black hooded sweatshirt, a hat, and big, gold-framed sunglasses. Kovacs also described the man as being around 5'9" and between 210–220 pounds. He described the other man as an African American in his teens, around 5'5", wearing a "red kind of shirt," though he could not remember the color exactly. VRP (Oct. 22, 2009) at 4. Several minutes later, based on Kovacs' description, a University of Washington patrol officer attempted to stop two African American men near the scene of the crime. One of the men, wearing a white T-shirt, fled. The other, Bryan Allen, did not. Seattle City Police detained Allen and Kovacs was transported to the location of the arrest for a showup identification procedure. Though Allen matched Kovacs' description of the man with the gun as to race, clothing, hat, and sunglasses, physically he was larger at 6′1″ and 280 pounds. Kovacs identified Allen as the man who threatened him. The police searched Allen incident to arrest but found no gun, marijuana, or cash.

The State charged Allen with felony harassment. Prior to trial, Allen requested the court to instruct the jury regarding cross-racial identifications.1 The court refused Allen's request. No expert testimony on the reliability of cross-racial eyewitness testimony was given at trial. The only testimony given on the subject was by Officer Bennett, the officer in charge of directing the showup identification, who, on cross-examination, agreed that he was "aware of studies suggesting that cross [-] racial identifications can be more difficult for people." VRP (Oct. 21, 2009) at 57. He also agreed that "sometimes people of different races will have a more difficult time identifying somebody of a different race," though he did not see any indication of difficulties in Kovacs' identification. VRP (Oct. 21, 2009) at 57. Allen's defense counsel, in closing argument, challenged the reliability of such evidence.

....

1. Cross–Racial Identification Instruction

Concerns and discussions over the reliability of eyewitness identifications, and more specifically cross-racial eyewitness identifications, have arisen in cases for some time. The United States Supreme Court focused on eyewitness identification problems in *United States v. Wade*, 388 U.S. 218, 228, 87 S.Ct. 1926, 18 L.Ed.2d 1149 (1967), noting that the "vagaries of eyewitness identification are well-known; the annals of criminal law are rife with instances of mistaken identification." The United States District Court for the District of Columbia, in *United States v. Telfaire*, 152 U.S.App. D.C. 146, 469 F.2d 552 (1972), cited to Wade and discussed the importance of, and need for, a special instruction on the issue of identification in order to safeguard the presumption of innocence. The court in Telfaire crafted a special identification instruction for use in future cases, to specifically instruct the jury to assess the value of eyewitness testimony based on several considerations. This model instruction did not specifically address cross-racial eyewitness identification; however, in his concurring opinion, Chief Judge Bazelon urged that juries be charged specifically on the pitfalls of cross-racial identification and also proposed sample instruction language. *Telfaire*, 469 F.2d at 559–61 (Bazelon, C.J., concurring).

After *Telfaire*, jurisdictions have developed three general approaches to address the problems perceived to be inherent in eyewitness identification testimony. Some have accepted the rationale underlying *Telfaire* and have required or encouraged a particularized instruction to be given. See *People v. Wright*, 45 Cal.3d 1126, 755 P.2d 1049, 248 Cal.Rptr. 600 (1988) (approving a condensed *Telfaire*-type instruction and requiring that such an instruction be given when requested in a case in which identification is a central issue and there is little corroborative evidence); *State v. Warren*, 230 Kan. 385, 635 P.2d 1236 (1981) (holding that where eyewitness identification is a critical part of the prosecution's case and there is serious doubt about the reliability of the identification, a cautionary instruction should be given); *State v. Henderson*, 208 N.J. 208, 27 A.3d 872 (2011) (requiring that an instruction on cross-racial identification be given whenever cross-racial identification is an issue at trial).

In other jurisdictions, the decision has been left up to the discretion of the trial court. See *United States v. Sambrano*, 505 F.2d 284, 287 (9th Cir.1974) (applying an abuse of discretion standard to the alleged error of failing to give an eyewitness identification instruction and holding the trial court had not abused its discretion where general instructions given by the court adequately directed the jury's attention to the identification issue); *Wallace v. State*, 306 Ga.App. 118, 701 S.E.2d 554 (2010) (holding the trial court did not abuse its discretion in refusing the defendant's requested jury instruction on the reliability of cross-racial eyewitness identification where, by general instructions, the jury was informed that it was required to determine whether the eyewitness identification was sufficiently reliable to help satisfy the State's burden of proof and other corroborating evidence existed).

The final approach adopted by some jurisdictions has been to reject outright a requirement for *Telfaire*-like instructions. The courts in these jurisdictions have held that the other general instructions on witness credibility and the government's burden of proof are adequate and/or that the identification instructions impermissibly comment on the evidence. See *State v. Valencia*, 118 Ariz. 136, 575 P.2d 335 (Ct.App.1977) (finding that the instruction on credibility of witnesses was sufficient and that part of *Telfaire*—type instruction constituted a comment on the evidence); *Nevius v. State*, 101 Nev. 238, 699 P.2d 1053 (1985) (holding that specific eyewitness identification instruction is duplicitous of general instructions on credibility of witnesses and proof beyond a reasonable doubt); *State v. Classen*, 31 Or.App. 683, 571 P.2d 527 (1977) (holding that specific *Telfaire*-type instruction overemphasized the identification issue and amounted to a comment on the evidence), rev'd on other grounds, 285 Or. 221, 590 P.2d 1198 (1979).

Our cases suggest we have aligned somewhere between the second and third categories mentioned above. In *State v. Laureano*, 101 Wash.2d 745, 682 P.2d 889 (1984), overruled on other grounds by *State v. Brown*, 111 Wash.2d 124, 132–33, 761 P.2d 588 (1988), adhered to on recons., 113 Wash.2d 520, 529, 782 P.2d 1013, 787 P.2d 906 (1989), we discussed, albeit briefly, a challenge to the trial court's *620 failure to instruct the jury on eyewitness identification, including cross-racial or ethnic eyewitness identification. In that case, we favorably cited to two Court of Appeals cases, *State v. Jordan*, 17 Wash.App. 542, 564 P.2d 340 (1977), and *State v. Edwards*, 23 Wash.App. 893, 600 P.2d 566 (1979), and found no reversible error.

In Jordan, the Court of Appeals reviewed a *Telfaire*-type instruction and held the trial judge did not err in rejecting the instruction. In that case the court recognized "the focus and 'emphasis' of the instruction is upon the credibility of identification witnesses.... Witness credibility is more properly tested 'by examination and cross-examination in the forum of the trial court.'" *Jordan*, 17 Wash.App. at 545, 564 P.2d 340 (quoting *State v. Johnson*, 12 Wash.App. 40, 45, 527 P.2d

1324 (1974)). Similarly, in *Edwards*, the Court of Appeals held the trial judge did not err in refusing an instruction charging the jury that it must " 'be satisfied beyond a reasonable doubt of the accuracy of the identification of defendant as the person who committed the offense before you may convict him.' " *Edwards*, 23 Wash.App. at 896, 600 P.2d 566. Although the instruction was not so "impermissibly slanted" as the *Telfaire*-type instruction rejected in Jordan, the court held "it nonetheless calls into question the credibility of particular witnesses." *Edwards*, 23 Wash.App. at 896, 600 P.2d 566.

After Laureano, the Court of Appeals continued to reject the requirement for a Telfaire-type instruction on eyewitness identification. In *State v. Hall*, 40 Wash.App. 162, 697 P.2d 597 (1985), the court noted that although this court has not ruled on whether a cautionary instruction on eyewitness identification testimony is always inappropriate, such instructions have been considered comments on the credibility of the identification witness and, in any case, the "court's general instructions on the 'beyond a reasonable doubt' standard enabled the defendant to argue his theory of the case and to attack the credibility of eyewitnesses." *Hall*, 40 Wash.App. at 167, 697 P.2d 597; see also *State v. Watkins*, 53 Wash.App. 264, 275, 766 P.2d 484 (1989). Thus, both prior to and following *Laureano*, our cases have held that an instruction on eyewitness identification is not constitutionally required.

Allen argues our case law, i.e., Laureano and the cases that preceded and followed it, is outdated. He argues the scientific data regarding the unreliability of eyewitness identification, and of cross-racial eyewitness identification in particular, is now irrefutable. He submits that since *Telfaire*, research and studies exposing problems inherent in eyewitness identification testimony have gained wide acceptance. While the State notes that some researchers have questioned the methodology used in the empirical studies in this field, and notes that publication in respected, peer-reviewed journals is not a guarantee of the validity of the underlying work, the State does not provide contrary evidence or research nor seriously question the scientific data relied upon by Allen. Based on this data, Allen asks us to adopt a rule of general application, founded in notions of due process, that in cases involving cross-racial eyewitness identification it is reversible error to fail to instruct on cross-racial identification when requested. Allen argues the world has changed, and we must change along with it. We are not convinced, however, that the constitutionality of our case law on this issue has changed.

A problem with the studies Allen relies upon is that none of them support the conclusion that the giving of a cautionary cross-racial identification instruction solves the purported unreliability of cross-racial eyewitness identification, any more than would cross-examination, expert evidence, or arguments to the jury. As the Supreme Court has recognized, the United States Constitution "protects a defendant against a conviction based on evidence of questionable reliability ... by affording the defendant means to persuade the jury that the evidence should be discounted as unworthy of credit." *Perry v. New Hampshire*, --- U.S. ----, 132 S.Ct. 716, 723, 181 L.Ed.2d 694 (2012). In Perry, the Supreme Court addressed the issue of whether due process requires judicial inquiry into the reliability of a suggestive eyewitness identification that was not the result of police arrangement, and held it does not. As part of its analysis, the Court listed safeguards, built into our adversary system, that caution juries against placing undue weight on eyewitness testimony of questionable reliability, including the right to confront witnesses, the right to counsel, eyewitness jury instructions adopted by many federal and state courts, expert evidence, the government's burden to prove guilt beyond a reasonable doubt, and state rules of evidence. Many of these safeguards were at work in Allen's trial.

For example, a defendant has a right to effective assistance of counsel, who can expose the unreliability in eyewitness' testimony during cross-examination and focus the jury's attention on the fallibility of eyewitness identification during opening and closing arguments. Allen's counsel did just that. On cross-examination he questioned Kovacs regarding his mental state during the encounter, regarding the time of day the encounter took place (dusk), and regarding the discrepancy between Allen's actual height and weight, and the description Kovacs gave the 911 dispatcher. Allen's counsel also questioned Officer Bennett regarding the potential suggestiveness of showup identifications, the problems associated with cross-racial identifications, and the lack of other witnesses to the crime. VRP (Oct. 21, 2009) at 54–59. Then, in closing argument, Allen's counsel discussed how emotion and stress can affect the reliability of identifications, and discussed the risk of police influence on identifications. He further discussed the " dangers of cross-racial identification" and explained how cross-racial identification may have impacted this case. VRP (Oct. 21, 2009) at 94–98.

The requirement that the State prove a defendant's guilt beyond a reasonable doubt also protects against convictions based on dubious identification evidence. The jury in Allen's case was instructed on the State's burden of proof and on witness credibility generally. Taken together, these instructions charged the jury with deciding whether the State has proved beyond a reasonable doubt that Kovacs correctly identified Allen as the man with the gun. In conjunction with competent defense counsel, the instructions focused the jury's attention to the issue of identification and the reliability of Kovacs' testimony.

Allen notes that in *Perry*, the Supreme Court identified eyewitness instructions, adopted by many federal and state courts, as one safeguard of several that can help focus the jury's attention on the fallibility of eyewitness testimony. Yet the Supreme Court has never required such an instruction. Nor have any of the jurisdictions we have aligned with on this issue reversed a conviction on due process grounds for failure to so instruct. Adopting a rule of general application, as Allen requests, would take us far afield from our jurisprudence and require us to revisit *Laureano* and the cases following it. *Laureano* does not support a rule of general application, but neither does it support a rigid prohibition against the giving of a cautionary cross-racial identification instruction. Indeed, such a prohibition would be inconsistent with the abuse of discretion standard, which we applied in *Laureano*, and which the Court of Appeals has applied in the cases following *Laureano*.

Applying that standard, we find no abuse of discretion here. Providing a cautionary cross-racial identification instruction would not have added to the safeguards operating in Allen's case, a case involving an eyewitness identification based on general physique, apparel, and sunglasses, and not on facial features. During the 911 call, Kovacs described the man with the gun by approximate age, height, and weight. Beyond these general characteristics, Kovacs' description was limited to the man's apparel: "black hoodie," "jeans," "baseball cap," and "big sunglasses" with "gold on the frames." VRP (Oct. 23, 2009) at 3. At trial, Kovacs testified, regarding the showup identification, that

> [the police officer] asked me to identify a gentleman standing on the street ... with some officers and some other people, and point him out....

> ....

> He was wearing the exact same clothes that he had on earlier, he was wearing the baseball hat, the black hood[ie], and he had the glasses.... And I said, yeah, definitely, that is one hundred percent him.

VRP (Oct. 21, 2009) at 16. Kovacs did not make an in-court identification of Allen. In fact, Kovacs testified Allen looked different at trial because he was not wearing the same clothes. Thus, Kovacs did not base the identification on facial features, specific physical characteristics, or merely the fact that Allen is African American.

The central premise of cross-race bias, the impetus for giving a cross-racial identification instruction, is that people are better able to remember faces of their own race than those of a different race. Kovacs' identification of Allen was less than ideal, as it was based largely on Allen's apparel and sunglasses and not on his facial appearance or other characteristics personal to Allen. However, a specific cross-racial identification instruction would not have been helpful in a case like this where the witness/victim's identification was based on identifying factors unrelated to cross-race bias. Indeed, Allen's proposed instructions, which alerted jurors to studies showing "it is more difficult to identify members of a different race than members of one's own," without explaining the scientific foundation for cross-race bias, would have been misleading and counterproductive under these circumstances.

We decline to adopt a general rule requiring the giving of a cross-racial instruction in cases where cross-racial identification is at issue, and the trial court did not abuse its discretion by refusing to give a cautionary cross-racial jury instruction under the facts of this case. We affirm the Court of Appeals.

Expert Testimony on Cross-Racial Identification

Note

Whether it is necessary or useful for jurors to be informed of the dangers of cross-racial eyewitness identification by way of expert testimony has been hotly contested. Psychology and Law Professor Elizabeth F. Loftus has suggested; " The psychologist could describe the studies that have been conducted on people's ability to perceive and recall complex events, and report the results. Factors that may have affected the accuracy of the particular identification in the case at hand could be related (sic) to the jury. In this way the jurors would have enough information with which to evaluate the identification evidence fully and properly", Elizabeth F. Loftus, EYEWITNESS TESTIMONY (Harvard Univ. Press 1996), p. 191.

Despite the support for expert testimony on cross-racial identification supported by Dr. Loftus and others, there has been concern and opposition expressed by both scholars and courts asserting that the reliability of eyewitness testimony, in general, is within the ability of jurors to consider without the aid of experts. See, Bryan Scott Ryan, Alleviating Own-Race Bias In Cross-Racial Identifications, 8 WASH. U. JURISPRUDENCE REV. 115, 137 (2015)

The American Bar Association has made the following observations:

> Those who favor the admissibility of expert testimony argue that it is crucial to the deliberative process that jurors are educated on the potential errors in cross-racial identifications. Jurors are more apt to comfortably discuss racial differences without fear of discord in the jury room when they have received testimony from an expert considering the possible influence of racial differences as affecting the accuracy of the identification. Also, they argue that the possibility of error in cross-racial identifications is not within the ordinary knowledge of many jurors. (See, e.g., People v. Beckford, 532 N.Y.S.2d 462, 465 (S. Ct. Kings Cty. 1988).)

> In Brodes v. State, 551 S.E.2d 757, 759 (Ga. Ct. App. 2002), the Georgia Court of Appeals stated that expert testimony would have aided the jury in evaluating the reliability of the identification because the expert would have testified about factors affecting the accuracy of the identification. The court suggested that those factors were highly relevant in the case, which involved cross-racial identifications by victims at gunpoint. The court also stated that producing an expert was the only way to present the proffered empirical evidence to the jury. (Id. at 759; see also Beckford, 532 N.Y.S.2d at 465.)

> On the other hand, in State v. Coley, 32 S.W. 3d 831 (Tenn. 2000), the Supreme Court of Tennessee held that expert testimony concerning eyewitness identification is per se inadmissible because the reliability of eyewitness identification is within the common understanding of jurors

aided by skillful cross-examination and an appropriate jury instruction. (Also, the court held that Tennessee Rule of Evidence 702, requiring that expert testimony be admissible only if it "substantially" assists the trier of fact, requires "a greater showing of probative force than the federal rules of evidence or the rules of evidence from those states that have followed the federal rules, making the per se exclusion appropriate." (Id. at 838.))

Opponents of expert witness testimony argue that expert testimony is not needed on the cross-racial identification issue because it is not too complicated an issue and jurors are able to understand and apply the judges' instructions. Deborah Bartolomey, deputy attorney general in the Criminal Division of the New Jersey Attorney General's Office, argues that experts may be costly for defendants, confuse the jury rather than clarify the issues, and take up time. (See Deborah Bartolomey, Cross-Racial Identification of Testimony and What Not to Do About It, 7 PSYCHOL. PUB. POL'Y & L. 247, 252 (2001).) A principal drawback of the use of expert witnesses is the lack of their availability, especially for indigent defendants. Stephen J. Saltzburg, Report to House of Delegates, 104D A.B.A. SEC. CRIM. J. 1, 6 (2008)

The following cases, are referred to in the above American Bar Association Report.

BRODES V. STATE.
250 Ga.App. 323 (2002)

A jury found J. Bodre Brodes guilty of two counts of armed robbery based on the victims' eyewitness identifications of him as the robber. Brodes contends that the trial court erred by (1) refusing to allow his expert witness to testify about the reliability of eyewitness identifications, (2) denying his motions to suppress the results of pretrial photographic and physical lineups, and (3) giving an erroneous pattern jury charge on eyewitness identification. He also claims that the evidence was insufficient to support the verdict. Because we agree that Brodes's expert witness should have been allowed to testify, we reverse.

On October 14, 1996, at around 11:00 p.m., Randy Barton and Greg Wilson were standing near their cars in the parking lot of a fast food restaurant in Hapeville. A man approached Barton, pointed a gun at him, and said, "I'll take all your f—ing money." Barton gave the man his wallet. The man then walked over to Wilson, pointed the gun at him, and demanded his money as well. After Wilson handed the man some money from his pocket, the man walked away. Both victims testified that the parking lot was well lit and that they got a good look at the robber's face, which was not obscured in any way.

Shortly after the incident, Barton described the robber to the police as a black male, aged 18 to 20, 5'8" to 5'10" tall, with a slender build, a "five o'clock shadow," and curly black hair that was short on the bottom and longer on top. Both victims told the police that the robber wore a red Bulls jacket.

Lieutenant Melissa Hughes of the Hapeville Police Department, who investigated the case, testified that she focused on Brodes as a suspect. She compiled a photographic array of six black men, including Brodes. On October 16, she showed the photographs to the two victims separately. Wilson immediately identified Brodes as the robber. At trial, he testified that he was positive about the identification. Barton told the police that he thought he recognized the robber but was not certain, and he requested a physical lineup.

On October 17, Hughes assembled a physical lineup of six black men, including Brodes. Both victims, viewing the lineup separately, identified Brodes as the robber. Barton testified that he was "absolutely certain" about his identification. Both victims also identified Brodes in court as the robber.

1. Before trial, the State filed a motion in limine to exclude the testimony of Brodes's expert witness, Dr. Stephen Cole, who had been called to testify about problems inherent in eyewitness identifications. At a pretrial hearing, defense counsel summarized the expected subject matter of Cole's testimony. The judge then granted the State's motion, explaining: "I think this is something the jurors can decide. I don't think they need expert testimony to help them with it. And I think that's what Georgia law intends and as it exists now." Later, the judge added, "I don't think that the issue of identification is beyond the ken of the jurors." Defense counsel sought permission to make a proffer of Cole's testimony. The judge granted that request but stated that it would not change his mind.

During the proffer, Cole testified, among other things, that cross-racial identifications are empirically less reliable than intra-racial identifications, particularly when—as was the case here—a white person is identifying a black person. Cole also testified that studies show that victims at gunpoint are less likely to remember their assailant's face and that the level of confidence an eyewitness places in his identification bears little relation to its accuracy. The judge ruled that Cole was an expert but reiterated without elaboration that he would exclude his testimony.

In Johnson v. State, our Supreme Court held that admission of expert testimony regarding eyewitness identification is in the discretion of the trial court. Where eyewitness identification of the defendant is a key element of the State's case and there is no substantial corroboration of that identification by other evidence, trial courts may not exclude expert testimony without carefully weighing whether the evidence would assist the jury in assessing the reliability of eyewitness testimony and whether expert eyewitness testimony is the only effective way to reveal any weakness in an eyewitness identification.

Brodes argues that the trial court abused its discretion by failing to consider whether Cole's testimony would have assisted the jury and would have provided Brodes's only means of revealing weaknesses in the victims' eyewitness identifications. We agree.

The State admitted that its case against Brodes hinged on the victims' eyewitness identifications. There was no other evidence tying Brodes to the crime and no evidence corroborating the victims' identifications. Under these circumstances, Cole's testimony should have been admitted.

First, the record shows that the testimony would have aided the jury in evaluating the reliability of the victims' identifications of Brodes. Cole would have testified about several factors affecting the accuracy of eyewitness identification that were otherwise not likely to be fully understood by jurors. Those factors are highly relevant in this case, which involves cross-racial identifications by victims who were at gunpoint and who professed confidence in their identifications.[5] Second, the record shows no other effective means for Brodes to illustrate the potential weaknesses of the victims' identifications. Although defense counsel cross-examined the victims, the testimony of an expert witness was the only way to put before the jury the empirical evidence proffered by Cole.

Moreover, we cannot say that the exclusion of Cole's testimony was harmless error. The only evidence against Brodes was the victims' identifications of him, and Brodes's only defense was mistaken identity. Thus, the reliability of the victims' identifications was the pivotal issue.

Note

State v. Coley, 32 S.W. 3d 831 (Tenn. 2000), referred to in the ABA Report as holding that expert testimony on the challenges of cross-racial identification was *per se* inadmissible, was overturned in the following case.

STATE V. COPELAND.

226 S.W.3d 287 (Tenn. 2007)

GARY R. WADE, J.

The Defendant, Arthur T. Copeland, was convicted of one count of first degree murder and sentenced to death. The jury found a single aggravating circumstance, that the Defendant previously had been convicted of one or more felonies involving violence to the person, see Tenn.Code Ann. § 39-13-204(i)(2) (1997), and further found that the aggravating circumstance outweighed the mitigating circumstances beyond a reasonable doubt, see Tenn.Code Ann. § 39–13–204(g)(1) (1997). The Court of Criminal Appeals held that the trial court properly excluded expert testimony on eyewitness identification but committed plain error by failing to conduct a hearing pursuant to *Momon v. State*, 18 S.W.3d 152, 157 (Tenn.1999), and ordered a remand for a determination of whether the error was harmless. Further, the Court of Criminal Appeals set aside the sentence of death as disproportionate. We granted the State's application for permission to appeal in order to resolve the dispositive issues. We first hold that the trial court erred by prohibiting the Defendant from offering expert testimony regarding eyewitness testimony and overrule *State v. Coley*, 32 S.W.3d 831 (Tenn.2000). Because the exclusion of the testimony cannot be classified as harmless under these circumstances, the Defendant must be granted a new trial. Although the trial court failed to conduct a Momon hearing, consideration of that issue is not necessary because of the grant of a new trial. Finally, we conclude that the Court of Criminal Appeals erred by finding that the death sentence was disproportionate; thus the State may choose to seek the death penalty upon remand. Accordingly, the judgment of the Court of Criminal Appeals is affirmed in part, reversed in part, and the cause is remanded for a new trial.

On April 7, 1998, the victim, Andre Jackson, was shot to death in Maryville, Tennessee. The shooting was apparently in response to the rape of Lynn Porter ("Porter"), the girlfriend of Reginald Stacy Sudderth ("Sudderth"). After learning of the rape, Sudderth purportedly offered a $10,000 "bounty" for the death of the perpetrator and warned, "[S]omeone is going to die tonight." There was evidence that the Defendant expressed an interest in the reward money and accompanied Sudderth and others to Maryville in search of the victim, whom they believed to be responsible for the rape. According to one State witness, the Defendant entered the victim's residence and ordered him outside. Moments later, the victim reentered the house, collapsed from gunshot wounds, and died. In the course of a lengthy trial over an eight-day period with contested factual and witness credibility issues, the Defendant claimed that he was mistakenly identified and suggested that Chris Knighton ("Knighton") was the perpetrator of the crime.

I. Exclusion of Expert Testimony Regarding Eyewitness Identification

The Defendant contends that the trial court erred by prohibiting expert testimony on the issue of the reliability of eyewitness identification. The record establishes that the defense sought to call as a witness John Brigham, a university professor of psychology, to testify as to the reliability of eyewitness identification, particularly related to cross-racial identification, an issue in this case. The trial court, relying on the Court of Criminal Appeals' decision in *State v. Wooden*, 658 S.W.2d 553 (Tenn.Crim.App.1983), ruled that the evidence was inadmissible. In *Wooden*, a case decided twenty-four years ago, the Court of Criminal Appeals concluded that "[w]hether an eyewitness's testimony is reliable is a matter which the jury can determine from hearing the witness's testimony on direct and cross-examination and which does not require expert testimony." Id. at 557. After conducting a hearing outside the presence of the jury and permitting an offer of proof, the trial judge concluded that but for the ruling in *Wooden* he would have admitted the expert testimony, observing, "I have to ... follow [*Wooden*] whether I personally agree with it or not."

Some three months after the conclusion of the trial in this case, this Court issued its opinion in *State v. Coley*, 32 S.W.3d 831 (Tenn.2000), adopting the holding in Wooden. In Coley, a majority of this Court concluded that Tennessee Rule of Evidence 702 precluded expert testimony concerning the reliability of eyewitness testimony, observing that "general and unparticularized expert testimony concerning the reliability of eyewitness testimony, which is not specific to the witness whose testimony is in question, does not substantially assist the trier of fact." Id. at 838. The majority determined that "[e]yewitness testimony has no scientific or technical underpinnings which would be outside the common understanding of the jury; therefore, expert testimony is not necessary to help jurors 'understand' the eyewitness's testimony." Id. at 833–34. Our ruling in *Coley* placed Tennessee in the minority of jurisdictions that have considered the issue. Id. at 838.6

The *Coley* dissenters concluded that the general rule established in *McDaniel v. CSX Transp.*, Inc., 955 S.W.2d 257 (Tenn.1997), wherein the trial court is afforded discretion as to the qualifications and relevancy of the testimony of an expert witness, was a sufficient guide to trial courts in determining whether to admit expert testimony on the issue of eyewitness identification. *Coley*, 32 S.W.3d at 838–39 (Holder, J., dissenting). Justice Holder, joined by then Chief Justice Anderson, observed that the majority's decision "exclud[ed] from consideration under *McDaniel* one class of proffered scientific evidence" and "foreclose[d] judicial recognition of future scientific advances." Id. at 839 (Holder, J., dissenting). Citing the sheer volume of "scientific study, scholarly debate, and comment" on the subject of eyewitness identification, the dissent, especially critical of the classification of the reliability of eyewitness identification as falling within the "common understanding" of jurors, concluded that it was unlikely that so much scholarly and scientific work had been "engendered by what is simply a matter of common knowledge." Id. (Holder, J., dissenting).

There have been advances in the field of eyewitness identification. In the article Behavioral Science Evidence in the Age of Daubert: Reflections of a Skeptic, Boston College Law Professor Mark S. Brodin, a self-described skeptic on the topic of behavioral science evidence, made the following observation:

Ironically, the form of social science evidence which is most solidly based in "hard" empirical science has met with the most resistance in the courts. Expert testimony concerning the limitations and weaknesses of eyewitness identification is firmly rooted in experimental foundation, derived from decades of psychological research on human perception and memory as well as an impressive peer review literature.

Mark S. Brodin, Behavioral Science Evidence in the Age of Daubert: Reflections of a Skeptic, 73 U. Cin. L.Rev. 867, 889–90 (2005) (footnotes omitted). Another author has observed that while experts are often not permitted to testify regarding eyewitness testimony, police officers and other law enforcement officials are regularly permitted to testify "concerning the general way criminal schemes and enterprises operate and the usual meaning of criminal slang and code words." D. Michael Risinger, Navigating Expert Reliability: Are Criminal Standards of Certainty Being Left on the Dock?, 64 Alb. L.Rev. 99, 132 (2000). The author contrasts the "technical" knowledge of the law enforcement officials with the educational and scientific credentials of experts on eyewitness identification. Id. at 131–35.

It is the educational training of the experts and empirical science behind the reliability of eyewitness testimony that persuades us to depart from the *Coley* rule. Times have changed. Today, many scholarly articles detail the extensive amount of behavioral science research in this area. See generally Gary L. Wells et al., Eyewitness Evidence: Improving Its Probative Value, 7 Psychol. Sci. Pub. Int. 45, 47–49 (2006) (for a brief history of psychological research of eyewitness testimony). There are literally hundreds of articles in scholarly, legal, and scientific journals on the subject of eyewitness testimony.

Our decision in *Coley* is also contrary to the modern trend:

> [S]tudies of DNA exonerations ... have validated the research of social scientists, particularly in the areas of mistaken eyewitness identification.... Courts traditionally tended to exclude scientific evidence from expert witnesses in these disciplines, primarily on the basis that the testimony addressed matters within the common understanding of jurors, was confusing, or that it invaded the province of the jury to make credibility determinations. However, with the increased awareness of the role that mistaken identification ... play[s] in convicting the innocent, a new trend is developing regarding the admissibility of expert testimony.

Jacqueline McMurtrie, The Role of the Social Sciences in Preventing Wrongful Convictions, 42 Am.Crim. L.Rev. 1271, 1273 (2005) (footnotes omitted). McMurtrie observes that "[r]esearch over the past thirty years has shown that expert testimony on memory and eyewitness identification is the only legal safeguard that is effective in sensitizing jurors to eyewitness errors." Id. at 1276. Studies have shown that erroneous identification accounted for as much as eighty-five percent of the convictions of those individuals later exonerated by DNA testing. Id. at 1275 n. 17.

Scientifically tested studies, subject to peer review, have identified legitimate areas of concern. See id. at 1277 n. 29 (citing Brian L. Cutler et al., Juror Sensitivity to Eyewitness Identification Evidence, 14 Law & Hum. Behav. 185, 190 (1990) (concluding that jurors were insensitive to many factors that influence eyewitness memory and give disproportionate weight to the confidence of the witness); Timothy P. O'Toole et al., District of Columbia Public Defender Eyewitness Reliability Survey, Champion, Apr. 2005, 28, 28–32 (finding, in a survey of approximately 1,000 potential jurors, that they overestimate the reliability of cross-racial identification); Gary Wells et al., Eyewitness Identification Procedures: Recommendations For Lineups and Photospreads, 22 Law & Hum. Behav. 603, 619–20 (1998); Richard A. Wise & Martin A. Safer, A Survey of Judges' Knowledge and Beliefs About Eyewitness Testimony, 40 Ct. Rev. 6, 8–14 (2003) (finding that judges had limited understanding regarding eyewitness accuracy and confidence and with studies indicating that half or more of all wrongful felony conviction are due to eyewitness misidentification)). The Utah Supreme Court has made the following observations in this regard:

Although research has convincingly demonstrated the weaknesses inherent in eyewitness identification, jurors are, for the most part, unaware of these problems. People simply do not accurately understand the deleterious effects that certain variables can have on the accuracy of the memory processes of an honest eyewitness. See K. Deffenbacher & E. Loftus, Do Jurors Share a Common Understanding Concerning Eyewitness Behavior?, 6 Law and Human Behavior 15 (1982); J. Brigham, R. Bothwell, The Ability of Prospective Jurors to Estimate the Accuracy of Eyewitness Identification, 7 Law and Human Behavior 19 (1983). Moreover, the common knowledge that people do possess often runs contrary to documented research findings. See Loftus, supra, at 171–77.

State v. Long, 721 P.2d 483, 490 (Utah 1986).

Further, the research also indicates that neither cross-examination nor jury instructions on the issue are sufficient to educate the jury on the problems with eyewitness identification, contrary to the conclusion reached by the majority in Coley. See, e.g., id. ("[E]ven when presented with an eyewitness who was quite thoroughly discredited by counsel, a full 68% still voted to convict.") (citing Elizabeth Loftus, Reconstructing Memory: The Incredible Eyewitness, 15 Jurimetrics J. 188, 189–90 (1975)). "Considered as a whole, the studies of juror knowledge and decision making indicate that expert psychological testimony can serve as a safeguard against mistaken identification." Steven D. Penrod & Brian L. Cutler, Preventing Mistaken Identification in Eyewitness Identification Trials, Psychology & Law: The State of the Discipline 89, 114 (1999).

In our view, it is far more likely for the jury to accredit the eyewitness than the expert. If eyewitness identification is a cornerstone of the criminal justice system, the jury is its foundation. It is also our view that the test in *McDaniel* is sufficient to allow the trial court to properly evaluate the admissibility of expert testimony on the reliability of eyewitness identification. To the extent that *Coley* holds otherwise, it is overruled. The essential role of the judge, as the neutral arbiter in the trial, is to govern the admission of the evidence within the rules, permitting only that expert testimony which substantially assists the jury in its consideration of the issue. The McDaniel test provides the trial judge with the necessary guidelines to properly exercise his or her discretion.

Because we have chosen to overrule *Coley's* conclusion that no one, regardless of credentials or experience and no matter how questionable the evidence, can provide testimony on the issue of eyewitness identification, we must next determine whether the trial court's failure to permit Dr. Brigham to testify was error. If so, a second question is whether the error can be classified as harmless. See Tenn. R.Crim. P. 52(a); Tenn. R.App. P. 36(b).

As indicated, the general rule is that "questions regarding the admissibility, qualifications, relevancy and competency of expert testimony are left to the discretion of the trial court." *McDaniel*, 955 S.W.2d at 263 (citing *State v. Ballard*, 855 S.W.2d 557, 562 (Tenn.1993)). A decision by the trial judge to admit or exclude expert testimony "may only be overturned if the discretion is arbitrarily exercised or abused." Id. at 263–64. Further, the admission of expert proof is governed by Tennessee Rules of Evidence 702 and 703. *Brown v. Crown Equip. Corp.*, 181 S.W.3d 268, 273 (Tenn.2005). Rule 702 provides as follows:

> If scientific, technical, or other specialized knowledge will substantially assist the trier of fact
> to understand the evidence or to determine a fact in issue, a witness qualified as an expert by
> knowledge, skill, experience, training, or education may testify in the form of an opinion or
> otherwise.

Tenn. R. Evid. 702 (emphasis added). Rule 703 provides:

> The facts or data in the particular case upon which an expert bases an opinion or inference
> may be those perceived by or made known to the expert at or before the hearing. If of a type
> reasonably relied upon by experts in the particular field in forming opinions or inferences
> upon the subject, the facts or data need not be admissible in evidence. The court shall disallow
> testimony in the form of an opinion or inference if the underlying facts or data indicate lack of
> trustworthiness.

Tenn. R. Evid. 703. Further, expert testimony must qualify as relevant: " 'Relevant evidence' means evidence having any tendency to make the existence of any fact that is of consequence to the determination of the action more probable or less probable than it would be without the evidence." Tenn. R. Evid. 401.

In *McDaniel*, this Court adopted a non-exclusive list of factors to consider when determining the reliability of expert testimony:

> whether scientific evidence has been tested and the methodology with which it has been tested;
> (2) whether the evidence has been subjected to peer review or publication; (3) whether a poten-
> tial rate of error is known; (4) whether, as formerly required by Frye,7 the evidence is generally

accepted in the scientific community; and (5) whether the expert's research in the field has been conducted independent of litigation.

McDaniel, 955 S.W.2d at 265. The trial court "must assure itself that the opinions are based on relevant scientific methods, processes, and data, and not upon an expert's mere speculation." Id. "The objective of the trial court's gatekeeping function is to ensure that 'an expert, whether basing testimony upon professional studies or personal experience, employs in the courtroom the same level of intellectual rigor that characterizes the practice of an expert in the relevant field.' " Brown, 181 S.W.3d at 275 (quoting *Kumho Tire Co. v. Carmichael*, 526 U.S. 137, 152, 119 S.Ct. 1167, 143 L.Ed.2d 238 (1999) (holding that a trial court may consider the *Daubert v. Merrell Dow Pharmaceuticals, Inc.*, 509 U.S. 579, 113 S.Ct. 2786, 125 L.Ed.2d 469 (1993), factors in assessing the reliability of non-scientific expert testimony in accordance with the Federal Rules of Evidence)). Rigid application of the *McDaniel* factors is not required. Id. at 277. This Court has observed that

> [t]he reasonableness of the *McDaniel* factors in assessing reliability depends upon the nature of the issue, the witness's particular expertise, and the subject of the expert's testimony. The *McDaniel* factors may apply, subject to the trial court's discretion, when they are reasonable measures of the reliability of the expert testimony.

Id. (citations omitted).

Because the trial judge in this case excluded Dr. Brigham's testimony on the basis of the decision in *Wooden,* there was no formal evaluation of the testimony under the Rules of Evidence. The trial judge did indicate, however, his preference to allow the testimony in the absence of binding precedent to the contrary.

Dr. Brigham, a psychology professor with more than thirty-five years' experience in the study of the accuracy of eyewitness identification, testified that since undertaking research on the subject in 1975, he had published forty-five studies and had read "many hundreds" more. He described his discipline as "mainstream" and "widely accepted" within the profession. While acknowledging that common sense suggests that the certainty of the identification is a good indicator of its reliability, he testified that "research has shown that there is little or no relationship between [the level of the eyewitness's] certainty and [its] accuracy." Dr. Brigham explained how extraneous factors such as "stress and arousal, presence of a weapon, race, age, opportunity to observe" can affect the accuracy of a memory.

Dr. Brigham's proffered testimony was directed primarily at the eyewitness identification by Delapp. He expressed particular concern about cross-racial identification in general and hers of the Defendant in particular. Dr. Brigham explained how in his opinion the subsequent events may have reinforced the correctness of Delapp's otherwise questionable identification. For example, after her identification of the Defendant in the photographic array, Detective Manuel commented that the person she had identified was the primary suspect. Shortly thereafter, she saw a photograph of the Defendant in the newspaper linking him to the crime.

In our view, Dr. Brigham's testimony satisfies the requirements of the *McDaniel* test in that it is reliable and would have been of substantial assistance to the jury. The proffered testimony was based upon solid empirical data gathered in a scientific setting. The information was subjected to a thorough peer review process. His opinions were formulated from extensive research and would have given the jury a valuable context within which to assess the eyewitness identification. Moreover, the trial judge, who saw and heard the witnesses firsthand, expressed a desire to allow the testimony as particularly helpful under the circumstances of this case.

It is also our view that the error cannot be classified as harmless. See Tenn. R.App. P. 36(b) ("A final judgment ... shall not be set aside unless, considering the whole record, error involving a substantial right more probably than not affected the judgment...."); Tenn. R.Crim. P. 52(a) ("No judgment shall be reversed on appeal except for errors that affirmatively appear to have affected the result of the trial on the merits."). "[T]he line between harmless and prejudicial error is in direct proportion to the degree ... by which proof exceeds the standard required to convict...." *Delk v. State*, 590 S.W.2d 435, 442 (Tenn.1979). In this case, the evidence of the Defendant's guilt was largely circumstantial. While the testimony of James, whose credibility was at issue, placed the Defendant in the car with Sudderth and others just prior to the shooting, only Delapp, a white woman, identified the Defendant, a black male, as the individual who entered her home and forced the victim outside. Delapp admitted, however, that she initially believed that Knighton, whom she had seen only hours earlier, had entered her home. She initially stated that her interior lights were off. Later, she told police that she had four, twenty-five-watt bulbs turned on as the perpetrator entered the residence. Some witnesses testified that the Defendant and Knighton bore a resemblance to each other. Delapp testified that the perpetrator's hair "stuck out" in twisted "horns" while Dean, who saw the Defendant later, and other witnesses, including Detective Wilburn, indicated a tight braid or plaited style. Delapp described the Defendant as being dressed in clothing different from that described by Kivett. There was testimony that Knighton and the Defendant had their hair styled similarly at the time of the shooting. Detective Manuel confirmed that Knighton was not included in the photographic array shown to Delapp. Afterward, the officer reinforced the identification by informing Delapp that she had identified the individual that police suspected of the crime.

As stated, Delapp's testimony was the only direct link to the Defendant's participation in the murder. She expressed certainty about her identification despite vigorous cross-examination. She did not, however, see the Defendant fire any shots. Moreover, there was evidence that Sudderth, who was said to have been involved in the shots fired at the Defendant two or three hours later, was present at the time of the shooting. Other proof indicated that Brown, also involved in the subsequent shooting, may have been there. All had a motive to do harm to the victim. Neither Kellogg nor James made a statement to police until well after the shooting.

Rainer testified that Knighton possessed a gun and had left her residence during the hours near the shooting for a purpose unknown to her. No weapon was found in the possession of the Defendant. The gun used to kill the victim was never found.

Dr. Brigham's testimony was designed to assist the jury in its evaluation of Delapp's testimony in terms of what is scientifically known about eyewitness identification, particularly that of a cross-racial nature. Under our rule, that assistance had to be "substantial" on a fact at issue in order to qualify for admission. The facts, especially on the question of identification, were contested at trial. There were conflicts in the testimony. There were significant challenges to the credibility of practically every State witness other than the law enforcement officers. Some witnesses had prior felony convictions and were evasive, perhaps even untruthful, as to collateral matters. Under these circumstances, we cannot say that the erroneous exclusion of Dr. Brigham's testimony was harmless. Accordingly, we must reverse the conviction and remand the cause for a new trial.

Note

For contrary views see *State v. McClendon*, 730 A. 2d 1107, 1114 (Conn. 1999) and *United States v. Larkin*, 978 F. 2d 964, 971 (7th Cir. 1992) (" [E]xpert testimony regarding the potential hazards of eyewitness identification – regardless of its reliability – will not aid the jury because it addresses an issue of which the jury already generally is aware, and it will not contribute to their understanding..").

Given the significance and the challenges of possible cross-racial misidentification, is it ever ineffective assistance of counsel for the defense not to consult an expert on cross-racial misidentification? See, *Wallace v. State*, 701 S.E. 2d 554 (Ga. 2010) (concluding that the defendant failed to show that counsel fell below the standard of a reasonably competent attorney by making a strategic decision not to consult and expert.)

Given the unsettled nature as to the admissibility of cross-racial identification experts, should an indigent defendant nonetheless be entitled to an appointed expert? Yes, concludes at least one author:

> Federal courts should establish a per se rule granting an expert witness on the unreliable nature
> of cross-racial identification in cases where the defendant is represented by a federal defender
> or indigent counsel and where the cross-racial identification is the primary piece of evidence
> against the defendant.

> Laura Connelly, *Cross-Racial Identifications: Solutions to the "They All Look Alike" Effect*, 21 MICH.
> J. RACE & L. 125, 143-144 (2015)

Other than a psychologist, who might qualify as an expert on the dangers of cross-racial identification? For an interesting alternative consider State v. Ayers, 1981 WL 3119 (10th Dist. Ct. of Appeals, Franklin County, Ohio, 1981, unreported), wherein the defendant unsuccessfully sought to qualify a forensic anthropologist on the difficulty of Caucasians distinguishing between African Americans.

Chapter Ten: Prosecutorial Misconduct and the Appealing to Racial Prejudice

Note

The importance of the role of the prosecutor in ensuring a fair trial cannot be overstated. The prosecutor has great discretion as to the initiation of investigations, the nature and extent of charges, plea negotiations and sentencing recommendations. See, Peter J. Henning, *Prosecutorial Misconduct and Constitutional Remedies*, 77 WASH. LAW. Q. 713,714 (1999)

The American Bar Association, in it adopted Standards for the Prosecution Function, concurs and state further:

> The primary duty of the prosecutor is to seek justice within the bounds of the law, not merely to convict. The prosecutor serves the public interest and should act with integrity and balanced judgment to increase public safety both by pursuing appropriate criminal charges of appropriate severity, and by exercising discretion to not pursue criminal charges in appropriate circumstances. The prosecutor should seek to protect the innocent and convict the guilty, consider the interests of victims and witnesses, and respect the constitutional and legal rights of all persons, including suspects and defendants. American Bar Association, CRIMINAL JUSTICE STANDARDS FOR THE PROSECUTION FUNCTION Standard 3-1.2 (b) Functions and Duties of the Prosecutor

The role of the prosecutor of prosecutor in combatting racism in the criminal trial is also addressed specifically in the ABA "Function" standards:

Standard 3-1.6 Improper Bias Prohibited

(a) The prosecutor should not manifest or exercise, by words or conduct, bias or prejudice based upon race, sex, religion, national origin, disability, age, sexual orientation, gender identity, or socioeconomic status. A prosecutor should not use other improper considerations, such as partisan or political or personal considerations, in exercising prosecutorial discretion. A prosecutor should strive to eliminate implicit biases, and act to mitigate any improper bias or prejudice when credibly informed that it exists within the scope of the prosecutor's authority.

Yet there has been concern expressed about the influence that the prosecutor has on the jury, particularly during opening and closing arguments, where there appears to be appeals to racial bias as the filter through which the jury should view the evidence. A classic example of such concern can be found in 1917 opinion in *Moulton v. State*, 74 So. 454 (Ala. 1917) where the prosecutor in his opening statement to the all-white jury said "Unless you hang this negro, our white people living out in the country won't be safe; to let such crimes go unpunished will cause riots in our land." (The Supreme Court of Alabama reversed and remanded the case for new trial. It is interesting to note that the Alabama Supreme Court was not unanimous in its opinion. A dissenting justice stated; "There was not in the remark to which the exception was reserved the slightest appeal to race prejudice.").

The following material looks at the question of appeal to racial prejudice in the opening , cross-examination, and closing statements. There is little debate that such conduct is prosecutorial misconduct, inconsistent with both prosecutorial standards and fair trial. The ultimate question is one of when such conduct is reversible error.

Opening Statements

PEOPLE V. ROBINSON
2019 Wl 6693197 (Colo. 2019)

A.M. and her roommate hosted a gathering for some co-workers in their apartment. A.M. drank heavily and eventually passed out on a couch. E.G., one of the guests at the party, fell ill after the alcohol that she drank reacted with a new medication that she was taking, and she fell asleep at the other end of the same couch on which A.M. had passed out.

Robinson arrived at the apartment later in the evening, when things were winding down. According to E.G., she woke to Robinson standing over her with his exposed penis in her face. She told him to get away from her, and he did. E.G. fell back asleep but subsequently woke to some motion on the couch. She then saw Robinson touching a still-unconscious A.M.'s breasts and leg. E.G. yelled at Robinson to leave A.M. alone and to get off of her, and he left the room. E.G. fell asleep again, but she claims to have been awakened a third time, this time by a "sexual motion, like a grinding." She allegedly saw Robinson vaginally penetrating the still-incapacitated A.M. E.G. screamed at Robinson, and after he left the apartment, she called 911 to report the sexual assault. Medical personnel arrived and attended to A.M., whom they found unconscious and with her leggings and underwear around her ankles. Ultimately, the medical personnel were able to rouse and treat her.

Robinson was arrested, and he admitted to the police that his initial intentions were to try to get A.M. to have sex with him. He, however, denied any sexual contact with her, claiming that she had said "no" several times and that he understood that "when you hear too many nos, that means no." Robinson also denied any sexual contact with E.G.

The People subsequently charged Robinson with multiple counts arising from the foregoing incidents. As to A.M., Robinson was charged with two counts of sexual assault (victim helpless), two counts of sexual assault (victim incapable), and two counts of unlawful sexual contact (victim helpless). People v. Robinson, 2017 COA 128M, ¶ 8, --- P.3d ----. As to E.G., Robinson was charged with one count of attempted sexual assault (victim incapable), one count of attempted sexual assault (victim helpless), and one count of attempted unlawful sexual contact (victim helpless). Id.

The case proceeded to trial, and during voir dire, defense counsel, who was apparently sensitive to the underlying racial issues in this case (Robinson is African American, and A.M. is white), inquired of the prospective jurors whether there was anything about the difference in the parties' races that made anyone uncomfortable. No one indicated any concern. Counsel then asked several of the prospective jurors whether they would be comfortable bringing any improper discussion of race in the jury room to the attention of the court. These jurors said that they would, and one of them noted that he understood that he could not allow racial considerations to influence him improperly.

Thereafter, during the prosecutor's opening statement, she described certain testimony that the jury purportedly would hear, stating:

> You're going to hear that [A.M.] is white. And she's actually pretty pasty. She's pasty white. And you obviously have seen Mr. Robinson is dark. He is an African American of dark complexion. [E.G.] looks over and she can see a dark penis going into a white body. That's how graphic she could see [sic].

Defense counsel did not object to these comments, and the trial court did not intervene sua sponte.

Later that day, E.G. took the stand and testified regarding her above-described allegations, including that when the medical personnel arrived, they found A.M. unconscious and with her leggings and underwear around her ankles (the prosecutor also introduced into evidence a photograph showing the condition in which the medical personnel had found A.M.). As pertinent here, after E.G. noted that A.M. was naked from the waist down, the prosecutor asked E.G. how she could see that in the dark room. E.G. responded, "[A.M.]—I hate to say it, but she's really, really white. So I could see that she was naked from the waist down." The prosecutor then asked

E.G. what was going on at that point, and E.G. responded, "He was inside of her. He was having sex with her." Notwithstanding the fact that the prosecutor had thus presented evidence of penetration without any reference to Robinson's race, the prosecutor proceeded to ask E.G. about Robinson's race and complexion. In response, E.G. described Robinson's complexion as "dark" and noted that he, too, was naked from the waist down and that she could see his butt clearly. The prosecutor then asked whether Robinson was "dark complected [sic]" at that location of his body as well, and E.G. answered, "Yes." In contrast to what the prosecutor suggested during her opening statement, however, E.G. did not testify to seeing "a dark penis going into a white body."

The following day, the sexual assault nurse examiner who had examined A.M. after the alleged assault testified that she found no injuries to A.M.'s genitalia, although she stated that this did not mean that A.M. was not sexually assaulted. In addition, a DNA analyst who had examined samples taken from A.M., Robinson, and the scene of the alleged assault testified that the test that she performed on the couch cushion did not detect any seminal fluid and that the amount of male DNA found on A.M.'s external genitalia was too small to allow her to draw any conclusions.

The jury ultimately acquitted Robinson of all of the charges related to E.G. and of all of the sexual assault counts against A.M., which included all of the counts that required proof of penetration. The jury convicted Robinson, however, of two counts of the lesser included offense of attempted sexual assault and two counts of unlawful sexual contact as to A.M. The trial court sentenced Robinson under the Sex Offender Lifetime Supervision Act to an indeterminate term of four years to life in the Department of Corrections, followed by ten years to life on parole.

Analysis

We begin by setting forth the appropriate analytical framework for a prosecutorial misconduct claim and the applicable standard of review. Applying this analytical framework, we consider whether the prosecutor's race-based comments were improper, and we conclude that they were because any probative value that they might have had was substantially outweighed by the danger of unfair prejudice to Robinson. Finally, we assess whether this error, which was unpreserved, was plain, and we conclude, on the facts before us, that even if the error could be deemed obvious (a matter that we need not decide), the error did not substantially undermine the fundamental fairness of the trial so as to cast serious doubt on the reliability of Robinson's judgment of conviction.

A. Analytical Framework and Standard of Review

We engage in a two-step analysis to review claims of prosecutorial misconduct. *Wend v. People*, 235 P.3d 1089, 1096 (Colo. 2010). First, we must determine whether the prosecutor's conduct was improper "based on the totality of the circumstances." Id. If we conclude that the conduct was improper, then we must decide whether such actions warrant reversal according to the proper standard of review. Id. Each step is analytically independent of the other. Id. Thus, we may conclude that a prosecutor's conduct was improper but nonetheless uphold the trial court's judgment because, for example, the error was harmless. Id.

When, as here, a defendant did not object at trial to the asserted misconduct, the plain error standard of review applies. *People v. Miller*, 113 P.3d 743, 745 (Colo. 2005). Plain error addresses error that was obvious and substantial and that so undermined the fundamental fairness of the trial itself as to cast serious doubt on the reliability of the judgment of conviction. Id. at 750. In the context of plain error review of prosecutorial misconduct, we will only reverse when the misconduct was "flagrantly, glaringly, or tremendously improper." *Domingo-Gomez v. People*, 125 P.3d 1043, 1053 (Colo. 2005) (quoting *People v. Avila*, 944 P.2d 673, 676 (Colo. App. 1997)); cf. *People v. Constant*, 645 P.2d 843, 847 (Colo. 1982) (noting that prosecutorial misconduct in closing argument rarely is so egregious as to constitute plain error).

B. The Race-Based Statements Were Improper

A prosecutor's interest in a criminal prosecution is not in winning a case, but in ensuring that justice is done. *Berger v. United States*, 295 U.S. 78, 88, 55 S.Ct. 629, 79 L.Ed. 1314 (1935). Accordingly, a prosecutor must refrain from using improper methods calculated to produce a wrongful conviction. *Harris v. People*, 888 P.2d 259, 263 (Colo. 1995). In particular, a prosecutor may not use arguments "calculated to inflame the passions or prejudice of the jury" or arguments that tend to influence jurors to reach a verdict based on preexisting biases rather than on the facts in evidence and the reasonable inferences to be drawn from those facts. *People v. Dunlap*, 975 P.2d 723, 758 (Colo. 1999).

Although all appeals to improper biases pose challenges to the trial process, the Supreme Court has observed that an appeal to racial bias should be treated with "added precaution" because "racial bias implicates unique historical, constitutional, and institutional concerns." *Peña-Rodriguez v. Colorado*, --- U.S. ----, 137 S. Ct. 855, 868–69, 197 L.Ed.2d 107 (2017).

Here, in her opening statement, the prosecutor noted the victim's "pasty white" skin tone, and she emphasized twice how Robinson is an African American of "dark" complexion. The prosecutor then stated that the jury would hear evidence that E.G. looked over and saw "a dark penis going into a white body," and she added, "That's how graphic she could see." Although the prosecutor's objective might have been to highlight a percipient witness's ability to see what the witness claimed to see, the prosecutor never directly explained the possible relevance of these race-based statements to the jury, nor did E.G. ultimately testify to the "graphic" image that the prosecutor painted for the jury.

Although the record here is insufficient to allow us to determine either what prompted the prosecutor to make these statements (e.g., the record does not reveal whether E.G. had made such statements prior to trial), or what the prosecutor hoped to achieve by them, it is not difficult to discern that when a prosecutor injects racial considerations into a trial, the risk of unfair prejudice rises dramatically. Indeed, the fact that racial considerations were introduced here, in the context of alleged sex crimes, made the risk of prejudice particularly acute, given the history of racial prejudice in this country. See *Miller v. North Carolina*, 583 F.2d 701, 707 (4th Cir. 1978) ("Concern about fairness should be especially acute where a prosecutor's argument appeals to race prejudice in the context of a sexual crime, for few forms of prejudice are so virulent."). Although in limited circumstances, the race of a defendant, victim, or witness may be relevant, when a race-based argument "shifts its emphasis from evidence to emotion," the statement is improper. *United States v. Doe*, 903 F.2d 16, 25 (D.C. Cir. 1990). In our view, even if the prosecutor's statements here had some evidentiary basis (and the record is insufficient to allow us to draw a conclusion in that regard), any probative value of these statements was substantially outweighed by the risks of unfair prejudice and the perception of an appeal to racial prejudice and stereotypes.

For several reasons, we are not persuaded otherwise by the People's assertion that the prosecutor's comments were proper because evidence of penetration was relevant and material to the prosecution's case in chief and that the prosecutor's statements merely explained how E.G. was able to observe the penetration in a darkened room.

First, at no time did the prosecutor directly explain that the contrast in skin tones between Robinson and A.M. was relevant to the issue of penetration, to how E.G. was able to see the penetration, or to any other evidentiary consideration. Nor did E.G.'s testimony suggest that it was. Indeed, E.G. said nothing in her testimony about Robinson's race or the darkness of his skin until the prosecutor inquired directly about those attributes (and the prosecutor did not ask about Robinson's race until after E.G. had testified that she saw Robinson inside of A.M., thereby making racial considerations irrelevant to the issue of penetration at that point).

Second, even if the prosecutor's race-based comments were premised on inferences drawn from E.G.'s anticipated testimony, the probative value of those comments was speculative at best and was substantially outweighed by the danger of unfair prejudice to Robinson. [footnote omitted]

For these reasons, we conclude that the prosecutor's race-based statements were unnecessary and therefore were improper.

C. The Error Was Not Plain

Having concluded that the prosecutor's race-based statements were erroneous, we next must decide whether the error was plain, which, as the division below observed, poses a more difficult question. Determining whether the error here was plain requires us to decide whether the error was obvious and substantial and whether it so undermined the fundamental fairness of Robinson's trial so as to cast serious doubt on the reliability of his judgment of conviction. *People v. Miller*, 113 P.3d at 750. We address these issues in turn.

The question of whether the impropriety of the prosecutor's conduct was obvious presents a close question. On the one hand, an error is obvious when, among other things, the challenged action contravenes a clear statutory command, a well-settled legal principle, or Colorado case law. *Scott v. People*, 2017 CO 16, ¶ 16, 390 P.3d 832, 835. Here, the prosecutor's repeated references to race arguably violated a settled legal principle because courts have routinely found error when a prosecutor has referred to the defendant's race when race was not a legitimate area of inquiry and when the prosecutor repeatedly emphasized the race of those involved. See, e.g., *State v. Rogan*, 984 P.2d 1231, 1240 (Haw. 1999) ("In this case, the deputy prosecutor's reference to Rogan as a 'black, military guy' was clearly inflammatory inasmuch as it raised the issue of and cast attention to Rogan's race. Because there was no dispute as to the identity of the perpetrator in this case, Rogan's race was not a legitimate area of inquiry inasmuch as race was irrelevant to the determination of whether Rogan committed the acts charged."); *Carter v. State*, 241 P.3d 476, 480 (Wyo. 2010) (noting that the prosecutor's repeated use of the terms "white guy" and "black guy" met the first prong of the plain error analysis).

On the other hand, "during opening statement, a prosecutor may refer to evidence that subsequently will be adduced at trial and draw inferences from that evidence." *People v. Estes*, 2012 COA 41, ¶ 23, 296 P.3d 189, 194. Here, the prosecutor's race-based comments were made in the context of suggesting to the jury what E.G. was apparently expected to say in her testimony. This testimony was at least possibly relevant to two evidentiary points, namely, (1) whether Robinson's alleged assault on A.M. included penetration and (2) how E.G. was able to see such penetration in a darkened room. In these circumstances, we can discern a reasonable argument that the impropriety of the prosecutor's comments may not have been so obvious as to require the trial court to intervene sua sponte. Indeed, such an argument has particular force here, where the comments were made in opening statement and defense counsel did not object, notwithstanding the fact that during voir dire, she had made clear that she was sensitive to the issues of race presented in this case. See *People v. Rodriguez*, 794 P.2d 965, 972 (Colo. 1990) (noting that the lack of a defense objection to asserted prosecutorial misconduct might indicate defense counsel's belief that the live argument, despite its appearance in a cold record, was not overly damaging).

We need not decide, however, whether the error at issue was obvious because even assuming, for the sake of argument, that it was, on the facts of this case, we cannot say that the error so undermined the fundamental fairness of Robinson's trial so as to cast serious doubt on the reliability of his judgment of conviction. We reach this conclusion for several reasons.

First, the trial judge instructed the jurors that they were not to allow bias or prejudice of any kind to influence their decisions in this case, and absent evidence to the contrary, we presume that the jury followed this instruction. *Bondsteel v. People*, 2019 CO 26, ¶ 62, 439 P.3d 847, 856.

Second, we note that the jury acquitted Robinson of every charge to which the improper statements were directed (i.e., every charge requiring proof of penetration). This indicates that the jury rejected the pertinent portions of E.G.'s testimony (and the prosecutor's assertions), and it tends to show that the jurors heeded the court's instruction not to allow bias or prejudice to influence their decisions. In addition, the fact that the jury acquitted Robinson of every charge to which the improper statements were directed tends to show that the jury could fairly and properly weigh and evaluate the evidence, notwithstanding the prosecutor's race-based comments. See *People v. Braley*, 879 P.2d 410, 414–15 (Colo. App. 1993) (noting that the fact that the jury acquitted the defendant of the charges for which allegedly improper evidence was offered indicates that the jury could fairly and properly weigh that evidence).

Accordingly, we conclude that the prosecutor's unnecessary and therefore improper race-based comments did not rise to the level of plain error.

Note

The type of appeal to racial fear and sex at the heart of *Robinson*, also arises in the context of closing argument in *State v. Rogan*, 984 P. 2d 1231 (Haw. 1999) with a different result from the court. Rogan, who was African American, was accused of sexual assault regarding a 12-year old White female. The defendant denied the accusation, and during rebuttal closing argument the Prosecutor stated; "complainant's parent's wanted a conviction, because "every mother's nightmare" is to "[l]eave your daughter for an hour and a half, and you walk back in, and here's some black, military guy on top of your daughter,". The Supreme Court of Hawaii, first noting that "Prosecution arguments which are contrived to stimulate racial prejudice represent a brazen attempt to subvert a criminal defendant's right to trial by an impartial jury, as guaranteed by both Federal and State Constitutions" went on to conclude that "References to race that do not have an objectively legitimate purpose constitute a particularly egregious form of prosecutorial misconduct", such misconduct required a mistrial and was not harmless error.

UNITED STATES V. GREY

422 F.2d 1043 (6th Cir. 1970)

These are direct appeals after jury trial in the United States District Court for the Northern District of Ohio, Western Division. Appellant Williams was charged with armed robbery of the Spicer Federal Credit Union of Toledo on November 21, 1968, in violation of 18 U.S.C. § 2113(d) (1964). He was found guilty and sentenced to twenty years.

Appellant Grey was charged with aiding and abetting in the same bank robbery, in violation of 18 U.S.C. §§ 2 and 2113(d) (1964). He was found guilty and sentenced to ten years.

....

A character witness for Grey was asked by the United States Attorney *1045 whether he knew that Grey, a Negro, and a married man, was 'running around with a white go-go dancer.' This question was objected to and the District Judge overruled the objection and subsequently denied a motion for mistrial based on this issue.

....

As to Grey's appeal, the evidence is much less adequate to support the jury finding of guilty. There was evidence, of course, that Grey had been with Williams before and after the robbery, and as we have noted, Grey had a $500 cash deposit the day after the robbery as to which the explanation appears doubtful. But, of themselves, these indicia of possible guilt would not constitute proof beyond reasonable doubt.

Further, there appears to be no direct support in this record for any identification of Grey as being at or near the Spicer Credit Union at the time of the robbery. Grey's conviction if sustained, would have to rest in large measure on Grey's admission that he had been in a maroon Rambler near the Credit Union on the morning of the day in question.

Under these circumstances, the claim of deliberate injection of race prejudice in the United States Attorney's cross-examination of one of Grey's character witnesses takes on greater significance. We find no nonprejudicial explanation for the 'white go-go dancer' question asked by the United States Attorney.

At best, the entire question was a magnificent irrelevance in a prosecution for bank robbery. No defense witness (character or otherwise) had put appellant's marital fidelity at issue. At worst, the gratuitous reference to the race of the go-go dancer may be read as a deliberate attempt to employ racial prejudice to strengthen the hand of the United States government. The United States needs and desires no such aid.

In *Berger v. United States*, 295 U.S. 78, 55 S.Ct. 629, 79 L.Ed. 1314 (1935), the Supreme Court said:

'The United States Attorney is the representative not of an ordinary party *1046 to a controversy, but of a sovereignty whose obligation to govern impartially is as compelling as its obligation to govern at all; and whose interest, therefore, in a criminal prosecution is not that it shall win a case, but that justice shall be done. As such, he is in a peculiar and very definite sense the servant of the law, the twofold aim of which is that guilt shall not escape or innocence suffer. He may prosecute with earnestness and vigor- indeed, he should do so. But, while he may strike hard blows, he is not at liberty to strike foul ones. It is as much his duty to refrain from improper methods calculated to produce a wrongful conviction as it is to use every legitimate means to bring about a just one.' *Berger v. United States, supra* at 88, 55 S.Ct. at 633.

Appeals to racial prejudice are foul blows and the courts of this country reject them. Where, as here, the facts are such as to indicate that such prejudicial tactics may have had a substantial influence upon the result of a trial, reversal for new trial is ordered. *Ross v. United States*, 180 F.2d 160 (6th Cir. 1950), cert. denied, 344 U.S. 832, 73 S.Ct. 40, 97 L.Ed. 648 (1952); *Fontanello v. United States*, 19 F.2d 921 (9th Cir. 1927); *People v. Hill*, 258 Mich. 79, 241 N.W. 873 (1932); *People v. Hoover*, 243 Mich. 534, 220 N.W. 702 (1928); *Manning v. State*, 195 Tenn. 94, 257 S.W.2d 6, 45 A.L.R.2d 299 (1953); *Roland v. State*, 137 Tenn. 663, 194 S.W. 1097 (1917). See also *Viereck v. United States*, 318 U.S. 236, 63 S.Ct. 561, 87 L.Ed. 734 (1943); *Berger v. United States*, 295 U.S. 78, 55 S.Ct. 629, 79 L.Ed. 1314 (1935).

The judgment in appellant Grey's appeal is vacated and the case is remanded to the District Court for a new trial.

Note

State v. Guthrie, 461 S.E.2d 163 (W.Va. 1995), presents an interesting factual twist, where both the defendant and the deceased victim were White.

STATE V. GUTHRIE

194 W.Va. 657 (1995)

It is undisputed that on the evening of February 12, 1993, the defendant removed a knife from his pocket and stabbed his co-worker, Steven Todd Farley, in the neck and killed him. The two men worked together as dishwashers at Danny's Rib House in Nitro and got along well together before this incident. On the night of the killing, the victim, his brother, Tracy Farley, and James Gibson were joking around while working in the kitchen of the restaurant. The victim was poking fun at the defendant who appeared to be in a bad mood. He told the defendant to "lighten up" and snapped him with a dishtowel several times. Apparently, the victim had no idea he was upsetting the defendant very much. The dishtowel flipped the defendant on the nose and he became enraged.

The defendant removed his gloves and started toward the victim. Mr. Farley, still teasing, said: "Ooo, he's taking his gloves off." The defendant then pulled a knife from his pocket and stabbed the victim in the neck. He also stabbed Mr. Farley in the arm as he fell to the floor. Mr. Farley looked up and cried: "Man, I was just kidding around." The defendant responded: "Well, man, you should have never hit me in my face." The police arrived at the restaurant and arrested the defendant. He was given his Miranda rights. The defendant made a statement at the police station and confessed to the killing.1 The police officers described him as calm and willing to cooperate.

It is also undisputed that the defendant suffers from a host of psychiatric problems. He experiences up to two panic attacks daily and had received treatment for them at the Veterans Administration Hospital in Huntington for more than a year preceding the killing. He suffers from chronic depression (dysthymic disorder), an obsession with his nose (body dysmorphic disorder), and borderline personality disorder. The defendant's father shed some light on his nose fixation. He stated that dozens of times a day the defendant stared in the mirror and turned his head back and forth to look at his nose. His father estimated that 50 percent of the time he observed his son he was looking at his nose. The defendant repeatedly asked for assurances that his nose was not too big. This obsession began when he was approximately seventeen years old. The defendant was twenty-nine years old at the time of trial.

....

During the cross-examination of the defendant's father, the prosecuting attorney inquired about prejudicial statements allegedly made by the defendant. Bobby Lee Guthrie was asked if the defendant told him that men were better than women and women should stay at home, that whites were better than blacks, and whether the two of them discussed the Ku Klux Klan. Defense counsel objected to this line of questioning because of its highly prejudicial effect, particularly with the women on the jury and the one African–American juror.

The State asserted it was proper cross-examination because the defense opened the door when it portrayed the defendant as a good, quiet, Bible-reading man when, in fact, he had made some bigoted comments to the State's psychiatrist, Dr. Ralph Smith. The State also argues the defendant was not prejudiced by these few questions concerning his views because Dr. Smith was not called as a witness and this issue was not raised further. Nevertheless, a curative instruction was not requested by either party and none was given.

....

Questions Relating to the Defendant's Prejudices

During the cross-examination of the defendant's father, the prosecuting attorney inquired about prejudicial statements allegedly made by the defendant. Bobby Lee Guthrie was asked if the defendant told him that men were better than women and women should stay at home, that whites were better than blacks, and whether the two of them discussed the Ku Klux Klan. Defense counsel objected to this line of questioning because of its highly prejudicial effect, particularly with the women on the jury and the one African–American juror.

The State asserted it was proper cross-examination because the defense opened the door when it portrayed the defendant as a good, quiet, Bible-reading man when, in fact, he had made some bigoted comments to the State's psychiatrist, Dr. Ralph Smith.30 The State also argues the defendant was not prejudiced by these few questions concerning his views because Dr. Smith was not called as a witness and this issue was not raised further. Nevertheless, a curative instruction was not requested by either party and none was given.

Although most rulings of a trial court regarding the admission of evidence are reviewed under an abuse of discretion standard, see McDougal v. McCammon, supra, an appellate court reviews de novo the legal analysis underlying a trial court's decision. See *Hottle v. Beech Aircraft Corp.*, 47 F.3d 106 (4th Cir.1995). A trial court's discretion is not unbounded, and the scope of the trial court's discretion varies according to the issue before it. In considering the admissibility **187 *681 of impeachment evidence, we apply the same standards of relevance that we apply to other questions of admissibility.

Appellate courts give strict scrutiny to cases involving the alleged wrongful injection of race, gender, or religion in criminal cases. Where these issues are wrongfully injected, reversal is usually the result. See *Miller v. N.C.*, 583 F.2d 701 (4th Cir.1978); *Weddington v. State*, 545 A.2d 607 (Del.Sup.1988). In *State v. Bennett*, 181 W.Va. 269, 274, 382 S.E.2d 322, 327 (1989), this Court condemned the practice of attorneys making unnecessary racial remarks in the presence of the jury:

> "Although Mr. Perrill referred to Dr. Arrieta as 'the colored lady' only once, it should not have been said for the obvious reason that it may be construed as an appeal to prejudice. 'To raise the issue of race is to draw the jury's attention to a characteristic that the Constitution generally

commands us to ignore. Even a reference that is not derogatory may carry impermissible connotations, or may trigger prejudiced responses in the listeners that the speaker might neither have predicted nor intended.' *McFarland v. Smith*, 611 F.2d 414, 417 (2d Cir.1979)."

The same rationale applies to the prosecuting attorney drawing the jury's attention to racial, gender, and political comments made by the defendant which in no way relate to the crime.

Under the first step of our inquiry, we must determine whether the evidence is relevant to an issue of consequence. Where race, gender, or religion is a relevant factor in the case, its admission is not prohibited unless the probative value of the evidence is substantially outweighed by the danger of unfair prejudice. See *Olden v. Kentucky*, 488 U.S. 227, 109 S.Ct. 480, 102 L.Ed.2d 513 (1988); *State v. Crockett*, 164 W.Va. 435, 265 S.E.2d 268 (1979). Normally, in order to be probative, evidence must be "relevant" under Rule 401, that is, it must tend to make an issue in the case more or less likely than would be so without the evidence. Other factors that bear on the probative value are the importance of the issue and the force of the evidence. 22 C. Wright & K. Graham, Federal Practice and Procedure § 5214 (1978). In this case, the State's most difficult problem throughout this appeal is explaining how this evidence is relevant to an issue of consequence in the case.

The prosecution argues that such evidence is relevant as impeachment evidence in light of the father's comments on direct examination when he portrayed the defendant as a good, quiet, Bible-reading man. In analyzing the contentions of the parties, we first observe that only the evidence of the defendant's quiet and peaceful character was admissible under Rule 404(a)(1) of the West Virginia Rules of Evidence.33 Quite clearly, evidence that the defendant was a "Bible-reading man" and his religious beliefs are not admissible under the same rule because they simply do not concern a pertinent character trait. See *State v. Marrs*, 180 W.Va. 693, 379 S.E.2d 497 (1989) (defendant's reputation for not selling drugs is inadmissible). See also W.Va.R.Evid. 610.34 This issue is in this case only because the prosecution chose not to object to the inadmissible evidence. Thus, we must decide whether the prosecution should have been permitted to rebut this evidence under our curative admissibility rule. We hold the prosecution evidence was barred under the doctrine of curative admissibility and Rule 403.

The doctrine of curative admissibility is to be evaluated under our relevancy rules. To some extent, this rule is a restatement of the general rule that when a party opens up a subject, there can be no objection if the opposing party introduces evidence on the same subject. The most significant feature of the curative admissibility rule, however, is that it allows a party to present otherwise inadmissible evidence on an evidentiary point where an opponent has "opened the door" by introducing similarly inadmissible evidence on the same point. Perhaps, the clearest statement of curative admissibility came in *Danielson v. Hanford,* 352 N.W.2d 758, 761 (Minn.App.1984), where the Minnesota court, quoting from *Busch v. Busch Construction, Inc.*, 262 N.W.2d 377, 387 (Minn.1977), stated:

"In order to be entitled as a matter of right to present rebutting evidence on an evidentiary fact: (a) the original evidence must be inadmissible and prejudicial, (b) the rebuttal evidence must be similarly inadmissible, and (c) the rebuttal evidence must be limited to the same evidentiary fact as the original inadmissible evidence." (Footnote omitted).

We believe the prosecution faces two hurdles in this case. First, was the evidence offered by the defendant prejudicial? This case was not one in which Bible reading had any relevancy. The defendant confessed to the killing and there were eyewitnesses. The only issue that the jury seriously had to consider was the degree of guilt. Certainly, whether the defendant read the Bible could have little impact on the degree of homicide. Second, the prosecution sought to go far beyond the evidence originally offered by the defendant. The fact that the defendant read the Bible and walked through the woods is hardly related to his affinity for Adolph Hitler, his dislike of African-Americans, and his chauvinistic feelings toward women.

The second inquiry under Rule 403 is whether the probity of the objected to evidence was substantially outweighed by its prejudice. In this regard, the defendant argues that even if the evidence had some probative value, it is clearly inadmissible under Rule 403. In *State v. Derr*, 192 W.Va. 165, 178, 451 S.E.2d 731, 744 (1994), we stated "that although Rules 401 and 402 strongly encourage the admission of as much evidence as possible, Rule 403 restricts this liberal policy by requiring a balancing of interests to determine whether logically relevant is legally relevant evidence." Rule 403 calls upon the trial court to weigh the probative evidence against the harm that it may cause—unfair prejudice, confusion, misleading the jury, delay, or repetition—and to exclude the evidence if the probative value is "substantially outweighed" by the harm.

Thus, to perform the Rule 403 balance, we must assess the degree of probity of the evidence, which, in turn, depends on its relation to the evidence and strategy presented at trial in general. The mission of Rule 403 is to eliminate the obvious instance in which a jury will convict because its passions are aroused rather than motivated by the persuasive force of the probative evidence. Stated another way, the concern is with any pronounced tendency of evidence to lead the jury, often for emotional reasons, to desire to convict a defendant for reasons other than the defendant's guilt. In *United States v. Ham*, 998 F.2d 1247, 1252 (4th Cir.1993), the court stated:

"We have defined undue prejudice as ' "a genuine risk that the emotions of the jury will be excited to irrational behavior, and that this risk is disproportionate to the probative value of the offered evidence." '...

"... When evidence of a defendant's involvement in several of these activities is presented to the jury, the risk of unfair prejudice is compounded. In such a case, we fear that jurors will convict a defendant based on the jurors' disdain or their belief that the defendant's prior bad acts make guilt more likely. Furthermore, we are especially sensitive to prejudice in a trial where defendants are members of an unpopular religion." (Citations omitted).

The prejudice that the trial court must assess is the prejudice that "lies in the danger of jury misuse of the evidence." *U.S. v. Brown*, 490 F.2d 758, 764 (D.C.Cir.1973). (Emphasis in original).

Prejudice is not the only threat. There is also a potential for confusing and misleading the jury. Quite apart from prejudice, there is a risk that undue emphasis on the defendant's racial, gender, and/or political views could direct the jury's attention from whether the defendant inflicted the fatal wound because of the "horseplay" or whether the defendant believed the victim was a threat to the defendant's philosophy or way of life. This deflection might seem like a minor matter easy to guard against in the instructions so far as confusion is concerned, but, when coupled with its potential for unfair prejudice, this evidence becomes overwhelmingly dangerous. Even if we concede that this evidence had some relevance on the impeachment issue, the risk of undue prejudice and the risk of confusion are alone enough to justify setting aside this verdict.

Our discussion thus far has not touched on the prosecution's need for this evidence and the closely related question of alternatives available. In note 15 of *Derr*, 192 W.Va. at 178, 451 S.E.2d at 744, we stated that "[o]ne important factor under Rule 403 is the prosecutor's need for the proffered evidence." Here, as discussed above, the evidence of the defendant's prejudices was not only unnecessary, but was not very helpful from a probative value standpoint. In applying Rule 403, it is pertinent whether a litigant has some alternative way to deal with the evidence that it claims the need to rebut that would involve a lesser risk of prejudice and confusion. 22 Wright & Graham, supra, § 5214 (citing cases). Obviously, we do not know what other means the prosecution had to prove the defendant was not a Bible reader or a person of peaceful character. What is important to us, however, is that the trial court failed to ascertain alternatives to this evidence before permitting the prosecution to use it. What we do know is that this issue arose because the prosecution did not object to some clearly irrelevant evidence. Nor did the trial court consider an instruction to the jury advising it to disregard all evidence of the defendant that the prosecution claimed needed rebutting. These failures strengthen our determination to declare error in this case.

To achieve substantial justice in our courts, a trial judge must not permit a jury's finding to be affected or decided on account of racial or gender bias and whether one holds an unpopular political belief or opinion. If Rule 403 is ever to have a significant and effective role in our trial courts, it must be used to bar the admission of this highly prejudicial evidence. See, e.g., *U.S. v. Kallin*, 50 F.3d 689 (9th Cir.1995) (reversible error under Rule 403 to allow witness to testify to defendant's dislike for Mexicans). While due process does not confer upon a criminal defendant a right to an error-free trial, see *U.S. v. Hasting*, 461 U.S. 499, 103 S.Ct. 1974, 76 L.Ed.2d 96 (1983),38 it unquestionably guarantees a fundamental right to a fair trial. See *Lutwak v. U.S.*, 344 U.S. 604,

73 S.Ct. 481, 97 L.Ed. 593 (1953). We emphasize that it is a fundamental guarantee under the Due Process Clause of Section 10 of Article III of the West Virginia Constitution that these factors—race, religion, gender, political ideology—when prohibited by our laws shall not play any role in our system of criminal justice.

Harmless Error Standard

Prosecutorial misconduct does not always warrant the granting of a mistrial or a new trial. The rule in West Virginia since time immemorial has been that a conviction will not be set aside because of improper remarks and conduct of the prosecution in the presence of a jury which do not clearly prejudice a defendant or result in manifest injustice. *State v. Beckett*, 172 W.Va. 817, 310 S.E.2d 883 (1983); *State v. Buck*, 170 W.Va. 428, 294 S.E.2d 281 (1982). Similarly, the United States Supreme Court has acknowledged that given "the reality of the human fallibility of the participants, there can be no such thing as an error-free, perfect trial, and that the Constitution does not guarantee such a trial." *U.S. v. Hasting*, 461 U.S. at 508–09, 103 S.Ct. at 1980, 76 L.Ed.2d at 106. Thus, the Supreme Court has held that an appellate court should not exercise its "[s]upervisory power to reverse a conviction ... when the error to which it is addressed is harmless since, by definition, the conviction would have been obtained notwithstanding the asserted error." *Hasting*, 461 U.S. at 506, 103 S.Ct. at 1979, 76 L.Ed.2d at 104.

The harmless error doctrine requires this Court to consider the error in light of the record as a whole, but the standard of review in determining whether an error is harmless depends on whether the error was constitutional or nonconstitutional. It is also necessary for us to distinguish between an error resulting from the admission of evidence and other trial error. As to error not involving the erroneous admission of evidence, we have held that nonconstitutional error is harmless when it is highly probable the error did not contribute to the judgment. *State v. Hobbs*, 178 W.Va. 128, 358 S.E.2d 212 (1987) (prosecutor's remarks although improper must be sufficiently prejudicial to warrant reversal); *State v. Brewster*, 164 W.Va. 173, 261 S.E.2d 77 (1979). On the other hand, when dealing with the wrongful admission of evidence, we have stated that the appropriate test for harmlessness articulated by this Court39 is whether we can say with fair assurance, after stripping the erroneous evidence from the whole, that the remaining evidence was independently sufficient to support the verdict and the jury was not substantially swayed by the error.

In determining prejudice, we consider the scope of the objectionable comments and their relationship to the entire proceedings, the ameliorative effect of any curative instruction given or that could have been given but was not asked for, and the strength of the evidence supporting the defendant's conviction. See *McDougal v. McCammon, supra*. As the United States Supreme Court explained "a criminal conviction is not to be lightly overturned on the basis of a prosecutor's comments [or conduct] standing alone, for the statements or conduct must be viewed in context[.]" *U.S. v. Young*, 470 U.S. 1, 11, 105 S.Ct. 1038, 1044, 84 L.Ed.2d 1, 9–10, on remand, 758 F.2d 514, on reconsideration, 767 F.2d 737 (1985) (finding harmless error where the prosecutor made an improper statement that the defendant was guilty and urged the jury to "do its job").

Notwithstanding the above discussion, this Court is obligated to see that the guarantee of a fair trial under our Constitution is honored. Thus, only where there is a high probability that an error did not contribute to the criminal conviction will we affirm. "High probability" requires that this Court possess a "sure conviction that the error did not prejudice the defendant." *U.S. v. Jannotti*, 729 F.2d 213, 220 n. 2 (3rd Cir.), cert. denied, 469 U.S. 880, 105 S.Ct. 243, 83 L.Ed.2d 182 (1984). Indeed, the United States Supreme Court recently stated that where there is " 'grave doubt' regarding the harmlessness of errors affecting substantial rights," reversal is required. *O'Neal v. McAninch*, 513 U.S. 432, ––––, 115 S.Ct. 992, 997, 130 L.Ed.2d 947, 956 (1995) ("grave doubt" about harmlessness of the error to be resolved in favor of the defendant). Therefore, we will reverse if we conclude that the prosecutor's conduct and remarks, taken in the context of the trial as a whole, prejudiced the defendant.

In this case, we have "grave doubt" as to whether the errors can be considered harmless. The primary issue in this case was not one of guilt or innocence, but was the degree of homicide for which the defendant would ultimately be convicted. To influence the jury's evaluation and decision, the prosecution was permitted to suggest that any conviction less than first degree murder would permit the defendant to be released in five years and the defendant was a racist, a sexist, a Nazi, and a KKK sympathizer. These errors in combination compel setting aside the verdict, and we do not hesitate to do so on these grounds alone. In fact, it is difficult to imagine any evidence that would have a more powerful impact upon a jury or which would be more likely to deter it from fairly finding the defendant guilty of a lesser offense.

However, there is more. On cross-examination, the prosecuting attorney asked the defendant if he, upon learning of the victim's death, replied to the police officer: "That's too bad, buddy. Do you think it'll snow?" Defense counsel objected because the alleged statement was not disclosed during discovery. Furthermore, the prosecuting attorney offered no factual basis for the question at trial. The defendant argues the State's nondisclosure of this statement, pursuant to Rule 16 of the West Virginia Rules of Criminal Procedure, was prejudicial because it hampered the preparation and presentation of his case. Syllabus Point 3 of *State v. Weaver*, 181 W.Va. 274, 382 S.E.2d 327 (1989), states:

> " 'When a trial court grants a pretrial discovery motion requiring the prosecution to disclose evidence in its possession, nondisclosure by the prosecution is fatal to its case where such nondisclosure is prejudicial. The nondisclosure is prejudicial where the defense is surprised on a material issue and where the failure to make the disclosure hampers the preparation and presentation of the defendant's case.' Syllabus Point 2, *State v. Grimm*, 165 W.Va. 547, 270 S.E.2d 173 (1980)."

See *State v. Myers*, supra. The defendant contends the issue of malice was critical at trial and the alleged statement was very damaging in proving a "heart regardless of social duty," as the jury was instructed on malice. We agree with the defendant. We conclude that this line of questioning was extremely inappropriate. There seems to have been little, if any, justification for this line of questioning other than to inflame the jury through insinuation. Although we would be hesitant to reverse on this error alone, when coupled with the other errors discussed above, our decision to reverse is fortified. Syllabus Point 5 of *State v. Walker*, 188 W.Va. 661, 425 S.E.2d 616 (1992), states:

> " 'Where the record of a criminal trial shows that the cumulative effect of numerous errors committed during the trial prevented the defendant from receiving a fair trial, his conviction should be set aside, even though any one of such errors standing alone would be harmless error.'

Summation/Closing Arguments

Note

While attorneys on both sides are sometimes given wide latitude in closing arguments, particularly where the trial court gives a cautionary instruction that such presentations are not evidence, it is at this stage that most concerns regarding the inappropriate injection of race occurs. Such appeals are almost always considered inappropriate and cover a wide range of racial suggestions including prosecutor singing in the following case.

STATE V. KIRK
157 Idaho 809 (Ct. App.2014)

LANSING, Judge.

James D. Kirk appeals from his convictions for lewd conduct with a minor child under sixteen and sexual battery of a minor sixteen or seventeen years old. Kirk contends that the prosecutor improperly injected race into his case by singing the first few lines of the song "Dixie" during closing argument. Kirk submits that the act unconstitutionally tainted his trial because the alleged victims were white, and he is African–American.

I.
BACKGROUND

On August 12, 2012, at about 6 p.m., four juvenile females, seventeen-year-old J.C., thirteen-year-old M.F., fifteen-year-old A.M., and fifteen-year-old M.G., ran away from the group home where they all resided. Outside a motel in downtown Nampa the four encountered defendant Kirk, who invited the girls into his room. They all spent the night there. A.M. and M.G. left the motel together early the next morning, and J.C. and M.F. departed together later that day.

When J.C. and M.F. were apprehended by Nampa police that evening, M.F. informed an officer that Kirk had raped her during the night in the motel room and that J.C. had participated in the rape by holding her down. M.F. further told the police that she was menstruating when the sexual assault occurred, so her blood would likely be found on the bed's comforter. J.C., although uncooperative at first, eventually told police that she and M.F. both had vaginal sex with Kirk while the three were in bed together, but J.C. denied holding M.F. down or forcing her to participate. Witnesses A.M. and M.G. turned themselves in to police a few days later and, when interviewed, said that they had observed Kirk, J.C., and M.F. having sex together and that M.F. was a willing participant. All of the girls said that Kirk offered them intoxicating prescription medication, which they ingested. A search warrant was obtained for the motel room, and police seized Kirk's cell phone and a blood-stained comforter. Kirk was arrested and admitted to a detective that the girls had been in his motel room, but he denied any sexual conduct.

Kirk was charged with one count of lewd conduct with a minor child under sixteen, Idaho Code § 18–1508, for sexual acts against thirteen-year-old M.F., and one count of sexual battery of a minor sixteen or seventeen years of age, I.C. § 18–1508A(1)(a), for sexual acts against seventeen-year-old J.C. The case was prosecuted primarily on the girls' testimony, which was in accord with what they had told the police, bolstered by the testimony of a sexual assault nurse who said that a physical examination of M.F. revealed vaginal tearing and abrasion consistent with sexual intercourse.

During closing argument, defense counsel focused on perceived weaknesses in the State's case, including the State's failure to gather physical evidence that might have corroborated or refuted the girls' testimony. Defense counsel pointed out that none of the girls were given a toxicology screen to confirm the presence of drugs in their systems and that no pills or pill bottles matching the medication that the girls described were found in the motel room. Defense counsel noted that although M.F. said that Kirk had taken cell phone photos of J.C. in her underwear, the police did not search Kirk's phone for photos. The defense also emphasized that the vaginal swabs taken from M.F. tested negative for male DNA and that J.C. was never asked to undergo a sexual assault examination. Similarly, the defense closing argument reminded the jury that a DNA test on a stain from the blood-stained comforter determined that the blood did not match either M.F. or Kirk, and counsel asserted that the State's failure to test other blood stains on the comforter and the failure to test the bedding for semen were further indicia of a lax investigation. All of this, the defense argued, left reasonable doubt as to guilt.

In her rebuttal closing argument, the prosecutor responded:

> Ladies and gentlemen, when I was a kid we used to like to sing songs a lot. I always think of this one song. Some people know it. It's the Dixie song. Right? Oh, I wish I was in the land of cotton. Good times not forgotten. Look away. Look away. Look away. And isn't that really what you've kind of been asked to do? Look away from the two eyewitnesses. Look away from the two victims. Look away from the nurse in her medical opinion. Look away. Look away. Look away. [footnote omitted]

Defense counsel did not object to this argument. The jury found Kirk guilty on both charges.

Kirk is a black man while the victims in this case were white females. Kirk's sole claim of error is that his constitutional rights to due process and equal protection were violated when the prosecutor sang or recited the lines from "Dixie," thereby injecting the risk of racial prejudice into the case.

II.
ANALYSIS

Under Idaho law, if a mistake that occurred during a criminal trial was not followed by a contemporaneous objection, the judgment of conviction will be reversed only if the appellant establishes that the mistake rose to the level of fundamental error. This requires that the defendant persuade the court that the alleged error: (1) violates one or more of the defendant's unwaived constitutional rights; (2) is clear or obvious without the need for reference to any additional information not contained in the appellate record and (3) there is a reasonable possibility that the error affected the outcome of the trial proceedings. *State v. Perry*, 150 Idaho 209, 226, 245 P.3d 961, 978 (2010). But see *State v. Skunkcap*, 157 Idaho 221, 235, 335 P.3d 561, 575 (2014) where, without expressly modifying or overruling *Perry*, the Idaho Supreme Court said that an appellant claiming fundamental error must show a reasonable likelihood that the error affected the verdict. Whether a prosecutor's comments during closing argument rise to the level of fundamental error is a question that must be analyzed in the context of the trial as a whole. *State v. Severson*, 147 Idaho 694, 720, 215 P.3d 414, 440 (2009). The relevant question is whether the prosecutor's comments so infected the trial with unfairness as to make the resulting conviction a denial of due process. *State v. Carson*, 151 Idaho 713, 718–19, 264 P.3d 54, 59–60 (2011) (citing *Darden v. Wainwright*, 477 U.S. 168, 181, 106 S.Ct. 2464, 2471–72, 91 L.Ed.2d 144, 157 (1986), and *Donnelly v. DeChristoforo*, 416 U.S. 637, 643, 94 S.Ct. 1868, 1871–72, 40 L.Ed.2d 431, 436–37 (1974)).

There is no question that a prosecutor's improper infusion of race into a criminal trial violates a defendant's constitutional rights. "The Constitution prohibits racially biased prosecutorial arguments." *McCleskey v. Kemp,* 481 U.S. 279, 309 n. 30, 107 S.Ct. 1756, 1776–77 n. 30, 95 L.Ed.2d 262, 290 n. 30 (1987). In *State v. Romero–Garcia,* 139 Idaho 199, 75 P.3d 1209 (Ct.App.2003), a case where the prosecutor emphasized the defendant's status as a noncitizen of the United States during closing argument, we said:

> [A] prosecutor is constitutionally prohibited from making racially or ethnically inflammatory remarks during its closing argument. See *McCleskey v. Kemp,* 481 U.S. 279, 309 n. 30, 107 S.Ct. 1756, 1770 n. 30, 95 L.Ed.2d 262, 289 n. 30 (1987); *Bains v. Cambra,* 204 F.3d 964, 974 (9th Cir.2000). Such comments violate a criminal defendant's due process and equal protection rights. *Bains,* 204 F.3d at 974. Appeals to racial or ethnic prejudice can distort the search for truth and drastically affect a juror's impartiality. *United States v. Doe,* 903 F.2d 16, 24 (D.C.Cir.1990).

Upon review of the prosecutor's comments in the case at bar, this Court concludes that the prosecutor's emphasis on Romero–Garcia's status as a non-citizen of the United States could be viewed as a subtle appeal to the jury's racial or ethnic prejudice. Even an artfully constructed appeal to a jury's prejudices cannot avoid application of the prohibition against such comments. *Romero–Garcia,* 139 Idaho at 203, 75 P.3d at 1213.

To support his argument that the song "Dixie" is racist in its origin and lyrics and is disparaging to black people, Kirk cites in his briefing a number of newspaper articles. The State objects to our consideration of these on the ground that the articles are "evidence" that this Court may not consider because the articles were not presented to the trial court. We need not resolve that dispute, for this Court does not require resort to articles or history books to recognize that "Dixie" was an anthem of the Confederacy, an ode to the Old South, which references with praise a time and place of the most pernicious racism. The prosecutor's mention of the title, "Dixie," as well as the specific lyrics recited by the prosecutor, referring to "the land of cotton," expressly evoke that setting with all its racial overtones.

The State maintains, however, that there was no "clear or obvious" constitutional error here because the prosecutor acted with innocent intent, presenting "simply a personal story of singing in her youth" to make a legitimate point that Kirk's closing argument asked the jury to "look away" from the prosecution's evidence. This was not, the State argues, an overt appeal to racial prejudice. We agree that the racial reference here was indirect and perhaps innocently made. This prosecutor may not have intended to appeal to racial bias, but a prosecutor's mental state, however innocent, does not determine the message received by the jurors or their individual responses to it. An invocation of race by a prosecutor, even if subtle and oblique, may be violative of due process or equal protection. As the Second Circuit Court of Appeals stated in *McFarland v. Smith,* 611 F.2d 414, 416–17 (2nd Cir.1979):

Race is an impermissible basis for any adverse governmental action in the absence of compelling justification.... To raise the issue of race is to draw the jury's attention to a characteristic that the Constitution generally commands us to ignore. Even a reference that is not derogatory may carry impermissible connotations, or may trigger prejudiced responses in the listeners that the speaker might neither have predicted nor intended.

See also *State v. Monday*, 171 Wash.2d 667, 257 P.3d 551 (2011) (finding constitutional infringement where the prosecutor several times pronounced "police" as "po-leese" while conducting examination of African–American witnesses). We conclude, therefore, that Kirk has demonstrated a clear violation of his unwaived constitutional right to due process and equal protection.

Whether Kirk has satisfied the third prong of the Perry fundamental error test, by showing a reasonable possibility (or likelihood) that the error affected the outcome of the trial, is a more difficult question. Kirk argues that when the constitutional error at issue is a prosecutor's improper introduction of race into a criminal trial, the defendant should be relieved of the burden of showing prejudice. He maintains we should treat this circumstance as structural error requiring automatic reversal or, alternatively, that the burden should be shifted to the State to demonstrate that the error is harmless.

The United States Supreme Court has described structural error as a constitutional deprivation that creates a structural defect affecting "the framework within which the trial proceeds, rather than simply an error in the trial process itself" and thus renders the trial so unfair that it is not subject to harmless error analysis. *Arizona v. Fulminante*, 499 U.S. 279, 310, 111 S.Ct. 1246, 1265, 113 L.Ed.2d 302, 331–32 (1991). Structural errors are to be distinguished from "trial errors" which, though depriving the defendant of a constitutional right, occur "during the presentation of the case to the jury, and which may therefore be quantitatively assessed in the context of other evidence presented" in order to determine whether the error was harmless beyond a reasonable doubt. Id. at 307–08, 111 S.Ct. at 1264, 113 L.Ed.2d at 330. Errors that have been identified by the United States Supreme Court as structural error include the complete denial of counsel (*Gideon v. Wainwright*, 372 U.S. 335, 83 S.Ct. 792, 9 L.Ed.2d 799 (1963)); a biased trial judge (*Tumey v. Ohio*, 273 U.S. 510, 47 S.Ct. 437, 71 L.Ed. 749 (1927)); racial discrimination in the selection of a grand jury (*Vasquez v. Hillery*, 474 U.S. 254, 106 S.Ct. 617, 88 L.Ed.2d 598 (1986)); denial of the right of self-representation at trial (*McKaskle v. Wiggins,* 465 U.S. 168, 104 S.Ct. 944, 79 L.Ed.2d 122 (1984)); denial of a public trial (*Waller v. Georgia*, 467 U.S. 39, 104 S.Ct. 2210, 81 L.Ed.2d 31 (1984)); a defective reasonable-doubt instruction (*Sullivan v. Louisiana*, 508 U.S. 275, 113 S.Ct. 2078, 124 L.Ed.2d 182 (1993)); and deprivation of the right to counsel of choice (*United States v. Gonzalez–Lopez*, 548 U.S. 140, 126 S.Ct. 2557, 165 L.Ed.2d 409 (2006)).

The Idaho Supreme Court's Perry decision leaves open the possibility that fundamental error review would not require a defendant to demonstrate prejudice in the event of structural error, see *Perry*, 150 Idaho at 225–26, 245 P.3d at 977–78, but to date neither the United States

Supreme Court nor the Idaho Supreme Court has held that an appeal to racial prejudice during the presentation of evidence or argument to a jury constitutes structural error.2 In our view, a prosecutor's improper reference to racial factors during the trial, though offensive and fraught with risk of prejudice to the defendant, does not amount to structural error, for it does not affect the entire framework or context within which the trial proceeds as do the circumstances that have heretofore been identified as structural error. Like other types of prosecutorial appeals to a jury's passion or prejudice, this conduct is trial error. In addition, we do not possess authority to modify Idaho Supreme Court precedent. Therefore, we are not at liberty to create an exception to the third prong of the Perry fundamental error test by shifting the burden to the State to establish that the error was harmless.

We thus arrive at the question whether Kirk has shown a reasonable possibility per Perry, 150 Idaho at 226, 245 P.3d at 978 (or likelihood, per *Skunkcap*, 157 Idaho at 235, 335 P.3d at 575), that the prosecutor's argument, raising the specter of racial prejudice, affected the outcome of the trial. In answering this inquiry for other types of fundamental error, we have often considered principally the weight of the evidence supporting the defendant's conviction to determine whether the trial outcome would have been the same absent the constitutional error. See *State v. Parton*, 154 Idaho 558, 568–69, 300 P.3d 1046, 1056–57 (2013); *State v. Galvan*, 156 Idaho 379, 386–87, 326 P.3d 1029, 1036–37 (Ct.App.2014); *State v. Betancourt*, 151 Idaho 635, 641, 262 P.3d 278, 284 (Ct.App.2011). We are not convinced, however, that a singular focus on the strength of the State's evidence is always appropriate where the constitutional error is State conduct that focuses the jury on racial factors. Although not deeming this error to be structural, we note that provocation of racial animus against a criminal defendant carries some of the characteristics of structural error in that racial bias implicates the defendant's right to a trial before an impartial jury. Like racial discrimination in the selection of jurors or grand jurors, the injection of racial considerations in closing arguments "casts doubt on the integrity of the judicial process," and "impairs the confidence of the public in the administration of justice." *Rose v. Mitchell*, 443 U.S. 545, 556, 99 S.Ct. 2993, 3000, 61 L.Ed.2d 739, 749 (1979).

Because of these considerations, courts from other jurisdictions have sometimes modified or relaxed the standards for determining whether the error was prejudicial where the prosecution invoked racial considerations. An example is Monday, a murder and assault case against an African–American defendant. During direct examination of two African–American witnesses who were not "enthusiastic proponents of the state's case," the prosecutor repeatedly pronounced "police" as "po-leese." Monday, 257 P.3d at 553–54. To discount the credibility of the same witnesses during closing argument, the prosecutor also suggested that there existed an anti-snitch code among African–Americans. The defense did not object to either of these tactics. The Washington Supreme Court found the prosecutor's acts to be appeals to racial stereotypes or racial bias that violated the defendant's right to an impartial jury. Id. at 556–57. Stating that the gravity of the violation "cannot be minimized or easily rationalized as harmless," the court abandoned its historical requirement that a defendant show "a substantial likelihood that the misconduct affected the verdict"; instead, the court cast the burden onto the state to show, beyond a reasonable doubt, that the misconduct did not affect the verdict. *Id.* at 558 (majority), 564–65 (Johnson, J., dissenting); see also *In re Gentry*, 179 Wash.2d 614, 316 P.3d 1020, 1025 (2014). Then, despite evidence against the defendant that included a videotape of the offense and the defendant's own confession, the court concluded that "we cannot say that the misconduct did not affect the jury's verdict" and reversed the conviction. Monday, 257 P.3d at 553, 558. Similarly, in *State v. Cabrera,* 700 N.W.2d 469 (Minn.2005), after finding that the prosecutor committed misconduct by wrongfully accusing defense counsel of asserting a racist defense, the Minnesota Supreme Court reversed the conviction despite acknowledging that given the strength of the state's evidence, including two eyewitnesses' identification and the defendant's admissions, "it would be difficult for us not to conclude that the prosecutor's comments were harmless beyond a reasonable doubt." Id. at 475. The court said that "[a]ffirming this conviction would undermine our strong commitment to routing out bias, no matter how subtle, indirect, or veiled," and that the court would therefore reverse the conviction and remand for a new trial "in the interest of justice and in the exercise of our supervisory powers." *Id.*

In the present case, nothing in the record suggests that the jurors harbored any racial prejudice or that they were actually influenced by the prosecutor's recitation of "Dixie," but the risk of prejudice to a defendant is magnified where the case is as sensitive as this one, involving alleged sexual molestation of minors. As the Fourth Circuit observed in *Miller v. North Carolina*, 583 F.2d 701, 707 (4th Cir.1978), "[c]oncern about fairness should be especially acute where a prosecutor's argument appeals to race prejudice in the context of a sexual crime, for few forms of prejudice are so virulent." In this circumstance, both the constitutional obligation to provide criminal defendants a fundamentally fair trial and the interest of maintaining public confidence in the integrity of judicial proceedings weigh against imposing a stringent standard for a defendant's demonstration that the error was harmful. Although the State's case here was a strong one, it was not so compelling that no rational juror could have voted to acquit, particularly with respect to the charge involving J.C., for which there was no physical evidence corroborating the charge. While there may be other cases where a prosecutorial remark with racial overtones would be harmless error, given the nature of this particular case, and considering the totality of the evidence and trial proceedings, we conclude that Kirk has demonstrated a reasonable possibility (or likelihood) that the error affected the outcome of the trial. Kirk is therefore entitled to a new trial.

The judgment of conviction is vacated and the case remanded for further proceedings.

Judge GRATTON and Judge MELANSON concur.

Note

As indicated in the *Kirk* case, courts have also had to address the question of whether and when appeals to racial prejudice is reversible error. As in *Kirk*, courts have often resolved this issue by application of the constitutional harmless error test annunciated in *Chapman v. California*, 386 U.S. 18 (1967). In the following cases the courts considered this question both in instances where the defendant objected to the prosecution's racist behavior and in instances where the issue was first raised on appeal. In *State v. Monday*, 171 Wash. 2d 667 (2011), which will also be discussed in the next chapter regarding race and the credibility of non-white witnesses, the trial court, while recognizing that the prosecutor improperly interjected his personal views regarding witness credibility, denied the defense request for a mistrial. On appeal the Supreme Court of Washington considers not only this ethical violation but the infusion of race by the prosecutor throughout the trial – including racially disparaging his own witnesses when he did not get the testimony wanted or expected. In granting relief to the defendant the Court states:

> A prosecutor serves two important functions. A prosecutor must enforce the law by prosecuting those who have violated the peace and dignity of the state by breaking the law. A prosecutor also functions as the representative of the people in a quasijudicial capacity in a search for justice.
>
> Defendants are among the people the prosecutor represents. The prosecutor owes a duty to defendants to see that their rights to a constitutionally fair trial are not violated. Thus, a prosecutor must function within boundaries while zealously seeking justice. Id. A prosecutor gravely violates a defendant's Washington State Constitution article I, section 22 right to an impartial jury when the prosecutor resorts to racist argument and appeals to racial stereotypes or racial bias to achieve convictions. 171 Wash. 2d at __ [citations and footnotes omitted]

UNITED STATES V. MCKENDRICK .
481 F.2d 152 (2nd Cir. 1973)

OAKES, Circuit Judge:

This case is surprising in this day and age since it presents, on appeal by the State from a conditional grant of the writ of habeas corpus in a proceeding under 28 U.S.C. § 2254, the question whether racially prejudicial remarks by a prosecutor in summation constitutionally infected the conviction of appellee. District Judge Motley held that they did so, that there was not harmless constitutional error, and accordingly granted the petition for the writ unless the State within 60 days retried petitioner, the appellee here. Her opinion is printed at 350 F.Supp. 990 (S.D.N.Y.1972). We agree and affirm.

On a rainy evening, December 11, 1965, three men robbed a Niagara, New York, delicatessen. In the process a robber wearing a beige trench coat, a black beret and a mask covering his mouth scooped up $132 from the cash register, hit a customer of the store with a gun, knocking him unconscious, and took his wallet and money. This robber ran out of the store, pursued by two policemen, but escaped. Meanwhile, two other officers came on the scene in a police car, and after briefly losing sight of the suspect, saw petitioner, Haynes, and arrested him. He was wearing a beige trench coat and black beret but he had no gun, no wallet and no $132. Two black stockings, one of which apparently fitted the description of the "mask," were, however, found in petitioner's pockets along with $25 in change and $73 in bills, 20 of which were and 53 of which were not in his wallet.

Petitioner was identified at the trial by four witnesses, three who saw him in lineups1 (two of whom said they had known him before the robbery) and one who testified he saw petitioner in front of the store before he put on his "mask." Petitioner's defense was based on an alibi supported by his own testimony, corroborated by three other players, that he had been playing poker and that the coins and bills were winnings. He explained his having the money in assorted pockets by saying that he had kept $17 rent money separately. The socks he and his wife said were put in his pocket when he had bought new gold ones that morning, to match his shirt. That the case was relatively a close one is partially evidenced by the fact that the jury retired at 6:07 p. m. on Friday, March 18, 1966, and returned at 10:42 p. m. with a series of questions concerning (1) the police log's data on the time of the call to the police car from which petitioner was ultimately seen and the time of the pick-up of petitioner; (2) from which of Haynes' pockets the arresting officer took the socks; and (3) the arresting officer's testimony as to mud on the shoes and pants of Haynes, coupled with a request to have the shoes and pants in the jury room. The jury retired at 11:16 p. m. and did not return with its guilty verdict until 12:55 a. m. on Saturday, March 19, 1966.

The appellant exhausted his remedies in the state courts, arguing in Point II of his brief to the Appellate Division of the State Supreme Court, 4th Department, entitled "Prosecutor's Remarks" that "allusions to race or ethnic background" were prejudicial and referring to the summation as being "replete with racial overtones, undertones, and explicit statements." Indeed, the State did not brief the exhaustion point here.2

What, then, were the remarks of the prosecutor to the all-white Niagara County jury, on which the trial court based its finding of a denial of due process? We repeat them here in extenso as we believe it necessary for better understanding of our decision (all quotations are from Volume 10 of the transcript of petitioner's trial):

. . . I know that [petitioner's counsel] Mr. Gold, in his experience, he has dealt with people for many years of the colored race. There is something about it, if you have dealt with colored people and have been living with them and see them you begin to be able to discern their mannerisms and appearances and to discern the different shades and so on. Any of you that have never been exposed to them would never be able to. I don't see, I have been exposed to some degree, that isn't what I am getting at. What I am getting at is those who are living with them, dealing with them, and working with them in a sense, have a much better opportunity to evaluate what they see to identify what they see. (27-28.)

******

Now, counsel for the defendants told you, and Attorney Gold is probably as well versed with the colored race as any man I know in the legal profession. He knows their weaknesses and inability to do certain things that maybe are commonplace for the ordinary person to do or remember or know certain things. (38.)

******

. . . Here she is, a young girl about 13 [referring to a prosecution witness who was black]. And I know that you have recalled this young McCray girl who is the tall sister of Jones. That young lady [also black] had her first baby at 15. She is now married at 16 with another baby on the way. The maturity among these people becomes quite evident quite quickly. Here is a young girl interested in all the young-or ought to be, in the young men of her circle of friends or environment . . . (40-41.)

******

It gets confusing when you talk to some of these youngsters like that because they don't express themselves as clearly as you and I might possibly be able to do so. (41-42.)

******

Eyvonne Martin true enough is 13 years old. Again I point to the fact she is a colored girl. She knows her own. She knows the young bucks in that neighborhood and she knew Terry Cox [petitioner's codefendant]. (43-44.)

******

I know that it is the custom and the habit of many colored people to try and straighten their hair. I don't know what the reason for it is. But in any event it is not uncommon to observe colored people with a heavy pomade grease or hair dressing in their hair. It is also not uncommon to find colored people with somewhat exotic hair-dos, male and female. Most of the exotic hair-dos take the form of a skull cap type hairdo, plastered down. You may have seen this. Others are taking the trend of the current day, of the long hair. It seems to be a fad. May I say that I cannot participate in that. The tendency on the part of these faddists, if I can call them that, is that they use this black bandana type, you have seen it, to hold the hair down. The effect of this grease is to straighten that hair out. And that would bring the hair down. The long hair as described by Mrs. Balon, being pulled down, plastered down on the side of the head and by Investigator Demler, who described it as long. This is not the type of sideburns that we usually think of when we think of sideburns. It probably operates much as bangs operate on a lady. They do not grow out of your forehead. They come off the top and dress down. . . . (79-81.)

We agree with the district court that the prosecutor's remarks introduced race prejudice into the trial and thereby denied petitioner his constitutional right under the due process clause to a fair trial. There can be no doubt that the prosecutor's remarks would have required reversal in a federal court appeal under the decisions of this and other federal courts. See *United States v. Grey*, 442 F.2d 1043 (6th Cir.), cert. denied sub nom. *Williams v. United States*, 400 U.S. 967, 91. S.Ct. 380, 27 L.Ed.2d 387 (1970).4 See also *United States v. Lamerson*, 457 F.2d 371 (5th Cir. 1972); *United States v. Grunberger*, 431 F.2d 1062, 1068 (2d Cir. 1970). *Skuy v. United States*, 261 F. 316 (8th Cir. 1919), contained a prosecutorial statement comparable in its instillation of racial prejudice with this one; in that case the prosecutor implied that the testimony of one Christian soldier should be believed even though disputed by four Jewish witnesses simply because of the different religious affiliations of the witnesses. In both Skuy and Grunberger, supra, reversal was had despite a failure on the part of the defendant to object properly (perhaps by virtue of unconscious acquiescence on the part of the defense attorney in the prosecutor's objectionable remarks), and here too defense counsel's failure to object does not dispose of the issues raised by this habeas petition. This case goes well beyond the classic *United States v. Antonelli Fireworks Co.*, 155 F.2d 631, 637-638 (2d Cir.), cert. denied, 329 U.S. 742, 67 S.Ct. 49, 91 L.Ed. 640 (1946), where the prosecutor's closing statement was an exhortation in wartime to the jury as patriotic Americans in disparagement of the Italian-American defendant. Judge Frank's eloquent dissent, it will be recalled, argued among many other things that a prosecutor "should not be permitted to summon that thirteenth juror, prejudice." 155 F.2d at 659.5 See also Annot., 45 A.L.R.2d 303, 322-68 (1956); ABA Project on Standards for Criminal Justice, The Prosecution Function and the Defense Function §§ 5.8(c) and (d), commentary at 128-29 (1970).

Racial prejudice can violently affect a juror's impartiality and must be removed from the courtroom proceeding to the fullest extent possible. See generally G. Allport, The Nature of Prejudice (1955); B. Bettelheim & M. Janowitz, Social Change and Prejudice (1964); S. Blackburn, White Justice; Black Experience Today in America's Courtroom (1971); J. Kovel, White Racism, A Psychohistory (1970). It negates the defendant's right to be tried on the evidence in the case and not on extraneous issues. ABA Standards, supra, at 129. More than just harm to the individual defendant is involved, however. For the introduction of racial prejudice into a trial helps further embed the already too deep impression in public consciousness that there are two standards of justice in the United States, one for whites and the other for blacks. Such an appearance of duality in our racially troubled times is, quite simply, intolerable from the standpoint of the future of our society.

Proceeding from the major premise that the remarks of the prosecutor were prejudicial and would have resulted in reversal had they been made in the federal courts, we must inquire whether, as the State seems to suggest, to result in reversal racially biased remarks of a prosecutor in a state court case must be shown to have had a greater probability of prejudice than remarks on a direct appeal in the federal courts.6 In our analysis we shall refer exclusively to federal court decisions which overturned state court decisions on fourteenth amendment grounds.

We commence our analysis of the application of the fourteenth amendment to prosecutorial summations in state courts with a considerable background of cases-none of them involving prosecutor's remarks, to be sure-overturning convictions on fourteenth amendment grounds where racial prejudice was a major factor in the fiber of the trial. [citations omitted]

....

Finally the State argues that there was harmless constitutional error13 in the sense that the evidence of guilt was so overwhelming that Haynes could not have been prejudiced by any of the prosecutor's remarks. Cf. *United States v. Benter, supra*, 457 F.2d at 1178; *United States v. Frascone*, 299 F.2d 824, 828 (2d Cir. 1962), cert. denied, 370 U.S. 910, 82 S.Ct. 1257, 8 L.Ed.2d 404 (1963). The short answer to this argument is that our review of the record satisfies us that the evidence was by no means so clear as the prosecution would have it. The identification of petitioner was not overwhelmingly persuasive-the black beret he was wearing was not uncommon in the neighborhood and many raincoats are "beige." Petitioner was not found with the robber's gun or customer's wallet or money in an amount similar to that taken. Petitioner presented, moreover, an alibi supported by the testimony of several witnesses. The jury, moreover was not so ready to convict, since it took several hours of deliberation before guilty verdicts were brought back. [footnote omitted] We totally disagree with the State's contention in the next to concluding sentence in its brief, that "It is clear from the evidence at trial that petitioner had a hopeless case." Rather, we think, the probability of prejudice was sufficiently great, and the case sufficiently close, that the defendant, appellee here, should be given a new trial as ordered by the district court under any applicable "harmless error" standard. *Harrington v. California*, 395 U.S. 250, 254, 89 S. Ct. 1726, 23 L.Ed.2d 284 (1969); *Chapman v. California*, 386 U.S. 18, 24, 87 S.Ct. 824, 17 L.Ed.2d 705 (1967). Accordingly we need not decide whether jury verdicts tainted by racially prejudicial statements by the prosecutor should be measured by the harmless error test, but rather should receive automatic reversal. Racially prejudicial remarks are, however, so likely to prevent the jury from deciding a case in an impartial manner and so difficult, if not impossible, to correct once introduced, that a good argument for applying a more abolute standard may be made. See Note, Harmless Constitutional Error: A Reappraisal, 83 Harv. L.Rev. 814, 820-24 (1970).

Thus, we affirm the judgment below.

Judgment affirmed.

Note

In the following case, the Court not only addresses the issue of review of prosecutorial racial misconduct during closing argument, in an instance where defense counsel failed to object, but also, in light of that failure, whether consideration in federal habeas corpus is barred by *Wainwright v. Sykes,* 433 U.S. 72 (1977).

MILLER, V. NORTH CAROLINA
583 F.2d 701 (4ᵗʰ Cir. 1978)

WINTER, Circuit Judge:

Appellants are three black men who, originally sentenced to death, are currently serving life sentences resulting from their North Carolina convictions, pursuant to N.C.Gen.Stat. s 14-21 (1977 Cum.Supp.), for first degree rape of a white woman. In their petition for federal habeas corpus relief, they alleged two principal constitutional errors in their convictions: first, that the trial court's insistence that one attorney represent all three defendants deprived them, because of conflicts among them, of the effective assistance of counsel, and second, that the racially inflammatory remarks in the prosecutor's closing argument before an all-white jury were so prejudicial as to make a fair trial impossible. The district court considered both claims to be without merit and denied relief.

We grant a certificate of probable cause and reverse. In our view, the prosecutor's summation, by deliberately injecting the issue of race into what was necessarily a racially sensitive prosecution, so infected the trial with unfairness as to deny appellants due process of law. Because we conclude that the prosecutor's argument invalidated the trial, we find it unnecessary to address appellants' contentions concerning the effectiveness of their representation. We direct that unless appellants are afforded a new trial, the writ should issue.

I.

We need state the facts relating to appellants' rape convictions only succinctly; they are stated more fully in the opinion of the Supreme Court of North Carolina which found no error in the convictions. See *State v. Miller,* 288 N.C. 582, 220 S.E.2d 326 (1975).

Deborah Case and her boyfriend, Michael Stumphey, hitchhiked to North Carolina so that they might attend a rock festival that was to be held in Charlotte on August 10, 1974. After arriving in Charlotte on August 9, however, the couple changed their plans, deciding to skip the concert and instead to travel to Colorado where they intended to get married. On the morning of August 10 they headed west. Shortly after starting, they accepted a ride in a car occupied by three black men, the appellants in this case. Once in route, the driver told them that he would take them as far as Hickory but that he first had to stop and see someone. On that supposed errand, he left the interstate and drove to the end of a remote country road. There, while Michael was held at bay at the point of a pistol, Deborah, allegedly at the point of a knife, was required to submit to sexual intercourse with each of the appellants in turn.

Later, Deborah and Michael were driven back to the interstate, where they were permitted to leave the car. They promptly hailed a state policeman. Acting on information supplied by the couple and others, the police arrested the appellants that same day and charged them with rape.

The state's case consisted chiefly of the testimony of Michael and Deborah. Each identified the three appellants as the occupants of the car and each testified to the use of the threat of force, although only Deborah could speak to the details of the assaults. Their identification of the appellants was corroborated by James Franklin, a hunter who had encountered the five of them while the car was parked at the end of the road. None of the defendants testified or offered any evidence in opposition to the state's case. From the tenor of the cross-examination, however, it was evident that the theory of the defense was that Deborah had consented to sexual intercourse with the defendants. The defense did elicit testimony that Deborah and Michael entered the car willingly and made no request to get out, that Deborah had previously engaged in acts of sexual intercourse, that both had taken drugs before the incident, that Deborah had no injuries other than a small bruise, and that she had offered no physical resistance during the several acts of sexual intercourse with appellants.

During closing arguments, the trial judge was not present on the bench. Under North Carolina practice, counsel for defendants had the opening and closing arguments. While counsel's opening argument was not transcribed, he apparently urged a theory of consent. In reply, the prosecutor made references to the defendants' race. He repeatedly referred to the defendants as "these black men" and ultimately argued that a defense based on consent was inherently untenable because no white woman would ever consent to having sexual relations with a black:

> Don't you know and I argue if that (i. e. consent) was the case she could not come in this court-
> room and relate the story that she has from this stand to you good people, because I argue to
> you that the average white woman abhors anything of this type in nature that had to do with a
> black man. It is innate within us, ...

No objection was voiced to the prosecutor's arguments nor was any attempt made to recall the judge from chambers. Defense counsel also voiced no objection when the judge returned to court.

The defendants were all convicted and were initially sentenced to death, but a change in the law caused their sentences later to be reduced to life imprisonment. An unsuccessful appeal was taken to the North Carolina Supreme Court. State v. Miller, supra. Briefs filed in that appeal urged reversal on several grounds; chief among them was that the prosecutor's remarks were so prejudicial as to constitute reversible error.

While the seven-member court was unanimous in affirming the convictions, the court split on the reasons for affirmance with respect to the prosecutor's argument. The opinion of the court, written by Justice Huskins, in which two other justices concurred completely and a third justice concurred in part, assigned alternative grounds for decision: that the error was harmless because the evidence against the defendants was overwhelming, and that the failure of counsel to object to the argument waived the point for purposes of review. In holding that the prosecutor's argument was harmless error, the majority expressed mild disapproval of the argument's content. Chief Justice Sharp's concurring opinion, joined by two other justices of the court, rested solely on the assertion that the error was harmless, but it characterized the prosecutor's argument as "an egregious blunder" which in a less one-sided case would have required a new trial. 220 S.E.2d at 341. The seventh justice who concurred mostly in the majority opinion wrote separately to express his view that no criticism of the prosecutor was justified because the remarks were not prejudicial since they simply stated a matter of common knowledge.

The appellants next brought this habeas corpus petition repeating the allegations that had been made in the state appeal. The district court denied relief. On the question of the prosecutor's remarks, it held, alternatively, that the failure to object constituted a waiver, that the remarks were not prejudicial, and that, if prejudicial, they were harmless beyond a reasonable doubt. This appeal followed.

II.

Before addressing the merits of appellants' contentions regarding the prosecutor's summation, we must first consider North Carolina's argument that *Wainwright v. Sykes,* 433 U.S. 72, 97 S.Ct. 2497, 53 L.Ed.2d 594 (1977), applies to this case by virtue of defense counsel's failure to object to the prosecutor's summation at the time it was delivered and that it bars habeas relief on this issue. Wainwright holds that a state procedural waiver rule may supply a state ground of decision adequate to foreclose federal habeas relief, absent a showing of cause for the failure to comply with the state rule and of prejudice from the failure to object.

We reject the argument. While we have no doubt that *Wainwright* binds us in federal habeas corpus proceedings to the North Carolina procedural rule concerning the preservation of error in a North Carolina criminal proceeding, we think that the instant case falls within an exception to the general North Carolina rule barring review where there has been no objection. The exception, as we have mentioned in n. 4, Supra, is that in a capital case " if argument of counsel . . . is so grossly improper that removal of its prejudicial effect, after a curative instruction, remains in doubt, the general rule requiring objection before verdict does not apply." 220 S.E.2d at 339. Accord: *State v. White*, 286 N.C. 395, 211 S.E.2d 445 (1975); *State v. Williams*, 276 N.C. 703, 174 S.E.2d 503 (1970); Rev'd on other grounds, 403 U.S. 948, 91 S.Ct. 2290, 29 L.Ed.2d 860 (1971); *State v. Miller*, 271 N.C. 646, 157 S.E.2d 335 (1967). Under this rule the first attention of the reviewing court is to consider if the challenged argument was improper and, if so, whether it was improper to the extent that doubt remains as to whether a curative instruction would remove its prejudicial effect. If a convicted defendant was so prejudiced, the failure to object is no bar and his claim may be decided on the merits. If, on the other hand, it can be said that the argument was not prejudicial or that a curative instruction would have removed any prejudice, his failure to object to the argument is treated as a bar to appellate relief. Thus, application of this exception entails an inquiry by the reviewing court into the merits of the claim; waiver is not automatic. This was the pattern of reasoning of the North Carolina Supreme Court in the instant case.

In the instant case, the North Carolina Supreme Court, while disapproving the prosecutor's choice of language, concluded that its use "in light of the facts and circumstances disclosed by the record" did not constitute prejudicial error requiring a new trial. The court added that the evidence of guilt was overwhelming and there was no reasonable basis on which to conclude that appellants would not have been convicted if the challenged argument had been entirely omitted. 220 S.E.2d 339. As we shall show, we are in disagreement with both of these conclusions. We think that there was prejudicial error of sufficient magnitude that even after a curative instruction there would remain doubt as to whether the prejudice was removed. Because the capital case exception to North Carolina's contemporaneous objection rule entails analysis both as to the degree of prejudice and to the consequences of the failure to object, we think that we too are authorized to consider the merits.

III.

We therefore turn to the merits of appellants' argument that the racial remarks of the prosecutor so prejudiced their trial as to deny them due process of law as guaranteed by the fourteenth amendment. The standard by which such claims are evaluated is a stringent one. Due process is not violated unless the error constitutes a "failure to observe that fundamental fairness essential to the very concept of justice." *Donnelly v. DeChristoforo*, 416 U.S. 637, 642, 94 S.Ct. 1868, 1871,

40 L.Ed.2d 431 (1974) (quoting *Lisenba v. California*, 314 U.S. 219, 236, 62 S.Ct. 280, 86 L.Ed. 166 (1941)). We think the prosecutorial misconduct in the instant case rose to that level.

Nothing is more fundamental to the provision of a fair trial than the right to an impartial jury. See *Aston v. Warden*, 574 F.2d 1169, 1172 (4 Cir. 1978). The impartiality of the jury must exist at the outset of the trial and it must be preserved throughout the entire trial. The device of Voir dire and the right to strike prospective jurors, both peremptorily and for cause, are the means by which an impartial jury is seated in the box. Thereafter, the law guarantees that every defendant may have his case decided strictly according to the evidence presented, not by extraneous matters or by the predilections of individual jurors. The law has developed an elaborate body of the law of evidence, the overall purpose of which is to restrict the deliberations of jurors to that which is trustworthy, probative and relevant. Where evidence is relevant but also prejudicial, the law requires that it not be received until it has been demonstrated that its relevance and probative value outweigh its collateral prejudicial effect. Thus, the objective of a fair trial is sought to be achieved.

A prejudicial argument by the prosecutor poses a serious threat to a fair trial. Not only does it undermine the jury's impartiality, but it also disregards the prosecutor's responsibility as a public officer. *Berger v. United States*, 295 U.S. 78, 85, 88, 55 S.Ct. 629, 79 L.Ed. 1314 (1935).6 Judge Jerome Frank's trenchant dissenting opinion in United States v. Antonelli Fireworks Co., 155 F.2d 631 (2 Cir. 1946), a case where the prosecutor appealed to the jury's sense of patriotism in a wartime prosecution, explains why such arguments are so objectionable.

Concern about fairness should be especially acute where a prosecutor's argument appeals to race prejudice in the context of a sexual crime, for few forms of prejudice are so virulent. Moreover, an appeal to racial prejudice impugns the concept of equal protection of the laws. One of the animating purposes of the equal protection clause of the fourteenth amendment, and a continuing principle of its jurisprudence, is the eradication of racial considerations from criminal proceedings. See *United States ex rel. Haynes v. McKendrick*, 481 F.2d 152, 158-59 (2 Cir. 1973). We agree with Judge Oakes, the author of Haynes, that "the purpose and spirit of the fourteenth amendment requires that prosecutions in state courts be free of racially prejudicial slurs in argument." 481 F.2d at 159.

On the facts as disclosed by this record, we are persuaded that the prosecutor's remarks so infected the proceeding as to deny appellants due process of law. Other courts have reached a similar conclusion where a prosecutor has made racially prejudicial comments, See *Kelly v. Stone*, 514 F.2d 18 (2 Cir. 1975); Haynes, supra; see generally Annot., 45 A.L.R.2d 303, 322-68 (1956). Of course where the legal standard is simply one of fairness, the resolution of each case must depend on its facts. There may be cases where a disputed remark is arguably not prejudicial or where it is plainly insignificant. There may also be instances where the curative instructions of the trial judge are so immediate and decisive that the prejudicial effects of the argument are effectively dispelled. But we see no saving features in the instant case. Here the comments were unquestionably prejudicial, and they related to the crucial issue of whether there was consent. Even if this were a case where prejudice could be dispelled by curative instructions, the efficacy of curative instructions is not in issue since none were given. We therefore hold that the prejudicial effects of the prosecutor's argument deprived appellants of their constitutional right to a fair trial.

IV.

There remains only the question of whether this constitutional deprivation was harmless error. In *Chapman v. California*, 386 U.S. 18, 87 S.Ct. 824, 17 L.Ed.2d 705 (1967), the Supreme Court observed that there might be some errors of constitutional magnitude that might, in a particular case, be so unimportant and insignificant as to be harmless. An error could not be so classified, however, unless the reviewing court were able to say, beyond a reasonable doubt, that there was no reasonable possibility that the disputed evidence might have contributed to the conviction. 386 U.S. at 23-24, 87 S.Ct. 824. And the Court recognized that "there are some constitutional rights so basic to a fair trial that their infraction can never be treated as harmless error." 386 U.S. at 23, 87 S.Ct. at 827. We do not think that there was harmless error in the instant case.

First, we cannot say beyond a reasonable doubt that the improper argument did not contribute to the convictions. The defense of consent admittedly was not a strong one. Yet by the same token, it was not frivolous. The evidence that the victim willingly entered the car, that she did not protest the deviation, that she and her male companion (to whom she was not then married) had consumed drugs, and that she was not inexperienced in sexual activity might have led the jury either to find consent or to deadlock on the issue of consent.8 The blatant appeal to racial prejudice in the assertion that no white woman would consent to sexual intercourse with a black man could not have had an insubstantial effect on the jury's verdict were it otherwise disposed to be persuaded by the defense.

Second, we incline to the view that the instant case falls into the category of constitutional violations to which, as *Chapman* recognizes, the harmless error rule does not apply. When the error is a coerced confession, denial of counsel, or lack of an impartial judge the examples cited in *Chapman,* 386 U.S. at 23, n. 8, 87 S.Ct. 824 the error infects the entire proceeding making it impossible to evaluate the effect of the error on the jury. As a consequence, with such errors reversal is automatic. See *Chapman, supra,* 386 U.S. at 23 n. 8, 87 S.Ct. 824; Mause, Harmless Constitutional Error: The Implications of Chapman v. California, 53 Minn.L.Rev. 519, 540-47 (1969); Note, Harmless Constitutional Error: A Reappraisal, 83 Harv.L.Rev. 814, 820-24 (1970).

Where the jury is exposed to highly prejudicial argument by the prosecutor's calculated resort to racial prejudice on an issue as sensitive as consent to sexual intercourse in a prosecution for rape, we think that the prejudice engendered is so great that automatic reversal is required. In such a case, the impartiality of the jury as a fact-finder is fatally compromised. Because that contamination may affect the jury's evaluation of all of the evidence before it, speculation about the effect of the error on the verdict is fruitless. Reversal must be automatic. See *Haynes, supra*, 481 F.2d at 161; Mause, Supra, 53 Minn.L.Rev. at 541-42.

For these reasons, the judgment of the district court is reversed and the case is remanded with directions to the district court to issue the writ unless North Carolina shall afford the appellants a new trial within such reasonable period as the district court shall prescribe.

REVERSED AND REMANDED.

[footnotes omitted]

Chapter Eleven: Race and Witness Testimony

Note

The impact of racism on both the competency and credibility of witnesses of color has longed plagued the American legal system. An example of the historic inability of non-whites to be considered competent to testify is demonstrated in the *United States v. Dow*, 25 F. Cas. 901(Md. 1840) Judge Taney, who would later in 1857 go on to author the *Dred Scot* decision as chief Justice of the United States Supreme Court, noted the prevailing view that as a general matter the right to be heard as a witness was largely a matter reserved for Whites. *See Also,* Thomas D. Morris, *Slaves and the Rules of Evidence in Criminal Trials*, 68 CHI-KENT L. REV. 1209 (1993)

UNITED STATES V. DOW.

Case No. 14,990, Taney, 34 (Cir. Ct. Md. 1840)

TANEY, Circuit Justice.

....

At the time of the murder, the captain was the only white person on board; the crew consisted of the Malay, three negroes, and one mulatto; two of the negroes were natives of Philadelphia, and one a native of the state of Delaware; the mulatto was a native of the British province of Nova Scotia; they were all free.

The first witness produced on behalf of the United States was one of these negroes. He was objected to by the counsel for the prisoner, upon the ground, that by the laws of Maryland, a free negro was not a competent witness in any case against the prisoner; or, at all events, not in a capital case.

In deciding upon the admissibility of this evidence, the court must be governed by the laws of Maryland, under the act of congress of 1789, c. 20, § 34 [1 Story's Laws, 67; 1 Stat. 92], which provides, 'that the laws of the several states, except where the constitution, treaties, or statutes of the United States shall otherwise require or provide, shall be regarded as rules of decision in trials at common law.' It will be necessary, therefore, to review the different acts of assembly, which have been passed by the state upon this subject; for, if the testimony offered is not admissible, it must be on the ground that it is excluded by some statute of the state. Upon general principles, there is certainly nothing in the case of the witness, or in his color, that would make him incompetent to give testimony in any case.

The first act of assembly upon this subject is that of May session 1717, c. 13. The second section of that law provides, that 'no negro or mulatto slave, free negro, or mulatto born of a white woman, during the time of his servitude by law, or any Indian slave, or free Indian, native of this or the neighboring provinces, be admitted or received as good and valid evidence in law, in any matter or thing whatsoever, depending before any court of record, or before any magistrate, within this province, wherein any Christian white person is concerned.' And the third section of this law makes the several persons excluded by the second section, witnesses against each other, where other sufficient evidence is wanting, 'provided such evidence or testimony do not extend to the depriving of them, or any of them, of life or member.'

It will be observed, that this act of assembly disqualifies the persons mentioned in it from giving testimony, in any case wherein a Christian white person is concerned; but permits them to be examined, in the discretion of the judge, against one another, in cases not extending to life or member. This qualified admission of their testimony against each other, was always held to be an implied exclusion of it in favor of one another; and this produced the act of assembly of 1801, c. 109, which permitted them to give testimony for, as well as against, each other, in prosecutions for stealing goods, or for receiving them knowing them to be stolen.

The act of 1808, c. 81, was the next in order, and made them witnesses in all criminal prosecutions, for and against one another. In this act, as well as in the act of 1801, before mentioned, 'Indian slaves,' and 'free Indian natives,' are not mentioned, because before the passage of these laws, that unfortunate race had disappeared from the state. And it is also proper to remark, that in the act of 1808, the expression used in the act of 1717, of 'mulatto born of a white woman, during the time of his servitude by law,' is altogether dropped, and the persons authorized to give testimony are, 'any negro or mulatto slave, or any mulatto descended of a white woman, or any negro or mulatto free or freed;' and the persons for or against whom it may be given, in any criminal prosecution, are described in precisely the same words. The acts of assembly that subjected a mulatto, born of a white woman, to a certain period of servitude, were not in force when the law of 1808, was passed; they were repealed by the act of 1790, and again in 1796, c. 67, § 14.

The result of these various acts of legislation is this: negroes and mulattoes, free or slave, are not competent witnesses, in any case wherein a Christian white person is concerned; but they are competent witnesses against all other persons. It is true, that the act of 1808 does not, in so many words, say that negroes and mulattoes shall be competent witnesses in all cases except those wherein a Christian white person is concerned; the language of the statute merely enables them to give testimony in the cases there specified. These were cases in which, among others, negroes and mulattoes had been made incompetent witnesses by the act of 1717; and the effect of the act of 1808 was to repeal so much *903 of this law. And as negroes and mulattoes, as well as persons of any other description, were competent witnesses upon the general principles of the common law, and as they had been disabled merely by the prohibitory provisions of the act of 1717; they are now competent witnesses in all cases, where the provisions of that statute are no longer in force; and the only disabling clause of that statute still in force, is the one which makes them incompetent where any Christian white person is concerned; the other disabling clauses have all been repealed.

We do not speak of the clauses in relation to Indian slaves, or native Indians; the silence of the laws of 1801 and 1808, in relation to this class of persons, has already been accounted for. The prisoner, however, is not an 'Indian slave, or a free Indian native of this or any of the neighboring provinces;' and if the provisions of the act of 1717, in relation to persons of that description, be regarded as still in force; and if negroes or mulattoes would be incompetent witnesses against them, in cases affecting life or member, yet the prohibition does not reach the case of the prisoner.

The only question is, whether he is to be regarded as a Christian white person? We think he is not; the Malays have never been ranked by any writer among the white races. But the act of 1717, which excludes the testimony of negroes and mulattoes, in cases where Christian white persons are concerned, did not look to the differences, moral or physical, which have been supposed to exist between the different races of mankind; the law was made for practical purposes, and grew out of the political and social condition of the colony. The colonists were all of the white race, and all professed the Christian religion; from the situation of the world at that time, no persons but white men professing the Christian religion could be expected to emigrate to Maryland; and if any person of a different color, or professing a different religion, had come into the colony, he would not, at that time, have been recognized as an equal by the colonists, or deemed worthy of participating with them in the privileges of this community. The only nations of the world which were then regarded, or perhaps entitled to be regarded, as civilized, were the white Christian nations of Europe; and certainly emigrants were not expected or desired from any other quarter.

The political community of the colony was composed entirely of white men professing the Christian religion; they possessed all the powers of government granted by the charter. Christian white men could not be reduced to slavery, or held as slaves in the colony; but they might, according to the laws of the colony, lawfully hold in slavery negroes or mulattoes, or Indians. The white race did not admit individuals of either of the other races to political or social equality; they were regarded and treated as inferiors, of whom it was lawful, under certain circumstances, to make slaves. These three races existing in the same territory, one possessing all the power, and holding the other two in a state of subjection and degredation, it was natural, that feelings should be created by such a state of things, that would make it dangerous for the white population to receive as witnesses against themselves the members of the two races which it had thus degraded; hence free negroes and mulattoes, and free Indians of this or the neighboring provinces, as well as those who were held in slavery, were disqualified from being witnesses against Christian white men. No one who belonged to either of the races of which slaves could be made, was allowed to be a witness where any one was concerned who belonged to the race of which the masters were composed.

In order, therefore, to make the negroes and the mulatto incompetent witnesses in this case, it must be shown that the prisoner belonging to the white race, that is to say, to that race of men who settled the colony of Maryland, and formed its political community, at the time the act of 1717 was passed. But it is admitted, that he is a Malay; and the Malays are not white men, and have never been classed with the white race. In Maryland, they were certainly regarded as belonging to one of those races of whom it was lawful to make slaves, and who, according to the laws of England and of the colony, were legitimate objects of the slave trade. This appears by the following case. By the act of assembly of Maryland of 1715, c. 44, § 22, it is declared, 'that all negroes and other slaves already imported, or hereafter to be imported into this province and all the children now born, or hereafter to be born of such negroes and slaves, shall be slaves during their natural lives.' It became a question, under this act, whether the descendant of a woman who was imported as a slave from Madagascar, could be held in slavery in Maryland. 3 Har. & McH. 501. This case is not fully stated in the report; I have examined the original papers. It was proved that the mother of the petitioner was a yellow woman with straight black hair, and that she was not of the negro race, and the testimony shows that it was upon this fact that the petitioner chiefly relied; she was undoubtedly a Malay, according to the description in the evidence. The court said that as Madagascar was a country where the slave trade is practised, the petitioner must show that her ancestor was free in her own country, in order to entitle her to freedom here. Now, it is well known that the Malay race form a part of the population of Madagascar (1 Maltebrun's Geography, 192, 586; 2 Murray's Geography, 525; McCul. Dict. 786; Wyatt, Nat. Hist. 22, 23; Ives' Voyage, 5; 2 Raynal's East & West Indies, 227); and consequently, under this decision, may be held in slavery in this state, if they were *904 slaves in their own country, and when imported here as slaves, they are presumed to have been slaves in their own country, till the contrary appears.

It follows, from this decision, that Malays might lawfully be held in slavery in the colony of Maryland, and consequently, are not embraced by the description of white men as mentioned in the act of 1717, and the testimony offered is not excluded by that law. The case before the court, therefore, stands upon the general principles of the common law, and the witnesses offered by the United States are competent witnesses.

It may be proper to say a few words in relation to the cases embraced by the third section of the act of 1717. By that section negroes, mulattoes and Indians were not witnesses against one another, in cases which might affect life or member. The policy of this section obviously stood upon very different principles from that which dictated the total exclusion of their testimony against white persons. It arose from the barbarous and brutal ignorance of the two excluded classes, and their crude and monstrous superstitions, which rendered them incapable of feeling or appreciating the obligation of an oath, as felt and appreciated in a Christian community; and it was not, therefore, deemed safe to receive them as witnesses, even against one another, in the more serious or grave offences, lest they should avail themselves of the privilege in order to obtain revenge for real or supposed injuries. Even the limited extent to which they might be heard was discretionary with the judge, and he might, if he deemed it proper to do so, refuse to hear them; and if he heard them at all, it must be against one another; they could in no case whatever be received as witnesses in behalf of each other.

In process of time, however, when the Indians had disappeared from the state, and the negro and mulatto population had become instructed in the doctrines of the Christian religion, and made aware of the sanctity and obligation of an oath, the reason which had excluded them as witnesses, even in cases where individuals of their own class were concerned, no longer existed; and the act of 1808, therefore, made them competent in all cases for and against one another. In other words, it made them competent in all cases in which they had been disabled by the act of 1717, except in the case where white persons or Indians were concerned; in the case of white persons, the reasons of policy which dictated the exclusion remained unchanged; and in the case of the Indians, the law had no longer any practical operation, as there were no Indians, free or slave, remaining within the borders of the state.

If the third section of the act of 1717 was still in force, we must have regarded it as an implied declaration that negroes or mulattoes, free or slave, were incompetent witnesses, in any case where life or member was at stake, and upon that principle have rejected the testimony now offered on behalf of the United States. But the act of 1808 having restored their competency in all cases except those above mentioned, and the case of the prisoner not being within either of those exceptions, the question must be determined upon common law principles, and the testimony of these witnesses must, therefore, be admitted.

The testimony was accordingly given to the jury, who found the prisoner guilty of murder.

[The defendant's Motion for Arrest of Judgment was sustained after consideration of other issues. He was re-indicted and sentenced to death which was commuted by Presidential Pardon]

Note

Although after the Civil War barriers to non-white witness competency to testify began to fade, the denigration of the credibility of non-white, particularly Black, witnesses because of race, continues into the 21st century. In Mikah K. Thompson's article *Blackness as Character Evidence*, 20 MICH. J. RACE & L. 321 (2015) concerning the much-publicized trial of George Zimmerman regarding the death of Trayvon Martin, and the treatment of the Black prosecution witness Rachel Jeantel.

The 2012 trial of George Zimmerman for the shooting death of Trayvon Martin, a 17-year old, unarmed African American teenager, on his way home from a store in Sanford, Florida, focused a nation on race and criminal justice in ways similar to the 1955 death by lynching of 14 – year old Emmit Till. The last person to speak to Martin, other than defendant Zimmerman, was 19 – year old Rachel Jeantel.

As Thompson's article points out her testimony was subjected race-infused perceptions of her character and credibility that extended to Trayvon Martin himself by way of proxy. Social media attacked Ms. Jentel by unfavorable comparison to black stereotypes such as the movie character "Precious" and the drag characterization of Black women as portrayed by Tyler Perry"s "Madea". Without much in the way of rehabilitation of this image by the prosecution, Jentel was perceived by many onlookers as ignorant and inarticulate, despite the fact that she spoke three languages with English not being the primary language. As Thompson's article also points out, these negative, race driven perception of witness credibility appears to have had a direct impact on the jury, as evidenced by post-trial interviews with at least one jury.

STATE V. MONDAY
171 Wash.2d 667 (2011)

CHAMBERS, J.

Kevin L. Monday Jr. was convicted of one count of first degree murder and two counts of first degree assault stemming from a shooting in Pioneer Square, Seattle, Washington. We granted review limited to two issues: whether prosecutorial misconduct deprived Monday of a fair trial and whether imposition of firearm enhancements violated Monday's jury trial right. Finding that his trial was fatally tainted by prosecutorial misconduct, we reverse.

FACTS AND PROCEDURAL HISTORY

A street musician was playing drums in Seattle's popular Pioneer Square early one Sunday morning in April 2006. He had mounted a digital video camera on his equipment. The camera captured a confrontation between several men, including one in a distinctive, long red shirt. The confrontation seemed to break up. Then, the red shirted man suddenly pulled out and rapidly fired a pistol as he walked backward and then as he turned and ran.

Francisco Green was shot four times. Two other men were also shot, though both survived. Green died upon arrival at the nearby Harborview Medical Center.

Once he was home, the street musician, who had wisely dropped to the ground when the shooting started, realized he had recorded the shooting. He gave the recording to the police that same day. Shortly after the shooting, a witness stopped an officer on the street to offer a description of the shooter and his very recent location. Following that tip, the officer found Antonio Saunders. Out of Saunders's hearing, the witness confirmed Saunders was the man he believed had committed the shooting, and the officer arrested Saunders for violating probation. Ultimately, Saunders told one of the homicide detectives investigating the murder that he saw Monday fire his gun at Green. Another witness picked Monday and another man out of a photomontage as possible shooters. Many of the other witnesses were more reluctant to cooperate or gave inconsistent responses to investigators. One witness gave a physical description of the shooter.

Monday was arrested three weeks after the murder. He was wearing a red shirt and hat that were strikingly similar to the ones in the video. He initially told the investigators that he had not been to Pioneer Square for years. After being shown some still shots from the video of people he knew, Monday admitted he had been to Pioneer Square recently, admitted he had gotten into a fight, and admitted that he heard a gun being fired. He denied that he had fired a gun himself. When the police showed Monday a picture of himself in a photographic still from the musician's video, Monday acknowledged it was him.

Not long afterward, the police suggested that they had found Monday's DNA (deoxyribonucleic acid) and fingerprints on shell casing recovered at the scene. This was not, in fact, true. Shortly afterward, Monday began to cry and said that "I wasn't trying to kill that man, I didn't mean to take his life." Verbatim Report of Proceedings (VRP) (May 29, 2007) at 32–33. Police searched Monday's home and found .40 caliber bullet cartridges and a gun holster. The gun was not recovered.

Monday was charged with one count of first degree murder and two counts of first degree assault, all while armed with a handgun, and second degree unlawful possession of a firearm. Trial began in April 2007 and lasted a month. During his opening statement, Prosecutor James Konat told the jury that the State takes great measures to ensure that no one is falsely accused or falsely convicted. Monday's counsel objected on the grounds that the State is not supposed to vouch for the credibility of its witnesses or its case. Judge Michael Hayden sustained the objection and stressed that "at no time during the trial will anyone be expressing their personal views as to the guilt or their personal views as to the truth-telling of anyone who takes the witness stand." VRP (May 10, 2007) at 8. The judge also reminded counsel that it was not their place to give their views on the "credibility of a witness or the guilt of anyone." Id. at 7. Judge Hayden denied Monday's motion for a mistrial. He invited Monday to submit a curative instruction but acknowledged that "would simply highlight what was said." *Id.*

Witness credibility was particularly at issue because many of the State's witnesses were not enthusiastic proponents of the State's case. For example, Saunders testified he had only identified Monday as the shooter because he thought Monday had blamed him. Saunders's former girl friend, Adonijah Sykes, had also told investigators that Monday was the shooter. On the stand, she testified that she had lied to police investigators.

During Sykes's second day of testimony, the following exchange took place between her and the prosecuting attorney:

Q. .... And would you agree or disagree with the notion that there is a code on the streets that you don't talk to the po-leese?

A. I mean, that's what some people say. That's what some people go by.

Q. Well, can you help us understand who these some people are?

A. I'm saying—I'm just saying that's how some people is. Some people talk to the police, some don't.

Q. And you're one of those that don't, right?

A. I'm saying—well, I don't—police ain't my friends or nothing.
....

Q. Does that mean that you're one of those people who don't talk to the police?

A. No, sometimes I don't talk to the po-leese. I mean, they got a question or something to ask me, I answer. I don't talk to them.

VRP (May 22, 2007) at 19. Monday did not immediately object to either the prosecutor's line of questioning or his potentially derogatory pronunciation. The examination continued:

Q. Let me ask you this about your conversation with the po-leese.
When did you figure out that that guy that got shot when you were on the corner on April 22nd, 2006[,] when did you find out that he was dead?

A. A couple weeks later.

Q. Really.

A. Yeah.

Mr. MINOR [defense counsel]: Objection, your honor.

Id. at 19–20. The judge asked, "Are you objecting to his tone of voice?" *Id.* at 20. When counsel demurred and said he was objecting to the comment itself, the judge said: "I think you're really objecting to the tone of voice that he's giving us. And I will ask him to try to ask your questions, let the jury decide whether this witness should be believed or not." Id. The prosecutor thanked the judge and continued. Not long after, the prosecutor used the term again:

Q. And fair to say that you didn't want your boyfriend to go to jail?

A. No.

Q. Right? And that's one of the reasons that you stayed away and tried to avoid the po-leese, right?

A. I just didn't want to have nothing to do with them.

Q. I mean, to be—to go back over your testimony yesterday for just one moment, you never called the police and told them you saw what happened down there, did you?

A. No. A lot of people was down there didn't call the police.

Q. That's right. And that's what I was asking you about, there's a code on the streets that you don't call the po-leese, right?

Id. at 22–23.

While Judge Hayden was clear that the prosecutor must refrain from any comments on the credibility of the witnesses, he was not without sympathy. He noted that "virtually every lay witness has been very reticent to testify in this case, and the memory of virtually every lay witness has had significant holes in places where one would not expect that they would have memory lapses." VRP (May 23, 2007) at 98.

Despite the court's earlier admonishment that it was not the State's role to vouch for the credibility of the State's witnesses or its case, in closing, the prosecutor argued:

Seventeen years and eleven months ago yesterday, I signed on, I signed on to serve at the pleasure of Norman K. Maleng. I never imagined in a million years I would get to try as many murder cases as I have in the last 15 years, and I never imagined I would ever get to try one, a doozy, like this one. Seventeen years and about ten months ago I started going to training sessions in the King County prosecutor's office on Saturday mornings that we just dreaded when we could be playing golf.... And two things stood out for me very shortly into my career as a prosecutor, two tenets that all good prosecutors, I think, believe. One is that when you have got a really, really, really strong case, it's hard to come up with something really, really, really compelling to say. And the other is that the word of a criminal defendant is inherently unreliable. Both of those tenets have proven true time and time again over the years, and they have done it specifically in this case over the last five weeks—four weeks.

I never imagined when I signed on to serve at the pleasure of Norm Maleng, this won't be the last murder case I will try, but it is the last one I will try under his name. I imagined I would call eight witnesses who simply will not or cannot bring themselves to admit what cannot be denied.

VRP (May 30, 2007) at 26–27. The prosecutor contended that Green was killed "for no reason. Francisco Green got killed because this messed up American male was trying to prove his macho. He stuck his nose in a fight that didn't have one damn thing to do with him." Id. at 28. The prosecutor acknowledged he was being selective in what part of his witnesses' testimony he wanted the jury to credit. He explained:

[T]he only thing that can explain to you the reasons why witness after witness after witness is called to this stand and flat out denies what cannot be denied on that video is the code. And the code is black folk don't testify against black folk. You don't snitch to the police. And whether it was the guy who was down there helping Francisco Green, trying to keep this killer off of him, or whether it was the people that were working with this killer to try and get to Francisco Green, none of them could bring themselves to recognize what cannot be denied.

Id. at 29–30. He returned to this point again and again throughout his closing argument. E.g., id. at 35 ("And there is only one conceivable explanation for this, and it is called code."); id. at 37 ("all of those witnesses are protecting Kevin Monday. Why? It's the same thing I'm going to say over and over before I sit down. Code. It's all about the code.").

The jury found Monday guilty of one count of first degree murder and two counts of first degree assault. The jury also answered "yes" to each of the special verdict form questions asking whether Monday committed the crimes with a firearm.

Monday appealed on numerous grounds, including that the prosecutor made a blatant and inappropriate appeal to racial prejudice and undermined the credibility of African American witnesses based on their race. The Court of Appeals affirmed Monday's conviction and sentence finding, among other things, that the prosecutor made a blatant appeal to racial prejudice but that any error was harmless under this court's established jurisprudence. *State v. Monday*, noted at 147 Wash.App. 1049, 2008 WL 5330824, 2008 Wash. App. LEXIS 2930. We granted review limited to whether prosecutorial misconduct deprived Monday of a fair trial and whether imposition of firearm enhancements violated Monday's jury trial right. *State v. Monday*, 166 Wash.2d 1010, 210 P.3d 1018 (2009).

Prosecutorial Misconduct

Prosecutorial misconduct is grounds for reversal if "the prosecuting attorney's conduct was both improper and prejudicial." *State v. Fisher*, 165 Wash.2d 727, 747, 202 P.3d 937 (2009) (citing *State v. Gregory*, 158 Wash.2d 759, 858, 147 P.3d 1201 (2006)). Instead of examining improper conduct in isolation, we determine the effect of a prosecutor's improper conduct by examining that conduct in the full trial context, including the evidence presented, " 'the context of the total argument, the issues in the case, the evidence addressed in the argument, and the instructions given to the jury.' " *State v. McKenzie*, 157 Wash.2d 44, 52, 134 P.3d 221 (2006) (quoting *State v. Brown*, 132 Wash.2d 529, 561, 940 P.2d 546 (1997)). Generally the prosecutor's improper comments are prejudicial " 'only where "there is a substantial likelihood the misconduct affected the jury's verdict." ' " *State v. Yates*, 161 Wash.2d 714, 774, 168 P.3d 359 (2007) (quoting *McKenzie*, 157 Wash.2d at 52, 134 P.3d 221 (quoting *Brown*, 132 Wash.2d at 561, 940 P.2d 546)). This has been the standard in this state for at least 40 years. See *State v. Music*, 79 Wash.2d 699, 714–15, 489 P.2d 159 (1971), judgment vacated in part by, 408 U.S. 940, 92 S.Ct. 2877, 33 L.Ed.2d 764 (1972). It is not clear from *Music* where this standard came from.

A prosecutor serves two important functions. A prosecutor must enforce the law by prosecuting those who have violated the peace and dignity of the state by breaking the law. A prosecutor also functions as the representative of the people in a quasijudicial capacity in a search for justice. *State v. Case*, 49 Wash.2d 66, 70–71, 298 P.2d 500 (1956) (quoting *People v. Fielding*, 158 N.Y. 542, 547, 53 N.E. 497 (1899)).[footnote omitted]

Defendants are among the people the prosecutor represents. The prosecutor owes a duty to defendants to see that their rights to a constitutionally fair trial are not violated. Id. at 71, 298 P.2d 500. Thus, a prosecutor must function within boundaries while zealously seeking justice. Id. A prosecutor gravely violates a defendant's Washington State Constitution article I, section 22 right to an impartial jury when the prosecutor resorts to racist argument and appeals to racial stereotypes or racial bias to achieve convictions.

Monday contends Prosecutor Konat injected racial prejudice into the trial proceedings by asserting that black witnesses are unreliable and using derogatory language toward a black witness, saying that "black folk don't testify against black folk." VRP (May 30, 2007) at 29–30.

He contends that the prosecutor made a variety of improper comments during opening statements and closing argument, including referencing his personal credibility, invoking popular former King County Prosecutor Norm Maleng, attacking Monday's credibility, the credibility of the State's own witnesses, and commenting on the strength of the State's case. Monday also contends the prosecutor acted improperly by stating that all good prosecutors believe "the word of a criminal defendant is inherently unreliable" and by adding that it was true in the present case. Id. at 26–27. The State concedes that some of these statements were improper but argues that any error was either not preserved by objection or was harmless given the overwhelming evidence against Monday.

A " '[f]air trial' certainly implies a trial in which the attorney representing the state does not throw the prestige of his public office ... and the expression of his own belief of guilt into the scales against the accused." *Case*, 49 Wash.2d at 71, 298 P.2d 500 (citing *State v. Susan,* 152 Wash. 365, 278 P. 149 (1929)). Turning first to the general issue of the State commenting on the credibility of its witnesses or its case, we agree with the Court of Appeals and Monday that the State crossed that line. It violates our jurisprudence for a prosecutor, a representative of the State, to comment on the credibility of the witnesses or the guilt and veracity of the accused.

[A]n attorney shall not

Assert his personal opinion as to the justness of a cause, as to the credibility of a witness, as to the culpability of a civil litigant, or as to the guilt or innocence of an accused; but he may argue, on his analysis of the evidence, for any position or conclusion with respect to the matters stated herein.

Applying the predecessor to this rule, this court has noted that it is just as reprehensible for one appearing as a public prosecutor to assert in argument his personal belief in the accused's guilt. *State v. Case,* 49 Wash.2d 66, 298 P.2d 500 (1956). Here, the prosecutor clearly violated CPR DR 7–106(C)(4) by asserting his personal opinion of the credibility of the witness and the guilt or innocence of the accused. First, he called the petitioner a liar no less than four times. Next, the prosecutor stated that the defense counsel did not have a case, and that the petitioner was clearly a "murder two". Finally, he implied that the defense witnesses should not be believed because they were from out of town and drove fancy cars.

These statements suggest not the dispassionate proceedings of an American jury trial, but the impassioned arguments of a character from Camus' "The Stranger".

State v. Reed, 102 Wash.2d 140, 145–46, 684 P.2d 699 (1984) (quoting former Code of Professional Responsibility DR 7–106(C)(4)). Plainly, the State violated these precepts. Monday has shown that the prosecutor's comments were improper.

Monday also contends, correctly, that the State committed improper conduct by injecting racial prejudice into the trial proceedings. The State repeatedly invoked an alleged African

American, antisnitch code to discount the credibility of his own witnesses. First, we find no support or justification in the record to attribute this code to "black folk" only. Commentators suggest the "no snitching" movement is very broad. Prosecutor Konat intentionally and improperly imputed this antisnitch code to black persons only. Second, this functioned as an attempt to discount several witnesses' testimony on the basis of race alone. It is deeply troubling that an experienced prosecutor who, by his own account, had been a prosecutor for 18 years would resort to such tactics. "[T]heories and arguments based upon racial, ethnic and most other stereotypes are antithetical to and impermissible in a fair and impartial trial." *State v. Dhaliwal*, 150 Wash.2d 559, 583, 79 P.3d 432 (2003) (Chambers, J., concurring).

Neither was it an isolated appeal to racism. Not all appeals to racial prejudice are blatant. Perhaps more effective but just as insidious are subtle references. Like wolves in sheep's clothing, a careful word here and there can trigger racial bias. See generally Elizabeth L. Earle, Note, Banishing the Thirteenth Juror: An Approach to the Identification of Prosecutorial Racism, 92 Colum. L.Rev. 1212, 1222–23 & nn. 67, 71 (1992) (citing Joel Kovel, White Racism: A Psychohistory 32 (1984); Thomas F. Pettigrew, New Patterns of Racism: The Different Worlds of 1984 and 1964, 37 Rutgers L.Rev. 673 (1985); Reynolds Farley, Trends in Racial Inequalities: Have the Gains of the 1960s Disappeared in the 1970s?, 42 Am. Soc. Rev. 189, 206 (1977)); see also A. Leon Higginbotham, Jr., Racism in American and South African Courts: Similarities and Differences, 65 N.Y.U. L.Rev. 479, 545–51 (1990). Among other things, the prosecutor in this case, on direct examination of a witness, began referring to the "police" as "po-leese." Monday contends, and we agree, that the only reason to use the word "po-leese" was to subtly, and likely deliberately, call to the jury's attention that the witness was African American and to emphasize the prosecutor's contention that "black folk don't testify against black folk." VRP (May 30, 2007) at 29. This conduct was highly improper.

The State contends that even if the conduct was improper, Monday still bears the burden of showing a substantial likelihood that the misconduct affected the verdict, and, it contends, given the overwhelming evidence of Monday's guilt, this is a burden he has not met. It also notes that Monday's counsel did not object and that we have held that without a timely objection, reversal is not required "unless the conduct is 'so flagrant and ill-intentioned that it causes an enduring and resulting prejudice that could not have been neutralized by a curative instruction to the jury.' " *State v. Warren*, 165 Wash.2d 17, 43, 195 P.3d 940 (2008) (quoting *Brown*, 132 Wash.2d at 561, 940 P.2d 546). We have also said that a defendant's failure to object to a prosecutor's remarks when they are made "strongly suggests" that the remark did not appear critically prejudicial in the trial's context. *State v. Swan*, 114 Wash.2d 613, 661, 790 P.2d 610 (1990). Similarly, objecting to improper conduct but failing to request a curative instruction does not warrant reversal if an instruction could have cured the prejudice. *Warren*, 165 Wash.2d at 26, 195 P.3d 940 (citing *Yates*, 161 Wash.2d at 774, 168 P.3d 359).

The notion that the State's representative in a criminal trial, the prosecutor, should seek to achieve a conviction by resorting to racist arguments is so fundamentally opposed to our founding principles, values, and fabric of our justice system that it should not need to be explained. The Bill of Rights sought to guarantee certain fundamental rights, including the right to a fair and impartial trial. The constitutional promise of an "impartial jury trial" commands jury indifference to race. If justice is not equal for all, it is not justice. The gravity of the violation of article I, section 22 and Sixth Amendment principles by a prosecutor's intentional appeals to racial prejudices cannot be minimized or easily rationalized as harmless. Because appeals by a prosecutor to racial bias necessarily seek to single out one racial minority for different treatment, it fundamentally undermines the principle of equal justice and is so repugnant to the concept of an impartial trial that its very existence demands that appellate courts set appropriate standards to deter such conduct. If our past efforts to address prosecutorial misconduct have proved insufficient to deter such conduct, then we must apply other tested and proven tests.

Such a test exists: constitutional harmless error. E.g., *State v. Evans*, 154 Wash.2d 438, 454, 114 P.3d 627 (2005) (citing *State v. Brown*, 147 Wash.2d 330, 340, 58 P.3d 889 (2002)); see also *State v. Evans*, 96 Wash.2d 1, 4, 633 P.2d 83 (1981). Under that standard, we will vacate a conviction unless it necessarily appears, beyond a reasonable doubt, that the misconduct did not affect the verdict. We hold that when a prosecutor flagrantly or apparently intentionally appeals to racial bias in a way that undermines the defendant's credibility or the presumption of innocence, we will vacate the conviction unless it appears beyond a reasonable doubt that the misconduct did not affect the jury's verdict. We also hold that in such cases, the burden is on the State. [footnote omitted]

In this case, we cannot say beyond a reasonable doubt that the error did not contribute to the verdicts. The prosecutor's misconduct tainted nearly every lay witness's testimony. It planted the seed in the jury's mind that most of the witnesses were, at best, shading the truth to benefit the defendant. Under the circumstances, we cannot say that the misconduct did not affect the jury's verdict. [footnote omitted]

CONCLUSION

It was improper for the prosecutor to cast doubt on the credibility of the witnesses based on their race. We cannot say beyond a reasonable doubt that the impropriety did not affect jury's work. We reverse.

Note

In *McFarland v. Smith*, 611 F. 2d 414 (2d cir. 1979) below, the prosecution sought to use race to suggest its witness, who was African American would not lie concerning the defendant, and because he was African American.

MCFARLAND V. SMITH
611 F.2d 414 (2nd Cir. 1979)

NEWMAN, Circuit Judge:

This is an appeal from a denial of a petition for a writ of habeas corpus brought by a state prisoner to challenge his conviction essentially on the ground that his constitutional rights were denied by the prosecutor's inclusion of improper racial remarks in the summation.

Petitioner was found guilty by a jury of criminal sale of a controlled substance (heroin) in the second degree, N.Y. Penal Law s 220.41, and sentenced on June 2, 1976 in the New York Supreme Court (Monroe County) to a term of eight years to life. The Appellate Division affirmed without opinion, *People v. McFarland*, 59 A.D.2d 1067, 399 N.Y.S.2d 828 (4th Dept. 1977), and the New York Court of Appeals denied permission to appeal. *People v. McFarland*, 43 N.Y.2d 836, 402 N.Y.S.2d 1042 (1977). A petition for a writ of habeas corpus was denied on May 30, 1978 by the United States District Court for the Western District of New York (Hon. Harold P. Burke, Judge).

At trial, the State's case depended almost entirely on the testimony of Patricia Dorman, a Rochester undercover police officer. She testified that she purchased $450 worth of heroin from petitioner in the bedroom of a second-floor apartment. She recognized petitioner as a person she had known in high school and had since seen occasionally. The defense case depended entirely on the testimony of petitioner's friend, Isaac Singletary. He testified that he and petitioner had come to the apartment house to see two prostitutes with whom they had earlier made a date. According to Singletary, he and petitioner went upstairs to the second-floor apartment together with a Puerto Rican man who had entered the building just after they did. Singletary further testified that he waited in a front room, petitioner used the bathroom, and the Puerto Rican man entered the bedroom along with a Black woman (Dorman) and another Puerto Rican man. Singletary heard a brief discussion in the bedroom, after which the Black woman left the building. Singletary said petitioner emerged from the bathroom, they both asked the Puerto Ricans where the girls were, and when they were told there were no girls, both left. The inference from

Singletary's testimony was that Dorman had purchased narcotics from the first Puerto Rican male, and not from petitioner.

Not surprisingly the summation of defense counsel contended vigorously that Officer Dorman's version was false and Singletary's version was true.

In the course of the prosecutor's summation the following occurred:

Mr. Pappalardo (the prosecutor): . . . The officer herself being, by the book, a young woman, black woman, by the way this Defendant is black also.

Mr. King (defense counsel): Objection to the racial connatation (Sic) of individuals.

The Court: Of course I'll instruct the jury now they shall not take into consideration to any extent and use that against any individual race, color, creed makes no difference whatsoever. You may continue.

Mr. Pappalardo: I'll also instruct the jury

Mr. King: Objection.

The Court: Yes, that's improper. You cannot instruct the jury.

Mr. Pappalardo: Excuse me, I seem to be interrupted before I finish my statement because the interruption is what the People believe the People's position, as in every single case, it makes no difference what color the Defendant is. I'll finish my point. Don't you convict anyone on color or race. It makes no difference. It makes no difference to me. I hope it makes no difference to Mr. King and anybody else, but the fact is that Officer Dorman is black and the Defendant is black. That's a fact. That's a fact like you consider any other fact. If she's lying she's lying against a member, a person that (Sic) is black.

Mr. King: Objection.

The Court: Overruled.

Mr. Pappalardo: That is a proper consideration for you to examine, to think about and now she's lying against another black person. You think about it because that's what Mr. King is telling you that she's lying. Someone she knows and that's (Sic) a member of her own race. You use your common sense to think about that.

(Tr. 369-71).

The prosecutor thus urged the jury to credit Officer Dorman's testimony on the theory that the probability of truthfulness was increased by the circumstance that a Black person was testifying against another Black person. The trial judge's overruling of defense counsel's objection assured the jury that the Court accepted the propriety of this argument.

In *United States ex rel. Haynes v. McKendrick*, 481 F.2d 152 (2d Cir. 1973), this Court ruled that racial remarks in a prosecutor's summation can constitute a violation of a defendant's right under the Due Process Clause to a fair trial. Judge Oakes' opinion drew upon the line of fair trial cases beginning with *Moore v. Dempsey*, 261 U.S. 86, 43 S.Ct. 265, 67 L.Ed. 543 (1923), and the line of equal protection cases beginning with *Strauder v. West Virginia*, 100 U.S. 303, 25 L.Ed. 664 (1879), and noted that when racial prejudice is injected into a criminal trial, "the due process and equal protection clauses overlap or at least meet . . . ." 481 F.2d at 159 (footnote omitted).

The Office of the Monroe County District Attorney, which has intervened to uphold petitioner's conviction, contends that the racial remarks of the prosecutor, while "imprudent" (Intervenor's Br. 12), were not racial slurs. The remarks in Haynes involved racial slurs, and the District Attorney argues that only remarks of that category are appeals to racial prejudice that can render a conviction invalid under the Fourteenth Amendment.

Neither Haynes nor the lines of authority on which it drew set the constitutional limits for improper prosecution argument at racial slurs. Race is an impermissible basis for any adverse governmental action in the absence of compelling justification. When a prosecutor's summation includes racial remarks in an effort to persuade a jury to return a guilty verdict, the resulting conviction is constitutionally unfair unless the remarks are abundantly justified. To raise the issue of race is to draw the jury's attention to a characteristic that the Constitution generally commands us to ignore. Even a reference that is not derogatory may carry impermissible connotations, or may trigger prejudiced responses in the listeners that the speaker might neither have predicted nor intended.

This is not to say that every race-conscious argument is impermissible. Indeed, in Haynes, defense counsel, with apparent court approval, had attacked identification testimony on the ground that the eyewitness, being White, was unlikely to be able to discern distinguishing characteristics of the face of the criminal, who was Black. 481 F.2d at 160. These remarks were race-conscious, but race-neutral, since presumably an argument could be made with equal force that a Black eyewitness would have difficulty discerning the features of a White criminal. And there is some basis for accepting the validity of both contentions. Chance, Goldstein & McBride, Differential Experience and Recognition Memory for Faces, 97 J. Soc. Psych. 243 (1975); Malpass, Racial Bias in Eyewitness Identification, 1 Personality & Soc. Psych. Bull. 42 (1974); Malpass & Kravitz, Recognition for Faces of Own and Other Race, 13 J. Personality & Soc. Psych. 330 (1969); Shepherd, Deregowski & Ellis, A Cross-Cultural Study of Recognition Memory for Faces, 9 Int'l J. Psych. 205 (1975). But given the general requirement that the race of a criminal defendant must not be the basis of any adverse inference, any reference to it by a prosecutor must be justified by a compelling state interest. The issue in this case is whether the racial remarks, even if not overt racial slurs, were sufficiently justified to be countenanced.

In *People v. Hearns*, 18 A.D.2d 922, 923, 238 N.Y.S.2d 173, 174-75 (2d Dept. 1963), the Appellate Division reversed a conviction because, as in this case, the prosecutor had urged the jury to credit the testimony of Black police officers partly on the basis of their membership in the same racial group as the defendant. That argument, the Court concluded, is predicated on a false and illogical premise and constitutes an appeal to racial prejudice. Some analysis is warranted to explore that conclusion. Since the prosecutor in this case did not spell out his reasoning, one is left to consider what possible lines of reasoning might support a valid argument that the testimony of Officer Dorman is entitled to some degree of enhanced probability of truthfulness because her race is the same as the defendant's.

The analysis may begin by recognizing the obvious fact that from any group, racial or otherwise, some persons called as witnesses will testify helpfully to a defendant and some will testify accusingly. It may well be that testimony is more frequently helpful than accusing when the testimony is given within group lines (witness and defendant members of the same group) than when testimony is given across group lines (witness and defendant not members of the same group). Two circumstances would seem to support this thesis. First, alibi and character witnesses normally come from those with whom the defendant spends time, and there is a reasonable likelihood that members of his group are a disproportionately large segment of his friends and associates. Victims and by-stander witnesses who testify accusingly are less likely to be drawn disproportionately from the defendant's group (though for some crimes, victims may be). Second, when testimony is given within rather than across group lines, the incidence of helpful testimony may be further increased because of lying. Of course, of all witnesses who testify helpfully, some percentage are lying, reflecting at least whatever extent mendacity is prevalent in the total population. But in the category of helpful testimony within group lines, an extra increment of lying might occur because of the tendency of some small percentage of the members of any group to lie in an effort to be helpful to a fellow member of their group.

The prosecutor in this case might have believed that both of these circumstances operate to make the incidence of helpful testimony higher within group lines than across them, and conversely that the incidence of accusing testimony is lower within group lines than across them. In other words, if 100 instances are randomly selected where a witness and a defendant are members of the same group, and another 100 instances are randomly selected where a witness and a defendant are not members of the same group, the percentage of witnesses giving accusing testimony may well be lower in the first 100 than in the second 100.

If this is what the prosecutor believed (and was urging the jury to believe), the premise might be sound, but the conclusion that Officer Dorman's accusing testimony is more likely to be credible because given within group lines rather than across them is completely illogical. All the premise indicates is that testimony within group lines, compared to testimony across group lines, is less likely to be Accusing. But this premise provides no basis whatever for reaching any conclusion as to the likelihood that accusing testimony within group lines is Credible. Specifically, it provides no logical basis for concluding that accusing testimony within group lines is more likely to be truthful than accusing testimony across group lines. Reduced frequency of occurrence is no indicator of credibility. The pertinent analysis is not a comparison of the Incidence of accusing testimony within and across group lines, but a comparison of the Truthfulness of accusing testimony within and across group lines.

As with witnesses giving helpful testimony, some percentage of all witnesses giving accusing testimony are lying. But when accusing testimony within and across group lines is compared, another circumstance may well be at work that might affect the likelihood of credibility. This is prejudice the hostility of some few members of any group against members of a different group to such a degree that they are willing to accuse falsely. It may well be that prejudice increases the probability of lying when accusing testimony is given across group lines to a greater degree than when accusing testimony is given within group lines. To whatever extent this is so, the converse effect would be to increase the probability of truthfulness when accusing testimony is given within group lines to a greater degree than when accusing testimony is given across group lines.

If the prosecutor was basing his argument on this reasoning, his argument might have some slight logical validity, but is nonetheless constitutionally impermissible for two reasons. First, the degree of validity is highly uncertain and may well be extremely slight. It is one thing to permit race-conscious arguments to be made when comparing the reliability of facial identifications within and across racial lines, but quite another to permit such arguments with respect to comparative rates of false accusations. While there is some reason to believe that identifications are more reliably made within racial lines than across them, there is no comparable basis for confidence in comparisons about false accusations. A race-conscious argument is not constitutionally permissible unless the basis for it has a sufficiently high degree of reliability to warrant the risks inevitably taken when racial matters are injected into any important decision-making. A major risk here is that the jury will totally fail to follow the narrow reasoning process that lends any possible validity to the prosecutor's argument and instead simply be influenced adversely to the defendant because of the prosecutor's reference to his race. A further risk is that the jury will wrongly conclude that the argument draws its validity from the previously discussed premise concerning the reduced incidence of accusing testimony within group lines. If the jury accepts that reasoning, it will be accepting an argument that is, as previously pointed out, completely illogical.

There is a second reason for disallowing the argument, to whatever extent it might have logical validity. The increased credibility of accusations within group lines compared to accusations across group lines results, if at all, from the degree to which some members of one group are so prejudiced against another group that they are willing to make false accusations. When a prosecutor argues for enhanced likelihood of credibility because the accusation is within group lines, he is asking the jury to give his witness some extra credit simply because the witness is lacking the prejudice that might prompt a witness of another group to accuse falsely. The credibility of the state's witnesses should depend on an assessment of many pertinent factors, but the state should not be entitled to have its witness's credibility enhanced simply because they are not members of a group that might be prejudiced against the defendant.

This point can best be appreciated by contemplating the minor premise the prosecutor would have to explain to the jury in order to develop his reasoning fully. If a Black officer is logically entitled to any enhanced credibility when testifying against a Black defendant, it can only be because White police officers are more likely than Black police officers to give false accusing testimony against a Black defendant. If the difference is true at all, it presumably is true for all police departments, including Officer Dorman's. If to the prosecutor's knowledge some White officers of her department would falsely accuse a Black defendant, such an outrageous circumstance surely cannot be a constitutionally valid basis for enhancing the credibility of this witness for the prosecution.

Furthermore, to whatever extent prejudice increases the incidence of false accusing testimony across compared to within group lines, this circumstance supports an argument that is not race-neutral. As the intervenor acknowledged at oral argument, it is inconceivable that a prosecutor would argue to a jury that one reason to believe the accusing testimony of a police officer is that both the officer and the defendant are White.

These considerations lead to the conclusion that the prosecutor's argument is constitutionally impermissible. It invokes race for a purpose that is either illogical or of very slight and uncertain logical validity, and does so at a distinct risk of stirring racially prejudiced attitudes. The evils of racial prejudice lurk too frequently throughout the administration of criminal justice. They must be condemned whenever they appear. The Constitution forbids the racial remarks in the summation that preceded petitioner's conviction.

....

[footnotes omitted]

Note

For an in-depth discussion of race and its influence on witness credibility, see Sheri Lynn Johnson, *The Color Of Truth: Race and The Assessment Of Credibility*, 1 MICH. J. RACE & L. 261, 318- 345 (1996). Professor Johnson's article not only analyzes the problem of race influence on witness credibility but also suggests mechanism for addressing the problem.

Chapter Twelve: Race and Change of Venue

Note

The issue of race and change of venue came to the forefront in 1991 as a result of the Rodney King beating and the subsequent civil upheaval. The image of Rodney King, an African American, being beaten and kicked by White Los Angeles police officers following a traffic stop, shocked and galvanized a nation. Following nationwide coverage of civilian videotape of the beating, LAPD Officers Laurence Powell, Theodore J. Briseno, Stacey C. Koon, and Timothy E. Wind were charged with assault by force likely to produce great bodily injury, among other offenses. The police officers quickly moved for a change of venue to move the trial outside of Los Angeles County, which had a significant number of African American and Latino perspective jurors, citing, among other things that national attention and pretrial publicity ,combined with racial turmoil, claiming that a fair trial was not possible.

The initial trial judge denied the request, finding that Los Angeles County had successfully tried numerous high-profile, notorious cases and that the county was sufficiently large and diverse to allow for a fair trial with the use of a thorough voir dire to eliminate bias. Subsequently the defendants sought a writ of mandamus from the Court of Appeals compelling the trial court to change venue.

In *Powell v. Superior Court*, 232 Cal. App. 3d 785 (1991) the Court of Appeals granted the petition for mandamus challenging the trial court's refusal to change venue. In doing so the Court found that the nature and extent of the publicity arising out of the conduct of the defendants in the arrest and apprehension of a Rodney King established more than a reasonable likelihood that a fair and impartial trial could not be held in Los Angeles County. In granting the petition the Court did not directly address or resolve the issue of the role that racial diversity should play in determining an appropriate new venue. Instead the Court stated:

> We leave the ultimate selection of a site for a fair trial to the trial court with directions to weigh
> the various factors bearing upon the selection of a forum free from the unacceptable risk that
> a fair trial cannot be conducted. 232 Cal. App. 3d at 803. In *Powell* the trial in the new venue
> resulted in an all-white jury

The concept of venue concerns itself with where geographically a case may be tried and is distinguishable from jurisdiction; which refers to the power of the court to try a case, and vicinage; which involves from where a jury may selected. Both venue and vicinage have constitutional roots in the United States Constitution, in its language which states : "the trial of all Crimes... shall be held in the State where the said Crimes shall have been committed... (venue) (United States Constitution Art. III, Sec. 2) and "by an impartial jury of the State and district wherein the crime shall have been committed" (Sixth Amendment, United States Constitution). Issues of venue and vicinage present "deep issues of public policy", *United States v. Johnson,* 323 U.S. 273 (1944), because of the concern that such trial settings may cause significant hardship and unfairness and thus negatively impact fair trial.

It is for that reason that all jurisdictions provide that a defendant may request a change of venue. As in *Powell* both the federal and state systems provide that upon motion of the defendant, the trial court may change venue if it is satisfied that there exists "so great a prejudice against the defendant that he cannot obtain a fair and impartial trial at any place fixed by law..." See, Rule 21 (a) FEDERAL RULES OF CRIMINAL PROCEDURE. There is a constitutional obligation to make available a change of venue in the presence of prejudicial pretrial publicity. *Groppi v. Wisconsin,* 400 U.S. 505 (1971).

Powell directly concerned itself with impact of pretrial pubilicity and media coverage of a racially volatile confrontation on fair trial. In *Rideau v. Louisiana,* 373 U.S. 723 (1963), *Estes v. Texas,* 381 U.S. 532 (1965) and more recently in *Skilling v. United States,* 561 U.S. 358 (2010), the Supreme Court sought to balance the First Amendment interest of free press with the guarantee off fair trial. As noted in *Skilling* a presumption of unfair trial may be found where it is determined that the trial atmosphere has been utterly corrupted by press coverage. While the corruption and unfair impact may be corrected by providing individual and extensive voir dire, such is not required in extreme cases, and is left to the trial judge to determine expanded voir dire is appropriate. *Mu'Min v. Virginia,* 500 U.S. 415 (1991).

The issue of relocation of trial following a change of venue, raises additional concerns regarding implementation of the "fair cross-section" requirement of the Sixth Amendment. Given that the interest in a diverse jury in order to afford fair public trial, is an interest shared by both the prosecution and the public, See, *In Re Winship,* 397 U.S. 358 (1970), *Taylor v. Louisiana,* 419 U.S. 522, 530 (1975).

The issue of potential exclusion or under-representation of persons of color in jury venires following a change of venue, and the defendant's right to fair trial is not only at the center of the *Powell* decision but takes on an additional complication in the following case where both the defendant is non-white (Latino) and the impacted community were the purported crime was committed has a different significant community of color (African American).

584 So.2d 19 (3rd Dist. Ct. App. 1991)

PER CURIAM.

Appellant, William Lozano (Lozano), appeals his convictions and sentences on two counts of manslaughter. We reverse for a new trial.

FACTS

Lozano was employed as a City of Miami police officer. On the day of the incident giving rise to the convictions, and unknown to Lozano, Clement Lloyd (Lloyd) and Allan Blanchard (Blanchard), two males riding a motorcycle, were committing a traffic infraction some distance away. Another police unit attempted to stop the motorcycle to issue a citation, but it sped away and a chase ensued.

The police unit followed the motorcycle as it travelled in the direction of Lozano. As the chase neared Lozano's location, Lozano and his partner could hear the siren of an approaching police vehicle, and could even see the flashing emergency lights.

As the vehicles approached, Lozano stepped into the street on which the vehicles travelled. Within seconds, the driver and passenger of the motorcycle lay dead: Lloyd, the driver, shot by Lozano; Blanchard, the passenger, dead from the resultant crash.

Within minutes, the neighborhood erupted into civil disturbances. Normal police procedures could not be followed. The scene of the shooting was not preserved, and vital physical evidence was lost.

The riots were extensively reported by the media. The media coverage was further increased by the presence of national and international reporters in Miami to cover the Super Bowl. The Miami riots became world news.

Because of the extensive media coverage and the facts that violence had followed both the incident itself and prior acquittals in similar so-called police brutality cases, Lozano sought a change of venue. In support of his motion for that relief, he provided the court with more than 375 affidavits, 500 newspaper articles, as well as with other supporting exhibits.

Lozano also sought a hearing on the motion, in order to present live testimony regarding the widespread concern over the prospect of unrest in the area if there were verdicts of not guilty. The trial court denied the motion for a change of venue, and it denied Lozano a full-scale hearing on the motion. The case proceeded to trial.

....

CHANGE OF VENUE

Appellant contends that the failure to grant the motion for a change of venue, and the denial of a hearing on the motion, constitute an abuse of discretion. Appellant argues that such abuse deprived him of a fair trial.

The courts of this State have steadfastly held to two major principles: (1) that the application for a change of venue is addressed to the sound discretion of the trial court; and, (2) that in determining a motion for a change of venue, of utmost consideration is whether the defendant can obtain a fair and impartial trial.3 In addressing these two considerations, the Florida Supreme Court stated:

> [A] determination must be made as to whether the general state of mind of the inhabitants of a community is so infected by knowledge of the incident and accompanying prejudice, bias, and preconceived opinions that jurors could not possibly put these matters out of their minds and try the case solely on the evidence presented in the courtroom.

Manning v. State, 378 So.2d at 276 (citing *McCaskill v. State*, 344 So.2d 1276 (Fla.1977)).
In determining the necessity for a change of venue, the court:

> Must liberally resolve in favor of the defendant any doubt as to the ability of the State to furnish a defendant a trial by fair and impartial jury.

Singer v. State, 109 So.2d at 14.

Where the evidence presented reflects prejudice, bias, and preconceived opinions, the trial court is bound to grant the motion. Manning v. State, 378 So.2d at 276.

The State correctly sets forth the test for judging a claim of prejudice in a denial for a change of venue:

> [T]he defendant has the burden of coming forward and showing that the setting of the trial is inherently prejudicial because of the general atmosphere and the state of mind of the inhabitants of the community.

Manning v. State, 378 So.2d at 276; see <u>Murphy v. Florida</u>, 421 U.S. 794, 95 S.Ct. 2031, 44 L.Ed.2d 589 (1975).

This case also invokes the doctrine, founded upon the Sixth Amendment right to an impartial jury, that every criminal defendant is entitled to a trial free of prejudice inherent in the circumstances which present an "unacceptable risk ... of impermissible factors coming into play." *Estelle v. Williams*, 425 U.S. 501, 505, 96 S.Ct. 1691, 1693, 48 L.Ed.2d 126, 131 (1976); *Sheppard v.*

Maxwell, 384 U.S. 333, 86 S.Ct. 1507, 16 L.Ed.2d 600 (1966); *Estes v. Texas*, 381 U.S. 532, 85 S.Ct. 1628, 14 L.Ed.2d 543, rehearing denied, 382 U.S. 875, 86 S.Ct. 18, 15 L.Ed.2d 118 (1965); *Rideau v. Louisiana*, 373 U.S. 723, 83 S.Ct. 1417, 10 L.Ed.2d 663 (1963); *Irvin v. Dowd*, 366 U.S. 717, 81 S.Ct. 1639, 6 L.Ed.2d 751 (1961); *Woods v. Dugger*, 923 F.2d 1454 (11th Cir.1991); *Norris v. Risley*, 918 F.2d 828 (9th Cir.1990).

Applying these principles, we must conclude that even the limited, yet uncontroverted, evidence presented by Lozano required a holding that the case could not then be fairly tried in Dade County. We simply cannot approve the result of a trial conducted, as was this one, in an atmosphere in which the entire community—including the jury—was so obviously, and, it must be said, so justifiably concerned with the dangers which would follow an acquittal, but which would be and were obviated if, as actually occurred, the defendant was convicted. Surely, the fear that one's own county would respond to a not guilty verdict by erupting into violence is as highly "impermissible [a] factor," *Estelle v. Williams*, 425 U.S. at 505, 96 S.Ct. at 1693, as can be contemplated. Surely too, there was an overwhelmingly "unacceptable risk," *Turner v. Louisiana*, 379 U.S. 466, 473, 85 S.Ct. 546, 550, 13 L.Ed.2d 424, 429 (1965), of its having adversely affected Lozano's—and every citizen's—most basic right under our system: the one to a fair determination of his guilt or innocence based on the evidence alone. The trial court's failure to grant the motion for a change of venue, therefore, mandates reversal for a new trial.

Although we find that the circumstances at the time of trial were such that the trial court erred in not granting a change of venue at that point, we do not mandate a transfer of venue after remand. Instead, that question will be resolved below, after hearing, on the basis of the conditions existing at the time of any such motion.

....

Note

Although a request for change of venue, in light of the mandates of the Sixth Amendment, are largely defense motions, the issue of racial diversity – specifically the underrepresentation of potential non-white jurors, can still be an issue where the defendant moves for a venue change for reasons the racial implications of the charge and is moved to a new venue where the defendant is no better, if not worse, off in terms of potential non-white jurors.

Opinion

RENDLEN, Judge.

Movant was convicted of first degree murder for killing Missouri State Highway Patrolman James Froemsdorf and was sentenced to death in the Circuit Court of Schuyler County. His conviction and sentence were affirmed on direct appeal in *State v. Mallett*, 732 S.W.2d 527 (Mo. banc 1987), where the facts surrounding the crime are detailed. Movant subsequently instituted this Rule 27.26 proceeding, and, after two written amendments by movant's counsel, an evidentiary hearing was held before the Honorable Ronald M. Belt, who was assigned the case as Special Judge. Finding three of movant's claims meritorious, Judge Belt entered an order vacating movant's sentence and requiring that movant be "tried in a venue where there is a possibility of blacks being on the jury." The state appealed the vacation of the sentence and movant cross-appealed, contending the motion court erred in not granting relief on other grounds alleged in his motion. The Court of Appeals, Western District transferred the appeal prior to opinion in compliance with our policy concerning 27.26 proceedings where the underlying conviction resulted in imposition of the death penalty. We reverse.

The state asserts on appeal that the motion court erred in concluding movant's due process and equal protection rights were violated by the trial court's selection of Schuyler County as the venue for movant's trial and in holding that movant did not receive effective assistance of counsel because of counsel's failure to object to a mitigating circumstances instruction that contained an erroneously numbered reference to another instruction. In examining the contentions of error, we bear in mind that appellate review of the motion court's decision in a 27.26 proceeding is limited to a determination of whether its findings, conclusions and judgment are clearly erroneous. *Sanders v. State*, 738 S.W.2d 856, 857 (Mo. banc 1987).

Initially we consider the questions raised concerning the trial court's transfer of venue to Schuyler County. Trooper Froemsdorf was murdered in Perry County, which is situated along the Mississippi River in Southeast Missouri, and movant was originally brought before the court in that county. Movant requested a change of venue, and after his counsel and the state were unable to reach agreement on venue, each party suggested certain counties of their own preference to Judge Murphy during argument on defendant's motion. The state mentioned Texas, Phelps, Clay, and Clinton Counties, while defense counsel named St. Louis City and the Counties of St. Louis, Jackson, and Boone, then added Buchanan and Adair. Movant's counsel expressed a concern that venue be moved to a community where there was a possibility of blacks appearing on the jury because movant is black. After the discussion Judge Murphy stated that he had in mind a county not included on either list and "very far and north of here." He subsequently entered an order transferring venue to Schuyler County, located along the Iowa border and containing, according to 1980 census statistics, 4964 white persons and three black persons. See U.S. Bureau of Census, Census of Population and Housing (1980). Judge Webber, who presided during the trial, testified at the 27.26 hearing he was not aware of any blacks living in Schuyler County at the time of movant's trial.

Movant asserted in his 27.26 motion that he was denied due process by the change of venue, and the motion court agreed, stating "an arbitrary choice of venue without giving the defense an opportunity to be heard; and the fact that the county chosen denies the movant of (sic) any opportunity of members of his own race being on the jury panel; and the fact that the case involves a black man killing a white trooper which has a high possibility for racial prejudice being a factor; violates the due process clause."

A fundamentally fair trial is the basic requirement of due process, and in most cases a showing of identifiable prejudice to the accused is necessary. *Estes v. State of Texas*, 381 U.S. 532, 85 S.Ct. 1628, 1633, 14 L.Ed.2d 543 (1965). It is also true that "at times a procedure employed by the State involves such a probability that prejudice will result that it is deemed inherently lacking in due process." Id.; see also *Sheppard v. Maxwell*, 384 U.S. 333, 86 S.Ct. 1507, 16 L.Ed.2d 600 (1966). However, in this case we believe the motion court clearly erred in concluding movant did not receive a fundamentally fair trial. The lack of potential black jurors and the issue of racial prejudice were discussed at length in our previous opinion on direct appeal of the conviction. In determining whether movant's death sentence was imposed under the influence of passion, prejudice, or the arbitrary factor of race, we stated that the voir dire examination provided "direct evidence that the jurors were not motivated by racism," and "[l]acking any other evidence, defendant urges that this Court assume racial bias because, while he is black and his victim was white, the county in which he was tried had no black residents, which resulted in a jury panel without blacks." *Mallett*, 732 S.W.2d at 539. We declined "to infer racial prejudice on the part of a jury which sentences a black killer of a white victim to death simply because that jury was drawn from a county which has no black residents[,]" and noted "[t]o hold that racial prejudice may be inferred from the absence of members of the defendant's race on the jury would be, in practical effect, to hold that the defendant has a right to members of his own race on the jury. A defendant, however, has no right to a jury of any particular racial composition. *Taylor v. Louisiana*, 419 U.S. 522, 538, 95 S.Ct. 692, 701, 42 L.Ed.2d 690 (1975); *State v. Blair*, 638 S.W.2d 739, 753 (Mo. banc 1982), cert. denied, 459 U.S. 1188, 103 S.Ct. 838, 74 L.Ed.2d 1030 (1983)." Id. at 540. We further rejected an argument that the trial of a black in a county with no black residents inherently results in a jury motivated by prejudice. *Id.* The fact that the murder victim was white and defendant was tried in a county without blacks is insufficient to establish identifiable prejudice to the defendant, and we do not find the change of venue procedure utilized here created such a high probability of prejudice that it was inherently lacking in due process;

indeed, as previously discussed, all the evidence, including the transcript of voir dire, indicates defendant received a fair trial by an impartial jury.

The third factor mentioned by the motion court was the purported lack of opportunity for the movant to be heard. We note in this regard that movant was able to, and did, express his venue preferences as well as his concern that there be potential black jurors. We see little significance in the fact there was no further hearing after venue was decided. The procedure here followed that specified in Rule 32.03. The motion court clearly erred in finding that movant was denied due process because the venue was changed to Schuyler County.

We next address the state's contention that the motion court erred in concluding movant was denied equal protection by the change of venue. To establish an equal protection violation, a defendant must prove the existence of purposeful discrimination and that the purposeful discrimination had a discriminatory effect on him. *McCleskey v. Kemp*, 481 U.S. 279, 107 S.Ct. 1756, 1766, 95 L.Ed.2d 262 (1987). Assuming arguendo that a change of venue from a county with few blacks to one with none has a discriminatory effect on a defendant for purposes of equal protection analysis, we find a complete void of evidence that Judge Murphy's venue decision was animated by a discriminatory purpose. Movant has not shown that Judge Murphy treated him differently than white defendants or that Judge Murphy systematically used the change of venue procedures to ensure that black defendants would be tried by white juries. Nor is there evidence indicating Judge Murphy was aware of the racial composition of Schuyler County; however, if so, "discriminatory purpose implies more than intent as volition or intent as awareness of consequences. It implies that the decisionmaker ... selected or reaffirmed a particular course of action at least in part 'because of,' not merely 'in spite of,' its adverse effects upon an identifiable group." Personnel Administrator of *Massachusetts v. Feeney*, 442 U.S. 256, 99 S.Ct. 2282, 2296, 60 L.Ed.2d 870 (1979). See also McCleskey, 107 S.Ct. at 1769; *Wayte v. United States*, 470 U.S. 598, 105 S.Ct. 1524, 1532, 84 L.Ed.2d 547 (1985).

The motion court relied on *Batson v. Kentucky*, 476 U.S. 79, 106 S.Ct. 1712, 90 L.Ed.2d 69 (1986), in concluding "this court need not find that Judge Murphy acted with a discriminatory purpose, [however,] this court finds that an inference of discriminatory purpose exists." (Emphasis in original.) Batson, of course, involved the use of peremptory strikes by prosecutors to exclude blacks from serving on juries, and the Supreme Court held there that a defendant may make a prima facia case of discrimination by establishing: 1) he is a member of a cognizable racial group and the prosecutor has exercised peremptory challenges to remove from the venire members of the defendant's race; 2) the practice in question permits "those who are of a mind to discriminate to discriminate," and 3) these facts and other relevant circumstances raise an inference that the prosecutor used that practice to exclude the veniremen from the jury on account of their race. Id. 106 S.Ct. at 1723. Once a prima facia case is established, the prosecution may come forward with a neutral explanation that rebuts the inference. *Id.* We find Batson of limited usefulness in analyzing movant's claim, which involves procedures for changing venue and has nothing to do with prosecutorial discretion or peremptory challenges.2 As noted in *McCleskey*, 107 S.Ct. at 1767, jury selection is one of the "limited contexts" in which statistics have been accepted as proof of intent to discriminate. Of course, we need not decide whether statistical proof may be accepted in the context of change of venue procedures, for movant has presented none.

The "facts" upon which the motion court based its decision were stated as follows: "1) the case involves a cross-racial murder of a state trooper; 2) the decision of Judge Murphy was made without giving counsel an opportunity to object; 3) counties which were of equal convenience to witnesses; equally free of pre-trial publicity; of equal, greater or less distance; and included blacks were tendered by the defense and prosecution; 4) no specific or compelling reason existed to send the case to Schuyler County; 5) there were no blacks living in Schulyer County at the time of trial; 6) movant is a black man; 7) the defense expressed concern that the county chosen include blacks." These "facts" are wholly inadequate under equal protection precedent to establish even an inference of discriminatory purpose when considered in the context of the "totality of relevant facts". *Batson*, 106 S.Ct. at 1721. As we stated in our previous opinion on direct appeal, "it can be assumed that venue was changed to Schuyler County in order to get the case moved as far north as possible to a county where reports of Trooper Froemsdorf's killing may have received less attention. There is not the slightest suggestion that race was a consideration in the decision to change the venue to Schuyler County." 732 S.W.2d at 540. Based upon the evidence adduced at the 27.26 hearing, we may now add that Judge Murphy selected a neutral site not suggested by either party. Movant's evidence falls short of the "exceptionally clear proof" required before it may be inferred that Judge Murphy abused his discretion, *McCleskey*, 107 S.Ct. at 1769, and the motion court clearly erred in concluding movant was denied equal protection.

We next address the state's contention that the motion court erred in determining movant was denied effective assistance of counsel by counsel's failure to specifically object to an erroneous reference in Instruction No. 24 (MAI–Cr2d 13.44) to Instruction No. 21 (MAI–Cr2d 13.40) instead of Instruction No. 23 (MAI–Cr2d 13.42). MAI–Cr2d 13.44 submits mitigating circumstances to the jury and provides in part: "If you decide that one or more sufficient aggravating circumstances exist to warrant the imposition of death, as submitted in Instruction No. ---, you must then determine whether one or more mitigating circumstances exist which outweigh the aggravating circumstance or circumstances so found to exist." The blank is to be filled in with the number given to the instruction patterned after MAI–Cr2d 13.42, which instructs the jury on weighing both statutory and nonstatutory aggravating factors, see MAI–Cr2d 13.44 note on use 2; however, the trial court erroneously inserted the number of the instruction patterned after MAI–Cr2d 13.40, which submits statutory aggravating factors.

In order to prevail on a claim of ineffective assistance of counsel, a defendant must establish that his attorney failed to exercise the customary skill and diligence that a reasonably competent attorney would perform under similar circumstances and that he was thereby prejudiced. *Sanders*, 738 S.W.2d at 857 (citing *Strickland v. Washington*, 466 U.S. 668, 104 S.Ct. 2052, 80 L.Ed.2d

674 (1984)). In reviewing such claims, a court need not determine the performance component before examining for prejudice, and if it is easier to dispose of the claim on the ground of lack of sufficient prejudice, the reviewing court is free to do so. Id. To establish prejudice, "the defendant must show that there is a reasonable probability that, but for counsel's unprofessional errors, the result of the proceeding would have been different. A reasonable probability is a probability sufficient to undermine confidence in the outcome." *Strickland v. Washington*, 466 U.S. 668, 104 S.Ct. 2052, 2068, 80 L.Ed.2d 674 (1984). The motion court apparently found prejudice because "movant was deprived of the right to have the Supreme Court review the error[,]" noting, "This Court cannot speculate as to how the Missouri Supreme Court might have ruled the matter." We hold that the motion court clearly erred in determining that movant was prejudiced by counsel's failure to object to the instruction.

Movant argues that the erroneous reference in Instruction No. 24 prevented the jury from weighing the mitigating circumstances against the nonstatutory aggravating circumstances and that several of the mitigating circumstances were submitted to address specific nonstatutory aggravating circumstances. The question is what a reasonable juror could have understood the charge as meaning, and if the specific instruction fails constitutional muster we review the instructions as a whole to see if the entire charge delivered a correct interpretation of the law. *California v. Brown*, 479 U.S. 538, 107 S.Ct. 837, 839, 93 L.Ed.2d 934 (1987). Movant's argument is untenable upon a reading of the instructions given the jury. Instruction No. 26 (MAI–Cr2d 13.46) informed the jury that: "You are not compelled to fix death as the punishment even if you do not find the existence of one or more mitigating circumstances sufficient to outweigh the aggravating circumstance or circumstances which you find to exist. You must consider all the circumstances in deciding whether to assess and declare the punishment at death. Whether that is to be your final decision rests with you." If not already clear from Instruction 24, Instruction No. 26 informed the jury they could consider all the circumstances in assessing punishment. Certainly they were not precluded from considering any of the mitigating factors and balancing them against any of the aggravating factors. Furthermore, accepting for the sake of argument movant's contention that the jury would have construed the references in Instruction 24 to "aggravating circumstances" as applying only to statutory aggravating circumstances, the jury would then have believed they must return a verdict of life imprisonment if they found the mitigating circumstances outweighed the statutory aggravating circumstances, making the nonstatutory aggravating circumstances superfluous at that point in the deliberation. MAI–Cr2d 13.44. Such a reading would be beneficial, not prejudicial, to movant. Movant totally failed to establish a reasonable probability that, but for the failure to object, the outcome would have been different, and the motion court clearly erred in determining that he received ineffective assistance of counsel.

We now turn to the issues raised by movant in his cross-appeal. First, movant contends the motion court erred in concluding his claim of denial of due process in connection with the trial judge's failure to recuse was not cognizable in this 27.26 proceeding because it was abandoned on direct appeal. Rule 27.26(b)(3). Alternatively, the motion court found that Judge Webber was not biased against movant. We believe the motion court did not clearly err in rejecting movant's claim. A proceeding under Rule 27.26 is not a substitute for appeal. *O'Neal v. State*, 486 S.W.2d 206, 207 (Mo.1972). "Trial errors cannot be brought within the scope of Rule 27.26 by simply alleging as a conclusion that they result in an unfair or impartial (sic) trial, or that they affected constitutional rights." *Id.* at 208. Although movant attempts to cloak his claim in constitutional attire, he alleges only that there was "an appearance of impropriety." Furthermore, the very issue movant now seeks to raise was presented in his motion for new trial. We find no clear error in the motion court's ruling on this point.

Movant also challenges the motion court's categorization of his claim concerning the trial court's failure to grant a change of venue from Schuyler County as trial error. Movant asserted he was denied his right to due process by the trial court's denial of his change of venue motion, which was filed on the first day of trial. The essence of movant's claim was addressed and rejected by this Court on direct appeal. *Mallett*, 732 S.W.2d at 539–40. "[A] matter decided on direct appeal may not be relitigated in post-conviction relief proceedings even if movant offers a different theory." *Schlup v. State*, 758 S.W.2d 715, 716 (Mo. banc 1988). The motion court did not clearly err in denying movant relief on this claim.

Movant further contends the motion court erred in ruling the statutory aggravating circumstance of "depravity of mind" was not unconstitutionally vague. On direct appeal we found sufficient evidence to support the jury's finding the murder outrageously or wantonly vile, horrible, or inhuman in that it involved depravity of mind. *Mallett*, 732 S.W.2d at 542. The evidence indicated the victim had been subjected to serious physical abuse and that movant's actions were in callous disregard for the sanctity of human life. *State v. Griffin*, 756 S.W.2d 475, 489–90 (Mo. banc 1988). The motion court did not err in ruling the aggravating circumstance of "depravity of mind" was not unconstitutionally vague in this context. *Jones v. State*, 767 S.W.2d 41 at 45 (Mo. banc 1989).

Finally, we address the purported failure of the motion court to rule on movant's claim of ineffective appellate counsel in connection with counsel's decision not to advance his claim concerning the trial court's failure to strike venireman Karen Long for cause. Although the motion court specifically mentioned the claim regarding juror Long, the ruling on that claim is not stated with particularity; however, we hold the findings and conclusions indicate the motion court's rejection of that claim and are sufficient for appellate review. The standard for reviewing a claim of ineffective appellate counsel is essentially the same as that employed with trial counsel; movant is expected to show both a breach of duty and resulting prejudice. *Blackmon v. White*, 825 F.2d 1263, 1265 (8th Cir.1987). There is "no duty to raise every possible issue asserted in the motion for new trial on appeal[,]" *Camillo v. State*, 757 S.W.2d 234, 241 (Mo.App.1988), and the motion court noted that appellate counsel has no duty to present non-frivolous issues where appellate counsel strategically decides to "winnow out" arguments in favor of other arguments, citing *Jones v. Barnes*, 463 U.S. 745, 103 S.Ct. 3308, 3312–13, 77 L.Ed.2d 987 (1983). The court stated: "In light of the fourteen issues presented by appellate counsel on direct appeal, this appears to be exactly what appellate counsel was doing." Despite counsel's decision to select and present the strongest contentions of error, the appellate brief submitted exceeded this Court's 100-page limitation, but was nonetheless accepted and considered. The motion court concluded with regard to the issues movant claimed should have been briefed, "counsel testified that she considered raising each one of them, but declined to do so. She considered those issues weaker than the issues she actually raised on direct appeal." We have examined the transcript of voir dire, as well as counsel's testimony at the 27.26 hearing, and find that appellate counsel did not breach her duty to movant.

For the reasons stated in this opinion, the motion court's order vacating movant's sentence is reversed and his 27.26 motion is overruled.

In *Hobbs v. State*, 617 S.W. 2d 347 (Ark. 1981) the Court reached a similar conclusion stating, "There is no constitutional right to a trial in a county most demographically like that in which the crime occurred. There is no right to a jury composed of a particular race." 617 S.W. 2d at 353. Similarly, Wisconsin although recognizing that an additional change of venue may be appropriate where the initial transferee district will not provide for a fair trial, has held that a defendant is not entitled to such relief unless it can be proven that there was systematic exclusion of potential jurors from the venire based on race. *Sanders v. State*, 230 N.W. 2d 845 (Wis. 1975).

Chapter Thirteen: Race and Jury Misconduct During Deliberations

Note

The prohibition against individual jurors impeaching the verdict of a jury has been a long-standing principle. It is embodied in Federal Rules of Evidence 606 which provides;

(b) During an Inquiry Into the Validity of a Verdict or Indictment.

(1) Prohibited Testimony or Other Evidence. During an inquiry into the validity of a verdict or indictment, a juror may not testify about any statement made or incident that occurred during the jury's deliberations; the effect of anything on that juror's or another juror's vote; or any juror's mental processes concerning the verdict or indictment. The court may not receive a juror's affidavit or evidence of a juror's statement on these matters.

(2) Exceptions. A juror may testify about whether:

(A) extraneous prejudicial information was improperly brought to the jury's attention;

(B) an outside influence was improperly brought to bear on any juror; or

(C) a mistake was made in entering the verdict on the verdict form.

The rationale behind such restrictions rest on policies supporting secret jury deliberations, the stability of verdicts, the finality of judgments, protection of jurors from harassment and preventing jurors from second-guessing their votes. Despite the long history of support for such policies, troubling examples of unchecked and un-remedied influence of racism in the jury deliberation process has plagued the criminal justice in numerous instances, including Native Americans, African Americans and Latinos. The tension between protecting the values associated with the principles represented in Fed. Rule of Evid. 606(b) and the concerns for fair trial, have led to a split in positions at both the federal and state levels. Symbolic of that split are the opinions below taken from the United States Court of Appeals for the Tenth Circuit and the United States Court of Appeals for the Ninth Circuit.

UNITED STATES V. BENALLY

546 F.3d 1230 (10th Cir. 2008)

McCONNELL, Circuit Judge.

On October 10, 2007, a jury convicted Kerry Dean Benally of forcibly assaulting a Bureau of Indian Affairs officer with a dangerous weapon, in violation of 18 U.S.C. § 111(b). The next day one of the jurors came forward with a charge that the jury deliberations had been tainted by racial bias and other inappropriate considerations. The district court held that Federal Rule of Evidence 606(b)'s general rule against jurors testifying about jury deliberations did not apply and that the evidence of juror misconduct was sufficient to warrant a new trial. We disagree. Rule 606(b)'s prohibition covers juror testimony of racial bias in jury deliberations of the kind alleged in Mr. Benally's trial, and the Sixth Amendment does not require an exception. The original conviction is reinstated.

I. BACKGROUND

Mr. Benally, a member of the Ute Mountain Ute tribe, was charged with forcibly assaulting a Bureau of Indian Affairs officer with a dangerous weapon. Prior to trial, he submitted several voir dire questions aimed at uncovering potential bias against Native Americans. The judge asked two of those questions at voir dire: "Would the fact that the defendant is a Native American affect your evaluation of the case?" and "Have you ever had a negative experience with any individuals of Native American descent? And, if so, would that experience affect your evaluation of the facts of this case?" No juror answered affirmatively to either question. The case proceeded to trial and the jury found Mr. Benally guilty.

The day after the jury announced its verdict, one juror approached defense counsel with unsettling information. This juror-"Juror K.C."-claimed that the jury deliberation had been improperly influenced by racist claims about Native Americans. The foreman, according to Juror K.C., told the other jurors that he used to live on or near an Indian Reservation, that "[w]hen Indians get alcohol, they all get drunk," and that when they get drunk, they get violent. Juror K.C. said that when she then argued with the foreman that not all Native Americans get drunk, the foreman insisted, "Yes, they do." Juror K.C. claimed that at that point a second juror chimed in to say that she had also lived on or near a reservation.

While Juror K.C. could not hear the rest of this juror's statement, it was "clear she was agreeing with the foreman's statement about Indians." Juror K.C. continued to argue with the foreman, going back and forth several times.

She also told defense counsel about another discussion in which some jurors discussed the need to "send a message back to the reservation." During this second discussion, Juror. K.C. says that one juror told how he had two family members in law enforcement and had "heard stories from them about what happens when people mess with police officers and get away with it."

Juror K.C. signed an affidavit attesting to both of these discussions. A defense investigator then contacted another juror who seems to have corroborated some of Juror K.C.'s claims, but this second juror was unwilling to sign an affidavit. The defense investigator did, however, sign an affidavit saying that the second juror "indicated that the jury foreman made a statement regarding Indians and drinking" and "said something like he had seen a lot of Indians that drink."

The investigator also testified that the juror recalled a statement about "sending a message back to the reservation."

Armed with these two affidavits, Mr. Benally moved to vacate the verdict and receive a new trial pursuant to Rule 33 of the Federal Rules of Criminal Procedure. He argued that the jurors had lied about their racial bias on voir dire and had improperly considered information not in evidence. The government opposed the motion on the ground that Mr. Benally's only evidence of misconduct was inadmissible under Rule 606(b). That rule states, in relevant part:

Upon an inquiry into the validity of a verdict or indictment, a juror may not testify as to any matter or statement occurring during the course of the jury's deliberations or to the effect of anything upon that or any other juror's mind or emotions as influencing the juror to assent to or dissent from the verdict or indictment or concerning the juror's mental processes in connection therewith.

Rule 606(b) provides three limited exceptions to this general prohibition against jurors testifying about jury deliberations:

But a juror may testify about (1) whether extraneous prejudicial information was improperly brought to the jury's attention, (2) whether any outside influence was improperly brought to bear upon any juror, or (3) whether there was a mistake in entering the verdict onto the verdict form.

The district court admitted the juror testimony under the exceptions that allow jurors to testify about "whether extraneous prejudicial information was improperly brought to the jury's attention" or "whether any outside influence was improperly brought to bear upon any juror." Dist. Ct.Op. 2. Relying upon this evidence, the judge found that two jurors had lied on voir dire when they failed to reveal their past experiences with Native Americans and their preconception that all Native Americans get drunk and then violent. He also found that the jury had improperly considered extrinsic evidence when the juror whose family was in law enforcement related stories that showed the need to send a message. The judge viewed each of these as sufficient evidence of misconduct and granted a new trial. The government then appealed.

II. ANALYSIS

"When the affidavit of a juror, as to the misconduct of himself or the other members of the jury, is made the basis of a motion for a new trial, the court must choose between redressing the injury of the private litigant and inflicting the public injury which would result if jurors were permitted to testify as to what happened in the jury room." *McDonald v. Pless*, 238 U.S. 264, 267, 35 S.Ct. 783, 59 L.Ed. 1300 (1915). This case illustrates the tension between those interests. A juror has offered testimony that the verdict may have been influenced by improper arguments predicated on racial stereotyping and a need to send a message; but Mr. Benally can obtain redress (in the form of a new trial) only if that juror's testimony is admissible. Rule 606(b)says it is not.

A. The History and Purpose of Rule 606(b)

The rule against impeachment of a jury verdict by juror testimony as to internal deliberations may be traced back to "Mansfield's Rule," originating in the 1785 case of *Vaise v. Delaval*, 99 Eng. Rep. 944 (K.B.1785). Faced with juror testimony that the jury had reached its verdict by drawing lots, Lord Mansfield established a blanket ban on jurors testifying against their own verdict. The rule was adopted by most American jurisdictions and "[b]y the beginning of [the twentieth] century, if not earlier, the near-universal and firmly established common-law rule in the United States flatly prohibited the admission of juror testimony to impeach a jury verdict." *Tanner v. United States*, 483 U.S. 107, 117, 107 S.Ct. 2739, 97 L.Ed.2d 90 (1987). This common-law principle, together with exceptions also developed by common law, was eventually codified into Federal Rule of Evidence 606(b).

Rule 606(b) is a rule of evidence, but its role in the criminal justice process is substantive: it insulates the deliberations of the jury from subsequent second-guessing by the judiciary. Jury decision-making is designed to be a black box: the inputs (evidence and argument) are carefully regulated by law and the output (the verdict) is publicly announced, but the inner workings and deliberation of the jury are deliberately insulated from subsequent review. Judges instruct the jury as to the law, but have no way of knowing whether the jurors follow those instructions. Judges and lawyers speak to the jury about how to evaluate the evidence, but cannot tell how the jurors decide among conflicting testimony or facts. Juries are told to put aside their prejudices and preconceptions, but no one knows whether they do so. Juries provide no reasons, only verdicts.

To treat the jury as a black box may seem to offend the search for perfect justice. The rule makes it difficult and in some cases impossible to ensure that jury verdicts are based on evidence and law rather than bias or caprice. But our legal system is grounded on the conviction, borne out by experience, that decisions by ordinary citizens are likely, over time and in the great majority of cases, to approximate justice more closely than more transparently law-bound decisions by professional jurists. Indeed, it might even be that the jury's ability to be *irrational*, as when it refuses to apply a law against a defendant who has in fact violated it, is one of its strengths. *See* John D. Jackson, Making Juries Accountable, 50 AM. J. COMP. L. 477, 515 (2002).

If what went on in the jury room were judicially reviewable for reasonableness or fairness, trials would no longer truly be by jury, as the Constitution commands. Final authority would be exercised by whomever is empowered to decide whether the jury's decision was reasonable enough, or based on proper considerations. Judicial review of internal jury deliberations would have the result that "every jury verdict would either become the court's verdict or would be permitted to stand only by the court's leave." *Carson v. Polley*, 689 F.2d 562, 581 (5th Cir.1982).

Defendants undoubtedly have a powerful interest in ensuring that the jury carefully and impartially considers the evidence. This case presents that interest to the highest degree. But there are compelling interests for prohibiting testimony about what goes on in the jury room after a verdict has been rendered. The rule protects the finality of verdicts. It protects jurors from harassment by counsel seeking to nullify a verdict. It reduces the incentive for jury tampering. It promotes free and frank jury discussions that would be chilled if threatened by the prospect of later being called to the stand. Finally, it preserves the "community's trust in a system that relies on the decisions of laypeople [that] would all be undermined by a barrage of postverdict scrutiny." *Tanner*, 483 U.S. at 121, 107 S.Ct. 2739; see also *Resolution Trust Corp. v. Stone*, 998 F.2d 1534, 1548 (10th Cir.1993) ("[T]he rule against jurors impeaching their own verdict is designed to promote the jury›s freedom of deliberation, the stability and finality of verdicts, and the protection of jurors against annoyance and embarrassment."); *Gov't of the V.I. v. Gereau*, 523 F.2d 140, 148 (3d Cir.1975) (listing these five policies behind the rule).

Like other rules of evidence protecting the confidentiality of certain communications, such as the attorney-client privilege or the priest-penitent privilege, Rule 606(b) denies the court access to what may be relevant information-information that might, for example, justify a motion for a new trial. But like these other privileges, the rule protects the deliberative process in a broader sense. It is essential that jurors express themselves candidly and vigorously as they discuss the evidence presented in court. The prospect that their words could be subjected to judicial critique and public cross examination would surely give jurors pause before they speak. *See Tanner*, 483 U.S. at 120, 107 S.Ct. 2739 ("If evidence thus secured could be thus used, the result would be to make what was intended to be a private deliberation, the constant subject of public investigation-to the destruction of all frankness and freedom of discussion and conference.") (quoting *McDonald v. Pless*, 238 U.S. at 267-68, 35 S.Ct. 783). Moreover, part of the urgency that comes from knowing that their decision is the final word may be lost if jurors know that their reasoning is subject to judicial oversight and correction. Had she known that the judge would review the jury›s reasoning process, for instance, Juror K.C. might not have argued so persistently with the foreman; she might have chosen instead to sit back and wait for the judge to correct the foreman›s unreasonableness.

B. Applicability of Rule 606(b) to the Juror Testimony in this Case

Against this background, we must consider whether Juror K.C.'s testimony, or the defense investigator's report of conversations with another juror, is inadmissible under Rule 606(b). The Rule provides: "Upon inquiry into the validity of a verdict or indictment, a juror may not testify as to any matter or statement occurring during the course of the jury's deliberations," with certain exceptions. The Rule goes on to say that "[a] juror's affidavit or evidence of any statement by the juror may not be received on a matter about which the juror would be precluded from testifying." Thus, if Juror K.C. or the other juror questioned by the defense investigator could not have testified on these matters, it was error for the district court to receive either an affidavit or other evidence of the testimony.

Juror K.C.'s testimony (along with the affidavit of the investigator reporting the statements of another juror) reported statements made by the jury foreman and other jurors in the jury room as part of the jury's discussion of the case. This evidence unquestionably falls within the category of testimony as to a "statement occurring during the course of the jury's deliberations." Mr. Benally does not argue otherwise.

He does argue, however, that the testimony concerning racial bias falls outside the ambit of the Rule because it is not being offered in connection with an "inquiry into the validity of a verdict or indictment." Fed.R.Evid. 606(b); see *McDonald*, 238 U.S. at 269, 35 S.Ct. 783 ("the principle is limited to those instances in which a private party seeks to use a juror as a witness to impeach the verdict"). The testimony was offered, he argues, only to show that a juror failed to answer questions honestly during voir dire. The jurors had been asked whether they had any negative experiences with Native Americans and whether the fact that Mr. Benally is a Native American would affect their evaluation of the case. All jurors answered "no." Yet the challenged testimony suggests that two jurors allowed preconceptions about Native Americans to color their evaluation.

We cannot accept this argument. Although the immediate purpose of introducing the testimony may have been to show that the two jurors failed to answer honestly during voir dire, the sole point of this showing was to support a motion to vacate the verdict, and for a new trial. That is a challenge to the validity of the verdict.

2It is true that juror testimony can be used to show dishonesty during voir dire, for purposes of contempt proceedings against the dishonest juror. *See Clark* v. *United States*, 289 U.S. 1, 12-14,

53 S.Ct. 465, 77 L.Ed. 993 (1933). Thus, if the purpose of the post-verdict proceeding were to charge the jury foreman or the other juror with contempt of court, Rule 606(b) would not apply. *McDonald*, 238 U.S. at 269, 35 S.Ct. 783. However, it does not follow that juror testimony that shows a failure to answer honestly during voir dire can be used to overturn the verdict.

There is a split in the Circuits on this point. The Ninth Circuit has held that "[s]tatements which tend to show deceit during voir dire are not barred by [Rule 606(b)]," even when the improper voir dire is the basis of a motion for a new trial. *Hard v. Burlington No. R.R.*, 812 F.2d 482, 485 (9th Cir.1987); *United States v. Henley*,238 F.3d 1111, 1121 (9th Cir.2001) ("Where, as here, a juror has been asked direct questions about racial bias during voir dire, and has sworn that racial bias would play no part in his deliberations, evidence of that juror›s alleged racial bias is indisputably admissible for the purpose of determining whether the juror›s responses were truthful."). At least one district court, in addition to the court below, has adopted a similar interpretation of the Rule. *See Tobias v. Smith*, 468 F.Supp. 1287, 1290 (W.D.N.Y.1979) (citing evidentiary treatise that suggested "where comments indicate prejudice or preconceived notions of guilt, statements may be admissible not under F.R.E. 606(b) but because they may prove that a juror lied during the voir dire.").

The Third Circuit, by contrast, has held that such an interpretation would be "plainly too broad," and that Rule 606(b) "categorically bar[s] juror testimony 'as to any matter or statement occurring during the course of the jury›s deliberations› even if the testimony is not offered to explore the jury›s decision-making process in reaching the verdict." *Williams v. Price*, 343 F.3d 223, 235 (3d Cir.2003) (Alito, J.). Then-Judge Alito acknowledged that the Ninth Circuit had held otherwise in *Hard* but that "it appears that [*Hard*] is inconsistent with Federal Rule of Evidence 606(b)." Id. at 236, n. 5.

The Third Circuit's approach best comports with Rule 606(b), and we follow it here. Mr. Benally seeks to use Juror K.C.'s testimony to question the validity of the verdict. The fact that he does so by challenging the voir dire does not change that fact. *Cf. Capps v. Sullivan*, 921 F.2d 260, 263 (10th Cir.1990) (rejecting defendant›s attempt to circumvent the rule by collaterally attacking the verdict with an ineffective assistance of counsel claim and asking what jurors would have thought had counsel requested a different jury instruction, noting that defendant "actually is probing their mental processes in their deliberations and using the results in an attempt to secure a new trial."). We agree with the government that allowing juror testimony through the backdoor of a voir dire challenge risks swallowing the rule. A broad question during voir dire could then justify the admission of any number of jury statements that would now be re-characterized as challenges to voir dire rather than challenges to the verdict. Given the importance that Rule 606(b) places on protecting jury deliberations from judicial review, we cannot read it to justify as large a loophole as Mr. Benally requests.

C. Whether the Juror Testimony in this Case Falls Within One of the Enumerated Exceptions to the Rule

Since the contested juror testimony falls under Rule 606(b)'s general proscription, we must ask whether Mr. Benally can take advantage of one of the Rule's limited exceptions. Rule 606(b) enumerates three exceptions: "a juror may testify about (1) whether extraneous prejudicial information was improperly brought to the jury›s attention, (2) whether any outside influence was improperly brought to bear upon any juror, or (3) whether there was a mistake in entering the verdict onto the verdict form." Fed.R.Evid. 606(b).

Mr. Benally argues that the juror statements in this case are about either "extraneous prejudicial information" or an "outside influence," falling under the first or second exception, respectively.2 These exceptions for extraneous influences cover misconduct such as jurors reading news reports about the case, jurors communicating with third parties, bribes, and jury tampering. *See Tanner,* 483 U.S. at 117, 107 S.Ct. 2739 (citing cases that identified "extraneous influences"); *United States v. Davis,* 60 F.3d 1479, 1482-83 (10ᵗʰ Cir.1995) (news reports as extraneous influence); *United States v. Scisum,* 32 F.3d 1479, 1483 (10ᵗʰ Cir.1994) (juror is permitted to testify that she had ex parte contact with judge but cannot testify about "mental processes in connection therewith"); *Mayhue v. St. Francis Hosp. of Wichita, Inc.,* 969 F.2d 919, 921-22 (10ᵗʰ Cir.1992) (dictionary as extraneous influence); *United States v. Dempsey,* 830 F.2d 1084, 1092 (10ᵗʰ Cir.1987) (interpreter›s misbehavior as extraneous influence); *Gereau,* 523 F.2d at 149 (listing situations that have been deemed "extraneous influences"). The exceptions do not extend to "discussions among jurors, intimidation or harassment of one juror by another, and other intra-jury influences on the verdict." *Gereau,* 523 F.2d at 150. They do not extend to evidence of drug and alcohol use during the deliberations. *Tanner,* 483 U.S. at 122, 107 S.Ct. 2739 ("However severe their effect and improper their use, drugs or alcohol voluntarily ingested by a juror seems no more an 'outside influence' than a virus, poorly prepared food, or a lack of sleep."). They do not extend even to questions of a juror›s sanity. *See United States v. Dioguardi,* 492 F.2d 70 (2d Cir.1974) (denying inquiry into state of mind of juror who claimed during trial to be cursed and able to see the future, because state of mind is internal rather than external).

If a juror were to conduct his own investigation and bring the results into the jury room, as the Henry Fonda character does in *Twelve Angry Men,* that behavior would constitute extraneous information, and Rule 606(b)would allow another juror to expose it. See *Southern Pac. Co. v. Klinge,* 65 F.2d 85, 87 (10ᵗʰ Cir.1933) for a real-world example. Courts must be careful, however, not to confuse a juror who introduces outside evidence with a juror who brings his personal experiences to bear on the matter at hand. *See Marquez v. City of Albuquerque,* 399 F.3d 1216, 1223 (10th Cir.2005) ("A juror›s personal experience, however, does not constitute 'extraneous prejudicial information.' "); 27 CHARLES ALAN WRIGHT & VICTOR JAMES GOLD, FEDERAL PRACTICE AND PROCEDURE: EVIDENCE 2D § 6074, 507 (2007) ("bias might not qualify as an 'outside influence' since it is imposed as a factor in decision-making by the jury itself, not some source extrinsic to the jury."). We have said that "the inquiry is not whether the jurors 'became witnesses' in the sense that they discussed any matters not of record, but whether they discussed specific extra-record *facts* relating to the defendant, and if they did, whether there was a significant possibility that the defendant was prejudiced thereby." *Marquez*, 399 F.3d at 1223 (quoting *United States ex rel. Owen v. McMann*, 435 F.2d 813, 818 n. 5 (2d Cir.1970)). In *Marquez*, the juror's personal experience was quite specific and relevant to the matter at hand: she discussed her own experience training police dogs to help the jury determine the issue before it, which was whether the use of a police dog had constituted excessive force. *Id.* Nevertheless, we held that this was not extraneous prejudicial information under Rule 606(b). Id.

None of the statements that Mr. Benally alleges his jurors made are "specific extra-record facts relating to the defendant." They are generalized statements, ostensibly based upon the jurors' personal experience. The statements might have been relevant to the matter before the jury, but that is not the inquiry. *See Marquez*, 399 F.3d at 1223. We instead ask whether the statements concerned specific facts about Mr. Benally or the incident in which he was charged, and they did not. *Cf. United States v. Humphrey*, 208 F.3d 1190, 1199 (10th Cir.2000)(holding a juror's statement about the personal reputation of the defendant to be extraneous information outside the scope of the Rule). We do not deny that the jurors' alleged statements were entirely improper and inappropriate. The statements about Native Americans in particular were gross generalizations built upon prejudice and had no place in the jury room. Impropriety alone, however, does not make a statement extraneous. That would unravel the internal/external distinction and make anything said in jury deliberations "extraneous information" so long as it was inappropriate. *See Martinez v. Food City, Inc.*, 658 F.2d 369, 373 (5th Cir.1981) ("[J]uror testimony regarding the possible subjective prejudices or improper motives of individual jurors has been held to be within the rule, rather than within the exceptions for 'extraneous influences.' "). *But see Tobias*, 468 F.Supp. at 1290 (conflating "improper" with "extraneous" by holding that "statements in the juror's affidavit are sufficient to raise a question as to whether the jury's verdict was discolored by improper influences and that they are not merely matters of jury deliberations."). It was an abuse of discretion for the district court to admit this testimony under Rule 606(b)'s exceptions.

D. Whether this Court Should Imply An Exception to Rule 606(b) for Evidence Touching on Racial Bias

Mr. Benally then urges us that if the foreman's statements are not extraneous and do not fall under one of Rule 606(b)'s explicit exceptions, they should fall under an *implicit* exception for evidence of racial bias. The Ninth Circuit adopted this approach in *United States v. Henley,* when it said it would seem "consistent with the text of the rule, as well as with the broad goal of eliminating racial prejudice from the judicial system, to hold that evidence of racial bias is generally not subject to Rule 606(b)'s prohibitions against juror testimony." 238 F.3d at 1120. Racial bias, according to *Henley*, is so "plainly a mental bias that is unrelated to any specific issue that a juror in a criminal case may legitimately be called upon to determine" that any statement indicative of such bias cannot be deemed protected by an evidentiary rule. *Id.* Other courts have refused to read such an exception into the text of Rule 606(b). *See, e.g., Shillcutt v. Gagnon*, 827 F.2d 1155 (7th Cir.1987) (applying Rule 606(b) to exclude a white juror›s statement that "[The Defendant›s] black and he sees a seventeen year old white girl-I know the type."); *Smith v. Brewer*, 444 F.Supp. 482 (S.D.Iowa 1978) (applying the Rule to exclude jurors› mimicking of black attorney during deliberations), *aff'd*, 577 F.2d 466 (8th Cir.1978).

To the extent the argument is made as a matter of policy, a court in a particular case is not the proper forum for making or enlarging exceptions to the rules of evidence. Our commission is to apply the Rules of Evidence as written and interpreted to the case at hand. Perhaps it would be a good idea to amend Rule 606(b) to allow testimony revealing racial bias in jury deliberations, but the body entrusted with making the Rules is Congress (advised by the Advisory Committee, which first considers proposed changes to the rules, takes public comment, and then recommends an appropriate action in a detailed report).

Congress deliberately rejected a version of Rule 606(b) with broader exceptions, which would have admitted the contested testimony in this case. The original House version of the rule would have allowed juror testimony regarding what was said in the jury room, while precluding testimony regarding the effect of those statements or anything else bearing on the subjective reasoning of the jurors. *See* H.R. 5463, 93d Cong., 2d Sess. (1974) ("Upon an inquiry into the validity of a verdict or indictment, a juror may not testify concerning the effect of anything upon his or any other juror›s mind or emotions as influencing him to assent to or dissent from the verdict or indictment or concerning his mental processes in connection therewith."). This would have adopted the so-called "Iowa Rule," in which jurors may testify about "any matter occurring during the trial or in the jury room" as long as it "does not essentially inhere in the verdict itself." *Wright v. Illinois & Miss. Tel. Co.*,20 Iowa 195, 210 (1866). The Senate rejected this "extension of the ability to impeach a verdict" as "unwarranted and ill-advised," S.REP. NO. 93-1277, 13 (1974), and its own version, which tracked the common-law rule, prevailed. *See Tanner*, 483 U.S. at 122-25, 107 S.Ct. 2739 (discussing the legislative history of Rule 606(b)). Notably, in the course of this discussion, one Senator referred to the problem of "bias" on the part of judges and juries, but noted: "I do not believe it would be possible to conduct trials, particularly criminal prosecutions, as we know them today, if every verdict were followed by a post-trial hearing into the conduct of the juror's deliberations." Letter from Senator McClellan to the Advisory Committee (August 12, 1971) 117 CONG. REC. 33642, 33655 (1971).

The fact that Congress "specifically understood, considered, and rejected a version of Rule 606(b) that would have allowed jurors to testify on juror conduct during deliberations," *Tanner*,

483 U.S. at 125, 107 S.Ct. 2739, reinforces our conviction that courts must adhere to the terms of the Rule. Judicial implication of a broader exception would be inconsistent with congressional intent. Courts no longer have common law authority to fashion and refashion rules of evidence as the justice of the case seems to demand, but must enforce the rules as enacted.

E. Whether Rule 606(b) Is Unconstitutional As Applied to Testimony that Would Support a Claim of a Sixth Amendment Violation

Mr. Benally's most powerful argument is that Rule 606(b) is unconstitutional as applied in this case, because it effectively precludes him from obtaining relief for what he regards as a violation of his Sixth Amendment right to an impartial jury. *See Tobias*, 468 F.Supp. at 1290 ("Whatever the scope of a jurisdiction›s non-impeachment rule, a court determination of whether particular jury events are open or closed to inquiry must consider a defendant›s sixth amendment rights to confront witnesses, to the assistance of counsel, and to an impartial jury.") (pre-dating *Tanner*); see also WRIGHT & GOLD, FEDERAL PRACTICE AND PROCEDURE: EVIDENCE 2D § 6074, 513 (suggesting that although racially biased statements do not fall within the exceptions to the Rule, in some cases the Sixth Amendment may require their admission).

This Court, however, has consistently "upheld application of the Rule 606(b) standards of exclusion of juror testimony even in the face of Sixth Amendment fair jury arguments." *Braley v. Shillinger*, 902 F.2d 20, 22 (10th Cir.1990); see, e.g., *Johnson v. Hunter*, 144 F.2d 565 (10th Cir.1944) (Constitution did not require court to admit black juror›s testimony that he was intimidated by other eleven white jurors, even though proof of that fact would require new trial and proof would be impossible without juror testimony). We continue to adhere to that view.

In its precedent most closely analogous to this case, the Supreme Court rejected the defendant's argument that his Sixth Amendment right to trial by a competent jury required the admission of evidence otherwise inadmissible under Rule 606(b). *Tanner*, 483 U.S. at 126-27, 107 S.Ct. 2739. In that case, after the jury had reached a guilty verdict, a juror voluntarily approached defense counsel and gave a sworn statement reporting heavy use of alcohol, marijuana, and cocaine by jurors during the trial. Id. at 115-16, 107 S.Ct. 2739. The Court "recognized that a defendant has a right to 'a tribunal both impartial and mentally competent to afford a hearing,'" id. at 127, 107 S.Ct. 2739 (quoting *Jordan v. Massachusetts*, 225 U.S. 167, 176, 32 S.Ct. 651, 56 L.Ed. 1038 (1912)), and did not question that juror intoxication, if proven through admissible evidence, would implicate that Sixth Amendment right. The Court reasoned, however, that in light of the "long-recognized and very substantial concerns [that] support the protection of jury deliberations from intrusive inquiry," *id.*, and the availability of other "aspects of the trial process" that protect the defendant›s "Sixth Amendment interests in an unimpaired jury," *id.*, the Sixth Amendment did not compel an exception to Rule 606(b), *id.*-even though, in the particular case, those other protections had failed to expose the problem, which therefore went uncorrected.

Tanner compels a similar result in this case. We must remember that the Sixth Amendment embodies a right to "a fair trial but not a perfect one, for there are no perfect trials." *McDonough Power Equipment, Inc. v. Greenwood*, 464 U.S. 548, 553, 104 S.Ct. 845, 78 L.Ed.2d 663 (1984) (internal quotations omitted). Where the attempt to cure defects in the jury process-here, the possibility that racial bias played a role in the jury›s deliberations-entails the sacrifice of structural features in the justice system that have important systemic benefits, it is not necessarily in the interest of overall justice to do so. As the Court said in *Tanner*, "There is little doubt that postverdict investigation into juror misconduct would in some instances lead to the invalidation of verdicts reached after irresponsible or improper juror behavior. It is not at all clear, however, that the jury system could survive such efforts to perfect it." *Tanner*, 483 U.S. at 120, 107 S.Ct. 2739.

The *Tanner* Court pointed out that there are a number of "aspects of the trial process," which, in most if not all cases, serve to protect the defendant›s Sixth Amendment right without breaching the ban on post-verdict juror testimony. *Id.* at 127, 107 S.Ct. 2739. The Court identified four such protections: voir dire, observation of the jury during court, reports by jurors of inappropriate behavior *before* they render a verdict, and post-verdict impeachment by evidence other than juror testimony. *Id.* Each protection might not be equally efficacious in every instance of jury misconduct. The judge will probably not be able to identify racist jurors based on trial conduct as easily as he could identify drunken jurors, for instance, and voir dire might be a feeble protection if a juror is determined to lie. This does not mean that defendants› interest in an impartial jury will go unprotected. Voir dire can still uncover racist predilections, especially when backed up by the threat of contempt or perjury prosecutions. Jurors can report to the judge during trial if racist remarks intrude on jury deliberations, enabling the judge to declare a mistrial or take other corrective measures. After the verdict is rendered, it could still be impeached if there is evidence of juror wrongdoing that does not depend on the testimony of fellow jurors in breach of Rule 606(b) confidentiality. And even trial observation could uncover racist attitudes if a juror openly wore his feelings on his sleeve. These protections might not be sufficient to eliminate every partial juror, just as in *Tanner* they proved insufficient to catch every intoxicated juror, but jury perfection is an untenable goal. The safeguards that the Court relied upon for exposing the drug and alcohol use amongst jurors in *Tanner* are also available to expose racial biases of the sort alleged in Mr. Benally›s case.

The defendant attempts to distinguish *Tanner* on the ground that racial bias is a more serious and fundamental danger to the justice system than intoxicated jurors. Perhaps that is so. But we do not see how the principle urged by the defendant in this case-that Rule 606(b) is unconstitutional as applied in a case where it prevents rectification of a Sixth Amendment violation-could be confined to the context of racial prejudice. It may well be true that racial prejudice is an especially odious, and especially common, form of Sixth Amendment violation. But once it is held that the rules of evidence must be subordinated to the need to admit evidence of Sixth Amendment violations, we do not see how the courts could stop at the "most serious" such violations. Indeed, it is hard to see why, under this theory, *Tanner* should not have been decided the other way.

Nor does there seem to be a principled reason to limit the exception only to claims of bias, when other types of jury misconduct undermine a fair trial as well. If a jury does not follow the jury instructions, or ignores relevant evidence, or flips a coin, or falls asleep, then surely that defendant's right to a fair trial would be aggrieved, just as Mr. Benally's was. *Cf. United States v. Voigt, 877 F.2d 1465, 1469 (10th Cir.1989)* (*Rule 606(b)* bars testimony that juror misunderstood jury instructions). How could we deny that defendant a chance to use juror testimony to seek a new trial, simply because the jury misconduct did not involve racial prejudice? But if every claim that, if factually supported, would be sufficient to demand a new trial warrants an exception to Rule 606(b), there would be nothing left of the Rule, and the great benefit of protecting jury decision-making from judicial review would be lost.

The defendant points out that no court of appeals has held, categorically, that Rule 606(b) is an absolute bar to the introduction of juror testimony regarding expressions of racial bias during jury deliberations. Other courts that have denied a general exception for racial bias have at the same time acknowledged that "further review may be necessary in the *occasional* case in order to discover the *extremely rare* abuse that could exist even after the court has applied the rule and determined the evidence incompetent." *Shillcutt*, 827 F.2d at 1159 (emphasis added); *see also Smith*, 444 F.Supp. at 490 ("[T]he Court does not suggest that the rule of juror incompetency embodied in Rule 606(b) should be applied dogmatically and in complete disregard of what is alleged to have occurred in the jury room."). We are skeptical of this approach. If confidentiality can be breached whenever a court, after the fact, thinks the advantages of doing so are important enough, much of the damage has already been done. We are inclined to think that in such a case other remedies can be found, without violating Rule 606(b). But here, it suffices to say that the case has not been made. According to Juror K.C.'s account, racially biased statements were made but she herself countered them. The verdict was unanimous, which means that Juror K.C., who protested the racially prejudiced statements, joined in finding Mr. Benally guilty beyond a reasonable doubt. This is not a case, therefore, where the verdict itself was shown to be based on the defendant's race rather than on the evidence and the law.

We therefore reject the defendant's argument that Rule 606(b) contains an implicit exception for racially biased statements made during jury deliberations, nor do we think the Rule is unconstitutional as applied in this case.

III. CONCLUSION

Because we hold that the district court erred in admitting both the juror testimony about racial bias and the juror testimony about sending a message under Rule 606(b), and because this was the only evidence that Mr. Benally presented to challenge the verdict, we REVERSE the district court's motion granting a new trial and REINSTATE the jury verdict.

UNITED STATES V. HENLEY

238 F.3d 1111 (9th Cir. 2001)

REINHARDT, Circuit Judge:

Rex Henley, Rafael Bustamante, Willie McGowan, and Garey West appeal their convictions for conspiracy to possess and distribute twelve kilograms of cocaine, in violation of 21 U.S.C. § 846, and possession with intent to distribute cocaine, in violation of 21 U.S.C. § 841(a)(1). They also appeal the denial of their motion for a new trial based on allegations of juror bias and tampering. We remand to the district court for further proceedings regarding the new trial motion. We reject appellants' other grounds for appeal in a memorandum disposition filed concurrently with this opinion.

I. Background

On June 23, 1994, a federal grand jury returned an indictment charging all four appellants, as well as Darryl Henley, Tracy Donaho, and Alejandro Cuevas, with conspiracy to distribute cocaine and possession with intent to distribute cocaine. The underlying conspiracy revolved around Darryl Henley, a professional football player for the Los Angeles Rams and the nephew of appellant Rex Henley. Appellant Bustamante supplied cocaine to Darryl Henley who, with the assistance of appellants West and McGowan, sought to distribute it in Memphis and Atlanta. Appellant Rex Henley helped prepare and conceal cocaine for transport and accompanied the couriers on some trips. Tracy Donaho, a Rams cheerleader who was romantically involved with Darryl Henley, served as a drug courier.

On July 15, 1993, Donaho was arrested at the Atlanta International Airport after agents from the Drug Enforcement Agency ("DEA") discovered twelve kilograms of cocaine in her bag. Soon thereafter, she agreed to cooperate with the DEA's investigation. At the subsequent trial, she provided testimony against all of the defendants.

On March 28, 1995, the appellants, along with Darryl Henley, were convicted on every count. One month later, juror Bryan Quihuis contacted the court and reported that he had been the subject of a bribery attempt orchestrated by Darryl Henley and former juror Michael

Malachowski. The parties were notified of the allegation and, on May 8, 1995, the appellants joined in a motion for a new trial, claiming that juror misconduct had deprived them of a fair trial. During several months of subsequent investigation, the following information came to light:

> Former juror Michael Malachowski, who had been excused from the jury during trial for reasons unrelated to the misconduct at issue here, paid an unsolicited visit to the home of Darryl and Rex Henley on March 20, 1995, while the trial was still in progress. He told the Henleys that they should contact him in the event that they were convicted, because he had information that might entitle them to a new trial. Specifically, Malachowski informed the Henleys that he had carpooled with two other jurors, Bryan Quihuis and Sean O'Reilly, and that the three jurors had discussed the evidence in violation of the court's instructions.

The following day, Darryl Henley contacted Malachowski and asked whether Malachowski knew any sitting juror who might be willing to vote not guilty on the charges against both of the Henleys.[3] Malachowski informed Henley that juror Quihuis had confessed to using methamphetamine on the weekends and that juror O'Reilly had made racist remarks. Henley instructed Malachowski to approach Quihuis and to "do anything it takes" to secure a not guilty vote. In exchange, Henley promised Malachowski a job with the Rams.

On the evening of March 21, Malachowski visited Bryan Quihuis at his home and asked Quihuis what he would want as payment for a not guilty vote. Quihuis professed shock and searched Malachowski for a recording device; only then did the two discuss money, settling conditionally on a figure of $25,000 to $50,000. Quihuis insisted on speaking directly to Henley. Malachowski and Quihuis then drove to a pay phone and placed a call to the Ram football player. Quihuis and Henley discussed the bribe, and Quihuis indicated that he wished to be paid half the money in advance.

Quihuis told Malachowski that he had tentatively decided to accept Henley's offer, but that he would like to consider the matter further and would contact Malachowski with his final answer. Quihuis had second thoughts soon thereafter. He called Malachowski later that night and informed him that he would not participate in the scheme.

Over the course of the next few days, as the jury entered deliberations, numerous efforts were made to persuade Quihuis to reconsider. Several phone calls were placed from Henley's cellular phone to Quihuis, but the two apparently did not speak again. Malachowski made frequent phone calls to Quihuis and even drove to Quihuis's home in an attempt to speak to him; Quihuis ultimately instructed his parents to tell Malachowski that he wasn't home. On Friday, March 24, two days after deliberations began, Quihuis informed the trial judge that he had seen a newspaper article about the case and had learned that Henley was facing a possible life sentence if convicted. Quihuis reported that the article had made a "big impact" on him and that he had had difficulty sleeping. After questioning Quihuis, the court determined that he need not be disqualified on account of his exposure to the article.

On Monday, March 27-the day before the jury returned its verdicts-Malachowski spoke to Quihuis and relayed Henley's concern that Quihuis was attempting to get himself excused from the jury. Malachowski made clear that Henley would pay $50,000 for a vote of not guilty. Quihuis once again declined the offer. The jury returned guilty verdicts against the defendants the next day.

Following the convictions, Malachowski provided a deposition to Rex Henley's counsel in which he swore-falsely, it seems-that Quihuis, not Malachowski, had initiated the bribery scheme and that Quihuis had attempted to extort money from Henley in exchange for a not guilty vote. Malachowski also alleged that juror Sean O'Reilly had made several racist remarks while carpooling to and from the trial, including the statement "All the niggers should hang." Finally, Malachowski reported that Quihuis had used drugs during the trial and that Malachowski, Quihuis, and O'Reilly had engaged in premature deliberations by discussing the evidence prior to the jury's deliberations.

After the allegations of misconduct had come to light, and after several months of investigation by the FBI, the district court conducted evidentiary hearings on the motions for a new trial. Malachowski and O'Reilly testified at the hearings, but Quihuis asserted his Fifth Amendment privilege against self-incrimination and refused to testify. The parties stipulated, however, that the transcripts of Quihuis's conversations with the court clerk, the FBI, and a defense investigator would be admitted into evidence.

The evidence pertaining to O'Reilly's alleged racist remarks was contradictory. Malachowski testified that he had embellished O'Reilly's statements and that, although O'Reilly had indeed used the word "nigger," he had not used it in reference to any of the defendants on trial. O'Reilly denied having made any racist statements and claimed to have dated an African-American woman in the past and to have befriended an African-American juror during the trial. Quihuis, however, provided a different account in his interviews with the FBI and the defense investigator. One of the FBI's reports recounts Quihuis's acknowledgment that at some point during the trial, "while either carpooling to or from the trial, O'Reilly stated, 'The niggers are guilty,' or 'Niggers are guilty.' " According to the report, Quihuis was unsure whether O'Reilly was referring to the defendants or to African-Americans in general. When asked by the defense investigator whether O'Reilly was likely to have been lying when he denied being racially biased in his juror questionnaire, Quihuis responded, "I would imagine so."

On August 29, 1996, the district court denied the motion for a new trial in a written order. The court held that the allegations of impropriety during trial-including the allegations of O'Reilly's racial prejudice-could not entitle the appellants to a new trial because Federal Rule of Evidence 606(b) barred virtually all juror testimony offered to impeach a jury's verdict. The court considered the allegations of O'Reilly's racial bias solely to the extent that they might reveal untruthful answers during voir dire. The court observed that prospective jurors were asked three race-related questions in their questionnaires: what their overall views were of interracial dating, whether they had ever had a bad experience with a person of a different race, and whether race would influence their decisions in any way. Without making any specific findings about the contents of O'Reilly's alleged racist remarks, the court stated: "[T]he court does not find that juror O'Reilly failed to answer honestly."

In considering the implications of the attempted bribe of Quihuis, the court acknowledged that such tampering with a sitting juror was presumptively prejudicial. However, citing our decision in *Hughes v. Borg*, 898 F.2d 695 (9th Cir.1990), the court found that the presumption of prejudice could be rebutted by a showing that "the judgment was not substantially swayed by the error." *Id.* at 701. In the present case, the court found that the presumption of prejudice had been rebutted by "overwhelming" evidence of the defendants' guilt, as demonstrated by the jury's "speedy" verdict.

The court further found, by a preponderance of the evidence, that Rex Henley had been aware of the bribery attempt before the verdict was rendered. Consequently, the court denied his motion for a new trial based on the jury tampering allegations as untimely under Federal Rule of Criminal Procedure 33, which requires new trial motions to be made within seven days after the verdict unless they are based on newly discovered evidence.

All four appellants timely appealed the district court's denial of their motion for a new trial.

II. Analysis

A. The Bribery Attempt

The Supreme Court announced the standard governing allegations of jury tampering in *Remmer v. United States,* 347 U.S. 227, 74 S.Ct. 450, 98 L.Ed. 654 (1954) ("*Remmer I*"). In that case, a juror had been approached during the trial by a man who suggested that the juror "could profit by bringing in a verdict favorable to the petitioner." *Id.* at 228, 74 S.Ct. 450. The Court held that "[a]ny private communication, contact, or tampering, directly or indirectly, with a juror during a trial about the matter pending before the jury is, for obvious reasons, deemed presumptively prejudicial.... The presumption is not conclusive, but the burden rests heavily upon the Government to establish, after notice to and hearing of the defendant, that such contact with the juror was harmless to the defendant." *Id.* at 229, 74 S.Ct. 450. The Court remanded the case to the district court for a hearing to determine whether the alleged contact had been harmless to the petitioner.

On remand, the district court concluded that the petitioner had not been prejudiced by the bribery attempt. The Court again granted certiorari and again reversed, finding that the bribery attempt might have affected the juror's "freedom of action" and had clearly left him "a disturbed and troubled man." *Remmer v. United States*, 350 U.S. 377, 381, 76 S.Ct. 425, 100 L.Ed. 435 (1956) (*"Remmer II"*). The Court reaffirmed that "it is the law's objective to guard jealously the sanctity of the jury's right to operate as freely as possible from outside unauthorized intrusions purposefully made." *Id.* at 382, 76 S.Ct. 425. The Court did not consider the weight of the government's case or indicate in any way whether the evidence of guilt was or was not overwhelming.

Since the *Remmer* cases, it has been clear that jury tampering creates a presumption of prejudice and that the government carries the heavy burden of rebutting that presumption. In *United States v. Dutkel*, 192 F.3d 893 (9th Cir.1999)-decided after the district court's order denying appellants' new trial motion-this court explained that allegations of jury tampering are qualitatively more prejudicial than other kinds of extraneous influence on the jury's deliberations: "Because jury tampering cuts to the heart of the Sixth Amendment's promise of a fair trial, we treat jury tampering cases very differently from other cases of jury misconduct." *Id.* at 894. *Dutkel*, like this appeal, involved allegations that one co-defendant in a joint trial had bribed a juror-in that case, successfully. The co-defendant who arranged the bribe secured a hung jury for himself, but Dutkel was convicted. We held that even though the bribery scheme had been carried out by and on behalf of Dutkel's co-defendant, the *Remmer* presumption of prejudice applied to Dutkel because the tampering "may have affected the juror in the exercise of his judgment." *Dutkel*, 192 F.3d at 897.

In evaluating allegations of jury tampering, *Dutkel* holds that we must first determine whether a defendant has made a prima facie showing that "the intrusion had such an adverse effect on the deliberations." *Id.* The "adverse effect" standard is a low one: "Unless the district court finds that this showing is entirely frivolous or wholly implausible, it must order a *Remmer* hearing to explore the degree of the intrusion and likely prejudice suffered by the defendant." *Id.* In evaluating such prejudice, the court "need not conclude that the verdict ... would have been different but for the jury tampering, but rather that the course of deliberations was materially affected by the intrusion." *Id.* at 899.

The district court, in rejecting appellants' new trial motion based on the attempted bribery of juror Quihuis, conducted the requisite hearing but applied what *Dutkel* has since made clear is an incorrect legal standard. Rather than examining whether the bribery attempt "interfered with the jury's deliberations by distracting one or more of the jurors," *id.* at 897, the court considered whether the jury was "substantially swayed" by the alleged misconduct. The standard applied by the district court derives from jury misconduct cases that do not involve allegations of jury tampering, but rather involve more common and less pernicious extraneous influences on jury deliberations. In fact, with the exception of *Remmer,* none of the cases cited by the district court involved jury tampering. *Dutkel* expressly distinguishes the "prosaic kinds of jury misconduct" cases cited by the district court from the "much more serious intrusion" of a bribe or threat. *Dutkel,* 192 F.3d at 895. Accordingly, the court erred in basing its decision on the "overwhelming evidence" of appellants' guilt rather than considering the effect of the bribery attempt on the course of deliberations.

Although, as mentioned earlier, juror Quihuis invoked his Fifth Amendment privilege against self-incrimination and declined to testify at the evidentiary hearing, sufficient evidence of the effect of the attempted bribe on Quihuis was introduced to convince us that the matter should be remanded to the district court for further consideration in light of *Dutkel.* For example, in an interview with defense investigator Jerry Mulligan, Quihuis described the impact of the bribery attempt:

Mulligan: Did you ever go to the judge [to report the bribery attempt]?

Quihuis: No I was scared. I was extremely extremely scared that if I went to the judge something would happen to me or my family.

Mulligan: Why were you scared?

Quihuis: Because what happened with uh earlier in the case so called I believe it was Alex Quevas uh Bustamante wanted Alex Quevas to do something on the stand or else he'd never see his son again. It kind of crossed my mind, freaked me out that maybe if I didn't cooperate maybe if I did do this something would happen to me so I was trying to be quiet and I was in fear that something would happen to me and my family and no way do I wanna go through a government relocation program and never see my family again.

In the same conversation, Quihuis insisted that the bribery attempt had not affected his judgment, but he conceded that "it screwed with me as far as I felt threatened that if I didn't cooperate, something would happen to me or my family because Mike [Malachowski] knew where I lived, and if he's talking to Darryl [Henley], what makes you think he hasn't given my address to Darryl, and like I said reflecting back to Bustamante and Quevas do you ever wanna see your son walk again crossed my mind. That if I don't cooperate, something's gonna happen to me and my family." Quihuis provided essentially the same account when he was interviewed by the FBI after the bribery scheme came to light, as recounted in the FBI's report:

QUIHUIS never told Judge TAYLOR about this incident because he feared that he or his family would be in jeopardy. He learned at the trial that defendant RAFAEL BUSTAMENTE threatened a witness, ALEX QUEVIS [sic], that he would kill his son if QUEVIS did not purger [sic] himself in the trial....

After the verdict, QUIHUIS mentioned [the bribery attempt] to his grandparents. His grandparents asked why he did not tell the judge about this. QUIHUIS explained his fear about he [sic] or his family members being hurt.

Under *Dutkel,* the appellants have made a prima facie showing that the intrusion "interfered with the jury's deliberations by distracting one or more of the jurors...." *Dutkel,* 192 F.3d at 897. As in *Dutkel,* there is evidence that Quihuis's contacts with Malachowski and Darryl Henley left him "a 'disturbed and troubled man,' deeply concerned about his own and his family's safety." *Id.* at 898 (quoting *Remmer II,* 350 U.S. at 381, 76 S.Ct. 425). As in *Dutkel,* Quihuis "stated that he was 'very scared' by the contacts." *Id.* Quihuis's fears "may well have prevented [him] from thinking about the evidence or paying attention to the judge's instructions." *Id.* Finally, because Quihuis did not report the incident to the court, he "had to worry not only about threats to his family, but also about concealing his predicament from the court and his fellow jurors. It is possible that [Quihuis] was hesitant about engaging in the normal give and take of deliberations, for fear of giving himself away." *Id.*

In its brief and at oral argument, the government stated that it did not oppose a "limited remand" so that the district court could hear Quihuis's sworn testimony. Because Quihuis has now pleaded guilty to charges relating to his conduct in this case, it is likely that he will no longer be able to invoke his Fifth Amendment right against self-incrimination and that he may be compelled to testify. We agree that, given the change in circumstances, remand is appropriate in order to afford the district court an opportunity to determine whether the presumption of prejudice can be rebutted under the recently explicated *Dutkel* standard. Because it is clear that the appellants have made a prima facie showing that the bribery scheme had an adverse effect on Quihuis's deliberations, the government now carries the "heavy burden" of demonstrating that "there is no reasonable possibility that [Quihuis] (or any other juror) 'was ... affected in his freedom of action as a juror' as to [appellants]." *Dutkel,* 192 F.3d at 899 (quoting *Remmer II,* 350 U.S. at 381, 76 S.Ct. 425). "Unless the district court is convinced that there is no reasonable possibility that the deliberations as to [appellants] were affected by the tampering, the court must vacate [their] conviction[s]." *Id.*

We are left with one further problem regarding the *Dutkel* remand. The appellants argue that Federal Rule of Evidence 606(b), when read with the *Remmer* cases, renders the presumption of prejudice effectively irrebuttable, because the rule precludes any testimony by a juror as to "any matter or statement occurring during the course of deliberations or to the effect of anything upon that or any other juror's mind or emotions as influencing the juror to assent or dissent from the verdict or indictment or concerning the juror's mental processes in connection therewith...." Fed R. Evid. 606(b). It is clear that the rule permits jurors to testify about whether "extraneous prejudicial information was improperly brought to the jury's attention or whether any outside influence was improperly brought to bear upon any juror." *Id.* Appellants contend, however, that juror testimony about the *effect* of extraneous information or improper contacts on a juror's state of mind is prohibited. Accordingly, appellants argue, if evidence of tampering is not uncovered prior to the verdict, *Remmer* 's presumption of prejudice becomes irrebuttable, because the court may not consider testimony tending to establish that the tampering had no material effect on the jury's deliberations. The appellants alternatively classify *Remmer* 's presumption as a "structural error" requiring per se reversal, because appellate review of the magnitude of the harm would be impossible without contravening Rule 606(b).

We have already rejected both of those arguments in *Dutkel* Although we did not discuss the tension between the government's burden of rebutting the presumption of prejudice and the constraints of Rule 606(b), we expressly noted Rule 606(b) when reaching our decision. Nevertheless, we relied on the fact that the juror in question had "himself stated that he was 'very scared' by the contacts," as well as testimony from other jurors that the juror was "distracted and expressed fear about his family," as support for our conclusion that the juror's deliberations might have been affected by the tampering. *Dutkel*, 192 F.3d at 898. Similarly, the Fourth Circuit, in a well-reasoned opinion that more squarely confronts the interplay between the *Remmer* presumption and Rule 606(b), has distinguished between testimony regarding the affected juror's mental processes in reaching the verdict-which is barred by Rule 606(b)-and testimony regarding the juror's more general fear and anxiety following a tampering incident, which is admissible for purposes of determining whether there is a "reasonable possibility that the extraneous contact affected the verdict." *United States v. Cheek*, 94 F.3d 136, 144 (4th Cir.1996).

Thus, statements such as those that Quihuis provided to the FBI and to the defense investigator-which reveal Quihuis's professed anxiety about his own and his family's well being-do not fall within Rule 606(b)'s "mental processes" prohibition and properly form the basis for the presumption that the government must now rebut. In attempting to do so, the government may not ask Quihuis whether, for example, he relied on the evidence introduced at trial in reaching his verdict. *See Cheek*, 94 F.3d at 143 ("By asking [the juror] whether he had listened to and considered all the evidence, the government was delving into [the juror's] mental processes about the sufficiency of the evidence in reaching his personal verdict. Such an inquiry exceeded the strict limits imposed by Rule 606(b)."). The government is free to question Quihuis, however, about his state of mind in general following the bribery attempt; the district court may then be called upon to evaluate the credibility of any testimony that contradicts Quihuis's earlier accounts.

The district court must be mindful that it "need not conclude that the verdict as to [the appellants] would have been different but for the jury tampering," *Dutkel*, 192 F.3d at 899, in order to reverse the convictions. The government has the burden of establishing not that the appellants would have been convicted with or without the bribery attempt, but rather, as *Dutkel* instructs, that there is no "reasonable possibility" that Quihuis was "affected in his freedom of action as a juror." *Id.* (quotations omitted). In directing district courts to consider such factors as whether the affected juror was frightened or distracted, and in placing the focus on the jury's deliberative process rather than on its verdict, *Dutkel* implicitly rejects the "overwhelming evidence of guilt" rationale that the district court applied below. In fact, *Dutkel,* like the two *Remmer* cases, does not so much as mention, anywhere in its analysis, the weight of the evidence at trial.

On remand, the district court shall conduct its review in light of these principles, and determine whether the government has carried its burden of rebutting the presumption of prejudice arising from the attempted bribery of juror Quihuis.

B. Allegations of Racism

All four appellants contend that their convictions must be reversed because their trial was tainted by juror Sean O'Reilly's racial bias, which appellants characterize as an "extraneous influence" not subject to Rule 606(b)'s prohibitions against juror testimony. In the alternative, appellants argue that even if Rule 606(b) bars the introduction of juror testimony regarding O'Reilly's racist statements in support of their claim that their right to an impartial jury was violated, that testimony may be considered as evidence that O'Reilly lied materially during voir dire, also compelling the grant of a new trial. Appellants emphasize that O'Reilly's alleged racism would have had a powerful impact in this trial, where three of the four appellants are African-American males and the prosecution's principal witness was a young white woman who had a sexual relationship with one of the African-American defendants.

The district court summarily rejected the appellants' claim that their trial was tainted by racial bias, holding that testimony regarding O'Reilly's "pre-verdict remarks" was foreclosed by Rule 606(b). The court did, however, consider the second question-whether O'Reilly's "claimed statements" demonstrated that he had failed to answer truthfully questions posed to him during voir dire. Without making any findings concerning the actual content of O'Reilly's statements-about which there was conflicting testimony and considerable dispute-the court ruled that it did "not find that juror O'Reilly failed to answer honestly."

Courts and commentators have struggled with the apparent conflict between protecting a defendant's right to a fair trial, free of racial bias, and protecting the secrecy and sanctity of jury deliberations. *See generally Developments in the Law-Race and the Criminal Process: VII. Racist Juror Misconduct During Deliberations,* 101 Harv. L. Rev. 1595 (1988); Victor Gold, *Juror Competency to Testify that a Verdict was the Product of Racial Bias,* 9 St. John's J. Legal Comment. 125 (1993). Although the broad language of Rule 606(b) could plausibly be read to exclude all juror testimony regarding racial bias during deliberations-at least to the extent that such testimony might reveal the influence of racial bias on a juror's verdict-"courts faced with the difficult issue of whether to consider evidence that a criminal defendant was prejudiced by racial bias in the jury room have hesitated to apply the rule dogmatically." Wright v. United States, 559 F.Supp. 1139, 1151 (E.D.N.Y.1983).

Appellants maintain that racial bias should be viewed as "extraneous prejudicial information" or as an "outside influence" that is expressly excluded from Rule 606(b)'s bar. Even without characterizing racial bias as "extraneous," a powerful case can be made that Rule 606(b) is wholly inapplicable to racial bias because, as the Supreme Court has explained, "[a] juror may testify concerning any mental bias in matters *unrelated to the specific issues that the juror was called upon to decide* ...." *Rushen v. Spain*, 464 U.S. 114, 121 n. 5, 104 S.Ct. 453, 78 L.Ed.2d 267 (1983) (per curiam) (citing Fed.R.Evid. 606(b)) (emphasis added). Racial prejudice is plainly a mental bias that is unrelated to any specific issue that a juror in a criminal case may legitimately be called upon to determine. It would seem, therefore, to be consistent with the text of the rule, as well as with the broad goal of eliminating racial prejudice from the judicial system, to hold that evidence of racial bias is generally not subject to Rule 606(b)'s prohibitions against juror testimony.

Some courts have suggested that Rule 606(b) should generally apply to racist statements made by jurors during deliberations, unless the resulting prohibition would deprive defendants of their right to a fair trial. The Seventh Circuit expressed that view as follows:

> The rule of juror incompetency cannot be applied in such an unfair manner as to deny due process. Thus, further review may be necessary in the occasional case in order to discover the extremely rare abuse that could exist even after the court has applied the rule and determined the evidence incompetent. In short, although our scope of review is narrow at this stage, we must consider whether prejudice pervaded the jury room, whether there is a substantial probability that the alleged racial slur made a difference in the outcome of the trial.

Shillcutt v. Gagnon, 827 F.2d 1155, 1159 (7th Cir.1987). Or, as another court explained, "if a criminal defendant could show that the jury was racially prejudiced, such evidence could not be ignored without trampling the sixth amendment's guarantee to a fair trial and an impartial jury." *Wright*, 559 F.Supp. at 1151. In order to apply Rule 606(b) in this limited manner, a court would first have to receive the juror testimony in question, and then determine whether the testimony established that "prejudice pervaded the jury room" or that "the jury was racially prejudiced." In our circuit, however, it would not be necessary to demonstrate that "prejudice pervaded the jury room" in order to establish a constitutional violation; we have made clear that the Sixth Amendment is violated by "the bias or prejudice of even a single juror." *Dyer v. Calderon*, 151 F.3d 970, 973 (9th Cir.1998) (en banc). One racist juror would be enough.

In this case, there would be even stronger reason to conclude that Rule 606(b) should not bar juror testimony regarding O'Reilly's alleged racist statements, because the statements in question were made *before* deliberations began and *outside* the jury room. Rule 606(b)'s primary purpose-the insulation of jurors' private deliberations from post-verdict scrutiny-would not be implicated by permitting juror testimony about what O'Reilly allegedly said while carpooling with other jurors.

While we find persuasive those cases that have exempted evidence of racial prejudice from Rule 606(b)'s juror incompetency doctrine, we need not decide today whether or to what extent the rule prohibits juror testimony concerning racist statements made during deliberations or, as in this case, outside of deliberations but during the course of the trial. Where, as here, a juror has been asked direct questions about racial bias during voir dire, and has sworn that racial bias would play no part in his deliberations, evidence of that juror's alleged racial bias is indisputably admissible for the purpose of determining whether the juror's responses were truthful. *Hard v. Burlington Northern R.R.*, 812 F.2d 482, 485 (9th Cir.1987) ("Statements which tend to show deceit during voir dire are not barred by [Rule 606(b)]."). If appellants can show that a juror "failed to answer honestly a material question on voir dire, and then further show that a correct response would have provided a valid basis for a challenge for cause," then they are entitled to a new trial. *McDonough Power Equipment, Inc. v. Greenwood,* 464 U.S. 548, 556, 104 S.Ct. 845, 78 L.Ed.2d 663 (1984).

The appellants contend that juror O'Reilly's racist statements establish conclusively that he answered questions untruthfully in his voir dire questionnaire. On that questionnaire, O'Reilly submitted that his overall view of interracial dating was "neutral," that he had never had a bad experience with a person of a different race, and that race would not influence his decision as a juror in any way. The district court rejected appellants' claim, finding that the record did not establish that O'Reilly had answered any questions untruthfully.

The government does not dispute that a juror who answered in the affirmative questions about whether race would influence his decision would be subject to a challenge for cause. Instead, the government argues that appellants' claim is based on an unsupportable inference that anyone who uses the word "nigger" must hold racial bias against all African-Americans, and that the district court was not obligated to draw that inference.

We have considerable difficulty accepting the government's assumption that, at this time in our history, people who use the word "nigger" are not racially biased. In the present case, however, it is necessary to determine precisely what O'Reilly did or did not say before evaluating the truthfulness of his voir dire responses. The district court erred by rejecting appellants' claim without making any findings concerning whether O'Reilly actually made a racist statement and, if so, its specific content. Because there is considerable dispute as to the facts, we are unable to review the district court's conclusion in the absence of a specific finding as to which, if any, of the various accounts is correct. For example, in Malachowski's first account, he maintained that O'Reilly had declared, "All the niggers should hang." Later, when Malachowski was pleading guilty to charges related to his role in the bribery scheme, he recanted his initial report and insisted that O'Reilly had simply used the word "nigger," but not in relation to the defendants in this case. Quihuis's version of events was different; it tended, however, to support Malachowski's original statement. Quihuis reported to the FBI that O'Reilly had stated, "The niggers are guilty," or simply "Niggers are guilty." Finally, O'Reilly himself denied having made any racist statements at all, although we note that O'Reilly's own denials may be entitled to less weight than the accounts of other witnesses. "Because the bias of a juror will rarely be admitted by the juror himself, partly because the juror may have an interest in concealing his own bias and partly because the juror may be unaware of it, it necessarily must be inferred from surrounding facts and circumstances." *McDonough*, 464 U.S. at 558, 104 S.Ct. 845 (Brennan, J., concurring) (citations omitted).

From the district court's order, it is not possible to determine whether the court concluded that O'Reilly had not made any racist statements, or whether it believed that while he did make such statements, that fact was not sufficient to establish that he answered untruthfully during voir dire. Resolution of the disputed question as to what O'Reilly did or did not say may well be determinative of whether his responses to the questionnaire were truthful. We therefore remand to the district court with instructions that the court enter detailed findings and make a specific determination regarding O'Reilly's alleged statements and racial bias.

C. Rex Henley

The district court found, by a preponderance of the evidence, that appellant Rex Henley was aware of the bribe attempt before the verdict was rendered; accordingly, the court ruled that Henley's motion for a new trial was untimely filed because it was not based on newly discovered evidence. The court recognized that there was no direct evidence of Henley's pre-verdict knowledge, but nevertheless concluded that "the strong circumstantial evidence compels that reasonable inference." Henley maintains that the district court's factual finding that he had pre-verdict knowledge of the bribery attempt was clearly erroneous, and that we should treat him in the same manner as the other three appellants for purposes of this appeal.

We need not resolve the question that Henley raises as to the correctness of the district court's untimeliness ruling, because we elect, for reasons of judicial economy, to consider Henley's jury tampering claim along with his admittedly timely juror bias claim and the identical tampering and bias claims raised by his co-appellants. Because we conclude that, as a matter of substantive law, all four appellants are entitled to the benefit of further proceedings with respect to both claims, it seems just and sensible to allow all of the claims to proceed together, rather than to require the district court to conduct a separate proceeding for one of the appellants on one of his claims.

Our decision to allow Henley to proceed with his appeal from the "untimely" portion of his new trial motion is supported by Rule 2 of the Federal Rules of Appellate Procedure, which vests in the court of appeals the discretionary authority to "suspend any provision of these rules in a particular case and order proceedings as it directs" in order to "expedite its decision or for other good cause...." Because we find ample "good cause" for facilitating the district court's resolution of all four appellants' claims in a single proceeding, we exercise that discretion here.

Accordingly, we instruct that, on remand, Henley's claim with respect to the jury tampering issue be adjudicated together with the identical claims of the other appellants on that point, and along with Henley's and the other appellants' claims regarding the racial bias question.

III. Conclusion

We remand this case to the district court so that it may determine whether, in light of *Dutkel,* the attempted bribery of juror Quihuis entitles the appellants to a new trial. We also remand so that the district court may reconsider its determination that juror O'Reilly failed to answer truthfully a material question or questions on voir dire. In this regard, the district court shall enter detailed findings concerning whether O'Reilly actually made racist remarks and, if so, their specific content.

REMANDED FOR FURTHER PROCEEDINGS CONSISTENT WITH THIS OPINION.

Note

In *United States v. Villar*, 586 F.3d 76 (1ˢᵗ Cir. 2009) the First Circuit, while seeming to side with the *Henley* position, expressed the view that the matter should be left to the discretion of the trial judge, under Fifth and Sixth Amendments, to inquire into validity of verdict due to alleged ethnic bias. In *Villar* the egregious juror conduct concerned a more generalized reference to "those people cause all the trouble" (interpreted by the reporting juror to refer to Hispanics) without any more specific derogatory reference to race. The *Villar* court, while affirming the validity of Rule 606(b), found that the trial court should only conduct an inquiry into alleged juror bias, misconduct, or extraneous influences when reasonable grounds exist to believe "there is clear, strong, substantial and incontrovertible evidence that a specific, nonspeculative impropriety has occurred which could have prejudiced the trial of a defendant". (586 F.3d at 83). The United States Supreme Court decision in *Pena-Rodriguez v. Colorado,* below suggests not just a resolution of the conflict among circuits but a constitutional mandate to inquire into the validity of the jury decision where the offending juror's comments are "egregious and unmistakable in their reliance on racial bias."

PEÑA-RODRIGUEZ V. COLORADO.

137 S.Ct. 855 (2017)

Justice KENNEDY delivered the opinion of the Court.

The jury is a central foundation of our justice system and our democracy. Whatever its imperfections in a particular case, the jury is a necessary check on governmental power. The jury, over the centuries, has been an inspired, trusted, and effective instrument for resolving factual disputes and determining ultimate questions of guilt or innocence in criminal cases. Over the long course its judgments find acceptance in the community, an acceptance essential to respect for the rule of law. The jury is a tangible implementation of the principle that the law comes from the people.

In the era of our Nation's founding, the right to a jury trial already had existed and evolved for centuries, through and alongside the common law. The jury was considered a fundamental safeguard of individual liberty. See The Federalist No. 83, p. 451 (B. Warner ed. 1818) (A. Hamilton). The right to a jury trial in criminal cases was part of the Constitution as first drawn, and it was restated in the Sixth Amendment. By operation of the Fourteenth Amendment, it is applicable to the States.

Like all human institutions, the jury system has its flaws, yet experience shows that fair and impartial verdicts can be reached if the jury follows the court's instructions and undertakes deliberations that are honest, candid, robust, and based on common sense. A general rule has evolved to give substantial protection to verdict finality and to assure jurors that, once their verdict has been entered, it will not later be called into question based on the comments or conclusions they expressed during deliberations. This principle, itself centuries old, is often referred to as the no-impeachment rule. The instant case presents the question whether there is an exception to the no-impeachment rule when, after the jury is discharged, a juror comes forward with compelling evidence that another juror made clear and explicit statements indicating that racial animus was a significant motivating factor in his or her vote to convict.

I

State prosecutors in Colorado brought criminal charges against petitioner, Miguel Angel Peña–Rodriguez, based on the following allegations. In 2007, in the bathroom of a Colorado horse-racing facility, a man sexually assaulted two teenage sisters. The girls told their father and identified the man as an employee of the racetrack. The police located and arrested petitioner. Each girl separately identified petitioner as the man who had assaulted her.

The State charged petitioner with harassment, unlawful sexual contact, and attempted sexual assault on a child. Before the jury was empaneled, members of the venire were repeatedly asked whether they believed that they could be fair and impartial in the case. A written questionnaire asked if there was "anything about you that you feel would make it difficult for you to be a fair juror." App. 14. The court repeated the question to the panel of prospective jurors and encouraged jurors to speak in private with the court if they had any concerns about their impartiality. Defense counsel likewise asked whether anyone felt that "this is simply not a good case" for them to be a fair juror. *Id.,* at 34. None of the empaneled jurors expressed any reservations based on racial or any other bias. And none asked to speak with the trial judge.

After a 3–day trial, the jury found petitioner guilty of unlawful sexual contact and harassment, but it failed to reach a verdict on the attempted sexual assault charge. When the jury was discharged, the court gave them this instruction, as mandated by Colorado law:

> "The question may arise whether you may now discuss this case with the lawyers, defendant, or other persons. For your guidance the court instructs you that whether you talk to anyone is entirely your own decision…. If any person persists in discussing the case over your objection, or becomes critical of your service either before or after any discussion has begun, please report it to me." *Id.,* at 85–86.

Following the discharge of the jury, petitioner's counsel entered the jury room to discuss the trial with the jurors. As the room was emptying, two jurors remained to speak with counsel in private. They stated that, during deliberations, another juror had expressed anti-Hispanic bias toward petitioner and petitioner's alibi witness. Petitioner's counsel reported this to the court and, with the court's supervision, obtained sworn affidavits from the two jurors.

The affidavits by the two jurors described a number of biased statements made by another juror, identified as Juror H.C. According to the two jurors, H.C. told the other jurors that he "believed the defendant was guilty because, in [H.C.'s] experience as an ex-law enforcement officer, Mexican men had a bravado that caused them to believe they could do whatever they wanted with women." *Id.,* at 110. The jurors reported that H.C. stated his belief that Mexican men are physically controlling of women because of their sense of entitlement, and further stated, "'I think he did it because he's Mexican and Mexican men take whatever they want.'" *Id.,* at 109. According to the jurors, H.C. further explained that, in his experience, "nine times out of ten Mexican men were guilty of being aggressive toward women and young girls." *Id.,* at 110. Finally, the jurors recounted that Juror H.C. said that he did not find petitioner's alibi witness credible because, among other things, the witness was " 'an illegal.' " *Ibid.* (In fact, the witness testified during trial that he was a legal resident of the United States.)

After reviewing the affidavits, the trial court acknowledged H.C.'s apparent bias. But the court denied petitioner's motion for a new trial, noting that "[t]he actual deliberations that occur among the jurors are protected from inquiry under [Colorado Rule of Evidence] 606(b)." *Id.,* at 90. Like its federal counterpart, Colorado's Rule 606(b) generally prohibits a juror from testifying as to any statement made during deliberations in a proceeding inquiring into the validity of the verdict. See Fed. Rule Evid. 606(b). The Colorado Rule reads as follows:

> "(b) Inquiry into validity of verdict or indictment. Upon an inquiry into the validity of a verdict or indictment, a juror may not testify as to any matter or statement occurring during the course

of the jury's deliberations or to the effect of anything upon his or any other juror's mind or emotions as influencing him to assent to or dissent from the verdict or indictment or concerning his mental processes in connection therewith. But a juror may testify about (1) whether extraneous prejudicial information was improperly brought to the jurors' attention, (2) whether any outside influence was improperly brought to bear upon any juror, or (3) whether there was a mistake in entering the verdict onto the verdict form. A juror's affidavit or evidence of any statement by the juror may not be received on a matter about which the juror would be precluded from testifying." Colo. Rule Evid. 606(b) (2016).

The verdict deemed final, petitioner was sentenced to two years' probation and was required to register as a sex offender. A divided panel of the Colorado Court of Appeals affirmed petitioner's conviction, agreeing that H.C.'s alleged statements did not fall within an exception to Rule 606(b) and so were inadmissible to undermine the validity of the verdict.

The Colorado Supreme Court affirmed by a vote of 4 to 3. The prevailing opinion relied on two decisions of this Court rejecting constitutional challenges to the federal no-impeachment rule as applied to evidence of juror misconduct or bias. After reviewing those precedents, the court could find no "dividing line between different *types* of juror bias or misconduct," and thus no basis for permitting impeachment of the verdicts in petitioner's trial, notwithstanding H.C.'s apparent racial bias. 350 P.3d, at 293. This Court granted certiorari to decide whether there is a constitutional exception to the no-impeachment rule for instances of racial bias. 578 U.S. ----, 136 S.Ct. 1513, 194 L.Ed.2d 602 (2016).

Juror H.C.'s bias was based on petitioner's Hispanic identity, which the Court in prior cases has referred to as ethnicity, and that may be an instructive term here. See, *e.g., Hernandez v. New York*, 500 U.S. 352, 355, 111 S.Ct. 1859, 114 L.Ed.2d 395 (1991) (plurality opinion). Yet we have also used the language of race when discussing the relevant constitutional principles in cases involving Hispanic persons. Petitioner and respondent both refer to race, or to race and ethnicity, in this more expansive sense in their briefs to the Court. This opinion refers to the nature of the bias as racial in keeping with the primary terminology employed by the parties and used in our precedents.

II

A

At common law jurors were forbidden to impeach their verdict, either by affidavit or live testimony. This rule originated in *Vaise v. Delaval*, 1 T.R. 11, 99 Eng. Rep. 944 (K.B. 1785). There, Lord Mansfield excluded juror testimony that the jury had decided the case through a game of chance. The Mansfield rule, as it came to be known, prohibited jurors, after the verdict was entered, from testifying either about their subjective mental processes or about objective events that occurred during deliberations.

American courts adopted the Mansfield rule as a matter of common law, though not in every detail. Some jurisdictions adopted a different, more flexible version of the no-impeachment bar known as the "Iowa rule." Under that rule, jurors were prevented only from testifying about their own subjective beliefs, thoughts, or motives during deliberations. See Wright v. Illinois & Miss. Tel. Co., 20 Iowa 195 (1866). Jurors could, however, testify about objective facts and events occurring during deliberations, in part because other jurors could corroborate that testimony.

An alternative approach, later referred to as the federal approach, stayed closer to the original Mansfield rule. See *Warger,* supra, at ––––, 135 S.Ct., at 526. Under this version of the rule, the no-impeachment bar permitted an exception only for testimony about events extraneous to the deliberative process, such as reliance on outside evidence—newspapers, dictionaries, and the like—or personal investigation of the facts.

This Court's early decisions did not establish a clear preference for a particular version of the no-impeachment rule. In *United States v. Reid,* 12 How. 361, 13 L.Ed. 1023 (1852), the Court appeared open to the admission of juror testimony that the jurors had consulted newspapers during deliberations, but in the end it barred the evidence because the newspapers "had not the slightest influence" on the verdict. Id., at 366. The *Reid* Court warned that juror testimony "ought always to be received with great caution." *Ibid.* Yet it added an important admonition: "cases might arise in which it would be impossible to refuse" juror testimony "without violating the plainest principles of justice." *Ibid.*

In a following case the Court required the admission of juror affidavits stating that the jury consulted information that was not in evidence, including a prejudicial newspaper article. *Mattox v. United States,* 146 U.S. 140, 151, 13 S.Ct. 50, 36 L.Ed. 917 (1892). The Court suggested, furthermore, that the admission of juror testimony might be governed by a more flexible rule, one permitting jury testimony even where it did not involve consultation of prejudicial extraneous information.

Later, however, the Court rejected the more lenient Iowa rule. In *McDonald v. Pless,* 238 U.S. 264, 35 S.Ct. 783, 59 L.Ed. 1300 (1915), the Court affirmed the exclusion of juror testimony about objective events in the jury room. There, the jury allegedly had calculated a damages award by averaging the numerical submissions of each member. Id., at 265–266, 35 S.Ct. 783. As the Court explained, admitting that evidence would have "dangerous consequences": "no verdict would be safe" and the practice would "open the door to the most pernicious arts and tampering with jurors." Id., at 268, 35 S.Ct. 783 (internal quotation marks omitted). Yet the Court reiterated its admonition from *Reid,* again cautioning that the no-impeachment rule might recognize exceptions "in the gravest and most important cases" where exclusion of juror affidavits might well violate "the plainest principles of justice." 238 U.S., at 269, 35 S.Ct. 783 (quoting *Reid, supra,* at 366; internal quotation marks omitted).

The common-law development of the no-impeachment rule reached a milestone in 1975, when Congress adopted the Federal Rules of Evidence, including Rule 606(b). Congress, like the *McDonald* Court, rejected the Iowa rule. Instead it endorsed a broad no-impeachment rule, with only limited exceptions.

The version of the rule that Congress adopted was "no accident." The Advisory Committee at first drafted a rule reflecting the Iowa approach, prohibiting admission of juror testimony only as it related to jurors' mental processes in reaching a verdict. The Department of Justice, however, expressed concern over the preliminary rule. The Advisory Committee then drafted the more stringent version now in effect, prohibiting all juror testimony, with exceptions only where the jury had considered prejudicial extraneous evidence or was subject to other outside influence. . The Court adopted this second version and transmitted it to Congress.

The House favored the Iowa approach, but the Senate expressed concern that it did not sufficiently address the public policy interest in the finality of verdicts. S.Rep. No. 93–1277, pp. 13–14 (1974). Siding with the Senate, the Conference Committee adopted, Congress enacted, and the President signed the Court's proposed rule. The substance of the Rule has not changed since 1975, except for a 2006 modification permitting evidence of a clerical mistake on the verdict form. See 574 U.S., at ––––, 135 S.Ct. 521.

The current version of Rule 606(b) states as follows:

"(1) *Prohibited Testimony or Other Evidence.* During an inquiry into the validity of a verdict or indictment, a juror may not testify about any statement made or incident that occurred during the jury's deliberations; the effect of anything on that juror's or another juror's vote; or any juror's mental processes concerning the verdict or indictment. The court may not receive a juror's affidavit or evidence of a juror's statement on these matters.

"(2) *Exceptions.* A juror may testify about whether:
   "(A) extraneous prejudicial information was improperly brought to the jury's attention;
   "(B) an outside influence was improperly brought to bear on any juror; or
   "(C) a mistake was made in entering the verdict on the verdict form."

This version of the no-impeachment rule has substantial merit. It promotes full and vigorous discussion by providing jurors with considerable assurance that after being discharged they will not be summoned to recount their deliberations, and they will not otherwise be harassed or annoyed by litigants seeking to challenge the verdict. The rule gives stability and finality to verdicts.

B

Some version of the no-impeachment rule is followed in every State and the District of Columbia. Variations make classification imprecise, but, as a general matter, it appears that 42 jurisdictions follow the Federal Rule, while 9 follow the Iowa Rule. Within both classifications there is a diversity of approaches. Nine jurisdictions that follow the Federal Rule have codified exceptions other than those listed in Federal Rule 606(b). See Appendix, *infra*. At least 16 jurisdictions, 11 of which follow the Federal Rule, have recognized an exception to the no-impeachment bar under the circumstances the Court faces here: juror testimony that racial bias played a part in deliberations. *Ibid.* According to the parties and *amici,* only one State other than Colorado has addressed this issue and declined to recognize an exception for racial bias. See *Commonwealth v. Steele,* 599 Pa. 341, 377–379, 961 A.2d 786, 807–808 (2008).

The federal courts, for their part, are governed by Federal Rule 606(b), but their interpretations deserve further comment. Various Courts of Appeals have had occasion to consider a racial bias exception and have reached different conclusions. Three have held or suggested there is a constitutional exception for evidence of racial bias. See *United States v. Villar,* 586 F.3d 76, 87–88 (C.A.1 2009) (holding the Constitution demands a racial-bias exception); *United States v. Henley,* 238 F.3d 1111, 1119–1121 (C.A.9 2001) (finding persuasive arguments in favor of an exception but not deciding the issue); *Shillcutt v. Gagnon,* 827 F.2d 1155, 1158–1160 (C.A.7 1987) (observing that in some cases fundamental fairness could require an exception). One Court of Appeals has declined to find an exception, reasoning that other safeguards inherent in the trial process suffice to protect defendants' constitutional interests. See *United States v. Benally,* 546 F.3d 1230, 1240–1241 (C.A.10 2008). Another has suggested as much, holding in the habeas context that an exception for racial bias was not clearly established but indicating in dicta that no such exception exists. See *Williams v. Price,* 343 F.3d 223, 237–239 (C.A.3 2003) (Alito, J.). And one Court of Appeals has held that evidence of racial bias is excluded by Rule 606(b), without addressing whether the Constitution may at times demand an exception. See *Martinez v. Food City, Inc.,* 658 F.2d 369, 373–374 (C.A.5 1981).

C

In addressing the scope of the common-law no-impeachment rule before Rule 606(b)'s adoption, the *Reid* and *McDonald* Courts noted the possibility of an exception to the rule in the "gravest and most important cases." *Reid,* 12 How., at 366; *McDonald,* 238 U.S., at 269, 35 S.Ct. 783. Yet since the enactment of Rule 606(b), the Court has addressed the precise question whether the Constitution mandates an exception to it in just two instances.

In its first case, *Tanner,* 483 U.S. 107, 107 S.Ct. 2739, 97 L.Ed.2d 90, the Court rejected a Sixth Amendment exception for evidence that some jurors were under the influence of drugs and alcohol during the trial. *Id.*, at 125, 107 S.Ct. 2739. Central to the Court's reasoning were the "long-recognized and very substantial concerns" supporting "the protection of jury deliberations from intrusive inquiry." *Id.*, at 127, 107 S.Ct. 2739. The *Tanner* Court echoed *McDonald*'s concern that, if attorneys could use juror testimony to attack verdicts, jurors would be "harassed and beset by the defeated party," thus destroying "all frankness and freedom of discussion and conference." 483 U.S., at 120, 107 S.Ct. 2739 (quoting *McDonald, supra*, at 267–268, 35 S.Ct. 783). The Court was concerned, moreover, that attempts to impeach a verdict would "disrupt the finality of the process" and undermine both "jurors' willingness to return an unpopular verdict" and "the community's trust in a system that relies on the decisions of laypeople." 483 U.S., at 120–121, 107 S.Ct. 2739.

The *Tanner* Court outlined existing, significant safeguards for the defendant's right to an impartial and competent jury beyond post-trial juror testimony. At the outset of the trial process, *voir dire* provides an opportunity for the court and counsel to examine members of the venire for impartiality. As a trial proceeds, the court, counsel, and court personnel have some opportunity to learn of any juror misconduct. And, before the verdict, jurors themselves can report misconduct to the court. These procedures do not undermine the stability of a verdict once rendered. Even after the trial, evidence of misconduct other than juror testimony can be used to attempt to impeach the verdict. *Id.*, at 127, 107 S.Ct. 2739. Balancing these interests and safeguards against the defendant's Sixth Amendment interest in that case, the Court affirmed the exclusion of affidavits pertaining to the jury's inebriated state. *Ibid.*

The second case to consider the general issue presented here was *Warger,* 574 U.S. ----, 135 S.Ct. 521, 190 L.Ed.2d 422. The Court again rejected the argument that, in the circumstances there, the jury trial right required an exception to the no-impeachment rule. *Warger* involved a civil case where, after the verdict was entered, the losing party sought to proffer evidence that the jury forewoman had failed to disclose prodefendant bias during *voir dire*. As in *Tanner,* the Court put substantial reliance on existing safeguards for a fair trial. The Court stated: "Even if jurors lie in *voir dire* in a way that conceals bias, juror impartiality is adequately assured by the parties' ability to bring to the court's attention any evidence of bias before the verdict is rendered, and to employ nonjuror evidence even after the verdict is rendered." 574 U.S., at ----, 135 S.Ct., at 529.

In *Warger,* however, the Court did reiterate that the no-impeachment rule may admit exceptions. As in *Reid* and *McDonald,* the Court warned of "juror bias so extreme that, almost by definition, the jury trial right has been abridged." 574 U.S., at ---- – ----, n. 3, 135 S.Ct., at 529, n. 3. "If and when such a case arises," the Court indicated it would "consider whether the usual safeguards are or are not sufficient to protect the integrity of the process." *Ibid.*

The recognition in *Warger* that there may be extreme cases where the jury trial right requires an exception to the no-impeachment rule must be interpreted in context as a guarded, cautious statement. This caution is warranted to avoid formulating an exception that might undermine the jury dynamics and finality interests the no-impeachment rule seeks to protect. Today, however, the Court faces the question that *Reid, McDonald,* and *Warger* left open. The Court must decide whether the Constitution requires an exception to the no-impeachment rule when a juror's statements indicate that racial animus was a significant motivating factor in his or her finding of guilt.

III

It must become the heritage of our Nation to rise above racial classifications that are so inconsistent with our commitment to the equal dignity of all persons. This imperative to purge racial prejudice from the administration of justice was given new force and direction by the ratification of the Civil War Amendments.

"[T]he central purpose of the Fourteenth Amendment was to eliminate racial discrimination emanating from official sources in the States." *McLaughlin v. Florida,* 379 U.S. 184, 192, 85 S.Ct. 283, 13 L.Ed.2d 222 (1964). In the years before and after the ratification of the Fourteenth Amendment, it became clear that racial discrimination in the jury system posed a particular threat both to the promise of the Amendment and to the integrity of the jury trial. "Almost immediately after the Civil War, the South began a practice that would continue for many decades: All-white juries punished black defendants particularly harshly, while simultaneously refusing to punish violence by whites, including Ku Klux Klan members, against blacks and Republicans." Forman, Juries and Race in the Nineteenth Century, 113 Yale L.J. 895, 909–910 (2004). To take one example, just in the years 1865 and 1866, all-white juries in Texas decided a total of 500 prosecutions of white defendants charged with killing African–Americans. All 500 were acquitted. *Id.,* at 916. The stark and unapologetic nature of race-motivated outcomes challenged the American belief that "the jury was a bulwark of liberty," *id.,* at 909, and prompted Congress to pass legislation to integrate the jury system and to bar persons from eligibility for jury service if they had conspired to deny the civil rights of African–Americans, *id.,* at 920–930. Members of Congress stressed that the legislation was necessary to preserve the right to a fair trial and to guarantee the equal protection of the laws. *Ibid.*

The duty to confront racial animus in the justice system is not the legislature's alone. Time and again, this Court has been called upon to enforce the Constitution's guarantee against state-sponsored racial discrimination in the jury system. Beginning in 1880, the Court interpreted the Fourteenth Amendment to prohibit the exclusion of jurors on the basis of race. *Strauder v. West Virginia,* 100 U.S. 303, 305–309, 25 L.Ed. 664 (1880). The Court has repeatedly struck down laws and practices that systematically exclude racial minorities from juries. To guard against discrimination in jury selection, the Court has ruled that no litigant may exclude a prospective juror on the basis of race. *Batson v. Kentucky,* 476 U.S. 79, 106 S.Ct. 1712, 90 L.Ed.2d 69 (1986);

Edmonson v. Leesville Concrete Co., 500 U.S. 614, 111 S.Ct. 2077, 114 L.Ed.2d 660 (1991); *Georgia v. McCollum,* 505 U.S. 42, 112 S.Ct. 2348, 120 L.Ed.2d 33 (1992). In an effort to ensure that individuals who sit on juries are free of racial bias, the Court has held that the Constitution at times demands that defendants be permitted to ask questions about racial bias during *voir dire. Ham v. South Carolina,* 409 U.S. 524, 93 S.Ct. 848, 35 L.Ed.2d 46 (1973); *Rosales–Lopez,* 451 U.S. 182, 101 S.Ct. 1629, 68 L.Ed.2d 22; *Turner v. Murray,* 476 U.S. 28, 106 S.Ct. 1683, 90 L.Ed.2d 27 (1986).

The unmistakable principle underlying these precedents is that discrimination on the basis of race, "odious in all aspects, is especially pernicious in the administration of justice." *Rose v. Mitchell,* 443 U.S. 545, 555, 99 S.Ct. 2993, 61 L.Ed.2d 739 (1979). The jury is to be "a criminal defendant's fundamental 'protection of life and liberty against race or color prejudice.' " *McCleskey v. Kemp,* 481 U.S. 279, 310, 107 S.Ct. 1756, 95 L.Ed.2d 262 (1987) (quoting *Strauder, supra,* at 309). Permitting racial prejudice in the jury system damages "both the fact and the perception" of the jury's role as "a vital check against the wrongful exercise of power by the State." *Powers v. Ohio,* 499 U.S. 400, 411, 111 S.Ct. 1364, 113 L.Ed.2d 411 (1991); cf. *Aldridge v. United States,* 283 U.S. 308, 315, 51 S.Ct. 470, 75 L.Ed. 1054 (1931); *Buck v. Davis,* ante, at 22.

IV

A

This case lies at the intersection of the Court's decisions endorsing the no-impeachment rule and its decisions seeking to eliminate racial bias in the jury system. The two lines of precedent, however, need not conflict.

Racial bias of the kind alleged in this case differs in critical ways from the compromise verdict in *McDonald,* the drug and alcohol abuse in *Tanner,* or the pro-defendant bias in *Warger.* The behavior in those cases is troubling and unacceptable, but each involved anomalous behavior from a single jury—or juror—gone off course. Jurors are presumed to follow their oath, cf. *Penry v. Johnson,* 532 U.S. 782, 799, 121 S.Ct. 1910, 150 L.Ed.2d 9 (2001), and neither history nor common experience show that the jury system is rife with mischief of these or similar kinds. To attempt to rid the jury of every irregularity of this sort would be to expose it to unrelenting scrutiny. "It is not at all clear … that the jury system could survive such efforts to perfect it." *Tanner,* 483 U.S., at 120, 107 S.Ct. 2739.

The same cannot be said about racial bias, a familiar and recurring evil that, if left unaddressed, would risk systemic injury to the administration of justice. This Court's decisions demonstrate that racial bias **implicates unique historical, constitutional, and institutional concerns.** An effort to address the most grave and serious statements of racial bias is not an effort to perfect the jury but to ensure that our legal system remains capable of coming ever closer to the promise of equal treatment under the law that is so central to a functioning democracy.

Racial bias is distinct in a pragmatic sense as well. In past cases this Court has relied on other safeguards to protect the right to an impartial jury. Some of those safeguards, to be sure, can disclose racial bias. *Voir dire* at the outset of trial, observation of juror demeanor and conduct during trial, juror reports before the verdict, and nonjuror evidence after trial are important mechanisms for discovering bias. Yet their operation may be compromised, or they may prove insufficient. For instance, this Court has noted the dilemma faced by trial court judges and counsel in deciding whether to explore potential racial bias at *voir dire*. See *Rosales–Lopez, supra*; *Ristaino v. Ross*, 424 U.S. 589, 96 S.Ct. 1017, 47 L.Ed.2d 258 (1976). Generic questions about juror impartiality may not expose specific attitudes or biases that can poison jury deliberations. Yet more pointed questions "could well exacerbate whatever prejudice might exist without substantially aiding in exposing it." *Rosales–Lopez, supra*, at 195, 101 S.Ct. 1629 (Rehnquist, J., concurring in result).

The stigma that attends racial bias may make it difficult for a juror to report inappropriate statements during the course of juror deliberations. It is one thing to accuse a fellow juror of having a personal experience that improperly influences her consideration of the case, as would have been required in *Warger*. It is quite another to call her a bigot.

The recognition that certain of the *Tanner* safeguards may be less effective in rooting out racial bias than other kinds of bias is not dispositive. All forms of improper bias pose challenges to the trial process. But there is a sound basis to treat racial bias with added precaution. A constitutional rule that racial bias in the justice system must be addressed—including, in some instances, after the verdict has been entered—is necessary to prevent a systemic loss of confidence in jury verdicts, a confidence that is a central premise of the Sixth Amendment trial right.

B

For the reasons explained above, the Court now holds that where a juror makes a clear statement that indicates he or she relied on racial stereotypes or animus to convict a criminal defendant, the Sixth Amendment requires that the no-impeachment rule give way in order to permit the trial court to consider the evidence of the juror's statement and any resulting denial of the jury trial guarantee.

Not every offhand comment indicating racial bias or hostility will justify setting aside the no-impeachment bar to allow further judicial inquiry. For the inquiry to proceed, there must be a showing that one or more jurors made statements exhibiting overt racial bias that cast serious doubt on the fairness and impartiality of the jury's deliberations and resulting verdict. To qualify, the statement must tend to show that racial animus was a significant motivating factor in the juror's vote to convict. Whether that threshold showing has been satisfied is a matter committed to the substantial discretion of the trial court in light of all the circumstances, including the content and timing of the alleged statements and the reliability of the proffered evidence.

The practical mechanics of acquiring and presenting such evidence will no doubt be shaped and guided by state rules of professional ethics and local court rules, both of which often limit counsel's post-trial contact with jurors. These limits seek to provide jurors some protection when they return to their daily affairs after the verdict has been entered. But while a juror can always tell counsel they do not wish to discuss the case, jurors in some instances may come forward of their own accord.

That is what happened here. In this case the alleged statements by a juror were egregious and unmistakable in their reliance on racial bias. Not only did juror H.C. deploy a dangerous racial stereotype to conclude petitioner was guilty and his alibi witness should not be believed, but he also encouraged other jurors to join him in convicting on that basis.

Petitioner's counsel did not seek out the two jurors' allegations of racial bias. Pursuant to Colorado's mandatory jury instruction, the trial court had set limits on juror contact and encouraged jurors to inform the court if anyone harassed them about their role in the case. Similar limits on juror contact can be found in other jurisdictions that recognize a racial-bias exception. See, *e.g.*, Fla. Standard Jury Instrs. in Crim. Cases No. 4.2 (West 2016) ("Although you are at liberty to speak with anyone about your deliberations, you are also at liberty to refuse to speak to anyone"); Mass. Office of Jury Comm'r, Trial Juror's Handbook (Dec. 2015) ("You are not required to speak with anyone once the trial is over.... If anyone tries to learn this confidential information from you, or if you feel harassed or embarrassed in any way, you should report it to the court ... immediately"); N.J. Crim. Model Jury Charges, Non 2C Charges, Dismissal of Jury (2014) ("It will be up to each of you to decide whether to speak about your service as a juror").

With the understanding that they were under no obligation to speak out, the jurors approached petitioner's counsel, within a short time after the verdict, to relay their concerns about H.C.'s statements. App. 77. A similar pattern is common in cases involving juror allegations of racial bias. See, *e.g.*, *Villar*, 586 F.3d, at 78 (juror e-mailed defense counsel within hours of the verdict); *Kittle v. United States*, 65 A.3d 1144, 1147 (D.C.2013) (juror wrote a letter to the judge the same day the court discharged the jury); *Benally*, 546 F.3d, at 1231 (juror approached defense counsel the day after the jury announced its verdict). Pursuant to local court rules, petitioner's counsel then sought and received permission from the court to contact the two jurors and obtain affidavits limited to recounting the exact statements made by H.C. that exhibited racial bias.

While the trial court concluded that Colorado's Rule 606(b) did not permit it even to consider the resulting affidavits, the Court's holding today removes that bar. When jurors disclose an instance of racial bias as serious as the one involved in this case, the law must not wholly disregard its occurrence.

C

As the preceding discussion makes clear, the Court relies on the experiences of the 17 jurisdictions that have recognized a racial-bias exception to the no-impeachment rule—some for over half a century—with no signs of an increase in juror harassment or a loss of juror willingness to engage in searching and candid deliberations.

The experience of these jurisdictions, and the experience of the courts going forward, will inform the proper exercise of trial judge discretion in these and related matters. This case does not ask, and the Court need not address, what procedures a trial court must follow when confronted with a motion for a new trial based on juror testimony of racial bias. See 27 Wright 575–578 Wright 575–578 (noting a divergence of authority over the necessity and scope of an evidentiary hearing on alleged juror misconduct). The Court also does not decide the appropriate standard for determining when evidence of racial bias is sufficient to require that the verdict be set aside and a new trial be granted. Compare, *e.g., Shillcutt*, 827 F.2d, at 1159 (inquiring whether racial bias "pervaded the jury room"), with, *e.g., Henley*, 238 F.3d, at 1120 ("One racist juror would be enough").

D

It is proper to observe as well that there are standard and existing processes designed to prevent racial bias in jury deliberations. The advantages of careful *voir dire* have already been noted. And other safeguards deserve mention.

Trial courts, often at the outset of the case and again in their final jury instructions, explain the jurors' duty to review the evidence and reach a verdict in a fair and impartial way, free from bias of any kind. Some instructions are framed by trial judges based on their own learning and experience. Model jury instructions likely take into account these continuing developments and are common across jurisdictions. See, *e.g.,* 1A K. O'Malley, J. Grenig, & W. Lee, Federal Jury Practice and Instructions, Criminal § 10:01, p. 22 (6th ed. 2008) ("Perform these duties fairly. Do not let any bias, sympathy or prejudice that you may feel toward one side or the other influence your decision in any way"). Instructions may emphasize the group dynamic of deliberations by urging jurors to share their questions and conclusions with their colleagues. See, *e.g., id.,* § 20:01, at 841 ("It is your duty as jurors to consult with one another and to deliberate with one another with a view towards reaching an agreement if you can do so without violence to individual judgment").

Probing and thoughtful deliberation improves the likelihood that other jurors can confront the flawed nature of reasoning that is prompted or influenced by improper biases, whether racial or otherwise. These dynamics can help ensure that the exception is limited to rare cases.

* * *

The Nation must continue to make strides to overcome race-based discrimination. The progress that has already been made underlies the Court's insistence that blatant racial prejudice is antithetical to the functioning of the jury system and must be confronted in egregious cases like this one despite the general bar of the no-impeachment rule. It is the mark of a maturing legal system that it seeks to understand and to implement the lessons of history. The Court now seeks to strengthen the broader principle that society can and must move forward by achieving the thoughtful, rational dialogue at the foundation of both the jury system and the free society that sustains our Constitution.

The judgment of the Supreme Court of Colorado is reversed, and the case is remanded for further proceedings not inconsistent with this opinion.

It is so ordered.

Note

The Supreme Court recognition of the seriousness of racial bigotry in the jury room has extended even so far as to allow a defendant the opportunity to raise such a challenge in post-conviction habeas corpus despite the existence of what might otherwise be considered procedural default. *See, Tharpe v. Sellers* below.

THARPE V. SELLERS

138 S.Ct. 545 (2018)

Opinion
PER CURIAM.

Petitioner Keith Tharpe moved to reopen his federal habeas corpus proceedings regarding his claim that the Georgia jury that convicted him of murder included a white juror, Barney Gattie, who was biased against Tharpe because he is black. See Fed. Rule Civ. Proc. 60(b)(6). The District Court denied the motion on the ground that, among other things, Tharpe's claim was procedurally defaulted in state court. The District Court also noted that Tharpe could not overcome that procedural default because he had failed to produce any clear and convincing evidence contradicting the state court's determination that Gattie's presence on the jury did not prejudice him. See *Tharpe v. Warden,* No. 5:10–cv–433 (MD Ga., Sept. 5, 2017), App. B to Pet. for Cert. 19.

Tharpe sought a certificate of appealability (COA). The Eleventh Circuit denied his COA application after deciding that jurists of reason could not dispute that the District Court's procedural ruling was correct. See *Tharpe v. Warden,* 2017 WL 4250413, (C.A.11, Sept. 21, 2017). The Eleventh Circuit's decision, as we read it, was based solely on its conclusion, rooted in the state court's factfinding, that Tharpe had failed to show prejudice in connection with his procedurally defaulted claim, *i.e.,* that Tharpe had "failed to demonstrate that Barney Gattie's behavior 'had substantial and injurious effect or influence in determining the jury's verdict.'" *Ibid.* (quoting *Brecht v. Abrahamson,* 507 U.S. 619, 637, 113 S.Ct. 1710, 123 L.Ed.2d 353 (1993)).

Our review of the record compels a different conclusion. The state court's prejudice determination rested on its finding that Gattie's vote to impose the death penalty was not based on Tharpe's race. See *Tharpe v. Warden,* No. 93–cv–144 (Super. Ct. Butts Cty., Ga., Dec. 1, 2008), App. F to Pet. for Cert. 102. And that factual determination is binding on federal courts, including this Court, in the absence of clear and convincing evidence to the contrary. See 28 U.S.C. § 2254(e) (1). Here, however, Tharpe produced a sworn affidavit, signed by Gattie, indicating Gattie's view that "there are two types of black people: 1. Black folks and 2. Niggers"; that Tharpe, "who wasn't in the 'good' black folks category in my book, should get the electric chair for what he did"; that "[s]ome of the jurors voted for death because they felt Tharpe should be an example to other blacks who kill blacks, but that wasn't my reason"; and that, "[a]fter studying the Bible, I have wondered if black people even have souls." App. B to Pet. for Cert. 15–16 (internal quotation marks omitted). Gattie's remarkable affidavit—which he never retracted—presents a strong factual basis for the argument that Tharpe's race affected Gattie's vote for a death verdict. At the very least, jurists of reason could debate whether Tharpe has shown by clear and convincing evidence that the state court's factual determination was wrong. The Eleventh Circuit erred when it concluded otherwise.

The question of prejudice—the ground on which the Eleventh Circuit chose to dispose of Tharpe's application—is not the only question relevant to the broader inquiry whether Tharpe should receive a COA. The District Court denied Tharpe's Rule 60(b) motion on several grounds not addressed by the Eleventh Circuit. We express no view of those issues here. In light of the standard for relief from judgment under Rule 60(b)(6), which is available only in "'extraordinary circumstances,'" *Gonzalez v. Crosby,* 545 U.S. 524, 536, 125 S.Ct. 2641, 162 L.Ed.2d 480 (2005), Tharpe faces a high bar in showing that jurists of reason could disagree whether the District Court abused its discretion in denying his motion. It may be that, at the end of the day, Tharpe should not receive a COA. And review of the denial of a COA is certainly not limited to grounds expressly addressed by the court whose decision is under review. But on the unusual facts of this case, the Court of Appeals' review should not have rested on the ground that it was indisputable among reasonable jurists that Gattie's service on the jury did not prejudice Tharpe.

We therefore grant Tharpe's motion to proceed *in forma pauperis,* grant the petition for certiorari, vacate the judgment of the Court of Appeals, and remand the case for further consideration of the question whether Tharpe is entitled to a COA.

It is so ordered.

Chapter Fourteen: Race and Sentencing

Race, Eight Amendment, Equal Protection and the Death Penalty

Note

Data supports the conclusion that race has, and continues to play a significant role in the imposition of capital punishment. People of color account for approximately 43 percent of the total executions since 1976 and 55 percent of the persons currently on death row, according to data presented by the American Civil Liberties Union https://www.aclu.org. Nearly 80% of the victims of homicide, resulting in the imposition of the death penalty have een white although Whites make up only 50 percent of all murder victims. This, combined with the disproportionate representation of persons of color on death row suggest both race of the victim and the race of the defendant have significant impact.

Justice Harry Blackmun stated in his dissent regarding the Court's refusal to hear *Callins v. Collins*, 510 U.S. 1141 (1994) "Perhaps it should not be surprising that the biases and prejudices that infect society generally would influence the determination of who is sentenced to death, even within the narrower pool of death eligible defendants selected according to objective standards." Whether this disproportionate imposition of the death penalty is the result race discrimination in the imposition of the penalty or the consequence of other aspects of race's impact on the criminal justice system as discussed elsewhere has been a matter of some conjecture. Race, and its role in jury selection, eyewitness identification, prosecutorial conduct, quality of defense counsel, and other factors, all likely have their role. The following material focuses on how and what role this disparity should play in determining of the death sentence itself is contrary to the Equal Protection Clause of the Fourteenth Amendment to the United States Constitution. This material begins first with the landmark decision of the United States Supreme Court in *McCleskey v. Kemp*.

MCCLESKEY V. KEMP

481 U.S. 279 (1987)

Justice POWELL delivered the opinion of the Court.

This case presents the question whether a complex statistical study that indicates a risk that racial considerations enter into capital sentencing determinations proves that petitioner McCleskey's capital sentence is unconstitutional under the Eighth or Fourteenth Amendment.

I

McCleskey, a black man, was convicted of two counts of armed robbery and one count of murder in the Superior Court of Fulton County, Georgia, on October 12, 1978. McCleskey's convictions arose out of the robbery of a furniture store and the killing of a white police officer during the course of the robbery. The evidence at trial indicated that McCleskey and three accomplices planned and carried out the robbery. All four were armed. McCleskey entered the front of the store while the other three entered the rear. McCleskey secured the front of the store by rounding up the customers and forcing them to lie face down on the floor. The other three rounded up the employees in the rear and tied them up with tape. The manager was forced at gunpoint to turn over the store receipts, his watch, and $6. During the course of the robbery, a police officer, answering a silent alarm, entered the store through the front door. As he was walking down the center aisle of the store, two shots were fired. Both struck the officer. One hit him in the face and killed him.

Several weeks later, McCleskey was arrested in connection with an unrelated offense. He confessed that he had participated in the furniture store robbery, but denied that he had shot the police officer. At trial, the State introduced evidence that at least one of the bullets that struck the officer was fired from a .38 caliber Rossi revolver. This description matched the description of the gun that McCleskey had carried during the robbery. The State also introduced the testimony of two witnesses who had heard McCleskey admit to the shooting.

The jury convicted McCleskey of murder. At the penalty hearing, the jury heard arguments as to the appropriate sentence. Under Georgia law, the jury could not consider imposing the death penalty unless it found beyond a reasonable doubt that the murder was accompanied by one of the statutory aggravating circumstances. Ga.Code Ann. § 17–10–30(c) (1982). The jury in this case found two aggravating circumstances to exist beyond a reasonable doubt: the murder was committed during the course of an armed robbery, § 17–10–30(b)(2); and the murder was committed upon a peace officer engaged in the performance of his duties, § 17–10–30(b)(8). In making its decision whether to impose the death sentence, the jury considered the mitigating and aggravating circumstances of McCleskey's conduct. § 17–10–2(c). McCleskey offered no mitigating evidence. The jury recommended that he be sentenced to death on the murder charge and to consecutive life sentences on the armed robbery charges. The court followed the jury's recommendation and sentenced McCleskey to death.

....

McCleskey next filed a petition for a writ of habeas corpus in the Federal District Court for the Northern District of Georgia. His petition raised 18 claims, one of which was that the Georgia capital sentencing process is administered in a racially discriminatory manner in violation of the Eighth and Fourteenth Amendments to the United States Constitution. In support of his claim, McCleskey proffered a statistical study performed by Professors David C. Baldus, Charles Pulaski, and George Woodworth, and (the Baldus study) that purports to show a disparity in the imposition of the death sentence in Georgia based on the race of the murder victim and, to a lesser extent, the race of the defendant. The Baldus study is actually two sophisticated statistical studies that examine over 2,000 murder cases that occurred in Georgia during the 1970's. The raw numbers collected by Professor Baldus indicate that defendants charged with killing white persons received the death penalty in 11% of the cases, but defendants charged with killing blacks received the death penalty in only 1% of the cases. The raw numbers also indicate a reverse racial disparity according to the race of the defendant: 4% of the black defendants received the death penalty, as opposed to 7% of the white defendants.

Baldus also divided the cases according to the combination of the race of the defendant and the race of the victim. He found that the death penalty was assessed in 22% of the cases involving black defendants and white victims; 8% of the cases involving white defendants and white victims; 1% of the cases involving black defendants and black victims; and 3% of the cases involving white defendants and black victims. Similarly, Baldus found that prosecutors sought the death penalty in 70% of the cases involving black defendants and white victims; 32% of the cases involving white defendants and white victims; 15% of the cases involving black defendants and black victims; and 19% of the cases involving white defendants and black victims.

Baldus subjected his data to an extensive analysis, taking account of 230 variables that could have explained the disparities on nonracial grounds. One of his models concludes that, even after taking account of 39 nonracial variables, defendants charged with killing white victims were 4.3 times as likely to receive a death sentence as defendants charged with killing blacks. According to this model, black defendants were 1.1 times as likely to receive a death sentence as other defendants. Thus, the Baldus study indicates that black defendants, such as McCleskey, who kill white victims have the greatest likelihood of receiving the death penalty.

The District Court held an extensive evidentiary hearing on McCleskey's petition. Although it believed that McCleskey's Eighth Amendment claim was foreclosed by the Fifth Circuit's decision in *Spinkellink v. Wainwright*, 578 F.2d 582, 612–616 (1978), cert. denied, 440 U.S. 976, 99

S.Ct. 1548, 59 L.Ed.2d 796 (1979), it nevertheless considered the Baldus study with care. It concluded that McCleskey's "statistics do not demonstrate a prima facie case in support of the contention that the death penalty was imposed upon him because of his race, because of the race of the victim, or because of any Eighth Amendment concern." *McCleskey v. Zant*, 580 F.Supp. 338, 379 (ND Ga.1984). As to McCleskey's Fourteenth Amendment claim, the court found that the methodology of the Baldus study was flawed in several respects.6 Because of these defects, the court held that the Baldus study "fail[ed] to contribute anything of value" to McCleskey's claim. Id., at 372 (emphasis omitted). Accordingly, the court denied the petition insofar as it was based upon the Baldus study.

....

II

McCleskey's first claim is that the Georgia capital punishment statute violates the Equal Protection Clause of the Fourteenth Amendment. He argues that race has infected the administration of Georgia's statute in two ways: persons who murder whites are more likely to be sentenced to death than persons who murder blacks, and black murderers are more likely to be sentenced to death than white murderers. As a black defendant who killed a white victim, McCleskey claims that the Baldus study demonstrates that he was discriminated against because of his race and because of the race of his victim. In its broadest form, McCleskey's claim of discrimination extends to every actor in the Georgia capital sentencing process, from the prosecutor who sought the death penalty and the jury that imposed the sentence, to the State itself that enacted the capital punishment statute and allows it to remain in effect despite its allegedly discriminatory application. We agree with the Court of Appeals, and every other court that has considered such a challenge,9 that this claim must fail.

A

Our analysis begins with the basic principle that a defendant who alleges an equal protection violation has the burden of proving "the existence of purposeful discrimination." *Whitus v. Georgia*, 385 U.S. 545, 550, 87 S.Ct. 643, 646, 17 L.Ed.2d 599 (1967).10 A corollary to this principle is that a criminal defendant must prove that the purposeful discrimination "had a discriminatory effect" on him. *Wayte v. United States*, 470 U.S. 598, 608, 105 S.Ct. 1524, 1531, 84 L.Ed.2d 547 (1985). Thus, to prevail under the Equal Protection Clause, McCleskey must prove that the decisionmakers in his case acted with discriminatory purpose. He offers no evidence specific to his own case that would support an inference that racial considerations played a part in his sentence. Instead, he relies solely on the Baldus study.11 McCleskey argues that the Baldus study compels an inference that his sentence rests on purposeful discrimination. McCleskey's claim that these statistics are sufficient proof of discrimination, without regard to the facts of a particular case, would extend to all capital cases in Georgia, at least where the victim was white and the defendant is black.

The Court has accepted statistics as proof of intent to discriminate in certain limited contexts. First, this Court has accepted statistical disparities as proof of an equal protection violation in the selection of the jury venire in a particular district. Although statistical proof normally must present a "stark" pattern to be accepted as the sole proof of discriminatory intent under the Constitution, *Arlington Heights v. Metropolitan Housing Dev. Corp.*, 429 U.S. 252, 266, 97 S.Ct. 555, 563, 50 L.Ed.2d 450 (1977), "[b]ecause of the nature of the jury-selection task, ... we have permitted a finding of constitutional violation even when the statistical pattern does not approach [such] extremes." Id., at 266, n. 13, 97 S.Ct., at 563, n. 13. Second, this Court has accepted statistics in the form of multiple-regression analysis to prove statutory violations under Title VII of the Civil Rights Act of 1964. Bazemore v. Friday, 478 U.S. 385, 400–401, 106 S.Ct. 3000, 3009, 92 L.Ed.2d 315 (1986) (opinion of BRENNAN, J., concurring in part).

But the nature of the capital sentencing decision, and the relationship of the statistics to that decision, are fundamentally different from the corresponding elements in the venire-selection or Title VII cases. Most importantly, each particular decision to impose the death penalty is made by a petit jury selected from a properly constituted venire. Each jury is unique in its composition, and the Constitution requires that its decision rest on consideration of innumerable factors that vary according to the characteristics of the individual defendant and the facts of the particular capital offense. See *Hitchcock v. Dugger*, 481 U.S. 393, 398–399, 107 S.Ct. 1821, 1824, 95 L.Ed.2d 347; *Lockett v. Ohio*, 438 U.S. 586, 602–605, 98 S.Ct. 2954, 2963–65, 57 L.Ed.2d 973 (1978) (plurality opinion of Burger, C.J.). Thus, the application of an inference drawn from the general statistics to a specific decision in a trial and sentencing simply is not comparable to the application of an inference drawn from general statistics to a specific venire-selection or Title VII case. In those cases, the statistics relate to fewer entities, and fewer variables are relevant to the challenged decisions.

Another important difference between the cases in which we have accepted statistics as proof of discriminatory intent and this case is that, in the venire-selection and Title VII contexts, the decisionmaker has an opportunity to explain the statistical disparity. See *Whitus v. Georgia*, 385 U.S., at 552, 87 S.Ct., at 647; *Texas Dept. of Community Affairs v. Burdine*, 450 U.S. 248, 254, 101 S.Ct. 1089, 1094, 67 L.Ed.2d 207 (1981); *McDonnell Douglas Corp. v. Green*, 411 U.S. 792, 802, 93 S.Ct. 1817, 1824, 36 L.Ed.2d 668 (1973). Here, the State has no practical opportunity to rebut the Baldus study. "[C]ontrolling considerations of ... public policy," *McDonald v. Pless*, 238 U.S. 264, 267, 35 S.Ct. 783, 784, 59 L.Ed. 1300 (1915), dictate that jurors "cannot be called ... to testify to the motives and influences that led to their verdict." *Chicago, B. & Q.R. Co. v. Babcock*, 204 U.S. 585, 593, 27 S.Ct. 326, 327, 51 L.Ed. 636 (1907). Similarly, the policy considerations behind a prosecutor's traditionally "wide discretion" suggest the impropriety of our requiring prosecutors to defend their decisions to seek death penalties, "often years after they were made." See *Imbler v. Pachtman*, 424 U.S. 409, 425–426, 96 S.Ct. 984, 992–993, 47 L.Ed.2d 128 (1976).18 Moreover, absent far stronger proof, it is unnecessary to seek such a rebuttal, because a legitimate and unchallenged explanation for the decision is apparent from the record: McCleskey committed an act for which the United States Constitution and Georgia laws permit imposition of the death penalty.

Finally, McCleskey's statistical proffer must be viewed in the context of his challenge. McCleskey challenges decisions at the heart of the State's criminal justice system. "[O]ne of society's most basic tasks is that of protecting the lives of its citizens and one of the most basic ways in which it achieves the task is through criminal laws against murder." *Gregg v. Georgia*, 428 U.S. 153, 226, 96 S.Ct. 2909, 2949, 49 L.Ed.2d 859 (1976) (WHITE, J., concurring). Implementation of these laws necessarily requires discretionary judgments. Because discretion is essential to the criminal justice process, we would demand exceptionally clear proof before we would infer that the discretion has been abused. The unique nature of the decisions at issue in this case also counsels against adopting such an inference from the disparities indicated by the Baldus study. Accordingly, we hold that the Baldus study is clearly insufficient to support an inference that any of the decisionmakers in McCleskey's case acted with discriminatory purpose.

B

McCleskey also suggests that the Baldus study proves that the State as a whole has acted with a discriminatory purpose. He appears to argue that the State has violated the Equal Protection Clause by adopting the capital punishment statute and allowing it to remain in force despite its allegedly discriminatory application. But " '[d]iscriminatory purpose' ... implies more than intent as volition or intent as awareness of consequences. It implies that the decisionmaker, in this case a state legislature, selected or reaffirmed a particular course of action at least in part 'because of,' not merely 'in spite of,' its adverse effects upon an identifiable group." *Personnel Administrator of Massachusetts v. Feeney*, 442 U.S. 256, 279, 99 S.Ct. 2282, 2296, 60 L.Ed.2d 870 (1979) (footnote and citation omitted). See *Wayte v. United States*, 470 U.S., at 608–609, 105 S.Ct., at 1531–1532. For this claim to prevail, McCleskey would have to prove that the Georgia Legislature enacted or maintained the death penalty statute because of an anticipated racially discriminatory effect. In Gregg v. Georgia, supra, this Court found that the Georgia capital sentencing system could operate in a fair and neutral manner. There was no evidence then, and there is none now, that the Georgia Legislature enacted the capital punishment statute to further a racially discriminatory purpose.

Nor has McCleskey demonstrated that the legislature maintains the capital punishment statute because of the racially disproportionate impact suggested by the Baldus study. As legislatures necessarily have wide discretion in the choice of criminal laws and penalties, and as there were legitimate reasons for the Georgia Legislature to adopt and maintain capital punishment, see *Gregg v. Georgia*, supra, at 183–187, 96 S.Ct., at 2929–2931 (joint opinion of Stewart, POWELL, and STEVENS, JJ.), we will not infer a discriminatory purpose on the part of the State of Georgia. **Accordingly, we reject McCleskey's equal protection claims.

III

McCleskey also argues that the Baldus study demonstrates that the Georgia capital sentencing system violates the Eighth Amendment. We begin our analysis of this claim by reviewing the restrictions on death sentences established by our prior decisions under that Amendment.

A

The Eighth Amendment prohibits infliction of "cruel and unusual punishments." This Court's early Eighth Amendment cases examined only the "particular methods of execution to determine whether they were too cruel to pass constitutional muster." *Gregg v. Georgia, supra*, at 170, 96 S.Ct., at 2923. See *In re Kemmler*, 136 U.S. 436, 10 S.Ct. 930, 34 L.Ed. 519 (1890) (electrocution); *Wilkerson v. Utah*, 99 U.S. (9 Otto) 130, 25 L.Ed. 345 (1879) (public shooting). Subsequently, the Court recognized that the constitutional prohibition against cruel and unusual punishments "is not fastened to the obsolete but may acquire meaning as public opinion becomes enlightened by a humane justice." *Weems v. United States*, 217 U.S. 349, 378, 30 S.Ct. 544, 553, 54 L.Ed. 793 (1910). In *Weems*, the Court identified a second principle inherent in the Eighth Amendment, "that punishment for crime should be graduated and proportioned to offense." Id., at 367, 30 S.Ct., at 549.

Chief Justice Warren, writing for the plurality in *Trop v. Dulles*, 356 U.S. 86, 99, 78 S.Ct. 590, 597, 2 L.Ed.2d 630 (1958), acknowledged the constitutionality of capital punishment. In his view, the "basic concept underlying the Eighth Amendment" in this area is that the penalty must accord with "the dignity of man." Id., at 100, 78 S.Ct., at 597. In applying this mandate, we have been guided by his statement that "[t]he Amendment must draw its meaning from the evolving standards of decency that mark the progress of a maturing society." Id., at 101, 78 S.Ct., at 598. Thus, our constitutional decisions have been informed by "contemporary values concerning the infliction of a challenged sanction," *Gregg v. Georgia*, 428 U.S., at 173, 96 S.Ct., at 2925. In assessing contemporary values, we have eschewed subjective judgment, and instead have sought to ascertain "objective indicia that reflect the public attitude toward a given sanction." Ibid. First among these indicia are the decisions of state legislatures, "because the ... legislative judgment weighs heavily in ascertaining" contemporary standards, id., at 175, 96 S.Ct., at 2926. We also have been guided by the sentencing decisions of juries, because they are "a significant and reliable objective index of contemporary values," id., at 181, 96 S.Ct., at 2928. Most of our recent decisions as to the constitutionality of the death penalty for a particular crime have rested on such an examination of contemporary values. E.g., *Enmund v. Florida*, 458 U.S. 782, 789–796, 102 S.Ct. 3368, 3372–3376, 73 L.Ed.2d 1140 (1982) (felony murder*); Coker v. Georgia*, 433 U.S. 584, 592–597, 97 S.Ct. 2861, 2866–2867, 53 L.Ed.2d 982 (1977) (plurality opinion of WHITE, J.) (rape); *Gregg v. Georgia*, supra, 428 U.S., at 179–182, 96 S.Ct., at 2928–2929 (murder).

B

Two principal decisions guide our resolution of McCleskey's Eighth Amendment claim. In *Furman v. Georgia*, 408 U.S. 238, 92 S.Ct. 2726, 33 L.Ed.2d 346 (1972), the Court concluded that the death penalty was so irrationally imposed that any particular death sentence could be presumed excessive. Under the statutes at issue in Furman, there was no basis for determining in any particular case whether the penalty was proportionate to the crime: "[T]he death penalty [was] exacted with great infrequency even for the most atrocious crimes and ... there [was] no meaningful basis for distinguishing the few cases in which it [was] imposed from the many cases in which it [was] not." *Id.*, at 313, 92 S.Ct., at 2764 (WHITE, J., concurring).

In *Gregg*, the Court specifically addressed the question left open in Furman—whether the punishment of death for murder is "under all circumstances, 'cruel and unusual' in violation of the Eighth and Fourteenth Amendments of the Constitution." 428 U.S., at 168, 96 S.Ct., at 2922. We noted that the imposition of the death penalty for the crime of murder "has a long history of acceptance both in the United States and in England." Id., at 176, 96 S.Ct., at 2926 (joint opinion of STEWART, POWELL, and STEVENS, JJ.). "The most marked indication of society's endorsement of the death penalty for murder [was] the legislative response to Furman." Id., at 179, 96 S.Ct., at 2928. During the 4–year period between Furman and Gregg, at least 35 States had reenacted the death penalty, and Congress had authorized the penalty for aircraft piracy. 428 U.S., at 179–180, 96 S.Ct., at 2928.23 The "actions of juries" were "fully compatible with the legislative judgments." Id., at 182, 96 S.Ct., at 2929. We noted that any punishment might be unconstitutionally severe if inflicted without penological justification, but concluded:

> "Considerations of federalism, as well as respect for the ability of a legislature to evaluate, in terms of its particular State, the moral consensus concerning the death penalty and its social utility as a sanction, require us to conclude, in the absence of more convincing evidence, that the infliction of death as a punishment for murder is not without justification and thus is not unconstitutionally severe." Id., at 186–187, 96 S.Ct., at 2931.

The second question before the Court in *Gregg* was the constitutionality of the particular procedures embodied in the Georgia capital punishment statute. We explained the fundamental principle of Furman, that "where discretion is afforded a sentencing body on a matter so grave as the determination of whether a human life should be taken or spared, that discretion must be suitably directed and limited so as to minimize the risk of wholly arbitrary and capricious action." 428 U.S., at 189, 96 S.Ct., at 2932. Numerous features of the then new Georgia statute met the concerns articulated in Furman. The Georgia system bifurcates guilt and sentencing proceedings so that the jury can receive all relevant information for sentencing without the risk that evidence irrelevant to the defendant's guilt will influence the jury's consideration of that issue. The statute narrows the class of murders subject to the death penalty to cases in which the jury finds at least one statutory aggravating circumstance beyond a reasonable doubt. Conversely, it allows the defendant to introduce any relevant mitigating evidence that might influence the jury not to impose a death sentence. See 428 U.S., at 163–164, 96 S.Ct., at 2920. The procedures also require a particularized inquiry into "'the circumstances of the offense together with the character and propensities of the offender.'" *Id.*, at 189, 96 S.Ct., at 2932 (quoting *Pennsylvania ex rel. Sullivan v. Ashe*, 302 U.S. 51, 55, 58 S.Ct. 59, 60, 82 L.Ed. 43 (1937)). Thus, "while some jury discretion still exists, 'the discretion to be exercised is controlled by clear and objective standards so as to produce non-discriminatory application.'" 428 U.S., at 197–198, 96 S.Ct., at 2936 (quoting *Coley v. State*, 231 Ga. 829, 834, 204 S.E.2d 612, 615 (1974)). Moreover, the Georgia system adds "an important additional safeguard against arbitrariness and caprice" in a provision for automatic appeal of a death sentence to the State Supreme Court. 428 U.S., at 198, 96 S.Ct., at 2936. The statute requires that court to review each sentence to determine whether it was imposed under the influence of passion or prejudice, whether the evidence supports the jury's finding of a statutory aggravating circumstance, and whether the sentence is disproportionate to sentences imposed in generally similar murder cases. To aid the court's review, the trial judge answers a questionnaire about the trial, including detailed questions as to "the quality of the defendant's representation [and] whether race played a role in the trial." Id., at 167, 96 S.Ct., at 2922.

C

In the cases decided after Gregg, the Court has imposed a number of requirements on the capital sentencing process to ensure that capital sentencing decisions rest on the individualized inquiry contemplated in *Gregg*. In *Woodson v. North Carolina*, 428 U.S. 280, 96 S.Ct. 2978, 49 L.Ed.2d 944 (1976), we invalidated a mandatory capital sentencing system, finding that the "respect for humanity underlying the Eighth Amendment requires consideration of the character and record of the individual offender and the circumstances of the particular offense as a constitutionally indispensable part of the process of inflicting the penalty of death." Id., at 304, 96 S.Ct., at 2991 (plurality opinion of Stewart, POWELL, and STEVENS, JJ.) (citation omitted). Similarly, a State must "narrow the class of murderers subject to capital punishment," *Gregg v.*

Georgia, supra, 428 U.S., at 196, 96 S.Ct., at 2936, by providing "specific and detailed guidance" to the sentencer. *Proffitt v. Florida*, 428 U.S. 242, 253, 96 S.Ct. 2960, 2967, 49 L.Ed.2d 913 (1976) (joint opinion of Stewart, POWELL, and STEVENS, JJ.).

In contrast to the carefully defined standards that must narrow a sentencer's discretion to impose the death sentence, the Constitution limits a State's ability to narrow a sentencer's discretion to consider relevant evidence that might cause it to decline to impose the death sentence. "[T]he sentencer ... [cannot] be precluded from considering, as a mitigating factor, any aspect of a defendant's character or record and any of the circumstances of the offense that the defendant proffers as a basis for a sentence less than death." *Lockett v. Ohio*, 438 U.S., at 604, 98 S.Ct., at 2964 (plurality opinion of Burger, C.J.) (emphasis in original; footnote omitted). See *Skipper v. South Carolina*, 476 U.S. 1, 106 S.Ct. 1669, 90 L.Ed.2d 1 (1986). Any exclusion of the "compassionate or mitigating factors stemming from the diverse frailties of humankind" that are relevant to the sentencer's decision would fail to treat all persons as "uniquely individual human beings." *Woodson v. North Carolina*, supra, 428 U.S., at 304, 96 S.Ct., at 2991.

Although our constitutional inquiry has centered on the procedures by which a death sentence is imposed, we have not stopped at the face of a statute, but have probed the application of statutes to particular cases. For example, in *Godfrey v. Georgia*, 446 U.S. 420, 100 S.Ct. 1759, 64 L.Ed.2d 398 (1980), the Court invalidated a Georgia Supreme Court interpretation of the statutory aggravating circumstance that the murder be "outrageously or wantonly vile, horrible or inhuman in that it involved torture, depravity of mind, or an aggravated battery to the victim." Ga.Code § 27–2534.1(b)(7) (1978). Although that court had articulated an adequate limiting definition of this phrase, we concluded that its interpretation in Godfrey was so broad that it may have vitiated the role of the aggravating circumstance in guiding the sentencing jury's discretion.

Finally, where the objective indicia of community values have demonstrated a consensus that the death penalty is disproportionate as applied to a certain class of cases, we have established substantive limitations on its application. In *Coker v. Georgia*, 433 U.S. 584, 97 S.Ct. 2861, 53 L.Ed.2d 982 (1977), the Court held that a State may not constitutionally sentence an individual to death for the rape of an adult woman. In *Enmund v. Florida*, 458 U.S. 782, 102 S.Ct. 3368, 73 L.Ed.2d 1140 (1982), the Court prohibited imposition of the death penalty on a defendant convicted of felony murder absent a showing that the defendant possessed a sufficiently culpable mental state. Most recently, in *Ford v. Wainwright*, 477 U.S. 399, 106 S.Ct. 2595, 91 L.Ed.2d 335 (1986), we prohibited execution of prisoners who are insane.

D

In sum, our decisions since Furman have identified a constitutionally permissible range of discretion in imposing the death penalty. First, there is a required threshold below which the death penalty cannot be imposed. In this context, the State must establish rational criteria that narrow the decisionmaker's judgment as to whether the circumstances of a particular defendant's case meet the threshold. Moreover, a societal consensus that the death penalty is disproportionate to a particular offense prevents a State from imposing the death penalty for that offense. Second, States cannot limit the sentencer's consideration of any relevant circumstance that could cause it to decline to impose the penalty. In this respect, the State cannot channel the sentencer's discretion, but must allow it to consider any relevant information offered by the defendant.

IV

A

In light of our precedents under the Eighth Amendment, McCleskey cannot argue successfully that his sentence is "disproportionate to the crime in the traditional sense." See *Pulley v. Harris*, 465 U.S. 37, 43, 104 S.Ct. 871, 876, 79 L.Ed.2d 29 (1984). He does not deny that he committed a murder in the course of a planned robbery, a crime for which this Court has determined that the death penalty constitutionally may be imposed. *Gregg v. Georgia*, 428 U.S., at 187, 96 S.Ct., at 2931. His disproportionality claim "is of a different sort." Pulley v. Harris, supra, 465 U.S., at 43, 104 S.Ct., at 876. McCleskey argues that the sentence in his case is disproportionate to the sentences in other murder cases.

On the one hand, he cannot base a constitutional claim on an argument that his case differs from other cases in which defendants did receive the death penalty. On automatic appeal, the Georgia Supreme Court found that McCleskey's death sentence was not disproportionate to other death sentences imposed in the State. *McCleskey v. State*, 245 Ga. 108, 263 S.E.2d 146 (1980). The court supported this conclusion with an appendix containing citations to 13 cases involving generally similar murders. See Ga.Code Ann. § 17–10–35(e) (1982). Moreover, where the statutory procedures adequately channel the sentencer's discretion, such proportionality review is not constitutionally required. *Pulley v. Harris*, supra, 465 U.S., at 50–51, 104 S.Ct., at 879.

On the other hand, absent a showing that the Georgia capital punishment system operates in an arbitrary and capricious manner, McCleskey cannot prove a constitutional violation by demonstrating that other defendants who may be similarly situated did not receive the death penalty. In *Gregg*, the Court confronted the argument that "the opportunities for discretionary action that are inherent in the processing of any murder case under Georgia law," 428 U.S., at 199, 96 S.Ct., at 2937, specifically the opportunities for discretionary leniency, rendered the capital sentences imposed arbitrary and capricious. We rejected this contention:

"The existence of these discretionary stages is not determinative of the issues before us. At each of these stages an actor in the criminal justice system makes a decision which may remove a defendant from consideration as a candidate for the death penalty. Furman, in contrast, dealt with the decision to impose the death sentence on a specific individual who had been convicted of a capital offense. Nothing in any of our cases suggests that the decision to afford an individual defendant mercy violates the Constitution. Furman held only that, in order to minimize the risk that the death penalty would be imposed on a capriciously selected group of offenders, the decision to impose it had to be guided by standards so that the sentencing authority would focus on the particularized circumstances of the crime and the defendant." *Ibid.*

Because McCleskey's sentence was imposed under Georgia sentencing procedures that focus discretion "on the particularized nature of the crime and the particularized characteristics of the individual defendant," id., at 206, 96 S.Ct., at 2940, we lawfully may presume that McCleskey's death sentence was not "wantonly and freakishly" imposed, id., at 207, 96 S.Ct., at 2941, and thus that the sentence is not disproportionate within any recognized meaning under the Eighth Amendment.

B

Although our decision in Gregg as to the facial validity of the Georgia capital punishment statute appears to foreclose McCleskey's disproportionality argument, he further contends that the Georgia capital punishment system is arbitrary and capricious in application, and therefore his sentence is excessive, because racial considerations may influence capital sentencing decisions in Georgia. We now address this claim.

To evaluate McCleskey's challenge, we must examine exactly what the Baldus study may show. Even Professor Baldus does not contend that his statistics prove that race enters into any capital sentencing decisions or that race was a factor in McCleskey's particular case. Statistics at most may show only a likelihood that a particular factor entered into some decisions. There is, of course, some risk of racial prejudice influencing a jury's decision in a criminal case. There are similar risks that other kinds of prejudice will influence other criminal trials. See *infra*, at 1776–1777. The question "is at what point that risk becomes constitutionally unacceptable," *Turner v. Murray*, 476 U.S. 28, 36, n. 8, 106 S.Ct. 1683, 1688, n. 8, 90 L.Ed.2d 27 (1986). McCleskey asks us to accept the likelihood allegedly shown by the Baldus study as the constitutional measure of an unacceptable risk of racial prejudice influencing capital sentencing decisions. This we decline to do.

Because of the risk that the factor of race may enter the criminal justice process, we have engaged in "unceasing efforts" to eradicate racial prejudice from our criminal justice system. *Batson v. Kentucky*, 476 U.S. 79, 85, 106 S.Ct. 1712, 1716, 90 L.Ed.2d 69 (1986).30 Our efforts have been guided by our recognition that "the inestimable privilege of trial by jury ... is a vital principle, underlying the whole administration of criminal justice," *Ex parte Milligan*, 4 Wall. 2, 123, 18 L.Ed. 281 (1866). See *Duncan v. Louisiana*, 391 U.S. 145, 155, 88 S.Ct. 1444, 1450, 20 L.Ed.2d 491 (1968). Thus, it is the jury that is a criminal defendant's fundamental "protection of life and liberty against race or color prejudice." *Strauder v. West Virginia*, 100 U.S. (10 Otto) 303, 309, 25 L.Ed. 664 (1880). Specifically, a capital sentencing jury representative of a criminal defendant's community assures a "'diffused impartiality,'" *Taylor v. Louisiana*, 419 U.S. 522, 530, 95 S.Ct. 692, 697, 42 L.Ed.2d 690 (1975) (quoting *Thiel v. Southern Pacific Co.*, 328 U.S. 217, 227, 66 S.Ct. 984, 989, 90 L.Ed. 1181 (1946) (Frankfurter, J., dissenting)), in the jury's task of "express[ing] the conscience of the community on the ultimate question of life or death," *Witherspoon v. Illinois*, 391 U.S. 510, 519, 88 S.Ct. 1770, 1775, 20 L.Ed.2d 776 (1968).

Individual jurors bring to their deliberations "qualities of human nature and varieties of human experience, the range of which is unknown and perhaps unknowable." *Peters v. Kiff*, 407 U.S. 493, 503, 92 S.Ct. 2163, 2168, 33 L.Ed.2d 83 (1972) (opinion of MARSHALL, J.). The capital sentencing decision requires the individual jurors to focus their collective judgment on the unique characteristics of a particular criminal defendant. It is not surprising that such collective judgments often are difficult to explain. But the inherent lack of predictability of jury decisions does not justify their condemnation. On the contrary, it is the jury's function to make the difficult and uniquely human judgments that defy codification and that "buil[d] discretion, equity, and flexibility into a legal system." H. Kalven & H. Zeisel, The American Jury 498 (1966).

McCleskey's argument that the Constitution condemns the discretion allowed decisionmakers in the Georgia capital sentencing system is antithetical to the fundamental role of discretion in our criminal justice system. Discretion in the criminal justice system offers substantial benefits to the criminal defendant. Not only can a jury decline to impose the death sentence, it can decline to convict or choose to convict of a lesser offense. Whereas decisions against a defendant's interest may be reversed by the trial judge or on appeal, these discretionary exercises of leniency are final and unreviewable. Similarly, the capacity of prosecutorial discretion to provide individualized justice is "firmly entrenched in American law." 2 W. LaFave & D. Israel, Criminal Procedure § 13.2(a), p. 160 (1984). As we have noted, a prosecutor can decline to charge, offer a plea bargain, or decline to seek a death sentence in any particular case. See n. 28, supra. Of course, "the power to be lenient [also] is the power to discriminate," K. Davis, Discretionary Justice 170 (1973), but a capital punishment system that did not allow for discretionary acts of leniency "would be totally alien to our notions of criminal justice." *Gregg v. Georgia*, 428 U.S., at 200, n. 50, 96 S.Ct., at 2937, n. 50.

C

At most, the Baldus study indicates a discrepancy that appears to correlate with race. Apparent disparities in sentencing are an inevitable part of our criminal justice system. The discrepancy indicated by the Baldus study is "a far cry from the major systemic defects identified in Furman," *Pulley v. Harris*, 465 U.S., at 54, 104 S.Ct., at 881. As this Court has recognized, any mode for determining guilt or punishment "has its weaknesses and the potential for misuse." *Singer v. United States*, 380 U.S. 24, 35, 85 S.Ct. 783, 790, 13 L.Ed.2d 630 (1965). *See Bordenkircher v. Hayes*, 434 U.S. 357, 365, 98 S.Ct. 663, 669, 54 L.Ed.2d 604 (1978). Specifically, "there can be 'no perfect procedure for deciding in which cases governmental authority should be used to impose death.'" *Zant v. Stephens*, 462 U.S. 862, 884, 103 S.Ct. 2733, 2746, 77 L.Ed.2d 235 (1983) (quoting *Lockett v. Ohio*, 438 U.S., at 605, 98 S.Ct., at 2965 (plurality opinion of Burger, C.J.)). Despite these imperfections, our consistent rule has been that constitutional guarantees are met when "the mode [for determining guilt or punishment] itself has been surrounded with safeguards to make it as fair as possible." *Singer v. United States*, supra, 380 U.S., at 35, 85 S.Ct., at 790. Where the discretion that is fundamental to our criminal process is involved, we decline to assume that what is unexplained is invidious. In light of the safeguards designed to minimize racial bias in the process, the fundamental value of jury trial in our criminal justice system, and the benefits that discretion provides to criminal defendants, we hold that the Baldus study does not demonstrate a constitutionally significant risk of racial bias affecting the Georgia capital sentencing process.

V

Two additional concerns inform our decision in this case. First, McCleskey's claim, taken to its logical conclusion, throws into serious question the principles that underlie our entire criminal justice system. The Eighth Amendment is not limited in application to capital punishment, but applies to all penalties. *Solem v. Helm*, 463 U.S. 277, 289–290, 103 S.Ct. 3001, 3009, 77 L.Ed.2d 637 (1983); *see Rummel v. Estelle*, 445 U.S. 263, 293, 100 S.Ct. 1133, 1149, 63 L.Ed.2d 382 (1980) (POWELL, J., dissenting). Thus, if we accepted McCleskey's claim that racial bias has impermissibly tainted the capital sentencing decision, we could soon be faced with similar claims as to other types of penalty. Moreover, the claim that his sentence rests on the irrelevant factor of race easily could be extended to apply to claims based on unexplained discrepancies that correlate to membership in other minority groups, and even to gender. Similarly, since McCleskey's claim relates to the race of his victim, other claims could apply with equally logical force to statistical disparities that correlate with the race or sex of other actors in the criminal justice system, such as defense attorneys, or judges. Also, there is no logical reason that such a claim need be limited to racial or sexual bias. If arbitrary and capricious punishment is the touchstone under the Eighth

Amendment, such a claim could—at least in theory—be based upon any arbitrary variable, such as the defendant's facial characteristics, or the physical attractiveness of the defendant or the victim, that some statistical study indicates may be influential in jury decisionmaking. As these examples illustrate, there is no limiting principle to the type of challenge brought by McCleskey. The Constitution does not require that a State eliminate any demonstrable disparity that correlates with a potentially irrelevant factor in order to operate a criminal justice system that includes capital punishment. As we have stated specifically in the context of capital punishment, the Constitution does not "plac[e] totally unrealistic conditions on its use." *Gregg v. Georgia*, 428 U.S., at 199, n. 50, 96 S.Ct., at 2937, n. 50.

Second, McCleskey's arguments are best presented to the legislative bodies. It is not the responsibility—or indeed even the right—of this Court to determine the appropriate punishment for particular crimes. It is the legislatures, the elected representatives of the people, that are "constituted to respond to the will and consequently the moral values of the people." *Furman v. Georgia*, 408 U.S., at 383, 92 S.Ct., at 2800 (Burger, C.J., dissenting). Legislatures also are better qualified to weigh and "evaluate the results of statistical studies in terms of their own local conditions and with a flexibility of approach that is not available to the courts," *Gregg v. Georgia*, supra, 428 U.S., at 186, 96 S.Ct., at 2931. Capital punishment is now the law in more than two-thirds of our States. It is the ultimate duty of courts to determine on a case-by-case basis whether these laws are applied consistently with the Constitution. Despite McCleskey's wide-ranging arguments that basically challenge the validity of capital punishment in our multiracial society, the only question before us is whether in his case, see supra, at 1761–1762, the law of Georgia was properly applied. We agree with the District Court and the Court of Appeals for the Eleventh Circuit that this was carefully and correctly done in this case.

....

Accordingly, we affirm the judgment of the Court of Appeals for the Eleventh Circuit.

....

Justice BLACKMUN, with whom Justice MARSHALL and Justice STEVENS join, and with whom Justice BRENNAN joins in all but Part IV–B, dissenting.

The Court today sanctions the execution of a man despite his presentation of evidence that establishes a constitutionally intolerable level of racially based discrimination leading to the imposition of his death sentence. I am disappointed with the Court's action not only because of its denial of constitutional guarantees to petitioner McCleskey individually, but also because of its departure from what seems to me to be well-developed constitutional jurisprudence.

Justice BRENNAN has thoroughly demonstrated, ante, that, if one assumes that the statistical evidence presented by petitioner McCleskey is valid, as we must in light of the Court of Appeals' assumption, there exists in the Georgia capital sentencing scheme a risk of racially based discrimination that is so acute that it violates the Eighth Amendment. His analysis of McCleskey's case in terms of the Eighth Amendment is consistent with this Court's recognition that because capital cases involve the State's imposition of a punishment that is unique both in kind and degree, the decision in such cases must reflect a heightened degree of reliability under the Amendment's prohibition of the infliction of cruel and unusual punishments. See *Woodson v. North Carolina*, 428 U.S. 280, 305, 96 S.Ct. 2978, 2991, 49 L.Ed.2d 944 (1976) (plurality opinion). I therefore join Parts II through V of Justice BRENNAN's dissenting opinion.

Yet McCleskey's case raises concerns that are central not only to the principles underlying the Eighth Amendment, but also to the principles underlying the Fourteenth Amendment. Analysis of his case in terms of the Fourteenth Amendment is consistent with this Court's recognition that racial discrimination is fundamentally at odds with our constitutional guarantee of equal protection. The protections afforded by the Fourteenth Amendment are not left at the courtroom door. *Hill v. Texas*, 316 U.S. 400, 406, 62 S.Ct. 1159, 1162, 86 L.Ed. 1559 (1942). Nor is equal protection denied to persons convicted of crimes. *Lee v. Washington*, 390 U.S. 333, 88 S.Ct. 994, 19 L.Ed.2d 1212 (1968) (per curiam). The Court in the past has found that racial discrimination within the criminal justice system is particularly abhorrent: "Discrimination on the basis of race, odious in all aspects, is especially pernicious in the administration of justice." *Rose v. Mitchell*, 443 U.S. 545, 555, 99 S.Ct. 2993, 2999, 61 L.Ed.2d 739 (1979). Disparate enforcement of criminal sanctions "destroys the appearance of justice and thereby casts doubt on the integrity of the judicial process." Id., at 555–556, 99 S.Ct., at 2999–3000. And only last Term Justice POWELL, writing for the Court, noted: "Discrimination within the judicial system is most pernicious because it is 'a stimulant to that race prejudice which is an impediment to securing to [black citizens] that equal justice which the law aims to secure to all others.' " *Batson v. Kentucky*, 476 U.S. 79, 87–88, 106 S.Ct. 1712, 1718, 90 L.Ed.2d 69 (1986), quoting *Strauder v. West Virginia*, 100 U.S. (10 Otto) 303, 308, 25 L.Ed. 664 (1880).

Moreover, the legislative history of the Fourteenth Amendment reminds us that discriminatory enforcement of States' criminal laws was a matter of great concern for the drafters. In the introductory remarks to its Report to Congress, the Joint Committee on Reconstruction, which reported out the Joint Resolution proposing the Fourteenth Amendment, specifically noted: "This deep-seated prejudice against color ... leads to acts of cruelty, oppression, and murder, which the local authorities are at no pains to prevent or punish." H.R. Joint Comm.Rep. No. 30, 39th Cong., 1st Sess., p. XVII (1866). Witnesses who testified before the Committee presented accounts of criminal acts of violence against black persons that were not prosecuted despite evidence as to the identity of the perpetrators.

I

A

The Court today seems to give a new meaning to our recognition that death is different. Rather than requiring "a correspondingly greater degree of scrutiny of the capital sentencing determination," *California v. Ramos*, 463 U.S. 992, 998–999, 103 S.Ct. 3446, 3451–3452, 77 L.Ed.2d 1171 (1983), the Court relies on the very fact that this is a case involving capital punishment to apply a lesser standard of scrutiny under the Equal Protection Clause. The Court concludes that "legitimate" explanations outweigh McCleskey's claim that his death sentence reflected a constitutionally impermissible risk of racial discrimination. The Court explains that McCleskey's evidence is too weak to require rebuttal "because a legitimate and unchallenged explanation for the decision is apparent from the record: McCleskey committed an act for which the United States Constitution and Georgia laws permit imposition of the death penalty." Ante, at 1769. The Court states that it will not infer a discriminatory purpose on the part of the state legislature because "there were legitimate reasons for the Georgia Legislature to adopt and maintain capital punishment." Ante, at 1770.

The Court's assertion that the fact of McCleskey's conviction undermines his constitutional claim is inconsistent with a long and unbroken line of this Court's case law. The Court on numerous occasions during the past century has recognized that an otherwise legitimate basis for a conviction does not outweigh an equal protection violation. In cases where racial discrimination in the administration of the criminal justice system is established, it has held that setting aside the conviction is the appropriate remedy. See, e.g., *Rose v. Mitchell*, 443 U.S., at 559, 99 S.Ct., at 3001; *Whitus v. Georgia*, 385 U.S. 545, 549–550, 87 S.Ct. 643, 646, 17 L.Ed.2d 599 (1967); *Strauder v. West Virginia*, 100 U.S. (10 Otto) 303, 25 L.Ed. 664 (1880). The Court recently reaffirmed the propriety of invalidating a conviction in order to vindicate federal constitutional rights. *Vasquez v. Hillery*, 474 U.S. 254, 106 S.Ct. 617, 88 L.Ed.2d 598 (1986). Invalidation of a criminal conviction on federal constitutional grounds does not necessarily preclude retrial and resentencing of the defendant by the State. *Hill v. Texas*, 316 U.S., at 406, 62 S.Ct., at 1162. The Court has maintained a per se reversal rule rejecting application of harmless-error analysis in cases involving racial discrimination that "strikes at the fundamental values of our judicial system and our society as a whole." *Rose v. Mitchell*, 443 U.S., at 556, 99 S.Ct., at 3000. We have noted that a conviction "in no way suggests that the discrimination did not impermissibly infect" earlier phases of the criminal prosecution "and, consequently, the nature or very existence of the proceedings to come." *Vasquez v. Hillery*, 474 U.S., at 263, 106 S.Ct., at 623. Hence, McCleskey's conviction and the imposition of his death sentence by the jury do not suggest that discrimination did not impermissibly infect the earlier steps in the prosecution of his case, such as the prosecutor's decision to seek the death penalty.

The Court's reliance on legitimate interests underlying the Georgia Legislature's enactment of its capital punishment statute is likewise inappropriate. Although that reasoning may be relevant in a case involving a facial challenge to the constitutionality of a statute, it has no relevance in a case dealing with a challenge to the Georgia capital sentencing system as applied in McCleskey's case. In *Batson v. Kentucky*, supra, we rejected such reasoning: "The Constitution requires ... that we look beyond the face of the statute ... and also consider challenged selection practices to afford 'protection against action of the State through its administrative officers in effecting the prohibited discrimination.'" 476 U.S., at 88, 106 S.Ct., at 1718, quoting *Norris v. Alabama*, 294 U.S. 587, 589, 55 S.Ct. 579, 580, 79 L.Ed. 1074 (1935).

B

In analyzing an equal protection claim, a court must first determine the nature of the claim and the responsibilities of the state actors involved to determine what showing is required for the establishment of a prima facie case. *Castaneda v. Partida*, 430 U.S. 482, 493–494, 97 S.Ct. 1272, 1279–1280, 51 L.Ed.2d 498 (1977). The Court correctly points out: "In its broadest form, McCleskey's claim of discrimination extends to every actor in the Georgia capital sentencing process, from the prosecutor who sought the death penalty and the jury that imposed the sentence, to the State itself that enacted the capital punishment statute and allows it to remain in effect despite its allegedly discriminatory application." Ante, at 1766. Having recognized the complexity of McCleskey's claim, however, the Court proceeds to ignore a significant element of that claim. The Court treats the case as if it is limited to challenges to the actions of two specific decisionmaking bodies—the petit jury and the state legislature. Ante, at 1767–1768, 1769–1770. This self-imposed restriction enables the Court to distinguish this case from the venire-selection cases and cases under Title VII of the Civil Rights Act of 1964 in which it long has accepted statistical evidence and has provided an easily applicable framework for review. See e.g., *Castaneda v. Partida, supra; Bazemore v. Friday*, 478 U.S. 385, 106 S.Ct. 3000, 92 L.Ed.2d 315 (1986) (BRENNAN, J., joined by all other Members of the Court, concurring in part). Considering McCleskey's claim in its entirety, however, reveals that the claim fits easily within that same framework. A significant aspect of his claim is that racial factors impermissibly affected numerous steps in the Georgia capital sentencing scheme between his indictment and the jury's vote to sentence him to death. The primary decisionmaker at each of the intervening steps of the process is the prosecutor, the quintessential state actor in a criminal proceeding. The District Court expressly stated that there were "two levels of the system that matter to [McCleskey], the decision to seek the death penalty and the decision to impose the death penalty." 580 F.Supp. 338, 379–380 (ND Ga.1984). I agree with this statement of McCleskey's case. Hence, my analysis in this dissenting opinion takes into account the role of the prosecutor in the Georgia capital-sentencing system. I certainly do not address all the alternative methods of proof in the Baldus study. Nor do I review each step in the process which McCleskey challenges. I concentrate on the decisions within the prosecutor's office through which the State decided to seek the death penalty and, in particular, the point at which the State proceeded to the penalty phase after conviction. This is a step at which the evidence of the effect of the racial factors was especially strong, see Supplemental Exhibits (Supp. Exh.) 56, 57; Transcript of Federal Habeas Corpus Hearing in No. C81-2434A (Tr.) 894–926, but is ignored by the Court.

II

A

A criminal defendant alleging an equal protection violation must prove the existence of purposeful discrimination. *Washington v. Davis*, 426 U.S. 229, 239–240, 96 S.Ct. 2040, 2047, 48 L.Ed.2d 597 (1976); *Whitus v. Georgia*, 385 U.S., at 550, 87 S.Ct., at 646. He may establish a prima facie case[4] of purposeful discrimination "by showing that the totality of the relevant facts gives rise to an inference of discriminatory purpose." *Batson v. Kentucky*, 476 U.S., at 94, 106 S.Ct., at 1721.[5] Once the defendant establishes a prima facie case, the burden shifts to the prosecution to rebut that case. "The State cannot meet this burden on mere general assertions that its officials did not discriminate or that they properly performed their official duties." Ibid. The State must demonstrate that the challenged effect was due to " 'permissible racially neutral selection criteria.' " Ibid., quoting *Alexander v. Louisiana*, 405 U.S. 625, 632, 92 S.Ct. 1221, 1226, 31 L.Ed.2d 536 (1972).

Under *Batson v. Kentucky* and the framework established in Castaneda v. Partida, McCleskey must meet a three-factor standard. First, he must establish that he is a member of a group "that is a recognizable, distinct class, singled out for different treatment." 430 U.S., at 494, 97 S.Ct., at 1280. Second, he must make a showing of a substantial degree of differential treatment.[6] Third, he must establish that the allegedly discriminatory procedure is susceptible to abuse or is not racially neutral. Ibid.

B

There can be no dispute that McCleskey has made the requisite showing under the first prong of the standard. The Baldus study demonstrates that black persons are a distinct group that are singled out for different treatment in the Georgia capital sentencing system. The Court acknowledges, as it must, that the raw statistics included in the Baldus study and presented by petitioner indicate that it is much less likely that a death sentence will result from a murder of a black person than from a murder of a white person. Ante, at 1764. White-victim cases are nearly 11 times more likely to yield a death sentence than are black-victim cases. Supp. Exh. 46. The raw figures also indicate that even within the group of defendants who are convicted of killing white persons and are thereby more likely to receive a death sentence, black defendants are more likely than white defendants to be sentenced to death. Supp. Exh. 47.

With respect to the second prong, McCleskey must prove that there is a substantial likelihood that his death sentence is due to racial factors. See *Hunter v. Underwood*, 471 U.S. 222, 228, 105 S.Ct. 1916, 1920, 85 L.Ed.2d 222 (1985). The Court of Appeals assumed the validity of the Baldus study and found that it "showed that systemic and substantial disparities existed in the penalties imposed upon homicide defendants in Georgia based on race of the homicide victim, that the disparities existed at a less substantial rate in death sentencing based on race of defendants, and that the factors of race of the victim and defendant were at work in Fulton County." 753 F.2d 877, 895 (CA11 1985). The question remaining therefore is at what point does that disparity become constitutionally unacceptable. *See Turner v. Murray*, 476 U.S. 28, 36, n. 8, 106 S.Ct. 1683, 1688, n. 8, 90 L.Ed.2d 27 (1986) (plurality opinion). Recognizing that additional factors can enter into the decisionmaking process that yields a death sentence, the authors of the Baldus study collected data concerning the presence of other relevant factors in homicide cases in Georgia during the time period relevant to McCleskey's case. They then analyzed the data in a manner that would permit them to ascertain the independent effect of the racial factors.

McCleskey demonstrated the degree to which his death sentence was affected by racial factors by introducing multiple-regression analyses that explain how much of the statistical distribution of the cases analyzed is attributable to the racial factors. McCleskey established that because he was charged with killing a white person he was 4.3 times as likely to be sentenced to death as he would have been had he been charged with killing a black person. Petitioner's Exhibit DB 82. McCleskey also demonstrated that it was more likely than not that the fact that the victim he was charged with killing was white determined that he received a sentence of death—20 out of every 34 defendants in McCleskey's midrange category would not have been sentenced to be executed if their victims had been black. Supp. Exh. 54.[8] The most persuasive evidence of the constitutionally significant effect of racial factors in the Georgia capital sentencing system is McCleskey's proof that the race of the victim is more important in explaining the imposition of a death sentence than is the factor whether the defendant was a prime mover in the homicide. Petitioner's Exhibit DB 82.[9] Similarly, the race-of-victim factor is nearly as crucial as the statutory aggravating circumstance whether the defendant had a prior record of a conviction for a capital crime.[10] Ibid. See Ga. Code Ann. § 17–10–30(b) (1982), ante, at 1762, n. 3. The Court has noted elsewhere that Georgia could not attach "the 'aggravating' label to factors that are constitutionally impermissible or totally irrelevant to the sentencing process, such as for example the race, religion, or political affiliation of the defendant." *Zant v. Stephens*, 462 U.S. 862, 885, 103 S.Ct. 2733, 2747, 77 L.Ed.2d 235 (1983). What we have held to be unconstitutional if included in the language of the statute surely cannot be constitutional because it is a de facto characteristic of the system.

McCleskey produced evidence concerning the role of racial factors at the various steps in the decisionmaking process, focusing on the prosecutor's decision as to which cases merit the death sentence. McCleskey established that the race of the victim is an especially significant factor at the point where the defendant has been convicted of murder and the prosecutor must choose whether to proceed to the penalty phase of the trial and create the possibility that a death sentence may be imposed or to accept the imposition of a sentence of life imprisonment. McCleskey demonstrated this effect at both the statewide level, see Supp. Exh. 56, Supp. Exh. 57, Tr. 897–910, and in Fulton County where he was tried and sentenced, see Supp. Exh. 59, Supp. Exh. 60, Tr. 978–981. The statewide statistics indicated that black-defendant/white-victim cases advanced to the penalty trial at nearly five times the rate of the black-defendant/black-victim cases (70% v. 15%), and over three times the rate of white-defendant/black-victim cases (70% v. 19%). See Supp. Exh. 56. The multiple-regression analysis demonstrated that racial factors had a readily identifiable effect at a statistically significant level. See id., at 57; Tr. 905. The Fulton County statistics were consistent with this evidence although they involved fewer cases. See Supp. Exh. 59, 60.

Individualized evidence relating to the disposition of the Fulton County cases that were most comparable to McCleskey's case was consistent with the evidence of the race-of-victim effect as well. Of the 17 defendants, including McCleskey, who were arrested and charged with homicide of a police officer in Fulton County during the 1973–1979 period, McCleskey, alone, was sentenced to death. The only other defendant whose case even proceeded to the penalty phase received a sentence of life imprisonment. That defendant had been convicted of killing a black police officer. See id., 61–63; Tr. 1050–1062.

As to the final element of the prima facie case, McCleskey showed that the process by which the State decided to seek a death penalty in his case and to pursue that sentence throughout the prosecution was susceptible to abuse. Petitioner submitted the deposition of Lewis R. Slaton, who, as of the date of the deposition, had been the District Attorney for 18 years in the county in which McCleskey was tried and sentenced. Deposition in No. 84–8176 of Lewis R. Slaton, Aug. 4, 1983, p. 5; see *McCleskey v. Zant*, 580 F.Supp. 338, 377, n. 15 (1984); Tr. 1316. As Mr. Slaton explained, the duties and responsibilities of that office are the prosecution of felony charges within the Atlanta Judicial Circuit that comprises Fulton County. Deposition 7–8. He testified that during his years in the office, there were no guidelines informing the Assistant District Attorneys who handled the cases how they should proceed at any particular stage of the prosecution. There were no guidelines as to when they should seek an indictment for murder as opposed to lesser charges, id., at 10–11; when they should recommend acceptance of a guilty plea to murder, acceptance of a guilty plea to a lesser charge, reduction of charges, or dismissal of charges at the postindictment-preconviction stage, id., at 25–26, 31; or when they should seek the death penalty, *id.*, at 31. Slaton testified that these decisions were left to the discretion of the individual attorneys who then informed Slaton of their decisions as they saw fit. Id., at 13, 24–25, 37–38.

Slaton's deposition proves that, at every stage of a prosecution, the Assistant District Attorney exercised much discretion. The only guidance given was "on-the-job training." *Id.*, at 20. Addressing plea bargaining, for example, Slaton stated that "through the training that the assistant DA's get, I think we pretty much think alike on the cases, on what we suggest." *Id.*, at 25. The sole effort to provide any consistency was Slaton's periodic pulling of files at random to check on the progress of cases. Id., at 28–29. Slaton explained that as far as he knew, he was the only one aware of this checking. *Id.*, at 28. The files contained information only as to the evidence in the case, not any indication as to why an attorney made a particular decision. The attorneys were not required to record why they sought an indictment for murder as opposed to a lesser charge, id., at 19, or why they recommended a certain plea, id., at 29–30.12 The attorneys were not required to report to Slaton the cases in which they decided not to seek the death penalty, *id.*, at 34–36, 38, or the cases in which they did seek the death penalty, id., at 41.

When questioned directly as to how the office decided whether to seek the death penalty, Slaton listed several factors he thought relevant to that decision, including the strength of the evidence, the atrociousness of the crime, and the likelihood that a jury would impose the death sentence. Id., at 59. He explained that the attorneys did not seek the death penalty in every case in which statutory aggravating factors existed. Id., at 38–39. Slaton testified that his office still operated in the same manner as it did when he took office in 1965, except that it has not sought the death penalty in any rape cases since this Court's decision in *Coker v. Georgia*, 433 U.S. 584, 97 S.Ct. 2861, 53 L.Ed.2d 982 (1977). Deposition 60.

In addition to this showing that the challenged system was susceptible to abuse, McCleskey presented evidence of the history of prior discrimination in the Georgia system. Justice BRENNAN has reviewed much of this history in detail in his dissenting opinion, ante, at 1786–1788, including the history of Georgia's racially based dual system of criminal justice. This historical background of the state action challenged "is one evidentiary source" in this equal protection case. *Arlington Heights v. Metropolitan Housing Development Corp.*, 429 U.S. 252, 267, 97 S.Ct. 555, 564, 50 L.Ed.2d 450 (1977); see also *Rogers v. Lodge*, 458 U.S. 613, 618, 623–625, 102 S.Ct. 3272, 3278–3279, 73 L.Ed.2d 1012 (1982). Although I would agree that evidence of "official actions taken long ago" could not alone establish that the current system is applied in an unconstitutionally discriminatory manner, I disagree with the Court's statement that such evidence is now irrelevant. Ante, at 1769, n. 20.

The above-described evidence, considered in conjunction with the other record evidence outlined by Justice BRENNAN, ante, at 1784–1786, and discussed in opinions dissenting from the judgment of the Court of Appeals, 753 F.2d, at 919 (Hatchett, J., dissenting in part and concurring in part); id., at 920–923 (Clark, J., dissenting in part and concurring in part), gives rise to an inference of discriminatory purpose. See *Washington v. Davis*, 426 U.S., at 239–242, 96 S.Ct., at 2047–2048. As in the context of the rule of exclusion, see n. 6, *supra*, McCleskey's showing is of sufficient magnitude that, absent evidence to the contrary, one must conclude that racial factors entered into the decisionmaking process that yielded McCleskey's death sentence. See *Castaneda v. Partida*, 430 U.S., at 494, n. 13, 97 S.Ct., at 1280, n. 13. The burden, therefore, shifts to the State to explain the racial selections. It must demonstrate that legitimate racially neutral criteria and procedures yielded this racially skewed result.

In rebuttal, the State's expert suggested that if the Baldus thesis was correct then the aggravation level in black-victim cases where a life sentence was imposed would be higher than in white-victim cases. See 580 F.Supp., at 373. The expert analyzed aggravating and mitigating circumstances "one by one, demonstrating that in life sentence cases, to the extent that any aggravating circumstance is more prevalent in one group than the other, there are more aggravating features in the group of white-victim cases than in the group of black-victim cases. Conversely, there were more mitigating circumstances in which black-victim cases had a higher proportion of that circumstance than in white-victim cases." Ibid. The District Court found that the State's suggestion was plausible. It concluded, however, that the State did not conclusively disprove McCleskey's case; yet it reasoned that the State's theory "stands to contradict any prima facie case." Ibid. I find that reasoning wrong as a matter of law, and the conclusion clearly erroneous.

The State did not test its hypothesis to determine if white-victim and black-victim cases at the same level of aggravating circumstances were similarly treated. Tr. 1613–1614, 1664. McCleskey's experts, however, performed this test on their data. Id., at 1297, 1729–1732, 1756–1761. They demonstrated that the racial disparities in the system were not the result of the differences in the average aggravation levels between white-victim and black-victim cases. See Supp. Exh. 72; Tr. 1291–1296; Petitioner's Exhibit DB 92. The State's meager and unsophisticated evidence cannot withstand the extensive scrutiny given the Baldus evidence. Here, as in *Bazemore v. Friday*, the State did not "demonstrate that when th[e] factors were properly organized and accounted for there was no significant disparity" between the death sentences imposed on defendants convicted of killing white victims and those imposed on defendants convicted of killing black victims. 478 U.S., at 403–404, n. 14, 106 S.Ct., at 3010, n. 14. In *Castaneda*, we rejected a similar effort by the State to rely on an unsupported countervailing theory to rebut the evidence. 430 U.S., at 500, 97 S.Ct., at 1283. In sum, McCleskey has demonstrated a clear pattern of differential treatment according to race that is "unexplainable on grounds other than race." *Arlington Heights v. Metropolitan Housing Development Corp.*, 429 U.S., at 266, 97 S.Ct., at 563.

III

The Court's explanations for its failure to apply this well-established equal protection analysis to this case are not persuasive. It first reasons that "each particular decision to impose the death penalty is made by a petit jury" and that the "application of an inference drawn from the general statistics to a specific decision in a trial and sentencing simply is not comparable to the application of an inference drawn from general statistics to a specific venire-selection or Title VII case." Ante, at 1768. According to the Court, the statistical evidence is less relevant because, in the two latter situations, there are fewer variables relevant to the decision and the "statistics relate to fewer entities." *Ibid.*

I disagree with the Court's assertion that there are fewer variables relevant to the decisions of jury commissioners or prosecutors in their selection of jurors, or to the decisions of employers in their selection, promotion, or discharge of employees. Such decisions involve a multitude of factors, some rational, some irrational. Second, I disagree with the comment that the venire-selection and employment decisions are "made by fewer entities." Certainly in the employment context, personnel decisions are often the product of several levels of decisionmaking within the business or government structure. The Court's statement that the decision to impose death is made by the petit jury also disregards the fact that the prosecutor screens the cases throughout the pretrial proceedings and decides to seek the death penalty and to pursue a capital case to the penalty phase where a death sentence can be imposed. McCleskey's claim in this regard lends itself to analysis under the framework we apply in assessing challenges to other prosecutorial actions. See *Batson v. Kentucky*, 476 U.S. 79, 106 S.Ct. 1712, 90 L.Ed.2d 69 (1986); see also *Wayte v. United States*, 470 U.S. 598, 608, n. 10, 105 S.Ct. 1524, 1531, n. 10, 84 L.Ed.2d 547 (1985) (applying Castaneda framework in challenge to prosecutor's allegedly selective enforcement of criminal sanction). It is appropriate to judge claims of racially discriminatory prosecutorial selection of cases according to ordinary equal protection standards. 470 U.S., at 608, 105 S.Ct., at 1531.

The Court's other reason for treating this case differently from venire-selection and employment cases is that in these latter contexts, "the decisionmaker has an opportunity to explain the statistical disparity," but in the instant case the State had no practical opportunity to rebut the Baldus study. Ante, at 1768. According to the Court, this is because jurors cannot be called to testify about their verdict and because policy considerations render it improper to require "prosecutors to defend their decisions to seek death penalties, 'often years after they were made.' " Ibid., quoting *Imbler v. Pachtman*, 424 U.S. 409, 425, 96 S.Ct. 984, 992, 47 L.Ed.2d 128 (1976).

I agree with the Court's observation as to the difficulty of examining the jury's decision-making process. There perhaps is an inherent tension between the discretion accorded capital sentencing juries and the guidance for use of that discretion that is constitutionally required. In his dissenting opinion, Justice BRENNAN demonstrates that the Eighth Amendment analysis is well suited to address that aspect of the case. Ante, at 1783. The Court's refusal to require that the prosecutor provide an explanation for his actions, however, is completely inconsistent with this Court's longstanding precedents. The Court misreads *Imbler v. Pachtman*. In that case, the Court held that a prosecutor who acted within the scope of his duties was entitled to absolute immunity in an action under 42 U.S.C. § 1983 for damages. We recognized that immunity from damages actions was necessary to prevent harassing litigation and to avoid the threat of civil litigation undermining the prosecutor's independence of judgment. We clearly specified, however, that the policy considerations that compelled civil immunity did not mean that prosecutors could not be called to answer for their actions. We noted the availability of both criminal sanctions and professional ethical discipline. 424 U.S., at 429, 96 S.Ct., at 994. Prosecutors undoubtedly need adequate discretion to allocate the resources of their offices and to fulfill their responsibilities to the public in deciding how best to enforce the law, but this does not place them beyond the constraints imposed on state action under the Fourteenth Amendment. Cf. *Ex parte Virginia*, 100 U.S. (10 Otto) 339, 25 L.Ed. 676 (1880) (upholding validity of conviction of state judge for discriminating on the basis of race in his selection of jurors).

The Court attempts to distinguish the present case from *Batson v. Kentucky*, in which we recently reaffirmed the fact that prosecutors' actions are not unreviewable. See ante, at 1768, n. 17. I agree with the Court's observation that this case is "quite different" from the Batson case. Ibid. The irony is that McCleskey presented proof in this case that would have satisfied the more burdensome standard of *Swain v. Alabama*, 380 U.S. 202, 85 S.Ct. 824, 13 L.Ed.2d 759 (1965), a standard that was described in *Batson* as having placed on defendants a "crippling burden of proof." 476 U.S., at 92, 106 S.Ct., at 1721. As discussed above, McCleskey presented evidence of numerous decisions impermissibly affected by racial factors over a significant number of cases. The exhaustive evidence presented in this case certainly demands an inquiry into the prosecutor's actions.

The Court's assertion that, because of the necessity of discretion in the criminal justice system, it "would demand exceptionally clear proof," ante, at 1769, before inferring abuse of that discretion thus misses the point of the constitutional challenge in this case. Its conclusory statement that "the capacity of prosecutorial discretion to provide individualized justice is 'firmly entrenched in American law,'" ante, at 1777, quoting 2 W. LaFave & J. Israel, Criminal Procedure § 13.2(a), p. 160 (1984), is likewise not helpful. The issue in this case is the extent to which the constitutional guarantee of equal protection limits the discretion in the Georgia capital sentencing system. As the Court concedes, discretionary authority can be discriminatory authority. Ante, at 1777. Prosecutorial decisions may not be "'deliberately based upon an unjustifiable standard such as race, religion, or other arbitrary classification.'" *Bordenkircher v. Hayes*, 434 U.S. 357, 364, 98 S.Ct. 663, 668, 54 L.Ed.2d 604 (1978), quoting *Oyler v. Boles*, 368 U.S. 448, 456, 82 S.Ct. 501, 505, 7 L.Ed.2d 446 (1962). Judicial scrutiny is particularly appropriate in McCleskey's case because "[m]ore subtle, less consciously held racial attitudes could also influence" the decisions in the Georgia capital sentencing system. *Turner v. Murray*, 476 U.S. 28, 35, 106 S.Ct. 1683, 1688, 90 L.Ed.2d 27 (1986); see n. 13, *supra*. The Court's rejection of McCleskey's equal protection claims is a far cry from the "sensitive inquiry" mandated by the Constitution.

IV

A

One of the final concerns discussed by the Court may be the most disturbing aspect of its opinion. Granting relief to McCleskey in this case, it is said, could lead to further constitutional challenges. Ante, at 1779–1781. That, of course, is no reason to deny McCleskey his rights under the Equal Protection Clause. If a grant of relief to him were to lead to a closer examination of the effects of racial considerations throughout the criminal justice system, the system, and hence society, might benefit. Where no such factors come into play, the integrity of the system is enhanced. Where such considerations are shown to be significant, efforts can be made to eradicate their impermissible influence and to ensure an evenhanded application of criminal sanctions.

B

Like Justice STEVENS, I do not believe acceptance of McCleskey's claim would eliminate capital punishment in Georgia. Post, at 1806. Justice STEVENS points out that the evidence presented in this case indicates that in extremely aggravated murders the risk of discriminatory enforcement of the death penalty is minimized. Ibid. I agree that narrowing the class of death-eligible defendants is not too high a price to pay for a death penalty system that does not discriminate on the basis of race. Moreover, the establishment of guidelines for Assistant District Attorneys as to the appropriate basis for exercising their discretion at the various steps in the prosecution of a case would provide at least a measure of consistency. The Court's emphasis on the procedural safeguards in the system ignores the fact that there are none whatsoever during the crucial process leading up to trial. As Justice WHITE stated for the plurality in *Turner v. Murray*, I find "the risk that racial prejudice may have infected petitioner's capital sentencing unacceptable in light of the ease with which that risk could have been minimized." 476 U.S., at 36, 106 S.Ct., at 1688. I dissent.

....

STATE V. LOFTIN

146 N.J. 295 (1996)

A jury convicted defendant, Donald Loftin, of the murder of Gary K. Marsh. At the penalty-phase hearing, a separately empanelled jury returned a death-penalty verdict, and the trial court sentenced defendant to death. Defendant appeals directly to this Court as of right. *See Rule* 2:2–1(a)(3). We affirm defendant's conviction for murder and his sentence of death.

A. Guilt Phase

1. The crime

On May 5, 1992, Gary Marsh was working the midnight to six-thirty a.m. shift at an Exxon service station located on Alternate Route One in Lawrenceville, New Jersey. Marsh had a key to the office that was located behind the gas pumps, away from the highway. At approximately 4:10 a.m., E. Thomas Citron stopped for gas at the station. He paid for his gas with a fifty-dollar bill.

David Paddock was scheduled to relieve Marsh at 6:30 a.m. Arriving early, at approximately 6:10 a.m., he waited in his parked truck. Paddock observed a customer pull up to the pumps, wait without service, and ultimately leave. Paddock then left his truck to find Marsh.

Approaching the station office, Paddock saw three large planters, a cola machine, a pile of pink slip receipts, and a half-eaten orange. The orange was found on the ground just outside the passenger door of Marsh's car. Paddock further observed the office keys in the door. The door was unlocked, but pulled closed. Marsh lay inside the office, his head in a puddle of blood. Paddock closed down the station and called the Lawrenceville Police. The murder had occurred between Citron's visit at 4:10 a.m. and Paddock finding Marsh at 6:10 a.m.

Marsh lay on his back with his head located three feet from the front doorway that was located in the northeast corner of the office. Officer Maple, one of the first police officers on the scene, observed that a large amount of blood was on the floor next to Marsh's head. His feet were pointed toward the southwest (back) corner of the office. Marsh's arms were at his side and his eyes were shut. His right eye was black and blue. Although still alive, Marsh was unconscious and struggling for breath.

Marsh's clothing did not appear to have been disturbed. His pockets were not turned out and he still was in possession of some personal items, including three dollar bills, some change, and lottery tickets. A spent brass shell casing was found on the office floor, four to six inches from Marsh's left ear. Further, the cash drawer sat empty on one of the counters and there was also some loose change on the floor. Closer examination of the station office revealed several crucial pieces of evidence. Although no fingerprints of defendant were found anywhere in or around the station, the bullet used to kill Marsh served a similar purpose. The bullet that killed Marsh was found behind a pegboard that hung on the back wall of the office. A few of Marsh's hairs were removed from the area of the bullet hole. Later ballistics testing traced that bullet to a .380 caliber Bryco Model 48 pistol, purchased by defendant from D & S Gun Supplies of Levittown, Pennsylvania, and subsequently discovered by the police in defendant's car under the dashboard.

Additionally, Mr. Peterson, the station owner, determined that approximately ninety dollars had been taken from that evening's revenue. Moreover, although Mr. Citron reported purchasing gas from Marsh with a fifty-dollar bill around 4:00 a.m., there was no fifty-dollar bill in the proceeds or on Marsh's person. Defendant was in possession of a fifty-dollar bill at the time of his arrest. However, the two fingerprints detected on that bill did not belong to Marsh, Loftin, or Citron.

Further examination of the office revealed the absence of a struggle, a significant fact because the office is particularly small and narrow. Without taking account of the furniture in the office, the dimensions of the room are nine feet seven inches by thirteen feet, five inches. The office furniture did, however, consume considerable floor space. As Officer Maple testified, "Nothing appeared to be touched or disturbed or moved or appeared out of place. I mean, it was ... the office was, to me appeared basically untouched. There was no signs of any struggle or anybody going through or gone through anything there."

Marsh never regained consciousness and died approximately nine and one half hours after he was discovered bleeding in the Exxon station. The next day, Mercer County's Chief Medical Examiner, Dr. Raafat Ahmad, conducted an autopsy and concluded that the cause of death was a gunshot wound to the head and that the manner of death was homicide. The entry wound was located in the left temporal region, with the bullet grazing the top of the left ear on entry. The bullet penetrated Marsh's skull, passed directly through both hemispheres of his brain, and exited on the opposite side at the right temporoparietal area, slightly above the right temple. Dr. Ahmad opined that the bullet's slight upward path through the skull was possibly caused by the tilting of the head on impact. The bullet caused fracturing lines to run from the top to the base of the skull on both sides. The doctor testified that Marsh's right eye was black and blue as a result of the bullet causing fractures inside the skull and the blood seeping into the eye area.

Dr. Ahmad observed that Marsh had no external injuries, cuts, or bruises. There were no "defense wounds" on the hands or arms that would have been indicative of a struggle.

....

We have previously held that when, as in this case, the trial involves an interracial murder, defendant is entitled to have the potential jurors questioned about prejudices and biases. *Ramseur, supra*, 106 N.J. at 243–48, 524 A.2d 188; see also *State v. Horcey*, 266 N.J.Super. 415, 418, 629 A.2d 1367 (App.Div.1993) ("Whenever there is a racial or ethnic difference between victim and accused, at defendant's request the trial judge should inquire of the prospective jurors as to whether the disparity will affect their ability to be impartial.").

Prior to *voir dire*, defense counsel requested that the trial court ask the following questions:

> Mr. Loftin is a black man, victim white, would that in any way prejudice or influence your sitting as a juror in this case?

> Do you know of any reason, such as prejudice, bias, or other opinion that you can think of that would prevent you from serving as a completely impartial juror?

The trial court agreed to ask the first question and noted that the other question would come out in the court's own extensive *voir dire*. The court informed defense counsel that "if at the end of the court's preliminary questioning of the jurors you still have additional questions that you'd like to raise from this list, we can address it at that time."

The trial court gave the following instruction to the prospective jurors:

> But in deciding what the facts are, you are to do so without bias, without prejudice, without sympathy, passion, or favor of any kind, and I'm going to talk a little bit more about bias and prejudice, because for most of us, when we hear the word prejudice, we get defensive because we don't want anybody to think or accuse us of being prejudiced. And that's why I asked that question yesterday.

> I pointed out to you that the defendant in this case is an African–American and that the victim in this matter is white, and I asked would any of you make a decision in this case based on the racial makeup, and you all answered no....

> We need to find a little bit about yours, so these attorneys can make a decision as to whether or not your bias or prejudice will impact on your ability to be fair and impartial in this case.

> So I'm going to give you an example. And it's a very simplistic example, but I don't want you to think that because the example is simplistic that I'm not trying to make a serious point. I keep emphasizing your responsibility as a juror is very, very critical....

> The example I'm going to use is a sports example. I am a diehard Cowboys fan.... Now, you know, the attorneys in this courthouse know where I'm going from. And some of them are real bold. They let me know, I don't like the Cowboys. How do I handle that?....

> Getting back to the attorneys, when they walk in here, do I tell them you can't get justice because you don't have the ... right attitude.... Do I take that kind of attitude and be open about my bias, or do I take the more subtle approach?....

> Obviously, isn't that how we deal with our biases and prejudices. This is 1994. We don't go out and openly tell people how we feel about things. Only you know that, but we ask you

if have a bias or if you have a prejudice that would affect your ability to be fair to the State of New Jersey and fair to the defendant, tell us about it. You don't—you can wait a couple of questions, you can do it at sidebar, but if you believe that you have any bias that could affect your ability to be fair and impartial, please raise your hand.

Defense counsel never objected to this explanation or sought to ask additional questions. Defendant now, however, claims that the trial court's failure to question jurors more extensively was plain error. First, defendant contends that the trial court's question invited only one answer, namely, that jurors are not racist. *See Moore, supra,* 122 N.J. at 449, 585 A.2d 864. Second, defendant argues that the football analogy trivialized the issue.

We find defendant's contentions to be without merit. We have often held that a general question about racial prejudice is sufficient absent a specific request or objection from defense counsel seeking more probing questions. *See, e.g., State v. Perry,* 124 N.J. 128, 157, 590 A.2d 624 (1991) (finding one general question investigating potential presence of "any passion, prejudice, sympathy or bias" is sufficient absent request from counsel for more specific inquiry); *State v. McDougald,* 120 N.J. 523, 550–51, 577 A.2d 419 (1990)(finding one general question sufficient to probe bias and prejudice where defense counsel also had freedom to inquire); *Ramseur, supra,* 106 N.J. at 244–48, 524 A.2d 188 (finding general question sufficient and commenting on ability of counsel to probe further). The trial court invited defense counsel to suggest additional questions if necessary, but defense counsel made no such request.

Justice Handler argues that the trial court had a duty to conduct a further inquiry because defendant was charged with an interracial crime. *Post* at 416–20, 680 A.2d at 737–39 (Handler, J., dissenting). However, that complaint ignores the basic principle of *Perry, McDougald,* and *Ramseur,* that "a capital defendant accused of an interracial crime ... cannot complain of a judge's failure to question the venire on racial prejudice unless the defendant has specifically requested such an inquiry." *Turner, supra,* 476 U.S. at 37, 106 S.Ct. at 1689, 90 L.Ed.2d at 37. Defense counsel asked for a general inquiry into bias, and the judge honored that request. "We in no way require or suggest that the judge broach the topic *sua sponte.*" Id. 476 U.S. at 37 n.10, 106 S.Ct. at 1688 n. 10, 90 L.Ed.2d at 37 n. 10.

We find that the trial court's question was proper and appropriate. The court's football example may not have been ideal, but it adequately conveyed the point.

....

Note

Justice Marshall maintained that the unconstitutionality of the death penalty as reflected by the disproportionate imposition on African Americans in particular, was more than an issue of Equal Protection. He argued forcibly for an Eight Amendment violation given the history of racial application. See his concurring opinion below in *Furman v. Georgia,* 408 U.S. 238 (1972).

FURMAN V. GEORGIA.
408 U.S. 238 (1972)

Mr. Justice MARSHALL, concurring.

....

VI

In addition, even if capital punishment is not excessive, it nonetheless violates the Eighth Amendment because it is morally unacceptable to the people of the United States at this time in their history.

In judging whether or not a given penalty is morally acceptable, most courts have said that the punishment is valid unless 'it shocks the conscience and sense of justice of the people.'

Judge Frank once noted the problems inherent in the use of such a measuring stick:

> '(The court,) before it reduces a sentence as 'cruel and unusual,' must have reasonably good assurances that the sentence offends the 'common conscience.' And, in any context, such a standard-the community's attitude-is usually an unknowable. It resembles a slithery shadow, since one can seldom learn, at all accurately, what the community, or a majority, actually feels. Even a carefully-taken 'public opinion poll' would be inconclusive in a case like this.'

While a public opinion poll obviously is of some assistance in indicating public acceptance or rejection of a specific penalty,its utility cannot be very great. This is because whether or not a punishment is cruel and unusual depends, not on whether its mere mention 'shocks the conscience and sense of justice of the people,' but on whether people who were fully informed as to the purposes of the penalty and its liabilities would find the penalty shocking, unjust, and unacceptable.

In other words, the question with which we must deal is not whether a substantial proportion of American citizens would today, if polled, opine that capital punishment is barbarously cruel, but whether they would find it to be so in the light of all information presently available.

This is not to suggest that with respect to this test of unconstitutionality people are required to act rationally; they are not. With respect to this judgment, a violation of the Eighth Amendment is totally dependent on the predictable subjective, emotional reactions of informed citizens.

It has often been noted that American citizens know almost nothing about capital punishment. Some of the conclusions arrived at in the preceding section and the supporting evidence would be critical to an informed judgment on the morality of the death penalty: e.g., that the death penalty is no more effective a deterrent than life imprisonment, that convicted murderers are rarely executed, but are usually sentenced to a term in prison; that convicted murderers usually are model prisoners, and that they almost always become lawabiding citizens upon their release from prison; that the costs of executing a capital offender exceed the costs of imprisoning him for life; that while in prison, a convict under sentence of death performs none of the useful functions that life prisoners perform; that no attempt is made in the sentencing process to ferret out likely recidivists for execution; and that the death penalty may actually stimulate criminal activity.

This information would almost surely convince the average citizen that the death penalty was unwise, but a problem arises as to whether it would convince him that the penalty was morally reprehensible. This problem arises from the fact that the public's desire for retribution, even though this is a goal that the legislature cannot constitutionally pursue as its sole justification for capital punishment, might influence the citizenry's view of the morality of capital punishment. The solution to the problem lies in the fact that no one has ever seriously advanced retribution as a legitimate goal of our society. Defenses of capital punishment are always mounted on deterrent or other similar theories. This should not be surprising. It is the people of this country who have urged in the past that prisons rehabilitate as well as isolate offenders, and it is the people who have injected a sense of purpose into our penology. I cannot believe that at this stage in our history, the American people would ever knowingly support purposeless vengeance. Thus, I believe that the great mass of citizens would conclude on the basis of the material already considered that the death penalty is immoral and therefore unconstitutional.

But, if this information needs supplementing, I believe that the following facts would serve to convince even the most hesitant of citizens to condemn death as a sanction: capital punishment is imposed discriminatorily against certain identifiable classes of people; there is evidence that innocent people have been executed before their innocence can be proved; and the death penalty wreaks havoc with our entire criminal justice system. Each of these facts is considered briefly below.

Regarding discrimination, it has been said that '(i)t is usually the poor, the illiterate, the underprivileged, the member of the minority group-the man who, because he is without means, and is defended by a court-appointed attorney-who becomes society's sacrificial lamb . . ..' Indeed, a look at the bare statistics regarding executions is enough to betray much of the discrimination. A total of 3,859 persons have been executed since 1930, of whom 1,751 were white and 2,066 were Negro. Of the executions, 3,334 were for murder; 1,664 of the executed murderers were white and 1,630 were Negro; 455 persons, including 48 whites and 405 Negroes, were executed for rape. It is immediately apparent that Negroes were executed far more often than whites in proportion to their percentage of the population. Studies indicate that while the higher rate of execution among Negroes is partially due to a higher rate of crime, there is evidence of racial discrimination. Racial or other discriminations should not be surprising. In *McGautha v. California*, 402 U.S., at 207, 91 S.Ct., at 1467, this Court held 'that committing to the untrammeled discretion of the jury the power to pronounce life or death in capital cases is (not) offensive to anything in the Constitution.' This was an open invitation to discrimination.

There is also overwhelming evidence that the death penalty is employed against men and not women. Only 32 women have been executed since 1930, while 3,827 men have met a similar fate. It is difficult to understand why women have received such favored treatment since the purposes allegedly served by capital punishment seemingly are equally applicable to both sexes.

It also is evident that the burden of capital punishment falls upon the poor, the ignorant, and the under privileged members of society. It is the poor, and the members of minority groups who are least able to voice their complaints against capital punishment. Their impotence leaves them victims of a sanction that the wealthier, better-represented, just-as-guilty person can escape. So long as the capital sanction is used only against the forlorn, easily forgotten members of society, legislators are content to maintain the status quo, because change would draw attention to the problem and concern might develop. Ignorance is perpetuated and apathy soon becomes its mate, and we have today's situation.

Just as Americans know little about who is executed and why, they are unaware of the potential dangers of executing an innocent man. Our 'beyond a reasonable doubt' burden of proof in criminal cases is intended to protect the innocent, but we know it is not foolproof. Various studies have shown that people whose innocence is later convincingly established are convicted and sentenced to death.

Proving one's innocence after a jury finding of guilt is almost impossible. While reviewing courts are willing to entertain all kinds of collateral attacks where a sentence of death is involved, they very rarely dispute the jury's interpretation of the evidence. This is, perhaps, as it should be. But, if an innocent man has been found guilty, he must then depend on the good faith of the prosecutor's office to help him establish his innocence. There is evidence, however, that prosecutors do not welcome the idea of having convictions, which they labored hard to secure, overturned, and that their cooperation is highly unlikely.

No matter how careful courts are, the possibility of perjured testimony, mistaken honest testimony, and human error remain all too real.We have no way of judging how many innocent persons have been executed but we can be certain that there were some. Whether there were many is an open question made difficult by the loss of those who were most knowledgeable about the crime for which they were convicted. Surely there will be more as long as capital punishment remains part of our penal law.

While it is difficult to ascertain with certainty the degree to which the death penalty is discriminatorily imposed or the number of innocent persons sentenced to die, there is one conclusion about the penalty that is universally accepted-i.e., it 'tends to distort the course of the criminal law.' As Mr. Justice Frankfurter said:

> 'I am strongly against capital punishment . . .. When life is at hazard in a trial, it sensational-izes the whole thing almost unwittingly; the effect on juries, the Bar, the public, the Judiciary, I regard as very bad. I think scientifically the claim of deterrence is not worth much. Whatever proof there may be in my judgment does not outweigh the social loss due to the inherent sensa-tionalism of a trial for life.'

The deleterious effects of the death penalty are also felt otherwise than at trial. For example, its very existence 'inevitably sabotages a social or institutional program of reformation.' In short '(t)he presence of the death penalty as the keystone of our penal system bedevils the adminis-tration of criminal justice all the way down the line and is the stumbling block in the path of general reform and of the treatment of crime and criminals.'

Assuming knowledge of all the facts presently available regarding capital punishment, the average citizen would, in my opinion, find it shocking to his conscience and sense of justice. For this reason alone capital punishment cannot stand.

....

UNITED STATES V. BARNES.

532 F.Supp.2d 625 (S.D. NY 2008)

MEMORANDUM DECISION AND ORDER

STEPHEN C. ROBINSON, District Judge.

Khalid Barnes ("Defendant"), along with two of his brothers, Dawud Barnes and Tuere Barnes, are charged with multiple crimes allegedly related to their participation in an enterprise the Government refers to as the "Barnes Brothers Organization." Defendant is charged with, *inter alia,* racketeering, narcotics distribution, and murder. On January 19, 2006, the Government served a Notice of Intent to Seek the Death Penalty against Khalid Barnes (the "Notice of Intent") for his alleged involvement in the murders of Demond Vaughan and Sergio Santana.

Defendant now challenges the constitutionality of the Federal Death Penalty Act, 18 U.S.C. §§ 3591 et seq. ("FDPA") and its application to this case. Further, the Government asks this Court to file an amended Notice of Intent. For the reasons set forth below, Defendant's motions are DENIED and the Government is granted leave to file its amended Notice of Intent.

I. Background

On November 1, 2004, a federal grand jury returned a twenty-nine count superceding indictment (the "S2 Indictment"), charging thirteen individuals, including Defendant, with crimes relating to their alleged participation in the Barnes Brothers Organization. The Government alleges that the Barnes Brothers Organization is a violent narcotics distribution ring that operated in and around Peekskill, New York. The S2 Indictment added four counts of capital murder against Khalid Barnes for the murders of Demond Vaughan and Sergio Santana. The S2 Indictment also included a Notice of Special Findings, alleging the existence of certain threshold factors rendering the capital counts eligible for punishment by death.

In its January 19, 2006 Notice of Intent, the Government specifically declared its intention to seek a sentence of death in the event the jury convicts Khalid Barnes of murder. The Notice of Intent also included the particular statutory proportionality factors, *see* 18 U.S.C. § 3591(a)(2), the statutory aggravating factors, *see* 18 U.S.C. § 3592(c), and the non-statutory aggravating factors, *see* 18 U.S.C. § 3593(a)(2), the Government intends to prove at trial to justify a sentence of death.

On August 7, 2006, a federal grand jury returned a thirty-eight count ninth superceding indictment (the "S9 Indictment"), charging Defendant and his two brothers with multiple crimes arising out of their alleged involvement with the Barnes Brothers Organization. The S9 Indictment charges Khalid Barnes with, *inter alia,* racketeering, in violation of 18 U.S.C. § 1962, racketeering conspiracy, in violation of 18 U.S.C. § 1962(d), various substantive narcotics distribution charges, various gun possession charges, in violation 18 U.S.C. § 924(c), and the murders of Demond Vaughan and Sergio Santana by the use of a firearm during and in relation to, or in furtherance of, a drug trafficking crime or a crime of violence, in violation of 18 U.S.C. § 924(j). The S9 Indictment also included a Notice of Special Findings, alleging the existence of certain threshold factors rendering the capital counts eligible for punishment by death.

The Government has asked this Court for permission to file an amended Notice of Intent that relates to the S9 Indictment. The Government provided this Court and Defendant a proposed amended Notice of Intent that it wishes to file.

....

C. Racial And Geographic Disparities In The Application Of The Federal Death Penalty

Defendant next asserts that the statistics from a 2000 Department of Justice study (the "the DOJ Report") on the federal death penalty show that it is disproportionately sought against minority group defendants and in the South. Using these statistics, he makes both constitutional and non-constitutional claims.

1. Racial Disparities

Defendant's arguments with respect to race are foreclosed by the Supreme Court's opinion in *McCleskey v. Kemp.* In *McCleskey,* the Court began its analysis "with the basic principle that a defendant who alleges an equal protection violation has the burden of proving 'the existence of purposeful discrimination.'" *McCleskey,* 481 U.S. at 292, 107 S.Ct. 1756 (quoting *Whitus v. Georgia,* 385 U.S. 545, 550, 87 S.Ct. 643, 17 L.Ed.2d 599 (1967)). The Court next observed that a "corollary to this principle is that a criminal defendant must prove that the purposeful discrimination 'had a discriminatory effect' on him." *Id.* (quoting Wayte v. United States, 470 U.S. 598, 608, 105 S.Ct. 1524, 84 L.Ed.2d 547 (1985)). Thus, the Court concluded, to prevail on a claim under the Equal Protection Clause, a defendant "must prove that the decisionmakers in *his* case acted with discriminatory purpose." *Id.* (emphasis in original). The defendant in *McCleskey* argued that a study, which showed that the death penalty in Georgia was imposed more often on black defendants and killers of white victim, showed that the decision-makers in his case acted with discriminatory purpose. The Court held, however, that statistical studies, such as the ones in this case, were "clearly insufficient to support an inference that any of the decision makers in McCleskey's case acted with discriminatory purpose." *Id.* at 297, 107 S.Ct. 1756; *see also Bin Laden,* 126 F.Supp.2d at 260 ("At its core, therefore, *McCleskey* stands for the notion that, by themselves, systemic statistics cannot prove racially discriminatory intent in support of an equal protection claim by a particular capital defendant"). Under *McCleskey,* Defendant cannot establish an equal protection violation using the statistics from the DOJ Report. *See Williams,* 2004 WL 2980027, *Sampson,* 275 F.Supp.2d at 89-93; *see also Bin Laden,* 126 F.Supp.2d at 260-62.

Defendant attempts to distinguish *McCleskey* on two grounds. First, Defendant argues that unlike the defendant in *McCleskey* who asserted that he was the victim of irrational government conduct, Defendant is being subjected to a system that "discriminates systemically." *Def. Mem.* at 68. Second, Defendant argues that unlike in *McCleskey,* where the statistics reflected the decisions of many actors, including individual prosecutors and juries, the statistics from the DOJ Report reflect the decision of only one entity, the Attorney General of the United States. As explained below, Defendant's attempts to distinguish McCleskey fail.

Defendant has not shown how the fact that he asserts that he is being subjected to a system that "discriminates systemically" changes the Court's conclusion that statistical studies are insufficient to show discriminatory purpose. In *McCleskey*, the Court observed that the defendant had standing to challenge the state's discrimination based on the statistics relating to the race of the victim because he was asserting his own right to be free from irrational government conduct. *McCleskey*, 481 U.S. at 291 n. 8, 107 S.Ct. 1756. Here, Defendant claims that in contrast to the defendant in *McCleskey*, he is a victim of a system that "discriminates systemically." Regardless of what is causing Defendant's alleged constitutional injury, however, he is still relying on statistics to support that injury. Accordingly, our analysis of his claim is no different from the Court's analysis in *McCleskey*. "In *McCleskey*, as here, the defendant was required to establish discriminatory intent, which, the Court held, systemic statistics could not do." *Williams*, 2004 WL 2980027. .

Defendant's second argument also fails. Defendant argues that unlike in *McCleskey*, where the Court was concerned about "deducing a consistent state-action 'policy' from the capital-sentencing performances of hundreds of juries and scores of local prosecutors," his "only claim here is prosecutorial discrimination, and, since 1988, all federal capital prosecutions have been personally authorized by a single officer of the United States, the Attorney General." *Def. Mem.* at 69, 70. However, this Court agrees with Judge Buchwald that:

In *McCleskey*, the Court noted that the statistics proffered in support of the equal protection claim had a different effect than they would have had in the context of a venire-selection or Title VII case. In a venire-selection or Title VII case, the Court noted, "statistics relate to fewer entities, and fewer variables are relevant to the challenged decisions." *McCleskey*, 481 U.S. at 295, 107 S.Ct. 1756. Defendants' argument that the *"fewer entities"* rationale is not present in this case-given defendants' contention that "[t]he only claim here is prosecutorial discrimination, and, since 1988, all federal capital prosecutions ... have been personally [sic] authorized by a single officer of the United States, the Attorney General"-has a basis in fact. However, defendants have not explained why the Court's *"fewer variables"* rationale is not sufficient to reach the same result. Nor have defendants explained how the statistics at issue here constitute the requisite "exceptionally clear proof of discriminatory intent, *McCleskey*, 481 U.S. at 297, 107 S.Ct. 1756, in light of the Courts determination that similar systemic statistics in *McCleskey* did not." Defendants' attempt to distinguish *McCleskey* must therefore be rejected.

Williams, 2004 WL 2980027 (footnote omitted). Accordingly, because *McCleskey* must guide this Court's decision, Defendant's arguments with respect to race are denied.

....

Note

Occasionally state legislatures have tried to address the issue of racial disparity in the imposition of the death penalty, as opposed to abolition of the death penalty completely. A notably attempt was that of North Carolina. The Racial Justice Act, N.C. Gen. Stat. Ann. § 15A-2011 (West 2009, was enacted as a response to the United States Supreme Court decision in *McCleskey*, (above) and its holding that an Equal Protection violation regarding racially discriminatory imposition of the death penalty can only successful if intent to discriminate is demonstrated. The 2009 North Carolina act, alternatively, allowed for the establishment of impermissible disparate impact based on statistical data.

In 2012, a North Carolina trial court found, pursuant to the Racial Justice Act, that an African American defendant, facing a death sentence, successfully demonstrated based on statistical impact, because "the imposition of capital punishment was impermissibly discriminatory [where] race was materially, practically, and statistically significant factor in the decision to exercise preemptory challenges during jury selection by prosecutors". The defendant Marcus Robinson, was sentenced to life imprisonment. *State v. Robinson*, No. 91-CRS-23143 (N.C. Sup. Ct. Div. Apr. 20, 2012).

Following three subsequent determinations wherein statistical date was used to support this *Batson v. Kentucky, supra*, attack on death sentences, the North Carolina legislature ultimately repealed the Racial Justice Act on June 5, 2013.

For a full discussion of the North Carolina Racial Justice Act *See,* John M. Powers, *State v. Robinson And the Racial Justice Act: Statistical Evidence Of Racial Discrimination In Capital Proceedings,* 29 HARV. J. RACIAL & ETHNIC JUST. 117 (2013).

Prior to the North Carolina effort, Kentucky enacted in 1998 a Racial Justice Act which provided:

(1) No person shall be subject to or given a sentence of death that was sought on the basis of race.

(2) A finding that race was the basis of the decision to seek a death sentence may be established if the court finds that race was a significant factor in decisions to seek the sentence of death in the Commonwealth at the time the death sentence was sought.

(3) Evidence relevant to establish a finding that race was the basis of the decision to seek a death sentence may include statistical evidence or other evidence, or both, that death sentences were sought significantly more frequently:

(a) Upon persons of one race than upon persons of another race; or

(b) As punishment for capital offenses against persons of one race than as punishment for capital offenses against persons of another race.

(4) The defendant shall state with particularity how the evidence supports a claim that racial considerations played a significant part in the decision to seek a death sentence in his or her case. The claim shall be raised by the defendant at the pre-trial conference. The court shall schedule a hearing on the claim and shall prescribe a time for the submission of evidence by both parties. If the court finds that race was the basis of the decision to seek the death sentence, the court shall order that a death sentence shall not be sought.

(5) The defendant has the burden of proving by clear and convincing evidence that race was the basis of the decision to seek the death penalty. The Commonwealth may offer evidence in rebuttal of the claims or evidence of the defendant.

Ky. Rev. Stat. Ann. § 532.300-309 (West 1998).

As indicated above, the defendant has the burden to prove by clear and convincing evidence that racial bias played a role in their individual case, which limited the use of statewide statistics. This is an extremely difficult burden for defendants to meet and although Kentucky has not reported data on the effectiveness of the Act, it appears that few if any have successfully avoided the death penalty under this provision. *See, in general,* Gennaro F. Vito, *The Racial Justice Act in Kentucky,* 37 NO. KY L. REV. 273 (2010).

....

Race and Disproportionate Sentencing in Drug Cases

UNITED STATES V. BLEWETT
Brief of Amicus Curiae NAACP Legal Defense & Educational Fund, Inc. in Support of Defendants-Appellants 2013 WL 5304321 (6th Cir. 2013)

ARGUMENT

The sentencing disparity between crack-cocaine and powder cocaine (the "100:1 ratio" or "100:1 classification")—and its particularized impact in the African-American community—have become notorious symbols of racial discrimination in the modern criminal justice system. Since the enactment of the 100:1 ratio, African Americans have suffered a panoply of direct and indirect harms, including pronounced disparities in rates of conviction and incarceration for drug offenses, disparities in lengths of sentences, and disparities in collateral consequences, as compared to whites. The unjust and arbitrary nature of the 100:1 ratio has provoked widespread criticism and gravely undermined the legitimacy of the criminal justice system. *See* Part II, *infra.*

In 2010, Congress enacted the Fair Sentencing Act ("FSA") which eliminated the 100:1 ratio, and replaced it with a much smaller disparity for crack and powder cocaine offenses. In enacting the law, Congress recognized that the 100:1 ratio lacked any penological justification; there was no evidence that crack cocaine was one hundred times more harmful than powder cocaine; and that the overwhelming majority of persons subject to excessive sentences under the 100:1 ratio were African American. *Id.*

The cases of Cornelius Blewett and Jarreous Blewitt ("the Blewetts") are an illustration. Both are serving ten-year mandatory minimums for offenses involving less than 30 grams of crack—offenses that would not have been subject to mandatory minimums had they involved powder cocaine. The FSA helps to remedy this unequal treatment: under the statute, the Blewetts are not subject to any mandatory minimum sentence. The Government, however, insists that the FSA should be interpreted so that the pre-FSA 100:1 classification keeps the Blewetts in prison. That interpretation raises grave constitutional problems, and this Court should reject it. The failure to apply the FSA to the Blewetts and similar cases will undermine the integrity of the criminal justice system in much the same way as the 100:1 ratio did prior to the enactment of the FSA.

I. The 100:1 Federal Sentencing Ratio Between Crack and Powder Cocaine Is Unjust and Discriminatory.

African Americans have suffered a vast array of well-documented and undisputed harms as a result of the application and the perpetuation of the 100:1 ratio. These harms include:

- African Americans have been incarcerated for federal crack-related offenses in substantially higher numbers and proportions than whites, even though whites use crack cocaine in greater numbers. Although more than 50% of reported crack users are white, whites represent less than 10% of federal convictions for crack offenses. Meanwhile African Americans comprise approximately 32% of reported crack cocaine users, but 82% of federal convictions for crack offenses.

- African Americans have been subject to longer federal prison sentences because of the 100:1 ratio. In 1986, prior to the institution of the 100:1 ratio, the average federal drug sentence for African Americans was 11% higher than it was for whites. Four years later, after the introduction of the 100:1 ratio, the average federal drug sentence for African Americans was 49% higher than for whites. As of 2003, African Americans served nearly as much time in prison for a drug offense in the federal system (58.7 months) as whites did for a violent offense (61.7 months).

- The exponentially longer prison terms stemming from the 100:1 ratio subject the broader African-American community to a host of negative consequences in excess of the initial sentence, including exclusion from labor markets, voting disenfranchisement, civic disengagement and damage to familial and social networks. Moreover, reintegration and reentry upon release are more difficult after prolonged incarceration because family and community relationships are often attenuated and support networks are typically deteriorated.

Given the fact that African Americans have been consistently overrepresented among those who have been prosecuted and sentenced under the 100:1 ratio, African Americans will certainly bear the brunt of any decision finding that the FSA is not retroactive. Before the FSA's enactment, African Americans comprised 78.5% of crack cocaine defendants and 78.8% of crack-cocaine offenders who received mandatory minimum penalties. United States Sentencing Comm'n ("USSC"), *2010 Annual Report*, 35-36 (2010).

II. Congress Enacted the FSA to Remedy the Arbitrary and Racially Discriminatory 100:1 Ratio.

In light of the overwhelming evidence that: (1) the 100:1 ratio was arbitrary and lacked any support in chemistry or penology; and (2) the classification imposed excessive sentences on African Americans, the USSC issued four reports to Congress where it repeatedly explained that the 100:1 ratio was "too high and unjustified," that it "reflected unjustified race based differences," and that it should be significantly modified. *Dorsey v. United States* 132 S. Ct. 2321, 2329 (2012). A wide range of voices echoed the USSC, including judges, civil rights advocates, and congressional leadership. Even the Department of Justice ("DOJ") recognized that "the current cocaine sentencing disparity is difficult to justify based on the facts and science" and that the racial "impact of these laws has fueled the belief across the country that federal cocaine laws are unjust." DOJ proposed formulating a policy that would "completely eliminate the sentencing disparity between crack and powder cocaine."

In 2010, Congress finally heeded these recommendations and enacted the FSA. *Dorsey*, 132 S. Ct. at 2329. The FSA's legislative history makes clear that the unfair sentencing of African Americans was a motivating factor behind the Act.

Thus, for example, Senator Dick Durbin, the author of the FSA, stated "[Ff]eavy [crack-cocaine] sentencing enacted years ago took its toll primarily in the African-American community. It resulted in the incarceration of thousands of people ... and a belief in the African-American community that it was fundamentally unfair." Steny Hoyer, Majority Leader of the House of Representatives explained that the:

> 100-to-1 disparity has had a racial dimension as well, helping to fill our prisons with African Americans disproportionately put behind bars for longer. The 100-to-1 disparity is counterproductive and unjust. That's not just my opinion, but the opinion of a bipartisan U.S. Sentencing Commission, the Judicial Conference of the United States, the National District Attorneys Association, the National Association of Police Organizations, the Federal Law Enforcement Officers Association, the International Union of Police Associations, and dozens of former Federal judges and prosecutors.

The concerns crossed political lines. For example, the FSA was co-sponsored by longtime conservative leader Senator Jeff Sessions. Additionally, Republican Representative Daniel Lungren, who helped author the original 100:1 ratio, supported the FSA and stated that the 100:1 ratio "has led to racial sentencing disparities which simply cannot be ignored in any reasoned discussion of this issue." Lungren also acknowledged the arbitrariness of the sentencing disparity: "We initially came out of committee with a 20-to-1 ratio. By the time we finished on the floor, it was 100-to-1. We didn't really have an evidentiary basis for it, but that's what we did, thinking we were doing the right thing at the time."

The Congressional intent behind the FSA was clear: to remedy the arbitrary and discriminatory 100:1 ratio.

III. The Panel Correctly Applied the Canon of Constitutional Avoidance in Interpreting the FSA.

Given the considerable record evidence that the 100:1 ratio was arbitrary and treats citizens unequally based on race—and Congress's knowledge of that record evidence—a failure to apply the FSA retroactively raises two significant constitutional questions. *First*, an interpretation of the FSA that denies retroactivity risks imputing a discriminatory purpose to Congress, which was aware that the ratio lacked a penological justification, and discriminated against African Americans, when the FSA was passed. *Second*, there is no legitimate state interest in imprisoning people under a sentencing classification that has been recognized as arbitrary and discriminatory. Retroactive application of the FSA, however, avoids these substantial constitutional concerns. *See United States v. Blewett,* 719 F.3d 482, 487 (6th Cir. 2013), *vacated,* pending rehearing, *U.S. v. Blewett* No. 12-5226 (6th Cir. July 11, 2013). ("'[W]here a statute is susceptible of two constructions, by one of which grave and doubtful constitutional questions arise and by the other of which such questions are avoided, our duty is to adopt the latter.'") (quoting *United States ex rel. Attorney General v. Delaware & Hudson Co.,* 213 U.S. 366, 40 (1909)) (additional citation omitted).

A. The Government's Interpretation of the FSA Raises Serious Questions of an Illicit Racial Purpose.

The Government insists Congress did not intend for the FSA to apply to persons already sentenced under the 100:1 classification. *See* Gov't Pet., DOC. 006111578150 at 11. But, as the Panel discussed, the Government's interpretation risks imputing an unconstitutional purpose to Congress's action. *See Blewett,* 719 F.3d at 487-88.

An examination of the equal protection principles at issue is instructive. The equal protection component of the Fifth and Fourteenth Amendments " 'requires that all persons subjected to legislation shall be treated alike, under like circumstances and conditions, both in the privileges conferred and in the liabilities imposed.' " *Engquist v. Oregon Dep't of Agric,* 553 U.S. 591, 602 (2008) (quoting *Hayes v. Missouri,* 120 U.S. 68, 71-72 (1887) (alteration omitted)). The judiciary must be particularly vigilant in enforcing this principle, which *amicus* refers to as the impartiality principle, where it has been the most often dishonored: the law's unequal treatment of African Americans, *See, e.g., Rose v. Mitchell,* 443 U.S. 545, 554 (1979) ("Discrimination on account of race was the primary evil at which the Amendments adopted after the War Between the States, including the Fourteenth Amendment, were aimed."); *Strauder v. West Virginia,* 100 U.S. 303, 306 (1880) (recognizing that the "common purpose" of the Reconstruction Amendments, including the Equal Protection Clause, was to "secur[e] to a race recently emancipated, a race that through many generations had been held in slavery, all the civil rights that [whites] enjoy"). Nowhere is impartiality more important than in the criminal justice system, because "[discrimination on the basis of race, odious in all respects, is especially pernicious in the administration of justice." *Rose,* 443 U.S. at 555.

A law violates the impartiality principle when it is motivated by a racially discriminatory purpose. *See, e.g., Hunter v. Underwood,* 471 U.S. 222, 233 (1985). Individuals subject to unduly harsh mandatory minimum sentences for crack offenses under the 100:1 ratio were overwhelmingly African-American. When the consequences of a legislative classification track race as closely as they do here, no additional evidence is necessary to support a finding of racial purpose. *See Till of Arlington Heights v. Metro Hous. Dev. Corp.,* 429 U.S. 252, 266 (1977) ("Sometimes a clear pattern, unexplainable on grounds other than race, emerges from the effect of the state action even when the governing legislation appears neutral on its face.") (citing, *inter alia, Yick Wo v. Hopkins,* 118 U. S. 356 (1886), and *Gomillion v. Lightfoot,* 364 U. S. 339 (1960)).

That principle applies with special force here because, by 2010, Congress recognized that the vast majority of those who received an excessive sentence due to the 100:1 classification were African-American. *See* Parts I & II, *supra.* As Judge Calabresi stated in 1995: "If Congress ... was made aware of both the dramatically disparate impact among minority groups of enhanced crack penalties and the limited evidence supporting such enhanced penalties," but were to allow the 100:1 classification to persist, "subsequent equal protection challenges based on claims of discriminatory purpose might well lie." *United States v. Then,* 56 F.3d 464, 468 (2d Cir. 1995) (concurring opinion).

For these reasons, the Government's interpretation of the FSA raises the prospect of assigning a discriminatory purpose to Congress. The Blewetts, by contrast, have offered a persuasive interpretation of the statute that raises none of these concerns and should therefore be adopted. *See* Blewetts' En Banc Br. Doc. 006111771993 at 3-14.

B. Interpreting the FSA to Deny Resentencing Would Implicate Equal Protection Regardless of Congress's Purpose.

The Government's interpretation of the FSA would raise serious equal protection concerns even if this Court concluded it would not impute a discriminatory purpose to Congress, because the impartiality principle does more than ensure that laws are not motivated by race. To withstand equal protection scrutiny, any "classification 'must be reasonable, not arbitrary, and must rest upon some ground of difference having a fair and substantial relation to the object of the legislation, so that all persons similarly circumstanced shall be treated alike.' " *Bowman,* 564 F.3d at 776 (quoting *Johnson v. Robison,* 415 U.S. 361, 374-75 (1974)) (additional citations omitted).

This standard, known as rational-basis review, is applied with more or less rigor depending on the context. It is applied deferentially in challenges to most social and economic legislation, where " 'the Constitution presumes that even improvident decisions will eventually be rectified by the democratic processes.' " *Northville Downs v. Granholm,* 622 F.3d 579, 586 (6th Cir. 2010) (quoting *City of Cleburne v. Cleburne Living Ctr.,* 473 U.S. 432, 440-41 (1985)). By contrast, courts have applied this review more rigorously to certain unusual classifications that raise doubts about the integrity of the democratic process. This more rigorous approach has been called " 'rational basis with a bite.' " *Am, Express Travel Related Servs. Co., v. Kentucky,* 641 F.3d 685, 692 (6th Cir. 2011). More generally, it can be seen as a type of heightened review that calls for " 'careful consideration' " of whether the legislature has fulfilled its duty to act impartially. *United States v. Windsor,* 133 S. Ct. 2675, 2692 (2013) (citation omitted); *see Cleburne,* 473 U.S. at 452 (Stevens, J., joined by Burger, C.J., concurring) (arguing that the tiered approach to equal protection scrutiny represents a single standard whose application varies with context, and explaining that the term " 'rational' " "includes elements of legitimacy and neutrality that must always characterize the performance of the sovereign's duty to govern impartially").

The Supreme Court has applied such heightened review to invalidate statutory classifications that discriminate against identifiable groups, even when classifications targeting the group are not categorically subject to heightened scrutiny. *See, e.g., Romer v. Evans*, 517 U.S. 620, 635 (1996) (discrimination against gays and lesbians); *Cleburne*, 473 U.S. at 450 (discrimination against people with intellectual disabilities); *see also Burstyn v. City of Miami Beach*, 663 F.Supp. 528, 536-37 (S.D. Fla. 1987) (discrimination against the elderly). Heightened review is also warranted where a classification is designed to entrench the privileged treatment of a favored group. *See Zobel v. Williams*, 457 U.S. 55, 63-64 (1974) (invalidating Alaska's dividend distribution scheme that provided more money to residents who had lived in the state longer); *Craigmiles v. Giles*, 312 F.3d 220, 224 (6th Cir. 2002) (invalidating an economic regulation aimed at "protecting a discrete interest group from economic competition"). In both of these circumstances, the democratic process has broken down, and the legislature has no legitimate justification for treating similarly-situated people differently.

These same principles apply here. As Judge Calabresi recognized in 1995, even if evidence concerning the 100:1 classification were insufficient to establish racially illicit purpose, that evidence "might nonetheless serve to support a claim of irrationality," given the more rigorous review that has been applied when "courts have reason to be concerned about possible discrimination." *Then*, 56 F.3d at 468 (citations omitted). By 2010, Congress knew that the 100:1 ratio lacked any evidence-based justification, even at the time it was enacted, and that the overwhelming majority of defendants who received excessively harsh sentences as a result were African American. If, as the Government contends, Congress nonetheless decided to maintain the arbitrary and discriminatory 100:1 classification for anyone already imprisoned, that would be a decision of an " 'unusual character,' " warranting " 'careful consideration to determine whether [it is] obnoxious' " to the constitutional requirement of equal protection. *Windsor*, 133 S. Ct. at 2692 (quoting *Romer*, 517 U.S. at 633) (additional quotation marks and citation omitted).

Careful scrutiny is especially warranted here given the long history of facially race-neutral laws targeting African Americans. *See, e.g., Shuttlesworth v. City of Birmingham*, 382 U.S. 87, 102 (1965) (Fortas, J., concurring) (explaining that "Shuttlesworth's arrest [for loitering] was an incident in the tense racial conflict in Birmingham"); Douglas A. Blackmon, *Slavery By Another Name: The Re-Enslavement of Black Americans from the Civil War to World War II*53 (2008) (detailing the historical use of facially neutral measures like vagrancy laws to subjugate African Americans).

The 100:1 classification cannot survive such careful scrutiny, because it is not supported by a legitimate, impartial state interest. *See, e.g.,Romer*, 517 U.S. at 632-33 (recognizing that a classification must be supported by "an independent and legitimate legislative end"); *see also Cleburne*, 473 U.S. at 446-47 (majority); *id.* at 452 (Stevens, J., concurring); *Zobel*, 457 U.S. at 63-64. This is not a case where the state proffered an independent, neutral justification for a classification (providing a benefit to veterans), which had adverse consequences on women. *See Personnel Adm. of Mass. v. Feeney,* 442 U.S. 256, 279 (1979). Here, the Government's proffered justification of finality, *see* En Banc Pet. at 10-11, is a euphemism for ossifying an arbitrary and discriminatory classification.

To be clear, *amicus* recognizes that finality can be a legitimate state interest. *See generally Penry v. Lynaugh,* 492 U.S. 302, 313-14 (1989) (citation omitted).[23] But not always, and not here. " 'As Justice Harlan wrote: 'There is little societal interest in permitting the criminal process to rest at a point where it ought properly never to repose.' " *Id.* at 330.

The Blewetts are imprisoned because of a 100:1 sentencing ratio, which, as Congress itself recognized, dramatically overstates the harm caused by crack as compared to powder cocaine, and thereby fails "to treat like offenders alike," or "treat different offenders (*e.g.*, major drug traffickers and low-level dealers) differently." *Dorsey,* 132 S. Ct. 2328, Not only is that classification arbitrary, it "reflects] unjustified race-based differences." *Id.* There is no legitimate state interest in keeping the Blewetts in prison because of a classification that Congress has recognized to be arbitrary and discriminatory. To do so would require their sentences to " 'rest at a point' " they " 'ought properly never to repose.' " *Penry,* 492 U.S. at 330.

C. The Government's Interpretation of the FSA Raises Eighth Amendment Concerns.

In addition to the arguments set forth here, LDF supports the argument made by *amicus curiae* National Association of Criminal Defense Lawyers. The Government's interpretation of the FSA raises substantial problems under the Eighth Amendment as well.

The Eighth Amendment is implicated when the law imposes a sentence in an arbitrary manner with what are known to be pronounced effects on a particular race. *See Furman,* 408 U.S. at 244-45 (Douglas, J., concurring) ("[I]t is 'cruel and unusual' to apply the death penalty— or any other penalty— selectively to minorities whose numbers are few, who are outcasts of society, and who are unpopular, but whom society is willing to see suffer though it would not countenance general application of the same penalty across the board."). Race cannot—and must not—play any role in the imposition of criminal sanctions. *Rose,* 443 U.S. at 555. Denying retroactive effect to the FSA, and continuing the well-documented racial discrimination associated with the 100:1 ratio, violates this basic precept.

CONCLUSION

"The concept of equal justice under law requires the State to govern impartially. The sovereign may not draw distinctions between individuals based solely on differences that are irrelevant to a legitimate governmental objective." *Lehr v. Robertson*, 463 U.S. 248, 265 (1983) (citations omitted). The Government's interpretation of the FSA conflicts with these principles, and the Panel properly rejected it in an appropriate exercise of constitutional avoidance.

....

DORSEY V. UNITED STATES
576 U.S. 260 (2012)

Justice BREYER delivered the opinion of the Court.

Federal statutes impose mandatory minimum prison sentences upon those convicted of federal drug crimes. These statutes typically base the length of a minimum prison term upon the kind and amount of the drug involved. Until 2010, the relevant statute imposed upon an offender who dealt in powder cocaine the same sentence it imposed upon an offender who dealt in one one-hundredth that amount of crack cocaine. It imposed, for example, the same 5–year minimum term upon (1) an offender convicted of possessing with intent to distribute 500 grams of powder cocaine as upon (2) an offender convicted of possessing with intent to distribute 5 grams of crack.

In 2010, Congress enacted a new statute reducing the crack-to-powder cocaine disparity from 100-to-1 to 18-to-1. Fair Sentencing Act, 124 Stat. 2372. The new statute took effect on August 3, 2010. The question here is whether the Act's more lenient penalty provisions apply to offenders who committed a crack cocaine crime before August 3, 2010, but were not sentenced until after August 3. We hold that the new, more lenient mandatory minimum provisions do apply to those pre-Act offenders.

I

The underlying question before us is one of congressional intent as revealed in the Fair Sentencing Act's language, structure, and basic objectives. Did Congress intend the Act's more lenient penalties to apply to pre-Act offenders sentenced after the Act took effect?

We recognize that, because of important background principles of interpretation, we must assume that Congress did *not* intend those penalties to apply unless it clearly indicated to the contrary. See *infra,* at 2330 – 2332. But we find that clear indication here. We rest our conclusion primarily upon the fact that a contrary determination would seriously undermine basic Federal Sentencing Guidelines objectives such as uniformity and proportionality in sentencing. Indeed, seen from that perspective, a contrary determination would (in respect to relevant groups of drug offenders) produce sentences less uniform and more disproportionate than if Congress had not enacted the Fair Sentencing Act at all. See *infra,* at 2332 – 2335.

Because our conclusion rests upon an analysis of the Guidelines-based sentencing system Congress has established, we describe that system at the outset and include an explanation of how the Guidelines interact with federal statutes setting forth specific terms of imprisonment.

A

The Guidelines originate in the Sentencing Reform Act of 1984, 98 Stat. 1987. That statute created a federal Sentencing Commission instructed to write guidelines that judges would use to determine sentences imposed upon offenders convicted of committing federal crimes. 28 U.S.C. §§ 991, 994. Congress thereby sought to increase transparency, uniformity, and proportionality in sentencing. United States Sentencing Commission (USSC or Commission), Guidelines Manual § 1A1.3, p. 2 (Nov. 2011) (USSG); see 28 U.S.C. §§ 991(b)(1), 994(f).

The Sentencing Reform Act directed the Commission to create in the Guidelines categories of offense behavior (*e.g.,* " 'bank robbery/committed with a gun/ $2500 taken' ") and offender characteristics (*e.g.,* "one prior conviction"). USSG § 1A1.2, at 1; see 28 U.S.C. § 994(a)–(e). A sentencing judge determines a Guidelines range by (1) finding the applicable offense level and offender category and then (2) consulting a table that lists proportionate sentencing ranges (*e.g.,* 18 to 24 months of imprisonment) at the intersections of rows (marking offense levels) and columns (marking offender categories). Sentencing Table, §§ 5E1.2, 7B1.4; see also § 1A1.4(h), at 11. The Guidelines, after telling the judge how to determine the applicable offense level and offender category, instruct the judge to apply the intersection's range in an ordinary case, but they leave the judge free to depart from that range in an unusual case. See. This Court has held that the Guidelines are now advisory.

The Guidelines determine most drug-crime offense levels in a special way. They set forth a Drug Quantity Table (or Table) that lists amounts of various drugs and associates different amounts with different "Base Offense Levels" (to which a judge may add or subtract levels depending upon the " specific" characteristics of the offender's behavior). The Table, for example, associates 400 to 499 grams of powder cocaine with a base offense level of 24, a level that would mean for a first-time offender a prison term of 51 to 63 months.

In 1986, Congress enacted a more specific, drug-related sentencing statute, the Anti–Drug Abuse Act (1986 Drug Act), 100 Stat. 3207. That statute sets forth mandatory minimum penalties of 5 and 10 years applicable to a drug offender depending primarily upon the kind and amount of drugs involved in the offense. See 21 U.S.C. § 841(b)(1)(A)–(C) (2006 ed. and Supp. IV). The minimum applicable to an offender convicted of possessing with intent to distribute 500 grams or more of powder cocaine is 5 years, and for 5,000 grams or more of powder the minimum is 10 years. § 841(b)(1)(A)(ii), (B)(ii). The 1986 Drug Act, however, treated crack cocaine crimes as far more serious. It applied its 5–year minimum to an offender convicted of possessing with intent to distribute only 5 grams of crack (as compared to 500 grams of powder) and its 10–year minimum to one convicted of possessing with intent to distribute only 50 grams of crack (as compared to 5,000 grams of powder), thus producing a 100–to–1 crack-to-powder ratio. § 841(b)(1)(A)(iii), (B)(iii) (2006 ed.).

The 1986 Drug Act, like other federal sentencing statutes, interacts with the Guidelines in an important way. Like other sentencing statutes, it trumps the Guidelines. Thus, ordinarily no matter what the Guidelines provide, a judge cannot sentence an offender to a sentence beyond the maximum contained in the federal statute setting forth the crime of conviction. Similarly, ordinarily no matter what range the Guidelines set forth, a sentencing judge must sentence an offender to at least the minimum prison term set forth in a statutory mandatory minimum. See 28 U.S.C. § 994(a), (b) (1); USSG § 5G1.1; *Neal v. United States*, 516 U.S. 284, 289–290, 295, 116 S.Ct. 763, 133 L.Ed.2d 709 (1996).

Not surprisingly, the Sentencing Commission incorporated the 1986 Drug Act's mandatory minimums into the first version of the Guidelines themselves. *Kimbrough, supra*, at 96–97, 128 S.Ct. 558. It did so by setting a base offense level for a first-time drug offender that corresponded to the lowest Guidelines range above the applicable mandatory minimum. USSC, Report to the Congress: Mandatory Minimum Penalties in the Federal Criminal Justice System 53–54 (Oct. 2011) (2011 Report). Thus, the first Guidelines Drug Quantity Table associated 500 grams of powder cocaine with an offense level of 26, which for a first-time offender meant a sentencing range of 63 to 78 months (just above the 5–year minimum), and it associated 5,000 grams of powder cocaine with an offense level of 32, which for a first-time offender meant a sentencing range of 121 to 151 months (just above the 10–year minimum). USSG § 2D1.1 (Oct. 1987). Further reflecting the 1986 Drug Act's 100–to–1 crack-to-powder ratio, the Table associated an offense level of 26 with 5 grams of crack and an offense level of 32 with 50 grams of crack. *Ibid.*

In addition, the Drug Quantity Table set offense levels for small drug amounts that did not trigger the 1986 Drug Act's mandatory minimums so that the resulting Guidelines sentences would remain proportionate to the sentences for amounts that did trigger these minimums. 2011 Report 54. Thus, the Table associated 400 grams of powder cocaine (an amount that fell just below the amount triggering the 1986 Drug Act's 5–year minimum) with an offense level of 24, which for a first-time offender meant a sentencing range of 51 to 63 months (the range just below the 5–year minimum). USSG § 2D1.1 (Oct. 1987). Following the 100–to–1 crack-to-powder ratio, the Table associated four grams of crack (an amount that also fell just below the amount triggering the 1986 Drug Act's 5–year minimum) with an offense level of 24. *Ibid.*

The Commission did this not because it necessarily thought that those levels were most in keeping with past sentencing practice or would independently have reflected a fair set of sentences, but rather because the Commission believed that doing so was the best way to keep similar drug-trafficking sentences proportional, thereby satisfying the Sentencing Reform Act's basic "proportionality" objective. See *Kimbrough*, 552 U.S., at 97, 128 S.Ct. 558; USSG § 1A1.3 (Nov. 2011); 2011 Report 53–54, 349, and n. 845. For this reason, the Commission derived the Drug Quantity Table's entire set of crack and powder cocaine offense levels by using the 1986 Drug Act's two (5– and 10–year) minimum amounts as reference points and then extrapolating from those two amounts upward and downward to set proportional offense levels for other drug amounts. *Ibid.*

B

During the next two decades, the Commission and others in the law enforcement community strongly criticized Congress' decision to set the crack-to-powder mandatory minimum ratio at 100–to–1. The Commission issued four separate reports telling Congress that the ratio was too high and unjustified because, for example, research showed the relative harm between crack and powder cocaine less severe than 100–to–1, because sentences embodying that ratio could not achieve the Sentencing Reform Act's "uniformity" goal of treating like offenders alike, because they could not achieve the "proportionality" goal of treating different offenders (*e.g.,* major drug traffickers and low-level dealers) differently, and because the public had come to understand sentences embodying the 100–to–1 ratio as reflecting unjustified race-based differences. *Kimbrough, supra,* at 97–98, 128 S.Ct. 558; see, *e.g.,* USSC, Special Report to the Congress: Cocaine and Federal Sentencing Policy 197–198 (Feb. 1995) (1995 Report); USSC, Special Report to Congress: Cocaine and Federal Sentencing Policy 8 (Apr. 1997) (1997 Report); USSC, Report to Congress: Cocaine and Federal Sentencing Policy 91, 103 (May 2002) (2002 Report); USSC, Report to Congress: Cocaine and Federal Sentencing Policy 8 (May 2007) (2007 Report). The Commission also asked Congress for new legislation embodying a lower crack-to-powder ratio. 1995 Report 198–200; 1997 Report 9–10; 2002 Report 103–107; 2007 Report 6–9. And the Commission recommended that the legislation "include" an "emergency amendment" allowing "the Commission to incorporate the statutory changes" in the Guidelines while "minimiz[ing]" the lag between any statutory and guideline modifications for cocaine offenders." *Id.,* at 9.

In 2010, Congress accepted the Commission's recommendations, see 2002 Report 104; 2007 Report 8–9, and n. 26, and enacted the Fair Sentencing Act into law. The Act increased the drug amounts triggering mandatory minimums for crack trafficking offenses from 5 grams to

28 grams in respect to the 5–year minimum and from 50 grams to 280 grams in respect to the 10–year minimum (while leaving powder at 500 grams and 5,000 grams respectively). § 2(a), 124 Stat. 2372. The change had the effect of lowering the 100–to–1 crack-to-powder ratio to 18–to–1. (The Act also eliminated the 5–year mandatory minimum for simple possession of crack. § 3, 124 Stat. 2372.)

Further, the Fair Sentencing Act instructed the Commission to "make such conforming amendments to the Federal sentencing guidelines as the Commission determines necessary to achieve consistency with other guideline provisions and applicable law." § 8(2), *id.,* at 2374. And it directed the Commission to "promulgate the guidelines, policy statements, or amendments provided for in this Act as soon as practicable, and in any event not later than 90 days" after the new Act took effect. § 8(1), *ibid.*

The Fair Sentencing Act took effect on August 3, 2010. The Commission promulgated conforming emergency Guidelines amendments that became effective on November 1, 2010. 75 Fed.Reg. 66188 (2010). A permanent version of those Guidelines amendments took effect on November 1, 2011. See 76 *id.,* at 24960 (2011).

C

With this background in mind, we turn to the relevant facts of the cases before us. Corey Hill, one of the petitioners, unlawfully sold 53 grams of crack in March 2007, before the Fair Sentencing Act became law. App. in No. 11–5721, pp. 6, 83 (hereinafter Hill App.). Under the 1986 Drug Act, an offender who sold 53 grams of crack was subject to a 10–year mandatory minimum. 21 U.S.C. § 841(b)(1)(A)(iii) (2006 ed.). Hill was not sentenced, however, until December 2010, after the Fair Sentencing Act became law and after the new Guidelines amendments had become effective. Hill App. 83–94. Under the Fair Sentencing Act, an offender who sold 53 grams of crack was subject to a 5–year, not a 10–year, minimum. § 841(b)(1)(B)(iii) (2006 ed., Supp. IV). The sentencing judge stated that, if he thought that the Fair Sentencing Act applied, he would have sentenced Hill to that Act's 5–year minimum. *Id.,* at 69. But he concluded that the Fair Sentencing Act's lower minimums apply only to those who committed a drug crime after August 3, 2010—the Act's effective date. *Id.,* at 65, 68. That is to say, he concluded that the new Act's more lenient sentences did not apply to those who committed a crime before August 3, even if they were sentenced after that date. Hence, the judge sentenced Hill to 10 years of imprisonment. *Id.,* at 78. The Court of Appeals for the Seventh Circuit affirmed. 417 Fed.Appx. 560 (2011).

The second petitioner, Edward Dorsey (who had previously been convicted of a drug felony), unlawfully sold 5.5 grams of crack in August 2008, before the Fair Sentencing Act took effect. App. in No. 5683, pp. 9, 48–49, 57–58 (hereinafter Dorsey App.). Under the 1986 Drug Act, an offender such as Dorsey with a prior drug felony who sold 5.5 grams of crack was subject to a 10–year minimum. § 841(b)(1)(B)(iii) (2006 ed.). Dorsey was not sentenced, however, until September 2010, after the new Fair Sentencing Act took effect. *Id.,* at 84–95. Under the Fair Sentencing Act, such an offender who sold 5.5 grams of crack was not subject to a mandatory minimum at all, for 5.5 grams is less than the 28 grams that triggers the new Act's mandatory minimum provisions. § 841(b)(1)(B)(iii) (2006 ed., Supp. IV). Dorsey asked the judge to apply the Fair Sentencing Act's more lenient statutory penalties. *Id.,* at 54–55.

Moreover, as of Dorsey's sentencing in September 2010, the unrevised Guidelines (reflecting the 1986 Drug Act's old minimums) were still in effect. The Commission had not yet finished revising the Guidelines to reflect the new, lower statutory minimums. And the basic sentencing statute, the Sentencing Reform Act, provides that a judge shall apply the Guidelines that "are in effect on the date the defendant is sentenced." 18 U.S.C. § 3553(a)(4)(A)(ii).

The sentencing judge, however, had the legal authority not to apply the Guidelines at all (for they are advisory). But he also knew that he could not ignore a minimum sentence contained in the applicable statute. Dorsey App. 67–68. The judge noted that, even though he was sentencing Dorsey after the effective date of the Fair Sentencing Act, Dorsey had committed the underlying crime prior to that date. *Id.,* at 69–70. And he concluded that the 1986 Drug Act's old minimums, not the new Fair Sentencing Act, applied in those circumstances. *Ibid.* He consequently sentenced Dorsey to the 1986 Drug Act's 10–year mandatory minimum term. *Id.,* at 80. The Court of Appeals for the Seventh Circuit affirmed, *United States v. Fisher,* 635 F.3d 336 (2011), and denied rehearing en banc, 646 F.3d 429 (2011) *(per curiam);* see also *United States v. Holcomb,* 657 F.3d 445 (C.A.7 2011).

The Courts of Appeals have come to different conclusions as to whether the Fair Sentencing Act's more lenient mandatory minimums apply to offenders whose unlawful conduct took place before, but whose sentencing took place after, the date that Act took effect, namely, August 3, 2010. Compare *United States v. Douglas,* 644 F.3d 39, 42–44 (C.A.1 2011) (Act applies), and *United States v. Dixon,* 648 F.3d 195, 203 (C.A.3 2011) (same), with 635 F.3d, at 339–340 (Act does not apply), *United States v. Sidney,* 648 F.3d 904, 910 (C.A.8 2011) (same), and *United States v. Tickles,* 661 F.3d 212, 215 (C.A.5 2011) *(per curiam)* (same). In light of that disagreement, we granted Hill's and Dorsey's petitions for certiorari. Since petitioners and the Government both take the position that the Fair Sentencing Act's new minimums do apply in these circumstances, we appointed as *amicus curiae* Miguel Estrada to argue the contrary position. He has ably discharged his responsibilities.

II

A

The timing issue before us is difficult in part because relevant language in different statutes argues in opposite directions. See Appendix A, *infra*. On the one hand, a federal saving statute, Act of Feb. 25, 1871 (1871 Act), § 4, 16 Stat. 432, phrased in general terms, provides that a new criminal statute that "repeal[s]" an older criminal statute shall not change the penalties "incurred" under that older statute "unless the repealing Act shall so expressly provide." . Case law makes clear that the word "repeal" applies when a new statute simply diminishes **2331 the penalties that the older statute set forth. See *Warden v. Marrero*, 417 U.S. 653, 659–664, 94 S.Ct. 2532, 41 L.Ed.2d 383 (1974); see also *United States v. Tynen*, 11 Wall. 88, 92, 20 L.Ed. 153 (1871). Case law also makes clear that penalties are "incurred" under the older statute when an offender becomes subject to them, *i.e.*, commits the underlying conduct that makes the offender liable. See *United States v. Reisinger*, 128 U.S. 398, 401, 9 S.Ct. 99, 32 L.Ed. 480 (1888); *Great Northern R. Co. v. United States*, 208 U.S. 452, 464–470, 28 S.Ct. 313, 52 L.Ed. 567 (1908).

On the other hand, the Sentencing Reform Act says that, regardless of when the offender's conduct occurs, the applicable Guidelines are the ones "in effect on the date the defendant is sentenced." 18 U.S.C. § 3553(a)(4)(A)(ii). And the Fair Sentencing Act requires the Commission to change the Guidelines in the wake of the Act's new minimums, making them consistent with "other guideline provisions and applicable law." § 8(2), 124 Stat. 2374.

Courts that have held that they must apply the old, higher 1986 Drug Act minimums to all pre-Act offenders, including those sentenced after the Fair Sentencing Act took effect, have emphasized that the 1871 Act requires that result unless the Fair Sentencing Act either expressly says or at least by fair implication implies the contrary. See 635 F.3d, at 339–340; *Sidney, supra*, at 906–908; *Tickles, supra*, at 214–215; see also *Holcomb, supra*, at 446–448 (opinion of Easterbrook, J.). Courts that have concluded that the Fair Sentencing Act's more lenient penalties apply have found in that Act, together with the Sentencing Reform Act and other related circumstances, indicia of a clear congressional intent to apply the new Act's minimums. See *Douglas*, supra, at 42–44; *Dixon, supra*, at 199–203; see also *Holcomb*, 657 F.3d, at 454–457 (Williams, J., dissenting from denial of rehearing en banc); *id.*, at 461–463 (Posner, J., dissenting from denial of rehearing en banc). We too take the latter view. Six considerations, taken together, convince us that Congress intended the Fair Sentencing Act's more lenient penalties to apply to those offenders whose crimes preceded August 3, 2010, but who are sentenced after that date.

First, *the 1871 saving statute permits Congress to apply a new Act's more lenient penalties to pre-Act offenders without expressly saying so in the new Act.* It is true that the 1871 Act uses the words "expressly provide." But the Court has long recognized that this saving statute creates what is in effect a less demanding interpretive requirement. That is because statutes enacted by one Congress cannot bind a later Congress, which remains free to repeal the earlier statute, to exempt the current statute from the earlier statute, to modify the earlier statute, or to apply the earlier statute but as modified. See, *e.g., Fletcher v. Peck*, 6 Cranch 87, 135, 3 L.Ed. 162 (1810); *Reichelderfer v. Quinn*, 287 U.S. 315, 318, 53 S.Ct. 177, 77 L.Ed. 331 (1932). And Congress remains free to express any such intention either expressly or by implication as it chooses.

Thus, the Court has said that the 1871 Act "cannot justify a disregard of the will of Congress as manifested either expressly or by *necessary implication* in a subsequent enactment." *Great Northern R. Co., supra*, at 465, 28 S.Ct. 313 (emphasis added). And in a comparable context the Court has emphasized that the Administrative Procedure Act's use of the word "expressly" does not require Congress to use any "magical passwords" to exempt a later statute from the provision. *Marcello v. Bonds*, 349 U.S. 302, 310, 75 S.Ct. 757, 99 L.Ed. 1107 (1955). Without requiring an "express" statement, the Court has described the necessary indicia of congressional intent by the terms "necessary implication," "clear implication," and "fair implication," phrases it has used interchangeably. *Great Northern R. Co., supra*, at 465, 466, 28 S.Ct. 313; *Hertz v. Woodman*, 218 U.S. 205, 218, 30 S.Ct. 621, 54 L.Ed. 1001 (1910); *Marrero, supra*, at 660, n. 10, 94 S.Ct. 2532. One Member of the Court has said we should determine whether "the plain import of a later statute directly conflicts with an earlier statute," and, if so, "the later enactment governs, *regardless* of its compliance with any earlier-enacted requirement of an express reference or other 'magical password.' " *Lockhart v. United States*, 546 U.S. 142, 149, 126 S.Ct. 699, 163 L.Ed.2d 557 (2005) (SCALIA, J., concurring).

Hence, the Court has treated the 1871 Act as setting forth an important background principle of interpretation. The Court has also assumed Congress is well aware of the background principle when it enacts new criminal statutes. *E.g., Great Northern R. Co., supra*, at 465, 28 S.Ct. 313; *Hertz, supra*, at 217, 30 S.Ct. 621; cf. *Marcello*, supra, at 310, 75 S.Ct. 757. And the principle requires courts, before interpreting a new criminal statute to apply its new penalties to a set of pre-Act offenders, to assure themselves that ordinary interpretive considerations point clearly in that direction. Words such as "plain import," "fair implication," or the like reflect the need for that assurance. And it is that assurance, which we shall assume is conveyed by the phrases "plain import" or "fair implication," that we must look for here.

Second, *the Sentencing Reform Act sets forth a special and different background principle.* That statute says that when "determining the particular sentence to be imposed" in an initial sentencing, the sentencing court "shall consider," among other things, the "sentencing range" established by the Guidelines that are "*in effect on the date the defendant is sentenced.*" 18 U.S.C. § 3553(a)(4)(A)(ii) (emphasis added). Although the Constitution's *Ex Post Facto* Clause, Art. I, § 9, cl. 3, prohibits applying a new Act's higher penalties to pre-Act conduct, it does not prohibit applying lower penalties. See *Calder v. Bull*, 3 Dall. 386, 390–391, 1 L.Ed. 648 (1798); *Collins v. Youngblood*, 497 U.S. 37, 41–44, 110 S.Ct. 2715, 111 L.Ed.2d 30 (1990). The Sentencing Commission has consequently instructed sentencing judges to "use the Guidelines Manual in effect on the date that the defendant is sentenced," regardless of when the defendant committed the offense, unless doing so "would violate the *ex post facto* clause." And therefore when the Commission adopts new, lower Guidelines amendments, those amendments become effective to offenders who committed an offense prior to the adoption of the new amendments but are sentenced thereafter. Just as we assume Congress was aware of the 1871 Act's background norm, so we assume that Congress was aware of this different background sentencing principle.

Third, *language in the Fair Sentencing Act implies that Congress intended to follow the Sentencing Reform Act background principle here.* A section of the Fair Sentencing Act entitled "Emergency Authority for United States Sentencing Commission" requires the Commission to promulgate "as soon as practicable" (and not later than 90 days after August 3, 2010) " conforming amendments" to the Guidelines that "achieve consistency with other guideline provisions and applicable law." § 8, 124 Stat. 2374. Read most naturally, "applicable law" refers to the law as changed by the Fair Sentencing Act, including the provision reducing the crack mandatory minimums. § 2(a), *id.*, at 2372. As the Commission understood this provision, achieving consistency with "other guideline provisions" means reducing the base offense levels for all crack amounts proportionally (using the new 18–to–1 ratio), including the offense levels governing small amounts of crack that did not fall within the scope of the mandatory minimum provisions. . And consistency with "other guideline provisions" and with prior Commission practice would require application of the new Guidelines amendments to offenders who committed their offense prior to the new amendments' effective date but were sentenced thereafter. See USSG § 1B1. 11(a); *e.g.,* USSG App. C, amdts. 706, 711 (Supp. Nov. 2004–Nov. 2007); see also Memorandum from G. Schmitt, L. Reed, & K. Cohen, USSC, to Chair Hinojosa et al., Subject: Analysis of the Impact of the Crack Cocaine Amendment if Made Retroactive 23 (Oct. 3, 2007). Cf. USSG App. C, amdt. 571 (amendment *increasing* restitution, which may present *ex post facto* and one-book-rule concerns, would apply only to defendants sentenced for post-amendment offenses), discussed *post,* at 2324 (SCALIA, J., dissenting).

Fourth, *applying the 1986 Drug Act's old mandatory minimums to the post-August 3 sentencing of pre-August 3 offenders would create disparities of a kind that Congress enacted the Sentencing Reform Act and the Fair Sentencing Act to prevent.* Two individuals with the same number of prior offenses who each engaged in the same criminal conduct involving the same amount of crack and were sentenced at the same time would receive radically different sentences. For example, a first-time post-Act offender with five grams of crack, subject to a Guidelines range of 21 to 27 months, could receive two years of imprisonment, while an otherwise identical pre-Act offender would have to receive the 5–year mandatory minimum. A first-time post-Act 50–gram offender would be subject to a Guidelines range of less than six years of imprisonment, while his otherwise identical pre-Act counterpart would have to receive the 10–year mandatory minimum.

Moreover, unlike many prechange/postchange discrepancies, the imposition of these disparate sentences involves roughly contemporaneous sentencing, *i.e.,* the same time, the same place, and even the same judge, thereby highlighting a kind of unfairness that modern sentencing statutes typically seek to combat. See, *e.g.*, 28 U.S.C. § 991(b)(1)(B) (purposes of Guidelines-based sentencing include "avoiding unwarranted sentencing disparities among defendants with similar records who have been found guilty of similar criminal conduct"); S.Rep. No. 98–223, p. 74 (1983)S.Rep. No. 98–223, p. 74 (1983) (explaining rationale for using same, current Guidelines for all roughly contemporaneous sentencings). Further, it would involve imposing upon the pre-Act offender a pre-Act sentence at a time after Congress had specifically found in the Fair Sentencing Act that such a sentence was unfairly long.

Finally, one cannot treat such problems as if they were minor ones. Given the 5–year statute of limitations for federal drug offenses, the 11–month median time between indictment and sentencing for those offenses, and the approximately 5,000 federal crack offenders convicted each year, many pre-Act offenders were not (and will not be) sentenced until after August 3, 2010, when the new, more lenient mandatory minimums took effect. See 18 U.S.C. § 3282(a); Administrative Office of United States Courts, Judicial Business of the United States Courts, p. 272 (2010) (Table D–10); 2011 Report 191.

Fifth, *not to apply the Fair Sentencing Act would do more than preserve a disproportionate status quo; it would make matters worse.* It would create new anomalies—new sets of disproportionate sentences—not previously present. That is because sentencing courts must apply new Guidelines (consistent with the Fair Sentencing Act's new minimums) to pre-Act offenders, see *supra*, at 2332 – 2333, and the 1986 Drug Act's old minimums would trump those new Guidelines for some pre-Act offenders but not for all of them—say, pre-Act offenders who possessed crack in small amounts not directly the subject of mandatory minimums.

Consider, for example, a first-time offender convicted of possessing with intent to distribute four grams of crack. No mandatory sentence, under the 1986 Drug Act or the Fair Sentencing Act, applies to an offender possessing so small an amount. Yet under the old law, the Commission, charged with creating proportionate sentences, had created a Guidelines range of 41 to 51 months for such an offender, a sentence proportional to the 60 months that the 1986 Drug Act required for one who trafficked five grams of crack. See *supra*, at 2327 – 2328 (Nov. 2009).

The Fair Sentencing Act, however, requires the Commission to write new Guidelines consistent with the new law. The Commission therefore wrote new Guidelines that provide a sentencing range of 21 to 27 months—about two years—for the first-time, 4–gram offender. See USSG § 2D1.1(c) (Nov. 2011). And the Sentencing Reform Act requires application of those new Guidelines to all offenders (including pre-Act offenders) who are sentenced once those new Guidelines take effect. See 18 U.S.C. § 3553(a)(4)(A)(ii). Those new Guidelines must take effect and apply to a pre-Act 4–gram offender, for such an offender was never subject to a trumping statutory 1986 Drug Act mandatory minimum. However, unless the Fair Sentencing Act's new, more lenient mandatory minimums apply to pre-Act offenders, an otherwise identical offender who possessed five grams would have to receive a 5–year sentence. See 21 U.S.C. § 841(b)(1)(B) (2006 ed., Supp. IV).

For example, imagine that on July 1, 2010, both Smith and Jones commit a crack crime identical but for the fact that Smith possesses with intent to distribute four grams of crack and Jones five grams. Both are sentenced on December 1, 2010, after the Fair Sentencing Act and the new Guidelines take effect. Smith's Guidelines sentence would be two years, but unless the Fair Sentencing Act applies, Jones's sentence would have to be five years. The difference of one gram would make a difference, not of only one year as it did before enactment of the Fair Sentencing Act, but instead of three years. Passage of the new Act, designed to have brought about fairer sentences, would here have created a new disparate sentencing "cliff."

Nor can one say that the new Act would produce disproportionalities like this in only a few cases. In fiscal year 2010, 17.8 percent of all crack offenders were convicted of offenses not subject to the 1986 Drug Act's minimums. 2011 Report 191. And since those minimums apply only to some drug offenders and they apply in different ways, one can find many similar examples of disproportionalities. See Appendix B, *infra*. Thus, application of the 1986 Drug Act minimums to pre-Act offenders sentenced after the new Guidelines take effect would produce a crazy quilt of sentences, at odds with Congress' basic efforts to achieve more uniform, more proportionate sentences. Congress, when enacting the Fair Sentencing Act, could not have intended any such result.

Sixth, *we have found no strong countervailing consideration. Amicus* and the dissent argue that one might read much of the statutory language we have discussed as embodying exceptions, permitting the old 1986 Drug Act minimums to apply to pre-Act offenders sentenced after August 3, 2010, when the Fair Sentencing Act took effect. The words "applicable law" in the new Act, for example, could, linguistically speaking, encompass the 1986 Drug Act minimums applied to those sentenced after August 3. *Post,* at 2340 – 2342 (SCALIA, J., dissenting). Moreover, Congress could have insisted that the Commission write new Guidelines with special speed to assure itself that new, post-August 3 offenders—but not old, pre-August 3 offenders— would receive the benefit of the new Act. *Post,* at 2341 – 2343. Further, *amicus* and the dissent note that to apply the new Act's minimums to the old, pre-August 3 offenders will create a new disparity—one between pre-Act offenders sentenced before August 3 and those sentenced after that date. *Post,* at 2343.

We do not believe that these arguments make a critical difference. Even if the relevant statutory language can be read as amicus and the dissent suggest and even if Congress *might* have wanted Guidelines written speedily simply in order to apply them quickly to new offenders, there is scant indication that this is what Congress *did* mean by the language in question nor that such was in fact Congress' motivation. The considerations we have set forth, *supra,* at 2332 – 2334 and this page, strongly suggest the contrary.

We also recognize that application of the new minimums to pre-Act offenders sentenced after August 3 will create a new set of disparities. But those disparities, reflecting a line-drawing effort, will exist whenever Congress enacts a new law changing sentences (unless Congress intends re-opening sentencing proceedings concluded prior to a new law's effective date). We have explained how in federal sentencing the ordinary practice is to apply new penalties to defendants not yet sentenced, while withholding that change from defendants already sentenced. *Supra*, at 2332; compare 18 U.S.C. § 3553(a)(4)(A)(ii) with § 3582(c). And we have explained how, here, continued application of the old 1986 Drug Act minimums to those pre-Act offenders sentenced after August 3 would make matters worse. *Supra*, at 2333 – 2335. We consequently conclude that this particular new disparity (between those pre-Act offenders already sentenced and those not yet sentenced as of August 3) cannot make a critical difference.

For these reasons considered as a whole, we conclude that Congress intended the Fair Sentencing Act's new, lower mandatory minimums to apply to the post-Act sentencing of pre-Act offenders. That is the Act's "plain import" or "fair implication."

....

We vacate the Court of Appeals' judgments and remand these cases for further proceedings consistent with this opinion.

It is so ordered.

CPSIA information can be obtained
at www.ICGtesting.com
Printed in the USA
LVHW100802010721
691624LV00001B/1